RECOVERY MECHANISMS IN DATABASE SYSTEMS

ISBN 0-13-614215-X

90000

9 780136 142157

RECOVERY MECHANISMS IN DATABASE SYSTEMS

Vijay Kumar and Meichun Hsu

Editors

To join a Prentice Hall PTR Internet mailing list, point to
http://www.prenhall.com/mail_lists/

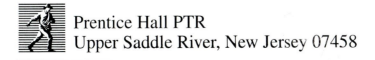
Prentice Hall PTR
Upper Saddle River, New Jersey 07458

Library of Congress Cataloging-in-Publication Data

Recovery mechanisms in database systems / Vijay Kumar and Meichun Hsu,
   editors.
        p.   cm.
    Includes bibliographical references and index.
    ISBN 0-13-614215-X
     1. Database management. 2. Fault-tolerant computing. I. Kumar,
Vijay. II. Hsu, Meichun.
    QA76.9.D3R424 1998   97-44452
    005.8'6--dc21   CIP

Cover design directors: *Jerry Votta and Amy Rosen*
Cover design: *Amy Rosen*
Cover illustration: *Wendy Grossman*
Manufacturing manager: *Alexis R. Heydt*
Acquisitions editor: *Mark L. Taub*
Editorial assistant: *Tara Ruggiero*
Marketing manager: *Dan Rush*

Published by Prentice Hall PTR
Prentice-Hall, Inc.
A Simon & Schuster Company
Upper Saddle River, New Jersey 07458

Prentice Hall books are widely used by corporations and government agencies for training, marketing,
and resale.

The publisher offers discounts on this book when ordered in bulk quantities. For more information,
contact Corporate Sales Department, Phone: 800-382-3419; FAX: 201- 236-7141;
E-mail: corpsales@prenhall.com
Or write: Prentice Hall PTR, Corporate Sales Dept., One Lake Street, Upper Saddle River, NJ 07458.

Product names mentioned herein are trademarks or registered trademarks of their respective owners.

Portions of this book have appeared in other publications. Permission acknowledgments are on p. xxx.

Printed in the United States of America
10 9 8 7 6 5 4 3 2 1

ISBN 0-13-614215-X

Prentice-Hall International (UK) Limited, *London*
Prentice-Hall of Australia Pty. Limited, *Sydney*
Prentice-Hall Canada Inc., *Toronto*
Prentice-Hall Hispanoamericana, S.A., *Mexico*
Prentice-Hall of India Private Limited, *New Delhi*
Prentice-Hall of Japan, Inc., *Tokyo*
Simon & Schuster Asia Pte. Ltd., *Singapore*
Editora Prentice-Hall do Brasil, Ltda., *Rio de Janeiro*

This book is dedicated to its contributors.

Contents

Foreword

Robust recovery is an essential feature of any database system. Who would trust their data to a system that didn't reliably recover from failures? Without a recovery subsystem, a database system would be virtually useless.

Database recovery is one of the best success stories of software fault tolerance. It has been successful because it is useful and efficient. It is useful because it factors system reliability concerns from the application programmer. It allows application programmers to use the simple transaction bracketing operations–Start Transaction, Commit, and Abort–with the result that either all of the transaction's work is permanently installed or none of it is, even in the face of application, operating system, and disk (media) failures. These atomicity and durability properties of transactions allow application programmers to focus on errors of application logic and ignore those of the underlying system. Moreover, it is efficient, so customers really want the feature. Thus, virtually all commercial database system products apply database recovery techniques.

Initial work on database recovery was done in the context of commercial product development, primarily at IBM in the 1970s. Since then, researchers have had a major impact on database recovery technology, refining and extending those techniques, and developing new ones, too. Many of these techniques developed by researchers are now standard approaches in commercial products. More of them are finding their way into commercial products every year.

This book brings together many of the most important research papers and articles on database recovery in the last decade in one volume. Although some of them have already appeared in print, they were spread over many research journals and conference proceedings and were therefore accessible only to the few people with time and energy to ferret them out. Some of them are expanded versions of those original papers, now including many important details left out of earlier versions. Many of them are new works: descriptions of commercial implementations, analyses of existing methods, and presentations of new techniques.

The first work on database system recovery was done in the context of a simple transaction model, implemented on a centralized system with expensive main memory and unreliable disks. Many logging-based algorithms to solve this problem are now well known, the best of which are variations of the ARIES algorithm developed by C. Mohan and colleagues at IBM; a comprehensive description of ARIES is included in this volume.

Most of the new work on database recovery is driven by recent changes in the system environment where database recovery is applied. Hardware improvements change the cost-benefit trade-offs in recovery algorithm design, such as the availability of large main memory, uninterruptible power supplies to backup main memory, and redundant arrays of inexpensive disks (RAID). Distributing processing between clients and servers changes the design space of recovery algorithms, since updates are performed on the client but stored persistently in the server. An extreme example of this is laptop computers, whose stable storage and communications subsystems have special properties that affect the performance of standard recovery algorithms. There are also changes in the time dimension of recovery. Workflow systems to manage long-running multi-step activities are now part of many application products and tools. Workflow mechanisms are finding their way into the underlying system platform, where they are likely to be a standard function in a few years' time.

This is hardly the end of the line in improving the performance and breadth of applicability of database recovery solutions. The new wave of object-relational database systems that will cover a wider variety of data types will undoubtedly place new demands on the flexibility of recovery algorithms, perhaps making it more important for recovery algorithms to handle multilevel atomic actions and a broader range of concurrency control protocols. The changing performance ratios of computing, disk access, and communications will lead to new problems and opportunities. So will the greatly expanding volume of Internet commerce, in which recovery actions may have to span heterogeneous systems and scale up to millions of interconnected server systems. There is no shortage of new challenges. This book includes ideas to seed new work in these exciting areas, and no doubt others yet to be contemplated.

The editors and publisher have done the field a real service in collecting so many of the best works on database recovery here in one volume. The book will be of great interest to the database system expert, since database recovery is one of those "must know" areas that affects many other aspects of database system implementation. It will also help engineers and researchers in related areas–such as operating systems, communications systems, and fault tolerance–to understand how database recovery works its magic and how they might better support and use database recovery techniques in their own work. It is an excellent summary of the state of the art of database recovery and where the field is headed.

Philip A. Bernstein
Microsoft Corporation
Redmond, Washington

Preface

Recovery is a process of restitution. In the spiritual world the recovery process restores and reveals our true self. When we arrive in this world, we *are* in our true self. Our interaction with the materialistic world then makes us believe that the world as we perceive with our senses *is* real and it is the absolute truth, thus falling into the state of ignorance (called MAYA in Indian philosophy). The recovery process salvages us from this state of ignorance and establishes us in the state of bliss, where duality does not exist.

The theme of this book, however, is recovery as practiced in database systems. We describe here the concept and the process of recovery to database systems. To some of us, database recovery has been made more obscure than recovery in the spiritual world. The book, therefore, has tried to provide both the theoretical and the applied aspects of database recovery. It covers recovery in traditional database systems, as well as in emerging technologies such as main memory databases, mobile computing, and workflow systems. It compiles valuable past and present works. Some of the chapters have been exclusively written for the book, and some have been selected from previously published works. One of our main goals is to gather together in one place the different perspectives on the subject currently scattered over time in many places.

The book begins with a historical perspective on database recovery. Ron Obermarck is the narrator, and he has done an excellent job in capturing most of the interesting events in the early evolution of the subject. Ron was one of the members of this "recovery gang" whose motto was "to recover from failure without loss of the customer's work." He takes us back to the fall of 1968, at some corner of an IBM laboratory, when database recovery was "born." He describes the advent of a number of "magics" such as "Write-Ahead-Log Tape," "Undo," and "Redo." It is interesting to note that mother nature did play an active role in the birth of database recovery by stimulating events such as lightning and thunderstorms that led to the development of some of these techniques. Chapter 1, therefore, serves as an appetizer. Ron's history of recovery also complements nicely the history of database concurrency control, as given by Jim Gray in an earlier book edited by one of us,

Performance of Concurrency Control Mechanisms in Centralized Database Systems, published by Prentice Hall, in 1996.

Since then, database recovery has become an important area of research. However, it lags behind concurrency control in the level of conceptual abstraction.

Every chapter of this book exposes some aspect of database recovery. We will only mention a few here as examples. In Chapter 4, Weihl lucidly exposes the intricate relationship between recovery and concurrency control, and shows how some recovery methods place a set of constraints on concurrency control. In Chapter 18, Hsu and Kleissner introduce and describe their perspectives on recovery in workflow systems, a subject still being debated in the research community and evolving in commercial systems. In Chapters 23 and 24, Krishna and colleagues and Bertino and colleagues take readers to the area of mobile recovery. In Chapters 25 through 28, veteran researchers who have worked intensively with commercial database systems describe database recovery in practice. In Chapter 30, Thomasian presents performance issues of the RAID5 disk arrays.

It is our sincere hope that, with the help of the experts who contributed to this volume, we have compiled a book on database recovery that our readers will enjoy reading and consider a valuable source of reference.

Acknowledgments

This book would not have been completed without the generous contributions from the authors. Practically every one of them accepted our invitation to contribute an article to the book with little persuasion. Their cooperation also made our lives much easier during manuscript preparation. Some even offered to help in formatting the manuscript, a very time-consuming task.

We are grateful to so many people for helping us to complete this project that we would not attempt to provide a complete list. We will, however, give a special mention to Ron Obermarck, Dave Lomet, Dave DeWitt, Jim Gray, Elisa Bertino, and Krithi Ramamritham. We especially enjoyed communicating with Ron Obermarck and Dave Lomet, who not only provided us technical guidance, but also generously offered moral support, which we at times greatly needed. Phil Bernstein was very kind in accepting our invitation to write a foreword.

Preparing the camera-ready copy of the book proved to be a very time-consuming process. It would have been worse had we not been rescued by Panos Chrysanthis; Bala Jayabalan and Yutong Wong, Vijay's Master and Ph.D. students; and Professor Gian Paolo Rossi's Ph.D. student Elena Pagani. Panos was generous with his help. Whenever we had a LATEX problem, we fired an e-mail to or called him and his response was immediate, and he never even threatened to change his e-mail address!

Bala laboriously incorporated copy editor's corrections to all chapters. Yutong helped us to redraw some of the graphs of our chapter, and Elena was very quick and precise in reformatting graphs of her chapter to fit in the book. We are thankful to these three wonderful students.

Our thanks also go to Mark Taub, Executive Editor, and Jane Bonnell at Prentice Hall PTR, and Cindy Kilborn, our representative at Prentice Hall. We communicated most of the time with Jane during the preparation of camera-ready chapters. Without her support and understanding we would not have succeeded in completing the camera-ready manuscript. Mark was very patient with us. Although he reminded us gently from time to time about the deadlines, he never exerted undue pressure, and was always kind enough to give us more time when we needed it. Cindy was instrumental in getting the project approved quickly.

Family members always play an important role in the completion of any project. Our children (Vijay's Krishna and Arjun, and Mei's baby Noelle) always greeted us with their wonderful smiles even when we stole some of their share of time in formatting the book chapters. The support and encouragement of Vijay's wife Elizabeth and Mei's husband Hoomin in completing this book have a special significance.

Finally, we wish to thank the Association for Computing Machinery, Institute of Electrical and Electronics Engineers, the VLDB Endowment, and Elsevier Science Publishing for granting permission to reprint the articles.

Vijay Kumar
University of Missouri
Kansas City, Missouri

Meichun Hsu
Hewlett-Packard Laboratories
Palo Alto, California

PERMISSION ACKNOWLEDGMENTS

Chapter 3. Haerder, T. and A. Reuter, "Principles of Transaction-Oriented Database Reccovery," *Computing Survey*, 15(4) (December 1983).

Chapter 5. Weihl, B. "The Impact of Recovery on Concurrency Control," *Journal of Computer and Systems Sciences*, 47(1) (August 1993).

Chapter 6. Lomet, D. and Mark R. Tuttle, "Redo Recovery after System Crashes," *Proceedings of Very Large Databases*, Zurich, September 1995.

Chapter 7. Lomet. D., "MLR: A Recovery Method for Multi-Level Systems," *ACM SIGMOD*, San Diego, 21(2) (June 1992).

Chapter 8. Mohan, C., Don Haderle, Bruce Lindsay, Hamid Pirahesh, and Peter Schwarz. "ARIES: A Transaction Recovery Method Supporting Fine-Granularity Locking and Partial Rollbacks Using Write-Ahead Logging," *ACM Transactions on Database Systems*, 17(1) (March 1992).

Chapter 9. Kumar, V. and Shown Moe. "Performance of Recovery Algorithms for Centralized Database Management Systems," *Information Sciences*, 86(1–3) (September 1995).

Chapter 10. Goes, P.B., and U. Sumita, "Stochastic Models for Performance Analysis of Database Recovery Control," *IEEE Transactions on Computers*, 44(4) (April 1995).

Chapter 12. Dan, A., Philip S. Yu, and A. Jhingran. "Recovery Analysis of Data Sharing Systems under Deferred Dirty Page Propagation Policies," *IEEE Transactions on Parallel and Distributed Systems*, 8(7) (July 1997).

Chapter 14. Franklin, M., Michael Zwilling, C.K. Tan, Michael Carey, and D. DeWitt, "Crash Recovery in Client-Server EXODUS," *ACM SIGMOD*, San Diego, 21(2) (June 1992).

Chapter 19. Copeland, G., T. Keller, R. Krishnamurthy, and M. Smith. "Case for Safe Ram," *Proc. of Very Large Databases*, Amsterdam, 1989.

Chapter 22. Kumar, V. and A. Bueger. "Performance Measurement of Main Memory Database Recovery Algorithms Based on Update-in-Place and Shadow Approaches," *IEEE Transactions on Knowledge and Data Engineering*, 4(6), (December 1992).

Chapter 23. Pradhan, D. K., P. Krishna, and N. H. Vaidya. "Recovery in Mobile Environment: Design and Trade-off Issues," *IEEE Proc. of Symposium for Fault-tolerant Computing*, June 1996.

Chapter 27. Gray, J., P. McJones, M. Blasgen, B. Lindsey, R. Lorie, T. Price, F. Putzolu, and I. Traiger. "The Recovery Manager of the System R Database Manager," *ACM Computing Surveys*, 13(2) (June 1981).

Chapter 28. White, Seth J., and David J. DeWitt. "Implementing Crash Recovery in QuickStore: A Performance Study," *ACM SIGMOD*, San Jose, 24(2)2 (May 1995).

Recovery Mechanisms in Database Systems

Chapter 1

IMS/360 and IMS/VS Recovery: Historical Recollections

Ron Obermarck

1.1 INTRODUCTION

International Business Machines Corporation (IBM) produced a program product called Information Management System (IMS/360)[1] in 1969. One of the main features of this new program product, was the ability to recover from failures without loss of the customer's work. IMS/ESA Version 6 Transaction and Database Servers was announced September 1996. The announcement included *Enhanced Enterprise Computing Systems Management, Availability, and ...*, continuing the evolution of nearly 30 years of recovery and availability innovation.

I was a member of the IMS development team from the fall of 1968 to the summer of 1976, and remained associated with the product in a support position for several years. Aspects of recovery and availability that have been formalized and documented in the literature are rooted in the pioneering efforts of products like IMS/360. There are several innovations that were the work of groups of people. Many things were not formally described until long after their implementation. This chapter brings a selection of the availability and recovery into perspective using IMS as an example. Most of the information in this chapter is from my own recollections. I will cover several aspects of recovery that are taken as totally

---

[1]IMS/360, IMS/VS, and IMS/ESA are registered trademarks of the International Business Machines Corp.

basic givens in today's designs and implementations, showing that the idea was not intuitively obvious to we who started.

IMS history begins well before 1968, when I joined the development group. IMS/360 Version 1.0 grew out of a joint development effort between IBM and several aerospace customers. When I joined, the joint development effort had come to a close. IMS/360 Version 1.0 was released at the end of 1968, IMS/360 Version 2 was announced in June 1970, and was a major redesign and rewrite of the original.

1.1.1   Basic Recovery Algorithms

Recovery by Replaying Transactions

IMS/360 Version 1 provided restart recovery from failures of the IMS system, and the operating system. Before-images of changes to the database were recorded on the log. Deletion of database segments was done by flagging the data segments as deleted. Recovery consisted of applying the before images of the *in-flight* transactions to the database, and putting the transactions back into the message queue for reprocessing.

The same kind of processing was done for recovery from failure of the database. In that case, the database was restored to a known point, and the logs would be replayed carefully, so that the transactions would be reprocessed in the same order as they had been originally. This had the advantage that logical errors to the database could be corrected by replacing an erroneous application program with a corrected version, and recovering the database.

There were also some disadvantages to this approach to recovery. Time dependent reporting, which relied on the system clock to time-stamp activities became unmanageable. Setting the system clock back was not feasible, so schedule reporting would show gaps of up to several days, with huge amounts of activity during the recovery period.

Almost as often as corrected application code could be used to correct logical errors, the corrected applications themselves would fail. Because there was no dynamic backout capability, partial changes would appear in the database. The attempts to ensure that the mix of transactions were the same when reprocessed as when originally executed were error-prone, and the recovered result never exactly matched the original.

Physical Image Logging

IMS/360 Version 2 introduced several new database organizations. Delete was no longer guaranteed to be a nondestructive operation. Direct access to data segments required pointer chain updates for insert and delete. The *Functional Specification for IMS/360 Version 2*, dated February 28, 1969, notes physical image logging as a release objective. In January 1971, additional recovery support was announced for Database recovery in the batch mode, increased performance in database recovery, and so on.

These features were the direct result of physical change logging of after-images. A set of utility programs had been created to use this information. A database image copy utility produced the base image from which recovery could be done. The performance of randomly applying the changes based on the after-image log records was poor, especially when tens to hundreds of 2400-foot reels of magnetic tape were involved. The increased performance part of the release corrected that problem.

A change accumulation utility was created, which did two things. First, it allowed the log tapes to be processed off-line, without the pressures of immediately getting a broken database on-line. Second, it reduced the volume of redo by sorting and merging the redo information by file and relative offset. As a result, the database recovery operation itself became the merge of the change accumulation and image copy while sequentially recreating the damaged files.

1.1.2   Write-Ahead Logging

Not Required

The initial release of IMS/360 used operating-system buffered I/O to write its log tapes. This was changed early to allow more control of when and how the log records were written. As the IMS control region was executed with a dump data set specified, a failure in which IMS was unable to properly close the log tape could be handled. A problem that caused OS/360 to hang was also covered, by requiring the system operator to execute a stand-alone dump program before restarting the system.

Before IMS was restarted, a utility program was executed that processed the dump data set. The processing extracted the contents of the IMS log buffers, translating them back to binary, and writing them to the tail of the IMS log tapes. Therefore, there was no need to write anything but full blocks to the IMS log.

This seemed to work quite well until IBM began producing computers with transistor memories. The computers with magnetic-core memories could lose power and still retain the information in core at the time of the outage.

OOPS

I was at the IBM plant in Burlington, Vermont, working on IMS/360 database corruption problems when a thunderstorm caused a power outage. The system operator was unable to run the stand-alone dump utility. The storm had caused a power spike that overrode the buffering in the power supply, and caused the core memory to be filled with parity errors.

One of the customers who had been involved in the original joint development effort suggested that we write the log records to the log before writing them to disk. I am sure he was not the only one who came up with the suggestion, but I still like the acronym he coined, *Write-Ahead Log Tape*, or *WALT*.

1.1.3   Duplex Logging

The need for duplex logging became apparent when some of the first customers encountered read errors when attempting to do restart recovery. Changing a reel of magnetic tape required the system operator to handle both the full tape and the new tape that replaced it. In addition, the number of tape volumes created per day of operation was becoming unmanageable. When a database required physical recovery, the number of reels of magnetic tape involved far exceeded the Mean Time to Failure (MTTF) of the tapes. Being able to write duplex logs was not sufficient without utility enhancements. Some of the enhancements that were found necessary were:

1. A utility to read two log tapes, skipping unreadable blocks, and create a single (it is hoped) readable tape, which could then be used as input to restart. This utility read and validated each logical log record.

2. A utility that dumped the unreadable blocks when both log tapes had an error at the same location, and allowed the content of the *best* block to be edited and inserted in the new log tape. This was demonstrated as necessary under two cases. Of course, it was necessary when both logs had errors at the same physical location relative to the beginning of the tape reel. It was also used to attempt repair when duplex logging was not used, and the single tape became unreadable.

3. Modifications to the IMS log writer to force an end of file on the second log tape when the first experienced an end of tape. This enhancement was necessary to allow volume substitution for bad tape volumes.

1.1.4   Dynamic Transaction Backout (Undo)

The integrity of the database was often breached by application failures that would leave partially updated information in the database. If the application handled the exceptions, or did not actually update the database until the last set of actions, the integrity hole was minimal. However, that was too seldom the way the application was designed.

With IMS/VS Version 1, in 1974, a feature called Program Isolation was released. Although the feature, called Exclusive Control Facility in the IMS/360 Version 2 Functional Specifications, was originally a concurrent scheduling enhancement, it had no way to handle potential deadlocks.

An internal version of the paper *Spheres of Control*, by Bjork and Davies, provided the base for the implementation of the Program Isolation feature. The paper showed that if all changes made by one process were isolated so that they could not be seen by any other process, they could be undone. Treating deadlock as a failure allowed the application to be aborted, and its changes rolled back, without involving the application design.

A disk log was created, and all undo records were written to that log in addition to the tape recovery log. This *dynamic backout data set* was disk backed, with the expectation that the information would be cached without actually writing it. Although created to handle deadlock situations, its applicability to other application program failures was seen almost immediately.

1.1.5   Conclusions

I selected some recovery-related developments from early IMS. In retrospect, the development of the preceding features was dictated by circumstance as much as by deep thought and study. The combination of requirements, restrictions, and inventive hard work brought them about. Looked at one way, we could say the following:

1. The transition of forward recovery from reprocessing transactions to application of physical redo information was done for performance and because the logical reprocessing could not restore the database precisely.

2. Log write-ahead was a pragmatic answer to the introduction of transistor memory. Had there been another way to retain a persistent copy of the log records, it would have been used.

3. The implementation of duplexing was done because magnetic-tape storage went through a stage of poor reliability, but was the only medium with the price-performance characteristics that could be used for logging.

4. The motivating factor for implementing dynamic backout was not database integrity, but resolution of deadlocks without requiring application involvement. The implications of dynamic backout on database integrity were seen once the idea had been broached.

On the other hand, the preceding items are key reliability and availability aspects of today's database and transaction processing systems. I make no claim that IMS development was the first, or only, discoverer and implementer of these features. However, the history of IMS contains a stream of innovation in recovery and availability in database and transaction processing worth studying. This is no more than a hint of the early history of recovery in the IMS program product set.

Chapter 2

Introduction to Database Recovery

Meichun Hsu and Vijay Kumar

2.1 INTRODUCTION

A database D is a representation of a part of the real world, such as a bank, a university, etc., as a set of data elements $\{d_1, d_2, ..., d_m\}$. For example, if the database represents a bank, then its employees, departments, accounts, and the relationships among these entities, can be represented as data elements. Data elements have implicit semantics and can be recorded on any storage medium.

The state of the part of the real world continuously changes; therefore, at any instant, the database must reflect the changes about the part of the real world it represents. The changes in the part of the real world are mapped to the database with appropriate modifications to a relevant subset of the data elements. Data elements are modified using a defined set of operations under a defined set of rules to maintain the *consistency* of the database.

A database is called consistent if at any time it is capable of projecting the facts about the part of the real world it represents. The consistency of a database is a time varying property because the state of the part of the real world is dynamic. Consistency is maintained by applying relevant modifications to the database under a set of "Consistency Constraints" or "Assertions." A consistency constraint can be regarded as a rule which validates the modifications to data elements to reflect the changes in the the part of the real world.

The Database Management System (DBMS) is responsible for implementing the relevant operations under the set of consistency constraints for maintaining the consistency of the database. An end user communicates with a database through a mechanism called a *transaction*. A transaction can be defined from a user viewpoint and from a system viewpoint. The end user (the operator, the system administrator, etc.) sees a transaction as a request/reply unit expressed in the form of a source program. The system, on the other hand, sees a transaction as a sequence of operations (reads, writes, etc.) on the data elements. The user conveys a change to the DBMS via a transaction and awaits a reply from the system. The DBMS then implements the set of operations (defined in the transaction) on a subset of data elements by executing the transaction under a set of consistency constraints. The DBMS guarantees the incorporation of the changes through a "successful" execution of the transaction. We will refer to such execution of a transaction as "commit."

A transaction T must possess a set of well-defined properties to be able to correctly reflect in the database the changes to the part of the real world. In executing a transaction, the system guarantees that all changes proposed in the transaction, not only a part of them, are incorporated correctly in the database. It guarantees that such modifications to the relevant data elements by a transaction are not affected by the execution of other concurrent transactions. Furthermore, if the changes are incorporated completely and correctly, then their presence will persist in the consistent database despite system failures that may occur subsequently.

While a user (database programmer) can attempt to provide the above set of guarantees by carefully coding the program that accesses the database, this approach would degrade performance and resource utilization and is often unreliable. Furthermore, this approach may force a user to know aspects of database implementation. This is not desirable. Therefore, the user defines transaction boundaries in the programs they write, and these guarantees are enforced by the system on transactions during their execution to reach a commit.

2.2   ACID PROPERTIES OF TRANSACTIONS

The properties of transactions informally described above are often referred to as the *ACID* (Atomicity, Consistency, Isolation, and Durability) properties.

Atomicity.   Refers to the "all or nothing" property. If a transaction succeeds (i.e., commits), then all its effect on the data is captured in the database. If the transaction does not succeed (i.e, aborts), then none of its effect on the data is captured in the database. In other words, the transaction processing algorithm guarantees that the database will not reflect a partial effect of a transaction.

Consistency.   Refers to the requirement that, given a consistent initial database state, the state of the database after the successful execution of a transaction is also consistent; that is, a transaction transforms a database from a consistent state to another consistent state. Database consistency may be defined as a set of rules or constraints. If the execution of a transaction causes the consistency constraints to be violated, the transaction is not accepted (and thus aborted) by the system.

Isolation.   Says that a transaction executes as if no other concurrent transactions are executing, and thus its execution results are equivalent to those obtained by executing database transactions serially. A system which maintains transaction isolation is also said to be enforcing serializability.

Durability. Says that, if a transaction succeeds, then its effect on the data is persistently captured and will survive subsequent system failures resulting in loss of data in volatile memory. Durability is usually enforced by first writing modified data to some non-volatile memory (usually disk) before a transaction is allowed to commit. If there is a system failure, upon recovery, the state of the non-volatile memory must be recovered to reflect the effect of all and only committed transactions.

Database recovery is about preserving the *atomicity* and the *durability* properties. It is primarily concerned about handling *transaction failures* and *system failures*, in other words, about *fault tolerance*:

- If a transaction should fail after it has been started, which may be caused by it violating database integrity constraints, or by the software program implementing the transaction encountering a fatal error, none of its operations already executed (i.e., the partial effects) should be allowed in the database. This is required to preserve the atomicity property.

- If a system should fail and lost the contents of its memory after it has successfully executed a number of transactions, the effects of those successfully executed transactions must not be lost, and must be reflected in the database when the system recovers. This is required to preserves the atomicity and the durability property.

Database concurrency control, on the other hand, is about preserving the *isolation* property, which is also referred to as *serializability*. Transactions can be executed serially where the commit of one transaction must precede the beginning of the next transaction. Such execution preserves the isolation property. However, it results in poor utilization of resources. To maximize resource utilization and system throughput, transactions are executed concurrently: individual operations (reads, writes, etc.) of transactions are interleaved. Interleaved execution allows interference which violates the isolation (i.e., serializability) property.

Undesirable interferences can be removed by regulating the interleaving of individual operations of concurrent transactions. Basically, it synchronizes the use of shared data items by concurrent transactions to produce a serializable execution order of their individual operations.

While concurrency control and database recovery have orthogonal goals, they are intertwined in implementation. We illustrate this point using the following example.

Two transactions, T_1 and T_2, want to modify a shared data item, say d. The initial consistent value of d is 10. If T_1 and T_2 are executed concurrently, then the following scenarios may arise.

Dirty read. Suppose T_1 modifies the value of d from 10 to 20. Later T_2 reads the value of d (= 20) and commits. Subsequently T_1 fails. To maintain atomicity, the value of d is restored to 10. However, the non-existent, partial-update value of d ($=$ 20) has been read by T_2.

Lost update.   Suppose T_1 modifies the value of d from 10 to 20. Later T_2 reads the value of d, changes it from 20 to 40, and commits. If T_1 now fails and is rolled back, and the value of d is restored to 10, then the database would have lost $T_2's$ update of d from the database. This violates the durability property.

This example illustrates that interleaved execution of transactions and handling of failure events often need to be examined together. In what follows, we focused on the basic concepts and mechanisms in database recovery; where applicable, we will also discuss these mechanisms' interactions with database concurrency control.

2.3   Principles of Database Recovery

The database recovery manager of a DBMS is responsible for ensuring consistency of the database under various failure scenarios: transaction failures, system failures where the contents of the main memory of the system is lost, and hard crash, where the storage media fails due to events such as a disk crash.

The atomicity and the durability properties of a transaction imply that each transaction must implement a unique, atomic *commit point*.

Definition.   The *commit point* of a transaction marks the successful execution of a transaction. The unit of work executed between the start of a transaction and the commit point of the transaction defines a unit of consistency. The *atomic* nature of a commit point says to the fact that at any point in time in the system state, a transaction that has started is either committed or not committed, and is never in an undetermined or ambiguous state with respect to its commit.

Definition.   A *consistent database state* is a database state in which all changes made by committed transactions are installed while none of the changes made by uncommitted transactions are installed.

Definition.   A *resilient database state* is a system database state from which a consistent database state can be constructed.

The main goal of the recovery manager is to ensure that the database is constantly in a resilient state in face of all potential failures, and, upon a failure (transaction failure or system failure), is always capable of restoring the database state to the consistent state defined as of the time of failure.

The notion of atomic commit point is instrumental to the implementation of recovery mechanism. The recovery manager makes use of the notion of atomic commit point to formulate its principles:

- Before a transaction T reaches its commit point, the system must ensure that it maintains enough information to allow T to be backed out, or *aborted*.

- After a transaction T reaches its commit point, its updates are captured in such a way that, despite subsequent system failures, these updates are not lost and will in any case be restored in the database state.

The above strategy is essentially implemented through maintaining redundant information and implementing the logic for restoring the database state. The basic mechanism for implementation consists of the following:

- Logging: The logging mechanism is used to maintain redundant information to ensure recoverability upon failures. Every time a change is made by a transaction to the database, the old value (referred to as the *before image*), the new value (referred to as the after image), or both values of the updated data item, is (are) written to a log.

- Redo and undo: The redo and undo logic is used to restore the database to a consistent state following a failure. The redo logic rolls the database forward to reflect all the changes made by committed transactions. The undo logic rolls the database backward to back out the changes made by aborted transactions.

- Checkpoint and database dump: Checkpoint is used to bound the size of the log that needs to be scanned for redo and undo when recovering from failures. Database dump refers to making a copy of the entire database periodically to guard against media failure.

2.4   Methods for Writing Updates to a Database

The logic of a database recovery manager depends on how a DBMS implements updates to the database as transactions execute. There are generally three methods for writing the updates:

- **In-place update**: When a transaction T executes a write operation on a data item d, the before image of d, $bef(d)$, in the database is immediately overwritten with the after image of d, $aft(d)$. This is also referred to as *dirty write*, since the change to d is not yet committed at the time it is reflected in the database.

  To guard against failures, $bef(d)$ must be written to the log when d is over-written. In case T commits later, this value in the log is not used. In case T is aborted later, or in case the system fails before T commits such that upon system recovery T is aborted, the before image $bef(d)$ in the log is used to back out the update, by replacing the value of d in the database with its before image.

  The in-place update method makes it easier to commit a transaction; however, aborting a transaction involves more work.

- **Update in private work space**: When a transaction T executes a write operation on a data item d, the before image of d, $bef(d)$, in the database is not overwritten. Instead, the after image $aft(d)$ is written to a private work space. If T or the system subsequently fails before T reaches its commit point, its private work space is discarded. When T commits, the contents of its private work space are installed into the database. This way, the database always contains only committed updates.

  The private work space method makes it easier to abort a transaction; however, committing a transaction involves more work.

- **Shadow-page**: This approach can be used when the database consists of logical pages as data items, and the pages are managed through a *page map* which maps a logical page to a physical page.

  When a transaction T starts, a shadow page map identical to the current page map is allocated. When T updates a page d, $bef(d)$ is copied to a new physical page (a *shadow page*) d', and the original page d is overwritten with the new value. The shadow page map is also updated such that it now points to d'. The shadow page map essentially maps to the before state, and the original page map maps to the after state or the dirty state. If T later commits, the shadow page map is discarded. If T later aborts, the shadow page map is installed as the current page map.

  The shadow page approach allows the commit or abort processing to be reduced to an atomic swapping of the page map.

These basic methods may also be combined to form hybrid methods. Most DBMS's today uses methods that are primarily based on the in-place update method. We will assume that the in-place update method is used in a DBMS for the remainder of this chapter.

2.5 Implementing Transaction Commit and Abort

A transaction is subject to abort before it commits; it cannot be aborted after it has committed. It is important that once a transaction has committed, it is not invalidated due to failures of other concurrent transactions. This section discusses the issue of interaction between recovery and concurrency control.

Assume that the DBMS implements in-place update, and it uses before image logging to ensure transaction recoverability. Consider the example in the first section, when we discussed the dirty read and lost update phenomenon. We rephrase the example formally below.

Example 1. Consider two transactions T_1 and T_2 as defined below. The two transactions share the data element d_i.

Consider the following interleaved execution sequence of T_1 and T_2:

$$R_{d_i}(T_1),\ W_{d_i}(T_1),\ R_{d_i}(T_2),\ W_{d_i}(T_2),\ Commit(T_2),\ R_{d_j}(T_1),\ Abort(T_1)...$$

$$T_1: \quad R_{d_i} \qquad\qquad\qquad T_2: \quad R_{d_i}$$
$$W_{d_i} \qquad\qquad\qquad\qquad\quad W_{d_i}$$
$$R_{d_j}$$
$$W_{d_j}$$

where $R_{d_i}(T_1)$ denotes the operation of reading d_i by T_1, $W_{d_i}(T_1)$ denotes writing d_i, $Commit(T_1)$ denotes the event of committing T_1, and so on. The schedule says that T_1, after updating d_i, is subsequently aborted, and T_2, after reading the updated d_i, is subsequently committed before T_1 fails. This interleaved execution will cause T_1's effect on d_i to be propagated to T_2. Aborting T_1 thus will require that T_2 be aborted, which contradicts the definition that a transaction, once committed, cannot be aborted.

This problem, referred to as the *cascaded abort* problem, is solved by having the recovery manager adhere to the following principles:

- Data written by uncommitted transactions are not revealed to other transactions.

- Once a transaction commits, *all* of its written data are revealed to other transactions simultaneously.

Interestingly, these principles jive well with the two phace locking protocol for concurrency control. We restate the behavior of the two transactions after inserting the two phace locking protocol as below:

$$T_1: \quad Lock_{d_i} \qquad\qquad\qquad T_2: \quad Lock_{d_i}$$
$$R_{d_i} \qquad\qquad\qquad\qquad\qquad R_{d_i}$$
$$W_{d_i} \qquad\qquad\qquad\qquad\qquad W_{d_i}$$
$$Lock_{d_j} \qquad\qquad\qquad\qquad\quad U_{d_j}$$
$$R_{d_j} \qquad\qquad\qquad\qquad\qquad Unlock_{d_j}$$
$$W_{d_j}$$
$$Unlock_{d_i}$$
$$Unlock_{d_j}$$

The two phase locking protocol ensures that T_2 will not perform any dirty read, and the cascaded abort problem is avoided. The atomic commit point in fact coincides with the *lock point* of the two phace locking protocol: the atomic commit point of a transaction T always occurs *after* T has reached its lock point, and *before* T releases any lock.

2.6   Commit Processing and System Recovery

A database management system caches the contents of the database in the main memory during transaction processing. The cached database contents are used to satisfy the read and write operations performed by transactions. Using in-place update, when a transaction performs a write operation, the after image is first cached in the main memory, and is written to the disk by the buffer manager of the DBMS at a later stage. Therefore, the contents of the database on the disk do not always reflect a consistent database state. When a system fails such that the contents of the main memory is lost, then upon system recovery, the database state must be reconstructed based on the contents that survive in the disk storage. This section describes the basic mechanism for system recovery.

We illustrate the task of system recovery using an example.

Example 2. Consider three non-conflicting transactions T_1, T_2 and T_3, each reading a data element and writing two data elements, as defined below.

$$
\begin{array}{lllll}
T_1: & R_{d_1} & T_2: & R_{d_3} & T_2: & R_{d_5} \\
     & W_{d_1} &   & W_{d_3} &   & W_{d_5} \\
     & W_{d_2} &   & W_{d_4} &   & W_{d_6}
\end{array}
$$

Consider the following execution sequence including disk events and failure events:

$R_{d_1}(T_1),\ W_{d_1}(T_1),\ R_{d_3}(T_2),\ W_{d_3}(T_2),$

$DiskWrite(d_1, d_3),$

$W_{d_2}(T_1),\ Commit(T_1),\ W_{d_4}(T_2),\ Abort(T_2),$

$R_{d_5}(T_3),\ W_{d_5}(T_3),\ W_{d_6}(T_3),\ Commit(T_3),$

$SystemCrash...$

where $DiskWrite(d_i, ..)$ refers to a buffer manager event where data elements d_i .. are written to the disk, and $SystemCrash$ refers to a system failure event where the content of the main memory is lost. Upon system recovery, the recovery manager must restore the consistent database state by performing the following:

- The after images of d_2, d_5, d_6, which were only cached in the main memory and not yet written to the disk when system crashes, must be installed to the database (redo).

- The disk image of d_3, which belongs to an aborted transaction T_2, must be rolled back to its before image (undo).

These operations must be performed based on information in the log, and thus the log entries for these data items must survive the system crash.

This example helps explain the following protocol:
The Write ahead Log Protocol.

- Before a disk write operation is performed on a dirty data element d, the log for undoing this write (i.e., its before image log entry) must first be written to the disk.

- Before committing a transaction T, the log for redoing any data element d written by T (i.e., its after image log entry) must first be written to the disk.

The write-ahead log protocol ensures that the information on the log needed for system recovery survives the system crash. Illustrating with our previous example, the before image logging and the write-ahead log protocols combined would have resulted in inserting the logging operations into the above execution schedule as follows (note that the Commit and Abort operations are essentially materialized through log operations, and we omit the two phase locking protocol operations):

$$R_{d_1}(T_1), \ LOG_{bef(d_1)}(T_1), \ W_{d_1}(T_1),$$
$$R_{d_3}(T_2), \ LOG_{bef(d_3)}(T_2), \ W_{d_3}(T_2),$$
$$ForceLog, \ DiskWrite(d_1, d_3),$$
$$LOG_{bef(d_2)}(T_1), \ W_{d_2}(T_1),$$
$$LOG_{aft(d_1)}(T_1), \ LOG_{aft(d_2)}(T_1), LOG_{Commit}(T_1), \ ForceLog,$$
$$LOG_{bef(d_4)}(T_2), \ W_{d_4}(T_2),$$
$$RestoreFromLog(bef(d_3), bef(d_4)), \ LOG_{Abort}(T_2),$$
$$R_{d_5}(T_3), \ LOG_{bef(d_5)}(T_3), \ W_{d_5}(T_3), \ LOG_{bef(d_6)}(T_3), \ W_{d_6}(T_3),$$
$$LOG_{aft(d_5)}(T_3), \ LOG_{aft(d_6)}(T_3), LOG_{Commit}(T_3), \ ForceLog,$$
$$SystemCrash...$$

The content of the log on the disk at the time of system crash would look like the following:

$$bef(d_1), bef(d_3), bef(d_2), aft(d_1), aft(d_2), Commit(T_1),$$
$$Abort(T_2), bef(d_5), bef(d_6), aft(d_5), aft(d_6), Commit(T_3)$$

With the write-ahead logging protocol, the commit point of a transaction T is defined as the point in time when its commit log record (i.e., $Commit(T)$) reaches the disk. Should the system crash before such a record has reached the disk, then upon recovery, T is aborted. Should the system crash after such a record has reached the disk, then upon recovery, T is considered committed. Upon system recovery, the recovery manager scans the log on the disk to first discover the status of each transaction. Then, it scans the log to restore the before images of aborted transactions, and to install the after images of committed transactions.

To reduce the size of the log that must be kept on-line and to ensure responsive system recovery processing, the *checkpoint* mechanism is used. Checkpointing involves establishing a point in the log (as the checkpoint log entry) such that transactions committed before that point will not have to be redone, and only transactions that are live or started after that point will have to be considered in the redo logic. This involves force writing the cached database to the disk at the checkpoint. At the checkpoint, the system also identifies the oldest log entry e recorded by active transactions. Log entries prior to e are no longer needed for the undo logic, and thus can be archived. Various optimized forms of this basic mechanism are used in practice.

Chapter 3

Principles of Transaction-Oriented Database Recovery

Theo Haerder and Andreas Reuter

Abstract

In this chapter, a terminological framework is provided for describing different transaction-oriented recovery schemes for database systems in a conceptual rather than an implementation-dependent way. By introducing the terms materialized database, propagation strategy, and checkpoint, we obtain a means for classifying arbitrary implementations from a unified viewpoint. This is complemented by a classification scheme for logging techniques, which are precisely defined by using the other terms. It is shown that these criteria are related to all relevant questions such as speed and the scope of recovery and amount of redundant information required. The primary purpose of this chapter, however, is to establish an adequate and precise terminology for a topic in which the confusion of concepts and implementation aspects still imposes a lot of problems.

3.1 INTRODUCTION

Database technology has seen tremendous progress during the past 10 years. Concepts and facilities that evolved in the single-user batch environments of the early days have given rise to efficient multiuser database systems with user-friendly interfaces, distributed data management,and so on From a scientific viewpoint, database systems today are established as a mature discipline with well-approved methods and technology. The methods and technology of such a discipline should be well represented in the literature by systematic surveys of the field. There are, in fact, a number of recent papers that attempt to summarize what is known about different aspects of database management [1, 2, 9, 17, 23, 33] These papers fall into two categories: (1) descriptions of innovative prototype systems and (2) thorough analyses of special problems and their solutions, based on a clear methodological and terminological framework. We are contributing to the second category in the field of database recovery. In particular, we are establishing a systematic framework for establishing and evaluating the basic concepts for fault-tolerant database operation This chapter is organized as follows. Section 3.3 contains a short description of what recovery is expected to accomplish and which notion of consistency we assume. This involves introducing the transaction, which has proved to be the major paradigm for synchronization and recovery in advanced database systems. This is also the most important difference between this paper and Verhofstadt's survey, in which techniques for file recovery are described without using a particular notion of consistency [38]. Section 3.2 provides an implementation model for database Systems, that is, a mapping hierarchy of data types. Section 3.4 introduces the key concepts of our framework, describing the database states after a crash, the type of log information required, and additional measures for facilitating recovery. Crash recovery is demonstrated with three sample implementation techniques. Section 3.5 applies concepts addressed in previous sections on media recovery, and Section 3.6 summarizes the scope of our taxonomy.

3.2 DATABASE RECOVERY: WHAT IT IS EXPECTED TO DO

Understanding the concepts of database recovery requires a clear comprehension of two factors:

- the type of failure the database has to cope with

- the notion of consistency that is assumed as eight criteria for describing the state to be reestablished.

Before beginning a discussion of these factors, we would like to point out that the contents of this section rely on the description of failure types and the concept of a transaction given by Gray et al. [17].

3.2.1 What Is a Transaction?

It was observed quite early that manipulating data in a multiuser environment requires some kind of isolation to prevent uncontrolled and undesired interactions. A user (or process) often does things when working with a database that are, up to a certain point in time, of tentative or preliminary value. The user may read some data and modify others before finding out that some of the initial input was wrong, invalidating everything that was done up to that point. Consequently, the user wants to remove what he or she has done from the system. If other users (or processes) have already seen the "dirty data" [17] and made decisions based upon it, they obviously will encounter difficulties. The following questions must be considered:

- How do they get the message that some of their input data have disappeared, when it is possible that they have already finished their job and left the terminal?

- How do they cope with such a situation? Do they also throw away what they have done, possibly affecting others in turn? Do they reprocess the affected parts of their program?

These situations and dependencies have been investigated thoroughly by Bjork and Davies in their studies of the so-called "spheres of control" [3, 11, 12]. They indicate that data being operated by a process must be isolated in some way that lets others know the degree of reliability provided for these data, that is,

- Will the data be changed without notification to others?

- Will others be informed about changes?

- Will the value definitely not change any more?

This ambitious concept was restricted to use in database systems by Eswaran et al. [15] and given its current name, the "transaction" The transaction basically reflects the idea that the activities of a particular user are isolated from all concurrent activities, but restricts the degree of isolation and the length of a transaction Typically, a transaction is a short sequence of interactions with the database, using operators such as FIND a record or MODIFY an item, which represents one meaningful activity in the user's environment. The standard example that is generally used to explain the idea is the transfer of money from one account to another. The corresponding transaction program is given in Figure 3.1

The concept of a transaction, which includes all database interactions between BT and CT in the preceding example, requires that all of its actions be executed *indivisibly*: Either all actions are properly reflected in the database or nothing has happened. No changes are reflected in the database if at any point in time before reaching the CT, the user enters the $ERROR$ clause containing the RT. To achieve this kind of indivisibility, a transaction must have four properties:

Atomicity. It must be of the all-or-nothing type described before, and the user must, whatever happens, know which state he or she is in.

Consistency. A transaction reaching its normal end (EOT, end of transaction), thereby committing its results, preserves the consistency of the database. In other words, each successful transaction by definition commits only legal results. This condition is necessary for the fourth property, durability.

Funds-Transfer: Procedure;
   Begin-Transaction (BT);
      On error DO; {in case of error}
         Restore-Transaction (RT); {undo all work}
         Get Input message; {require input}
         Put message (`Transfer failed`*'); {report failure}*
         Go to Commit;
      End;
      Get Input message; {get and parse input}
      Extract Account-Debit, Account-Credit, Amount from message;
      Update Accounts {do debit}
         Set Balance = Balance - Amount where
                        Accounts.Number = Account - Debit;
      Update Accounts {do credit}
         Set Balance = Balance + Amount where
                        Account.Number = Account - Credit;
      Insert into History <Date, Message>; {keep audit trail}
      Put message (`Transfer done`*'); {report success}*
      Commit: {commit updates}
   Commit-Transaction (CT)
End; {end program}

Figure 3.1. Example of a transaction program [17].

```
BEGIN        BEGIN        BEGIN
READ         READ         READ
WRITE        WRITE        WRITE
READ         READ         READ
  .            .            .

  .            .            .
WRITE        ABORT        ⇐══ SYSTEM ABORTS TRANSACTIONS
COMMIT
```

Figure 3.2. The three possible outcomes of a transaction [17].

Isolation. Events within a transaction must be hidden from other transactions running concurrently. If this were not the case, a transaction could not be reset to its beginning for the reasons sketched earlier. The techniques that achieve isolation are known as synchronization, and since Gray et al. [18] there have been numerous contributions to this topic of database research [23].

Durability. Once a transaction has been completed and has committed its results to the database, the system must guarantee that these results survive any subsequent malfunctions. Since there is no sphere of control constituting a set of transactions, the database management system (DBMS) has no control beyond transaction boundaries. Therefore, the user must have a guarantee that the things the system says have happened have actually happened. Since, by definition, each transaction is correct, the effects of an inevitable incorrect transaction (i.e., the transaction containing faulty data) can only be removed by countertransactions.

These four properties, atomicity, consistency, isolation, and durability (*ACID*), describe the major highlights of the transaction paradigm, which has influenced many aspects of development in database systems. We therefore consider the question of whether the transaction is supported by a particular system to be the ACID test of the system's quality.

In summary, a transaction can terminate in the three ways illustrated in Figure 3.2. It is hoped that the transaction will reach its commit point, yielding the all case (as in the all-or-nothing dichotomy). Sometimes the transaction detects bad input or other violations of consistency, preventing a normal termination, in which case it will reset all that it has done (abort). Finally, a transaction may run into a problem that can only be detected by the system, such as a timeout or deadlock, in which case its effects are aborted by the DBMS.

In addition to the preceding events occurring during normal execution, a transaction can also be affected by a system crash. This is discussed in the next section

3.2.2   Which Failures Have to Be Anticipated

In order to design and implement a recovery component, one must know precisely which types of failures are to be considered, how often they will occur, how much time is expected for recovery, and so on One must also make assumptions about the reliability of the underlying hardware and storage media, and about dependencies between different failure modes. However, the list of anticipated failures will never be complete for these reasons:

- For each set of failures that one can think of, there is at least one that was forgotten.

- Some failures are extremely rare. The cost of redundancy needed to cope with them may be so high that it may be a sensible design decision to exclude these failures from consideration If one of them does occur, however, the system will not be able to recover from the situation automatically, and the database will be corrupted. The techniques for handling this catastrophe are beyond the scope of this paper.

We shall consider the following types of failure.

Transaction Failure.   The transaction of failure has already been mentioned in the previous section For various reasons, the transaction program does not reach its normal commit and has to be reset back to its beginning, either at its own request or on behalf of the DBMS. Gray indicates that percent of all transactions terminate abnormally, but this rate is not likely to be a constant [17]. From our own experiences with different application databases, and from Gray's result [13, 17], we can conclude that

- Within one application, the ratio of transactions that abort themselves is rather constant, depending only on the amount of incorrect input data, the quality of consistency checking performed by the transaction program, and so on

- The ratio of transactions being aborted by the DBMS, especially those caused by deadlocks, depends to a great extent on the degree of parallelism, the granularity of locking used by the DBMS, the logical schema (there may be hot spot data, or data that are very frequently referenced by many concurrent transactions), and the degree of interference between concurrent activities (which is, in turn, very application-dependent).

For our classification, it is sufficient to say that transaction failures occur 10 to100 times per minute, and that recovery from these failures must take place within the time required by the transaction for its regular execution

System Failure.   The system failures that we are considering can be caused by a bug in the DBMS code, an operating system fault, or a hardware failure. In each of these cases, processing is terminated in an uncontrolled manner, and we assume that the contents of main memory are lost. Since database-related secondary (nonvolatile) storage remains unaffected, we require that a recovery take place in the same amount of time that would have been required for the execution of all interrupted transactions. If one transaction is executed within the order of 10 milliseconds to 1 second, the recovery should take no more than a few minutes. A system failure is assumed to occur several times a week, depending on the stability of both the DBMS and its operational environment.

Media Failure.   Besides these more or less normal failures, we have to anticipate the loss of some or all of the secondary storage holding the database. There are several causes for such a problem, the most common of which are

- bugs in the operating system routines for writing the disk

- hardware errors in the channel or disk controller

- head crash

- loss of information due to magnetic decay

Such a situation can only be overcome by full redundancy, that is, by a copy of the database and an audit trail covering what has happened since then. Magnetic storage devices are usually very reliable, and recovery from a media failure is not likely to happen more often than *once* or *twice* a year. Depending on the size of a database, the media used for storing the copy, and the age of the copy, recovery of this type will take on the order of 1 hour.

3.2.3   Summary of Recovery Actions

As we mentioned in Section 3.2.1, the notion of consistency that we use for defining the targets of recovery is tied to the transaction paradigm, which we have encapsulated in the "ACID principle." According to this definition, a database is consistent *if and only if* it contains the results of successful transactions. Such a state will hereafter be called *transaction consistent* or *logically consistent*. A transaction, in turn, must not see anything but effects of complete transactions (i.e., a consistent database in those parts that it uses), and will then, by definition, create a consistent update of the database. What does that mean for the recovery component?

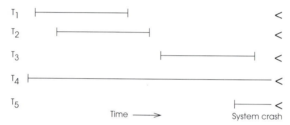

Figure 3.3. Scenario for discussing transaction-oriented recovery [17].

Let us for the moment ignore transactions being aborted during normal execution and consider only a system failure (a crash). We might then encounter the situation depicted in Figure 3.3. Transactions T_1, T_2, and T_3 have committed before the crash, and therefore will survive. Recovery after a system failure must ensure that the effects of all successful transactions are actually reflected in the database. But what is to be done with T_4 and T_5? Transactions have been defined to be atomic; they either succeed or disappear as though they had never been entered. There is therefore no choice about what to do after a system failure; the effects of all incomplete transactions must be removed from the database. Clearly, a recovery component adhering to these principles will produce a transaction-consistent database. Since all successful transactions have contributed to the database state, it will be the most recent transaction-consistent state. We now can distinguish four recovery actions coping with different situations [16]:

Transaction UNDO.   If a transaction aborts itself or must be aborted by the system during normal execution, this will be called "transaction $UNDO$." By definition, UNDO removes all effects of this transaction from the database and does not influence any other transaction

Global UNDO.   When recovering from a system failure, the effects of all incomplete transactions have to be rolled back.

Partial REDO.   When recovering from a system failure, since execution has been terminated in an uncontrolled manner, results of complete transactions may not yet be reflected in the database. Hence, they must be repeated, if necessary, by the recovery component.

Global REDO.   Gray calls this recovery action "archive recovery" [17]. The database is assumed to be physically destroyed; we therefore must start from a copy that reflects the state of the database some days, weeks, or months ago. Since transactions are typically short, we need not consider incomplete transactions over such a long time. Rather we have to supplement the copy with the effects of all transactions that have committed since the copy was created.

With these definitions, we have introduced the transaction as the *only unit of recovery* in a database system. This is an ideal condition that does not exactly match reality. For example, transactions might be nested, that is, composed of smaller subtransactions. These subtransactions also are atomic, consistent, and isolated—but they are not durable. Since the results of subtransactions are removed whenever the enclosing transaction is undone, durability can only be guaranteed for the highest transaction in the composition hierarchy. A two-level nesting of transactions can be found in System R, in which an arbitrary number of save points can be generated inside a transaction [17]. The database and the processing state can be reset to any of these savepoints by the application program. Another extension of the transaction concept is necessary in fields like CAD. Here the units of consistent state transitions, that is, the design steps, are so long (days or weeks) that it is not feasible to treat them as indivisible actions. Hence, these *long* transactions are consistent, isolated, and durable, but they are not atomic [17]. It is sufficient for the purpose of our taxonomy to consider "ideal" transactions only.

3.3   THE MAPPING HIERARCHY OF A DBMS

There are numerous techniques and algorithms for implementing database recovery, many of which have been described in detail by Verhofstadt [38]. We want to reduce these various methods to a small set of basic concepts, allowing a simple, yet precise classification of all reasonable implementation techniques; for the purposes of illustration, we need a basic model of the DBMS architecture and its hardware environment. This model, although it contains many familiar terms from systems like INGRES, SystemR, or those of the CODASYL [8, 7] type, is in fact a rudimentary database architecture that can also be applied to unconventional approaches like CASSM or DIRECT [32], although this is not our purpose here.

3.3.1   The Mapping Process: Objects and Operations

The model shown in Table 3.1 describes the major steps of dynamic abstraction from the level of physical storage up to the user interface. At the bottom, the database consists of some billions of bits stored on disk, which are interpreted by the DBMS into meaningful information on which the user can operate. With each level of abstraction (proceeding from the bottom up), the objects become more complex, allowing more powerful operations and being constrained by a larger number of integrity rules. The uppermost interface supports one of the well-known data models, whether relational, networklike, or hierarchical.

Table 3.1. Description of the DB-Mapping Hierarchy

Level of abstraction	Objects	Auxiliary mapping data
Nonprocedural or algebraic access	Relations, views tuples	Logical schema description
Record-oriented, navigational access	Records, sets, hierarchies, networks	Logical and physical schema description
Record and access path management	Physical records, access paths	Free-space tables, DB-key translation tables
Propagation control	Segments, pages	Page tables, Bloom filters
File management	Files, blocks	Directories, VTOCs, and so on

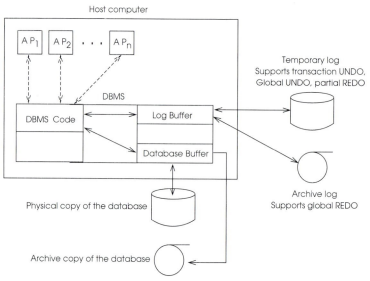

Figure 3.4. Scenario for discussing transaction-oriented recovery [17].

Note that this mapping hierarchy is virtually contained in each DBMS, although for performance reasons, it will hardly be reflected in the module structure. We shall briefly sketch the characteristics of each layer, with enough detail to establish our taxonomy. For a more complete description, see Haerder and Reuter [20].

File Management.   The lowest layer operates directly on the bit patterns stored on some nonvolatile, direct access device like a disk, drum, or even magnetic bubble memory. This layer copes with the physical characteristics of each storage type and abstracts these characteristics into fixed-length blocks. These blocks can be read, written, and identified by a (relative) block number. This kind of abstraction is usually done by the data management system (DMS) of a normal general-purpose operating system.

Propagation Control.[1]   This level is not usually considered separately in the current database literature, but for reasons that will become clear in the following sections we strictly distinguish between *pages* and *blocks*. A page is a fixed-length partition of a linear address space and is mapped into a physical block by the propagation control layer. Therefore, a page can be stored in different blocks during its lifetime in the database, depending on the strategy implemented for propagation control.

Access Path Management.   This layer implements mapping functions much more complicated than those performed by subordinate layers. It has to maintain all physical object representations in the database (records, fields, and so on), and their related access paths (pointers, hash tables, search trees, and so on) in a *potentially unlimited* linear virtual address space. This address space, which is divided into fixed-length pages, is provided by the upper interface of the supporting layer. For performance reasons, the partitioning of data into pages is still visible on this level.

Navigational Access Layer.   At the top of this layer, we find the operations and objects that are typical for a procedural data manipulation language (DML). Occurrences of record types and members of sets are handled by statements like STORE, MODIFY, FIND NEXT, and CONNECT [7]. At this interface, the user navigates one record at a time through a hierarchy, through a network, or along logical access paths.

Nonprocedural Access Layer.   This level provides a nonprocedural interface to the database. With each operation, the user can handle sets of results rather than single records. A relational model with high-level query languages like SQL or QUEL is a convenient example of the abstraction achieved by the top layer [4, 34].

On each level, the mapping of higher objects to more elementary ones requires additional data structures, some of which are shown in Table 3.1.

3.3.2   The Storage Hierarchy: Implementation Environment

Both the number of redundant data required to support the recovery actions described in Section 3.2 and the methods of collecting such data are strongly influenced by various properties of the different storage media used by the DBMS. In particular, the dependencies between volatile and permanent storage have a strong impact

---

[1]This term is introduced in Section 3.3.4; its meaning is not essential to the understanding of this paragraph.

on algorithms for gathering redundant information and implementing recovery measures [6]. As a descriptional framework, we shall use a storage hierarchy, as shown in Figure 3.4. It closely resembles the situation that must be dealt with by most of today's commercial database systems. The host computer, where the application programs and DBMS are located, has a main memory, which is usually volatile.[2] Hence, we assume that the contents of the database buffer, as well as the contents of the output buffers to the log files, are lost whenever the DBMS terminates abnormally. Below the volatile main memory, there is a two-level hierarchy of permanent copies of the database. One level contains an on-line version of the database in direct access memory; the other contains an archive copy as a provision against loss of the on-line copy. Although both are functionally situated on the same level, the on-line copy is almost always up to date, whereas the archive copy can contain an old state of the database. Our main concern here is database recovery, which, like all provisions for fault tolerance, is based on redundancy. We have mentioned one type of redundancy: the archive copy, kept as a starting point for reconstruction of an up-to-date on-line version of the database (global $REDO$). This is discussed in more detail in Section 4. To support this, and other recovery actions introduced in Section 1, two types of log files are required:

Temporary Log. The information collected in this file supports crash recovery; that is, it contains information needed to reconstruct the most recent database (DB) buffer. Selective transaction $UNDO$ requires random access to the log records. Therefore, we assume that the temporary log is located on disk.

Archive Log. This file supports global $REDO$ after a media failure. It depends on the availability of the archive copy and must contain all changes committed to the database after the state reflected in the archive copy. Since the archive log is always processed in sequential order, we assume that the archive log is written on magnetic tape.

3.3.3   Different Views of a Database

In Section 3.3.1, we indicated that the database looks different at each level of abstraction, with each level using different objects and interfaces. But this is not what mean by "different views of a database" in this section We have observed that the process of abstraction really begins at Level 3, up to which there is only a more convenient representation of data in external storage. At this level, abstraction is dependent on which pages actually establish the linear address space, that is, which block is read when a certain page is referenced. In the event of a failure, there are different possibilities for retrieving the contents of a page. These possibilities are denoted by different views of the database:

---

[2]In some real-time applications, main memory is supported by a battery backup. It is possible that in the future mainframes will have some stable buffer storage. However, we are not considering these conditions here.

The *current database* comprises all objects accessible to the DBMS during normal processing. The current contents of all pages can be found on disk, except for those pages that have been recently modified. Their new contents are found in the DB buffer. The mapping hierarchy is completely correct.

The *materialized database* is the state that the DBMS finds at restart after a crash without having applied any log information There is no buffer. Hence, some page modifications (even of successful transactions) may not be reflected in the on-line copy. It is also possible that a new state of a page has been written to disk, but the control structure that maps pages to blocks has not yet been updated. In this case, a reference to such a page will yield the old value. This view of the database is what the recovery system has to transform into the most recent logically consistent current database.

The *physical database* is composed of all blocks of the on-line copy containing page images–current or obsolete. Depending on the strategy used on Level 2, there may be different values for one page in the physical database, none of which is necessarily the current contents. This view is not normally used by recovery procedures, but a salvation program would try to exploit all information contained therein.

With these views of a database, we can distinguish three types of updates all of which explain the mapping function provided by the propagation control level. First, we have the *modification of page contents* caused by some higher-level module. This operation takes place in the DB buffer and therefore affects only the current database. Second, there is the write operation, transferring a modified page to a block on disk. In general, this affects only the physical database. If the information about the block containing the new page value is stored in volatile memory, the new contents will not be accessible after a crash; that is, it is not yet part of the materialized database. The operation that makes a previously written page image part of the materialized database is called *propagation*. This operation writes the updated control structures for mapping pages to blocks in a safe, nonvolatile place, so that they are available after a crash.

If pages are always written to the same block (the so-called "update-in-place" operation, which is done in most commercial DBMS), writing implicitly is the equivalent of propagation However, there is an important difference between these operations if a page can be stored in different blocks. This is explained in the next section

3.3.4 Mapping Concepts for Updates

In this section, we define a number of concepts related to the operation of mapping changes in a database from volatile to nonvolatile storage. They are directly related to the views of a database introduced previously. The key issue is that each modification of a page (which changes the current database) takes place in the database buffer and is allocated to *volatile* storage. In order to save this state, the corresponding page must be brought to nonvolatile storage, that is, to the physical database. Two different schemes for accomplishing this can be applied, as shown in

Figure 3.5.

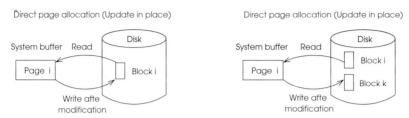

Figure 3.5. Page allocation principles.

With *direct page allocation*, each page of a segment is related to exactly one block of the corresponding file. Each output of a modified page causes an update in place. By using an *indirect page allocation* scheme, each output is directed to a new block, leaving the old contents of the page unchanged. It provides the option of holding n successive versions of a page. The moment when a younger version definitively replaces an older one can be determined by appropriate (consistency-related) criteria; it is no longer bound to the moment of writing. This update scheme has some very attractive properties in case of recovery, as is shown later on Direct page allocation leaves no choice as to when to make a new version part of the materialized database; the output operation destroys the previous image. Hence, in this case, writing and propagating coincide.

There is still another important difference between direct and indirect page allocation schemes, which can be characterized as follows:

- In *direct* page allocation, each single propagation (physical write) is inter- ruptable by a system crash, thus leaving the materialized, and possibly the physical, database in an inconsistent state.

- In *indirect* page allocation, there is always a way back to the old state. Hence, propagation of an arbitrary set of pages can be made uninterruptable by system crashes. References to such algorithms will be given.

On the basis of this observation, we can distinguish two types of propagation strategies:

ATOMIC.   Any set of modified pages can be propagated as a unit, such that either all or none of the updates becomes part of the materialized database.

$\neg ATOMIC$.   Pages are written to blocks according to an update-in-place policy. Since no set of pages can be written indivisibly (even a single write may be inter- rupted somewhere in between), propagation is vulnerable to system crashes.

Of course, many details have been omitted from Figure 3.5. In particular, there is no hint of the techniques used to make propagation take place atomically in case of indirect page mapping. We have tried to illustrate aspects of this issue in Figure 3.6. The figure contains a comparison of the current and the materialized database

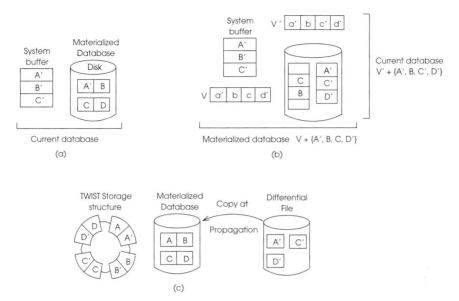

Figure 3.6. Current versus materialized database in (a) $\neg ATOMIC$ and (b and c) $ATOMIC$ propagation

for the update-in-place scheme and three different implementations of indirect page mapping allowing for $ATOMIC$ propagation Figure 3.6(b) refers to the well-known shadow page mechanism [26]. The mapping of page numbers to block numbers is done by using page tables. These tables have one entry per page containing the block number where the page contents are stored. The *shadow pages*, accessed via the shadow page table V, preserve the old state of the materialized database. The current version is defined by the current page table V'. Before this state is made stable (propagated), all changed pages are written to their new blocks, and so is the current page table. If this fails, the database will come up in its old state. When all pages have been written related to the new state, $ATOMIC$ propagation takes place by changing one record on disk (which now points to V' rather than V) in a way that cannot be confused by a system crash. Thus, the problem of indivisibly propagating a set of pages has been reduced to safely updating one record, which can be done in a simple way. For details, see [26].

There are other implementations for $ATOMIC$ propagation One is based on maintaining two recent versions of a page. For each page access, both versions have to be read into the buffer. This can be done with minimal overhead by storing them in adjacent disk blocks and reading them with chained I/O. The latest version, recognized by a time stamp, is kept in the buffer; the other one is immediately discarded. A modified page replaces the older version on disk. $ATOMIC$ propagation is accomplished by incrementing a special counter that is related to the time stamps in the pages. Details can be found in [27]. Another approach to $ATOMIC$

propagation has been introduced under the name "differential files" by Severance and Lohman [31]. Modified pages are written to a separate (differential) file. Propagating these updates to the main database is not $ATOMIC$ in itself, but once all modifications are written to the differential file, propagation can be repeated as often as wished. In other words, the process of copying modified pages into the materialized database can be made to appear $ATOMIC$. A variant of this technique, the "intention list," is described by Lampson and Sturgis [24] and Sturgis et al. [35]. Thus far, we have shown that arbitrary sets of pages can be propagated in an $ATOMIC$ manner using indirect page allocation In the next section, we discuss how these sets of pages for propagation should be defined.

3.4 CRASH RECOVERY

In order to illustrate the consequences of the concepts introduced thus far, we shall present a detailed discussion of crash recovery. First, we consider the state in which a database is left when the system terminates abnormally. From this, we derive the type of redundant (log) information required to reestablish a transaction-consistent state, which is the overall purpose of DB recovery. After completing our classification scheme, we give examples of recovery techniques in currently available database systems. Finally, we present a table containing a qualitative evaluation of all instances encompassed by our taxonomy (Table 3.4).

Note that the results in this section also apply to transaction $UNDO$–a much simpler case of global $UNDO$, which applies when the DBMS is processing normally and no information is lost.

3.4.1 State of the Database after a Crash

After a crash, the DBMS has to restart by applying all the necessary recovery actions described in Section 3.2. The DB buffer is lost, as is the *current database*, the only view of the database to contain the most recent state of processing. Assuming that the on-line copy of the database is intact, there are the *materialized database* and the *temporary log file* from which to start recovery. We have not discussed the contents of the log files for the reason that the type and number of log data to be written during normal processing are dependent on the state of the materialized database after a crash. This state, in turn, depends on which method of page allocation and propagation is used.

In the case of direct page allocation and $\neg ATOMIC$ propagation, each write operation affects the materialized database. The decision to write pages is made by the *buffer manager* according to buffer capacity at points in time that appear arbitrary. Hence, the state of the materialized database after a crash is unpredictable: When recent modifications are reflected in the materialized database, it is not possible (without further provisions) to know which pages were modified by complete transactions (whose contents must be reconstructed by partial $REDO$) and which pages were modified by incomplete transactions (whose contents must be returned to their previous state by global $UNDO$). Further possibilities for providing against this situation are briefly discussed in Section 3.2.1.

In the case of indirect page allocation and $ATOMIC$ propagation, we know much more about the state of the materialized database after crash. $ATOMIC$ propagation is indivisible by any type of failure, and therefore we find the materialized database to be exactly in the state produced by the most recent successful propagation This state may still be inconsistent in that not all updates of complete transactions are visible, and some effects of incomplete transactions are. However, $ATOMIC$ propagation ensures that a set of related pages is propagated in a safe manner by restricting propagation to points in time when the current database fulfills certain consistency constraints. When these constraints are satisfied, the updates can be mapped to the materialized database all at once. Since the current database is consistent in terms of the access path management level where propagation occurs, this also ensures that all internal pointers, tree structures, tables, and so on, are correct. Later, we also discuss schemes that allow for transaction-consistent propagation

The state of the materialized database after a crash can be summarized as follows:

$\neg ATOMIC$ **Propagation.**   Nothing is known about the state of the materialized database; it must be characterized as "chaotic."

$ATOMIC$ **Propagation.**   The materialized database is in the state produced by the most recent propagation Since this is bound by certain consistency constraints, the materialized database will be consistent (but not necessarily up to date) at least up to the third level of the mapping hierarchy.

In the case of $\neg ATOMIC$ propagation, one cannot expect to read valid images for all pages from the materialized database after a crash; it is inconsistent on the propagation level, and all abstractions on higher levels will fail. In the case of $ATOMIC$ propagation, the materialized database is consistent at least on Level 3, thus allowing for the execution of operations on Level 4 (DML statements).

3.4.2   Types of Log Information to Support Recovery Actions

The temporary log file must contain all the information required to transform the materialized database "as found" into the most recent transaction-consistent state (see Section 3.2). As we have shown, the materialized database can be in more or less defined states, may or may not fulfill consistency constraints, and so on. Hence, the number of log data will be determined by what is contained in the materialized database at the beginning of restart. We can be fairly certain of the contents of the materialized database in the case of $ATOMIC$ propagation, but the result of $\neg ATOMIC$ schemes have been shown to be unpredictable. There are, however, additional measures to somewhat reduce the degree of uncertainty resulting from $\neg ATOMIC$ propagation, as discussed in the following section

Dependencies between the Buffer Manager and the Recovery Component

Buffer Management and $UNDO$ **Recovery Actions.**   During the normal mode of operation, modified pages are written to disk by some replacement algorithm managing the database buffer. Ideally, this happens at points in time determined solely by buffer occupation and, from a consistency perspective, seem to be arbitrary. In general, even dirty data, that is, pages modified by incomplete transactions, may be written to the physical database. Hence, the $UNDO$ operations described earlier will have to recover the contents of both the materialized database and the external storage media. The only way to avoid this requires that the buffer manager be modified to prevent it from writing or propagating dirty pages under all circumstances. In this case, $UNDO$ could be considerably simplified:

- If no dirty pages are propagated, global $UNDO$ becomes virtually unnecessary that is, if there are no dirty data in the materialized database.

- If no dirty pages are written, transaction $UNDO$ can be limited to main storage (buffer) operations.

The major disadvantage of this idea is that very large database buffers would be required (e.g., for long batch-update transactions), making it generally incompatible with existing systems. However, the two different methods of handling modified pages introduced with this idea have important implications with $UNDO$ recovery. We shall refer to these methods as:

$STEAL$. Modified pages may be written and/or propagated at any time.

$\neg STEAL$. Modified pages are kept in buffer at least until the end of the transaction (EOT).

The definition of $STEAL$ can be based on either writing or propagating, which are not discriminated in $\neg ATOMIC$ schemes. In the case of $ATOMIC$ propagation both variants of $STEAL$ are conceivable, and each would have a different impact on $UNDO$ recovery actions; in the case of $\neg STEAL$, no logging is required for $UNDO$ purposes.

Buffer Management and $REDO$ **Recovery Actions.**   As soon as a transaction commits, all of its results must survive any subsequent failure (*durability*). Committed updates that have not been propagated to the materialized database would definitely be lost in case of a system crash, and so there must be enough redundant information in the log file to reconstruct these results during restart (partial $REDO$). It is conceivable, however to avoid this kind of recovery by the following technique. During Phase 1 of EOT processing, all pages modified by this transaction are propagated to the materialized database; that is, their writing and propagation are enforced. Then we can be sure that either the transaction is complete, which means that all of its results are safely recorded (no partial $REDO$), or in case of a crash, some updates are not yet written, which means that the transaction is not successful and must be rolled back (UNDO recovery actions). Thus, we have another criterion concerning buffer handling, which is related to the necessity of $REDO$ recovery during restart:

$FORCE$. All modified pages are written and propagated during EOT processing.

$\neg FORCE$. No propagation is triggered during EOT processing.

The implications with regard to the gathering of log data are quite straight-forward in the case of $FORCE$. No logging is required for partial $REDO$; in the case of $\neg FORCE$ such information is required. Although FORCE avoids partial $REDO$, there must still be some $REDO$-log information for global $REDO$ to provide against loss of the on-line copy of the database.

3.4.3   Classification of Log Data

Depending on which of the write and propagation schemes introduced before are being implemented, we will have to collect log information for the purpose of

- removing invalid data (modifications effected by incomplete transactions) from the materialized database

- supplementing the materialized database with updates of complete transactions that were not contained in it at the time of crash

In this section, we briefly describe what such log data can look like and when such data are applicable to the crash state of the materialized database.

Table 3.2. Classification Scheme for Log Data

	State	**Transition**
Logical	- - -	Actions (DML statements)
Physical	Before images, After images	EXOR differences

Log data are redundant information, collected for the sole purpose of recovery from a crash or a media failure. They do not undergo the mapping process of the database objects, but are obtained on a certain level of the mapping hierarchy and written directly to nonvolatile storage, that is, the log files. There are two different, albeit not fully orthogonal, criteria for classifying log data. The first is concerned with the type of objects to be logged. If some part of the physical representation, that is, the bit pattern, is written to the log, we refer to it as *physical logging*; if the operators and their arguments are recorded on a higher level, this is called *logical logging*. The second criterion concerns whether the state of the database–before or after a change–or the transition causing the change is to be logged. Table 3.2 contains some examples for these different types of logging, which are explained what follows.

Physical State Logging on the Page Level.   The most basic method, which is still applied in many commercial DBMSs, uses the page as the unit of log information Each time a part of the linear address space is changed by some modification, insertion, and so on, the whole page containing this part of the linear address space is written to the log. If $UNDO$ logging is required, this will be done before the change takes place, yielding the so-called *before image*. For $REDO$ purposes, the resulting page state is recorded as an *after image*.

Physical Transition Logging on Page Level.   This logging technique is based also on pages. However, it does not explicitly record the old and new states of a page; rather it writes the *difference between them* to the log. The function used for computing the "difference" between two bit strings is the exclusive-OR, which is both commutative and associative as required by the recovery algorithm. If this difference is applied to the old state of a page, again using the exclusive-or, the new state will result. On the other hand, applying it to the new state will yield the old state. There are some problems in the details of this approach, but these are beyond the scope of this chapter.

The two methods of page logging that we have discussed can be compared as follows:

- Transition logging requires only one log entry (the difference), whereas state logging uses both a before image and an after image. If there are multiple changes applied to the same page during one transaction, transition logging can express these either by successive differences or by one accumulated difference. With state logging, the first before image and the last after image are required.

- Since there are usually only a small number of data inside a page affected by a change, the exclusive-OR difference will contain long strings of 0's, which can be removed by well-known compression techniques. Hence, transition logging can potentially require much less space than does state logging.

Physical State Logging on Access Path Level.   Physical logging can also be applied to the objects of the access path level, namely, physical records, access path structures, tables, and so on. The log component has to be aware of these storage structures and record only the changed entry, rather than blindly logging the whole page around it. The advantage of this requirement is obvious: By logging only the physical objects actually being changed, space requirements for log files can be drastically reduced. One can save even more space by exploiting the fact that most access path structures consist of fully redundant information For example, one can completely reconstruct a $B^* - tree$ from the record occurrences to which it refers. In itself, this type of reconstruction is certainly too expensive to become a standard method for crash recovery. But if only the modifications in the records are logged, after a crash, the corresponding $B^* - tree$ can be recovered consistently, provided that an appropriate write discipline has been observed for the pages containing the tree. This principle, stating that changed nodes must be written bottom up, is a special case of the "careful replacement" technique explained in detail by Verhofstadt [38]. For our taxonomy, it makes no difference whether the principle is applied or not.

Transition Logging on the Access Path Level. On the access path level, we are dealing with the entries of storage structures, but do not know how they are related to each other with regard to the objects of the database schema. This type of information is maintained on higher levels of the mapping hierarchy. If we look only at the physical entry representation (*physical* transition logging), state transition on this level means that a physical record, a table entry, and so on, is *added* to, *deleted* from, or modified in a page. The arguments pertaining to these operations are the entries themselves, and so there is little difference between this and the previous approach. In the case of physical state logging on the access path level, we placed the physical address together with the entry representation Here we place the operation code and object identifier with the same type of argument. Thus, physical transition logging on this level does not provide anything essentially different.

We can also consider logical transition logging, attempting to exploit the syntax of the storage structures implemented on this level. The logical addition, a new record occurrence, for example, would include all the redundant table updates such as the record ID index, the free space table, and so on, each of which was explicitly logged with the physical schemes. Hence, we again have a potential saving of log space. However, it is important to note that the logical transitions on this level generally affect *more than one page*. If they (or their inverse operators for $UNDO$) are to be applied during recovery, we must be sure that all affected pages have the same state in the materialized database. This is not the case with direct page allocation, and using the more expensive indirect schemes cannot be justified by the comparatively few benefits yielded by logical transition logging on the access path level. Hence, logical transition logging on this level can generally be ruled out, but will become more attractive on the next higher level.

Logical Logging on the Record-Oriented Level. At one level higher, it is possible to express the changes performed by the transaction program in a very compact manner by simply recording the update DML statements with their parameters. Even if a nonprocedural query language is being used above this level, its updates will be decomposed into updates of single records or tuples equivalent to the single record updates of procedural DB languages. Thus, logging on this level means that only the $INSERT$, $UPDATE$, and $DELETE$ operations, together with their record IDs and attribute values, are written to the log. The mapping process discerns which entries are affected, which pages must be modified, and so on. Thus recovery is achieved by reexecuting some of the previously processed DML statements. For

UNDO recovery, of course, the inverse DML statement must be executed, that is, a *DELETE* to compensate an *INSERT* and vice versa, and an *UPDATE* returned to the original values. These inverse DML statements must be generated automatically as part of the regular logging activity, and for this reason, this approach is not viable for network oriented DBMSs with information-bearing interrecord relations. In such cases, it can be extremely expensive to determine, for example, the inverse for a *DELETE*. Details can be found in [29].

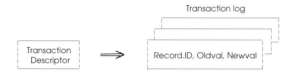

Figure 3.7. Logical transaction logging as implemented in System R [17].

System R is a good example of a system with logical logging on the record-oriented level. All update operations performed on the tuples are represented by one generalized modification operator, which is not explicitly recorded. This operator changes a tuple identified by its tuple identifier (TID) from an old value to a new one, both of which are recorded. Inserting a tuple entails modifying its initial null value to the given value, and deleting a tuple entails the inverse transition. Hence the log contains the information shown in Figure 3.7.

Logical transition logging obviously requires a materialized database that is consistent up to Level 3; that is, it can only be combined with *ATOMIC* propagation schemes. Although the number of log data written is very small, recovery will be more expensive than that in other schemes, because it involves the reprocessing of some DML statements, although this can be done more cheaply than the original processing.

Table 3.3. Qualitative Comparison of Various Logging Techniques

Logical technique	Level number	Expenses during normal processing	Expenses for recovery operations
Physical state	2	High	Low
Physical transition	2	Medium	low
Physical state	3	Low	low
Logical transition	4	Very low	Medium

Table 3.3 is a summation of the properties of all logging techniques that we have described under two considerations: What is the cost of collecting the log data during normal processing? How expensive is recovery based on the respective

type of log information? Of course, the entries in the table are only very rough qualitative estimations; for more detailed quantitative analysis see [28].

Writing log information, no matter what type, is determined by two rules:

- $UNDO$ information must be written to the log file *before* the corresponding updates are propagated to the materialized database. This has come to be known as the *write-ahead-log (WAL)* principle [16].

- $REDO$ information must be written to the temporary and the archive log file *before* EOT is acknowledged to the transaction program. Once this is done, the system must be able to ensure the transaction's durability.

We return to different facets of these rules in Section 3.4.

3.4.4   Examples of Recovery Techniques

Optimization of Recovery Actions by Checkpoints

An appropriate combination of redundancy provided by log protocols and mapping techniques is basically all that we need for implementing transaction-oriented database recovery, as described in Section 3.2. In real systems, however, there are a number of important refinements that reduce the amount of log data required and the costs of crash recovery. Figure 3.8 is a very general example of crash recovery. In the center, there is the temporary log containing $UNDO$ and $REDO$ information and special entries notifying the begin and end of a transaction (BOT and EOT, respectively). Below the temporary log, the transaction history preceding the crash is shown, and above it, recovery processing for global $UNDO$ and partial $REDO$ is related to the log entries. We have not assumed a specific propagation strategy. There are two questions concerning the costs of crash recovery:

- In the case of the materialized DB being modified by incomplete transactions, to what extent does the log have to be processed for $UNDO$ recovery?

- If the DBMS does not use a FORCE discipline, which part of the log has to processed for REDO recovery?

The first question can be easily answered: If we know that updates of incomplete transactions can have affected the materialized database (STEAL), we must scan the temporary log file back to the BOT entry of the oldest incomplete transaction to be sure that no invalid data are left in the system. The second question is not as simple. In Figure 3.8, $REDO$ is started at a point that seems to be chosen arbitrarily. Why is there no $REDO$ recovery for object A? In general, we can assume that in the case of a FORCE discipline, modified pages will be written eventually because of buffer replacement. One might expect that only the contents of the most recently changed pages have to be redone–if the change was caused by a complete transaction But look at a buffer activity record shown in Figure 3.9.

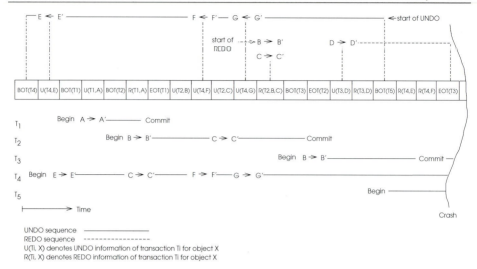

Figure 3.8. A crash recovery scenario.

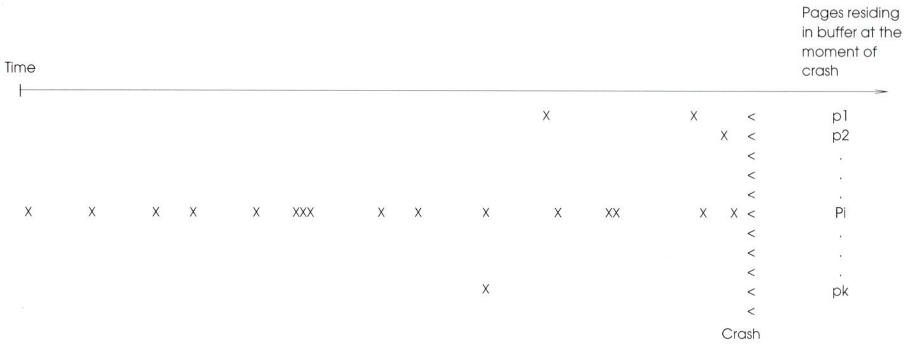

Figure 3.9. Age of buffer page modificaitons (× indicates a modification).

The situation depicted in Figure 3.9 is typical of many large database applications. Most of the modified pages will have been changed "recently," but there are a few hot spots like pages that are modified again and again, and, since they are referenced so frequently, have not been written from the buffer. After a while, such pages will contain the updates of many complete transactions, and *REDO* recovery will therefore have to go back very far on the temporary log. This makes restart expensive. In general, the amount of log data to be processed for partial *REDO* will increase with the interval of time between two subsequent crashes. In other words, the higher the availability of the system, the more costly recovery will become. This is unacceptable for large, demanding applications. For this reason, additional measures are required for making restart costs independent of mean time between failure. Such provisions will be called checkpoints, and are defined as follows. Generating a checkpoint means collecting information in a safe place, which has the effect of defining and limiting the amount of $REDO$ recovery required after a crash. Whether this information is stored in the log or elsewhere depends on which implementation technique is chosen; we give some examples in this section Checkpoint generation involves three steps [16]:

- Write a BEGIN_CHECKPOINT record to the temporary log file.

- Write all checkpoint data to the log file and/or the database.

- Write an END_CHECKPOINT record to the temporary log file.

During restart, the BEGIN-END bracket is a clear indication as to whether a checkpoint was generated completely or interrupted by a system crash. Sometimes checkpointing is considered to be a means for restoring the whole database to some previous state. Our view, however, focuses on transaction recovery. Therefore, to us, a checkpoint is a technique for optimizing crash recovery rather than a definition of a distinguished state for recovery itself. In order to effectively constrain partial $REDO$, checkpoints must be generated at well-defined points in time. In the following sections, we shall introduce four separate criteria for determining when to start checkpoint activities.

Transaction-Oriented Checkpoints

As previously explained, a FORCE discipline will avoid partial $REDO$. All modified pages are propagated before an EOT record is written to the log, which makes the transaction durable. If this record is not found in the log after a crash, the transaction will be considered incomplete and its effects will be $UNDO$ne. Hence, the EOT record of each transaction can be interpreted as a BEGIN_CHECKPOINT and END_CHECK-POINT, since it agrees with our definition of a checkpoint in that it limits the scope of $REDO$. Figure 3.10 illustrates transaction-oriented checkpoints (TOC).

As can be seen in Figure 3.10, transaction-oriented checkpoints are implied by a FORCE discipline. The major drawback to this approach can be deduced from Figure 3.9. Hot spot pages like will be propagated each time they are modified by a transaction even though they remain in the buffer for a long time. The reduction of recovery expenses with the use of transaction-oriented checkpoints is accomplished by imposing some overhead on normal processing. This is discussed in more detail in Section 3.4.6. The cost factor of unnecessary write operations performed by a FORCE discipline is highly relevant for very large database buffers. The longer a page remains in the buffer, the higher is the probability of multiple updates to the same page by different transactions. Thus, for DBMSs supporting large applications, transaction-oriented checkpointing is not the proper choice.

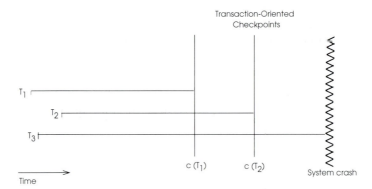

Figure 3.10. Scenario for transaction-oriented checkpoints.

Transaction-Consistent Checkpoints

The following transaction-consistent checkpoints (TCCs) are global in that they save the work of all transactions that have modified the database. The first TCC, when successfully generated, creates a transaction-consistent database. It requires that all update activities on the database be quiescent. In other words, when the checkpoint generation is signaled by the recovery component, all incomplete update transactions are completed and new ones are not admitted. The checkpoint is actually generated when the last update is completed. After the END_CHECKPOINT record has been successfully written, normal operation is resumed. This is illustrated in Figure 3.11.

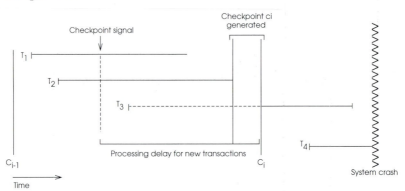

Figure 3.11. Scenario for transaction-consistent checkpoints.

Checkpointing connotes propagating all modified buffer pages and writing a record to the log, which notifies the materialized database of a new transaction-consistent state, hence, the name "transaction-consistent checkpoint." By propagating all modified pages to the database, TCC establishes a point past which partial *REDO* will not operate. Since all modifications prior to the recent checkpoint are reflected in the database, $REDO$-log information need only be processed back to the youngest END_CHECKPOINT record found on the log. We shall see later that the time between two subsequent checkpoints can be adjusted to minimize overall recovery costs.

In Figure 3.11, T_3 must be $REDO$ne completely, whereas T_4 must be rolled back. There is nothing to be done about T_1 and T_2, since their updates have been propagated by generating. Favorable as that may sound, the TCC approach is quite unrealistic for large multiuser DBMSs, with the exception of one special case, which is discussed in Section 3.4.5. There are two reasons for this:

- Putting the system into a quiescent state until no update transaction is active may cause an intolerable delay for incoming transactions.

- Checkpoint costs will be high in the case of large buffers, where many changed pages will have accumulated. With a buffer of 6 megabytes and a substantial number of updates, propagating the modified pages will take about 10 seconds.

For small applications and single-user systems, TCC certainly is useful.

Action-Consistent Checkpoints

Each transaction is considered a sequence of elementary actions that affect the database. On the record-oriented level, these actions can be seen as DML statements. Action-consistent checkpoints (ACC) can be generated when no update action is being processed. Therefore, signaling an ACC means putting the system into quiescence on the action level, which impedes operation here much less than on the transaction level. A scenario is shown in Figure 3.12.

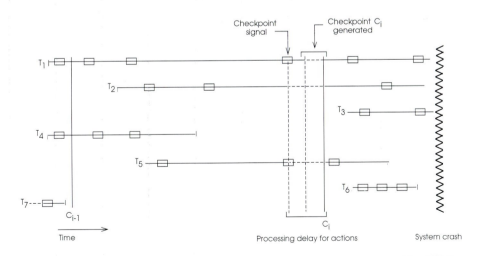

Figure 3.12. Scenario for action-consistent checkpoint.

The checkpoint itself is generated in the very same way as was described for the TCC technique. In the case of ACC, however, the END_CHECKPOINT record indicates an action-consistent[3] rather than a transaction-consistent database. Obviously, such a checkpoint imposes a limit on partial $REDO$. In contrast to TCC, it does not establish a boundary to global $UNDO$; however, it is not required by definition to do so. Recovery in the above scenario means global $UNDO$ for T_1, T_2, and T_3. $REDO$ has to be performed for the last action of T_5 and for all of T_6. The changes of T_4 and T_7 are part of the materialized database because of checkpointing. So again, $REDO$-log information prior to the recent checkpoint is irrelevant for crash recovery. This scheme is much more realistic, since it does not cause long delays for incoming transactions. Costs of checkpointing, however, are still high when large buffers are used.

Fuzzy Checkpoints

In order to further reduce checkpoint costs, propagation activity at the checkpoint time has to be avoided whenever possible. One way to do this is indirect checkpointing. Indirect checkpointing means that information about the buffer occupation is written to the log file rather than the pages themselves. This can be done with two or three write operations, even with very large buffers, and helps to determmine which pages committed data were actually in the buffer at the moment of a crash. However, if there are hot-spot pages, their $REDO$ information will have to be traced back very far on the temporary log. So, although indirect checkpointing does reduce the costs of partial $REDO$, this does not in general make partial $REDO$ independent of the mean time between failure. Note also that this method is only applicable with $\neg ATOMIC$ propagation In the case of $ATOMIC$ schemes, propagation always takes effect at one well-defined moment, which is a checkpoint; pages that have only been written (not propagated) are lost after a crash. Since this checkpointing method is concerned only with the temporary log, leaving the database as it is, we call it "fuzzy." A description of a particular implementation of indirect, fuzzy checkpoints is given by Gray [16].

The best of both worlds, low checkpoint costs with fixed limits to partial $REDO$, is achieved by another fuzzy scheme described by Lindsay et al. [25]. This scheme combines ACC with indirect checkpointing: At checkpoint time, the numbers of all pages (with an update indicator) currently in buffer are written to the log file. If there are no hot-spot pages, nothing else is done. If, however, a modified page is found at two subsequent checkpoints without having been propagated, it will be propagated during checkpoint generation Hence, the scope of partial $REDO$ is limited to two checkpoint intervals. Empiric studies show that the I/O activity for checkpointing is only about 3% percent of what is required with ACC [29]. This scheme can be given general applicability by adjusting the number of checkpoint intervals for modified pages in buffer.

---

[3]This means that the materialized database reflects a state produced by complete actions only; that is, it is consistent up to Level 3 at the moment of checkpointing.

Another fuzzy checkpoint approach has been proposed by Elhardt [14]. Since a description of this technique, called database cache, would require more details than we can present in this chapter, readers are referred to the literature.

3.4.5   Examples of Logging and Recovery Concepts

The introduction of various checkpoint schemes has completed our taxonomy. Data base recovery techniques can now be classified as shown in Figure 3.13. In order to make the classification more vivid, we have added the names of a few existing DBMSs and implementation concepts to the corresponding entries.

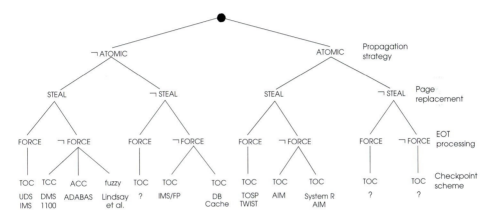

Figure 3.13. Classification scheme for recovery concepts.

In this section, we attempt to illustrate the functional principles of three different approaches found in well-known database systems. We particularly want to elaborate on the cooperation between mapping, logging, and recovery facilities, using a sample database constituting four pages, A, B, C, and D, which are modified by six transactions. What the transactions do is shown in Figure 3.14. The indicated checkpoint is relevant only to those implementations actually applying checkpoint techniques. Prior to the beginning of T_1, the DB pages were in the states A, B, C, and D, respectively.

Implementation Technique: $\neg ATOMIC$, $\neg STEAL$, $\neg FORCE$, **and** TCC

An implementation technique involving the principles of $\neg ATOMIC$, $STEAL$, $FORCE$, and TOC can be found in many systems, for example, IMS [22] and UDS [37]. The temporary log file contains only $UNDO$ data (owing to FORCE), whereas $REDO$ information is written to the archive log. According to the write rules introduced in Section 3.4.2, we must be sure that $UNDO$ logging has taken effect before a changed page is either replaced in the buffer or forced at EOT. Note that in $\neg ATOMIC$ schemes EOT processing is interruptable by a crash.

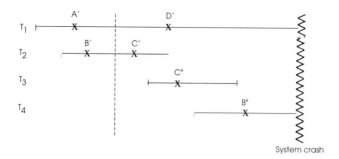

Figure 3.14. Transaction scenario for illustrating recovery techniques.

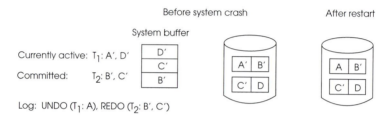

Figure 3.15. Page allocation principles.

In the scenario given in Figure 3.15, we need only consider T_1 and T_2; the rest is irrelevant to the example. According to the scenario, A' has been replaced from the buffer, which triggered an $UNDO$ entry to be written. Pages B' and C' remained in buffer as long as T_2 was active. T_2 reached its normal end before the crash, and so the following had to be done:

- Write $UNDO$ information for B and C (in case the $FORCE$ fails).

- Propagate B' and G'.

- Write $REDO$ information for B' and C' to the archive log file.

- Discard the $UNDO$ entries for B and C.

- Write an EOT record to the log files and acknowledge EOT to the user.

Of course, there are some obvious optimizations as regards the $UNDO$ data for pages that have not been replaced before EOT, but these are not our concern here. After the crash, the recovery component finds the database and the log files as shown in the scenario. The materialized database is inconsistent owing to $\neg ATOMIC$ propagation, and must be made consistent by applying all $UNDO$ information in reverse chronological order.

Implementation Technique: $\neg ATOMIC$, $\neg STEAL$, $\neg FORCE$, **and** TCC

Applications with high transaction rates require large DB buffers to yield satisfactory performance. With sufficient buffer space, a $\neg STEAL$ approach becomes feasible; that is, the materialized database will never contain updates of incomplete transactions. $\neg FORCE$ is desirable for efficient EOT processing, as discussed previously. The IMS/Fast Path in its "main storage database" version is a system designed with this implementation technique [10, 22]. The $\neg STEAL$ and $\neg FORCE$ principles are generalized to the extent that there are no write operations to the database during normal processing. All updates are recorded to the log, and propagation is delayed until shutdown (or some other very infrequent checkpoint), which makes the system belong to the TCC class. Figure 3.16 illustrates the implications of this approach.

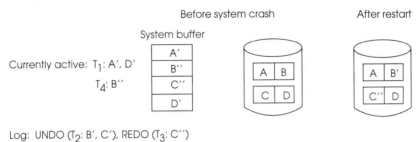

Figure 3.16. Recovery scenario for $\neg ATOMIC$, $\neg STEAL$, $\neg FORCE$, and TCC.

With $\neg STEAL$, there is no UNDO information on the temporary log. Accordingly, there are only committed pages in the materialized database. Each successful transaction writes $REDO$ information during EOT processing. Assuming that the crash occurs as indicated in Figure 3.14, the materialized database is in the initial state, and, compared with the former current database, is old. Everything that has been done since startup must therefore be applied to the database by processing the entire temporary log in chronological order. This, of course, can be very expensive, and hence the entire environment should be as stable as possible to minimize crashes. The benefits of this approach are extremely high transaction rates and short response times, since physical I/O during normal processing is reduced to a minimum.

The database cache, mentioned in Section 3.3, also tries to exploit the desirable properties of $\neg STEAL$ and $\neg FORCE$, but, in addition, attempts to provide very fast crash recovery. This is attempted by implementing a checkpointing scheme of the "fuzzy" type.

Implementation Technique: $ATOMIC$, $STEAL$, $\neg FORCE$, **and** ACC

$ATOMIC$ propagation is not yet widely used in commercial database systems. This may result because indirect page mapping is more complicated and more expensive

than the update-in-place technique. However, there is a well-known example of
this type of implementation, based on the shadow-page mechanism in System R.
This system uses action-consistent checkpointing for update propagation, and hence
comes up with a consistent materialized database after a crash. More specifically,
the materialized database will be consistent up to Level 4 of the mapping hierarchy
and reflect the state of the most recent checkpoint; everything occurring after the
most recent checkpoint will have disappeared. As discussed in Section 3.4.2, with
an action-consistent database, one can use logical transition logging based on DML
statements, which System R does. Note that in the case of $ATOMIC$ propagation,
the WAL principle is bound to the propagation, that is, to the checkpoints. In
other words, modified pages can be written, but not propagated, without having
written an $UNDO$ log. If the modified pages pertain to incomplete transactions, the
$UNDO$ information must be on the temporary log before the pages are propagated.
The same is true for $STEAL$: Not only can dirty pages be written, in the case of
System R, they can also be propagated. Consider the scenario in Figure 3.17.

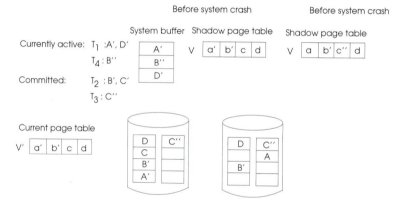

Figure 3.17. Recovery scenario for $ATOMIC$, $STEAL$, $\neg FORCE$, and ACC.

T_1 and T_2 were both incomplete at checkpoint. Since their updates (A′ and b′)
have been propagated, $UNDO$ information must be written to the temporary log.
In System R, this is done with logical transitions, as described in Section 3.4.2.
EOT processing of T_2 and T_3 includes writing $REDO$ information to the log, again
using logical transitions. When the System crashes, the current database is in the
state depicted in Figure 3.17; at restart the materialized database will reflect the
most recent checkpoint state. Crash recovery involves the following actions:

- $UNDO$ the modification of A′. Because of the STEAL policy in System R,
  incomplete transactions can span several checkpoints. Global $UNDO$ must
  be applied to all changes of failed transactions prior to the recent checkpoint.

- $REDO$ the last action of T_2 (modification of C$\prime$) and the whole T_3 (modification of C$\prime\prime$). Although they are committed, the corresponding page states are not yet reflected in the materialized database.

- Nothing has to be done with D$\prime$ since this has not yet become part of the materialized database. The same is true of T_4. Since it was not present when C_i was generated, it has had no effect on the materialized database.

3.4.6 Evaluation of Logging and Recovery Concepts

Combining all possibilities of propagating, buffer handling, and checkpointing, and considering the overall properties of each scheme that we have discussed, we can derive the evaluation given in Table 3.4.

Table 3.4. Evaluation of Logging and Recovery Techniques Based on the Introduced Taxonomy.

Propagation strategy	$\neg A$							A				
Buffer replacement	s				$\neg s$			s			$\neg s$	
EOT processing	F	$\neg F$			F	$\neg F$		F	$\neg F$		F	$\neg F$
Ckpting type	T	C	A_C	FZ	T	C	FZ	T	C	A_C	T	C
Materialized DB state after system failure	D	D	D	D	D	D	D	C	C	AC	C	C
Cost of tran. UNDO	+	+	+	- -	- -	- -	-	-	+	+	- -	- -
Cost of partial REDO at restart	- -	-	-	+	- -	-	-	- -	-	-	- -	-
Cost of global UNDO at restart	+	+	+	+	- -	- -	- -	- -	- -	+	- -	- -
Overhead during normal processing	- -	- -	- -	- -	- -	- -	- -	- -	+	+	+	+
Frequency ckpts	+	-	-	-	+	-	-	+	-	-	+	-
Checkpoint cost	+	++	++	-	+	++	+	+	++	++	+	++

Abbreviations

A = $ATOMIC$; F = $FORCE$; T = TOC; C = TCC; A_C = ACC; FZ = FUZZY; S = $STEAL$; D = Device-Consistent (chaotic); AC = Action-Consistent; TC = Transaction-Consistent.

Evaluation symbols

- - = Very low; - = Low; + = High; ++ = Very high.

Table 3.4 can be seen as a compact summary of what we have discussed up to this point. Combinations leading to inherent contradictions have been suppressed (e.g., $\neg STEAL$ does not allow for ACC). By referring the information in Table

3.4 to Figure 3.13; one can see how existing DBMSs are rated in this qualitative comparison

Some criteria of our taxonomy divide the world of DB recovery into clearly distinct areas:

- *ATOMIC* propagation achieves an action- or transaction-consistent materialized database in the event of a crash. Physical as well as logical logging techniques are therefore applicable. The benefits of this property are offset by increased overhead during normal processing caused by the redundancy required for indirect page mapping. On the other hand, recovery can be cheap when ATOMIC propagation is combined with TOC schemes.

- $\neg ATOMIC$ propagation generally results in a chaotic materialized database in the event of a crash, which makes physical logging mandatory. There is almost no overhead during normal processing, but without appropriate checkpoint schemes, recovery will more expensive.

- All transaction-oriented and transaction-consistent schemes cause high checkpoint costs. This problem is emphasized in transaction-oriented schemes by a relatively high checkpoint frequency.

It is, in general, important when deciding which implementation techniques to choose for database recovery to carefully consider whether optimizations of crash recovery put additional burdens on normal processing. If this is the case, it will certainly not pay off, since crash recovery, it is hoped, will be a rare event. Recovery components should be designed with minimal overhead for normal processing, provided that there is fixed limit to the costs of crash recovery.

This consideration rules out schemes of the *ATOMIC*, *FORCE*, and TOC type, which can be implemented and look very appealing at first sight. According to the classification, the materialized database will always be in the most recent transaction-consistent state in implementations of these schemes. Incomplete transactions have not affected the materialized database, and successful transactions have propagated indivisibly during EOT processing. However appealing the schemes may be in terms of crash recovery, the overhead during normal processing is too high to justify their use [21, 27].

There are, of course, other factors influencing the performance of a logging and recovery component: The granule of logging (pages or entries), the frequency of checkpoints (it depends on the transaction load), and so on, are important. Logging is also tied to concurrency control in that the granule of logging determined the granule of locking. If page logging is applied, DBMS must not use smaller granules of locking than pages. However, a detailed discussion of these aspects is beyond the scope of this chapter; detailed analyses can be found in Chandy et al. [5] and Reuter [28].

3.5   ARCHIVE RECOVERY

Throughout this chapter we have focused on crash recovery, but in general there are two types of DB recovery, as is shown in Figure 3.18. The first path represents the standard crash recovery, depending on the physical (and the materialized) database as well as on the temporary log. If one of these is lost or corrupted because of hardware or software failure, the second path, archive recovery, must be tried. This presupposes that the components involved have independent failure modes, for example, if temporary and archive logs are kept on different devices. The global scenario for archive recovery is shown in Figure 3.19; it illustrates that the component "archive copy" actually depends on some dynamically modified subcomponents. These subcomponents create new archive copies and update existing ones. The following is a brief sketch of some problems associated with this.

Figure 3.18. Two ways of DB recovery and the components involved.

Creating an archive copy, that is, copying the on-line version of the database, is a very expensive process. If the copy is to be consistent, update operation on the database has to be interrupted for a long time, which is unacceptable in many applications. Archive recovery is likely to be rare, and an archive copy should not be created too frequently, both because of cost and because there is a chance that it will never be used. On the other hand, if the archive copy is very old, recovery starting from such a copy will have to $REDO$ too much work and will take too long. There are two methods to cope with this. First, the database can be copied on the fly, that is, without interrupting processing, in parallel with normal processing. This will create an inconsistent copy, a so-called "fuzzy dump."

The other possibility is to write only the changed pages to an incremental dump, since a new copy will be different from an old one only with respect to these pages. Either type of dump can be used to create a new, more up-to-date copy from the previous one. This is done by a separate off-line process with respect to the database and therefore does not affect DB operation In the case of DB applications running 24 hours per day, this type of separate process is the only possible way to maintain archive recovery data. As shown in Figure 3.19, archive recovery in such an environment requires the most recent archive copy, the latest incremental modifications to it (if there are any), and the archive log. When recovering the database itself, there is little additional cost in creating an identical new archive

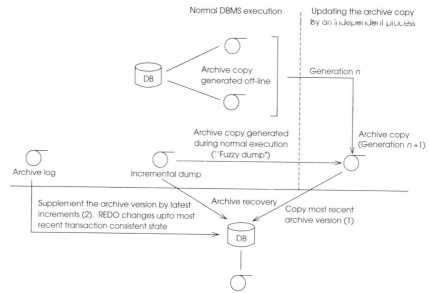

Figure 3.19. Scenario for archive recovery (global REDO).

copy in parallel.

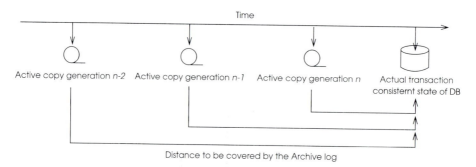

Figure 3.20. Consequences of multigeneration archive copies.

There is still another problem hidden in this scenario: Since archive copies are needed very infrequently, they may be susceptible to magnetic decay. For this reason, several generations of the archive copy are usually kept. If the most recent one does not work, its predecessor can be tried, and so on. This leads to the consequences illustrated in Figure 3.20.

We must anticipate the case of starting archive recovery from the oldest generation, and hence the archive log must span the whole distance back to this point in time. That makes the log susceptible to magnetic decay, as well, but in this case,

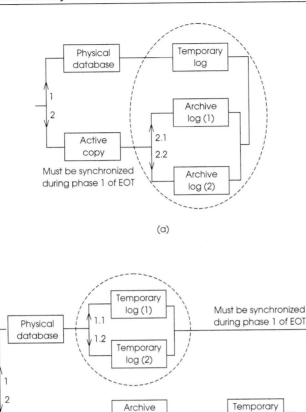

Figure 3.21. The possibilities for duplicating the archive log.

generations will not help; rather we have to duplicate the entire archive log file. Without taking storage costs into account, this has severe impact on normal DB processing, as is shown in Figure 3.21.

Figure 3.21(a) shows the straightforward solution: Two archive log files that are kept on different devices. If this scheme is to work, all three log files must be in the same state at any point in time. In other words, writing to these files must be synchronized at each EOT. This adds substantial costs to normal processing and particularly affects transaction response times. The solution in Figure 3.21b assumes that all log information is written only to the temporary log during normal processing. An independent process is one that runs asynchronously and then copies the *REDO* data to the archive log. Hence, archive recovery finds most of the log entries in the archive log, but the temporary log is required for the most recent information In such an environment, temporary and archive logs are no longer independent from a recovery perspective, and so we must make the temporary log very reliable by duplicating it. The resulting scenario looks much more complicated than the first one, but in fact the only additional costs are those for temporary log storage, which are usually small. The advantage here is that only two files have to be synchronized during EOT, and moreover–as numerical analysis shows–this environment is more reliable than the first one by a factor of 2.

These arguments do not, of course, exhaust the problem of archive recovery. Applications demanding very high availability and fast recovery from a media failure will use additional measures such as duplexing the whole database and all the hardware (e.g., see TANDEM [36]). This aspect of database recovery does not add anything conceptually to the recovery taxonomy established in this chapter.

3.6   CONCLUSION

We have presented a taxonomy for classifying the implementation techniques for database recovery. It is based on four criteria:

Propagation.   We have shown that update propagation should be carefully distinguished from the write operation The $ATOMIC/\neg ATOMIC$ dichotomy defines two different methods of handling low-level updates of the database, and also gives rise to different views of the database, both the materialized and the physical database. This proves to be useful in defining different crash states of a database.

Buffer Handling.   We have shown that interfering with buffer replacement can support $UNDO$ recovery. The $STEAL/\neg STEAL$ criterion deals with this concept.

EOT Processing.   By distinguishing $FORCE$ policies from $\neg FORCE$ policies, we can distinguish whether successful transactions will have to be redone after a crash. It can also be shown that this criterion heavily influences the DBMS performance during normal operation.

Checkpointing.   Checkpoints have been introduced as a means for limiting the costs of partial REDO during crash recovery. They can be classified with regard to the events triggering checkpoint generation and the number of data written at a checkpoint. We have shown that each class has some particular performance characteristics.

Some existing DBMSs and implementation concepts have been classified and described according to the taxonomy. Since the criteria are relatively simple, each system can easily be assigned to the appropriate node of the classification tree. This classification is more than an ordering scheme for concepts: Once the parameters of a system are known, it is possible to draw important conclusions as to the behavior and performance of the recovery component.

Acknowledgments

We would like to thank Jim Gray for his detailed proposals concerning the structure and contents of this chapter, and his enlightening discussions of logging and recovery. Thanks are also due to our colleagues Flaviu Cristian, Shel Finkelstein, C. Mohan, Kurt Shoens, and Irv Traiger (IBM Research Laboratory) for their encouraging comments and critical remarks.

References

[1] Astrahan, M. M., Blasgen, M. W., Chamberlin, D. D., Gray, J. N., W. F., Lindsay, B. G., Lorie, R., Mehl, J. W., Price, T. G., Putzolu, F., selinger, P. G., schkolnick, M., Slutz, D. R., Traiger, I. L., Wade, B. W., and Yost, R. A. 1981. "History and evolution of system R," *Communications of the ACM*, 24(10) (October 1991).

[2] Bernstein, P. A., and Goodman, N. 1981. "Concurrency control in distributed database systems," *ACM Computing Survey*, 13(2) (June 81).

[3] Bjork, L. A. 1973. "Recovery scenario for DB/DC system," In *Proceedings of the ACM 73 National Conference*, Atlanta, Georgia, August 1973.

[4] Chamberlin, D. D. 1980. "A summary of user experience with SQL data sublanguage," In *Proceeding of the international conference on Databases*, Aberdeen, Scotland, S. M. Deen and P. Hammersely, (Eds.), July 1980.

[5] Chandy, K. M., Brown, J. C., Dissley, C. W., and Uhrig, W. R. 1975. "Analytic models for rollback and recovery strategies in data base systems," *IEEE Transactions on Software Engineering* SE-1(1) (March 1975).

[6] Chen, T. C. 1978. "'Computer technology and the database user," In *Proceedings of the 4th International Conference on Very Large Database systems* Berlin, October 1978.

[7] "Codasyl: Report of the data description Language Committee," *Information Systems*, 3(4), 1978.

[8] "Codasyl DDL," *Journal of Development*, Data Processing Group, 40 Paulus Potterstraat, Amsterdam, 1973.

[9] Codd, E. F. "Relational database: A practical foundation for productivity," *Communications of the ACM*, 25(2) (February 1982).

[10] Date, C. J. *An Introduction to database systems*, 3rd ed. Addison-wesley, Reading, MA:1981.

[11] Davies, C. T. "Data processing spheres of control," *IBM System Journal*, 17(2), 1978.

[12] Davies, C. T. "Recovery semantics for DB/DC system," In *Proceedings of the ACM 73 National Conference*, Atlanta, Ga., August 1973.

[13] Effelsberg, W., Hearder, T., Reuter, A., and Schulze-Bohl, J. "Performance measurement in database systems-Modeling, interpretation and evaluation," In *Informatik Fachberichte 41*, Springer-Verlag, Berlin, (in German).

[14] Elhardt, K. *The database cache-Principles of operation*, Ph.D. dissertation, Technical University of Munich, Munich, West Germany (in German).

[15] Eswaran, K. P., Gray, J. N., Lorie, R. A., and Traiger, I. L. "The notions of consistency and predicate locks in a database systems," *Communication of the ACM*, 19(11) (November 1976).

[16] Gray, J. N., *Notes on data base operating systems*, Lecture notes on Computer Science, 60, R. Bayer, R. N. Graham, and G. seegmueller, Eds. Springer-Verlag, New York, 1978.

[17] Gray, J. N., "The Transaction concept; Virtues and limitations," In *Proceedings of the 7th International Conference on Very Large Database Systems*, Cannes, France, ACM , New York, September 9-11, 1981.

[18] Gray, J. N., Lorie, R., Putzolu, F., and Traiger, I. L. "Granularity of locks and degrees of consistency in a large shared data base," In *Modeling in Data Base Management Systems*. Elsevier North-Holland, New York, 1976.

[19] Gray, J. N., Mcjones, P., Blasgen, M., Lindsay, B., Lorie, R., Price, T., Putzolu, F., and Traiger, I. L. "The recovery manager of the systems R database manager," *ACM Computing Survey* 13(2) (June 1981).

[20] Hearder, T., and Reuter, A. " Concepts for implementing a centralized database management system," In *Proceedings of the International Computing Symposium* (Invited Paper) (Nuernberg, W. Germany, Apr.), H. J Scheneider, Ed. German Chapter of ACM, B. G. Teubner, Stuttgart, 1983.

[21] Haerder, T., and Reuter, A. *Optimization of logging and recovery in a database system*, Database Architecture, G. Bracchi, Ed. Elsevier North-Holland, New York, 1979.

[22] *IMS/VS-DB N.d. IMS/VS-DB Primer*, IBM World Trade Center, Palo Alto, July 1976.

[23] Kohler, W. H. 1981. "A survey of techniques for synchronization and recovery in decentralized computer systems," *ACM Computing Survey* 13(2) (June 1981).

[24] Lampson, B. W., and Sturgis, H. E. 1979. Crach recovery in a distributed data storage system. XEROX Research Report Palo Alto, CA, 1979.

[25] Lindsay, B. G., Selinger, P. G., Galtieri, C., Gray, J. N., Lorie, R., Price, T. G., Putzolu, F., Traiger, I. L., and Wade, B. W. 1979. "Notes on distributed databases," *IBM Research Report*, RJ 2571, San Jose, 1979.

[26] Lorie, R. A. 1977. "Physical integrity in a large segmented database," *ACM Transactions on Database SYS.* , 2(1) (March 1977).

[27] Reuter, A. 1980. "A fast transaction-oriented logging scheme for UNDO-recovery," *IEEE Transactions on Software Engineering* SE-6 (July 1980).

[28] Reuter, A. 1982. *Performance Analysis of Recovery techniques*, Research Report, Computer Science Department, Univ. of Kaiserslautern, 1982.

[29] Reuter, A. 1981. *Recovery in Database systems.* Carl Hanser Verlag, Munich (in German).

[30] Senko, M. E., Altman, E. B., Astrahan, M. M., and Fehber, P. L. 1973. "Data structures and accessing in data base systems," *IBM Systems Journal* 12(1) (January 1973).

[31] Severance, D. G., and Lohman, G. M. "Differential files: Their application to the maintenance of large databases," *ACM Transactions on Database Systems* 1(3) (September 1976).

[32] Smith, D. D. P., and Smith, J. M. 1979. "Relational database machines," *IEEE Computing* 12(3), 1979.

[33] Stonebraker, M. 1980. "Retrospection on a database system," *ACM Transactions on Database Systems* 5(2) (June 1980).

[34] Stonebraker, M., Wong, E., Kreeps, P., and Held, G. 1976. "The design and implementation of INGRES," *ACM Transactions on Database Systems* 1(3) (September 1976).

[35] Sturgis, H., Mitchell, J., and Israel, J., "Issues in the design and use of a distributed file system," *ACM Operating Systems Review* 14(3) (July 1980).

[36] TANDEM. N.d. TANDEM 16, *ENSCRIBE Data base Record Manager, Programming Manual*, TANDEM Computer Inc., Cupertino.

[37] UDS, N.d. UDS, *Universal Data Base Management System*, UDS-V2 Reference Manual Package, Siemens AG, Munich, West Germany.

[38] Verhofstadt, J. M. "Recovery techniques for database systems," *ACM Computing Survey* , 10(2) (June 1978).

Chapter 4

Recovery-Enhanced, Reliability, Dependability, and Performability

Abdelsalam Heddaya, Abdelsalam Helal,and Ahmed Elmagarmid

Abstract

Reliability and availability have long been considered twin system properties that could be enhanced by distribution. Paradoxically, the traditional definitions of these properties do not recognize the positive impact of *recovery*—as distinct from simple repair and restart—on reliability, nor the negative effect of recovery, and of internetworking of clients and servers, on availability. As a result of employing the standard definitions, reliability would tend to be underestimated, and availability overestimated.

We offer revised definitions of these two critical metrics, which we call *service reliability* and *service availability*, that improve the match between their formal expression and intuitive meaning. A fortuitous advantage of our approach is that the product of our two metrics yields a highly meaningful figure of merit for the overall *dependability* of a system. But techniques that enhance system dependability exact a performance cost, so we conclude with a cohesive definition of *performability* that rewards the system for performance that is delivered to its client applications, after discounting the following consequences of failure: service denial and interruption, lost work, and recovery cost.

4.1 INTRODUCTION

What good is a fast but brittle system? What good is a reliable but slow system? What good is an available but unreliable system? We could go on, enumerating the eight binary permutations of three of the most critical descriptors of system value: *availability, reliability,* and *performance,* questioning whether each permutation is meaningful and desirable. But, we are interested in more than simple enumeration: We would like to examine each of these properties carefully, so as to ensure that its definition matches the expectations of the system's user. This scrutiny enables us to refine the definitions of availability and reliability to account for network and service states that affect the end user, and to reward software recovery procedures for their positive impact on reliability. Equally importantly, we elucidate the relationships and trade-offs between these pivotal system qualities, to the point of deriving expressions that quantitatively capture the composite system features of *dependability* and *performability* [18]. Dependability combines availability and reliability, and performability adds performance to the mix. We believe that any reasonable comparison between fault-tolerant systems must attempt to measure and compare all of the above four quantities.

The subject of this chapter is becoming increasingly important despite the continuous improvements in the reliability and overall quality of hardware components [11]. A very large distributed computing system, being composed of a large number of computers and communication links, almost always functions with some part of it broken. Over time, only the identity and number of the failed components change. Failures arise from software bugs, human operator errors, performance overload, severe congestion, magnetic media failures, electronic component failures, or malicious subversion [7]. Additionally, scheduled maintenance and environmental disasters such as fires, floods, and earthquakes shut down portions of distributed systems.

We can achieve fault tolerance by *recovering* from failures when they occur, or by *masking* failures on-the-fly. In the recovery approach, failed components are repaired or replaced, and once they become operational, the interrupted services are resumed by recovering as much state information as needed to enable the system to execute the services to completion. By contrast, the masking approach prepares for failures by keeping on-line redundant components that replicate the state of execution of services. Failed components can be replaced or repaired in the background, but service execution is not interrupted by failures. Failure masking is expensive, however, and is sometimes not available as a design option. Moreover, under large extents of failures (e.g., total failures), and under particular types of failures (e.g., network partitioning), failure masking may be inadequate to achieve fault tolerance.

From the point of view of applications, it matters not what the sources of failures are, nor the design schemes employed to combat them; what matters is the end result in terms of the reliability and availability properties of the distributed system services these applications need. The widespread use of mission-critical applications in areas such as banking and online transaction processing (OLTP), manufacturing, video conferencing, air traffic control, and space exploration has demonstrated a great need for highly available and reliable computing systems. These systems typically have their resources geographically distributed and are required to remain *available* for use with very high probability at all times. Long-lived computations and long-term data storage place the additional burden of *reliability*.

We extend the notion of reliability to require that either the system not fail at all for a given length of time—which is the standard definition—or that it recover enough state information after a failure for it to resume its service as if it were not interrupted. This definition, which we call *service reliability*, differs from the traditional definition in that the latter does not reward recovery by accounting for its positive effect on reliabilty, as perceived by the user. We say that for a system to be reliable, either its failures must be rare or the system must be capable of fully recovering from them. The difference between the full recovery required to enhance reliability and the fast restart needed to heighten availability is that recovery must reconstruct the state of the service after failures to what it was just before the failure. Activities interrupted by the failure thus can be resumed exactly as if no failure had occurred.

In the classical definition, a system is highly available if the fraction of its down-time is very small, either because failures are rare or because it can restart very quickly after a failure. However, as a result of recovery activity after a repair, system services may not become accessible to users immediately after restoration to an operational state. We therefore deviate from the classical definition by stressing a more relevant measure, which we call *service availability*.

Given our views on how availability and reliability should be defined, much of the commonly construed relationships between both definitions simply vanishes. Under the classical definitions, availability is always a superior quality to reliability; it is simply an enhanced measure of reliability with lifetime being augmented by the repair process. Under our definitions, however, availability does not always relate to reliability. The superiority relationship holds only up till the occurrence of the first failure. This will become apparent in Section 4.5.

A reliable system is not necessarily highly available. For example, a reliable system that overcomes frequent failures by always recovering, and always completing all operations in progress, will spend a significant amount of time performing the recovery procedure, during which the system may deny new service requests. Another example is a system that is periodically brought down to perform backup procedures that facilitate future recovery. During the backup, which is done to enhance the reliability of the data storage operation, the system is not available to initiate the storage of new data.

Conversely, a system that does not use recovery can be highly available, but not necessarily reliable. For instance, a system that restarts itself quickly upon failures, without performing recovery actions, is more available than a system that performs recovery. Yet, the absence of recovery will render the system less reliable, especially if the failure has interrupted ongoing operations. Another available but unreliable system is one without any downtime due to backups, because it is not backed up at all.

An important question, whose answer determines the end-user requirements of the system, is: Which is more significant? For frequently submitted, short-duration operations, availability may be more significant than reliability, given the very low probability of a failure interrupting the small duration of activity. Such operations are therefore better served by a high probability of being admitted into the system than by a long time to failure. For long-duration, relatively infrequently requested services and long-running transactions, reliability represents a property more critical than availability. A highly available system can be useless for a very long-duration service that is always admitted into the system, but never completes successfully because it is unable to run long enough before a failure aborts it in midstream.

In this chapter, we quantify the effect of recovery on reliability and availability. We also address systems whose mixed workload requires both reliability and availability. In this case, a composite measure can more effectively assist the end user in specifying the requirements of the system. We define *dependability* as the product of our refined reliability and availability, because their multiplication yields the probability that a service can be both initiated successfully and terminated correctly. Also, we address complex systems that sustain partial states of failure (as opposed to either up or down binary states), in which case the system's performance degrades even though its full range of functionality remains intact. In these systems, reliability and availability definitions are not directly utilizable in a straightforward manner. To capture partial failures, we define system performability that rewards the system for every interval of time it is operational, at a reward rate proportional to its level of performance during that interval.

This chapter is organized as follows. In Section 4.2, we describe how systems fail. We enumerate the various sources of failures and characterize the failure and operational states of a distributed system. Section 4.3 introduces our refined definition of reliability, which we call *service reliability*, and compares it to the classical definition of reliability. Similarly Section 4.4 presents *service availability* and contrasts it against the classical definition of availability. In Section 4.5, a brief derivation of dependability is presented, followed in Section 4.6 by a similar, more elaborate derivation of performability. Finally, a conclusion and a discussion are presented in Section 4.7.

4.2   HOW SYSTEMS RESPOND TO FAILURE

The rich variety of possible failure events and system responses to them gives rise to an equally wide range of system states that are relevant to its ability to accept and successfully carry out its tasks. Figure 4.1 shows the system states that we distinguish in this chapter, and their structure. The states are hierarchically categorized as *operational* or *failed*. An operational state is further classified into *recovering* or *ready*. That is, a system can be operational but not quite ready to be accessed as it performs recovery procedures. A ready state is classified, in turn, into *accessible* or *inaccessible*. For example, a system can be ready to accept requests, but network failure renders the system inaccessible to some, or all, potential clients. Similarly, a failed state is either *dead* or *underrepair*. An underrepair state is further subdivided into *recoverable* and *nonrecoverable*. In the former state, repair or replacement as well as recovery procedures are used to resume the state the system was in right before the failure. In the latter state, only restart is possible through repair or replacement.

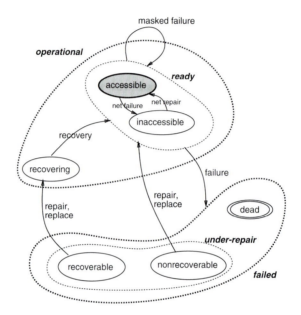

Figure 4.1. Failure states of a distributed system.

For a particular failure state, we define corresponding probabilistic events that take place instantaneously or over a time interval. For a state Q, $Q(t)$ denotes the event that the system is in state Q at time t, and $Q(t, t')$ denotes the event of the system being in state Q continuously in the time interval $[t, t']$. We use this notation throughout the chapter.

4.3   RELIABILITY

With the emergence of critical business applications, such as global commerce, and with the advent of mission-critical systems, such as the space shuttle, the traditional definition of reliability needs to be extended to account for systems that commit to completing a system operation, despite failures, once the operation is accepted by the system. In pursuit of such a commitment, a reliable system will take all needed *recovery actions* after a failure occurs, to detect it, restore operation and system states, and resume the processing of the temporarily interrupted tasks. Unfortunately, the traditional definition of reliability does not reward recovery actions. It only captures the ability of the system to operate continuously without interruption. Realizing that the field has not yet produced unified metrics to quantify recovery-enhanced reliability, we make an attempt in that direction. First, we review the standard definition of reliability, then refine it, and rename it as *system reliability*, R_y. Second, we propose a new definition of reliability, which we dub *service reliability*, R_s, that is similar in spirit to task-based reliability [15].

4.3.1 System Reliability

Reliability refers to the ability of the system to operate continuously without interruption. By tradition, *reliability* is defined as the probability that the system functions properly and continuously in the interval $[0, \tau]$, assuming that it was operational at time 0. We call this property *system reliability*, R_y. In a system without repair, $R_y(\tau)$ is the probability that the system's lifetime exceeds τ. Given the time-to-failure cumulative probability distribution function, $F(x)$, we can write $R_y(\tau) = 1 - F(\tau)$, where $F(\tau)$ is the probability that the time-to-failure is less than or equal to τ.

A system is perfectly reliable if it never fails. This can be attributed to the unlikely event that the constituent components are themselves perfectly reliable and the system's design suffers from no latent errors, or it can arise from the more likely event that component failures are *masked* so that they do not prevent the system as a whole from completing an ongoing service.

We refine system reliability so that (1) it is defined starting from any point t in time, instead of from time 0, and (2) it is conditioned explicitly on the system being operational at time t. Thus, $R_y(t, \tau)$ is the conditional probability that the system does not fail in the interval $[t, t + \tau]$, given that it is operational to start with, at time t. This definition is only slightly more general than the traditional definition, but allows us to tie it smoothly with *availability*, as shown in Section 4.5. Formally,

$$R_y(t, \tau) = \Pr\left[ready(t, t + \tau) \setminus ready(t)\right]$$

where $ready(t, t')$ is the event of the system being continuously in the *ready* state from time t to t'.

4.3.2 Service Reliability

From the point of view of the service requester, it is not always necessary that the system run continuously for the requested service to be completed successfully. Our notion of service reliability, R_s, reflects the ability of the system to complete successfully a service, even in the presence of failures, given that the system accepted the service request in the first place. Successful completion can certainly be achieved by a perfectly reliable system, but it also can be attained more realistically and cheaply by a system that can detect, repair, and *recover* from component failures and design errors. We define service reliability, $R_s(t, \tau)$, as the conditional probability that a request for service s that requires τ time units to complete be successfully finished by the system at some time $t' \geq t+\tau$, given that s was properly initiated at time t. If the system experiences no failures in the interval $[t, t+\tau]$, then $t' = t+\tau$. However, we allow the system to accumulate the requisite τ units of execution time by aggregating work performed between failures, as long as the system is able to recover from each of these failures. When failures interrupt the processing of s, we have $t' > t+\tau$, to account for downtime, repair time, recovery time, and any work done just before the failure that is lost.

From the preceding discussion, it follows immediately that, in a system that does not employ recovery,

$$R_s(t, \tau) = R_y(t, \tau) \tag{4.1}$$

but that, when recovery's contribution to reliability is accounted for, we have

$$R_s(t, \tau) \geq R_y(t, \tau) \tag{4.2}$$

An accurate formalization of R_s that captures the recovery aspect of the system must account for two random phenomena: the *recoverability* of failures and the ability of the system to accumulate at least τ time units before it fails fatally. Certain types of failures can be fatal, or unrecoverable, such as undetected malicious subversion, failures of the recovery subsystem itself, and catastrophic failures that wipe out all resources that may be used for repair or replacement. Let $U_i(t)$ denote the *uptime* between the recovery from f_{i-1}, the $(i-1)$st failure after time t, and f_i, the ith failure. If failure f_{i-1} is unrecoverable, then $U_k(t) = 0$, for all $k \geq i$. We can now define service reliability, assuming that no work is lost and that the system is restored to its full capacity when a failure is recovered from:

$$R_s(t, \tau) = \Pr\left[\sum_i U_i(t) \geq \tau \setminus ready(t)\right] \tag{4.3}$$

In other words, service reliability is the conditional probability that the system will eventually be able to accumulate enough uptime to perform the τ units of time required by service s, given that the system was available to start work on s at time t. Since not all failures are recoverable, $R_s(t, \tau)$ must decay as a function of τ. As τ increases, more failures are likely to occur, and the probability that a fatal unrecoverable failure will strike grows. Conversely, $R_s(t, 0) = 1$, always.

The conditional probability in the definition limits R_s to the case in which the system is operational at time t and the service is admitted to the system. This excludes the situation where the system is in a failure state at time t or is recovering at time t after being repaired. This is not an arbitrary choice, for the fundamental intuition underlying reliability focuses on the system's capacity to finish what it starts.

As an example, we calculate R_s in the simple case where execution of s can be interrupted by at most one failure, then generalize our analysis to any number of failures. Figure 4.2 shows the case of the one failure occurring, which must necessarily

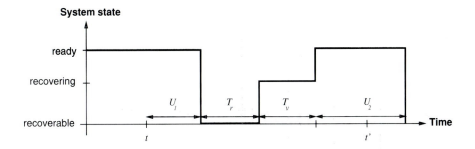

Figure 4.2. An example execution that is interrupted by one failure.

happen before $t+\tau$ to have any effect on the service s that is assumed to have begun at time t. Assume that all $\{U_i(t)\}$ are independent random variables with identical stationary (time-independent) cumulative distributions $F(u) = \Pr[U \leq u]$.

$$
\begin{aligned}
R_s(t,\tau) &= \Pr[U_1(t) \geq \tau \text{ or } \{U_1(t) < \tau \text{ and } U_1(t) + U_2(t) \geq \tau \text{ and } f_1 \text{ recoverable}\}] \\
&= \Pr[U \geq \tau \text{ or } \{U < \tau \text{ and } 2U \geq \tau \text{ and } f_1 \text{ recoverable}\}] \\
&= \Pr\left[U \geq \tau \text{ or } \left\{\frac{\tau}{2} \leq U < \tau \text{ and } f_1 \text{ recoverable}\right\}\right] \\
&= 1 - F(\tau) + c \cdot \left[F(\tau) - F\left(\frac{\tau}{2}\right)\right] \quad\quad (4.4)
\end{aligned}
$$

where c is the probability that a failure is recoverable.[1] Noting that $R_y(t,\tau) = 1 - F(\tau)$, we express R_s in terms of R_y and c, using $R(\tau)$ as a shorthand for $R_y(t,\tau)$ to avoid clutter.

$$
R_s(t,\tau) = c \cdot R\left(\frac{\tau}{2}\right) + (1-c) \cdot R(\tau) \quad\quad (4.5)
$$

when at most one failure can occur. In general, for an arbitrary number of n or fewer failures,

$$
\begin{aligned}
R_s(t,\tau) &= R(\tau) + c \cdot \left[R\left(\frac{\tau}{2}\right) - R(\tau)\right] + \cdots + c^n \cdot \left[R\left(\frac{\tau}{n+1}\right) - R\left(\frac{\tau}{n}\right)\right] \\
&= c^n \cdot R\left(\frac{\tau}{n+1}\right) + (1-c) \cdot \sum_{k=1}^{n} c^{k-1} \cdot R\left(\frac{\tau}{k}\right) \\
&\geq c^n \cdot R\left(\frac{\tau}{n+1}\right) + (1-c^n) \cdot R(\tau) \quad\quad (4.6)
\end{aligned}
$$

The preceding equations yield insight into the relationship between our definition of service reliability and that of system reliability. In the case of a system that cannot recover from any failure, $c = 0$ and $R_s(t,\tau) = R(\tau)$, as would be expected.

---

[1] The quantity c is sometimes called *coverage*.

At the other extreme, a perfectly recoverable system has $c = 1$, which yields perfect service reliability; $R_s(t, \tau) \to R(0) = 1$, as $n \to \infty$, no matter how low system reliability may be. In the region that lies between these two extremes, we rely for our interpretation on the fact that $R(\tau/2) \geq R(\tau)$ always. As the failure coverage of the recovery component of a system increases, so does c, which can dramatically raise service reliability by allowing the service to aggregate progressively more numerous, and hence smaller and more likely, uptime intervals (times-to-failure).

For very long missions, where τ can be so large that $R(\tau)$ becomes negligible, our formulation quantifies the precise advantage to be gained by recovery, in rendering the effective reliability (i.e., service reliability) acceptable. Recovery can, measurably and dramatically reduce the coupling between mission duration and system lifetime.

The above analysis and discussion illustrates how our definition of service reliability R_s recognizes the impact of repair and recovery processes on reliability, by rewarding the ability to recover from a high percentage of failures. At the same time, R_s preserves and reflects any improvements in system reliability, although the quantitative extent to which such gains contribute to R_s is inversely proportional to the quality of the recovery subsystem!

4.4   AVAILABILITY

Availability refers to the accessibility of the system to users. A system is available if its users' requests for service are accepted at the time of their submission. Unlike reliability, availability is instantaneous. The former focuses on the duration of time a system is expected to remain in continuous operation—or effectively so in the case of recovery-enhanced reliability—starting in a normal state of operation. The latter concentrates on the fraction of time instants where the system is operational in the sense of being accessible to the end user.

4.4.1   System and Service Availability

The traditional definition of availability captures only overall failure and repair characteristics of the distributed system hardware. It neither captures the *readiness* of the system to perform a particular operation or service nor the system's *accessibility* over the network. This can lead to overestimating the availability of systems that may not always be ready to accept new service requests when operational, for example, systems that use recovery to enhance reliability. During recovery, new service requests may be blocked while the system is necessarily operational and accessible. Furthermore, if the "system" is narrowly construed to contain the minimal set of server and network resources that is sufficient for proper operation, then it is still possible for the rest of the network to experience difficulties that prevent communication between clients and the system. As a result, availability can degrade well beyond the estimate of the traditional definition, as far as service *users* are concerned.

Availability, therefore, needs to be redefined for recovery-enhanced reliable systems that are internetworked with clients. In this chapter, we make an attempt in that direction. We define *service availability*, A_s, and distinguish it from the traditional definition of availability, which we rename as *system availability*, and denote it by A_y. With reference to the state diagram of Figure 4.1, we write

$$A_y(t) \;=\; \Pr\left[operational(t)\right] \tag{4.7}$$

$$A_s(t) \;=\; \Pr\left[ready(t)\right] \tag{4.8}$$

$$\;=\; \frac{1}{t}\sum_i U_i(0,t) \tag{4.9}$$

where $U_i(t_1,t_2)$ is the *uptime* between the recovery from f_{i-1}, the $(i-1)$st failure in the time interval $[t_1,t_2]$, and f_i, the ith failure in the same interval. In addition, we can also define *customer availability*, which is similar to Larry Raab's *site availability* [9].

$$A_c(t) \;=\; \Pr\left[accessible(t)\right] \tag{4.10}$$

All three measures reflect *instantaneous availability* [19]. The definitions immediately imply that $A_c \le A_s \le A_y$, which is what we mean by saying that A_y overestimates availability. This arises because system availability A_y does not reward fast recovery, since the system is already considered operational once it is repaired, even though it may yet have to recover. Similarly, service availability ignores the possibility that the system may be ready, but inaccessible to some of its customers.

Assuming at most one failure can occur in the interval $[0,t]$, we can express A_y and A_s with reference to Figure 4.2, after setting $t \leftarrow 0$, and $t' \leftarrow t$. By following an analysis similar to that used to express R_s in Section 4.3, and writing $R(t)$ as a shorthand for $R_y(0,t)$,

$$A_y(t) \;=\; R(t) + [1 - R(t)] \cdot [1 - R(t - T_r)] \tag{4.11}$$

$$A_s(t) \;=\; R(t) + [1 - R(t)] \cdot [1 - R(t - T_r - T_v)] \tag{4.12}$$

The preceding expressions seem to indicate that availability improves as t increases, but this is only because we artificially constrained the number of failures to a maximum of one during time interval $[0,t]$. What remedies this is the measure, $\lim_{t\to\infty} A(t)$—known as the *limiting availability*—that can be shown to depend only on the mean time to fail and the mean time to repair.

$$\lim_{t\to\infty} A_y(t) \;=\; \frac{U}{U + T_r}$$

$$\lim_{t\to\infty} A_s(t) \;=\; \frac{U}{U + T_r + T_v} \tag{4.13}$$

but not on the nature of the distributions of failure times, repair times [19], or, by analogy, recovery time.

Service and customer availability as defined before are scalar measures that necessarily induce a total ordering on any systems that are compared in these terms. Other measures that are more complex, but that lead to more detailed design insights, have been proposed in the literature [3, 6, 8, 12, 13]. For example, availability can be measured in a combinatoric sense by the size, composition, and number of the various alternative sets of resources that suffice to keep the system ready to accept new service requests. Such metrics are invented to help reveal information about the impact and relative merit of certain design choices and load conditions, such as the number and placement of replicas, degree of concurrency, transaction length, data access distribution, operation mix, and so on. The scalar and combinatoric availability metrics, however, do not conflict, since it should always be possible, and, we believe, extremely desirable, to compute the scalar metrics from the combinatoric ones. This enables fair across-the-board comparisons between whole systems, accounting for such critical phenomena as recovery and failure-prone internetworking of remote clients with the systems that serve them.

4.5 DEPENDABILITY

The overall success of service s depends both on its correct initiation on demand *and* on its successful termination. Therefore, we define the *dependability*[2] of s, $D_s(t, \tau)$, as the probability of the conjunction of the two events, that of $ready(t)$ and that of accumulating enough work in the duration from t to $t' \geq t + \tau$ to complete the τ units of work required by s (as defined in Section 4.3). Let $T_s(t, \tau)$ denote the latter event. Recall that

$$
\begin{aligned}
A_s(t) &= \Pr[ready(t)] \\
R_s(t, \tau) &= \Pr[T_s(t, \tau) \setminus ready(t)]
\end{aligned}
$$

Bayes' law of conditional probability dictates that dependability be the product of availability and reliability, as follows:

$$
\begin{aligned}
D_s(t, \tau) &= \Pr[ready(t) \wedge T_s(t, \tau)] \\
&= A_s(t) \cdot R_s(t, \tau) \tag{4.14}
\end{aligned}
$$

So we have in this definition of dependability the happy coincidence of a single scalar metric that measures the full *initiation-to-termination probability* of successful service. We ommit discussion of *customer dependability*, except to state that it can be defined, in terms of customer availability instead of service availability, simply as $D_c(t, \tau = A_c(t) \cdot R_s(t, \tau)$.

---

[2]Other researchers include into the notion of dependability additional dimensions such as security against malicious attack and safety from disasterous consequences of failure.

4.6   PERFORMABILITY

The implicit assumption in the preceding analysis of availability and reliability is that the relevant system states are binary: Either the system is up and running or it is not. This simplistic view does hold true for systems that cannot tolerate failures, but for fault-tolerant systems, many more system states become important, one for every possible masked failure pattern. Under such partial failures, the system's *performance* degrades, even as its full range of functionality remains intact. One way to measure the consequences is to reward the system for every time unit it is ready, at a rate proportional to its performance during that interval.

The resulting metric is called *performability*, since it combines both performance and dependability [18]. To arrive at a quantitative measure of performability, $Y_s(t, \tau)$, we reward the system for dependable performance in the time interval $[t, t']$, where $t' \gg t + \tau$. We denote the reward rate during that interval by $r_s(g(x))$, $t \le x \le t'$, which is the performance at time x when the system's failure configuration is $g(x)$. The traditional definition of performability [14, 18, 20] is the simple integration of the reward function.

$$\frac{1}{t' - t} \int_t^{t'} r(g(x))dx$$

A shortcomming of this definition is that it rewards the system for every subinterval of $[t, t']$ in which it has a positive reward rate, regardless of whether this subinterval can contribute toward the successful initiation, and execution to completion, of any service of the system. We prefer to use the more realistic

$$Y_s(t, \tau) \quad = \quad D_s(t, \tau) \cdot \frac{1}{t' - t} \int_t^{t'} r(g(x))dx \qquad (4.15)$$

whose mean value is

$$\overline{Y}_s(t, \tau) \quad = \quad A_s(t) \cdot R_s(t, \tau) \cdot \overline{r} \cdot A_s(t) \qquad (4.16)$$

$$= \quad [A_s(t)]^2 \cdot R_s(t, \tau) \cdot \overline{r} \qquad (4.17)$$

where $\overline{r}$ is the average performance[3] while the system is *ready*, and $\overline{r} \cdot A_s(t)$ is the average performance after discounting downtime. We can view this definition as dependability weighted by performance, or as performance weighted by dependability. A curious consequence of this definition is that availability has a higher impact on performability than does reliability.

Here, too, we make only quick mention of *customer performability*, which emerges by substituting customer availability A_c for service availability A_s in the preceding formulas.

---

[3] For systems whose steady-state probability distribution of failure configuration is stationary, we have $\overline{r} = \sum_i \pi_i \cdot r(g_i)$, where π_i is the probability of the system being in partial failure configuration g_i. Note that this includes only configurations in which the system is *ready*, that is, able to function, albeit at lower performance.

4.7   DISCUSSION

In this chapter, we revised the classical definitions of reliability and availability. We considered the positive effect of recovery on reliability and the potentially negative effect on availability. Our revised definitions, which we call *service reliability*, and *service availability* improve the match between their formal expression and intuitive meaning. A natural definition of *dependability* fortuitously results from adopting a conditional probability framework. This definition is meaningful in systems that require both high reliability and high availability, or in which trading off one for the other is an acceptable route to maximizing dependability. Air traffic control systems are a famous example [4, 10] that can benefit from our dependability metric. Finally, we reformulated the definition of *performability* as a composite measure of dependability and performance for systems that exhibit smooth degradation in performance in response to failures, ranging from fully operational, to slowly or partially operational, to completely failed. An expression for evaluating performability is derived, which recognizes the joint contributions of unavailability, unreliability, and low performance, in determining the net level of service that is deliverable to clients of a distributed system.

The ultimate test of a new modeling or evaluation framework rests on whether it influences design decisions. Our work paves the way for a systematic trade-off of reliability against availability in order to optimize dependability or performability, an approach that has proven successful in a more limited context [16, 17]. For example, consider two different recovery subsystems, V, W. V is more sophisticated, and hence has a higher coverage $c_v > c_w$. By the same token, V takes longer to recover from a failure, and incurs more overhead during normal operation, thus, $A_v < A_w$, and $\bar{r}_v < \bar{r}_w$. Clearly, if reliability is the only concern, then V is the better choice, but if overall dependability and performability are computed, it may well turn out to be more advantageous to adopt W.

The traditional definitions are valuable because of their mathematical tractability, and the large body of results and software [2, 5] that exists for them. Even though our revised definitions may prove more difficult for analytic evaluation, they are all directly measurable by simulation and system monitoring studies.[4] Finally, we note that adding to our suite of definitions, a real-time deadline interval δ, such that a request for service submitted at time t must be completed by time $t + \delta$, is a straightforward and worthwhile exercise.

References

[1] Bhargava, B., Helal, A. and Friesen, K. Analyzing Availability of Replicated Database Systems, *International Journal of Computer Simulation*, 1(4), (December 1991):

---

[4]Admittedly, simulating for *customer* availability, dependability, and performability will be more costly than for *service*-based metrics.

[2] Blum, Alvin M., Ambuj, Goyal., Philip, Heidelberger., Stephen, Lavenberg., Marvin K, Nakayama., and Perwez, Shahabuddin. Modeling and Analysis of System Dependability Using the System Availability Estimator. In *Digest 24th IEEE International Symposium on Fault-Tolerant Computing*, 1994.

[3] Coan, B. M, Oki and E. K. Kolodner. Limitations on Database Availability When Networks Partition, In *Proc. 5th ACM Symp. on Principles of Distributed Computing*, Calgary, Canada, August 1986.

[4] F. Cristian and B. Dancey and J. Dehn. Fault-Tolerance in Air Traffic Control Systems. *ACM Trans. on Computer Systems*, 14(3) (August 1996).

[5] Stacy A. Doyle and Joanne Bechta Dugan. Dependability Assessment using Binary Decision Diagrams (BDDs). In *Digest 25th IEEE int. Symp. on Fault-tolerant Computing*, 1995.

[6] H. Garcia-Molina and J. Kent. Performance Evaluation of Reliable Distributed Systems. In Concurrency Control and Reliability in Distributed Systems, B. Bhargava (ed), Van Nostrand Reinhold, 1987.

[7] Jim Gray. A Census of Tandem System Availability Between 1985 and 1990. *IEEE Trans. on Reliability*, 39(4) (October 1990).

[8] Helal, A. Modeling Database System Availability Under Network Partitioning. *Information Sciences*, 83(1–2) (March 1995).

[9] D.B. Johnson and L.J. Raab. A Tight Upper Bound on the Benefits of Replication and Consistency Control Protocols. *ACM PODS*, May 1991.

[10] K. Kanoun and M. Borrel and T. Morteveille and A. Peytavin. Modeling the Dependability of the French Air Traffic Control System. In Digest 26th IEEE Ann. Int. Symp. on Fault-tolerant Computing, Sendai, Japan, June 1996.

[11] Jean-Claude Laprie. Dependable Computing: Concepts, Limits, Challenges. In Digest 25th IEEE Ann. Int. Symp. on Fault-tolerant Computing, 1995.

[12] G. Martella and B. Ronchetti and F. Shreiber. Availability Evaluation in Distributed Database Systems. *Performance Evaluation*, 1981.

[13] Mukkamala, R. Measuring the effect of data distribution and replication policies on performance evaluation of distributed database systems. February 1989.

[14] H. Nabli and B. Sericola. Performability analysis of fault-tolerant computer systems. Technical Report 805, IRISA, Campus de Beaulieu, Rennes, France, 1994.

[15] Pradhan, D. K. and Vaidya, N. H. Roll-Forward and Rollback Recovery: Performance-Reliability Trade-Off. In Digest 24th IEEE Ann. Int. Symp. on Fault-tolerant Computing, 1994.

[16] R.M. Smith and K.S. Trivedi. A Performability Analysis of Two Multiprocessor Systems. In Digest 17th IEEE Ann. Int. Symp. on Fault-tolerant Computing, Pittsburgh, July 1996.

[17] Tai, Ann T. Performability-Driven Adaptive Fault Tolerance. In Digest 24th IEEE Ann. Int. Symp. on Fault-tolerant Computing, 1994.

[18] A.T. Tai and J.F. Meyer and A. Avizienis. Software Performability: From Concepts to Applications. 347. International Series in Engineering and Computer Science. Kluwer Academic Publisher, 1996.

[19] K. S. Trivedi. Probability & Statistics with Reliability, Queuing, and Computer Science Applications. Prentice-Hall, 1982.

[20] K.S. Trivedi and G. Ciardo and M. Malhotra and R.A. Sahner. Dependability and Performability Analysis. Technical Report ICASE 93-85, NASA Langley Research Center, November 1993.

Chapter 5

The Impact of Recovery on Concurrency Control

William E. Weihl

Abstract

It is widely recognized by practitioners that concurrency control and recovery for transaction systems interact in subtle ways. In most theoretical work, however, concurrency control and recovery are treated as separate, largely independent problems. In this chapter, we investigate the interactions between concurrency control and recovery. We consider two general recovery methods for abstract data types, update in place and deferred update.

Although each requires operations to conflict if they do not "commute," the two recovery methods require subtly different notions of commutativity. We give a precise characterization of the conflict relations that work with each recovery method, and show that each permits conflict relations that the other does not. Thus, the two recovery methods place incomparable constraints on concurrency control. Our analysis applies to arbitrary abstract data types, including those with operations that may be partial or nondeterministic.

5.1 INTRODUCTION

It is widely recognized by practitioners that concurrency control and recovery for transaction systems interact in subtle ways. In most theoretical work, however, concurrency control and recovery are treated as separate, largely independent problems. For example, most theoretical paperpapers on concurrency control tend to ignore recovery, assuming that some unspecified recovery mechanism ensures that aborted transactions have no effect, and then considering only executions in which no transactions abort. In this chapter, we investigate the interactions between concurrency control and recovery. We show that the choice of recovery method constrains the possible choices for concurrency control algorithms, and that different recovery methods place incomparable constraints on concurrency control. Existing work on concurrency control is not invalidated by these results; rather, implicit assumptions about recovery in prior work are identified and made explicit.

Atomic transactions have been widely studied for over a decade as a mechanism for coping with concurrency and failures, particularly in distributed systems [1, 10, 17, 32]. A major area of research during this period has involved the design and analysis of concurrency control algorithms, for which an extensive theory has been developed (e.g., see [4, 24]). Initial work in the area left the data uninterpreted, or viewed operations as simple reads and writes. Recently, a number of researchers have considered placing more structure on the data accessed by transactions, and have shown how this structure can be used to permit more concurrency [1, 3, 14, 22, 23, 29, 36, 38, 40, 41, 42]. For example, in our own work, we have shown how the specifications of abstract data types can be used to permit high levels of concurrency [36, 38], by designing type-specific concurrency control algorithms that take advantage of algebraic properties of a type's operations. Such techniques have been used in existing systems to deal with "hot spots." In addition, such techniques are useful in general distributed systems, and may also prove useful in object-oriented database systems.

In contrast to the vast theoretical literature on concurrency control, there has been relatively little theoretical work on recovery, although some work does exist [11]. Hadzilacos analyzes several crash recovery methods and addresses the question of what constraints are needed on concurrency control for the recovery methods to work. However, he assumes an update-in-place model for recovery, and analyzes only single-version read-write databases. In addition, the recovery methods studied by Hadzilacos, based on logging values, will not work with concurrency control algorithms that permit concurrent updates. More complex recovery algorithms, based on intentions lists or undo operations, have been designed for these more sophisticated concurrency control algorithms that permit concurrent updates. However, a theory of their interactions is sadly lacking.

This chapter is part of an effort to develop a better understanding of the interactions between concurrency control and recovery. Our analysis indicates that there is no single notion of correctness such that any "correct" concurrency control algorithm can be used with any "correct" recovery algorithm and guarantee that transactions are atomic. Our approach in this chapter is formal in part because the interactions between concurrency control and recovery are very subtle. It is easy to be informal and wrong, or to avoid stating critical assumptions that are necessary for others to be able to build on the work.

We focus in this chapter on recovery from transaction aborts, and ignore crash recovery. Crash recovery mechanisms are frequently similar to abort recovery mechanisms, but are also usually more complex due to the need to cope with the uncertainties about exactly what information might be lost in a crash. Thus, we expect a similar analysis to apply to many crash recovery mechanisms. To simplify the problem, however, we ignore crash recovery here, and leave its analysis for future work.

We consider two general recovery methods, update in place and deferred update, and show that they place incomparable constraints on concurrency control. Although each requires operations to conflict if they do not "commute," the two recovery methods require subtly different notions of commutativity. We give a precise characterization of the conflict relations that work with each recovery method, and show that each permits conflict relations that the other does not. Our analysis applies to arbitrary abstract data types, including those with operations that may be partial or nondeterministic. In addition, our analysis covers concurrency control algorithms in which the lock required by an operation may be determined by the results returned by the operation, as well as by its name and arguments.

We use dynamic atomicity [36, 38] as our correctness criterion. Dynamic atomicity characterizes the behavior of many popular concurrency control algorithms, including most variations of two-phase locking [8, 14, 29, 40]. Dynamic atomicity is a local atomicity property, which means that if every object in a system is dynamic atomic, transactions will be atomic (i.e., serializable and recoverable).[1] This means that different concurrency control and recovery algorithms can be used at different objects in a system, and as long as each object is dynamic atomic, the overall system will be correct.

The remainder of this chapter is organized as follows. In Section 5.2, we summarize our computational model, and in Section 5.3, we summarize the definitions of atomicity and dynamic atomicity. Then, in Section 5.4, we describe a high-level model for concurrency control and recovery algorithms that permits us to focus on their interactions while ignoring many implementation details. In Section 5.5, we describe the two recovery methods, and in Section 5.6, we define several different notions of commutativity. Next, in Section 5.7, we give a precise characterization of the conflict relations that work with each of the two recovery methods defined in Section 5.5. In Section 5.8, we analyze several restricted classes of locking algorithms. Finally, in Section 5.9, we conclude with a brief summary of our results.

5.2 COMPUTATIONAL MODEL

Our model of computation is taken from [36, 38]; we summarize the relevant details here. There are two kinds of entities in our model: *transactions* and *objects*. Each object provides operations that can be called by transactions to examine and modify the object's state. These operations constitute the sole means by which transactions can access the state of the object. We will typically use the symbols A, B, and C for transactions, and X, Y, and Z for objects. We use ACT to denote the set of transactions.

---

[1] Dynamic atomicity is in fact an *optimal* local atomicity property: No strictly weaker property of individual objects suffices to ensure global atomicity of transactions.

Our model of computation is event-based, focusing on the events at the interface between transactions and objects. There are four kinds of events of interest:

- Invocation events, denoted <inv, X, A>, occur when a transaction A invokes an operation of object X. The "inv" field includes both the name of the operation and its arguments.

- Response events, denoted <res, X, A>, occur when an object returns a response res to an earlier invocation by transaction A of an operation of object X.

- Commit events, denoted <commit, X, A>, occur when object X learns that transaction A has committed.

- Abort events, denoted <abort, X, A>, occur when object X learns that transaction A has aborted.

We say that event <e, X, A> *involves* X and A.

We introduce some notation here. If H is a sequence of events, let *Committed*(H) be the set of transactions that commit in H; similarly, define *Aborted*(H) to be the set of transactions that abort in H. Define *Active*(H) to be the set of active transactions in H; that is, Active(H) = ACT − Committed(H) − Aborted(H). Also, if H is a sequence of events and X is a (set of) object(s), define H|X to be the subsequence of H consisting of the events involving (the objects in) X; similarly define H|A for a (set of) transaction(s) A.

A computation is modeled as a sequence of events. To simplify the model, we consider only finite sequences. The properties of interest in this chapter are safety properties, and finite sequences suffice for analyzing such properties. Not all finite sequences, however, make sense. For example, a transaction should not commit at some objects and abort at others, and should not continue executing operations at objects after it has committed. To capture these constraints, we introduce a set of *well-formedness* constraints. A well-formed finite sequence of events is called a *history*. We summarize the well-formedness constraints here; details can be found in [36, 38]:

- Each transaction A must wait for the response to its last invocation before invoking the next operation, and an object can generate a response for A only if A has a pending invocation.

- Each transaction A can commit or abort in H, but not both; that is, aborted(H|A) ∩ committed(H|A) = ∅.

- A transaction A cannot commit if it is waiting for the response to an invocation, and cannot invoke any operations after it commits.

These restrictions on transactions are intended to model the typical use of transactions in existing systems. A transaction executes by invoking operations on objects, receiving results when the operations finish. Since we disallow concurrency within a transaction, a transaction is permitted at most one pending invocation at any time. After receiving a response from all invocations, a transaction can commit at one or more objects. A transaction is not allowed to commit at some objects and abort at others; this requirement, called *atomic commitment*, can be implemented using well–known commitment protocols [9, 16, 31].

We will typically use juxtaposition (e.g., $\alpha\beta$) to denote concatenation of sequences, but will use the symbol $\bullet$ to denote concatenation when juxtaposition is too hard to read. We use Λ to denote the empty sequence.

5.3   ATOMICITY

In this section, we define atomicity and several related properties. Most of the definitions are abstracted from [36, 38]; complete details can be found there.

5.3.1   I/O Automata

I/O automata [19, 20] are a convenient tool for describing concurrent and distributed systems. We will use I/O automata in several ways in this chapter. For example, we will model an implementation of an object as an I/O automaton. We will also use I/O automata as a way of describing specifications of objects: We model a specification as a set of sequences (or traces), which is just a language, and an automaton is a convenient tool for describing a language.

We assume minimal familiarity with the details of I/O automata; we summarize the relevant details here. An I/O automaton consists of a *state set*, a subset of which are designated as *initial states*; a set of *actions*, partitioned into *input* and *output* actions; and a *transition relation*, which is a set of triples of the form (s',π,s), where s' and s are states and π is an action.[2] The elements of the transition relation are called *steps* of the automaton.

If there exists a state s such that (s',π,s) is an element of the transition relation, we say that π is enabled in s'. An I/O automaton is required to be *input-enabled*: Every input action must be enabled in every state.

A finite sequence $\alpha = \pi_1, \ldots, \pi_n$ of actions is said to be a *schedule* of an I/O automaton if there exist states $s_0, \ldots, s_n$ such that s_0 is a start state, and each triple (s_{i-1},π_i,s_i) is a step of the automaton for $1 \leq i \leq n$. We define the *language* of an I/O automaton M, denoted L(M), to be the set of schedules of M.

5.3.2   Specifications

Each object has a *serial specification*, which defines its behavior in the absence of concurrency and failures, as well as a *behavioral specification*, which characterizes its behavior in the presence of concurrency and failures. The behavioral specification of an object X is simply a set of histories that contains only events involving X.

---

[2]An I/O automaton also can have internal actions and an additional component characterizing the fair executions; we omit these here since we do not need them in the rest of the chapter.

The serial specification of an object X, denoted Spec(X), is intended to capture the acceptable behavior of X in a sequential, failure-free environment. We could model the serial specification of X as a set of histories, where the histories satisfy certain restrictions (e.g., all transactions commit and events of different transactions do not interleave). We have found it convenient, however, to use a slightly different model for serial specifications. Instead of a set of histories, we will use a prefix-closed set of *operation sequences*. (Prefix closure means that if a sequence α is in the set, any prefix β of α is also in the set.) An *operation* is a pair consisting of an invocation and a response to that invocation; in addition, an operation identifies the object on which it is executed.

We often speak informally of an "operation" on an object, as in "the insert operation on a set object." An operation in our formal model is intended to represent a single execution of an "operation" as used in the informal sense. For example, the following might be an operation (in the formal sense) on a set object X:

$$X:[\text{insert}(3), \text{ok}]$$

This operation represents an execution of the insert operation (in the informal sense) on X with argument "3" and result "ok."

If an operation sequence α is in Spec(X), we say that α is *legal according to* Spec(X). If Spec(X) is clear from context, we will simply say that α is legal.

We will typically use I/O automata to describe serial specifications, by defining Spec(X) to be the language of some I/O automaton whose actions are the operations of X. For example, consider a bank account object BA, with operations to deposit and withdraw money, and to retrieve the current balance. Assume that a withdrawal has two possible results, "ok" and "no." Spec(BA) is the language of an I/O automaton M(BA), defined as follows. A state s of M(BA) is a nonnegative integer; the initial state is 0. The output actions of M(BA) are the operations of BA; there are no input actions. The steps (s', π, s) of M(BA) are defined by the preconditions and effects that follow for each action π. We follow the convention that an omitted precondition is short for a precondition of true, and an omitted effects indicates that s = s'.

$$\pi \;=\; \text{BA} : [deposit(i), ok], i > 0$$
$$\textbf{Effects:} s = s' + i$$

$$\pi \;=\; \text{BA} : [withdraw(i), ok], i > 0$$
$$\textbf{Precondition:} s' \geq i$$
$$\textbf{Effects:} s = s' - -i$$

$$\pi \;=\; \text{BA} : [withdraw(i), no], i > 0$$
$$\textbf{Precondition:} s' < i$$

$$\pi \;=\; \text{BA} : [balance, i]$$
$$\textbf{Precondition:} s' = i$$

Spec(BA) includes the following sequence of operations:

$$BA:[deposit(5), ok]$$
$$BA:[withdraw(3), ok]$$
$$BA:[balance,2]$$
$$BA:[withdraw(3), no].$$

However, it does not include the following sequence:

$$BA:[deposit(5), ok]$$
$$BA:[withdraw(3), ok]$$
$$BA:[balance,2]$$
$$BA:[withdraw(3), ok].$$

The withdraw operation returns "ok" if and only if the current balance is not less than the argument of the operation; the first preceding sequence satisfies this constraint, and the second does not.

5.3.3   Global Atomicity

Informally, a history of a system is atomic if the committed transactions in the history can be executed in some serial order and have the same effect. In order to exploit type-specific properties, we need to define serializability and atomicity in terms of the serial specifications of objects.

Since serial specifications are sets of operation sequences, not sets of histories, we need to establish a correspondence between histories and operation sequences. We do this by defining a function $Opseq$ from histories to operation sequences. Opseq is defined inductively as follows. First, $Opseq(\Lambda) = \Lambda$. Second, $Opseq(H \bullet e)$, where e is a single event, is just $Opseq(H)$ if e is an invocation, commit or abort event; if e is a response event $<R,X,A>$, and $<I,X,A>$ is the pending invocation for A in H, then $Opseq(H \bullet e) = Opseq(H) \bullet X:[I,R]$. In other words, $Opseq(H)$ is the operation sequence that contains the operations in H in the order in which they occur (i.e., the order of the response events); commit and abort events and pending invocations are ignored.

We say that a serial failure-free history H (one in which events for different transactions are not interleaved, and in which no transaction aborts) is *acceptable* at X if $Opseq(H|X)$ is legal according to $Spec(X)$; in other words, if the sequence of operations in H involving X is permitted by the serial specification of X. A serial failure-free history is *acceptable* if it is acceptable at every object X.

We say that two histories H and K are *equivalent* if every transaction performs the same steps in H as in K; that is, if $H|A = K|A$ for every transaction A. If H is a history and T is a partial order on transactions that totally orders the transactions that appear in H, we define $Serial(H,T)$ to be the serial history equivalent to H in which transactions appear in the order T. Thus, if $A_1, \ldots, A_n$ are the transactions in H in the order T, then Serial(H,T) = $\Pi | A_1 \bullet \ldots \bullet \Pi | A_n$.

If H is a failure-free history and T is a partial order on transactions that totally orders the transactions that appear in H, we then say that H is *serializable in the order T* if Serial(H,T) is acceptable. In other words, H is serializable in the order T if, according to the serial specifications of the objects, it is permissible for the transactions in H, when run in the order T, to execute the same steps as in H. We say that a failure-free history H is *serializable* if there exists an order T such that H is serializable in the order T.

Now, define *permanent*(H) to be H|committed(H). We then say that H is *atomic* if permanent(H) is serializable. Thus, we formalize recoverability by throwing away events for noncommitted transactions, and requiring that the committed transactions be serializable.

For example, the following history involving a bank account object BA is atomic:

$$
\begin{array}{c}
<\text{deposit}(3), \text{BA}, \text{A}> \\
<\text{ok}, \text{BA}, \text{A}> \\
<\text{withdraw}(2), \text{BA}, \text{B}> \\
<\text{ok}, \text{BA}, \text{B}> \\
<\text{balance}, \text{BA}, \text{A}> \\
<3, \text{BA}, \text{A}> \\
<\text{balance}, \text{BA}, \text{B}> \\
<\text{commit}, \text{BA}, \text{A}> \\
<1, \text{BA}, \text{B}> \\
<\text{commit}, \text{BA}, \text{B}> \\
<\text{withdraw}(2), \text{BA}, \text{C}> \\
<\text{no}, \text{BA}, \text{C}> \\
<\text{commit}, \text{BA}, \text{C}>.
\end{array}
$$

The history contains only committed transactions, and is serializable in the order A followed by B followed by C.

5.3.4 Local Atomicity

The definition of atomicity previously given is global: It applies to a history of an entire system. To build systems in a modular, extensible fashion, it is important to define local properties of objects that guarantee a desired global property such as atomicity. A *local atomicity property* is a property $\mathcal{P}$ of specifications of objects such that the following is true: If the specification of every object in a system satisfies $\mathcal{P}$, then every history in the system's behavior is atomic. To design a local atomicity property, one must ensure that the objects agree on at least one serialization order for the committed transactions. This problem can be difficult because each object has only *local* information; no object has complete information about the *global* computation of the system. As illustrated in [36, 38], if different objects use "correct" but incompatible concurrency control methods, nonserializable executions can result. A local atomicity property describes how objects agree on a serialization order for committed transactions.

In this section, we define a particular local atomicity property, which we call *dynamic atomicity*. Most concurrency control algorithms, including two-phase locking [8, 5, 14], determine a serialization order for transactions *dynamically*, based on the order in which transactions invoke operations and obtain locks on objects. Dynamic atomicity characterizes the behavior of algorithms that are dynamic in this sense. Informally stated, the fundamental property of protocols characterized by dynamic atomicity is the following: If the sequence of operations executed by one committed transaction conflicts with the operations executed by another committed transaction, then some of the operations executed by one of the transactions must occur after the other transaction has committed. In other words, if two transactions are completely concurrent at the object (neither executes an operation after the other commits), they must not conflict. Locking protocols (and all pessimistic protocols) achieve this property by *delaying* or *refusing* conflicting operations; optimistic protocols [15] achieve this property by allowing conflicts to occur, but *aborting* conflicting transactions when they try to commit to prevent conflicts among committed transactions.

We can describe dynamic atomicity precisely as follows. If H is a history, define *precedes*(H) to be the following relation on transactions: $(A,B) \in precedes(H)$ if and only if there exists an operation invoked by B that responds after A commits in H. The events need not occur at the same object. The relation precedes(H) captures the concept of one transaction occurring after another: if $(A,B) \in precedes(H)$, then some operation executed by B occurred in H after A committed. This could have happened because B started after A finished or ran more slowly than A, or because B was delayed because of a conflict with A. We note that the well-formedness constraints on histories are sufficient to guarantee that precedes(H) is a partial order.

The following lemma from [36, 38] provides the key to our definition of dynamic atomicity.

Lemma 1: If H is a history and X is an object, then precedes(H|X) $\subseteq$ precedes(H).

If H is a history of the system, each object has only partial information about precedes(H). However, if each object X ensures local serializability in *all* orders consistent with precedes(H|X), then by Lemma 1, we are guaranteed global serializability in all orders consistent with precedes(H). To be precise, we have the following definition of dynamic atomicity: We say that a history H is *dynamic atomic* if permanent(H) is serializable in every total order consistent with precedes(H). In other words, every serial history equivalent to permanent(H), with the transactions in an order consistent with precedes(H), must be acceptable.

The following theorem, taken from [36, 38], justifies our claim that dynamic atomicity is a local atomicity property:

Theorem 1: If every local history in the behavioral specification of each object in a system is dynamic atomic, then every history in the system's behavior is atomic.

As an example, the history H illustrated at the end of Section 5.3.3 is dynamic atomic as well as atomic: It is serializable in the order A–B–C, and since a response event for B occurs after the commit event for A, and similarly a response event for C occurs after the commit event for B, this is the only total order consistent with precedes(H). However, if the last response event for B occurred before the commit event for A, the history would not be dynamic atomic, since then (A,B) would not be in precedes(H), but the history is not serializable in the order B–A–C.

5.4   CC AND RECOVERY ALGORITHMS

We adopt the following as the correctness criterion for an implementation of an object. First, we view an implementation of an object as an I/O automaton I whose actions are the events involving the object. Now, we say that I is *correct* if every history in L(I) is dynamic atomic. Our goal in this chapter is to explore which combinations of concurrency control and recovery algorithms lead to correct implementations.

Different implementations of objects differ greatly in the details of the steps they perform to execute an operation invoked by a transaction. Viewed at a high level, an implementation might do the following:

1. Acquire any locks needed (waiting if there are conflicts).

2. Determine the "state" of the object.

3. Choose a result consistent with the state found in the previous step.

4. Update the state if necessary.

5. Record recovery data.

6. Return the result chosen in step 3.

Some implementations might execute these steps in a different order, or might use a completely different breakdown. For example, some implementations might use the result of an operation, as well as its name and arguments, to determine the locks required by the operation. Other implementations might allow several operations to run concurrently, relying on short-term locks (e.g., page locks) held for the duration of each operation to prevent them from interfering with each other.

Most of these differences among implementations are irrelevant as far as the interactions between concurrency control and recovery are concerned. To be reasonably general, and to avoid getting bogged down in complex implementation details, we adopt the following more abstract model of an object's implementation: We view an implementation of an object X as an I/O automaton I(X, Spec, View, Conflict), where Spec is the serial specification of X, View is an abstraction of the recovery algorithm to be used, and Conflict is an abstraction of the concurrency control algorithm to be used. Spec is a set of operation sequences; the types of View and Conflict are defined more precisely in what follow.

The actions of I(X, Spec, View, Conflict) are simply the events involving X. More precisely, the input actions of I(X, Spec, View, Conflict) are the invocation, commit, and abort events involving X; the outputs are the response events involving X. Thus, the object receives invocations, commits, and aborts from transactions, and can generate responses to invocations.

We use perhaps the most abstract model possible for the states of I(X, Spec, View, Conflict): A state of I(X, Spec, View, Conflict) is simply a sequence of events. The initial state is the empty sequence. When an event involving the object takes place, it is appended to the state. Thus, the state of the object records the events involving the object in the order they happen. Of course, an actual implementation would use a much more efficient representation for the state of an object, but such implementation details are not relevant for our analysis.

The input events are always enabled, since they are controlled by the transactions. However, we will assume that transactions preserve the well-formedness constraints discussed earlier. Response events are enabled if there are no concurrency conflicts, and if the response being returned is consistent (according to the serial specification Spec(X)) with the current state of the object.

More precisely, let *Conflict* be a binary relation on operations. The relation Conflict is used by I(X,Spec,View,Conflict) to test for conflicts: A response $<R,$ X, A> can occur for an invocation $<I, X, A>$ only if the operation $X:[I,R]$ does not conflict with any operation already executed by other active transactions. The conflict relation between operations is the essential variable in conflict-based locking.

Recovery is modeled by a function *View* from histories and active transactions to operation sequences. The function View can be thought of as defining the "serial state" (represented as an operation sequence) used to determine the legal responses to an invocation. View models recovery from aborts in the sense that the serial state used by an operation to determine its response should ignore the operations executed by aborted transactions. We will show in the next section how View can be used to model different recovery methods. First, however, we present the transitions of I(X,Spec,View,Conflict) more formally.

Formally, the transitions (s',π,s) of I(X,Spec,View,Conflict) are described by the preconditions and effects given in what follows for each action π:

> π is an invocation event $<I,X,A>$
> > **Effects:** $s = s'\pi$

> π is a response event $<R,X,A>$
> > **Precondition:**
> > > A has a pending invocation I in s
> > > $\forall$ transactions $B \in$ Active(s),
> > > > $\forall$ operations P in Opseq(s|B),
> > > > > $(X:[I,R],P) \notin$ Conflict
> > > View(s,A) $\bullet$ X:[I,R] $\in$ Spec(X)

Effects: s = s'π

π is a commit event <commit,X,A>
      Effects: s = s'π

π is an abort event <abort,X,A>
      Effects: s = s'π

As stated before, each event is simply recorded in the state when it occurs. The first precondition for response events ensures that I(X,Spec,View,Conflict) preserves well-formedness: A response event is generated only for transactions with pending invocations. The second precondition tests whether the locks required by the operation can be obtained. The locks acquired by a transaction are implicit in the operations it has executed; locks are released implicitly when a transaction commits or aborts (since then it is no longer active). The third precondition constrains the responses that can be generated: They must be legal according to Spec(X) after the operation sequence View(s,A).

An actual implementation could test the preconditions on response events in any order, and if there are several legal responses might always choose a particular one. Our model abstracts from such details. We note that not all algorithms can be modeled in this way. For example, the test for concurrency conflicts considered here is independent of the current state of the object. Nevertheless, many interesting algorithms, including most published type-specific concurrency control and recovery algorithms (e.g., [3, 14, 29, 40, 41]), fit into this framework. In the remainder of this chapter, we will explore constraints on Conflict and View that guarantee that I(X,Spec,View,Conflict) is correct. We will consider two different recovery methods, and show that they place incomparable constraints on conflict relations.

5.5   RECOVERY

In this section, we present two different recovery methods, and show how to model them in terms of a View function. The first method is called "update in place" (or UIP). UIP is an abstraction of recovery algorithms in which a single "current" state is maintained. When a transaction executes an operation, the current state is used to determine the response to the operation, and is modified to reflect any changes (e.g., inserting a tuple) performed by the operation. When a transaction commits, nothing needs to be done, since the current state already reflects the effects of the transaction's operations. When a transaction aborts, however, the effects of the transaction's operations on the current state must be "undone" in some fashion. Most database systems, including System R [10], use an update-in-place strategy for recovery from transaction aborts.

The details of undoing operations can be complex. We abstract from them by defining the view based on the entire history. More precisely, we define the function UIP for a history H and a transaction A∈Active(H) as follows: UIP(H,A) = Opseq(H | ACT–Aborted(H)). In other words, UIP computes a serial state by including all the operations executed by nonaborted transactions, in the order in which they were executed (i.e., the order in which their responses occurred).

The second recovery method is called "deferred update" (or DU). DU is an abstraction of recovery algorithms based on intentions lists, in which the base copy of the database is not updated until a transaction commits [16]. Alternatively, one can think of each transaction as having its own private workspace with a copy of the database in which it makes changes; these changes are not seen by other transactions until they commit. The way in which a transaction executes an operation depends on the implementation. If we use private workspaces, the state in the transaction's private workspace is used to determine the response to the operation, and the private workspace is updated to reflect any changes performed by the operation. If we use intentions lists, the base copy of the database is used to determine the response to the operation, except that the effects of the operations already in the transaction's intentions list must be accounted for; the intentions list is updated simply by appending the new operation. Aborts are simple for DU, since the intentions list or private workspace can just be discarded. Commits can be harder, depending on the implementation. If we use intentions lists, we simply have to apply the transaction's intentions list to the base copy of the database. If we use private workspaces, we have to update the base copy appropriately, but may also have to update the private workspaces of other active transactions to ensure that the effects of committed transactions are made visible to active transactions. Relatively few systems seem to use a deferred-update strategy for recovery from transaction aborts, perhaps because executing an operation and committing a transaction can be more expensive than when an update-in-place strategy is used. Nevertheless, this strategy has been used in some systems, notably XDFS and CFS [21].

More precisely, we define the function DU for a history H and a transaction $A \in Active(H)$ as follows. First, define the total order *Commit-order*(H) on transactions that commit in H to contain exactly those pairs (A,B) such that the first commit event for A occurs in H before the first commit event for B.[3] Now, define DU(H,A) = Opseq(Serial(H|Committed(H), Commit-order(H))) • Opseq(H|A). In other words, DU computes a serial state by including all the operations of committed transactions, in the order in which they committed, followed by the operations already executed by the transaction A itself.

DU and UIP both include the effects of the operations of committed transactions, and of the particular active transaction A. They differ in the order of these operations: UIP includes them in the order in which the operations occurred, whereas DU includes them in the order in which the transactions committed, followed by A. They also differ in whether the effects of other active transactions are included: UIP includes the effects of *all* nonaborted transactions, both committed and active, whereas DU includes the effects of only the committed transactions and the particular active transaction A.

A simple example serves to illustrate the differences between DU and UIP. Con-

---

[3]Commit-order(H) is defined for all histories H; however, we will make use of the definition only for histories involving a single object. The same is true of UIP and DU.

sider the following history H involving a bank account object BA:

<deposit(5), BA, A>
<ok, BA, A>
<commit, BA, A>
<withdraw(3), BA, B>
<ok, BA, B>

UIP(H,B) is the following operation sequence (corresponding to an account balance of 2):

BA:[deposit(5), ok]
BA:[withdraw(3), ok]

Since UIP gives the same result regardless of the transaction, UIP(H,C), for some other transaction C, is the same operation sequence. Since B is the only active transaction in H, DU(H,B) is also the same operation sequence. However, DU(H,C) is the sequence

BA:[deposit(5), ok]

which contains only the operations executed by the committed transactions.

One might think that these rather subtle differences between DU and UIP are irrelevant. Indeed, much of the literature on concurrency control seems to be based on the implicit assumption that concurrency control and recovery can be studied independently, and that different recovery methods such as DU and UIP all can be regarded as implementations of some more abstract notion of recovery. For example, recovery is typically handled by assuming that there is some recovery method that ensures that aborted transactions "have no effect," and then considering only executions in which no transactions abort when analyzing concurrency control. In the process, however, most people seem to assume a model for recovery similar to UIP. As we will show, this assumption is nontrivial: DU and UIP work correctly with different, in fact, incomparable, classes of concurrency control algorithms.

We note that many other View functions are possible. We have begun by studying UIP and DU because they are abstractions of the two most common recovery methods in use. One interesting question for future work is whether there are other View functions that place fewer constraints on concurrency control than UIP or DU.

5.6 COMMUTATIVITY

Each of the recovery methods described in the previous section works in combination with a conflict relation based on "commutativity": two operations conflict if they do not "commute." However, the different recovery algorithms require subtly different notions of commutativity. In this section, we describe the two definitions and give some examples to illustrate how they differ.

It is important to point out that we define the two notions of commutativity as binary relations on operations in the sense of our formal definition, rather than simply for invocations as is usually done. Thus, the locks acquired by an operation can depend on the results returned by the operation. In addition, it is convenient to phrase our definitions in terms of sequences of operations, not just individual operations.

5.6.1 Equieffectiveness

To define commutativity, it is important to know when two operation sequences lead to the same "state." Rather than defining commutativity in terms of the "states" of objects, however, we take a more abstract view based on the sequence of operations applied to an object.

First, if Spec is a set of operation sequences and α and β are operation sequences, we say that α *looks like* β *with respect to* Spec (written $\alpha \leq_{Spec} \beta$, or $\alpha \leq \beta$ when Spec is clear from context) if for every operation sequence γ, $\alpha\gamma \in$Spec only if $\beta\gamma \in$Spec. In other words, $\alpha \leq \beta$ if, after executing α, we will never see a result of an operation that allows us to distinguish β from α. Notice that the relation "looks like" is not necessarily symmetric (although it is reflexive and transitive).

Second, if Spec is a set of operation sequences and α and β are operation sequences, we say that α and β are *equieffective with respect to* Spec (written $\alpha \cong_{Spec}$ β, or $\alpha \cong \beta$ when Spec is clear from context) if $\alpha \leq_{Spec} \beta$ and $\beta \leq_{Spec} \alpha$. In other words, α and β are indistinguishable by future operations.

We include here some simple properties of these definitions.

Lemma 2: The relation $\leq_{Spec}$ is reflexive and transitive.

Lemma 3: The relation $\cong_{Spec}$ is an equivalence relation.

Lemma 4: If $\alpha \in$Spec and either $\alpha \leq_{Spec} \beta$ or $\alpha \cong_{Spec} \beta$, then $\beta \in$Spec.

Lemma 5: If $\alpha \leq \beta$, then $\alpha\gamma \leq \beta\gamma$ for all γ.

Lemma 6: If $\alpha \cong \beta$, then $\alpha\gamma \cong \beta\gamma$ for all γ.

5.6.2 Forward Commutativity

If Spec is a set of operation sequences, and β and γ are operation sequences, we say that β and γ *commute forward with respect to* Spec if, for every operation sequence α such that $\alpha\beta \in$Spec and $\alpha\gamma \in$Spec, $\alpha\beta\gamma \cong_{Spec} \alpha\gamma\beta$ and $\alpha\beta\gamma \in$Spec. The motivation for the terminology is that whenever β and γ each can be executed after some sequence α, each can be "pushed forward" past the other. (Also, conflict relations based on forward commutativity work with a deferred-update recovery method, which is a kind of "forward recovery.")

Define the relation FC(Spec) to be the binary relation on operations containing all pairs (β, γ) such that β and γ commute forward with respect to Spec. Define the relation NFC(Spec) to be the complement of FC(Spec).

Lemma 7: FC(Spec) and NFC(Spec) are symmetric relations.

For example, the forward commutativity relation on operations of the bank account object BA is given by Table 5.1. Deposits and successful withdrawals do not commute with balance operations, since the former change the state. Similarly, successful withdrawals do not commute with each other; for example, each of BA:[withdraw(i), ok] and BA:[withdraw(j), ok] is legal after any operation sequence α that results in a net balance greater than or equal to max(i,j), but if the net balance after α is less than i + j, then the two withdrawal operations cannot be executed in sequence after α. However, successful withdrawals commute with deposits: If P = BA:[withdraw(i), ok] and Q = BA:[deposit(j), ok], and αP and αQ are both legal, then αQP is legal since the balance after αQ is bigger than the balance after α; αPQ is legal since deposits are always legal; and αPQ $\cong$ αQP since addition is commutative.

Table 5.1. Forward Commutativity Relation for BA

	BA:[dep(j),ok]	BA:[wd(j),ok]	BA:[wd(j),ok]	BA:[bal(j),ok]
BA:[dep(i),ok]			×	×
BA:[wd(i),ok]		×		×
BA:[wd(i),no]	×			
BA:[bal,i]	×	×		

× *indicates that the operations for the given row and column do* <u>*not*</u> *commute forward.* **dep** *indicates* *deposit,* **wd** *indicates* **withdrawal** *and* **bal** *indicates* **balance**.

5.6.3 Backward Commutativity

If Spec is a set of operation sequences, and β and γ are operation sequences, we say that β *right commutes backward with* γ *with respect to* Spec if, for every operation sequence α, $\alpha\gamma\beta \leq_{Spec} \alpha\beta\gamma$. The motivation for the terminology is that whenever β can be executed immediately after (i.e., to the right of) γ, it can be "pushed backward" so that it is before γ. (Also, conflict relations based on backward commutativity work with an update-in-place recovery method, which is a kind of "backward recovery.")

Define the relation RBC(Spec) to be the binary relation on operations containing all pairs (β,γ) such that β right commutes backward with γ with respect to Spec. Define the relation NRBC(Spec) to be the complement of RBC(Spec).

Notice that RBC(Spec) and NRBC(Spec) are not necessarily symmetric. Most previous work (including some of our own) assumes, sometimes implicitly, that conflict relations must be symmetric. We will show that UIP works with *Conflict* if and only if NRBC(Spec)$\subseteq$*Conflict*. If we required conflict relations to be symmetric, we would be forced to include additional conflicts that are not necessary. (In particular, *Conflict* would have to contain the symmetric closure of NRBC(Spec).)

The right backward commutativity relation for the bank account object BA is described in Figure 5.2. For example, suppose P = BA:[withdraw(j), ok] and Q = BA:[deposit(i), ok], let α be such that $\alpha QP \in$ Spec(BA), and let s' be the state of M(BA) after α. Then by the precondition for P, s'+i $\geq$ j, so s' $\geq$ j–i. If α is such that s' < j, then $\alpha PQ \notin$ Spec(BA), so P does not right commute backward with Q. However, Q does right commute backward with P: If the withdrawal (P) can be executed before the deposit (Q), it can also be executed after the deposit since the deposit increases the balance (and the two sequences are equieffective since addition commutes).

Table 5.2. Right Backward Commutativity Relation for BA

	BA:[dep(j),ok]	BA:[wd(j),ok]	BA:[wd(j),no]	BA:[bal,j]
BA:[dep(i),ok]			×	×
BA:[wd(i),ok]	×			×
BA:[wd(i),no]		×		
BA:[bal,i]	×	×		

× *indicates that the operation for the given row does not right commute backward with the operation for the column.* **dep** *indicates* **deposit**, **wd** *indicates* **withdrawal**, *and* **bal** *indicates* **balance**.

5.6.4   Discussion

The rather subtle differences between the two notions of commutativity are shown by comparing Table 5.2 to Table 5.1: The forward and right backward commutativity relations are incomparable. We will show that UIP works in combination with exactly those conflict relations that contain NRBC(Spec), whereas DU works in combination with exactly those conflict relations that contain NFC(Spec). Since in general NRBC(Spec) and NFC(Spec) are incomparable, this implies that these two recovery methods place incomparable constraints on concurrency control.

5.7   INTERACTION OF RECOVERY AND CONCURRENCY CONTROL

In this section, we characterize the conflict relations that work with UIP and with DU. The proofs make use of the following additional definitions. First, if H is a history and CS is a set of transactions, we say that CS is a *commit set* for H if committed(H) $\subseteq$ CS and CS $\cap$ aborted(H) = $\emptyset$. In other words, CS is a set of transactions that have already committed or might commit. Second, we say that H is *on line dynamic atomic* if, for every commit set CS for H, H|CS is serializable in every total order consistent with precedes(H|CS). It is immediate that H is dynamic atomic if it is on line dynamic atomic.

The conflict relations that work with an update-in-place recovery method are characterized by the following theorem:

Theorem 2: I(X,Spec,UIP,Conflict) is correct iff NRBC(Spec)⊆Conflict.

Proof: For the if direction, suppose NRBC(Spec)⊆Conflict, and let H be a history in L(I(X,Spec,UIP,Conflict)). We show that H is online dynamic atomic, which implies that H is dynamic atomic. The proof is by induction on the length of H. If H = Λ, the result is immediate. Otherwise, suppose H = K•<e,X,A>, and let CS be a commit set for H. By induction, K is online dynamic atomic. There are now two cases. First, if e is an invocation of an operation, e = commit, e = abort, or A∉CS, then CS is also a commit set for K, and Opseq(H|CS) = Opseq(K|CS) and precedes(H|CS) = precedes(K|CS), so the result holds by induction.

Second, suppose e is the response R to an invocation I, and A∈CS. Let Q be the operation X:[I,R]. By the precondition for e, UIP(H,A)•Q is legal. We need to show that Serial(H|CS,T) is legal for every T consistent with precedes(H|CS). Let α = Serial(H|CS∪Active(H),T'), where T' is consistent with T on CS but orders the elements of Active(H)–CS after the elements of CS. Serial(H|CS,T) is a prefix of α. Since Spec(X) is prefix-closed, it suffices to show that α is legal. It is easy to show that there is a sequence UIP(H,A)•Q = $α_0, α_1, \ldots, α_n = α$ of operation sequences such that $α_i$ can be obtained from $α_{i-1}$ by swapping two adjacent operations, that is, $α_{i-1} = βPQγ$, and $α_i = βQPγ$, and (Q,P)∉Conflict. Since NRBC(Spec)⊆Conflict, (Q,P)∈RBC(Spec), so $α_{i--1}$ looks like $α_i$. By Lemma 2, UIP(H,A)•Q looks like α. By Lemma 4, α is legal.

For the only if direction, suppose (P,Q)∈NRBC(Spec) but (P,Q)∉Conflict. We show that there is a history H in L(I(X,Spec,UIP,Conflict)) that is not dynamic atomic. Since (P,Q)∈NRBC(Spec), there exists an α such that αQP does not look like αPQ with respect to Spec. Then there must be some ρ such that αQPρ∈Spec but αPQρ∉Spec. Let H be the history constructed as follows:

> A executes the operation sequence α at X
> A commits at X
> B executes Q at X
> C executes P at X
> B commits at X
> C commits at X
> D executes the operation sequence ρ at X
> D commits at X

H is permitted by I(X,Spec,UIP,Conflict). However, it is not dynamic atomic, since neither B nor C precedes the other, yet it is not serializable in the order A–C–B–D (because αPQρ ∉Spec). □

The conflict relations that work with a deferred-update recovery method are characterized by the following theorem:

Theorem 3: I(X,Spec,DU,Conflict) is correct if and only if NFC(Spec)⊆Conflict.

Proof: The if direction is a relatively straightforward induction; proofs can be found in [36, 40]. For the only if direction, suppose (P,Q)∈NFC(Spec) but (P,Q) ∉ Conflict. We show that there is a history H in L(I(X,Spec,DU,Conflict)) that is not dynamic atomic. Since (P,Q)∈NFC(Spec), there exists an α such that αP∈Spec and αQ∈Spec, and either αPQ∉Spec or αPQ is not equieffective to αQP with respect to Spec.

There are two cases. First, if αPQ∉Spec, let H be the history constructed as follows.

> A executes the operation sequence α at X
> A commits at X
> B executes P at X
> C executes Q at X
> B commits at X
> C commits at X

H is permitted by I(X,Spec,DU,Conflict). However, it is not dynamic atomic. Since neither B nor C precedes the other, dynamic atomicity requires that H be serializable in the orders A–B–C and A–C–B. But αPQ∉Spec, so H is not serializable in the order A–B–C.

Second, suppose αPQ is not equieffective to αQP with respect to Spec. Then there is some ρ such that either αPQρ∈Spec and αQPρ∉Spec, or αQPρ∈Spec and αPQρ∉Spec. Without loss of generality, suppose αPQρ∈Spec and αQPρ∉Spec. Let H be the history constructed as follows:

> A executes the operation sequence α at X
> A commits at X
> B executes P at X
> C executes Q at X
> B commits at X
> C commits at X
> D executes the operation sequence ρ at X
> D commits at X

H is permitted by I(X,Spec,DU,Conflict). However, it is not dynamic atomic, since neither B nor C precedes the other, yet it is not serializable in the order A–C–B–D (because αQPρ∉Spec). □

5.8   RESTRICTED LOCKING ALGORITHMS

In this section, we consider two restricted classes of locking algorithms: read/write locking and invocation-based locking (in which the lock acquired by an operation depends only on its inputs, and not on its results). We show that the differences between DU and UIP are irrelevant for read/write locking. For invocation-based locking, the differences between DU and UIP are irrelevant if all invocations are total and deterministic.

5.8.1 Read/Write Locking

In read/write locking [8], operations on an object are classified as either reads or writes, with the requirement that a read operation does not change the state of the object. There are two lock modes, read and write; write locks conflict with read and write locks (and vice versa). Read operations acquire read locks, and write operations acquire write locks. We show here that read/write locking works in combination with either DU or UIP, for the simple reason that the conflict relation contains both NFC and NRBC.

Let X be an object with serial specification Spec, and let P be an operation on X. We say that P is a *read operation* if for all operation sequences α such that αP is legal, $\alpha P \cong_{Spec} \alpha$. In other words, executing P has no effect on the results of future operations.

The following lemmas show that read operations commute forward and backward.

Lemma 8: If P and Q are read operations, then $(P,Q) \in$ FC.

Proof: Suppose that αP and αQ are legal. Since P is a read operation, $\alpha P \cong \alpha$. By Lemma 6, $\alpha PQ \cong \alpha Q$. Since Q is a read operation, $\alpha Q \cong \alpha$. By Lemma 3, $\alpha PQ \cong \alpha$. Since αP is legal, so is α, so by Lemma 4, αPQ is legal. A symmetric argument shows that $\alpha QP \cong \alpha$, and that αQP is legal. Then by Lemma 3, $\alpha PQ \cong \alpha QP$. $\square$

Lemma 9: If P and Q are read operations, then $(P,Q) \in$ RBC.

Proof: We must show that $\alpha QP \leq \alpha PQ$ for all α. Suppose $\alpha QP\beta$ is legal. By the definition of $\leq$, it suffices to show that $\alpha PQ\beta$ is legal. Since P and Q are read operations, it follows from Lemma 3 that $\alpha QP\beta \cong \alpha\beta$, and that $\alpha PQ\beta \cong \alpha\beta$. Thus, $\alpha QP\beta \cong \alpha PQ\beta$, so by Lemma 4, $\alpha PQ\beta$ is legal. $\square$

Since the read/write locking conflict relation contains all operation pairs (P,Q) except when P and Q are both read operations, it follows that read/write locking works with both DU and UIP. The differences between DU and UIP are irrelevant for read/write locking because read/write locking does not allow any transaction to access an object concurrently with one that is updating the object. Thus, the concurrency control restricts executions so that at any point in time either all active transactions are readers, and the view given by DU and by UIP is simply the "committed state," or there is a single writer, and the view given it *both* by DU *and* by UIP is the committed state modified by the writer's operations. (DU and UIP order the update operations of the committed transactions in the same way because there is only one writer active at a time, so that the commit order on writers used by DU is the same as the execution order used by UIP.)

5.8.2 Invocation-Based Locking

We use the term *invocation-based locking* to mean a locking algorithm in which the lock acquired by an operation depends only on its inputs and not on its results. The general commutativity-based locking algorithms studied earlier allow the lock acquired by an operation to depend on the results of the operation, as well as on its inputs. The bank account object BA illustrates how this can be useful: successful withdrawals commute forward with deposits, and unsuccessful withdrawals do not (see Table 5.1). If we used invocation-based locking, then every withdrawal operation would have to conflict with deposit operations.

More precisely, an invocation-based locking algorithm uses a conflict relation on operations derived from one on invocations as follows. If RI is a binary relation on invocations, let RI_{op} denote the binary relation on operations defined by ([I,Q],[J,R]) $\in RI_{op}$ iff (I,J) $\in$ RI. In other words, all operations with the same invocation have equivalent conflicts.

Even though invocation-based locking algorithms permit less concurrency than the general algorithms studied earlier, they are still interesting, in part because they form a subclass of the more general algorithms that corresponds naturally to the techniques used in many systems, and in part because under certain conditions, the differences between DU and UIP are irrelevant for invocation-based locking.

The results in this section can be summarized as follows: If all invocations are total and deterministic (i.e., every invocation has exactly one possible result in every state), then the conflict relations on invocations that work with DU are exactly the same as those that work with UIP. However, if operations can be partial or nondeterministic, then DU and UIP differ in their constraints on invocation-based locking. Notice also that the bank account object BA illustrates that even if all invocations are total and deterministic, UIP and DU differ when the results of operations are used to choose locks (since NFC and NRBC are incomparable; see Tables 5.1 and 5.2). Thus, the differences between DU and UIP can be ignored if the lock acquired by an operation depends only on its inputs, *and* if all invocations are total and deterministic.

Total Deterministic Invocations

Objects with partial and nondeterministic invocations are important in some applications [37]; for example, the allocation operation on a pool of resources is typically nondeterministic, and may be specified to be partial when the resource pool is empty (i.e., to have no possible result in the serial specification, which might correspond to blocking in a concurrent system until some other transaction makes a resource available for allocation). However, many objects have invocations that are total and deterministic. For example, the invocations on the bank account object BA described earlier are total and deterministic. In this section, we show that for the restricted class of objects whose invocations are total and deterministic, DU and UIP place identical constraints on invocation-based locking algorithms.

Let X be an object with serial specification Spec, and let I be an invocation on X. We say that I is *deterministic* if, for every legal operation sequence α, there is at most one response R such that $\alpha \bullet X:[I,R]$ is legal. We say that I is *total* if, for every legal operation sequence α, there is at least one response R such that $\alpha \bullet X:[I,R]$ is legal. Thus, if an invocation is both total and deterministic, then in any state (represented by a legal operation sequence), there is a unique response for the invocation. If I is both total and deterministic, we denote its response in state α by $R(I,\alpha)$. We use $I(\alpha)$ to denote the new state resulting from executing I in state α (i.e., $\alpha \bullet X:[I,R(I,\alpha)]$).

If I and J are invocations, we say that I *commutes forward with* J if, for all responses Q and R, [I,Q] commutes forward with [J,R]. We say that I *right commutes backward with* J if, for all responses Q and R, [I,Q] right commutes backward with [J,R].

In the remainder of this subsection, we assume that all invocations are total and deterministic.

We say that I and J *commute* if, for every legal operation sequence α, $I(J(\alpha)) \cong J(I(\alpha))$, $R(I,\alpha) = R(I,J(\alpha))$, and $R(J,\alpha) = R(J,I(\alpha))$. In other words, the state produced by executing the two invocations does not depend on the order, and neither influences the response returned by the other.

Let FCI denote the binary relation on invocations containing all pairs (I,J) such that I commutes forward with J. Similarly, let RBCI denote the binary relation on invocations containing all pairs (I,J) such that I right commutes backward with J, and let CI denote the binary relation on invocations containing all pairs (I,J) such that I commutes with J.

The following are straightforward:

Lemma 10: $I(X,Spec,UIP,RI_{op})$ is correct if and only if $NRBCI(Spec) \subseteq RI$.

Lemma 11: $I(X,Spec,DU,RI_{op})$ is correct if and only if $NFCI(Spec) \subseteq RI$.

We show that FCI = CI and RBCI = CI, thus implying that FCI = RBCI, and hence that $FCI_{op} = RBCI_{op}$. Thus, DU and UIP work with the same class of invocation-based locking algorithms, as long as all invocations are total and deterministic.

Lemma 12: FCI = CI.

Proof: First, we show that FCI $\subseteq$ CI. Suppose (I,J) $\in$ FCI. Then for all operation sequences α, and for all responses Q and R such that $\alpha \bullet X:[I,Q]$ is legal and $\alpha \bullet X:[J,R]$ is legal, $\alpha \bullet X:[I,Q] \bullet X:[J,R]$ and $\alpha \bullet X:[J,R] \bullet X:[I,Q]$ are legal and equieffective. Therefore, if α is legal, $J(I(\alpha)) \cong I(J(\alpha))$. Furthermore, $R(I,\alpha) = R(I,J(\alpha)) = Q$, and similarly for J. Therefore, (I,J) $\in$ CI.

Now we show that CI $\subseteq$ FCI. Suppose (I,J) $\in$ CI. Let α be a legal operation sequence, and let $Q = R(I,\alpha)$ and $R = R(J,\alpha)$. Thus, $\alpha \bullet X:[I,Q]$ and $\alpha \bullet X:[J,R]$ are legal. We need to show that $\alpha \bullet$X:[I,Q]$\bullet$X:[J,R] and $\alpha \bullet$X:[J,R]$\bullet$X:[I,Q] are legal and equieffective. By the definition of CI, R(I,α) = R(I,J(α)), and R(J,α) = R(J,I(α)). Therefore, $\alpha \bullet$X:[I,Q]$\bullet$X:[J,R] and $\alpha \bullet$X:[J,R]$\bullet$X:[I,Q] are legal. Furthermore, I(J(α)) $\cong$ J(I(α)), so $\alpha \bullet$X:[I,Q]$\bullet$X:[J,R] $\cong$ $\alpha \bullet$X:[J,R]$\bullet$X:[I,Q]. Thus, (I,J) $\in$ FCI. $\square$

To show that RBCI = CI, we will use the following additional notation: If β_I is a sequence of invocations, and β_R is a sequence of responses such that the two sequences have the same length, we use X:[β_I,β_R] to denote the sequence of operations obtained by pairing corresponding elements of β_I and β_R and concatenating the resulting operations in their original order.

Lemma 13: RBCI = CI.

Proof: First, we show that RBCI $\subseteq$ CI. Suppose (I,J) $\in$ RBCI. Let α be an operation sequence. Then for all Q and R, $\alpha \bullet$X:[J,R]$\bullet$X:[I,Q] $\le$ $\alpha \bullet$X:[I,Q]$\bullet$X:[J,R]; that is, for all β such that $\alpha \bullet$X:[J,R]$\bullet$X:[I,Q]$\bullet\beta$ is legal, $\alpha \bullet$X:[I,Q]$\bullet$X:[J,R]$\bullet\beta$ is also legal. Suppose $\alpha \bullet$X:[J,R]$\bullet$X:[I,Q] is legal; then R = R(J,α) and Q = R(I,J(α)). Since $\alpha \bullet$X:[J,R]$\bullet$X:[I,Q] $\le$ $\alpha \bullet$X:[I,Q]$\bullet$X:[J,R], $\alpha \bullet$X:[I,Q]$\bullet$X:[J,R] is also legal, so Q = R(I,α) and R = R(J,I(α)). It remains to show that I(J(α)) $\cong$ J(I(α)).

We know that I(J(α)) $\le$ J(I(α)); we must show that J(I(α)) $\le$ (I(J(α)). Let β be such that $\alpha \bullet$X:[I,Q]$\bullet$X:[J,R]$\bullet\beta$ is legal. Let β_I be the sequence of invocations in β, and let β_R be the sequence of responses. Since all invocations are total, there exists a sequence of responses γ_R such that $\alpha \bullet$X:[J,R]$\bullet$X:[I,Q]$\bullet$X:[β_I,γ_R] is legal. Since I(J(α)) $\le$ J(I(α)), $\alpha \bullet$X:[I,Q]$\bullet$X:[J,R]$\bullet$X:[β_I,γ_R] is also legal. Since all invocations are deterministic, γ_R = β_R. Therefore, $\alpha \bullet$X:[J,R]$\bullet$X:[I,Q]$\bullet\beta$ is legal. Hence, J(I(α)) $\le$ I(J(α)).

Now we show that CI $\subseteq$ RBCI. Suppose (I,J) $\in$ CI. Then for all α, I(J(α)) $\cong$ J(I(α)), R(I,α) = R(I,J(α)), and R(J,α) = R(J,I(α)). We must show that for all α, Q, and R, $\alpha \bullet$X:[J,R]$\bullet$X:[I,Q] $\le$ $\alpha \bullet$X:[I,Q]$\bullet$X:[J,R]. If $\alpha \bullet$X:[J,R]$\bullet$X:[I,Q] is illegal, the result is immediate. So assume that $\alpha \bullet$X:[J,R]$\bullet$X:[I,Q] is legal. Then Q = R(I,J(α)) and R = R(J,α). Therefore, $\alpha \bullet$X:[I,Q]$\bullet$X:[J,R] is legal. But then I(J(α)) = $\alpha \bullet$X:[J,R]$\bullet$X:[I,Q] and J(I(α)) = $\alpha \bullet$X:[I,Q]$\bullet$X:[J,R]. Hence, $\alpha \bullet$X:[J,R]$\bullet$X:[I,Q] $\cong$ $\alpha \bullet$X:[I,Q]$\bullet$X:[J,R], which implies the desired result. $\square$

Thus, if the lock acquired by an operation depends only on its inputs, *and* if all invocations are total and deterministic, UIP and DU work with the same class of conflict relations on invocations, namely, any relation containing CI.

Partial or Nondeterministic Invocations

We showed earlier that FCI and RBCI are equal if all invocations are total and deterministic. If we relax either assumption, that is, allow invocations to be either partial or nondeterministic, then FCI and RBCI need not be equal. In this section, we present several simple examples illustrating the differences between FCI and RBCI that arise because of partial or nondeterministic invocations. First, we consider objects whose invocations are partial but deterministic. Then we consider objects whose invocations are nondeterministic but total. Finally, we show that these effects are nonlocal, in the sense that if an object has any partial or nondeterministic invocations, FCI and RBCI can differ even when restricted to only those invocations that are total and deterministic.

Partial (Deterministic) Invocations: We consider objects for which some invocations are partial (but deterministic).

First, we show that RBCI need not be contained in FCI. Consider an object with the following serial specification. There are two invocations, I and J. There are three legal operation sequences: Λ, [I,Q], and [J,R]. In other words, either I or J can be executed in the object's initial state, but neither operation can be executed after that. The sequences [I,Q] and [J,R] are both legal, but neither of the sequences [I,Q]•[J,R] and [J,R]•[I,Q] is legal. Therefore, (I,J) $\notin$ FCI. However, I right commutes backward with J: For all α, x, and y, α•[I,x]•[J,y] and α•[J,y]•[I,x] are illegal, and hence equieffective.

We now show that FCI need not be contained in RBCI. Consider an object with the following serial specifiation. As before, there are two invocations, I and J. The legal operation sequences are the prefixes of the sequence [J,R]•[I,Q]. In other words, J can be executed only in the initial state, and I can be executed only immediately after J. I and J commute forward because at least one is illegal in each state. However, (I,J) $\notin$ RBCI: [J,R]•[I,Q] is legal, but [I,Q]•[J,R] is not.

Nondeterministic (Total) Invocations: We consider objects for which some invocations are nondeterministic (but total).

First, we show that RBCI need not be contained in FCI. Consider an object with the following serial specification. As above, there are two invocations, I and J. The legal operation sequences are described by the following regular expression: ([I,Q] | [J,Q])* | ([I,R] | [J,R])*. In other words, the first operation makes a nondeterministic choice of a result for itself and all subsequent operations. First, we claim that (I,J) $\notin$ FCI. Consider [I,Q] and [J,R]. Each is legal in the initial state, yet neither sequence of both is legal in the initial state. Second, we claim that (I,J) $\in$ RBCI. Consider a legal operation sequence α[J,y][I,x]. From the, regular expression earlier we see that x = y. But then α[I,x][J,y] is also legal, and is easily seen to be equieffective to α[J,y][I,x].

We now show that FCI need not be contained in RBCI. Consider an object with the following serial specification. As before, there are two invocations, I and J. The legal operation sequences are described by the following regular expression: [I,Q]* [J,T] ([I,Q] | [I,R] | [J,T])*. In other words, I has a single possible result, Q, until J has been invoked; once J has been invoked for the first time, I has two possible results, Q and R. First, we claim that (I,J) $\in$ FCI. We consider the possible combinations of results for I and J:

1. [I,Q] and [J,T]: Each is legal after any sequence α. Also, α[I,Q][J,T] and α[J,T][I,Q] are both legal. Furthermore, all sequences containing [J,T] are equieffective. Thus, [I,Q] commutes forward with [J,T].

2. [I,R] and [J,T]: Both are legal only after a sequence α containing [J,T]. If α contains [J,T], then α[I,R][J,T] and α[J,T][I,R] are both legal. Finally, as above, all sequences containing [J,T] are equieffective. Thus, [I,R] commutes forward with [J,T].

Second, we claim that (I,J) $\notin$ RBCI, since [J,T][I,R] is legal, but [I,R][J,T] is not.

Nonlocal Effects: Notice that the earlier proof that FCI = CI actually suffices to prove the following stronger result:

Lemma 14: Suppose I and J are total and deterministic (but other invocations may be partial or nondeterministic). Then (I,J) $\in$ FCI iff (I,J) $\in$ CI.

However, the proof that RBCI = CI relies on the assumption that *all* invocations are total and deterministic. This assumption is necessary, as the following example shows.

We show that even if I and J are total and deterministic, it is possible to have (I,J) $\in$ RBCI and (I,J) $\notin$ CI if some other invocation is partial or nondeterministic. Consider an object with the following serial specification. There are three invocations, I, J, and K. I and J are total and deterministic; K is partial. The legal operation sequences are described as follows. The response for I in all states is Q; that for J is R; and that for K is S (in all states in which K is legal). The sequences are those generated by the automaton described by the state transition Table 5.3 (Since each invocation has only one possible result, we have omitted the results).

Table 5.3. State Transitions

s	I(s)	J(s)	K(s)
0	1	2	
1	3	4	
2	5	3	
3	3	3	
4	3	3	4
5	3	3	

I and J are clearly total and deterministic; each has a single legal response in every state. K is partial (but deterministic); it is legal only in state 4. We claim that I right commutes backward with J. From every state except state 0, executing J followed by I (or I followed by J) yields state 3. From state 0, executing J followed by I yields state 5, and executing I followed by J yields state 4. Furthermore, 5 looks like 4 (but not vice versa). Therefore, I right commutes backward with J (but not vice versa). However, I does not commute with J, since in state 0, executing I followed by J is not equieffective to executing J followed by I.

This example can be modified fairly simply to give one in which the existence of a nondeterministic (but total) operation causes the same problem. Allow K to have two possible results, S and T. In every state s, have the next state for K be s. In state 4, let both S and T be possible results for K; in other states, let S be the only possible result for K. As before, 5 looks like 4, but not vice versa.

If I and J are total and deterministic and $(I,J) \in CI$, then it must also be that $(I,J) \in RBCI$ (regardless of whether other operations are partial or nondeterministic). The last part of the proof of Lemma 13 shows this claim.

5.9 CONCLUSIONS

We have analyzed two general recovery methods for abstract data types, and have given necessary and sufficient conditions for conflict relations to work with each. The classes of conflict relations that work in combination with the two recovery methods are incomparable, implying that choosing between these two recovery methods involves a trade-off in concurrency: Each permits conflict relations that the other does not, and thus there may be applications for which one or the other is preferable on the basis of the level of concurrency achieved.

Most of the concurrency control literature assumes an update-in-place model for recovery. The results in this chapter show that this is not just a technical assumption: Other recovery methods permit conflict relations not permitted by update-in-place, and thus cannot be viewed simply as implementations of update-in-place.

For the two particular recovery methods studied in this chapter, namely, update-in-place and deferred-update, we have also shown that, if locks for operations are chosen based only on the inputs to the operations, and all invocations are total and deterministic, then the two recovery methods place identical constraints on concurrency control.

Most, if not all, approaches to recovery of which we are aware can be viewed as implementations of either update-in-place or deferred-update, so we believe that the analysis of these specific methods is quite important. However, there are interesting algorithms that combine aspects of both of these two methods, or in which concurrency control and recovery are more tightly integrated. For example, O'Neil has presented a type-specific concurrency control and recovery algorithm in which concurrency control and recovery are tightly coupled, and in which the test for conflicts depends on the current state of the object [23]. Further work is required to characterize the recovery algorithms that can be modeled using the framework presented in this chapter, and to generalize our approach to accommodate other algorithms. It would be interesting to consider concurrency control algorithms other than the conflict-based locking algorithms considered here, and to consider correctness conditions other than dynamic atomicity.

The material presented here grew out of earlier work [40], in which we presented two locking algorithms for abstract data types. One of the two algorithms in [40] is essentially a combination of DU with a conflict relation of NFC; the other is a combination of UIP with a more restrictive conflict relation than NRBC. In [40] we proved the correctness of the two algorithms, and conjectured that it was impossible to do better for either recovery method. In addition, the model of an implementation used in [40] is relatively low-level, containing many details that turn out not to be important; the model of an implementation presented in this chapter more clearly highlights the interactions between concurrency control and recovery. The results here provide a precise characterization of the conflict relations that work with each recovery method, confirming our earlier conjecture for DU but disproving it for UIP. The algorithm consisting of the combination of UIP and NRBC(Spec) presented in this chapter is interesting in itself, since it requires fewer conflicts than previous algorithms, and also because it is impossible to do better.

References

[1] Allchin, J. E., *An architecture for reliable decentralized systems*, Technical Report GIT-ICS-83/23, Georgia Institute of Technology, September, 1983.

[2] Allchin, J. E., and McKendry, M. S., "Synchronization and recovery of actions", in *Proceedings of the Second Annual ACM Symposium on Principles of Distributed Computing*, Canada, August, 1983.

[3] Beeri, C., et al., "A concurrency control theory for nested transactions", *Proceedings of the Second Annual ACM Symposium on Principles of Distributed Computing*, Canada, August, 1983.

[4] Bernstein, P. A., and Goodman, N., "Concurrency control in distributed database systems", *ACM Computing Surveys*, 13(2) (June 1981).

[5] Bernstein, P., Goodman, N., and Lai, M.-Y., "Analyzing concurrency control when user and system operations differ", *IEEE Transactions on Software Engineering*, SE-9(3) (May 1983).

[6] Bernstein, P., V. Hadzilacos, N. Goodman, *Concurrency control and recovery in database systems*. Addison-Wesley, 1987.

[7] Chan, A., et al., *The implementation of an integrated concurrency control and recovery scheme*, Computer Corporation of America, Technical Report CCA-82-01, March, 1982.

[8] Eswaran, K. P., Gray, J. N., Lorie, R. A., and Traiger, I. L., "The notions of consistency and predicate locks in a database system", *CACM*, 19(11) (November 1976).

[9] Gray, J., *Notes on Database Operating Systems*, Operating Systems – An Advanced Course, Springer-Verlag, Lecture Notes in Computer Science, Vol. 60, 1978.

[10] Gray, J.N., et al., "The recovery manager of the System R database manager", *ACM Computing Surveys*, 13(2) (June 1981).

[11] Hadzilacos, V., "A theory of reliability in database systems", *Journal of the ACM*, 35(1) (January 1988).

[12] Korth, H. F., *Locking protocols: general lock classes and deadlock freedom*, Princeton University, 1981.

[13] Korth, H. F. "A deadlock-free, variable granularity locking protocol", *Proceedings of the Fifth Berkeley Workshop on Distributed Data Management and Computer Networks*, February, 1981.

[14] Korth, H. F., "Locking Primitives in a Database System", *Journal of the Association for Computing Machinery*, 30(1) (January 1983).

[15] Kung, H.T., and Robinson, J.T., "On optimistic methods for concurrency control", *ACM Transactions on Database Systems*, 6(2) (June 1981).

[16] Lampson, B., Atomic transactions, "In Distributed Systems: Architecture and Implementation", Springer-Verlag Lecture Notes in Computer Science, ed. by Goos and Hartmanis, Vol. 105, 1981.

[17] Liskov, B., and Scheifler, R., "Guardians and actions: linguistic support for robust, distributed programs", *ACM Transactions on Programming Languages and Systems*, 5(3) (July 1983).

[18] Lynch, N.A., "Concurrency control for resilient nested transactions", *Proceedings of the 2nd ACM Symposium on Principles of Database Systems*, March, 1983.

[19] Lynch, N. A., and M. R. Tuttle, *Hierarchical correctness proofs for distributed algorithms*, Technical Report MIT/LCS/TR-387, MIT Laboratory for Computer Science, April, 1987.

[20] Lynch, N. and Tuttle, M., *An Introduction to Input/Output Automata*, Technical Memo, MIT/LCS/TM-373, Lab for Computer Science Massachusetts Institute of Technology, November 1988.

[21] Mitchell, J. G. and Dion, J., A comparison of two network-based file servers, *Communications of the ACM*, 25(4) (April 1982).

[22] Moss, J., N. Griffeth, M. Graham, *Abstraction in concurrency control and recovery management (revised)*, Technical Report 86-20, University of Massachusetts at Amherst, May 1986.

[23] O'Neil, P. E., The escrow transactional method, *ACM Transactions on Database Systems*, 11(4) (December 1986).

[24] Papadimitriou, C.H., The serializability of concurrent database updates, *Journal of the ACM*, 26(4) (October 1979).

[25] Reed, D. P., Implementing Atomic Actions on Decentralized Data, *ACM Transactions on Computer Systems*, 1(1), 1983.

[26] Reuter, A., Concurrency on high-traffic data elements, *Proceedings of the Symposium on Principles of Database Systems*, Los Angeles, CA, March, 1982.

[27] Rosenkrantz, D. J., Stearns, R. E., and Lewis, P. M., System level concurrency control for distributed database systems, *ACM Transactions on Database Systems*, 3(2) (June 1978).

[28] Schwarz, P., and Spector, A., *Synchronizing shared abstract types*, Technical Report CMU-CS-82-128. Pittsburgh: Carnegie Mellon University, 1982.

[29] Schwarz, P. M., and Spector, A. Z., Synchronizing shared abstract types, *ACM Transactions on Computer Systems*, 2(3) (August 1984).

[30] Schwarz, P., *Transactions on typed objects*, Technical Report CMU-CS-84-166. Pittsburgh: Carnegie Mellon University, 1984.

[31] Skeen, M. D., *Crash recovery in a distributed database system*, Technical Report UCB/ERL M82/45. Berkeley: University of California, 1982.

[32] Spector, A. Z., et al., Support for distributed transactions in the TABS prototype, *IEEE Transactions on Software Engineering*, SE-11(6) (June 1985).

[33] Verhofstad, J.S.M., *Recovery for multi-level data structures*, Technical Report 96. England: University of Newcastle upon Tyne, December, 1976.

[34] Verhofstad, J. S. M., Recovery techniques for database systems, *ACM Computing Surveys*, 10(2) (June 1978).

[35] Weihl, W. and Liskov, B., Specification and implementation of resilient, atomic data types, *Proceedings of the Symposium on Programming Language Issues in Software Systems*, San Francisco, CA, June, 1983.

[36] Weihl, W.E., Specification and implementation of atomic data types, Technical Report, MIT/LCS/TR-314, 1984.

[37] Weihl, W., and Liskov, B., Implementation of resilient, atomic data types, *ACM Transactions on Programming Languages and Systems*, April, 1985.

[38] Weihl, W.E., Local atomicity properties: modular concurrency control for abstract data types, *ACM Transactions on Programming Languages and Systems*, 11(2) (April 1989).

[39] Weihl, W. E., Commutativity-based Concurrency Control for Abstract Data Types, Memo, MIT Laboratory for Computer Science, October, 1987.

[40] Weihl, W.E., Commutativity-based Concurrency Control for Abstract Data Types, *IEEE Transactions on Computers*, 37(12) (December 1988).

[41] Weikum, G., and H.-J. Schek, Architectural issues of transaction management in multi-layered systems, *Proceedings of the 10th International Conference on Very Large Data Bases*, Singapore, Auugust, 1984.

[42] Weikum, G., A theoretical foundation of multi-level concurrency control, *Proceedings of the Fifth ACM Symposium on Principles of Database Systems*, 1986.

Chapter 6

Redo Recovery After System Crashes

David Lomet and Mark R. Tuttle

Abstract

This chapter defines a framework for explaining redo recovery after a system crash. In this framework, an installation graph explains the order in which operations must be installed into the stable database if it is to remain recoverable. This installation graph is a significantly weaker ordering on operations than the conflict graph from concurrency control. We use the installation graph to devise (1) a cache management algorithm for writing data from the volatile cache to the stable database, (2) the specification of a REDO test used to choose the operations on the log to replay during recovery, and (3) an idempotent recovery algorithm based on this test; and we prove that these cache management and recovery algorithms are correct. Most pragmatic recovery methods depend on constraining the kinds of operations that can appear in the log, but our framework allows arbitrary logged operations. We use our framework to explain pragmatic methods that constrain the logged operations to reading and writing single pages, and then using this new understanding to relax these constraints. The result is a new class of logged operations having a recovery method with practical advantages over current methods.

6.1 INTRODUCTION

Explaining how to recover from a system crash requires answering some fundamental questions.

- How can the stable state be explained in terms of what operations have been installed and what operations have not?

- How should recovery choose the operations to redo in order to recover an explainable state?
- How should the cache manager install operations into the stable state in order to keep the state explainable, and hence recoverable?

The answers to these questions can be found in the delicately balanced and highly interdependent decisions an implementor must make. One of these decisions is the choice of operations to be recorded in the log. Many systems rely on page-oriented operations where operations write a single page and read at most that page, but how would the answers to the three preceding questions change if the operations could read or write other pages? The goal of this work is to understand the impact the choice of logged operations has on crash recovery.

The foundation for this work is an *installation graph* that constrains the order in which changes by operations can be installed into the stable state, and provides a way of explaining what changes have been installed. This graph uses edges to order conflicting operations like the conflict graph from concurrency control, but the installation ordering is much weaker. We prove that if, at the time of a crash, the state can be explained in terms of this graph, then we can use the log to recover the state. We then design a *cache management algorithm* that guarantees that the stable state remains explainable and a *recovery algorithm* that recovers any explainable state, and we prove that these algorithms are correct. Both cache management and recovery algorithms are based on conditions derived from the installation graph. In this sense, it is the installation graph that captures the impact of the choice of logged operations on the recovery process.

One pragmatic impact of our work is a concise explanation of redo recovery. Our work makes it easy to compare recovery methods and to understand how changing the logged operations will change the algorithms needed for crash recovery. For example, given a database using one class of logged operations, we can see exactly how using another class of logged operations forces the cache manager to change. Our work also has the potential for identifying generalizations of known logging strategies. Indeed, we generalize the logged operations used in physiological logging to a class we call *tree operations* that improves the efficiency of logging changes like B-tree splits while introducing only minor changes to cache management.

To the best of our knowledge, this is the first treatment of crash recovery that is both formal and general. Formal treatments of recovery from aborts via transaction rollback are quite general [13], but the only formal treatment of recovery from crashes we know about [10] is specific to ARIES [14]. In the remainder of this introduction, we explain in more detail how the choice of logged operations can affect recovery, and how our framework exposes this impact.

6.1.1   The Basics of Redo Recovery

When a computer crashes, the contents of the memory are presumed to be lost or corrupted. Only the contents of the disk are trusted to remain. In order to guarantee that the database state can survive a crash, it is stored on disk in the *stable database.* Reading and writing the disk is slow, however, so parts of the state are kept in memory in the *database cache.* Each change an operation makes to the state is made in the cache, and the *cache manager* is responsible for writing these changes into the stable database at some later point in time.

The cache manager may not be able to write all of the changes into the stable database before a crash, so information about each operation is written to a record in a *log,* and the log is used to reconstruct the database state after a crash. The log is typically a sequence of log records (but see [11, 15]). The head of the log is kept on disk in the *stable log,* the tail of the log is kept in memory, and the *log manager* is responsible for moving log records from memory to disk. We assume the log manager is following the *write-ahead log protocol* WAL. This is a well-understood way of managing the log. It has the property that before any state change made by an operation O is written into the stable state, the log record for O and all records preceding this record are written into the stable log.

The recovery process uses the stable state and the stable log to recover the database after a crash. There are many methods for recovery that appear in the literature. These methods provide many specific techniques for ensuring transaction atomicity and durability, including write-ahead logging, the do/undo/redo paradigm, forcing log records at commit, forcing pages at commit, and so on [2, 3, 4, 5, 8, 14], and much of this work has found its way into textbooks [1, 6]. In addition, general methods exist for undoing nested transactions [18] and multi-level transactions [12, 19, 20].

We focus on *redo recovery.* This technique starts at some point in the log and reads to the end of the log. As it examines each log record, it either reinvokes the logged operation on the current state or passes it by. Although redo recovery is just one form of recovery, it is an important technique because every efficient recovery method uses it. Redo recovery is efficient in the sense that it does not require the cache manager to write all changes to the stable state when a transaction commits. Redo recovery also has applications in areas like word processing and file editing that are independent of the transactional setting. Furthermore, ARIES [14] suggests understanding recovery after a crash as performing redo recovery followed by undo recovery. With this, redo recovery must solve the hardest parts of recovery: making sense of the state at the time of the crash, and determining what operations in the log to reexecute to rebuild the state. These are the kinds of problems we want to study.

6.1.2   The Problem

The operations a user invokes on the database can be quite different from the operations appearing in the log. For example, inserting a record into a B-tree may be a single operation to the user, but may be recorded as a sequence of write operations in the log if the insert involves splitting a node. The only requirement is that the combined effect of the logged operations be equal to the effect of the user operation. There are many ways that a user operation can be split into logged operations. How this split is made can affect many aspects of recovery. To see that this is true, let us examine two common logging strategies.

In the simplest form of *after-image logging* (also called *state* or *physical logging*), each log record consists of a variable name and a value written to that variable. Each logged operation is effectively of the form $x \leftarrow v$ describing a blind write to a single variable (typically, a disk page). This technique has the advantage that cache management and recovery are quite easy. The cache manager can install changes into the stable database in any order, and recovery is still possible.

Figure 6.1. Recovery based on after-image logging.

In the example in Figure 6.1, variables in the stable database can have any value at the start of recovery. The recovery process merely needs to start scanning the log at a point where all uninstalled operations will be included in the scan, and then write values into variables one after another in log (or conflict graph) order. At the end of recovery, each variable will be set to its final logged value and the state will be recovered.

In *logical logging*, each log record consists of the name of the operation and the parameters with which it was invoked. This technique has the advantage that the log records are much smaller (an operation's name and parameters are typically much smaller than a copy of a disk page), but now cache management is tricky.

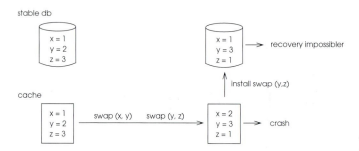

Figure 6.2. Recovery based on logical logging.

In the scenario of Figure 6.2, the stable database and the database cache begin in the same state, then two swap operations are performed, their changes are made in the cache, and the two log records for the swaps are written to the stable log. Suppose that the effect of the first swap is written to the stable database just before a crash. The recovery process can redo the second swap and recover the state of the database. On the other hand, suppose the effect of the second swap is installed just before a crash, and the effect of the first is never installed. Now the recovery process is stuck. There is no way that it can recover by redoing one or both of the swap operations appearing in the log: It cannot swap the value 2 into x since the value 2 does not even appear in the stable state. The cache manager *must* install the first swap before the second.

Given a class of logged operations, how much flexibility does the cache manager have in the order it installs database changes? At one extreme, the cache manager could install changes in the order they occur, but this ordering is too strict to be efficient. At the other extreme, the cache manager could install changes in any order. This does not work with logical logging. On the other hand, it does work with after-image logging. This causes us to ask the following question: Given a set of logged operations, what is the weakest possible ordering that the cache manager can use when installing changes and still guarantee that the stable database remains recoverable?

Identifying this weakest ordering is interesting for many reasons. It gives the cache manager more flexibility to install changes in a more efficient order, perhaps making cache management simpler. It also may lead to new logging strategies making use of new kinds of logged operations that reduce logging cost but preserve cache efficiency and database recoverability. Finally, it can lead to improved understanding and comparison of known recovery strategies.

6.1.3   The Solution

Given a class of logged operations, we represent the amount of flexibility the cache manager has to install the changes made by these operations with an *installation graph* giving a partial order on the operations. We prove that if a database state can be "explained" as the result of installing operations in a prefix of this graph, and if the database log contains the remaining uninstalled operations, then the database is recoverable. One well-known partial order on operations is the *conflict graph*. Two operations O and P conflict if one writes a variable x that the other reads or writes, and every pair of conflicting operations is ordered by an edge in the graph from one to the other. The edges are classified into sets of read-write, write-read, and write-write edges depending on how the operations O and P access x. It is easy to see that if operations are installed in a sequential order consistent with the conflict graph, then the state remains recoverable: Redoing the uninstalled operations in a sequential order consistent with the graph will recover the state. Are all of the edges in the conflict graph needed? The answer is no.

We do not need write-read edges. The example in Figure 6.3 involves one operation O setting $x \leftarrow 1$ followed by a second operation P setting $y \leftarrow x$, and there is clearly a write-read edge from O to P in the conflict graph since O writes x before P reads it.

O and P are invoked on the database and their changes are made in the cache, but P is installed first in the stable database just before a crash. The recovery

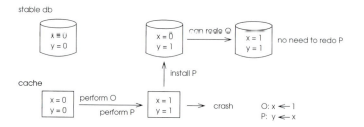

Figure 6.3. Write-read edges can be ignored.

process can redo O, and since redoing O does not reset the effect of P (O does not write to the variable y written by P), recovery is accomplished.

In many cases, we do not need write-write edges either. This observation is related to the Thomas write rule in the special case of blind writes to single pages, but it is also true in more general situations. In the example of Figure 6.4, an operation O setting $x \leftarrow 1$ and $z \leftarrow 2$ is followed by an operation P setting $y \leftarrow x$ and $z \leftarrow 3$, so there is a write-write edge from O to P since both write to the variable z.

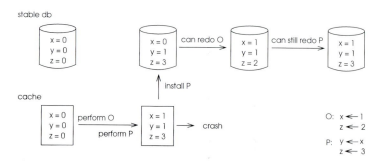

Figure 6.4. Write-write edges can often be ignored.

Again, O and P are invoked on the database and their changes are made in the cache, but only P is installed in the stable database before a crash, and not O. The recovery process can redo O and this resets a change made by P, but redoing O has the effect of reconstructing the read set of P, so the recovery process can redo P as well.

We can generalize this last example to the case where redoing a sequence of operations beginning with O reconstructs the read set of P during recovery, and hence enables the redo of P. Given an operation O, we define the *must redo set of O*, denoted by $must(O)$, that contains O and all operations following O in the conflict graph whose changes would be reset by redoing O during recovery, and hence would have to be redone themselves. This is effectively the transitive closure of the write-write edges in the conflict graph starting from O. We also define the *can redo set of* O, denoted by $can(O)$, containing operations reset by redoing O that can be redone ultimately as a result of redoing O. These operations can be ordered in a way consistent with the conflict graph and beginning with O so that redoing the first operation rebuilds the read set of the second, redoing the first two operations rebuilds the read set of the third, and so on.

The *installation graph* is obtained from the conflict graph by keeping all read-write edges, throwing away all write-read edges, and keeping write-write edges from O to P when $P \in must(O)\backslash can(O)$.[1] This reflects our earlier observation that all of the write-read edges and many of the write-write edges are unnecessary. In the case of write-write edges, there is an edge from O to P if redoing O during recovery forces us to redo P, but redoing O does not guarantee that P can actually be redone. This definition of an installation graph is quite simple, but it is already enough to demonstrate differences between logging strategies.

First, consider after-image logging, where the logged operations are blind writes of the form $x \leftarrow v$. In this case, the installation graph has no edges at all, which corresponds to our earlier observation that changes resulting from these operations can be installed in any order. This is because the read set of every operation is empty. There are obviously no read-write edges for this reason. To see that there are no write-write edges, notice that if P is in O's must redo set then P is in O's can redo set, since P's read set is null and does not need reconstruction.

Now consider the case of physiological logging [6], where each logged operation $x \leftarrow f(x)$ reads the value of a single page and writes some function of this value back to the same page. In this case, the installation graph consists of chains of read-write edges, one chain for each variable x that orders the operations accessing x. Once again there are no write-write edges because every operation P in O's must redo set is also in O's can redo set. To see this, notice that if O reads and writes x, then O's must redo set consists of all operations P reading and writing x that follow O in the conflict graph. We can redo all of these operations after redoing O by redoing them in conflict graph order.

The installation graph we have defined so far is quite simple because we have made some simplifying assumptions. We have assumed that when an operation O's changes are installed into the stable database, that all of its changes are installed atomically, but this is frequently not necessary. Atomic installation may even be problematic if an operation O can write multiple pages. We allow O's write set to be partitioned into *updates* that represent the units of atomic installation. We have also assumed that when an operation O is redone during recovery, that the entire write set of O is recomputed and installed, but this may not be true either. There are recovery methods that can test during recovery which of O's changes are uninstalled and recompute only a portion of O's write set. One example is recovery based on log sequence numbers (LSNs), where every page is tagged with the LSN of the log record of the last operation to write to the page. During recovery, any page

---

[1]We denote the set difference of two sets A and B by $A\backslash B$. This is the set of elements in A and not in B.

having an LSN greater than the LSN associated with an operation's log record must already contain the changes made by this operation, so no change needs to be made to the page. We allow O's write set to be partitioned into *redos* that represent the units of recovery. Incorporating these notions into the installation graph is delicate, but we do so in a clean way, and this enables us to capture more general logging strategies.

6.1.4   The Consequences

Given our installation graph, we prove that if the state of the stable database can be "explained" by a prefix of the installation graph, then we can use the stable log to recover the state. A state S can be explained by a prefix of the graph if there is an ordering of the operations in the prefix that (among other things) assigns certain "exposed" variables the same values they have in S. If we consider the operations in the prefix to be installed and the rest of the operations to be uninstalled, then the exposed variables are (roughly speaking) all variables that are read by one uninstalled operation before being written by any other. Assuming these exposed variables have the right values, then we can recover the state simply by redoing the uninstalled operations in conflict graph order.

Since an explainable state is a recoverable state, all the cache manager has to do is install operations one after another in a way that guarantees that the stable state remains explainable. Of course, in reality, a cache manager does not install operations, it installs variables. If two operations happen to write two values to a variable x between two successive installations of x, then the cache manager writes the second value back to the stable state and effectively installs changes made by both operations at once. Nonetheless, the installation graph ordering of operations can be used to construct an ordering on variables so that if the cache manager installs variables in this order, then the state remains explainable in terms of a set of installed operations.

Recovering an explainable state can be as simple as going through the log and redoing an operation if it is uninstalled, but this requires a test for whether an operation is installed. On the other hand, some recovery methods redo many more operations than this. Some recovery methods go through the log and redo every operation that can be redone, but this requires knowing whether an operation is applicable in the current state. This also requires knowing whether redoing an installed operation O will reset the effects of another installed operation P, and if so, whether it will be possible to redo P when it is reached in the log. We abstract away these details by assuming the existence of a test REDO(O) for whether the recovery procedure should redo the operation O. The specification of REDO(O) is stated in terms of the installation graph, and it is an abstraction of many implementation techniques like log sequence numbers used to determine during recovery whether the operation O should be redone. We give an algorithm that goes through the log and redoes O whenever REDO(O) returns true, and we prove that this is an idempotent recovery algorithm when started in an explainable (and hence recoverable) state.

The installation graph is also a criterion for the correctness of checkpointing algorithms. The process of checkpointing need only identify (perhaps after flushing portions of the cache to disk) a prefix of the installation graph that explains the stable state, and then remove a prefix of the stable log that contains only operations in this prefix, always leaving all uninstalled operations on the log.

Finally, we can exploit the installation graph to generalize existing logging strategies. We show how the logged operations used in physiological logging can be generalized to what we call *tree operations*. A tree operation reads one page and writes that page together with a set of "new pages" that have never been written before. Cache management for tree operations is only slightly more difficult than for physiological operations. Tree operations, however, enable us to log the splitting of a B-tree node with a single operation rather than with a sequence of physiological operations. In addition, we can use checkpointing as a kind of garbage collection that allows us to reclaim used-and-discarded pages as "new pages" that can be written by future tree operations. In ways like these, the installation graph gives us a graph-theoretic technique for understanding many aspects of redo recovery methods that appear in the literature.

6.2 DATABASE MODEL

We sketch our model of a database here, and give the complete statement in the technical report [22]. A *state* is a function mapping variables in a set V to values in a set $\mathcal{V}$, and one state is chosen as the *initial state*. An *operation* is a function mapping states to states. We consider only the logged operations in this model, and do not explicitly model the user operations. An *operation invocation* describes a particular invocation of an operation. It is a tuple including the operation invoked, the read and write sets for the invocation, and their before and after images. When it will cause no confusion, we denote an operation invocation by the name of the operation invoked, and we shorten "operation invocation" to "operation."

We mentioned in the introduction that the changes an operation makes to its write set need not be installed into the database atomically, since they may be installed as a sequence of atomic installations instead, perhaps one page at a time. We model this by assuming that the write set of an operation O is partitioned into a collection $U_1, \ldots, U_u$ of disjoint subsets. Our interpretation of U_i is that the changes O makes to variables in U_i must be installed atomically. We refer to the pair $\langle O, U_i \rangle$ as an *update*. We assume that the intersection of O's read and write sets is contained in just one of the sets U_i, which means that O's changes to its read set must be installed atomically. We note that O's changes to its read set must be installed after all of O's other changes, or it may be impossible to redo O after a crash. Informally, we think of an operation O as being a set of updates whose write sets partition O's write set.

We also mentioned in the introduction that it may not be necessary or desirable to reconstruct the entire write set of an operation during recovery, since it may be possible to apply some test during recovery to determine which of the operation's updates need to be reinstalled. The more specific this test can be about which updates need to be reinstalled, the smaller the reconstructed portion of the write set needs to be. We model this by assuming that an operation O's set of updates is partitioned into a collection of *redos*. The recovery process may choose to redo only a few of an operation's redos, but redoing one redo means reinstalling all of that redo's updates. During recovery, a redo is an all-or-nothing thing: Either all of the updates in the redo are reinstalled or none are. Given an update $\langle O, U \rangle$, we let $[O, U]$ denote the redo that contains it.

Two operation invocations *conflict* if the write set of one intersects the read or write set of the other. A *conflict graph* orders conflicting invocations O and P with a path from O to P if O occurs before P, in which case we write $O \leq P$. We consider only *serializable* conflict graphs, which means they can be totally ordered. A *history* H is a conflict graph describing a database execution, that is, a conflict graph that contains all operation ever invoked on the database. A *log* L for H is a subgraph of H induced by some nodes in H giving a partial description of the history, and possibly including some additional edges to impose a stricter ordering (like a sequence) on invocations.

A *database system* D is a triple (S, L, H) consisting of a state S, a history H, and a log L for H. Of course, no real database implementation would explicitly represent the history since the state and the log contain all of the information about the history needed by the implementation. For us, the history is just the correctness condition for the recovery process. We say that D is *recovered* if its state S is the result of starting with the initial state and applying the operations in its history H in a sequence consistent with H. We say that D is *recoverable* if it can be transformed into a recovered database by installing some redos for some operations appearing in the log in some order consistent with the log. The recovery process should be *idempotent*, meaning that the database remains recoverable throughout the recovery process.

We can assume that the log is always a suffix of the history for two reasons. First, we assume that the log manager is following the *write-ahead log protocol* WAL. In our model, this means that when an operation is added to the stable history, the operation is also added to the stable log. Second, we assume that the *checkpointing* process, which speeds recovery by shortening the log, removes installed operations from the front of the log. The result is that the log forms a suffix of the history that contains all uninstalled operations of the history. For example, this means the log of a recovered database can be empty.

A database implementation splits a database into stable and volatile components, as illustrated in Figure 6.5.

The *stable database* is a database (S_s, L_s, H_s) as defined before, and represents the disk resident part of the database (i.e., the final copy of the database). The *volatile database*, or *cache*, is a partial database $(S_v, L_v, H_v, U_v, B_v)$, meaning that the volatile state is a partial mapping from variables to values, with two additional data structures:

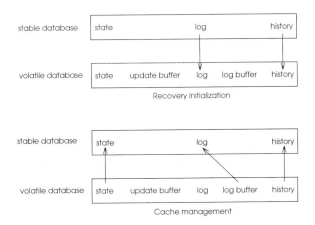

Figure 6.5. Normal operation and recovery in a database.

- the *update buffer* U_v is a set of updates not yet installed in the stable state S_s, and

- the *log buffer* B_v is a working log consisting of operations not yet posted to the stable log L_s.

The logical database is a database (S_ℓ, L_ℓ, H_ℓ) where the state S_ℓ is a merge of the volatile and stable states, the log L_ℓ is the volatile log, and the history H_ℓ is the volatile history. The value of a variable x in the logical state is the value of x in the volatile state if defined, and the value of x in the stable state otherwise.

During normal operation, invoking an operation O on the database changes the volatile state by changing the values of variables in O's write set to the values given by O's after image, adds O's updates to the update buffer, adds O to the log buffer, and adds O to the volatile history. The volatile log is empty during normal operation; it is used only during recovery, implying that the logical log is also empty.

At the start of recovery, the volatile database is reset as follows (see Figure 6.5). The volatile log and history are set equal to the stable log and history; and the volatile state, update buffer, and log buffer are set to empty. One after another, operations O are chosen from the front of the log, and some collection of O's redos $[O, U]$, perhaps none, is chosen. For each chosen redo $[O, U]$, one after another, the updates $\langle O, V \rangle$ in $[O, U]$ are used to modify the volatile state and then are added to the update buffer. Finally, O is removed from the log. Notice that O already appears in the stable history and log, so there is no need to add it to the volatile history and log buffer.

It is the cache manager that moves information from the volatile database to the stable database (see Figure 6.5). It does so as follows:

1. It chooses a variable x to write to the stable state, and then chooses a set

X of variables including x. How this choice is made is the subject of a later section.

2. It updates the stable log by following the write-ahead log protocol. This means that it identifies all operations O with updates $\langle O, U \rangle$ in the volatile update buffer writing to a variable in X, it identifies prefixes of the volatile log buffer and volatile history so that no such operation O appears in the remaining suffixes, it adds these prefixes to the stable log and stable history, and it removes the log buffer prefix from the log buffer.

3. It writes X atomically to the stable state and removes the updates $\langle O, U \rangle$ from the volatile update buffer.

This description is consistent with our use of the WAL protocol and our checkpointing requirement, and guarantees that the stable log is always a suffix of the stable history.

6.3   CONDITIONS FOR RECOVERABILITY

The main results of this section are the definition of the installation graph and what it means for a state to be explainable in terms of this graph. Then, in later sections, we will use this graph to construct recovery and cache management algorithms.

6.3.1   Must Redo and Can Redo

As in the introduction, the definition of the installation graph begins with the definition of the must and can redo sets.

In the introduction, we defined $must(O)$ to be the set of all operations following O in the conflict graph whose changes would be reset by redoing O during recovery, and hence would have to be redone themselves. This was effectively the transitive closure of the write-write edges in the conflict graph starting with O. Now that redos are the unit of recovery, and not operations, we want to define this set in terms of updates and redos.

Assuming that we must reinstall an update $\langle O, U \rangle$ during recovery, what is the set of updates that will be deinstalled when we reinstall $\langle O, U \rangle$? First, reinstalling $\langle O, U \rangle$ during recovery requires that we reinstall every update in its redo set $[O, U]$. Next, reinstalling the updates in $[O, U]$ may overwrite variables written by operations following O in the conflict graph, effectively deinstalling updates for later operations. Each of these deinstalled updates $\langle P, V \rangle$ and their associated redos $[P, V]$ will have to be reinstalled, and reinstalling them will in turn deinstall updates for later operations, and so on.

With this intuition, we define $|O, P|$ to be the length of the longest path from O to P in the conflict graph, and we define $\textsc{must}\langle O, U \rangle$ by induction as follows.

1. $\textsc{must}_0\langle O, U \rangle = [O, U]$.
2. $\textsc{must}_d\langle O, U \rangle = \textsc{must}_{d-1}\langle O, U \rangle \cup [P, V]$ for all updates $\langle P, V \rangle$ such that $d = |O, P|$ and V intersects the set of variables written by updates in $\textsc{must}_{d-1}\langle O, U \rangle$.

The set MUST$\langle O, U \rangle$ is the union or limit of the sets MUST$_d\langle O, U \rangle$, and MUST$\langle O, U \rangle$ \\[O, U] [2] is the set of updates that must be reinstalled as a result of reinstalling $\langle O, U \rangle$. Notice how the size of the redos $[P, V]$ affects the size of the must redo sets MUST$\langle O, U \rangle$: The more updates in a redo $[P, V]$, the more updates that have to be reinstalled after $\langle O, U \rangle$.

In the introduction, we defined $can(O)$ to be the operations in $must(O)$ that we know can ultimately be redone once O has been redone. These operations can be ordered in a way consistent with the conflict graph and beginning with O so that redoing the first operation rebuilds the read set of the second, redoing the first two operations rebuilds the read set of the third, and so on. This is because the second operation reads the variables just written by the first one, the third operation reads the variables just written by the first two, and so on. Since each operation will read the same values from its read set during recovery as it saw during normal operation, it will write the same values to its write set. We can make a similar definition in terms of updates and redos. We proceed by induction and define

1. CAN$_0\langle O, U \rangle = [O, U]$.
2. CAN$_d\langle O, U \rangle = $ CAN$_{d-1}\langle O, U \rangle \cup [P, V]$ for all updates $\langle P, V \rangle$ in the set MUST$_d$ $\langle O, U \rangle$ with $d = |O, P|$ such that the read set of P is contained in the set of variables written by updates in CAN$_{d-1}\langle O, U \rangle$.

The set CAN$\langle O, U \rangle$ is the union or limit of the CAN$_d\langle O, U \rangle$.

Having thought so hard about how installing one update during recovery can deinstall a second, let us formally define an installed update. Suppose we have a state that is the result of installing some sequence σ of updates, where σ may describe alternating periods of normal operation and recovery. Which of the updates in σ do we consider installed? We have already noted that MUST$\langle O, U \rangle$\\[O, U] is the set of updates that must be redone as a result of reinstalling $\langle O, U \rangle$, so it seems natural to define *installed subsequence* of σ to be the subsequence of σ obtained as follows:

1. Select an update $\langle O, U \rangle$ in σ and delete from σ all but the last instance of $\langle O, U \rangle$ in σ.
2. Delete from σ all instances of updates in MUST$\langle O, U \rangle$\\[O, U] that precede this last appearance of $\langle O, U \rangle$ in σ.
3. Repeat this for all updates in σ.

The result of this construction is well-defined, that is, if σ_1 and σ_2 are installed subsequences of σ, then $\sigma_1 = \sigma_2$. We define the set of *installed updates* in σ to be those appearing in the installed subsequence. A sequence σ is an *installed sequence* if it is equal to its own installed subsequence.

---

[2]Remember that we write $A \backslash B$ to denote the set of elements in A that are not in B.

6.3.2   Installation Graph

In the introduction, we defined the installation graph by observing that in the conflict graph, all of the write-read edges and many of the write-write edges are unneeded. We defined the installation graph to be the result of keeping all read-write edges, throwing away all write-read edges, and keeping write-write edges from O to P when $P \in must(O)\backslash can(O)$. Keeping the write-write edge from O to P meant that redoing O meant we must redo P, but that redoing O is no guarantee that we can ever redo P. Since must and can redo sets have exactly the same interpretation when defined in terms of updates and redos, we can define the installation graph in exactly the same way now.

The *installation graph* for a history (or conflict graph) is a directed graph where each node is labeled with an update $\langle O, U \rangle$, and for distinct updates $\langle O, U \rangle$ and $\langle P, V \rangle$, there is an edge from $\langle O, U \rangle$ to $\langle P, V \rangle$ if $O \leq P$ in the history and either

1. *read-write edges*: the intersection of the read set of O and V is nonempty, or
2. *write-write edges*: $\langle P, V \rangle$ is contained in MUST$\langle O, U \rangle$ but not in CAN$\langle O, U \rangle$.

We write $\langle O, U \rangle \prec \langle P, V \rangle$ if there is a path from $\langle O, U \rangle$ to $\langle P, V \rangle$. A *prefix* of the installation graph is an update sequence σ such that (1) σ is an installed sequence, and (2) if $\langle O, U \rangle$ appears in σ, then every update $\langle P, V \rangle \prec \langle O, U \rangle$ appears in σ. We will also refer to a set I of updates as a prefix if there is a prefix σ consisting of the updates in I.

The updates for an operation O are unordered by $\prec$ for the most part, the only exception being when O writes to its own read set. In this case, there is a read-write edge from every update $\langle O, V \rangle$ to the (single) update $\langle O, U \rangle$ writing to O's read set. These read-write edges represent the fact that O's changes to its read set must be installed last, or it may be impossible to redo O after a crash. We say that $\langle O, U \rangle$ is the *final* update for O if U contains O's read set, and we say that $[O, U]$ is the *final* redo for O if $[O, U]$ contains O's final update. A *consistent* ordering of O's updates is any sequence that ends with O's final update or does not include O's final update, and we define a *consistent* sequence of O's redos in the same way. Ordering updates in this way has been referred to as "careful replacement" in the recovery literature [1, 6].

Another useful ordering on updates respects both the installation graph and conflict graph orderings: We define $\langle O, U \rangle \sqsubset \langle P, V \rangle$ iff $\langle O, U \rangle \prec \langle P, V \rangle$ or $O < P$. It is convenient to extend $\sqsubset$ to redos: we define $[O, U] \sqsubset [P, V]$ iff $[O, U]$ and $[P, V]$ contain $\langle O, U' \rangle$ and $\langle P, V' \rangle$ satisfying $\langle O, U' \rangle \sqsubset \langle P, V' \rangle$. When we say that an update $\langle O, U \rangle$ or redo $[O, U]$ is minimal with respect to some set of updates or redos, we mean minimal with respect to $\sqsubset$. The idea here is that we will be redoing operations in conflict order during recovery because we read the log in this sequence. We install the updates of these operations in an order consistent with the installation graph.

6.3.3 Explainable States

During recovery, certain important variables must have the right values in them. These are the variables whose values must be correct in order to reconstruct the read sets of the uninstalled updates. We define a variable x to be *exposed* by σ iff one of the following conditions is true:

1. no update uninstalled after σ reads or writes x, or
2. some update uninstalled after σ reads or writes x, and the minimal such update reads x.

The exposed variables have some very nice properties. For example, if σ and τ have the same set of installed updates, then they have the same set of exposed variables, and every exposed variable x has the same value after σ and τ.

A prefix σ *explains* a state S if for every variable x exposed by σ, the value of x in S is the value of x after σ. A set of installed updates I *explains* a state S if some σ explains S and I is the set of installed updates in σ, in which case we can prove that any τ with this set of installed updates explains S. Thus, if S is the state of the stable database at the start of recovery, then the exact sequence of updates used to construct S is unimportant. Only the set of updates considered installed in S is important. This is crucial as it is impossible in general to determine the exact installation sequence that leads to a database state, a task that is made even more difficult by the fact that crashes can occur that require multiple invocations of recovery and hence produce arbitrarily complex installation sequences.

6.3.4 Minimal Uninstalled Updates

An operation O is *applicable* to a state S if for every variable x in O's read set, the value of x in S is given by O's before image. This means that O reads the same values during recovery as it did during normal operation, so it will write the same values as well. An update $\langle O, U \rangle$ is *installable* in a state S if the database state $S' = S\langle O, U \rangle$ obtained by installing the effects of $\langle O, U \rangle$ into S is explainable by a prefix of the installation graph. We can extend this definition to sequences of updates in the obvious way.

A prefix σ can be *extended* by an update $\langle O, U \rangle$ if (1) there is no write-write edge from $\langle O, U \rangle$ to any update in σ, and (2) σ contains every update $\langle P, V \rangle \prec \langle O, U \rangle$. We define $extend(\sigma, \langle O, U \rangle)$ to be the result of deleting every update in MUST$\langle O, U \rangle \backslash [O, U]$ from σ, and then appending $\langle O, U \rangle$ if it does not appear in the result. This is the result of removing all updates that $\langle O, U \rangle$ deinstalls, and then making sure that $\langle O, U \rangle$'s effects are present.

The following theorem is the basis of our informal intuition that an explainable state can be recovered by installing uninstalled updates in conflict-graph order.

Theorem: 1 *Let S be an explainable state. If $[O, U]$ is a minimal redo with an uninstalled update and τ is any consistent ordering of $[O, U]$, then O is applicable to S and $extend(\sigma, \tau)$ explains $S\tau$, so τ is installable in S.*

6.4 GENERAL RECOVERY METHOD

Theorem 1 suggests a procedure for recovering a database with an explainable state: choose a minimal redo $[O, U]$ with an uninstalled update, install it, and repeat. In order for this to work, of course, O must appear in the log. Informally, we say that a database is explainable if its state is explainable and its log contains the uninstalled operations. Formally, we say that a database $D = (S, L, H)$ is *explainable* if there is a prefix σ of the installation graph of the history H such that σ explains the state S and σ contains every update of every operation that is in the history H but not in the log L.

---

procedure Recover(D, σ)
  while the log L is nonempty do
    choose a minimal operation O in the log L
    choose a consistent ordering of O's redos
    for each redo $[O, U]$ satisfying REDO($D, \sigma, [O, U]$) do
      compute the after image of $[O, U]$
      choose a consistent ordering of $[O, U]$'s updates
      for each update $\langle O, V \rangle$ do atomically
        install $\langle O, V \rangle$
        replace σ with $extend(\sigma, \langle O, V \rangle)$
    delete O from the log L

Figure 6.6. Recovering a database D explained by σ.

The procedure Recover(D, σ) in Figure 6.6 captures the procedure described earlier for recovering a database D explained by a prefix σ. The algorithm considers all operations O in log order, considers all redos for O in a consistent order, and then invokes a test REDO($D, \sigma, [O, U]$) to determine whether $[O, U]$ should be installed into the state of a database D explained by a prefix σ.

But under what conditions should this test REDO($D, \sigma, [O, U]$) return true? At the very least, it must return true if $[O, U]$ contains an uninstalled update. Since the log is read in conflict-graph order, such a $[O, U]$ would be a minimal redo with an uninstalled update, and in this case Theorem 1 says that $[O, U]$ is guaranteed to be applicable and installable. Sometimes it is hard to tell that a redo contains an uninstalled update, so a recovery method may end up redoing many installed redos all over again. In fact, whenever $[O, U]$ is applicable and installable, it is okay for the test to return true. Since the log is read in conflict-graph order, we know that installing $[O, U]$ is not going to deinstall things the recovery process has just installed, and deinstalled things will be reinstalled when we reach them later in the log.

With this in mind, we require that the test REDO($D, \sigma, [O, U]$) satisfies the following conditions:

1. Safety: If the test returns true, then (a) O is applicable to S, and (b) there

are no write-write edges from updates in $[O, U]$ to updates in σ

2. Liveness: If $[O, U]$ is a minimal redo containing an uninstalled update in σ, then the test returns true.

Theorem 1 says that the liveness condition implies the safety condition, and the safety condition essentially says that $[O, U]$ must be applicable and installable: Since operations are considered in conflict-graph order, condition (1b) will imply that $[O, U]$ extends σ and hence is installable. This test need only be defined for a database D that is explainable by a prefix σ and for a redo $[O, U]$, where O is a minimal operation on D's log, since these are the only conditions under which the test is used. The safety condition guarantes that an operation is redone only when it sees the read set seen originally, and when installing, its redos will reset the state such that operations that are deinstalled by it can be redone. The liveness condition guarantes that the uninstalled operations will always be redone and reinstalled during recovery.

One property of the algorithm Recover that will bother some is that it maintains a sequence σ of updates. No recovery algorithm actually does this. Fortunately, σ is only used when evaluating the test REDO$(D, \sigma, [O, U])$. Since testing for applicability is usually much easier than testing for installability, most practical methods restrict their operations so that applicable operations are always installable. For example, page-oriented and tree-structured operations that we study later in this chapter restrict their operations so that there are effectively no write-write edges in the installation graph. Thus, REDO$(D, \sigma, [O, U])$ can ignore σ and return true whenever O is applicable. (This becomes a particularly easy test for blind writes as they are always applicable. For page-oriented read/write operations, we can exploit state identifiers to determine when a page is in the state in which the operation was originally done.) Since σ is unneeded by the test, maintenance of σ can be removed from the algorithm. We can prove that the invariant "D is explained by σ" holds after each step of Recover(D, σ), and conclude that an explainable database is recoverable.

Theorem: 2 *If database D is explained by σ, then Recover(D, σ) is an idempotent recovery process that recovers D.*

6.5   GENERAL CACHE MANAGEMENT

The main result of the previous section was that an explainable database is a recoverable database. To prove that crash recovery is possible, we need to show how to keep the stable database explainable; that is, so that the stable state is explainable and the stable log contains all of the uninstalled operations. Fortunately, the WAL protocol and our checkpointing requirement guarantee that the all uninstalled operations appear in the stable log. Specifically, the WAL protocol guarantees that an operation is added to L_s the moment it is added to H_s, and our checkpointing requirement guarantees that only installed operations are removed from L_s, so together they guarantee that operations in $H_s \backslash L_s$ are installed. Consequently, in this section, we just need to show how to keep the stable state S_s explainable. We give an algorithm for managing the cache during normal operation and recovery that keeps the stable state in an explainable state.

We have assumed that the volatile update buffer is a set of updates whose effects appear in the volatile state. Here, we must assume that the update buffer is actually the subgraph of the installation graph induced by the updates in the update buffer. We discuss how to avoid explicitly maintaining this subgraph in the technical report [22].

A cache manager effectively partitions the volatile state into a "dirty" part and a "clean" part (which we do not discuss here). A variable enters the dirty volatile state when an operation updates it, can be the subject of multiple updates while there, and leaves the dirty volatile state only and immediately upon being written to the stable database. Variables of the dirty volatile state are written to the stable database for two reasons. First, the volatile state can be (nearly) full, requiring that variables currently present be removed to make room for new variables. Second, it may be desired to shorten recovery by checkpointing the stable log. Since only installed operations can be removed from the log, it may be necessary to install some of their updates before removing them from the log. Systematic installation permits a prefix of the log to be truncated while preserving stable database recoverability.

The central problem for cache management is that installation graph nodes are *updates* but the cache manager writes *variables*. The cache manager must write sets of variables in such a way that update atomicity and update installation order are observed. The cache manager computes a *write graph* for this purpose. Each write-graph node v has an associated set $updates(v)$ of updates in the volatile update buffer and a set $variables(v)$ of the variables these updates write. The variables of a write-graph node must be written atomically in order to guarantee update atomicity. These sets must be written in write-graph order to guarantee update installation order. There is an edge from v to w in the write graph if there is an edge from any $\langle P, V \rangle$ in $updates(v)$ to any $updateQ, W$ in $updates(w)$ in the installation graph. (Page-oriented operations result in a degenerate write graph, each node of which is associated with the updates of a single variable and with no edges between nodes and hence with no restrictions on installation order of cache pages.)

---

procedure WriteGraph(I)

   $T \leftarrow$ the transitive closure of "$\langle O, U \rangle \sim_I \langle P, V \rangle$ iff $U \cap V$ is nonempty" for nodes of I

   $\mathcal{I} \leftarrow$ the graph I after replacing each $\langle O, U \rangle$ with $\{\langle O, U \rangle\}$

   $\mathcal{V} \leftarrow$ collapse $\mathcal{I}$ with respect to the equivalence classes of T

   $S \leftarrow$ the strongly connected components of $\mathcal{V}$

   $\mathcal{W} \leftarrow$ collapse $\mathcal{V}$ with respect to the equivalence classes of nodes in S

   return($\mathcal{W}$)   /* collapsing $\mathcal{V}$ made $\mathcal{W}$ acyclic */

Figure 6.7. Computing the write graph.

The write graph is computed from the volatile update buffer by the algorithm WriteGraph(U_v) in Figure 6.7. In this algorithm, we use the idea of collapsing a graph $\mathcal{A}$ with respect to a partition Π of its nodes. Each set of the partition represents variables that must be written atomically. The result is the graph $\mathcal{B}$, where each node w corresponds to a class π_w in the partition Π and an edge exists between nodes v and w of $\mathcal{B}$ if there is an edge between nodes a and b of $\mathcal{A}$ contained respectively in π_v and π_w. This idea is used twice in computing the write graph, once to collapse intersecting updates, and again to make the write graph acyclic. In the technical report [22], we discuss incremental methods of maintaining the write graph $\mathcal{W}$ so that it evolves as new updates are added to the cache.

---

procedure PurgeCache
    compute the write graph $\mathcal{W}$
    choose a minimal v node in $\mathcal{W}$
    write operations from the log buffer with updates in $updates(v)$ to the stable log in
        conflict order
    (this adds these operations to the stable history)
    atomically write values of variables in $variables(v)$ to the stable state
    delete operations with updates in $updates(v)$ from the log buffer
    delete updates in $updates(v)$ from the volatile update buffer
    delete variables in $variables(v)$ from the dirty volatile state
    return

Figure 6.8. The cache management algorithm PurgeCache.

The cache manager uses the algorithm PurgeCache in Figure 6.8 to write to the stable state. We can prove that using this algorithm during normal operation and recovery preserves some simple properties of the stable state. For example, if the stable state S is explainable by a prefix σ, then for every update $\langle O, U \rangle$ in the volatile update buffer,

1. there are no write-write edges in the volatile history's installation graph from $\langle O, U \rangle$ to updates in σ and
2. every update $\langle P, V \rangle \prec \langle O, U \rangle$ is in σ or in the volatile update buffer.

In the special case that $\langle O, U \rangle$ is a minimal update in the update buffer, these conditions imply that σ can be extended by $\langle O, U \rangle$, so installing $\langle O, U \rangle$ in the stable state will yield an explainable state. These conditions are invariant because operations are added to the update buffer in conflict order during normal operation, and the REDO test skips over updates that violate condition 1 during recovery. We can also prove that these conditions are preserved by the algorithm PurgeCache. Thus, the stable state remains explainable, and the database remains recoverable.

Theorem: 3 *PurgeCache preserves the recoverability of the stable database.*

6.6 PRACTICAL RECOVERY METHODS

There are three hard problems that a practical recovery method must solve:

1. **Atomicity**, since multiple pages may have to be installed atomically.
2. **Write Order**, since the cache manager must compute the write-graph dependencies between cached variables in real time.
3. REDO **test**, since this test determines which logged operations are redone during recovery.

Practical methods usually cope with these problems by constraining logged operations to syntactically simple forms. In this section, we discuss common constraints used by existing methods, and propose a less restrictive constraint that preserves most of the simplicity of these methods.

6.6.1 Existing Methods

Most practical recovery methods permit only *page-oriented operations* that access exactly one page. Such operations yield installation graphs without any write-write edges. This is because if O writes x and P writes x, then P reads either x or nothing at all, so P is in the can redo of O. Consequently, such operations are always installable during recovery, and the REDO test need only test for applicability. Each node of the write graph is associated with a single page, and there are no edges at all between nodes of the graph. This means that the atomicity problem is solved since each page can be installed atomically,[3] and the write-order problem is solved since the pages can be installed in any order. Only the REDO test poses a problem.

One example of page-oriented operations is *after-image writes* which that have empty read sets and single-page write sets. This single-page write might write to the entire page [3] or to selected records or bytes on the page [2, 4]. These methods differ in the trade-off they make between log record size and the need to access a page before replaying the operation during recovery. These operations are always applicable, and hence the REDO test can always return true.

Another example is *physiological* operations as described in [6] and used in ARIES [14]. These are state-transition operations that require reading the before-image of a page and then computing its after-image. These operations are *not* always applicable, so the REDO test must test for applicability. This is usually implemented by storing a state identifier in the written page and associating the state identifier in some way with the operation's log record. The address of the log record (called a log sequence number, or LSN) is often used as the state identifier [6]. The REDO test simply compares the log record's state identifier with the state identifier stored in the page to determine applicability.

---

[3]Actually, this is only true if we are guaranteed that a disk write does not fail in the middle. When such a failure occurs, media failure recovery must be invoked. For single page writes, a subsequent read can readily detect such a failure.

6.6.2   A New Method: Tree Operations

Understanding installation graphs and their resulting write graphs allows us to generalize page-oriented methods with what we call *tree operations*. A tree operation O reads one page x, and then writes x and possibly other pages in NEW. NEW is the set of pages that have never been written before, and writing a page in NEW removes it from NEW. Although O may write multiple pages, the write set of each update U is a single page. We call these tree operations because their conflict graph is a tree.

Like page-oriented operations, tree operations solve the atomicity problem by defining the write set of each update to be a single page. Like page-oriented operations, tree operations yield installation graphs with no write-write edges, so these operations are also always installable and the REDO test need only test for applicability. Testing for applicability is easy to implement using log sequence numbers.

Cache management, however, is more difficult since the write graph is now nontrivial: If O reads x and writes x and y, then there is an edge from y to x in the write graph because there is a read-write edge from $\langle O, y \rangle$ to $\langle O, x \rangle$ in the installation graph since both updates read x. The cache manager needs to do "careful replacement" of these pages, that is, write the pages in a constrained order. These read-write edges in the write graph are simple to compute, since no cycles ever occur for the second "collapse" to process, so a simple incremental computation of the write graph is possible [22].

Tree operations can improve logging performance for practical problems like splitting the node of a B-tree. Splitting a node requires reading the page containing the old node and splitting its contents by writing back to the old node and a new node, as well as reading and updating the parent node. "B-link-tree" concurrency and recovery techniques [21] link the old and new nodes together. This link preserves the accessibility of the moved data in the new node until the parent is updated. As a consequence, we can log the split of the node and the update of the parent as two separate atomic operations. Let us compare logging the split of the node using page-oriented operations and tree operations:

- Page-oriented operations: Two logged operations are required, one for each node. One is a blind write to the new page, requiring that we log the entire contents of this new page. The other is a rewrite of the original page, which only requires that we log the split key and instructions to remove all entries greater than the split key from the node.
- Tree operations: One logged operation can deal with the updating of both new and original nodes. This operation reads the old value of the original node and, using the result of this read, writes both original and new nodes. In particular, the new node's contents need not be logged in its entirety because it is derived from the old value in the original node, that is, the entries greater than the split key.

Logging tree operations yields in a smaller log at the cost of requiring "careful replacement": The value of the new node must be installed in the stable database before the the updated value of the old node can be installed.

6.6.3   Recycling Pages

It is important to be able to replenish NEW with pages that have been freed, effectively recycling them and reclaiming space. Recycling an old page, however, can introduce a write-write edge in the installation graph between the last update writing the page prior to its being freed and the first update writing the same page after reallocation. The operation performing the new update does not read the page, and hence this operation is not guaranteed to be in the *can-redo* of the earlier operation.

Because of these write-write edges, redoing operations in the log during recovery threatens to violate the cache management invariant concerning the absence of write-write edges. This threat can be removed without complicating the REDO test. The trick is simply to take a checkpoint.

We recycle freed pages by *scrubbing* them before reusing them. Scrubbing is done by checkpointing. A checkpoint "cuts" write-write edges from prior incarnations of a freed page by removing from the log all operations that have written to the page x prior to it being freed. Since x will never be reset to a value prior to the checkpoint during recovery, the page can be added back to NEW. Scrubbing is appropriate for recycling pages in any recovery technique and avoids any change to the technique's REDO test.

6.6.4   Future Directions

Our framework provides a clean decomposition of the recovery problem that allows us to identify and focus on the three hard problems a practical recovery method must solve: atomicity, the write order, and the REDO test. We hope that the clearer understanding of recovery that we provide here will transform what has been an arcane art into the realm of skilled engineering. We anticipate that this clearer understanding will shortly lead to a number of interesting and practical new recovery.

Acknowledgments

We would like to thank Rakesh Agrawal for urging the first author to demystify recovery and Butler Lampson for his enthusiastic interest.

References

[1] Bernstein, P., and V. Hadzilacos and N. Goodman *Concurrency Control and Recovery in Database Systems*. Addision Wesley, Reading, MA, 1987.

[2] Crus, R. Data recovery in IBM Database 2," *IBM System Journal*, 23(2) (1984).

[3] Elhardt, K., and R. Bayer. A database cache for high performance and fast restart in database systems," *ACM TODS*, 9(4) (December 1984).

[4] Gray, J. Notes on Database Operating Systems," in *Operating Systems—An Advanced Course*, Vol. 60, Lecture Notes in Computer Science, ed. by R. Bayer and R. Graham and G. Seegmuller. Springer-Verlag, 1978.

[5] Gray, J., and P. McJones and M. Blasgen and B. Lindsay and R. Lorie and T. Price and F. Putzolu. The Recovery Manager of the System R Database Manager," *ACM Computing Survey*, 13(2) (June 1981).

[6] Gray, J., and A. Reuter. *Transaction Processing: Concepts and Techniques.* Morgan Kaufmann, 1993.

[7] Hadzilacos, V. A theory of reliability in database systems," *Journal of the ACM*, 35(1) (January 1988).

[8] Haerder, T., and A. Reuter. Principles of transaction oriented database recovery: A Taxonomy," *ACM Computing Survey*, 15(4) (December 1983).

[9] Haskin, R., and Y. Malachi and W. Sawdon and G. Chan. Recovery Management in Quicksilver," *ACM Transactions on Computer Systems*, 6(1) (February 1988).

[10] Kuo, D. Model and Verification of a Data Manager Based on ARIES,". *Proceedings of the 4th International Conference on Database Theory*, October 1992.

[11] Lomet, D. *Recovery for shared disk systems using multiple redo logs.* Technical Report No. 90/4. DEC Cambridge Research Laboratory, October 1990.

[12] Lomet, D. MLR: A recovery method for multi-level systems," *Proceedings of the 1992 ACM SIGMOD International Conference on Management of Data*, June 1992.

[13] Lynch, N., M. Merritt, W. Weihl and A. Fekete. *Atomic Transactions*, Morgan Kaufman, 1993.

[14] Mohan, C., D. Haderle, B. Lindsay, H. Pirahesh and P. Schwarz. ARIES: A Transaction Recovery Method Supporting Fine-Granularity Locking and Partial Rollbacks Using Write-Ahead Logging," *ACM TODS*, 17(1) (March 1992).

[15] Mohan, C., I. Narang and J. Palmer. *A case study of problems in migrating to distributed computing: Page recovery using multiple logs in the shared disks environment*, Research Report RJ7343, IBM Almaden Research Center, August 1991.

[16] Mohan, C., and H. Pirahesh. ARIES-RRH: Restricted repeating of history in the ARIES transaction recovery method," *Proceedings of the Seventh International Conference on Data Engineering*, April 1991.

[17] Rosenblum, M., and J. Ousterhout. The Design and Implementation of a Log-Structured File System," *Proceedings of the 13th Annual ACM Symposium on Operating System Principles*, October 1991.

[18] Rothermel, K., and C. Mohan. ARIES/NT: A recovery method based on write-ahead logging for nested transactions," *Proceedings of the 15th International Conference on Very Large Data Bases*, August 1989.

[19] Weikum, G. A theoretical foundation of multi-level concurrency control," *Proceedings of the 5th Annual ACM Symposium on Principles of Database Systems*, March 1986.

[20] Weikum, G., C. Hasse, P. Broessler and P. Muth. Multi-level recovery," *Proceedings of the 9th Annual ACM Symposium on Principles of Database Systems*, April 1990.

[21] Lomet, D., and B. Salzberg. Access method concurrency with recovery," *ACM SIGMOD*, June 1992.

[22] Lomet, D., and M. Tuttle. *Redo Recovery after System Crashes*, DEC Cambridge Research Lab. Technical Report No. 95/5, 1995.

Chapter 7

MLR: A Recovery Method for Multilevel Systems

David B. Lomet

Abstract

To achieve high concurrency in a database system has meant building a system that copes well with important special cases. Recent work on multilevel systems suggests a systematic way of providing high concurrency. A multilevel system using locks permits restrictive low-level locks of a subtransaction to be replaced with less restrictive high-level locks when a subtransaction commits, hence enhancing concurrency. This is possible because subtransactions can be undone by executing high-level compensation actions rather than by restoring a prior lower-level state. We describe a recovery scheme, called multilevel recovery (**mlr**), that logs this high-level undo operation with the commit record for the subtransaction that it compensates, posting log records to only a single log. A variant of the method copes with nested transactions, and both nested and multilevel transactions can be treated in a unified fashion.

7.1 INTRODUCTION

7.1.1 Precursor Multilevel Methods

Most of our understanding of concurrency control and recovery, for example, two-phase locking [5], serializability theory [3], and before-image/after-image recovery [9], is based on treating disjoint resources in a uniform "single-level" way. But, when examined in detail, database systems support multiple levels of abstraction and exploit the levels to improve concurrency. A few of the multilevel cases exploited by some existing systems follows:

- Mutual exclusion via a semaphore guarantees atomicity of page writes.

125

- B-tree concurrency methods hold locks on index nodes only for the duration of a tree structure change [12, 15].

- The ARIES recovery method [14] logs operations that update disk pages, but are reinterpreted (if necessary) during recovery to undo a record update even if the record has moved to a different page.

7.1.2   Explicit Multilevel Systems

Multilevel transactions were made explicit in [2, 19, 18].   Theoretical work was reported in [1, 10, 13], and special cases were described in [6, 9, 17, 14].   An implementation of multilevel system recovery, restricted to two levels, is described in [20]. Here we briefly characterize multilevel systems.

We begin by describing "layers" of a multilayer system, and then distinguish two kinds of layers, a "multilevel" layer and a nested transaction layer. Each layer of a multilayer system realizes a set of abstract states, each represented by a number of lower-layer states. Each layer sees state transitions in the form of atomic operations provided by the next lower-layer, and uses them to provide atomic operations to the next higher layer. A layer thus transforms the sequence of operations that were supplied to it into operations that it supplies to its users.

A multilevel (ml) system exploits the layers of abstraction common in most systems to enhance concurrency. Concurrency control and recovery are concerned ultimately with ensuring that the system behavior at the highest layer is correct. By defining a layer to be a *level* of a multilevel system, an ml system can exploit the flexibility of choosing among the lower-layer states that realize a desired high-layer state. ml concurrency control need only ensure that committed transactions finish in one of the low-level states that realizes a high-level state providing high-level serializability. More importantly, on abort, a level of an ml system need only be returned to the starting high-level state, but not necessarily the starting low-level state.

The lowest-layer of an ml system directly provides abstractions on which succeeding layers can be built. The system also provides a set of services to the implementor of a level. If an implementor desires to define his layer as a level, these enable the tailoring of concurrency control and recovery to the needs of the level. An implementor also can ignore these services and use nested transactions, thus exploiting the capabilities provided by the recoverable abstractions of the lower-levels. Such a nested transaction layer is not a level.

The level-oriented services provided an implementor permit, for example, the definition of lock modes, the requesting of locks, and the specification of compensation operations. The ml system framework is responsible for the interactions between layers, for controlling implicit release or retention of locks, for staging the recovery process that aborts transactions or recovers from system crashes, for assuring that these operations are applied only to an "operation consistent" database state and that idempotency of recovery is assured, and so on.

An operation's level number is determined when it is defined. A multilevel layer's

Table 7.1. List of Acronyms

L_i	Level i of a multilevel system
OP_i	Normal forward database operation at L_i
OP_i^{-1}	Inverse(undo) operation for OP_i
ML	Multilevel
MLT	Multilevel transaction
NT	Nested transaction (transaction or system)
CT	Compensation transaction
$LOCK_i$	A lock at L_i
CLR	Compensation log record (recording undo progress)
LL_i	Level list (of undo actions for L_i)
$TransT$	Transaction table

(see Section 7.3) level is L_{i+1}, where L_i is the level of the layer for the operations that it uses. We denote operations at a level L_i as OP_is. We require here that all operations of a layer be at the same level, that is, that the leveling be uniform, as it would be in a hierarchy of "virtual machines" as described in [18]. (In Section 7.1, we discuss briefly a "layers of abstraction" generalization that does not require this uniformity of level.) Lowest-level operations are defined to be L_0. (Table 7.1 contains a list of the notation used in this chapter.)

7.1.3   Our Effort

In this chapter, we present an algorithm for recovery in multilevel systems. Our recovery method, called MLR, is reminiscent of ARIES/NT [16] and enjoys many of the same desirable features of that scheme. MLR copes correctly with both nested transactions (NTs) and with multilevel transactions (MLTs). It uses a single log for all levels, and thus presents a unified way of dealing with all levels.

Multilevel systems are discussed in Section 7.2. Section 7.3 introduces the fundamentals of layered recovery. Section 7.4 shows the way that the log is used to prepare for MLR recovery, and Section 7.5 describes the rolling back of transactions both during normal operation and as a result of system crash recovery. Section 7.6 discusses our results and suggests some generalizations.

7.2   MULTILEVEL SYSTEMS

7.2.1   High-level Compensation

The essence of multilevel recovery for a new level is that a completed OP_{i+1} is "undone" by the execution of its inverse operation (OP_{i+1}^{-1}) called a *compensation operation.* The OP_{i+1}^{-1} returns a system to a high-level state in which the effect of the original OP_{i+1} has disappeared. OP_{i+1}^{-1}s require the reacquisition of $LOCK_j$s, where $j < i + 1$, and some of these may conflict with (possibly implicit) $LOCK_j$s held by currently active OP_js. MLR must be prepared to deal with this. It does this by executing each OP_{i+1}^{-1} within a compensation transaction (CT). The CT holds the locks required and can be rolled back should deadlocks occur. It is this use of CTs that clearly distinguishes MLR from prior methods.

It is also possible to undo a OP_{i+1} by execution in reverse order of inverse low-level operations OP_i^{-1}s for the OP_is that constituted its original execution. This also returns the system to the same high-level state, that is, it does this by returning the system to the original low-level state. Low-level recovery requires retention of $LOCK_i$s for the duration of the higher-level subtransaction to guarantee that the OP_i^{-1}s can be executed without deadlock. In an *ml* system, $LOCK_i$s are retained until their containing OP_{i+1} completes. An interrupted OP_{i+1} cannot be compensated by its OP_{i+1}^{-1} because only complete executions of a forward operation can be so compensated. Hence, an abort within an OP_{i+1} operation can and must be recovered by execution of lower-level compensation operations.

7.2.2   Concurrency Control

Concurrency control requirements for recovery are nicely characterized in [2] as: "Recovery actions must participate in concurrency control protocols, just like ordinary actions." We assume that locking is used so as to ensure serializability and recoverability. Thus, operations executed during recovery must honor all locks held

- explicitly by other transactions during explicit rollback;

- implicitly by other interrupted transactions during crash recovery.

Redo recovery can repeat history, that is, execute the original operations in an order equivalent to their original order. These operations will honor both implicit and explicit locks because their original execution honored them. Undo operations are newly executed during recovery. Ensuring that they correctly obey the concurrency control protocol is more difficult.

Locks must guarantee not only serializability, but also absence from deadlock during rollback. Completing an abort of a subtransaction is not optional. An "abort of the abort" is not an acceptable outcome. Absence of deadlock during rollback ordinarily requires that locks acquired for an operation cover both its original execution and its undoing.

In traditional single-level systems, the recovery process executes inverse (undo) operations in reverse order of the original sequence of operations. The locks for the forward operations are sufficient for the execution of the inverse operations, and hence recovery requires no additional locking. Hence, single-level system recovery satisfies the concurrency control protocols while guaranteeing that recovery will not deadlock.

For an *ml* system, we assume that each level performs strict two-phase locking such that the locks acquired for the level are sufficient for both serializability and for execution of inverse operations at that level. At level L_{i+1}, high-level locks ($LOCK_{i+1}$s) will be acquired during OP_{i+1} execution. Once an OP_{i+1} is completed and its $LOCK_{i+1}$s acquired, the low-level locks $LOCK_i$s used by its implementation OP_is are released. There should be fewer conflicts with the $LOCK_{i+1}$s than with the $LOCK_i$s.

The previous locking protocol is an instance of an order-preserving, conflict-based scheduler. In [2], these schedulers were shown to correctly serialize multilevel systems. The order-preserving condition simply means that lower-level transactions of a single higher-level transaction must be scheduled in the order determined by the higher-level transaction, not in an arbitrary serializable order.

7.2.3 Layers in a Multilevel System

A New Level

When an abstraction implementor cannot achieve the concurrency he needs when using lower-level operations, he can define a new multilevel transaction (MLT) layer that is a new level. This involves:

1. defining for each OP_{i+1} an OP_{i+1}^{-1} that compensates the OP_{i+1};

2. specifying the $LOCK_{i+1}$s that are needed by OP_{i+1}s to ensure that subtransactions using OP_{i+1}s can be serialized and recovered. This includes defining the lock-mode conflict matrix for the $LOCK_{i+1}$s. Locks are compatible exactly when the operations that use the locks on the same resource commute;

3. implementing each OP_{i+1} as a subtransaction over the OP_is that acquires the appropriate $LOCK_{i+1}$s during its execution. (The *ml* system will then release all acquired $LOCK_i$s when an OP_{i+1} "commits.")

A Nested Transaction Layer

An implementor need not introduce a new MLT layer in the *ml* system to export atomic and recoverable operations. If the concurrency achieved by using $LOCK_i$s is satisfactory, the definer can realize his operations using traditional nested transactions. A nested transaction retains $LOCK_i$s across the operations that it defines instead of replacing them with newly defined $LOCK_{i+1}$s. And a nested transaction is recovered by undoing each of the OP_is that was used to realize it.

Thus, completed NTs that are parts of aborted transactions are rolled back in a similar way to the rollback of incomplete subtransactions, that is, using lower-level inverse operations. The level of an NT layer is the same as the level of the operations that it uses.

Implementing an NT layer is easier than introducing a new MLT layer. An implementor must balance his concurrency needs against the increased cost of an MLT layer. What is important here is that *ml* systems provide the choice between

NT and MLT at every level of abstraction, independently of how other layers of the system have made the choice.

7.3   RECOVERY FUNDAMENTALS

7.3.1   Recovery Predicates

Recovery applies the actions specified in log records to whatever happens to be the available system state. Crashes can occur at arbitrary times, independent of operation boundaries. In addition, recovery must cope with the fact that the preserved system state (in stable storage) is not usually the same as the system state at the time of the crash. The stable system state after a crash may include the effects of some operations while not including the effects of others. And those included or excluded may be in no particular order on the log. All recovery schemes must be prepared to deal with these difficulties. To help in organizing the recovery process, we introduce two properties that, once established, greatly simplify further recovery. These properties are essential when non-idempotent operations need recovery. These are described in what follows.

Operation Consistency

The operation consistency property (OC) states that the system state is such that an operation has either been

- executed and the system state reflects all of the results; or

- not executed and the system state reflects none of the results.

Essentially, an OC state is one in which no logged operation is currently active, that is, partially executed. In an ml system, a level L_i is said to be OC if no logged OP_i is partially executed.

The OC property solves two problems in ml recovery.

Partial Results: Correct redo requires that the part of the system state seen by the operation be the same as seen by the original execution. Correct undo requires that the results from the original operation all be present. With partially executed operations, recovery can leave the system state undefined.

Implicit Locks: If an ml system is not OC at L_i when undo recovery attempts to execute OP_i^{-1} operations, there may be $LOCK_i$s held (implicitly) by interrupted OP_is that conflict with locks needed to execute these inverse operations.

Determinable Execution

In order to guarantee recovery idempotence for nonidempotent operations, it must be known which operations have been executed and are reflected in the system state. We call this property *determinable execution*, or DE.

If a logged operation must be executed because it is part of a committed transaction and it does not have its effects reflected in the available system state, then the DE property enables us to detect this and to schedule the redo of that operation. If an operation has been done and it is part of a transaction that needs to be aborted, DE permits us to detect its execution and to schedule an undo operation that purges the system state of the effects of the operation.

7.3.2 Higher-level Undo Recovery

At levels above L_0, hardware atomicity will not normally guarantee OC. Further, it is very difficult and/or expensive to guarantee the DE property by direct examination of system state. For these reasons, lower-levels of the system are recovered before higher-levels. Recovery prior to L_i will be responsible for guaranteeing that

1. all logged operations have been executed, hence that operations are DE;

2. all lower-level interrupted transactions have been rolled back, and hence the system is L_i OC;

3. only OP_js, for $j > i$ are in need of undo and those are indicated on the log as incompletely executed subtransactions.

L_i recovery undoes (compensates) the OP_is, as indicated on the log that are part of incomplete OP_{i+1}s and logs what it has accomplished. This ensures that the system becomes OC at level L_{i+1}. The DE property is also preserved and the set of operations in need of undo is now restricted to operations in incomplete transactions at levels above L_{i+1}.

Logging undo recovery operations is essential because it permits redo recovery (see what follows) to reestablish the system state as reflected in what has been written to the log, and hence to reestablish OC and DE should a crash interrupt recovery. And it does thiswhile not constraining the posting of an updated system state to stable storage.

In the detailed description of Section 7.4, we choose to write a compensation log record (CLR) that documents that an OP_i^{-1} has been executed that compensates for a specific prior OP_i. When we have completed the compensation of all OP_is within an OP_{i+1}, we mark the OP_{i+1} operation as aborted. This records the fact that this operation is complete and no longer needs undo recovery.

7.3.3 Level L_0 Recovery

Recovery at L_0 is responsible for "breaking the recursion" in which higher-levels assume that the lower-levels provide serializable and recoverable operations and that guarantees the OC and DE properties. Lowest-level recovery must be prepared to deal with the part of the database state that is stable at the time of a system crash. Its goals are to transform whatever is in the stable system state into a system state that is L_1 OC, to establish the DE property, and to make sure that only the operations in incomplete transactions above L_0 need undoing.

We perform redo recovery at L_0. Redo is responsible for making sure that all logged operations are installed in the system state. It establishes the DE property. The paradigm of performing redo first and repeating history, as in ARIES, works well with L_0 logging. When this is done, the L_0 undo precondition is the same as the precondition for higher-level undo. Hence, it can simply remove the effects of incomplete L_1 operations by compensating all their constituent OP_0s, hence making the state L_1 OC.

ml systems can be built on top of a number of different L_0 recovery methods. We describe two possible L_0 techniques here, one that requires both OC and DE, and the other that does not.

Operation Logging

The nonidempotent operations that cause state transitions are logged. In order for this to be effective, we must be able to guarantee the OC and DE properties at the start of recovery, before L_0 recovery begins.

L_0 is the only level for which OC is needed as of the time of a crash. Several approaches have been used. For example, System R [9] achieved RSS operation consistency by installing RSS operation consistent shadows during checkpoints. However, maximum flexibility in checkpointing and buffer management is achieved by having the OP_0s act on single blocks that can be atomically written to disk. Blocks in the cache can be written to disk at any time, and in any order. Only the need to observe the write-ahead-log (WAL) protocol constrains the writing to stable storage.

The DE property also needs to be guaranteed. This is usually done by a form of testable state (TS). The TS property states that whether an operation has been executed or not can be determined by testing the system state that is available (this can be done in conjunction with information that is stored in the log). An easy way to do this is to write a state identifier [11] in each block, write the state identifier seen by an operation in the log record for the operation, and increase the value of the state identifier to a new unique value as a consequence of executing the operation. Then, by comparing the state identifier in a block to the state identifier in a log record, one can determine whether or not the block includes the effects of the execution of the operation.

Before-Image/After-Image Logging

When before and after images of the portions of the state modified by an operation are logged, applying these "operations" to the designated parts of the system state is idempotent. That is, one can "execute" these "state installation" operations more than once without changing the result. No effort need be made to ensure that the system state is OC and DE at time of crash with this state-based logging.

Only the order of installation of before and after images is important, and this is determined from the placement of log records on the log. During redo recovery, the after images of completed operations, as recorded in the log, are installed, independent of the stable system state at time of crash. Again, once redo recovery is completed via repeating history, the system state meets the necessary precondition for our standard undo recovery. Undo by before-image installation can be treated just like any other undo operation.

An L_0 abstraction might be persistent virtual memory. Such an abstraction is very flexible, and perhaps is ideally suited for extendible or object-oriented systems. The operations on persistent virtual memory are reads or writes of byte strings, without concern for disk block boundaries. Blocks are written to disk freely, without regard to the boundaries of write operations. Hence, should the system crash, it is possible that parts of a logged write operation are reflected in the stable database whereas other parts are not. Using before-image and after-image logging permits us to support this abstraction without the need for the testable state property. This is important because it permits the entire disk block to be available to support the virtual-memory abstraction. We do not need any part of it to store a state identifier.

7.4 LOGGING FOR MLR

7.4.1 Forward Operations

When a transaction at any level is initiated, it is entered into the Transaction Table ($TransT$) used to keep track of system operation. In the $TransT$, its parent transaction and its level are recorded. Its initiation is documented durably by writing a start-transaction record to the log.

MLR logs forward operations of subtransactions as if they were operations of an independent transaction. As each of its operations completes, a log record is added to the transaction's chain of log records to document its execution. When a subtransaction commits, its commit record links it to the chain of log records of its parent transaction, similar to ARIES/NT. MLR does this by writing a log record that both commits the subtransaction and that causes the committed subtransaction to be logged as an operation in the parent. The format of this record is as a pair consisting of an operation log record for the parent transaction and a commit record for the child subtransaction. This is illustrated in Figure 7.1(a).

Whether a subtransaction is an NT or an MLT is only distinguished by whether the commit record for the subtransaction contains an inverse operation in the UNDO field of the operation part of the log record pair. This inverse operation is used to execute high-level compensation should the completed MLT need to be rolled back. NTs have no such operation as they will be rolled back by compensation of each of their constituent operations.

As an example, the log records for two subtransactions executing in parallel during normal system operation are shown in Figure 7.2. This will serve as a running example. One subtransaction has committed and becomes linked with the parent (top-level) transaction. The other hasnot yet committed and hence is indistinguishable from an active top-level transaction.

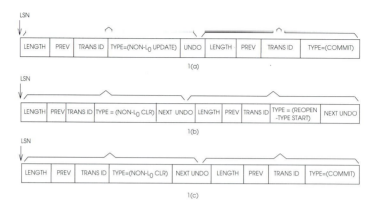

Figure 7.1. (a) MLR operation log record and subtransaction commit record, which handles both NT and MLT subtransactions. (b) MLR CLR and CT subtransaction start record for NTs. (c) MLR CLR and CT subtransaction commit record for MLTs.

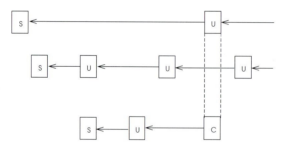

Figure 7.2. Normal operation logging for subtransactions. S denotes a start record, U an update (operation) record, and C a commit record. Log records are back linked within (sub)transactions and are shown from left to right as recorded on the log, left being earlier than right. When completed, a subtransaction is linked to its parent by its commit record, which is paired with an update record for its parent. These two components of a single log record are shown linked by dashed lines. Prior to commit, one cannot distinguish, based on log records, whether a transaction is an incomplete subtransaction or an incomplete top-level transaction.

7.4.2 Interrupted Transaction Undo

We call a transaction that cannot finish normally and hence must be rolled back an interrupted transaction. MLR rolls back interrupted transactions of any level in exactly the same way, whether they are top-level transactions or orphaned subtransactions of a parent transaction that is itself interrupted. Each such interrupted transaction must have its constituent operations (completed subtransactions or operations) compensated.

MLR durably records undo recovery progress by writing compensation log records. During rollback, a transaction's chain of log records is scanned backwards. Each operation encountered on the chain has its compensation operation stored as the UNDO operation in the log record, executed, and logged with a CLR. Once compensation is complete, an abort record is written for the interrupted transaction. The abort record documents that the transaction is complete and needs no further undo recovery. Its effects have been completely purged from the system state.

As in the ARIES method, we distinguish CLRs from other log records, and indicate in them the next logged operation of a transaction on which to perform undo. This is useful (but not essential) in that CLRs are never undone, and undo recovery can continue from where it was interrupted should the system crash during recovery. The pointer to the next operation to be rolled back is copied into the CLR. This permits undo recovery to proceed from the point where it left off should a crash occur during recovery. CLRs do not need to be themselves undone. Thus, undo recovery progress always advances.

We do not need the ARIES ability to support so-called "nested top-level actions" via distinguished CLRs whose pointer structure bypasses their logged operations during undo. This can be achieved via explicit multilevel subtransactions.

7.4.3   Completed Subtransaction Undo

For each completed subtransaction, we initiate a separate compensation transaction that undoes its effects. The CT is added to the $TransT$, as if it were a normal subtransaction. Compensation for a subtransaction occurs entirely in its CT, with the added proviso that once compensation is assured, a CLR describing the compensation performed by the CT is written as a log record of the parent transaction. The form of this CLR differs depending on whether a subtransaction is an NT or an MLT.

Nested Transaction Compensation

A nested transaction CT executes in the "backward" direction, and executes only compensation operations, which are logged as CLRs. CLRs are written as CT log records as compensation operations are executed. Each compensation operation is performed when its forward operation from the original completed NT is encountered in the backward undo scan of the log. CTs for nested transactions contain only CLRs, and these CLRs always point to a next operation to be undone, which is in the original completed NT.

Nested transaction CTs can always be completed. They never deadlock since all needed locks have been acquired during forward operation. Should recovery be interrupted, the last CLR written for each transaction points to the next operation that is to be undone. Hence, the CT can be continued after a crash, without needing rollback.

Because a nested transaction's CT is guaranteed to complete, an NT is effectively compensated once its CT is initiated. Hence, we pair the CLR for the NT with the

start record for its CT. This permits parent transaction rollback to proceed to its
next operation. This record is shown in Figure 7.1(b).

By initiating a CT, handling multiple pointers in CLRs, as is done in ARIES/NT,
is avoided. Each transaction consists of only a single threaded chain of log records
keeping track of undo progress in a single level. The next CLR of the parent points
to the the paired record CLR as if it were a simple atomic compensation operation
that was part of flat transaction recovery. In the start subtransaction part of the
preceding log record is posted a next-undo pointer to the first (next) operation of
the NT to be undone. This is the last operation logged for the completed NT.

The NT chain of log records is scanned backwards, and CLRs are written for
each encountered operation. When the start record for an NT is reached, a commit
record for the CT is written. This commit record need not be paired with a parent
transaction record since the start subtransaction record for the CT is already paired
with the CLR for the original NT.

Figure 7.3 illustrates nested transaction recovery using the MLR approach, applied to our running example.

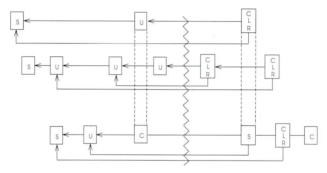

Figure 7.3. MLR log records for nested transaction recovery. The rollback of
both interrupted and completed NTs is illustrated. A system crash is indicated
by the jagged solid line. In addition to the normal back linking of log records,
compensation log records (CLRs also contain "next-undo" pointers, denoted by the
arrows out of the bottom of these records.

Multilevel Transaction Compensation

When a completed MLT subtransaction, representing the execution of an OP_{i+1},
needs to be rolled back, the OP_{i+1}^{-1} stored as the UNDO field of its commit record
pair is executed as a FORWARD operation in a CT. It is not rolled back by compensating each of its OP_is or included subtransactions.

An OP_{i+1}^{-1} CT executes in the forward direction during rollback, must observe
concurrency control protocols, and hence may deadlock. Further, it cannot be
continued across a system crash. In both these cases, it must be rolled back. An
OP_{i+1}^{-1} CT is made recoverable via the logging of its constituent OP_is as forward

operations or lower-level subtransactions. The effects of an interrupted OP_{i+1}^{-1} CT are undone by compensating each of its OP_is, and logging undo progress via CLRs, just as when undoing a forward subtransaction. We need not know that it is a CT.

Because OP_{i+1}^{-1} CTs are not guaranteed to complete, an MLT's CT does not compensate an OP_{i+1} until it commits. As we do with forward operations, we pair the OP_{i+1}^{-1} operation log record with the L_i CT commit record. Since this is a CT, its L_{i+1} log record is a CLR. See Figure 7.1(c).

Until its CT commits, a CLR for the original MLT subtransaction has not been written. Hence, we will start another CT to compensate this MLT when we again undo operations at L_{i+1}. This limits special processing for MLTs to that required for log records describing their commit, whether they be forward subtransactions or CTs. Handling of their other log records is as if they were independent and flat.

Figure 7.4 illustrates the appearance of the log for our running example, interpreted now as having multilevel transactions instead of nested transactions.

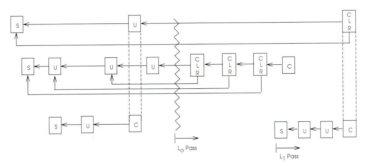

Figure 7.4. MLR log records for multilevel transaction recovery. The rollback of both interrupted and completed MLTs is illustrated.

7.4.4 Another CLR Logging Strategy

The logging we described for CLRs is consistent with how ARIES handles CLRs. That is, CLRs are distinguished from forward operation log records and are never undone. Recovery is made slightly simpler when CLRs are indistinguishable from forward operation log records. This has three effects.

1. CLRs can then be treated during recovery just like forward operations, reducing the number of cases to be handled.

2. Compensation operations for an NT can be logged as operations of the higher-level interrupted transaction, rather than as operations of a CT.

3. Failures during recovery require the undo of already compensated operations and subtransactions. It can be argued that crashes during recovery do not occur sufficiently often to justify trying to avoid the rollback of compensation operations.

The unique property of MLR recovery, namely, the initiation of a compensation transaction for a completed multilevel subtransaction within an interrupted higher-level transaction, works regardless of which CLR logging method is used.

7.5   MLR ROLLBACK

We describe here both the rollback that can occur via user or system-initiated aborts, for example, because of deadlock, during normal execution, and the roll-back necessary when the system crashes and the transactions interrupted by the crash need to be aborted. The important issue for both forms of rollback is that rollback must succeed, despite deadlocks or system crashes and while honoring the normal concurrency control protocol. Completion of rollback, including completion of inverse operations, is not optional. Inverse operations that are halted by deadlock or system crash can be rolled back, but they must then be reexecuted to ensure that recovery of the original forward transaction completes.

7.5.1   Rollback in Normal Operation

In an ml system, rollback for incomplete subtransactions at any level is achieved by executing inverse operations at the next lower-level.

While any subtransaction is active, it retains the $LOCK_i$s needed by its OP_is, and these $LOCK_i$s permit the corresponding OP_i^{-1}s to be executed. Deadlock during rollback is not possible *at this level*. But the execution of an OP_i^{-1} can require the acquisition of new $LOCK_j$s for $j < i$ that enforce serialization at that lower-levels of the system. The attempt to acquire these lower-level locks can result in deadlock during rollback. Of course, deadlocks can arise during normal forward operation as well.

Rolling back to subtransaction start can be exploited to overcome deadlocks, whether for forward or CT subtransactions. Once a subtransaction is rolled back, all locks that it holds can be released. Subtransaction start is a "savepoint" permitting partial rollback of a transaction. The subtransaction can be reexecuted once the partial effects of its prior execution have been removed.

This technique has different implications depending on whether a subtransaction is an NT or an MLT.

- NT: Rollback of an L_j subtransaction does not guarantee the release of all $LOCK_j$s held by its top-level transaction. Previously completed subtransactions may have passed their $LOCK_j$s to the parent. Another subtransaction holding and requesting $LOCK_j$s might remain blocked waiting for this parent to release these $LOCK_j$s. Hence, clearing of the deadlock is not guaranteed. Overcoming the deadlock might require rollback at even higher-levels. Rollback is, however, always possible without deadlock since locks are not acquired during rollback. NT deadlocks occur only during forward operation.

- MLT: Rollback of an L_j subtransaction guarantees the release of all $LOCK_j$s held by its top level transaction. (This is not quite true, but can be made true by waiting for any concurrently executing subtransactions at L_j to complete.) Hence, any other subtransactions holding and requesting $LOCK_j$s will no longer be blocked, thus clearing the deadlock. The rolled back MLT can then be reexecuted. Although it may deadlock again, repetitions of this process will ensure that the MLT will eventually complete if the scheduling is fair.

Systems where transactions need to acquire locks during rollback and that lack a subtransaction capability must make sure that a rolling back transaction is not itself subject to further rollback. System R [9] is an example. In special cases, it releases "low-level" locks before commit, and then needs to reacquire them should the transaction roll back. It designates the rolling back transaction as GOLDEN, constrains the system to permit only one GOLDEN transaction at a time, and never victimizes GOLDEN transactions in a deadlock. Rollback is hence single-threaded. With an MLT subtransaction capability, one can abort a CT subtransaction and clear the deadlock. Hence, multiple transactions can be permitted to rollback concurrently.

7.5.2 Rollback for Crash Recovery

After a system crash, redo recovery is performed first and only at L_0. We then perform undo recovery level by level. To do this, we need to know the level of each logged operation. One simple way to recover the level of an operation is to record an operation's level in its log record. Another, since all operations of a subtransaction are at the same level, is to record the level in the $TransT$ during redo, and whether it is an NT or an MLT subtransaction. NTs are at the same level as their highest-level operations whereas MLTs are at a level one more than the level of their highest-level operations.

Multiple-Scan Multilevel Undo

The simplest multilevel undo by levels is to scan the log backward multiple times, once for each level. After redo recovery has completed, we first do L_0 undo by scanning the log backwards performing undo for L_0 operations that occur within interrupted L_1 subtransactions. On each subsequent backward pass of the log, we increment the level by one and perform undo for that level. For L_i undo, we begin at the tail of the log as of the time of the crash, and scan the log until there are no more interrupted L_{i+1} subtransactions in the $TransT$. There are no more undo scans when the $TransT$ is empty of interrupted transactions.

We distinguish three sets of log records.

1. **Log Records for Operations in Completed Transactions and MLT Subtransactions:** Ignore these. These never require compensation.

2. OP_js, $j \geq i$, **Active Transaction:** Ignore these. These operations will be undone in subsequent undo scans.

3. OP_is, **Active Transaction:** Perform undo recovery for these log records.

The undo recovery in case 3. includes recovery for OP_is that occur within completed NTs of active transactions as well as OP_is that are directly in active transactions. Those within an NT are compensated within a CT for the NT. Above L_0, OP_i undo requires execution of a CT. These CTs execute when no lower-level locks are held, since lower-level undo recovery has already been performed, making the system state OC at L_i. Further, the OP_i^{-1}s execute in reverse order of the original OP_i execution order, thus forming the required "palindromic" sequence. Each CT executes serially to completion, and its operations are logged as indicated previously.

Should the system crash during recovery, redo and undo phases of recovery are repeated. The state of the log is different, however. Already recovered subtransactions will not be active. However, lower-level operations logged as part of MLT CTs must be rolled back, so, in general, it is not possible to skip levels during undo recovery. However, the previously completed levels of undo can be greatly shortened (see what follows).

Reducing Multiple Scans to One

We can avoid multiple passes over the log by recording during each undo pass what it is that still needs undo (case 2) but that is at a higher-level. Instead, we write these log records in main memory into separate lists for each level, which we call Level Lists or LLs). LLs must be linked in the same direction that the log records are encountered during the backward scan of the log. That means that each log record encountered at L_i that needs compensation is appended to LL_i. Undo recovery for L_i begins by scanning LL_i and initiating CTs for each operation in the order encountered on LL_i, just as if it had been encountered while scanning the log.

For each interrupted transaction at L_i, there will usually be an interrupted parent transaction at L_{i+1} that started before it. Thus, we expect to usually finish the undo of all L_i interrupted transactions before all the log records for interrupted L_{i+1} transactions have been seen. During the L_i undo phase, we may exhaust LL_i without having compensated all active L_{i+1} transactions. The backward scan of the log is then resumed where it left off during the L_{i-1} undo–level scan and continues until all active L_{i+1} transactions are aborted. When continuing the log scan, we once again add log records to the higher-level LLs. Since we can discard an operation on an LL_i as soon as it is undone, this "staggered" backward undo scan of the log reduces the sizes of the LLs simultaneously needed in main memory.

7.6   DISCUSSION

7.6.1   Characterization of MLR

MLR is an integrated industrial strength multilevel recovery algorithm that works for systems with arbitrary numbers of levels. Like ARIES, it supports operation logging and provides flexible cache management, and so on. During normal forward system operation, the additional MLR requirements are modest. Essentially, extra

overhead is incurred to acquire higher-level LOCKs, and, as with ARIES/NT, to link subtransactions with their parents upon subtransaction commit. It is these, of course, that enable the substantial increase in concurrency.

Rolling back a (sub)transaction is more complex in MLR than with flat or NT systems because one must deal with multilevel concurrency control and operation consistency. Undo recovery must be done level by level. MLR minimizes the impact of this by performing only a single backward scan of the log. We speculate that undo recovery is less than a factor of 2 longer than for flat transaction undo. When the cost of the redo phase, which is usually much more expensive and is essentially unchanged in MLR, is factored in, the relative performance difference should be much smaller than that.

An ml layer implementor does not need a detailed understanding of MLR. He need only supply a set of OPs and OP^{-1}s, a set of LOCK definitions, and a compatibility matrix for these locks, and then implement his operations. He need not be concerned with whether an operation is executing as a forward or rollback operation. The ml system can determine this. Hence, variations in logging and locking needs between normal and rollback execution can be made invisible to the layer implementor.

7.6.2 General Multilevel Systems

MLR is useful in a wider setting than when only top-level transactions are durable and contain nondurable subtransactions.

- MLR is not sensitive to the constraints being enforced by the concurrency control protocol. Only locking needed for compensatability is required and the MLR framework holds these locks until subtransaction completion. Whether the locks involved enforce other constraints is at the discretion of the implementor, including whether they enforce serializability.

- Although the write-ahead log protocol must be observed, whether the log is forced at (sub)transaction commit is optional. An ml-layer implementor can determine the durability of the layer's transactions. Durability can be a declarative part of each layer's definition and can be enforced by the ml framework.

For example, MLR can be used in a system that supports sagas [8, 7]. Transactions of a saga must be durable. But sagas need not be serializable. Compensatability is sufficient, and this may need substantially weaker locks. Traditionally, no locks are held between constituent transactions. Saga compensation is assumed to be possible regardless of other system activity.

In general, some locks may be needed to ensure compensatability. Consider that a possible insurance company claims saga. The company wishes to expose intermediate states of a claim saga to its headquarters employees. Hence, locks held by the saga are compatible with locks used by headquarters operations. On the other hand, agents should not know these internal states, and hence locks of agent operations conflict. Possible rationales are (1) compensation, where all agents are informed that a saga has been rolled back, is difficult and expensive because of the large number of agents and the cost of communication, and (2) agents might leak information to claimants, which the company views with alarm. MLR can accommodate concurrency control of this form.

7.6.3   Layered Abstraction Systems

The *ml* system discussed thus far is structured as a strictly layered hierarchical system. Each layer must use only the operations provided by the layer immediately below it. More flexibility is possible. A system may permit the definer of an abstraction (which exports atomic and recoverable operations) to use instances of any abstraction previously defined. The abstractions so used might not all be at the same level. Hence, the lower-level OPs used in the new abstraction's OPs have different levels. Can MLR work for such a system?

The answer is yes, MLR will work, provided that the specific instances of abstractions used to realize a new abstraction are not accessible outside of the new abstraction. This constraint is frequently satisfied as a natural result of our desire to hide the representation of an abstraction. For example, if some instances of a disk block abstraction are used to support a record abstraction, the constraint requires that those disk blocks only be accessed in operations supporting the accessing of records. Then, the lower-level operations can be recovered first even though this may not be a palindromic ordering of forward and undo operations within a transaction. The ordering can be made palindromic by commutativity, that is, operations on disjoint resources commute.

One example of the use of the layered abstraction technique is for building recoverable queues [4] on top of a database system. MLR solves two significant problems that arise in this.

1. Once an element is enqueued/dequeued from the queue, the low-level database locks for these operations can be released. Only enqueue or dequeue locks need be retained, which can be defined to commute. That is, for example, a dequeue operation for one transaction need not conflict with the dequeue operation on the same queue by another transaction. This avoids the head of queue (tail of queue) bottleneck that arises if only single-level database locks are used. This exploits the natural capabilities of multilevel locking.

2. The abort of a containing transaction will usually cause a dequeued element to be returned to the queue via the defined compensation operation. However, this compensation operation can do more, for example, the number of times the queue element was dequeued and its transaction failed can be counted. After some number of failures, the queue element can be placed on an error queue. This exploits user defined compensation operations that do not need to exactly undo their forward operations.

Layered abstraction functionality, coupled with a persistent virtual memory abstraction for level L_0 may make MLR recovery ideal for extendible and object-oriented transaction systems. Persistent virtual memory is a very flexible basis from which to work. Layered abstractions with MLR recovery permit implementors to achieve high concurrency while preserving transactionality.

Acknowledgements

In 1976, Michael Melliar-Smith suggested to me that recovery for high-level operations might be accomplished in a hierarchically structured system by executing inverses of higher-level operations rather than inverses of the low-level operations that implement them. Recently, in conversations with Butler Lampson, I became convinced that the low-level redo, high-level undo model of recovery was the correct model to provide operation consistency and maximum concurrency.

References

[1] Beeri, C., Bernstein, P., Goodman, N., Lai, M., and Shasha, D. "A concurrency control theory for nested transactions", *Proc. PODC* (August 1983).

[2] Beeri, C., Schek, H.-J., and Weikum, G. *Multilevel transaction management, theoretical art or practical need? Lecture Notes in Computer Science*, Vol. 303, Springer-Verlag, 1988.

[3] Bernstein, P., Hadzilacos, V., and Goodman, N. *Concurrency Control and Recovery in Database Systems*, Addison Wesley (Reading, MA) 1987.

[4] Bernstein, P., Hsu, M. and Mann, B. Implementing "Recoverable Requests Using Queues," *Proc. ACM SIGMOD Conf.* (June 1989).

[5] Eswaran, K., Gray, J., Lorie, R., Traiger, I. "The notions of consistency and predicate locks in a database system," *Comm ACM*, 19(11) (Nov 1975).

[6] Garcia-Molina, H. "Using semantic knowledge for transaction processing in a distributed database," *ACM TODS*, 8(2) (June 1983).

[7] Garcia-Molina, H. and Salem, K. "Sagas," *Proc. ACM SIGMOD Conf.* (June, 1987), San Francisco, CA.

[8] Gray, J. "The transaction concept: virtues and limitations," *Proc. VLDB Conf.* (Sept. 1981) Cannes, France.

[9] Gray, J., McJones, P., Blasgen, M., Lindsay, B., Lorie, R., Price, T., Putzulo, F., Traiger, I. "The recovery manager of the System R database manager," *ACM Computing Surveys* 13(2) (June 1981).

[10] Korth, H., Levy, E. and Silberschatz, A. "A formal approach to recovery by compensating transactions," *Proc. VLDB Conf.*, Brisbane, Australia, (August 1990).

[11] Lomet, D. *Recovery for shared disk systems using multiple redo logs*, DEC Tech Report CRL90/4, Cambridge Research Lab, Cambridge, MA. (Oct 1990).

[12] Lomet, D. and Salzberg, B. *Concurrency and recovery for index trees*, Draft report (Dec 1990).

[13] Lynch, N. "Multilevel atomicity–a new correctness criterion for database concurrency control," *ACM TODS* 8(4) (December 1983).

[14] Mohan, C., Haderle, D., Lindsay, B., Pirahesh, H., and Schwarz, P. "ARIES: A transaction recovery method supporting fine-granularity locking and partial rollbacks using write-ahead logging," *ACM TODS*, 17(1) (March 1992).

[15] Mohan, C. and Levine, F. "ARIES/IM: an efficient and high concurrency index management method using write-ahead logging," *IBM Research Report* RJ 6846, IBM Almaden Research Center, San Jose, CA. (Aug 1989).

[16] Rothermel, K. and Mohan, C. "ARIES/NT: A recovery method based on write-ahead logging for nested transactions," *Proc. VLDB Conf.*, Amsterdam, Netherlands, (August 1989).

[17] Traiger, I. "Trends in systems aspects of database management," *Proc. ICOD Conf.*, Cambridge, MA (1983).

[18] Weikum, G. and Schek, H.-J. "Architectural issues of transaction management in multilayered systems," *Proc. VLDB Conf.*, Singapore. (August, 1984).

[19] Weikum, G. "A theoretical foundation of multilevel concurrency control," *Proc. ACM PODS Conf.*, Cambridge, MA. (March 1986).

[20] Weikum, G., Hasse, C., Broessler, P., and Muth, P. "Multilevel recovery," *Proc. ACM PODS Conf.*, Nashville, Tenn (April 1990).

Chapter 8

ARIES: A Transaction Recovery Method Supporting Fine-Granularity Locking and Partial Rollbacks Using Write-Ahead Logging

*C. Mohan, Don Haderle, Bruce Lindsay, Hamid Pirahesh,
and Peter Schwarz*

Abstract

In this chapter we present a simple and efficient method, called ARIES-*Algorithm for Recovery and Isolation Exploiting Semantics*-which supports partial rollbacks of transactions, fine-granularity (e.g., record) locking and recovery using write-ahead logging (WAL). We introduce the paradigm of *repeating history* to redo all missing updates *before* performing the rollbacks of the loser transactions during restart after a system failure. ARIES uses a log sequence number in each page to correlate the state of a page with respect to logged updates of that page. All updates of a transactions are logged, including those performed during rollbacks. By appropriate chaining of the log records written during rollbacks to those written during forward progress, a bounded amount of logging is ensured during rollbacks even in the face of repeated failures during restarts or of nested rollbacks. We deal with a variety of features that are very important in building and operating an *industrial-strength*, transsaction processing system. ARIES supports fuzzy checkpoints, selective and deferred restart, fuzzy image copies, media recovery, and high-concurrency lock modes (e.g., increment/decrement) that exploit the semantics of the operations and require the ability to perform the operation logging. ARIES is flexible with respect to the kinds of buffer management policies that can be implemented. It supports objects of varying length efficiently. By enabling parallelism during restart, page-oriented redo, and logical undo, it enhances concurrency and performance. We show why some of the System R paradigm for logging and recovery, which were based on the shadow-page technique, need to be changed in the context of WAL. We compare ARIES to the WAL-based recovery methods of DB2[1], IMS, and Tandem systems. ARIES is applicable not only to database management systems but also to persistent object-oriented languages, recoverable file systems and transaction based operating systems. ARIES has been implemented, to varying degrees, in IBM's OS/2 Extended Edition Database Manager, DB2, Workstation Data Save Facility/VM, Starbust and Quicksilver, and in the University of Wisconsin's EXODUS and Gamma database machine.

8.1   INTRODUCTION

In this section, first we introduce some basic concepts relating to recovery, concurrency control and buffer management, and then we outline the organization of the rest of the chapter.

8.1.1   Logging, Failures, and Recovery Methods

The transaction concept, which is well understood by now, has been around for a long time. It encapsulates the *ACID* (Atomicity, Consistency, Isolation, and Durability) properties [38]. The application of the transaction concept is not limited to the data base area [6, 17, 23, 25, 32, 42, 43, 55, 80, 94, 98, 110]. Guaranteeing the atomicity and durability of transactions, in the face of concurrent execution of multiple transactions and various failures, is a very important problem in transaction processing. Although many methods have been developed in the past to deal with this problem, the assumptions, performance characteristics, and the complexity and the ad hoc nature of such methods have not always been acceptable. Solutions to this problem may be judged using several metrics: degree of concurrency supported within a page and across pages, complexity of the resulting logic, space overhead on nonvolatile storage and in memory for data and the log, overhead in terms of the number of synchronous and asynchronous I/Os required during restart recovery and normal processing, kinds of functionality supported (partial transaction rollbacks, etc.), amount of processing performed during restart recovery, degree of

---

[1]ADSM, ADSTAR, AS/400, DB2, DB2/2, DB2/6000, IBM, and OS/2 are trademarks of the International Business Machines Corp. NonStop SQL and Tandem are trademarks of Tandem Computers, Inc. DEC, VAX DBMS, VAX, VAXcluster, and Rdb/VMS are trademarks of Digital Equipment Corp. DBC/1012 is a trademark of Teradata Corp. Encina and Transarc are trademarks of Transarc Corp. Informix is a registered trademark of Informix Software, Inc.

concurrent processing supported during restart recovery, extent of system-induced transaction rollbacks because of deadlocks, restrictions placed on stored data (e.g., requiring unique keys for all records, restricting maximum size of objects to the page size, etc.), ability to support novel lock modes that allow the concurrent execution, based on commutativity and other properties [2, 28, 41, 49, 94, 95], of operations like increment/decrement on the same data by different transactions, and so on.

In this chapter, we introduce a new recovery method, called $ARIES^2$ (*Algorithm for Recovery and Isolation Exploiting Semantics*), which fares very well with respect to all these metrics. It also provides a great deal of flexibility to take advantage of some special characteristics of a class of applications for better performance (e.g., the kinds of applications that IMS Fast Path [30, 45] supports efficiently).

To meet transaction and data recovery guarantees, ARIES records in a *log* the progress of a transaction, and its actions that cause changes to recoverable data objects. The log becomes the source for ensuring either that the transaction's committed actions are reflected in the database despite various types of failures, or that its uncommitted actions are undone (i.e., rolled back). When the logged actions reflect data object content, then those log records also become the source for reconstruction of damaged or lost data (i.e., media recovery). *Conceptually*, the log can be thought of as an ever growing *sequential* file. In the actual implementation, multiple physical files may be used in a serial fashion to ease the job of archiving log records [15]. Every log record is assigned a unique *log sequence number (LSN)* when that record is appended to the log. The LSNs are assigned in ascending sequence. Typically, they are the *logical* addresses of the corresponding log records. At times, version numbers or timestamps are also used as LSNs [73]. If more than one log is used for storing the log records relating to *different* pieces of data, then a form of two-phase commit protocol (e.g., the current industry-standard, presumed abort protocol, [57, 68, 69] must be used.

Logical page LP1 is read from physical page P1 and after modification is written to physical page P1*ı*. P1*ı* is the *current* version and P1 is the *shadow* version. During a checkpoint, the shadow version is discarded and the current version becomes the shadow version also. On a failure, database recovery is performed using the log and the shadow version of the database.

The nonvolatile version of the log is stored on what is generally called *stable storage*. Stable storage means nonvolatile storage that remains intact and available across system failures. Disk is an example of nonvolatile storage and its stability is generally improved by maintaining synchronously two identical copies of the log on different devices. We would expect the on-line log records stored on direct access storage devices to be archived to a cheaper and slower medium like tape at regular intervals. The archived log records may be discarded once the appropriate image copies (archive dumps) of the database have been produced and those log records are no longer needed for media recovery.

---

[2]The choice of the name ARIES, besides its use as an acronym that describes certain features of our recovery method, is also supposed to convey the relationship of our work to the Starburst project at IBM, since Aries is the name of a constellation.

Whenever log records are written, they are placed first only in the *volatile storage* (i.e., virtual storage) buffers of the log file. Only at certain times (e.g., at commit time) are the log records up to a certain point (LSN) written, in log-page sequence, to stable storage. This is called *forcing* the log up to that LSN. Besides forces caused by transaction and buffer manager activities, a system process may, in the background, periodically force the log buffers as they fill up.

For ease of exposition, we assume that each log record describes the update performed to only a single page. This is not a requirement of ARIES. In fact, in the Starburst [93] implementation of ARIES, sometimes a single log record might be written to describe updates to two pages. The *undo* (respectively, *redo*) portion of a log record provides information on how to undo (respectively, redo) changes performed by the transaction. A log record that contains both the undo and the redo information is called an *undo-redo log record*. Sometimes, a log record may be written to contain only the redo information or only the undo information. Such a record is called a *redo-only log record* or an *undo-only log record*, respectively. Depending on the action that is performed, the undo-redo information may be recorded *physically* (e.g., before the update and after the update images or values of specific fields within the object) or *operationally* (e.g., add 5 to field 3 of record 15, subtract 3 from field 4 of record 10). Operation logging permits the use of high-concurrency lock modes, which exploit the semantics of the operations performed on the data. For example, with certain operations, the same field of a record could have uncommitted updates of many transactions. These permit more concurrency than what is permitted by the *strict executions* property of the model of [3], which essentially says that modified objects must be locked exclusively (X mode) for commit duration.

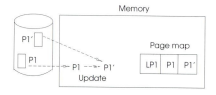

Logical page LP1 is read from physical page P1 and after modification is written to physical page P1', P1' is the *current* version and P1 is the *shadow* version. During a checkpoint the shadow version is discarded and the current version becomes the shadow version also. On a failure, database recovery is performed using the log and the shadow version of the database

Figure 8.1. Shadow-page technique.

ARIES uses the widely accepted write-ahead logging (WAL) protocol. Some of the commercial and prototype systems based on WAL are IBM's AS/400 [9, 22], CMU's Camelot [25, 98], IBM's DB2 [1, 10, 11, 12, 13, 14, 15, 20, 37, 104], Unisys' DMS/1100 [29], Tandem's Encompass [4, 40], IBM's IMS [45, 47, 58, 82, 86, 102], Informix's Informix-Turbo [16], Honeywell's MRDS [99], Tandem's NonStop SQL [103], MCC's ORION [31], IBM's OS/2 Extended Edition Database Manager [7], IBM's Quicksilver [43], IBM's Starburst [93], SYNAPSE [84], IBM's System38 [108], and DEC's VAX DBMS and VAX Rdb/VMS [87]. In WAL-based systems, an updated page is written back to the same nonvolatile storage location from where it was read. That is, *in-place updating* is performed on nonvolatile storage. Contrast this with what happens in the shadow-page technique that is used in systems such as System R [33] and SQL/DS [5] and that is illustrated in Figure 8.1. There, the updated version of the page is written to a different location on nonvolatile storage and the previous version of the page is used for performing database recovery if the system were to fail before the next checkpoint.

The *WAL protocol* asserts that the log records representing changes to some data must already be on stable storage *before* the changed data is allowed to replace the previous version of that data on nonvolatile storage. That is, the system is not allowed to write an updated page to the nonvolatile storage version of the database until at least the undo portions of the log records that describe the updates to the page have been written to stable storage. To enable the enforcement of this protocol, systems using the WAL method of recovery store in every page the LSN of the log record that describes the *most recent* update performed on that page. The reader is referred to [33, 105] for discussions about why the WAL technique is considered to be better than the shadow page technique. Methods are discussed in [16, 84] which shadowing is performed using a separate log. While these avoid some of the problems of the original shadow-page approach, they still retain some of the important drawbacks and they introduce some new ones. Similar comments apply to the methods suggested in [88, 94]. Later, in Section 8.10, we show why some of the recovery paradigms of System R, which were based on the shadow-page technique, are inappropriate in the WAL context, when we need support for high levels of concurrency and various other features that are described in Section 8.2.

Transaction status is also stored in the log and no transaction can be considered complete until its committed status and all its log data is safely recorded on stable storage by forcing the log up to the transaction's commit log record's LSN. This allows a restart recovery procedure to recover any transactions that completed successfully but whose updated pages were not physically written to nonvolatile storage before the failure of the system. This means that a transaction is not permitted to complete its *commit* processing (see [68, 69]) until the redo portions of all log records of that transaction have been written to stable storage.

We deal with three types of failures: transaction or process, system, and media or device. When a transaction or process failure occurs, typically, the transaction would be in such a state that its updates would have to be undone. It is possible that the transaction had corrupted some pages in the buffer pool if it was in the middle of performing some updates when the process disappeared. When a system failure occurs, typically, the virtual storage contents would be lost and the transaction system would have to be restarted and recovery would have to be performed using the nonvolatile storage versions of the database and the log. When a media or device failure occurs, typically the contents of that media would be lost and the lost data would have to be recovered using an image copy (archive dump) version of the lost data and the log.

Forward processing refers to the updates performed when the system is in normal (i.e., not restart recovery) processing and the transaction is updating the database because of the data manipulation (e.g., SQL) calls issued by the user or the application program. That is, the transaction is not rolling back and using the log to generate the (undo) update calls. *Partial rollback* refers to the ability to set up *savepoints* during the execution of a transaction and later in the transaction request the rolling back of the changes performed by the transaction since the establishment of a previous savepoint [1, 33]. This is to be contrasted with *total rollback* in which *all* the updates of the transaction are undone and the transaction is terminated. Whether the savepoint concept is exposed at the application level is immaterial to us since we are dealing with only database recovery in this chapter. A *nested rollback* is said to have taken place if a partial rollback were to be later followed by a total rollback or another partial rollback whose point of termination is an *earlier* point in the transaction than the point of termination of the first rollback. *Normal undo* refers to total or partial transaction rollback when the system is in normal operation. A normal undo may be caused by a transaction request to rollback or it may be system-initiated because of deadlocks or errors (e.g., integrity constraint violations). *Restart undo* refers to transaction rollback during restart recovery after a system failure. To make partial or total rollback efficient and also to make debugging easier, all the log records written by a transaction are linked via the *PrevLSN* field of the log records in reverse chronological order. That is, the most recently written log record of the transaction would point to the previous most recent log record written by that transaction, if there is such a log record.[3] In many WAL-based systems, the updates performed during a rollback are logged using what are called *compensation log records (CLRs)* [15]. Whether a CLR's update is undone, if that CLR is encountered during a rollback, depends on the particular system. As we will see later, in ARIES, a CLR's update is never undone and hence CLRs are viewed as redo-only log records.

Page-oriented redo is said to occur if the log record whose update is being redone describes which page of the database was originally modified during normal processing and the same page is modified during the redo processing also. No internal descriptors of tables or indexes need to be accessed to redo the update. That is, no other page of the database needs to be examined. This is to be contrasted with *logical redo*, which is required in System R, SQL/DS and AS/400, for indexes [22, 67]. In those systems, since index changes are not logged separately but are redone using the log records for the data pages, performing a redo requires accessing several descriptors and pages of the database. The index tree would have to be retraversed to determine the page(s) to be modified and, sometimes, the index page(s) that is modified because of this redo operation may be different from the index page(s) that was originally modified during normal processing. Being able to perform page-oriented redo allows the system to provide *recovery independence amongst objects*. That is, the recovery of one page's contents does not require accesses to any other (data or catalog) pages of the database. This makes media recovery very simple, as we will describe later.

---

[3]The AS/400, Encompass, and NonStop SQL do not explicitly link all the log records written by a transaction. This makes undo inefficient since a *sequential* backward scan of the log must be performed to retrieve all the desired log records of a transaction.

In a similar fashion, we can define *page-oriented undo* and *logical undo*. Being able to perform logical undos allows the system to provide higher levels of concurrency than what would be possible if the system were to be restricted to only page-oriented undos. This is because the former, with appropriate concurrency control protocols, would permit uncommitted updates of one transaction to be moved to a different page by another transaction. If one were restricted to only page-oriented undos, then the latter transaction would have had to wait for the former to commit. Page-oriented redo and page-oriented undo permit faster recovery since pages of the database other than the pages mentioned in the log records are not accessed. ARIES supports, in the interest of efficiency, page-oriented redo and it supports, in the interest of high concurrency, logical undos. In [67], we introduce the ARIES/IM method for concurrency control and recovery in B^+-tree indexes and show the advantages of being able to perform logical undos by comparing ARIES/IM with other index methods.

8.1.2   Latches and Locks

Normally, latches and locks are used to control access to shared information. Locking has been discussed to a great extent in the literature. Latches, on the other hand, have not been discussed that much. *Latches* are like semaphores. Usually, latches are used to guarantee physical consistency of data, and *locks* are used to assure logical consistency of data. We need to worry about physical consistency since we need to support a multiprocessor environment. Latches are usually held for a much shorter period than are locks. Also, the deadlock detector is not informed about latch waits. Latches are requested in such a manner so as to avoid deadlocks involving latches alone, or involving latches and locks.

Acquiring and releasing a latch is much cheaper than acquiring and releasing a lock. In the no-conflict case, the overhead amounts to 10's of instructions for the former versus 100's of instructions for the latter. Latches are cheaper because the *latch control information* is always in virtual memory in a fixed place, and direct addressability to the latch information is possible given the latch name. As the protocols presented later in this chapter and those in [62, 67] show, each transaction holds at most two or three latches simultaneously. As a result, the *latch request blocks* can be permanently allocated to each transaction and initialized with transaction ID, and so on, right at the start of that transaction. On the other hand, typically, storage for individual locks has to be acquired, formatted, and released dynamically, causing more instructions to be executed to acquire and release locks. This is advisable because, in most systems, the number of lockable objects is many orders of magnitude greater than the number of latchable objects. Typically, all information relating to locks currently held or requested by all the transactions is stored in a single, central hash table; addressability to a particular lock's information is gained by first hashing the lock name to get the address of the hash anchor and then, possibly, following a chain of pointers. Usually, in the process of trying to locate the *lock control block*, because multiple transactions may be simultaneously

reading and modifying the contents of the lock table, one or more latches will be acquired and released—one latch on the hash anchor and, possibly, one on the specific
lock's chain of holders and waiters.

Table 8.1. Lock mode compatibility

	S	X	IS	IX	SIX
S	√		√		
X					
IS	√		√	√	√
IX			√	√	
SIX			√		

Locks may be obtained in different *modes* such as S (Shared), X (eXclusive),
IX (Intention eXclusive), IS (Intention Shared), and SIX (Shared Intention eXclusive), and at different *granularities* such as record (tuple), table (relation), and file
(tablespace) [34]. The S and X locks are the most common ones. S provides the
read privilege and X provides the read and write privileges. Locks on a given object
can be held simultaneously by different transactions only if those locks' modes are
compatible. The compatibility relationships amongst the above modes of locking
are shown in Table 8.1. A check mark ($\sqrt{}$) indicates that the corresponding modes
are compatible. With *hierarchical locking*, the intention locks (IX, IS, and SIX) are
generally obtained on the higher levels of the hierarchy (e.g., table), and the S and
X locks are obtained on the lower levels (e.g., record). The nonintention mode locks
(S and X), when obtained on an object at a certain level of the hierarchy, *implicitly*
grant locks of the corresponding mode on the lower level-objects of that higher level
object. The intention mode locks, on the other hand, only give the privilege of
requesting the corresponding intention or nonintention mode locks on the lower
level objects. For example, SIX on a table *implicitly* grants S on all the records of
that table, and it allows X to be requested *explicitly* on the records. Additional,
semantically rich lock modes have been defined in the literature [2, 41, 49, 60] and
ARIES can accommodate them.

Lock requests may be made with the *conditional* or the *unconditional* option.
A *conditional* request means that the requestor is not willing to wait if, when
the request is processed, the lock is not grantable immediately. An *unconditional*
request means that the requestor is willing to wait until the lock becomes grantable.
Locks may be held for different *durations*. An unconditional request for an *instant
duration* lock means that the lock is not to be actually granted, but the lock manager
has to delay returning the lock call with the *success* status until the lock becomes
grantable. *Manual duration* locks are released some time after they are acquired

and, typically, long before transaction termination. *Commit duration* locks are released only when the transaction terminates, that is, after commit or rollback is completed. The preceding discussions concerning conditional requests, different modes, and durations, except for commit duration, apply to latches also.

8.1.3   Fine-Granularity Locking

Fine-granularity (e.g., record) locking has been supported by nonrelational database systems (e.g., IMS [58, 82, 86]) for a long time. Surprisingly, only a few of the commercially available relational systems provide fine-granularity locking, even though IBM's System R [34], S/38 [108], and SQL/DS [5], and Tandem's Encompass [40] supported record and/or key locking from the beginning.[4] Although many interesting problems relating to providing fine-granularity locking in the context of WAL have remained to be solved, the research community has not been paying enough attention to this area [3, 81, 94]. Some of the System R solutions worked only because of the use of the shadow-page recovery technique in combination with locking (see Section 8.10). Supporting fine-granularity locking and variable-length records in a flexible fashion requires addressing some interesting storage management issues that have never really been discussed in the database literature. Unfortunately, some of the interesting techniques that were developed for System R and that are now part of SQL/DS are not documented in the literature. At the expense of making this chapter long, we will be discussing here some of those interesting problems and their solutions.

As supporting high concurrency gains importance (see [85] for the description of an application requiring very high concurrency) and as object-oriented systems gain more popularity, it becomes necessary to invent concurrency control and recovery methods that take advantage of the semantics of the operations on the data [2, 28, 41, 94, 95], and that support fine-granularity locking efficiently. Object-oriented systems may tend to encourage users to define a large number of small objects and users may expect object instances to be the appropriate granularity of locking. In the object-oriented logical view of the database, the concept of a page, with its physical orientation as the container of objects, becomes unnatural to think about as the unit of locking during object accesses and modifications. Also, object-oriented system users may tend to have many terminal interactions during the course of a transaction, thereby increasing the lock hold times. These will aggravate the lock wait times and deadlock possibilities, if the unit of locking were to be a page. Other discussions concerning transaction management in an object-oriented environment can be found in [23, 31].

As more and more customers adopt relational systems for production applications, it becomes all the more important to handle *hotspots* [30, 36, 83, 85, 89] and storage management without requiring too much tuning by the system users or administrators. Since relational systems have been welcomed to a great extent

---

[4]Encompass and S/38 had only X locks for records and no locks were acquired *automatically* by these systems for reads.

because of their ease of use, it is important that we pay greater attention to this area than what has been done in the context of the nonrelational systems. Apart from the need for high concurrency for user data, the ease with which on-line data definition operations can be performed in relational systems by even ordinary users requires the support for high concurrency of access to, at least, the catalog data. Since a single leaf page in an index typically describes data in hundreds of data pages, page-level locking of index data is just not acceptable. A flexible recovery method that allows the support of high levels of concurrency during index accesses is needed.

The preceding argues for supporting semantically rich modes of locking, such as increment/decrement, which allow multiple transactions to concurrently modify even the same piece of data. In funds-transfer applications, increment and decrement operations are frequently performed on the branch and teller balances by numerous transactions. If those transactions are forced to use only X locks, then they will be serialized, even though their operations commute.

8.1.4   Buffer Management

The buffer manager (BM) is the component of the transaction system that manages the buffer pool and does I/Os to read/write pages from/to the nonvolatile storage version of the database. The fix primitive of the BM may be used to request the buffer address of a logical page in the database. If the requested page is not in the buffer pool, BM allocates a buffer slot and reads the page. There may be instances (e.g., during a B^+-tree page split, when the new page is allocated) where the current contents of a page on nonvolatile storage are not of interest. In such a case, the fix_new primitive may be used to make the BM allocate a $free$ slot and return the address of that slot, if BM does not find the page in the buffer pool. The fix_new invoker will then format the page as desired. Once a page is fixed in the buffer pool, the corresponding buffer slot is not available for page replacement until the $unfix$ primitive is issued by the data manipulative component. Actually, for each page, BM keeps a fix count that is incremented by one during every fix operation and that is decremented by one during every unfix operation. A page in the buffer pool is said to be $dirty$ if the buffer version of the page has some updates that are not yet reflected in the nonvolatile storage version of the same page. The fix primitive is also used to communicate the intention to modify the page. Dirty pages can be written back to nonvolatile storage when no fix with the modification intention is held, thus allowing read accesses to the page while it is being written out. The role of BM is discussed in [104] in writing in the background, on a continuous basis, dirty pages to nonvolatile storage to reduce the amount of redo work that would be needed if a system failure were to occur. BM also keeps a certain percentage of the buffer pool pages in the nondirty state so that they may be replaced with other pages without synchronous write I/Os having to be performed at the time of replacement. While performing those writes, BM ensures that the WAL protocol is obeyed. As a consequence, BM may have to force the log up to the LSN of the dirty page before writing the page to nonvolatile storage. Given the large buffer pools that are common today, we would expect a force of this nature to be very rare. We would expect most log forces to occur because of transactions committing or entering the prepare state.

BM also implements the support for latching pages. To provide direct address-ability to page latches and to reduce the storage associated with those latches, the latch on a logical page is actually the latch on the corresponding buffer slot. This means that a logical page can be latched only after it is fixed in the buffer pool and the latch has to be released before the page is unfixed. These are highly accept-able conditions. The latch control information is stored in the buffer control block (BCB) for the corresponding buffer slot. The BCB also contains the identity of the logical page, what the fix count is, the dirty status of the page, and so on.

Buffer management policies differ amongst the many systems in existence (see Section 8.11). If a page modified by a transaction is allowed to be written to the permanent database on nonvolatile storage before that transaction commits, then the *steal* policy is said to be followed by the buffer manager (see [38] for such terminologies). Otherwise, a *nosteal* policy is said to be in effect. Steal implies that during normal or restart rollback, some undo work might have to be performed on the nonvolatile storage version of the data base. If a transaction is *not* allowed to commit until all *pages* modified by it are written to the permanent version of the database, then a *force* policy is said to be in effect. Otherwise, a *noforce* policy is said to be in effect. With a force policy, during restart recovery, no redo work will be necessary for committed transactions. *Deferred updating* is said to occur if, even in the virtual-storage database buffers, the updates are not performed in place when the transaction issues the corresponding database calls. The updates are kept in a pending list elsewhere. The updates are performed in place, using the pending list information, only after it is determined that the transaction is definitely committing. If the transaction needs to be rolled back, then the pending list is discarded or is ignored. The deferred updating policy has implications on whether a transaction can "see" its own updates or not, and on whether partial rollbacks are possible or not. For more discussions concerning buffer management, see [8, 15, 26, 104].

8.1.5   Organization

The rest of the chapter is organized as follows. After stating our goals in Section 8.2 and giving an overview of the new recovery method ARIES in Section 8.3, we present, in Section 8.4, the important data structures used by ARIES during normal and restart recovery processing. Next, in Section 8.5, the protocols followed during normal processing are presented followed, in Section 8.6, by the description of the processing performed during restart recovery. The latter section also presents ways to exploit parallelism during recovery and methods for performing recovery selectively or postponing the recovery of some of the data. Then, in Section 8.5.4, algorithms are described for taking checkpoints during the different log passes of restart recovery to reduce the impact of failures during recovery. This is followed, in Section 8.8, by the description of how fuzzy-image copying and media recovery are supported. Section 8.9 introduces the significant notion of *nested top actions* and presents a method for implementing them efficiently. Then, in Section 8.10, we describe and critique some of the existing recovery paradigms that originated in the context of the shadow page technique and System R. We discuss the problems caused by using those paradigms in the WAL context. Section 8.11 describes in detail the characteristics of many of the WAL-based recovery methods in use in different systems like IMS, DB2, Encompass and NonStop SQL. Section 8.12 outlines the many different properties of ARIES. We conclude by summarizing, in Section 8.13, the features of ARIES that provide flexibility and efficiency, and by describing the extensions and the current status of the implementations of ARIES.

Besides presenting a new recovery method, by way of motivation for our work, we also describe some previously unpublished aspects of recovery in System R. For comparison purposes, we also do a survey of the recovery methods used by other WAL-based systems and collect information appearing in several publications, many of which are not widely available. One of our aims in this chapter is to show the intricate and unobvious interactions resulting from the different choices made for the recovery technique, the granularity of locking and the storage management scheme. One cannot make arbitrarily independent choices for these and still expect the combination to function together correctly and efficiently. This point needs to be emphasized, as it is not always dealt with adequately in most papers and books on concurrency control and recovery. In this chapter, we have tried to cover, as much as possible, all the interesting recovery-related problems that one encounters in building and operating an *industrialstrength* transaction processing system.

8.2 GOALS

This section lists the goals of our work and outlines the difficulties involved in designing a recovery method that supports the features that we aimed for. The goals relate to the metrics for comparison of recovery methods that we discussed earlier, in Section 8.1.1.

Simplicity.   Concurrency and recovery are complex subjects to think about and program for, compared to other aspects of data management. The algorithms are bound to be error-prone, if they are complex. Hence, we strived for a simple, yet powerful and flexible, algorithm. Although this chapter is long because of the comprehensive discussion of numerous problems that are mostly ignored in the literature, the main algorithm itself is quite simple. It is hoped that the overview presented in Section 8.3 gives the reader that feeling.

Operation Logging.   The recovery method had to permit operation logging (and value logging) so that semantically rich lock modes could be supported. This would let one transaction modify the same data that were modified earlier by another transaction that has not yet committed, when the two transactions' actions are se-

mantically compatible (e.g., increment/decrement operations – see [2, 28, 49, 94]).
As it should be clear, recovery methods that *always* perform *value or state logging*
(i.e., logging before images and afterimages of modified data) cannot support operation logging. This includes systems that do very physical – *byteoriented* – logging
of all changes to a page [6, 82, 87]. The difficulty in supporting operation logging
is that we need to track precisely, using a concept like the LSN, the exact state of
a page with respect to logged actions relating to that page. An undo or a redo of
an update should not be performed without being sure that the original update is
present or is not present, respectively. This also means that if one or more transactions that had modified a page earlier start rolling back, then we need to know
precisely how the page has been affected during the rollbacks and how much of the
rollbacks has been accomplished so far. This requires that updates performed during rollbacks also be logged via the so-called *compensation log records* (*CLRs*). The
LSN concept lets us avoid attempting to redo an operation when the operation's
effect is already present in the page. It also lets us avoid attempting to undo an
operation when the operation's effect is not present in the page. Operation logging
lets us perform, if found desirable, *logical logging*, which means that not everything
that was changed on a page needs to be logged explicitly, thereby saving log space.
For example, changes of control information, like the amount of free space on the
page, need not be logged. The redo and the undo operations can be performed
logically. For a good discussion of operation and value logging, see [94].

Flexible Storage Management. Efficient support for the storage and manipulation
of varying length data is important. In contrast to systems like IMS, the intent here
is to be able to avoid the need for off-line reorganization of the data to garbage collect
any space that might have been freed up because of deletions and updates that
caused data shrinkage. It is desirable that the recovery method and the concurrency
control method be such that the logging and locking are *logical* in nature so that
movements of the data within a page for garbage collection reasons do not cause
the moved data to be locked or the movements to be logged. For an index, this
also means that one transaction must be able to split a leaf page even if that page
currently has some uncommitted data inserted by another transaction. This may
lead to problems in performing page-oriented undos using the log – *logical undos*
may be necessary. Further, we would like to be able to let a transaction that has
freed up some space be able to use, if necessary, that space during its later insert
activity [54]. System R, for example, does not permit this in data pages.

Partial Rollbacks. It was essential that the new recovery method support the concept of savepoints and rollbacks to savepoints (i.e., partial rollbacks). This is crucial
for handling, in a user-friendly fashion (i.e., without requiring a total rollback of
the transaction), integrity constraint violations (see [1, 33]), and problems arising
from using obsolete cached information (see [53]).

Flexible Buffer Management. The recovery method should make the least number
of restrictive assumptions about the buffer management policies (*steal*, *force*, etc.)

in effect. At the same time, the method must be able to take advantage of the characteristics of any specific policy that is in effect, for example, with a force policy, there is no need to perform any redos for committed transactions. This flexibility could result in increased concurrency, decreased I/Os, and efficient usage of buffer storage. Depending on the policies, the work that needs to be performed during restart recovery after a system failure or during media recovery may be more or less complex. Even with large main memories, it must be noted that a steal policy is still very desirable. This is because, with a no-steal policy, a page may never get written to nonvolatile storage if the page always contains *uncommitted* updates due to fine-granularity locking and overlapping transactions' updates to that page. The situation would be further aggravated if there are long-running transactions. Under those conditions, either the system would have to frequently reduce concurrency by quiescing all activities on the page (i.e., by locking all the objects on the page) and then writing the page to nonvolatile storage or by doing nothing special and then paying a huge restart redo recovery cost if the system were to fail. Also, a no-steal policy incurs additional bookkeeping overhead to track whether a page contains any uncommitted updates. We believe that given our goal of supporting semantically rich lock modes, partial rollbacks, and varying-length objects efficiently, in the general case, we need to perform undo logging and in-place updating. Hence, methods like the transaction workspace model of AIM [50] are not general enough for our purposes. Other problems relating to no-steal policy are discussed in Section 8.11 with reference to IMS Fast Path.

Recovery Independence. It should be possible to image copy (archive dump), and perform media recovery or restart recovery at different granularities, rather than only at the entire database level. The recovery of one object should not force the concurrent or lock-step recovery of another object. Contrast this with what happens in the shadow-page technique as implemented in System R, where index and space management information are recovered *lock step* with user and catalog table (relation) data by starting from an internally consistent state of the *whole* database and redoing changes to all the related objects of the data base simultaneously, as in normal processing. Recovery independence means that during the restart recovery of some object, catalog information in the database cannot be accessed for descriptors of that object and its related objects, since that information itself may be undergoing recovery in parallel with the object being recovered and the two may be out of synchronization [14]. During restart recovery, it should be possible to do selective recovery and defer recovery of some objects to a later point in time to speed up restart and also to accommodate some off-line devices. *Page-oriented recovery* means that even if one page in the data base is corrupted because of a process failure or a media problem, it should be possible to recover that page alone. To be able to do this efficiently, we need to log every page's change individually, even if the object being updated spans multiple pages and the update affects more than one page. This, in conjunction with the writing of CLRs for updates performed during rollbacks, will make media recovery very simple (see Section 8.8). This will also permit the image copying of different objects to be performed independently and at different frequencies.

Logical Undo. This relates to the ability, during undo, to affect a page that is different from the one modified during forward processing, as is needed in the earlier-mentioned context of the split by one transaction of an index page containing uncommitted data of another transaction. Being able to perform logical undos allows higher levels of concurrency to be supported, especially in search structures [62, 64, 67]. If logging is not performed during rollback processing, logical undos would be very difficult to support if we also desired recovery independence and page-oriented recovery. System R and SQL/DS support logical undos, but at the expense of recovery independence.

Parallelism and Fast Recovery. With multiprocessors becoming very common and greater data availability becoming increasingly important, the recovery method has to be able to exploit parallelism during the different stages of restart recovery and during media recovery. It is also important that the recovery method be such that recovery can be very fast, if in fact a *hot standby* approach is going to be used (a la IBM's IMS/VS XRF [47] and Tandem's NonStop [4, 40]). This means that redo processing and, whenever possible, undo processing should be page-oriented (cf. always logical redos and undos in System R and SQL/DS for indexes and space management). It should also be possible to let the backup system start processing new transactions, even before the undo processing for the interrupted transactions completes. This is necessary because undo processing may take a long time if there were long update transactions.

Minimal Overhead. Our goal is to have good performance both during normal and restart recovery processing. The overhead (log data volume, storage consumption, etc.) imposed by the recovery method in virtual and nonvolatile storages for accomplishing the preceding goals should be minimal. Contrast this with the space overhead caused by the shadow-page technique. This goal also implied that we should minimize the number of pages that are modified (*dirtied*) during restart. The idea is to reduce the number of pages that have to be written back to nonvolatile storage and also to reduce CPU overhead. This rules out methods that, during restart recovery, first undo some committed changes that had already reached the nonvolatile storage before the failure and then redo them; see for example, [16, 22, 78, 84, 94]. It also rules out methods in which updates that are not present in a page on nonvolatile storage are undone unnecessarily; see for example, [44, 77, 94]. The method should not cause deadlocks involving transactions that are already rolling back. Further, the writing of CLRs should not result in an unbounded number of log records having to be written for a transaction because of the undoing of CLRs if there were nested rollbacks or repeated system failures during rollbacks. It should also be possible to take checkpoints and image copies without quiescing significant activities in the system. The impact of these operations on other activities should be minimal. To contrast, checkpointing and image copying in System R cause major perturbations in the rest of the system [33].

As the reader would have realized by now, some of these goals are contradictory. Based on our knowledge about different developers' existing systems' features, experiences with IBM's existing transaction systems, and contacts with customers, we made the necessary trade-offs. We were keen on learning from past successes *and* mistakes involving many prototypes and products.

8.3   OVERVIEW OF ARIES

The aim of this section is to provide a brief overview of the new recovery method ARIES, which satisfies quite reasonably the goals that we set forth in Section 8.2. Issues like deferred and selective restart, parallelism during restart recovery, and so on will be discussed later in the chapter.

After performing three actions, the transaction performs a partial rollback by undoing actions 3 and 2, writing the compensation log records $3'$ and $2'$, and then starts going forward again and performs actions four and five.

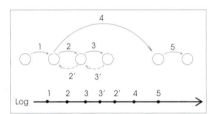

After performing 3 actions, the transaction performs a partial rollback by undoing actions 3 and 2, writing the compensation log records 3' and 2', and then starts going forward again and performs actions 4 and 5.

Figure 8.2. Partial rollback example.

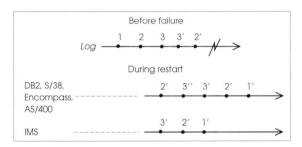

I' is the CLR for I and I'' is the CLR for I'

Figure 8.3. Problem of compensating compensations or duplicate compensations, or both.

ARIES guarantees the atomicity and durability properties of transactions in the face of process, transaction, system and media failures. For this purpose, ARIES keeps track of the changes made to the database by using a log and it does write-

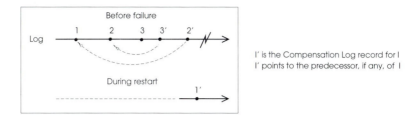

Figure 8.4. ARIES's technique for avoiding compensating compensations and duplicate compensations.

ahead logging (WAL). Besides logging, on a per-affected-page basis, update activities performed during forward processing of transactions, ARIES also logs, typically using compensation log records (CLRs), updates performed during partial or total rollbacks of transactions during both normal and restart processing. Figure 8.2 gives an example of a partial rollback in which a transaction, after performing three updates, rolls back two of them, and then starts going forward again. Because of the undo of the two updates, two CLRs are written. In ARIES, CLRs have the property that they are redo-only log records. By appropriate chaining of the CLRs to log records written during forward processing, a bounded amount of logging is ensured during rollbacks, even in the face of repeated failures during restart or of nested rollbacks. This is to be contrasted with what happens in IMS, which may undo the same non-CLR multiple times, and in AS/400, DB2, and NonStop SQL, which, besides undoing the same non-CLR multiple times, may also undo CLRs one or more times (see Figure 8.3). These have caused severe problems in real-life customer situations.

In ARIES, as Figure 8.4 shows, when the undo of a log record causes a CLR to be written, the CLR, besides containing a description of the compensating action for redo purposes, is made to contain the $UndoNxtLSN$ pointer that points to the *predecessor* of the just undone log record. The predecessor information is readily available since every log record, including a CLR, contains the $PrevLSN$ pointer that points to the most recent preceding log record written by the same transaction. The UndoNxtLSN pointer allows us to determine precisely how much of the transaction has not been undone so far. In Figure 8.3, log record 3', which is the CLR for log record 3, points to log record 2, which is the predecessor of log record 3. Thus, during rollback, the UndoNxtLSN field of the *most recently written CLR* keeps track of the progress of rollback. It tells the system from where to continue the rollback of the transaction if a system failure were to interrupt the completion of the rollback or if a nested rollback were to be performed. It lets the system bypass those log records that had already been undone. Since CLRs are available to describe what actions are actually performed during the undo of an original action, the undo action need not be, in terms of which page(s) is affected, the exact inverse of the original action. That is, logical undo, which allows very high concurrency to be supported, is made possible. For example, a key inserted on page 10 of a B^+ tree by one transaction may be moved to page 20 by *another* transaction *before* the key insertion is committed. Later, if the first transaction were to roll back, then the key will be located on page 20 by retraversing the tree and deleted from there. A CLR will be written to describe the key deletion on page 20. This permits page-oriented redo, which is very efficient. ARIES/LHS and ARIES/IM which exploit this logical undo feature are described in [64, 67].

ARIES uses a single LSN on each page to track the page's state. Whenever a page is updated and a log record is written, the LSN of the log record is placed in the *page_LSN* field of the updated page. This tagging of the page with the LSN allows ARIES to precisely track, for restart and media recovery purposes, the state of the page with respect to logged updates for that page. It allows ARIES to support novel lock modes, using, before an update performed on a record's field by one transaction is committed, another transaction may be permitted to modify the *same data* for specified operations.

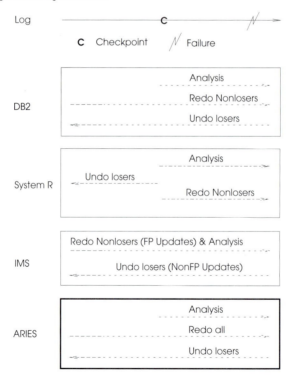

Figure 8.5. Restart processing in different methods.

Periodically during normal processing, ARIES takes checkpoints. The checkpoint log records identify the transactions that are active, their states, and the LSNs of their most recently written log records, and also the modified data (*dirty* data) that is in the buffer pool. The latter information is needed to determine from where the redo pass of restart recovery should begin its processing.

During restart recovery (see Figure 8.5), ARIES first scans the log, starting from the first record of the last checkpoint, up to the end of the log. During this *analysis pass*, information about dirty pages and transactions that were in progress at the time of the checkpoint is brought up to date as of the end of the log. The analysis pass using the dirty pages information determines the starting point (*RedoLSN*) for the log scan of the immediately following redo pass. The analysis pass also determines the list of transactions that are to be rolled back in the undo pass. For each in-progress transaction, the LSN of the most recently written log record will also be determined. Then, during the *redo pass*, ARIES *repeats history*, with respect to those updates logged on stable storage, but whose effects on the database pages did not get reflected on nonvolatile storage before the failure of the system. This is done for the updates of ALL transactions, *including* the updates of those transactions that had neither committed nor reached the in-doubt state of two-phase commit by the time of the system failure (i.e., even the missing updates of the so-called *loser* transactions are redone). This essentially reestablishes the state of the database as of the time of the system failure. A log record's update is redone if the affected page's page_LSN is *less than* the log record's LSN. No logging is performed when updates are redone. The redo pass obtains the locks needed to protect the uncommitted updates of those distributed transactions that will remain in the *in doubt* (*prepared*) state [68, 69] at the end of restart recovery.

The next log pass is the *undo pass* during which all loser transactions' updates are rolled back, in reverse chronological order, in a single sweep of the log. This is done by continually taking the maximum of the LSNs of the next log record to be processed for each of the yet-to-be-completely-undone loser transactions, until no transaction remains to be undone. Unlike during the redo pass, during the undo pass (and during normal undo), performing undos is not a conditional operation. That is, ARIES does *not* compare the page_LSN of the affected page to the LSN of the log record to decide whether to undo the update. When a non-CLR is encountered for a transaction during the undo pass, if it is an undo-redo or undo-only log record, then its update is undone. In any case, the next record to process for that transaction is determined by looking at the PrevLSN of that non-CLR. Since CLRs are never undone (i.e., CLRs are not compensated; see Figure 8.4), when a CLR is encountered during undo, it is used just to determine the next log record to process by looking at the UndoNxtLSN field of the CLR.

For those transactions that were already rolling back at the time of the system failure, ARIES will rollback only those actions that had not already been undone. This is possible since history is repeated for such transactions and since the last CLR written for each transaction points (directly or indirectly) to the next non-CLR record that is to be undone. The net result is that if only page-oriented undos are involved or logical undos generate only CLRs, then, for rolled-back transactions, the number of CLRs written will be exactly equal to the number of (undoable) log records written during forward processing of those transactions. This will be the case even if there are repeated failures during restart or there are nested rollbacks.

8.4   DATA STRUCTURES

This section describes the major data structures that are used by ARIES.

8.4.1   Log Records

In what follows, we describe the important fields that may be present in different types of log records.

LSN.   Address of the first byte of the log record in the ever-growing log address space. This is a monotonically increasing value. This is shown here as a field only to make it easier to describe ARIES. The LSN need not actually be stored in the record.

Type.   Indicates whether this is a compensation record ("compensation"), a regular update record ("update"), a commit protocol-related record (e.g., "prepare"), or a nontransaction-related record (e.g., "OSfile_return").

TransID.   Identifier of the transaction, if any, that wrote the log record.

PrevLSN.   LSN of the preceding log record written by the same transaction. This field has a value of zero in nontransaction-related records and in the first log record of a transaction, thus avoiding the need for an explicit begin-transaction log record.

PageID.   Present only in records of type "update" or "compensation." The identifier of the page to which the updates of this record were applied. This PageID will normally consist of two parts: an objectID (e.g., tablespaceID) and a page number within that object. ARIES can deal with a log record that contains updates for multiple pages. For ease of exposition, we assume that only one page is involved.

UndoNxtLSN.   Present only in CLRs. It is the LSN of the next log record of this transaction that is to be processed during rollback. That is, UndoNxtLSN is the value of PrevLSN of the log record that the current log record is compensating. If there are no more log records to be undone, then this field contains a zero.

Data.   This is the redo and/or undo data that describe the update that was performed. CLRs contain only redo information since they are never undone. Updates can be logged in a logical fashion. Changes to some fields (e.g., amount of free space) of that page need not be logged since they can be easily derived. The undo information and the redo information for the entire object need not be logged. It suffices if the changed fields alone are logged. For increment or decrement kinds of operations, before and after images of the field are not needed. Information about the type of operation and the decrement or increment amount is enough. The information here would also be used to determine the appropriate action routine to be used to perform the redo and/or the undo of this log record.

8.4.2   Page Structure

One of the fields in every page of the database is the *page_LSN/ field*. It contains the LSN of the log record that describes the latest update to the page. This record may be a regular update record or a CLR. ARIES expects the buffer manager to enforce the WAL protocol. Except for this, ARIES does not place any restrictions on the buffer-page replacement policy. The steal-buffer management policy may be used. In-place updating is performed on nonvolatile storage. Updates are applied immediately and directly to the buffer version of the page containing the object. That is, no deferred updating as in INGRES [92] is performed. If it is found desirable, deferred updating and, consequently, deferred logging can be implemented. ARIES is flexible enough not to preclude those policies from being implemented.

8.4.3   Transaction Table

A table called the *transaction table* is used during restart recovery to track the state of active transactions. The table is initialized during the analysis pass from the most recent checkpoint's record(s) and is modified during the analysis of the log records written after the beginning of that checkpoint. During the undo pass, the entries of the table are also modified. If a checkpoint is taken during restart recovery, then the contents of the table will be included in the checkpoint record(s). The same table is also used during normal processing by the transaction manager. A description of the important fields of the transaction table follows:

TransID.   Transaction ID.

State.   Commit state of the transaction: *prepared* ("P"; also called *in doubt*) or unprepared ("U").

LastLSN.   The LSN of the latest log record written by the transaction.

UndoNxtLSN.   The LSN of the next record to be processed during rollback.

   If the most recent log record written or seen for this transaction is an undoable non-CLR log record, then this field's value will be set to LastLSN. If that most recent log record is a CLR, then this field's value is set to the UndoNxtLSN value from that CLR.

8.4.4   Dirty_Pages Table

A table called the *dirty_pages table* is used to represent information about dirty buffer pages during normal processing. This table is also used during restart recovery. The actual implementation of this table may be done using hashing or via the deferred-writes queue mechanism of [104]. Each entry in the table consists of two fields: PageID and RecLSN. During normal processing, when a nondirty page is being fixed in the buffers with the intention to modify, the buffer manager records in the *buffer pool* (BP) dirty_pages table, as *RecLSN* (recovery LSN), the current end-of-log LSN, which will be the LSN of the next log record to be written. The value of RecLSN indicates from what point in the log there may be updates which are, possibly, not yet in the nonvolatile storage version of the page. Whenever pages are written back to nonvolatile storage, the corresponding entries in the BP dirty_pages table are removed. The contents of this table are included in the checkpoint record(s) that is written during normal processing. The *restart* dirty_pages table is initialized from the latest checkpoint's record(s) and is modified during the analysis of the other records during the analysis pass. The minimum RecLSN value in the table gives the starting point for the redo pass during restart recovery.

8.5   NORMAL PROCESSING

This section discusses the actions that are performed as part of normal transaction processing. Section 8.6 discusses the actions that are performed as part of recovering from a system failure.

8.5.1   Updates

During normal processing, transactions may be in forward processing, partial rollback, or total rollback. The rollbacks may be system- or application-initiated. The causes of rollbacks may be deadlocks, error conditions, integrity-constraint violations, unexpected database state, and so on.

   If the granularity of locking is a record, then, when an update is to be performed on a record in a page, after the record is locked, that page is fixed in the buffer and latched in the X mode, the update is performed, a log record is appended to the log, the LSN of the log record is placed in the page_LSN field of the page and in the transaction table, and the page is unlatched and unfixed. The page latch is held during the call to the logger. This is done to ensure that the order of logging of updates of a page is the same as the order in which those updates are performed on the page. This is very important if some of the redo information is going to be logged physically (e.g., amount of free space in the page) and repetition of history has to be guaranteed for the physical redo to work correctly. The page latch must be held during read and update operations to assure physical consistency of the page contents. This is necessary because inserters and updaters of records might move records around within a page to do garbage collection. When such garbage collection is going on, no other transaction should be allowed to look at the page since they might get confused. Readers of pages latch in the S mode and modifiers latch in the X mode.

   The data page latch is not held while any necessary index operations are performed. *At most*, two page latches are held simultaneously (also see [62, 67]). This means that two transactions, T1 and T2, that are modifying *different pieces of data* may modify a particular data page in one order (T1, T2) and a particular index page in another order (T2, T1).[5] This scenario is impossible in System R and SQL/DS,

---

[5]The situation gets very complicated if operations like increment/decrement are supported

since in those systems, locks, instead of latches, are used for providing physical consistency. Typically, *all* the (physical) page locks are released only at the end of the RSS (data manager) call. A single RSS call deals with modifying the data and all the relevant indexes. This may involve waiting for many I/Os and locks. This means that deadlocks involving (physical) page locks alone or (physical) page locks and (logical) record/key locks are possible. They have been a major problem in System R and SQL/DS.

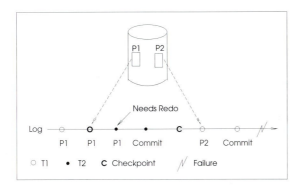

Figure 8.6. Database state as of a failure.

Figure 8.6 depicts a situation at the time of a system failure that followed the commit of two transactions. The dashed lines show how up to date the states of pages P1 and P2 are on nonvolatile storage with respect to logged updates of those pages. During restart recovery, it must be realized that the most recent log record written for P1, which was written by a transaction that later committed, needs to be redone and that there is nothing to be redone for P2. This situation points to the need for having the LSN to relate the state of a page on nonvolatile storage to a particular position in the log and the need for knowing where restart redo pass should begin by noting some information in the checkpoint record (see Section 8.5.4). For the example scenario, the restart redo log scan should begin at least from the log record representing the most recent update of P1 by T2 since that update needs to be redone.

It is not assumed that a single log record can always accommodate all the information needed to redo or undo the update operation. There may be instances when more than one record needs to be written for this purpose. For example, one record may be written with the undo information and another one with the redo information. In such cases, (1) the undo-only log record should be written *before* the redo-only log record is written and (2) it is the LSN of the redo-only log record that should be placed in the page_LSN field. The first condition is enforced to make sure that we do not have a situation in which the redo-only record and not the undo-

---

with high-concurrency lock modes and indexes are allowed to be defined on fields on which such operations are supported. We are currently studying those situations.

only record is written to stable storage before a failure and during restart recovery, the redo of that redo-only log record is performed (because of the repeating history feature) only to realize later that there is not an undo-only record to undo the effect of that operation. Given that the undo-only record is written before the redo-only record, the second condition ensures that we do not have a situation in which even though the page in nonvolatile storage already contains the update of the redo-only record, that same update is redone unnecessarily during restart recovery because the page contained the LSN of the undo-only record instead of that of the redo-only record. This unnecessary redo could cause integrity problems if operation logging is being performed.

There may be some log records written during forward processing that cannot or should not be undone (prepare, free-space inventory update, etc., records). These are identified as *redo only* log records. See Section 8.10.3 for a discussion of this kind of situation for free-space inventory updates.

Sometimes, the identity of the (data) record to be modified or read may not be known before a (data) page is examined. For example, during an insert, the record ID is not determined until the page is examined to find an empty slot. In such cases, the record lock must be obtained after the page is latched. To avoid waiting for a lock while holding a latch, which could lead to an undetected deadlock, the lock is requested *conditionally*, and if it is not granted, then the latch is released and the lock is requested *unconditionally*. Once the unconditionally requested lock is granted, the page is latched again, and any previously verified conditions are rechecked. This rechecking is required because, after the page was unlatched, the conditions could have changed. The page_LSN value at the time of unlatching could be remembered to detect quickly, on relatching, if any changes could have possibly occurred. If the conditions are still found to be satisfied for performing the update, the update is performed as described before. Otherwise, corrective actions are taken. If the conditionally requested lock is granted immediately, then the update can proceed as before.

If the granularity of locking is a page or something coarser than a page, then there is no need to latch the page since the lock on the page will be sufficient to isolate the executing transaction. Except for this change, the actions taken are the same as in the record-locking case. But, if the system is to support unlocked or *dirty* reads, then, even with page locking, a transaction that is updating a page should be made to hold the X latch on the page so that readers who are not acquiring locks are assured physical consistency if they hold an S latch while reading the page. Unlocked reads may also be performed by the image-copy utility in the interest of causing the least amount of interference to normal transaction processing.

Applicability of ARIES is not restricted to only those systems in which locking is used as the concurrency control mechanism. Even other concurrency control schemes that are similar to locking, like the ones in [2], could be used with ARIES.

ROLLBACK *(SaveLSN, TransID);*
UndoNxt := Trans_Table[TransID].UndoNxtLSN; {addr of 1st record to undo}
WHILE SaveLSN ¡ UndoNxt DO; {loop thru all relevant records}
  LogRec := Log_Read(UndoNxt); {read record to be processed}
  SELECT (LogRec.Type)
    WHEN("update") DO;
      IF LogRec is undoable THEN DO;
        Page := fix&latch(LogRec.PageID, "X");
        Undo_Update(Page,LogRec);
        Log_Write("compensation",LogRec.TransID, Trans_Table[TransID].LastLSN,
          LogRec.PageID,LogRec.PrevLSN, ...,LgLSN,Data); {write CLR}
        Page.LSN := LgLSN;
        Trans_Table[TransID].LastLSN := LgLSN;
        unfix&unlatch(Page);
      END;
      UndoNxt := LogRec.PrevLSN;
    END; {WHEN("update")}
    WHEN("compensation") UndoNxt := LogRec.UndoNxtLSN; {a CLR - nothing to undo}
    OTHERWISE UndoNxt := LogRec.PrevLSN {skip record and go to previous one}
  END; {SELECT}
  Trans_Table[TransID]. UndoNxtLSN := UndoNxt;
END; {WHILE}
RETURN;

Figure 8.7. Pseudocode for rollback.

8.5.2   Total or Partial Rollbacks

To provide flexibility in limiting the extent of transaction rollbacks, the notion of a
savepoint is supported [1, 33]. At any point during the execution of a transaction,
a savepoint can be established. Any number of savepoints could be outstanding at
a point in time. Typically, in a system like DB2, a savepoint is established before
every SQL data manipulation command that might perform updates to the data.
This is needed to support SQL statement-level atomicity. After executing for a
while, the transaction or the system can request the undoing of all the updates
performed after the establishment of a still outstanding savepoint. After such a
partial rollback, the transaction can continue execution and start going forward
again (see Figure 8.2). A particular savepoint is no longer outstanding if a rollback
has been performed to that savepoint or to a preceding one. When a savepoint
is established, the LSN of the latest log record written by the transaction, called
SaveLSN, is remembered in virtual storage.

If the savepoint is being established at the beginning of the transaction (i.e.,
when it has not yet written a log record), SaveLSN is set to zero. When the
transaction desires to roll back to a savepoint, it supplies the remembered SaveLSN.
If the savepoint concept were to be exposed at the user level, then we would expect
the system not to expose the SaveLSNs to the user but use some symbolic values
or sequence numbers and do the mapping to LSNs internally, as it is done in IMS
[45] and INGRES [18].

Figure 8.7 describes the routine, *ROLLBACK* which is used for rolling back to a savepoint. The input to the routine is the SaveLSN and the TransID. No locks are acquired during rollback, even though a latch is acquired during undo activity on a page. Since we have always ensured that latches do not get involved in deadlocks, a rolling-back transaction cannot get involved in a deadlock, unlike as in System R and R* [33, 69] and in the algorithms of [109]. During the rollback, the log records are undone in reverse chronological order, and for each log record that is undone, a CLR is written. For ease of exposition, assume that all the information about the undo action will fit in a single CLR. It is easy to extend ARIES to the case where multiple CLRs need to be written. It is possible that when a logical undo is performed, some non-CLRs are sometimes written, as described in [64, 67]. As mentioned before, when a CLR is written, its UndoNxtLSN field is made to contain the PrevLSN value in the log record whose undo caused this CLR to be written. Since CLRs will never be undone, they do not have to contain undo information (e.g., before images). Redo-only log records are ignored during rollback. When a non-CLR is encountered, after it is processed, the next record to process is determined by looking up its PrevLSN field. When a CLR is encountered during rollback, the UndoNxtLSN field of that record is looked up to determine the next log record to be processed. Thus, the UndoNxtLSN pointer helps us skip over already undone log records. This means that if a nested rollback were to occur, then, because of the UndoNxtLSN in CLRs, during the second rollback, none of the log records that were undone during the first rollback would be processed again. Even though Figures 8.3, 8.4, and 8.11 describe partial-rollback scenarios in conjunction with restart undos in the various recovery methods, it should be easy to see how nested rollbacks are handled efficiently by ARIES.

Being able to describe, via CLRs, the actions performed during undo gives us the flexibility of not having to force the undo actions to be the exact inverses of the original actions. In particular, the undo action could affect a page that was not involved in the original action. Such logical undo situations are possible in, for example, index management [67] and space management (see Section 8.10.3).

ARIES's guarantee of a bounded amount of logging during undo allows us to deal safely with small computer systems situations in which a circular on-line log might be used and log space is at a premium. Knowing the bound, we can keep in reserve enough log space to be able to rollback all currently running transactions under critical conditions (e.g., log space shortage). The implementation of ARIES in the OS/2 Extended Edition Database Manager takes advantage of this.

When a transaction rolls back, the locks obtained after the establishment of the savepoint that is the target of the rollback may be released *after* the partial or total rollback is completed. In fact, systems like DB2 do not and cannot release any of the locks after a partial rollback because, after such a lock release, a later rollback may still cause the same updates to be undone again, thereby causing data inconsistencies. System R does release locks after a partial rollback completes. But, because ARIES never undoes CLRs and because it never undoes a particular non-CLR more than once, because of the chaining of the CLRs using the UndoNxtLSN field, during a (partial) rollback, when the transaction's very *first* update to a particular object is undone and a CLR is written for it, the system can release the lock on that object. This makes it possible to consider resolving deadlocks using partial rollbacks rather than always resorting to total rollbacks.

8.5.3   Transaction Termination

Assume that some form of two-phase commit protocol (e.g., Presumed Abort or Presumed Commit; see [57, 68, 69]) is used to terminate transactions and that the *prepare* record that is *synchronously* written to the log as part of the protocol includes the list of update-type locks (IX, X, SIX, etc.) held by the transaction. The logging of the locks is done to ensure that if a system failure were to occur after a transaction enters the in-doubt state, then those locks could be reacquired, during restart recovery, to protect the uncommitted updates of the in-doubt transaction.[6] When the prepare record is written, the read locks (e.g., S and IS) could be released if no new locks would be acquired later as part of getting into the prepare state in some other part of the distributed transaction (at the same site or a different site). To deal with actions like dropping of objects that may cause files to be erased, for the sake of avoiding the logging of such objects' complete contents, we postpone performing actions like erasing files until we are sure that the transaction is definitely committing [20]. We need to log these *pending actions* in the prepare record.

Once a transaction enters the $in-doubt$ state, it is committed by writing an *end* record and releasing its locks. Once the end record is written, if there are any pending actions, then they must be performed. For each pending action that involves erasing or returning a file to the operating system, we write an $OSfile\_return$ redo-only log record. For ease of exposition, we assume that this log record is not associated with any particular transaction and that this action does not take place when a checkpoint is in progress.

A transaction in the $in-doubt$ state is rolled back by writing a *rollback* record, rolling back the transaction to its beginning, discarding the pending actions list, releasing its locks, and then writing the end record. Whether or not the rollback and end records are *synchronously* written to stable storage will depend on the type of two-phase commit protocol used. Also, the writing of the prepare record may be avoided if the transaction is not a distributed one or is read-only.

8.5.4   Checkpoints

Periodically, checkpoints are taken to reduce the amount of work that needs to be performed during restart recovery. The work may relate to the extent of the log that needs to be examined, the number of data pages that have to be read from nonvolatile storage, ans so on. Checkpoints can be taken asynchronously (i.e., while transaction processing, including updates, is going on). Such a *fuzzy checkpoint* is

---

[6]Another possibility is not to log the locks, but to regenerate the lock names during restart recovery by examining all the log records written by the in-doubt transaction–see Sections 8.6.1 and 8.6.4, and item 18 (Section 8.12) for further ramifications of this approach.

initiated by writing a *begin_chkpt* record. Then, the *end_chkpt* record is constructed by including in it the contents of the normal transaction table, the BP dirty_pages table, and any file-mapping information for the objects (like tablespace, indexspace, etc.) that are "open" (i.e., for which BP dirty_pages table has entries). Only for simplicity of exposition, we assume that all the information can be accommodated in a single end_chkpt record. It is easy to deal with the case where multiple records are needed to log this information. Once the end_chkpt record is constructed, it is written to the log. Once that record reaches stable storage, the LSN of the begin_chkpt record is stored in the *master record*, which is in a well-known place on stable storage. If a failure were to occur before the end_chkpt record migrates to stable storage, but after the begin_chkpt record migrates to stable storage, then that checkpoint is considered an *incomplete checkpoint*. Between the *begin_chkpt* and *end_chkpt* log records, transactions might have written other log records. If one or more transactions are likely to remain in the $in - doubt$ state for a long time because of prolonged loss of contact with the commit coordinator, then it is a good idea to include in the end_chkpt record, information about the update-type locks (e.g., X, IX, and SIX) held by those transactions. This way, if a failure were to occur, then, during restart recovery, those locks could be reacquired without having to access the prepare records of those transactions.

Since latches may need to be acquired to read the dirty_pages table correctly while gathering the needed information, it is a good idea to gather the information a little at a time to reduce contention on the table. For example, if the dirty_pages table has 1000 rows, during each latch acquisition, 100 entries can be examined. If the already examined entries change before the end of the checkpoint, still the recovery algorithms remain correct (see Figure 8.9). This is because, in computing the restart redo point, besides taking into account the minimum of the RecLSNs of the dirty pages included in the end_chkpt record, ARIES also takes into account the log records that were written by transactions since the beginning of the checkpoint. This is important because the effect of some of the updates that were performed since the initiation of the checkpoint might not be reflected in the dirty-page list that is recorded as part of the checkpoint.

ARIES does not require that any dirty pages be forced to nonvolatile storage during a checkpoint. The assumption is that the buffer manager is, on a continuous basis, writing out dirty pages in the background using system processes. The buffer manager can batch the writes and write multiple pages in one I/O operation.Details about how DB2 manages its buffer pools in this fashion are found in [104]. Even if there are some hot-spot pages that are frequently modified, the buffer manager has to ensure that those pages are written to nonvolatile storage reasonably often to reduce restart redo work, just in case system failure was to occur. To avoid the prevention of updates to such hot-spot pages during an I/O operation, the buffer manager could make a copy of each of those pages and perform the I/O from the copy. This minimizes the data unavailability time for writes.

8.6 RESTART PROCESSING

When the transaction system restarts after a failure, recovery needs to be performed to bring the data to a consistent state and ensure the atomicity and durability properties of transactions. Figure 8.8 describes the *RESTART* routine that gets invoked at the beginning of the restart of a failed system. The input to this routine is the LSN of the master record that contains the pointer to the begin_chkpt record of the last complete checkpoint taken before site failure or shutdown. This routine invokes the routines for the analysis pass, the redo pass, and the undo pass in that order. The buffer-pool dirty_pages table is updated appropriately. At the end of restart recovery, a checkpoint is taken.

RESTART (Master_Addr);
Restart_Analysis(Master_Addr, Trans_Table, Dirty_Pages, RedoLSN);
Restart_Redo(RedoLSN, Trans_Table, Dirty_Pages);
buffer pool Dirty_Pages table := Dirty_Pages;
remove entries for non-buffer-resident pages from the buffer pool Dirty_Pages table;
Restart_Undo(Trans_Table);
reacquire locks for prepared transactions;
checkpoint();
RETURN;

Figure 8.8. Pseudo-code for restart.

For high availability, the duration of restart processing must be as short as possible. One way of accomplishing this is by exploiting parallelism during the redo and undo passes. Only if parallelism is going to be employed, is it necessary to latch pages before they are modified during restart recovery. Ideas for improving data availability by allowing new transaction processing during recovery are explored in [65].

8.6.1 Analysis Pass

The first pass of the log that is made during restart recovery is the *analysis pass*. Figure 8.9 describes the *RESTART_ANALYSIS* routine that implements the analysis-pass actions. The input to this routine is the LSN of the *master* record. The outputs of this routine are the transaction table, which contains the list of transactions that were in the $in - doubt$ or the unprepared state at the time of system failure or shutdown the dirty_pages table, which contains the list of pages that were potentially dirty in the buffers when the system failed or was shut down and the *RedoLSN*, which is the location on the log from which the redo pass must start processing the log. The only log records that may be written by this routine are end records for transactions that had totally rolled back before system failure, but for whom end records are missing.

During this pass, if a log record is encountered for a page whose identity does not already appear in the dirty_pages table, then an entry is made in the table with the current log record's LSN as the page's RecLSN. The transaction table is modified to

RESTART_ANALYSIS (Master_Addr, Trans_Table, Dirty_Pages, RedoLSN);
Initialize this Trans Table and Dirty Pages to empty; Master_Rec := Read_Disk(Master_Addr);
Open_Log_Scan(Master_Rec.ChkptLSN); {open log scan at Begin_Chkpt rec.}
LogRec := Next_Log(); {read in the Begin_Chkpt rec.}
LogRec := Next_Log(); {read log rec. following Begin_Chkpt}
WHILE NOT(End_of_Log) DO;
  IF trans related rec. & LogRec.TransID NOT in Trans_Table THEN {not chkpt/OSfile_return}
    insert (LogRec.TransID, "U",LogRec.LSN,LogRec.PrevLSN) into Trans_Table;
  SELECT(LogRec.Type)
    WHEN("update"| "compensation") DO;
      Trans_Table[LogRec.TransID].LastLSN := LogRec.LSN;
      IF LogRec.Type = "update" THEN
        IF LogRec is undoable THEN
          Trans_Table[LogRec.TransID].UndoNxtLSN := LogRec.LSN;
        ELSE Trans_Table[LogRec.TransID].UndoNxtLSN := LogRec.UndoNxtLSN;
          {next record to undo is the one pointed to by this CLR}
      IF LogRec is redoable & LogRec.PageID NOT IN Dirty_Pages THEN
        insert (LogRec.PageID, LogRec.LSN) into Dirty_Pages;
    END; {WHEN("update"| "compensation")}
    WHEN("Begin_Chkpt"); {found an incomplete chkpt's Begin_Chkpt rec., ignore it}
    WHEN("End_Chkpt") DO;
      FOR each entry in LogRec.Tran_Table DO;
        IF TransID NOT IN Trans_Table THEN DO;
          insert entry(TransID,State,LastLSN,UndoNxtLSN) in Trans_Table;
        END;
      END; {FOR}
        FOR each entry in LogRec.Dirty_PagLst DO;
          IF PageID NOT IN Dirty_Pages THEN insert entry(PageID,RecLSN) in Dirty_Pages;
          ELSE set RecLSN of Dirty_Pages entry to RecLSN in Dirty_PagLst;
        END; {FOR}
    END; {WHEN("End_Chkpt")}
    WHEN("prepare"|"rollback") DO;
      IF LogRec.Type = "prepare" THEN Trans_Table[LogRec.TransID].State := "P";
      ELSE Trans_Table[LogRec.TransID].State := "U";
      Trans_Table[LogRec.TransID].LastLSN := LogRec.LSN;
    END; {WHEN("prepare"| "rollback")}
    WHEN("end") delete Trans_Table entry for which TransID = LogRec.TransID;
    WHEN("OSfile_return") delete from Dirty_Pages all pages of returned file;
  END; {SELECT}
  LogRec := Next_Log();
END; {WHILE}
  FOR each Trans_Table entry with (State="U") & (UndoNxtLSN = 0) DO; {rolled-bk trans }
    write end record and remove entry from Trans_Table; {with missing end record}
END; {FOR}
RedoLSN := minimum(Dirty_Pages.RecLSN); {return start position for redo}
RETURN;

Figure 8.9. Pseudo-code for restart analysis.

track the state changes of transactions and also to note the LSN of the most recent log record that would need to be undone if it were determined ultimately that the transaction had to be rolled back. If an OSfile_return log record is encountered, then any pages belonging to that file that are in the dirty_pages table are removed from the latter in order make sure that no page belonging to that version of that file is accessed during the *redo* pass. The same file may be recreated and updated later, once the original operation causing the file erasure is committed. In that case, some pages of the recreated file will reappear in the dirty_pages table later with RecLSN values *greaterthan* the end_of_log LSN when the file was erased. The RedoLSN is the *minimum* RecLSN from the dirty_pages table at the *end* of the analysis pass. The redo pass can be skipped if there are no pages in the dirty_pages table.

It is not necessary that there be a separate analysis pass, and in fact in the ARIES implementation in the OS/2 Extended Edition Database Manager, there is no analysis pass. This is especially because, as we mentioned before (see also Section 8.6.2), in the redo pass, ARIES unconditionally redoes all missing updates. That is, it redoes them irrespective of whether they were logged by loser or nonloser transactions, unlike as in System R, SQL/DS, and DB2. Hence, redo does not need to know the loser or nonloser status of a transaction. That information is, strictly speaking, needed only for the undo pass. This would not be true for a system (like DB2) in which for in-doubt transactions their update locks are reacquired by inferring the lock names from the log records of the in-doubt transactions, as they are encountered during the redo pass. This technique for reacquiring locks forces the RedoLSN computation to consider the Begin_LSNs of in-doubt transactions, which in turn requires that we know, before the start of the redo pass, the identities of the in-doubt transactions.

Without the analysis pass, the transaction table could be constructed from the checkpoint record and the log records encountered during the *redo* pass. The RedoLSN would have to be the minimum(minimum(RecLSNs from the dirty_pages table in the end_chkpt record), LSN(begin_chkpt record)). Suppression of the analysis pass would also require that other methods be used to avoid processing updates to files that have been returned to the operating system. Another consequence is that the dirty_pages table used during the redo pass cannot be used to filter update log records that occur *after* the begin_chkpt record. For in-doubt transactions, if locks to be reacquired are to be determined by analyzing all the log records of such transactions during the redo pass, as DB2 does it today, then clearly the analysis pass needs to be performed to determine, before the redo pass starts, which transactions are in the in-doubt state.

8.6.2   Redo Pass

The second pass of the log that is made during restart recovery is the *redo pass*. Figure 8.10 describes the *RESTART_REDO* routine that implements the redo pass actions. The inputs to this routine are the RedoLSN and the dirty_pages table supplied by the restart_analysis routine. No log records are written by this

```
RESTART_REDO (RedoLSN, Dirty_Pages);
Open_Log_Scan(RedoLSN); {open log scan and position at restart pt}
LogRec := Next_Log(); {read log record at restart redo point }
WHILE NOT(End_of_Log) DO; {look at all records till end of log}
  IF LogRec.Type = ('update' | 'compensation') & LogRec is redoable &
     LogRec.PageID IN Dirty_Pages & LogRec.LSN ≥ Dirty_Pages[LogRec.PageID].RecLSN
  THEN DO;{a redoable page update. updated page might not have made it to}
        {disk before sys failure. need to access page and check its LSN}
    Page := fix&latch(LogRec.PageID, "X");
    IF Page.LSN < LogRec.LSN THEN DO {update not on page. need to redo it}
      Redo_Update(Page,LogRec); {redo update}
      Page.LSN := LogRec.LSN;
    END; {redid update}
    ELSE Dirty_Pages[LogRec.PageID].RecLSN := Page.LSN+1;
        {update dirty page list with correct info. this will happen if this page was}
        {written to disk after the chkpt but before sys failure}
    unfix&unlatch(Page);
  END; {LSN on page had to be checked}
  LogRec := Next_Log(); {read next log record}
END; {reading till end of log}
RETURN;
```

Figure 8.10. Pseudo-code for restart redo.

routine. The redo pass starts scanning the log records from the RedoLSN point.
When a redoable log record is encountered, a check is made to see if the referenced
page appears in the dirty_pages table. If it does and if the log record's LSN is
greater than or equal to the RecLSN for the page in the table, then it is suspected
that the page state might be such that the log record's update might have to be
redone. To resolve this suspicion, the page is accessed. If the page's LSN is found
to be *less than* the log record's LSN, then the update is redone. Thus, the RecLSN
information serves to limit the number of pages that have to be examined. This
routine reestablishes the database state as of the time of system failure. Even
updates performed by loser transactions are redone. The rationale behind this
repeating of history is explained in Section 8.10.1. It turns out that some of that
redo of loser transactions' log records may be unnecessary. In [75], we have explored
further the idea of restricting the repeating of history to possibly reduce the number
of pages that get dirtied during this pass.

Since redo is page-oriented, only the pages with entries in the dirty_pages table
may get modified during the redo pass. Only the pages listed in the dirty_pages table
will be read and examined during this pass. Not all the pages that are read may
require redo. This is because, some of the pages that were dirty at the time of the
last checkpoint or which became dirty later might have been written to nonvolatile
storage before the system failure. Because of reasons like reducing log volume and
saving some CPU overhead, we do not expect systems to write log records that
identify the dirty pages that were written to nonvolatile storage, although that
option is available and such log records can be used to eliminate the corresponding
pages from the dirty_pages table when those log records are encountered during the

analysis pass. Even if such records were to be written usually, a system failure in a narrow window could prevent them from being written. The corresponding pages will not get modified during this pass.

For brevity, we do not discuss here as to how, if a failure were to occur after the logging of the end record of a transaction, but before the execution of all the pending actions of that transaction, the remaining pending actions are redone during the redo pass.

```
RESTART_UNDO (Trans_Table);
WHILE EXISTS(Trans with State = "U" in Trans_Table) DO;
  UndoLSN := maximum(UndoNxtLSN) from Trans_Table entries with State = "U";
    {pick up UndoNxtLSN of unprepared trans with maximum UndoNxtLSN}
  LogRec := Log_Read(UndoLSN); {read log record to be undone or a CLR}
  SELECT(LogRec.Type)
    WHEN("update") DO;
      IF LogRec is undoable THEN DO; {record needs undoing (not redo-only record)}
        Page := fix&latch(LogRec.PageID,"X");
        Undo_Update(Page,LogRec);
        Log_Write("compensation",LogRec.TransID,Trans_Table[LogRec.TransID].LastLSN,
            LogRec.PageID,LogRec.PrevLSN, ...,LgLSN,Data); {write CLR}
        Page.LSN := LgLSN; {store LSN of CLR in page}
        Trans_Table[LogRec.TransID].LastLSN := LgLSN; {store LSN of CLR in table}
        unfix&unlatch(Page);
      END; {undoable record case}
      ELSE; {record cannot be undone - ignore it}
      Trans_Table[LogRec.TransID].UndoNxtLSN := LogRec.PrevLSN;
          {next record to process is the one preceding this record in its backward chain}
      IF LogRec.PrevLSN = 0 THEN DO; {have undone completely - write end}
        Log_Write("end",LogRec.Trans ID,Trans_Table[LogRec.TransID].LastLSN,...);
        delete Trans_Table entry where TransID = LogRec.TransID; {delete trans from table}
      END; {trans fully undone}
    END; {WHEN("update")}
    WHEN("compensation")
      Trans_Table[LogRec.TransID].UndoNxtLSN := LogRec.UndoNxtLSN;
          {pick up addr of next record to examine}
    WHEN('rollback'|'prepare')
      Trans_Table[LogRec.TransID].UndoNxtLSN := LogRec.PrevLSN;
          {pick up addr of next record to examine}
  END; {SELECT}
END; {WHILE}
RETURN;
```

Figure 8.11. Pseudo-code for restart undo.

For exploiting parallelism, the availability of the information in the dirty_pages table gives us the possibility of initiating asynchronous I/Os in parallel to read all these pages so that they may be available in the buffers possibly before the corresponding log records are encountered in the redo pass. Since updates performed during the redo pass are not logged, we can also perform sophisticated things like building in-memory queues of log records that potentially need to be reapplied (as dictated by the information in the dirty_pages table) on a per page or group-of-pages basis and, as the asynchronously initiated I/Os complete and pages come into the buffer pool, processing the corresponding log-record queues using multiple processes. This requires that each queue be dealt with by only one process. Updates to *different* pages may get applied in different orders from the order represented in the log. This does not violate any correctness properties since for a given page all its missing updates are reapplied in the same order as before. These parallelism ideas are also applicable to the context of supporting disaster recovery via remote backups [79].

8.6.3   Undo Pass

The third pass of the log that is made during restart recovery is the *undo pass*. Figure 8.11 describes the *RESTART_UNDO* routine that implements the undo pass actions. The input to this routine is the restart transaction table. The dirty_pages table is *not* consulted during this undo pass. Also, since history is repeated before the undo pass is initiated, the LSN on the page is *not* consulted to determine whether an undo operation should be performed or not. Contrast this with what we describe in Section 8.10.1 for systems like DB2, which do not repeat history but perform selective redo.

The restart_undo routine rolls back loser transactions, in reverse chronological order, in a single sweep of the log. This is done by continually taking the maximum of the LSNs of the next log record to be processed for each of the yet-to-be-completely-undone loser transactions, until no loser transaction remains to be undone. The next record to process for each transaction to be rolled back is determined by an entry in the transaction table for each of those transactions. The processing of the encountered log records is exactly as we described before in Section 8.5.2. In the process of rolling back the transactions, this routine writes CLRs. The buffer manager follows the usual WAL protocol while writing dirty pages to nonvolatile storage during the undo pass.

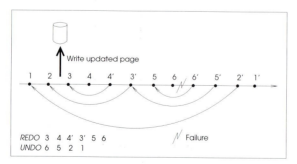

Figure 8.12. Restart recovery example with ARIES.

To exploit parallelism, the undo pass can also be performed using multiple processes. It is important that each transaction be dealt with completely by a single process because of the UndoNxtLSN chaining in the CLRs. This still leaves open the possibility of writing the CLRs first, without applying the undos to the pages (see Section 8.6.4 for problems in accomplishing this for objects that may require logical undos), and then redoing the CLRs in parallel, as explained in Section 8.6.2. In this fashion, the undo work of actually applying the changes to the pages can be performed in parallel, even for a single transaction.

Figure 8.12 depicts an example restart recovery scenario using ARIES. Here, all the log records describe updates to the same page. Before the failure, the page was written to disk after the second update. After that disk write, a partial rollback was performed (undo of log records 4 and 3) and then the transaction went forward (updates 5 and 6). During restart recovery, the missing updates (3, 4, 4', 3', 5, and 6) are first redone and then the undos (of 6, 5, 2, and 1) are performed. Each update log record will be matched with at most one CLR, regardless of how many times restart recovery is performed.

With ARIES, we have the *option* of allowing the continuation of loser transactions after restart recovery is completed. Since ARIES repeats history and supports the savepoint concept, we could, in the undo pass, instead of totally rolling back the loser transactions, roll back each loser only to its latest savepoint. Later, we could resume the transaction by invoking its application at a special entry point and passing enough information about the savepoint from which execution is to be resumed. Doing this correctly would require (1) the ability to generate lock names from the transaction's log records for its uncommitted, not undone updates, (2) reacquiring those locks before completing restart recovery, and (3) logging enough information whenever savepoints are established so that the system can restore cursor positions, application program state, and so on.

8.6.4 Selective or Deferred Restart

Sometimes, after a system failure, we may wish to restart the processing of new transactions as soon as possible. Hence, we may wish to defer doing some recovery work to a later point in time. This is usually done to reduce the amount of time during which some critical data are unavailable. It is accomplished by recovering such data first and then opening the system for the processing of new transactions. In DB2, for example, it is possible to perform restart recovery even when some of the objects for which redo and/or undo work needs to be performed are off-line when the system is brought up. If some undo work needs to be performed for some loser transactions on those off-line objects, then DB2 is able to write the CLRs alone and finish handling the transactions. This is possible because the CLRs can be generated based solely on the information in the non-CLR records written during the forward processing of the transactions [15]. Because page (or minipage, for indexes) is the smallest granularity of locking, the undo actions will be exact inverses of the original actions. That is, there are no logical undos in DB2. DB2 remembers, in an exceptions table (called the database allocation [DBA] table) that is maintained in the log and in virtual storage, the fact that those off-line objects need to be recovered when they are brought on-line, *before* they are made accessible to other transactions [14]. The LSN ranges of log records to be applied are also remembered. Unless there are some in-doubt transactions with uncommitted updates to those objects, no locks need to be acquired to protect those objects since accesses to those objects will not be permitted until recovery is completed. When those objects are brought on-line, then recovery is performed efficiently by rolling forward using the log records in the remembered ranges. Even during *normal* rollbacks, CLRs may be written for off-line objects.

In ARIES also, we can take similar actions, provided none of the loser transactions has modified one or more of the offline objects that *may* require logical undos. This is because logical undos are based on the *currentstate* of the object. Redos are not at all a problem, since they are always page-oriented. For logical undos involving space management (see Section 8.10.3), generally we can take a conservative approach and generate the appropriate CLRs. For example, during the undo of an insert-record operation, we can write a CLR for the space-related update stating that the page is 0% full. But for the high concurrency, index management methods of [67], this is not possible, since the effect of the logical undo (e.g., retraversing the index tree to do a key deletion), in terms of which page may be affected, is unpredictable; in fact, we cannot even predict when page-oriented undo will not work and hence logical undo is necessary.

It is not possible to handle the undos of some of the records of a transaction during restart recovery and handle the undos (possibly, logical) of the rest of the records at a later point in time if the two sets of records are interspersed. Remember that in all the recovery methods, undo of a transaction is done in reverse chronological order. Hence, it is enough to remember, for each transaction, the next record to be processed during the undo; from that record, the PrevLSN and/or the UndoNxtLSN chain leads us to all the other records to be processed.

Even under the circumstances where one or more of the loser transactions have to perform potentially logical undos on some off-line objects, if deferred restart needs to be supported, then we suggest the following algorithm:

1. Perform the repeating of history for the $on-line$ objects, as usual; postpone it for the $off-line$ objects and remember the log ranges.

2. Proceed with the undo pass as usual, but stop undoing a loser transaction when one of its log records is encountered for which a CLR cannot be generated for the preceding reasons. Call such a transaction a *stopped transaction*. But, continue undoing the other, unstopped transactions.

3. For the stopped transactions, acquire locks to protect their updates that have not yet been undone. This could be done as part of the undo pass by continuing to follow the pointers, as usual, even for the stopped transactions and acquiring locks based on the encountered $non-CLRs$ that were written by the stopped transactions.

4. When restart recovery is completed and later the previously off-line objects are made on-line, first repeat history based on the remembered log ranges and

then continue with the undoing of the stopped transactions. After each of the stopped transactions is totally rolled back, release its still held locks.

5. Whenever an off-line object becomes on-line, when the repeating of history is completed for that object, new transactions can be allowed to access that object in parallel with the further undoing of all of the stopped transactions that can make progress.

The preceding requires the ability to generate lock names based on the information in the update (non-CLR) log records. DB2 is doing that already for in-doubt transactions.

Even if none of the objects to be recovered is off-line, but it is desired that the processing of new transactions start before the rollbacks of the loser transactions are completed, then we can accommodate it by doing the following: (1) first repeat history and reacquire, based on their log records, the locks for the uncommitted updates of the loser and in-doubt transactions, and (2) then start processing new transactions even as the rollbacks of the loser transactions are performed in parallel. The locks acquired in step (1) are released as each loser transaction's rollback completes. Performing step (1) requires that the restart RedoLSN be adjusted appropriately to ensure that *all* the log records of the loser transactions are encountered during the *redo* pass. If a loser transaction was already rolling back at the time of the system failure, then, with the information obtained during the analysis pass for such a transaction, it will be known as to which log records remain to be undone. These are the log records whose LSNs are *lessthanorequalto* the UndoNxtLSN of the transaction's last CLR. Locks need to be obtained during the redo pass only for those updates that have not yet been undone.

If a long transaction is being rolled back and we would like to release some of its locks as soon as possible, then we can mark specially those log records that represent the *first* update by that transaction on the corresponding object (e.g., record, if record locking is in effect) and then release that object's lock as soon as the corresponding log record is undone. This works only because we do not undo CLRs and because we do not undo the same non-CLR more than once; hence, it will not work in systems that undo CLRs (e.g., Encompass, AS/400, DB2) or that undo a non-CLR more than once (e.g., IMS). This early release of locks can be performed in ARIES during normal transaction undo to possibly permit resolution of deadlocks using partial rollbacks.

8.7 CHECKPOINTS DURING RESTART

In this section, we describe how the impact of failures on CPU processing and I/O can be reduced by optionally taking checkpoints during different stages of restart recovery processing.

Analysis Pass. By taking a checkpoint at the end of the analysis pass, we can save some work if a failure were to occur during recovery. The entries of the transaction table of this checkpoint will be the same as the entries of the transaction table at the end of the analysis pass. The entries of the dirty_pages list of this checkpoint will be the same as the entries that the *restart* dirty_pages table contains at the end of the analysis pass. This is different from what happens during a *normal* checkpoint. For the latter, the dirty_pages list is obtained from the *buffer-pool* (BP) dirty_pages table.

Redo Pass.   At the beginning of the redo pass, the buffer manager (BM) is notified so that, whenever it writes out a modified page to nonvolatile storage during the redo pass, it will change the restart dirty_pages table entry for that page by making the RecLSN be equal to the LSN of that log record such that *all* log records up to that log record had been *processed*. It is enough if BM manipulates the restart dirty_pages table in this fashion. BM does not have to maintain its own dirty_pages table as it does during normal processing. Of course, it should still be keeping track of what pages are currently in the buffers. The preceding allows checkpoints to be taken any time during the redo pass to reduce the amount of the log that would need to be redone if a failure were to occur before the end of the redo pass. The entries of the dirty_pages list of this checkpoint will be the same as the entries of the *restart* dirty_pages table at the time of the checkpoint. The entries of the transaction table of this checkpoint will be the same as the entries of the transaction table at the end of the *analysis* pass. This checkpointing is not affected by whether parallelism is employed in the redo pass.

Undo Pass.   At the beginning of the undo pass, the restart dirty_pages table becomes the BP dirty_pages table. At this point, the table is cleaned up by removing those entries for which the corresponding pages are no longer in the buffers. From then onwards, the BP manager manipulates this table as it does during normal processing–removing entries when pages are written to nonvolatile storage, adding entries when pages are about to become dirty, and so on. During the undo pass, the entries of the transaction table are modified as during normal undo. If a checkpoint is taken any time during the undo pass, then the entries of the dirty_pages list of that checkpoint are the same as the entries of the BP dirty_pages table at the time of the checkpoint. The entries of the transaction table of this checkpoint will be the same as the entries of the transaction table at that time.

During restart recovery in System R, sometimes it may be *required* that a checkpoint be taken to free up some physical pages (the shadow pages) for more undo or redo work to be performed. This is another consequence of the fact that history cannot be repeated in System R. This complicates the restart logic since the view depicted in Figure 8.16 would no longer be true after a restart checkpoint completes. The restart checkpoint logic and its effect on a restart following a system failure *during* an earlier restart were considered too complex to be describable in [33]. ARIES is able to easily accommodate checkpoints during restart. Although these checkpoints are optional in our case, they may be forced to take place in System R.

8.8   MEDIA RECOVERY

We will assume that media recovery will be required at the level of a file or some such entity (like DBspace, tablespace, etc.). A *fuzzy-image copy* (also called a *fuzzy archive dump*) operation involving such an entity can be performed concurrently with modifications to the entity by other transactions. With such a high-concurrency image-copy method, the image copy might contain some uncommitted updates, in contrast to the method of [56]. Of course, if desired, we could also easily produce an image copy with no uncommitted updates. Let us assume that the image copying is performed *directly* from the nonvolatile storage version of the entity. This means that more recent versions of some of the copied pages may be present in the transaction system's buffers. Copying directly from the nonvolatile storage version of the object would usually be much more efficient since the device geometry can be exploited during such a copy operation and since the buffer manager overheads will be eliminated. Since the transaction system does not have to be up for the direct copying, it may also be more convenient than copying via the transaction system's buffers. If the latter is found desirable (e.g., to support incremental image copying, as described in [13]), then it is easy to modify the presented method to accommodate it. Of course, in that case, some minimal amount of synchronization will be needed. For example, latching at the page level, but no locking will be needed.

When the fuzzy-image-copy operation is initiated, the location of the begin_chkpt record of the most recent complete checkpoint is noted and remembered along with the image-copy data. Let us call this checkpoint the *image-copy checkpoint*. The assertion that can be made based on this checkpoint information is that all updates that had been logged in log records with LSNs less than minimum(minimum(RecLSNs of dirty pages of the image copied entity in the image copy checkpoint's end_chkpt record), LSN(begin_chkpt record of the image copy checkpoint)) would have been externalized to nonvolatile storage by the time the fuzzy-image-copy operation began. Hence, the image-copied version of the entity would be *atleast* as up to date as of that point in the log. We call that point the *media recovery redo point*. The reason for taking into account the LSN of the begin_chkpt record in computing the media recovery redo point is the same as the one given in Section 8.5.4 when discussing the computation of the restart redo point.

When media recovery is required, the image-copied version of the entity is reloaded and then a redo scan is initiated starting from the media recovery redo point. During the redo scan, all the log records relating to the entity being recovered are processed and the corresponding updates are applied, unless the information in the image-copy checkpoint record's dirty_pages list or the LSN on the page makes it unnecessary. Unlike during *restart* redo, if a log record refers to a page that is *not* in the dirty_pages list and the log record's LSN is *greater than* the LSN of the begin_chkpt log record of the image-copy checkpoint, then that page *must* be accessed and its LSN compared to the log record's LSN to check if the update must be redone. Once the end of the log is reached, if there are any in-progress transactions, then those transactions that had made changes to the entity are undone, as in the undo pass of restart recovery. The information about the identities, and so on, of such transactions may be kept separately somewhere (e.g., in an exceptions table like the DBA table in DB2, see Section 8.6.4) or may be obtained by performing an analysis pass from the last complete checkpoint in the log until the end of the log.

Page-oriented logging provides recovery independence amongst objects. Since, in ARIES, every database page's update is logged separately, even if an arbitrary database page is damaged in the nonvolatile storage and the page needs recovery, the recovery can be accomplished easily by extracting an earlier copy of that page from an image copy and rolling forward that version of the page using the log, as described before. This is to be contrasted with systems like System R in which, for some pages (e.g., index and space management pages), updates for log records are not written, recovery from damage to such a page may require the expensive operation of reconstructing the entire object (e.g., rebuilding the complete index even when only one page of an index is damaged). Also, even for pages for which logging is performed explicitly (e.g., data pages in System R), if CLRs are not written when undo is performed, then bringing a page's state up to date by starting from the image-copy state would require paying attention to the log records representing the transaction state (commit, partial, or total rollback) to determine what actions, if any, should be undone. If any transactions had rolled back partially or totally, then backward scans of such transactions would be required to see if they made any changes to the page being recovered so that they are undone. These backward scans may result in useless work being performed if it turns out that some rolled-back transaction had not made any changes to the page being recovered. An alternative would be to preprocess the log and place forward pointers to skip over rolled-back log records, as it is done in System R during the analysis pass of restart recovery (see Section 8.10.2 and Figure 8.17).

Individual pages of the database may be corrupted not only because of media problems, but also because of an abnormal process termination while the process is actively making changes to a page in the buffer pool and before the process gets a chance to write a log record describing the changes. If the database code is executed by the application process itself, which is what performance-conscious systems like DB2 implement, such abnormal terminations may occur because of the user's interruption (e.g., by hitting the *attention* key) or due to the operating system's action on noting that the process had exhausted its CPU time limit. It is generally an expensive operation to put the process in an uninterruptable state before every page update. Given all these circumstances, an efficient way to recover the corrupted page is to read the uncorrupted version of the page from the nonvolatile storage and bring it up to date by rolling forward the page state using all the relevant log records for that page. The roll-forward redo scan of the log is started from the RecLSN remembered for the buffer by the buffer manager. DB2 does this kind of internal recovery operation automatically [15]. The corruption of a page is detected by using a bit in the page header. The bit is set to "1" after the page is fixed and X-latched. Once the update operation is complete (i.e., page

updated, update logged, and page LSN modified), the bit is reset to "0". Given this, whenever a page is latched, for read or write, first this bit is tested to see if its value is equal to "1", in which case automatic page recovery is initiated. From an availability viewpoint, it is unacceptable to bring down the entire transaction system to recover from such a *brokenpage* situation by letting restart recovery redo all those logged updates that were in the corrupted page but were missing in the uncorrupted version of the page on nonvolatile storage. A related problem is to make sure that for those pages that were left in the fixed state by the abnormally terminating process, unfix calls are issued by the transaction system. By leaving enough *footprints* around before performing operations like fix, unfix, and latch, the user process aids system processes in performing the necessary cleanups.

For the variety of reasons mentioned in this section and elsewhere, writing CLRs is a very good idea even if the system is supporting only page locking. This is to be contrasted with the no-CLRs approach, suggested in [56], which supports only page locking.

8.9   NESTED TOP ACTIONS

There are times when we would like some updates of a transaction to be committed, irrespective of whether later the transaction commits. We do need the atomicity property for these updates themselves. This is illustrated in the context of file extension. After a transaction extends a file that causes updates to some system data *in the database*, other transactions may be allowed to use the extended area *prior to* the commit of the extending transaction. If the extending transaction were to roll back, then it would not be acceptable to undo the effects of the extension. Such an undo might very well lead to a loss of updates performed by the other committed transactions. On the other hand, if the extension-related updates to the system data in the database were themselves interrupted by a failure before their completion, it is necessary to undo them. These kinds of actions have been traditionally performed by starting independent transactions, called *top actions* [55]. A transaction initiating such an independent transaction waits until that independent transaction commits before proceeding. The independent transaction mechanism is, of course, vulnerable to lock conflicts, between the initiating transaction and the independent transaction, which would be unacceptable.

In ARIES, using the concept of a *nested top action*, we are able to support the preceding requirement very efficiently, without having to initiate independent transactions to perform the actions. A nested top action, for our purposes, is taken to mean any subsequence of actions of a transaction that should not be undone once the sequence is complete and some later action that is dependent on the nested top action is logged to stable storage, irrespective of the outcome of the enclosing transaction.

A transaction execution performing a sequence of actions that define a nested top action consists of the following steps:

1. Ascertaining the position of the current transaction's last log record

2. Logging the redo and undo information associated with the actions of the nested top action

3. On completing the nested top action, writing a *dummy CLR* whose UndoNxtLSN points to the log record whose position was remembered in step 1

We assume that effects of any actions like creating a file and their associated updates to system data normally resident *outsidethedatabase* are externalized, before the dummy CLR is written. When we discuss redo, we are referring to only the system data that are resident in the database itself. By using this nested top action approach, if the enclosing transaction were to rollback after the completion of the nested top action, then the dummy CLR will ensure that the updates performed as part of the nested top action are not undone. If a system failure were to occur before the dummy CLR is written, then the incomplete nested top action will be undone since the nested top action's log records are written as undo-redo (as opposed to redo-only) log records. This provides the desired atomicity property for the nested top action. Unlike for the normal CLRs, there is nothing to redo when a dummy CLR is encountered during the redo pass. The dummy CLR in a sense can be thought of as the commit record for the nested top action. The advantage of our approach is that the enclosing transaction need not wait for this record to be forced to stable storage before proceeding with its subsequent actions.[7] Also, we do not pay the price of starting a new transaction. Nor do we run into lock conflict problems. This is to be contrasted with the costly independent-transaction approach.

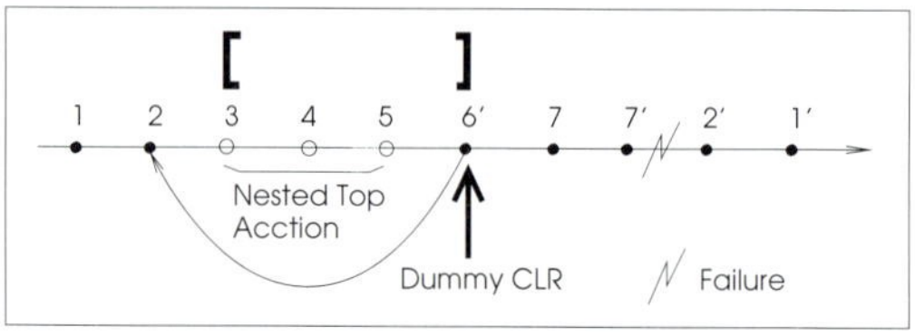

Figure 8.13. Nested top action example.

Figure 8.13 gives an example of a nested top action consisting of the actions 3, 4 and 5. Log record 6′ acts as the dummy CLR. Even though the enclosing transaction's activity is interrupted by a failure and hence it needs to be rolled back, 6′ ensures that the nested top action is not undone.

It should be emphasized that the nested top action implementation relies on repeating history. If the nested top action consists of only a single update, then we can log that update using a single *redo only* log record and avoid writing the dummy

---

[7]The dummy CLR may have to be forced if some *unlogged* updates may be performed later by other transactions which depended on the nested top action having completed.

CLR. Applications of the nested top action concept in the context of a hash-based storage method and index management can be found in [64, 67].

8.10 RECOVERY PARADIGMS

This section describes some of the problems associated with providing fine-granularity (e.g., record) locking and handling transaction rollbacks. Some additional discussion can be found in [105]. Our aim is to show how certain features of the existing recovery methods caused us difficulties in accomplishing our goals and to motivate the need for certain features that we had to include in ARIES. In particular, we show why some of the recovery paradigms of System R, which were developed in the context of the shadow-page technique, are inappropriate when WAL is to be used and there is a need for high levels of concurrency. In the past, one or more of those System R paradigms have been adopted in the context of WAL, leading to the design of algorithms with limitations and/or errors [3, 15, 16, 56, 77, 78, 84, 88, 94]. The System R paradigms that are of interest are

- selective redo during restart recovery

- undo work preceding redo work during restart recovery

- no logging of updates performed during transaction rollback (i.e., no CLRs)

- no logging of index and space management information changes

- no tracking of the page state on the page itself to relate it to logged updates (i.e., no LSNs on pages)

8.10.1 Selective Redo

The goal of this subsection is to introduce the concept of selective redo that has been implemented in many systems and to show the problems that it introduces in supporting fine granularity locking with WAL-based recovery. The aim is to motivate why ARIES repeats history.

When transaction systems restart after failures, they generally perform database recovery updates in 2 passes of the log: a redo pass and an undo pass (see Figure 8.5). System R first performs the undo pass and then the redo pass. As we will show later, the System R paradigm of *undo preceding redo is incorrect with WAL and fine-granularity locking*. The WAL-based DB2, on the other hand, does just the opposite. During the redo pass, System R redoes only the actions of committed and *prepared* (i.e., *in−doubt*) transactions [33]. We call this *selective redo*. Although the selective redo paradigm of System R intuitively seems to be the efficient approach to take, it has many pitfalls, as we discuss in what follows.

Some WAL-based systems, such as DB2, support only page locking and perform selective redo [15]. This approach will lead to data inconsistencies in such systems if record locking were to be implemented. Let us consider a WAL technique in which each page contains an LSN as described before. During the redo pass, the page LSN is compared to the LSN of a log record describing an update to the page to determine whether the log record's update needs to be reapplied to the page. If the page LSN is *lessthan* the log record's LSN, then the update is redone and the page's LSN is set to the log record's LSN (see Figure 8.14). During the undo pass, if the page LSN is *less than* the LSN of the log record to be undone, then no undo action is performed on the page. Otherwise, undo is performed on the page. Whether or not undo needs to be actually performed on the page, a CLR describing the updates that would have been performed as part of the undo operation is always written, when the transaction's actions are being rolled back. The CLR is written even when the page is not containing the update just to make media recovery simpler and not force it to handle rolled-back updates in a special way. Writing the CLR when an undo is not actually performed on the page turns out to be necessary also to handle a failure of the system during restart recovery. This will happen if there were an update U2 for page P1 that did not have to be undone, but there were an earlier update U1 for P1 that had to be undone, resulting in U1' (CLR for U1) being written and P1's LSN being changed to the LSN of U1' (>LSN of U2). After that, if P1 were to be written to nonvolatile storage before a system failure interrupts the completion of this restart, then, during the next restart, it would appear as if P1 contains the update U2 and an attempt would be made to undo it. On the other hand, if U2' had been written, then there would not be any problem. It should be emphasized that this problem arises even when only page locking is used, as is the case with DB2 [15].

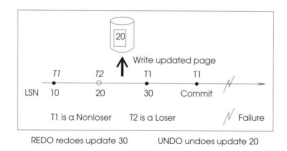

Figure 8.14. Selective redo with WAL : problem-free scenario.

Given these properties of the selective-redo WAL-based method under discussion, we would lose track of the state of a page with respect to a losing (in-progress or in-rollback) transaction in the situation where the page modified first by the losing transaction (say, update with LSN 20 by T2) was subsequently modified by a nonloser transaction's update (say, update with LSN 30 by T1) that had to be redone. The latter would have pushed the LSN of the page beyond the value established by the loser. So, when the time comes to undo the loser, we would not know if its update needs to be undone or not. Figures 8.14 and 8.15 illustrate this

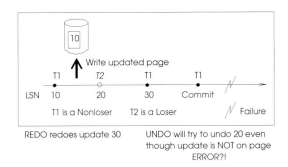

Figure 8.15. Selective redo with WAL : problem scenario.

problem with selective redo and fine-granularity locking. In the latter scenario, not redoing the update with LSN 20 since it belongs to a loser transaction, but redoing the update with LSN 30 since it belongs to a nonloser transaction, causes the undo pass to perform the undo of the former update even though it is not present in the page. This is because the undo logic relies on the page_LSN value to determine whether or not an update should be undone (undo if page_LSN is *greater than or equal to* the log record's LSN). By not repeating history, the page_LSN is no longer a true indicator of the current state of the page.

Undoing an action even when its effect is not present in a page will be harmless only under certain conditions, for example, with physical/byte-oriented locking and logging, as they are implemented in IMS [82], VAX DBMS and VAX Rdb/VMS [87], and other systems [6], no automatic reuse of freed space, and unique keys for all records. With operation logging, data inconsistencies will be caused by undoing an original operation whose effect is not present in the page.

Reversing the order of the selective redo and the undo passes will not solve the problem either. This *incorrect* approach is suggested in [3]. If the undo pass were to precede the redo pass, then we might lose track of which actions need to be redone. In Figure 8.14, the undo of 20 would make the page LSN become greater than 30, because of the writing of a CLR and the assignment of that CLR's LSN to the page. Since, during the redo pass, a log record's update is redone only if the page_LSN is *less than* the log record's LSN, we would not redo 30 even though that update is not present on the page. Not redoing that update would violate the durability and atomicity properties of transactions.

The use of the shadow-page technique by System R makes it unnecessary to have the concept of page_LSN in that system to determine what needs to be undone and what needs to be redone. With the shadow-page technique, during a checkpoint, an action-consistent version of the database called the *shadow version*, is saved on nonvolatile storage. Updates between two checkpoints create a new version of the updated page, thus constituting the *current version* of the database (see Figure 8.1).

During restart, recovery is performed from the *shadow* version and shadowing

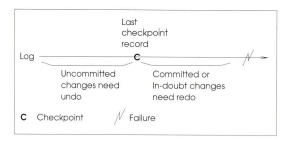

Figure 8.16. Simple view of recovery processing in system R.

is done even during restart recovery. As a result, there is no ambiguity about which updates are in the data base and which are not. All updates logged after the last checkpoint are *not* in the database and all updates logged before the checkpoint are in the data base.[8] This is one reason the System R recovery method functions correctly even with selective redo. The other reason is that index and space management changes are not logged, but are redone or undone logically.[9]

As was described before, ARIES does not perform selective redo, but *repeats history*. Apart from allowing us to support fine-granularity locking, repeating history has another beneficial side effect. It gives us the ability to commit some actions of a transaction irrespective of whether the transaction ultimately commits or not, as was described in Section 8.9

8.10.2   Rollback State

The goal of this subsection is to discuss the difficulties introduced by rollbacks in tracking their progress and how writing CLRs that describe updates performed during rollbacks solves some of the problems. Although the concept of writing CLRs has been implemented in many systems and has been around for a long time, in the literature, there has not really been, in the literature, a significant discussion of CLRs, problems relating to them and the advantages of writing them. Their utility and the fundamental role that they play in recovery have not been well recognized by the research community. In fact, whether undone actions could be undone and what additional problems these would present were left as open questions in [61]. In this section and elsewhere in this chapter, in the appropriate contexts, we try to

---

[8]This simple view, as it is depicted in Figure 8.16, is not completely accurate; see the Section 8.10.2.

[9]In fact, if index changes had been logged, then selective redo would not have worked. The problem would have come from structure modifications (like page split) that were performed after the last checkpoint by *loser* transactions that were taken advantage of later by transactions that ultimately committed. Even if logical undo were performed (if necessary), if redo was page-oriented, selective redo would have caused problems. To make it work, the structure modifications could have been performed using separate transactions. Of course, this would have been very expensive. For an alternate, efficient solution, see [67].

note all the known advantages of writing CLRs. We summarize these advantages
in the section 8.13

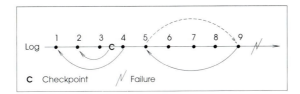

Figure 8.17. Partial rollback handling in system R

A transaction may totally or partially rollback its actions for any number of
reasons. For example, a unique key violation will cause only the rollback of the
update statement causing the violation and not of the entire transaction. Figure 8.2.
illustrates a partial rollback. Supporting partial rollback [1, 33], at least internally,
if not also at the application level, is a very important requirement for current day
transaction systems. Since a transaction may be rolling back when a failure occurs
and since some of the effects of the updates performed during the rollback might
have been written to nonvolatile storage, we need a way to keep track of the state
of progress of transaction rollback. It is relatively easy to do this in System R.
The only time we care about the transaction state in System R is at the time a
checkpoint is taken. So, the checkpoint record in System R keeps track of the next
record to be undone for each of the active transactions, some of which may already
be rolling back. The rollback state of a transaction at the time of a system failure
is unimportant since the database changes performed after the last checkpoint are
not *visible* in the database during restart. That is, restart recovery starts from
the state of the database as of the last checkpoint before the system failure – this
is the shadow version of the database as of the time of system failure. Despite
this, since CLRs are never written, System R needs to do some special processing
to handle those committed or in-doubt transactions that initiated and completed
partial rollbacks after the last checkpoint. The special handling is to avoid the need
for multiple passes over the log during the redo pass. The designers wanted to avoid
redoing some actions only to undo them a little later with a backward scan, when
the information about a partial rollback having occurred is encountered.

Figure 8.17 depicts an example of a restart recovery scenario for System R. All
log records are written by the same transaction, say, T1. In the checkpoint record,
the information for T1 points to log record 2, since by the time the checkpoint was
taken, log record 3 had already been undone because of a partial rollback. System
R not only does not write CLRs, but it also does not write a separate log record to
say that a partial rollback took place. Such information must be inferred from the
breakage in the chaining of the log records of a transaction. Ordinarily, a log record
written by a transaction points to the record that was most recently written by that
transaction via the PrevLSN pointer. But the first forward processing log record
written after the completion of a partial rollback does not follow this protocol.

When we examine, as part of the analysis pass, log record 4 and notice that its Prev_LSN pointer is pointing to 1, instead of the immediately preceding log record 3, we conclude that the partial rollback that started with the undo of 3 ended with the undo of 2. Since, during restart, the database state from which recovery needs to be performed is the state of the database as of the last checkpoint, log record 2 definitely needs to be undone. Whether 1 needs to be undone or not will depend on whether T1 is a losing transaction or not.

During the analysis pass, it is determined that log record 9 points to log record 5 and hence it is concluded that a partial rollback had caused the undo of log records 6, 7, and 8. To ensure that the rolled-back records are not redone during the redo pass, the log is patched by putting a forward pointer during the analysis pass in log record 5 to make it point to log record 9.

If log record 9 is a commit record, then during the undo pass log record 2 will be undone and during the redo pass log records 4 and 5 will be redone. Here, the same transaction is involved both in the undo pass and in the redo pass. To see why the undo pass has to precede the redo pass in System R,[10] consider the following scenario: Since a transaction that deleted a record is allowed to reuse that record's ID for a record inserted later by the same transaction, in the preceding case, a record might have been deleted because of the partial rollback, which had to be dealt with in the undo pass, and that record's ID might have been reused in the portion of the transaction that is dealt with in the redo pass. To repeat history with respect to the original sequence of actions before the failure, the undo must be performed before the redo is performed.

If 9 is neither a commit record nor a prepare record, then the transaction will be determined to be a loser, and during the undo pass, log records 2 and 1 will be undone. In the redo pass, none of the records will be redone.

Since CLRs are not written in System R and hence the exact way in which one transaction's undo operations were interspersed with other transactions' forward processing or undo actions is not known, the processing, for a given page as well as across different pages, during restart may be quite different from what happened during normal processing (i.e., *repeating history* is impossible to guarantee). Not logging index changes in System R also further contributes to this.(see footnote 8). These could potentially cause some space management problems such as a split that did not occur during normal processing being required during the restart redo or undo processing (see also the section 8.5.4). Not writing CLRs also prevents logging of redo information from being done physically (i.e., the operation performed on an object has to be logged – not the after image created by the operation). Let us consider an example: A piece of data has value 0 *after* the last checkpoint. Then, transaction T1 adds 1, T2 adds 2, T1 rolls back, and T2 commits. If T1 and T2 had logged the after image for redo and the operation for undo, then there will be a data integrity problem because after recovery, the data will have the value

---

[10] In the other systems, because CLRs are written and that, sometimes, page LSNs are compared with log record's LSNs to determine whether redo needs to be performed, the redo pass *precedes* the undo pass–see the Section 8.10.1 and Figure 8.6

3 instead of 2. In this case, in System R, undo for T1 is being accomplished by not redoing its update. Of course, System R did not support the fancy lock mode that would be needed to support 2 concurrent updates by different transactions to the same object. Allowing the logging of redo information physically will let redo recovery be performed very efficiently using *dumb* logic. This does not necessarily mean byte-oriented logging; that will depend on whether or not flexible storage management is used (see Section 8.10.3). Allowing the logging of undo information logically will permit high concurrency to be supported (see [64, 67] for examples). ARIES supports these.

WAL-based systems handle this problem by logging actions performed during rollbacks using CLRs. So, as far as recovery is concerned, the state of the data is always "marching" forward, even if some original actions are being rolled back. Contrast this with the approach, suggested in [56], in which the state of the data, as denoted by the LSN, is "pushed" back during rollbacks. That method works only with page-level (or coarser-granularity) locking. The immediate consequence of writing CLRs is that if a transaction were to be rolled back, then some of its original actions are undone more than once and, worse still, the compensating actions are also undone, possibly more than once. This is illustrated in Figure 8.3, in which a transaction had started rolling back even before the failure of the system. Then, during recovery, the previously written CLRs are undone and already undone non-CLRs are undone again. ARIES avoids such a situation while still retaining the idea of writing CLRs. Not undoing CLRs has benefits relating to deadlock management and early release of locks on undone objects also (see item 22, Section 8.12, and Section 8.6.4). Additional benefits of CLRs are discussed in the next section and in [75]. Some were already discussed in Section 8.8.

Unfortunately, recovery methods like the one suggested in [100] do not support partial rollbacks. We feel that this is an important drawback of such methods.

8.10.3 Space Management

The goal of this subsection is to point out the problems involved in space management when finer than page-level granularity of locking and varying-length records are to be supported efficiently.

A problem to be dealt with in doing record locking with flexible storage management is to make sure that the space released by a transaction during record deletion or update on a data page is not consumed by another transaction until the space releasing transaction is committed. This problem is discussed briefly in [82]. We do not deal with solutions to this space reservation problem here. The interested reader is referred to [54]. For index updates, in the interest of increasing concurrency, we do not want to prevent the space released by one transaction from being consumed by another before the commit of the first transaction. The way undo is dealt with under such circumstances using a logical undo approach is described in [67].

Since flexible storage management was a goal, it was not desirable to do physical

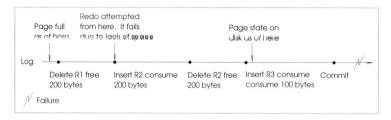

Figure 8.18. Wrong redo point causing problem with space for insert.

(i.e., byte-oriented) locking and logging of data within a page, as some systems do (see [6, 82, 87]). That is, we did not want to use the address of the first byte of a record as the lock name for the record. We did not want to identify the specific bytes that were changed on the page. The logging and locking have to be logical within a page. The record's lock name looks something like (page#, slot#), where slot# identifies a location on the page that then points to the actual location of the record. The log record describes how the contents of the data record were changed. The consequence is that garbage collection that collects unused space on a page does not have to lock or log the records that are moved around within the page. This gives us the flexibility of being able to move records around within a page to store and modify variable-length records efficiently. In systems like IMS, utilities have to be run quite frequently to deal with storage fragmentation. These reduce the availability of data to users.

Figure 8.18 shows a scenario in which not keeping track of the actual page state (by, e.g., storing the LSN in the nonvolatile storage version of the page) and attempting to perform redo from an *earlier* point in the log leads to problems, when flexible storage management is used. Assuming that all updates in Figure 8.18 involve the same page and the same transaction, an insert requiring 200 bytes is attempted on a page that has only 100 bytes of free space left in it. This shows the need for exact tracking of page state using an LSN to avoid attempting to redo operations that are already applied to the page.

Typically, each file containing records of one or more relations has a few pages called free-space inventory pages (FSIPs). They are called space map pages (SMPs) in DB2. Each FSIP describes the space information relating to many data or index pages. During a record-insert operation, possibly based on information obtained from a clustering index about the location of other records with the same key (or closely related keys) as that of the new record, one or more FSIPs are consulted to identify a data page with enough free space in it for inserting the new record. The FSIP keeps only approximate information (e.g., information like at least 25% of the page is full, at least 50% is full, etc.) to make sure that not every space releasing or consuming operation to a data page requires an update to the space information in the corresponding FSIP. To avoid special handling of the recovery of the FSIPs during redo and undo, and also to provide recovery independence, updates to the FSIPs must also be logged.

Transaction T1 might cause the space on the page to change from 23% full to 27% full, thereby requiring an update to the FSIP to change it from 0% full to 25% full. Later, T2 might cause the space to go to 35% full, which does not require an update to the FSIP. Now, if T1 were to rollback, then the space would change to 31% full and this should *not* cause an update to the FSIP. If T1 had written its FSIP change log record as a redo/undo record, then T1's rollback would cause the FSIP entry to, say, 0% full, which would be wrong, given the *current* state of the data page. This scenario points to the need for logging the changes to the FSIP as *redo — only* changes and for the need to do logical undos with respect to the free-space inventory updates. That is, while undoing a data page update, the system has to determine whether that operation causes the free space information to change and if it does cause a change, then update the FSIP and write a CLR that describes the change to the FSIP. We can easily construct an example in which a transaction does not perform an update to the FSIP during forward processing, but needs to perform an update to the FSIP during rollback. We can also construct an example in which the update performed during forward processing is not the exact inverse of the update during the rollback.

8.10.4 Multiple LSNs

Noticing the problems caused by having one LSN per page when trying to support record locking, it may be tempting to suggest that we track each object's state precisely by assigning a separate LSN to each object. Next, we explain why it is not a good idea.

DB2 already supports a granularity of locking that is less than a page. This happens in the case of indexes where the user has the option of requiring DB2 to physically divide each *leaf* page of the index into 2 to 16 minipages and do locking at the granularity of a minipage [10, 12]. The way DB2 does recovery properly on such leaf pages, despite not redoing actions of loser transactions during the redo pass, is as follows. DB2 tracks each minipage's state separately by associating an LSN with each minipage, besides having an LSN for the leaf page as a whole. Whenever a minipage is updated, the corresponding log record's LSN is stored in the minipage LSN field. The page LSN is set equal to the *maximum* of the minipage LSNs. During undo, it is the minipage LSN and not the page LSN that is compared to the log record's LSN to determine if that log record's update needs to be actually undone on the minipage. This technique, besides incurring too much space overhead for storing the LSNs, tends to fragment (and therefore waste) space available for storing keys. Further, it does not carry over conveniently to the case of record and key locking, especially when varying-length objects have to be supported efficiently. Maintaining LSNs for deleted objects is cumbersome at best. We desired to have a *single* state variable (LSN) for each page, even when minipage locking is being done, to make recovery, especially media recovery, very efficient. The simple technique of repeating history during restart recovery *before* performing the rollback of loser transactions turns out to be sufficient, as we have seen in ARIES.

Since DB2 *physically* divides up a page into a fixed number of minipages, no special technique is needed to handle the space reservation problem. Methods like the one proposed in [66] for fine-granularity locking do not support varying-length objects (*atoms* in the terminology of that paper).

8.11   OTHER WAL-BASED METHODS

In the following, we summarize the properties of some other significant recovery methods that also use the WAL protocol. Recovery methods based on the shadow-page technique (like that of System R) are not considered here because of their well-known disadvantages, for example, very costly checkpoints; extra nonvolatile storage space overhead for the shadow copies of data, disturbing the physical clustering of data; and extra I/Os involving page map blocks (see the previous sections of this chapter and [33] for additional discussions). First, we briefly introduce the different systems and recovery methods that we will be examining in this section. Next, we compare the different methods along various dimensions. We have been informed that the DB-cache recovery method of [27] has been implemented with significant modifications by Siemens. But, because of lack of information about that implementation, we are unable to include it here.

IBM's IMS/VS [44, 45, 47, 52, 58, 82, 86, 102], which is a hierarchical database system, consists of two parts: IMS Full Function (FF), which is relatively flexible, and IMS Fast Path (FP) [30, 45, 101], which is more efficient but has many restrictions (e.g., no support for secondary indexes). A single IMS transaction can access both FF and FP data. The recovery and buffering methods used by the two parts have many differences. In FF, depending on the database types and the operations, the granularities of the locked objects vary. FP supports two kinds of databases: main storage databases (MSDBs) and data entry databases (DEDBs). MSDBs support only fixed-length records, but FP provides the mechanisms (i.e., *field calls*) to make the lock hold times be the minimum possible for MSDB records. Only page locking is supported for DEDBs. But, DEDBs have many high-availability and parallelism features and large database support. IMS, with XRF, provides *hot − standby* support [47]. IMS, via global locking, also supports data sharing across two different systems, each with its own buffer pools [86, 102].

DB2 is IBM's relational database system for the MVS operating system. Limited distributed data access functions are available in DB2. The DB2 recovery algorithm has been presented in [1, 13, 14, 15, 20]. It supports different locking granularities (tablespace, table and page for data, and minipage and page for indexes) and consistency levels (*cursor stability, repeatable read*) [10, 11, 12]. DB2 allows logging to be turned off temporarily for tables and indexes only during utility operations like loading and reorganizing data. A single transaction can access both DB2 and IMS data with atomicity. The Encompass recovery algorithm [4, 40] with some changes has been incorporated in Tandem's NonStop SQL [103]. With NonStop, Tandem provides *hot − standby* support for its products. Both Encompass and NonStop SQL support distributed data access. They allow multisite updates within a single transaction using the Presumed Abort two-phase commit protocol of [57, 68, 69]. NonStop SQL supports different locking granularities (file, key prefix and record) and consistency levels (*cursor stability*), *repeatable read*, and unlocked or dirty read). Logging can be turned off temporarily or permanently even for nonutility operations on files.

Schwarz [94] presents two different recovery methods based on value logging (a la IMS) and operation logging. The two methods have several differences, as will be outlined in what follows. The value logging method (VLM), which is much less complex than the operation logging method (OLM), has been implemented in CMU's Camelot [25, 98].

Buffer Management. Encompass, NonStop SQL, OLM, VLM, and DB2 have adopted the steal and no-force policies. During normal processing, VLM and OLM write a *fetch* record whenever a page is read from nonvolatile storage and an $end - write$ record every time a dirty page is successfully written back to non-volatile storage. These are written during restart processing also in OLM alone. These records help in identifying the super set of dirty pages that might have been in the buffer pool at the time of system failure. DB2 has a sophisticated buffer manager [10, 104]. DB2 writes a log record whenever a tablespace or an indexspace is opened and another record whenever such a space is closed. The close operation is performed only after all the dirty pages of the space have been written back to nonvolatile storage. DB2's analysis pass uses these log records to bring the dirty objects information up to date as of the failure.

For MSDBs, IMS FP does deferred updating. This means that a transaction does not *see* its own MSDB updates. For DEDBs, a no-steal policy is used. FP writes, at commit time, *all* the log records for a given transaction in a single call to the log manager. After placing the log records in the *log buffers* (*not* on stable storage), the MSDB updates are applied and the MSDB record locks are released. The MSDB locks are released even before the commit log record is placed on stable storage. This is how FP minimizes the amount of time locks are held on the MSDB records. The DEDB locks are transferred to system processes. The log manager is given time to let it force the log records to stable storage ultimately (i.e., group commit logic is used; see [30]). After the logging is completed (i.e., *after* the transaction has been committed), all the pages of the DEDBs that were modified by the transaction are forced to nonvolatile storage using system processes that, on completion of the I/Os, release the DEDB locks. This does not result in any uncommitted updates being forced to nonvolatile storage since page locking with a no-steal policy is used for DEDBs. The use of separate processes for writing the DEDB pages to nonvolatile storage is intended to let the user process go ahead with the next transaction's processing as soon as possible and also to gain parallelism for the I/Os. IMS FF follows the steal and force policies. *Before* committing a transaction, IMS FF forces to nonvolatile storage all the pages that were modified by that transaction. Since finer than page locking is supported by FF, this may result in some uncommitted data being placed on nonvolatile storage. Of course, all the recovery algorithms considered in this section force the log during commit processing.

Normal Checkpointing.   Normal checkpoints are the ones that are taken when the system is not in the restart recovery mode. OLM and VLM quiesce all activity in the system and take, similar to System R, an operation consistent (not necessarily transaction consistent) checkpoint. The contents of the checkpoint record are similar to those of ARIES. DB2, IMS, NonStop SQL, and Encompass do take (fuzzy) checkpoints even when update and logging activities are going on concurrently. DB2's checkpoint actions are similar to what we described for ARIES. The major difference is that instead of writing the dirty_pages table, it writes the dirty objects (tablespaces, indexspaces, etc.) list with a RecLSN for each object [104]. For MSDBs alone, IMS writes their complete contents alternately to one of two files on nonvolatile storage during a checkpoint. Since deferred updating is performed for MSDBs, no uncommitted changes will be present in their checkpointed version. Also, it is ensured that no partial committed changes of a transaction are present. Care is needed since the updates are applied after the commit record is written. For DEDBs, any *committed* updated pages that have not yet been written to nonvolatile storage are included in the checkpoint records. These together avoid the need for examining, during restart recovery, any log records written before the checkpoint for FP data recovery. Encompass and NonStop SQL might force some dirty pages to nonvolatile storage during a checkpoint. They enforce the policy that requires that a page once dirtied must be written to nonvolatile storage *before* the completion of the *second* checkpoint following the dirtying of the page. Because of this policy, the completion of a checkpoint may be delayed waiting for the completion of the writing of the old dirty pages.

Partial Rollbacks.   Encompass, NonStop SQL, OLM, and VLM do not support partial transaction rollback. From Version 2 Release 1, IMS supports partial rollbacks. In fact, the savepoint concept is exposed at the application-program level. This support is available only to those applications that do not access FP data. The reason FP data are excluded is because FP does not write undo data in its log records and because deferred updating is performed for MSDBs. DB2 supports partial rollbacks for internal use by the system to provide statement-level atomicity [1].

Compensation Log Records.   Encompass, NonStop SQL, DB2, VLM, OLM, and IMS FF write CLRs during normal rollbacks. During a normal rollback, IMS FP does not write CLRs since it would not have written any log records for changes to such data until the decision to roll back is made. This is because FP is always the coordinator in two-phase commit and hence it never needs to get into the prepared state. Since deferred updating is performed for MSDBs, the updates kept in pending (to-do) lists are discarded at rollback time. Since a no-steal policy is followed and page locking is done for DEDBs, the modified pages of DEDBs are simply purged from the buffer pool at rollback time. Encompass, NonStop SQL, DB2, and IMS (FF and FP) write CLRs during restart rollbacks also. During restart recovery, IMS

FP might find some log records written by (at the most) one in-progress transaction. This transaction must have been in commit processing, that is, about to commit, with some of its log records already having been written to nonvolatile storage, when the system went down. Even though, because of the no-steal policy, none of the corresponding FP updates would have been written to nonvolatile storage and hence there would be nothing to be undone, IMS FP writes CLRs for such records to simplify media recovery [101]. Since FP log records contain only redo information, just to write these CLRs, for which the undo information is needed, the corresponding unmodified data on nonvolatile storage are accessed during restart recovery. This should illustrate to the reader that even with a no-steal policy and without supporting partial rollbacks, there are still some problems to be dealt with at restart for FP. Too often, people assume that the no-steal policy eliminates many problems. Actually, it has many shortcomings.

VLM does not write CLRs during restart rollbacks. As a result, a bounded amount of logging will occur for a rolled-back transaction, even in the face of repeated failures during restart. In fact, CLRs are written only for normal rollbacks. Of course, this has some negative implications with respect to media recovery. OLM writes CLRs for undos and *redos* performed during restart (called *undomodify* and *redomodify* records, respectively). This is done to deal with failures during restart. OLM might write multiple undomodify and redomodify records for a given update record if failures interrupt restart processing. No CLRs are generated for CLRs themselves. During restart recovery, Encompass and DB2 undo changes of CLRs, thus causing the writing of CLRs for CLRs and the writing of multiple, identical CLRs for a given record written during forward or restart processing. In the worst case, the number of log records written during repeated restart failures grows exponentially. Figure 8.4 shows how ARIES avoids this problem. IMS ignores CLRs during the undo pass and hence does not write CLRs for them. The net result is that, because of multiple failures, like the others, IMS might wind up writing multiple times the same CLR for a given record written during forward processing. In the worst case, the number of log records written by IMS and OLM grows linearly. Because of its force policy, IMS will need to redo the CLRs' updates only during media recovery.

Log Record Contents.   IMS FP writes only redo information (i.e., the after image of records) because of its no-steal policy. As mentioned before, IMS does value (or state) logging and physical (i.e., byte-range) locking (see [82]). IMS FF logs both the undo information and the redo information. Since IMS does not undo CLRs' updates, CLRs need to have only the redo information. For providing the XRF hot-standby support, IMS includes enough information in its log records for the backup system to track the lock names of updated objects. IMS FP also logs the address of the buffer occupied by a modified page. This information is used during a backup's takeover or restart recovery to reduce the amount of redo work of DEDBs' updates. Encompass and VLM also log complete undo and redo information of updated records. DB2 and NonStop SQL log only the before and after images of the updated fields. OLM logs the description of the update operation. The CLRs of Encompass and DB2 need to contain both the redo and the undo information since their CLRs might be undone. OLM periodically logs an operation consistent *snapshot* of each object. OLM's undomodify and redomodify records contain no redo or undo information but only the LSNs of the corresponding modify records. But OLM's modify, redomodify, and undomodify records also contain a page map that specifies the set of pages where parts of the modified object reside.

Page Overhead. Encompass and NonStop SQL use one LSN on each page to keep track of the state of the page. VLM uses no LSNs, but OLM uses one LSN. DB2 uses one LSN and IMS FF no LSN. Not having the LSN in IMS FF and VLM to know the exact state of a page does not cause any problems because of IMS's and VLM's value logging and physical locking attributes. It is acceptable to redo an already present update or undo an absent update. IMS FP uses a field in the pages of DEDBs as a version number to handle redos correctly after all the data sharing systems had failed [73]. When DB2 divides an index leaf page into minipages then it uses one LSN for each minipage, besides one LSN for the page as a whole.

Log Passes During Restart Recovery. Encompass and NonStop SQL make two passes (redo and then undo), and DB2 three passes (analysis, redo, and then undo; see Figure 8.5. Encompass and NonStop SQL start their redo passes from the beginning of the penultimate successful checkpoint. This is sufficient because of the buffer management policy of writing to disk a dirty page within two checkpoints after the page became dirty. They also seem to repeat history before performing the undo pass. They do not seem to repeat history if a backup system takes over when a primary system fails [4]. In the case of a takeover by a hot standby, locks are first reacquired for the losers' updates and then the rollbacks of the losers are performed in parallel with the processing of new transactions. Each loser transaction is rolled back using a separate process to gain parallelism. DB2 starts its redo scan from that point determined using information recorded in the last successful checkpoint, as modified by the analysis pass. As mentioned before, DB2 does selective redo (see Section 8.10.1).

VLM makes one backward pass and OLM makes three passes (analysis, undo, and then redo). Many lists are maintained during OLM's and VLM's passes. The undomodify and redomodify log records of OLM are used only to modify these lists, unlike in the case of the CLRs written in the other systems. In VLM, the one backward pass is used to undo uncommitted changes on nonvolatile storage and also to redo missing committed changes. No log records are written during these operations. In OLM, during the undo pass, for each object to be recovered, if an operation-consistent version of the object does not exist on nonvolatile storage, then it restores a snapshot of the object from the snapshot log record so that, starting from a consistent version of the object, (1) in the remainder of the undo pass, any to-be-undone updates that precede the snapshot log record can be undone logically and (2) in the redo pass, any committed or in-doubt updates (modify records only) that follow the snapshot record can be redone logically. This is similar to the shadowing performed in [16, 84] using a separate log–the difference is in the database wide checkpointing being replaced by object-level checkpointing and the use of a single log instead of two logs.

IMS first reloads MSDBs from the file that received their contents during the latest successful checkpoint before the failure. The dirty DEDB buffers that were included in the checkpoint records are also reloaded into the same buffers as before. This means that during the restart after a failure, the number of buffers cannot be altered. Then, it makes just one forward pass over the log (see Figure 8.5. During that pass, it accumulates log records in memory on a per transaction basis and redoes, if necessary, completed transactions' FP updates. Multiple processes are used in parallel to redo the DEDB updates. As far as FP is concerned, only the updates starting from the last checkpoint before the failure are of interest. At the end of that one pass, in-progress transactions' FF updates are undone (using the log records in memory), in parallel, using one process per transaction. If the space allocated in memory for a transaction's log records is not enough, then a backward scan of the log will be performed to fetch the needed records during that transaction's rollback. In the XRF context, when a hot-standby IMS takes over, the handling of the loser transactions is similar to the way Tandem does it. That is, rollbacks are performed in parallel with new transaction processing.

Page Forces During Restart. OLM, VLM, and DB2 force all dirty pages at the end of restart. Information on Encompass and NonStop SQL is not available.

Restart Checkpoints. IMS, DB2, OLM, and VLM take a checkpoint only at the end of restart recovery. Information on Encompass and NonStop SQL is not available.

Restrictions on Data. Encompass and NonStop SQL require that every record have a unique key. This unique key is used to guarantee that if an attempt is made to undo a logged action that was never applied to the nonvolatile storage version of the data, then the latter is realized and the undo fails. In other words, idempotence of operations is achieved using the unique key. IMS in effect does byte-range locking and logging and hence does not allow records to be moved around freely within a page. This results in the fragmentation and the less efficient usage of free space. IMS imposes some additional constraints with respect to FP data. VLM requires that an object's representation be divided into fixed-length (less than one page sized) unrelocatable quanta. The consequences of these restrictions are similar to those for IMS.

Recovery from system failures is not discussed in [2, 28, 61], where as the theory of [35] does not include semantically rich modes of locking (i.e., operation logging). In other sections of this chapter, we have pointed out the problems with some of the other approaches that have been proposed in the literature.

8.12 ATTRIBUTES OF ARIES

ARIES makes few assumptions about the data or its model and has several advantages over other recovery methods. While ARIES is simple, it possesses several interesting and useful properties. Each of most of these properties has been demonstrated in one or more existing or proposed systems, as summarized in the last section. However, we know of no single system, proposed or real, that has all of these properties. Some of these properties of ARIES are as follows:

1. *Support for finer-than-page-level concurrency control and multiple granularities of locking.* ARIES supports page-level and record-level locking in a uniform fashion. Recovery is not affected by what the granularity of locking is. Depending on the expected contention for the data, the appropriate level of locking can be chosen. It also allows multiple granularities of locking (e.g., record, table, and tablespace level) for the same object (e.g., tablespace). Concurrency control schemes other than locking (e.g., the schemes of [2]) can also be used.

2. *Flexible buffer management during restart and normal processing.* As long as the write-ahead logging protocol is followed, the buffer manager is free to use any page replacement policy. In particular, dirty pages of incomplete transactions can be written to nonvolatile storage before those transactions commit (steal policy). Also, it is not required that all pages dirtied by a transaction be written back to nonvolatile storage before the transaction is allowed to commit (i.e., no-force policy). These properties lead to reduced demands for buffer storage and fewer I/Os involving frequently updated ("hot-spot") pages. ARIES does not preclude the possibilities of using deferred-updating and force-at-commit policies and benefitting from them. ARIES is quite flexible in these respects.

3. *Minimal space overhead–only one LSN per page.* The permanent (excluding log) space overhead of this scheme is limited to the storage required on each page to store the LSN of the last logged action performed on the page. The LSN of a page is a monotonically increasing value.

4. *No constraints on data to guarantee idempotence of redo or undo of logged actions.* There are no restrictions on the data with respect to unique keys, and so on. Records can be of variable length. Data can be moved around within a page for garbage collection. Idempotence of operations is ensured since the LSN on each page is used to determine whether an operation should be redone or not.

5. *Actions taken during the undo of an update need not necessarily be the exact inverses of the actions taken during the original update.* Since CLRs are being written during undos, any differences between the inverses of the original actions and what actually had to be done during undo can be recorded in the former. An example of when the inverse might not be correct is the one that relates to the free-space information (like at least 10% free, 20% free, etc.) about data pages that are maintained in space map pages. Because of finer-than-page-level granularity locking, while no free space information

change takes place during the initial update of a page by a transaction, a free-space information change might occur during the undo (from 20% free to 10% free) of that original change because of intervening update activities of other transactions (see Section 8.10.3).

Other benefits of this attribute in the context of hash-based storage methods and index management can be found in [64, 67].

6. *Support for operation logging and novel lock modes.* The changes made to a page can be logged in a logical fashion. The undo information and the redo information for the entire object need not be logged. It suffices if the changed fields alone are logged. Since history is repeated, for increment or decrement kinds of operations, before and after images of the field are not needed. Information about the type of operation and the decrement or increment amount is enough. Garbage collection actions and changes to some fields (e.g., amount of free space) of that page need not be logged. Novel lock modes based on commutativity and other properties of operations can be supported [2, 28, 94].

7. *Even redo-only and undo-only records are accommodated.* Although it may be efficient (single call to the log component) sometimes to include the undo and redo information about an update in the same log record, at other times it may be efficient (from the original data, the undo record can be constructed and, after the update is performed *inplace* in the data record, from the updated data, the redo record can be constructed) and/or necessary (because of log record size restrictions) to log the information in two different records. ARIES can handle both situations. Under these conditions, the undo record must be logged before the redo record.

8. *Support for partial and total transaction rollback.* Besides allowing transactions to be rolled back totally, ARIES also allows the establishment of savepoints and the partial rollback of transactions to such savepoints. Without the support for partial rollbacks, even logically recoverable errors (e.g., unique key violation, out-of-date cached catalog information in a distributed database system) will require total rollbacks and result in wasted work.

9. *Support for objects spanning multiple pages.* Objects can span multiple pages (e.g., an IMS "record" that consists of multiple segments may be scattered over many pages). When an object is modified, if log records are written for every page affected by that update, ARIES works fine. ARIES itself does not treat multipage objects in any special way.

10. *Allows files to be acquired or returned, any time, from or to the operating system.* ARIES provides the flexibility of being able to return files dynamically and permanently to the operating system (see [20] for the detailed description of a technique to accomplish this). Such an action is considered to be one that cannot be undone. It does not prevent the same file from being reallocated to

the data base system. Mappings between objects (tablespaces, etc.) and files are not required to be defined statically as in System R.

11. *Some actions of a transaction may be committed even if the transaction as a whole is rolled back.*

    This refers to the technique of using the concept of a dummy CLR to implement nested top actions. File extension has been given as an example situation that could benefit from this. Other applications of this technique, in the context of hash-based storage methods and index management, can be found in [64, 67].

12. *Efficient checkpoints (including during restart recovery).* By supporting fuzzy checkpointing, ARIES makes taking a checkpoint an efficient operation. Checkpoints can be taken even when update activities and logging are going on concurrently. Permitting checkpoints even during restart processing will help reduce the impact of failures during restart recovery. The dirty_pages information written during checkpointing helps reduce the number of pages that are read from nonvolatile storage during the redo pass.

13. *Simultaneous processing of multiple transactions in forward processing and/or in rollback accessing of the same page.* Since many transactions could simultaneously be going forward or rolling back on a given page, the level of concurrent access supported could be quite high. Except for the short-duration latching that has to be performed any time a page is being physically modified or examined, be it during forward processing or during rollback, rolling back transactions do not affect one another in any unusual fashion.

14. *No locking or deadlocks during transaction rollback.* Since no locking is required during transaction rollback, no deadlocks will involve transactions that are rolling back. Avoiding locking during rollbacks simplifies not only the rollback logic, but also the deadlock detector logic. The deadlock detector need not worry about making the mistake of choosing a rolling-back transaction as a victim in the event of a deadlock (cf. System R and R* [33, 53, 69]).

15. *Bounded logging during restart in spite of repeated failures or of nested rollbacks.* Even if repeated failures occur during restart, the number of CLRs written is unaffected. This is also true if partial rollbacks are nested. The number of log records written will be the same as that written at the time of transaction rollback during normal processing. The latter again is a fixed number and is, usually, equal to the number of undoable records written during the forward processing of the transaction. No log records are written during the redo pass of restart.

16. *Permits exploitation of parallelism and selective/deferred processing for faster restart.*

Restart can be made faster by not doing all the needed I/Os synchronously one at a time while processing the corresponding log record. ARIES permits the early identification of the pages needing recovery and the initiation of asynchronous parallel I/Os for the reading of those pages. The pages can be processed concurrently as they are brought into memory during the redo pass. Undo parallelism requires complete handling of a given transaction by a single process. Some of the restart processing can be postponed to speed up restart or to accommodate off-line devices. If desired, undo of loser transactions can be performed in parallel with new transaction processing.

17. *Fuzzy-image copying (archive dumping) for media recovery.* Media recovery and image copying of the data are supported very efficiently. To take advantage of device geometry, the actual act of copying can even be performed outside the transaction system (i.e., without going through the buffer pool). This can happen even while the latter is accessing and modifying the information being copied. During media recovery, only one forward traversal of the log is made.

18. *Continuation of loser transactions after a system restart.* Since ARIES repeats history and supports the savepoint concept, we could, in the undo pass, instead of totally rolling back the loser transactions, roll back each loser only to its latest savepoint. Locks must be acquired to protect the transaction's uncommitted, not undone updates. Later, we could resume the transaction by invoking its application at a special entry point and passing enough information about the savepoint from which execution is to be resumed.

19. *Only one backward traversal of the log during restart or media recovery.* Both during media recovery and restart recovery, one backward traversal of the log is sufficient. This is especially important if any portion of the log is likely to be stored in a slow medium like tape.

20. *Need only redo information in compensation log records.* Since compensation records are never undone, they need to contain only redo information. So, on the average, the amount of log space consumed during a transaction rollback will be half the space consumed during the forward processing of that transaction.

21. *Support for distributed transactions.* ARIES accommodates distributed transactions. Whether a given site is a coordinator or a subordinate site does not affect ARIES.

22. *Early release of locks during transaction rollback and deadlock resolution using partial rollbacks.* Because ARIES never undoes CLRs and because it never undoes a particular non-CLR more than once, during a (partial) rollback, when the transaction's very *first* update to a particular object is undone and a CLR is written for it, the system can release the lock on that object. This makes it possible to consider resolving deadlocks using partial rollbacks.

It should be noted that ARIES does not prevent the shadow-page technique from being used for selected portions of the data to avoid logging of only undo information or both undo and redo information. This maybe useful for dealing with long fields, as is the case in the OS/2 Extended Edition Database Manager. In such instances, for such data, the modified pages would have to be forced to nonvolatile storage before commit. Whether or not media recovery and partial rollbacks can be supported will depend on what is logged and for which updates shadowing is done.

8.13   SUMMARY

In this chapter, we presented the ARIES recovery method and showed why some of the recovery paradigms of System R are inappropriate in the WAL context. We dealt with a variety of features that are very important in building and operating an *industrial − strength* transaction processing system. Several issues regarding operation logging, fine-granularity locking, space management, and flexible recovery were discussed. In brief, ARIES accomplishes the goals that we set out with by logging all updates on a per page basis, using an LSN on every page for tracking page state, repeating history during restart recovery before undoing the loser transactions, and chaining the CLRs to the predecessors of the log records that they compensated. Use of ARIES is not restricted to the database area alone. It can be used for implementing persistent object-oriented languages, recoverable file systems, and transaction-based operating systems. In fact, it is being used in the QuickSilver distributed operating system [43] and in a system designed to aid the backing up of workstation data on a host [48].

In this section, we summarize as to which specific features of ARIES lead to which specific attributes that give us flexibility and efficiency.

Repeating history exactly, which in turn implies using LSNs and writing CLRs during undos, permits the following, irrespective of whether CLRs are chained using the UndoNxtLSN field:

1. Record-level locking to be supported and records to be moved around within a page to avoid storage fragmentation without the moved records having to be locked and without the movements having to be logged.

2. Use only one state variable, a log-sequence number, per page.

3. Reuse of storage released by one transaction for the same transaction's later actions or for other transactions' actions once the former commits, thereby leading to the preservation of clustering of records and the efficient usage of storage.

4. The inverse of an action originally performed during forward processing of a transaction to be different from the action(s) performed during the undo of that original action (e.g., class changes in the space map pages). That is, logical undo with recovery independence is made possible.

5. Multiple transactions may undo on the same page concurrently with transactions going forward.

6. Recovery of each page independently of other pages or of log records relating to transaction state, especially during media recovery.

7. If necessary, the continuation of transactions that were in progress at the time of system failure.

8. Selective or deferred restart, and undo of losers concurrently with new transaction processing to improve data availability.

9. Partial rollback of transactions.

10. Operation logging and logical logging of changes within a page. For example, decrement and increment operations may be logged, rather than the before and after images of modified data.

Chaining, using the UndoNxtLSN field, CLRs to log records written during forward processing permits the following, provided the protocol of repeating history is also followed:

1. The avoidance of undoing CLRs' actions, thus avoiding writing CLRs for CLRs. This also makes it unnecessary to store undo information in CLRs.

2. The avoidance of the undo of the same log record written during forward processing more than once.

3. As a transaction is being rolled back, the ability to release the lock on an object when all the updates to that object had been undone. This may be important while rolling back a long transaction or while resolving a deadlock by partially rolling back the victim.

4. Handling partial rollbacks without any special actions like patching the log, as in System R.

5. Making permanent, if necessary via nested top actions, some of the changes made by a transaction, irrespective of whether the transaction itself subsequently rolls back or commits.

Performing the analysis pass before repeating history permits the following:

1. Checkpoints to be taken any time during the redo and undo passes of recovery.

2. Files to be returned to the operating system dynamically, thereby allowing dynamic binding between database objects and files.

3. Recovery of file-related information concurrently with the recovery of user data, without requiring special treatment for the former.

4. Identifying pages possibly requiring redo, so that asynchronous parallel I/Os could be initiated for them even before the redo pass starts.

5. Exploiting opportunities to avoid redos on some pages by eliminating those pages from the dirty_pages table on noticing, for example, that some empty pages have been freed.

6. Exploiting opportunities to avoid reading some pages during redo, for example, by writing end_write records after dirty pages have been written to nonvolatile storage and by eliminating those pages from the dirty_pages table when the end_write records are encountered.

7. Identifying the transactions in the in-doubt and in-progress states so that locks could be reacquired for them during the redo pass to support selective or deferred restart, the continuation of loser transactions after restart, and undo of loser transactions in parallel with new transaction processing.

8.13.1   Implementations and Extensions

ARIES forms the basis of the recovery algorithms used in the IBM research proto-type systems Starburst [39, 93] and QuickSilver [43], in the University of Wisconsin's EXODUS and Gamma database machine [21], and in the IBM program products OS/2 Extended Edition Database Manager [7] and Workstation Data Save Facility/VM [48]. One feature of ARIES, namely, *repeatinghistory*, has been implemented in DB2 Version 2 Release 1 to use the concept of nested top action for supporting segmented tablespaces. A simulation study of the performance of ARIES is reported in [106, 107]. The following conclusions from that study are worth noting: "Simulation results indicate the success of the ARIES recovery method in providing fast recovery from failures, and thus scoring availability figures close to unity. Even though considerably long redo spans are caused by long intercheckpoint intervals, efficient use of page LSNs, log LSNs, and RecLSNs avoids redoing updates unnecessarily, and the actual recovery load is reduced skillfully. Besides, the overhead incurred by the concurrency control and recovery algorithms on transactions is very low, as indicated by the negligibly small difference between the mean transaction response time and the average duration of a transaction if it ran alone in a never failing system. This observation also emerges as evidence that the recovery method goes well with concurrency control through fine-granularity locking, an important virtue."

We have extended ARIES to make it work in the context of the nested transaction model (see [76, 91]). Based on ARIES, we have developed new methods, called ARIES/KVL, ARIES/IM and ARIES/LHS, to efficiently provide high concurrency and recovery for B^+-tree indexes [62, 67] and for hashing based storage structures [64]. We have also extended ARIES to restrict the amount of repeating of history that takes place for the loser transactions [75]. We have designed concurrency control and recovery algorithms, based on ARIES, for the N-way data sharing (i.e., shared disks) environment [70, 71, 72, 73, 74]. A method, called *Commit_LSN*, which takes advantage of the page_LSN which exists in every page to reduce the locking, latching and predicate reevaluation overheads and also to improve concurrency has been presented in [59, 63, 65]. Although messages are an important part of transaction processing, we did not discuss message logging and recovery in this chapter.

Acknowledgments

We have benefitted immensely from the work that was performed in the System R project and in the DB2 and IMS product groups. We have learned valuable lessons by looking at the experiences with those systems. Access to the source code and internal documents of those systems was very helpful. The Starburst project gave us the opportunity to begin from scratch and design some of the fundamental algorithms of a transaction system, taking into account experiences with the prior systems. We would like to acknowledge the contributions of the designers of the other systems. We would also like to thank our colleagues in the research and product groups that have adopted our research results. Our thanks also go to Klaus Kuespert, Brian Oki, Erhard Rahm, Andreas Reuter, Pat Selinger, Dennis Shasha and Irv Traiger for their detailed comments.

References

[1] Baker, J., Crus, R., Haderle, D. "Method for Assuring Atomicity of Multi-Row Update Operations in a Database System", U.S. Patent 4,498,145/, IBM, February 1985.

[2] Badrinath, B.R., Ramamritham, K. "Semantics-Based Concurrency Control: Beyond Commutativity," *Proc. 3rd IEEE International Conference on Data Engineering*, February 1987.

[3] Bernstein, P., Hadzilacos, V., Goodman, N. *Concurrency Control and Recovery in Database Systems*, Addison-Wesley, 1987.

[4] Borr, A. "Robustness to Crash in a Distributed Database: A Non Shared-Memory Multi-Processor Approach," *Proc. 10th International Conference on Very Large databases*, Singapore, August 1984.

[5] Chamberlin, D., Gilbert, A., Yost, R. "A History of System R and SQL/Data System," *Proc. 7th International Conference on Very Large databases*, Cannes, France, September 1981.

[6] Chang, A., Mergen, M. "801 Storage: Architecture and Programming," *ACM Transactions on Computer Systems*, 6(1) (February 1988).

[7] Chang, P.Y., Myre, W.W. "OS/2 EE Database Manager Overview and Technical Highlights," *IBM Systems Journal*, 27(2) (1988).

[8] Copeland, G., Khoshafian, S., Smith, M., Valduriez, P. "Buffering Schemes for Permanent Data," *Proc. International Conference on Data Engineering*, Los Angeles, February 1986.

[9] Clark, B.E., Corrigan, M.J. "Application System/400 Performance Characteristics," *IBM Systems Journal*, 28(3) (1989).

[10] Cheng, J., Loosely, C., Shibamiya, A., Worthington, P. "IBM Database 2 Performance: Design, Implementation, and Tuning," *IBM Systems Journal*, 23(2) (1984).

[11] Crus, R., Haderle, D., Herron, H. "Method for Managing Lock Escalation in a Multiprocessing, Multiprogramming Environment," U.S. Patent 4,716,528, IBM, December 1987.

[12] Crus, R., Malkemus, T., Putzolu, G.R. "Index Mini-Pages," *IBM Technical Disclosure Bulletin*, 26(4) (April 1983).

[13] Crus, R., Putzolu, F., Mortenson, J.A. Incremental database Log Image Copy, *IBM Technical Disclosure Bulletin*, 25(7B) (December 1982).

[14] Crus, R., Putzolu, F. "Database Allocation Table," *IBM Technical Disclosure Bulletin*, 25(7B) (December 1982).

[15] Crus, R. "Data Recovery in IBM Database 2," *IBM Systems Journal*, 23(2) (1984).

[16] Curtis, R. "Informix-Turbo," *Proc. IEEE Compcon Spring*, February-March 1988.

[17] Dasgupta, P., LeBlanc Jr., R., Appelbe, W. "The Clouds Distributed Operating System," *Proc. 8th International Conference on Distributed Computing Systems*, San Jose, June 1988.

[18] Date, C. *A Guide to INGRES*, Addison-Wesley Publishing Company, 1987.

[19] Detlefs, D., Herlihy, M., Wing, J. *Inheritance of Synchronization and Recovery Properties in Avalon/C++*, Technical Report CMU-CS-87-133, Carnegie-Mellon University, March 1987.

[20] Dey, R., Shan, M., Traiger, I. "Method for Dropping Data Sets," *IBM Technical Disclosure Bulletin*, 25(11A) (April 1983).

[21] DeWitt, D., Ghandeharizadeh, S., Schneider, D., Bricker, A., Hsiao, H.-I, Rasmussen, R. "The Gamma Database Machine Project," *IEEE Transactions on Knowledge and Data Engineering*, 2(1) (March 1990).

[22] DeLorme, D., Holm, M., Lee, W., Passe, P., Ricard, G., Timms, Jr., G., Youngren, L. "Database Index Journaling for Enhanced Recovery," U.S. Patent 4,819,156, IBM, April 1989.

[23] Dixon, G.N., Parrington, G.D., Shrivastava, S., Wheater, S.M. "The Treatment of Persistent Objects in Arjuna," *The Computer Journal*, 32(4) (1989).

[24] DuBourdieu, D.J. "Implementation of Distributed Transactions," *Proc. 6th Berkeley Workshop on Distributed Data Management and Computer Networks*, May 1982.

[25] Duchamp, D. *Transaction Management*, PhD Thesis, Technical Report CMU-CS-88-192, Carnegie-Mellon University, December 1988.

[26] Effelsberg, W., Haerder, T. "Principles of Database Buffer Management," *ACM Transactions on Database Systems*, 9(4) (December 1984).

[27] Elhardt, K., Bayer, R. "A Database Cache for High Performance and Fast Restart in Database Systems," *ACM Transactions on Database Systems*, 9(4) (December 1984).

[28] Fekete, A., Lynch, N., Merritt, M., Weihl, W. *Commutativity-Based Locking for Nested Transactions*, Technical Report MIT/LCS/TM-370, MIT, July 1989.

[29] Fossum, B. *Database Integrity as Provided for by a Particular database Management System, In database Management*, J.W. Klimbie and K.L. Koffeman (Eds.), North-Holland Publishing Co., 1974.

[30] Gawlick, D., Kinkade, D. "Varieties of Concurrency Control in IMS/VS Fast Path," *IEEE Database Engineering*, 8(2) (June 1985).

[31] Garza, J., Kim, W. "Transaction Management in an Object-Oriented Database System," *Proc. ACM-SIGMOD International Conference on Management of Data*, Chicago, June 1988.

[32] Gheith, A., Schwan, K. "CHAOS:sup/art/: Support for Real-Time Atomic Transactions," *Proc. 19th International Symposium on Fault-Tolerant Computing*, Chicago, June 1989.

[33] Gray, J., McJones, P., Blasgen, M., Lindsay, B., Lorie, R., Price, T., Putzolu, F., Traiger, I. "The Recovery Manager of the System R Database Manager," *ACM Computing Surveys*, 13(2) (June 1981).

[34] Gray, J. *Notes on database Operating Systems, In Operating Systems - An Advanced Course*, R. Bayer, R. Graham, and G. Seegmuller (Eds.), LNCS Volume 60, Springer-Verlag, 1978.

[35] Hadzilacos, V. "A Theory of Reliability in Database Systems," *Journal of the ACM*, 35(1) (January 1988).

[36] Haerder, T. "Handling Hot Spot Data in DB-Sharing Systems," *Information Systems*, 13(2) (1988).

[37] Haderle, D., Jackson, R. "IBM Database 2 Overview," *IBM Systems Journal*, 23(2) (1984).

[38] Haerder, T., Reuter, A. "Principles of Transaction Oriented Database Recovery - A Taxonomy," *Computing Surveys*, 15(4) (December 1983).

[39] Haas, L., Chang, W., Lohman, G., McPherson, J., Wilms, P., Lapis, G., Lindsay, B., Pirahesh, H., Carey, Shekita, E. "Starburst Mid-Flight: As the Dust Clears," *IEEE Transactions on Knowledge and Data Engineering*, 2(1) (March 1990).

[40] Helland, P. *The TMF Application Programming Interface: Program to Program Communication, Transactions, and Concurrency in the Tandem NonStop System*, Tandem Technical Report TR89.3, Tandem Computers, Inc., February 1989.

[41] Herlihy, M., Weihl, W. "Hybrid Concurrency Control for Abstract Data Types," *Proc. 7th ACM SIGACT-SIGMOD-SIGART Symposium on Principles of Database Systems*, Austin, March 1988.

[42] Herlihy, M., Wing, J.M. "Avalon: Language Support for Reliable Distributed Systems," *Proc. 17th International Symposium on Fault-Tolerant Computing*, Pittsburgh, July 1987.

[43] Haskin, R., Malachi, Y., Sawdon, W., Chan, G. "Recovery Management in QuickSilver," *ACM Transactions on Computer Systems*, 6(1) (February 1988).

[44] *IMS/VS Version 1 Release 3 Recovery/Restart*, Document Number GG24-1652, IBM, April 1984.

[45] *IMS/VS Version 2 Application Programming*, Document Number SC26-4178, IBM, March 1986.

[46] *IMS/VS Version 2 Release 1 database Administration Guide*, Document Number SC26-4179, IBM, March 1986.

[47] *IMS/VS Extended Recovery Facility (XRF): Technical Reference*, Document Number GG24-3153, IBM, April 1987.

[48] *IBM Workstation Data Save Facility/VM: General Information*, Document Number GH24-5232, IBM, 1990.

[49] Korth, H. "Locking Primitives in a Database System," *Journal of the ACM*, 30(1) (January 1983).

[50] Lum, V., Dadam, P., Erbe, R., Guenauer, J., Pistor, P., Walch, G., Werner, H., Woodfill, J. "Design of an Integrated DBMS to Support Advanced Applications," *Proc. International Conference on Foundations of Data Organization*, Kyoto, May 1985.

[51] Levine, F., Mohan, C. "Method for Concurrent Record Access, Insertion, Deletion and Alteration Using an Index Tree," United States Patent 4,914,569, IBM, April 1990.

[52] Lewis, R.Z., *IMS Program Isolation Locking*, Document Number GG66-3193, IBM Dallas Systems Center, December 1990.

[53] Lindsay, B., Haas, L., Mohan, C., Wilms, P., Yost, R. "Computation and Communication in R*: A Distributed Database Manager," *ACM Transactions on Computer Systems*, 2(1) (February 1984). Also in *Proc. 9th ACM Symposium on Operating Systems Principles*, Bretton Woods, October 1983.

[54] Lindsay, B., Mohan, C., Pirahesh, H. "Method for Reserving Space Needed for "Rollback" Actions," *IBM Technical Disclosure Bulletin*, 29(6) (November 1986).

[55] Liskov, B., Scheifler, R. "Guardians and Actions: Linguistic Support for Robust, Distributed Programs," *ACM Transactions on Programming Languages and Systems*, 5(3) (July 1983).

[56] Lindsay, B., Selinger, P., Galtieri, C., Gray, J., Lorie, R., Putzolu, F., Traiger, I., Wade, B. *Notes on Distributed Databases*, IBM Research Report RJ2571, San Jose, July 1979.

[57] Mohan, C., Britton, K., Citron, A., Samaras, G. "Generalized Presumed Abort: Marrying Presumed Abort and SNA's LU 6.2 Commit Protocols," *IBM Research Report*, IBM Almaden Research Center, November 1991.

[58] McGee, W.C. "The Information Management System IMS/VS - Part II: database Facilities; Part V: Transaction Processing Facilities," *IBM Systems Journal*, 16(2) (1977).

[59] Mohan, C., Haderle, D., Wang, Y., Cheng, J. Single Table Access Using Multiple Indexes: Optimization, Execution, and Concurrency Control Techniques, *Proc. International Conference on Extending database Technology*, Venice, March 1990. An expanded version of this chapter is available as *IBM Research Report* RJ7341, IBM Almaden Research Center, March 1990.

[60] Mohan, C., Fussell, D., Silberschatz, A. Compatibility and Commutativity of Lock Modes, *Information and Control*, Volume 61, Number 1, April 1984. Also available as *IBM Research Report* RJ3948, San Jose, July 1983.

[61] Moss, E., Griffeth, N., Graham, M. Abstraction in Recovery Management, *Proc. ACM SIGMOD International Conference on Management of Data*, Washington, D.C., May 1986.

[62] Mohan, C. ARIES/KVL: A Key-Value Locking Method for Concurrency Control of Multiaction Transactions Operating on B-Tree Indexes, *Proc. 16th International Conference on Very Large databases*, Brisbane, August 1990. Another version of this chapter is available as *IBM Research Report* RJ7008, IBM Almaden Research Center, September 1989.

[63] Mohan, C. Commit_LSN: A Novel and Simple Method for Reducing Locking and Latching in Transaction Processing Systems, *Proc. 16th International Conference on Very Large databases*, Brisbane, August 1990. Also available as *IBM Research Report* RJ7344, IBM Almaden Research Center, February 1990.

[64] Mohan, C. ARIES/LHS: A Concurrency Control and Recovery Method Using Write-Ahead Logging for Linear Hashing with Separators, *IBM Research Report*, IBM Almaden Research Center, November 1990.

[65] Mohan, C. A Cost-Effective Method for Providing Improved Data Availability During DBMS Restart Recovery After a Failure, *Proc. 4th International Workshop on High Performance Transaction Systems*, Asilomar, September 1991. Also available as *IBM Research Report* RJ8114, IBM Almaden Research Center, May 1991.

[66] Moss, E., Leban, B., Chrysanthis, P. Fine Grained Concurrency for the Database Cache, *Proc. 3rd IEEE International Conference on Data Engineering*, Los Angeles, February 1987.

[67] Mohan, C., Levine, F. ARIES/IM: An Efficient and High Concurrency Index Management Method Using Write-Ahead Logging, To appear in *Proc. ACM SIGMOD International Conference on Management of Data*, San Diego, June 1992. A longer version of this chapter is available as *IBM Research Report* RJ6846, IBM Almaden Research Center, August 1989.

[68] Mohan, C., Lindsay, B. Efficient Commit Protocols for the Tree of Processes Model of Distributed Transactions, *Proc. 2nd ACM SIGACT/SIGOPS Symposium on Principles of Distributed Computing*, Montreal, Canada, August 1983. Also available as *IBM Research Report* RJ3881, IBM San Jose Research Laboratory, June 1983.

[69] Mohan, C., Lindsay, B., Obermarck, R. Transaction Management in the R* Distributed database Management System, *ACM Transactions on Database Systems*, (11(4, December 1986.

[70] Mohan, C., Narang, I. Efficient Locking and Caching of Data in the Multisystem Shared Disks Transaction Environment, *IBM Research Report* RJ8301, IBM Almaden Research Center, August 1991. To appear in *Proc. International Conference on Extending Data Base Technology*, Vienna, March 1992.

[71] Mohan, C., Narang, I. Recovery and Coherency-Control Protocols for Fast Intersystem Page Transfer and Fine-Granularity Locking in a Shared Disks Transaction Environment, *Proc. 17th International Conference on Very Large databases*, Barcelona, September 1991. A longer version is available as *IBM Research Report* RJ8017, IBM Almaden Research Center, March 1991.

[72] Mohan, C., Narang, I. database Recovery in Shared Disks and Client-Server Architectures, To appear in *Proc. 12th International Conference on Distribute Computing Systems*, Yokohama, June 1992.

[73] Mohan, C., Narang, I., Palmer, J. A Case Study of Problems in Migrating to Distributed Computing: Page Recovery Using Multiple Logs in the Shared Disks Environment, *IBM Research Report* RJ7343, IBM Almaden Research Center, March 1990.

[74] Mohan, C., Narang, I., Silen, S. Solutions to Hot Spot Problems in a Shared Disks Transaction Environment, *Proc. 4th International Workshop on High Performance Transaction Systems*, Asilomar, September 1991. Also available as *IBM Research Report* RJ8281, IBM Almaden Research Center, August 1991.

[75] Mohan, C., Pirahesh, H. ARIES-RRH: Restricted Repeating of History in the ARIES Transaction Recovery Method, *Proc. 7th International Conference on Data Engineering*, Kobe, April 1991. Also available as *IBM Research Report* RJ7342, IBM Almaden Research Center, February 1990.

[76] Mohan, C., Rothermel, K. Recovery Protocol for Nested Transactions Using Write-Ahead Logging, *IBM Technical Disclosure Bulletin*, (31(4, September 1988.

[77] Moss, E. Checkpoint and Restart in Distributed Transaction Systems, *Proc. 3rd Symposium on Reliability in Distributed Software and Database Systems*, Clearwater Beach, October 1983.

[78] Moss, E. Log-Based Recovery for Nested Transactions, *Proc. 13th International Conference on Very Large databases*, Brighton, September 1987.

[79] Mohan, C., Treiber, K., Obermarck, R. Algorithms for the Management of Remote Backup databases for Disaster Recovery, *IBM Research Report* RJ7885, IBM Almaden Research Center, November 1990.

[80] Nett, E., Kaiser, J., Kroger, R. Providing Recoverability in a Transaction Oriented Distributed Operating System, *Proc. 6th International Conference on Distributed Computing Systems*, Cambridge, May 1986.

[81] Noe, J., Kaiser, J., Kroger, R., Nett, E. The Commit/Abort Problem in Type-Specific Locking, *GMD Technical Report* 267, GMD mbH, Sankt Augustin, September 1987.

[82] Obermarck, R. IMS/VS Program Isolation Feature, *IBM Research Report* RJ2879, San Jose, July 1980.

[83] O'Neil, P. The Escrow Transaction Method, *ACM Transactions on Database Systems*, (11(4, December 1986.

[84] Ong, K. SYNAPSE Approach to Database Recovery, *Proc. 3rd ACM SIGACT-SIGMOD Symposium on Principles of Database Systems*, Waterloo, April 1984.

[85] Peinl, P., Reuter, A., Sammer, H. High Contention in a Stock Trading Database: A Case Study, *ACM SIGMOD International Conference on Management of Data*, Chicago, June 1988.

[86] Peterson, R.J., Strickland, J.P. Log Write-Ahead Protocols and IMS/VS Logging, *Proc. 2nd ACM SIGACT-SIGMOD Symposium on Principles of Database Systems*, Atlanta, March 1983.

[87] Rengarajan, T.K., Spiro, P., Wright, W. High Availability Mechanisms of VAX DBMS Software,

[88] Reuter, A. A Fast Transaction-Oriented Logging Scheme for UNDO Recovery, *IEEE Transactions on Software Engineering*, (SE-6(4, July 1980.

[89] Reuter, A. Concurrency on High-Traffic Data Elements, *Proc. ACM SIGACT-SIGMOD Symposium on Principles of Database Systems*, Los Angeles, March 1982.

[90] Reuter, A. Performance Analysis of Recovery Techniques, *ACM Transactions on Database Systems*, (9(4, p526-559, December 1984.

[91] Rothermel, K., Mohan, C. ARIES/NT: A Recovery Method Based on Write-Ahead Logging for Nested Transactions, *Proc. 15th International Conference on Very Large databases*, Amsterdam, August 1989. A longer version of this chapter is available as *IBM Research Report* RJ6650, IBM Almaden Research Center, January 1989.

[92] Rowe, L., Stonebraker, M. (Ed.) The Commercial INGRES Epilogue, Chapter 3 in *The INGRES Papers*, Stonebraker, M. (Ed.), Addison-Wesley Publishing Company, Inc., 1986.

[93] Schwarz, P., Chang, W., Freytag, J., Lohman, G., McPherson, J., Mohan, C., Pirahesh, H. Extensibility in the Starburst Database System, *Proc. Workshop on Object-Oriented database Systems*, Asilomar, September 1986. Also available as *IBM Research Report* RJ5311, San Jose, September 1986.

[94] Schwarz, P. Transactions on Typed Objects, PhD Thesis, Technical Report CMU-CS-84-166, Carnegie-Mellon University, December 1984.

[95] Shasha, D., Goodman, N. Concurrent Search Structure Algorithms, *ACM Transactions on Database Systems*, (13(1, March 1988.

[96] Shekita, E., Zwilling, M. Cricket: A Mapped, Persistent Object Store, *Proc. 4th International Workshop on Persistent Object Systems*, Martha's Vineyard, September 1990, Morgan Kaufmann Publishers, Inc.

[97] Spector, A. Open, Distributed Transaction Processing with Encia *Proc. 4th International Workshop on High Performance Transaction Systems*, Asilomar, September 1991.

[98] Spector, A., Pausch, R., Bruell, G. Camelot: A Flexible, Distributed Transaction Processing System, *Proc. IEEE Compcon Spring '88*, San Francisco, March 1988.

[99] Spratt, L. The Transaction Resolution Journal: Extending the Before Journal, *ACM Operating Systems Review*, (19(3, July 1985.

[100] Stonebraker, M. The Design of the POSTGRES Storage System, *Proc. 13th International Conference on Very Large databases*, Brighton, September 1987.

[101] Stillwell, J.W., Rader, P.M. IMS/VS Version 1 Release 3 Fast Path Notebook, *Document Number G320-0149-0*, IBM, September 1984.

[102] Strickland, J., Uhrowczik, P., Watts, V. IMS/VS: An Evolving System, *IBM Systems Journal*, (21(4, 1982.

[103] The Tandem Database Group NonStop SQL: A Distributed, High-Performance, High-Availability Implementation of SQL, In *Lecture Notes in Computer Science*, (359, D. Gawlick, M. Haynie, A. Reuter (Eds.), Springer-Verlag, 1989.

[104] Teng, J., Gumaer, R. Managing IBM Database 2 Buffers to Maximize Performance, *IBM Systems Journal*, (23(2, 1984.

[105] Traiger, I. Virtual Memory Management for database Systems, *ACM Operating Systems Review*, (16(4, p26-48, October 1982.

[106] Vural, S., Dogac, A., A Performance Analysis of the ARIES Recovery Method through Simulation, *Proc. 5th International Symposium on Computer and Information Sciences*, Cappadocia, November 1990, pp.53-65.

[107] Vural, S. A Simulation Study for the Performance Analysis of the ARIES Transaction Recovery Method, M. Sc. Thesis, Middle East Technical University, Ankara, February 1990.

[108] Watson, C.T., Aberle, G.F. System/38 Machine database Support, In *IBM System/38 Technical Developments*, Document Number G580-0237, IBM, July 1980.

[109] Weikum, G. Principles and Realisation Strategies of Multi-Level Transaction Management, *ACM Transactions on Database Systems*, (16(1, March 1991.

[110] Weinstein, M., Page, Jr., T., Livezey, B., Popek, G. Transactions and Synchronization in a Distributed Operating System, *Proc. 10th ACM Symposium on Operating Systems Principles*, Orcas Island, December 1985.

Chapter 9

Performance of Recovery Algorithms for Centralized Database Management Systems

Vijay Kumar and Shawn D. Moe

9.1 INTRODUCTION

Database recovery preserves database consistency in the presence of a failure. A database may get corrupted by a *transaction* failure, by a system failure, or by a media failure. The effect of a transaction failure is usually localized to its execution domain (the number of data items it accessed so far), thus the portion of the database needing recovery is identifiable. A system or a media failure may corrupt a subset of the database, but the corrupted portion is not easily identifiable. For this reason, one generally assumes that entire database may be inconsistent and, therefore, must be recovered.

Database recovery is performed with two main operations: *undo* and *redo*. An undo operation removes the effects of a failed transaction from the database and a redo operation preserves the *ACID* (*Atomicity, Consistency, Isolation, and Durability*) [4] properties of transactions, i.e., a redo completes the leftover portion of a transaction commit. Undo and redo operations can be combined to define four different basic recovery algorithms, which are referred to as U-R (undo-redo), NU-R (no undo-redo), U-NR (undo-no redo), and NU-NR (no undo-no redo) [2].

This chapter investigates the relative performance of these four algorithms through simulation. The purpose of this study is (a) to verify the findings of earlier works,

219

and (b) to identify the algorithm that offers the best performance in most of the transaction processing environments. The experiment has investigated the effect of redos, undos, log management, and checkpointing frequency on recovery time (time to complete the entire recovery process). The results show that in most cases, undo-redo and no undo-redo deliver similar recovery performance but better than undo-no redo and no undo-no redo. Recovery times increase with *multiprogramming* level, but generally decrease as the number of *checkpoints* increases. The undo-no redo algorithm results in a greater number of transaction *rollbacks* and thus its recovery time is longer. Its performance increases against undo-redo and no undo-redo as input/output performance improves. Slow input/output performance is also attributed as one of the reasons for relatively poor performance of no undo-no redo algorithm.

A brief survey of earlier works on the performance of recovery algorithms is presented here. In [3], a mathematical model of a transaction-oriented system has been used to study the effect of checkpointing on recovery. A mathematical model is presented in [5], which compares several recovery protocols, but uses overall transaction throughput, as opposed to the length of recovery, as its method of comparison. Recovery performance for special-purpose dedicated algorithms is presented in [6]. In [8], it was reported that a version of the U-R outperformed the U-NR algorithm. In [1], it was shown that a version of the U-NR algorithm outperformed the U-R algorithm. In summary, there is no single work that presents a detailed performance study of these four algorithms and compares their behavior under a variety of failure environments.

9.2 RECOVERY ALGORITHMS

The four recovery algorithms that we have investigated are adopted from [2] and presented here in some pseudo-code. The TM-DM (Transaction Manager-Data Manager) architecture model [2] of database systems has been used to describe the working of these algorithms. The TM in conjunction with a *schedular* is responsible for managing concurrent transactions, and the DM is responsible for implementing the effects of transactions in the database. The Recovery Manager (RM), which is a part of DM, uses various schemes to restore the consistent state of the database after a system failure. It determines whether values from uncommitted transactions can update the database, when to declare a transaction committed, and when transaction modifications are transferred to the stable database. These decisions are made during forward processing of a transaction and have a direct effect on the type of processing that must be performed during database recovery.

A transaction may exist in any of the following states during its execution life: *active*, *abort*, *finished*, and *committed*. A transaction that has sent its requests for a data item to the schedular is regarded as active and remains in an *active list* (AL). A transaction that is unable to remain active because of some error goes to an abort state and enters an *abort list* (AbL). A transaction which has completed all its modifications and has logged its execution history but has not yet installed all its updates into the database is in a finished state. A transaction that has completed all its modifications and has installed them into the database is ready to be committed, and waits in a *commit list* (CL). The DM of a database system interacts frequently with the underlying operating system; interested readers should refer to [2] for detail. The initial value of a data item is identified as $BFIM$ (BeFore IMage) and its new value as $AFIM$ (AFter IMage). A *fetch* operation transfers data from disk to cache and a *flush* moves data from cache to disk. We have used "ckpt" to denote checkpointing and T_i for a transaction.

9.2.1 The U-R Algorithm

The U-R algorithm uses both undo and redo for recovering the database from a failure. An undo is required since the system allows intermediate modifications of a transaction to be installed in the database, and a redo is required because all modifications by committed transactions are in the log but may not be present in the stable database.

If T_i wants to write a new value into data item x then
Begin
    if T_i not in AL, then add it there;
    if x not in the cache then fetch it, and write its BFIM and AFIM to the log;
    overwrite the contents of x by its AFIM in the cache;
End
Else if T_i wants to read x then fetch it in the cache and returns its value to T_i
    Else if T_i wants to commit then
    Begin
        Add T_i to CL;
        {if the system fails before T_i is appended to CL, T_i is not
        committed, regardless of the status of the T_i's modifications to the
        stable database, T_i must be undone. Similarly if a failure occurs
        after T_i is added to CL but before its modifications have
        been transferred to stable storage, T_i must be redone.}
        acknowledge the commit of T_i and delete it from AL
    End
Else if T_i is to be aborted then {this is an undo}
    Begin
        for each x updated by T_i copy its BFIM to the cache;
        add T_i to AbL;
        acknowledge the abortion of T_i and delete it from AL
    end
Else if there is a system failure then {start recovery}
    Begin
        discard all cache slots, fetch log and start backward processing of log;
        if x not in cache then get a cache slot for it and fetch CL;
        if T_i is in CL then copy AFIM of x to a cache slot; {begin redo}

if T_i is in AbL then copy its BFIM of x to cache; {begin undo}
repeat until log records up to the last checkpoint have been processed;
  {this completes the undo and redo operations}
for each T_i in CL, if it is in AL, then remove it from there;
   End;

9.2.2   The U-NR Algorithm

This class of algorithms requires only undo. To accomplish this, all updates of a transaction are forced to the stable database before the transaction commits. The read, write, and abort operations are identical to the U-R case. Only the commit and restore operations are presented here because other steps are similar to U-R.

If a transaction T_i wants to commit then
Begin
    if data item x modified by T_i is in the cache then force a flush;
     {this guarantees that an undo will be performed during recovery}
    add T_i to the commit list;
     {all its modifications have been flushed to the database}
    acknowledge the commitment of T_i and delete it from AL;
End
Else if there is a system failure then
    Begin
        discard all cache slots, fetch log and start backward log processing; {undo}
        if T_i is in CL, then skip this log record
        Else
        Begin
           copy BFIM of x to a cache slot;
           repeat until all log records up to the last ckpt have been processed;
           remove T_i from AL;
        End;
    End;

9.2.3   The NU-R Algorithm

This class of algorithms requires only redo. To achieve this, RM *pins* and *unpins* data in the cache for managing fetch and flush.

If T_i wants to write the new value v into data item x then
Begin
    add T_i to AL and fetch x in the cache if they is not there;
    write BFIM $(=x)$ and AFIM $(=v)$ to the log;
    overwrite x by v in the cache;
    pin the cache slot so that it cannot be flushed and acknowledge write
End
Else if T_i wants to read x then

Begin
    if x is not in the cache then fetch it and return its value to T_i;
End
Else if T_i is ready to commit then
    Begin
        add T_i to CL and for each x modified by T_i unpin its cache slot;
        acknowledge the commitment of T_i and delete it from AL
    End
    Else if T_i fails then {abort T_i}
        Begin
            for each x updated by T_i copy the BFIM of x into x's cache slot;
            unpin the cache slot of x and add T_i to the abort list;
            acknowledge the abortion of T_i and delete it from AL;
        End
    Else if the system fails then {begin recovery}
        Begin
            discard all cache slots and fetch log;
            start backward log processing;
            copy AFIM of x to a cache slot if it is not there;
            repeat until all log records up to the last ckpt are processed;
        End;

9.2.4 The NU-NR Algorithm

This class of algorithms requires neither undo nor redo. To avoid undo, no modifications from a transaction are forced to the stable database before it commits, and to avoid redo, all modifications from a transaction must be in the stable database before it commits. This is achieved by the *shadow* scheme. The location of each data item's last committed value is recorded in a directory maintained on stable storage. When T_i writes x, a new version of x is created in stable storage and the scratch directory is updated to point to this version of x. When T_i commits, the directory that defines the committed database state is updated to point to the versions that T_i wrote. T_i's modifications are added to the stable database, thus committing T_i. Together, these directories point to all of the BFIMs and AFIMs on stable storage; thus a transaction execution log is not necessary.

As indicated earlier, data in cache slots are pinned until the transaction that updated the item is committed or aborted. In this algorithm, writing updates to database may be implemented without pinning cache slots or in some other way. For example, in some implementations, pinning is avoided by using versioning in stable storage. This work, however, did not use a particular implementation technique because the performance of any algorithms may vary with implementation strategies. It, therefore, modeled the operations that were right conceptually.

9.3   CHECKPOINTING

Checkpointing is an activity that *markes* modified data values to be written to
a stable storage database during forward processing to reduce the number of log
records that the recovery operation must examine. Although checkpointing does reduce the amount of log processing, it impedes normal transaction processing since
the database remains unavailable to new transactions during this process. In most
commercial systems, checkpointing and normal transaction processing can go concurrently. This, however, has not been modeled here because the study aims to
investigate the effect of checkpointing on recovery. RM decides at what intervals to
perform checkpointing, which may be measured in time or in terms of the number
of committed transactions since the last checkpoint.

9.4   EXPECTED BEHAVIOR OF RECOVERY ALGORITHMS

The expected behavior of these algorithms is presented in this section and are then
verified by simulation. It is expected that U-R would provide the best overall
forward processing of transactions, while delivering a slower recovery. One of the
main reasons for this seems to be the lack of control of RM over cache. RM does not
direct or force CM to flush the cache. This lack of control allows CM to implement
the most efficient scheme to swap cache pages. The penalty for this freedom appears
during recovery, where both undo and redo operations must be performed; however,
it is expected that a frequent checkpointing may improve its performance.

It is expected that the NU-R algorithm will deliver the best overall recovery
performance. The NU-R algorithm requires only redos. At the time of a system
failure, under normal circumstances, a large number of transactions are likely to be
active, and a much smaller number would be on the commit list. Thus, algorithms
that use undo (U-R, U-NR) should have more transactions requiring undo. The NU-
R algorithm, on the other hand, only has to process the smaller set of transactions
residing on the commit list.

The recovery times required for performing the actual undo and redo operations
for each data item are the same since the work required is similar. Since NU-R
should have fewer transactions to process, the NU-R algorithm should reflect the
best recovery time of the log-based algorithms.

It is expected that with each additional checkpoint the overall recovery time
will reduce since each checkpoint reduces the number of log records that must be
examined during recovery. It is also expected that the recovery time will increases
with MP L. With each higher MPL value there should be more transactions (active,
to be aborted and to be committed) at the time of failure which will increase the
recovery time.

The flexibility of the U-R and NU-R algorithms allow a transaction to become
committed faster than with the U-NR algorithm because there is no need to wait
until the cache is flushed before the data items are unlocked. Locked data items
result in CCM conflicts, which lead to transaction rollbacks and additional records

written to the log. The logs produced by the NU-R algorithm should be very similar in size to those of U-R, because both algorithms allow transactions to commit before waiting for the cache to be flushed. It is assumed that NU-R logs may be slightly larger than U-R because a few more data item conflicts are possible due to the delay necessary to unpin the data items during the commit process.

An algorithm that causes more transactions to be aborted should result in a longer recovery time since aborted transactions create additional entries to be written to the log, whose additional records must be transferred to memory and then examined. For this reason, the flexibility of U-R should produce the smallest number of aborted transactions. Since U-NR keeps data items locked for a longer period of time, should result in the highest number of aborted transactions. The NU-R algorithm should abort a few more transactions than U-R. This is because NU-R is delayed slightly during the commit process in order to unpin the transaction's data items. This delay is minimal and should not result in a significant difference from U-R.

It is expected that decreasing the I/O transfer time shall also decrease the recovery times in all three algorithms. With better I/O performance, the transaction logs should be transferred to memory faster, resulting in better recovery performance.

The NU-NR algorithm saves its master directory on disk, and so must transfer it and any scratch directori es to memory, and then create a new shadow directory. The size of the master directory is likely to be equal to the number of items in the database. With a slow I/O, the directory transfer may take a long time. It is expected that with faster I/O the overall recovery performance of all four algorithms would improve. The relationships between the algorithms' performance, however, should not change dramatically. With the NU-NR algorithm, the directory sizes that must be transferred are constant in size, and thus would not show any relative improvement. The log-based algorithms, on the other hand, will show an improvement in their relative performance.

The NU-NR algorithm seems to suffer performance and resource degradation during forward processing. Several factors contribute to this situation. Access to the stable database is through the directory structure maintained by RM, and thus provides another level of indirection to access data items. The scratch directories, created for each transaction to contain uncommitted versions for each data item, require some management in order to reclaim the space. The most important consideration with this algorithm is the constant fragmentation of the stable database. Since multiple copies of each data item appear in stable storage, it is unlikely that all versions are stored in proximity to each other. Thus, a new stable version of a data item may appear in a much different physical location in stable storage, and may even appear in a different physical storage device from where it was previously stored. A database originally created to occupy contiguous storage for I/O efficiency will eventually fragment all over the available disk storage.

With the previous factors in mind, it can be argued that the performance of a NU-NR will slowly degrade over the life of the database. It is believed that NU-NR would perform better in situations where the percentage of query transactions far outnumbers the update transactions.

U-NR and NU-R algorithms seem very similar since RM exerts control over the timing of CM's activities. During forward processing, CM is instructed when to flush each modified data item and when to unpin cache slots. The action of unpinning cache slots should require less work than flushing; unpinning requires only CPU resources, and flushing requires CPU and I/O resources. If the cache is of sufficient size to eliminate massive contention arising from a large number of slots that are pinned and thus cannot be swapped, the NU-R algorithm arguably can provide better forward processing performance.

The same relationship should exist during a restart as well. In a normal situation, the number of transactions requiring undo should be larger than the number of transactions requiring redo. This situation is assumed because prior to a system failure, the number of active and aborted transactions could outnumber the number of committed transactions, especially at a higher concurrency. The action of undoing or redoing is logically the same. The difference in restart time must then be found in the number of data items to be undone or redone. With this in mind, it is expected that NU-R would perform the restart faster than U-NR.

With checkpointing, U-NR and NU-R could recover faster than U-R. Logically, restart for either U-NR or NU-R should take less than half the time required for U-R, because (at most) only half the work is required. It is assumed that if the frequency of failure is high, the recovery must be very fast in order to compensate for the unavailability of the database to the users.

9.5   SIMULATION MODEL AND PARAMETERS

In this section modeling assumptions and parameters are introduced. The set of assumptions and parameters for the simulation experiment has been kept consistent with earlier studies for a meaningful comparison of the behavior of these algorithms.

It is assumed that the database is a set of data items each of which is a lockable unit. Transaction size (number of data items accessed by a transaction) is exponentially distributed around a mean and the selection of data items is uniformly distributed. The model depicts a closed system where predetermined number of transactions are created and processed after some predefined delay. If a transaction aborts, the same transaction is submitted for processing after a delay of an average response time. *WAL (write ahead logging)* [4] has been used for managing the log. The model uses a strict two-phase locking policy for managing concurrent transactions. In Table 9.1, some of the important parameters are listed with their meaning.

The transaction log is implemented as a sequential list of log records. Each log record contains the transaction's identifier, data item identifier, location of the log record (memory or disk), type of log record (read, write, commit, etc.), BFIM, AFIM, and pointers to link the log records for one transaction together.

Table 9.1. Simulation Parameters and Their Meaning.

Name	Meaning
DatabaseSize	Number of data items in the database
NumTrans	Number of transactions in the transaction set
NumItems	Average transaction size
WriteReadPct	Percentage write transactions
MinimumTransactionSize	Number of items a transaction accesses

9.5.1 Failure Criteria

To investigate the effect of database failure on recovery, it is simulated using the following criteria.

ActiveBased: failure occurs once the number of active transactions is greater or equal to the supplied threshold value.

CommitBased: failure occurs once the number of committed transactions is greater or equal to the supplied threshold value.

TimeBased: failure occurs once the elapsed simulation time surpasses the threshold value.

TransBased: failure occurs once the number of transactions launched surpasses the threshold value.

CPFullMPL: failure occurs after the first checkpoint is completed and the number of active transactions is equal to the MPL. This criterion was established to always ensure a fully loaded system at the time of failure.

The criteria to flush the log for (U-R, NU-R and U-NR) are also determined by ActiveBased, CommitBased, TimeBased and TransBased, as described before. The time to checkpoint the log is also determined using these same criteria. For added flexibility, the models contain a flag that identifies whether the transaction log-flushing criteria is described for the model. If the flag indicates no criteria, the log is flushed immediately. Otherwise, the criteria are checked to see whether to flush the log. In addition to the log-flush flag, the model allows various types of checkpoint criteria. These criteria are used to determine what values determine whether the checkpoint threshold has been met. The models for the log-based algorithms assume that a commit consistent checkpointing scheme is used to perform checkpointing at the appropriate time.

9.5.2   Common Forward Processing

Since the forward processing of transactions under a recovery scheme shares considerable functionality, it is useful to follow a common transaction scheme. Therefore, first, the set of common features is explained and then specifics of forward processing for each recovery schemes are identified.

The main simulation process adds transactions to the active list, each after waiting a length of time, which is set to a random derivate drawn from an exponential distribution with a mean of the ThinkTime (see Section 9.6.) parameter. The main process is also responsible for determining if the system failure, log-flushing, or checkpoint criteria have been met, and then initiating those actions.

The processing of an active transaction includes obtaining the lock on the data item and its manipulation. For simulation purposes, some delays were introduced in the data manipulation in order to keep a transaction active for a period of time. This is necessary to eventually capture active transactions at the time of system failure. In U-R, U-NR and NU-R, the log record is created to reflect the data item modification. After all data items are acquired and modified, the transaction prepares to commit. The commit process is unique for each algorithm and will be described with the algorithm specific information.

Transaction rollback is performed by releasing data items and updating the lock table. The release of each data item expends simulation time, which simulates the Cache Manager (CM) processing to determine if the slot needs to be flushed to stable storage. To simulate a realistic CM, a random number of the held items are determined that require flushing to stable storage and thus expend additional simulation time. An abort record is written to the transaction log after all of the items have been processed. The transaction is removed from the active list and added to the abort list. The aborted transaction is delayed a random length of time and then it joins the set of transactions available for processing at the head of the list. This delay is necessary in order to keep the transaction from repeatedly conflicting with the same transaction.

For U-R, NU-R, and U-NR, the time to flush the transaction log is also determined by the main simulation process. A FlushCheck flag system parameter determines whether the threshold criteria should be checked to determine if the flush should occur. If the FlushCheck flag is false, the flush will always occur. If the flag is true, the threshold criteria are checked against the various simulation counters. The criteria ActiveBased, CommitBased, TimeBased, and TransBased as described earlier are also used to describe the log-flush criteria. The time to checkpoint the transaction log is also determined using these same criteria definitions.

Commit-consistent checkpointing is implemented in the main simulation process, once the checkpoint threshold has been met, by suspending the release of new transactions to the active list and waiting until all of the currently processing transactions to terminate normally either though commit or rollback. Once all of the transaction activity has completed, a checkpoint record is appended to the transaction log, and the transaction suspension is removed, thus allowing the active list to fill from the transactions available for processing. Normal processing then resumes.

Specifics of the U-R Model

Transaction commit in the Undo/Redo model is performed once all of the data items have been manipulated. Query transactions are not committed; they are just marked as completed. The action of committing an update transaction is accomplished by writing a commit record to the transaction log, and marking the transaction as "Committing". As the recovery algorithm goes, the transaction is technically committed at this point, but for the simulation, it is necessary to identify which transactions still have modifications contained in the cache. During the committing state, the CM is assumed to be flushing the modifications to stable storage. Since the CM is not directed to flush the cache in U-R, the transaction stays in this state until a predetermined minimal amount of simulation time elapses. After this period, it is assumed that CM has flushed the modifications to stable storage, and no undo or redo will ever be required for this transaction and the transaction's effects become durable.

Specifics of the U-NR Model

Each data item is forced to disk, and the item is unlocked. Once all of the data items have been processed, the commit record is written to the log and the transaction state is marked committed. This model does not use the committing state because CM does flush the cache as part of the normal course of events. As with U-R, transactions that are committed require no redo.

Specifics of the NU-R Model

Transaction commit with NU-R is also similar to the U-R implementation. A commit record is appended to the log and the transaction is marked as committing while the data items are processed. Each data item is unlocked, and the data item is unpinned. As with U-R, the transaction is marked as committing until enough simulation time has elapsed for the cache slots to have been flushed to stable storage. At that time, the transaction state is changed to committed, which identifies the transaction as one in which redo operations are not required.

Specifics of the NU-NR Model

The implementation of the NU-NR model differs from the other models because it does not rely on a transaction log.

9.5.3   Common Recovery Processing Features

Database recovery is initiated after a system failure. For U-R, NU-R, and U-NR, the general recovery process first simulates transferring the transaction log to memory. The log is then scanned from the last record until the first (last occurred) checkpoint record is found. Each log record is then a candidate for undo or redo based on the particular recovery algorithm. Once all of the log records are processed, the log is flushed to stable storage, and the recovery process is terminated.

In recovery, the activities of undoing and redoing individual data items are common between the three log-based algorithms. In real computer systems, the underlying operating systems "know" which cache slots have been flushed to stable storage. These items do not need to be undone or redone. This knowledge of which slots have been flushed must also be simulated in the model to achieve realistic results. It is not desirable to redo all the effects of a committed transaction when in fact all of the modifications have been flushed to stable storage. In our simulation, the recovery process accomplishes this by randomly determining a number of data items for each transaction that must be undone or redone for those transactions that have recently committed or aborted.

The action of undoing a data item first determines if the action should be performed on the particular data item using the logic described earlier. If the undo should proceed, the BFIM, which was part of the log record, is written to the cache, the update is forced to stable storage, and the data item is unlocked. The redo operation is performed in a similar manner. It must be first determined if the redo should take place at all. If so, the AFIM, which is part of the log record, is written to the cache, and the update is forced to stable storage.

The NU-NRCommitList is a mechanism that ensures only one transaction committing at a time. The master bit is implemented as a global storage location that contains the identifier for one of the two primary directories. The current and shadow directories are implemented as direct access structures each constrained at DatabaseSize items. Recovery using this model is accomplished by first retrieving the master directory bit and then transferring the current and scratch directories contents to memory. A new shadow directory is allocated, and then each item is copied from the current directory to the new shadow directory. Each scratch directory is then traversed, unlocking any data items found. The new current and shadow directories are then forced to stable storage. The recovery is then completed.

9.5.4　Simulation Models

This section presents the simulation model for all recovery algorithms and describes the flow of transactions through it. This description is useful for simulation purposes and complements recovery algorithms given earlier. Some repetition of information in presenting the flow of transaction through these models has been deliberately introduced for improving the description of the approach taken here. The entire simulation is divided into two parts: forward processing of transactions and database recovery from a system failure. The forward processing of transactions is explained first followed by the recovery model.

Forward Processing in U-R

Figure 9.1 presents the forward processing model of the U-R algorithm.

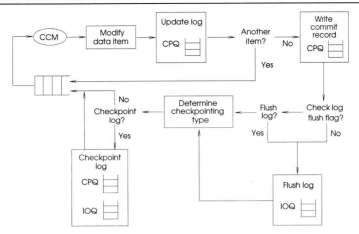

Figure 9.1. U-R model (forward transaction processing).

1. Select a transaction from the head of the the Active List

2. For each data item in the transaction:

    (a) Get an exclusive lock on the data item.

    (b) Process the data item (i.e., write AFIM to the cache slot).

    (c) Update the log record of this transaction.

3. Once all the data items are modified, write a Commit record in the log.

4. If the log-flush flag is to be checked, check it; otherwise, flush the log to stable storage.

5. If the log-flush flag is checked and the conditions are met to flush the log, flush the transaction log to stable storage.

6. Determine the type of checkpoint criteria. If the checkpoint threshold has been met, then perform a checkpoint.

7. End of transaction.

Recovery in U-R. Figure 9.2 presents the recovery model of the U-R algorithm.

1. Transfer the transaction log from stable storage to memory.

2. If the system recovery is not complete, then read the last log record.

3. If the transaction that wrote the log record is in the commit list, then find the AFIM in the log and redo the modification by writing it to the cache or else locate the BFIM in the log and undo the modification by writing it to the cache.

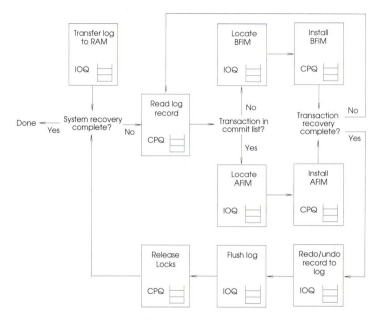

Figure 9.2. Recovery model for the U-R algorithm.

4. If the transaction recovery that wrote the log record is not complete, then read the next log record and repeat step 3.

5. At the end of transaction, write an undone or redone (as applicable) record to the transaction log.

6. Flush the transaction log to stable storage.

7. Release locks on the data items held by the transaction.

8. End of transaction recovery.

Forward Processing in U-NR.   Figure 9.3 presents forward processing in the U-NR model.

1. Select a transaction from the head of the Active List.

2. For each data item in the transaction:

    (a) Get an exclusive lock on the data item.

    (b) Process it (i.e., write AFIM to the cache slot).

    (c) Update the log record of this transaction.

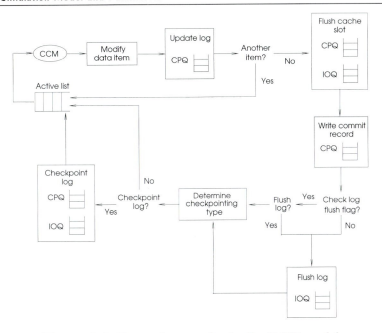

Figure 9.3. Forward processing in the U-NR model.

3. Once all the data items for the transaction are modified, direct the CM to flush the cache slots containing the transaction's modifications.

4. Write a Commit record to the transaction log.

5. If the log-flush flag is to be checked, check it, otherwise, flush the log to stable storage.

6. If the log-flush flag is set and the conditions are met to flush the log, then flush it to stable storage.

7. Determine the type of checkpoint criteria. If the checkpoint threshold is met, then perform a checkpoint.

8. End of transaction.

Recovery in U-NR.   Figure 9.4 presents recovery in the U-NR model.

1. Transfer the log from stable storage to memory.

2. If system recovery is not complete, then read the last log record.

3. If the transaction that wrote the log record is in the commit list then remove the transaction from the active list if it is there. Read the next log record and repeat step 3. Otherwise, locate the BFIM in the log and undo the modification by writing the BFIM to the cache.

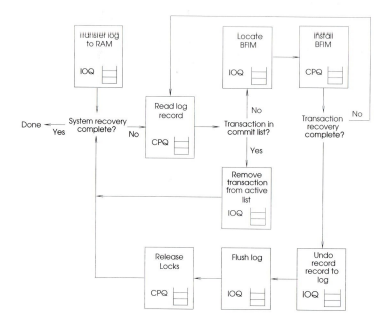

Figure 9.4. Recovery in the U-NR model.

4. If the recovery for the transaction that wrote the log record is not complete, then read the next log record and repeat step 3.

5. At the end of transaction recovery, write an undone record to the log.

6. Flush the transaction log to stable storage and release locks on data items.

7. End of transaction.

Forward Processing in NU-R.   Figure 9.5 presents forward processing in NU-R Model.

1. Select a transaction from the head of the Active List.

2. For each data item in the transaction:

   (a) Get an exclusive lock on the data item.

   (b) Process it (i.e., write AFIM to the cache slot defined for the data item.

   (c) Pin the cache slot so that it cannot be flushed prematurely.

   (d) Update the log

3. Once all data items are modified, then write a commit record in the log.

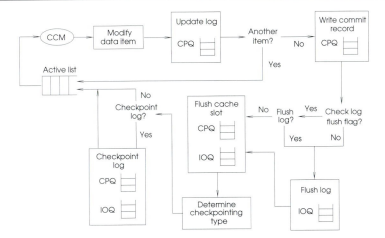

Figure 9.5. Forward processing in the NU-R model.

4. If the log-flush flag is to be checked, check it. Otherwise, flush the transaction log to stable storage.

5. If the log-flush flag is checked and the conditions are met to flush the log, flush the transaction log to stable storage.

6. Unpin the cache slots containing the modifications made by the transaction, thus allowing CM to flush the slots.

7. Determine the type of checkpoint criteria and if the checkpoint is met, then perform a checkpoint.

8. End of transaction.

Recovery in NU-R.   Figure 9.6 describes recovery in the NU-R model.

1. Transfer the log from stable storage to memory.

2. If the system recovery is not complete, then read the last log record.

3. If the transaction that wrote the log record is not in the commit list, then remove the transaction from the active list if it is there. Read the next log record and repeat step 3. Otherwise, locate the AFIM in the log and redo by writing the AFIM to the cache.

4. If the recovery for the transaction that wrote the log record is not complete, then read the next log record and repeat step 3.

5. Since the recovery for the particular transaction is complete, write a redone record to the log.

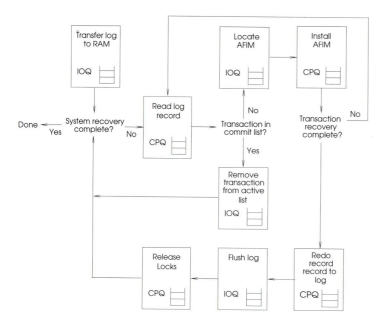

Figure 9.6. Recovery in the NU-R model.

6. Flush the log to disk and release locks on data items.

7. End of transaction.

Forward Processing in the NU-NR: Figure 9.7 describes forward processing in the NU-NR model.

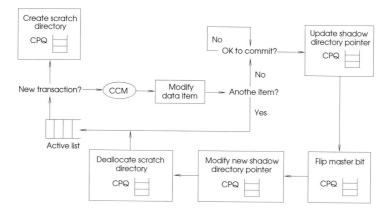

Figure 9.7. Forward processing in the NU-NR model.

1. Select a transaction from the head of the Active List.

2. Create a scratch directory in memory for data items modified by the transaction.

3. For each data item in the transaction, get an exclusive lock on the data item and modify it (i.e., write the AFIM to the scratch directory created for the transaction).

4. Once all data items are modified, determine if another transaction is in the process of committing. Only one transaction may commit at a time. Transactions desiring to commit when another is in the commit phase are queued in a first-in-first-out (FIFO) basis until the next transaction can commit.

5. If it can commit, then identify the current and shadow directories. Update the shadow directory with the contents of the transaction's scratch directory.

6. Flip the master directory bit, thus committing the transaction The master bit is stored in stable storage at a known location (fixed address). This allows the RM to "know" where to find the information describing the master directory. The master bit information must also be forced to stable storage.

7. Modify the new shadow directory pointers to reflect the changes made in the transaction's scratch directory.

8. Deallocate the transaction's scratch directory

9. End of transaction.

Recovery in the NU-NR. Figure 9.8 illustrates recovery in the NU-NR model.

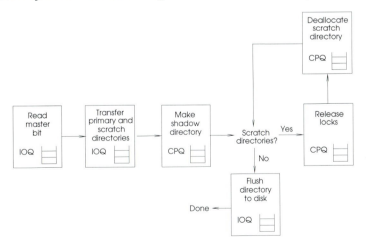

Figure 9.8. Recovery in the NU-NR model.

1. Locate the Master Directory Bit at the fixed location in stable storage.

2. Transfer the directory described by the master bit and any scratch directories from stable storage to memory.

3. Create a new shadow directory by duplicating the current master directory to a new directory structure.

4. For (any) scratch directories retrieved, release locks held by transactions creating the scratch directory and deallocate the scratch directory.

5. Flush the new master and shadow directories to stable storage.

6. Transaction recovery is complete

9.6   SIMULATION RESULTS AND DISCUSSION

The basis of the performance comparison for each of the experiments is total recovery time from a random system failure. The total recovery time is the time spent in the actual database recovery and not the time expended in forward processing for the purposes of an eventual recovery. These values are measured in time units, which can represent milliseconds if desired.

Three parameters–multiprogramming level (MPL), checkpoint threshold, and failure threshold–were selected for this series of experiments. The upper and lower threshold values for each of these parameters were chosen. The constant values used for establishing the recovery time were initially set and then modified with successive runs of the model. Table 9.2 presents the parameter values and the timing constants used.

Experiment 1: The effect of checkpoints on the recovery time

The experiment is conducted by processing a set of transactions against U-R, NU-R, and U-NR models. For each model, separate simulation runs are conducted while varying the MPL values. For each model and MPL value, the transaction log is checkpointed various times before the system failure is encountered. Since MPL is defined as the number of concurrently executing transactions, it is desired to show the differences between MPL values by making the number of active transactions equal to the MPL at the time of the failure. This ensured that the maximum number of transactions are active with respect to the MPL, and thus more transactions are susceptible to recovery processing as the MPL increases. Number of Checkpoints ranges from 0 to 5. In order to have the desired number of checkpoints occur using *Commit Based* checkpoint criteria, it is necessary to determine the number of committed transactions that must occur between checkpoints. Table 9.3 shows the Checkpoint Thresholds for each of the MPL values that is used to ensure the desired number of checkpoints occur before the Failure Threshold is reached. For the higher MPL values, the threshold values must be reduced in order to secure the

Table 9.2. Simulation Parameters and Their Values

Parameter	Description	Value
Checkpoint Criteria	To initiate a checkpoint	CommitBased
Checkpoint Threshold	Time for a checkpoint	Dynamic
MPL	Transaction workload	25 to 150
Failure Criteria	To initiate a failure	CommitBased
Failure Threshold	Time for a failure	1000
Average Think Time	Average transaction delay	10-(exponential)
Database Size	No. of items in the database	10000
No. of Transactions	No. of transactions processed	5000
Transaction Size	No. of items per transaction	15-(exponential)
W/R Percentage	Percentage of write:read	100% (write only)
Flush Criteria	Log flushing criteria	CommitBased
Flush Threshold	Log flush point	1
Lock Time	Time to lock a data item	25
Unlock Time	Time to unlock a data item	10
Rollback Delay	Mean restart delay	100 - (exponential)
Flush Delay	Time to flush a cache slot	1000 - (exponential)
I/O Transfer Time	I/O time for an item	25
Log Access Time	Time to access the log	2
Log Update Time	Time to update the log	5
Undo/Redo Time	Time to update a cache slot	2

desired number of checkpoints. The failure is introduced after 1000 transactions have committed.

Figures 9.9 through 9.14 show that the recovery times increase with MPL for different number of checkpoints. This relationship holds for all three of the algorithms at all levels of checkpointing. Since it was desired for the active count to be equal to the MPL at the time of failure, each higher MPL has more transactions to recover than the immediately preceding (smaller) MPL. A greater number of transactions to be recovered results in greater recovery time. The results also show that first recovery time reduces with number of checkpoints and then it begins to increase (Figures 9.15 through 9.20; UR-25 means UR with MPL of 25).

The best recovery times were delivered where three equally distributed checkpoints (at 1000 commits) were performed before the failure is introduced. A possible explanation is that four and five checkpoints do not increase the recovery performance. Checkpointing tends to increase the size of the transaction log. With the simulation time value for I/O transfers of 25 units, the time spent transferring the larger log from disk may outweigh the savings of processing (undoing and redoing)

Table 9.3. Checkpointing Thresholds

MPL	1 CP	2 CP	3 CP	4 CP	5 CP
25	500	333	250	200	160
50	500	333	250	200	150
50	500	333	250	180	120
100	500	333	250	160	120
125	500	333	200	150	100
150	500	333	200	120	80

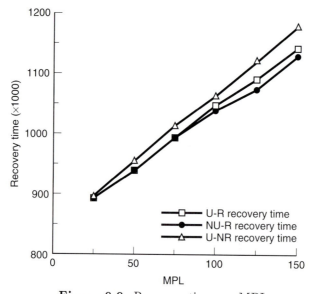

Figure 9.9. Recovery time vs. MPL.

a smaller number of data items.

This log-size differential assumption can explain why the NU-R and the U-R performance is so similar when the number of transactions that must be recovered with U-R exceeds that of NU-R. In this experiment, all three of the algorithms record both BFIMs and AFIMs in the log, so this fact should have no bearing on the overall log sizes. In order to explain the results, the U-R logs must be smaller than the NU-R logs, and thus are transferred to memory faster. Once transferred, however, U-R must recover more transactions, performing both undo and redo operations, than NU-R, which only performs redo operations. The overall effect is that these two stages of the recovery operation (log transfer and transaction

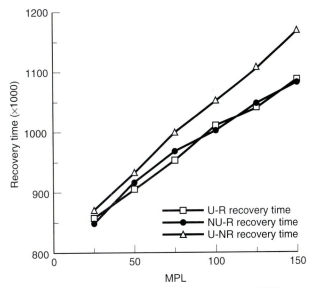

Figure 9.10. Recovery time vs. MPL.

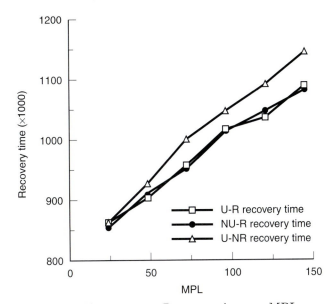

Figure 9.11. Recovery time vs. MPL.

recovery) balance each other with respect to recovery time. Another experiment deals with the size of the transaction log and its effect on recovery times.

The results for U-R and NU-R are very similar for all levels of checkpointing. These two algorithms consistently produce the lowest recovery times. In all situ-

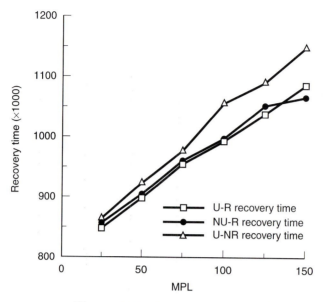

Figure 9.12. Recovery time vs. MPL.

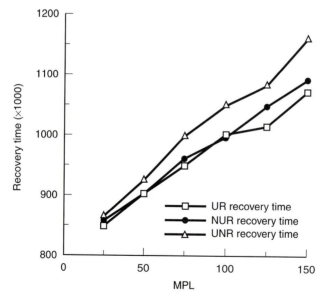

Figure 9.13. Recovery time vs. MPL.

ations, the U-NR recovery times are the longest. At MPL 100 (Figure 9.18), for example, the NU-R algorithm delivers the best performance at checkpoint levels of 0, 1, 2, and 4 checkpoints. The U-R algorithm delivers the best recovery time at

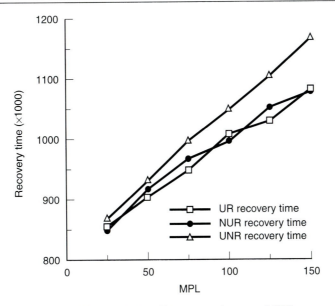

Figure 9.14. Recovery time vs. MPL.

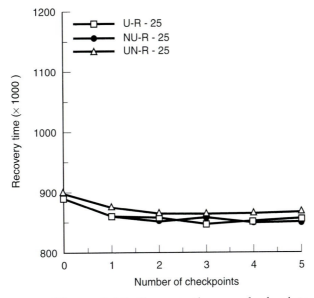

Figure 9.15. Recovery time vs. checkpoints.

the 3 and 5 checkpoint levels. The recovery times for the U-NR algorithm range from 2.5% to 6.2% longer than the other two algorithms at MPL 100.

The gap between the U-NR recovery times and those of the other algorithms

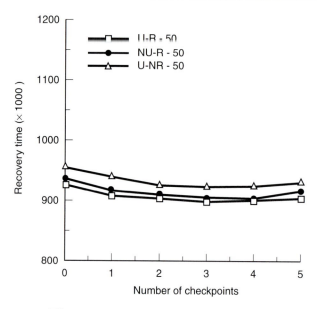

Figure 9.16. Recovery time vs. checkpoints.

appears to widen at the highest MPL values and at the highest level of checkpointing. For example, at MPL 25 (Figure 9.15), U-NR ranges from 0.7% to 2.2% longer recovery times, while at MPL 150 (Figure 9.20), U-NR ranges from 4.3% to 8.2% longer recovery times. It can be assumed that this trend would continue as the MPL or level of checkpointing increases.

The rate of growth in the U-R recovery times appears to slow between MPL values of 100 and 125 for all levels of checkpointing. Perhaps this is the "optimum" MPL for this algorithm given the other constraints of the experiment. A possible explanation as to the reason for the comparatively poor U-NR recovery times may lie in the behavior of the algorithm, and, as described before, the length of time required to transfer the log from disk to memory. The U-NR algorithm keeps data items locked for a longer period of time than U-R or NU-R. A greater number of CCM conflicts will occur when data items are locked for a greater length of time. A larger number of rolled-back transactions is the result of the CCM conflicts. Rolled-back transactions must update the transaction log, thus increasing its size. With the rather high I/O transfer time in the experiment, the cost of transferring the larger logs could possibly cancel the benefits of processing a smaller number of data items as defined in the U-NR and NU-R algorithms. Another experiment will deal with the time required to transfer the log from disk and its effect on the performance of the models.

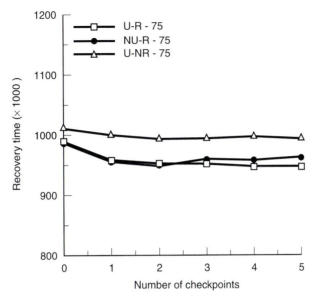

Figure 9.17. Recovery time vs. checkpoints.

Experiment 2: Relationship between log size and recovery time

The intent of this experiment is to determine if there is a relationship between log size and recovery time. In the previous experiment, it was speculated that the U-NR algorithm created a larger transaction log because it keeps data items locked for a longer period of time, resulting in a greater number of aborted transactions. Larger logs, it was argued, in a system with a very slow I/O transfer time could have an impact on recovery time. This experiment will attempt to validate the assumption.

The experiment is conducted using the setup of Experiment 1, with the additions of measuring the size of the transaction log at the time of failure and counting the number of records that are examined upon recovery. To simplify the experiment, it is conducted keeping the MPL constant at 100. This is a median value, and from the results of Experiment 1, should be able to correctly represent the model in the experiment. Table 9.3 describes the Checkpoint Thresholds used in the experiment. The thresholds found in the MPL = 100 row are used in the experiment and the failure threshold and criteria were the same as in Experiment 1.

Results and Interpretation

The total log sizes are presented in Figure 9.21 and the number of log records processed is shown in Figure 9.22. Figure 9.21 indicates that the log sizes increase as the number of checkpoints increases. The logs produced by the U-NR algorithm range from 3.2% to 7.5% larger than those of U-R or NU-R. U-R and NU-R logs are very similar in size at all levels of checkpointing. Figure 9.22 shows that, as

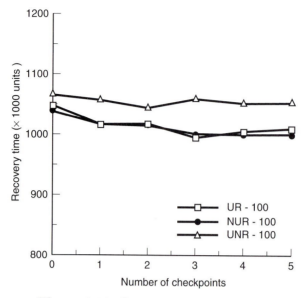

Figure 9.18. Recovery time vs. checkpoints.

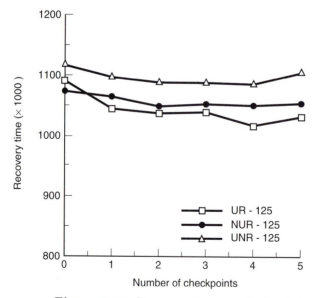

Figure 9.19. Recovery time vs. checkpoints.

expected, the number of log records to be processed decreases as the number of checkpoints increases. Because of the scale of the graph and the fact that the U-R and NU-R results are so similar, only one set of points can be observed. U-R and NU-R consistently have a smaller number of log records to process, except in the

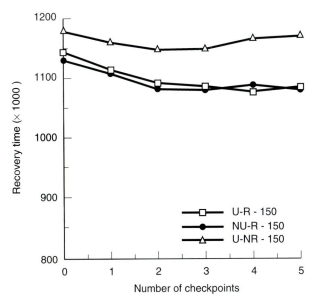

Figure 9.20. Recovery time vs. checkpoints.

case of two checkpoints, where all three algorithms have virtually the same number of log records to process.

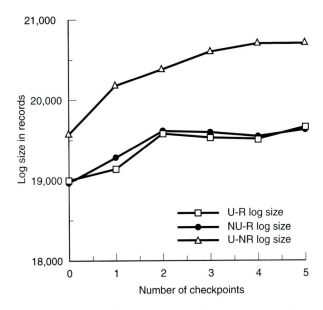

Figure 9.21. Total log size (MPL = 100).

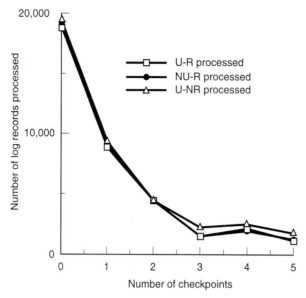

Figure 9.22. Total log size (MPL = 100).

By comparing the results of Figure 9.22 and Figure 9.18, there is a correlation between the number of log records processed and the total recovery time. The number of log records processed decreases as the recovery time decreases. The total log sizes for the U-R and NU-R algorithms are smaller and thus it takes less time to transfer them to memory. The recovery process requires the entire log to be transferred to memory, before it determines which records are to be processed. This means that regardless of how small the number of records to be processed, the overall recovery time must include the (rather lengthy) time required to transfer the entire log from disk.

Experiment 3: Rolled-back transactions and recovery time

The intent of this experiment is to determine if a larger number of rolled back transactions in forward processing results in a longer recovery time. In the first experiment, it was speculated that the U-NR algorithm aborted more transactions, creating a larger transaction log, which, as verified in the second experiment, should result in longer recovery times.

It was speculated that since U-NR exercises control over when a transaction is added to the commit list, the transaction's data items remain locked for a longer period of time. The extra "lock time" causes additional conflicts between transactions over the locked data items. These conflicts are resolved by the CCM by rolling back one of the offending transactions. The experiment is conducted using the situation created for Experiments 1 and 2, with the addition of counting the number of transactions that must be rolled back in forward processing and MPL = 100. Table 9.3 describes the checkpoint thresholds used in the experiment (same as Experiment 1).

Results and Interpretation

The total number of aborted transactions is depicted graphically in Figure 9.23. U-NR shows the largest number of aborted transactions, ranging from 30% to 47% more aborts than NU-R. NU-R consistently aborts more (4.2% to 13%) transactions than U-R. Comparing Figures 9.23 and 9.18, it is possible to explain the much higher recovery times (Figure 9.18) for the U-NR algorithm by noting the much larger number of aborted transactions (Figure 9.18) for the same algorithm. The algorithm that causes the greatest number of transactions to abort in forward processing will result in the worst overall recovery performance.

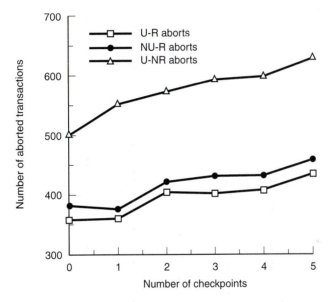

Figure 9.23. Number of aborted transactions (MPL = 100).

As expected, the NU-R algorithm aborts slightly more transactions than the U-R algorithm. The difference between these two algorithms is not great enough to cause noticeable differences in recovery time (Figure 9.18). In Figure 9.18, the NU-R algorithm delivers slightly better recovery performance at most checkpoint levels, even though it creates more aborted transactions in forward processing. This situation exists because the slightly longer I/O transfer time required to transfer the NU-R log from disk does not outweigh the greater number of data items that must be recovered with the U-R algorithm. The amount of data items that must be recovered with each algorithm will be explored in the next experiment.

Experiment 4: Number of transactions in a recovery

The intent of this experiment is to determine the number of transactions that must be recovered for each algorithm under the same circumstances. In the third experiment, it was speculated the U-R algorithm must recover a greater number of transactions than the NU-R algorithm, and thus could explain why the NU-R algorithm delivers slightly better performance than the U-R algorithm even after causing slightly more transactions to abort in forward processing (Figure 9.23). The experiment is conducted using the situation created for Experiment 1 with the addition of counting the number of transactions that are undone and redone during recovery operations. Table 9.3 describes the checkpoint thresholds used in the experiment and the thresholds found in the MPL = 100 row are used in the experiment.

Results and Interpretation

The number of recovered transactions is depicted graphically in Figure 9.24, which shows the number of transactions undone and redone with the U-R algorithm, the number of redone transactions with the NU-R algorithm, and the number of undone transactions with the U-NR algorithm. It is clear from Figure 9.24, that the U-R algorithm processes a relatively constant 100 transactions during the recovery process. Compared to both NU-R and U-NR, the U-R must recover between 30% and 40% more transactions than the next closest algorithm.

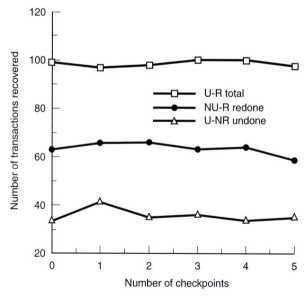

Figure 9.24. Number of recovered transactions (MPL = 100).

What is unexpected is that NU-R algorithm recovers between 59 and 66 out of the 100 transactions as compared to U-NR, which only must recover between 28 and 41. The simulation constant Flush Delay (Table 9.3) can explain this result. Flush Delay simulates the time required for the Cache Manager to determine which cache slots to flush to stable storage during the commit process. The simulation uses a value of 1000 time units for this constant. This appears to hold the transactions a lengthy period of time during the commit process, and thus exposing the transactions to the redo operation when the failure occurs. Since the system is fully loaded (active count = MPL), no additional transactions can become active until a transaction either aborts or is committed. Transactions appear to spend a longer time in the process of committing than they do in actual transaction processing.

The U-NR algorithm performs the least amount of recovery processing (Figure 9.24) and yet delivers the worst overall recovery performance (Figure 9.18) for MPL = 100. The results obtained in Experiment 2 (Figure 9.21) and Experiment 3 (Figure 9.23) provide an explanation for this. The U-NR algorithm creates more aborted transactions, and thus a larger transaction log. The time required to transfer this larger log from disk to memory outweighs any savings gained in processing the least number of transactions during recovery.

Experiment 5: I/O time and recovery

The intent of this experiment is to determine if decreasing the I/O transfer time, and thus increasing the I/O performance, has an effect on recovery performance. It was shown in the earlier experiments that I/O performance has a significant impact on the overall recovery performance. The transaction logs maintained by all three of the algorithms must be transferred from disk to memory at the onset of the recovery process. The previous experiments showed that even though the U-NR algorithm requires less work in the form of undoing the effects of the transactions, its performance suffers because of the length of time required to transfer the log from disk. This experiment will try to determine whether a host computer system with faster I/O transfer speeds would result in different recovery performance than that presented in Experiment 1. Variable timing values were the same as in Experiment 1, with the exception of the I/O transfer time constant. This value is reduced from 25 to 15 units. Table 9.3 describes the checkpoint thresholds used in the experiment and the thresholds found in the MPL = 100 row are used in the experiment.

Results and Interpretation

The recovery performance using the I/O transfer time value of 15 time units is shown in Figure 9.25. It shows that better I/O performance (lower I/O transfer times) does improve the recovery performance for all three algorithms. At three checkpoints with an I/O transfer time of 15 units, the average recovery time between the algorithms is 609. With the I/O transfer time of 25 units, the average recovery time is 1017. Reducing the I/O transfer time by 40% reduces the overall recovery time by about 40%.

The performance of the U-NR algorithm improves against the U-R and NU-R algorithms. In Figure 9.25, the performance of the U-NR algorithm is almost equal to that of the other algorithms, ranging from showing better performance at two and four checkpoints to 1.8% greater at three checkpoints. This performance can be compared with Figure 9.18, where the U-NR performance is consistently higher than the other algorithms, ranging from 1.6% to 5.7% higher than the next closest algorithm's performance.

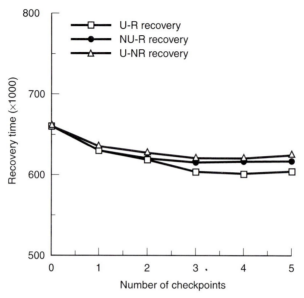

Figure 9.25. Recovery performance (I/O time 15; MPL = 100).

Faster I/O performance delivers better recovery performance. In addition, after reducing the effects of transferring the log to disk, the recovery performance starts to reflect each of the algorithm's actual recovery characteristics - undoing and redoing the affected transactions. Lowering the I/O transfer rates even further should result in recovery performance reflecting the number of recovered transactions relationship presented in Figure 9.24.

Experiment 6: Failure threshold and recovery

The intent of this experiment is to determine if increasing the failure threshold changes the overall relationship between the recovery performance established in the earlier experiments. It is necessary to determine whether the performance described in the previous experiments reflects that of a stable database and not fringe values captured when the database is at its limits. Increasing the failure threshold allows additional transactions to be created and flow through the system, giving it additional time to stabilize. The experiment is conducted using the situation created for Experiment 1 with MPL = 100. The I/O transfer time remains at 25 time units (as opposed to 15 time units from Experiment 5). Because of the higher failure threshold, the checkpoint thresholds must be adjusted accordingly. The failure threshold is increased from 1000 committed transactions to 2500 committed

transactions.
Results and Interpretation

The recovery performance using the new failure threshold of 2500 committed trans-actions and MPL = 100 transactions is depicted graphically in Figure 9.26. As expected, Figure 9.26 shows that the length of the recovery period increases when the failure threshold is increased. The relationship between each of the algorithm's performance stays the same as with the lower failure threshold and is presented in Figure 9.18. The U-NR consistently delivers the worst overall performance, whereas U-R and NU-R are very similar.

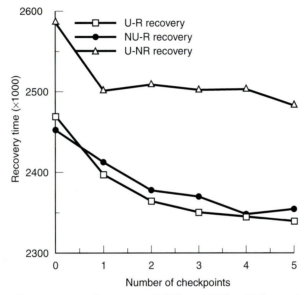

Figure 9.26. Recovery performance (MPL = 100). Failure threshold is 2500 commits.

In Figure 9.18, the U-NR performance ranged from 1.6% to 5.7% worse than the other algorithms. With the higher failure threshold, in Figure 9.26, the U-NR performance ranged from 3.7% to 6.7% worse than the other algorithms. As the failure threshold increases, U-NR will have aborted even more transactions at the time of failure, and thus created a proportionally larger log than U-R and NU-R at the time of failure. The increase in the relative recovery times for U-NR can be attributed to transferring this log from disk. It is expected that U-NR performance will get progressively worse as the failure threshold increases, given the current simulation parameter set.

Experiment 7: NU-NR versus log-based algorithms

The intent of this experiment is to provide a basis on which to compare the NU-NR algorithm with the three log-based algorithms. Checkpointing was a key component of the previous experiments, and since a transaction log is not maintained by NU-NR, it was not practical to include this algorithm in the previous experiments. This experiment is conducted in order to compare the performance of the four algorithms using the various MPL values used in the previous experiments. The experiment is conducted using the situation created for Experiment 1 with the addition of the NU-NR algorithm. The log-based algorithms are configured so that there is no checkpointing of the transaction logs. For each algorithm, the MPL values are varied, and the performance for each is collected and presented for comparison. As with the first experiment, in order to fully explore the potential differences between the MPL values, it is desired to have the number of active transactions equal to the MPL at the time of failure.

Results and Interpretation

The recovery performance for the MPL values 25 through 150 with no checkpoints is depicted graphically in Figure 9.27. It shows that the NU-NR performance is significantly worse than the other three algorithms. The NU-NR recovery times range from 41% to 46% greater than U-NR, the closest algorithm in terms of performance. The relationships between the performance of the three log-based algorithms were discussed in detail in the first experiment.

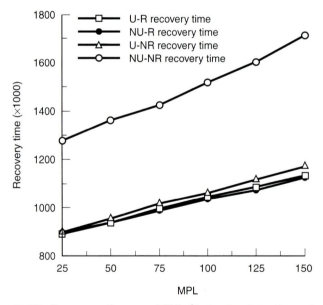

Figure 9.27. Recovery time vs. MPL (0 checkpoints; four algorithms).

The failure threshold is 1000 committed transactions, with the average number of data items per transaction set to 15 items. The logs for U-R, U-NR, and NU-R should contain a minimum of 15,000 records. Transferring the logs and transferring the master directory from disk to memory are similar operations, and if the log and the database sizes are equal, should take the same amount of time. NU-NR must transfer at least a 10,000-item master directory from disk. Assuming that the log sizes are similar in size to the master directory, the extra work required to create the shadow directory and then reestablish the master and shadow directory structures on disk cause the NU-NR recovery performance to suffer, using the timing constants of this experiment. Once again, the I/O transfer time appears to have significant impact on overall recovery performance.

Experiment 8: I/O and NU-NR

The intent of this experiment is to determine if decreasing the I/O transfer time from that of Experiment 7 causes the NU-NR algorithm's recovery performance to improve in comparison to the three log-based algorithms. It was assumed that the much larger I/O requirements of the NU-NR algorithm and the slow I/O transfer time of Experiment 7 explained the performance depicted in Figure 9.27. This experiment, as with Experiment 5 was conducted between the log-based algorithms, is intended to determine if the relationships between the overall recovery performance of all four algorithms changes when I/O performance is improved. The experiment is conducted using the situation created for Experiment 7, and variable timing values were the same as Experiment 7, with the exception of the I/O transfer time constant. This value is reduced from 25 to 15 units.

Results and Interpretation

The recovery performance for the MPL values 25 through 150 with no checkpoints and an I/O transfer time of 15 time units is presented in Figure 9.28. Comparing Figure 9.28 with Figure 9.27, it is clear that the recovery times decrease for all four algorithms when the I/O transfer time is lowered to 15 time units. The performance increase of the log-based algorithms was discussed fully in Experiment 5. As expected, since the NU-NR directories that must be transferred from disk are constant in size, an improvement in I/O transfer time does not improve its performance relative to the other algorithms. NU-NR recovery times exceed those of U-NR by 39% to 42%. With the longer I/O transfer time in Experiment 7, NU-NR recovery times exceeded those of U-NR by 41% to 46%. This does not appear to be a significant improvement.

In a situation where the log sizes of the log-based algorithms are significantly larger than the NU-NR directory structures, NU-NR should deliver better performance simply because of fewer I/O transfers. With no checkpoints, this situation should exist if the failure threshold is increased past the 1000 committed transactions level of this experiment.

9.7   CONCLUSIONS

This chapter investigated four algorithms, undo-redo (U-R), undo-no redo (U-NR), no undo-redo (NU-R), and no undo-no redo (NU-NR). U-R, U-NR, and NU-R are

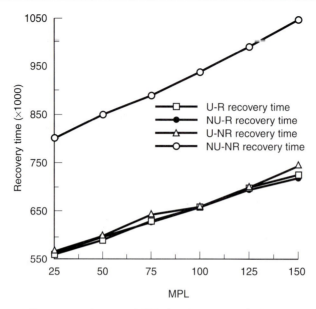

Figure 9.28. Recovery time vs. MPL (0 checkpoints) algorithms (I/O time = 15).

similar algorithms in that they each maintain a stable storage log of each transaction's modifications to the database. During recovery, the logs are examined and the transactions' effects can be undone, redone, or left intact, depending on the algorithm and the state of the transaction at the time of failure. The NU-NR algorithm relies on maintaining various stable storage directory structures that describe the current database location of each data item. The recovery process using this algorithm involves restoring the last directory structure from stable storage.

The simulation results showed that, in general, the recovery times increase as the MPL increases. The results also showed that for the log-based algorithms (U-R, NU-R, and U-NR), the recovery times generally decrease as the number of checkpoints increases. They also suggest that U-R and NU-R deliver very similar performance, and, in all cases, better than U-NR. It is observed that U-NR delivers slower recovery times than U-R and NU-R, and that with most MPL values and across all levels of checkpointing, U-R delivers the best recovery times. It is interesting to note that U-R must recover more transactions than either NU-R or U-NR. These results were explained by the smaller transaction log generated by the U-R algorithm and the relatively slow I/O transfer time. In the simulation, the amount of information that was required to be transferred from disk was often the key factor in the overall recovery performance.

It was shown that the U-NR algorithm causes more transactions to be rolled back in forward processing and thus creates a larger transaction log than either U-R or NU-R. As the I/O performance is improved, the performance of the U-NR algorithm improves relative to U-R and NU-R. This improved performance trend is assumed to continue as the I/O performance increases. Since U-NR is shown to require the fewest number of transactions to be recovered, once the I/O performance is improved to make it less of a factor on overall performance, the overall U-NR recovery performance could surpass that of U-R and NU-R. Increasing failure threshold does not change relationships between U-NR and other log-based algorithms.

The NU-NR algorithm delivered the worst overall recovery performance because of the large number of I/O transfers necessary to restore the current database directory in memory. Again, the speed of I/O transfers has a dramatic effect on an algorithm's recovery performance. It was speculated that this algorithm's performance could be improved by using it with a smaller database or with a system capable of much faster I/O transfer rates.

The results showed that the U-R and NU-R algorithms deliver very similar performance, and in all cases, better than U-NR or NU-NR. The slow I/O transfer rate in the simulation must account for the similarity of the U-R and NU-R recovery performance. NU-R's forward processing creates a slightly larger transaction log than U-R. Although NU-R must process fewer transactions during recovery than UR, the savings in transaction recovery processing are offset by the time required to transfer the slightly longer log from disk. The performance of the NU-R algorithm over the U-R algorithm should be much greater if I/O performance can be increased.

References

[1] Antani, S. "A Performance Study of Undo-Redo and Undo No-Redo Recovery Algorithms in Centralized Database System." MS thesis, University of Missouri-Kansas City, Missouri, 1992.

[2] Bernstein, P. A., V. Hadzilacos, and N. Goodman, *Concurrency Control and Recovery in Database Systems*. Reading, MA: Addison-Wesley, 1987.

[3] Gelenbe, E, and D. Derochette, "Performance of Rollback Recovery Systems under Intermittent Failure," *Communication of the ACM*, 21(6), 1978.

[4] Gray, Jim. "Notes on Database Operating Systems," in *Operating Systems, An Advanced Course*, ed. by Bayer, Graham and Seegmuller. Springer Verlag, 1978.

[5] Griffith, N, and J. A. Miuller, "Performance Modeling of Database Recovery Protocols," *IEEE Transactions on Software Engineering*, SE-11(6) 1985.

[6] Kent, J., H. garcia-Molina, and J. Chung. "An Experimental Evaluation of Crash Recovery Mechanisms," in *Proceedings of the 4th ACM SIGACT-SIGMOD on Principles of Database Systems*, Portland, Oregan, March 1985.

[7] *Oracle User Manual. Database Administrator's Guide*. Oracle.

[8] Reuter, A. "Performance Analysis of Recovery Techniques," *ACM Transactions on database systems*, 9(4) (December 1984).

[9] Schwetman, H. *CSIM User's Guide.* Austin, TX: Microelectronics and Technology Computer Company.

Chapter 10

Stochastic Models for Performance Analysis of Database Recovery Control

Paulo B. Goes and Ushio Sumita

Abstract

In this chapter we develop three analytical models for a comprehensive analysis of database recovery. These models, based on Semi-Markov stochastic analysis and queueing networks, not only capture the details of modern recovery mechanisms, but take the complex stochastic behavior of the system into account. Furthermore, we use multiple performance measures to analyze different recovery mechanisms, the impact of environment characteristics, and the effect of tunable system parameters, thus offering database designers and administrators a better understanding of the recovery system to be designed or managed. A special case of database recovery that has been studied by previous researchers is analyzed in detail; numerical experiments offer evidence of the effectiveness of our approach. The models developed in this chapter, however, are applicable to much more general systems and environments.

10.1 INTRODUCTION

Computer systems are subject to a variety of failures that can cause loss and corruption of the data in their databases. If a Database Management System (DBMS) through its recovery control subsystem cannot reconstruct the lost or corrupted data in an efficient way, the organization's operations may be seriously compromised. Businesses such as airlines, telecommunication companies, and banks, for example, are virtually unable to function if their on line database systems are down.

Simply stated, recovery control consists of generating and keeping redundancy of the data subject to loss in a safe place while the system is up and using this redundancy to recover when the system is down. Several methods have been proposed to address the issues of how to generate redundant data in efficient ways and how to provide fast recovery. The fundamental trade-off that governs the choice of methods for recovery control is between the effort expended during up time to generate redundancy and the ease of recovery after failures occur.

There is no question that recovery methods affect the overall performance of database systems and that there is an explicit need to develop good performance evaluation methods that can be used both at the design and the management of recovery control. When designing the recovery components, it is extremely important to choose the right combination of recovery operations that best suits a database environment with given operational parameters. Additionally, database administrators can use these tools to fine-tune system parameters to enhance the overall system performance.

In this research, we develop three analytical models for a comprehensive performance evaluation of database recovery. Analytical models provide flexibility for evaluating performance of complex, sophisticated systems with tightly coupled multiple components and typically outperform practical simulations in the ability to swiftly evaluate different parameters and scenarios. This ability provides analytical models with great power to generate insights in performance evaluation and sensitivity analysis of complex systems such as modern databases.

Our first two models are based on Semi-Markov analysis of the database operations. Under considerably general assumptions, we model the stochastic behavior of the system under various recovery environments. The third model uses a closed network of queues that incorporates the details of database transaction processing and recovery-related operations. It considers queueing delays and congestion effects ignored by previous simpler nonstochastic models.

Multiple performance measures are considered, such as availability, time to recover, transaction processing time and system throughput. By using multiple measures, one can better analyze the fundamental trade-off between ease of recovery after failures and the overhead imposed by the recovery mechanisms during up time. We demonstrate the effectiveness of our approach by conducting numerical experiments with extensive sensitivity analyses of various parameters for a specific environment of database recovery, commonly used in a number of commercial systems. General insights and conclusions are obtained.

This chapter is organized as follows. Section 10.2 overviews the basic concepts of database recovery and highlights the fundamental issues involved with its performance management. We also present an extensive literature review of analytical modeling of database recovery and position the contributions of our research. Sections 10.3 and 10.4 introduce models 1 and 2, respectively. We then use these models to investigate database recovery under specific conditions in Section 10.5. Section

10.6 is dedicated to model 3 based on a closed queueing network. Extensive numerical experiments are conducted in Section 10.7 for the case presented in Section 10.5. Finally, we conclude the chapter in Section 10.8 with an overall assessment of the models and directions for future research.

10.2   ANALYTICAL MODELING OF DATABASE RECOVERY

10.2.1   Recovery Concepts

We focus on *system* failures that interrupt the execution of transactions and cause loss of the contents of main memory. Several events may be responsible for system failures, such as a fault in the operating system, a bug in an application software, power outage, hardware failure, or a virus attack. It is estimated that these failures occur at a rate of "several times a week" in major database installations, depending on the stability of both the DBMS and its operational environment [21].

In the main memory of a database server, one finds a special data storage area called the database cache, or *buffer*, whose main purpose is to hold those pages (data blocks) that are frequently referenced so that excessive I/O operations are avoided. Since the buffer is in volatile storage, its contents are subject to loss due to system failures.

To better understand how recovery control works, it is useful to classify the overall database operational cycle in the stages *normal operation*, *checkpointing* and *recovery*. Associated with each stage, there are special recovery-oriented activities. During normal operation database transactions read and update pages in the buffer. In addition, redundant information about the effects of transactions is written to secondary storage. Usually, a *log* file is employed, as shown in Figure 10.1 [21]. Periodically, during checkpointing, the state of the system is saved on stable storage. The objective of checkpointing is to reduce the amount of information to be processed during recovery. Finally, during recovery, the redundant information collected during normal operation is processed in conjunction with the database on disk, so that the proper actions *undo* and *redo* are taken [20].

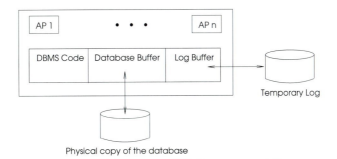

Figure 10.1. Database storage hierarchy.

Several methods have been proposed to address the various recovery activities outlined earlier. Haerder and Reuter [21], for example, identify a dozen different general strategies for recovery control, each one being a feasible combination of various recovery techniques proposed for the stages' normal operation, checkpointing, and recovery. Another good survey of different methods appears in [2]. The following are examples of choices that have to be made, for which analytical models can be used for evaluating their performance impact.

10.2.2 Buffer Management in Normal Operation

Keeping pages that are highly referenced (*hot* pages) in the buffer without writing them back to secondary storage after each successful update can save considerable amount of I/O costs at the expense of extra recovery efforts upon failures. One would like to investigate the costs and benefits of the so called force and noforce buffer management strategies. Under force, an updated page is written to secondary storage when the corresponding transaction successfully terminates and *commits*. Under noforce, the updated page is kept in the buffer and written to disk only when it is necessary to make room to bring a new page to the buffer. Redundant information is written to a log file. Under noforce, the overhead during normal processing is smaller because writing entries to the log, usually a sequential file, is less costly than writing a page to the database disk. However, recovery costs are higher due to log processing.

10.2.3 Checkpointing Schemes

A simple strategy for implementing checkpointing is to periodically stop accepting new transactions and then flush all committed pages from buffer to disk. Variations of this scheme are Transaction Consistent Checkpointing (TCC) and Action Consistent Checkpointing (ACC) [2, 21]. When using such a strategy, the system is unavailable during the period that corresponds to the writing of all committed pages to the database disk. Fuzzy Checkpointing tries to overcome this delay by using the following approach. At checkpointing, time information identifying all committed pages that are still in the buffer is written to the log, with pointers to their redo information, which is already in the log. The system only writes to disk those committed pages that were already in the buffer since the previous checkpoint. The idea is that normal buffer replacement between two consecutive checkpoints naturally performs most of the writing of the committed pages to disk. As a result of this strategy, only a fraction of the buffer is actually written to the database disk during the checkpointing period, thus reducing the unavailable period.

10.2.4 Final Destination of Recovery Actions

The decision here is whether to write all the recovered pages to the database on disk after reconstructing them from the information in the log file or just restore them to the buffer. Some authors (e.g., [2, 10]) present strategies in which recovery is done only in the buffer. Under this alternative, during recovery no "redone" pages are written to the database disk. Under other systems, in particular some of the commercial DBMS's such as IBM's DB2 [23], the entire database in secondary storage is brought to the latest consistent state during the recovery operations. The idea is that since the system is already unavailable, it should take this opportunity and write all lost committed pages back to the database disk.

10.2.5   Operational Parameters

In addition to the previous major decisions, which are made at the design stage of the recovery components, there are several operational parameters that can affect the performance of database recovery. Database administrators should be aware of the impact of these parameters, and how they can be tuned in different operation environments, so that the performance of the database is enhanced. These parameters include the buffer size, the page size, the log record size, the log buffering scheme, and the frequency of checkpointing. Also, the parameters associated with the disk subsystem are extremely important: access times, degree of locality, channel speed, and so on.

10.2.6   Analytical Modeling of Database Recovery

For exposition purposes, we classify the analytical models for database recovery in the literature in two types, as shown in Table 10.1.

Table 10.1. Macro and Micro Models of Database Recovery

	MACRO MODELS	MICRO MODELS
Author(s)	Young [37] Chandy et al. [6] Gelenbe and Derochette [13] Gelenbe [14] Tantawi and Ruschitzka [36] L'Ecuyer and Malenfant [29] Sumita et al. [35] Grassi et al. [19]	Reuter [30] Agrawal and Dewitt [1]
Perf. Measures	System Availability	I/O Costs
Remarks	Broad stochastic modeling of states *normal operation, recovery,* and *checkpointing.* Limited modeling of actual recovery methods.	Mean value analysis of recovery operations. No stochastic aspects.

Macro models are stochastic models that broadly analyze how the system alternates among the general states of normal operation, checkpointing, and recovery.

These models are usually based on Markov or Semi-Markov analysis, whose main objective is to derive general measures of the system availability, defined as the long-run proportion of time the database is operating normally. They also investigate the problem of defining optimal intercheckpointing intervals that maximize the availability or production cycle. These models are usually based on very simplistic rollback strategies. The major shortcoming of these models is that they make no effort to capture the actual details of the various components of database recovery methods, such as buffer management, transaction processing, logging, and checkpointing. In real systems, availability alone is not an adequate measure of the performance of recovery control. Time to recover and the overhead imposed by recovery-related activities to normal processing are extremely important.

Micro models have attempted to study how the various recovery components are actually implemented and how database transactions are processed. Due to the complexity of these micro-level operations, these models are typically deterministic and have only derived mean value measures of I/O costs. Agrawal and Dewitt [1] present an interesting study of the integration of concurrency and recovery mechanisms, which however does not consider important aspects such as buffer management and checkpointing. Reuter [30] conducts a detailed study of the costs involved in the different recovery techniques that have appeared in the taxonomy of [21]. A shortcoming of this second group of works is that they do not consider the stochastic aspects of the operation of database management systems: the obvious stochastic nature of fault-tolerant systems, arrivals and processing of transactions, disk accesses, internal queues, and so on.

In this chapter we develop both macro and micro models that overcome the deficiencies of previous models. Our macro models (models 1 and 2) are based on Semi-Markov analysis of the database operational cycle and make less restrictive assumptions than previous macro models. In model 1, recovery techniques that reconstruct only the buffer are analyzed. Model 2 considers the case where both the buffer and the database disk are affected by the recovery operations. Under this latter condition, both checkpointing and recovery constitute renewal points of the stochastic process used to model the database operations. This feature has not been captured by previous macro models. Our macro models provide measures of the ease of recovery after failure and the system availability and are shown to capture the behavior of real recovery methods.

To our best knowledge, our model 3 represents the first time a queuing network model is used to analyze the micro behavior of recovery-related activities during the normal transaction processing. The advantage of such an approach is that the derived measures capture the overhead imposed to the normal transaction processing by the recovery-related operations. The transaction response time and the system throughput in the presence of various alternatives and parameters are obtained.

Considered together, the multiple performance measures offered by our macro and micro models provide a comprehensive way to analyze database recovery.

10.3 RECOVERY AT BUFFER LEVEL: MODEL 1

The model developed in this section considers that at recovery time, the *redo* operations reconstruct lost updates at the buffer only, so that if a new failure occurs after this last recovery operation, the log file will have to be processed as far back as the last checkpoint.

We consider a database system where checkpoints are established from time to time. During normal operation-log files are created with entries for transactions that have arrived since the last checkpoint. We define $X(t)$ as the cumulative operation time since the last checkpoint. The length of the recovery period depends on the number of entries in the log, and hence on the value of $X(t)$ at the time of failure. We employ a generic random variable V_x denoting the length of the recovery period given that a failure occurred at time t with $X(t) = x$. The distribution of V_x is denoted by $B_x(y) = P[V_x \le y]$. Failures occur according to an inhomogeneous Poisson process with intensity $\lambda(x)$.

Intervals between two consecutive checkpoints are determined by the total operation time in the interval excluding recovery periods. The ith checkpoint is created as soon as the total operation time since the $(i-1)$st checkpoint reaches the length T_1^i. We assume that (T_1^i) constitutes a sequence of random variables with common distribution $A_1(x) = P[T_1^i \le x]$. It should be noted that T_1^i may be deterministic. Times required for creating checkpoints also form a sequence of i.i.d. random variables (T_0^i) with $A_0(x) = P[T_0^i \le x]$.

Let T^i be the actual time interval between the $(i-1)$st and the ith checkpoint. It is then clear that (T^i) is a sequence of i.i.d. random variables that agrees with the fact that checkpoints are regenerative points of our model.

Let I(t) be a stochastic process defined by

$$I(t) = \begin{cases} 0, & \text{if a checkpoint is being created at time } t \\ 1, & \text{if the database is operating normally at time } t \\ 2, & \text{if the database is recovering from a failure at time } t \end{cases} \tag{10.1}$$

We define $Y(t)$ as the elapsed time in the recovery period, given $I(t) = 2$. Since checkpoints are regenerative points in our model, it is clear that the trivariate process $[X(t), Y(t), I(t)]$ has a cyclic stochastic behavior, as depicted in Figure 10.2, and it suffices to study the model in one cycle. We therefore drop the discrete time index i.

The analysis of the trivariate stochastic process $[X(t), Y(t), I(t)]$ provides the performance measures of interest and is developed in Sumita et al. [35]. Gelenbe [13] presented results for the case failures that occur according to a simple Poisson process. We present here the result from [35] in the form of the following.

Theorem 1: If $E[T_1] < \infty$, $E[T_0] < \infty$ and $R = \int_0^\infty dA(x) \int_0^x \lambda(\tau) E[V_\tau] d\tau < \infty$, then the process $I(t); t \ge 0$ is ergodic. Furthermore, $\pi_i = \lim_{t \to \infty} P[I(t) = i], 0 \le i \le 2$ are given by

$$\pi_0 = \frac{E[T_0]}{E[T_1] + R + E[T_0]} \tag{10.2}$$

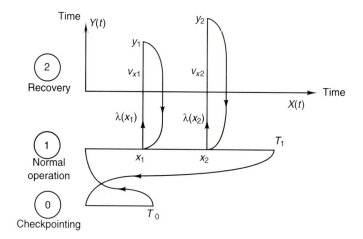

Figure 10.2. Model 1 : Posssible sample path.

$$\pi_1 = \frac{E[T_1]}{E[T_1] + R + E[T_0]} \tag{10.3}$$

$$\pi_2 = \frac{R}{E[T_1] + R + E[T_0]} \tag{10.4}$$

Notice that the preceding results have very general applicability. The residence times in each state follow general distributions, and the failure process is inhomogeneous Poisson. Also, in the formula for R, which represents the expected time per cycle that the system spends in recovery, the component $E[V_x]$ can be a general function on x, the time the system failure occurs during normal operation.

For database systems that follow a physical logging scheme [2, 21], it is usually appropriate to have $E[V_x]$ as a linear function on x. The main activity during the recovery period relates to sequentially scanning the log file to redo or undo updates from the before images and after images written to the log. However, if logical logs are used, the information in the log relates to the operations that need to be reexecuted in order to update the data items. These update operations may be complex operations such as indexed access to the database on disk, relational joins, selections, and projections. In these cases, a linear function may no longer be appropriate. Furthermore, recovery of more advanced and complex data objects may require more general functions for $E[V_x]$. Theorem 1 is sufficiently general to accommodate various functional forms of $E[V_x]$.

Of possible interest to database administration is the appropriate selection of the frequency of the checkpointing operation. We recall that checkpointing starts as soon as the cumulative operation time since the last checkpoint exceeds a random level T_1. It has been proved [35] that if the expression $\lambda(x)E[V_x]$ is nondecreasing in x, then triggering checkpoints deterministically, that is, $P[T_1 \le x] = U(x - \kappa)$ maximizes the ergodic availability π_1. Similar results have appeared in [12] and [13], under the assumption of Poisson failures. Strategies of deterministically starting checkpointing have been named equidistant and have been also analyzed by [29] and [36]. The idea has been to choose the optimal value of the intercheckpoint production time that maximizes the ergodic availability.

In real systems, instead of triggering checkpoints after a fixed time has elapsed, it is customary to initiate the checkpointing activity after a fixed number of total transactions have arrived to the system since the last checkpoint. The two approaches are equivalent if transactions follow a random (Poisson) arrival pattern with constant arrival rate. In Section 9.5, the issue of controlling the intercheckpointing interval will be further investigated under specific conditions.

10.4 RECOVERY AT BUFFER AND DISK LEVELS: MODEL 2

Model 2 has been developed for recovery methods that bring the *secondary storage* to the latest consistent state immediately after each system failure. For such alternative, not only *undo* but also *redo* operations are extended to the *database disk* during the recovery period. We then have operation "renewal" points being established after both checkpoints and failure recoveries.

In order to simplify the analysis, we assume in this case that system failures occur according to a Poisson process with parameter λ. Let $J(t)$ be a stochastic process defined by

$$J(t) = \begin{cases} 0, & \text{if a checkpoint is being created at time } t \\ 1, & \text{if the database is operating normally at time } t \\ 2, & \text{if the database is recovering from a failure at time } t \end{cases} \qquad (10.5)$$

We denote the elapsed time since either the last checkpoint or the last recovery period, whichever is the most recent, by $X(t)$. In other words, $X(t)$ keeps track of the elapsed time since the last *transition* to normal processing. Let $Y(t)$ be the elapsed time in the recovery period, given $J(t) = 2$.

Checkpoints are triggered whenever normal processing time since the last transition reaches the random level T_1. T_1 is a random variable with distribution $A_1(x) = P[T_1 \leq x]$ with hazard function $\eta_1(x)$. Checkpointing takes a random time T_0 that follows a distribution $A_0(x) = P[T_0 \leq x]$ with hazard function $\eta_0(x)$. As in model 1, the length of the recovery period, given the occurrence of a failure at time t, with $X(t) = x$, is represented by the random variable V_x. The distribution of V_x is denoted by $B_x(y) = P[V_x \leq y]$, with hazard function $\zeta_x(y)$. Because of the renewal nature of both checkpointing and recovery, the stochastic behavior of the trivariate process $[X(t), Y(t), J(t)]$ has a cyclic structure as depicted in Figure 10.3.

The analysis of the trivariate process is presented in Appendix A. We summarize the results through the following

Theorem 2: The ergodic probabilities π_i, $i = 0, 1, 2$, of the process $J(t)$ are given

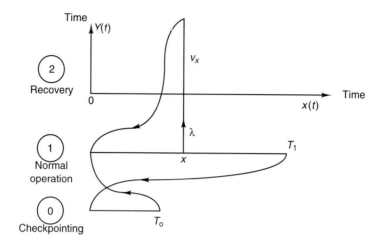

Figure 10.3. Possible sample path.

by

$$\pi_0 = \frac{E[T_0]\alpha_1(\lambda)}{E[T_0]\alpha_1(\lambda) - \lambda G(\lambda) - \dot{\alpha}_1(\lambda)}$$

$$\pi_1 = \frac{1 - \alpha_1(\lambda)}{\lambda[E[T_0]\alpha_1(\lambda) - \lambda G(\lambda) - \dot{\alpha}_1(\lambda)]}$$

$$\pi_2 = \frac{\alpha_1(\lambda) - \lambda^2 G(\lambda) - \lambda\dot{\alpha}_1(\lambda) - 1}{\lambda[E[T_0]\alpha_1(\lambda) - \lambda G(\lambda) - \dot{\alpha}_1(\lambda)]}$$

where

$$\alpha_1(s) = \int_0^\infty e^{-st} a_1(t)dt, \ \dot{\alpha}_1(\lambda) = \frac{\partial}{\partial s}\alpha_1(s)|_{s=\lambda}$$

$$G(\lambda) = -G_1(\lambda) - G_2(\lambda), \ G_1(\lambda) = \frac{\lambda\dot{\alpha}_1(\lambda) - \alpha_1(\lambda) + 1}{\lambda^2}$$

and

$$G_2(\lambda) = \int_0^\infty e^{-\lambda x}\bar{A}_1(x)E[V_x]dx$$

As with Theorem 1, we emphasize the generality of the results in Theorem 2. The closedform solutions for the ergodic probabilities are based on general distributions of the residence times and a general function for $E[V_x]$. However, the expressions obtained here are a little more complex than the ones in Theorem 1, because they directly involve $\alpha_1(s)$, the Laplace transform of the distribution of the time spent in normal operation. This transform can be evaluated exactly for some known probability distributions or approximated via numerical methods. In Section 10.5, we evaluate the results of Theorem 2 under special conditions.

10.5   PHYSICAL LOGS, LINEAR RECOVERY PERIODS AND DETERMINISTIC CHECKPOINTS

As defined in [21], a physical log contains before and/or after images of the pages that are updated. The recovery period then consists of processing the images written on the log file and redoing lost updates, as well as possibly undoing updates already reflected in the database disk. Due to the sequential nature of the log file, it is usual [13, 19, 29, 36] to assume that $E[V_x]$, the expected recovery time given a failure occurred at time x, has a linear form consisting of a fixed component and a variable component that depends on the time elapsed since the last checkpoint, and consequently on the total number of before and after images in the log:

$$E[V_x] = a + bx, \ a, b \geq 0 \tag{10.6}$$

We now evaluate the effect of the assumption expressed in Eq. 10.1 on models 1 and 2.

10.5.1   Model 1

Consider a constant failure rate, that is, $\lambda(x) = \lambda, \ \forall x$. From Theorem 1 and Eq. 10.1, the ergodic state probabilities of the process $I(t)$ are given by

$$\pi_0(\kappa) = \frac{E[T_0]}{\kappa + E[T_0] + \lambda\kappa(a + b\kappa/2)} \tag{10.7}$$

$$\pi_1(\kappa) = \frac{\kappa}{\kappa + E[T_0] + \lambda\kappa(a + b\kappa/2)} \tag{10.8}$$

$$\pi_2(\kappa) = \frac{\lambda\kappa(a + \frac{b\kappa}{2})}{\kappa + E[T_0] + \lambda\kappa(a + b\kappa/2)} \tag{10.9}$$

The maximum system availability is achieved at the level κ^*, the best choice among all deterministic possibilities. κ^* is obtained by setting $\frac{\partial \pi_1(\kappa)}{\partial \kappa} = 0$ from Eq. 10.3 as

$$\kappa^* = \sqrt{\frac{2E[T_0]}{\lambda b}} \tag{10.10}$$

Asymptotic Behavior

We proceed to investigate the ergodic behavior of the database system under two extreme conditions. The first one is related to a situation in which checkpoints are never triggered so we make $\kappa \to \infty$. From Eq. 10.8 we obtain

$$\lim_{\kappa \to \infty} \pi_1(\kappa) = 0 \tag{10.11}$$

This result indicates that with logging and no checkpoints, the system availability yielded by buffer-only consistent recovery drops to zero at ergodicity. This is not surprising because the recovery mechanism would have to scan all the images in the log since the database creation every time there is a system failure. At ergodicity ($t \to \infty$), the log would be of infinite size.

The second limiting condition is total absence of system failures, that is,

$$\lim_{\lambda \to 0} \pi_1(\kappa) = \frac{\kappa}{\kappa + E[T_0]} \tag{10.12}$$

in which case the system follows an alternate renewal process that oscillates between normal operation and checkpointing.

10.5.2   Model 2

Here we explicitly evaluate Theorem 2 considering the linear function of Eq. 10.6. It can be readily seen that

$$G_2(\lambda) = G_3(\lambda) + G_4(\lambda),$$

where

$$G_3(\lambda) = a \int_0^\infty e^{-\lambda x} \bar{A}_1(x)dx = \frac{a}{\lambda}[1 - \alpha_1(\lambda)]$$

$$G_4(\lambda) = b \int_0^\infty x e^{-\lambda x} \bar{A}_1(x)dx = bG_1(\lambda) = \frac{b}{\lambda^2}[\lambda \dot{\alpha}_1(\lambda) - \alpha_1(\lambda) + 1]$$

which lead to the following.

Corollary 3: Let $E[V_x] = a + bx$. Then the ergodic probabilities π_i, $0 \leq i \leq 2$, are given by

$$\pi_0 = \frac{\lambda \alpha_1(\lambda)E[T_0]}{[1 - \alpha_1(\lambda)](1 + \lambda a + b) + \lambda \alpha_1(\lambda)E[T_0] + \lambda b \dot{\alpha}_1(\lambda)}$$

$$\pi_1 = \frac{1 - \alpha_1(\lambda)}{[1 - \alpha_1(\lambda)](1 + \lambda a + b) + \lambda \alpha_1(\lambda)E[T_0] + \lambda b \dot{\alpha}_1(\lambda)}$$

$$\pi_2 = \frac{[1 - \alpha_1(\lambda)](\lambda a + b) + b \lambda \dot{\alpha}_1(\lambda)}{[1 - \alpha_1(\lambda)](1 + \lambda a + b) + \lambda \alpha_1(\lambda)E[T_0] + \lambda b \dot{\alpha}_1(\lambda)}$$

where

$$\alpha_1(\lambda) = \alpha_1(s)|_{s=\lambda} \quad \alpha_1(s) = \int_0^\infty e^{-st} dA_1(t)\, dt$$

and

$$\dot{\alpha}_1(\lambda) = \frac{\partial}{\partial s} \alpha_1(s)|_{s=\lambda}$$

Assuming that checkpoints are triggered by the system whenever the operative time since either the last checkpoint or the last recovery period, whichever comes first, reaches the *deterministic* level κ, we have

$$\alpha_1(\lambda) = e^{-\lambda \kappa} \quad \dot{\alpha}_1(\lambda) = -\kappa e^{-\lambda \kappa}$$

Hence, from Corollary 3 the ergodic probabilities π_i, $i = 0, 1, 2$, are given by

$$\pi_0(\kappa) = \frac{\lambda e^{-\lambda \kappa} E[T_0]}{(1 - e^{-\lambda \kappa})(1 + \lambda a + b) + \lambda e^{-\lambda \kappa}(E[T_0] - b\kappa)} \tag{10.13}$$

$$\pi_1(\kappa) = \frac{1 - e^{-\lambda \kappa}}{(1 - e^{-\lambda \kappa})(1 + \lambda a + b) + \lambda e^{-\lambda \kappa}(E[T_0] - b\kappa)} \tag{10.14}$$

$$\pi_2(\kappa) = \frac{(1 - e^{-\lambda \kappa})(\lambda a + b) - \lambda b\kappa e^{-\lambda \kappa}}{(1 - e^{-\lambda \kappa})(1 + \lambda a + b) + \lambda e^{-\lambda \kappa}(E[T_0] - b\kappa)} \tag{10.15}$$

Asymptotic Behavior

Eq. 10.14 enables us to evaluate the availability behavior of buffer-and-disk consistent recovery policies under the following extreme conditions:

$$\lim_{\kappa \to \infty} \pi_1(\kappa) = \frac{1}{1 + \lambda a + b} \tag{10.16}$$

and

$$\lim_{\lambda \to 0} \pi_1(\kappa) = \frac{\kappa}{\kappa + E[T_0]} \tag{10.17}$$

We note from Eq. 10.16 that in the absence of checkpoints, the long-run availability of the database system drops to the constant $(1 + \lambda a + b)^{-1}$. This result differs from the corresponding result for buffer-only recovery policies in Eq. 10.12 because under buffer-and-disk consistent policies, recovery periods also play the role of regenerative actions, which means that after the next failure, the log files have to be processed back to the previous failure mark.

When system failures cease to exist, the limit in Eq. 10.17 tells us that the system performs as an alternating renewal process. Under such condition, it is interesting to notice that models 1 and 2 present the same limiting behavior.

10.6 TRANSACTION PROCESSING IN NORMAL OPERATION: MODEL 3

In this section, we present a micro model for the processing of transactions during normal operation. We consider a closed network of queues consisting of three nodes: the CPU/Main Memory (CM), the Log Disk (LOG), and the database disk subsystem (DBD), as depicted in Figure 10.4.

10.6.1 Input Parameters

The following input parameters are needed:

$$P \quad = \quad \text{degree of multiprogramming or parallelism}$$
$$n_i \quad = \quad \text{number of visits to node } i \text{ per transaction,}$$

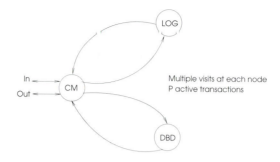

Figure 10.4. Model 3 : closed network of queues.

$$i = CM, LOG, DBD$$

$$V_{it} = \text{visit ratio per transaction at node } i, \text{ visit } t,$$
$$i = CM, LOG, DBD, \ t = 1, ..., n_i$$

$$s_{it} = \text{mean service time per transaction at node } i, \text{ visit } t,$$
$$i = CM, LOG, DBD, \ t = 1, ..., n_i.$$

The parameter P corresponds to the total number of active transactions allowed in the system. This is usually a value that can be appropriately set by database administration [23].

The parameters n_i and V_{it} depend on the buffer management technique and recovery-oriented activities that are selected for normal operation. They can be determined by tracing the sequence of steps involved by a transaction execution under a given recovery control environment. V_{it} can be interpreted as the expected number of times a transaction will visit node i for the tth visit. In this context, a *visit* to a node corresponds to an operation such as read an item, write an item, write a log entry, lock an item, and so on.

The mean service times s_{it} at each node are determined from the system characteristics, mainly the hardware configuration, and constitute the principal input to the queuing network model. For determining the service times to nodes LOG and SBD, we use a disk subsystem model based on [7, 11]. For the CM node, CPU operations such as scheduling, synchronization and locking could be evaluated in terms of MIPS (millions of instructions per second) so that the corresponding values for $s_{CM,t}$ can be determined.

10.6.2   Output of the Model

The main output measures are, for $i = CM, LOG, DBD$, and $1 \leq t \leq n_i$:

$$\lambda_{it} = \text{throughput at node } i \text{ measured in number of type } t$$
$$\text{visits per unit of time}$$

$$w_{it} = \text{mean sojourn time at node } i, \text{ either on queue or in}$$

$$
\begin{aligned}
&\quad\quad\quad \text{service, for one type } t \text{ visit} \\[4pt]
N_{it} \;&=\; \text{mean number of transactions at node } i, \text{ either on queue or in} \\
&\quad\quad\quad \text{service, for type } t \text{ visit} \\[4pt]
N_i \;&=\; \sum_{t=1}^{n_i} N_{it} \;\; \text{mean number of transactions at node } i, \\[4pt]
U_i \;&=\; \sum_{t=1}^{n_i} \lambda_{it} s_{it} \;\; \text{utilization at server } i, \\[4pt]
\lambda_i \;&=\; \sum_{j=1}^{n_i} \lambda_{it} \;\; \text{total number of visits per unit time at node } i, \\[4pt]
\bar{s} \;&=\; \sum_{i} \sum_{t=1}^{n_i} V_{it} w_{it} \;\; \text{mean transaction processing time,} \\[4pt]
TH \;&=\; P/\bar{s} \;\; \text{overall system throughput (Little's law)}
\end{aligned}
$$

Although the queuing network consists of only 3 nodes, because there are multiple visits at each node, it does not lend itself to closedform solutions (see e.g. [9]); interactive solution procedures are appropriate. We employ a modification of Schweitzer's MVA analysis [31] and incorporate the special characteristics of the DBD node as an aggregation of multiple devices and several communication channels. In our extensive numerical experiments, the solution procedure presented very fast convergence. Details of the analysis and implementation of model 3 can be found in [16] and [18].

10.7 NUMERICAL RESULTS

In this section, we illustrate the effectiveness of the models presented in this chapter through numerical experiments and sensitivity analyses for the case of physical logs, linear recovery time, and deterministic checkpointing. Even though our models can be used in more general contexts, we chose to use the same special environment that has been modeled by most previous research in performance evaluation of database recovery. Not only does this environment provide a common ground for comparison between our models and previous studies, but it also represents many actual commercial implementations of DBMSs [22, 23].

The experiments are designed around a base case, whose fixed parameters are given in Table 10.2.

Using the preceding system configuration, we look into the following alternatives for recovery methods and their impact on database performance:

- Destination of the recovery operations: buffer only versus buffer and database disk

Table 10.2. Base Case: Parameter Values

Parameter	Value
Database Disk Subsystem	IBM 3390 (8 devices)
Database Page Size	4096 bytes
Log Device	Dedicated IBM 3390
Log Record Size	512 bytes
Log Buffer Size (b_l)	10 records

- Checkpointing schemes

- Recovery-oriented activities and strategies for buffer management during normal operation

The first two sets of decisions refer primarily to the recovery operations that take place outside the normal operation periods (recovery and checkpointing). Their impact is evaluated through models 1 and 2 using the measures system availability and mean recovery time. The third set of alternatives impacts all three periods of database operation: normal operation, recovery, and checkpointing. We evaluate these alternatives using all three models developed in this chapter. In addition to availability and recovery time, the measures of system throughput and transaction processing time are utilized in the performance comparison.

We also conduct sensitivity analyses on the following operational parameters:

1. *System Tunable Parameters:*

   - Database buffer size B (number of pages)

   - Degree of multiprogramming P (number of active transactions at a time)

   - Intercheckpointing interval κ (seconds)

2. *Environment Parameters:*

   - Transaction arrival rate γ (transactions per second)

   - Transaction configuration (n_r, n_w) (number of reads and number of writes per transaction)

   - System failure rate γ (failures per second)

10.7.1 Recovery at Buffer versus Recovery at Buffer and Disk

In order to compare these two alternatives, we consider that during normal operation, the buffer management uses noforce and steal strategies. Steal buffers give more flexibility to the buffer manager and have been implemented by most commercial systems [2]. With a steal buffer, one may find pages in the disk reflecting uncommitted updates. Consequently, before images of pages need to be logged during normal operation so that the "dirty" pages on disk can be undone. Therefore, under noforce and steal, a log file is created, which contains both before and after images for the recovery operations.

We start by estimating parameters a and b, which are needed in the linear recovery Eq. 10.6 for each one of the strategies. In the following expressions, a_1 refers to the fixed cost of recovery as used in model 1 and a_2 is the value used in model 2. These estimates are

$$a_1 = B(t_d + \frac{t_l}{b_l}) + Pn_w(2t_d + \frac{t_l}{b_l}) \tag{10.18}$$

$$a_2 = B(2t_d + \frac{t_l}{b_l}) + Pn_w(2t_d + \frac{t_l}{b_l}) \tag{10.19}$$

The two components of each formula are the fixed redo and undo costs, respectively. t_d and t_l represent the disk and log access times when no new transactions are being accepted and processed. These values are obtained from a disk subsystem model for the case where is little contention for the utilization of the disk channels since there is no normal transaction activity (see Appendix B).

For model 1, the redo operations are limited to the buffer. Therefore, for each page to be recovered, there is the time to bring the old page from the disk (t_d) and the time to bring the after image from the log (t_l/b_l). For model 2, with the need to write the redone page back to the database disk, there is an extra t_d in the first component of Eq. 10.19. In both models, the time to undo pages prematurely written to the database disk is estimated in the same way: For each one of the P active transactions, there are n_w pages to be undone. Each page is read into the buffer, appropriately changed, and written back to disk.

The coefficient b of Eq. 10.6 is estimated in both models as

$$b = 2n_l\gamma\frac{t_l}{b_l} \tag{10.20}$$

Where b expresses the time required to process the log per unit of time elapsed in normal processing. During normal operation, γ transactions are processed per unit of time. Each transaction is responsible for writing n_l records to the log file, so that the number of log entries generated per unit of operational time is given by $n_l\gamma$. During log processing, each log entry takes t_l/b_l units of time to be transferred to main memory. We also consider that the log is read twice.

The value of n_l can be determined as a function of the number of writes per transaction n_w, for the case of noforce / steal buffer management as

$$n_l = 2 + 2n_w \tag{10.21}$$

Each transaction writes one beginning of transaction record, one before image and one after image for each page written, and one end of transaction record.

Effect of Transaction Arrival Rates

Numerical results for the first set of experiments are presented in Figures 10.5. The impact of varying the transaction load is investigated for the two recovery strategies: buffer only (B) and buffer and disk (B/D). We also varied the size of the buffer, since this is a parameter that affects both the recovery time, as seen in Eqs. 10.18 and 10.19, and the checkpointing duration. For this set of experiments, $E[T_0]$ is obtained as Bt_d (the entire buffer is flushed). The system failure rate is fixed at 0.00001 per second and the transaction configuration is 10 reads and 10 writes per transaction.

In Figure 10.5(a) the values for optimal intercheckpointing intervals determined by the models are shown. As expected, these values are higher for the buffer and disk method, with the largest differences presented when the arrival rate is smallest (50 transactions per second). Also, the optimal intercheckpointing intervals increase as the buffer size increases. To maximize the availability of the system, longer periods are taken between checkpoints, for more time is spent in recovery and checkpointing due to the larger buffer.

The maximized availability for the two methods is displayed in Figure 10.5(b). Buffer-only recovery dominates buffer-and-disk. At small buffer sizes, little difference is noted between the two methods.

Figure 10.5(c) depicts the effect of varying the buffer size and the arrival rate on the mean recovery time. Again, buffer-only methods dominate for the entire range in which we varied the parameters. This dominance increases with the buffer size. From Figures 10.5(b) and 10.5(c), it is apparent that the extra effort to extend the recovered pages to the database disk does not pay off in terms of gaining on the availability of the system: Recovery should be done at the buffer only.

Effect of Failure Rates

Using the base case parameters and fixing the arrival rate at 100 per second, we investigated the effect of varying the system failure rate while also varying the buffer size. Each transaction reads and writes 10 pages. The results are shown in Figures 10.6. The optimal values for the intercheckpointing intervals are very close for both methods, as displayed by Figure 10.6(a). Figure 10.6(b) shows that the availability of the system drops substantially when the failure rate is at 0.0001 per second (~1 failure every 3 hours), which fortunately is very unrealistic for real database systems. Overall, buffer-only strategies dominate buffer and disk strategies. The same conclusion can be verified from Figure 10.6(c), where the effect on the mean recovery times is presented.

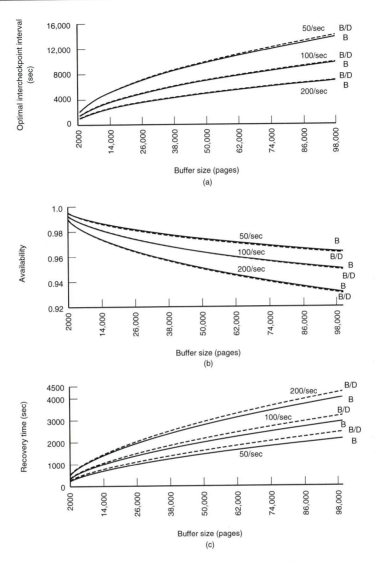

Figure 10.5. Effect of transaction arrival rates.

10.7.2 Checkpointing Strategies

Checkpointing strategies vary according to the duration taken during the check-pointing period. It is well known that fuzzy strategies are faster than traditional ACC or TCC strategies because only a fraction of the database buffer is flushed to permanent storage. The question to investigate is how much better the overall performance of the system becomes as smaller fractions of the buffer are flushed. The outcome of this set of experiments for the base case parameters is presented in

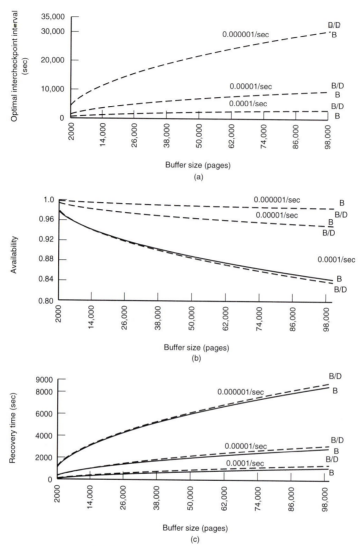

Figure 10.6. Effect of failure rates.

Figures 10.7. Since the buffer size is crucial in the determination of the duration of the checkpointing operations, the results are again plotted for different buffer sizes We also look at how the duration of the checkpointing period affects the buffer-only and buffer-and-disk recovery strategies. The arrival rate is 100 per second and the system failure rate is 0.00001 per second. Each transaction reads and writes 10 pages.

It is clear that flushing smaller fractions of the buffer during checkpointing al-

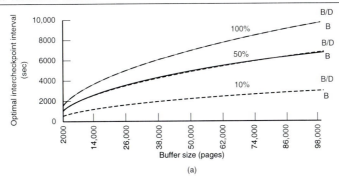

(a)

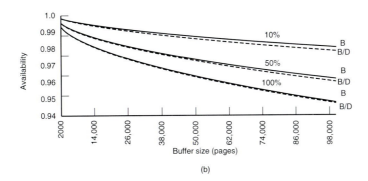

(b)

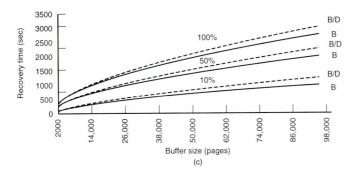

(c)

Figure 10.7. Effect of checkpointing duration.

lows the system to optimally trigger checkpoints at shorter intervals. Since the checkpointing operation becomes less costly, the system can trigger checkpoints more frequently so that the availability is maximized, as demonstrated by Figures

10.7(a) and 10.7(b). It is also evident from these graphs that availability is greater at small buffer sizes. The effect of the duration of checkpoints on the mean recovery time is shown in Figure 10.7(c). Because checkpointing occurs more frequently, the amount of recovery information to be processed after a failure is reduced. Consequently, the beneficial effect of shorter checkpointing periods is also felt at recovery time. Also, as confirmed previously, buffer-only strategies dominate buffer-and-disk recovery under the various scenarios investigated.

10.7.3   Recovery-Oriented Activities During Normal Operation

The recovery-related activities that take place during normal operation have direct impact on all phases of the operational cycle. First, they impose extra overhead to the processing of transactions in normal operation. Second, the performance of recovery is a function of how the redundant data are collected and organized. Finally, the work that is done during checkpointing of flushing pages from the buffer depends on the way the buffer is managed during normal operation.

We designed a set of numerical experiments to evaluate buffer management activities. Models 1 and 2 are used to assess the effect of these activities on the "off-line" stages (checkpointing and recovery) through the measures availability and mean recovery time. Model 3 is used to determine how recovery-related activities during normal operation impact the transaction processing time and system throughput.

Determination of Model 3 Parameters

For the sake of simplicity, we assume that all visits to each secondary storage node DBD and LOG have the same time requirements. In other words,

$$s_{DBD,t} = s_{DBD}, \ t = 1, ..., n_{DBD} \quad s_{LOG,t} = s_{LOG}, \ t = 1, ..., n_{LOG}.$$

The input parameters for model 3 that need to be determined are the visit ratios V_{ij}'s, the total number of database disk visits n_{DBD}, and the total number of log visits n_{LOG}. Tables 9.3 and 9.4 present these parameters for force and no force strategies, respectively. The first column of each table shows the detailed visits to the database disk node. The second column has the corresponding information for the log node. The third column displays the derivation of the visit ratios. The last row in each table has the values of the total number of visits to each device. Notice that we are not considering visits to the main memory node: We assume an I/O bound system in which processing times are dominated by disk accesses. Also for the sake of simplicity, in these experiments, individual transactions do not fail during their execution. Transaction failures can be easily accommodated in the model by defining extra "restart" visits to the nodes according to the transaction failure probabilities.

The processing of a transaction in a force environment can be traced by reading Table 10.3. The first operation is to write to the log a BOT (beginning of transaction) mark. Since log entries are buffered before written, the visit ratio for this

Table 10.3. Model 3 Input Parameters: Force Strategy

Force		
Disk Access $(i = DBD)$	**Log Access** $(i = LOG)$	**Visit Ratio** V_{ij}
	BOT $(j = 1)$	$1/b_l$
Bring Page $(j = 1)$		$(1 - C_b)n_r$
	Before Image $(j = 2)$	n_w/b_l
Write Page $(j = 2)$		n_w
	EOT $(j = 3)$	$1/b_l$
$n_{DBD} = 2$	$n_{LOG} = 4$	

operation is $1/b_l$. The next operation is to bring the pages to the buffer, if they are not already there. With probability $(1 - C_b)$, a page will be brought to the buffer, where C_b is the buffer communality, a parameter that is a function of the page replacement strategy in place[1]. Before pages are updated, before images in the log need to be created. Due to the force strategy, all n_w pages are then written to the database disk. Upon reaching the transaction commit point, an EOT (end of transaction) mark is written to the log.

In Table 10.4, one can see that because of the noforce nature, one needs to make room for the requested pages before they are brought into the buffer. Therefore, the first operation to the database disk is to write $(1 - C_b)n_w$ old pages. In addition, under no force, after images have to be written to the log file. Pages are not written back to the database disk after they are updated.

Results

Four transaction configurations (n_r, n_w) were considered: (5, 5), (10, 5), (10, 10), and (20, 5); the degree of multiprogramming was also varied due to its importance as a tunable parameter and as a measure of capacity in the queueing network model. Figures 10.8(a) and 10.8(b) show the values of response time (in msec) for the alternatives considered. It is salient that the force discipline is outperformed by no force. Forcing updated pages to the database disk is way too costly. The queuing network model shows that the utilization of the database disk is rather high for the

---

[1] For example, the popular LRU (Least Recently Used) algorithm. Based on analyses of [5] and [10], we adopted a value of $C_b = 0.85$ in the experiments.

Table 10.4. Model 3 Input Parameters: No Force Strategy

No Force		
Disk Access ($i = DBD$)	**Log Access** ($i = LOG$)	**Visit Ratio** V_{ij}
	BOT ($j = 1$)	$1/b_l$
Write Page ($j = 1$)		$(1 - C_b)n_w$
Bring Page ($j = 2$)		$(1 - C_b)n_r$
	Before Image ($j = 2$)	n_w/b_l
	After Image ($j = 3$)	n_w/b_l
	EOT ($j = 4$)	$1/b_l$
$n_{DBD} = 2$	$n_{LOG} = 5$	

force strategy, which translates into substantial overhead and congestion delays to the transaction processing. This observation is overwhelmingly true for transactions with higher update demands, for example, configuration (10 reads, 10 writes). The difference in response time between force and no force becomes wider as the degree of multiprogramming increases, that is, as the database is required to handle a larger number of simultaneous transactions. The demands on the database disk are too high and the congestion delays are excessive.

Figures 10.8(c) and 10.8(d) are the most revealing about the differences in normal operation performance between force and no force. As expected, the transaction throughput increases with the degree of multiprogramming P. However, the maximum throughput attained by the force strategy is considerably lower than the maximum throughput of no force strategies under the same transaction loads and configurations. For example, the maximum throughput attained by force for 10 reads and 10 writes under the base case environment is approximately 10 transactions per second. For the same parameters, a no force strategy yields over 50 transactions per second, a fivefold difference! The conclusion is obvious: Force disciplines should not be used in environments subject to a high level of on-line database transactions.

The positive side of force disciplines is nonetheless displayed in Figures 10.9(a) and 10.9(b) for the base case parameters, a failure rate of 0.00001 per second, and a transaction configuration of 5 reads and 5 writes. For low transaction activity (less than 20 per second), force outperforms no force both in availability and mean

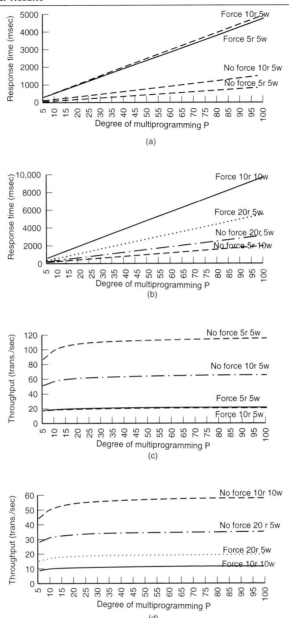

Figure 10.8. Response time and throughput analysis: Force versus no force.

recovery time. Since all updated pages are immediately written to the database disk, upon system failures, the recovery operations under force are minimal. For arrival rates above 20 transactions per second, a force discipline is inappropriate for the system becomes totally congested.

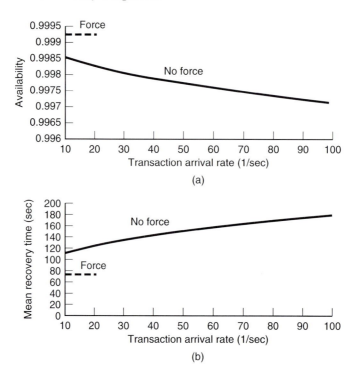

Figure 10.9. Availability and recovery time analysis: Force versus no force.

10.7.4 Comparison with Previous Models and Summary of Results

The three models proposed in this chapter provide a comprehensive tool to assess performance of recovery mechanisms. For the sake of gaining perspective on the effectiveness of our approach, Table 9.5 displays the main features of several models followed by our major conclusion regarding the recovery case studied in this section.

From Table 10.4, we notice that Reuter [30] addresses several performance features. His work is commonly accepted in the literature as state-of-the-art analytical modeling of a variety of proposed recovery methods [2]. Contrasting his approach to ours, we identify the following simplifications in his model:

- The performance measure used is the number of I/O operations. No differentiation is made between log and database disk accesses or access during normal operation and access during checkpointing or recovery. The different nature of these I/O accesses implies rather different access times.

Table 10.5. Comparison of Analytical Models

Feature	[6]	[15]	[39]	[41]	[30]	This chapter
Stochastic analysis	√	√	√	√		√
Availability measure	√	√	√	√		√
Optimum checkpoint interval	√	√	√	√	√	√
I/O modeling					√	√
Buffer management					√	√
Checkpointing operations					√	√
Buffer-only recovery	√	√	√	√	√	√
Buffer-and-disk recovery					√	√
Congestion effects						√

- No congestion or queuing effects are taken into account during normal operation. We have seen in the previous subsection (see, e.g., Figure 10.9.) that the throughput yielded in normal operation is not linearly proportional to the number of active transactions in the system due to inherent resource contention delays.

- The failure process and the transaction arrival process are not considered in a stochastic sense.

Despite the preceding simplifications, Reuter's work deserves merit for outlining the detailed processes of the various recovery mechanisms. His conclusions regarding the case of physical logs, linear recovery periods, and deterministic checkpointing are (a) force should be ruled out in applications with high update frequencies, and (b) if logs with redo information are used because of no force disciplines, checkpointing must be used.

Among other results, our models corroborate Reuter's two conclusions and tend to agree with empirical observations reported by practitioners [4, 12, 15]. In addition, we also provide new observations that cannot be reached by the previous models and are able to explain properly the behavior of various components of the recovery methods under different operational and environment parameters. Our main conclusions for the specific recovery case studied are summarized in what followed.

Design Issues

- Buffer-only recovery dominates buffer-and-disk recovery in terms of system availability and mean recovery time for the systems and environments studied.

The extra effort to write recovered pages to the database disk during recovery does not produce extra benefits for the overall system performance.

- Strategies that flush only a fraction of the buffer, such as fuzzy checkpointing should be preferred for systems with relatively high update intensity. In addition to decreasing the checkpointing time, gains in the system availability and mean recovery time are generated.

- Force disciplines are beneficial only for very low arrival rates, in which case they can achieve higher system availability and shorter recovery times. No force should always be used for high update intensity.

Administration Issues: Effect of Tunable Parameters

- The system availability can be maximized by an optimal choice of the interval between checkpointing operations. A relatively large leeway for this choice is allowed due to the "shallow bowl" shape of the availability function.

- Although a larger buffer can speed up normal operation activities, it affects negatively the system availability because more time is spent during checkpointing and recovering the buffer.

- Increasing the number of allowed active transactions increases the system processing capacity. However, due to queuing effects, the gains diminish rapidly with the increase in the multiprogramming level. The transaction processing time increases with larger number of active transactions.

Effect of Application Environment

- If failures are very rare, little impact is felt at the system availability. The recovery time should be used as a primary performance measure.

- High update intensity has the largest impact on all components of the recovery control subsystem: Recovery periods are longer because of the increase in redo information to be processed, checkpointing has to occur more frequently and the normal operations need to be designed such that the system throughput is able to handle the high update rate.

10.8   CONCLUDING REMARKS AND FUTURE RESEARCH

In this chapter, we have developed stochastic models to analyze the performance of recovery control of database systems. These models are considerably more general than the previous models in the literature. Not only do they adequately capture the dynamics of the underlying stochastic processes, but are also able to incorporate important details of the many recovery mechanisms that have been proposed. By deriving several important performance measures, the models do provide the ability to compare the different factors that affect performance, thus facilitating the identification of the most important design features, operational parameters and environment parameters. The effect of these key parameters then can be investigated and explained in a convenient way.

We used experiments based on a specific case of database recovery that utilizes physical logs, linear recovery periods, and deterministic checkpoints in order to assess the effectiveness of the models and contrast their reach against previous studies. Our observations tend to agree with empirical conclusions achieved by practitioners, corroborate some of the conclusions of the previous analytical models, but essentially provide newer and more comprehensive ways of analyzing the performance of database recovery methods.

We caution that the models are not intended to yield *exact* performance predictions in terms of system availability, response time, or recovery time with a defined error margin. To obtain this degree of precision, one must include many details about the implementation of the recovery algorithm itself and other components of the DBMS it has to cooperate with. As analytical models based on certain assumptions, their main objective is to gain quick insights and conduct sensitivity analyses. They offer more flexibility and are far less costly than constructing real prototype systems or even developing simulation models.

In addition to the analyses presented in this research the authors have extended the three models of this chapter to further investigate database recovery. A more detailed analysis of recovery-related operations during normal processing, which includes the study of log buffering schemes and the impact of the size of the log buffer appears in [18]. In [17], the concept of a database buffer is taken to the extreme of main memory resident systems. An extension of model 1 is used for the analysis of recovery of such systems.

Finally, modern databases will have to deal with new, nontraditional data or objects, in the form of documents, image, video, voice, knowledge, and so on, which will considerably impact the way database transactions are processed [32]. New database architectures are being developed, which make better use and combine different storage media, so that new kinds of data can be integrated. Underlying all these developments is the enormous challenge of designing and managing the recovery component of database systems. We believe that the models developed in this chapter can be very useful as a tool for analysis of recovery of the newer, emerging database architectures designed to handle complex data objects.

10.9   Appendix A - Analysis of the Database Recovery Model 2

The derivations of this appendix refer to the definitions of Section 10.4 and Figure 10.3. We start by defining

$$F_0(x,t) = P[X(t) \leq x, J(t) = 0 | J(0^+) = 1, X(0^+) = 0]; \quad f_0(x,t) = \frac{\partial}{\partial x} F_0(x,t)$$

$$F_1(x,t) = P[X(t) \leq x, J(t) = 1 | J(0^+) = 1, X(0^+) = 0]; \quad f_1(x,t) = \frac{\partial}{\partial x} F_1(x,t)$$

$$F_2(x, y, t) = P[X(t) \le x, Y(t) \le y, J(t) = 2 | J(0^+) = 1, X(0^+) = 0];$$

$$f_2(x, y, t) = \frac{\partial^2}{\partial x \partial y} F_2(x, y, t)$$

For the trivariate process to be at $(x, 0, 0)$ at time t, it had to be at $(0, 0, 0)$ at time $t - x$, and during the period of length x, no transition to normal processing has taken place. This condition can be expressed as

$$f_0(x, t) = f_0(0^+, t - x)\bar{A}_0(x) \tag{10.22}$$

where a bar over the distribution function denotes the corresponding survival function. For the process to be at $(x, 0, 1)$ at time t, it had to be at $(0, 0, 1)$ at time $t - x$, with neither a transition to checkpointing nor a failure occurring during the normal operation period of length x. We then get

$$f_1(x, t) = \{f_1(0^+, t - x) + \delta(t - x)\}\bar{A}_1(x)e^{-\lambda x} \tag{10.23}$$

where $\delta(t)$ is the delta function corresponding to the initial condition of the system. Similarly, we can write the condition for the system to be at $(x, y, 2)$ as

$$f_2(x, y, t) = f_2(x, 0, t - y)\bar{B}_x(y) = \lambda f_1(x, t - y)\bar{B}_x(y) \tag{10.24}$$

The entry conditions at the states $(0, 0, 0)$ and $(0, 0, 1)$ are expressed respectively by

$$f_0(0^+, t) = \int_0^\infty f_1(x, t)\eta_1(x)dx \tag{10.25}$$

and

$$f_1(0^+, t) = \int_0^\infty f_0(x, t)\eta_0(x)dx + \int_0^\infty dx \int_0^\infty f_2(x, y, t)\zeta_x(y)dy \tag{10.26}$$

Substituting (A.2) into (A.4), one obtains

$$f_0(0^+, t) = \int_0^\infty f_1(0^+, t - x)a_1(x)e^{-\lambda x}dx + a_1(t)e^{-\lambda t} \tag{10.27}$$

where $a_1(x)$ is the p.d.f. associated with T_1. Taking the Laplace transform of both sides of (A.6) with respect to t, it can be readily seen that

$$\hat{f}_0(0^+, s) = \hat{f}_1(0^+, s)\alpha_1(s + \lambda) + \alpha_1(s + \lambda) \tag{10.28}$$

where $\hat{f}_i(0^+, s) = \int_0^\infty e^{-st} f_i(0^+, t)dt$, $i = 0, 1$, and $\alpha_1(s) = \int_0^\infty e^{-st}a_1(t)dt$
Working out from (A.1),(A.2),(A.3) and (A.5), we can write

$$f_1(0^+, t) = \int_0^\infty f_0(0^+, t - x)a_0(x)dx$$
$$+\lambda \int_0^\infty dx \int_0^\infty \{f_1(0^+, t - x - y) + \delta(t - x - y)\}\bar{A}_1(x)e^{-\lambda x}b_x(y)dy,$$

$a_0(x)$ where the p.d.f. associated with T_0. Taking the Laplace transform with respect to t on both sides, and defining $\alpha_0(s) = \int_0^\infty e^{-st} a_0(t) dt$, we obtain

$$
\begin{aligned}
\hat{f}_1(0^+, s) &= \hat{f}_0(0^+, s) \alpha_0(s) \\
&+ \lambda \int_0^\infty dx\, e^{-sx} \bar{A}_1(x) e^{-\lambda x} \int_0^\infty dy\, e^{-sy} b_x(y) \\
&\quad \int_0^\infty e^{-s(t-x-y)} \{ f_1(0^+, t-x-y) + \delta(t-x-y) \} dt
\end{aligned}
$$

After some algebra this leads to

$$
\hat{f}_1(0^+, s) = \hat{f}_0(0^+, s) \alpha_0(s) + \lambda \{ \hat{f}_1(0^+, s) + 1 \} \int_0^\infty e^{-(s+\lambda)x} \bar{A}_1(x) \beta_x(s) dx
$$

where $\beta_x(s)$ is the Laplace transform of $b_x(t)$ with respect to t. By defining

$$
\gamma(s, \lambda) = \int_0^\infty e^{-(s+\lambda)x} \bar{A}_1(x) \beta_x(s) dx \tag{10.29}
$$

we can finally obtain

$$
\{ 1 - \lambda \gamma(s, \lambda) \} \hat{f}_1(0^+, s) = \hat{f}_0(0, s) \alpha_0(s) + \lambda \gamma(s, \lambda) \tag{10.30}
$$

Equations (A.7) and (A.8) together provide means for deriving

$$
\hat{f}_1(0^+, s) = \frac{\lambda \gamma(s, \lambda) + \alpha_0(s) \alpha_1(s+\lambda)}{1 - \{ \lambda \gamma(s, \lambda) + \alpha_0(s) \alpha_1(s+\lambda) \}}
$$

and

$$
\hat{f}_0(0^+, s) = \frac{\alpha_1(s+\lambda)}{1 - \{ \lambda \gamma(s, \lambda) + \alpha_0(s) \alpha_1(s+\lambda) \}}
$$

We now define the double transform

$$
\hat{\hat{f}}_1(w, s) = \int_0^\infty dt\, e^{-st} \int_0^\infty e^{-wx} f_1(x, t) dx \tag{10.31}
$$

By substituting (A.2) into (A.10), the following is obtained:

$$
\hat{\hat{f}}_1(w, s) = [\hat{f}_1(0^+, s) + 1] \frac{1 - \alpha_1(s+w+\lambda)}{s+w+\lambda}
$$

The ergodic availability of the system is given by $\pi_1 = \lim_{s \to 0^+} s \hat{\hat{f}}_1(0, s)$, which can be explicitly evaluated from the preceding expression after some algebraic manipulation with L'Hospital as

$$
\pi_1 = \frac{1 - \alpha_1(\lambda)}{\lambda [E[T_0] \alpha_1(\lambda) - \lambda G(\lambda) - \dot{\alpha}_1(\lambda)]} \tag{10.32}
$$

where

$$G(\lambda) = \frac{\partial}{\partial s}\gamma(s,\lambda)|_{s=0}; \quad \dot{\alpha}_1(\lambda) = \frac{\partial}{\partial s}\alpha_1(s)|_{s=\lambda} \tag{10.33}$$

In a similar fashion, the double transform $\hat{\hat{f}}_0(w,s)$ can be computed as

$$\hat{\hat{f}}_0(w,s) = \hat{f}(0^+,s)\frac{1-\alpha_0(s+w)}{s+w}$$

The ergodic probability of $J(t)$ being in state 0 (checkpointing) is therefore given by

$$\pi_0 = \lim_{s\to 0^+} s\hat{\hat{f}}_0(0,s) = \frac{E[T_0]\alpha_1(\lambda)}{E[T_0]\alpha_1(\lambda) - \lambda G(\lambda) - \dot{\alpha}_1(\lambda)} \tag{10.34}$$

The ergodic probability of $J(t)$ being in a recovery period, given by π_2, is directly obtained from (A.11) and (A.13), as $1 - \pi_0 - \pi_1$:

$$\pi_2 = \frac{\alpha_1(\lambda) - \lambda^2 G(\lambda) - \lambda\dot{\alpha}_1(\lambda) - 1}{\lambda\{E[T_0]\alpha_1(\lambda) - \lambda G(\lambda) - \dot{\alpha}_1(\lambda)\}} \tag{10.35}$$

From (A.8) and (A.12), $G(\lambda)$ can be written as

$$G(\lambda) = -G_1(\lambda) - G_2(\lambda)$$

where

$$G_1(\lambda) = \int_0^\infty xe^{-\lambda x}\bar{A}_1(x)dx \text{ and } G_2(\lambda) = \int_0^\infty e^{-\lambda x}\bar{A}_1(x)E[V_x]dx$$

Recognizing that the RHS of the expression for the preceding $G_1(\lambda)$ is $-\frac{\partial}{\partial\lambda}\mathcal{L}(\bar{A}_1(x))$, where $\mathcal{L}(\bar{A}_1(x))$ stands for the Laplace transform of $\bar{A}_1(x)$, $G_1(\lambda)$ can be easily obtained as

$$G_1(\lambda) = \frac{\lambda\dot{\alpha}_1(\lambda) - \alpha_1(\lambda) + 1}{\lambda^2}$$

10.10   Appendix B : Disk Subsystem Operational Parameters

The parameter values in Table 10.6 were used in the disk subsystem performance evaluation model [7, 11], which gives input values for the database disk and log I/O recovery times t_d and t_l. These parameters are also used as input to model 3.

Table 10.6. IBM 3390 Disk Subsystem : Parameter Values

Parameter	Value
Time to send a command	100 μsec
Seek time fixed parameter	1490 μsec
Seek time variable parameter	10 μsec/cylinder
Number of cylinders per device	2226
Rotational speed	14100 μsec/revolution
Disk density	56664 bytes/track
Disk locality of Reference	0.9
Data transfer rate	5.2 Mbytes/sec
Disk cache read hit ratio	0.82

References

[1] Agrawal, R. and Dewitt, D. J., "Integrated Concurrency Control and Recovery Mechanisms: Design and Performance Evaluation," *ACM Transactions on Database Systems*, 10(4) (1985).

[2] Bernstein, P. A., Hadzilacos, V. and Goodman, N., *Concurrency Control and Recovery in Database Systems*, Addison-Wesley (1987).

[3] Brooks, R. C., "An Approach to High Availability in High Transaction Rate Systems," *IBM Systems Journal* 24(3/4) (1985).

[4] Burman, M., "Aspects of a High-Volume Production On-Line Banking System," *IEEE COMPCON*, Spring (1985).

[5] Casas, I. R. and Sevcik, K. C., "A Buffer Management Model for Use in Predicting Overall Database System Performance," proceedings of the *IEEE Conference on Data Engineering*, (1989).

[6] Chandy, K. M., Browne, J. C., Dissly, C. W. and Uhrig, W. R., "Analytic Models for Rollback and Recovery Strategies," *IEEE Trans. on Software Engineering*, SE-1(1) (March 1975).

[7] Coffman, E. G. and Hofri, M., "Queueing Models of Secondary Storage Devices" in *Stochastic Analysis of Computer and Communication Systems*, Takagi (Ed.) Elsevier (1990).

[8] de Souza e Silva, E. and Gail, H. R., "Calculating Availability and Performability Measures of Repairable Computer Systems Using Randomization", *Journal of the ACM*, 36(1) (1989).

[9] de Souza e Silva, E. and Muntz, R. R., "Queueing Networks: Solutions and Applications," in *Stochastic Analysis of Computer and Communication Systems*, Takagi (Ed.), Elsevier (1990).

[10] Elhardt, K. and Bayer, R., "A Database Cache for High Performance and Fast Restart in Database Systems," *ACM Transactions in Database Systems*, 9(4) (December 1984).

[11] Gavish, B. and Sumita, U., "Analysis of Channel and Disk Subsystems in Computer Systems," *Queueing Systems: Theory and Applications*, 3(1) (1988).

[12] Gawlick, "Processing 'Hot Spots' in High Performance Systems," *IEEE COMPCON*, Spring (1985).

[13] Gelenbe, E., "On the Optimum Checkpoint Interval," *Communications of the ACM*, 22(2) (April 1979).

[14] Gelenbe, E. and Derochette, D., "Performance of Rollback Recovery Systems Under Intermittent Failures," *Communications of the ACM*, 21(6) (June 1978).

[15] Gifford, D. and Spector, A., "The TWA Reservation System," *Communications of the ACM* 27 (7), July (1984).

[16] Goes, P. B., *Performance of Recovery Control for Database Systems: a Hierarchical Analysis*, Ph.D. Thesis, William E. Simon Graduate School of Business Administration, University of Rochester, (1991).

[17] Goes, P. B., "A Stochastic Model for Performance Evaluation of Main Memory Resident Database Systems," to appear in *ORSA Journal on Computing*, (1995).

[18] Goes, P. B. and Sumita, U., *A Closed Queueing Network Model to Evaluate the Impact of Recovery Operations on the Performance of Database Servers*, Working Paper, University of Connecticut, (1994).

[19] Grassi, V., Donatiello, L., and Tucci, S., "On the Optimal Checkpointing of Critical Tasks and Transaction-Oriented Systems", *IEEE Transactions on Software Engineering*, 18(1) (January 1992).

[20] Gray, J., *Notes on Database Operating Systems*, Technical Report RJ 3120, IBM Research Center, San Jose, CA. (1978).

[21] Haerder, T. and Reuter, A., "Principles of Transaction-Oriented Database Recovery," *ACM Computing Surveys* 15(4) (December 1983).

[22] IBM, *IMS/VS Version 1 Fast Path Feature General Information Manual*, (1984).

[23] IBM, *Database 2 Version 2 General Information*, (1988).

[24] IBM, *IBM 3390 Direct Access Storage Introduction*, (1989).

[25] Jain, R., *The Art of Computer Systems Performance Analysis*, John Wiley and Sons, (1991).

[26] Kent, J., Garcia-Molina, H. and Chung, J., "An Experimental Evaluation of Crash Recovery Mechanisms," *4th ACM SIGACT-SIGMOD Symp. Principles Database Systems*, (1985).

[27] Lavenberg, S. S. (Ed.), *Computer Performance Modelling Handbook*, Academic Press, (1983).

[28] Lazowska, E. D., Zahorjan, J., Graham, G. S. and Sevcik, K. C., *Quantitative System Performance–Computer System Analysis Using Queueing Network Models*, Prentice-Hall (1984).

[29] L'Ecuyer, P. and Malenfant, J., "Computing Optimal Checkpointing Strategies for Rollback and Recovery Systems", *IEEE Transactions on Computers*, 37(4) (April 1988).

[30] Reuter, A., "Performance Analysis of Recovery Techniques," em ACM Transactions on Database Systems, 9(4) (December 1984).

[31] Schweitzer, P. J., "Approximate Analysis of Multiclass Closed Network of Queues," *Proceedings of the International Conference on Stochastic Control and Optimization*, Free University, Amsterdam, (1979).

[32] Silberschatz, A., Stonebraker, M., and Ullman, J., "Database Systems: Achievements and Opportunities," *Communications of the ACM*, 34(10) (October 1991).

[33] Stonebraker, M., "Operating System Support for Database Management," *Communications of the ACM*, 24(7) (July 1981).

[34] Stonebraker, M., "The Design of the POSTGRES Storage System," in proceedings of *13th Very Large Database Conference*, Brighton (1987).

[35] Sumita, U., Kaio, N. and Goes, P. B., "Analysis of Effective Service Time with Age Dependent Interruptions and Its Application to Optimal Rollback Policy for Database Management," *Queueing Systems: Theory and Applications*, Vol. 4, (1989).

[36] Tantawi, A. N. and Ruschitzka, M., "Performance Analysis of Checkpointing Strategies", *ACM Transactions on Computer Systems*, 2(2) (May 1984).

[37] Young, J. W., "A First Order Approximation to the Optimum Checkpoint Interval," *Communications of the ACM* 17(9) (September 1974).

Chapter 11

Analytical Modeling and Comparison of Buffer Coherency and Dirty-Page Propagation Policies under Different Recovery Complexities

Asit Dan and Philip S. Yu

Abstract

In a multinode shared disk environment, buffer coherency control can be achieved through retaining a lock on each page in the buffer, even after the requesting transaction has committed. In addition to tracking the validity of the buffered pages, additional capabilities can be provided through lock retention such as deferred writes to disk on commit, (node) location identification of valid pages to support internode page transfer, and restricting the number of replications of a page across buffers of different nodes. However, these can have serious implications, not only on the performance but also on the recovery complexity. In this chapter, six different integrated coherency and dirty-page propagation policies are considered. We classify these policies into three different categories according to their recovery requirements. A performance study based on analytic models is provided to understand the trade-offs on both throughputs and response times of the policies with a similar level of recovery complexity and the performance gain achievable through increasing the level of recovery complexity. The analytic model is able to capture the buffer composition in terms of the different lock modes retained on the buffer pages and the intricacies of the different coherency polices. A detailed simulation model is also developed to validate the analytic models.

11.1 INTRODUCTION

Coupling multiple microprocessors to form a powerful data server has become increasingly popular. Data sharing (see Figure 11.1) is one of the coupling architectures where multiple processing nodes share common disks and each node maintains a local buffer to reduce the number of I/Os [6, 24, 26, 25, 29, 36]. It is the coupling architecture used by DEC VAX-Cluster (or Alpha-Cluster) [17] and IBM S/390 Parallel Sysplex [16]. Data sharing is supported by various commercial database products, including Oracle, IBM DB2, and IMS. In this chapter, we focus on the transaction processing application in a multi-node data sharing environment.

In the data sharing environment, global concurrency control is needed for maintaining serializability across multiple concurrently executed transactions on different nodes. Here a centralized global lock manager (GLM) is assumed, referred to as the concurrency controller in Figure 11.1. An example of this type of data sharing system is the IBM S/390 Parallel Sysplex. The presence of high-speed interconnect is also assumed among the nodes for message exchange and data transfer.

The issue of buffer coherency control arises in this environment. Some coherency policy is needed to ensure that the data pages present in multiple local buffers are up to date, where a page is the unit of transfer between memory and disks. There are many different approaches to devise buffer coherency control policies. One way to maintain coherency is via *lock retention*, that is, to retain a lock on each buffer page at GLM by the buffer manager, even after the transaction accessing the page is committed [15, 23, 25, 32].

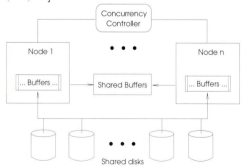

Figure 11.1. Database sharing architecture.

This lock for coherency control is in addition to the lock on each data granule required by transactions for the purpose of concurrency control. The locks for coherency control (respectively, concurrency control) are sometimes referred to as *physical* (respectively, *logical*) locks [23]. The concurrency and coherency control can be integrated by combining the two locks to reduce the message overhead between the processing node and GLM, if the data granule for logical locking is also a page [2, 12, 22, 26, 25, 27]. (This combined lock is referred to as LP lock in [22].) In this chapter, we develop analytical models to study the relative performance of six different coherency policies that are based on lock retention of this combined lock.

Depending on the lock mode (e.g., shared vs. exclusive) held for retention, different coherency control policies can be devised. In addition to tracking the validity of the buffered pages, additional capabilities can be provided, including

- deferred writes to support the *no-force* scheme[1] on commit [23],

- (node) location identification of valid granules to support internode page transfer for remote memory access,[2] (as in [14] in a client-server database environment)

- restriction on the number of replications across buffers

- shared/exclusive lock retention to reduce the number of global lock requests for concurrency control

In [26, 32], a shared lock retention approach (called *read optimization* policy) is used to provide coherency control under the *force* scheme. The approach saves the global lock request message for a read access if the lock is already retained in the executing node. Retention of exclusive locks (also known as *sole interest*) is also proposed in [25]. Mohan and Narang [23] have proposed and detailed several buffer coherency policies based on exclusive lock retention to support a *no-force* scheme at commit. These policies differ on the time when an updated page is forced out to disk and the way remote memory transfer is carried out. The ways by which the writes are deferred can have serious implications to *recovery complexity* in terms of processing overhead and recovery time. It is assumed that each node maintains its own log. Deferred writes within a single node require going back further into the log of that node to redo the missing updates during recovery. This is referred to as the *medium* recovery characteristic in contrast to the *simple recovery* characteristic of the policies under the *force* scheme. Deferred writes across multiple nodes, that is, letting a page accumulate updates from multiple nodes before it is written back to disk, would require a log merge across nodes before the recovery can be started. This is referred to as the *complex recovery* characteristic.

---

[1] Under a *force* scheme, updated pages are propagated to the disk at most by the transaction commit time, whereas they can be deferred under a *no-force* scheme.

[2] With the advent of high-bandwidth interconnection technology, the time to obtain a data page buffered in another node through internode page transfer is expected to be far less than the disk I/O time. This is referred to as remote caching in [19].

11.1.1   Primary Focus

In this chapter, we consider six different integrated concurrency coherency policies under the three recovery characteristics mentioned earlier. Depending on the
lock modes retained, these policies also differ in another dimension, which is the
mechanism for invalidation: notification-vs. detection-oriented approach, where the
notification-oriented approach requires each node being explicitly notified of the invalidation, and the detection-oriented approach only determines the validity of a
page at the next access time [9]. Two of the policies with lock retention (based
on the notification-oriented approach) are variants of the policies considered in [23]
with medium and complex recovery characteristics, respectively. We consider additional variation to restrain the proliferation of the number of buffered copies of
a page. We further examine extension of the detection-oriented policies to support
deferred writes. Without loss of generality, we consider these two variations only
for the policies with the complex recovery characteristic. For the policies with the
simple recovery characteristic, besides a detection-oriented policy [2, 12, 26], we
also examine a shared lock retention policy under the force scheme [26, 32]. Apart
from the differences in recovery complexity, there are obvious performance trade-offs
among the policies. While increasing the recovery complexity, the deferred write
or no-force scheme obviously reduces the number of disk writes. But an additional
number of messages are incurred to maintain coherency when a dirty page, that
is, an updated page not yet written to disk, is needed by another node. *Thus, the
major contribution of this chapter is to provide an understanding of the trade-offs
on both throughputs and response times of these polices with a similar level of recovery complexity and the performance gain achievable through increasing the level
of recovery complexity.* (The recovery-time analysis is a separate subject in its own
right and is studied in [11].)

*Another contribution in this chapter is to develop a general analytical framework
that can be used to analyze and compare the relative performance of the various policies under different recovery characteristics.* The analytic buffer model developed is
able to capture the buffer composition in terms of the different lock modes retained
on the buffer pages and the intricacies of the different coherency policies. We also
model the notion of affinity, which is shown in this chapter to have a strong impact
on the performance of these policies. The modeling methodology is based on extensions of the methodologies developed in [6, 8, 9] where a simpler case of the buffer
composition in terms of the logical groupings based on access frequencies, like hot
set and cold set, is addressed. The LRU analysis methodology in [6, 8, 9] sets up a
set of forward recurrence relations by decomposing the LRU stack into substacks.
In this chapter we extend the LRU analysis methodology to the cases where such
substack decomposition is not applicable (detailed later).

We next describe briefly related earlier performance studies. The remainder of
the chapter is organized as follows. Section 11.2 describes the details of the the six
buffer coherency policies that are considered in this chapter. The analytical models
to estimate the local and remote buffer hit probabilities, the CPU overhead due to

various types of coherency messages, and the overall transaction response time are developed in Section 11.3. The performance comparisons are presented in Section 11.4. A summary and concluding remarks appear in Section 11.5.

11.1.2   Related Performance Study

In [25], a trace-driven simulation study was conducted to compare the performance of the shared lock retention policy to that of the policies that do not retain any lock, and the shared lock retention policy was found to perform better. In [9], six different policies with only the simple recovery characteristic (i.e., based on the force scheme) and no logical lock retention are examined. The policies are classified broadly into three categories: *detection* of invalidated pages, *notification* of invalidated pages, and *propagation* of updated pages, and analytic models are developed to compare the performance trade-offs. It was found that a detection-oriented policy shows the most robust performance. Except for the broadcast invalidation and propagation policies, the buffer coherency control is integrated with concurrency control at the global lock manager, in that work. Several policies considered in the simulation studies in [33, 4, 32] for a client-server architecture fall under the category of the simple recovery characteristic. The primary concern of these papers is the efficient resolution of conflict across the active transactions in the system. In [14], several integrated data and lock caching algorithms are compared in a client-server architecture, where, in addition to the client buffers, server buffers can also be used to cache data. The trade-offs of shared/exclusive lock retention was studied for the client-server environment in [13].

11.2   BUFFER COHERENCY POLICIES

Here, we will describe the data sharing environment (Figure. 11.1) and the various integrated concurrency coherency policies in detail. Standard two-phase locking is used for concurrency control by GLM. The GLM can be implemented through some specialized processor [16, 28]. The access conflicts across transactions executing in different nodes are resolved by the GLM and the access conflict across transactions executing in the same node is resolved by the local lock manager (LLM) in each node. To access a data granule (which is assumed to be a page in this chapter), a transaction requires a *logical* lock (shared or exclusive) on that granule as well as an up-to-date (valid) version of that data granule in its executing node. Each node maintains a local buffer and caches a part of the database in this buffer to reduce the transaction response time. An LRU (Least Recently Used) buffer replacement scheme is used by each node for its local buffer management.

The copies of the same page may be present at more than one node. Therefore, a coherency control mechanism is needed to prevent obsolete pages from being accessed. The concurrency and coherency messages should be combined whenever possible to reduce the CPU overhead. The GLM can provide an integrated concurrency-coherency management through additional *physical* locks on buffer pages to guarantee buffer validity. The number of messages to the GLM can be reduced by combining the logical and physical locks into one lock. The retained combined lock is released and the associated buffer copy is purged if either there is a conflicting request or the buffer copy is pushed out of the buffer. Note that the lock can be either shared(S) or exclusive(X). A shared lock implies that only the shared read requests can be granted to a local transaction, and the page can be present in other buffer. On the other hand, an exclusive lock ensures that no other node has a copy of this page and update requests can be granted locally. Additional lock modes may be required for some of the policies, as described in what follows. We will first discuss the performance issues resulting from variations along several dimensions, and then describe in detail the six selected policies.

11.2.1   Buffer Coherency Performance Issues

At transaction commit time, *write-ahead logs* are forced to the disk to guarantee that the updates can be permanently reflected onto the database. However, the updated pages need not be immediately propagated to the disk if exclusive locks on the updated pages are retained by the LLM.[3] This is referred to as deferred write [31]. If the updated pages are further updated by any subsequent transactions in the same node, only the final versions need to be propagated to the disk before releasing the exclusive locks. This way many write I/Os may be saved, improving system throughput and response time. However, the deferred-write scheme increases the recovery complexity, as the updates in the write-ahead logs that need to be examined and applied may go back for a long period of time in case of a node failure.

A retained X lock needs to be either downgraded to an S lock or released if a lock on the same page is requested by a remote node in S or X mode, respectively. To keep the recovery scheme simpler in the medium recovery scheme, an updated page can accumulate updates only from a single node and, hence, the updated page needs to be propagated to the disk before the X lock is downgraded or released. Upon the failure of a node, to recreate the dirty pages, only the log entries of the failed node need to be applied. However, this forced propagation during an inter-system page transfer results in additional I/O delay and larger transaction response time. A copy of the updated page is transferred directly to the requesting node after the propagation to the disk is completed. This type of schemes with *medium* recovery complexity is referred to as the *Medium* scheme in [23] due to performance consideration. (Note that in [23], the logical and physical locks are two different entities (page and record) and hence separate. The focus there is on data or physical lock retention. Here the logical and physical locks are combined as in [22] and the retention of these combined locks are considered [22].)

The write I/O can be further deferred (and perhaps saved) at the expense of increasing the recovery complexity by not propagating the updated pages to the disk on transfer. Since the deferred write now involves updates by transactions across

---

[3] Note that locks cannot be downgraded or released by the node until the pages are propagated to the disk to guarantee that other nodes see the most recent copy of these pages.

multiple nodes, a more complex recovery scheme that uses merged logs of all nodes is required. This type of schemes with *complex* recovery is referred to as the *Fast* scheme in [23] for its ability to have faster page transfer and the most reduction in write I/O. Aperiodic checkpointing scheme can be used to asynchronously write out long-time dirty pages to reduce recovery time [21]. Assuming the disk is not the bottleneck, this should have little impact on normal performance. (Recovery-time analysis for schemes corresponding to the complex and medium recovery characteristics is beyond the scope of this chapter. The recovery issue is discussed in detail in [23] and analyzed in [11].)

Within each level of recovery complexity, there are additional dimensions that result in many different coherency control schemes. For example, in [9], six different coherency schemes are evaluated that are all with the *simple* recovery characteristic and no logical lock retention. The focus there is on the invalidation mechanisms (i.e., detection vs. notification). The schemes trade off response time and throughput in different ways. The detection-oriented scheme (referred to as the check-on-access scheme) was found to provide shorter response time as well as higher throughput for a wide range of system and workload parameters. Here our focus is on the *data and lock* retention. Apart from the recovery aspect, another new dimension considered here is to restrict the number of in-buffer replications to fully exploit the advantage of remote memory accesses. This can improve the buffering efficiency, and, hence, reduce the number of disk reads, but increase the local buffer misses, and, hence, increase the number of messages, and memory-to-memory transfers. Even without resorting to deferred writes to keep the recovery simple, an S lock retention on previously accessed pages can be used to save the number of lock requests if subsequent accesses to these pages are from the same node. Otherwise, additional messages will incur. Thus, the number of messages needed to resolve the coherency and serialization requirements and the number of I/Os are quite different for these schemes. Therefore, in addition to a detection-oriented scheme, we select five alternative schemes (choice of them should be clear, as the results are presented) to explore data lock retention and evaluate their relative performance through analytical models.

11.2.2 Schemes with Simple Recovery

As mentioned earlier, under this recovery scheme, writes are forced at the transaction commit time. However, the propagation delay of write I/Os is not included in the transaction response time. We choose two different policies under this recovery scheme: One retains no lock and the other retains only the shared lock.

Check-on-Access (CA) Policy. Under this policy, the obsolete pages are detected at the page access time by a transaction. At the transaction commit time, all locks are released while the GLM continues to track the nodes buffering each page using a valid bit per node and mark their copies invalid on subsequent updates by another node [12]. Before accessing any page, the processing node of the transaction makes a global lock request to the GLM. In response, the integrated GLM returns not only the requested lock, but also the result of the associated buffer validity check based on the valid bit. Note that the page is valid at the lock release time at the executing node. At the lock release time, if the page has been updated, the valid bits corresponding to all other nodes except the updating node (which is the only node with an up-to-date version of that page) will be turned off. The policy certainly saves the overhead of sending immediate notification of page invalidations to other nodes, but it also reduces the buffer hit probability as the obsolete pages continue to reside in the local buffer [9].

Shared Lock Retention (SLR) Policy.   Here the S locks are retained by the node even after the transaction has completed, but until the associated data page is flushed out of buffer. The X locks are downgraded to S locks, so that an S lock request by a remote node can be granted by the GLM immediately. Retention of an S lock has two advantages. First, an S lock request by a subsequent local transaction can be granted without the overhead of an GLM lock request, if it has been retained. Otherwise, a lock request is made to the GLM. This is in contrast to CA, where no lock is retained and every lock request for a page causes a message to the GLM. Second, through the retained S lock, the GLM can identify the nodes with a valid buffer copy, and notify it to forward a copy to the requesting node. However, if an X lock is requested by a remote node, GLM has to revoke all the S locks retained (also the pages are purged from buffers) before the X lock is granted. This can incur a large message overhead, negating the advantage of retention. If the lock is held by an active transaction, the change of lock ownership or lock mode will be delayed until the end of the transaction. Hereon, to simplify the explanation, we only present the case where conflicting locks are retained for coherency control purposes.

11.2.3   Schemes with Medium Recovery

Deferred until Transfer or Flushing (DTF) Policy.   Here the writes (or dirty pages) are deferred as long as the X locks are retained. The writes are forced to the disk before a node-to-node page transfer occurs due to a lock request by a remote node either in an S or X mode. If the remote request is for an S lock, then the local X lock retained is downgraded to an S mode. Otherwise, if the remote request is for an X lock, the local X lock retained is released and the local buffer copy is purged. The writes are also propagated to the disk if an updated page is pushed out of buffer, referred to as buffer flushing. When a page is pushed out of the buffer, its associated lock (S or X) is also released. In actual implementation, the write propagation can be initiated once the updated page is close to the bottom of the LRU stack, so that no synchronous I/O delay is incurred due to buffer flushing. Note that to avoid a race condition (i.e., out-of-order write propagation from different nodes), an X lock is not released by a node until the write I/O is completed. Note also that after flushing, the lock release messages can be piggybacked with other GLM communications (e.g., lock request message). Figure 11.1 describes the details of the DTF policy. There is a chance of deadlock between nodes if multiple nodes concurrently try to upgrade from S to X mode. One possibility is that during upgrade, a node only asks for X mode conditionally. If it cannot get it, the S lock is released and then an X lock will be requested unconditionally. Since the other policies share a lot of similarity, we will focus only on their differences.

11.2.4 Schemes with Complex Recovery

Deferred until Flushing (DF) Policy. This is similar to the DTF policy as far as propagation of updated pages to the disk as the buffer flushing goes. However, on a lock request by a remote node, updates are not propagated to the disk. If the remote request is for an X lock, similar to the DTF policy, both the updated page as well as the X lock are transferred to the requesting node. On the other hand, if the remote request is for an S lock, the local node downgrades its X lock to the shared mode, and a copy of the page is also send to the requesting node. Note that the updated page still needs to be propagated to the disk by one of the nodes eventually. Therefore, a new form of shared lock, called a U lock, is introduced [23]. The local shared lock is in the U mode, implying a pending update propagation. Therefore, at the buffer flushing time, not only the pages associated with X locks, but also the ones with U locks are propagated to the disk.

Restricted Proliferation along with Deferred until Flushing (ODF) Policy. In both DTF and DF policies, one can restrain the proliferations of buffered copies for a page. One simple implementation is to only allow one node at a time to buffer a page. This can improve the buffer efficiency as replications in multiple buffers are disallowed. However, the policy can be inefficient if there are enough buffers available in the system, since replications of hot data can substantially reduce node-to-node page transfer. We can easily extend the implementation to apply the restrictions on proliferations only to certain relations and allow the hot relations to be buffered at multiple buffers. Since restricting proliferation is a separate dimension, we consider this policy only for the case with complex recovery to illustrate the idea.

Check-on-Access with Deferred until Flushing (CADF) Policy. This policy integrates deferred write and remote memory-access features of the DF policy with the validity-checking mechanism of the check-on-access (CA) policy. As in the CA policy, the GLM maintains a valid bit corresponding to each of the buffer pages in all the nodes, and this bit is checked during the time of an access to this page. The GLM also maintains a dirty bit, in addition to the valid bit, for each of the buffer pages. Before a page is replaced out of any of the buffer, it needs to be propagated to the disk if it is valid and dirty. We will assume that the checking of a dirty bit message is piggy backed with other lock request messages and a write I/O is scheduled for a page on flushing. To avoid race condition, a temporary X lock is obtained on a page before scheduling its I/O.

11.3   PERFORMANCE MODEL

We first describe the details of the data sharing environment, and then develop the buffer model under the LRU replacement policy, which provides an estimation of the number of pages holding various types of locks (S, X, and U locks) retained in a particular buffer. We will then present the estimation of local and remote buffer hit probabilities and the overall system model for the estimation of response time.

11.3.1   Data Sharing Environment and Model Assumptions

The data sharing system considered consists of N loosely coupled nodes. Each node maintains a local buffer of size B. Transactions arrive at each node according to a Poisson process with rate λ. We assume that each transaction accesses L pages from the shared database. Each page access is assumed to be independent of all other page accesses (Independent Reference Model, IRM) [9]. Such a model holds for many database transaction processing applications where each transaction accesses a relatively small set of pages.

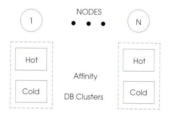

Figure 11.2. Database affinity clusters.

In a transaction processing environment, there are generally multiple transaction classes and relations [5]. Each transaction class may exhibit affinity to certain relations. To reduce the intersystem interference and improve the local buffer hit probability, the related transactions (that reference mostly the same set of relations) can be grouped logically into *affinity clusters* (AC) [34] and the transactions associated with an affinity cluster are routed to the same node by the front-end router. The relations associated with each AC is referred to as a DB cluster (see Figure 11.2). Let η be the fraction of pages accessed by a transaction from its associated DB cluster. We will assume each transaction accesses the remaining fraction, $(1 - \eta)$, of its data from the nonassociated DB clusters uniformly. Let each DB cluster consists of D pages. The database accesses within each DB cluster need not be uniform, that is, some pages are accessed more often than others. The skewed access pattern is modeled in an earlier work as access to two kinds of data [30] (*hot* data and *cold* data). A common model is the so-called 80:20 rule, where 80% of the accesses go to a hot set that comprises 20% of the database. In general, the access pattern can be approximated as consisting of multiple such partitions [6, 8], as shown in [7], based on real workload traces. Based on the frequency of data access, the data pages within each cluster are grouped into P partitions, such that the probability of accessing any page within a partition is uniform (see Figure 11.2). Let β_p denote the fraction of the DB cluster pages in partition p, that is, the size of partition p is $\beta_p D$. Let α_p be the probability of accessing a page of the pth partition of this cluster, given that a page is accessed from this DB cluster. The probability that an accessed page is also updated is denoted as γ.

For the purpose of analysis, the entire database can be divided into NP partitions, that is, N DB clusters and P partitions within each cluster (see Figure 11.2). Each partition is identified by the subscript pair $(n,p), n \in \{1, \ldots, N\}, p \in \{1, \ldots, P\}$. Define $D_{n,p}$ to be the size of partition (n,p). Then, $D_{n,p}$ is given by $D\beta_p$. Note that transactions at node m have a higher affinity to the partitions $(m, p), p = 1, \ldots, P$, although pages in partition (m, p) can be accessed and buffered by transactions in any node. Taking the view from node m, let $\lambda_{n,p,m}^{lcl}$ be the rate at which data from partition (n,p) are accessed by the local transactions of node m, and $\lambda_{n,p,m}^{rem}$ be the rate at which they are accessed by the remote transactions, that is, transactions executed at nodes other than node m. Now, for $p = 1, \ldots, P$,

$$\lambda_{n,p,m}^{lcl} = \begin{cases} \lambda L \alpha_p \eta, & \text{if } n = m \\ \lambda L \alpha_p \frac{1-\eta}{N-1} & \text{otherwise} \end{cases}$$

and

$$\lambda_{n,p,m}^{rem} = \begin{cases} \lambda L \alpha_p (N-1) \frac{1-\eta}{N-1} & \text{if } n = m \\ \lambda L \alpha_p \left\{ \eta + \frac{(N-2)(1-\eta)}{N-1} \right\} & \text{otherwise} \end{cases} \qquad (11.1)$$

We now explain how the expression for $\lambda_{n,p,m}^{rem}$ is obtained, whereas that for $\lambda_{n,p,m}^{lcl}$ is straightforward. Note that the partitions (m,p), for $p = 1, \ldots, P$ (i.e., partitions of the DB cluster m), are nonaffinity partitions to the transactions executed at the $(N-1)$ remote nodes. These remote transactions access the partition (m,p) with probability $(1-\eta)/(N-1)$ for each page access, and the total transaction rate due to these transactions is $(N-1)\lambda$. For each of the remaining partitions, (n,p), only the transactions at node n have an affinity to this partition (i.e., they access this partition with a probability η), and the transactions executed at the other $(N-2)$ remote nodes access this partition with a probability of $(1-\eta)/(N-1)$ for each access.

11.3.2 Buffer Model

To estimate the steady-state buffer hit probability, we first derive the average number of pages of each partition in the local buffer holding S, X, or U locks, respectively (see Figure 11.3). Let us focus our attention to the buffer at the mth node. The parameter m is fixed for the following set of equations, and the analysis can be repeated for all other nodes. Our analysis extends the methodology used in [8, 9] for estimating the buffer hit probabilities under the broadcast invalidation and check-on-access policies. Here the analysis methodology is extended to set up a set of recursive equations for estimating the number of pages of each partition holding each type of locks in the top $(k+1)$ locations of the LRU stack.

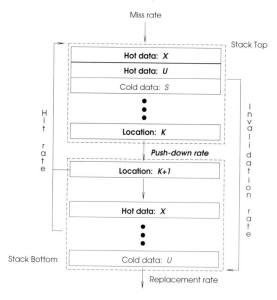

Figure 11.3. LRU buffer management policy.

As shown in Figure 11.3, for any k, the LRU buffer can be viewed as consisting of two parts: the stack top, consisting of the top k locations, and the stack bottom, containing the rest of the stack. Let $Y_{n,p,m}(k)$ denote the average number of pages of partition (n,p) present in the top k buffer locations of the mth node. (Table 11.1 provides a summary of the symbols used in this chapter.) Similarly, let $S_{n,p,m}(k)$, $X_{n,p,m}(k)$, and $U_{n,p,m}(k)$ denote the average number of pages holding S, X, and U locks, respectively, in the top substack at node m. Under the CADF and CA policies, there are also some buffer pages that are invalid, and we denote $Z_{n,p,m}(k)$ as the average number of invalid pages in the top substack at node m. We say an analysis is *substack decomposable* if the recurrence equation for the $(k+1)$th location only involves these quantities relating to the top substack. This simplifies the analysis as it involves only a forward recurrence. Another important factor in simplifying the LRU analysis is the *node isolatable* property, where the buffer contents at each node can be analyzed separately. All the previous work on LRU analysis in [6, 8, 9] satisfies both the *substack decomposable* and *node isolatable* properties. Here the recurrence equations for $Y_{n,p,m}(k+1)$ and $Z_{n,p,m}(k+1)$ also satisfy these properties.

The recurrence equations for $X_{n,p,m}(k+1)$ and $U_{n,p,m}(k+1)$, however, involve not only these quantities in the top substack, but also those of the bottom substack. For example, under the DTF policy, the dirty pages (i.e., pages holding X locks) can be brought to the top substack from the bottom substack due to a read hit on a dirty page. The recurrence equation for $X_{n,p,m}(k+1)$ needs to relate to

Table 11.1. Summary of the Symbols Used.

System Environment

N	Number of nodes
B	Buffer size per node
M_{cpu}	Processor speed in MIPS
T_{io}	I/O access delay
T_{log}	Log I/O delay

Workload

D	Number of database pages per cluster
P	Number of database partitions within each DB cluster
α_p	Probability of accessing the pth partition of a cluster given that the page lies in this cluster
β_p	Fraction of database pages that lies in partition p of any DB cluster
γ	Probability of updating an accessed page
L	Average number of pages accessed by a transaction
λ	Mean transaction arrival rate per node
I_{trx}	Base instructions executed per transaction
I_{io}	Instruction overhead per I/O operation
I_{GLM}	Overhead per communication with the GLM
I_{page}	Overhead per page transfer

Other symbols: Subscript (n,p,m) stands for activity to partition (n,p) as viewed by transactions at node m.

$\lambda_{n,p,m}^{lcl}$	Access rate to pages of partition (n,p) by local transactions at node m
$\lambda_{n,p,m}^{rem}$	Access rate to pages of partition (n,p) by remote transactions to node m
$f_{n,p,m}$	Average number of pages of accessed from partition (n,p) by a transaction
$Y_{n,p,m}(k)$	Average number of pages of partition (n,p) in the top k buffer locations at node m ($X_{n,p,m}(k)$, $S_{n,p,m}(k)$, and $U_{n,p,m}(k)$ are defined similarly for the pages holding X, S, and U locks)
$y_{n,p,m}(k)$	Probability that the kth buffer location at node m holds a page of partition (n,p) ($x_{n,p,m}(k)$ and $u_{n,p,m}(k)$ are defined similarly for the X and U lock holding pages)
$r_{n,p,m}(k)$	Pushdown rate of partition (n,p) pages from the kth buffer location at node m ($r_{n,p,m}^X(k)$ and $r_{n,p,m}^U(k)$ are defined similarly for the X an d U lock holding pages)
$h_{n,p,m}^{X,lcl}$	Buffer hit probability for local exclusive pages of partition (n,p) at node m ($h_{n,p,m}^{X,rem}$, $h_{n,p,m}^{SU,lcl}$, and $h_{n,p,m}^{SU,rem}$ are defined similarly for the remote exclusive, local shared, and remote shared pages)
$h_{n,p,m}$	Overall buffer hit probability for the pages of partition (n,p)
$N_{n,p,m}^{SU,rem}$	Average number of SU locks revoked per page update
I_{syn}	Total CPU demand as a part of response time
I_{asyn}	Additional CPU demand per transaction (not part of response time)
ρ	CPU utilization
R_{cpu}	CPU component of mean transaction response time
R_{io}	I/O component of mean transaction response time
R	Mean transaction. response time

the rate of bringing up new dirty pages to the top substack (detailed later). The estimation of the read hit probability on a dirty page in the bottom substack requires knowledge of its contents. (Note that in estimating $Y_{n,p,m}(k+1)$, we need the buffer miss probability in the top substack, but there is no need to distinguish between whether the missed granule is brought back from the bottom substack or the disk.) Therefore, the recurrence equation for $X_{n,p,m}(k+1)$ does not satisfy the substack decomposable property. Furthermore, as we shall see, certain schemes like the ODF policy even violate the node isolatable property. Hence, *an important methodological contribution of this chapter is to provide LRU analysis methodology for the quantities that do not satisfy the substack decomposable property and/or the node isolatable property.* The solution method is based on multiple iterations of the LRU analysis. For example, in solving a recurrence equation that requires both the quantities of the top and bottom substacks, the quantities for the bottom substack from the previous iteration are used in solving the recurrence equation for the current iteration step. The values of the quantities in the bottom substack are assumed to be zero for the first iteration step. Note that an approximation of this analysis is reported in [10], where the values of the quantities in the bottom substack are ignored, and thus no iterations are required. Such an approximation is accurate only for smaller buffer sizes.

General Overview of the LRU Analysis. We will now provide the general overview of this analysis, followed by the specific details for each of the policies. Let $y_{n,p,m}(k)$ be the probability that the kth buffer location from the top of the LRU stack at node m contains a (valid or invalid) page of partition (n,p). Let $z_{n,p,m}(k)$, $x_{n,p,m}(k)$, and $u_{n,p,m}(k)$ be the probabilities that the page is of partition (n,p) and is invalid, is X lock holder, and is U lock holder, respectively. Note that $z_{n,p,m}(k)$ is zero for all policies except the CA and the CADF policies. Then,

$$Y_{n,p,m}(k) = \sum_{l=1}^{k} y_{n,p,m}(l),$$

$$Z_{n,p,m}(k) = \sum_{l=1}^{k} z_{n,p,m}(l),$$

$$X_{n,p,m}(k) = \sum_{l=1}^{k} x_{n,p,m}(l),$$

$$U_{n,p,m}(k) = \sum_{l=1}^{k} u_{n,p,m}(l),$$

$$S_{n,p,m}(k) = Y_{n,p,m}(k) - Z_{n,p,m}(k) + X_{n,p,m}(k) + U_{n,p,m}(k) \qquad (11.2)$$

We will set up a recursive formulation to determine $y_{n,p,m}(k+1)$, $z_{n,p,m}(k+1)$, $x_{n,p,m}(k+1)$, and $u_{n,p,m}(k+1)$, for $k \geq 1$. The buffer location $(k+1)$ receives the page that is pushed down from location k (i.e., from the top stack in Figure 11.3). Let $r_{n,p,m}(k)$ be the rate at which pages of partition (n,p) are pushed down from location k. Similarly, let $r_{n,p,m}^{Z}(k)$, $r_{n,p,m}^{X}(k)$, and $r_{n,p,m}^{U}(k)$ be the rates at which pages of partition (n, p) that are invalid, holding an X lock and holding an U lock, respectively, are pushed down from location k. Our estimations of $y_{n,p,m}(k)$, $z_{n,p,m}(k)$, $x_{n,p,m}(k)$, and $u_{n,p,m}(k)$ are based on the following two observations.

Conservation of Flow: Under steady state conditions, the long term rate at which pages of the (n, p)th partition get pushed down from the top k locations of the buffer equals the difference in rates at which they are brought into the top k locations and at which they are purged from the top k locations due to invalidation, or transfer. Hence, the pushdown rate, $r_{n,p,m}(k)$ is given by

$$
r_{n,p,m}(k) = \begin{cases} \lambda^{lcl}_{n,p,m} \left[1 - \frac{Y_{n,p,m}(k)}{D_{n,p}}, \right] - \lambda^{rem}_{n,p,m} \gamma \frac{Y_{n,p,m}(k)}{D_{n,p}} & \text{for the SLR, DTF} \\ & \text{and DF policies} \\ \lambda^{lcl}_{n,p,m} \left[1 - \frac{Y_{n,p,m}(k)}{D_{n,p}}, \right] - \lambda^{rem}_{n,p,m} \frac{Y_{n,p,m}(k)}{D_{n,p}} & \text{for the ODF policy} \\ \lambda^{lcl}_{n,p,m} \left[1 - \frac{Y_{n,p,m}(k)}{D_{n,p}}, \right] & \text{for CADF and CA} \\ & \text{policies} \end{cases}
$$

(11.3)

Note that under the ODF policy, even a remote read results in the purge of the local copy due to the one-copy constraint. Under CADF and CA policies, notification is delayed and, hence, remote update does not result in a buffer purge.[4]

Using a similar conservation of flow argument for the pages holding X or U locks, we can derive the rate at which these pages of the $(n, p)^{th}$ partition get pushed down from the top k locations of the buffer. However, the quantities $r^X_{n,p,m}(k)$ and $r^U_{n,p,m}(k)$ do not satisfy the substack decomposable property, and, hence, their derivations are more complex (discussed later) for the DTF, DF, and SLR policies, and Section ?? for the ODF policy. As mentioned earlier, $r^Z_{n,p,m}(k)$ is zero for all policies except for the CA and CADF policies. Its derivation for the CA and CADF policies will be provided in Section 11.3.2.

Relative Pushdown Rate: The probability of finding a page of the (n, p)th partition in the $(k + 1)^{st}$ buffer location over all time, $y_{n,p,m}(k + 1)$, is approximately the same as the probability of finding a page of the (n, p)th partition in the $(k + 1)$st buffer location in the event that a page is pushed down from location k to location $(k + 1)$. That is to say, the relative down push rate of a (n, p)th partition page from location k to $k + 1$ determines the probability of location $(k + 1)$ containing a

---

[4]Strictly speaking, when remote buffer lookup is integrated with the CA policy, if the current access mode is updated, the buffer copy can be purged from the node from which it is read, while the notification to other nodes is delayed. However, this makes the analysis somewhat more complex, since several nodes simultaneously may hold such a copy, and only one of them will be read, and purged. Alternatively, the analysis can be viewed as the conservative estimate of its performance.

(n,p)th partition page. Hence, for $k = 0, \ldots, B - 1$,

$$y_{n,p,m}(k+1) \approx \frac{r_{n,p,m}(k)}{\sum_{i \in \{1,\ldots,N\}, j \in \{1,\ldots,P\}} r_{i,j,m}(k)} \tag{11.4}$$

Furthermore, the probabilities that the page at the $(k+1)^{st}$ location is of partition (n,p), and it is invalid, holds an X lock, and holds an U lock, respectively, are given in what follows, for $k = 0, \ldots, B - 1$:

$$z_{n,p,m}(k+1) \approx \frac{r^Z_{n,p,m}(k)}{r_{n,p,m}(k)} y_{n,p,m}(k+1)$$

$$x_{n,p,m}(k+1) \approx \frac{r^X_{n,p,m}(k)}{r_{n,p,m}(k)} y_{n,p,m}(k+1)$$

$$u_{n,p,m}(k+1) \approx \frac{r^U_{n,p,m}(k)}{r_{n,p,m}(k)} y_{n,p,m}(k+1) \tag{11.5}$$

Equations (11.2) through (11.4) can be solved iteratively with the base conditions of $y_{n,p,m}(0) = 0$. At the point when $Y_{n,p,m}(k)$ is very close to its limit $D_{n,p}$, $Y_{n,p,m}(k)$ may exceed $D_{n,p}$ because of the approximation in the preceding equations. This is corrected by resetting $Y_{n,p,m}(k)$ to $D_{n,p}$ whenever $Y_{n,p,m}(k)$ exceeds $D_{n,p}$, and $r_{n,p,m}(k)$, $r^X_{n,p,m}(k)$, and $r^U_{n,p,m}(k)$ are taken to be zero for all subsequent steps for that partition.

Analyses of the DF, DTF, and SLR Policies.   Let us first consider the DF policy. We need to estimate the number of buffer pages in each lock mode. The tracking of pages with an X or U lock is somewhat similar to the tracking of pages with any lock in the top k locations, $Y_{n,p,m}(k)$. The main difference lies in the fact that estimating the replacement rate, $r_{n,p,m}(k)$, for the pages of (n,p) partition with any lock needs to consider only the miss rate in the top k locations (i.e., the top substack), whereas that for the X or U pages requires also the knowledge of the state of the buffer pages outside the top substack (i.e., locations in the bottom substack). For example, the pages with an X lock can be brought from outside the top substack in two ways: (1) update access on a page that is not present in the top substack, and (2) read access on a page with an X lock that is present in the bottom substack, that is, the buffer hit on the pages in the set of size $\{X_{n,p,m}(B) - X_{n,p,m}(k)\}$, where B is the buffer size. Let $h^{X,bot}_{n,p,m}(k)$ represent a buffer hit on an X page in the bottom substack. Note that $X_{n,p,m}(B)$ and, therefore, $h^{X,bot}_{n,p,m}(k)$ are known only after the recursion step B. We therefore set up a second-level iteration over the LRU recursion analysis. At the jth iteration, the value of $X_{n,p,m}(B)$ obtained from the previous iteration (referred to as $X^{j-1}_{n,p,m}(B)$) is used to compute the new values of $X^j_{n,p,m}(k)$. Therefore, at the kth recursion step of the jth iteration,

$$h^{X,bot}_{n,p,m}(k) = \begin{cases} \frac{X^{j-1}_{n,p,m}(B) - X^j_{n,p,m}(k)}{D_{n,p}}, & \text{if } X^{j-1}_{n,p,m}(B) > X^j_{n,p,m}(k) \\ 0, & \text{otherwise} \end{cases} \tag{11.6}$$

Finally,

$$r_{n,p,m}^{X}(k) = \lambda_{n,p,m}^{lcl}\left(\gamma\left[1 - \frac{X_{n,p,m}(k)}{D_{n,p}}\right] + (1-\gamma)h_{n,p,m}^{X,bot}(k)\right) - \lambda_{n,p,m}^{rem}\frac{X_{n,p,m}(k)}{D_{n,p}}(11.7)$$

Here the first two terms provide the rate at which dirty pages are brought to the top substack due to write and read, and the last term is the rate they are depleted due to accesses from remote nodes. Note that X locks are lost not only on a remote exclusive lock request but also on a remote shared lock request, (converted to U locks). For the first iteration, step $X_{n,p,m}^{0}(B)$ is set to zero.

Similarly, $r_{n,p,m}^{U}(k)$ can be estimated. Let $h_{n,p,m}^{U,bot}(k)$ represent a buffer hit on an U page outside the top substack consisting of the top k locations. At the kth recursion step of the jth iteration,

$$h_{n,p,m}^{U,bot}(k) = \begin{cases} \frac{U_{n,p,m}^{j-1}(B)-U_{n,p,m}^{j}(k)}{D_{n,p}}, & \text{if } U_{n,p,m}^{j-1}(B) > U_{n,p,m}^{j}(k) \\ 0, & \text{otherwise} \end{cases} \qquad (11.8)$$

Now, the replacement rate for the pages holding an U lock is given by

$$\begin{aligned} r_{n,p,m}^{U}(k) &= \lambda_{n,p,m}^{rem}(1-\gamma)\frac{X_{n,p,m}(k)}{D_{n,p}} + \lambda_{n,p,m}^{lcl}(1-\gamma)h_{n,p,m}^{U,bot}(k) \\ &\quad -(\lambda_{n,p,m}^{lcl} + \lambda_{n,p,m}^{rem})\gamma\frac{U_{n,p,m}(k)}{D_{n,p}} \end{aligned} \qquad (11.9)$$

The first term represents the rate at which X locks are converted U locks due to remote read access, and the second term provides the rate at which the pages with a U lock are brought from the bottom substack to the top substack due to local read access. Finally, the last term provides the combined rate at which the U locks are either converted to X locks due to local write access or deleted due to remote write access.

The preceding set of equations hold for both the SLR and DTF policies, with the following exceptions. Under the DTF policy, there are no U locks, as writes are not allowed to be deferred after a remote S lock request. Here U locks are interpreted as S locks that is, the corresponding writes are already propagated. Under the SLR policy, additionally, there are no X locks, as writes are never deferred, and X locks are downgraded to S locks. Therefore, both X and U locks are interpreted as S locks for the purpose of analysis. Note that the pages that would have retained X locks are mutually disjoint in different buffers, and this distinction is important for the estimation of the overall buffer hit probability.

Analysis of the ODF policy. Under the ODF policy, only a single copy of a page can be retained in the buffers across all nodes. Therefore, a dirty page along with propagation responsibility is transferred across nodes, even on a read request. (Note

that under the DF policy, the dirty-page propagation responsibility is not transferred.) This nonisolatable property on nodes introduces additional complexity in
the LRU analysis on top of the complexity for the nondecomposable stack property.
The recurrence equation now requires not only the knowledge of the content of the
local bottom substack, but also that of the buffers in the remote nodes. This is
handled as follows. In each iteration step, the LRU analysis is carried out independently for each of the nodes, using the values pertaining to remote nodes from the
previous iteration. As before, in the first iteration step, the terms pertaining to the
local bottom substack and the remote buffers are assumed to be zero.

Let $h_{n,p,m}^{X,rem}$ denote the probability that the page of partition (n,p) lies in one of
the remote buffers (i.e., in buffers other than node m), and the page is holding an
X lock. At the jth iteration step,

$$h_{n,p,m}^{X,rem} = \frac{\sum_{i=1,i\neq m}^{N} X_{n,p,i}^{j-1}(B)}{D_{n,p}} \tag{11.10}$$

Now the replacement rate for the pages holding an X lock is given by

$$
\begin{aligned}
r_{n,p,m}^{X}(k) &= \lambda_{n,p,m}^{lcl}\left(\gamma\left[1-\frac{X_{n,p,m}(k)}{D_{n,p}}\right]+(1-\gamma)\left[h_{n,p,m}^{X,bot}(k)+h_{n,p,m}^{X,rem}\right]\right)\\
&\quad -\lambda_{n,p,m}^{rem}\frac{X_{n,p,m}(k)}{D_{n,p}}
\end{aligned}
\tag{11.11}
$$

Note the additional term relating to the read hit on the dirty pages in the remote
buffers. Under the ODF policy, there are no U pages.

Analyses of the CA and CADF policies

The analysis for the CADF policy captures both the complexities of the basic CA
and DF policies. The number of valid pages in a buffer, and, hence, the local buffer
hit probability are the same under both the CADF and basic CA policies. The
analysis of the CADF policy, in addition, provides an estimate of the number of
valid pages that are dirty with or without a replica of theses pages in other nodes.
Therefore, the analysis for the basic CA policy presented in [9] is a special case of
this analysis. Note that under the CADF and CA policies, no locks are retained
in any node, and invalidation notifications for a page are delayed until access time
in a remote node to that page. From the point of view of the overall buffer hit
probability, we need to distinguish between two types of dirty pages: (1) the ones
that have no other copies in remote nodes, and (2) the ones that have (clean)
replicas in remote nodes. These two types of pages are similar to the pages with X
and U locks, respectively, under the DF policy. Hence, under the CADF policy, we
will refer to these pages as pages with weak X locks and weak U locks, respectively.
These weak locks are not real locks, but correspond to status bit settings used by
the GLM to keep track of not only the validity but also the dirty-page propagation
responsibility.

The equations for the pushdown rates for the pages with weak X and U locks, $r_{n,p,m}^X(k)$ and $r_{n,p,m}^U(k)$, are the same as those under the DF policy, holding a lock in modes X and U, respectively. The equation for $r_{n,p,m}(k)$ has also already been provided by Equation(11.3.) Hence, we derive only the down push rate for the invalid pages. This is given by

$$r_{n,p,m}^Z(k) = \lambda_{n,p,m}^{rem} \gamma \frac{Y_{n,p,m}(k) - Z_{n,p,m}(k)}{D_{n,p}} - \lambda_{n,p,m}^{lcl} \frac{Z_{n,p,m}(k)}{D_{n,p}} \qquad (11.12)$$

The updates at the remote nodes invalidate all valid (clean or dirty) pages, and local accesses replace invalid pages with their valid copies. The first term provides the rate at which invalid pages are generated due to remote write access, and the second term provides the rate at which invalid pages are made valid due to local access.

11.3.3   Estimation of Local and Remote Buffer Hit Probabilities

In this subsection, we will show how to estimate the local, remote, and overall buffer hit probabilities from the point of view of the transactions at the mth node given the composition of buffers at all nodes. These probabilities provide not only the estimates of the average number of read I/O operations saved, but also the average number of messages of various types incurred (depending on the policy), and the average number of write propagations to disks. We will first focus our analysis on the DF policy, and then discuss the modifications needed for the other policies. The U locks are different from the S locks only from the point of view of write propagation at the time the page is pushed out of the buffer. Hence, from the transaction lock conflict resolution point of view (i.e., the average number of messages needed to revoke all shared locks, etc.), the same actions are taken for both S and U locks. Note that the sets of pages holding X locks in different buffers are mutually disjoint, and more than one copy of the other pages may be present in different buffers. Therefore, the computation of remote buffer hit probabilities for the pages with X locks is different from those of the pages with S or U locks.

Let $f_{n,p,m}$ be the average number of pages accessed from the partition (n,p) by a transaction executing at the mth node. Then $f_{n,p,m}$ is given by the equation

$$f_{n,p,m} = \frac{\lambda_{n,p,m}^{lcl}}{\lambda} \qquad (11.13)$$

Given that the next page accessed by a transaction at node m lies in partition (n,p), we need to estimate the following probabilities:

1. the probability that the page is found in the local buffer of the mth node holding an X lock, $h_{n,p,m}^{X,lcl}$

2. the probability that the page is found in one of the remote buffers holding an X lock, $h_{n,p,m}^{X,rem}$

3. the probability that the page is found in the local buffer of the mth node holding an S or U lock, $h_{n,p,m}^{SU,lcl}$

4. the joint probability that the page is found in one of the remote buffers holding an S or U lock, and it is not found locally, $h_{n,p,m}^{SU,rem}$

The probabilities $h_{n,p,m}^{X,lcl}$ and $h_{n,p,m}^{X,rem}$ can be estimated in a straightforward way, since the events are mutually disjoint. Therefore,

$$h_{n,p,m}^{X,lcl} = \frac{X_{n,p,m}(B)}{D_{n,p}} \tag{11.14}$$

The expression for $h_{n,p,m}^{X,rem}$ is given by Equation(11.10). The pages with shared locks can be present in multiple buffers, but cannot lie in the set of pages holding X locks. Therefore,

$$
\begin{aligned}
h_{n,p,m}^{SU,lcl} &= \left[1 - \left(h_{n,p,m}^{X,lcl} + h_{n,p,m}^{X,rem}\right)\right] \left[\frac{Y_{n,p,m} - (X_{n,p,m} + Z_{n,p,m})}{D_{n,p} - \sum_{i=1}^{N} X_{n,p,i}(B)}\right] \\
&= \frac{Y_{n,p,m} - (X_{n,p,m} + Z_{n,p,m})}{D_{n,p}}
\end{aligned}
\tag{11.15}
$$

The second term in the Equation 11.15 is the conditional probability that a valid page is found locally given that it does not lie in the set of pages holding an X lock. Note that $Z_{n,p,m}$ is zero for all policies except the CA and CADF policies. Similarly,

$$
\begin{aligned}
h_{n,p,m}^{SU,rem} = & \left[1 - \left(h_{n,p,m}^{X,lcl} + h_{n,p,m}^{X,rem}\right)\right] \left[1 - \frac{Y_{n,p,m} - (X_{n,p,m} + Z_{n,p,m})}{D_{n,p} - \sum_{i=1}^{N} X_{n,p,i}(B)}\right] \\
& \left\{1 - \prod_{j=1,j\neq m}^{N} \left[1 - \frac{Y_{n,p,j} - (X_{n,p,j} + Z_{n,p,j})}{D_{n,p} - \sum_{i=1}^{N} X_{n,p,i}(B)}\right]\right\}
\end{aligned}
\tag{11.16}
$$

As before, the first term is the probability that the page does not lie in the set of pages holding an X lock. Given that the page does not lie in the set of pages holding an X lock, it can still appear in both local and remote buffers independently. The second term is the conditional probability that the page is not present in the local buffer given the first condition. And the third term is the conditional probability that the page appears in one of the remote buffers given the first condition (the second condition has no effect on this term since the events are independent). After combining the first two terms in the preceding equation, it can be rewritten as

$$
\begin{aligned}
h_{n,p,m}^{SU,rem} = & \left[1 - \left(h_{n,p,m}^{X,lcl} + h_{n,p,m}^{X,rem} + h_{n,p,m}^{SU,lcl}\right)\right] \times \\
& \left\{1 - \prod_{j=1,j\neq m}^{N} \left[1 - \frac{Y_{n,p,j} - (X_{n,p,j} + Z_{n,p,j})}{D_{n,p} - \sum_{i=1}^{N} X_{n,p,i}(B)}\right]\right\}
\end{aligned}
\tag{11.17}
$$

One more related entity is the average number of shared (S or U) locks revoked per access, $N_{n,p,m}^{SU,rem}$. This will happen if the next access is an update and the page does not lie in the set of pages holding an X lock. Therefore,

$$N_{n,p,m}^{SU,rem} = \gamma \left[1 - \left(h_{n,p,m}^{X,lcl} + h_{n,p,m}^{X,rem}\right)\right] \left[\sum_{j=1,j\neq m}^{N} \frac{Y_{n,p,j} - (X_{n,p,j} + Z_{n,p,j})}{D_{n,p} - \sum_{i=1}^{N} X_{n,p,i}(B)}\right] \quad (11.18)$$

Finally, the overall buffer hit probability for a page of partition (n,p) for all policies (except the CA policy, which does not make use of remote buffers), $h_{n,p,m}$, can be written as

$$h_{n,p,m} = h_{n,p,m}^{X,lcl} + h_{n,p,m}^{X,rem} + h_{n,p,m}^{SU,lcl} + h_{n,p,m}^{SU,rem} \quad (11.19)$$

The preceding equations for the local and remote buffer hit probabilities and hence, for the overall buffer hit probability also hold for the DTF, SLR, and CADF policies. The expression for the average number of shared lock revocation messages also holds for the DTF and SLR policies. As mentioned earlier, no X locks are retained under the SLR policy, however, the interpretation in the preceding analysis of the pages with X locks in reality is that those pages with S locks are recently updated and are not yet replicated in other buffers.

Under the ODF policy, each page can be present in at most one buffer, irrespective of the lock mode retained on that page. Therefore, all events are independent and the equations for $h_{n,p,m}^{SU,lcl}$ and $h_{n,p,m}^{SU,rem}$ are modified as

$$h_{n,p,m}^{SU,lcl} = \frac{Y_{n,p,m} - X_{n,p,m}}{D_{n,p}}, \quad h_{n,p,m}^{SU,rem} = \sum_{i=1,i\neq m}^{N} \frac{Y_{n,p,i} - X_{n,p,i}}{D_{n,p}} \quad (11.20)$$

11.3.4 Integrated System Model

The execution time of a transaction depends on three main factors: (1) the private and remote buffer hit probabilities that determine the number of synchronous read and write I/O operations to be performed by the transaction, (2) the effect of the concurrency control (locking) schemes on resolving conflict in accessing data pages, and (3) the processing time and the queuing delay in accessing system resources such as CPU, and so on. We will use a hierarchical modeling approach where the buffer hit probabilities, concurrency control, and system resource access times are modeled separately and the interactions amongst the submodels are captured via a higher-level model [6, 8, 9]. This higher-level model relates quantities from the lower level models through a set of non-linear equations. The solution of the higher level model corresponds to the solution of a fixed-point problem, which we solve through an iterative process.

Since the concurrency control and the CPU resource models are similar to those used in previous studies [8, 9] of various coherency control policies with simple recovery, we will focus here on the CPU overhead of various concurrency-coherency messages under the different polices due to lock retentions and direct memory-to-memory transfers the buffer models for these policies were given in the previous subsection. The transaction response time can be broken down into three parts: (1) synchronous I/O delay (due to read or write), R_{io}, (2) CPU queuing delay and service time for application processing and synchronous concurrency-coherency overhead, R_{cpu}, and (3) lock contention wait time, R_{cont}. Thus, the average transaction response time, R, can be expressed as

$$R = R_{io} + R_{cpu} + R_{cont} \tag{11.21}$$

To estimate R_{cpu} for each of these policies, we have to estimate the average number of CPU instructions executed by a transaction across all nodes and the CPU utilizations in each node. Since the system is homogeneous, the CPU utilization is the same in all nodes. Let I_{syn} be the total number of instructions executed synchronously by a transaction as a part of its response time. In addition to I_{syn}, each transaction may incur an additional CPU overhead in the form of asynchronous write propagation overhead. Let I_{asyn} be the average number of instructions executed by all nodes on behalf of a transactions. Since the system is homogeneous, the average number of instructions executed on each node is $\lambda(I_{syn} + I_{asyn})$. Therefore, the CPU utilization on each node, ρ, is given by $\rho = \lambda(I_{syn} + I_{asyn})/M_{cpu}$, where M_{cpu} is the MIPS per node. By using a M/M/1 queuing model, the R_{cpu} is now given by

$$R_{cpu} = \frac{I_{syn}}{M_{cpu}(1 - \rho)} \tag{11.22}$$

In the next subsection, we will provide the estimates of I_{syn} and I_{asyn} under all policies.

The R_{io} under all policies consists of read I/O and log I/O delays, except under the DTF policy, where a fraction of write propagation (due to read or write on a remote dirty page) is also synchronous. Note that write propagation even under the simple recovery scheme is not included in the transaction response time, and hence can be viewed as asynchronous. Therefore, R_{io} can be written as

$$R_{io} = \begin{cases} \sum_{n=1, \ldots, N, p=1 \ldots P} f_{n,p,m}(1 - h_{n,p,m})T_{io} + T_{log} \\ \text{except for DTF policy} \\ \sum_{n=1, \ldots, N, p=1, \ldots, P} f_{n,p,m} \left[(1 - h_{n,p,m}) + h_{n,p,m}^{X,rem}\right] T_{io} + T_{log} \\ \text{only for DTF policy} \end{cases}$$

$$\tag{11.23}$$

where T_{io} and T_{log} are the I/O delays for random read/write and log write, respectively.

Let $P_{n,p}^{cont}$ be the contention probability encountered by each lock request to the (n, p) partition and R_{wait} be the average waiting time for a contended lock. Furthermore, define $\lambda_{n,p}$ to be the page request rate to the (n, p) partition, that is,

$\lambda_{n,p} = L\lambda\alpha_p$. Then R_{cont} is given by

$$R_{cont} = \sum_{n=1, \ldots, N, p=1,\ldots,P} f_{n,p,m} P_{n,p}^{cont} R_{wait} \qquad (11.24)$$

Based on the CC model in [36, 35], $P_{n,p}^{cont}$ can be estimated as proportional to the lock request rate to the (n,p) partition and the average lock hold time, R_{hold}, and inversely proportional to the size of the (n,p) partition. Thus,

$$P_{n,p}^{cont} = \frac{\lambda_{n,p} R_{hold}}{D_{n,p}} [\gamma + (1 - \gamma)\gamma] \qquad (11.25)$$

Note that a request for update conflicts with all ongoing access modes (read or write) on the same page, whereas a read request conflicts only with an ongoing update-access mode.

Assume that the granule accesses are spread uniformly across the execution time of a transaction. If the commit phase is short, as in all coherency policies with deferred writes, the average lock hold time, R_{hold}, would be $R/2$, and R_{wait} would be roughly equal to one-third of R [36] while a more elaborate estimate for and R_{hold} and R_{wait} can be found in [35]. Since R and R_{cont} in Equations (11.21) and (11.24), respectively, depend on each other, this corresponds to a fixed-point problem that we solve through an iterative process. We note that for the schemes with simple recovery characteristics, since the transactions are committed after the log writes, the propagation delay of write I/Os is not included in the transaction response time, but it is included in the lock hold time.

Estimation of CPU Utilization. We will show the estimation of I_{syn} and I_{asyn} for the DTF policy (which is the most complex policy), and it is done for the other policies in a very similar way. Let I_{trx} be the base number of instructions executed per transaction excluding the I/O and coherency overhead. Let I_{io} be the number of CPU instructions required per disk I/O operation. Also, let I_{GLM} be the number of instructions executed by a node per communication (e.g., lock request) with the GLM, and I_{page} be the total number of instructions executed (combined overhead of the sender and receiver nodes) to transfer a page between two nodes.

The next page to be accessed by a transaction may be in one of the five states (4 buffer states as enumerated in the earlier subsection and the buffer miss state), and different actions are taken depending on the state. The action also depends on the access mode of the current transaction. The actions are enumerated as follows:

1. **Local Exclusive.** No action is needed for this state as both the highest mode of a lock and up-to-date data are retained.

2. **Remote Exclusive.** Local node requests the GLM for an S or X lock depending on the access mode. The GLM requests the node holding the X lock to downgrade it to an S mode or revoke the X lock depending on the lock request mode. (These are the first and second GLM messages.) After

receiving the request from the GLM (if the lock is in the retention mode), the remote node first propagates the dirty page to the disk and then sends a copy directly to the requesting node. It then downgrades or releases its lock as per request, and, subsequently, the GLM grants the requested lock to the local node. (These are the third and fourth GLM messages.)

3. **Local Shared.** No action is needed for an S lock request, but all remote S lock revocations through the GLM are required if the next access is in X mode.

4. **Remote Shared.** Request for an S lock is granted by the GLM immediately. The GLM also requests one of the remote nodes holding an S lock on this page to transfer a copy of the page to the requesting node. In case of an X lock request, all the remote S locks are revoked before the X lock is granted by the GLM, and one of the S lock holding node also transfers a copy of that page. Note that the request for page transfer and the lock revocation can be combined into a single message by the GLM.

5. **Buffer Miss.** The lock request is granted by the GLM immediately, as no node is holding a lock. The page is read from the disk.

The I_{syn} can now be expressed as

$$
\begin{aligned}
I_{syn} \;=\; & I_{trx} + \sum_{n\in\{1,\,\ldots,\,N\},p\in\{1,\,\ldots,\,P\}} f_{n,p,m}\left[h_{n,p,m}^{X,rem}(4I_{GLM} + I_{page} + I_{io})\right. \\
& + N_{n,p,m}^{SU,rem}2I_{GLM} + h_{n,p,m}^{SU,lcl}\gamma 2I_{GLM} \\
& + h_{n,p,m}^{SU,rem}\{I_{GLM}(2 + (1-\gamma)) + I_{page}\} \\
& \left. + (1 - h_{n,p,m})(2I_{GLM} + I_{io})\right].
\end{aligned}
\tag{11.26}
$$

Here, the first term is for the remote exclusive case, and it involves four communications to the GLM (two on the requester side and two on the remote node), a page transfer, and a disk I/O propagation. The second term includes all revocations of remote shared locks (two per lock holding node). The third term is for the local shared case, and it includes only the request for upgrade to the X mode, since the remote S lock revocation is already included in the second term. The fourth term is for the remote shared hit case. It includes two communications for the requester (send and receive), one page transfer, and one communication to the remote node for read. Note that for the write request, the page transfer request to one of the remote node, can be combined with an invalidation message reflected in the second term. Finally, the last term is for the case of buffer miss.

I_{asyn} involves only the propagation of deferred writes at the buffer flushing time. Note that the release of the associated lock can be piggybacked with the next communication with the GLM, and, therefore, incurs no extra overhead. The additional CPU overhead per transaction, I_{asyn}, can be written as

$$I_{asyn} = \frac{\sum_{n \in \{1, \ldots, N\}, p \in \{1, \ldots, P\}} r_{n,p,m}^X(B) I_{io}}{\lambda} \qquad (11.27)$$

Recall from Equation(11.4) that $r_{n,p,m}^X(B)$ is the rate of flushing of the dirty pages from the buffer. For the DF policy, the numerator in Equation(11.27) also includes additional terms on the flushing of pages with an U lock, and the I_{io} term associated with a remote exclusive lock hit (i.e., the $h_{n,p,m}^{X,rem}$ term) in Equation(11.26) for the DF policy is eliminated. Under the SLR policy, downgrading of all X locks to S locks can be batched together, and, hence, requires only two GLM communications. Similarly, under the CA and CADF policies, the release of all the locks held by a committed transaction can be batched together. For the CADF policy, we have

$$
\begin{aligned}
I_{syn} = \quad I_{trx} + \sum_{n \in \{1, \ldots, N\}, p \in \{1, \ldots, P\}} & f_{n,p,m} + \left[2I_{GLM} + (h_{n,p,m}^{X,rem} + h_{n,p,m}^{SU,rem}) \right. \\
& \left. (2I_{GLM} + I_{page}) + (1 - h_{n,p,m}) I_{io} \right]
\end{aligned}
\qquad (11.28)
$$

11.4 PERFORMANCE COMPARISONS

We will first validate the buffer submodels for predicting the overall buffer hit probability seen by a transaction. We then use the integrated system models that combine the buffer submodels for various policies with the concurrency control and CPU queuing submodels to compare their transaction response times and maximum throughputs.

11.4.1 Validation of the Buffer Analyses

A discrete event simulator is developed specifically for validating the buffer analyses under various coherency policies. Each node manages its local buffer under the LRU replacement policy. A lock mode associated with each buffer page is explicitly maintained. Upon a remote request, lock modes are appropriately downgraded and/or buffer pages are purged (depending on the policy) in the simulator, as described in Section 10.2. The free buffer slots are put at the bottom of the LRU chain. Under the CADF and CA policies, at the transaction commit time, the remote buffer copies of the updated pages are marked invalid (but not purged). We focus on the validation of the buffer model. Other aspects of the integrated system model have been extensively validated in previous studies [8, 6, 9] under other coherency control policies with simple recovery characteristics and no lock retention, including CA [9].

The synthetic workload that is used to drive the simulator is as follows. Transactions executing at a particular node have an affinity to a part of the database (DB cluster), that is, they have a higher probability of accessing a part of the database associated with that node. To simulate a skewed access pattern within each DB cluster, we assume that each DB cluster consists of two partitions ($P = 2$), namely, the hot set and the cold set, and the the access pattern follows the 80:20 rule. Each DB cluster consists of 20,000 pages (D_p), and each node is assumed to have a local buffer size of 10,000 pages (unless otherwise

specified). Without any loss of generality, we will consider for the validation purpose only
a system consisting of four nodes.

Figure 11.4 shows the composition of a particular node buffer (specifically, the number
of X pages) under the DF policy for an affinity (η) of 0.9 and an update probability (γ)
of 0.5. The buffer size is varied from a small buffer size to a buffer size larger than the
size of the associated DB cluster. From the viewpoint of a transaction executing at a
particular node, the pages of the entire database can be divided into four groups: the
hot and cold sets of its associated DB cluster and the hot and cold sets of the remaining
database pages. Figure 11.4 shows the number of X pages of the four groups retained in
a particular buffer under the DF policy. We emphasize the match between the simulation
and analysis predictions (solid and dotted curves) are strikingly close. A similar close
match is also observed for other policies and workloads.

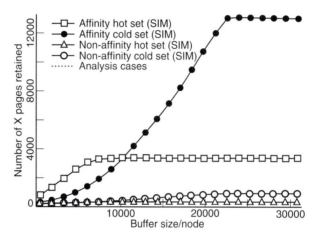

Figure 11.4. Validation of the DF policy ($N = 4$, $\gamma = 0.5$, $\eta = 0.9$).

Figure 11.5 shows the validation of local buffer hit probability under all of the proposed
policies for two sets of parameters. The solids curves (referred to as set 1) are for an affinity
(η) of 0.9 and an update probability (γ) of 0.5, and the dashed curves (referred to as set
2) are for an affinity of 0.7 and an update probability of 0.2. The analysis predictions
show a striking match for all cases, even the minute details of crossover amongst the
curves. In Figure 11.5, only three curves are shown for each parameter set, since the local
buffer hit probabilities of the remaining policies (SLR, DTF, and CA policies) fall on these
curves. The local buffer hit probabilities of the SLR, DTF, and DF polices are the same,
even though the compositions of the buffer in terms of lock modes under these policies
are different. These different compositions result in different response times and CPU
utilizations. Similarly, the local buffer hit probabilities under the CA and CADF policies
are the same.

The local buffer hit probability under the CADF policy is always smaller than that
under the DF policy, since some of the buffer pages are wasted (occupied by invalid pages)
under the CADF policy. Given enough buffer space, however, their buffer hit probabilities
eventually become the same, since the maximum number of valid hot pages of the affinity
DB cluster that can be retained in a particular buffer is limited by the invalidation rate

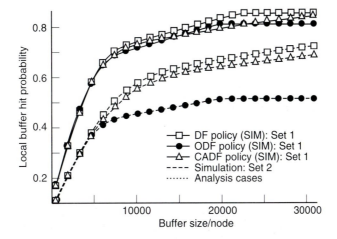

Figure 11.5. Validation of the local buffer hit probabilities.

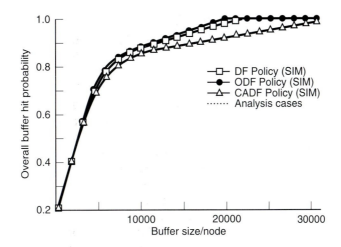

Figure 11.6. Validation of overall buffer hit probabilities

[8]. Therefore, increasing the buffer space under the DF policy implies more cold pages are retained and/or some buffer pages remain empty. The observation was also confirmed in an earlier study [9], where the coherency policies based on detection are compared against those based on immediate notification of invalidation messages. Finally, the local buffer hit probability under the ODF policy is smaller than those under the DF and CADF policies in most cases, since pages are not allowed to be replicated in multiple buffers, and, hence, are purged frequently. However, the overall buffer hit probability under the ODF policy is the highest since the buffer space is best utilized by avoiding replication. Figure 11.6 shows the validation of the corresponding overall buffer hit probabilities. The match is also very close for the overall buffer hit probability. Since the curves for the second parameter

set ($\eta = 0.7$, $\gamma = 0.2$) are very close to those for the first set, they are not shown for the sake of clarity of presentation.

11.4.2   Comparison of Response Time and Maximum Throughput

We now use the analytic integrated system models for the comparison of the performance of various policies. Various other parameters required for the prediction of the overall response times are as follows. We assume a transaction profile similar to that of a relational transaction workload based on the inventory tracking and stock control application used in [36, 34]. The transaction has a path length of 250K instructions (I_{trx}) and requests 14 locks. The overhead for communication with the GLM (I_{GLM}) is assumed to be 2K instructions and the overheads for transferring a page (I_{page}) and disk I/O (I_{io}) are both taken to be 5K instructions. The coupled system or cluster consists of eight nodes where each node has a 20-MIPS processor. The I/O time for read or write is 25 milliseconds and that for writing the log is 5 milliseconds.

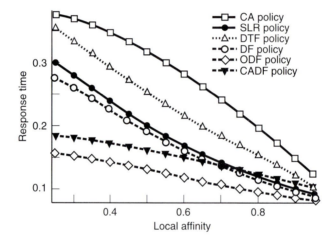

Figure 11.7. Effect of affinity (access rule of 80:20, $\gamma = 0.2$, $\lambda = 40$ tps/node).

Effect of Transaction Affinity. Figures 11.7 and 11.8 compare the response times of all six policies for an update probability of 0.2 and 0.5, respectively, as the transaction affinity to its associated DB cluster is changed. In both figures, the dashed curves represent the policies with complex recovery characteristics (DF, ODF, and CADF policies). The response times of these three policies are substantially lower than those of the other policies in most cases. With a high affinity, the response-time gaps among various policies are narrowed substantially. However, the CPU utilization under various policies could still be significantly different. Figures 11.9 and 11.10 compare their corresponding CPU utilizations, and Figures 11.11 and 11.12 compare their corresponding local and overall buffer hit probabilities, respectively.

To understand the effects of affinity and update probability on the response times, we need to first understand their effects on the buffer hit probability and CPU utilization components. The local buffer hit probability of a transaction increases with the increase

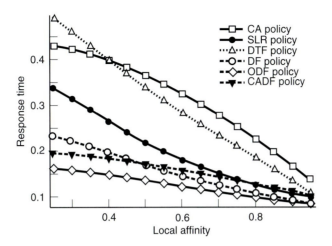

Figure 11.8. Effect of affinity (access rule of 80:20, $\gamma = 0.5$, $\lambda = 40$ tps/node).

in affinity, under all policies (see Figure 11.11). The narrow gaps in local buffer hit probability amongst the various policies do not depend on the buffer composition in terms of lock modes, but do depend on the underlying invalidation mechanism (detection vs. notification), and on whether replication is allowed. Therefore, the gap in the local buffer hit probabilities depends primarily on the combination of buffer size, update probability, and access skew. (The presence of invalid granules in the detection-oriented policy, like CADF, could reduce the buffer hit probability significantly for certain buffer sizes if the access within a DB cluster is less skewed [9].)

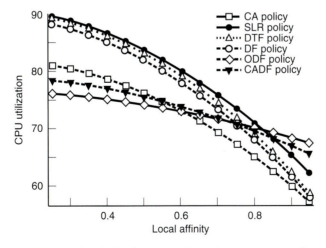

Figure 11.9. Effect of affinity (access rule of 80:20, $\gamma = 0.2$, $\lambda = 40$ tps/node).

The overall buffer hit probabilities under various policies are quite sensitive to the

affinity factor, and the gaps among them are significant. The overall buffer hit probability
under the ODF policy remains unchanged with the change in affinity, since the buffer pages
are not replicated, and a low affinity only implies that the hot pages of a particular DB
cluster is spread over multiple nodes. The CADF policy with delayed purging of invalid
pages has the worst overall buffer hit probability. The overall buffer hit probabilities of
the SLR and DTF policies are the same as that of the DF policy. Note that with an
increase in update probability, the overall buffer hit probability of the DF policy improves
significantly, particularly for the low-affinity case (compare solid and dashed curves marked
with F in Figure 11.12). This can be explained as follows. With an increase in update
probability, a larger number of pages are held in the X mode under the DF policy. Since
the X pages are not replicated, this implies a higher overall buffer utilization. Without
a high update probability, there will be a lot of replication of buffer pages across nodes,
particularly under a lower affinity.

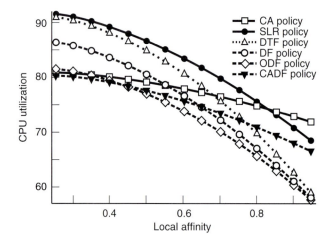

Figure 11.10. Effect of affinity (access rule of 80:20, $\gamma = 0.5$, $\lambda = 40$ tps/node).

A second component that has a strong effect on the response time, particularly under
a high transaction rate/node, is the CPU utilization. Figure 11.9 compares the CPU
utilizations under all six policies for an update probability of 0.2. With a lower transaction
affinity, the policies cluster into two groups:(1) the SLR, DTF, and DF policies that have
a higher CPU utilization due to a large number of messages revoking the retained locks
and (2) the CA and CADF policies that require no such messages. The ODF also falls
in the group of policies with smaller utilizations for two reasons. First, since a page
can be retained only in a single node, revocation messages need to be sent to at most
one node. Second, with the highest overall buffer hit probability among all polices, its
CPU utilization also reduces. Nevertheless, ODF operates less efficiently for the case
with low affinity under small update probability due to the one-copy constraint. As the
affinity increases, it has only a small impact on the utilizations of the CA and CADF
policies through the improvement in local and overall buffer hit probabilities. However,
all the policies that retain locks can benefit from not only the reduction of lock revocation
messages, but also the reduced number of lock request messages. The trend is quite similar

for the 0.5 update probability (see Figure 11.10), except that the DF policy improves its CPU utilization due to the reduction in read disk I/Os. This reduction in disk I/Os is nullified by the increase in write I/Os under the SLR and DTF policies. The SLR policy further suffers from less effective lock retentions. Figure 11.13 shows the increase in write I/Os with the decrease in affinity. (For the SLR policy, the write I/Os per access is a constant, i.e., the update probability, 0.5.) Note that the DTF policy suffers the most from the increase in write I/Os as affinity decreases.

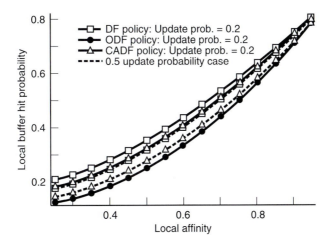

Figure 11.11. Effect of affinity (access rule of 80:20, $\lambda = 40$ tps/node).

Summing up the effects on buffer hit probability and CPU utilization, it is easy to follow the effects of affinity on the response times. The response times of all the policies improve with the increase in affinity due to reduction in read and/or write disk I/Os. The increase in local buffer hit probability is the only reason for the reduction of response time in CA policy. Under the DTF policy, there is also a substantial reduction in the number of synchronous write I/Os with the increase in transaction affinity. Note that with a high update probability this effect of synchronous write I/Os becomes very dominant for a lower affinity (see Figure 11.8) and there is even a crossover between the DTF and CA policies. The SLR policy, on the other hand, provides the best response time amongst these three policies. The SLR also has a simpler recovery complexity than the DTF policy. By comparing Figures 11.7 and 11.8, it can be seen that the DF policy improves substantially at lower affinity for a higher update rate due to the higher overall buffer hit probability (Figure 11.12) and also the lower CPU utilization (Figures 11.9 and 11.10).

Generally, increase in recovery complexity can improve both response time and maximum throughput due to reduction in write I/Os. However, as we have seen before this may not always be the case. Even a policy with a higher recovery complexity (the DTF policy with the medium recovery complexity) can have a worse response time in comparison with a policy with a lower recovery complexity (the SLR policy with the simple recovery complexity). Note also that in an open system, a lower response time does not imply a higher throughput. Therefore, we will compare these policies in more detail to understand the trade-off between response time and maximum throughput. We will group these policies

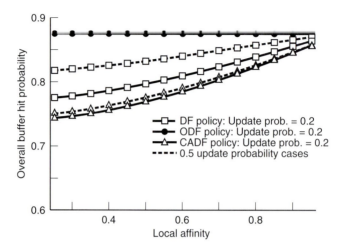

Figure 11.12. Effect of affinity (access rule of 80:20, $\lambda = 40$ tps/node).

by comparable response times. We first compare the policies with simple and medium recovery complexities, namely, the CA, SLR, and DTF policies. We will select one policy from this group as a reference policy, and compare it with the remaining policies that have a complex recovery characteristic.

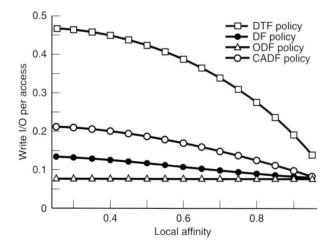

Figure 11.13. Effect of affinity (access rule of 80:20, $\gamma = 0.5$, $\lambda = 40$ tps/node).

Comparison of the CA, SLR, and DTF Policies. Figure 11.14 compares the response times of the CA, SLR, and DTF policies under two different values of affinity as the transaction rate/node is varied. For a low transaction rate, the SLR provides the lowest response time for both cases. For the high-affinity case, the response-time gap amongst these policies is very small. However, the SLR policy provides a higher maximum through-put than the CA policy as it benefits from the remote memory access and reduction of lock request messages (due to the retention of S locks). The DTF policy further benefits from the reduction in write I/Os. These same factors, however, turn against them with a lower affinity. The increase in CPU utilization due to the (lock) revocation messages reduces their maximum throughputs, which can be even lower than that of the CA policy. From this point of view, the throughputs of the policies that do not retain any locks (like CA and CADF policies) are less sensitive to the affinity factor. Note that the SLR policy still provides the best response time before reaching its maximum throughput. The DTF policy suffers also from a larger increase in response time, since a large number of remote requests will occur with additional delay due to synchronous write I/O propagation (see Figure 11.13).

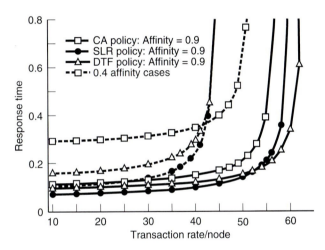

Figure 11.14. Comparison of policies ($\gamma = 0.2$, access rule of 80:20).

The update probability also has a strong impact on the response times and throughputs of these policies. Figures 11.15 through 11.17 show the effect of update probability on the response time, CPU utilization, and write I/O per access, respectively, under these policies. In the high-affinity case, all three policies are not sensitive to the update probability. With a lower affinity (0.4), the response times of both the CA and DTF policies are sensitive to the update probability due to a lower buffer hit probability under the CA policy, and for a higher synchronous write I/Os under the DTF policy. The response time of the SLR policy is not very sensitive to the update probability unless the CPU utilization is very high (note the abrupt rise in the dashed curve marked with S in Figure 11.15).

The effects of an increase in update probability on the utilization curves for these policies are even more interesting. For a higher affinity (0.9), the DTF policy benefits substantially by reducing the number of write I/O operations, and, hence, the utilization remains quite stable with the increase in update probability. The CPU utilizations of both the CA and SLR policies (policies with a simple recovery) increase linearly with the update probability. Under a lower affinity (0.4), the trend is still very similar for the CA policy. However, the CPU utilizations of the SLR and DTF policies are much higher than

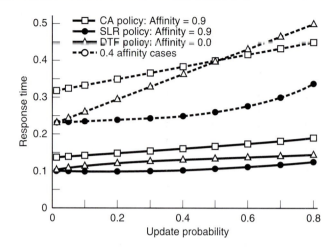

Figure 11.15. Effect of update probability, γ (access rule of 80:20, $\lambda = 40$ tps/node).

that of the CA policy, and the increase in update probability does not have much effect on their CPU utilizations. The increase in update probability improves the overall buffer hit probability, and counterbalances the increase in write I/O operations. The write I/Os per access under the SLR policy increase linearly with the update probability by definition, and the write I/Os also increase linearly with the update probability for the DTF policy (see Figure 11.17). Summarizing the preceding discussion, there is not a single policy in this group that can provide both the lowest response time and the highest maximum throughput, under all parameter sets.

Comparison of the SLR, DF, ODF, and CADF Policies. We include the SLR policy in the following comparison graphs as a reference policy since it has the lowest response time amongst the earlier compared policies. Figures 11.18 and 11.19 compare the response times of the SLR, DF, ODF, and CADF policies for an update probability of 0.2 and 0.5, respectively, as the transaction rate/node is varied. Note that both the response time and throughput of the SLR policy are comparable to those of the other policies with a complex recovery characteristic. The ODF policy provides the best response time as well as the highest maximum throughput in all cases. With a higher affinity (0.9), the performance curves for the DF policy is very close to those of the ODF policy (see the solid curves in both Figures 11.18 and 11.19). This is due to the fact that with a high affinity, there is very little replication of pages across node buffers, and, hence, explicit replica control is not required. However, under a lower affinity, there will be a significant amount of replication of buffer pages. This not only reduces the overall buffer hit probability, but also incurs a lot of message overhead. Therefore, both the response time and maximum throughput of the DF policy suffer from it. Note that the replication effect reduces the overall buffer hit probability of all the policies except the ODF policy, and hence, under a lower affinity (0.4), all other policies have a higher response time. This replication also depends on the update probability. The replication generally decreases with an increase in update probability. This can lead to not only a better overall buffer utilization, but also

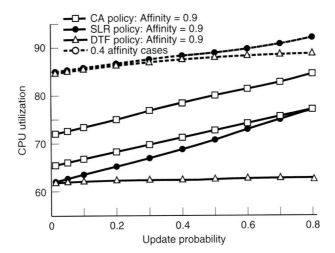

Figure 11.16. Effect of update probability, γ (access rule of 80:20, $\lambda = 40$ tps/node).

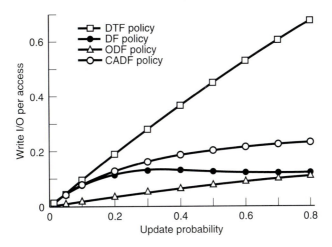

Figure 11.17. Effect of update probability, γ (access rule of 80:20, $\eta = 0.4$, $\lambda = 40$ tps/node).

in a flattening of the write I/O count per access due to buffer flushing (see Figure 11.17).

The performance curves for the CADF policy are quite interesting. Under a high affinity, the performance of the CADF policy is comparable to that of the SLR policy. This is because their buffer hit probabilities are comparable, as the CADF policy suffers very little from the invalidation effect. The difference in their maximum throughputs depends primarily on the update probability. The SLR policy incurs very little lock revocation messages (because of a high affinity), but incurs write I/O propagation and lock upgrade

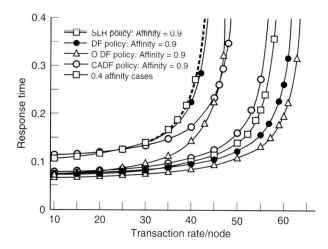

Figure 11.18. Comparison of policies ($\gamma = 0.2$, access rule of 80:20).

messages. On the other hand, the CADF saves on write I/O propagations, but incurs more lock request messages. Therefore, the ordering on their maximum throughputs get reversed with a change in update probability (see Figures 11.18 and 11.19). With a low affinity, the throughput of the CADF policy becomes comparable to that of the ODF policy. This is because the various overheads incurred by these policies are comparable. The CADF policy has a slightly worse overall buffer hit probability in comparison with the ODF policy, and, hence, it incurs somewhat more read disk I/Os, which also results in a higher response time. On the other hand, the ODF policy under a low affinity incurs somewhat more lock revocation messages.

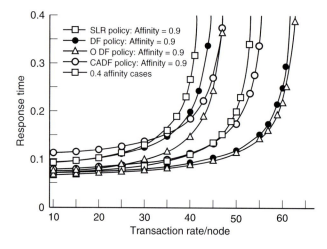

Figure 11.19. Comparison of policies ($\gamma = 0.5$, access rule of 80:20).

Summarizing the preceding discussion, the ODF policy shows that even with a simple replica control, the performance can be improved both in terms of response time and maximum throughput. We note that ODF can be easily modified to allow for certain (hot) relations to be buffered in multiple nodes if that can further improve the performance. DF also performs well under high affinity. The performance of the SLR policy that has a simple recovery complexity is quite comparable to those of the policies with a complex recovery characteristic. Finally, the performance of the CADF policy is relatively less sensitive to the affinity factor.

11.5   SUMMARY AND CONCLUSIONS

In a data sharing environment, buffer coherency control is needed to ensure that the data pages present in multiple local buffers are up to date. This can be achieved through retaining a lock on each page in the buffer, even after the requesting transaction has committed. In addition to tracking the validity of the buffered pages, additional capabilities can be provided through lock retention such as deferred writes to support the no-force scheme on commit, (node) location identification of valid granules to support internode page transfer, and restriction on the number of replications across buffers. However, these can have serious implications not only on the performance, but also on the recovery complexity.

In this chapter, six different integrated coherency policies are considered. We classify these policies into three different categories according to their recovery requirements. Analytic models are developed to study the trade-offs on both throughputs and response times of the policies with a similar level of recovery complexity and the performance gain achievable through increasing the level of recovery complexity. The analysis extends previous work on buffer modeling, which only captures the buffer composition based on the logical grouping on access frequencies like hot and cold sets, to track the average number of pages holding each type of locks, like S, X, and U locks. Some of the nice properties that simplify the previous analysis no longer hold in the lock mode analysis. These include the properties that the LRU stack can be decomposed and the top substack of the LRU stack can be analyzed independent of the bottom substack (*substack decomposable property*) and each node can be considered separately (*node isolatable property*). A detailed simulation model is developed to validate the analytic model. Various factors including buffer size, transaction rate, update probability, and data access pattern are examined. We also capture the notion of affinity that is shown in this chapter to have a strong impact on the performance of these policies.

For the policies with a simple recovery characteristic, besides the check-on-access (CA) policy that serves as our base policy, we also consider a shared lock retention (SLR) policy under the force scheme. The remaining four policies considered use deferred writes to save write I/O propagation at the expense of increased recovery complexity, and they fall in two categories: deferred until transfer or flushing (DTF) and deferred until flushing (DF) polices. Two variations of the basic DF policy considered explore separate dimensions: (1) the ODF policy uses replica control to improve overall buffer hit probability, and (2) the CADF policy combines the CA policy with the deferred write approach.

References

[1] Bellew, M., M. Hsu, and V-O. Tam, "Update Propagation in Distributed Memory Hi-

erarchy," *6th International Conference on Data Engineering*, Los Angeles, in preceding of the February, 1000.

[2] Bennett, B. T., P. A. Franaszek, J. T. Robinson, and P. S. Yu, "Check on Access Via Hierarchical Block Validation," *IBM Technical Disclosure Bulletin*, 27(7A) (December 1984).

[3] Bennett, J. K., J. B. Carter, and W. Zwaenepoel, "Distributed Shared Memory Based on Type-Specific Memory Coherence," *2nd ACM SIGPLAN Symposium on Principles and Practices of Parallel Programming*, Seattle, 25(3) (March 1990).

[4] Carey, M. J., M. J. Franklin, M. Livny, and E. J. Shekita, "Data Caching Tradeoffs in Client-Server DBMS Architectures," *ACM SIGMOD*, Denver, May 1991.

[5] Cornell, D.W., D. M. Dias, and P. S. Yu, "On Multisystem Coupling Through Function Request Shipping," *IEEE Transactions on Software Engineering*, 12(10) (October 1986).

[6] Dan, A., "Performance Analysis of Data Sharing Environments," PhD Dissertation, University of Massachusetts, Amherst, September 1990.

[7] Dan, A., J.Y. Chung, and P. S. Yu, "Characterization of Database Access Pattern for Analytic Prediction of Buffer Hit Probability," *VLDB Journal*, 4(1) (1995).

[8] Dan, A., D. M. Dias, and P. S. Yu, "Buffer Analysis for a Data Sharing Environment with Skewed Data Access," *IEEE Trans. Knowledge and Data Engineering*, 6(2) (April 1994).

[9] Dan, A., and P. S. Yu, "Performance Analysis of Buffer Coherency Policies in a Multi-System Data Sharing Environment," *IEEE Trans. on Parallel and Distributed Systems*, 4(3) (March 1993).

[10] Dan, A., and P. S. Yu, "Performance Analysis of Coherency Control Policies through Lock Retention," *ACM SIGMOD*, San Diego, June 1992.

[11] Dan, A., P. S. Yu, and A. Jhingran, "Recovery Analysis of Data Sharing Systems under Deferred Dirty Page Propagation Policies," IBM Research Report 18553, 1992.

[12] Dias, D. M., B. R. Iyer, J. T. Robinson, and P. S. Yu, "Integrated Concurrency-Coherency Controls for Multisystem Data Sharing," *IEEE Transactions on Software Engineering*, 15(4) (April 1989).

[13] Franklin, M. J., and M. J. Carey, "Client-Server Caching Revisited," *International Workshop on Distributed Object Management*, Edmonton, Canada, August 1992.

[14] Franklin, M. J., M. J. Carey, and M. Livny, "Global Memory Management in Client Server DBMS Architectures," *18th International Conference on Very Large Databases*, Vancouver, Canada, August 1992.

[15] Howard, J. H. and et al, "Scale and Performance in a Distributed File System," *ACM Transactions on Computer System*, 6(1) (February 1988).

[16] IBM Corporation, "Sysplex Overview: Introducing Data Sharing and Parallelism in a Sysplex," Technical Report GC28-1208, April 1994.

[17] Kronenberg, N., H. Levy and W. D. Strecker, "VAXcluster: a Closely-Coupled Distributed System," *ACM Transactions on Computer System*, 4(2) (May 1986).

[18] Lavenberg, S. S. (Ed.), Computer Performance Modeling Handbook. New York, Academic Press, 1983.

[19] Leff, A., J. L. Wolf, and P. S. Yu, "Replication Algorithms in a Remote Caching Architecture," *IEEE Transactions Parallel and Distributed Systems*, 4(11) (November 1993).

[20] Li, K., and P. Hudak, "Memory Coherence in Shared Virtual Memory Systems," *ACM Transactions on Computer System*, 7, (November 1989).

[21] Mohan, C., D. Haderle, B. Lindsay, H. Pirahesh, and P. Schwarz, "ARIES: A Transaction Recovery Method Supporting Fine-Granularity Locking and Partial Rollbacks Using Write-Ahead Logging," *ACM Trans. on Database Systems*, 17(1) 1992.

[22] Mohan, C., and I. Narang, "Efficient Locking and Caching of Data in the Multisystem Shared Disks Transaction Environment," *Intl. Conf. on Extending Database Technology*, Vienna, Austria, March 1992.

[23] Mohan, C., and I. Narang, "Recovery and Coherency Control Protocols for Fast Intersystem Page Transfer and Fine Granularity Locking in a Shared Disks Transaction Environment," *17th International Conference on Very Large Databases*, Barcelona, Spain, Sept. 1991.

[24] Mohan, C., I. Narang and J. Palmer, "A Case Study of Problems in Migrating to Distributed Computing: Page Recovery Using Multiple Logs in the Shared Disks Environment," IBM Research Report RJ 7343, March 1990.

[25] Rahm, E., "Empirical Performance Evaluation of Concurrency and Coherency Control Protocols for Data Sharing Systems," *ACM Trans. on Database Systems*, 18(2) (June 1993).

[26] Rahm, E., "Primary Copy Synchronization for DB-Sharing," *Information Systems*, 11(4), 1986.

[27] Ramachandran, U., M. Ahamad and M. Y. A. Khalidi, "Coherence of Distributed Shared Memory: Unifying Synchronization and Data Transfer," *18th International Conference on Parallel Processing*, St. Charles, Ill., August 1989.

[28] Robinson, J.T., "A Fast General-Purpose Hardware Synchronization Mechanism," *SIGMOD Record*, 1985.

[29] Strickland, J. P., P. P. Uhrowczik and V. L. Watts, "IMS/VS: An Evolving System," *IBM Systems Journal*, 21(4), 1982.

[30] Tay, Y. C., N. Goodman, and R. Suri, "Locking Performance in Centralized Databases," *ACM Trans. Database Systems*, 10(4) (December1985).

[31] Teng, J., and R. Gumaer, "Managing IBM Database 2 Buffers to Maximize Performance," *IBM Systems Journal*, 24(2), 1984.

[32] Wang, Y. and L. A. Rowe, "Cache Consistency and Concurrency Control in a Client/Server DBMS Architectures," *ACM SIGMOD*, Denver, CO, May 1991.

[33] Wilkinson, K., and M. A. Neimat, "Maintaining Consistency of Client-Cached Data," *16th Very Large Database Conference*, Brisbane, Australia, August 1990.

[34] Yu, P. S., and A. Dan, "Performance Analysis of Affinity Clustering on Transaction Processing Coupling Architectures," IEEE Trans. Knowledge and Data Engineering, 6(5) (October 1994).

[35] Yu, P. S., D.M. Dias, and S. S. Lavenberg, "On the Analytical Modelling of Database Concurrency Control," *Journal of the ACM*, 40(4) (September 1993).

[36] Yu, P. S., Dias, D. M., Robinson, J. T., Iyer, B. R. and Cornell, D. W., "On Coupling Multi Systems Through Data Sharing," *Proceedings of the IEEE*, 75(5) (May 1987).

Chapter 12

Recovery Analysis of Data Sharing Systems under Deferred Dirty Page Propagation Policies

Asit Dan, Philip S. Yu, and Anant Jhingran

Abstract

In a multi-node data sharing environment, different buffer coherency control schemes based on various lock retention mechanisms can be designed to exploit the concept of deferring the propagation or writing of dirty pages to disk to improve normal performance. Two types of deferred write polices are considered. One policy only propagates dirty pages to disk at the times when dirty pages are flushed out of the buffer under LRU buffer replacement. The other policy also performs writes at the times when dirty pages are transferred across nodes. The dirty page propagation policy can have significant implications on the database recovery time. In this paper, we provide an analytical modeling framework for the analysis of the recovery times under the two deferred write policies. We demonstrate how these policies can be mapped onto a unified analytic modeling framework. The main challenge in the analysis is to obtain the pending update count distribution which can be used to determine the average numbers of log records and data I/Os needed to be applied during recovery. The analysis goes beyond previous work on modeling buffer hit probability in a data sharing system where only the average buffer composition, not the distribution, needs to be estimated, and recovery analysis in a single node environment where the complexities on tracking the propagation of dirty pages across nodes and the buffer invalidation effect do not appear. A clipping mechanism can be employed to improve recovery time where the number of pending update on a dirty page is limited by forcing a dirty page to disk after the number of updates accumulated on this page exceeds a certain threshold. The analysis captures the effect of clipping also. Finally, we show the sensitivities of the recovery time and normal performance to the clipping count.

12.1 INTRODUCTION

In transaction processing systems, there are stringent requirements on not only performance but also availability. These two requirements can often result in conflicting design goals. To improve the performance, the approach of deferring the propagation of updated or dirty pages to disk is often used to reduce the I/O overhead as multiple updates may accumulate on the same page. Since the performance of transaction processing systems is often disk arm limited, reducing the number of write I/Os can also result in substantial saving on the system cost as the storage cost today often dominates the overall system cost. This deferred write strategy is used in various commercial and prototype systems [27], including IBM DB2 database system [38], IMS Fast Path [13], Tandem Encompass [16], NonStop SQL [37], and CMU's Camelot [36, 35]. However, deferred writes can also increase the database recovery time upon system failure as all dirty pages need to be derived from the database log and applied to the database. The larger the number of deferred writes, the longer the recovery time. With the current trend in larger main memory database buffer, controlling recovery time becomes very important.

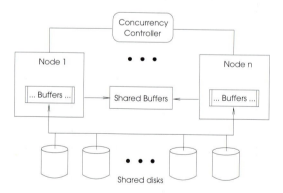

Figure 12.1. Recovery time vs. MPL.

Coupling multiple microprocessors to form a powerful data server has become increasingly popular. Data sharing (see Figure 12.1) is one of the coupling architectures [39, 41], where multiple processing nodes share common disks and each node maintains a local buffer to reduce the number of I/O's. It is the coupling architecture used by DEC VAX-Cluster (or Alpha-Cluster) [22] and IBM S/390 Parallel

Sysplex [19]. Data Sharing is supported by various commercial database products, including Oracle, IBM DB2 and IMS. In this paper, we examine the data sharing environment. In this environment, updating a data block causes other buffered copies of that block to become invalid or obsolete. A buffer coherency control mechanism is needed to guarantee that only valid copies are referenced by transactions. Deferring the update propagation of dirty pages further complicates the coherency control. With deferred writes, the disk copy may no longer be the most up-to-date version. That is to say, not only buffered copies but also the disk copy can become obsolete. The coherency control mechanism needs to track where the valid copy of each data block resides. This can be done by using some lock retention mechanisms at each of the processing nodes [28]. The basic idea is to have the buffer manager in each node retain some type of locks on each buffered page (even after the last transaction accessing the page is committed). So upon data page updates the lock manager can use the lock holder information to determine which nodes to invalidate and upon read accesses, it can determine where to get a (valid) copy of the page for the requesting node. The timing on when the dirty pages are reflected onto disk has a significant implication to recovery complexity in a multi-node data sharing environment.

Three types of dirty page propagation polices with different recovery complexities are considered in this paper. The first policy pushes out the dirty pages at the times of transaction commit. In this case, only the updates from the last committed transaction, and those from the uncommitted transactions may need to be recovered upon node failure, i.e. very little log scan is required. This is considered to be a simple recovery which is the base case with no deferred writes. In the second scenario, dirty pages are pushed out to disk at the times of page transfer between nodes. Thus a dirty page can accumulate updates only from a single node, and database recovery would require scanning only the log of the failed node (but not of any other nodes) to rederive the missing updates on the node. This results in medium recovery complexity. In the third scenario, update propagation to disk is done at the times of page flushing from buffer due to LRU replacement. Since a dirty page can accumulate updates from multiple nodes, the recovery would require scanning the logs of all nodes. This is referred to as a complex recovery scenario. Furthermore, a clipping (of pending update count) mechanism as in [21] is also considered which improves the recovery time by forcing a dirty page to disk after the number of updates accumulated exceeds a certain threshold, referred to as *Clipping Count*. The clipping mechanism will avoid going back too far in the log during recovery and can be applied to the policies with either the medium or complex recovery complexity.

In this paper, we develop an analytic modeling framework for analyzing the recovery times under different dirty page propagation schemes. We show how these complicated schemes can be mapped onto the analytic modeling framework capturing all significant factors such as clipping (i.e. limiting the maximum pending update count per page), local and remote buffer hit, skewed access pattern, affinity factor (i.e. different nodes can show distinct access affinities to different set of

pages in the database), and multiple access modes (read and update). The main
challenge in the analysis is to obtain the pending update count distribution which
can be used to determine the average number of log records and data I/Os that
need to be applied during recovery. The analysis also estimates the average number
of write I/Os during normal operation under various schemes.

Section 12.2 provides preliminary information on the general database recovery
process in a single node environment. It then introduces the data sharing environment and the various dirty page propagation policies and their recovery process in
that environment. The analytic model is described in Section 12.3. We present
the model validation and performance results in Section 12.4. Finally, Section 12.5
summarizes the results.

12.1.1   Related Work

The analysis methodology relates to two sets of previous work. The first set of work
is on buffer hit analysis in a data sharing environment. In [7], various coherency
control schemes are considered with no deferred writes and remote caching, while
in [8], the LRU analysis methodology is further extended to capture the effects of
deferred writes and remote caching. Here the analysis needs to capture not only the
buffer composition of various data types (hot set, cold set, etc.) and the lock mode
held on these pages but also the probability distribution of pending update count
which depends upon various factors such as local and remote buffer hit on dirty
pages, write propagation policy, clipping of pending update count, etc.. In [8, 7],
the performance trade-offs of various coherency control policies under each recovery
scenario are analyzed. Generally speaking, the policies under the complex recovery
scenario achieve the most write I/O savings and yield the best performance.

The second set of work examines the recovery time in a single node environment
[20, 21], and provides a recursive formulation approach for estimating pending update count albeit in a much simpler single node environment. The recovery time
is decomposed into several components: log read time, data I/O, log application
and undo processing time. Similar decomposition is followed here. However, in the
data sharing environment the buffer invalidation effect and remote buffer accesses
substantially complicate the analysis.

12.2   PRELIMINARY

We first summarize the issues and mechanisms involved in database recovery in a
single node environment in Section 12.2.1. An excellent paper on this is [27]. Then
the data sharing environment and the different failure scenarios are discussed in
Section 12.2.2. Finally, we describe the different dirty page propagation policies
and recovery process in section 12.2.3.

12.2.1   Database Recovery in A Single Node Environment

Typical transaction processing systems use write-ahead logging (WAL) for recovery wherein a transaction commits by forcing its logs to the disk. If deferred write is not used, the updated pages will be forced to disks at commit time after the logging is completed. This is the simple recovery scenario. Upon processing node failure, the recovery is basically the *undo* of the uncommitted transactions [2].

Deferred write improves performance as the log write is generally fast and the response-time penalty of dirty data page I/O's is avoided [15]. A data page can be written to disk anytime after all the logs describing changes to it have been forced to disk. Th deferred write complicates the recovery process as it can result in a sequence of updates to a page not reflected on disk when the processing node fails. A *redo* phase is thus required to re-caputre these missing updates. The undo of uncommitted transactions is exactly the same as in the simple recovery scenario with no deferred write. The undo work only involves the currently on-going not yet committed transactions while the redo work can potentially involve a huge number of transactions where some of them may be executed a long time back. That is to say redo is the dominating component[1]. In any case, compared with the simple recovery scenario with no deferred write, the penalty of the deferred write polices on the recovery time is on the redo work. Hence we focus the analysis of this paper on the various components associated with redo and generally ignore the undo phase.

Whereas many flavors of such WAL to support deferred writes are possible, here we describe some general features:

- The log is an append-only file, consisting of log records. Each log record has a *log sequence number* (or LSN) which is the physical address of the beginning of the log record (it may or may not be stored with the log record).

- If a crash occurs, the only log records that need to be applied to a page to redo the actions lost in the volatile memory are those that reflect updates since the time the page was last forced to the disk. Consequently, the system maintains an equivalent of what is called a *dirty page table* (or DPT) in the memory. The DPT records, for each page that is dirty and in the memory, the LSN of the earliest log record describing an update to it, since the page was last written to the disk.[2] The minimum of the LSNs of all the dirty page entries in the DPT is referred to as *MinRecLSN*.

- Each update to a page, in addition to updating the database record, also updates an entry in its header (called *updateLSN*) by recording the LSN of the log record that describes that update.

- Periodically, a *checkpoint* is taken, where, in the log, the current DPT is recorded.

---

[1] The recovery time study presented in [20] found that in a single node environment, undo work is insignificant compared with redo, and data I/O is the dominating component in redo for typical "light"- and "medium"-weight transactions.

[2] As a corollary, this entry is deleted when the page is forced to the disk.

- After a crash, the recovery proceeds in three phases:

  - In the *analysis* phase, if the latest DPT was lost due to the failure, it is reconstructed by scanning the log from last checkpoint of the DPT onwards. However, this step is not required in this paper as described later due to the proposed recovery scheme where the information about the dirty pages of the crashed node is readily available in the global lock manager.

  - In the *redo* phase, the log is scanned forward from the MinRecLSN of the latest DPT, i.e., a point sufficiently far back, so that all the log records that reflect changes to the pages in the memory at the time of the crash are encountered. In the redo phase, when a log record is scanned, its corresponding data page is read into memory if it is in the latest DPT (and is not already in the memory). Furthermore, the corresponding log record needs to be applied to the page *if the updateLSN on the page header is less than the LSN of this log record.*

    There are therefore three components of redo: *log scan, data page read I/O* and *log application.*

  - In the *undo* phase, for each transaction that needs to be aborted because of the crash (the list of these transactions and their associated pages can be constructed during the redo or analysis phase), its updates need to be undone. For each such transaction, all its log records are read in reverse order, the corresponding pages brought back in (if not already in memory), and the changes undone.

12.2.2 Data Sharing Architecture

We first describe the data sharing system architecture [19, 22, 28, 32, 39, 40], and then its failure scenarios. The multi-node data sharing system considered here consists of multiple loosely coupled processing nodes sharing a common database at the disk level (see Figure 12.1). The processing nodes are used to run transaction applications. Each of which contains local volatile memory for buffering. Each node generates its own log stream, based on the WAL protocol described above.[3] The presence of a fast speed interconnect is assumed amongst the nodes, such that propagation delay (not the CPU overhead) in transferring a page between two nodes is negligible.

We assume a centralized global lock manager (GLM) for the purpose of concurrency control across multiple concurrently executing transactions [1, 10, 34]. The GLM may physically reside in a separate processor (or be partitioned across a set of separate processors), referred to in Figure 12.1 as the concurrency controller, with nonvolatile shared memory [10]. (Alternatively, GLM can be implemented on the

---

[3]The log streams are assumed to be stored separately, and must be merged, if required, during recovery.

disk controller [1].) An example of this type of data sharing system is the IBM S/390 Parallel Sysplex [19].

The most common failure scenario is the processing node failure which can either be due to hardware or software. When a processing node fails, its buffer contents (including all the dirty pages) are lost. The node needs to be restarted. The remaining nodes and GLM can continue to operate. (We note that in a data sharing system or any other types of coupled system, the objective on availability is to allow the rest of the system to continue to function upon a processing node failure.) Since all disks are shared, they are continued accessible by the operating nodes. Under a deferred write policy, any dirty page in the failed node buffer will need to be fenced out, as the most recent version of the page is not yet reflected on disk. (The dirty pages in each node is tracked by the GLM.) It cannot be accessed by transactions running on the unfailed nodes until restored from the log, i.e. the processing of these transactions will be delayed until recovery is competed. The recovery time from processing node failure is thus important and is the focus on the analysis of this paper.

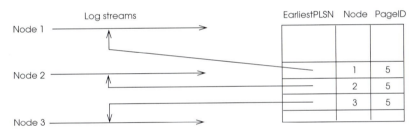

Figure 12.2. Recovery time vs. MPL.

GLM can be augmented to also facilitate "recovery", by keeping an additional table. Figure 12.2 describes the information kept *solely* for recovery purposes. This table records, for each page that currently has an X lock on one of the nodes, the corresponding entry from the DPT on each of the nodes (if such an entry exists). We refer to this table as the "global" DPT in the rest of the paper. The LSN recorded in this table is the *physical* LSN (PLSN, i.e. the physical address on the logging disk)–this is to be distinguished from a logical LSN (described later). Note that when the X lock on a page is transferred to another node, a new entry on the page will be added to the global DPT for that node, if not already exists, to indicate the earliest PLSN. For example, Figure 12.2 presents the entries for page 5, which have been updated by nodes 1, 2 and 3. The entries indicate the earliest PLSN of the logs for each node on page 5. When recovering page 5 due to the failure of either of these nodes, we would need to get the update information from all three nodes recorded in their logs. The PLSN entries corresponding to a dirty page are purged once the page is propagated to the disk.

12.2.3   Dirty Page Propagation Polices and Recovery under Data Sharing

To maintain consistent (buffer) images across multiple nodes a coherency mechanism is required. Various integrated concurrency-coherency mechanisms using the GLM are described in [7, 8]. Typically this is achieved by retaining a lock on a data page in the buffer even after the transaction accessing it has committed. An appropriate lock on a dirty page guarantees that other nodes will not access an old copy of that page and hence, the propagation of that page to the disk can be deferred. The lock on a page can be of several modes: (1) an X mode implies the page is updated (dirty) and no other node currently holds a copy, (2) an S mode implies the page is clean and other nodes may also hold a copy, and (3) an U mode implies the page is dirty and the present node need to propagate the page to the disk before flushing out of buffer, however, other nodes may hold a copy of this page in S mode.

Under the various dirty page propagation policies, the recovery algorithms differ only in the redo phase. Based on our assumption that the GLM is always available, the analysis phase is not required. Furthermore, the undo phase requires replaying, in reverse order, the log records associated with all the transactions that need to be aborted because of the crashed node. Since a transaction lives on only one node throughout its life, this undo is exactly identical to the WAL undo described in 12.2.1.

Medium Recovery.   In this scheme, a dirty page is forced out to disk before it can be transferred to a new node, or be pushed out from the buffer. The transferred page will then be considered a clean page due to the forced disk write. Below we describe a representative dirty page propagation policy.

Deferred until Transfer or Flushing (DTF) Policy.   Here, the dirty pages are deferred as long as the X locks are retained. The dirty pages are forced to the disk before a node to node page transfer occurs due to a lock request by a remote node either in an S or X mode. If the remote request is for an S lock then the local X lock is downgraded to S mode. Otherwise, if the remote request is for an X lock, the local X lock is released and the local buffer copy is purged. Either way, after the forced write, a copy of the page is directly sent to the other node to avoid disk read. A dirty page also needs to be propagated to the disk if it is pushed out of buffer, referred to as buffer flushing. When a page is pushed out of the buffer, its associated lock (S or X) is also released. In actual implementation, the dirty propagation can be initiated once the dirty page is close to the bottom of the LRU stack, so that no synchronous I/O delay is incurred due to buffer flushing and multiple disk writes can be batched together[4].

Redo in Medium Recovery: Since a page is forced to the disk whenever it is transferred, redo involves logs *only* from the failed nodes. Furthermore, each log can be applied independently, *because the logs from the node which had the exclusive copy of the page before the crash only need be applied.*

Complex Recovery. In this, the dirty page is transferred directly to the new node, without forcing a write to the disk. The redo part of the recovery might now involve several nodes, and hence this policy is termed "complex". This is also referred to as the *Fast* scheme in [28] for its ability to have faster page transfer and the most reduction in write I/O. (Recovery issues corresponding to the fast and medium schemes are discussed in detail in [28].) One such dirty page propagation policy is described below.

Deferred until Flushing (DF) Policy. This is similar to DTF policy as far as propagation of dirty pages to the disk at the buffer flushing goes. However, on a lock request by a remote node, dirty pages are not propagated to the disk. If the remote request is for an X lock, like the DTF policy both the dirty page as well as the X lock is transferred to the requesting node. On the other hand, if the remote request is for an S lock, the local node downgrades its X lock to the shared mode, and a copy of the page is also sent to the requesting node. Note, that the dirty page still needs to be propagated to the disk by one of the nodes eventually. Therefore, a new form of shared lock called U lock is introduced [28]. The local shared lock is in U mode implying a pending update. Therefore, at the buffer flushing time, not only the pages associated with X locks but also the ones with U locks are propagated to the disk.

Redo in Complex Recovery. In this, a merge of logs is required in order to correctly recover the state of the database. The merge of the log requires *synchronization points* between different log streams. A synchronization point occurs when the control of the X lock on the page is transferred from one node to the other. There are various schemes possible for this [25, 29, 33], we propose an alternative scheme modeled on Lamport's clock scheme [23].

Basically, each node maintains a logical log sequence number (LLSN) which is a monotonically increasing sequence. Whenever the control of a page is passed from node i to node j, the LLSN of node j is set to the maximum of its current LLSN and the LLSN of node i when the page was transferred. Every other log record increments the LLSN by 1. This ensures that the LLSN order of the logs associated with a page follows the update order. Log merge is then based on LLSN, and ties are broken arbitrarily. Furthermore, by maintaining an LLSN per node, rather than per page (as suggested by [25]), we minimize the state information that needs to be kept during recovery.

The standard LSN assumed by WAL protocol in Section 12.2.1 is now termed PLSN (physical LSN), because it reflects the actual byte address of the log record. Recall that during redo processing, we need this physical address in order to determine from where to start playing a particular log. That is where the global DPT table of GLM helps – it records, for each page, the corresponding earliest update PLSN, which is physical and not logical. During recovery, then, we start with an empty recovery DPT for each node. For each page p that was held exclusively by the crashed node, an entry is added for the page in the recovery DPT of node j, if an entry for page p, node j exists in the global DPT table. At the end of this processing, the starting point for each log is obtained by the minimum value in the LSN field of the corresponding recovery DPT.

Table 12.1. Summary of the major symbols

$D_{n,p}$	Size of partition (n,p)
$Z_{n,p,m}$	Average number of dirty pages in the (n,p,m) substack
$P_{n,p,m}^k(j)$	Prob. of jth ranked page of the (n,p,m) substack with a pending update count of k
$P_{n,p,m}^k$	Prob. of a page of the (n,p,m) substack with a pending update count of k
$\zeta_{n,p,m}$	Prob. of next access to (n,p,m) substack
$\theta_{n,p,m}$	Buffer hit prob. on dirty pages of the (n,p,m) substack $(= \frac{Z_{n,p,m}}{D_{n,p}})$
$K_{n,p,m}$	Pending update count on (n,p,m) substack
A_m	Total log application count at node m
W_m	Total number of write propagations per access at node m
$N_{m,dirty}$	Number of dirty pages at node m
α_p	Prob. of accessing a partition p granule
β_p	Fractional size of partition p
γ	Update prob. of a granule access
η	Fraction of accesses within the affiliated DB cluster
C	Pending update count threshold
N	Number of nodes in the data sharing environment
B	Local buffer size at each node
D	Number of pages in each DB cluster

All subscript pair (n,p) refers to the granules of partition p of node n
All subscript triplet (n,p,m) refers to the (n,p) partition pages appeared in node m buffer.

12.3   PERFORMANCE MODEL

In this section, we develop a unified analytical modeling framework for analyzing the recovery times under different dirty page propagation policies. We show how these complicated schemes can be mapped onto the modeling framework capturing all significant factors like clipping, local and remote buffer hit, skewed access pattern, affinity factor, multiple access/lock modes, and the intricacies of resetting versus preserving the pending update count upon page transfer between nodes. The analytic models provide estimates of the various redo components of the recovery process, i.e., the number of log entries that need to be applied and the number of dirty pages that need to be recreated. They also estimate the average number of write I/O during normal operation under various schemes. These analyses are independent of whether a GLM or other mechanism is used to track the buffer content. In the next section, we will then combine various redo components to estimate overall cost of recovery process. Summary of the notations used in this section is given in Table 12.1.

12.3.1 Overview on Methodology

The redo component of recovery time under each of the policies can be broken down into three parts: (1) time for disk I/O to bring back the clean earlier versions of the dirty pages on which the logs will be applied, (2) time for application of the log entries to recreate the latest versions of the dirty pages, and (3) time for scanning the log entries to select the appropriate entries that need to be applied. The first component is given by the number of dirty pages in the buffer of the failed node at the time of failure. The log application time is given by the total number of pending update count over all dirty pages. The log scan time is less significant particularly under skewed data access [20] and is also difficult to estimate. (It requires estimating the oldest entry in the log that need to be applied.) Also, the log scan time is overlapped with the log application time. We will assume the log scan time as proportional to the number of log entries that need to be applied.

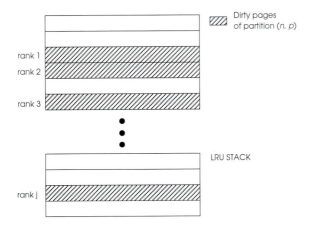

Figure 12.3. Recovery time vs. MPL.

Thus the recovery time analysis of redo component in essence is an analysis of the number of dirty pages and the pending update counts in the buffer. Our approach consists of several major elements. First, we decompose the LRU stack (of each node) into separate substacks according to some page set classification or partitioning based on access frequencies and focus on the relative positions of the dirty pages within the substack, where the dirty pages are reflected by the lock mode held. As shown in Figure 12.3, the dirty pages belonging to a particular database logical partition (e.g. hot set, cold set, etc.) form a separate substack interwoven with other substacks. The analysis of the pending update count for pages in each substack is then separated into two sub-problems: estimating the average number of dirty pages in each substack in the buffer, and analyzing the pending update count distribution for each page in the substack. The clipping process is modeled by developing an equivalent process which can coupled with the dirty page substack analysis. We also provide an estimation of the number of extra write I/O due to clipping (in addition to the write I/O due to buffer flushing, or due to intersystem page transfer under DTF policy).

Estimation of the average number of pages held at different lock modes under all policies considered here is detailed in the previous work [6], and is also described in brief in the Appendix. We therefore focus on the estimation of the pending update count distribution for each dirty page. A key observation is made that the pending update count distribution of each page is independent of its relative position in the substack. We derive a difference equation on the pending update count based on *balancing the LRU substack state transition probabilities*. A closed form formula is obtained in terms of the average number of dirty pages. In analyzing the LRU substack state transition, we concentrate on the pending update count of the page at the top of the LRU substack (of the dirty pages of a specific class). For a specific probability state of the pending update count of the top page, we estimate the different ways of transition into that state. The steady state probability at a particular state equals to the sum of the various local and remote read or update access rate multiplied by the corresponding steady state probabilities of the states that can transition into the desired state due to these accesses. The issue is to identify all the transitions that affect the state of a particular substack under various dirty page propagation policies.

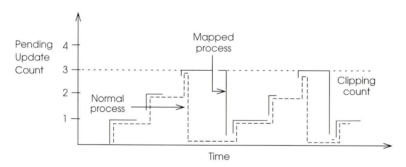

Figure 12.4. Recovery time vs. MPL.

Finally, we comment on the mapping of the clipping process (see Figure 12.4). The clipping process sets a pending update count threshold after which the dirty page is written out to disk. The count is then reset to zero. In the mapped process, the disk write (and hence the resetting of update count) will be delayed until just before the next update. Also, the count will be reset to 1 implying the last update is not reflected in the propagated version (i.e., the passing through state 0 is assumed to be instantaneous). This is required since in the following derivation of the probability distribution of pending update count, only the dirty pages are considered. Resetting the count to zero will make the page clean and hence, make it drop out from the LRU substack. The only difference between the two clipping processes is that in the mapped process, the pages with the maximum pending update count is in fact a clean page in the normal process. Since we have the probability distribution of each count state, proper adjustment can be made at the final result to address this difference so that the numbers of pending update counts and dirty pages in the buffer can be derived.

Below we describe various assumptions about system parameters and workload models. We first provide the estimate for the average total log application count, and the time required to apply these logs. We will then estimate the time required to bring back the earlier version of the dirty pages from the disk, as well as the number of write I/O operations during normal operations.

12.3.2   Model Assumption

The data sharing system considered here consists of N loosely coupled nodes. Each node maintains a local buffer of size B. Transactions arrive at each node according to a Poisson process. The access pattern over the entire database is not the same for all transactions. First, we assume the related transactions (i.e., transactions that reference the same set of pages or relations in the database) can be grouped logically into *affinity clusters* (AC) [41] (See Figure 12.5) and the transactions affiliated with an affinity cluster are routed to the same node by the front end router. This reduces the inter-system interference and improve the local buffer hit probability. The set of pages or relations affiliated with each AC is referred to as a DB cluster. Let η be the fraction of pages accessed by a transaction from its affiliated DB cluster. We will assume each transaction accesses the remaining fraction, $(1 - \eta)$, of its data from the non-affiliated DB clusters uniformly. Let each DB cluster consists of D pages. Secondly, we assume that the database accesses within each DB cluster is skewed. We model skewed access pattern by assuming P logical partitions within each cluster such that the probability of accessing any page within a partition is uniform. In Figure 12.5, each DB cluster is shown to have two partitions: Hot and Cold sets. Let β_p denote the fraction of the DB cluster pages in partition p, i.e., the size of partition p is $\beta_p D$. Let α_p be the probability of accessing a page of the pth partition of this cluster, given that a page is accessed from this DB cluster. The probability that an accessed page is also updated is denoted as γ.

Note that under certain conditions, (combination of one or more of the following factors: large buffer size, high affinity, skewed access and DF policy) certain data pages (hot sets) will not be propagated to the disk and will accumulate large pending update counts. In order to bound the recovery time, the (normal) clipping process forces an update to the disk after the pending update count of a page reaches a pre-specified threshold. (The page will continue to be retained in the buffer as a clean page.) Let C be the pending update count threshold. The parameter C is

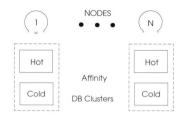

Figure 12.5. Recovery time vs. MPL.

also referred to as the *Clipping age*. Note that clipping age of 1 implies a simple recovery scheme.

For the purpose of analysis, the entire database can be divided into NP partitions, i.e., N DB clusters and P partitions within each cluster (based on the hotness of the data). Each partition is identified by the subscript pair $(n,p), n \in \{1...N\}, p \in \{1...P\}$. Define $D_{n,p}$ to be the size of partition (n,p). Then, $D_{n,p}$ is given by $D\beta_p$. Note that transactions at node m have higher affinity to the partitions (m,p), $p = 1...P$. Let $Z_{n,p,m}$ denote the average number of dirty pages of partition (n,p) present in the buffer of the mth node. Estimation of $Z_{n,p,m}$ is required for estimating both log application count as well as data I/O count. As mentioned earlier, the estimation of $Z_{n,p,m}$ is described in brief in the Appendix. Under DTF policy, $Z_{n,p,m}$ includes only the pages holding X locks while under DF policy, this includes also the pages holding U locks.

12.3.3   Estimation of Log Application Count

We first derive the probability distribution of pending update count, for each type of dirty pages, and then estimate the average total pending update count.

Medium Recovery Complexity   Here, before transferring a dirty page from one node to another a copy of the page is propagated to the disk. To derive the probability distribution of pending update count of the pages of partition (n,p) in the buffer of node m, we will focus only on the dirty pages of that partition (see Figure 12.3), that is the LRU substack of the dirty pages. We will refer to this set of pages by (n,p,m). The pages within this set are ranked by their relative distance from the stack stop. Note that any access to pages of partitions other than partition (n,p) changes the state of the LRU stack, but it does not change the relative distance or rank of the dirty buffer pages of partition (n,p) in the LRU substack. Therefore, in deriving the probability distribution of the pending update count of the pages of partition (n,p), we will ignore the events corresponding to the access to the pages of other partitions. Let $P^k_{n,p,m}(j)$ be the probability that the jth ranked page of the (n,p,m) LRU substack has a pending update count of k. Since, within each (n,p,m) set, the access distribution is assumed to be uniform, $P^k_{n,p,m}(j)$ will be independent of j as in [20] for the uniform access case. We therefore derive only $P^k_{n,p,m}(1)$.

The pending update count of the top dirty page of the LRU substack (n, p, m) changes its value in the following events: 1) a new dirty page is brought to the top, 2) top dirty page is updated or 3) after a remote access the top dirty page is purged due to invalidation or become clean due to page transfer and hence, the second ranked dirty page becomes the top page. We will set up a recursive formulation for $P_{n,p,m}^k(1)$ in terms of $P_{n,p,m}^{k-1}(1)$ by focussing only on the events that access a page of partition (n, p) in any node (local or remote). The other events are neutral for this substack as they have no impact on the distribution of $P_{n,p,m}^k(1)$. Let $\zeta_{n,p,m}$ be the probability that the next access to partition (n, p) is from node m. $\zeta_{n,p,m}$ can be easily derived from the access rates to each node. Hence, $(1 - \zeta_{n,p,m})$ is the probability that the next access to this partition is from a remote node.

To analyze the LRU substack state transitions leading to $P_{n,p,m}^k(1)$ for $k > 1$, the state transitions can be decomposed into local access events and other access events from remote nodes. The local access events can be further decomposed into *update hit, read hit and read miss events on the LRU substack* for the dirty pages. (Note that for an update miss on the substack, a clean page is brought in and the pending update count is set to 1. Hence, an update miss only affects the case with $k = 1$.) The accesses from remote nodes can be further decomposed according to *miss and hit events on the top dirty page*. For $k > 1$,

$$
\begin{aligned}
P_{n,p,m}^k(1) \;=\; &\zeta_{n,p,m} \left[\frac{1}{D_{n,p}} \sum_{j=1}^{Z_{n,p,m}} P_{n,p,m}^{k-1}(j)\gamma + \frac{1}{D_{n,p}} \sum_{j=1}^{Z_{n,p,m}} P_{n,p,m}^k(j)(1-\gamma) \right. \\
&\left. + (1 - \frac{Z_{n,p,m}}{D_{n,p}})P_{n,p,m}^k(1)(1-\gamma) \right] \\
&+ (1 - \zeta_{n,p,m}) \left[(1 - \frac{1}{D_{n,p}})P_{n,p,m}^k(1) + \frac{1}{D_{n,p}}P_{n,p,m}^k(2) \right] \quad (12.1)
\end{aligned}
$$

Here, the first part of the right hand side expression is due to local access events and the second part is due to the access events from remote nodes. The first term of the first part of the expression is the (update hit) probability that the next access is update and the page brought to the top has already a pending update count of $k - 1$. Similarly, the second term, the read hit term, is due to a read on an existing page with a pending update count of k. The third term, the read miss term, is the probability that the next access is a read and it doesn't fall on a dirty page, and hence, it does not change the update count of the top dirty page of the set (n, p, m). The first term of the second part is the probability that the remote access does not fall on the top dirty page, while the second term is the probability that the remote access fall on this page. Since the remote access results either in purge or forced propagation of write, the second ranked page becomes the top page. By replacing $P_{n,p,m}^k(2)$ by $P_{n,p,m}^k(1)$ (based on our assumption that $P_{n,p,m}^k(j)$ is independent of j) the last term reduces to $(1 - \zeta_{n,p,m})P_{n,p,m}^k(1)$. Therefore, Equation 12.1 can be rewritten as

$$P_{n,p,m}^k(1) = \frac{1}{D_{n,p}} \sum_{j=1}^{Z_{n,p,m}} P_{n,p,m}^{k-1}(j)\gamma + \frac{1}{D_{n,p}} \sum_{j=1}^{Z_{n,p,m}} P_{n,p,m}^k(j)(1-\gamma)$$

$$+ (1 - \frac{Z_{n,p,m}}{D_{n,p}}) P_{n,p,m}^k(1)(1-\gamma) \qquad (12.2)$$

That is to say in writing down the balance equation for the LRU substack transition probability, the effect of accesses from remote nodes can be ignored and the transitions only need to be decomposed over the local events: update hit, read hit and read miss (corresponding to the three terms in Equation 12.2, respectively).

Since $P_{n,p,m}^k(j)$ is independent of j, by replacing the term $P_{n,p,m}^k(j)$ by $P_{n,p,m}^k$ and after simplification we get

$$P_{n,p,m}^k = \frac{Z_{n,p,m}}{D_{n,p}} P_{n,p,m}^{k-1}, \quad k > 1. \qquad (12.3)$$

Note that the above equation is independent of the probability of update, γ. It implies that in fact only the update events need to be considered in writing down the balance equation for the LRU substack transition probability. The way to get k updates on the top page of the substack is to have an update hit on the local stack position with $k-1$ updates, where the buffer hit probability on the dirty pages is $\frac{Z_{n,p,m}}{D_{n,p}}$ and the probability that a dirty page has $k-1$ updates is $P_{n,p,m}^{k-1}$. Let us represent the term $\frac{Z_{n,p,m}}{D_{n,p}}$ as $\theta_{n,p,m}$. Then, $P_{n,p,m}^k = (\theta_{n,p,m})^{k-1} P_{n,p,m}^1$. Now, $P_{n,p,m}^1$ can be obtained after normalization from the expression $\sum_{i=1}^{C} P_{n,p,m}^k = 1$. After further simplification,

$$P_{n,p,m}^1 = \frac{1 - \theta_{n,p,m}}{1 - (\theta_{n,p,m})^C}. \qquad (12.4)$$

Now the expected number of pending updates on a page of set (n,p,m) is $K_{n,p,m}$ is given by

$$K_{n,p,m} = \sum_{k=1}^{C-1} k P_{n,p,m}^k = \frac{1}{1 - \theta_{n,p,m}} - \frac{C(\theta_{n,p,m})^{C-1}}{1 - (\theta_{n,p,m})^C}. \qquad (12.5)$$

Note that in the above equation the probability state with pending update count of C is not included, since this probability state corresponds to a clean page state in the normal clipping process (See the dashed line in Figure 12.4). The total log application count at node m, A_m, can now be expressed as

$$A_m = \sum_{n \in \{1...N\}, p \in \{1...P\}} K_{n,p,m} Z_{n,p,m}. \qquad (12.6)$$

Complex Recovery Here, the dirty pages are transferred to other nodes if requested by remote nodes and hence, a larger number of updates are accumulated on each page. A page is propagated to the disk only when it is flushed out of buffer and it holds an X or U lock. Since a dirty page is moved from one node to another without resetting its update count, the probability distribution of update count for the pages of partition (n, p) will be independent of node in which it is present. The probability distribution is also independent of the rank of the page in the LRU substack. Therefore, we can set up the following recursive formulation similar to Equation 12.2. (We omit similar derivations to show that the access events from remote nodes can be ignored as before.) For $k > 1$,

$$
P_{n,p,m}^k = \frac{1}{D_{n,p}} \sum_{l=1}^{N} \sum_{j=1}^{Z_{n,p,l}} P_{n,p,l}^{k-1} \gamma
$$

$$
+ \frac{1}{D_{n,p}} \sum_{j=1}^{Z_{n,p,m}} P_{n,p,m}^k(j)(1 - \gamma) + (1 - \frac{Z_{n,p,m}}{D_{n,p}}) P_{n,p,m}^k(1)(1 - \gamma) \quad (12.7)
$$

There are several points to note here. First, the dirty pages include both types of pages holding X and U locks, respectively. Second, update on a page simply increases its update count even if the page is found in a remote node, and hence, the first term of the right hand side expression includes the remote dirty pages. The second and third terms represent the read hit and read miss events on the LRU substack of dirty pages, and therefore are the same as that in Equation 12.2.[4] After further simplification, Equation 12.7 can be rewritten as, for $k > 1$,

$$
P_{n,p,m}^k = \frac{1}{D_{n,p}} \sum_{l=1}^{N} Z_{n,p,l} P_{n,p,l}^{k-1}. \quad (12.8)
$$

The expression is similar in form to that of the earlier case, except that $\theta_{n,p,m}$ for the current policy is expressed as

$$
\theta_{n,p,m} = \frac{1}{D_{n,p}} \sum_{l=1}^{N} Z_{n,p,l}. \quad (12.9)
$$

(Note that $P_{n,p,l}^k$ is independent of l.) It again implies that in fact only the update events need to be considered in writing the balance equation for the LRU substack

---

[4]In case of a read access, if it falls on a dirty page in the remote buffer, one of two cases are possible. If the remote page is holding an X lock, it is downgraded to an U lock (retaining the propagation responsibility) and a copy of the page holding S lock is brought to the local node. Therefore, the new page in the local node is considered clean, i.e., the local node can flush it out of the buffer without propagating it to the disk. If on the other hand, the remote page is holding an U lock a copy of that page holding S lock is brought to the local buffer and no further action is needed. In either case, it does not change the state of the top dirty page of that partition. Also, as before, the hit on a local clean page for read access doesn't change the state of the top dirty page.

transition probability. The way to get k updates on the top page of the substack is to have an update hit on either the local or remote (n, p, m) substack position with $k - 1$ updates.

12.3.4   Estimation of Data I/O Count

We now estimate the number of dirty pages in the buffer of the failed node as well as the number of write I/Os propagated to the disk during normal operations. The number of dirty pages, $N_{m,dirty}$,

$$N_{m,dirty} = \sum_{n \in \{1...N\}, p \in \{1...P\}} Z_{n,p,m}(1 - P^C_{n,p,m}). \qquad (12.10)$$

Note that pages with pending update count of C are not included since they will be clean in the normal clipping process due to early clipping. Under the DF policy, an optimization can reduce the above data I/O component. A page holding U lock implies that an up-to-date version of this page has been transferred to another node in the recent past. The copies of this page may or may not exist in the remote nodes since they can be flushed out of the remote buffers without propagating a copy of the page to the disk. The GLM can identify the nodes that currently hold an S lock on this page, and can save an I/O during recovery by copying this page. It is not difficult to estimate the reduction in I/O due to this optimization, since 1) the number of pages holding U locks is known, and 2) the probability that such a page is retained in S mode in another node can be computed given the composition of the buffer of each node. However, for the sake of simplicity we will not consider this improvement here.

The write I/O propagation count during normal operations under the DTF policy includes three types of write propagations: 1) the flushing of dirty pages out of buffer as a result of LRU buffer replacement policy, 2) forcing of write I/Os during inter-system page transfer, and 3) write I/O propagations due to clipping of pending update counts. The second component is zero under the DF policy, i.e., there is no forcing of write I/O operations during transfer of a dirty page across nodes. Note also that under the DF policy, the flushing component includes also the pages holding U locks.

The estimation of component (1) and (2) of the write I/O propagation count is detailed in the previous work [6], and is also described in brief in the Appendix. Note that under the mapped clipping process (dashed line in Figure 12.4), a slightly larger number of dirty pages can get flushed out of the LRU buffer due to the delayed clipping. However, the clipping I/O's of the flushed out pages is also saved with delayed clipping. Hence, the total write I/O under steady state is the same for both the clipping processes. We therefore, estimate the write I/O under the mapped process. Under this process, a page is propagated to the disk due to clipping if it has a pending update count of C and the next access is an update. Let $w_{n,p,m}$ be the number of write I/O propagations to disk of the pages of partition (n, p) from the buffer of node m per database access due to events (1) and (2). Therefore, the total number of write I/O propagations per database access at the node m, W_m, is given by

$$W_m = \begin{cases} \sum_{n \in \{1...N\}, p \in \{1...P\}} \left(w_{n,p,m} + \zeta_{n,p,m} \gamma P_{n,p,m}^C \frac{Z_{n,p,m}}{D_{n,p}} \right) & \text{DTF policy} \\ \sum_{n \in \{1...N\}, p \in \{1...P\}} \left(w_{n,p,m} + \zeta_{n,p,m} \gamma P_{n,p,m}^C \frac{\sum_{l=1}^{N} Z_{n,p,l}}{D_{n,p}} \right) & \text{DF policy} \end{cases}$$
$$(12.11)$$

where $\zeta_{n,p,m}$ is the probability that the next database access at node m falls on partition (n,p), and $w_{n,p,m}$ is given in the Appendix.

12.4 PERFORMANCE COMPARISON

We will first validate the analytic models against simulation results and then use the analytic models to study the recovery time requirements of the different deferred page propagation policies. These include the DTF policy of the medium recovery scenario and the DF policy of the complex recovery scenario. We then demonstrate how the analysis can be used to select the clipping count to support recovery time and performance requirements. Various sensitivity analyses on the buffer size, affinity factor (η), update probability, etc, are also conducted, while only a subset is shown.

We now detail the cost model used to estimate the recovery time, given the various redo components. Let #DIO be the dirty page count in the buffer (given by Eq. 12.10). Let #UPD be the total log application count (given by Eq. 12.6) and #LOGS be the number of log entries that need to be scanned during recovery. Clearly the REDO component of the recovery time depends on all three factors. However, without an explicit system model the recovery time can not be estimated. For example, if the identities of the dirty pages are known (from the unfailed GLM, or in [30] from the primary, etc.) the reading of the old versions of the dirty pages can be done in parallel if the database is spread over multiple disks [30]. The disk I/O itself depends on the disk scheduling policy (ordered fetch vs. random I/O, etc.) [3, 4, 31]. Additionally, one or more of these REDO components, #DIO, #UPD and #LOGS, can be overlapped. However, the recovery time will increase with the increase in the values of one or more components. Therefore, without any loss of generality, we will express the recovery time as a function of the three components, i.e.,

$$Recovery \ time = W1 * \#DIO + W2 * \#UPD + W3 * \#LOGS \qquad (12.12)$$

where $W1$, $W2$ and $W3$ are the effective time (after reflecting the parallelism in the system) for a disk I/O operation to read an old copy of a page, application of a log entry and scanning of a log entry, respectively. The system pathlength parameters are chosen based on estimate from DB2 and are similar to those used in [20, 21] as follows. The pathlength for each log application is around 10K CPU instructions and that for scanning a log entry (reading and examining, etc.) is 500 instructions.

Assuming a 15 MIPS processor, $W2$ and $W3$ will take 0.666 ms. and 0.033 ms, respectively. We make following further assumptions as in [20, 21]

- We will assume the entries (dirty page ids) in the DPT are sorted in order and the older version of these pages are read from the disk to the buffer in one pass at the beginning of the Redo step. This will reduce the disk seek time. As a general rule of thumb, the I/O time will be reduced by a factor of 3 [31], and we will assume time for each disk I/O, $W1$, as 8 ms.

- We further assume the number of log entries scanned is proportional to the number of log entries applied. Note that most of the pending updates are on hot entries since they are flushed less often. Therefore, for the medium recovery case (where only the logs of the failed node needs to be scanned), assuming a $80 - 20$ access rule, a conservative estimate of the number of log entries scanned, #LOGS, is 1.25*#UPD. Note that the overall contribution of the log scan component is small compared to the dirty page I/O and log application components. For a complex recovery case, the log scan is somewhat larger as the merged log of multiple nodes is scanned. For a conservative estimate we assume the effective log scan under the DF policy for a N node system is N*1.25*#UPD.

Next we discuss the workload parameters considered. To study the impact of affinity, we consider two types of workload: one with high affinity ($\eta = 0.9$) and the other with low affinity ($\eta = 0.4$). The high affinity workload models the TPCA-type debit-credit application in the banking environment [14], where the databases and transactions can easily be partitioned [17] (according to the branch number). The low affinity workload models inventory tracking and stock control applications in a manufacturing environment [18] where partitioning into DB clusters can not be done without sacrificing the affinity as shown in [5]. For the update probability, we use a default value of 0.2, as it is usually observed that the update to read ratio is 1 to 4 [18]. Sensitivity to higher update probability will also be considered. The database access pattern often exhibits high degree of skewness [9]. We assume the access pattern within each DB cluster is given by a 80-20 rule, i.e., 80% of all accesses to a cluster goes to 20% of the pages of the cluster.

12.4.1 Validation of Analytical Models

Since the analytic model is an approximate analysis based on the steady state composition of the buffer contents,[5] a detailed buffer simulation program is developed to validate the analyses. The simulation explicitly tracks not only the buffer pages with various lock modes (S, X, and U), but also the number of pending updates (since it was first brought in or since the last update propagation) on each page. Note that we do not simulate actual failure of a node; instead the simulation keeps

---

[5]See Equations 12.13, 12.14 and 12.15 in the Appendix on the approximations for the probability of the lock type held on a page.

track of the number of dirty pages and the number of pending update counts on all pages under steady state situation. We gather in the simulation not only the aggregate statistics, but also statistics per data class (affinity hot set, etc.) basis, as well as the detailed probability distribution of pending update count. As the simulation time increases with the number of nodes and the buffer size per node of the simulated configuration, we show the validation results with a smaller configuration and explore the larger configuration with the analytic results. The validation results are shown only for a 2 node case with a DB cluster size ($D_{n,p}$) of 1000 pages (4MB) under the DTF and DF policies, however, we have found a similar match for 4 and 6 node cases.

The pending update count under the DTF policy is first considered with a clipping count of 25 for a two node system and for an affinity of 0.9. From the view point of each node, the database pages can be grouped into four sets. These are the hot and cold sets of its affiliated DB cluster, and the hot and cold sets of all the other DB clusters. We refer to these four page sets of a node as its affinity hot and cold sets and its non-affinity hot and cold sets, respectively.

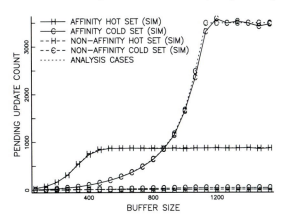

Figure 12.6. Recovery time vs. MPL.

In Figure 12.6, we show the pending update counts over these four sets of pages for each node. The analysis and simulation results match closely. Note that the pending update count on the affinity cold set can become very large for large buffer sizes. This is due to the presence of a large number of dirty pages from the affinity cold set as the buffer size increases. The affinity pages do not get much references from other nodes, hence once updated they continue to stay on as dirty pages in the buffer for a long time, if the buffer size is large. This is in contrast to the non-affinity dirty pages which tends to get more frequent references from other nodes and become clean again.

The probabilities that a page has exactly a single pending update under DTF are shown in Figure 12.7 again for the four sets of pages: the affinity hot and cold set pages and the non-affinity hot and cold set pages, respectively. The pages in

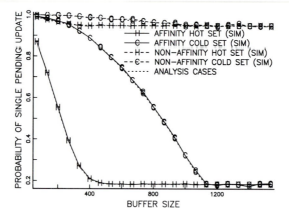

Figure 12.7. Recovery time vs. MPL.

the non-affinity hot and cold sets tend to get only one update during its life time in the buffer of a non-affinity node as the next update would most likely comes from another node. When the buffer size is small, the pages in the affinity cold set tend to get flushed out before the next update. Hence the probability of a single pending update is quite high. This probability decreases as the buffer size increases. As the buffer size becomes large (more than 1,200 pages in this case), the probability that an affinity cold page has exactly a single pending update levels off and becomes very low. This occurs at a much smaller buffer size (around 400 pages) for an affinity hot page of which the probability drops much faster as the buffer size increases.

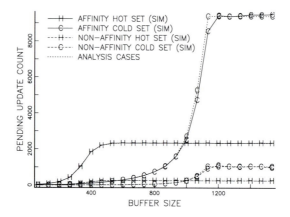

Figure 12.8. Recovery time vs. MPL.

We next consider the DF policy under the same set of parameters (i.e., a clipping count of 25, 2 nodes system and an affinity of 0.9). Figure 12.8 shows the pending update counts over all pages of the affinity hot and cold sets and the non-affinity

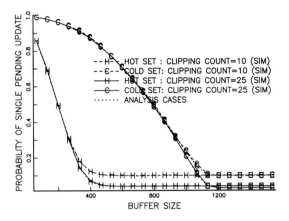

Figure 12.9. Recovery time vs. MPL.

hot and cold sets, respectively. This is similar to Figure 12.6 with one exception. Now the curve for the non-affinity cold set also can rise and level off for large buffer sizes. This is due to the fact the pending update count is not reset to zero upon transfer under DF in contrast to DTF. The probabilities that a page has exactly a single pending update are shown in Figure 12.9 for the hot and cold pages under the DF policy. Two different clipping counts of 10 and 25 are considered (the remaining parameters are same the as before). Note that the curves for the affinity hot set (respectively, cold set) and non-affinity hot set (respectively, cold set) are not distinguishable. This is due to the fact that dirty pages get moved around the nodes with their update counts preserved. (Recall that under the DTF policy, the update count gets reset to zero when a dirty page is transferred to another node.) Hence the pending update count distribution of a page (or a page class) is independent of its node (or affinity) location. (Figure 12.8 shows the pending update count for a set of pages instead of a single page. Hence, it would be location dependent as the buffer content, i.e. how may pages of that set is in the buffer, becomes relevant.) As in the DTF case, the probability of a single pending update decreases with buffer size and eventually levels off. For the cold set, it comes down at a slower rate and levels off at a much larger buffer size. Note that the clipping count only has an effect on the level that it settles upon, but has little effect on the slope of the curve and the buffer size where it levels off.

12.4.2 Comparison of Recovery Times

We now use the analytical model to estimate recovery times under the DTF and DF policies. All the results presented here as well as in the next subsection are for a 6 node case. Note that the recovery time of a failed node is dependent only on the content of its buffer. The content of a node buffer depends on the affinity factor and the coherency policy, and not directly on on the number of nodes. The number of nodes may play a role in partitioning an workload and therefore, in determining the affinity. The size of each affinity DB cluster is assumed to be 10,000 pages (40MB),

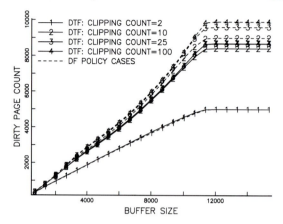

Figure 12.10. Recovery time vs. MPL.

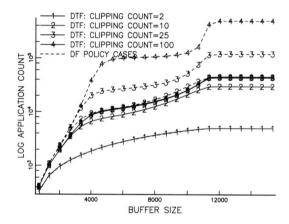

Figure 12.11. Recovery time vs. MPL.

Figure 12.10 shows the dirty page counts for both the DTF and DF polices under different clipping counts. (The two policies overlap for the case of $C = 2$ and the cases for $C = 25$ and 100 under DTF also overlap.) The number of dirty pages increases with the clipping count for both the DTF and DF policies. However, beyond a clipping count of 10, the dirty page counts are not much affected by the clipping process. Note however the large differences in the dirty page counts between smaller clipping counts. The difference between the DTF and DF policies on dirty page counts is mainly on the large buffer sizes where the curves are close to leveling off.

Figure 12.11 shows the numbers of log records that need to be applied during recovery for both the DF and DTF polices under different clipping counts. (The two policies again overlap for the case of $C = 2$.) As the clipping count increases, the number of log applications increases much more rapidly under the DF policy than the DTF policy. (Note that the Y-axis is in logarithmic scale.) Initial sharp rise is due to the increase in the number of hot dirty pages, and the second sharp rise corresponds to the buffer size (12000 approx.) when most of the cold affinity sets are retained such that they build up high pending update counts. Under the DTF policy, this rise in pending update count is less sharp since the accesses from remote nodes effectively act as a clipping process.

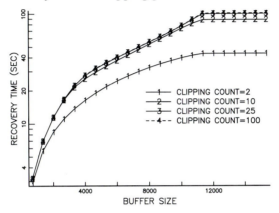

Figure 12.12. Recovery time vs. MPL.

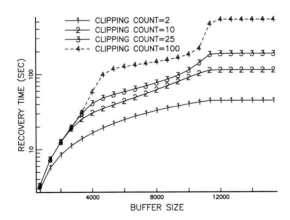

Figure 12.13. Recovery time vs. MPL.

For the DTF and DF policies, Figures 12.12 and 12.13 show, respectively, the recovery times which are the sum of the corresponding components in Figures 12.10

and 12.11. Recovery time for smaller buffer sizes is dominated by the I/O component while for larger buffer sizes it is dominated by the log application count. Note that log application component is an order of magnitude higher for the DF policy for larger buffer sizes and clipping counts. In comparison, we note that for a scheme with the simple recovery scenario, the dirty pages can mainly come from the uncommitted transactions. The average log application count is also very small. Thus the recovery time for the simple recovery type scheme is only on the order of a second.

12.4.3   Recovery Time Vs. Performance Trade-off

One of the ways the analysis can be very helpful to a system designer is to choose the right clipping count given various other system parameters and the dirty page propagation policy. In some system design, quick recovery may be of the utmost importance while in others recovery time can be traded for better on line system performance. Figures 12.14 through 12.16 show the effect of clipping count on both recovery time and write I/O reduction due to deferred write under DTF and DF policies for various system and workload parameters. The reduction in write I/O is estimated as the percentage savings in write I/O relative to that under no deferred write. The various points on each curve corresponds to different clipping counts (2, 3, 4, 8, 16, 32, 64, etc.). Increase in clipping count moves left to right on each curve of Figures 12.14 through 12.16 increasing both recovery time and reduction in write I/O operations.

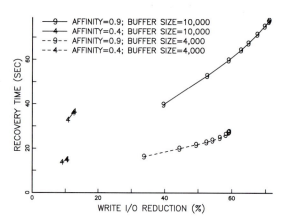

Figure 12.14. Recovery time vs. MPL.

   Two different buffer sizes, 4,000 and 10,000 pages are considered. For each buffer size, two different affinity factors, 0.9 and 0.4, are examined. Generally speaking, the system takes a longer time to recover for a larger buffer size. Higher affinity also results in longer recovery time due to higher pending update counts. Consider Figure 12.14 under the DTF policy. For a low affinity (0.4) very few dirty pages accumulate multiple pending updates before they are transferred to another node and hence flushed (cleaned). Therefore, clipping count has no effect on the trade-off between write I/O reduction and recovery time. However, for a higher affinity (0.9) this trade-off appears linear for both large and small buffer sizes. The difference in the slopes of the two curves can be explained as follows. For the smaller buffer size most of the pages are hot while the larger buffer retains both hot and cold pages. If only the hot pages are retained in the buffer, the write I/O reduction is given by $p_u - \{(1 - \alpha) + \alpha/C\}p_u$, where α fraction of the accesses goes to the hot set, p_u is the update probability and C is the clipping count. On the other hand, if both the hot and cold pages are retained in the buffer the reduction in write I/O is $p_u - p_u/C$. Note that by increasing the clipping count the change in write I/O reduction in both the cases are comparable if α is close to 1. However, the change in recovery time for the second case is much larger, since it has a larger number of dirty pages. Therefore, larger the number of cold dirty pages in the buffer steeper the slope.

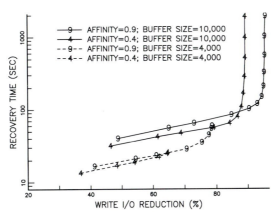

Figure 12.15. Recovery time vs. MPL.

Next consider Figure 12.15 under the DF policy. Now both the high and low affinity cases are sensitive to the clipping count. For a smaller buffer size the trade-off is still close to linear since no page remains indefinitely in the buffer. However, for a larger buffer size the hot pages may never be flushed out of buffer by the LRU replacement policy, and hence, a good choice of clipping count is very important. A moderate clipping count (say around 16, i.e., the 5th point from the left on each curve) will achieve good reduction on recovery time and savings on write I/Os for all cases. Note that without clipping (i.e. with very large clipping count), the recovery time can grow extremely large. A clipping count much higher than 16 increases the recovery time significantly without increasing substantially the reduction write I/O.

Figure 12.16 shows the corresponding curves for a lower update probability (0.2) under the DF policy. The sensitivity to the clipping count is substantially reduced,

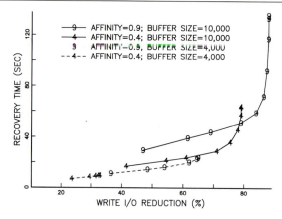

Figure 12.16. Recovery time vs. MPL.

especially for large clipping counts under a large buffer size. However, the knee of the curves occur still for a clipping count around 16. The reduction of sensitivity to the clipping count can be explained as follows. Compare the recovery times for a buffer size of 10,000 pages and for an affinity of 0.9, (solid curves marked by 9) in Figures 12.15 and 12.16. The recovery time is bounded for the lower update probability (0.2) while that for the higher update probability (0.5) is unbounded. For a higher update probability, a larger number of pages hold an X lock and hence, there is less replication of pages across multiple nodes. Therefore, the hot pages can be retained in the buffers across all nodes with that buffer size. Since, the pages do not reset their pending update counts when moved across nodes, the hot pages can build up high pending update counts, unless they are clipped. For a lower update probability a larger amount of buffer is required for retaining all hot pages so that the hot pages can build up high pending update counts. This shows the dependency of clipping count to limit recovery time not only on the buffer size but also on the probability of update and the overall buffer hit probability. The analysis provides the means to select the appropriate clipping count based on the system configuration and workload parameters.

12.5   SUMMARY

In a data sharing environment, the concept of deferring the propagation of dirty pages to disk can be explored to improve normal performance. However, this can have a negative impact on the recovery time. In this paper, analytic models are developed to analyze the recovery times under different dirty page propagation policies. We show how these complicated schemes can be mapped onto analytic models capturing all significant factors like clipping (i.e. limiting the maximum pending update count per page), local and remote buffer hit, skewed access pattern, affinity factor, multiple access modes (read and update) and lock modes, and the intricacies of resetting versus preserving the pending update count upon page transfer between nodes. The recovery time analysis in essence is an analysis of the number of dirty pages and the pending update counts in the buffer. Our approach consists of several major elements. First of all, we decompose the LRU stack (of each node) into separate substacks according to some page set classifications based on access frequencies and focus on the relative positions of the dirty pages within the substack. The analysis of the pending update count for each class of pages is then separated into two sub-problems, where one is on estimating the number of dirty pages in the substack, and the other is on analyzing the the pending update count distribution for each page. The clipping process is modeled by developing an equivalent process which can be combined with the dirty page substack analysis.

The major contribution of the paper is to provide an analytic modeling methodology on recovery analysis. The analytic model is validated extensively through detailed simulations. The impact on recovery times under various dirty page propagation policies is studied. These include the DTF policy for medium recovery scenario and the DF policy for complex recovery scenario. The model provides a framework to understand the factors affecting the recovery time. We show the sensitivity of the recovery time to the clipping count selection. Our analysis also gives insights on the trade-offs between recovery time and I/O saving during normal operations. It provides a means for the system administrators to select the appropriate operating parameters such as clipping count and buffer size to satisfy the recovery and performance requirements.

Acknowledgments: We like to thank P. Shahabuddin for many helpful discussions.

Appendix

In this appendix, we outline the analysis of the LRU replacement policy [7, 6] which is used to derive the number of dirty pages. Under the DTF policy, the dirty pages include only the pages holding X lock while under the DF policy, pages holding either X or U lock are included. We will outline the derivation for the DF policy, and a very similar process can be followed for the DTF policy (see, [6, 8]).

Let $Y_{n,p,m}(k)$ denote the average number of pages of partition (n,p) present in the top k buffer locations of the mth node. Similarly, $S_{n,p,m}(k)$, $X_{n,p,m}(k)$ and $U_{n,p,m}(k)$ denote the average number of pages holding S, X and U locks, respectively, in the top k locations of the LRU stack at node m. Let $\lambda^l_{n,p,m}$ be the rate at which data of partition (n,p) are accessed by the local transactions of node m, and $\lambda^r_{n,p,m}$ be the rate at which they are accessed by the remote transactions. Recall that α_p is the access probability to partition p. Now, for $p = 1, ..., P$,

$$\lambda^l_{n,p,m} = \begin{cases} \lambda L \alpha_p \eta, & \text{if } n = m \\ \lambda L \alpha_p \frac{(1-\eta)}{(N-1)}, & \text{otherwise,} \end{cases}$$

$$and \quad \lambda^r_{n,p,m} = \begin{cases} \lambda L \alpha_p (N-1) \frac{(1-\eta)}{(N-1)}, & \text{if } n = m \\ \lambda L \alpha_p \left\{ \eta + \frac{(N-2)(1-\eta)}{(N-1)} \right\} & \text{otherwise.} \end{cases}$$

where λ is the transaction rate, and L is the number of pages accessed by each transaction. Let $y_{n,p,m}(k)$ be the probability that the kth buffer location from the top of the LRU stack at node m contains a page of partition (n,p). Let $x_{n,p,m}(k)$ and $u_{n,p,m}(k)$ be the probabilities that the page is of partition (n,p) and is holding an X and U lock, respectively. Then,

$$Y_{n,p,m}(k) = \sum_{l=1}^{k} y_{n,p,m}(l), \quad X_{n,p,m}(k) = \sum_{l=1}^{k} x_{n,p,m}(l), \quad U_{n,p,m}(k) = \sum_{l=1}^{k} u_{n,p,m}(l),$$

$$and \quad S_{n,p,m}(k) = Y_{n,p,m}(k) - (X_{n,p,m}(k) + U_{n,p,m}(k)).$$

We will set up a recursive formulation to determine $y_{n,p,m}(k+1)$, $x_{n,p,m}(k+1)$ and $u_{n,p,m}(k+1)$ for $k \geq 1$ given $y_{n,p,m}(l)$, $x_{n,p,m}(l)$ and $u_{n,p,m}(l)$, for $l = 1, ..., k$. Consider a smaller buffer consisting of the top k locations only. The buffer location $(k+1)$ receives the page that is pushed down from location k. Let $r_{n,p,m}(k)$ be the rate at which pages of partition (n,p) are pushed down from location k. Similarly, let $r_{n,p,m}^{X}(k)$ and $r_{n,p,m}^{U}(k)$ be the rates at which pages of partition (n,p) holding X and U locks, respectively, are pushed down from location k. Our estimation of $y_{n,p,m}(k+1)$, $x_{n,p,m}(k+1)$ and $u_{n,p,m}(k+1)$ is based on the following: (1) the relative push down rate for each data type from location k is approximated as the expected value of finding a page of the $(n,p)^{th}$ partition in the $(k+1)^{st}$ buffer location over all time, and (2) push down rate for each data type at location k can be derived using the conservation of flow argument for each data type separately. Therefore, using the conservation of flow for the pages holding any lock, we equate the long term rate at which these pages of the $(n,p)^{th}$ partition get pushed down from the top k locations of the buffer, as

$$r_{n,p,m}(k) = \lambda_{n,p,m}^{l} \left[1 - \frac{Y_{n,p,m}(k)}{D_{n,p}} \right] - \lambda_{n,p,m}^{r} \gamma \frac{Y_{n,p,m}(k)}{D_{n,p}}.$$

Estimation of $r_{n,p,m}^{X}(k)$ and $r_{n,p,m}^{U}(k)$ is somewhat subtle, and is explained later. Now, the probability $y_{n,p,m}(k+1)$, can be approximated as

$$y_{n,p,m}(k+1) \approx \frac{r_{n,p,m}(k)}{\sum_{i \in \{1..N\}, j \in \{1...P\}} r_{i,j,m}(k)}. \tag{12.13}$$

The probabilities that the page at the $(k+1)^{st}$ location is of partition (n,p), and it holds an X and U locks, respectively, are given by their joint probabilities. Therefore,

$$x_{n,p,m}(k+1) \approx \frac{r_{n,p,m}^{X}(k)}{r_{n,p,m}(k)} y_{n,p,m}(k+1), \tag{12.14}$$

$$u_{n,p,m}(k+1) \approx \frac{r_{n,p,m}^{U}(k)}{r_{n,p,m}(k)} y_{n,p,m}(k+1). \tag{12.15}$$

The above equations are solved iteratively, with the base conditions of $y_{n,p,m}(0) = 0$, $x_{n,p,m}(0) = 0$, and $u_{n,p,m}(0) = 0$. At the point, when $Y_{n,p,m}(k)$ is very close to its limit $D_{n,p}$, $Y_{n,p,m}(k)$ may exceed $D_{n,p}$ because of the approximation in the above equations. This is corrected by resetting $Y_{n,p,m}(k)$ to $D_{n,p}$ whenever $Y_{n,p,m}(k)$ exceeds $D_{n,p}$ and $r_{n,p,m}(k)$, $r_{n,p,m}^X(k)$ and $r_{n,p,m}^U(k)$ are taken to be zero for all subsequent steps for that partition. The above approximations are very accurate and particularly for a large buffer size. Thus the $Z_{n,p,m}$ defined in Section 4 is given by

$$Z_{n,p,m} = X_{n,p,m}(B) + U_{n,p,m}(B)$$

Also, the write I/O probability per database access, $w_{n,p,m}$ (defined in Section 4), under DF is given by $(r_{n,p,m}^X(B) + r_{n,p,m}^U(B))/\lambda L$. Here, the numerator is the flush rate of the dirty pages from the buffer.

The tracking of pages with an X or U lock is somewhat similar to the tracking of pages with any lock, $Y_{n,p,m}(k)$. The main difference lies in the fact that estimating the replacement rate, $r_{n,p,m}(k)$, for the pages of (n,p) partition with any lock needs to consider only the miss rate in the smaller buffer consisting of the top k locations, while that for the X or U pages requires also the knowledge of the state of the buffer pages outside the smaller buffer (i.e., locations with index higher than k). For example, the pages with an X lock can be brought from outside the smaller buffer in two ways: (1) update access on a page which is not present in the smaller buffer, and (2) read access on a page with an X lock that is present outside the smaller buffer i.e., the buffer hit on pages in the set of size $X_{n,p,m}(B) - X_{n,p,m}(k)$, where B is the buffer size. Let $h_{n,p,m}^{X,out}(k)$ represent a buffer hit on an X page outside the smaller buffer consisting of k locations. Note that $X_{n,p,m}(B)$ and therefore, $h_{n,p,m}^{X,out}(k)$ are known only after the recursion step B. We therefore set up a second level iteration over the LRU recursion analysis. At the lth iteration, the value of $X_{n,p,m}(B)$ obtained from the previous iteration (referred to as $X_{n,p,m}^{l-1}(B)$) is used to compute the new values of $X_{n,p,m}^l(k)$. Therefore, at the lth iteration of the kth recursion step,

$$h_{n,p,m}^{X,out}(k) = \begin{cases} \frac{X_{n,p,m}^{l-1}(B) - X_{n,p,m}^l(k)}{D_{n,p}} & \text{if } X_{n,p,m}^{l-1}(B) > X_{n,p,m}^l(k) \\ 0 & \text{otherwise.} \end{cases}$$

Finally,

$$\begin{aligned} r_{n,p,m}^X(k) &= \lambda_{n,p,m}^l \left(\gamma \left[1 - \frac{X_{n,p,m}(k)}{D_{n,p}} \right] + (1-\gamma) h_{n,p,m}^{X,out}(k) \right) \\ &\quad - \lambda_{n,p,m}^r \frac{X_{n,p,m}(k)}{D_{n,p}} \end{aligned}$$

Here, the first two terms provide the rate at which dirty pages are brought to the smaller buffer due to write and read, and the last term is the rate they are depleted due to accesses from remote nodes. For the first iteration step $X_{n,p,m}^0(B)$ is set to zero. Similarly, $r_{n,p,m}^U(k)$ can be estimated. Further details of the analysis can be found in [6].

References

[1] Behman, S.B., T.A. DeNatale, and R.W. Shomler, *Limited Lock Facility in a DASD Control Unit*, Tech. Report TR 02.859, IBM General Products Division, San Jose, CA, Oct. 1979.

[2] Berstein, P., V. Hadzilacos, and N. Goodman, *Concurrency Control and Recovery in Database Systems*, Addison-Wesley, Reading, Mass., 1987.

[3] Biswas, P., K. K. Ramakrishnan and D. Towsley, "Trace Driven Analysis of Write Caching Policies for Disks," *ACM SIGMETRICS*, Santa Clara, CA, May 1993.

[4] Carson., S. D., and S. Setia, "Analysis of Periodic Update Write Policy," *IEEE Trans. on Software Eng.*, 18(1) 1992.

[5] Cornell, D.W., D.M. Dias, and P.S. Yu, "On Multisystem Coupling through Function Request Shipping," *IEEE Trans. on Software Eng.*, 12(10) (October 1986).

[6] Dan, A. and P. S. Yu, *Analytic Modeling and Comparison of Buffer Coherency Policies based on Lock Retention*, IBM research Report, RC 18664, Yorktown Heights, 1993.

[7] Dan, A., and P. S. Yu, "Performance Analysis of Buffer Coherency Policies in a Multi-System Data Sharing Environment," *IEEE Transactions on Parallel and Distributed Systems*, 4(3) (March 1993).

[8] Dan, A. and P. S. Yu, "Performance analysis of coherency control policies through lock retention," *Proc. of the ACM SIGMOD Intl. Conf. on Management of Data*, San Diego, CA, June 1992.

[9] Dan, A., P. S. Yu, and J.Y. Chung, "Characterization of Database Access Pattern for Analytic Prediction of Buffer Hit Probability," *VLDB Journal*, Vol. 4, 1995.

[10] Dias, D. M., B. R. Iyer, J. T. Robinson, and P. S. Yu, "Integrated Concurrency-Coherency Controls for Multisystem Data Sharing," *IEEE Trans. Software Eng.*, 15(4) (April 1989).

[11] Franklin, M. J., M. J. Carey, and M. Livny, "Global Memory Management in Client Server DBMS Architectures," *18th International Conference on Very Large Databases*, Vancouver, Canada, Aug. 1992.

[12] Franklin, M.J., et al., "Crash Recovery in Client-Server EXODUS," *Proc. of the ACM SIGMOD Intl. Conf. on Management of Data*, San Diego, CA, June 1992.

[13] Gawlick, D. and D. Kinkade, "Varieties of Concurrency Control in IMS/VS Fast Path," *IEEE Database Engineering,* 2(8) (June 1985).

[14] Gray, J. (ed.), *The Benchmark Handbook for Database and Transaction Processing Systems,* Morgan Kaufmann, San Mateo, CA, 1991.

[15] Haerder, T. and A. Reuter, "Principles of Transaction-Oriented Database Recovery," ACM Comput. Surv., 15(4) (December 1983).

[16] Helland, P., *The TMF Application Programming Interface: Program to Program Communication, Transactions, and Concurrency in the Tandem NonStop System,* Tandem Tech. Rep. TR89.3, Tandem Computers, Feb. 1989.

[17] Horst, R.W., and T.C.K. Chow, "An Architectue for High Volume Transaction Processing," *12th International Symposium on Computer Architecture,* Boston, MA, June 1985.

[18] IBM Corp., *DB2 V2R2 Performance Report,* Technical Report GG24-3461, 1989.

[19] IBM Corp., *Sysplex Overview: Introducing Data Sharing and Parallelism in a Sysplex,* Technical Report GC28-1208, April 1994.

[20] Jhingran, A. and P. Khedkar, "Analysis of Recovery in a Database System Using a Write-Ahead Log Protocol," *Proc. of the ACM SIGMOD Intl. Conf. on Management of Data,* San Diego, CA, June 1992.

[21] Jhingran, A. and P. Khedkar, *Analysis of Run-Time v Recovery-Time Tradeoffs for Database Management Systems,* IBM research Report, Yorktown Heights, 1992.

[22] Kronenberg, N., H. Levy and W. D. Strecker, "VAXcluster: a Closely-Coupled Distributed System," *ACM Transactions on Computer System,* 4, May 1986.

[23] Lamport, L., "Time, Clocks, and the Ordering of Events in a Distributed System," *Communications of the ACM,* 21(7), 1978.

[24] Leff, A., J.L. Wolf, and P.S. Yu, "Replication Algorithms in a Remote Caching Architecture," *IEEE Trans. Parallel and Distributed Systems,* 4(11) (November 1993).

[25] Lomet, D., *Recovery for Shared Disk Systems using Multiple Redo Logs,* DEC Tech. Report, CRL90/4, Cambridge Research Lab, MA, October 1990.

[26] Mohan, C., Personal Communication.

[27] Mohan, C., D. Haderle, B. Lindsay, H. Pirahesh, and P. Schwarz, "ARIES: A Transaction Recovery Method Supporting Fine-Granularity Locking and Partial Rollbacks Using Write-Ahead Logging," *ACM Trans. on Database Systems,* 17(1), 1992.

[28] Mohan, C., and I. Narang, "Recovery and Coherency Control Protocols for Fast Intersystem Page Transfer and Fine Granularity Locking in a Shared Disks Transaction Environment," *Proc. 17th Intl. Conf. on Very Large Databases*, Barcelona, Spain, Sept. 1991.

[29] Mohan, C., I. S. Narang, and J. D. Palmer, *Page Recovery Using Multiple Logs in a Data Sharing Environment*, IBM Technical Disclosure Bulletin, 33(3B), 1990.

[30] Mohan, C., K. Treiber, and R. Obermarck, "Algorithms for the Management of Remote Backup Data Bases for Disaster Recovery," *Ninth Int. Conf. on Data Engineering*, Vienna, April 1993.

[31] Polyzois, C., A. Bhide, and D. Dias, "Disk Mirroring with Alternating Deferred Updates," *18th International Conference on Very Large Databases*, Dublin, Ireland, Aug. 1993.

[32] Rahm, E., "Empirical Performance Evaluation of Concurrecy Control Protocols for Databse Sharing Systems," *ACM Transactions on Database Systems*, 18(2) (June 1993).

[33] Rahm, E., "Recovery Concepts for Data Sharing Systems," *Proc. 17th Intl. Conf. on FTCS*, 1991.

[34] Robinson, J. T., "A Fast General Purpose Hardware Synchronization Mechanism", *SIGMOD Record*, 1985.

[35] Schwarz, P., *Transactions on Typed Objects*, Technical Report CMU-CS-84-166, Carnegie Mellon Univ., Dec. 1984.

[36] Spector, A., R. Pausch, and G. Bruell, "Camelot: A Flexible, Distributed Transaction Processing Systems," *IEEE Compcon Spring'88*, San Francisco, CA, March 1988.

[37] The Tandem Database Group, *NonStop SQL: A Distributed, High Performance, High-Availability Implementation of SQL*, Lecture Notes in Computer Science, No. 359, D. Gawlick, M. Haynie, and A. Reuter, Eds., Springer-Verlag, New York, 1989.

[38] Teng, J., and R. Gumaer, "Managing IBM Database 2 Buffers to Maximize Performance," *IBM Systems Journal*, 24(2), 1984.

[39] Yu, P. S., and A. Dan, "Performance Evaluation of Transaction Processing Coupling Architectures for Handling System Dynamics," *IEEE Trans. Parallel and Distributed Systems*, 5(2) (Februry 1994).

[40] Yu, P. S., D. M. Dias, J. T. Robinson, B. R. Iyer, and D. W. Cornell, "On Coupling Multi-Systems Through Data Sharing," *Proceedings of the IEEE*, 75(5) (May 1987).

[41] Yu, P. S., and A. Dan, "Performance Analysis of Affinity Clustering on Transaction Processing Coupling Architectures," IEEE Trans. Knowledge and Data Eng, 6(5) (October 1994).

Chapter 13

Recovery and Performance of Atomic Commit Processing in Distributed Database Systems

P. K. Chrysanthis, G. Samaras, and Y. J. Al-Houmaily

Abstract

A transaction is traditionally defined so as to provide the properties of atomicity, consistency, integrity, and durability (ACID) for any operation it performs. In order to ensure the atomicity of distributed transactions, an atomic commit protocol needs to be followed by all sites participating in a transaction execution to agree on the final outcome, that is, commit or abort. A variety of commit protocols have been proposed that either enhance the *performance* of the classical *two-phase commit* protocol during normal processing or reduce the cost of *recovery* processing after a failure. In this chapter, we survey a number of two-phase commit variants and optimizations, including some recent ones, providing an insight in the performance trade-off between normal and recovery processing. We also analyze the performance of a representative set of commit protocols both analytically as well as empirically using simulation.

13.1 INTRODUCTION

Transactions are powerful abstractions that facilitate the structuring of database systems, and distributed systems in general, in a reliable manner. Each transaction represents a task or a logical function that involves access to a shared database and assumes that it executes as if no other transactions were executing concurrently and as if there were no program and system failures. In this way, programmers are relieved from dealing with the complexity of concurrent programming and failures, and can focus on designing the applications and developing correctly the individual transactions of the applications.

A transaction provides reliability guarantees by implementing a state transformation with four important properties, commonly known as ACID properties [23, 24, 27]: (1) *atomicity*, (2) *consistency*, (3) *isolation* and (4) *durability*. *Atomicity* ensures that either all or none of the transaction's operations are performed. Thus, all the operations of a transaction are treated as a single, indivisible, atomic unit. *Consistency* requires that a transaction maintains the integrity constraints on the database. *Isolation* demands that a transaction executes (as though) without any interference from other concurrent transactions. *Durability* ensures that all the changes made by a successfully terminated (committed) transaction become permanent in the database, surviving any subsequent failures.

The ACID properties are usually ensured by combining two different sets of algorithms. The first set, referred to as *concurrency control protocols*, ensures the isolation property, whereas the second one, referred to as *recovery protocols*, ensures atomicity and durability properties. Commonly, consistency is satisfied by designing transactions such that each transaction preserves the consistency of the database at its boundaries and is enforced by specifying integrity constraints on a database using *triggers* and *alerters*.

In a *distributed database system* (DDBS) in which the data items are stored at multiple sites interconnected via a communication network, transactions are executed in a distributed fashion at different sites based on the location of the data that they require to access. Since sites and communication links can fail independently, the atomicity property of a distributed transaction cannot be guaranteed without taking additional measures besides concurrency control and recovery protocols. Specifically, for a distributed transaction that executes across multiple sites, the sites need to agree about *when* and *how* the transaction should terminate. That is, all the sites participating in a transaction execution need to (1) *eventually* reach an agreement; and (2) all agree to either *commit* the transaction, making all its effects persistent, or *abort* the transaction, obliterating all its effects as if the transaction had never executed. A protocol that achieves this kind of agreement is called an *atomic commit protocol* (ACP).

Three important performance issues are associated with ACPs.

- *Efficiency during Normal Processing*: This refers to the cost of an ACP to provide atomicity in the absence of failures. Traditionally, this is measured using three metrics [10, 38, 39]. The first metric is *message complexity*, which deals with the number of messages that are needed to be exchanged between the systems participating in the execution of a transaction to reach a consistent decision regarding the final status of the transaction. The second metric is *log complexity*, which accounts for the amount of information that needs to be recorded at each participant site in order to achieve resiliency to failures. The

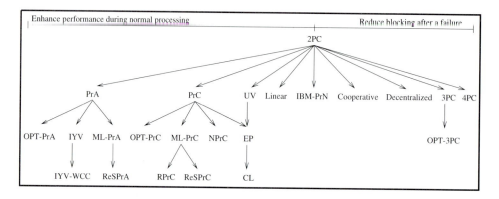

Figure 13.1. Significant steps in the evolution of ACPs.

2PC: Two-Phase Commit [1978], Linear 2PC [1978], UV: Unsolicited-vote [1979], Decentralized 2PC [1981], 3PC: Three-Phase Commit [1981], 4PC: Four-Phase Commit[1981], Cooperative 2PC [1981], PrA: Presumed Abort [1983], ML-PrA: multi-level PrA [1983], PrC: Presumed Commit [1983], ML-PrC: multi-level PrC [1983], IBM-PrN: IBM's 2PC [1990], EP: Early Prepare [1990], CL: Coordinators Log [1990], NPrC: New PrC [1993], IYV: Implicit YES-Vote [1995], IYV-WCC: IYV with Commit Coordinator [1996], RPrC: Rooted PrC [1997], ReSPrC: Restructured PrC [1997], OPT: Optimistic ACPs [1997].

third metric is *time complexity*, which corresponds to the number of rounds or sequential exchanges of messages that are required in order for a decision to reach the participants.

- *Resilience to Failures:* This refers to the failures an ACP can tolerate and the effects of failures on operational sites. A ACP is *non-blocking* if it allows transactions being processed at a failed site to be terminated at the operational sites without waiting for the failed site to recover [24, 55].

- *Independent Recovery:* This refers to the speed of recovery, that is, the time required for a site to recover its database and become operational accepting new transactions after a system crash. A site can *independently* recover, if it has all the necessary information for recovering stored locally (in its log) and does not require any communication with any other site.

The *two-phase commit* protocol (2PC) [22, 32] is the first proposed and simplest ACP. The basic idea behind the design of all other ACPs is to enhance either (1) the efficiency of the 2PC for the normal processing case or (2) the reliability of 2PC by either reducing 2PC's blocking aspects or enhancing the degree of independent recovery. In this chapter, we survey a number of key ACPs and discuss the rationale behind their designs, hence tracing the significant steps in the evolution of ACPs (Figure 13.1). In a way, all ACPs can be regarded as optimizations to the basic 2PC. However, we distinguish between a 2PC variant and a 2PC optimization. As it will become evident in what follows, 2PC variants make conflicting assumptions and hence, only a single 2PC variant can be used in a DDBS with any number of compatible optimizations. By this, we do not imply that conflicting 2PC variants cannot be made to interoperate [4, 66].

Although message complexity, log complexity and time complexity are very useful in analyzing the best and worst case performance behavior of ACPs, they neither can be used to completely characterize the performance of some protocols (e.g., Coordinator Log (CL) [60, 61], Implicit Yes-Vote (IYV) [3] and the set of OPT ACPs [26]) nor are able to capture the impact of ACPs on the *overall* performance of a system. To illustrate this, we present the results of a recent simulation study that shows the relative performance differences among CL, IYV, 2PC and two of 2PC's common variants in a distributed database system over a wide-area network [2, 9]. This study has been motivated by the fact that, in the near future due to the recent advances in networking technologies, it is expected that very large distributed databases systems will be deployed over high-speed wide-area networks. The study also captures the performance gains when read-only optimizations are used.

The rest of this chapter is structured as follows. After introducing the different distributed database system models in the next section, we discuss the basic 2PC in section 13.3. *Presumed-abort* (PrA) and *presumed commit* (PrC) are the best known 2PC variants. In section 13.4, we focus on PrA-based and PrC-based ACPs and analytically evaluate and compare them. In section 13.5, we discuss six more 2PC variants developed with specific environments in mind whereas in section 13.6, we discuss the six most significant optimizations that reduce the cost of commit processing. In section 13.7, we deal with the issue of blocking and present ways to reduce its negative effects. In section 13.8, we present an ACP simulator and discuss the results of the study of the five ACPs mentioned above with regard to their impact on transaction throughput. This chapter ends with some concluding remarks.

13.2 DISTRIBUTED DATABASE SYSTEM MODEL

In a distributed database environment, each transaction is associated with a *coordinator* that is responsible for coordinating the different aspects of the transaction execution. In a *client-server* environment, the coordinator of a transaction is assumed to be the *transaction manager* at the site where the transaction has been initiated. For example, in Figure 13.2, the coordinator of transaction T_i is the transaction manager, which is a component of the database management system (DBMS), at site 1. In the figure, T_i accesses data located at sites 1, 2, and 3 and transaction T_j accesses data located at sites 2, 3, and n. The data distribution is transparent to submitted transactions. A transaction accesses data by submitting its data operations to its coordinator. Depending on the location of the data objects, the coordinator determines the appropriate *participant* site to which it submits each data operation received from the transaction for execution. Hence, each transaction is decomposed by its coordinator into several *subtransactions*, each of which exe-

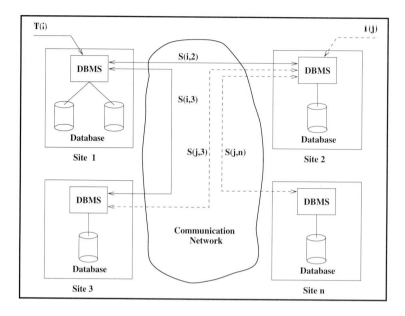

Figure 13.2. A distributed database environment.

cutes at a single site. For example, the subtransactions of T_i are $S_{i,1}$ executing at the site where T_i has been initiated and $S_{i,2}$, and $S_{i,3}$ sent for execution to sites 2 and 3, respectively. When a transaction finishes its execution and submits its commit request, its coordinator initiates an ACP that is carried out by the transaction managers at the participanting sites, to ensure that all its subtransactions either commit or abort at all sites.

In the standards and in a number of commercial database systems, the basic two-level distributed transaction execution model is generalized to a multi-level transaction execution model, called the *tree-of-processes* model [39]. In this model, a transaction manager at a participating site can decompose a subtransaction further into new subtransactions to be executed at its site or different sites. Hence, a distributed transaction can be represented by a multi-level execution tree where the coordinator resides at the root of the tree. The interactions between the coordinator and any participant transaction manager TM_i have to go through all the intermediate participants which are called *cascaded coordinators* between the coordinator and TM_i.

Each transaction manager maintains a *protocol table* in its main memory. For each (sub)transaction at its site, it records the identities of the sites that need to participate in the commitment of the transaction and the progress of the protocol once it is initiated. The protocol table also enables a root or cascaded coordinator to respond to any inquiries pertaining to a transaction very quickly. In order to be able to recover after failures, part of the information in the protocol table is also recorded in a log on a stable storage (*stable log*) that survives system failures. This includes the identities of the sites that might need to be contacted during recovery and the different states of the ACPs in progress.

An alternative to the *client-server* environment is the *peer-to-peer* environment. In this environment, any participant in the transaction can decide to initiate the commit protocol and thus become the coordinator at the root of the transaction commit tree [50].

All ACPs discussed in this chapter with the exception of *IBM's presumed nothing* protocol (IBM-PrN) [48, 50] (Section 13.7.2), are only targeted for a client-server environment. Further, unless otherwise stated, all ACPs are based on the assumptions that (1) each site is *sane* [46, 47] and (2) each site can cause only *omission* failures. That is, each site is assumed to be *fail stop* [53] where it never deviates from the specification of the protocol that it is using, and when it fails, it will, eventually, recover.

13.3   THE BASIC TWO-PHASE COMMIT PROTOCOL

The basic *two-phase commit* protocol (2PC) [22, 32], as the name implies, consists of two phases, namely, a *voting phase* and a *decision phase* (Figure 13.3). During the voting phase, the coordinator of a distributed transaction requests that all sites participating in the transaction's execution *prepare-to-commit*, whereas, during the decision phase, the coordinator either decides to commit the transaction if *all* participants are *prepared to commit* (voted "yes") or to abort if any participant has decided to abort (voted "no"). On commit decision, the coordinator sends out a commit message to all participants whereas on abort decision, it sends out abort messages only to those participants which voted "yes".

When a participant receives a "prepare" request for a transaction, it validates the transaction with respect to data consistency (e.g., executes all integrity constraint evaluations deferred for commit time). If the transaction is validated, then the participant replies with a "yes" vote; otherwise it sends a "no" vote and aborts the transaction releasing all the resources held by the transaction. Even when a participant votes "yes", it may release some of the resources held by the transaction, in particular those not needed for rolling back the transaction in case of an abort decision (e.g., read locks).

If a participant has voted "yes," it can neither commit nor abort the transaction until it receives the final decision from the coordinator. When a participant receives the final decision, it complies with the decision, *acknowledges* the decision, and releases all the resources held by the transaction.

When the coordinator receives acknowledgments from all theparticipants that voted "yes", it completes the protocol and *forgets* the transaction by discarding all information pertaining to the transaction from its protocol table.

The resilience of 2PC to system and communication failures is achieved by recording the progress of the protocol in the logs of the coordinator and the participants. The coordinator force writes a *decision* record prior to sending its final

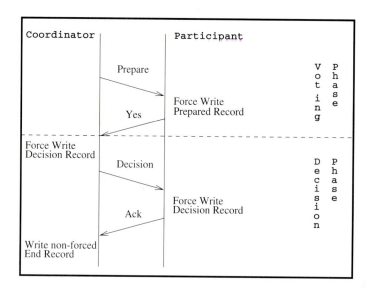

Figure 13.3. The basic two-phase commit protocol.

decision to the participants. Since a force write ensures that a log record is written into a stable storage that survives system failures, the final decision is not lost if the coordinator fails.[1] Similarly, each participant force writes a *prepared* record before sending its "yes" vote and force writes a *decision* record before acknowledging a final decision. In the case that different logs are used to record update operations and the progress of commit protocols, a participant must force all update log records pertaining to the transaction on a stable log before force writing a *prepare* log record. When the coordinator completes the protocol, it writes a non-forced *end* record, indicating that the log records pertaining to the transaction can be garbage collected from the stable log when necessary. Note that the end log record as well as the "acknowledgment" message is required for resource management purposes.

From the above it follows that, during normal processing, the cost to commit or to abort a transaction executing at n participants is the same. 2PC requires $2n + 1$ forced log writes (log complexity), one forced write at the coordinator's site and two at each participant, and $4n$ messages (message complexity). The time complexity of 2PC is 3 rounds, first one is the sending of "prepare" requests, second one is the sending of votes and third one is the sending of decision messages.

Clearly, in the absence of failures, 2PC ensures the atomicity of each transaction because all the sites participating in a transaction's execution will reach a consistent decision regarding the transaction and enforce it. Now, let us consider the behavior

---

[1] In contrast, a non-forced log write is written into the log buffer in main memory and its cost is negligible compared to a forced write that requires a disk access. However, a non-forced log write might be lost in the case of a site failure.

of 2PC in the case of communication and site failures.

13.3.1 Recovery in 2PC Protocol

Site and communication failures are usually detected by *timeouts*. In 2PC, there are four situations where a communication failure might occur. The first situation is when a participant is waiting for a "prepare" message from the coordinator. Since this can occur before the participant has voted, the participant may unilaterally decide to abort if it times out. The second situation is when the coordinator is waiting for the votes of the participants. Since the coordinator has not made a final decision yet and no participant could have decided to commit, the coordinator can decide to abort. The third situation is when a participant has voted "yes" but has not received a commit or an abort final decision message. In this case, the participant cannot make any unilateral decision because it is *uncertain* about the coordinator's final decision. The participant, in this case, is *blocked* until it reestablishes communication with the coordinator. The fourth situation is when the coordinator is waiting for the acknowledgments of the participants. In this case, the coordinator resubmits its final decision to those participants that have not acknowledged the decision once it reestablishes communication with them. Notice that the coordinator cannot simply discard the information pertaining to a transaction from its protocol table or its stable log until it receives acknowledgments from all the participants.

To recover from site failures, there are two cases to consider: coordinator's failure and participant's failure. In the case of a coordinator's failure, the coordinator, upon its restart, scans its stable log and rebuilds its protocol table to reflect the progress of 2PC for all the pending transactions prior to the failure. The coordinator has to consider only those transactions that have started the protocol and have not finished prior to the failure (that is, transactions associated with decision log records without corresponding end log records in the stable log). Once the coordinator rebuilds its protocol table, it completes the protocol for each of these transactions by resubmitting its final decision to all the participants whose identities are recorded in the decision record and are waiting for their acknowledgment. Since some of the participants might have already received the decision prior to the failure and enforced it, these participants might have already forgotten that the transaction had ever existed. In this case, these participants simply reply with *blind* acknowledgments, indicating that they have already received and enforced the final decision.

In the case of a participant's failure, the participant, as part of its recovery procedure, checks whether there exists any transaction in a prepared-to-commit state (that is, has a prepared log record without a corresponding final decision log record). For each prepared-to-commit transaction, the participant reestablishes communication with the transaction's coordinator and inquires it about its final decision. When the participant receives the final decision from the coordinator, it enforces the decision and completes the protocol by acknowledging the coordinator. Once the participant recovers the database, it re-acquires the locks of the prepared-to-commit transactions (in accordance to their write log records) and resumes normal transaction processing.

13.4 ENHANCING THE PERFORMANCE OF THE 2PC PRO-TOCOL

By using today's technology, a disk access requires 10 to 20 milliseconds, whereas the propagation latency of a message from one site to another is typically of the order of hundreds of milliseconds in wide-area networks. These costs do not take into consideration the queuing delays over the CPUs and disks, which are much higher than these basic costs especially in high-volume transactional systems. Because of this, 2PC has been found to consume a substantial amount of a transaction's execution time during normal processing [59]. Hence, eliminating the need for a disk access or a message from the commit processing of transactions greatly reduces queuing delays and congestion over the system resources including contention over the data objects that are stored in a database.

In this section, we discuss the two most notable 2PC variants, namely, *presumed abort* (PrA) and *presumed commit* (PrC) that reduce the message complexity of 2PC by eliminating a single message from each participant site for aborting and committing transactions, respectively. Our discussion also includes the *new PrC* and *rooted PrC* protocols.

13.4.1   The Presumed Abort Protocol

The basic 2PC protocol is also referred to as the *presumed nothing* 2PC (PrN) protocol [33] because it treats all transactions uniformly, whether they are to be committed or aborted, requiring information to be explicitly exchanged and logged at all times. However, in case of a coordinator's failure, there is a *hidden presumption* in PrN by which the coordinator considers all active transactions at the time of the failure as aborted transactions. This presumption allows a coordinator in 2PC not to force write any log records prior to the decision phase. Note that a force write involves a disk access that suspends the protocol until the disk access is completed. If a participant inquires the coordinator about an active transaction after the coordinator has failed and recovered, the coordinator, not remembering the transaction, will direct the participant to abort the transaction, by presumption.

The *presumed abort* (PrA) protocol makes the abort presumption of PrN explicit in order to reduce the cost associated with aborted transactions further [38, 39]. When the coordinator of a transaction decides to abort the transaction, in PrA, the coordinator discards all information about the transaction from its protocol table and sends out abort messages to all the participants without having to log an abort decision record as it would be the case in PrN (see Figure 13.4). After a coordinator failure, if a participant inquires about the outcome of a transaction, the coordinator, not finding any information regarding the transaction will direct the participant to abort the transaction. Furthermore, in PrA, the coordinator of a transaction does

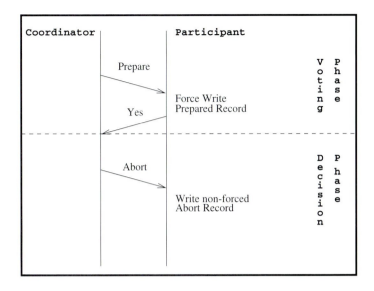

Figure 13.4. The presumed abort 2PC protocol (abort case).

not require abort acknowledgments from the participants because it can discard all information pertaining to the transaction from its protocol table once an abort decision is made. Since the participants are not required to acknowledge abort decisions, they do not have to force write abort log decisions either. Instead, they write non-forced abort records.

Compared to PrN, PrA saves a forced log write at the coordinator's site and, a forced log write and an acknowledgment message from each participant for the abort case. For the commit case, the cost of PrA remains the same as in PrN. Failures in PrA are handled as in PrN.

The PrA can be extended in the tree-of-processes model as follows. The behavior of the root coordinator and each leaf participant in the transaction execution tree remains the same as in two-level transactions. Cascaded coordinators (i.e., non-root and non-leaf participants) are made to behave as leaf participants with respect to their direct ancestors and as root coordinators with respect to their direct descendants. Specifically, when a cascaded coordinator receives a "prepare" message, in *multi-level PrA*, it forwards the message to its descendent participants and waits for their votes. If all descendants have voted "yes", the cascaded coordinator force writes a prepared log record and then sends a "yes" vote to its coordinator. If any descendant has voted "no", the cascaded coordinator sends an abort decision to its descendants and a "no" vote to its coordinator. When a cascaded coordinator receives an abort decision, it writes a non-forced abort record, forwards the decision to its direct descendants and forgets the transaction. On the other hand, when a cascaded coordinator receives a commit decision, it forwards the decision to its direct descendants and force writes a commit record. Afterwards, the cascaded coordinator sends an acknowledgment to its coordinator. Once the direct descendants of the cascaded coordinator acknowledge the decision, it writes a non-forced end record and forgets the transaction.

It should be pointed that PrA is the current choice of the ISO-OSI [67, 30] and X/Open [12, 19] distributed transaction processing standards. Along with 2PC, PrA has been implemented in a number of commercial products such as DECdtm Services [59, 68], DEC VMS [11, 31], Transarc's Encina [54, 58] and TUXEDO of Unix System Laboratories [43].

13.4.2   The Presumed Commit Protocol

As opposed to PrA protocol that favors aborted transactions, the *presumed commit* (PrC) protocol is designed to reduce the cost of committed transactions [38, 39]. It is based on the assumption that a transaction is most probably going to be committed once it has finished its execution and submitted its commit request to its coordinator.

In PrC, instead of interpreting missing information about transactions as abort decisions, which is the case in PrA, coordinators interpret missing information about transactions as commit decisions. However, in this 2PC variant, a coordinator of a transaction has to force write an *initiation* record (which is also called *collecting* record in [39]) for the transaction before sending out "prepare" messages to the participants (Figure 13.5). The initiation record ensures that missing information about a transaction will not be misinterpreted as a commit after a coordinator's site failure. Thus, this record is necessary for the correctness of this variant. In addition, the initiation record facilitates recovery by recording the identities of the participants, which in the case of PrN and PrA are recorded in the decision records.

To commit a transaction (Figure 13.5(a)), the transaction's coordinator force writes a commit record to logically eliminate the initiation record of the transaction and then sends out its commit decision to all the participants. When a participant receives the commit message, it writes a non-forced commit record and commits the transaction, releasing all its resources. Since the coordinator can discard all information about a committed transaction without the acknowledgments of the participants, a participant does not have to acknowledge a commit decision.

To abort a transaction (Figure 13.5(b)), on the other hand, the transaction's coordinator does not force write an abort record. Instead, the coordinator sends out abort messages to all the participants that voted "yes", and waits for their acknowledgments. Once the coordinator receives the acknowledgments, it discards all information pertaining to the transaction from its protocol table and writes a non-forced end record. Each participant, in this case, force writes an abort record and then acknowledges the coordinator's abort decision.

In the case of a coordinator's site failure, the coordinator rebuilds its protocol table by scanning its log as part of its recovery procedure and includes each transaction with an initiation record that is without an associated end record. For each

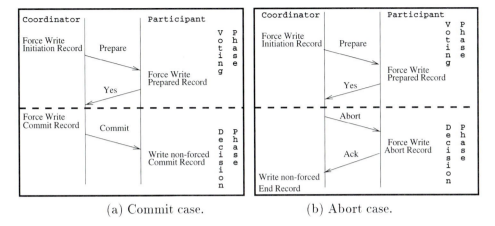

(a) Commit case.   (b) Abort case.

Figure 13.5. The presumed commit 2PC protocol.

of these transactions, the coordinator sends out an abort message to each participating site and waits for acknowledgments. A participant has either received and enforced the abort decision prior to the coordinator's failure or has been left blocked awaiting the final decision. In the former case, the participant will not have any recollection about the transaction and it will blindly acknowledge the decision. In the latter case, the participant force writes an abort log record, as if the coordinator did not fail, and then acknowledges the decision. Once all the required acknowledgments arrive, the coordinator writes a non-forced end record and forgets about the transaction.

In the case of a participant failure, the participant inquires about the outcome of each transaction that has a prepared log record but without a final decision record. When a coordinator receives an inquiry message pertaining to a transaction, the coordinator either has an entry including an initiation record in its protocol table for this transaction or it does not have any entry, which means that the coordinator has forgotten the transaction. In the former case, the coordinator sends an abort and waits for an acknowledgment. In the latter case, not remembering the transaction, the coordinator sends a commit final decision message (hence, the presumed commit presumption holds).

Compared to PrN, PrC saves a forced log write and an acknowledgment message from each participant for the commit case at the expense of an extra forced log write at the coordinator (that is, the initiation log record). For the abort case, PrC incurs one extra forced log write at the coordinator compared to PrN.

PrC can be extended in the tree-of-processes model in two ways. The first extension provides for a speedy recovery in the case of failures accompanied by slow commitment during normal processing, while the second one provides for fast commitment during normal processing accompanied by slow recovery in the presence of failures.

In both resulting protocols, the root coordinator and each leaf participant behave as in PrC, both during normal processing and in the presence of failures. The first protocol, called *multi-level PrC* [38, 39] extends PrC in a manner similar to PrA with the commit presumption to hold between any adjacent levels in the transaction tree in the case of failures. Since a cascaded coordinator behaves as a PrC coordinator for its direct descendent participants, each cascaded coordinator has to force write an initiation record before propagating the "prepare" message to its descendents. If the final decision is to abort the transaction, a cascaded coordinator propagates the decision to its descendants, force writes an abort record and, then, acknowledges its ancestor. Once the acknowledgments arrive from the descendents, a cascaded coordinator writes a non-forced end record and forgets the transaction. If the final decision is a commit decision, a prepared-to-commit cascaded coordinator propagates the decision to its direct descendants, writes a non-forced commit record and, then, forgets the transaction.

The second protocol, called the *rooted presumed commit* protocol (RPrC) [8], eliminates *all* the intermediate initiation records from cascaded coordinators, and, consequently, reduces the cost of commitment during normal processing. But, as opposed to multi-level PrC, RPrC does not realize the two-level presumption of PrC on every adjacent level [8]. Consequently, in the presence of multiple failures, cascaded coordinators cannot provide a fast reply to inquiring messages from recovering participants by presuming commitment in the case that they do not remember a transaction due to a failure. If a cascaded coordinator does not remember a transaction, it needs to inquire its direct ancestor about the outcome of the transaction which in turn might have to inquire its own ancestor. Eventually, either one of the cascaded coordinators in the path of ancestors will remember the transaction and provide a reply, or the inquiry message will finally reach the root coordinator. The root coordinator will respond with the appropriate decision if it remembers the outcome of the transaction or will respond with a commit decision by presumption. RPrC supports efficient propagation of inquiring messages, by requiring each participant to store the list of ancestors of a transaction as part of the transaction's prepare log record and include it in any inquiring message. In this way, if the direct ancestor of a prepared transaction does not remember the transaction, it uses the list of ancestors to find out its own direct ancestor.

It order to facilitate recovery after a coordinator failure and in particular, the failure of the root coordinator, RPrC also requires that, for each transaction, the root coordinator stores in the initiation record and each cascaded coordinator stores in the prepare record all the direct descendants along with their lists of descendants in the transaction's execution tree. Thus, for example, a recovering root coordinator can abort transactions that have not completed their commitment by sending an abort message to its direct descendants, as recorded in the initiation record, along with their lists of descendants in the transaction execution tree to be used by any descendant cascaded coordinator which does not remember the transaction due to a failure, to propagate the abort decision further down the tree.

The list of descendants is constructed by requiring each participant to append its identifier in the acknowledgment of the *first* operation that executes on behalf of a transaction whereas the list of and ancestors is constructed by requiring each coordinator, including the root, to append its identifier in the "prepare" message.

13.4.3   The New Presumed Commit Protocol

Although PrC is more efficient than PrN, its major drawback, as alluded above, is the forcing of the initiation record which prolongs the voting phase and delays the sending of the "prepare" message. This means, for example, the participants in PrA receive the "prepare" message which allows them to release the read locks, earlier than the participants in PrC.

The *new presumed commit* 2PC variant (NPrC) [33], eliminates the initiation record of the PrC by (1) giving up precise knowledge about the active transactions prior to a coordinator's site failure and (2) making the garbage collection of the stable log more expensive. In order to distinguish between committed and aborted or active transactions in the absence of the initiation record after a failure, the coordinator in NPrC maintains two sets of transactions: the set of *recent transactions* (RECT) and the set of *potentially initiated transactions* (PIT). Specifically, in NPrC, a coordinator does not interpret lack of information in its log as commitment but instead, it presumes that a transaction is committed if it is not in a PIT set stored on its stable storage. A PIT contains those transactions that were either aborted or possibly active prior to a failure. After a coordinator crash, the corresponding PIT is derived from RECT as follows.

NPrC assigns transactions monotonically increasing identifiers. Any transaction whose identifier tid is less that the lower-bound tid_l of RECT has completed the commit protocol whereas no transaction with tid greater than the upper bound tid_u of RECT has started its execution. Whenever the transaction with tid_l completes the protocol, tid_l is advanced and is either forced written as part of the transaction's log records if the transaction is committed, or written into the log buffer if the transaction is aborted to be propagated to the stable log when a subsequent force log write is performed. On the other hand, tid_u is periodically increased and force written on the log.

After a failure, the coordinator reads from its log the values of tid_l and tid_u and, by scanning its log for explicit commit records, determines all committed transactions prior to the failure whose tid lies between tid_l and tid_u. By excluding these committed transactions from RECT, PIT is constructed. Once PIT is determined, it is recorded in the stable storage and the coordinator resumes processing with a new tid_l, that is greater than the tid_u of the previous crash, and a new tid_u.

When stable memory space becomes full, the PIT sets can be garbage collected by propagating them to all possible participants. When all the participants acknowledge the reception of PIT sets, the coordinator can discard them knowing that no participant will inquire about the outcome of any of the transactions contained in these sets.

2PC Variants	Commit Decision						Abort Decision					
	Coordinator			Participant			Coordinator			Participant		
	r	f	p	r	f	q	r	f	p	r	f	q
PrN	2	1	2	2	2	2	2	1	2	2	2	2
PrA	2	1	2	2	2	2	0	0	2	2	1	1
PrC	2	2	2	2	1	1	2	1	2	2	2	2
NPrC	1	1	2	2	1	1	1	1	2	2	2	2

Table 13.1. The complexities of 2PC and its standard variants.

13.4.4 Efficiency of Presumed Abort and Presumed Commit variants

The cost of the common 2PC variants discussed above during normal processing, as shown in Table 13.1, can be compared in terms of the message and log complexities of the coordinator and a participant which votes "yes". Recall that the basic 2PC is also referred to as Presumed Nothing (PrN). In the Table, r is the total number of log records, f is the number of forced log writes, p is the number of messages received by a participant from the coordinator and q is the number of messages sent back to the coordinator by the participant.

In section 13.3, we saw that, in PrN, the cost to commit or to abort a two-level transaction executing at n participants is the same. PrN has log complexity $2n + 1$, message complexity $4n$ and time complexity 3 rounds. PrA and the two PrC variants also have the same time complexity as PrN.

To abort a transaction in PrA requires n forced log writes, one at each participant, and $3n$ messages. The cost to commit a transaction in PrA is the same as in PrN. That is, $2n + 1$ forced log writes and $4n$ messages. In PrC, the cost to commit a transaction is $n + 2$ forced log writes and $3n$ messages. To abort a transaction, the cost is $2n + 1$ forced log writes and $4n$ coordination messages. In NPrC, there is a reduction of a forced log write for both the commit as well as the abort case[2] (i.e., the initiation record at the coordinator's site) when compared with PrC.

It follows, from the above, that it is cheaper to use PrA in a system where transactions are most probably going to abort, while it is cheaper to use PrC, or preferably NPrC, if transactions have higher probability of being committed. In a system where transactions have the same probability of being aborted as of being committed, it is cheaper to use PrA. This is because the costs of the two variants are not exactly symmetric. Whereas the cost to commit a transaction in PrA is the same as to abort a transaction in PrC and NPrC, the cost to abort a transaction in PrA is not the same as to commit a transaction in neither PrC nor NPrC. PrC requires two forced log writes at the coordinator's site and NPrC requires one forced

---

[2]In NPrC, an **abort** record is forced only if the transaction is the oldest (i.e., has the least tid in its RECT set) so that the tid_l is advanced. Here, we assume that an aborted transaction is always the oldest as a worst case scenario in order to simplify performance analysis.

	Commit		Abort	
	Forced Log Writes	#Messages	Forced Log Writes	#Messages
ML-PrA	$2l + 2c + 1$	$4n$	$l + c$	$3n$
ML-PrC	$l + 2c + 2$	$3n$	$2l + 3c + 1$	$4n$
RPrC	$l + c + 2$	$3n$	$2l + 2c + 1$	$4n$

Table 13.2. The complexities of multi-level PrA, multi-level PrC and RPrC.

write for the commit case while PrA does not require any log writes for the abort case.

Multi-level PrA (ML-PrA) and multi-level PrC (ML-PrC) retain the relative advantages of PrA and PrC. They also retain the relative message complexity of PrA and PrC. However, due to the extra forced **initiation** log records at the cascaded coordinators, the difference between the cost of aborting a transaction in multi-level PrC and multi-level PrA is greater than the difference between PrC and PrA, whereas the difference between the cost of committing a transaction in multi-level PrC and multi-level PrA is less than the difference between PrC and PrA. Let us illustrate this by considering a transaction with n participants of which c are cascaded coordinators and l are leaf participants.

Multi-level PrA involves $l + c$ (or n) forced log writes to abort a transaction whereas multi-level PrC involves $2l + 3c + 1$ (or $2n + c + 1$). That is, multi-level PrC incurs $n + c + 1$ more forced log writes than multi-level PrA while PrC incurs only $n + 1$ more forced log writes than PrA to abort a transaction. To commit a transaction, multi-level PrC involves $l + 2c + 2$ (or $n + c + 2$) forced log writes whereas multi-level PrA incurs $2l + 2c + 1$ (or $2n + 1$). That is, multi-level PrA requires $n - c - 1$ more forced log writes than multi-level PrC while PrA incurs $n - 1$ more forced log writes than PrC.

RPrC is more efficient that multi-level PrC and the relative advantage of RPrC and multi-level PrA is reduced to the relative advantage of PrC and PrA. To commit a transaction in RPrC requires $l + c + 2$ (or $n + 2$) forced log writes whereas, to abort a transaction requires $2l + 2c + 1$ (or $2n + 1$) forced log writes, which is the same as in PrC. Table 13.2 summarizes the complexities of the multi-level 2PC variants.

13.5   OTHER TWO-PHASE COMMIT VARIANTS

In this section, we discuss six more 2PC variants that have been proposed for specific environments. The common characteristic of these protocols is that they exploit the semantics of the communication networks, the database management systems and/or the transactions to enhance the performance of 2PC.

13.5.1   Network Topology Specific 2PCs

The *linear* 2PC [22, 45] exploits the communication topology to reduce message complexity at the expense of time complexity compared to the basic 2PC, making it suitable for token-ring local-area networks. In linear 2PC, the participants are linearly ordered with the coordinator being the first in the linear order. The coordinator initiates the commitment of a transaction by sending a "prepare" message to the site that follows it in the linear order. The message also includes the coordinator's vote. Thus, if the vote is a "yes", the coordinator prepares itself to commit before sending the message.

When a participant receives a vote from its predecessor in the linear order, it prepares itself to commit if the vote that it has received is a "yes" vote and its own vote is also a "yes" vote and sends a message to its successor. If a participant receives a "no" vote or its own vote is a "no", it aborts the transaction and sends an abort message to its predecessor if it has voted "yes". The participant also sends a "no" vote to its successor if it has one.

Eventually, the last participant will receive the collective vote of all its predecessors. On a commit decision, the participant commits the transaction and sends a commit message to its predecessor, which in turn commits the transaction and sends a commit message to its predecessor, and so on. If the last participant decides to abort the transaction, it sends an abort message to its predecessor, which in turn aborts the transaction and sends an abort message to its predecessor, and so on. The commit or abort acknowledgments are also propagated to the site that has made the final decision (that is, the last site in the linear order) in a manner similar to the way the vote messages are propagated. That is, each message is sent in a different round and thus, linear 2PC has the same message and time complexities $2n$, for n participants. Compared to 2PC, linear 2PC has the same log complexity as 2PC, reduces the message complexity of 2PC from $3n$ to $2n$ but it increases the time complexity of 2PC from 3 to $2n$ rounds.

In *decentralized* 2PC (d2PC) [55], the interconnecting communication network is assumed to be fully connected and contrast to linear 2PC, d2PC reduces time complexity at the expense of message complexity. As in linear 2PC, the coordinator in d2PC includes in the "prepare" message it own vote. Furthermore, it includes the identities of all the participants. When a participant receives the "prepare" message, it broadcasts its vote to all participants. If a participant has voted "yes", it can locally decide about the outcome of the transaction when a participant receives the votes from all other participants. If all votes are "yes", the participant commits the transaction, otherwise it aborts it.

In d2PC, two rounds of messages are required for a participant to make a final decision. The first round is the coordinator's vote, whereas the second is the other participants' votes. By reducing the time complexity from three rounds of messages which is the case in 2PC, to two rounds, it becomes less likely for a participant to be blocked during commit processing in the case of a coordinator failure. This is another advantage of d2PC. On the other hand, d2PC requires $n^2 + n$ messages compared to $3n$ required by 2PC, where n is the number of participants.

13.5.2   Transaction Type Specific 2PCs

The common goal of all four protocols below is to improve both the message and time complexities of 2PC by eliminating the explicit voting phase of 2PC, which polls the votes of the participants. Specifically, these protocols eliminate the "prepare" messages and their corresponding sequential rounds of messages.

The *unsolicited-vote* protocol (UV) [62] shortens the voting phase of 2PC based on the assumption that each participant knows when it has executed the last operation on behalf of a transaction. In this case, a participant does not have to wait for the "prepare" message. Instead, it sends its vote on its own initiative once it recognizes that it has executed the last operation. When the coordinator receives the vote from each participant, it proceeds with the decision phase.

The applicability of UV is limited to database environments in which a coordinator either submits to a participant all the operations of a transaction at the same time or indicates to the participant the last operation at the time that this operation is submitted. The former is a form of predeclaration while the latter implies that each transaction has knowledge about data distribution and can indicate to its coordinator when it has finished accessing a participant site.

Another 2PC variant that eliminates the voting phase of 2PC is the *early prepare* protocol (EP) [60, 61] in which the "prepare" messages are traded for force written log records. EP is based on the following three assumptions: (1) the cost of accessing a stable storage in some systems is as cheap as accessing main memory, (2) each site implements the *strict two-phase locking* protocol [20] which is used in most commercial systems for concurrency control, and (3) transactions do not require deferred consistency constraints validation at commit time.

EP combines UV with PrC without assuming that a participant can recognize the last operation of a transaction. Every operation, therefore, is treated as the last operation and its acknowledgment is interpreted as a "yes" vote. This means that a participant has to prepare a transaction each time it executes an operation of that transaction and prior to acknowledging the operation[3] When the participant receives a new operation for execution, the transaction becomes active again. While the transaction is active, the participant can abort it, for example, if it causes a deadlock. When a transaction is aborted by a participant, the participant responds to an operation with a *negative acknowledgment* (NACK) which the coordinator interprets as a "no" vote and decides to abort the transaction at all participants.

Since, EP requires each acknowledgment to be preceded by a force log write, the number of forced prepared records pertaining to a transaction at a participant is equal to the number of operations submitted sequentially by the transaction and

---

[3]This is possible based on the assumption that each site employs the strict two-phase locking protocol in which it is impossible for a participant in a transaction's execution to abort the transaction due to a deadlock or serializability violation once all the operations received by the participant have been successfully executed and acknowledged [6, 2].

executed by the participant. Furthermore, since PrC requires the identities of the participants to be explicitly recorded at the coordinator's log as part of a forced initiation record, the coordinator must update and force write an initiation record each time a new participant is involved in the execution of the transaction. In the worst case, when the participants become known dynamically, the number of forced initiation records pertaining to a transaction is equal to the number of the participants that executed the transaction.

Two other protocols, namely, the *coordinator log* protocol (CL) [60, 61] and the *implicit yes-vote* protocol (IYV) [2, 3, 6], share the same basic idea with EP but they eliminate the need for the forced log writes at the participants. CL which is derived from PrC, eliminates logging at the participants by implementing *distributed write-ahead logging* (DWAL) [17] whereas IYV which is based on PrA, by implementing *replicated write-ahead logging* (RWAL). Both CL and IYV assume high speed communication network and highly reliable sites.

In CL, only the coordinators maintain stable logs. When a participant executes an operation, as part of its acknowledgment, the participant propagates any redo and undo log records generated during the execution of the operation to the transaction's coordinator to write them in its log. This means that participants cannot independently recover after a system failure and need to communicate with all possible coordinators in order to reconstruct their logs. CL also eliminates the forced initiation log record of PrC at the expense of independent recovery. That is, after a failure, during its recovery, the coordinator needs to communicate with all possible participants in the system in order to determine the set of active transactions prior to the failure and to abort them instead of wrongly assuming commitment. Thus, in CL, the execution of transactions is distributed across multiple database sites, whereas WAL logging and commit processing are centralized at the coordinators' sites.

To commit a transaction, in CL, the coordinator first force writes a commit log record and then sends out commit messages to all participants. When a participant receives a commit message, it commits the transaction by releasing all the resources held by the transaction and without sending an acknowledgment according to PrC. On the other hand, when the coordinator of a transaction decides to abort the transaction, it writes a non-forced abort record and sends out abort messages to all participants. Each abort message includes the undo records of the aborted transaction.[4] When a participant receives an abort message, it rolls back the transaction, releases all the resources held by the transaction, and sends an acknowledgment message that includes all the new log records generated during the transaction rollback. When the coordinator receives the acknowledgment messages, it writes both the received log records and an end record in in its log in a non-forced manner and forgets the transaction.

As opposed to CL, in IYV participants maintain a log and can independently

---

[4]The assumed underlying recovery scheme of CL is ARIES [40], in which transactions are undone logically (that is, undoing an operation is another operation that needs to be executed and acknowledged).

rollback an aborted transaction. IYV eliminates only the forced prepare records at the participants by using RWAL, that is, replicating the redo part of its log pertaining to a transaction at the transaction's coordinator site. Furthermore, IYV proposes logging of state information (e.g., read locks) along with redo records at the coordinator site in order to support *forward recovery*.

On a commit decision, the coordinator in IYV first force writes a commit log record, then sends out commit messages to all participants and waits for their acknowledgments. When a participant receives a commit message, it commits the transaction releasing all its resources and writing a non-forced commit log record. When the commit log record is flushed into stable storage, due to a periodic flushing of the log, the participant acknowledges the commit decision since it follows PrA. When the coordinator receives acknowledgments from all participants, it writes a non-forced end log record and forgets the transaction.

On an abort decision, the coordinator sends out abort messages to all participant except for the participants that have sent NACKs and forgets the transaction without writing any log records. When a participant receives an abort message, it undoes the effects of the transaction using its local log and writes a non forced abort log record. Once the effects of the transaction are undone, the participant releases the resources held by the transaction without sending any messages back to the coordinator.

Although, as opposed to CL, coordinators in IYV can independently recover, participants in IYV, as in CL, cannot. Recovering participants need to communicate with all potential coordinators in order to reconstruct the redo part of their log and determine which of the active transactions in its site have been committed and which are still in progress. Because of this, a participant cannot resume normal transaction processing until it receives replies from all the coordinators. Thus, the applicability of IYV as well as CL is curtailed in the presence of unreliable and slow coordinators.

Even though, due to local logging, a recovering participant in IYV can overlap the undo phase with the resolution of the status of active transactions and the repairing of the redo part of the log that partially masks the effects communication delays, it is imperative that all participants become operational in a bounded amount of time, in a similar manner as in 2PC. For this reason, another IYV variant, called *implicit yes-vote with delegation of commitment* (IYV-WCC) has been proposed in [2, 5] that reduces the blocking aspects of IYV by combining the delegation of commitment technique, found in open commit protocols [46, 47] (section 13.7), with a novel timestamp coordination mechanism. Although, the new IYV variant requires extra messages and log writes, it still maintains the cost of commit processing during normal processing below that of 2PC, PrA and PrC. (For a detail analytical comparison of EP, CL, IYV, IYV-WCC with 2PC and its common variants see [2, 5].)

Thus far, we have reviewed some of the protocols that have been proposed in order to minimize the cost of commit processing during normal processing by reducing the message complexity, the log complexity, or the time complexity. In what follows, after discussing the most common 2PC optimizations, we review some of the efforts that have been made in order to eliminate the blocking aspects of 2PC by adding extra coordination messages and forced log writes.

13.6   ATOMIC COMMIT PROTOCOL OPTIMIZATION

In this section, we focus on the six most significant optimizations proposed in the literature, namely, *read-only, last agent, group commit, sharing the log, flattening the transaction tree* and optimistic, that can reduce the cost associated with commit processing. With the exception of the optimistic optimization which was only recently proposed (1997), all others have been implemented in commercial systems. These can be combined and used together with a number of 2PC variants as well as other ACPs. For a survey of the most common optimizations implemented in commercial transactional systems, including within a peer-to-peer environment can be found in [48, 50].

13.6.1   Read-Only

Traditionally, a transaction is called (completely) *read-only* if all the operations it has submitted to all the participants are read operations. On the other hand, a transaction is called *partially* read-only if only some of the participants in its execution have executed read operations. Otherwise, a transaction is called an *update* transaction.

In the traditional read-only optimization [39], when a participant that has executed only read operations on behalf of a transaction receives a "prepare" message from the transaction's coordinator, it either replies with a "no" or read-only vote instead of a "yes" and immediately releases all the resources held by the transaction without writing any log records.

From a coordinator's perspective, the read-only vote means that the transaction has read consistent data. Furthermore, the read-only participant does not need to be involved in the second phase of the protocol because it does not matter whether the transaction is finally committed or aborted to ensure its atomicity at the participant.

If a transaction is read-only, it does not matter whether the transaction is finally committed or aborted since it has not modified any data. Hence, the coordinator of a read-only transaction, in both PrA and PrC, treats the transaction as an aborted one. This is because it is cheaper to abort than to commit a read-only transaction with respect to logging. Recall that a coordinator does not write any log records in PrA, whereas abort records are written in a non-forced manner in PrC.

The read-only optimization can be considered as the most significant optimization, given that read-only transactions are the majority in any general database system. In fact, the performance gains allowed by the read-only optimization provided the argument in favor of PrA to become the current choice of ACP in the standards and commercial systems.

From the evaluation in section 13.4.4, it is clear the PrC variants are the best choice for committing transactions only in systems in which the majority of the transactions are update transactions and are finally committed. However, in general, and in systems in which the majority of the transactions are read-only in particular, the PrA variants are the choice. This is because the costs of aborting a transaction in PrA variants are less than the costs of committing a transaction in PrC variants. This asymmetry in their costs is due primarily to initiation log records forced in PrC variants for both update and read-only transactions. Not knowing whether a transaction is going to be read-only, a coordinator in PrC has to force write an initiation record.

This motivated the development of new read-only optimization, called *unsolicited update-vote* (UUV) [7, 8] that eliminates the initiation record for read-only transactions using a similar idea as the UV and EP protocols (see section 13.5). In UUV, a participant is assumed as a read-only one until it sends an *unsolicited update-vote* to the coordinator as part of the acknowledgement of the first update operation (which is recognized by the generation of undo/redo log record(s)) that it has executed. When a coordinator receives a final commit request for a transaction, it checks for any update votes pertained to the transaction and if none is found, the transaction is recognized as read-only and the coordinator sends out a read-only message to all the participants indicating that the transaction can be terminated. UUV can also be used to reduce the cost of committing partial read-only transactions by excluding read-only participants from voting by sending them a *read-only* message and allowing them to release all the resources held by the transaction without writing any log record.

From the performance point of view, the cost of PrA variants combined with UUV is the same as in PrC variants combined with UUV while PrC combined with UUV is cheaper than PrA combined with the traditional read-only optimization that requires the voting phase.

13.6.2 Last Agent

The *last agent* optimization has been implemented by a number of commercial systems to reduce the cost of commit processing in the presence of a *single remote* participant [50]. In this optimization, a coordinator first prepares itself and the nearby participants for commitment (fast first phase), and then delegates the responsibility of making the final decision to the remote participant. Once the remote participant receives the request for final decision, if it is prepared to commit, it sends out a commit decision, otherwise, it sends out an abort one. In this way, it reduces the communication required with the faraway participant to one slow round-trip message exchange.

This optimization yields the greatest benefit, especially if sending messages to the remote participant involves long network delays (i.e., connection through satellite). Clearly, its benefit is also depended on the time required to prepare the nearby participants. For example, in the case of a deep transaction tree, if the time required to prepare the nearby participants is sufficient to send a "prepare" message to the remote participant and get back its vote, last agent is not applicable. In such cases, it actually delays the decision by sequencing the "prepare" messages to the nearby participants and to the remote one.

13.6.3   Group Commit

The group commit optimization [18, 21] has been also implemented by a number of commercial products to reduce the cost associated with the forcing of the log records. In the context of centralized database systems, a commit record pertaining to a transaction is not forced on an individual basis. Instead, a single force write to the log is performed when a number of transactions are to be committed or when a timer has expired. The latter technique is used in order to limit the response time of a transaction when the system becomes lightly loaded (that is, not many activities are going on in the system). Thus, the cost of a single access to the stable log is amortized among several transactions.

In the context of distributed database systems, this technique is used at the participants' sites *only* for the commit records of transactions during commit processing. The *lazy commit* optimization is a generalization of the *group commit* in which not only the commit records at the participants are forced in a group fashion, but *all* log records are lazily forced written on stable storage during commit processing. In addition, the coordination messages pertaining to different transactions are also propagated in a grouped fashion. For example, a single message from a participant might contain the acknowledgments of several decisions pertaining to different transactions as well as votes for some other transactions. In this way, the cost of sending a single message is also amortized among several transactions.

13.6.4   Sharing the Log

A local data manager (DM) uses a log to keep track of updates so that it can either abort or commit a transaction. Before a DM votes "yes", it ensures that this information has been forced to stable storage. When it learns of a commit outcome, it also force writes a commit record.

The DM can share the same log with the transaction manager (TM) at its site [39]. With this optimization, the DM takes advantage of the sequential nature of the log and of the knowledge that the TM will force write a commit record. The DM does not force write the prepared record because the TM's force write of the commit record causes the local DM's earlier non-forced write to be written to the log. If the transaction successfully commits, the TM's commit record and the DM's prepared record will both be on the log. This ensures successful recovery processing. If the system fails before the commit is forced, the prepared record may be lost. This does not change the outcome of the transaction, since the TM aborts the transaction if it does not find a commit record on the log. Similarly, the DM does not need to force write the commit record. If the system fails and the non-forced commit record is lost, since TM's commit record and the DM's prepared record are both on the log, the recovery process will successfully commit the transaction.

This optimization saves two forced writes per DM that shared the log. The more DMs that share the log with the TM, the more savings per transaction. CL and IYV, discussed in section 13.5, can be viewed as extending this optimization to include remote data/resource managers.

13.6.5 Flattening the transaction tree

As discussed in the previous section, in a multi-level 2PC variant, coordination messages are propagated down and up the transaction tree in a sequential manner, level by level. Clearly, this serialization of messages increases the duration of commit processing as the tree depth grows.

The *flattening the transaction tree* optimization transforms the transaction execution tree of *any* depth into a two-level commit tree at commit initiation time [50]. In this way, the root coordinator sends coordination messages directly to, and receives messages directly from, any participant. This is achieved by (1) propagating the identity of the root coordinator to each participant as part of the first operation request and (2) propagating the identity of each participant to the root coordinator as part of the acknowledgement of the first operation the participant has executed.

Since messages in a flatten, two-level commit tree can be sent in parallel, this optimization avoids the propagation delays and can be a big performance winner in distributed transactions that contain deep trees. This optimization has been effectively used in [8] to optimize the performance of the multi-level PrC by reducing, in addition to time complexity, its log complexity. That is, it (1) reduces the number of initiation records, (2) allows forced log records to be performed in parallel and (3) reduces the number of non-forced log writes.

This optimization cannot be used in an environment where a participant is prohibited to directly communicate with the root coordinator or vice versa for security reasons. In general, it also cannot be used when the communication topology does not support direct interaction between a root coordinator and the leaf participants. Similarly, it is not feasible when the establishment of new direct communication channels (i.e., sessions) between the coordinator and the participants are expensive and should be avoided as much as possible, a situation that exists in some commercial systems [24].

Another limitation is in protocols that do not require acknowledgement, such as some message based protocols, and conversational protocols (i.e., LU6.2 [29, 65]). In these, the identities of all the participants may not be known prior to the first phase. However, for these protocols it is possible to flatten the tree during the second phase.

13.6.6 Optimistic

The most recently proposed optimization is *optimistic* (OPT) [26] which enhances the overall system performance by reducing blocking arising out of locks held by prepared transactions.

OPT shares the same assumption as PrC, that is, transactions tend to commit when they reach their commit points. Under this assumption, OPT relaxes the *strictness* requirement of recovery [10, 44], allowing a transaction to *borrow* data that have been modified by another transaction that has entered a prepared to commit state and has not committed. That is, when a transaction enters its prepared to commit state, other transactions can observe its effects at the expense of aborting them if the prepared to commit transaction is aborted. OPT prevents cascading aborts and complex recovery after failures by limiting the abort chain to one. It allows only prepared transactions to lend their data while borrowers cannot enter the prepared state until the borrowing is terminated, a rule which is consistent with the notion of prepared state in ACPs.

OPT can be combined with the other optimizations and integrated with most of the ACPs. Its power to enhance the overall system performance due to the early release of data held by prepared to commit transactions has been demonstrated through simulation using OPT-2PC, OPT-PrC, OPT-PrA and OPT-3PC. An interesting result of these simulations is that, although 3PC (three-phase commit protocol, discussed in the next section) is more expensive than any of the 2PC variants, OPT-3PC exhibits better peak throughput than all the 2PC variants in high contention situations. This means that in such situations is better to use OPT-3PC that offers superior performance during normal processing and non-blocking properties in the presence of failures.

13.7 REDUCING THE BLOCKING EFFECTS OF 2PC PROTOCOL

All the proposed ACPs involve blocking [10, 56]. They just differ in the size of the window during which a site might be blocked [16]. In this section, we focus on ACPs that have been designed with different non-blocking features that reduce the size of this window. These protocols can be classified into whether they preserve the prepare state or allow *unilateral or heuristic* decisions in the presence of unbearable delays. Below, we first briefly review four protocols in the first category which we call *non-blocking ACPs*, namely, *cooperative* 2PC, *three-phase*, *four-phase*, and *open* commit protocols. Interestingly, perhaps, due to their increased overheads, none of the non-blocking ACPs has been implemented in commercial systems. Then, we discuss IBM's Presumed Nothing protocol, which has been designed to take into consideration the necessity of heuristics decisions.

13.7.1 Non-blocking Atomic Commit Protocols

The *cooperative* 2PC [34] reduces the *likelihood* of blocking in case of a coordinator failure. In cooperative 2PC, the identities of all participants are included in the "prepare" message so that each participant becomes aware of the other participants. In the case of a coordinator or a communication failure, a participant does not block waiting until it reestablishes communication with the coordinator. Instead, it inquires the other operational participants in the transaction's execution. If any of the operational participants have received the final decision from the coordinator prior to the failure, it informs the inquiring participant about the final decision, thus, reducing the time for which a participant is blocked waiting for recovery from a failure.

Cooperative 2PC is still subject to blocking in the event of a coordinator's site failure when all other participants are in their prepared to commit state. In contrast, the *three-phase commit* (3PC) [55] and the *four-phase commit* (4PC) [28] protocols eliminate the blocking aspects of a 2PC that are due to site failures. That is, if a coordinator fails, the participants can make their own decision.

In 3PC, a preliminary decision is reached before the final decision is made. For this reason, in 3PC, an extra phase is inserted between the two phases of 2PC and the *precommit* state, an intermediate buffering state between the prepared to commit and the final commit (or abort) states at the participants' sites, is introduced. If the coordinator fails during commit processing, the operational sites exchange the status of the transaction among themselves and elect a new coordinator. The new coordinator commits the transaction if any operational site has the transaction in the precommit state. Otherwise, the new coordinator aborts the transaction.

In 4PC, on the other hand, the coordinator of a transaction initiates the 2PC with a number of back up sites that are linearly ordered. The back up sites do not participate in the transaction execution per se but they increase the number of sites that might have status information about the transaction in the case of a coordinator's failure. Once the back up sites have acknowledged the commitment of the transaction, the coordinator initiates the 2PC with rest of the participants. Thus, in the case of a coordinator failure, the back up site with the least identifier in the order that is still operational takes over as the new coordinator and commits the transaction as in 2PC.

All the protocols that we have discussed thus far have been designed assuming no *commission* failures. But this assumption does not hold in *open distributed systems*. In such an environment, a participant site is classified as, *trusted* or *nontrusted* node. A trusted node is one that fails only transiently, and when it fails, it does not send misleading messages. Otherwise, the node is considered nontrusted in the sense that it may never recover or it may deviate from the algorithm of the commit protocol by sending different messages, including misleading ones, causing a commission failure.

The *open commit protocols* [46, 47] (OCPs) have been proposed in the context of *open distributed systems* to ensure the atomicity of transactions *at least* across trusted nodes and despite the existence of nontrusted ones. This goal is achieved by delegating the commit processing (that is, transferring the commit responsibilities) from a nontrusted node to a trusted one and transforming the execution tree of a transaction through restructuring into a different commit tree. Thus, OCPs guarantee that all trusted nodes will reach an agreement about the outcome of transactions despite the participation of nontrusted nodes.

13.7.2   IBM's Presumed Nothing Protocol

In some real-world applications, in the event that a transaction's outcome is bloked due to failures or long delays, certain participants might be required not to wait for recovery processing to discover the outcome because of valuable locks being held [36, 50]. Depending on business needs, these participants might unilaterally commit or abort the transaction. The decision to allow heuristic decisions involves business trade-offs between the cost of fixing database inconsistencies and the cost of missed opportunities. This heuristic decision may damage the consistency of the transaction and data. The IBM's *Presumed Nothing* protocol (IBM-PrN) [51, 65] is a 2PC variant that detects and reports heuristic damage (i.e., conflicting heuristic decisions) simplifying the task of identifying problems that must be fixed. IBM-PrN is part of the SNA LU6.2 architecture [48, 50] that defines the *peer-to-peer* distributed transaction environment, the commit protocols and their synchronization.

In IBM-PrN, a participant site might unilaterally decide to commit or abort a transaction to avoid any unbearable delays while in a prepared to commit state, especially in case of failures involving the coordinator. Once a heuristic decision is made, a participant force writes its decision for comparison during recovery and reports it to the site's systems control operator (since a heuristic decision may result in loss of synchronization among the distributed resources that has to be repaired by an operator action).

The scope of heuristic decisions depends on the participant's role in the transaction commit protocol. In general, heuristic decisions should be propagated to subordinates (descendants) and reported to the coordinator. The subordinates take the same action as the participant that propagated the decision. If recovery is required with some of them, it is performed and completed (so the subordinates can be informed of the heuristic decision of their coordinator) before their coordinator's coordinator (if any) is informed. This permits full and accurate reporting to the root coordinator.

A coordinator in IBM-PrN does not make any presumptions about the outcome of a prepared to commit transaction after a site failure. This is because some participants might have decided to commit, whereas the others have decided to abort the transaction. Therefore, in IBM-PrN, a coordinator force writes an initiation record before it sends out the prepare to commit messages, and each participant has to acknowledge the final decision regardless of whether the decision is to commit or to abort the transaction. In this way, the coordinator will be able to detect any heuristic damages and to correct it. Of course, as mentioned above, the intervention of a human (or automated) operator is required for the restoration of consistency in the event of a heuristic decision. Hence, IBM-PrN retains its performance close to 2PC while, reducing the blocking effects of 2PC in the case of failures.

Different heuristic situations are described in [51, 65]. The detailed description of these scenarios demonstrated the complexity of incorporating heuristic decisions in the basic 2PC. This resulted in a very similar to IBM-PrN 2PC variant called in [51] Presumed Nothing (PN), that reliable handles Heuristic Decisions. In [52], it was showed that all commit variants (PrA- or PrC-based) once enhanced with heuristic decisions collapsed onto the PrN commit variant. This led to a classification of commit protocols around heuristic processing. This classification is quite significant in that it simplifies, for example, the task of evaluating the performance of any commit protocol variant when heuristic decisions are to be considered. One can simply evaluate the IBM-PrN. At IBM, another effort to enhance SNA's LU6.2 with PrA that also includes heuristic decisions resulted in a protocol, called *generalized presumed abort* (GPA) [41, 49], that when recognition of heuristic decisions is required collapses to PN. [51, 52] generalizes and extends that effort.

13.8   SIMULATION-BASED PERFORMANCE EVALUATION

The traditional method of performance evaluation is useful, as we have seen in the previous sections, in analyzing best- and worst-case scenarios to highlight the performance differences among different ACPs. However, to compare and determine the best ACP for a particular database environment, quantitative performance evaluations with respect to the overall system performance, such as *mean response time* or *peak throughput*, are required as is the case with other database protocols (e.g., [1, 14, 15, 42]). Surprisingly, as it was pointed out in [26], very few such performance evaluations exists [2, 9, 26, 35].

In this section, we report on a simulation study [2, 9] that evaluates the performance implications of five ACPs on *transaction throughput* in wide-area, gigabit-networked, distributed database systems. These protocols are 2PC (section 13.3), PrA (section 13.4.1), PrC (section 13.4.2, CL and IYV (section 13.5.2). The study under consideration considers CL and IYV because they can exploit the characteristics of a gigabit network to enhance the performance of a database system. In particular, they can exploit the fact that, in gigabit networks, the size of a message is less of a concern than the number of sequential phases of message passing.

To isolate the impact of ACPs on the overall performance of the system, the study also simulates the behavior of the system when *distributed-execution centralized-commit* (DECC) is used as in [26]. DECC simulates the distributed execution of operations and centralized commit processing (that is, no ACP is used). Though artificial, DECC shows the *highest attainable* system performance in the absence of failures. In this way, one can better relate the performance enhancement of ACPs and optimizations to the highest attainable performance while at the same time comparing their performance to each other.

Since read-only transactions are the majority of transactions in any general database system, the study also evaluates the performance gains when the traditional read-only (TRO) and unsolicited update-vote (UUV) optimizations (section 13.6.1) are incorporated into the protocols under evaluation.

In contrast to other recent comparative performance evaluations of 2PC variants in local-area networks [35, 26], the study under consideration explicitly model, (1) the propagation latency of the communication network, (2) the overhead of the management of the database buffer and of flushing the transaction and protocol execution log records, and (3) the overhead of recovery from site failures. Previous studies did not consider these issues based on the belief that these issues should not affect the relative performance of the common 2PC variants. On the other hand, the results of the study show that these issues do have a direct impact on the performance of IYV and CL. Previous studies have also adopted a parallel model of execution of transactions' operations at the participant sites, whereas the study that we discuss adopted the more realistic sequential execution model of the operations of transactions since transactions, being programs that are usually written in ad hoc fashion, have behaviors that cannot be determined a priori [39] with respect to either their execution patterns or the sites participating in their execution.

In the rest of this section, we first present the simulation system model that is used in the study and its associated parameters, and then present only the results of the study during normal processing and in the absence of failures. The results in the presence of one or two failed sites at any given time can be found in [9, 2]. We summarize these results in the last subsection.

13.8.1   Simulation System Model

The simulation model can be expressed by four logical sets of parameters as shown in Table 13.3: (1) *database parameters*, (2) *transaction parameters*, (3) *site parameters*, and (4) *resource parameters*.

In the model which is similar to the database simulation model in [1], a database is a collection of objects that are uniformly distributed across a number of sites without data replication. A data object is uniquely identified by the tuple $< Site_{id}, Object_{No} >$. The database parameters that are the number of sites ($NumSites$) and objects ($NumObjects$) are specified as parameters to the simulating system.

The sites are interconnected via a *high-speed*, wide-area communication network. The propagation latency ($PropLatency$) of the network is specified as a resource parameter.

Each site consists of (1) a *transaction manager* (TM), (2) a *data manager* (DM), (3) a *lock manager* (LM), (4) a *communication manager* (CM), (5) a *resource manager* (RSM), and (6) a *database cache manager* (DCM).

At a site, the TM manages transaction identifiers, dispatches operations for execution to the appropriate DMs, and coordinates the commit processing for transactions initiated at its site. A TM maintains its own log for those transactions that it coordinates.

A DM receives operation requests from both the local TM and remote TMs, accesses the resources necessary to fulfill these requests, acknowledges the requesting TM on the completion of the request, and participates in the commit processing of those transactions that have performed operations at its site. A DM maintains a log for all database operations that it executes and for transactions in which it participates in their commitment.

Strict two-phase locking is used for concurrency control. An LM at a site is

Database Parameters		
1	*NumSites*	The number of database sites
2	*NumObjs*	The number of data items per database site
Transaction Parameters		
3	*ExecPattern*	Sequential
4	*DistDegree*	Number of participants
5	*ParticipantSize*	Transaction's average access per participant
6	*ThinkTime*	Think time between database operations
7	*PercRead-OnlyTrx*	Percentage of read-only transactions
Site Parameters		
8	*NumCPUs*	Number of CPUs
9	*NumDisks*	Number of disks
10	*MPL*	Degree of multiprogramming per site
11	*HitRate*	Buffer pool hit probability
12	*LogFlushRate*	Log pool flush probability due to WAL
13	*LogSize*	Maximum log buffer size in pages
Resource Parameters		
14	*CPUTime(MESG)*	CPU time for processing a message
15	*CPUTime(READ)*	CPU time for processing a read operation
16	*CPUTime(WRITE)*	CPU time for processing a write operation
17	*DiskTime*	Disk access time
18	*DiskTransfTime*	Page transfer time
19	*PropLatency*	Propagation time for a message
20	*Timeout*	Message timeout

Table 13.3. Simulation system parameters.

responsible for the granting and releasing of locks at its site in accordance to the used ACP. If the lock manager cannot satisfy a request for a lock on a data object, the requesting transaction is immediately aborted to avoid deadlocks.

An RSM is a logical entity that represents the set of physical resources available at any given site. Access to all physical resources within a site is served on a first-come-first-serve (FCFS) basis without any preference to the type of service requested from a resource. The physical resources available at a site consist of a number of CPUs ($NumCPUs$) and disks ($NumDisks$). All CPUs within a site share a common queue and are responsible for the processing of messages and database operations. When a message is received or about to be sent by a CM, it consumes some $CPUTime(MESG)$ of CPU time. Furthermore, the receipt of a message may require additional CPU time. For example, receiving a message requesting a database operation will require $CPUTime(READ)$ of CPU time for a read operation or $CPUTime(WRITE)$ for a write operation. Additionally, some messages will be need to be acknowledged requiring another $CPUTime(MESG)$ of CPU time.

At a site, there are one or more disks dedicated to storing data, and separate disks dedicated to storing logs. The RSM maintains a separate queue for each disk at its site. For log disks, the log buffer may be limited to $LogSize$. When the log buffer reaches $LogSize$, the log buffer must be flushed to disk. The cost of flushing to or reading from disk is represented by the access time ($DiskTime$) and a transfer rate ($DiskTransfTime$) for each page moved to/from the disk.

A DCM at a site is responsible for the management of the data transfer between database cache and data disk(s). A DCM determines whether a page resides in the database cache or needs to be fetched from the data disks based on a $HitRate$ parameter. Similarly, a DCM is responsible for locating an available slot in the cache to swap the requested database page in the case of a miss. If the page to be replaced in the cache is dirty, the page must first be flushed to disk before it is replaced. However, before flushing the replaced page to disk, the DCM must ensure that WAL has been performed for the dirty page. Based on the $LogFlushRate$, the DCM determines whether WAL needs to be performed or not. If WAL must be performed, the DCM requests that the DM at its site flush its log. Once the DM has flushed its log, the DCM flushes the dirty page to disk and fetches the requested database page from disk.

13.8.2   Transactions and Their Execution Model

While still adhering to the traditional ACID, a distributed transaction is modeled as a sequence of read and write operations that is terminated by a commit or an abort transaction management primitive. The execution model adopted in the study is *two-level sequential*. In the two-level sequential execution model, (1) a participant never decomposes a subtransaction further and (2) before a transaction submits an operation, it waits until the previous submitted operation has been executed and acknowledged by the corresponding participant. In other words, a transaction submits an operation only if it has no other operations pending, irrespective of the type of the pending operation. When a transaction receives the results of an operation, it spends some $ThinkTime$, which represents the processing time of the received results before it sends the next operation for execution.

13.8.3   Workload Model

Each site is associated with a multiprogramming level (MPL) that is specified as a parameter to the system. The MPL parameter is used to limit the number of active transactions at a site at any given time. At the beginning of a simulation run, a trace of transactions is generated and used with all protocols. The trace is generated based on the $ExecPattern$ of transactions, the number of sites participating in a transaction's execution, which is specified by the $DistDegree$ parameter, the number of data operations that a transaction performs at each participant site, which is uniformly distributed between 0.5 and 1.5 of the *ParticipantSize* parameter, and the percentage of read-only transactions (*PercRead-OnlyTrx*).

The simulator is run at full capacity (that is, peak load). That is, when a transaction terminates, a new transaction enters the system and starts executing at the site where the previous transaction has terminated. For aborted transactions, *fake* restart is used. By using fake restart, an aborted transaction is restarted as an independent transaction after a delay time that is equal to the mean response time of transactions. For each run, the simulator executes until 10,000 transactions are committed. This translates to a total of 12,000 to 40,000 transactions that are processed by the system, depending on the transaction length. This number of transactions ensures that the system is operating within its steady state. This is confirmed by comparing runs of 10,000, 12,000, and 15,000 committed transactions. The comparison did not show any statistically significant differences between these runs. Hence, in all experiments, the system executes for 10,000 committed transactions. The performance curves of all experiments represent the statistical mean of three independent runs with a confidence half-length interval of no more than 2.7 at the 90% confidence level and no more than 3.5% relative precision (that is, relative error).

13.8.4 Performance of Atomic Commit Protocols

This section includes discussion about the performance of ACPs. The parameter settings for the different experiments are as shown in Table 13.8.3. Since there are no failures, it is assumed that when a transaction reaches its commit point (that is, all its operations have been executed and acknowledged), the transaction commits. Also, since 2PC and PrA behave exactly the same in the absence of failures for committing transactions, for the clarity of the figures, only the performance curves of PrA are included.

Given the size of the simulated database, long transactions execute, on average, 6 operations at each participant site, whereas short transactions execute, on average, 2 operation at each participant site. The first experiment deals with the performance impact of ACPs for long- and short-update transactions. The second experiment deals with the performance impact of ACPs when read-only transactions are introduced. The last experiment deals with the performance gains when read-only optimizations are used.

Performance of ACPs with Update Transactions

In this experiment, as well as all the other two experiments, the system throughput, which is the total number of committed transactions per second with varying multiprogramming levels (MPLs), is measured. The MPL represents the total number of transactions executing at any given site and at any given point in time (since the system operates at full capacity).

As shown in Figure 13.6, the x axis is used for the MPL and the y axis is used for the system throughput. As shown in the figure, the performance curves of all

Database Parameters		
1	*NumSites*	8
2	*NumObjs*	1000
Transaction Parameters		
3	*ExecPattern*	Sequential
4	*DistDegree*	3
5	*ParticipantSize*	6 (long) and 2 (short)
6	*ThinkTime*	0
7	*PercRead-OnlyTrx*	0 (update), 70 %
Site Parameters		
8	*NumCPUs*	1
9	*NumDisks*	1 for each log and 2 for data
10	*MPL*	4-14 (long), 5-50 (short)
11	*HitRate*	80 %
12	*LogFlushRate*	50 %
13	*LogSize*	10 pages
Resource Parameters		
14	*CPUTime(MESG)*	1 msec
15	*CPUTime(READ)*	5 msec
16	*CPUTime(WRITE)*	5 msec
17	*DiskTime*	20 msec
18	*DiskTransfTime*	0.1 msec
19	*PropLatency*	50 msec

Table 13.4. Simulation parameter settings.

ACPs start to increase from the MPL of 4 up to the peak MPL (that is, MPL of 8) and then they start to decline. This *thrashing* behavior of the system is due to the contention of transactions over the data objects as well as the system resources (that is, CPU, disk, log buffer, and the flushing and fetching of data objects) and appears in all three experiments. Due to this contention, at high MPLs, transactions tend to abort because of the high percentage of conflicts over the data objects, reducing the overall system performance.

Figure 13.6 shows the performance of the different protocols when all the operations of transactions are update operations and transactions are long. At the peak MPL (MPL of 8), the difference in the performance of the system in the ideal case (that is, distributed-execution centralized-commit, DECC) and the worst case (that is, using the coordinator log CL protocol) is about 2.5 transactions per second which translates to about 15% performance difference. In the case of implicit yes vote (IYV), DECC outperforms IYV about by 5%. At the same time, IYV

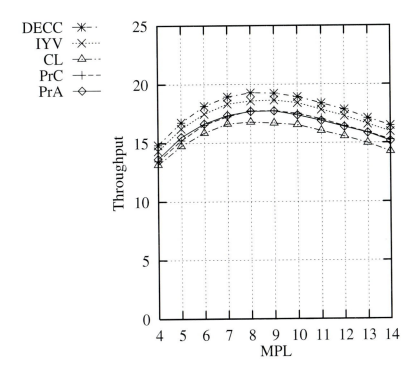

Figure 13.6. The performance of ACPs for long update transactions.

outperforms all other protocols. Also, all three 2PC variants have about the same throughput. IYV outperforms two-phase commit variants at the peak performance by about 5% performance enhancement in throughput with no less than 2.5% enhancement over all multiprogramming levels. Similarly, IYV outperforms CL by about 10% at the peak performance with no less than 9% performance enhancement across all multiprogramming levels.

One interesting observation in this experiment and the other two experiments is the existence of a cross-over point between the performance curves of PrA and PrC even though all transactions are committed once they reach their commit point. Based on the traditional performance evaluation, this point should not exist since PrC will always have the least number of coordination messages and forced log writes. However, this result reveals that under low system loads, the initiation records of PrC affect its performance and makes it worse than PrA. At higher MPLs, the effects of the forced log writes at the participants in PrA as well as the acknowledgment messages of the commit decisions overshadow the cost of the initiation records of PrC, making PrC performance better than PrA performance.

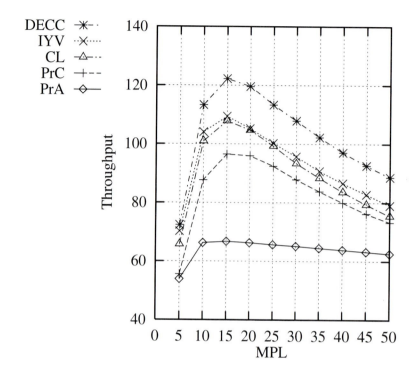

Figure 13.7. The performance of ACPs for short update transactions.

Figure 13.7 shows the impact of the different ACPs on the performance of the system for short update transactions. Comparing the different protocols to DECC, DECC outperforms IYV by about 12% while it outperforms CL by about 13%. With respect to PrA and PrC, DECC outperforms PrC by about 27%, whereas DECC outperforms PrA by about 83%.

The results of this experiment also show three interesting observations. The first observation is that CL is a clear winner compared to the three 2PC variants as opposed to being the loser in the case of long update transactions. This result clearly supports the motivation behind the design of CL [61] which assumes short transactions with high probability of being committed once they reach their commit point. However, the performance of CL starts to degrade more quickly after an MPL of 25 where its performance enhancement over PrC is about 3% at an MPL of 50 after it was about 12% at the peak MPL. On the other hand, IYV performance enhancement over PrC degrades to about 8% at an MPL of 50 from about 13% at an MPL of 15. The reason behind the quick degradation in the CL's performance is due to its *distributed write-ahead logging* (DWAL), which requires a participant that aborts a transaction to wait until it receives the undo log records pertaining to the transaction from the transaction's coordinator before it can release the locks held by the transaction. In contrast, the other protocols do not suffer from such an overhead since the undo records of an aborting transaction at a participant is available locally in its own log.

The second observation is that the performance of PrC has increased from a negligible one in the case of long transactions to about a 45% enhancement over the performance of PrN and PrA at peak performance (MPL of 15). Similarly, by comparing the results of this experiment to the results of long transactions, one notices that the maximum performance difference in the first experiment was about 15% (DECC versus CL), whereas in this experiment, it is about 83% (DECC versus PrA). Thus, not only the relative performance order of the protocols have changed (CL became a winner in this experiment compared to the 2PC variants after it was a loser in the previous experiment), but also the magnitude in the performance differences have greatly changed. These two results clearly show that the traditional way of evaluating the performance of ACPs does not only fail to reflect their relative performance, but it also fails to reflect the magnitude in performance differences.

The third observation is regarding PrA's low thrashing behavior compared to the other protocols after it reaches its peak performance. With respect to this issue, it is noticed that the PrA reaches its performance peak very quickly because the system becomes highly congested due to the excessive forced log writes and coordination messages. This has a consequence that makes PrA less sensitive to increased MPL compared to the other protocols.

Performance of ACPs with Read-Only Transactions

Since read-only transactions are the majority of transactions in any general database system, traces of long and short transactions containing 70% read-only transactions were used in this experiment.

Figure 13.8 shows the performance of ACPs for log, majority read-only transactions. By comparing Figure 13.8 to Figure 13.6, one notices that when read-only transactions are introduced, the performance of all the evaluated ACPs has been enhanced by at least 10% across all multiprogramming levels. Furthermore, the peak performance point of all protocols has been shifted from an MPL of 9 to an MPL of 10. This is consistent with the fact that the system resources are still underutilized and transactions do not conflict at the same rate as in Experiment 1.

In this experiment, IYV still exhibits the best performance over all other protocols and across all multiprogramming levels. In addition, the CL's performance has been enhanced to become better than all 3 two-phase commit variants at low MPLs and about the same as PrC at peak performance (i.e., around an MPL of 10) due to the reduced distributed write-ahead logging (DWAL) of CL when the majority of transactions are read-only.

Figure 13.9 shows the performance of ACPs for short transactions where the performance of all ACPs has been enhanced by at least 7% across all multiprogramming

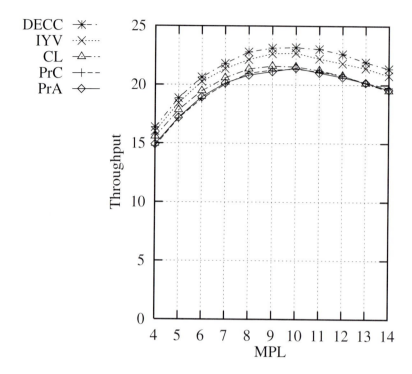

Figure 13.8. The performance of ACPs with long 70% read-only transactions.

levels (which is the case in the PrA protocol). Interestingly, the performance of the CL became better than, IYV in this experiment. This is because DWAL does not add much extra overhead in the case of short transactions dominated by read-only transactions and the extra non-forced (commit) log records of IYV become more significant given the limited log buffers of the participants.

Another interesting result is that PrA reaches a steady state for a period longer than that in the case short update transactions. This is because the 70% read-only transactions do not conflict over locks with each other, and, therefore, a read-only transaction is not aborted unless it conflicts over a lock with an update transaction, resulting in fewer aborted transactions with less system thrashing.

Performance Gains When Using Read-Only Optimizations

As in the previous experiment, in this experiment, traces containing 70% read-only are used to evaluate the performance gains when the traditional read-only (TRO) optimization and unsolicited update-vote (UUV) optimization are incorporated into the system. For IYV and CL, a special case of UUV in the case IYV and CL is

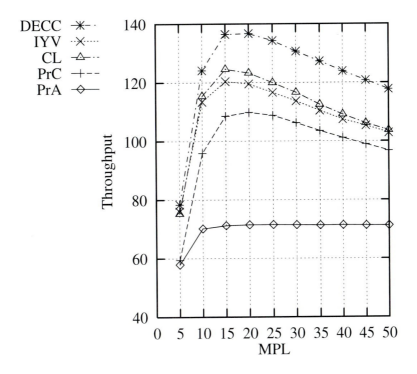

Figure 13.9. The performance of ACPs with short 70% read-only transactions.

applied. Since a coordinator in both protocols can determine if a transaction is read-only at a participant's site based on whether it has received any log records from the participant during the execution of the transaction, participants do not have to send unsolicited update-votes. Thus, in this special case, which is called *read-only (RO)*, the coordinator sends a read-only message to each read-only participant without waiting until the commit record is in its stable log, thereby releasing the resources at read-only participants earlier than their update counterparts.

As shown in Figure 13.10, neither the IYV nor the CL have benefited significantly from RO (that is, about 1% performance enhancement), whereas the 2PC variants have benefited more from TRO and UUV, reducing the performance gap with IYV at high MPLs to 3%. For the CL, at low MPLs, its performance is about the same as the 2PC variants whereas, at high MPLs, CL performance became worse than PrN, PrA, and PrC due to DWAL.

As reasoned in the previous experiments, any extra coordination messages or forced log writes in the case of short transactions by an ACP have a significant impact on its performance compared to long transactions. Conversely, any reduction

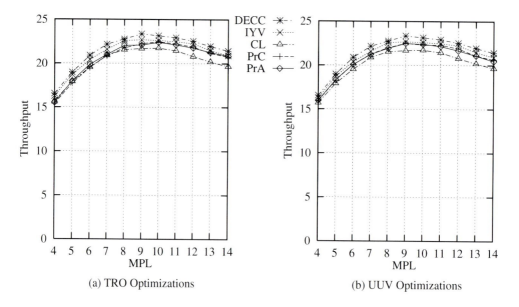

Figure 13.10. The performance of ACPs for long transactions with read-only optimizations.

in the coordination messages or forced log writes greatly enhances the performance of an ACP in the case of short transactions as opposed to long ones. Thus, unlike the results of long transactions, the performance of all protocols has been enhanced with a PrA gaining the most and CL the least, as shown in Figure 13.11. PrA has gained about 60% performance enhancement using TRO, bringing its performance comparable to PrC. It also made PrA as sensitive as the other protocols to the MPL level as opposed to its behavior in Experiments 2 and 4. By factoring in the effects of RO, the performance of IYV is again better than CL since it has gained more by the reduction of the logging activities than CL using RO. By comparing UUV with TRO, PrA has gained about 70% with UUV instead of 60% with TRO, whereas PrC has gained 12% using UUV instead of 6% using TRO. Hence, the UUV has closed the gap between the performance of PrC and IYV to about 3% in favor of IYV.

13.8.5   Summary of results

The results of the above study show that IYV is better or performs equally to the other evaluated protocols in almost all cases of long and short, update transactions

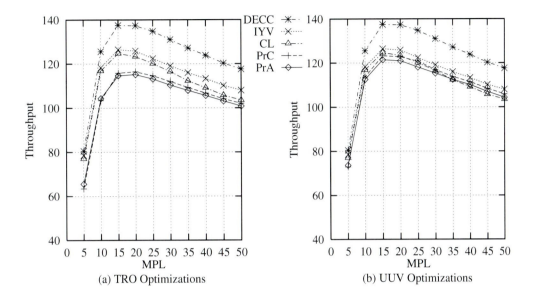

Figure 13.11. The performance of ACPs for short transactions with a read-only optimization.

as well as of long and short, majority read-only transactions with and without using a read-only optimization. This also holds in the presence of single and two overlapping site failures, although the results in the present of failures were not discussed here.

With the exception of the case of short, majority read-only transactions without a read-only optimization (in which CL performed better than IYV), CL is the worst among all the evaluated protocols under the specified conditions and in particular, the usage of the immediate abort strategy for deadlock avoidance. This has revealed the fact that in CL, recovering from aborted transactions is very expensive due to DWAL. This is also supported by the facts that (1) the performance of CL is greatly influenced by the length of the transactions and (2) its performance degrades significantly for high multiprogramming levels. This has also been confirmed in a recent evaluation of the same protocols in which deadlock avoidance was replaced by deadlock detection. In this, CL consistently exhibits the second best performance after IYV.

Interestingly, with respect to the two-phase commit variants, the choice of a protocol has very little impact on performance for the case of long transactions as opposed to short ones. When there is a performance difference between 2PC variants, PrC is always the winner, exhibiting the best peak throughput. This is especially the case for short transactions. Further, performance enhancements due to a read-only optimization are more pronounced with short transactions.

Another very interesting result is that the impact on performance of the initiation log record associated with PrC becomes significant in light loaded systems. This can be concluded by the fact that PrA is the winner only in low multiprogramming levels. One can observe in all experiments a cross-over point between the performance curves of PrA and PrC even under the assumption that all transactions are to be committed when they reach their commit points. The location of the cross-over point varies depending on the length of transactions, the transaction mix (i.e., the percentage of read-only transactions) and whether or not a read-only optimization is used. In contrast to the general belief, these results shows that PrC, in general, is better than PrA.

In summary, this study leads to the conclusion that IYV should be the choice for the future gigabit network database systems and only replaced by PrC whenever IYV's assumptions are not applicable.

13.9   CONCLUSIONS

Research in the area of database systems is one of the most active areas in computer science and technology. This is because current and future application software systems require controlled access to data with enhanced reliability guarantees despite concurrency and failures. These guarantees are provided by database management systems that support the traditional ACID (e.g., atomicity, consistency, isolation, and durability) transaction properties.

The atomicity property of distributed transactions can only be ensured with the use of an atomic commit protocol. Atomic commit protocols received extensive work in the late 1970s to the mid 1980s. After that, the database system industry took over and the standardization organizations picked what was seemingly the best choice among the available atomic commit protocols at that time.

Due to the great impact of atomic commit protocols on the performance of any distributed database system and given recent advances in hardware, software and network technology, recently there has been a renewed interest in the search for efficient atomic commit protocols in the context of traditional database systems as well as in emerging ones such as real-time database systems [25, 57] and multi-database systems [4, 13, 37, 66]. In this chapter, we have discussed both previous and recent proposals of atomic commit protocols and evaluated the performance of a representative subset of them, both analytically as well as empirically using simulation, providing an insight in the performance trade-off between normal and recovery processing. We hope that it will provide the stimulus for further research and development of efficient atomic commit protocols.

Acknowledgments

We are grateful to Sujata Banerjee, George Kyrou and Susan Lauzac for their comments on previous versions of this chapter, and especially to Rob Conticello who participated in the design of the ACP simulator and helped in the writing of the corresponding section. Support for our database research from our respective institutions (University of Pittsburgh, University of Cyprus and Institute of Public Administration, Saudi Arabia) and from the National Science Foundation grants IRI-9210588 and IRI-95020091 is gratefully acknowledged.

References

[1] Agrawal, R., M. Carey and M. Livny. "Concurrency Control Performance Modeling: Alternatives and Implications," *ACM Transactions on Database Systems*, 12(4) (December 1987).

[2] Al-Houmaily, Y. J. *Commit Processing in Distributed Database Systems and in Heterogeneous Multidatabase Systems*, Ph.D. Thesis, Department of Electrical Engineering, University of Pittsburgh, Pittsburgh, Pennsylvania, April 1997.

[3] Al-Houmaily, Y. and P. Chrysanthis. "Two-Phase Commit in Gigabit-Networked Distributed Databases," *Proc. of the 8th Int'l Conference on Parallel and Distributed Computing Systems*, Sept. 1995.

[4] Al-Houmaily, Y. J. and P. K. Chrysanthis. "Dealing with Incompatible Presumptions of Commit Protocols in Multidatabase Systems," *Proc. of the 11th ACM Annual Symposium on Applied Computing*, February 1996.

[5] Al-Houmaily, Y. and P. Chrysanthis. "The Implicit Yes-Vote Commit Protocol with Delegation of Commitment," *Proc. of the 9th Int'l Conference on Parallel and Distributed Computing Systems*, September 1996.

[6] Al-Houmaily, Y. and P. Chrysanthis. "An Atomic Commit Protocol for Gigabit-Networked Distributed Databases," *Journal of Systems Architecture, The EUROMICRO Journal*, (To Appear), 1998.

[7] Al-Houmaily, Y., P. Chrysanthis and S. Levitan. "Enhancing the Performance of Presumed Commit Protocol," *Proc. of the 12h ACM Annual Symposium on Applied Computing*, Feb. 1997.

[8] Al-Houmaily, Y., P. Chrysanthis and S. Levitan. "An Argument in Favor of the Presumed Commit Protocol," *Proc. of the 13th Int'l Conference on Data Engineering*, April 1997.

[9] Al-Houmaily, Y., R. Conticello and P. K. Chrysanthis. *Performance of Atomic Commit Protocols in Gigabit-Networked Database Systems*, Technical report TR-97-15, Department of Computer Science, University of Pittsburgh, Pittsburgh, Pennsylvania, Mar. 1997.

[10] Bernstein P. A., V. Hadzilacos, and N. Goodman. *Concurrency Control and Recovery in Database Systems*. Addison-Wesley, Reading, MA, 1987.

[11] Bernstein, P., W. Emberton, V. Trehan. "DECdta - Digital's Distributed Transaction Processing Architecture," *Digital Technical Journal*, 3(1) (Winter 1991).

[12] Braginski, E. The X/Open DTP Effort. *Proc. of the 4th Int'l Workshop on High Performance Transaction Systems*, Asilomar, California, Sept. 1991.

[13] Breitbart, Y., H. Garcia-Molina, and A. Silberschatz. Overview of Multi-database Transaction Management. *VLDB Journal*, 1(2) (October 1992).

[14] Carey, M. and M. Livny. "Distributed Concurrency Control Performance: A Study of Algorithms, Distribution, and Replication," *Proc. of the 14th Int'l Conference on Very Large Data Bases*, August 1988.

[15] Carey, M. and M. Livny. "Parallelism and Concurrency Control in Distributed Database Machines," *Proc. of the ACM SIGMOD Int'l Conference on the Management of Data*, June 1989.

[16] Cooper, E. "Analysis of Distributed Commit Protocols," *Proc. of the ACM SIGMOD Int'l Conference on Management of Data*, June 1992.

[17] DeWitt, D., S. Ghandeharizadeh, D. Schneider, A. Bricker, H. Hsiao and R. Rasmussen. "The Gamma Database Machine Project," *IEEE Transactions on Knowledge and Data Engineering*, 2(1) (June 1990).

[18] DeWitt, D., R. Katz, F. Olken, L. Shapiro, M. Stonebraker and D. Wood. "Implementation Techniques for Main Memory Database Systems," *Proc. of the ACM SIGMOD Int'l Conference on Management of Data*, 1984.

[19] Distributed TP: a) The TX specification P209, b) The XA Specification C193 6/91, c) The XA+ SpecificationS201, *X/Open Consortium*, Nov. 1992, Feb. 1992, April 1993

[20] Eswaran K., J. Gray, R. Lorie and I. Traiger. "The Notion of Consistency and Predicate Locks in a Database System," *Communications of the ACM*, 19(11) (November 1976).

[21] Gawlick, D. and D. Kinkade. "Varieties of Concurrency Control in IMS/VS Fast Path.," *IEEE Database Engineering*, 8(2) (June 1985).

[22] Gray, J. Notes on Data Base Operating Systems. In Bayer R., R.M. Graham, and G. Seegmuller (Eds), *Operating Systems: An Advanced Course, Lecture Notes in Computer Science*, Volume 60, Springer-Verlag, 1978.

[23] Gray, J. "The Transaction Concept: Virtues and Limitations," *Proc. of the 7th Int'l Conference on Very Large Databases*, September 1981.

[24] Gray, J. N. and A. Reuter. *Transaction Processing: Concepts and Techniques.* Morgan Kaufmann, 1993.

[25] Gupta, R., J. Haritsa, K. Ramamritham and S. Seshadri. "Commit Processing in Distributed Real-Time Database Systems. *Proc. of the 17th IEEE Real-Time Systems Symposium,* Dec. 1996.

[26] Gupta, R., J. Haritsa and K. Ramamritham. "Revisiting Commit Processing in Distributed Database Systems," *Proc. of the ACM SIGMOD Int'l Conference on the Management of Data,* May 1997.

[27] Haerder, T. and A. Reuter. "Principles of Transaction-Oriented Database Recovery," *ACM Computing Surveys,* 15(4) (Dec. 1983).

[28] Hammer M. and D. Shipman. "Reliability Mechanisms for SDD–1: A System for Distributed Databases," *ACM Transactions on Database Systems,* 8(4) (Dec. 1980).

[29] Helland, P. "The LU6.2 protocol boundary: The 'L' stands for 'Lightweight'," *Proc. 3th Int'l Workshop on High Performance Transaction Systems,* Sept. 1989.

[30] *Information Technology - Open Systems Interconnection - Distributed Transaction Processing - Part 1: OSI TP Model; Part 2: OSI TP Service,* ISO/IEC JTC 1/SC 21 N, April 1992.

[31] Laing, W., Johnson, J. and R. Landau. "Transaction Management Support in the VMS Operating System Kernel," *Digital Technical Journal,* 3(1) (Winter 1991).

[32] Lampson, B. Atomic Transactions. *Distributed Systems: Architecture and Implementation - An Advanced Course,* B. Lampson (Ed.), *Lecture Notes in Computer Science,* Volume 105, pp. 246-265, Springer-Verlag, 1981.

[33] Lampson, B. and D. Lomet. "A New Presumed Commit Optimization for Two Phase Commit," *Proc. of the 19th Conference on Very Large Databases,* August 1993.

[34] LeLann, G. Error Recovery. *Distributed Systems: Architecture and Implementation - An Advanced Course, Lecture Notes in Computer Science,* Vol. 105, Springer-Verlag, 1981.

[35] Liu, M. L., D. Agrawal and A. El Abbadi. "The Performance of Two-Phase Commit Protocols in the Presence of Site Failures," *Proc. of the 24th Int'l Symposium on Fault-Tolerant Computing,* 1994.

[36] Maslak, B., Showalter, J. and T. Szczygielski. "Coordinated Resource Recovery in VM/ESA," *IBM Systems Journal,* 30(1), 1991

[37] Mehrotra, S., R. Rastogi, H. Korth and A. Silberschatz. "A Transaction Model for Multidatabase System," *Proc. of the Int'l Conference on Distributed Computing Systems*, June 1992.

[38] Mohan, C. and B. Lindsay. "Efficient Commit Protocols for the Tree of Processes Model of Distributed Transactions," *Proc. of the 2nd ACM SIGACT/SICOPS Symposium on Principles of Distributed Computing*, Aug. 1983.

[39] Mohan, C., B. Lindsay and R. Obermarck. "Transaction Management in the R^* Distributed Data Base Management System," *ACM Transactions on Database Systems*, 11(4) (Dec. 1986).

[40] Mohan, C., D. Hderle, B. Lindsay, H. Pirahesh and P. Schwarz. "ARIES: A Transaction Recovery Method Supporting Fine-Granularity Locking and Partial Rollbacks Using Write-Ahead Logging," *ACM Transaction on Database Systems*, 17(1) (March 1992).

[41] Mohan, C., K. Britton, A. Citron and G. Samaras. "Generalized Presumed Abort: Marrying Presumed Abort and SNA's LU6.2 Commit Protocols.," *An Int'l Workshop on Advance Transaction Models and Architectures*, India, Sept. 1996.

[42] *Performance of Concurrency Control Mechanisms in Centralized Database Management Systems*, V. Kumar, ed., Prentice Hall, 1996.

[43] Primatesta, F. *TUXEDO, An Open Approach to OLTP*. Prentice Hall, 1995.

[44] Ramamritham, K. and P. K. Chrysanthis. *Advances in Concurrency Control and Transaction Processing*, IEEE Computer Society Press, 1997.

[45] Rosenkrantz D., R. Stearns and P. M. Lewis II. "System Level Concurrency Control for Distributed Database Systems," *ACM Transactions on Database Systems*, 3(2) (June 1978).

[46] Rothermel, K. and S. Pappe. "Open Commit Protocols for the Tree of Processes Model," *Proc. of the 10th Int'l Conference on Distributed Computer Systems*, 1990.

[47] Rothermel, K. and S. Pappe. "Open Commit Protocols Tolerating Commission Failures," *ACM Transactions on Database Systems*, 18(2) (June 1993).

[48] Samaras, G., K. Britton, A. Citron and C. Mohan. "Two-Phase Commit Optimizations and Tradeoffs in the Commercial Environment," *Proc. of the 9th Int'l Conference on Data Engineering*, Feb. 1993.

[49] Samaras, G., Britton, K., Citron, A. and C. Mohan. *Enhancing SNA's LU6.2 Sync Point to Include Presumed Abort Protocol*, IBM Technical Report TR29.1751, IBM Research Triangle Park, Aug. 1993.

[50] Samaras, G., K. Britton, A. Citron and C. Mohan. "Two-Phase Commit Optimizations in a Commercial Distributed Environment," *Distributed and Parallel Databases*, 3(4) (October 1995).

[51] Samaras, G., S.D. Nikolopoulos. "Algorithmic Techniques Incorporating Heuristic Decisions in Commit Protocols," *Proc. of the 25th Euromicro Conference*, Sept. 1995.

[52] Samaras, G. *Heuristic Decisions and Commit Protocols, University of Cyprus Technical Report CS-TR96-17*, Dec. 1996.

[53] Schlighting, R. and F. Schneider. "Fail-Stop Processors: An Approach to Designing Fault-Tolerant Computing Systems," *ACM Transactions on Computing Systems*, 1(3) (September 1983).

[54] Sherman, M. "Architecture of the Encina Distributed Transaction Processing Family. *Proc. of the ACM SIGMOD Int'l Conference on Management of Data*, May 1993.

[55] Skeen D. "Non-blocking Commit Protocols," *Proc. of the ACM SIGMOD Int'l Conference on the Management of Data.*, May 1981.

[56] Skeen D., and M. Stonebraker. "A Formal Model of Crash Recovery in a Distributed System," *IEEE Transactions on Software Engineering*, 9(3) (May 1983).

[57] Soparkar N., E. Levy, H. Korth and A. Silberschatz. *Adaptive Commitment for Real-time Distributed Transactions*, Dept. of Computer Science TR92-15, Univ. of Texas-Austin, 1992.

[58] Spector, A. "Open Distributed Transaction Processing with Encina," *Proc. 4th Int'l Workshop on High Performance Transaction Systems*, Sept. 1991.

[59] Spiro, P., A. Joshi and T. K. Rengarajan. "Designing an Optimized Transaction Commit Protocol," *Digital Technical Journal*, 3(1) (Winter 1993).

[60] Stamos, J. and F. Cristian. "A Low-Cost Atomic Commit Protocol," *Proc. of the 9th Symposium on Reliable Distributed Systems*, 1990.

[61] Stamos, J. and F. Cristian, "Coordinator Log Transaction Execution Protocol," *Distributed and Parallel Databases*, Vol. 1, 1993.

[62] Stonebraker, M. "Concurrency Control and Consistency of Multiple of Data in Distributed INGRES," *IEEE Transactions on Software Engineering*, 5(3) (May 1979).

[63] *Systems Network Architecture LU 6.2 Reference: Peer Protocols*, Document Number SC31-6808-1, IBM, Sept. 1990.

[64] *Systems Network Architecture Transaction Programmer's Reference Manual for LU Type 6.2*, Document Number SC30-3084-5, IBM, June 1993.

[65] *Systems Network Architecture. SYNC Point Services Architecture Reference*, Document Number SC31-8134, IBM, Sept. 1994.

[66] Tal, A. and Alonso, R. "Commit Protocols for Externalized–Commit Heterogeneous Databases," *Distributed and Parallel Databases*, 2(2) (April 1994).

[67] Upton IV, F. "OSI Distributed Transaction Processing, An Overview," *Proc. of the 4th Int'l Workshop on High Performance Transaction Systems*, Sept. 1991.

[68] Zimran, E. "The Two-Phase Commit Performance of The DECdtm Services," *Proc. of the 11th Symposium on Reliable Distributed Systems*, 1992.

Chapter 14

Crash Recovery in Client-Server EXODUS

Michael J. Franklin, Michael J. Zwilling, C. K. Tan,
Michael J. Carey, and David J. DeWitt

Abstract

In this chapter, we address the correctness and performance issues that arise when implementing logging and crash recovery in a page-server environment. The issues result from two characteristics of page-server systems: (1) the fact that data are modified and cached in client database buffers that are not accessible by the server, and (2) the performance and cost trade-offs that are inherent in a client-server environment. We describe a recovery system that we have implemented for the client-server version of the EXODUS storage manager. The implementation supports efficient buffer management policies, allows flexibility in the interaction between clients and the server, and reduces the server load by generating log records at clients. We also present a preliminary performance analysis of the implementation.

14.1 INTRODUCTION

Networks of powerful workstations and servers have become the computing environment of choice in many application domains. As a result, most recent commercial and experimental DBMSs have been constructed to run in such environments. These systems are referred to as *client-server DBMSs*. Recovery has long been studied in centralized and distributed database systems [1, 10, 17, 12, 20, 11] and more recently in architectures such as *shared-disk* systems [19, 21, 24] and distributed transaction facilities [6, 13]. However, little has been published about recovery issues for client-server database systems. This chapter describes the implementation challenges and performance trade-offs involved in implementing recovery in such a system, based on our experience in building the client-server implementation of the EXODUS storage manager [2, 8].

Client-server DBMS architectures can be categorized according to whether they send requests to a server as queries or as requests for specific data items. We refer to systems of the former type as *query-shipping* systems and to those of the latter type as *data-shipping* systems. Data-shipping systems can be further categorized as *page servers*, which interact using physical units of data (e.g., individual pages or groups of pages such as segments), and *object servers*, which interact using logical units of data (e.g., tuples or objects) [5]. There is still much debate about the relative advantages of the different architectures with respect to current technology trends [26, 4, 5]. Most commercial relational database systems have adopted query-shipping architectures. Query-shipping architectures have the advantage that they are similar in process structure to a single-site database system, and, hence, provide a relatively easy migration path from an existing single-site system to the client-server environment. They also have the advantage of minimizing communication, since only data that satisfy the query are sent from the server to the requesting clients.

In contrast to the relational DBMS systems, virtually all commercial object-oriented database systems (OODBMSs) and many recent research prototypes have adopted some variant of the data-shipping approach (e.g., O2 [7], ObjectStore [18], and ORION [16]). Data-shipping architectures have the potential advantage of avoiding bottlenecks at the server by exploiting the processing power and memory of the client machines. This is important for performance, since the majority of the processing power and memory in a client-server environment is likely to be at the clients. Moreover, as network bandwidth improves, the cost of the additional communication as compared to query-shipping architectures will become less significant. Also, the data-shipping approach is a good match for many OODBMSs in which database objects can be accessed directly in the client's memory.

Implementing recovery in query-shipping architectures raises few new issues over traditional recovery approaches since the architecture of the database engine remains largely unchanged. In contrast, data-shipping architectures present a new set of problems and issues for the design of the recovery and logging subsystems of a DBMS. These arise from four main architectural features of data-shipping architectures, which differentiate them from traditional centralized and distributed systems and from other related architectures such as shared-disk systems. These features are

1. Database updates are made primarily at clients, and the server keeps the stable copy of the database and the log.

2. Each client manages its own local buffer pool.

3. Communication between clients and the server is relatively expensive (e.g., compared to local IPC).

4. Client machines tend to have different performance and reliability characteristics than server machines.

The client-server EXODUS Storage Manager (ESM-CS) is a data-shipping system which employs a page-server architecture. The implementation of recovery
in ESM-CS involves two main components. The *logging subsystem* manages and
provides access to an append-only log on stable storage. The *recovery subsystem*
uses the information in the log to provide transaction rollback (e.g., abort) and
system restart (i.e., crash recovery). The recovery algorithm is based on ARIES
[20]. ARIES was chosen because of its simplicity and flexibility, its ability to support the efficient STEAL/NO FORCE buffer management policy [14], its support
for savepoints, nested top-level actions, and logical Undo. However, the algorithm
as specified in [20] cannot be directly implemented in a page-server system because
the architecture violates some of the explicit and implicit assumptions on which
the original algorithm is based. In this chapter we describe our recovery manager,
paying particular attention to the modifications to ARIES that were required due
to the correctness and efficiency concerns of recovery in a page-server system. We
also discuss several engineering decisions that were made in the design of the logging
and recovery subsystems.

It should be noted that the ARIES algorithm has recently been extended in
ways that are similar to some of the extensions we describe in this chapter. [23]
describes an extension of the algorithm that can reduce the work performed during
system restart. The algorithm used in ESM-CS required a similar extension, not for
efficiency, but in order to operate correctly in the page-server environment. [21] and
[22] describe extensions to ARIES for the shared-disk environment. As would be
expected, some of the solutions in that environment are applicable to the page-server
environment, whereas others are not (for both correctness and efficiency reasons).
We discuss these extensions and other related work in Section 14.6.

The remainder of the chapter is structured as follows: Section 14.2 describes
the ESM-CS architecture. Section 14.3 provides a brief overview of ARIES. Section
14.4 motivates and describes the modifications made to ARIES for the page-server
environment. Section 14.5 presents a study of the performance of the ESM-CS
logging and recovery implementation. Section 14.6 describes related work. Section
14.7 presents our conclusions.

14.2 THE CLIENT-SERVER ENVIRONMENT

14.2.1 Architecture Overview

ESM-CS is a multiuser system with full support for indexing, concurrency control,
and recovery that is designed for use in a client-server environment. In addition
to supporting these new features, ESM-CS provides support for all of the features
provided previously by the EXODUS storage manager, such as large and versioned
objects [2]. ESM-CS can be accessed through a C procedure call interface or through
E [25], a persistent programming language based on C++.

Figure 14.1 shows the architecture of ESM-CS. The system consists of a client library, which is linked into the user's application, and the server, which runs as a separate process. Clients perform all data and index manipulation during normal (i.e., nonrecovery or rollback) operation. Each client process (i.e., each application that is linked with the client library) has its own buffer pool and lock cache and runs a single transaction at a time. The server is the main repository for the database and the log, and provides support for lock management, page allocation, and recovery/rollback. The server is multithreaded so that it can handle requests from multiple clients, and it uses separate disk processes for asynchronous I/O. Communication between clients and the server uses reliable TCP connections and UNIX sockets. All communication is initiated by the client and is responded to by the server. There is no mechanism for the server to initiate contact with a client.

As stated earlier, ESM-CS employs a page-server architecture in which the client sends requests for specific data and index pages to the server. ESM-CS uses strict two-phase locking for data and non-two-phase locking for indexes. Data are locked at a page or coarser granularity. Index page splits are logged as nested top-level actions [20] so they are committed regardless of whether or not their enclosing transaction commits. During a transaction, clients cache data and index pages in their local buffer pool. Before committing a transaction, the client sends all the pages modified by the transaction to the server. In the current implementation, a client's cache is purged on completion (commit or abort) of a transaction. Future enhancements will allow intertransaction caching of pages [3].

Clients initiate transactions by sending a *start transaction* message to the server and can request the commit or abort of a transaction by sending a message to the server. The server can decide to abort a transaction due to a system error or deadlock. After aborting a transaction, the server informs the client of the abort in response to the next message it receives from the client. During the execution of a transaction, the client generates log records for all updates to data and index pages. The server manages the log as a circular buffer, and will abort executing transactions if it is in danger of running out of log space.

14.2.2 Logging Subsystem

One of the main challenges in designing a recovery system is to minimize the negative performance impact of logging during normal operation. As stated in the previous section, the log in ESM-CS is kept at the server. This decision was made for two reasons: (1) we do not want to lose access to data as the result of a client failure, and (2) it is not economical to require that clients have log disks. Given that the log is kept at the server while the operations on data and indexes on behalf of application programs are performed at the clients, an efficient interface for shipping log records from the clients to the server is required. The logging subsystem is an extension of a centralized logging subsystem that is intended to work efficiently in the client-server environment.

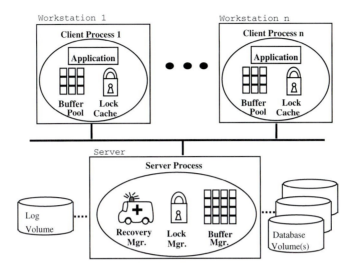

Figure 14.1. The architecture of client-server EXODUS.

Log Records and Data Pages: Our ARIES-based recovery algorithm depends on the use of the write-ahead-logging (WAL) protocol [10] at the server. The WAL protocol ensures that (1) all log records pertaining to an updated page are written to stable storage before the page itself is overwritten on stable storage, and (2) a transaction cannot commit until all of its log records have been written to stable storage. The WAL protocol enables the use of a steal/no-force buffer management policy, which means that pages on stable storage can be overwritten with uncommitted data (steal), and that data pages do not need to be forced to disk in order to commit a transaction (no force).

In order to implement the WAL protocol at the server, we enforce a similar protocol between clients and the server. That is, a client must send log records to the server prior to sending the pages on which the updates were performed. This policy is enforced for two reasons. First, it simplifies transaction rollback by ensuring that the server has all log records necessary to roll back updates to pages at the server that contain uncommitted updates. If the policy were not enforced, transaction rollback caused by a client crash could require performing restart recovery on the affected pages at the server since necessary log records could be lost due to the client crash. Second, it simplifies the server's buffer manager by freeing it from having to manage dependencies between the arrival of log records from clients and the flushing of dirty pages to stable storage.

Log Record Generation and Shipping: The client generates one or more log records for each operation that updates a data or index page. These log records contain redo and/or undo information specific to the operation performed, rather than entire before and/or after images of pages. This decision was motivated by the desire to reduce two overheads: (1) the expense of sending data from clients to the server, especially because some of the pages are quite large (e.g., 8K bytes or longer) and (2) the expense of writing to the log. Another decision that was made in this regard was to not allow log records generated at the client to span log page boundaries. That is, all log records generated by clients are smaller than a log page and are wholly contained in a single log page when sent to the server. This restriction simplifies both the sending of log records at the client and the handling of log record pages at the server. The restriction sometimes requires operations to be logged slightly differently from the way they were actually performed. For example, the creation of a data object that is larger than the size of a log page is logged as the *create* of the first portion of the object followed by the *append* of any remaining data.

As a result of the client-server WAL protocol and/or the boundary-spanning restriction, a client may at times be forced to send partially filled log pages to the server. This could result in wasted log space and unnecessary writes to the log. The server, however, is not subject to the restrictions imposed on clients and can therefore combine log records received from different clients onto the same log page and can write log records received from a given client across multiple pages in order to conserve log writes. However, the server must preserve the ordering of the log records received from a particular client and must maintain the WAL protocol between the updated pages in its buffer and the corresponding log pages. In addition to log records received from clients, the server also generates certain log records of its own. Server log records are not subject to the size constraint that is imposed on client log records and can span multiple log pages.

14.3   OVERVIEW OF ARIES

In this section, we present a brief overview of the ARIES recovery method, concentrating on the features of the algorithm that are pertinent to the ESM-CS environment (see [20] for a more complete treatment). ARIES is a fairly recent refinement of the WAL protocol. As with other WAL implementations, each page in the database contains a log sequence number (LSN) that uniquely identifies the log record for the latest update applied to the page. This LSN (referred to as the *pageLSN*) is used during recovery to determine whether an update for a page must be redone. LSN information is also used to determine the point in the log from which the redo pass must commence during restart from a system crash. Log records belonging to the same transaction are linked backwards in time using a *prevLSN* field in each log record.

ARIES uses a three-pass algorithm for restart recovery (see Figure 14.2). *Analysis* first processes the log forward from the most recent checkpoint, determining information about dirty pages and active transactions for use in the later passes. The second pass, *redo*, processes the log forward from the earliest log record that could require redo, ensuring that all logged operations have been applied. The third pass, *undo*, proceeds backwards from the end of the log, removing the effects of all uncommitted transactions from the database. ARIES employs a redo paradigm called *repeating history*, in which it redoes updates for *all* transactions, including those that will eventually be undone. Repeating history simplifies the implementation of fine-grained locking and the use of logical undo, as described in [20, 23].

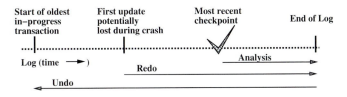

Figure 14.2. The three passes of ARIES restart.

14.3.1 Normal Operation

ARIES maintains two important data structures during normal operation. The first is the *transaction table*, which contains an entry for each transaction that is currently running. Each entry includes a *lastLSN* field, which is the LSN of the transaction's most recent log record. The second data structure, called the *dirty page table* (DPT), contains an entry for each "dirty" page. A page is dirty if it contains updates that are not reflected on stable storage. Each entry in the DPT includes a *recoveryLSN* field, which is the LSN of the log record that caused the associated page to become dirty. The *recoveryLSN* is the LSN of the earliest log record that might need to be redone for the page during restart.

During normal operation, checkpoints are taken periodically. ARIES uses an inexpensive form of fuzzy checkpoints [1] that requires only the writing of a checkpoint record. Checkpoint records include the contents of the transaction table and the DPT. Checkpoints are efficient since no operations need be quiesced and no database pages are flushed. However, the effectiveness of checkpoints in allowing reclamation of log space is limited in part by the earliest *recoveryLSN* of the dirty pages at checkpoint time. Therefore, it is helpful to have a background process that periodically writes dirty pages to stable storage.

14.3.2 Analysis

The job of the analysis pass of restart recovery is threefold: (1) it determines the point in the log at which to start the redo pass, (2) it determines which pages could have been dirty at the time of the crash in order to avoid unnecessary I/O during the redo pass, and (3) it determines which transactions had not committed at the time of the crash and will therefore need to be undone. Analysis begins at the most recent checkpoint and scans forward to the end of the log. It reconstructs the transaction table and DPT to determine the state of the system as of the time of the crash. It begins with the copies of those structures that were logged in the checkpoint record. Then, the contents of the tables are modified according to the log records that are encountered during the forward scan. At the end of the analysis pass, the DPT is a conservative (since pages may have been flushed to stable storage) list of all pages that could have been dirty at the time of the crash, and the transaction table contains entries for those transactions that will actually require undo processing during the undo phase. The earliest *recoveryLSN* in the DPT is called the *firstLSN* and is used as the spot in the log from which to begin the redo phase.

14.3.3 Redo

As stated earlier, ARIES employs a redo paradigm called *repeating history*. That is, it redoes updates for *all* transactions, committed or otherwise. Therefore, at the end of redo, the database is in the same state with respect to the logged updates that it was in at the time that the crash occurred. The redo pass begins at the log record whose LSN is the *firstLSN* determined by analysis and scans forward. To redo an update, the logged action is reapplied and the *pageLSN* on the page is set to the LSN of the redone log record. No logging is performed as a result of a redo. A logged action must be redone if its LSN is greater than the *pageLSN* of the affected page. To avoid unnecessary disk I/O, the *pageLSN* is not checked if the page is not in the DPT, or if the *recoveryLSN* for the page is greater than the record LSN.

14.3.4 Undo

The undo pass scans backwards from the end of the log, removing the effects of all transactions that had not committed at the time of the crash. In ARIES, undo is an *unconditional* operation, so the *pageLSN* of an affected page is not checked because it is always the case that the undo must be performed. To undo an update, the undo operation is applied to the page and is logged using a *compensation log record* (CLR). In addition to the undo information, a CLR contains a *UndoNxtLSN* field, which is the LSN of the next log record that must be undone for the transaction. It is set to the value of the *prevLSN* field of the log record being undone. CLRs enable ARIES to avoid ever having to undo the effects of an undo (e.g., due to a crash during an abort), thereby limiting the amount of undo work and bounding the amount of logging done in the event of multiple crashes. When a CLR is encountered during undo, no operation is performed on the page, and the value of the *UndoNxtLSN* field is used as the next log record to be undone for the transaction, thereby skipping any previously undone updates of the transaction.

For example, in Figure 14.3, a transaction logged three updates (LSNs 10, 20, and 30) before the system crashed for the first time. During redo, the database was brought up to date with respect to the log, but since the transaction was in progress at the time of the crash, it must be undone. During the undo pass, update 30 was undone, resulting in the writing of a CLR with LSN 40, which contains an *UndoNxtLSN* value that points to 20. Then, 20 was undone, resulting in CLR

(LSN 50) with an *UndoNxtLSN* value of 10. However, the system then crashed for
a second time before 10 was undone. Once again, history is repeated during redo,
which brings the database back to the state it was in after the application of LSN 50
(the CLR for 20). When undo begins during this second restart, it will first examine
the log record 50. Since the record is a CLR, no modification will be performed on
the page, and undo will skip to the record whose LSN is stored in the *UndoNxtLSN*
field of the CLR. Therefore, it will continue by undoing the update whose log record
has LSN 10. This is where undo was interrupted at the time of the second crash.
Note that no extra logging was performed as a result of the second crash.

In order to undo multiple transactions, restart undo keeps a list containing the
next LSN to be undone for each transaction being undone. When a log record is
undone, the *prevLSN* (or *UndoNxtLSN*, in the case of a CLR) is entered as the next
LSN to be undone for that transaction and undo moves on to the log record whose
LSN is the most recent in the list. Undo continues until all of the transactions in
the list have been completely undone. Undo for *transaction rollback* (for transaction
aborts or savepoints) works similarly to restart undo.

14.4   RECOVERY IN ESM-CS

14.4.1   ARIES and the Page-Server Environment

In this section, we describe the problems that arise when adapting ARIES to a page-
server environment and outline the solutions that we implemented. These issues
stem mainly from two features of the page-server environment: (1) the modification
of data in client database buffers, while the log and recovery manager are at the
server and (2) the expense of communicating between the clients and the server.
The first issue violates several important assumptions of the ARIES algorithm, and
thus had to be addressed for correctness of the implementation. The second issue
results in performance trade-offs that have a significant impact on the algorithm
design.

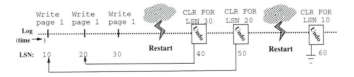

Figure 14.3. The use of CLRs for undo.

The presence of separate buffers on the clients is a fundamental departure from
the environment for which ARIES was originally specified. This difference creates
problems with both transaction rollback and system restart. In ARIES, rollback
undo is an unconditional operation since it is known that at rollback, the effects
of all logged updates appear in the copies of pages either on stable storage or in
the server's buffer pool. However, in the page-server environment, *the server can*

have log records for updates for which it does not have the affected database pages. During rollback, unconditional undo could result in corruption of the database and system crashes due to attempts to undo operations that are not reflected in the server's copy of a page.

This difference in buffering also causes a related problem for system restart. The correctness of the restart algorithm depends on the ability to determine all pages that could have possibly been dirty (i.e., different from their copy on stable storage) at the time of a crash. As described in Section 14.2, this information is gathered by starting with the DPT that was logged at the most recent checkpoint, and augmenting it based on log records that are encountered during the analysis pass. In a page-server system, this process is not sufficient, since *there may be pages that are dirty at a client but not at the server*, and hence, do not appear in any checkpoint's DPT. This problem, if not addressed, would result in incorrect recovery due to the violation of the repeating history property of redo.

A problem that arises due to the expense of communication between clients and the server is the inability of clients to efficiently assign LSNs. ARIES expects that LSNs are unique within a log, and that log records are added to the log in monotonically increasing LSN order. In a centralized or shared memory system, this is easily achieved, since a single source for generating LSNs can be cheaply accessed each time a log record is generated. However, in a page-server environment, clients generate log records in parallel, making it difficult for them to efficiently assign unique LSNs that will arrive at the server in monotonically increasing order. Furthermore, if the LSNs are to be physical (e.g., based on log record addresses), then the server would be required to be involved in the generation of LSNs.

To summarize, the issues that must be addressed in a page-server environment are the following:

1. The assignment of state identifiers (e.g., LSNs) for pages.

2. The need to make undo a *conditional* operation.

3. Changes to analysis to ensure correctness.

We next describe these issues and their effects on the algorithm. The algorithm is then summarized in Section 14.4.5.

14.4.2 Log Record Counters (LRCs)

As described in Section 14.3, ARIES requires that each log record be identified by an LSN and that each page contain a *pageLSN* field that indicates the LSN of the most recent log record applied to that page. These LSNs must be unique and monotonically increasing. It is useful for LSNs be the physical addresses of records in the log. However, as discussed earlier, it is not possible to efficiently generate such LSNs in a page-server system. In general, the problem with LSNs in a page-server system is that their use is overloaded: (1) they identify the state of a page with respect to a particular log record, (2) they identify the state of a page with respect to a position in the log (e.g., an LSN is used to determine the point from which to begin redo for a page), and (3) they identify where in the log to find a relevant record.

Since clients do not have inexpensive access to the log, they can only be responsible for the preceding point 1. Therefore, our solution was to separate the functionality of point 1 from the others by introducing the notion of a log record counter (LRC). An LRC is a counter that is associated with each page. The LRC *for a particular page* is monotonically increasing and uniquely identifies an operation that has been applied to the page. Instead of storing an LSN on the page, we store the LRC (called the *pageLRC*). In order to map between LRCs and entries in the log, the log record structure is augmented to include an LRC field that indicates the LRC that was placed on the page as a result of the logged operation. Note that for reasons to be explained in the following sections, LRCs have the same size and structure as LSNs (currently, an 8-byte integer).

LRCs are used in the following way: When a page is modified, the LRC on the page (*pageLRC*) is updated and then copied into the corresponding log record. When the server examines a page to see if a particular update has been applied to the page, the current *pageLRC* is compared to the LRC contained in the log record corresponding to the modification. If the *pageLRC* is *greater than or equal to* the LRC in the log record, then the update is known to be reflected in the page. LRCs have the advantage that, since they are private to a particular page, they can be manipulated at the client without intervention by the server. There are two main disadvantages of using LRCs, however. First, since they are not physical log pointers, they cannot be directly used to serve as an access point into the log. Second, care must be taken to ensure that each combination of page id and LRC refers to a unique log record. Our approaches to handling these two problems are addressed in the following sections.

14.4.3 Conditional Undo

In ESM-CS, log records for operations performed on clients arrive at the server before the dirty pages containing the effects of those operations, and, thus, when aborting a transaction it is possible to encounter log records for operations whose effects are not reflected in the pages at the server. Attempting to undo such an operation could result in corrupted data. Therefore, we implement undo as a *conditional* operation. When scanning the log backwards during rollback (or restart undo) the page associated with each log record is examined and undo is performed only for logged operations that had actually been applied.

As described in Section 14.3.4, undo in ARIES is an *unconditional operation*. This is possible in ARIES for two reasons. First, in ARIES, all dirty pages are located in the system's buffer pool, so at rollback time, all logged operations are reflected in the pages at the server. Second, history is always repeated during restart redo. Therefore, it is assured that all of the operations up to the time of the crash are reflected in either the pages on stable storage or in the buffer pool when restart undo begins.

With conditional undo, CLRs must still be written for all undo operations, including those that are not actually performed. However, the *pageLRCs* of the affected pages must not be updated unless the undo operation is actually performed. The reasons for these requirements can be seen in the example shown in Figure 14.4. In the figure, a transaction logged three updates (LRCs 10, 11, and 12) for a page, and the page was sent to the server after the first update had been applied but before the others had been applied. When the transaction rolls back, a conditional undo results in only LRC 10 being undone. If only the CLR pertaining to that update is written, a problem can arise if the server crashes after logging the CLR but before the page reflecting the undo is written to stable storage (as shown in the figure). Restart redo repeats history, thereby redoing LRCs 10, 11, and 12 and the CLR. The undo pass encounters the CLR, and since the UndoNxtLSN is NIL, considers the transaction completely undone. This incorrectly leaves the effects of LRCs 11 and 12 on the page. Therefore, rollback must log CLRs for the second and third updates as well, even though the updates were never applied to the page. However, if the *pageLRC* is updated when the fake undo is performed for LRC 12, then rollback would not work properly since when it encounters the log record for LRC 11, it would erroneously infer that the update had been applied to the page and would attempt to undo the update, resulting in a corrupted page.

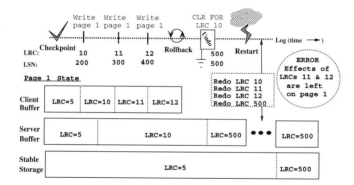

Figure 14.4. Error due to missing CLRs in conditional undo.

Up to this point, the solution described is to log undo operations, even if they are not performed, but not to update the LRC on the page unless an undo is actually performed on the page. Unfortunately, there is one additional complication that is due to the use of LRCs rather than LSNs. The problem is that in the case where no logged updates to a page are truly undone, the value of the *pageLRC* will still be less than some of the LRCs in the log records of the rolled-back transaction. If this *pageLRC* is simply incremented by updates in subsequent transactions, there will then be values of the *pageLRC* that map to multiple log records. This is a violation of an important invariant and can result in problems in both redo and undo.

The preceding problem could not occur if LSNs were being used, since they are guaranteed to be unique and monotonically increasing, making it impossible to generate a duplicate LSN. This problem is solved by taking advantage of the fact that, whereas LRCs must be unique and monotonically increasing for a page, they need not be consecutive. The solution requires that the server send the *LSN of the current end-of-log* (i.e., the LSN of the next log record to be written) every time it sends a page to a client. It does this by piggybacking the end-of-log LSN in the message header. When the client receives a data or index page from the server, it initializes the *pageLRC* field of the received page to be the end-of-log LSN that is sent along with the page. When a client updates a page, it increments the *pageLRC* on the page. When the server updates a page (e.g., for page formatting, compensation for undo, etc.), it places the LSN of the corresponding log record in the page's *pageLRC* field. The resulting *pageLRC*s are guaranteed to be unique and monotonically increasing (but not necessarily consecutive) with respect to each page.

14.4.4   Performing Correct Analysis during Restart

The remaining issue to be addressed is to ensure that the analysis pass of system restart produces the correct information about the state of pages at the time of a crash. There are three related problems to be solved in this regard:

1. Maintaining *recoveryLSN*s for dirty pages

2. Determining which pages may require redo

3. Determining the point in the log at which to start redo

Maintaining the RecoveryLSN for a Page: During the analysis pass of the restart algorithm, ARIES computes the LSN of the earliest log record that could require redo. As explained in Section 14.3.2, this LSN, called the *firstLSN*, is computed by taking the minimum of the *recoveryLSN*s of all of the pages considered dirty at the end of analysis. In a centralized system, the *recoveryLSN* for each page can be kept by storing the LSN of the update that causes a page to become dirty in the buffer-pool control information for that page. Unfortunately, in the page-server environment, clients do not have access to the LSN of an update's corresponding log record when the update is performed (for the reasons described previously).

This problem is solved by having clients attach an *approximate recoveryLSN* to a page when they initially dirty the page. To implement this, we extend the mechanism described in Section 14.4.3 so that the server piggybacks the LSN of the current end-of-log on *every* reply that it sends to a client. When a client initially dirties a page, it attaches the most recent end-of-log LSN that it received from the server, as the *recoveryLSN* for the page. This LSN is guaranteed to be less than or equal to the LSN of the log record that will eventually be generated for the operation that actually dirties the page. Since the client must communicate with the server in order to initiate a transaction, and since clients must send dirty pages to the server on commit, the approximate *recoveryLSN* will be no earlier than the end-of-log LSN at the time when the transaction that dirties the page was initiated. Typically, it will be more recent than this. When the client returns a dirty page to the server, it sends the approximate *recoveryLSN* for the page in the message along with the page. If the page is not already considered dirty at the server, then it is marked dirty and the approximate *recoveryLSN* is entered in the buffer-pool control information for the page at the server.

Determining Which Pages May Require Redo: As described earlier, a fundamental problem with implementing the ARIES algorithm in the page-server environment is the presence of buffer pools on the clients. One manifestation of this difference is the problem of determining which pages were dirty at the time of a crash, and hence may require redo. A page is *not* considered dirty by the basic ARIES analysis algorithm if it satisfies *both* of the following criteria:

1. It does not appear in the DPT logged in the most recent complete checkpoint prior to the crash.

2. No log records for updates to the page appear in the log after that checkpoint.

There are two reasons that a page updated at a client might not appear in the checkpoint's DPT. The first is simply that the page was sent back to the server and written to stable storage before the checkpoint was taken. This causes no problems since the page is no longer dirty at this point. The second reason is that the page may have been updated at the client but not sent back to the server prior to the taking of the checkpoint. (Note that even if the page is sent to the server after the checkpoint has been taken, it will be lost during the crash.) In this case, there may have been log records for updates to the page that appeared before the checkpoint. These updates will be skipped by the Redo pass because it will not consider the page to be dirty.

Figure 14.5 shows an example of this problem. In the figure, a transaction updated a page (page 1) and sent the corresponding log record (LRC 10) to the server without sending the page to the server. After a checkpoint had occurred, the client sent the dirtied page (with LRC = 10) to the server followed by a commit request. The server wrote a commit record and forced it to disk, thereby committing the transaction. The server then crashed before page 1 was flushed to disk. In this case, restart will not redo LRC 10 because according to the ARIES analysis algorithm, page 1 is not considered dirty (since it neither appears in the most recent checkpoint's DPT nor is referenced by any log records that appear after the checkpoint), and, therefore, does not require redo. This would violate the durability of committed updates since the update of LRC 10 would be lost.

Fortunately, the problem of missed dirty pages only has correctness implications for updates of transactions that commit before the system crashes. The reason for this is that the updates of any transactions that had not committed prior to the crash will be undone during the undo pass of restart. The conditional undo of our

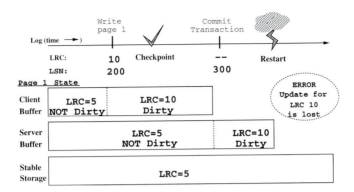

Figure 14.5. Lost update due to missed dirty pages.

algorithm (Section 14.3) can tolerate the absence of the effects of logged updates on a page, providing that all of the missing updates occur later in the log than any updates that were applied to the page. That condition holds in this case, since the problem arises only when the most recent image of the dirty page was lost during the crash.

Given that the problem of missing dirty pages arises only for committed transactions, we solve the problem by logging dirty-page information at transaction commit time. When a client sends a dirty page to the server, this page and its *recoveryLSN* are added to a list of dirty pages for the transaction. When a page is flushed to stable storage, it is removed from the list. We refer to this list as a *commit dirty-page list*. Before logging a commit record for a transaction, the server first logs the contents of the list for the committing transaction. During restart analysis, when a commit dirty page list is encountered, each page that appears in the list is added (along with its *recoveryLSN*) to the DPT if it does not already have an entry in the table.

An alternative solution we considered was to log the receipt of dirty pages at the server (similar to the logging of buffer operations in [17]), and then during restart analysis, to add pages encountered in such log records to the dirty page table. Although this solution is also a correct one, we felt that the additional log overhead during normal operation could prove to be unacceptable. We also investigated solutions that involved the clients in the checkpointing process. These solutions were rejected because they violate a system design constraint that prohibits the server from depending on clients for any crucial functions.

Determining Where to Begin the Redo Pass: The final problem to be addressed in this section is that of determining the proper point in the log at which to begin redo. Recall that in ARIES, the LSN at which to begin redo (called the *firstLSN*) is determined to be the minimum of the *recoveryLSN*s of all of the pages in the DPT at the end of the analysis phase. If a page is not dirty at the time of a checkpoint, then it is known that all updates logged prior to the checkpoint are reflected in the copy of the page that is on stable storage, and, thus, it is safe to begin redo for the page at the first log record for the page that is encountered during analysis, or anywhere earlier. In the page-server environment, however, this is not the case. For example, in Figure 14.6, a transaction logged two updates to page 1. One log record arrived at the server before a checkpoint, and one arrived after the checkpoint, and the dirty page containing the effects of the updates was not shipped to the server until after the checkpoint. Therefore, page 1 does not appear in the DPT recorded in the checkpoint. If the server crashes at the point shown in the figure, then during analysis, when the log record for LRC 11 is encountered, page 1 will be added to the DPT with the LSN of that record as its *recoveryLSN* (LSN = 300). Starting redo for page 1 at this point would result in LRC 11 being redone without LRC 10 having been applied, thus corrupting page 1.

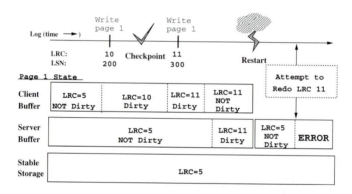

Figure 14.6. Inconsistent redo due to missed log record.

For pages that are dirtied by a transaction that eventually commits, the commit dirty-page list contains conservative *recoveryLSN*s, which ensure that redo will begin at a proper point in the log for such pages. Also, for pages dirtied by a transaction that does not commit, but that appear in the DPT recorded in the most recent checkpoint, the *recoveryLSN* in the DPT entry is valid. Therefore, the problem that must be addressed is that of pages dirtied by a transaction that does not commit and are added to the DPT during analysis (as shown in Figure 6). To solve this problem, we augment the transaction table structure (described in Section 14.3.2) to include a field for the first LSN generated by each transaction (called the *startLSN*). Then, during analysis, when a page is added to the DPT, it is marked as a newly added page and tagged with the transaction ID of the transaction that dirtied it. At the end of analysis, entries for pages that were added to the dirty-page table due to an update by an uncommitted transaction have their *recoveryLSN* replaced by that transaction's *startLSN*. This conservative approximation results in correct behavior, but it may cause extra I/O during redo because pages may have to be read from stable storage to determine whether a logged update must be redone. However, the number of pages for which this conservative approximation is required can be kept small by taking (inexpensive) checkpoints.

14.4.5   Summary of the Algorithm

Although the preceding discussion was fairly detailed, the resulting algorithm requires only the following changes to ARIES:

During Normal Operation

- The LSN of the first log record generated by a transaction is entered in the transaction table as the transaction's *startLSN*.

- Each client keeps an estimate of the current end-of-log LSN updated on receipt of every message from the server.

- When a data or index page arrives at the client, the *pageLRC* of the page is initialized to be the estimated end-of-log LSN. The page is *not* marked dirty as a result of this initialization.

- When a client updates a page, it increments the *pageLRC* on the page and places the new *pageLRC* value in the log record. If this update causes the page to be marked "dirty", the current estimated end-of-log LSN is entered as the *recoveryLSN* in the page's buffer-control information at the client.

- When the server updates a page, it places the LSN of the log record it generates as the *pageLRC* on the page and in the log record. If this update causes the page to be marked "dirty", then the LSN is also entered as the *recoveryLSN* in the page's buffer-control information at the server.

- When a client sends a dirty page to the server, it includes the page's *recoveryLSN* in the message.

- When the server receives a dirty page from a client, the page is added to a list of dirty pages for the transaction that dirtied it. If the transaction commits, this list is logged as the commit dirty-page list for the transaction.

During Restart Analysis

- When a transaction is added to the transaction table as the result of encountering a log record, the LSN of the log record is entered as the transaction's *startLSN*.

- When a commit dirty-page list is encountered, the pages that appear in it are added to the DPT. The *recoveryLSN* in the DPT entry for each page is set to the minimum of the *recoveryLSN* for the page in the DPT (if the page already has an entry) and that in the commit dirty-page list.

- At the end of analysis, all pages that were added to the DPT by analysis due to log records generated by noncommitting transactions are given a conservative *recoveryLSN*, namely, the *startLSN* of the transaction that dirtied the page.

During Restart Redo

- Redo is unchanged except for the use of LRCs for comparisons between log records and pages rather than LSNs.

During Undo (for Restart or Rollback):

- To undo a log record, the LRC stored in the record is compared to the *pageLRC* of the affected page. If the log record LRC is *greater than or equal to* the *pageLRC*, then an actual undo is performed otherwise, a "fake" undo is performed.

- Actual undo is performed by logging a CLR for the undone operation, performing the undo on the page, and placing the LSN of the CLR in the *pageLRC* of the affected page.

- Fake undo is performed simply by logging a CLR for the undone operation. The page itself is not modified, is not marked as dirty, and its it pageLRC is not changed.

14.5   PERFORMANCE

In this section, we describe an initial study of the performance of logging and recovery in ESM-CS. The performance experiments described in this section were run on two SPARCstation ELCs, each with 24 MB of memory, running Version 4.1.1 of SunOS. The client and server processes were run on separate machines that were connected by an Ethernet. The log and database were stored on separate disks, and raw disk partitions were used to avoid operating system buffering. The log page size was 8 KB and database page size was 4 KB. All times were obtained using *gettimeofday*() and *getusage*() and are reported in seconds.

14.5.1   Logging Experiments

In the first set of experiments, we investigated the overhead imposed on transactions by the logging subsystem during normal operation. Three different databases were used for the experiments and are described in Table 14.1. All three databases initially contain 2 MB of data on pages that are approximately 504 MB of physical space. We describe the results for two types of transactions applied to the three databases: *write*, which sequentially scans the database and writes (updates) half of the bytes in each object, updating a total of 1 MB of data and *insert*, which sequentially scans the database and inserts new data at the beginning of each object to increase its size by 50%, resulting in the insertion of 1 MB of new data. *Insert* does not increase the number of pages in the database since each page has enough free space to accommodate the inserted data.[1]

Table 14.1. Description of Experimental Database.

DB Name	Objects in DB	Object Size (bytes)	Objects/Page	Pages in DB
FewLg	1,000	2,000	1	1,000
SomeMd	10,000	200	10	1,000
ManySm	100,000	20	100	1,000

Table 14.2. Loggging Experiment Results.

Experiment Name	Execution Time (sec)		Logging overhead
	Logging on	Logging off	
Write_FewLg	17.37	13.55	3.82 (28%)
Write_SomeMd	18.43	14.46	3.97 (27%)
Write_ManySm	32.32	21.36	10.96 (51%)
Insert_FewLg	14.29	12.49	1.80 (14%)
Insert_SomeMd	15.74	13.05	2.69 (21%)

Table 14.2 shows the results from running the five experiments with and without logging. These numbers were obtained by running each transaction five times and taking the average of the last four runs. They include the time to initiate, execute, and commit a transaction, including the time to send dirty pages to the server. In these experiments the server buffer pool was 5 MB, so the entire database was cached in the server's buffer pool for the measured runs. The client buffer pool is also 5 MB so that the entire database fits in the client buffer pool during a transaction, however, it is empty at the beginning of each transaction. The large buffer pools were used in order to help us isolate the effects of logging by removing sources of variability (e.g., other disk I/O) and by making logging a more significant part of the total work performed in the tests. The write-intensiveness of the transactions also accentuates the impact of logging. For these reasons, the overhead of

---

[1] This does not hold for the ManySm database due to the overhead of object headers, thus we do not show the results from running *Insert* on the ManySm database.

logging reflected in Table 14.2 is much higher than would be expected in an actual application.

As shown in Table 14.2, the overhead of logging increased with the number of operations for which log records were generated even though the amount of actual data that was updated remained constant. This increase was due to the size overhead added for each log record. In ESM-CS, this overhead is 64 bytes: 56 bytes for the record header and 8 bytes for the operation information. As a result of this overhead, the number of log pages generated and written increased considerably when a larger number of smaller operations were performed per transaction. For example, the 1000 operations of the Write_FewLg experiment generated 2.7 MB of log records in 337 log pages, and the 100,000 operations of the Write_ManySm experiment generated 8.9 MB of log records in 1090 log pages. When comparing the two transaction types, the logging time overhead of the *insert* tests was less than that of the *write* tests. This difference is because *insert* logs only the inserted data, whereas *write* logs both the before *and* after images, resulting in a larger volume of logged data for *write*.

Table 14.3. Logging Cost Breakdown (seconds)

Experiment name	General Log recs	Ship Log Pages act/obsv	Write Log Pages act/obsv	Total Overhead act/obsv
Write				
fewlg	0.48	2.57/2.45	6.18/0.78	9.23/3.71
SomeMd	0.92	2.57/2.03	6.18/0.87	9.67/3.82
ManySm	5.19	8.37/4.24	20.36/1.35	33.92/10.78
Insert				
FewLg	0.31	1.10/1.05	3.03/0.26	4.44/1.62
SomeMd	0.89	1.57/1.23	3.75/0.44	6.21/2.56

In order to better understand these results, we analyzed the costs of the three main components of logging: (1) generating log records at the client, (2) shipping log pages from the client to the server, and (3) writing log pages from the server's buffer to the log disk. To obtain this breakdown, we altered ESM-CS to allow these three logging components to be selectively turned on and off. Because the shipping and writing of log pages can occur in parallel with other client and server activity, these costs were measured in two ways. The first was to separately measure the actual time it took to ship or write a certain number of pages. The second was to selectively turn off the shipping and writing of log pages and compute the differences in time observed by the client. These results are shown in Table 14.3

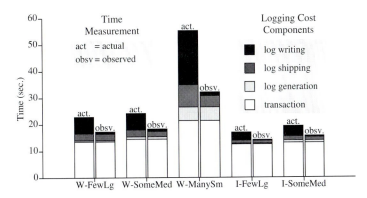

Figure 14.7. Actual and observed logging cost.

(and graphically in Figure 14.7) as *actual* and *observed*, respectively. As would be expected, the highest actual cost was the writing of log records to disk. Shipping the log pages to the server took about 41to write the pages to disk. The cost of generating the log records was small in the FewLg cases but became more significant in the transactions that generated more log records, as the number of log records generated grew faster than the number of log pages.

From the client's point of view, the observed cost of shipping was more significant than the writing cost since most of the writing was performed in parallel with other client and server activity. In principle, the shipping of log pages can also be performed in parallel with other activity, but with the small compute time of these tests, the network was kept busy by client data page and lock requests. One exception to this was the Write_ManySm case, which had more significant compute time due to the generation of log records, and thus obtained some parallelism between log page shipping and log record generation.

Although comparable published performance results for logging systems are difficult to find, the results from these write-intensive experiments lead us to conclude that the performance of our initial logging implementation is reasonable. The results also indicate two areas for improvement. First, reducing the amount of logged information can result in significant performance improvements, especially for small updates. The current log record overhead size of 64 bytes is slightly larger than the typical log record header size of approximately 50 bytes [12]. With sufficient coding effort, the ESM-CS log record overhead could be reduced to 56 bytes (but not much smaller). A different approach would be to reduce the number of log records generated in special cases like Write_ManySm (where most or all of the objects on a page are updated) by logging entire pages. Second, by performing shipping and writing of log pages in parallel with other activity, the observed cost for logging can be reduced considerably. We plan to investigate ways of further exploiting such parallelism.

14.5.2   Transaction Rollback and Recovery Performance

We also ran some simple experiments to gain insight into the performance of roll-back and recovery. These experiments used the databases and *write* transactions described in the previous section. Table 14.4 shows the results of these experiments and also shows the execution times of the transactions with logging turned on (from Table 2) for comparison. To measure the cost of transaction rollback, we aborted each transaction after all the dirty pages and log records had been shipped back to the server. In this experiment, rollback did not perform any I/O for data pages since the database was cached in the server buffer, and thus, the transaction rollback results were primarily determined by the time to read the log, to gener-ate compensation log records, and to write those log records to disk. The cost of actually performing the undo operations was only several seconds in the longest case. Compensation log records for write operations only require the logging of redo information, so CLRs for writes contain only half as much operation informa-tion as normal write log records. However, the fine granularity of the updates in the Write_ManySm case results in much of the log space being used for log record headers. Therefore, although undoing the Write_FewLg case generated about half as many log pages as the original transaction, undoing the Write_ManySm case required almost as much log space as the original transaction. The generation of CLRs also results in significant log disk arm movement, as these new records must be appended to the log while rollback is trying to scan the log backwards. Disk arm movement is especially expensive in the Write_ManySm case, due to the amount of compensation log space generated. A way to reduce disk arm movement is to batch newly written log pages and write them out in groups.

For restart, Table 14.4 shows the analysis and redo times when the server was crashed immediately after the transaction committed. Since the server buffer could hold the entire database, no data pages had been written to stable storage prior to the crash, and, thus, all data pages had to be reread from disk during recovery. The restart tests showed a significant increase in the cost of analysis and redo as the volume of log data increased. Note that no checkpoints were taken during these tests, so analysis scanned the entire log. The Analysis times can be improved by taking more frequent checkpoints. Redo also scanned the log and read all the data pages from stable storage. The cost of actually performing the redo operations was small. One way to speed up system restart would be to use Most Recently Used (MRU) buffering (instead of LRU) for the log pages during analysis, as redo scans the log in the same direction as analysis. Also, restart performance could be improved by prefetching log pages and the pages in the DPT. Still, although improvements can be made, the transaction rollback and system restart performance of the current implementation seem to be acceptable.

Table 14.4. Rollback and Recovery Times (seconds)

Experiment Name	Execution Time	Rollback time	Analysis Time	Redo Time
Write_FewLg	17.37	13.24	2.06	5.65
Write_SomeMd	18.43	15.86	2.07	6.26
Write_ManySm	32.32	62.86	8.17	15.32

14.6 RELATED WORK

In this section, we briefly cover related work, including ARIES extensions and recovery algorithms for shared-disk and client-server systems (see [9] for a more detailed discussion).

The recent ARIES/RRH (Restricted Repeating of History) algorithm [23] relaxes the repeating of history during restart redo. ARIES/RRH requires the notion of conditional undo *during restart* and writes fake CLRs to simplify media recovery. The differences between ARIES/RRH and ESM-CS conditional undo result from the fact that ARIES/RRH was designed to enhance the performance of ARIES during restart, whereas ESM-CS conditional undo was developed in order to correctly implement transaction rollback in a page-server system. Thus, whereas conditional undo is an option in ARIES, it is a requirement in ESM-CS.

Extensions to ARIES for the shared disk environment are also related to our algorithm extensions. [22] addresses the problems of migrating a single-site database system to the shared disk environment. The problem relevant to our work is the lack of monotonically increasing LSNs due to the use of a separate log for each node in the system. The given solution is to store update sequence numbers (USNs) on pages, rather than LSNs. USNs are initialized based on a clock value at the time the page is formatted, requiring that the clocks be synchronized to within an acceptable limit. We used LRCs to solve a similar problem in ESM-CS, but due to the lack of synchronized clocks and local logs, we used the estimated end-of-log LSN and approximate *recoveryLSNs*, as described in Section 14.4. In [23], protocols for transferring a page between nodes without writing the page to disk are discussed; these protocols are subject to recovery issues similar to those that arise in ESM-CS, as a node can have log records for a page that is not dirty at that node. The solutions use a global lock manager (GLM) whose entries are extended with LSN information, such as the *recoveryLSNs*. There are two disadvantages to implementing a similar solution in a page-server system: It would negate many of the performance benefits of using coarse-grained locking (e.g., as in [15]), and it would preclude the use of some noncentralized locking algorithms in the page-server environment. As was shown in [3, 27], the overhead of centralized locking in the page-server environment can have a major performance impact.

Several other proposals for recovery in shared-disk systems have been published. [19] describes an algorithm that allows multiple logs to be easily merged during redo. The algorithm does not require synchronized clocks, and, thus, may prove useful in a client-server environment in which clients perform their own logging. As described in Section 2.2, we chose not to implement client logging because of the unreliability of clients compared to the server and the expense of extra client disks. In [24], an algorithm is defined for use with a no steal buffer management policy. The algorithm differs from the ones described previously in that it assigns responsibility for recovery of certain partitions of the database to particular systems. It may require substantial communication to perform redo for a failed node, which can be costly in a client-server system. All of these algorithms depend on the individual logs of crashed systems being available to other nodes, which is not possible with local logs in a client-server system. [19] suggests approaches toward addressing this problem.

As stated earlier, few details about recovery in page-server and object-server architectures have been published. This is due in part because many of the systems have proprietary implementations. The O2 system [7] employs an ARIES-based approach that uses shadowing in order to avoid undo. The ORION-1SX system [16] uses a FORCE policy and therefore keeps only an undo log. We are unaware of any systems that have implemented the steal/no force policy for a page-server (or object-server) system.

14.7 CONCLUSIONS

In this chapter, we have described the problems that arise when implementing recovery in a page-server environment, and have presented a recovery method that addresses these problems. The recovery method was designed with the goal of minimizing the impact of recovery-related overhead during normal processing, while still providing reasonable rollback and system restart times. In particular, the method supports efficient buffer management policies, allows flexibility in the interaction between clients and the server, and allows clients to offload the server by performing much of the work involved in generating log records. We described the implementation of the method in ESM-CS, and presented measurements of the implementation. The measurements obtained so far appear promising. Overhead for many cases was reasonable, and the study raised issues to be addressed in order to improve the performance of the system, including reducing log record size, batching writes to the log disk, prefetching from the log during recovery, and exploiting additional parallelism between logging operations on the server and other operations on the client during normal processing. Additional studies of realistic workloads will be required in order to better understand the performance impact of the logging and recovery subsystems. In addition, we plan to extend the system to include media recovery, restricted repeating of history, and intertransaction caching. Finally, this work has raised a number of interesting possibilities for alternative recovery system designs, and we plan to investigate the performance trade-offs among these alternatives.

Acknowledgments

We thank C. Mohan for a number of informative discussions regarding ARIES and our algorithm, and for suggesting improvements that made our implementation much simpler. Dave Haight did much of the initial work of converting the original EXODUS storage manager to a client-server system. Nancy Hall and Zack Xu helped build the new version of the system. Praveen Seshadri provided helpful comments on an earlier draft of this chapter.

References

[1] Bernstein, P., Hadzilacos, V., and Goodman, N., *Concurrency Control and Recovery in Database Systems*, Addison-Wesley, 1987.

[2] Carey, M., DeWitt, D., Richardson, J., Shekita, E., "Storage Management for Objects in EXODUS," in *Object-Oriented Concepts, Databases, and Applications*, W. Kim and F. Lochovsky, eds., Addison-Wesley, 1989.

[3] Carey, M., Franklin, M., Livny, M., Shekita, E., "Data Caching trade-offs in Client-Server DBMS Architectures", *Proc. ACM SIGMOD Conf.*, Denver, June 1991.

[4] The Committee for Advanced DBMS Function, "Third Generation Data Base System Manifesto", *SIGMOD Record*, Vol. 19, No. 3, Sept. 1990.

[5] DeWitt, D., Futtersack, P., Maier, D., Velez, F., "A Study of Three Alternative Workstation-Server Architectures for Object-Oriented Database Systems," *Proc. 16th VLDB Conf.*, Brisbane, Aug. 1990.

[6] Daniels, D., Spector, A., Thompson, D., "Distributed Logging for Transaction Processing", *Proc. ACM SIGMOD Conf.*, San Francisco, May,

[7] Deux, O., *et al.*, "The O2 System", *CACM*, 34(10) (Oct. 1991).

[8] EXODUS Project Group, "EXODUS Storage Manager Architectural Overview", *EXODUS Project Document*, University of Wisconsin at Madison, Nov. 1991.

[9] Franklin, M., Zwilling, M., Tan, C., Carey, M., DeWitt, D., "Crash Recovery in Client-Server EXODUS", *TR No. 1081*, Comp Sci Dept., Univ. of Wisconsin - Madison, Mar. 1992.

[10] Gray, J., "Notes on Data Base Operating Systems", *Operating Systems - An advanced Course*, R. Bayer, R.M. Graham, G. Seegmuller, eds. Springer-Verlag, N.Y., 1978.

[11] Gray, J., *et al.*, "The Recovery Manager of the System R Database Manager", *ACM Comp. Srv.*, 13(2) (June 1981).

[12] Gray, J., Reuter, A., *Transaction Processing: Concepts and Techniques*, Morgan Kaufmann, San Mateo, to appear, 1992.

[13] Haskin, R., Malachi, Y., Sawdon, W., Chan, G., "Recovery Management in QuickSilver", *ACM Trans. on Comp. Sys.*, 6(1) (Feb. 1988).

[14] Haerder, T., Reuter, A., "Principles of Transaction Oriented Database Recovery - A Taxonomy", *Computing Surveys*, 15(4) (Dec. 1983).

[15] Joshi, A., "Adaptive Locking Strategies in a Multi-Node Data Sharing Environment", *Proc. 17th VLDB Conf.*, Barcelona, Sept., 1991.

[16] Kim, W., Garza, J., Ballou, N., Woelk, D., "Architecture of the ORION Next-Generation Database System", *IEEE Trans. on Knowledge and Data Eng.*, 2(1) (March 1990).

[17] Lindsay, B. *et al*, "Notes on Distributed Databases, *IBM Research Report RJ2571*, San Jose, July 1979.

[18] Lamb, C., Landis, G., Orenstein, J. Weinreb, D., "The ObjectStore Database System", *CACM*, 34(10) (Oct. 1991).

[19] Lomet, D., "Recovery for Shared Disk Systems Using Multiple Redo Logs", *TR CRL 90/4*, DEC CRL, Oct. 1990.

[20] Mohan, C., Haderle, D., Lindsay, B., Pirahesh, H., Schwarz, P., "ARIES: A Transaction Method Supporting Fine-Granularity Locking and Partial Rollbacks Using Write-Ahead Logging", *IBM Research Report RJ6649, IBM ARC*, Nov., 1990.

[21] Mohan, C., Narang, I., "Recovery and Coherency-Control Protocols for Fast Intersystem Page Transfer and Fine-Granularity Locking in a Shared Disks Transaction Environment", *Proc. 17th VLDB Conf.*, Barcelona, Sept., 1991.

[22] Mohan, C., Narang, I., Palmer, J., "A Case Study of Problems in Migrating to Distributed Computing: Page Recovery Using Multiple Logs in the Shared Disks Environment", *IBM Research Report RJ7343, Almaden Research Ctr.*, March, 1990.

[23] Mohan, C., Pirahesh, H., "ARIES-RRH: Restricted Repeating of History in the ARIES Recovery Method", *Proc. 7th Int'l Conference on Data Engineering*, Kobe, April 1991.

[24] Rahm, E. , "Recovery Concepts for Data Sharing Systems", *Proc. 21st Int'l Symp. on Fault-Tolerant Computing*, Montreal, June, 1991.

[25] Richardson, J., Carey, M., "Persistence in the E Language: Issues and Implementation", *Software Practice and Experience*, Vol. 19, Dec. 1989.

[26] Stonebraker, M., "Architecture of Future Data Base Systems", *Data Eng.*, 13(4) (Dec. 1990).

[27] Wang, Y., Rowe, L., "Cache Consistency and Concurrency Control in a Client/Server DBMS Architecture", *Proc. ACM SIGMOD Conf.*, Denver, June 1991.

Chapter 15

A Formal Approach to Recovery by Compensating Transactions

Henry F. Korth, Eliezer Levy, and Abraham Silberschatz

Abstract

Compensating transactions are intended to handle situations where it is required to undo either committed or uncommitted transactions that affect other transactions, without resorting to cascading aborts. This stands in sharp contrast to the standard approach to transaction recovery where cascading aborts are avoided by requiring transactions to read only committed data, and where committed transactions are treated as permanent and irreversible. We argue that this standard approach to recovery is not suitable for a wide range of advanced database applications, in particular those applications that incorporate long-duration or nested transactions. We show how compensating transactions can be effectively used to handle these types of applications. We present a model that allows the definition of a variety of types of correct compensation. These types of compensation range from traditional undo, at one extreme, to application-dependent, special-purpose compensating transactions, at the other extreme.

15.1 INTRODUCTION

The concept of transaction atomicity is the cornerstone of today's transaction management systems. Atomicity requires that an aborted transaction will have no effect on the state of the database. The most common method for achieving this is to maintain a recovery log and provide the $undo(T_i)$ operation that restores the data items updated by T_i to the value they had just prior to the execution of T_i. However, if some other transaction, T_j, has read data values written by T_i, undoing T_i is not sufficient. The (indirect) effects of T_i must be removed by aborting T_j. Aborting the affected transaction may trigger further aborts. This undesirable phenomenon, called *cascading aborts*, can result in uncontrollably many transactions being forced to abort because some other transaction happened to abort.

Since a committed transaction, by definition, cannot abort, it is required that if transaction T_j reads the values of data items written by transaction T_i, then T_j does not commit before T_i commits. A system that ensures this property is said to be *recoverable* [2]. One way of avoiding cascading aborts and ensuring recoverability is to prohibit transactions from reading *uncommitted* data values–those produced by transactions that have not committed yet. This principle has formed the basis for standard recovery in most contemporary database systems.

Unfortunately, there is a large range of database applications for which the standard recovery approach is excessively restrictive and even not appropriate. The common denominator of such applications is the need to allow transactions to read *uncommitted data* values.

In general, as indicated by Gray [6], early exposure of uncommitted data is essential in the realm of long-duration and nested transactions. When transactions are long-lived, it is unreasonable to prevent access to uncommitted data by forcing other transactions to wait until the updating transaction commits, since the wait will be of long duration. Also, long-duration and nested transactions are often used to model collaborative design activities [9]. In order to promote the cooperative nature of design environments, there is a need to expose incomplete (i.e., uncommitted) design objects. Such applicatons, and others that incorporate transactions of that nature, cannot be accommodated by the standard recovery approach since their executions entail cascading aborts and some of them are even nonrecoverable.

An additional restriction imposed by standard recovery is the inability to undo an already committed transaction. Suppose that a transaction was committed "erroneously." By committed erroneously, we mean that from the system's point of view, there was nothing wrong with the committed transaction. However, external reasons, which were discovered later, rendered the decision to commit the transaction erroneous. Under the standard recovery approach, there is no support for undoing such transactions.

This chapter presents the method of *compensating transactions* as a recovery mechanism in applications where exposure of uncommitted data and undoing of committed transactions must be facilitated. Our goals are to develop a better understanding of what compensation really is, when it is possible to employ it, and what the implications are on correctness of executions when compensation is used.

This chapter is organized as follows. We give an informal introduction to compensating transactions in Section 15.2. In Section 15.3, we present a transaction model suitable for the study of compensation. We then use this model in Section 15.4 to define criteria for "reasonable" compensation. After illustrating our definitions with examples in Section 15.5, we examine the theoretical consequences of our model in Section 15.6. Implementation issues are discussed in Section 15.7, and related work is described in Section 15.8.

15.2   OVERVIEW OF COMPENSATION

When the updates of a (committed or uncommitted) transaction T are read by some other transaction, we say that T has been *externalized*. The sole purpose of *compensation* is to handle situations where we want to undo an externalized transaction T, without resorting to cascading aborts. We refer to T as the *compensated-for transaction*. The transactions that are affected by (reading) the data values written by T are referred to as *dependent transactions* (of T), and are referred to as a set using the notation $dep(T)$. The key point of our recovery paradigm is that we would like to *leave the effects of the dependent transactions intact* while preserving the consistency of the database, when undoing the compensated-for transaction. Compensation undoes T's effects in a *semantic* manner, rather than by physically restoring a prior state. All that is guaranteed by compensation is that a consistent state is established based on semantic information. This state may not be identical to the state that would have been reached had the compensated-for transaction never taken place.

We propose the notion of *compensating transactions* as the vehicle for carrying out compensation. We use the notation CT to denote the compensating transaction for transaction T. A compensating transaction has the fundamental properties of a transaction along with some special characteristics. It appears atomic to concurrently executing transactions (i.e., transactions do not observe partially compensated states), it conforms to consistency constraints; and its effects are durable. However, a compensating transaction is a very special type of transaction. Under certain circumstances, it is required to *restore* consistency, rather than merely preserve it. It is durable in the strong sense that once a decision is made to initiate compensation, the compensating transaction must complete, since it does not make any sense to abort it. The choice of either to abort or to commit is present for the original transaction. A compensating transaction offers the ability to reverse this choice, but we do not go any further by providing the capability to abort the compensation. There are other special characteristics. Above all, a compensating transaction does not exist by its own right; it is always regarded within the context of the compensated-for transaction. It is always executed after the compensated-for transaction. Its actions are derivative of the actions of the compensated-for and the dependent transactions. In some situations, the actions of a compensating transaction can be extracted automatically from the program of the compensated-for transaction, the current state of the database, and the current state of the log. In other situations, it is the system programmer's responsibility to predefine a compensating transaction.

A mundane example taken from "real life" exemplifies some of the characteristics of compensation. Consider a database system that deals with transactions that represent purchasing of goods. Consider the act of a customer returning goods after they have been sold. The compensated-for transaction in that case is a particular purchase, and the compensating transaction encompasses the activity caused by the cancellation of the purchase. The compensating transaction is bound to the compensated-for transaction by the details of the particular sale (e.g., price, method of payment, date of purchase). The purchasing transaction's effects might have been externalized in different ways. For instance, it might have triggered a dependent transaction that issued an order to the supplier in an attempt to replenish the inventory of the sold goods. Furthermore, the customer might have been added to the store's mailing list as a result of that particular sale. The actual compensation depends on the relevant policy. For example, the customer may be given store credit, or full refund. Whether to cancel the order from the supplier and whether to retain the customer in the mailing list are other application-dependent issues with which the compensating transaction must deal.

15.3   A TRANSACTION MODEL

In the classical transaction model [2, 14], transactions are viewed as sequences of read and write operations that map consistent database states to consistent states when executed in isolation. The correctness criterion of this model is called *serializability*. A concurrent execution of a set of transactions is represented as an interleaved sequence of read and write operations, and is said to be serializable if it is equivalent to a serial (nonconcurrent) execution.

This approach poses severe limitations on the use of compensation. First, sequences of uninterpreted reads and writes are of little use when the semantically rich activity of compensation is considered. Second, the use of serializability as the correctness criterion for applications that demand interaction and cooperation among possibly long-duration transactions was questioned by the work on concurrency control in [3, 9, 11]. Since we target compensation as a recovery mechanism for these kind of applications, our model does not rely on serializability as the correctness notion.

15.3.1   Transaction and Programs

A transaction is a sequence of operations that are generated as a result of the execution of some program. The exact sequence that the program generates depends on the database state "seen" by the program. In the classical transaction model, only the sequences are dealt with, whereas the programs are abstracted and are of little use. Given a concurrent execution of a set of transactions (i.e., an interleaved sequence of operations), compensation for one of the transactions, T, can be modeled as an attempt to cancel the operations of T while leaving the rest of the sequence intact. The validity of what remains from that execution is now in serious doubt, since originally transactions read data items updated by T and acted accordingly, whereas now T's operations have vanished but its indirect impact on its dependent transactions. The only formal way to examine a compensated execution is by comparing it to a hypothetical execution of only the dependent transactions, without the compensated-for transaction. We use the comparison of the compensated execution with the hypothetical execution that does not include the compensated-for transaction, as a key criterion in our exposition. However, the generation and study of this hypothetical execution requires the introduction of a *transaction program* that is, therefore, indispensable for our purposes.

A *transaction program* can be defined in any high-level programming language. Programs have local (i.e., private) variables. In order to support the private (i.e., nondatabase) state space of programs, we define the concept of an *augmented state*. The augmented state space is the database state space unioned with the private state spaces of the transactions' programs. The provision of an augmented state allows one to treat reading and updating the database state in a similar manner. Reading the database state is translated to an update of the augmented state, thereby modeling the storage of the value read in a local variable.

Thus, a *database*, denoted as *db*, is a set of data *entities*. The *augmented database*, denoted as *adb*, is a set of entities that is a superset of the database, that is, $db \subset adb$. An entity in the set $(adb - db)$ is called a *private entity*. Entities have identifying *names* and corresponding *values*. A *state* is a mapping of entity names to entity values. We distinguish between the *database state* and the state of the augmented database, which is referred to as the *augmented state*. We use the notation $S(e)$, to denote the value of entity e in a state S. The symbols S and e (and their primed versions, S', e', etc.) are used hereafter to denote a state and an entity, respectively.

Another deviation from the classical transaction model is the use of operations that are semantically richer than the primitive read and write operations. Having such operations allows us to refine the notion of conflicting versus commutative operations [1, 16]. That is, we are able to examine whether two operations commute, and, hence, can execute concurrently. The classical model, in contrast, allows little scope for such considerations, since a write operation conflicts with any other operation on the same entity.

An *operation* is a function from augmented states to augmented states that is restricted as follows:

- An operation updates at most one entity (either a private or a database entity).

- An operation reads at most one *database* entity, but it may read an arbitrary number of private entities.

- An operation can both update and read only the same database entity.

We use the following notation for a single operation f: $e_0 := f(e_1, \ldots, e_k)$. We say that f *updates* entity e_0 and *reads* entities $e_1, \ldots, e_k$. The *arguments* of an operation are all the entities it reads. There are two special termination operations, *commit* and *abort*, that have no effect on the augmented state. Operations are assumed to be executed *atomically*.

We assume implicitly that all the arguments of an operation are meaningful, that is, a change in their value causes a change in the value computed by the operation.

The operations in our model reconcile two contradictory goals. On the one hand, operations are functions from augmented states to augmented states, thereby giving the flexibility to define complex and semantically rich operations. On the other hand, the mappings are restricted so that at most one database entity is accessed in the same operation, thereby making it feasible to allow atomic execution of an operation. Although only one database entity may be accessed by an operation, as many local variables (i.e., private entities) as needed may be used as arguments for the mapping associated with the operation. Having private entities as arguments to operations adds more semantics to operations. Having functions for operations allows us to compose conveniently operations by functional composition, thereby making sequences of operations functions too.

We are in a position now to introduce the notion of a transaction as a program. A *transaction program* is a sequence of *program statements*, each of which is either:

- An operation

- A *conditional statement* that takes the form

  if b **then** $SS1$ **else** $SS2$

  where $SS1$ and $SS2$ are sequences of program statements, and b is a predicate that mentions only private entities and constants

We impose the following restrictions on the operations that are specified in the statements:

- The set of private entities is *partitioned* among the transaction programs. An operation in a program cannot read nor update a private entity that is not in its own partition.

- Private entities are updated only once.

- An operation reads a private entity only after another operation has updated that entity.

Example 1: Consider the following sets of entities: $db = \{a, b, c\}$, and $adb = db \cup \{u, v, w\}$, and the following two transaction programs, T_1 and T_2:

```
T1    begin
         u:=a;
         v:=b;
         if u > v then c:= f(c,v)
         else  begin
                  w:=c;
                  b:= g(u,w)
               end
      end
```

```
T2   begin
       a:=0;
       b:=1
     end
```

Observe that operation f both updates and reads entity c. T_2 demonstrates operations that read no entities.

15.3.2 Histories and Correctness

We use the framework for alternative correctness criteria set forth in [11]. Explicit *input* and *output predicates* over the database state are associated with transactions. The input predicate is a precondition of transaction execution and must hold on the state that the transaction reads. The output condition is a postcondition that the transaction guarantees on the database state at the end of the transaction provided that there is no concurrency and the database state seen by the transaction satisfies the input condition. Thus, as in the standard model, transactions are assumed to be generated by correct programs, and responsibility for correct concurrent execution lies with the concurrency control protocol.

Observe that the input and output predicates are excellent means for capturing the semantics of a database system. We use the convention that predicates (and hence semantics) can be associated with a set of transactions, similarly to the way predicates are associated with nested transactions in [11]. That is, a set of transactions is supposed to collectively establish some desirable property, or complete a coherent task. This convention is most useful in domains where a set of subtransactions are assigned a single complex task.

We do not elaborate on the generation of interleaved or concurrent executions of sets of transaction programs, since this is not central to understanding our results. However, the notion of a history–the result of this interleaving–is a central concept in our model. A *history* is a sequence of operations that defines both a total order among the operations, and a function from augmented states to augmented states that is the functional composition of the operations. We use the notation $X = <f_1, \ldots, f_n>$ to denote a history X in which operation f_i precedes f_{i+1}, $1 \leq i < n$. Alternatively, we use the functional composition symbol "∘" to compose operations as functions. That is, $X = f_1 \circ \ldots \circ f_n$ denotes the function from augmented states to augmented states that is defined by the same history X. We use the uppercase letters at the end of the alphabet, e.g., X, Y, Z, to denote both the sequence and the function that a history defines.

The equivalence symbol "≡" is used to denote equality of histories as functions. That is, if X and Y are histories, then $X \equiv Y$ means that for all augmented states S, $X(S) = Y(S)$. Observe that since histories and operations alike are functions, the function composition symbol "∘" is used to compose histories as well as operations.

When a (concurrent) execution of a set of transaction programs A is initiated on a state S and generates a history X, we say that X is a *history of A* whose *initial* *state* is S.

Example 2:   Consider the transaction program T_1 of Example 1. Since T_1 has a conditional statement, there are two histories, X and Y, that can be generated when T_1 is executed in isolation. We list the histories as sequences of operations:

$$X \;=\; < u := a, v := b, c := f(c,v) >$$
$$Y \;=\; < u := a, v := b, w := c, b := g(u,w) >$$

Let $S = \{\, a = 1\,,\; b = 0\,,\; c = 2 \,\}$ be the database state, then S is an initial state for X. $X(S) = S'$, where $S'(c) = f(2,0)$. Consider a *concurrent* execution of T_1 and T_2 of the previous example. We show two (out of the many possible) histories, Z and W, whose initial state is S given before. Each operation is prefixed with the name of the transaction that issued it.

$$Z = < T_2 : a := 0, \;\; T_1 : u := a, \;\; T_2 : b := 1,$$
$$T_1 : v := b, \;\; T_1 : w := c, \;\; T_1 : b := g(u,w) >$$
$$W = < T_2 : a := 0, \;\; T_2 : b := 1, \;\; T_1 : u := a,$$
$$T_1 : v := b, \;\; T_1 : w := c, \;\; T_1 : b := g(u,w) >$$

Observe that $Z(S) = W(S) = S''$, where $S'' = \{a = 0, b = g(0,2), c = 2\}$. Observe that $Z \equiv W$.

A key notion in the treatment of compensation is *commutativity*. We say that two sequences of operations, X and Y, *commute* if $(X \circ Y) \;\equiv\; (Y \circ X)$. Two operations *conflict* if they do not commute. Observe that defining operations as functions, regardless of whether they read or update the database, leads to a very simple definition of the key concept of commutativity.

Part of the orderings implied by the total order in which operations are composed to form a history are arbitrary, since only conflicting operations must be totally ordered. In essence, our equivalence notion (when restricted to database state) is similar to final-state equivalence [14]. However, in what follows, we shall need to equate histories that are not necessarily over the same set of transactions, which is in contrast to final-state equivalence (and actually to all familiar equivalence notions).

A *projection* of a history X on an entity e is a subsequence of X, which consists of the operations in X that updated e. We denote the projection of X on e as X_e. We use the same notation for a projection on a set of entities.

We impose very weak constraints on concurrent executions in order to exclude as few executions as possible from consideration. In this chapter we consider the following types of histories:

- A history X is *serial* if for every two transactions T_i and T_j that appear in X, either all operations of T_i appear before all operations of T_j or vice versa.

- A history X is *serializable* (SR) if there exists a serial history Y such that $X \equiv Y$.

- Let $C = c_1 \wedge \ldots \wedge c_n$ be a predicate over the database state. For each conjunct c_i, let d_i denote the set of database entities mentioned in c_i, A history X is *predicatewise serializable* with respect to a predicate C (PWSR$_C$) if for every set of entities d_i, there exists a serial history Y such that $X_{d_i} \equiv Y_{d_i}$.

- A history X is *entitywise serializable* (EWSR) if for every entity e, there exists a serial history Y such that $X_e \equiv Y_e$.

The definition of PWSR histories is adapted from [9]. As we shall see shortly, EWSR histories are going to be quite useful in our work. The following lemma is given without proof.

Lemma 1: Let C be a predicate that mentions all database entities, and let ewsr, pwsr$_C$, and sr denote the set of EWSR histories, PWSR$_C$ histories, and SR histories, respectively. Then, $sr \subset pwsr_C \subset ewsr$. $\square$

We denote by X_T the sequence of operations of a transaction T in a history X, involving possibly other transactions. The same notation is used for sets of transactions. When X_T is projected on entity e, the resulting sequence is denoted $X_{T,e}$.

15.4 COMPENSATING TRANSACTIONS

With the aid of the tools developed in the last section, we are in a position to define compensation more formally.

15.4.1 Specification Constraints

Although compensation is an application-dependent activity, there are certain guidelines to which every compensating transaction must adhere. After introducing some notation and conventions, we present three specification constraints for defining compensating transactions. These constraints provide a broad framework for defining concrete compensating transactions for concrete applications, and can be thought of as a generic specification for all compensating transactions.

We say that transaction T_j is *dependent on* transaction T_i in a history if there exists an entity e such that

- T_j reads e after T_i has updated e

- T_i does not abort before T_j reads e

- Every transaction (if any) that updates e between the time T_i updates e and T_j reads e is aborted before T_j reads e

This definition is adapted from [2].

A dependent transaction T_i may be either a committed transaction, or an active transaction. In either case, if we want to support the undo of T_i, then the corresponding compensating transaction, CT_i, must be predefined. The key point is that admitting nonrecoverable histories and supporting the undo of committed transactions are predicated on the existence of the compensatory mechanisms needed to handle undoing externalized transactions. In the rest of the chapter, T denotes a compensated-for transaction, CT denotes the corresponding compensating transaction, and $dep(T)$ denotes a set of transactions dependent on T. This set of dependent transactions can be regarded as a set of related (sub)transactions that perform some coherent task.

Constraint 1: *For all histories X, if $X_{T,e} \circ X_{CT,e}$ is a contiguous subsequence of X_e, then $(X_{T,e} \circ X_{CT,e}) \equiv I$, where I is the identity mapping.* $\square$

The simplest interpretation of Constraint 1 is that for all entities e that were updated by T but read by no other transaction (since $X_{CT,e}$ follows $X_{T,e}$ in the history), CT amounts simply to undoing T. Consequently, if there are no transactions that depend on T (i.e., no transaction reads T's updated data entities), then CT is just the traditional $undo(T)$. The fact that CT does not always just undo T is crucial, since the effects of compensation depend on the span of history from the execution of the compensated-for transaction until its own initiation. If such a span exists, and T has dependent transactions, the effects of compensation may vary and can be very different from undoing T. For instance, compensation may include additional activity that is not directly related to undoing. A good example here is the cancelation of a reservation in an airline reservation system; this action is handled as a compensating transaction that causes the transfer of a pending reservation from the waiting list to the confirmed list.

There are certain operations on certain entities that cannot be undone, or even compensated for, in the form of inverting the state. In [6], these type of operations and entities are called *real* (e.g., dispensing money, firing a missile). For simplicity's sake, we omit discussion of such entities.

Constraint 2: Given a history X involving T and CT, there must exist X' and X'' subsequences of X, such that no transaction has operations both in X' and in X'', and $X \equiv X' \circ X_{CT} \circ X''$. $\square$

This constraint represents the atomicity of compensation. That is, a transaction should either see a database state affected by T (and not by CT), or see a state following CT's termination. More precisely, transactions should not have operations that conflict with CT's operations scheduled both before and after CT's operations, or in between CT's first and last operations. It is the responsibility of the concurrency control protocol to implement this constraint (see Section 15.7 for implementation discussion).

In what follows, we use the notation O_T and I_T to denote the output and input predicate of transaction T, respectively. The same notation is used for a set of transactions. These predicates are predicates over the database state.

Constraint 3: Let Q be a predicate defined over the database state, and if $(O_{dep(T)} \Rightarrow Q) \wedge (I_T \Rightarrow Q)$, then $O_{CT} \Rightarrow Q$. $\square$

Constraint 3 is appropriate when Q is either a general consistency constraint or a specific predicate that is established by $dep(T)$ (i.e., one of the collective tasks of the transactions in $dep(T)$ was to make Q true). Informally, this constraint says that if Q was established by $dep(T)$, and is not violated by undoing T, then it should be preserved by CT. Observe that the assumption that Q holds initially (i.e., $I_T \Rightarrow Q$) is crucial since T's effects are undone by CT, and, hence, predicates established by T and preserved by $dep(T)$ do not persist after the compensation. It is the responsibility of whoever defines CT to enforce Constraint 3.

Constraints 1 and 2 will be assumed to hold for all compensating transactions hereafter. Constraint 3, which is more intricate and captures more of the semantics of compensation, will be discussed further in Section 15.6.

15.4.2   Types of Compensation

For some applications, it is acceptable that an execution of the dependent transaction, without the compensated-for and the compensating transactions, would produce different results than those produced by the execution with the compensation. On the other hand, other applications might forbid compensation unless the outcome of these two executions is the same. Next, we make explicit the preceding criterion that distinguishes among types of compensation by defining the notion of compensation soundness.

Definition 1:   *Let X be the history of T, CT, and $dep(T)$ whose initial state is S. Let Y be some history of only the transactions in $dep(T)$ whose initial state is also S. The history X is sound if $X(S) = Y(S)$.* □

The history Y can be any history of $dep(T)$. As far as the definition goes, different sets of (sub)transactions of $dep(T)$ may commit in X and in Y, and conflicting operations may be ordered differently. The key point is that $X(S) = Y(S)$. If a history is sound, then compensation does not disturb the outcome of the dependent transactions. The database state after compensation is the same as the state after an execution of only the dependent transactions in $dep(T)$. All direct and indirect effects of the compensated-for transaction T have been erased by the compensation.

Transactions in $dep(T)$ see different database states when T and CT are not executed, and therefore generate a history Y that can be totally different than the history X. This distinction between the histories X and Y, which is the essence of the important notion of soundness, would not have been possible had we viewed a transaction merely as sequence of operations rather than a program.

Soundness may be compromised when S does not satisfy $I_{dep(T)}$. Such a situation may occur when T establishes $I_{dep(T)}$ for $dep(T)$ in such a manner that $dep(T)$ *must* follow T in any history. Hence, if T is compensated for, there is no history of $dep(T)$, Y, that can satisfy the soundness requirement. We model such situations by postulating that if $I_{dep(T)}(S)$ does not hold, then $Y(S)$ results in a special state that is not equal to any other state (the *undefined* state), and hence X is indeed not sound.

We illustrate Definition 1 by considering the following two histories over read and write operations (the notation $r_i[e]$ denotes reading e by T_i, and, similarly, $w_i[e]$ for write and c_i for commit):

$$W = <w_j[e], r_i[e], c_j, c_i>$$
$$Z = <w_j[e], r_i[e], w_i[e'], c_i>$$

The history W is recoverable. History Z is not recoverable. If, however, CT_j is defined, T_j can still be aborted. Let us extend Z with the operations of CT_j and call the extended history Z'. Z' is sound provided that Z'_{T_i} would have been generated by T_i's program, and the same value would have been written to e' had T_i run in isolation starting with the same initial state as in Z'.

The key notion in the context of compensation, as we defined it, is the *commutativity* of compensating operations with operations of dependent transactions. Significant attention has been devoted to the effects of commutative operations on concurrency control [1, 8, 16]. Our work parallels these results as it exploits commutativity with respect to recovery. Because CT is less exposed to users than is T, we prefer to impose commutativity requirements on CT, rather than on T, in our theorems. Predicated on commutativity, the operations of the compensated-for transaction and the corresponding compensatory operations can be "brought together", and then cancel each other's effects (by the enforcement of Constraint 1), thereby ensuring sound histories. The following theorem formalizes this idea.

Theorem 1: *Let X be a history involving $T, dep(T)$ and CT. If each of the operations in $X_{dep(T)}$ commutes with each of the operations in X_{CT}, then X is sound.* □

We illustrate this theorem by the following simple example.

Example 3: Let T_i, T_j, and CT_i be a compensated-for transaction, a dependent transaction, and the compensating transaction, respectively. Let the programs of all these transactions include no condition statements (i.e., they are sequences of operations). We give a history X, in which each operation is prefixed by the name of the issuing transaction. $X = <T_i : a := a + 2, T_j : u := b, T_j : a := a + u, CT_i : a := a - 2)>$. Clearly, every operation of T_j commutes with every operation of CT_i in X. Hence, X is sound, and the history that demonstrates soundness is simply $Y = X_{T_j} = <T_j : u := b, T_j : a := a + u>$. As will become clear in Section 15.6, the fact that no condition statements appear in T_j is important.

Our main emphasis in this chapter is on more liberal forms of compensation soundness, where the results of executing the dependent transactions in isolation may be different from their results in the presence of the compensated-for and the compensating transactions. One way of characterizing these weaker forms of soundness is by qualifying the set of entities for which the equality in Definition 1 holds. In Section 15.5, we define a type of compensating transaction that ensures sound compensation with respect to some set of entities. Alternatively, in Section 6, we investigate other weak forms of soundness that approximate (pure) soundness.

15.5   EXAMPLES AND APPLICATIONS

In this section, we present several examples to illustrate the various concepts we have introduced so far. Throughout this section, we use the symbols T, $dep(T)$, CT, X, and S to denote, respectively, a compensated-for transaction, its compensating transaction, the corresponding set of dependent transactions, the history of all these transactions, and the history's initial state.

15.5.1   A Generic Example

In this example, we present a generic compensation definition. Let $update(T, X)$ denote the set of database entities that were updated by T in history X. The same notation is used for a set of transactions.

Definition 2:   *Let $X(S) = S'$ and $X \equiv X' \circ X_{CT}$ (by Constraint 2). We define the generic compensating transaction CT by characterizing S' for all entities e:*

$$S'(e) = \begin{cases} S(e), & \text{if } e \notin update(dep(T), X) \\ (X'(S))(e), & \text{if } e \in update(dep(T), X) \\ & \wedge\ e \notin update(T, X) \\ X_{dep(T),e}(S), & \text{if } e \in update(dep(T), X) \\ & \wedge\ e \in update(T, X) \end{cases}$$

Before proceeding, we explain informally the meaning of this type of compensation. If no dependent transaction updates an entity that T updates, CT undoes T's updates on that entity. The value of entities that were updated only by dependent transactions is left intact. The value of entities updated by both T and its dependents should reflect only the dependents' updates.

Next, we illustrate a certain subtlety in the second case of the definition. Assume that T updated e. The modified e is read by a transaction in $dep(T)$ and the value read determines how this transaction updates e'. After compensation, even though the initial value of e is restored (by the first case of the definition), the indirect effect it had on e' is left intact (by the second case of the definition). We use this definition as a precise specification of what CT should accomplish.

We now give a concrete example of this type of compensation. Consider an airline reservation system with the entity *seats* that denotes the total number of seats in a particular flight, the entity *rs* that denotes the number of already reserved seats in that flight, and the entity *reject* that counts the number of transactions whose reservations for that flight have been rejected. Let **reserve(x)** be a simplified seat reservation transaction for x seats defined as:

```
if (rs + x) <= seats then rs := rs + x
                    else reject := reject + 1
```

The consistency constraint Q in this case is $Q(S)$ *iff* $S(rs) \leq S(seats)$. Assume that

$$S = \{seats = 100, rs = 95, rejects = 10\}$$
$$T = \mathbf{reserve(5)}, \; dep(T) = \{\mathbf{reserve(3)}\}$$

Let the history be $X \equiv X_T \circ X_{dep(T)} \circ X_{CT}$, where CT is defined by Definition 2. We would like to have after X: $S' = \{rs = 95, rejects = 11\}$, that is, T's reservations were made and later canceled by running CT, and $dep(T)$'s reservations were rejected. And that is exactly what we get by our definition. Observe how T's reservations were canceled, but still its indirect impact on $rejects$ persists (since T caused $dep(T)$'s reservations to be rejected).

Hence, this example demonstrates a history that is not sound but is nevertheless intuitively acceptable. Had the transaction in $dep(T)$ been executed alone, it would result in successful reservations. Notice how in this example the operation of CT can be implemented as a inverse of T's operation (addition and subtraction). The less interesting case, where there are enough seats to accommodate both T and $dep(T)$, also fits nicely. In this case, CT's subtraction on the entity $seats$ commutes with $dep(T)$'s addition to this entity.

15.5.2 Storage Management Examples

The following example is from [13], though the notion of compensation is not used there. Consider transactions T_1 and T_2, each of which adds a new tuple to a relation in a relational database. Assume the added tuples have different keys. A tuple addition is processed by first allocating and filling in a slot in the relation's tuple file, and then adding the key and slot number to a separate index. Assume that T_i's slot updating (S_i) and index insertion (I_i) steps can each be implemented by a single page read followed by a single page write (written $r_i[tp]$, $w_i[tp]$ for a tuple file page p, and $r_i[ip]$, $w_i[ip]$ for an index file page p).

Consider the following history of T_1 and T_2 regarding the tuple pages tq, tr, and the index page ip:

$$< r_1[tq] \, , \; w_1[tq] \, , \; r_2[tr] \, , \; w_2[tr],$$
$$r_2[ip] \, , \; w_2[ip] \, , \; r_1[ip] \, , \; w_1[ip] \; >$$

This is a serial execution of $< S_1, S_2, I_2, I_1 >$, which is equivalent to the serial history of executing T_1 and then T_2. Assume, now, that we want to abort T_2. The index insertion I_1 has seen and used page p, which was written by T_2 in its index insertion step. The only way to abort T_2, without aborting T_1, is to compensate for T_2. Fortunately, we have a very natural compensation CT_2, which is a delete key operation. Observe that a delete operation as compensation, satisfies Constraint 1, commutes with insertion of a tuple with a different key, and encapsulates composite compensation for the slot updating and index insertion. The resulting history is sound.

15.6 APPROXIMATING SOUNDNESS

In this section, we introduce weak forms of compensation soundness, where the results of an execution that includes compensation only *approximate* the results of executing the dependent transactions in isolation.

Let us denote the history of transactions T, $dep(T)$, and CT as X, and the history without compensation, that is, a history of only $dep(T)$, as Y. In an approximated form of soundness, the final state of X is only *related* to the final state of Y.

The relation should serve to constrain CT, and prevent it from violating consistency constraints and other desirable predicates established by $dep(T)$. Thus, the relation should have some "goodness" properties, for instance: "If a consistency constraint predicate holds on the final state of Y, it should also hold on the final state of X."

Achieving even approximated soundness is an intricate problem when the histories are nonserializable, as we allow them to be. The obstacle is, as mentioned before, that the programs of transactions in $dep(T)$ see different database states when T and CT are not executed, and therefore may generate a history Y that can be totally different than the original history X. Hence, X and Y may not be related as required.

We state several theorems that formalize the interplay among the approximated soundness notion, concurrency control constraints, restrictions on programs of dependent transactions, and commutativity. Each theorem is followed by a simplified example that serves to illustrate at least part of the theorem's premises and consequences. Proofs of the theorems can be found in [10]. Throughout this section, we assume that a compensating transaction complies with Constraints 1 and 2 of Section 4. We start with definitions of weaker forms of commutativity and weaker forms of compensation soundness.

Definition 3: *Two sequences of operations, X and Y, commute with respect to a relation $\mathcal{R}$ on augmented states (in short, R-commute), if for all augmented states S, $(X \circ Y)(S) \; \mathcal{R} \; (Y \circ X)(S)$.* □

Observe that when $\mathcal{R}$ is the equality relation, we have regular commutativity.

Definition 4: *Let X be a history of T, $dep(T)$, and CT whose initial state is S, and let $\mathcal{R}$ be a reflexive relation on augmented states. The history X is sound with respect to R (in short R-sound), if there exists a history Y of $dep(T)$ whose initial state is S such that $Y(S) \; \mathcal{R} \; X(S)$.* □

Observe that regular soundness is a special case of R-soundness when $\mathcal{R}$ is the equality relation. Since $\mathcal{R}$ is reflexive, the empty history is always R-sound, regardless of the choice of R.

We motivate the preceding definitions by considering adequate relations $\mathcal{R}$ in the context of R-commutativity and R-soundness. Let Q be a predicate on database states such that $O_{dep(T)} \Rightarrow Q$. Q can be regarded as either a consistency constraint, or a desired predicate that is established by $dep(T)$ (similarly to the predicate Q in Constraint 3). Therefore, we would like to guarantee that compensation does not violate Q. Define $\mathcal{R}$ (in the context of X, Y, and S) as follows:

$$Y(S) \; \mathcal{R} \; X(S) \;\; iff \;\; (Q(Y(S)) \Rightarrow Q(X(S)))$$

An R-sound history with such $\mathcal{R}$ has the advantageous property that predicates like Q are not violated by the compensation. Such R-sound histories yield states that approximate states yielded by sound histories in the sense that both states satisfy some desirable predicates. In the examples that follow the theorems, we use relations $\mathcal{R}$ of that form.

Definition 5: *Let $\mathcal{R}$ be a relation on states, and let v_e and v_e' denote values of an arbitrary entity e. We define the relations R_e on values of e for every entity e as follows:*

$$v_e \; R_e \; v_e' \; iff$$
$$(\exists S', S'' : \; S'(e) = v_1 \; \wedge \; S''(e) = v_2 \; \wedge \; S' \; \mathcal{R} \; S'')$$

Definition 6: *Let X be a history of T, $dep(T)$, and CT whose initial state is S, and let $\mathcal{R}$ be a reflexive relation on augmented states. The history X is partially R-sound if there exists a history Y of $dep(T)$ whose initial state is S such that $(\forall e \in db : (Y(S))(e) \; R_e \; (X(S))(e))$.* $\square$

Definition 7: *A program of a transaction is fixed if it is a sequence of operations that uses no private entities as arguments.* $\square$

If T's program is fixed, then it has no conditional branches. Moreover, T cannot use local variables to store values for subsequent referencing. A sequence of operations, where each operation reads and updates a single database entity (without storing values in local variables) is a fixed transaction. A transaction that uses a single operation to give a raise to a certain employee recorded in a salary management database is an example for a fixed transaction.

Theorem 2: *Let X be a history of T, $dep(T)$, and CT whose initial state is S. If the histories $X_{dep(T)}$ and X_{CT} R-commute, X is EWSR, and all programs of transactions in $dep(T)$ are fixed, then X is partially R-sound.* $\square$

Example 4: Consider a database system with the following entities, parametric operations, and reflexive relation:

$$db = \{a : integer, \; b : integer\},$$
$$f(e) :: \;\; \textbf{if } e > 2 \;\; \textbf{then} \;\; e := e - 2$$
$$g(e) :: \;\; \textbf{if } e > 10 \, \textbf{then} \;\; e := e - 10$$
$$S' \; \mathcal{R} \; S'' \; iff \; (((S'(b) \geq 0 \wedge S'(a) \geq 10) \vee (S'(a) = 4))$$
$$\Rightarrow ((S''(b) \geq 0 \wedge S''(a) \geq 10) \vee (S''(a) = 4)))$$

(The predicates on a are present only to demonstrate partial R-soundness.) We emphasize that f and g are (atomic) operations. The history X is as follows (there is no need to give the program of $dep(T)$ since it is fixed):

$$X = < dep(T) : A := a + 2, \ T : f(a), \ T : g(b),$$
$$dep(T) : g(b), \ CT : a := a + 2, \ CT : b := b + 10 >$$

Observe that $X_{dep(T)}$ and X_{CT} do not commute but they do R-commute for the given relation $\mathcal{R}$. Let the initial state be $S = \{a = 2, \ b = 15\}$. We have that $X(S) = \{a = 4, \ b = 15\}$, whereas $Y(S) = \{a = 4, \ b = 5\}$, and indeed X is *partially* R-sound.

The inherent problem with (the proofs of) compensation soundness is that they equate two histories that are *not* over the same set of transactions, which is in contrast to all the equivalence notions in the traditional theory of concurrency control. The obstacle is that the history Y may be generated by different executions of the programs of $dep(T)$, and may be totally different from $X_{dep(T)}$, which is just a syntactic derivative of the history X. In Theorem 2, this problem was solved only because $dep(T)$ was fixed. This obstacle can be removed by posing more assumptions, as is done next.

Definition 8: *A transaction T is a serialization point in a history X if $X \equiv X' \circ X_T \circ X''$.* □

Observe that no restrictions are imposed on X' and X''. Also notice that a compensating transaction is a serialization point, as implied by Constraint 2.

Theorem 3: *Let X be a history of T, $dep(T)$, and CT. Let Z be a history of the transactions in $dep(T)$ and CT such that $Z \equiv Z_{dep(T)} \circ Z_{CT}$. If for all states S and for all histories Z, there exists a history Y of $dep(T)$ such that $(Z_{CT} \circ Y)(S) \ \mathcal{R} \ (Z_{dep(T)} \circ Z_{CT})(S)$, then every history X where T is a serialization point is R-sound.* □

Note that it is required that $dep(T)$'s programs be such that executing CT before $dep(T)$ would result in a state that is related by $\mathcal{R}$ to the state resulting when executing $dep(T)$ first and then CT. Observe that this requirement is stronger than R-commutativity.

This theorem is quite useful since it specifies a concurrency control policy that guarantees R-soundness. Namely, we need to ensure that every potential compensated-for transaction be isolated (i.e., T is a serialization point) in order to guarantee R-soundness in case of compensation.

Example 5: Consider the set entities of Example 4, with the addition of a private entity u that belongs to some transaction in $dep(T)$. Let the programs of T, $dep(T)$, CT, and the relation $\mathcal{R}$ be defined as follows:

$$T \ = \ a := a + 1, \quad CT \ = \ a := a - 1$$
$$dep(T) \ = \ \{ \ u := a; \ \text{if } u \geq 5 \text{ then } f(b) \text{ else } g(b) \}$$
$$S' \ \mathcal{R} \ S'' \ \textit{iff} \ (S'(b) \geq 0 \Rightarrow S''(b) \geq 0)$$

Even though $dep(T)$'s history can branch differently when run alone and in the presence of T and CT, the two different histories produce final states that are related by $\mathcal{R}$.

Definition 9:   *A program of a transaction is linear if it is a sequence of operations.* Programs are sequences, but we allow operations to read multiple entities, that is, use local variables. Therefore, programs may not be fixed. An example for a linear transaction program is a program that gives a raise to all employees, where the raise based on some aggregated computation (for instance, 10% of the minimum salary).

Definition 10:   *Let $\mathcal{R}$ be a reflexive relation on augmented states. An operation f that updates e preserves $\mathcal{R}$, if $(\forall e' \in adb : (S(e') \, \mathcal{R}_{e'} \, S'(e')) \Rightarrow (f(S) \, \mathcal{R}_e \, f(S'))$* □

Theorem 4:   *Let X be a history of T, $dep(T)$, and CT whose initial state is S. If the histories $X_{dep(T)}$ and X_{CT} R-commute, X is EWSR, the programs of all transactions in $dep(T)$ are linear, R is transitive, and the operations of $dep(T)$ preserve $\mathcal{R}$, then X is partially R-sound.* □

Example 6:   Consider the set entities of Example 4, with the addition of a private entity u that belongs to some transaction in $dep(T)$. We use the relation $S' \, \mathcal{R} \, S''$ *iff* $((S'(b) \geq S'(a)) \Rightarrow (S''(b) \geq S''(a)))$. The history X is as follows:

$$X \;=\; < T : a := a + 1, \;\; dep(T) : u := a,$$
$$dep(T) : b := u + 10, \;\; CT : a := a - 1 \; >$$

Observe that X_{CT} and $X_{dep(T)}$ R-commute (but do not commute), $dep(T)$ is linear (but not fixed), and X is (partially) R-sound.

Finally, based on Lemma 1 from Section 2, we derive the following corollary.

Corollary 1.   *Theorems 2 and 4 hold when X is $PWSR_C$ or SR instead of EWSR.* The requirements from the dependent transactions in Theorems 2, 3, and 4 are quite severe. Besides the R-commutativity requirement imposed on the operations of the dependent transactions, there are restrictions on the shape of the programs (e.g., fixed or linear programs) in each of the theorems' premises. Clearly, in practical systems, there are many transactions that do not stand up to any of these criteria. The practical ramification of this observation is that externalization of uncommitted data items should be done in a controlled manner if a degree of soundness is of importance. That is, uncommitted data should be externalized only to transactions that do satisfy the requirements specified in the premises of the theorems. In the context of locks, locks should be released only to qualified transactions, that is, those transactions that do satisfy the requirements. Other transactions must be delayed and are subject to the standard concurrency control and recovery policies.

15.7   IMPLEMENTATION ISSUES

In this section, we discuss several implementation issues that need to be considered in order for compensation to be of practical use. We envision that a compensating transaction would be driven by a scan of the log starting from the first record of the compensated-for transaction and up to its own begin-transaction log record. It is important to provide convenient on-line access to the log information for these purposes. Without a suitable logging architecture, these accesses might translate to

I/O traffic that would interrupt the sequential log I/O that is performed on behalf of executing transactions. In addition, log records should contain enough semantic information to guide the execution of the compensating transaction. Therefore, it is likely that some form of operation logging will be used [7].

Next, we discuss subtle ramifications on concurrency control in the context of locking. We have required that CT's execution is serializable with respect to other concurrent transactions (Constraint 2). Also, if we reasonably assume that $update(CT, X) \subseteq update(T, X)$, we can conclude that the compensating transaction and the dependent transactions should follow a 2-phase locking protocol [2] with respect to entities in $update(T, X)$. Otherwise, it possible to violate Constraint 2. A viable strategy that might simplify matters for the implementation follows. Once CT is invoked, the entities in $update(T, X)$ should be identified by analyzing the log and then CT should exclusively lock all entities in this set. After performing the necessary updates, CT can release these locks.

The recovery issues of compensating transactions themselves must be considered also. As was noted earlier, we should disallow a compensating transaction to be aborted either externally (by user, or an application), or internally (e.g., as a deadlock resolution victim). Still, there is the problem of system failures. We think that the preferred way to handle this problem is to resume uncompleted compensating transactions rather than to undo them. To accomplish this, we need to resume a compensating transaction from a point where its internal state was saved along with the necessary concurrency control information. We emphasize that the principle for recovery of a compensating transaction is that once a begin-transaction record of CT appears in stable storage, CT must be completed. An implementation along the lines of the ARIES system [12] can support the persistence of compensating transactions across system crashes. In ARIES, undo activity is logged using compensating log records (CLRs). It is guaranteed that actions are not undone more than once, and that undo actions are not undone, even if the undo of a transaction is interrupted by a system crash.

15.8   RELATED WORK

Compensating transactions as semantically rich recovery mechanisms are mentioned, or at least referred to, in several papers. However, to the best of our knowledge, a formal and comprehensive treatment of the issue and its ramifications is lacking.

Strong motivation for our work can be found in Gray's early paper [6]. The notion of compensation (countersteps) is mentioned in the context of histories that preserve consistency without being serializable in [4, 3].

Compensating transactions are also mentioned in the context of a *saga*, a long-duration transaction that can be broken into a collection of subtransactions that can be interleaved in any way with other transactions [5]. A saga must execute all its subtransactions, hence compensating transactions are used to amend partial execution of sagas. In [4] and in [5], the idea that a compensating transaction cannot voluntarily abort itself is introduced.

A noteworthy approach, which can be classified as a simple type of compensation, is employed in the XPRS system [15]. There, a notion of *failure commutativity* is defined for complete transactions. Two transaction failures, commute if they commute, and if they can both succeed, then a unilateral abort by either transaction cannot cause the other to abort. Transactions that are classified as failure commutative can run concurrently without any conflicts. Handling the abort of such a transaction is done by a log-based special undo function, which is a special case of compensation as we define it.

In [1], semantics of operations on abstract data types are used to define *recoverability*, which is a weaker notion than commutativity. Conflict relations are based on recoverability rather than commutativity. Consequently, concurrency is enhanced since the potential for conflicts is reduced. When an operation is recoverable with respect to an uncommitted operation, the former operation can be executed; however, a commit dependency is forced between the two operations. This dependency affects the order in which the operations should commit, if they both commit. If either operation aborts, the other can still commit, thereby avoiding cascading aborts. This work is more conservative than ours in the sense that it narrows the domain of interest to serializable histories.

15.9 CONCLUSIONS

We have argued that exposing uncommitted data is useful for many database applications employing long-duration, nested, and collaborative transactions. We proposed compensating transactions as the means for recovery management in the presence of early externalization. We introduced several types of compensation-soundness criteria and found them to be predicated on notions of commutativity. Even the approximated forms of soundness can be used to guarantee that compensation results in desirable consequences and does not abrogate dependent transactions' outcome. We set up a semantically rich model that is adequate for dealing with nonserializable and nonrecoverable histories; we offered this model as a viable tool for the understanding of these intricate history and compensation issues.

We believe that future database applications will require the rethinking of the traditional transaction model that is founded on serializability and permanence of commitment. Contemporary applications in the domains of CAD and CASE exemplify our belief. The work presented in this chapter is a step toward establishing this new model.

References

[1] B. R. Badrinath and K. Ramamritham. "Semantic-based concurrency control: Beyond commutativity," In *Proceedings of the Third International Conference on Data Engineering*, Los Angeles, 1987.

[2] P. A. Bernstein, V. Hadzilacos, and N. Goodman. *Concurrency Control and Recovery in Database Systems.* Addison-Wesley, Reading, MA, 1987.

[3] A. A. Farrag and M. T. Ozsu. "Using semantic knowledge of transactions to increase concurrency," *ACM Transactions on Database Systems,* 12(4) (December 1989).

[4] H. Garcia-Molina. "Using semantic knowledge for transaction processing in a distributed database," *ACM Transactions on Database Systems,* 8(2) (June 1983).

[5] H. Garcia-Molina and K. Salem. "Sagas," In *Proceedings of the ACM-SIGMOD 1987 International Conference on Management of Data,* San Francisco, 1987.

[6] J. N. Gray. "The transaction concept: Virtues and limitations," In *Proceedings of the Seventh International Conference on Very Large Databases,* Cannes, 1981.

[7] T. Haerder and A. Reuter. "Principles of transaction oriented database recovery–a taxonomy," *ACM Computing Surveys,* 15(4) (December 1983).

[8] H. F. Korth. "Locking primitives in a database system," *Journal of the ACM,* 30(1) (Jan. 1983).

[9] H. F. Korth and W. Kim and F. Bancilhon. "On long duration CAD transactions," *Information Sciences,* October 1988.

[10] H. F. Korth, E. Levy, and A. Silberschatz. *A formal approach to recovery by compensating transactions,* Technical Report TR-90-14, The University of Texas at Austin, Computer Sciences Department, 1990.

[11] H. F. Korth and G. Speegle. "Formal model of correctness without serializability," In *Proceedings of the ACM-SIGMOD 1988 International Conference on Management of Data,* Chicago, June 1988.

[12] C. Mohan, D. Haderle, B. Lindsay, H. Pirahesh, and P. Schwarz. "ARIES: A transaction recovery method supporting fine-granularity locking and partial rollbacks using write-ahead logging," *ACM Transactions on Database Systems,* 17(1) (March 1992).

[13] J. E. B. Moss, N. D. Griffeth, and M. H. Graham. "Abstractions in recovery management," In *Proceedings of the ACM-SIGMOD 1986 International Conference on Management of Data,* Washington, 1986.

[14] C. Papadimitriou. *The Theory of Database Concurrency Control.* Computer Science Press, Rockville, Maryland, 1986.

[15] M. R. Stonebraker, R. H. Katz, D. A. Patterson, and J. K. Ousterhout. "The design of XPRS," In *Proceedings of the Fourteenth International Conference on Very Large Databases,* Los Angeles, 1988.

[16] W. E. Weihl. "Commutativity-based concurrency control for abstract data types," *IEEE Transactions on Computers,* C-37(12) (December 1988).

Chapter 16

Coordinating Multitransaction Activities with Nested Sagas

Hector Garcia-Molina, Deiter Gawlick, Johannes Klein,
Charly Kleissner, and Kenneth Salem

Abstract

Data processing applications must often execute collections of related transactions. We propose a set of services that can be used to support such applications. The services include creation and monitoring of persistent transactions, communication between transactions, and compensation for committed transactions whose effects must be undone. We illustrate the use of these services with examples.

16.1 INTRODUCTION

In this chapter we study so-called business data processing applications. These applications contain programs that perform computing functions necessary for running a business or enterprise. The functions may include, for instance, inventory control, accounting, market projections, and so on. The persistent data required by these programs are typically stored in databases. The programs execute transactions that are the elementary or atomic units of work (e.g., record a new purchase order). However, there is more to an application than simply a set of independent transactions. It is also necessary to manage the flow of data and control between the transactions.

To illustrate what we mean, consider the processing of a "purchase order" at some company. This activity can be represented as a collection of steps, as shown in Figure 16.1. This is a very simplified version of what may occur. The activity starts when a phone call is received to place a new order (step `phone_call`). A clerk enters the required information into an electronic form. The next step is to run a transaction (step `enter_order`) to record the new order in the database. Note that the first step was not a transaction: There is no need to save the data permanently until the entire request has been made. After the order is entered, two parallel steps are executed. The `billing` step charges the customer and the `inventory` step updates the inventory. Each of these steps involves a transaction that reads and updates the database. After these transactions complete, a final `shipping` step is executed to generate the appropriate shipping orders.

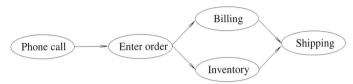

Figure 16.1. A purchase order activity.

We are concerned with defining an environment in which activities such as this can be easily specified and executed. What services should this environment provide? The purchase order example suggests some answers to this question.

Concurrent Database Access. Steps should be able to access shared databases concurrently. In our example, the databases may contain information about items in stock, their prices, and customer histories. Concurrency can arise among the steps of a single activity, for example, the `billing` and `inventory` steps of Figure 16.1, or between steps of different activities.

Communication. There should be some mechanism for communication among steps. Steps within an activity are related, and may need to share information. For example, the `enter_order` step may provide a purchase order number to the `billing` step, for use on the customer's bill. Communication can be accomplished through the shared databases, or steps could send data explicitly to each other. There may also be an activity context, accessible from all steps, that holds temporary data used by the activity.

Modularity and Reuse. It should be possible to define modular, reusable steps. A step may be useful in several types of activities. For example, the `shipping` step from the purchase order activity may also be useful in another activity that accomplishes a transfer of stock between two company warehouses. Since a given step will be connected to different steps within the two activities, the connections between steps should not be part of their static definitions.

Recovery from Step Failures. There should be some facility for coping with failed steps, and for aborting activities. A step may be unable or unwilling to complete its task. For example, the `inventory` step may find insufficient stock available to fill the order, or the `billing` step may discover that the customer has a bad credit history with the company. There are many possible techniques for coping with the failure. Steps can be retried, or an alternative step can be initiated. Sometimes a step is critical, and the failure of a step and its alternatives should cause the entire activity to fail. For example, discovery of a bad credit history might result in the cancelation of the entire purchase order. In this case, it may be desirable to undo or compensate for other steps in the activity as a result of the failure. Failure-induced activities can be initiated automatically by the system, or the necessary information can be provided so that the application can handle the failure as it chooses.

Recovery from System Failures.   Activities should not be aborted because of system failures. Activities may be long-running, so aborting and restarting the entire activity may be costly. Instead, we would prefer to restart where we left off before the failure, for example, simply redo (or complete) the missing steps. We refer to this property as *forward progress* of activities.

Several types of systems provide some of this functionality. Transaction processing systems implement atomic transactions [1, 15] to support reliable concurrent access to shared databases. Programming languages with embedded transaction constructs [11, 12] may, in addition, provide mechanisms for communication between transactions and for failure notification. Software engineers have constructed systems to facilitate "programming-in-the-large" [4], including support for modular programming and the reuse of code [8]. Research in the area of office information systems has also suggested mechanisms for dealing with activities [5]. Our model can be seen as a blend of ideas from each of these domains. There have also been a number of papers dealing with multitransaction activities [3, 6, 13]. The work presented here can be thought of as a low-level framework on which some of those concepts could be implemented. Also, the concept of nested sagas that we introduce here could be incorporated into some of those proposals.

Our goal, then, is to describe an environment that will provide these services. So that we can give concrete examples of how the environment can be used to support activities, we have chosen to do so by defining the environment's interface. We can then write pseudo-code to illustrate how the interface can be used to implement activities. We will present the interface as a set of "system calls." We do not mean to suggest that the details of these calls, as we present them, are important. Nor do we intend that the pseudo-coded examples represent the right way for an application developer to code an activity. Our intention is to provide a concrete illustration of a simple environment that can provide the services required by business data processing applications.

We will present the interface in two stages. First, we describe a basic set of system calls that can be used to satisfy some, but not all, of the application requirements listed before. In particular, the basic set of calls provides for the creation and termination of persistent, atomic steps, and for communication among steps. Next, in Section 16.3, we refine the basic calls, and add one new one, so that the remaining requirements can be satisfied. At that point, we introduce *nested sagas* as a model for activities.

16.2   BASIC SERVICES

The basic services provide support for application steps. At this point, we have not really defined what a step is. Intuitively, a step is an execution of a program that accomplishes some part of a data processing activity (e.g., `billing`). In our model, a step is an instance of a *module*. Modules, in turn, are code fragments.

To keep our presentation concrete and simple, we will assume that each module consists of an interface and a body. The body contains the code to be executed. The interface defines a name for the module, as well as a set of module *ports*. Ports support direct communication between steps. Ports in different steps can be connected at run time (using the `Bind` service described in what follows) through persistent message queues [2]. Once its ports are connected, a step can use them to send and receive messages. The important features of this mechanism are run-time binding of one step to another (allowing one module to be reused in several different activities) and persistent, transactional messages. Other communications facilities that provide these features could be substituted for the one described here. The following six calls constitute the basic service interface:

`Create.` This command takes a module name and a port as parameters. It creates a new step, an instance of the specified module, and returns a unique step identifier. The identifier can be used as an argument to subsequent calls that are to affect the new step. When the new step terminates, the system will deliver a message indicating its termination status (committed or aborted) to the port specified as the second parameter.

`Commit.` Step execution is atomic, and steps terminate either by committing or by aborting. This call terminates the calling step's execution and commits its actions. A step is implicitly committed after executing its last statement if it has not explicitly committed or aborted.

`Abort.` This call aborts the calling step, terminating its execution. Optionally, a step other than the calling one can be aborted by specifying a step identifier as a parameter. Actions taken by the aborted step are rolled back and undone.

`Bind.` This call takes two ports as parameters, and links them together through a persistent message queue. If neither port is currently bound, then a new empty queue is created and both ports are linked to it. If one or the other port is already bound to an existing queue, then this command links the unbound port to the same queue. If both ports are already bound to different queues, an error occurs.

`Send.` This call is used to send a message through a specified port. The port must already be bound, and the message is placed into the persistent queue to which it is linked.

`Receive.` This call receives a message through a specified port, which must be bound. The message is taken from the queue to which the port is linked.

Although we do not discuss it further here, Receive may be blocking or non-blocking.

Steps execute as persistent atomic transactions. Because a step is a transaction, the effects of any system calls it makes are not visible to others until the step commits. Specifically, newly created steps do not exist until their creator commits, messages cannot be received until the sender commits, and ports are not considered bound until the binding step commits. Should a step abort, any system calls it has made are rolled back so that they have no effect. The one exception to this rule is for self-abort. That is, a call to Abort with no parameter takes effect immediately, and obviously the effect of this call is not undone during the abort.

The system implementing these calls may fail, for example, because of a power outage. Any steps that are active when the system fails will be rolled back and aborted when it recovers. Because steps are persistent, such steps will then be restarted (from the beginning) automatically by the system.

Note that to enforce atomicity of steps, the system must control concurrent accesses to its data structures. For instance, if one step is attempting to commit while another step is trying to abort it, the system must ensure that these calls appear to execute sequentially. For persistent message queues, concurrency can be improved by treating them as sets of messages rather than FIFO queues [14, 10, 16]. That is, for a FIFO queue, if one step reads the first message, no other step can read from that queue until that first step commits. With a set, several steps can concurrently read.

To illustrate the use and behavior of the basic services, let us return to the purchase order example of Figure 16.1 and see how it can be implemented. We start by writing a module for each of the five steps of the purchase order. For example, the billing module is shown in Figure 16.2. The modules for the other steps are similar. Note incidentally that the phone_call step will be executed as a transaction even though in our initial description of the example we stated that this was not necessary.

```
Module Billing:
[ port:  input, status
    ...
  Receive(port:input, msg:m)
  extract order number from m
  access database to read purchase order
  do billing
  marshall results into r
  Send(port:status, msg:r)
]
```

Figure 16.2. Pseudo-code for the billing module.

To implement the purchase order, we need to write a module that creates instances of each of the modules that comprise the purchase order activity, and binds them together so that they can communicate. Such a module is shown in Figure 16.3, and its graphical representation in Figure 16.4.

```
Module PO;
[ port:  trigger

    ...
    pc ← Create(module:phone_call)
    eo ← Create(module:enter_order)
    bi ← Create(module:billing)
    in ← Create(module:inventory)
    sh ← Create(module:shipping)
    Bind(port:trigger,port:pc.in)
    Bind(port:pc.out,port:eo.in)
    Bind(port:eo.tobill,port:bi.input)
    Bind(port:eo.toinv,port:in.input)
    Bind(port:bi.status,port:sh.in1)
    Bind(port:in.out,port:sh.in2)
]
```

Figure 16.3. Pseudo-code for the purchase order module.

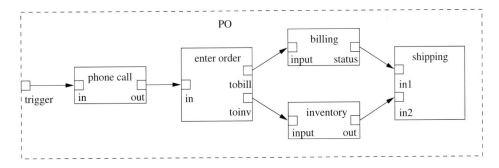

Figure 16.4. Graphical representation of the purchase order module.

Let us now walk through the execution of this activity. First, some other step creates an instance of module PO. We will refer to this new step also by the name PO to avoid generating a new name for our sample step. We will do the same for other steps. The step that creates PO also binds port trigger to some port, associating trigger with a message queue, say, Q. When PO executes, it creates the five steps necessary for the activity. The in port of the phone_call step is bound to trigger, which links in to Q. Thus, any messages that were written to Q for PO can actually be read by the phone_call step. Notice that this is not visible from the outside: Steps that send messages into Q do not know, and need not care, that the PO activity consists of several steps. The rest of the binds in PO will create new queues. For example, the output of the phone_call step will be written into one of these queues, to be read later as input for enter_order.

The steps created by PO do not start until PO commits. When PO commits, the phone_call step then can read from Q and start processing. The rest of the steps block waiting to receive input. When phone_call commits, its output becomes visible and enter_order starts processing it. When enter_order commits, both the billing and inventory steps proceed in parallel, and so on.

If a system failure occurs, the system aborts pending transactions and restarts them. For instance, suppose that the system fails after the billing and inventory steps have read their input and are processing it. These steps are aborted, returning the inputs to their queues. (Since the steps never committed, the input messages were never actually received, and therefore are still available in their queues.) After recovery, the persistent system data structures will indicate that there are three steps, billing, inventory, and shipping, that must be restarted. When billing and inventory restart, each will be able to read the messages it had read before the crash.

A second scenario is that one of the steps of PO voluntarily aborts. For example, billing may decide that the customer credit is not good. One possible reaction to this is to terminate the entire PO activity if this occurs. Since some steps of PO may already have committed, their effects will have to be compensated for. We will discuss this option further in Section 16.3.

In other cases, it may be desirable to take some other action, such as executing an alternative to the failed step. The notification service provided by the system makes this possible. When PO creates each step, it can use a command like:

```
bi ← Create(module:billing,notification_port:ppp)
```

This causes the system to send a (persistent) message to the notification_port when billing terminates. The notification port should not be in the PO step itself. Recall that the PO step must terminate and commit for the rest of the PO activity's steps to execute. Hence, PO will not be around when billing aborts. The solution is for PO to create a monitor step containing the notification port. The same is done for other steps. Figure 16.5 is a graphical representation of the PO module with a monitor step. In the figure, the monitor is set up to receive notification from all other steps in PO through its port ppp. The code of the monitor step checks at run time (by making calls to Receive) that all of the steps in the PO activity commit, and takes appropriate action (such as creating alternatives) if any do not.

These basic services satisfy many of the requirements of data processing activities. They allow steps to be created and connected to implement activities. They provide a mechanism through which related steps can communicate. They support concurrent access to shared databases, since steps execute as atomic transactions.

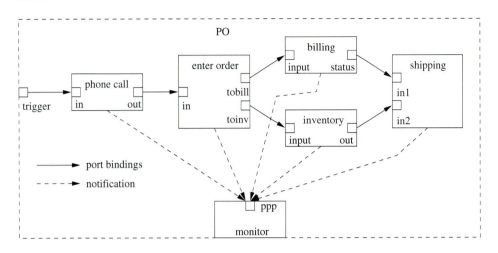

Figure 16.5. The monitor and notification in the PO activity.

Because steps are persistent, forward progress through activities is achieved despite system failures.

The basic services also provide some support for modular design of activities. Ports and run-time port binding allow the same module to be connected to other modules a variety of ways. It is also possible to build higher-level modules by composing lower-level ones. For example, the multistep implementation of the purchase order activity shown in Figure 16.3 behaves much like a single-module implementation would. In both cases, new purchase order instances can be created, and can communicate with the outside world through ports. Both implementations provide a guarantee of forward execution progress.

However, there are several differences between a multistep implementation of the purchase order and a single-step implementation. One difference is that the single-step implementation is atomic, whereas the multistep implementation is not. In the multistep implementation shown in Figure 16.3, partial results may be visible before the order is fully processed. For example, after enter_order commits, the order becomes visible in the database to any other transaction. Another difference is that individual steps can be aborted, but there is no mechanism for aborting multistep activities. A cosmetic reason for this is that there are identifiers only for individual steps, and not for groups of steps. Thus, there is no way to use Abort to abort a multistep activity. A more fundamental reason is that a multistep activity is not atomic. For example, if a problem is discovered during the billing step of Figure 16.4, we cannot simply roll back the entire activity since phone_call and enter_order (and possibly inventory) may have committed already.

16.3   NESTED SAGAS

In this section, we refine and enhance the basic services to so that the application requirements can be fully met. In particular, we add support for sagas [9]. Sagas define how to treat multistep activities as a single entity. Like individual steps, sagas can be created, aborted, and committed, and they have identifiers. We permit sagas to be nested, which allows previously defined activities to be used as component steps of new activities.

Before defining nested sagas more precisely, we will try to motivate them by showing how the purchase order activity might be implemented using the improved services. The new version of module PO is shown in Figure 16.6 (compare to Figure 16.3). The five sub steps that will process the order are created as before. Now, however, we assume that the Create command by default links parent step (PO) and its children (phone_call, enter_order, billing, inventory, shipping) into a saga. The identifier of the saga is the same as the identifier of the step PO, the saga's parent step. By using the saga identifier, it will be possible to abort the saga in a manner we will describe.

```
Module PO;
[ port:  trigger
   ...
   pc ← Create(module:phone_call)
   eo ← Create(module:enter_order)
   bi ← Create(module:billing)
   in ← Create(module:inventory)
   sh ← Create(module:shipping)
   Bind(port:trigger,port:pc.in)
   Bind(port:pc.out,port:eo.in)
   Bind(port:eo.tobill,port:bi.input)
   Bind(port:eo.toinv,port:in.input)
   Bind(port:bi.status,port:sh.in1)
   Bind(port:in.out,port:sh.in2)
   eo' ← Create(module:delete_order,type:independent)
   bi' ← Create(module:crediting,type:independent)
   in' ← Create(module:add_stock,type:independent)
   Compensation_Bind(forward:eo,compensation:eo')
   Compensation_Bind(forward:bi,compensation:bi')
   Compensation_Bind(forward:in,compensation:in')
]
```

Figure 16.6. Pseudo-code for the purchase order module (as a Saga).

The six Bind commands are as before and set up the communication structure for the activity. They are followed by three new Create commands. These create *com-*

pensating steps, which may be used in the event that the PO saga is aborted. Each compensating step is associated with a forward step via the `Compensation_Bind` command. We are assuming here that the compensating steps contain the application code necessary to compensate for their corresponding forward steps. For example, `delete_order` would erase the customer order placed by the `enter_order` step. Not all steps require compensation. In our example, we have not created compensating steps for the `phone_call` and `shipping` substeps. Note that the compensating steps are created using a new, optional `type` parameter to `Create`. Their type is specified as `independent` to indicate they are not actually part of the PO saga. Later, we will elaborate further on this parameter.

Let us now walk through an execution of the new module by supposing that some step creates an instance of PO by calling `Create`. When it does so it receives an identifier. This identifier identifies both the PO step itself and the PO step's saga. This saga includes the PO step as the parent, and will include any new child steps created by PO as it runs. When the PO step is finished, it will commit, thereby activating each of its child steps. (The compensating steps will be activated only if compensation is required.) Although the PO step has committed at this point, the PO saga is not finished until all of its children finish.

The PO identifier can be passed to the `Abort` command to cause the saga to abort. Let us suppose that this occurs while the `inventory` and `shipping` steps are still active, and the others have committed. The `Abort` will cause the still-active `inventory` and `shipping` steps to be aborted and rolled back. The compensating steps `crediting` and `delete_order` will be automatically initiated to compensate for `billing` and `enter_order`, which have already committed.

Now let us briefly consider a different execution scenario. Suppose that PO is not aborted as described before. Instead, the step `billing` voluntarily aborts (e.g., because customer credit was bad) by making an `Abort` call without a parameter. Since `billing` is member of the PO saga, the PO saga itself is aborted as a result. This proceeds as described before, with the abort of active steps in PO and the compensation of committed ones. In some cases, it may be undesirable to have a saga abort automatically when one of its components aborts. Later, we discuss how this default behavior can be changed.

It is important to note that sagas can be nested. For example, what PO thinks is a simple atomic `billing` step, may actually generate substeps of its own. Thus, in general, a saga will contain a parent step, plus zero or more children, each of which is itself a saga. Figure 16.7 illustrates the nesting of sagas.

Aborts are propagated down and up the tree defined by the saga parent/child relationship. To illustrate, say that PO is aborted and that the `billing` step is written to create substeps to do its work, as in Figure 16.7. If PO is aborted before the `billing` step itself commits, that is, before its children have been created, then the billing step itself is simply rolled back. If PO is aborted while `billing`'s children are still active (but the `billing` step itself is committed), then the `billing` saga is still active, and it is aborted recursively, aborting each of its children. If PO is aborted after the `billing` saga is committed (i.e., all of `billing`'s children

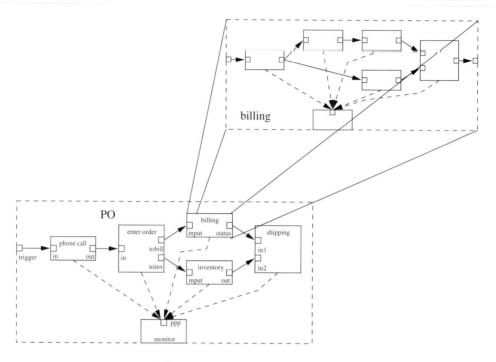

Figure 16.7. Nesting of sagas.

are committed), then the compensating step for `billing`, `crediting`, would be executed. Going in the opposite direction now, if a child of `billing` aborts, then the `billing` saga would be aborted, which would in turn cause the PO saga to abort.

As our example illustrates, the interface supports sagas through refinements to the behavior of the `Create`, `Abort` and `Commit` calls, and through the introduction of the new `Compensation_Bind` call. The `Bind`, `Send`, and `Receive` calls remain unchanged. The modified interface is as follows:

`Create.` This call creates a new saga containing one new step. The new step is considered to be the parent step of the new saga. When we refer to a "step's saga," we are refering to the saga of which the step is the parent step. `Create` returns an identifier that is used to refer both to the new step and to its saga. The `Create` call has a parameter `type` that is used to define the relationship between the new saga and its creator's saga. This relationship controls the propagation of aborts, as will be described in what follows.

`Commit.` As before, `Commit` causes the calling step to commit. If the step has no children, then its saga is also committed. If the step does have children, then the step is committed but its saga is not. Its saga is committed when all of its children's sagas have committed.

Abort. As before, `Abort` can be used with or without a parameter. If the specified step (or the calling step, if no parameter is used) is still active, it is aborted and rolled back by this call, and its saga is considered to be aborted as well. If the specified step is committed, but its saga is still active, then this call causes its saga to abort. If both the specifed step and its saga are committed, then this call causes the step's compensation (if one has been specified via `Compensation_Bind`) to be executed, and the status of the saga to change from committed to aborted. The abort of a saga may propagate automatically to the saga's parents or children, as described in what follows.

Compensation_Bind. Compensation bind takes two parameters, which are `forward` and `compensate`. Both are step identifiers. This function makes `compensate` the compensating step for `forward`, that is, if `forward`'s saga is aborted after committing, then `compensate` will be executed. A compensating step is executed only under this condition. Thus, it does not automatically begin executing when its creator commits. It is an error to make a step into a compensating step if it is already running therefore, only a step's creator can specify that it is to be used for compensation. Compensating steps are always considered to be of type `independent`.

As described in our example, saga aborts may propagate from parents to children, and vice versa. Propagation depends on how sagas are created. Suppose that a step P creates a child C. If no type is specified when C is created, then an abort of P's saga causes C's saga to abort as well, and an abort of C's causes P's to abort. This is the default behavior. In some cases, it is desirable to permit some additional flexibility in the way aborts are cascaded. For example, consider an instance of the PO activity in which the `inventory` step fails because sufficient parts are not available to satisfy the customer's order. In this case, it may be possible to substitute a similar part to complete the order. Thus, in the case of a failed inventory step, the corrective action desired by the application would be the invocation of an alternate instance of the `inventory` step, without affecting the other steps of the PO activity.

If P creates C with type `non-vital`, the an abort of C does not propagate to P. However, an abort of P does propagate to C. This is the desired behavior in the case of the PO and `inventory` sagas, since it allows recovery from a failure of the `inventory` saga to be customized through the creation of a monitor step for `inventory`. The monitor can wait for notification of the termination (abort or commit) of the `inventory` saga, and then take the appropriate action, such as creating an alternative step, if `inventory` fails.

A third option is to use the `independent` type. If C is independent, the C's abort will not propate to P, and P's will not propagate to C. A common use of the `independent` type is for creating compensating steps, as shown in Figure 16.6. The `independent` type can also be used to define steps that are not sagas. For instance, in Figure 16.3, we illustrated an activity that was not a saga, using our initial version of the `Create` command. With our refined version of `Create`, we can obtain that effect by using the type `independent` in all `Create` calls.

16.4 DISCUSSION

Our proposal can be thought of as an operating system for activities. A conventional operating system provides the notion of processes and interprocess communication facilities. Processes use the system interface to start up other processes, to communicate, or to request other services. In our environment, a step is analogous to a process. The calls we defined are used by steps to request services from the system.

In our model, the concept of module (or its instance, a step) now embodies five concepts:

1. Modules are the units of program composition. That is, we build complex programs (activities) by linking together modules.

2. Modules are the units of execution. As processes are in an operating system, module instances are created and executed.

3. Modules are the units of atomicity. That is, modules are executed as transactions.

4. Modules are the units of compensation. To compensate for a committed activity, a step is executed.

5. Modules are the units of checkpointing. At the end of each step, we essentially take a checkpoint (by making relevant system structures and message queues persistent), so that a completed step will never have to be rerun because of a system failure.

One can argue whether combining all these concepts into a single one is the right thing to do. There are cases where this is not appropriate. For example, it may be desirable to execute several steps within a single transaction. However, we believe that this will be more of the exception. In a majority of the examples we have studied, the various concepts naturally overlap. For instance, consider the `billing` step in our running example. There is no need for it to share its local, volatile data with other steps. If there is a problem, this is the natural unit of work to abort or to compensate, and so on. Thus, we opted for a simple model, with few concepts and a simple interface, that could be useful for describing the most common activities.

As discussed in the introduction, one of our goals was to facilitate the reuse of steps. We believe that our model successfully decouples the internals of a step from environment in which the step will run. The step's environment is specified by the its creator, which determines how the steps ports will be bound, and what actions should occur when the step commits or aborts, and how the step should be compensated for, if compensation proves necessary. It even should be relatively simple to use legacy programs as modules. For example, suppose we are handed a C procedure that does the `billing` step. This procedure is a set of input and output parameters. We can simply write a shell module around the given procedure. The shell will receive the necessary data, transferring them to local C variables. The shell then calls the C procedure, and on return, packages the results into an output message.

Another goal for our model was to provide a communication mechanism. We have chosen persistent queues, as opposed to more conventional mechanisms where a connections are established directly from one process to another, and where messages are not persistent. Our belief is that persistent queues make it easier to decouple steps. A step can even exchange data with steps that are not active concurrently (or may not even be created yet). One case when this occurs is when a step passes information to its compensating step, in case compensation is eventually required. For example, the `enter_order` step might pass an order number to `delete_order`, its compensation.

16.5   CONCLUSIONS

In this chapter we have presented a simple set of services to support multitransaction activities. Let us briefly return to the application requirements we hoped to meet with these services.

Concurrency.   Steps are executed as transactions, a well-understood mechanism for supporting concurrent access to shared databases.

Communication.   Communication is achieved in a flexible way through the `Bind`, `Send`, and `Receive` commands. Steps can also communicate via the shared database.

Modularity.   The use of ports and dynamic binding makes it possible for a module to be used as part of several activities without modification. This capability is similar in philosophy to the standard input/standard output facility provided for UNIX processes. Collections of cooperating steps can be made to look like a single step. Like single steps, they can be created, committed, and aborted. This facilitates the composition of activities to produce more complex, higher-level activities.

Step Failure Recovery.   Facilities are provided for coping with failed steps. A collection of steps can be treated as a monolithic computation, where the failure of one element causes the abortion of the entire activity. Alternatively, it is possible customize the handling of subactivity failures.

System Failure Recovery.   By making system structures persistent, forward progress is achieved despite system failures. After a system failure, the system restarts activities where they were suspended.

We have illustrated how nested sagas can be used in the design of multistep activities. Such activities are common in business data processing environments, but are difficult to support using only the existing atomic transaction model.

References

[1] P. A. Bernstein, V. Hadzilacos, and N. Goodman. "Concurrency Control and Recovery in Database Systems," Addison-Wesley, 1987.

[2] P. Bernstein, M. Hsu, and B. Mann. "Recoverable queues," In *Proceedings of the ACM SIGMOD International Conference on Management of Data*, 1990.

[3] U. Dayal, M. Hsu, and R. Ladin. "Organizing long-running activities with triggers and transactions," In *Proceedings of the ACM SIGMOD International Conference on Management of Data*, June 1990.

[4] F. DeRemer and H. H. Kron. "Programming-in-the-large versus programming-in-the-small," *IEEE Transactions on Software Engineering*, SE-2(2) (June 1976).

[5] Clarence A. Ellis. "Formal and informal models of office activity," In R.E.A. Mason, editor, *Information Processing 83*, Elsevier Science Publishers B.V., 1983.

[6] Ahmed K. Elmagarmid, editor. *Database Transaction Models for Advanced Applications*. Morgan Kaufmann, 1992.

[7] H. Garcia-Molina, D. Gawlick, J. Klein, K. Kleissner, and K. Salem. *Coordinating multi-transaction activities*, Technical Report CS-TR-2412, Computer Science Department, University of Maryland, College Park, MD, February 1990.

[8] R. Hayes and R. Schlichting. "Facilitating mixed language programming in distributed systems," *IEEE Transactions on Software Engineering*, SE-13(12) (December 1987).

[9] Hector Garcia-Molina and Kenneth Salem. "Sagas", In *Proceedings of the ACM SIGMOD International Conference on Management of Data*, May 1987.

[10] M. P. Herlihy and W. E. Weihl. *Hybrid concurrency control for abstract data types*, Technical Report MIT/LCS/TM-368, Laboratory for Computer Science, Massachusetts Inst. of Technology, August 1988.

[11] M. P. Herlihy and J. Wing. "Avalon: Language support for reliable distributed systems", In *Proc. 17th International Symposium on Fault Tolerant Computing*, July 1987.

[12] Barbara Liskov. "Distributed programming in Argus," *Communications of the ACM*, 31(3) (March 1988).

[13] A. Reuter. "Contracts: A means for extending control beyond transaction boundaries," In *Proc. Third International Workshop on High Performance Transaction Systems*, September 1989.

[14] Peter M. Schwarz and Alfred Z. Spector. "Synchronizing shared abstract types," *ACM Transactions on Computer Systems*, 2(3) (August 1984).

[15] Alfred Z. Spector and Peter M. Schwarz. "Transactions: A construct for reliable distributed computing," *Operating Systems Review*, 17(2) (April 1983).

[16] W. E. Weihl. "Local autonomy properties: Modular concurrency control for abstract data types," *ACM Transactions on Programming Languages and Systems*, 11(2) (April 1989).

Chapter 17

Recovery Options in Directory-Based Software Coherency Schemes

Lory D. Molesky and Krithi Ramamritham

Abstract

Directory-based coherency (DBC) has proven to be a popular and effective means for making a collection of local memories appear as one large global memory. Database systems composed of multiple nodes, such as client-server and shared-disk systems, often use DBC to achieve coherency. In this chapter, we present a method for achieving failure atomicity of transactions in DBC systems, which support fine-granularity locking, and that avoid unnecessary transaction aborts. We use the term *Isolated Failure Atomicity* (IFA) to denote this property because it ensures failure atomicity while isolating node failures. IFA is achieved through schemes that allow surviving nodes to recover from the effects of transactions that were executing on failed nodes and hence were aborted without waiting for the crashed node(s) to recover first. To this end, we have developed techniques (a) to reconstruct directory information and (b) to recover the data touched by transactions that were running on crashed nodes. One of the novel ingredients of our techniques is the idea of *undo log shipping*, which adds only minimal space and time overheads to normal processing. A by-product of this systematic development of recovery techniques is that it helps to demystify some of the facets of multiple-node recovery.

17.1 INTRODUCTION

Hardware-based cache coherence protocols in shared-memory multiprocessors (SMPs) use the convenience of a broadcast bus to achieve coherency. On the other hand, *directory-based approaches* implement coherency without relying on the broadcast properties of a shared bus. To accomplish this, *directory* information is distributed among the nodes, indicating the location and access rights of *pages*[1] that make up the distributed shared memory. To ensure coherent access, it is often necessary to send messages between nodes to obtain the most recent copy of a page. As in cache-coherent SMPs, performance advantages are achieved via replication, which reduces the average cost of read operations by allowing simultaneous reads to the same page by multiple nodes.

Even though coherent shared memory can improve performance and has programming advantages, data sharing applications, such as in database and transaction processing (TP) systems, may suffer from recovery problems due to side effects of coherency. When a node crash occurs (whereby the contents of the physical memory on the failed node are destroyed), correctly recovering from the crash may require aborting otherwise independent transactions that execute on the *surviving* nodes. These unnecessary transaction aborts can be avoided by appropriate design of recovery protocols. When one or more nodes crash, our *recovery objective* is to

- abort all transactions running on crashed nodes.
- avoid aborting transactions running on surviving nodes.

We use the term *Isolated Failure Atomicity* (IFA), to denote the previous property because it ensures failure atomicity while isolating node failures.

Because of data sharing between transactions, mechanisms to detect and isolate node failures essential to achieve the fail-stop assumption [22] alone are not enough to guarantee that transactions are not unnecessarily aborted due to node failures. Ensuring IFA is especially difficult in systems that support *fine-granularity locking* (FGL), which is used because it allows for high degrees of transaction concurrency. For example, when a page (containing multiple data items) is the unit of data sharing (between nodes), and the data item is the unit of logical locking, multiple active data items may be shipped between nodes. In the context of FGL, it was shown in [16] that additional protocols are necessary to achieve IFA in cache-coherent SMPs, that is, systems that use cache-coherence *hardware*.

In this chapter, we consider ensuring IFA in the context of directory-based coherency (DBC) schemes. IFA in such systems implies recovering not only the data modified by transactions that were running on crashed nodes but also reconstructing the directory information made inconsistent due to node crashes. DBC has been used in many system architectures, including distributed shared-memory (DSM) architectures [11, 24], client-server database systems that employ data shipping and

---

[1]Whereas the *cache line* is the unit of data sharing in cache-coherent multiprocessors, the *page* is typically the unit of sharing in directory-based systems.

local caching [5, 15, 17], and also in shared disk-database systems [12, 14]. Client-server data shipping is very similar to distributed shared-memory architectures, with the following exception. Unlike in client-server systems, many distributed shared-memory architectures require kernel modifications in order to determine efficiently whether a page is resident in the local memory of the requesting processor.

In DBC, coherency is typically implemented in software. This makes it feasible to change the coherency protocol to support independent recovery of surviving nodes. We achieve IFA through schemes that allow surviving nodes to recover from the effects of transactions that were executing on failed nodes and hence were aborted *without waiting for the crashed node(s) to recover first*. The key features of our recovery protocols to achieve IFA are (a) *logging-before-migration* (LBM) protocols, which enforce specific logging policies prior to the migration of uncommitted data from one node to another, and (b) recovery mechanisms for ensuring that the appropriate undos and redos are performed upon a node failure.

Loosely coupled DSM systems are generally configured with *private disks*. Unlike SMP and shared-disk systems, where many nodes may share a disk, in systems with private disks, it is not possible to access the crashed node's stable storage until the crashed node reboots. An obvious simple way to ensure the availability of information needed to *undo* the effects of transactions on a crashed node is to move the needed information to stable storage. This proposition not only increases run-time overheads (due to stable writes to disk), but also delays recovery until the disk attached to the failed node becomes accessible. Recovery mechanisms of course must be able to *recover the data* modified by transactions that were running on crashed nodes. In the case of DBC, they must also *reconstruct the directory information*. The latter is essential to produce consistent information about the location and state of the data across nodes.

Instead, we use a novel technique called *undo log shipping*, whereby when data migrates from one node to another, the associated (and usually required) undo log information is also migrated. This obviates the need to access the stable storage (if any) of the crashed node and enables surviving nodes to eliminate the effects of transactions that were executing on failed nodes quickly, thus minimizing the time that a surviving node is unavailable for processing transactions. As a result, existing transactions are allowed to make progress, and new transactions can begin execution as well.

For many loosely coupled systems supported by directory-based architectures with private disks, it is important to consider support for *disconnected operation*. In the event of a node crash or disconnection, there may be no guarantee that the connection with a crashed node can be reestablished in a timely manner. Our techniques do not require such a guarantee and hence allow a surviving node to recover independently from a crashed node.

In summary, the main contributions of this chapter as follows:

- A systematic derivation of the requirements imposed on recovery in DBC systems

- Development of techniques to achieve Isolated Failure Atomicity in DBC systems, in particular (a) to reconstruct directory information and (b) to recover the data modified by transactions that were running on crashed nodes

- Development of the simple but effective technique of log shipping to minimize run-time overheads entailed by recovery

Section 17.2 provides an overview of owner-based DBC protocols. Section 17.3 describes our transaction and failure model. To set the stage to discuss recovery issues that arise in DBC systems, we review in Section 17.4 the anomalous behaviors that occur, in the form of lost and spurious updates, when data are stored in shared memory. The specific recovery issues that arise in DBC systems are discussed in Section 17.5. Section 17.6 is devoted to showing how (1) directories structures and (2) data items are recovered in DBC systems. Related work is discussed in Section 17.7. Section 17.8 summarizes the chapter.

17.2   OVERVIEW OF OWNER-BASED DIRECTORY COHERENCEY PROTOCOLS

In owner-based directory schemes, each page in the global memory has a node designated as the owner. For example, in client-server DBC database system, the server would own all pages corresponding to its database. When loaner (nonowner or client) nodes require access to a page owned by some other node, the page is transferred to the requesting node by an underlying coherency protocol. We assume a *single-writer* coherency protocol, where prior to updating a page, a node must obtain exclusive access to the page. However, many nodes may simultaneously access a page for reading, and this is achieved by allowing many nodes to simultaneously cache a page. This single-write/multiple-reads protocol is achieved with the following mechanisms:

Write Invalidation.   A write to a page invalidates all other copies.

Read Replication.   A read issued to a page that is not locally cached, but is in another cache, will cause the page to be replicated in the reading node's cache.

In the context of DBC, these mechanisms are implemented as follows: The owner maintains *location* information and the *mode* of the page. The mode of the page is either X (exclusive), S (shared), or I (invalid). For X pages, the owner maintains the node that has the writable copy (denoted the *writer*). For S pages, the owner maintains the list of nodes that have read-only copies of the page (denoted by the *readers*). The owner will have a copy of the page if either the owner holds the page in the X mode or if any node holds the page in the S mode. This information is maintained in the owning node's global directory, denoted *GDir*. Loaner nodes maintain local directory (*LDir*) information for pages that they possess but for which they are not the owners. The contents of an I page are invalid in that another node has modified the page, but the modifications are not reflected on this node's page. Hence, they must not be read.

An example of DBC follows. Suppose node x owns p. After node y requests to write p, p will be cached on node y and $LDir^y$ will have an entry indicating that p is held in the X mode. A node that needs access to page p first checks either its $GDir$ or $LDir$ to determine if p is cached locally in a compatible mode (X for write, X or S for read). Note that we assume that ownership can be determined statically, for example, via a simple function on the page identifier (such as a hash function). If p is cached locally in a compatible mode, then it can be accessed without any internode communication. Otherwise, when either a *read miss* or *write miss* occurs, it triggers internode communication to bring the necessary pages into the local buffer.

In summary, a $GDir$ maintains complete location information for all pages owned by that node, and an $LDir$ maintains location information for pages that it does not own. This $LDir$ information is redundant, since each $LDir$ entry mirrors location information contained in one of the $GDir$s. Because location information is distributed, with local and global directories storing potentially redundant information, directory inconsistencies may arise due to node crashes. These inconsistencies must be resolved during recovery. How this can be done is discussed in Section 17.6.1. In the rest of this section, we discuss the protocols for handling read and write misses. These protocols are similar to those described in [3, 4, 26, 14, 19].

Handling a READ MISS:

1. A read request for p is sent to the owner.

2. Upon receipt of the request, the owner does the following:
   If the current mode of p is X, then

   (a) The owner sends a downgrade message to current holder, requesting that the current mode of p be set to S.

   (b) The current holder downgrades its mode of p to S and then sends a copy of p to the owner.

   (c) Upon receipt of p, the owner assigns the mode of its local copy to S.

3. The owner adds the requesting node to the *readers* of p and then sends a copy of the page to the requester.

4. The requester caches p locally, and makes an entry it its $LDir$ indicating p is held in S mode.

Figure 17.1 graphically illustrates the messages transmitted and the resulting state changes for the case where a loaner (other than the requester) holds the exclusive copy. Three different nodes are shown: a *requestor, owner,* and a *holder. Send()* denotes a message send, and the direction of the arrow indicate the sender (source) and the receiver (destination). The labels on the directed arrows correspond to conditional operations based on the states of the sender's cache and the action taken by the sender. The resulting change in the mode of the page, due to these coherency messages, is shown at the bottom of each node. In the figure, the mode of the page is denoted as either I (invalid), S (shared), or X (exclusive).

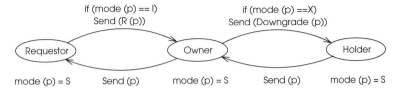

Figure 17.1. Resolving a read miss.

A similar strategy is employed on a write miss. In this case, in order to obtain an X copy of p, ownership must be transferred from the current holder to the node requesting the write operation. Next, we show the steps for resolving a write miss when there is a single holder.

Handling a WRITE MISS:

1. A write request for p is sent to the owner.

2. The owner sends an invalidation message to current holder.

3. The current holder supplies p to the owner, and invalidates its copy.

4. The owner supplies p to the requestor and makes the requestor the writer.

5. The requestor receives and caches p, and updates $LDir$ to indicate that p is held in the X mode.

Figure 17.2 graphically illustrates the write miss protocol for the case where one loaner (other than the requestor) holds a shared copy (and the owner also has a copy in a shared mode). Note that in the case where many nodes hold p in a shared mode, invalidate messages must be sent to each holder (steps 2 and 3).

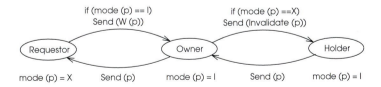

Figure 17.2. Resolving a write miss.

This section has described the basic protocols for owner-based DBC. Next we present our failure and transaction model, and then discuss the recovery issues that arise in shared-memory systems in general. Recovery issues in DBC systems are presented subsequently.

17.3   FAILURE AND TRANSACTION MODEL

In the context of DBC, we assume that node crashes are *fail-stop* [22]. The visible effects of the failure of node x are (a) node x stops executing, (b) the internal state and the contents of volatile storage on node x are lost, and (c) other nodes detect the failure of node x. Once a node failure is detected, transaction processing is halted, and a restart recovery procedure is executed to restore system consistency. We assume that the failed node eventually reboots successfully and that the crash of a particular node does not affect the physical contents of *volatile* memory on other (surviving) nodes. We also assume that the underlying interconnection network remains fully operational. In context coherency, we assume that message sends and receives are atomic with respect to recovery.

In our model of transaction execution, transaction and buffer management functions are implemented symmetrically at each node. In this context, we make a number of assumptions that are consistent with most commercial database implementations. All data are updated in place and updates follow the write-ahead log (WAL) protocol [2]. Each node maintains a log. All update operations to this log take place in the node's memory. This in-memory log is volatile, but can be made stable by writing it to the local private disk. Log records are typically written in conjunction with the data item updates–this is referred to as an *update protocol*.

We assume that locking-based concurrency control is used to enforce serializable execution histories.[2] Whereas coherency control ensures correctness at an operation level, *concurrency control* is used to ensure correctness between groups of operations, defined as transactions. In locking-based concurrency control, the basic lock modes are shared and exclusive. An exclusive lock on a data item i guarantees that no other transaction will read or modify i, whereas a shared lock on i ensures that no other transaction will modify i. Note that several shared requests on i can be granted concurrently. We also assume the most flexible buffer management policy, no-force/steal [8]. We also assume that lock management is performed at the node which *owns* the data to be locked.

Our recovery algorithms are designed to work correctly when *fine-granularity locking* (FGL) [14] is used. For example, although pages are the grain of coherency, multiple data items may be stored in a page, and the data item is the unit of logical (database) locking. FGL allows high concurrency of transactions, but complicates recovery. These complications arise when a page containing multiple active data items are transferred between nodes.

We focus on transaction workloads where independent transactions execute entirely on a single node. Although a database system implemented on multiple nodes is well suited for applications where a single (parallelized) transaction executes on multiple nodes, the presentation of the recovery strategies is simplified under the assumption that each transaction executes on a single node. However, the results can be extended to handle parallel transactions by treating each component of a

---

[2]The recovery anomalies we address arise also in nonserializable executions, but we focus on serializable execution histories in this chapter.

parallel transaction as a separate transaction for the purposes of recovery.

17.4 RECOVERY ISSUES IN COHERENT SHARED-MEMORY SYSTEMS

Traditional database recovery only ensures that the results of *committed* transactions are unaffected by crashes. In the event of a node crash, most protocols in use today (see Section 7) will abort *all running transactions*, even those running on surviving nodes. Under our recovery objective of IFA, in addition to ensuring that *committed* transactions are unaffected by crashes, we must also ensure that *active transactions running on surviving nodes are unaffected by crashes*. Our approaches to achieving IFA are based on volatile logging, and thus incur little or no additional run-time cost to the DBMS (which is done anyways in traditional DBMSs). In this section, we summarize the causes of recovery anomalies in shared-memory systems. In subsequent sections, we show how these anomalies affect DBC systems, and discuss approaches to resolving these anomalies.

As a result of the write-invalidate and read-replication coherency mechanisms, updates performed by one node may (1) *migrate* to some other node or (2) be *replicated* on another node. If node crashes occur after migration or replication, recovery anomalies may arise [16]. In particular, spurious updates may arise due to either write invalidation or read replication, and lost updates may arise due to write invalidation. Consider the following two histories, where the superscripts x and y denote *different* nodes, and data items i and j are stored in page p.

$$H^{ww1} \;\; = \;\; w^x[i]; \; w^y[j]; \; Crash^y$$

In the history, a write by node x is executed on data item i and then a write by node y is executed on data item j. After these two operations, due to write invalidation, *the only copy* of line p resides on node y. Note that this history is serializable, and, when using FGL, the page migration will occur due to write invalidation. At this point, if node y crashes, a lost update occurs.

A *lost update* occurs if a node crash destroys an update that was made by an active transaction running on a surviving node. When node y crashes (denoted $Crash^y$) in H^{ww1}, the contents of all volatile memory on node y are lost. This includes the update performed by node x ($w^x[i]$). Our recovery objective requires that transactions running on surviving nodes must remain unaffected. Thus, we must restore the lost update ($w^x[i]$).

A *spurious update* occurs if a node where some active transaction was executing crashes, but an update made by this transaction remains in the cache of some other node. Spurious updates may arise due to either write invalidation or read replication. These cases are exemplified in the following histories:

$$H^{ww2} = w^x[i]; \; w^y[j]; \; Crash^x \qquad H^{wr} = w^x[i]; \; r^y[j]; \; Crash^x$$

When node x crashes in H^{ww2}, the contents of volatile memory on node x are lost and thus all transactions executing on node x must be aborted. However, the update made by node x $(w^x[i])$ remains in the cache of node y, since p had migrated to node y prior to the crash of node x.

In H^{wr}, as in H^{ww2}, the crash of node x only partially aborts t^x, failing to eliminate $w^x[i]$. Note that read replication does not lead to lost updates, since invalidation occurs only on a write. For example, after $w^x[i]$; $r^y[j]$, since p remains on node x, if node y were to crash, all copies of p are not destroyed.

17.5   RECOVERY ISSUES IN DIRECTORY-BASED COHERENCY PROTOCOLS

Directories can become inconsistent when either (i) p's global directory ($GDir(p)$) is destroyed due to a node crash, but one or more local directory entries ($LDir(p)$) of p survive, or (ii) when one or more $LDir(p)$'s are destroyed, but $GDir(p)$ survives. With respect to a particular page, we classify these cases as *owner crashes* and *loaner crashes* respectively. [3] Owner crashes may lead to lost $GDir(p)$ entries, whereas loaner crashes may lead to spurious $GDir(p)$ entries:

- Lost $GDir(p)$
  A Lost $GDir(p)$ occurs when the owner's directory entry for p ($GDir(p)$) is destroyed, but the loaner's directory entry for p ($LDir(p)$) remains unaffected by the crash.

- Spurious $GDir(p)$
  A Spurious $GDir(p)$ occurs when the loaner's directory entry for p ($LDir(p)$) is destroyed, but the owner's directory entry for p ($GDir(p)$) remains unaffected by the crash.

Next, we consider the details of owner and loaner crashes.

17.5.1   Owner Crashes

Table 17.1 illustrates the possible directory inconsistencies and update anomalies that may arise due to *owner* crashes. For completeness, the table also includes the associated lost and spurious updates to data. In all entries of the table, given page p, $owner(p) = x$, data items $i, j \in p$. In all histories, node x crashes, destroying x's global directory $GDir^x$. Node y, and its associated $LDir^y$, exemplify local directories that survive the crash of node x. The four histories O1, O2, O3, and O4 illustrate the possible directory inconsistencies that may arise due to different patterns of read (r) and write(w):

These four cases exemplify all the recovery problems that may arise *due to the crash of the owning node*. Cases O1 and O2 exemplify uncommitted data migration and replication from the owner to a loaner, respectively, and cases O3 and

---

[3]Note that if more than one node crashes, causing the loss of both $GDir(p)$ and $LDir(p)$, then the only possible directory inconsistency for p arises if one or more $LDir(p)$ survive. This still belongs to the category of owner crashes.

Table 17.1. Directory Inconsistencies and Update Anomalies When x, the Owner of p, Crashes

Case/ Type	History	Destroyed $GDir^x$	Destroyed $LDir^y$	Update Anomaly	Directory Inconsistency
O1	$w^x[i];\ w^y[j];\ Crash^x$	Yes	No	Spurious w^x	Lost $GDir^x(p)$
O2	$w^x[i];\ r^y[j];\ Crash^x$	Yes	No	Spurious w^x	Lost $GDir^x(p)$
O3	$w^y[j];\ w^x[i];\ Crash^x$	Yes	No	Lost w^y	—
O4	$w^y[j];\ r^x[i];\ Crash^x$	Yes	No		Lost $GDir^x(p)$

Table 17.2. Directory Inconsistencies and Update Anomalies When y, the Loaner of p, Crashes

Case	History	Destroyed $GDir^x$	Destroyed $LDir^y$	Update Anomaly	Directory Inconsistency
L1	$w^x[i];\ w^y[j];\ Crash^y$	No	Yes	Lost w^{x4}	Spurious $GDir^x(p)$
L2	$w^x[i];\ r^y[j];\ Crash^y$	No	Yes	—	Spurious $GDir^x(p)$
L3	$w^y[j];\ w^x[i];\ Crash^y$	No	Yes	Spurious w^y	—
L4	$w^y[j];\ r^x[i];\ Crash^y$	No	Yes	Spurious w^y	—

O4 exemplify uncommitted data migration and replication from a loaner node to the owner. Since these cases exemplify general patterns of update anomalies and directory inconsistencies, they are also referred to as *types* of inconsistencies.

17.5.2 Loaner Crashes

Table 17.2 illustrates the possible directory inconsistencies and update anomalies that may arise due to *loaner* crashes: The histories shown are abbreviated L1, L2, L3, and L4. These four cases exemplify all recovery problems that may arise *due to the crash of a loaner node.* Cases L1 and L2 exemplify uncommitted data migration and replication from the owner to a loaner, respectively, and cases L3 and L4 exemplify uncommitted data migration and replication from a loaner node to the owner.

17.6   RECOVERY IN DIRECTORY-BASED COHERENCY

Since a node crash destroys the volatile memory on the crashed node, recovery in DBC requires that *directories* and *data* be recovered.

- Recovery on Survivor Nodes

---

[4]We show later in this section how this update anomaly can be avoided by extending the DBC protocol.

```
RecoverSurvivor()
{
    /* Cleanup Directories */
    CrashPageList = SurvivorCleanupLDir();
    SurvivorCleanupGDir();

    /* Restore Lost Updates of type O3 (type L1 are fixed with OLV) */
    if (CrashPageList != 0)
        for (i=StartLSN, i<LastLSN, i++)
            if ((Log[i].page ∈ CrashPageList) AND RedoCondition(Log[i]))
                RedoUpdate(i);

    EliminateSpuriousUpdates();
}
```

Figure 17.3. Recovery on surviving nodes.

1. Directories must be cleaned up so as to eliminate spurious references to pages on the crashed node(s).

2. Lost updates are restored.

3. Spurious updates are eliminated.

- Recovery of Crashed Nodes

    1. The $GDir$ must be reconstructed to include entries for pages held on surviving nodes.

    2. Traditional recovery follows to ensure FA.

After a survivor node recovers but during recovery of the crashed node, transactions executing on survivors can continue to make progress until they need to lock data items owned by the crashed node. Figures 17.3 and 17.4 summarize the steps for recovering directories on surviving and crashed nodes.

Section 17.6.1 shows how directories can be recovered, Section 17.6.2 shows how run-time extensions can be employed to eliminate some types of update anomalies, and Section 17.6.3 shows how data can be recovered.

17.6.1   Recovering Directory Structures

In this section, we show how lost $GDir$ entries can be recovered and how spurious $GDir$ entries can be eliminated after the failure of a node.

Recovering Lost $GDir$ Entries.   Consider the lost $GDir$ entry problem, which arises in cases O1, O2, and O4. Our basic approach is to reconstruct, when x recovers, the $GDir$ of x based on any $LDir$ entries that mirror the entries that were on x prior to the crash. This is performed as follows:

1. Each surviving node y examines its $LDir$ and then sends (to node x) a list of pages owned by x.

2. Upon the reception of these lists from all survivors, x initializes its $GDir$ to contain entries for all the pages in the receive list.

The pseudo-code for step 1 of the preceding strategy is illustrated in Figure 17.5, denoted $SurvivorCleanupLDir()$. The figure also includes the definition of the $GDir$ and $LDir$ data structures. To simplify the presentation, $GDir$ and $LDir$ are represented as arrays (of structures) indexed by a page identifier in practice, for performance reasons, hash tables are preferable to arrays.

After each survivor completes SurvivorCleanupLDir(), the recovering (crashed) node performs step 2. That is, cases where $GDir(p)$ was destroyed but $LDir(p)$ survived (as in O1, O2, and O4), at recovery time, $GDir(p)$ is reconstructed to reflect all $LDir(p)$s. Recall that O3 causes no directory inconsistencies. Thus, this strategy resolves all lost $GDir$ entries. Note that this algorithm can easily handle multiple node crashes, simply by invoking SurvivorCleanupLDir() once for each crashed node.

Eliminating Spurious $GDir$ Entries.   Our approach is to eliminate $GDir$ references that indicate that a page is held by a node that crashed.

To this end, for all surviving nodes x:

- Examine $GDir^x$ and eliminate references to pages held by crashed nodes. These references fall into two categories:

  1. Those of type L1.
     Resolving these and the related lost update of type L1 is potentially expensive. Even though the redo log for the update done by w^x is likely

```
RecoverCrashed()
{
     ∀ s ∈ Survivors
        Receive(s,Pagelist);

     Reconstruct_GDir();

     Follow Traditional Recovery.
}
```

Figure 17.4. Recovery on crashed nodes.

```
typedef struct GDir {              typedef struct LDir {
    int pid;                           int pid;
    int mode;                          int mode;
    int readers[];                     int owner;
    int writer[];                      int *p;
    int *p;                        } LDir[MAX_LOCAL_PAGES];
} GDir[MAX_GLOBAL_PAGES];

    /*
        The surviving node constructs a list of all pages in the
        local directory (LDir) which were owned by the crashed node,
        then sends this list to the crashed node.
    */
    SurvivorCleanupLDir()
    {
        CrashPageList = ∅;
        ∀ page ∈ LDir
          if (LDir[page].owner == CrashedNode)
              Append(CrashPageList,LDir[page].pid);
        Send(CrashedNode,CrashPageList);
        return(CrashPageList);
    }
```

Figure 17.5. Resolving local directory inconsistencies on survivors.

to be in x, it is possible that no node has page p in its memory to apply this redo log. It is possible that y may have written p to its stable storage, but this can be resolved only after y recovers, and in that case, it will require access to the disk of the failed node to obtain the most recent version of p. As we show in the next section, lost updates of type L1 and the related Spurious GDir entry of type L1 can be avoided with a simple extension to DBC.

2. Those of type L2.
   If the crashed node is one of many holders of p (i.e., in a shared mode), then the crashed node is merely deleted from the *readers* of $GDir^x(p)$.

17.6.2 Run-Time Recovery Extensions for DBC

Masking lost updates of type L1 can be potentially expensive if performed at restart recovery time. This is because of the need to obtain the previous version of p, which must either be reconstructed from the log (this is feasible if entire pages are logged), or otherwise the page must be fetched from disk. In [15], it was shown that a software coherency protocol can be extended (in the case of a write miss) in order to avoid going to disk at restart recovery time.

> COHERENCY PROTOCOL EXTENSION: **Owner Last Version (OLV)**
> Whenever the owner grants X access to another node, the owner main-
> tains a copy of the previous version of the page. This version is not used
> unless the current holder of the page crashes.

Given this extension, the resolution of spurious *GDir* entries of type L1 can be
performed very quickly as follows.

> OLV RECOVERY:
> If the only (loaner) holder of p crashes, *writers* is reinitialized to be
> the owner node (and *readers* is assigned to null). At this point, the old
> version of p stored at the owner becomes the current version of the page.

By using OLV, the pseudo-code for resolving global directory inconsistencies on
surviving nodes is given in Figure 17.6. Note that SurviviorCleanupGDir() can
easily handle the case where multiple nodes crash by invoking it once for each
crashed node.

To see how OLV avoids update anomalies of type L1, consider the history
corresponding to type L1, $(w^x[i]; \; w^y[j]; \; Crash^y)$. During normal runtime, after
$w^x[i]; \; w^y[j]$, node x retains the version of p produced by $w^x[i]$. After $Crash^y$, since
the only holder (node y) crashed, node x (the owner node of p), installs the previous
version of p ($v^{-1}(p)$). Thus, no lost updates arise (i.e., w^x is not lost).

Note that this mechanism may introduce additional cases where spurious updates may arise, but these cases are handled by the restart recovery protocols of
Section 17.6.3. This may occur when two loaner nodes alternately update a page,
and then one of these nodes crashes, such as in the following history, where $i, j, k \in p$,
and $owner(p) = x$:

$$w^z[i]; \; w^y[j]; \; w^z[k]; \; Crash^z$$

In this case, the restoration of $v^{-1}(p)$ by the owner results in $w^z[i]$ and $w^y[j]$
being reflected in the recovery post version of p. Of these two writes, $w^z[i]$ is
spurious. However, this does not present any additional problems, since spurious
undos by transactions executing on failed nodes are eliminated with the logging and
restart recovery protocols described in Section 17.4.

17.6.3   Recovering Data in Directory-Based Coherency

In the previous section, we have described how software-based coherency protocols
can be extended to deal with lost update in L1. Here we give general solutions to
deal with lost and spurious updates to data in DBC systems. An important issue
is that in DBC systems, the use of private (nonshared) disks affects the design of
recovery strategies (in contrast with SMPs). To this end, we consider extensions
to the *selective redo* restart recovery scheme [16], originally proposed for handling

```
/*
    Remove from readers and writers of the survivor (s) any pages owned by s
    that were resident on the crashed node. If this results in empty writers
    or readers, then restore the previous version of p at the owner node.
    This is accomplished by setting the mode of GDir to be exclusive.
*/
SurvivorCleanupGDir()
{
      ∀ p ∈ GDir
        if (GDir[p].mode == shared)
            if (CrashedNode ∈ GDir[p].readers {
                Delete(GDir[p].readers,CrashedNode);
                if (GDir[p].readers == ∅)
                    GDir[p].mode = exclusive;
            }
        else if (GDir[p].mode == exclusive)
            if (CrashedNode ∈ GDir[p].writer {
                Delete(GDir[p].writer,CrashedNode);
                GDir[p].mode = exclusive;
            }
}
```

Figure 17.6. Resolving global directory inconsistencies on survivors.

recovery in shared-memory database systems, since it enables independent recovery on survivors. In selective redo, the restart recovery strategy for surviving nodes consists of two basic steps.

1. Each surviving node performs redo for only those data item updates that were made by the local node, but that were exclusively resident on the crashed node.

2. Each surviving node undoes the updates of aborted transactions using the undo information (described in what follows) stored along with each data item.

Selective redo minimizes the number of redos; only updates made by surviving nodes which were present *exclusively* on the crashed node may need redo.

As a result of the first step of the selective redo protocol, all updates made by surviving nodes will be restored. However, the caches of surviving nodes may also contain spurious updates, those made by transactions that were running on crashed nodes. Thus, we need an additional mechanism to identify the *active* data items, that is, data items updated by active transactions, that require undo. This is described earlier in this chapter, which explained how spurious updates on crashed nodes can be masked without requiring access to the crashed node's stable storage. We also discussed additional issues related to recovery on the crashed node. First, we deal with the restoration of lost updates.

Handling Lost Updates in DBC. As Tables 17.1 and 17.2 show, lost updates of type O3 or L1 may arise due to node crashes. We have already shown how OLV can be used to mask lost updates of type L1, thus, in this section, we focus on the resolution of lost updates of type O3. To accomplish this, the directory structure of DBC is used to efficiently support selective redo for surviving nodes. This is illustrated in the RecoverySurvivor() procedure of Figure 17.3. The Survivor-CleanupLDir() routine returns a list of pages that were owned by the crashed node and were locally cached. Since we only need to mask lost updates of type O3, for a specific surviving node, these are the only pages that could possibly need redo. If the CrashPageList is empty, then no redo need be performed.

Note that Figure 17.3 refers to a *RedoCondition*, which is necessary to avoid the redo of pages that already reflect the logged update. For an update U, *Redo-Condition* evaluates to true if either of the following conditions is true: (a) U was performed by a surviving active transaction, and U has not been propagated to the stable database (as may arise due to steal) or (b) U was performed by a committed transaction, and U has not been propagated to the stable database. These conditions can be efficiently evaluated by using techniques and data structures that are already maintained for use in traditional restart recovery [7, 13]. These data structures are used to (a) determine the earliest point in the log to begin forward processing the log, and (b) for a given page, determine whether a particular update needs to be redone.

Handling Spurious Updates with Page Logging. We seek recovery strategies for surviving nodes that are *independent* of crashed node recovery. If the crashed node manages a private disk, surviving nodes must wait for the crashed node to reboot before fetching the undo log records from the crashed node's disk. Moreover, the crashed node may require substantial disk I/O for its own local recovery, causing a bottleneck for access to the crashed node's disk. In loosely coupled systems, one extreme example of recovery delay on the crashed node arises when a node disconnection occurs and surviving nodes lose contact with the crashed node, possibly for hours or days.

Dealing with fine-granularity sharing is another significant challenge, since it allows a single page to contain multiple active updates.

To address these problems, we propose techniques for eliminating spurious updates based on an *undo log shipping* mechanism. Each data page has an associated undo log page. *Whenever a data page containing active data is transferred to another node, the associated undo log page is also transferred.*[5]

For each active data item in the data page, the before image (BI) is stored in

---

[5] Log shipping also has been proposed for other purposes, such as optimizing 2PC commit [1].

the undo log page, as shown in Figure 17.7.[6]. The figure graphically illustrates this data structure and also provides the C language definition of the data structure. Associated with each BI in the log page is the ID (the *tag*) of the node that performed the active update. This undo log page is initialized as follows:

- When a page is first loaded in to the database buffer from disk, the undo log page is initialized. That is, the BI's are assigned to the current values of the data items in the data page, and all Node IDs in the undo log page are assigned to the local node.

- When a page is forced to disk, the undo log page is discarded from volatile memory.

- At commit time, all after images are copied to the corresponding undo log page for subsequent use.

Note that the BI/AI logging technique, and its adaptation to the undo log page, is appropriate when strict two-phase locking is used for writes, where any active data item reflects the updates of at most one transaction, and locks on these data items are not released until transaction commit. This is typically the assumption of commercial database systems. If strict two-phase locking were not used, an active data item could reflect the updates of more than one transaction, and correct recovery would be more complex.

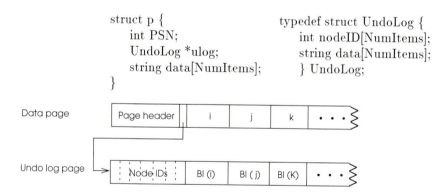

Figure 17.7. Masking Spurious Updates with Page Logging.

Note that to simplify the presentation, the pointer to the undo log page is shown as a field of the data page. To avoid maintaining this pointer in the data page, an alternative representation, which stores the pointer to the undo log page in the directory structure, is also feasible.

---

[6] Note that undo logs also need to be maintained in traditional DBMS that allow buffer steals.

Figure 17.8 shows the pseudo-code for accomplishing the elimination of spurious updates. Pages in either the *LDir* or the *GDir* could contain spurious updates. These pages are examined, and if the updating node (the *Node ID*) was the crashed node, undo is accomplished by assigning the before image (stored in the undo log page) to the data page's data item.

Clearly, the use of the undo log page requires that twice the amount of data is sent between nodes during coherency operations for database pages. However, in many cases, this may be an acceptable trade-off because of the independent recovery of survivor nodes facilitated by log shipping.

```
/*
    Eliminate Spurious Updates.
    Any Active Updates made by the Crashed
    Node are assigned the before image.
*/
EliminateSpuriousUpdates()
{
    ∀ p ∈ (LDir ∪ GDir) {
        ∀ item ∈ p
            if (p->ulog.nodeID[item] == CrashedNode)
                p.data[item] = p->ulog.data[item];
    }
}
```

Figure 17.8. Eliminating Spurious Updates.

Additional Considerations for Recovery on the Crashed Node.   We consider some additional issues related to recovery on the crashed node. These additional issues are related to the maintenance of dirty-page tables (DPTs) on each node. For example, because of the way that the dirty-page table is managed on client and server nodes, pages owned by the crashed node that were not present in the cache of any surviving node may be missed with the basic ARIES restart recovery algorithm. For example, consider page p at server s. Suppose p was updated by a client transaction, then was transferred back to the server's cache after the server's last logged checkpoint, and then the server crashes. This results in a dirty page that (a) was present only in the cache of the server, (b) is not in the crashed server's last checkpointed dirty-page table, and (c) was not updated by the crashed node after the last checkpoint was written.[7]

---

[7] These are essentially the same conditions for which *missing redos* may result in ESM-CS [5] and ARIES/CSA [15], which we discuss in Section 17.7.

To recover these pages in the event of a server crash, *coordinated recovery* [17][8] can be used, where information from the DPTs (dirty-page tables) of all clients are merged at recovery time, in order to determine which pages need redo. Specifically, the protocol involves each remote node sending (to the crashed node) (a) its list of cached pages owned by the crashed node, and (b) all entries in the DPT owned by the crashed node. After this is complete, the crashed node merges these and its own DPT to determine which pages are dirty. In order to support an ARIES style recovery method, these methods for determining which pages are dirty and for determining where to start the redo log scan can be adopted to support IFA.

17.7   RELATED WORK

Directory-based coherency has been implemented in basically two types of database systems, SD (shared-disk) and client-server systems. We cover this work in chronological order, starting with SD systems.

Some of the earliest published work on recovery in SD systems includes Digital Equipment Corporation's recovery in VAXcluster systems [10, 21, 23]. This recovery architecture has shaped the basic strategies for handling issues that arise in many other multiple node recovery systems. For example, in the VAXcluster, each node can manage a lock table for a partition of the database. In the event of a node failure, the strategy for recovering lock tables is as follows: All cluster nodes must complete the recovery of their lock managers before cluster operation can continue. First, a lock manager deallocates all locks acquired on behalf of other nodes. Next, a lock manager reacquires each of the locks it had when the transition began. The net result is to release locks held by a node if that node has left the cluster. This can be viewed as one instance of our more general notion of undo's of changes to the state of data. However, there are at least three significant differences between recovery in a VAXcluster and our recovery approach. The VAXcluster architecture employs a single log (as opposed to multiple local logs), an undo/no-redo recovery strategy (i.e., at commit, force is employed), and prior to migration, a page is forced to the stable database. Even though these polices simplify recovery, they degrade performance because of the disk writes caused by the force policy.

Issues of interest to us have also been examined in [13, 14, 19, 20] where coherency is implemented in software by transferring *pages* between nodes. But there are some significant differences:

- Most of these systems do not support fine-granularity (data item) locking [19, 20]. Instead, page granularity locking is used in conjunction with strict two-phase locking. The main drawback of this approach is the loss of concurrency resulting from page granularity locking.

- The SD proposals that support fine-granularity (data item) locking [12, 14] ensure FA. They can ensure IFA only by performing stable logging to disk prior

---

[8]Note that in this design, both locking and sharing are done at the page level, which restricts concurrency.

to the migration of uncommitted data. Our protocols ensure IFA without this negative performance impact.

Given these differences, in this section, we review the proposals of [12, 14], and consider how the FA ensuring mechanisms defined for these systems can be adapted to achieve IFA. These SD recovery proposals are based on ARIES [13], which uses the repeating history paradigm followed by undos to recover from failures.

The SD system in [14] addresses some of the issues related to the migration of uncommitted data. In order to ensure internode coherency, [14] defines four internode page transfer schemes, two of which allow the migration of uncommitted data, called *fast*, and *superfast* schemes. In the fast scheme, all updates to page p must be stable logged prior to p's migration. This, in conjunction with traditional recovery approaches, satisfies IFA. In the superfast scheme, all updates to page p must be volatile logged prior to p's migration. The superfast scheme does not support IFA, since no provision is made for handling the undo of active updates, performed by transactions running on crashed nodes - necessary in case these active updates had migrated to another node. Similarly, the approach of [12] does not define an undo approach for these cases.

Finally, some client-server systems [18] allow a page to be updated simultaneously by many client nodes (multiple writers). Allowing multiple writers requires that the server eventually merges the updates. The main disadvantage of this approach is that additional bookkeeping must be done in order to track the portions of a page that have been updated by a client and to recover properly from either client or server crashes. For example, to handle recovery properly, servers must remember the current PSN (page sequence number) of p each time p is sent to a client. To handle server crashes, prior to forcing a page to the server's disk, a list of the PSN values that the server remembered is first logged. Thus, allowing clients to simultaneously update a page imposes additional overheads on the run time and the logging system.

For a client-server system allowing multiple simultaneous writers, under some conditions, some of the recovery problems discussed in this chapter can be avoided. For example, if clients only send committed updates back to the server, and the server does not perform updates, uncommitted data will not migrate. However, in the absence of these conditions, uncommitted data will migrate, and additional measures must be employed to ensure IFA. This is necessary if the additional performance that can be derived from relaxing these conditions can be exploited by the application.

17.8 SUMMARY

In this chapter, we have presented protocols for ensuring IFA recovery in DBC systems that allow fine-granularity locking. In contrast with our previous work in the area of recovery in shared-memory database systems [16], in DBC systems, directory recovery must also be addressed, and the fact that software coherency protocols allow for runtime modifications must be exploited to facilitate recovery. In this chapter, we have analyzed the possible directory inconsistencies that may arise in DBC systems due to node crashes, and presented protocols that resolve these inconsistencies. These protocols require no additional run time overheads, directory resolution is performed entirely at recovery time, and no additional logging (beyond what is normally done to ensure FA) is needed.

We have also investigated extensions to coherency that enable independent recovery of surviving nodes. During recovery of the crashed node, transactions executing on survivors can continue to make progress until they need to lock data items owned by the crashed node. We showed how OLV avoids lost updates of type L1. In DBC, OLV is an inexpensive optimization, requiring only that the owner node cache a copy of any page that contains an uncommitted update. We also proposed a novel mechanism for eliminating spurious updates, *undo log shipping*, that has the advantage that communication with the crashed node is not needed during recovery of surviving nodes. By eliminating spurious updates from a surviving node independently of the crashed node, IFA can be ensured, while allowing new transactions to begin on surviving nodes with minimal delay. A by-product of our systematic development of recovery techniques is that it helps to demystify some of the facets of multiple-node recovery.

Some distributed shared-memory architectures enforce sequential consistency [25], whereas others support more relaxed memory consistency models, such as *release consistency* [6] or *lazy release consistency* [9]. Here we have assumed that sequential consistency, which is equivalent to serializability, is the desired correctness. Achieving IFA under a relaxed memory consistency model is worthy of examination.

References

[1] Y. Al-Houmaily and P. Chrysanthis. A Two Phase Commit Optimization for Gigabit-Networked Databases. *Proceedings of the 8th International Conference on Parallel and Distributed Computing Systems (PDCS)*, September 1995.

[2] P. A. Bernstein, V. Hadzilacos, and N. Goodman. *Concurrency Control and Recovery in Database Systems.* Addison-Wesley, Reading, MA, 1987.

[3] I. Censier and P. Feautrier. A New Solution to Coherence Problems in Multi-Cache Systems. *IEEE Transactions on Computers*, 27(12) (1978).

[4] D. Chaiken, C. Fields, K. Kurihara, and A. Agarwal. Directory-Based Cache Coherence in Large-Scale Multiprocessors. *IEEE Computer*, June 1990.

[5] M. Franklin, M. Zwilling, C. Tan, M. Carey, and D. DeWitt. Crash Recovery in Client-Server EXODUS. *Proceedings of the 1992 ACM SIGMOD International Conference on Management of Data*, June 1992.

[6] K. Gharachorloo, D. Lenoski, J. Laudon, P. Gibbons, A. Gupta, and J. Hennessy. Memory Consistency and Event Ordering in Scalable Shared-Memory

Multiprocessors. *Proceedings of the 17th International Symposium on Computer Architecture*, May 1990.

[7] J. Gray and A. Reuter. *Transaction Processing: Concepts and Techniques.* Morgan Kaufmann, 1993.

[8] T. Haerder and A. Reuter. Principles of Transaction-Oriented Database Recovery. *ACM Computing Surveys*, 15(4) (December 1983).

[9] P. Keleher, A. Cox, and W. Zwaenepoel. Lazy Release Consistency for Software Distributed Shared Memory. *Proceedings of the 19th International Symposium on Computer Architecture*, May 1992.

[10] N. Kronenberg, H. Levy, and W. Streker. Vaxclusters: A Closely-Coupled Distributed System. *ACM Transactions on Computer Systems*, 4(2) (May 1986).

[11] K. Li and P. Hudak. Memory Coherence in Shared Virtual Memory Systems. *ACM Transactions on Database Systems*, 7(4) (November 1989).

[12] D. Lomet. Recovery for Shared Disk Systems Using Multiple Redo Logs. *Digital Equipment Cambridge Research Laboratory Technical Report*, No. 4, October 1990.

[13] C. Mohan, D. Haderle, B. Lindsay, H. Pirahesh, and P. Schwarz. ARIES: A Transaction Recovery Method Supporting Fine-Granularity Locking and Partial Rollbacks Using Write-Ahead Logging. *ACM Transactions on Database Systems*, 17(1) (March 1992).

[14] C. Mohan and I. Narang. Recovery and Coherency-Control Protocols for Fast Intersystem Page Transfer and Fine-Granularity Locking in a Shared-Disk Transaction Environment. *Proceedings of the 17th International Conference on Very Large Data Bases*, Vol. 17, 1991.

[15] C. Mohan and I. Narang. ARIES/CSA: A Method for Database Recovery in Client-Server Architectures. *Proceedings of the 1994 ACM SIGMOD International Conference on Management of Data*, Vol. 23, 1994.

[16] L. Molesky and K. Ramamritham. Recovery Protocols for Shared Memory Database Systems. *Proceedings of the 1995 ACM SIGMOD International Conference on Management of Data*, May 1995.

[17] E. Panagos, A. Biliris, H. Jagadish, and R. Rastogi. Client-Based Logging for High Performance Distributed Architectures. *Proceedings of the 13th IEEE Conference on Data Engineering*, 1996.

[18] E. Panagos, A. Biliris, H. Jagadish, and R. Rastogi. Fine-granularity Locking and Client-Based Logging for Distributed Architectures. *Proceedings of the Seventh Conference on Extended Database Technology*, 1996.

[19] E. Rahm. Concurrency and Coherency Control in Database Sharing Systems. *Technical Report, University of Kaiserslautern, Germany,* December 1991.

[20] E. Rahm. Use of Global Extended Memory for Distributed Transaction Processing. *Proceedings of the 4th Int. Workshop on High Performance Transaction Systems, Asilomar, CA.,* September 1991.

[21] T. Rengarajan, P. Spiro, and W. Wright. High Availability Mechanisms of VAX DBMS Software. *Digital Technical Journal,* Vol.8, February 1989.

[22] R. Schlichting and F. Schnieder. Fail-Stop Processors: An Approach to Designing Fault-Tolerant Computing Systems. *ACM Transactions on Computing Systems,* 1(3) (August 1983).

[23] W. Snaman and D. Thiel. The VAX/VMS Distributed Lock Manager. *Digital Technical Journal,* Vol. 5, September 1987.

[24] M. Stumm and S. Zhou. Algorithms Implementing Distributed Shared Memory. *IEEE Computer,* May 1990.

[25] M. Tam. CapNet – Using Gigabit Networks as a High Speed Backplane. *PhD. Thesis, Department of Computer and Information Science, University of Pennsylvania,* 1994.

[26] C. K. Tang. Cache Design in the Tightly Coupled Multiprocessor System. *AFIPS National Computer Conference,* 1976.

Chapter 18

ObjectFlow and Recovery in Workflow Systems

Meichun Hsu and Charly Kleissner

Abstract

A number of business and technical trends have prompted the emergence of a new kind of infrastructure, workflow enabler, that provides a model for business processes, and a foundation on which to build solutions supporting the execution and management of business processes. This chapter provides an introduction to workflow systems, describes an open framework for such systems, and distinguishes between business-process-level recovery and system-level recovery. It positions ObjectFlow, a software product, within this framework to illustrate the concepts.

18.1 INTRODUCTION

A number of business and technical trends of the last few years have attracted researchers and developers to the area of workflow systems. As businesses feel competitive and economic pressures to automate and streamline their operations, they examine their business processes and look to business process reengineering (BPR) practices to provide solutions [9]. Increased adoption of and migration to open systems have created an opportunity for businesses to examine their Information Technology (IT) practices and look for ways to coordinate and automate the flow of work between people and groups in an organization. Improved networking capabilities and widespread deployment and usage of personal computers have enabled knowledge workers as well as clerical workers to be increasingly interconnected. Emergence of industrial strength middleware, for example, open transaction managers, reliable and secure communication and queuing mechanisms, and distributed object technology, enable the construction of workflow systems based on an open architecture. Workflow systems have surfaced as a foundation on which to build solutions supporting the execution and management of business processes.

Workflow systems have a complementary relationship with database systems. The database research community has long pursued the notion of extended transaction models and is exploring the applicability of such models to business processes (also known as "business transactions"). Workflow systems require an infrastructure for reliably capturing the states of business processes and tying together distributed applications, and DBMSs have been found by many to be the most natural choice for this infrastructure. As workflow systems scale to the enterprise level, the requirements on robustness, scalability, and distributability are likened to those required and developed in TP monitors and distributed DBMSs.

Workflow as extended transactions inevitably raises the question of its recovery semantics. Many have argued that the isolation and atomicity properties in the classic transaction model are not practical and cannot be realized in a business process, and other new models must be defined for workflow systems (see, e.g., [21].) On the other hand, a process execution consists of multiple state transitions, each of which must be recoverable despite of system failures once "committed."

We separate the workflow system recovery issue into two levels. The first level deals with business process rollback and recovery on workflow exceptions (e.g., detection of a human error or an unexpected business event). The second level deals with the rollback and recovery of atomic state transitions contained in a process execution to guard such state transitions against system failures. We denote the first type of recovery issue as the business-level recovery, and the second as the system-level recovery.

Section 18.2 describes the flow model, or how business processes are modeled and specified in a workflow system. It formally defines ObjectFlow's flow model. Instead of the ACID property, it discusses the *progress* property as a more relevant business-level property to be associated with a flow model. In particular, ObjectFlow employs the notion of "redo" to model business process recovery.

Section 18.4 describes the logical structure of an open workflow system as a set of components with well-defined interfaces. Within this framework, this section also describes implementation of the ObjectFlow Engine. In particular, it describes distributability and transactional robustness of ObjectFlow and how ObjectFlow defines and implements system-level recovery. Section 18.5 summarizes the chapter and discusses future directions. Although the contents focus on describing the approaches taken in ObjectFlow, we hope to illuminate the basic concepts and rationales behind a workflow system in general.

18.1.1   Introduction to Workflow Computing

The main business problem that a workflow system addresses is to enable flexible and repeatable business process automation and reengineering. A workflow system supports integration of three types of business entities: *processes, organizational re-*

sources, and *business data*. A *process* is a set of activities executed by resources and driven by a set of rules and milestones to achieve specific business goals. Processes range from simple activities (e.g., route a document) to very complex activities (e.g., design an aircraft). Processes might have a very rigid structure that is carefully planned or a very loose structure that allows for ad hoc changes at execution time.

An *organization* is a set of objects containing resources, capabilities, roles, and relationships. Resources have capabilities and assume roles. Processes are sensitive to changes in organizations (e.g., events like business trips and vacations influence execution of processes).

Business data objects are used in processes. Business data range from very simple data items (e.g., records in a file, tuples in a database) to complex work objects (e.g., health records, expense reports, general forms). Changes in data can influence the execution of processes (e.g., conditional routing based on business data contents).

Figure 18.1 shows the life-cycle phases of a typical workflow application. They are iterative in nature to support continuous business process improvements.

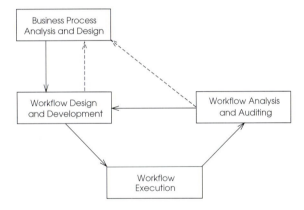

Figure 18.1. Life cycle phase of a workflow.

Workflow application development starts with business process analysis and modeling. This phase provides input for the next phase, "workflow design and development," where a *flow designer* utilizes the output of business process design and, with refinement on data, organization, and process requirements, creates formal executable flow descriptions that are installed into workflow systems. In addition, *application developers* develop new applications or adapt existing applications and integrate them with the workflow system. These applications are to be executed in steps in a flow. Application developers might put an invocation wrapper around legacy applications, thus making it easier for workflow system to invoke them. Wrappers can be normalized using a single methodology like Common Object Request Broker.

During workflow execution, the workflow system notifies appropriate resources to perform tasks in the process. The workflow system gathers the information regarding the execution of processes and the usage of resources. This information is then used by workflow analysis and auditing tools. Administrators manage the daily operations of the business and perform workflow analysis and auditing. They maintain current information on their organization's resources, and determine when to cut over to a new business process. In addition, business analysts can use the history data to optimize the business process. The data gathered during execution may be fed back directly into the business process analysis and design tools or the workflow design and development tools.

There are many business benefits of workflow automation (see, e.g., [11]). First, workflow systems provide independence of applications, business policies, and information flow. Changes in procedures can be made using workflow tools without having to rewrite the applications. Second, workflow automation captures the performance of operational systems, which can be fed back into the analysis and design phase, thus effectively implementing a continuous business process optimization loop. Third, workflow systems provide just-in-time information to the workers and increase the productivity of these workers. They encourage reuse of application components and reduce maintenance costs. Managers spend less time collecting information on the status of processes and resources that is automatically collected by the workflow system. Workflow systems also have the potential to dramatically improve the quality of service with respect to timeliness and accuracy by taking advantage of the state information that is easily accessible to authorized personnel. Finally, workflow supports policy-driven allocation of resources and can therefore adapt dynamically to changing workloads, thus maximizing asset utilization. One must also guard against some pitfalls, such as automating ineffective processes ("paving the cowpath"), automating departments instead of business processes across functions, and overlooking the possible organizational resistance to change.

18.1.2   Evolution of Workflow Systems

The last few years have seen some important changes in the approach to workflow systems. We summarize the evolution of workflow systems by identifying three generations of systems:[1]

First Generation: Homegrown Workflow (–1992). The first generation of workflow systems were monolithic in nature. All information flow (control and data flow) was hard-coded into the applications. These systems were hard to maintain and harder to enhance. Typical examples of this generation are factory automation systems and order-entry systems.

Second Generation: Rudimentary Workflow (1992–1995). The second generation of workflow systems were driven by imaging/document management systems

---

[1][15] offered this notion of three-generation evolution. [6] elaborated the notion further.

or desktop object management systems. The workflow components of these products are usually tightly coupled and not separable from the rest of the product. Typical examples of this generation are off-the-shelf workflow products for object routing, for example, document routing systems (e.g., route design documents), case folder management systems (e.g., handle insurance claims), and smart forms systems (e.g., expense report forms, hiring request forms).

Third Generation: Architected Workflow (1994–). The third generation of workflow systems have generic, open workflow engines that provide an infrastructure for robust production-oriented workflow. Examples of this genre of workflow combine predefined workflow with ad hoc changes, use database and repository technologies for sharing of information, use middleware technology for notification and distribution, and take advantage of object-oriented technologies to provide customization. ObjectFlow is an example of the third generation of workflow systems.[2] Third-generation workflow systems are also referred to as *process managers*.[3]

18.2 THE FLOW MODEL

18.2.1 Flow Definition Model

A *flow* is an abstract, active business object, representing an instance of a business process. It contains nested flows and steps. A step is a primitive unit of processing, and it represents individual business activities required to complete the business process. The *flow procedure* that a flow executes is defined in a flow definition language. To support business processes effectively, a flow definition model needs to offer an intuitive and visually amenable representation of a business process, and its *progress* in execution, to end users. Traditional petri-nets have been used to model office procedures (e.g., see [22, 4, 15]). However, the generality of petri-nets does not lend itself to ease of analysis. Database trigger-based models, such as the ones proposed in [2] embed the relationships among activities in action statements that are associated with database update events, and thus it is difficult to use them to achieve an intuitive understanding of the progression of a business process. [14] contains an extensive review of recent work in the use of high-level petri-nets for process models, and the application of process models to various problem areas.

The flow definition model used in ObjectFlow is a graph-based model and can be seen as a constrained petri-net model. Activities are abstracted as nodes in the graph, and a node is triggered when it receives sufficient signals from its predecessors *and* if certain conditions in the *context* of the flow are satisfied. This approach is very similar to that used in FlowMark [14]. One important characteristic of this flow

---

[2]There are other products that can be argued to be in this space. Xerox's InConcert [18] is among the early ones on the market. IBM's Flow Mark [14] and Action Technology's Action Workflow [3, 19] offer different flow models. All three offer open interfaces to a large extent. REI's Plexus and Reach's Workman have also positioned themselves as workflow enablers.

[3]Gartner's group, in particular, has written about the potential transition from TP monitors to process managers. See, for example, [17].

definition model is that it is possible to rigorously define a notion of progress as the flow executes. We have also generalized the idea of "redo" in the ECHO flow model [8, 17] to accommodate *business process recovery*. "Redo" rolls the current state of the process back to a previous state, effectively undoing part of the progress made by the process. In contrast to compensation transactions ([7]), our model relies on restoring the process state to effect business process recovery.

We have chosen to separate data flow from control flow in our flow definition model, by first focusing on defining the control flow of the business process and then addressing the data flow dimension as data passing relationships between the context data of a flow and the applications that perform the activities. This leads to a simpler representation of the business process. The following concepts are also used in the flow definition model:

Resource. An accountable performer of work. A resource can be a person, a computer process, or machine that plays a role in the workflow system. A resource has a name and various attributes defining its characteristics. Typical examples of these attributes are job code, skill set, organization unit, and availability.

Policy. A set of rules that relate resources to work within a business process. It specifies assignment and authorization of work to resources.

Domain. A unit of autonomy that owns a collection of flow procedures and their instances. Therefore, flows are grouped by domains, and each domain also manages a set of flow procedures installed in the domain. In practical terms, a domain might define the scope of a department or division in an organization. A domain is not defined or limited by networks, processors, or peripherals. A domain can span several processors in a network, and a single processor can host several domains.

In the following three subsections, we introduce our flow definition model in stages:

1. **Noncyclic Model.** This basic model is sufficient for the definition and execution of a noncyclic business process, including conditional branching and parallel work.

2. **Cyclic Model.** We extend the model to accommodate process rollback or rework.

3. Complex Flow Model. We refine the node types in the base model to allow nested subflows, iteration and dynamic fanout in a flow procedure.

4. **Execution Control.** We describe how the model accommodates run-time exceptions.

To illustrate the flow definition model, we use a patient care process in a hospital. A synopsis of the example is described in what follows (see Figures 18.2 and 18.3):[4]

---
[4]This example is based on a design by Keith Bartell.

A patient enters the hospital and registers with an admitting nurse (the Register step). The doctor examines the patient and orders some tests (the Exam step). Each test is carried out by hospital personnel as a step. On completion of all prescribed tests, the doctor analyzes the test results (the Analysis step) and determines if the patient needs to be hospitalized (the InPatient nested flow), treated as an outpatient (the OutPatient nested flow), or discharged (the Case_Closed step). If the patient goes through inpatient treatment, then at the end of inpatient care, a decision is made whether to continue the patient as an outpatient. If the patient goes through the outpatient treatment, then at the end of outpatient care, a decision is made whether to reexamine the patient (back to the Exam step) or to be discharged (to the CaseClosed step).

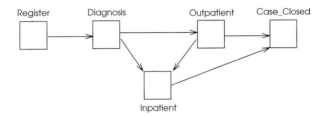

Figure 18.2. The patient care mainflow.

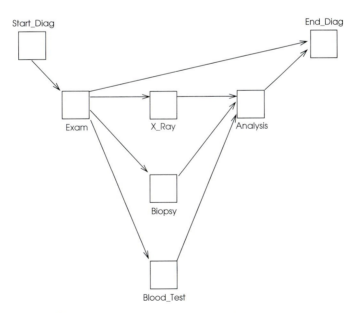

Figure 18.3. The diagnosis subflow.

18.2.2   Noncyclic Flows

A flow procedure consists of a set of nodes that represents individual business activities and a set of arcs, representing signals among the nodes. Each node in a flow procedure is annotated with a trigger expression.[5] The trigger defines the condition required to fire the node upon receiving a signal from another node. Each flow procedure has exactly one start node and one end node. When a flow is instantiated, its start node is triggered. When the end node of a flow is triggered, the flow terminates.

Definition 1.   *A noncyclic flow procedure g is a 4-tuple* $\langle N, A, D, T \rangle$, *where*

- $N = \{n_1, n_2, ...\}$ is a set of nodes s.t. there is a distinct *start node*, denoted as *startnode*, and an *end node*, denoted as *endnode*;

- $A = \{a_1, a_2, ...\}$ is a set of arcs of the form $n_i \rightarrow n_j n_i \neq endnode$, and $n_j \neq startnode$, and for all n, there is a path from startnode to n, and there is a path from n to *endnode*; and the graph $\langle N, A \rangle$ is acyclic. We use α_g to denote the transitive reduction of $\langle N, A \rangle$. (Terminology: Given an arc $a = n_i \rightarrow n_j, n_i$ is the *origin* of a, n_j the *target* of a, a is an *output arc* of n_i, and an *input arc* of n_j.)

- $D = \{d_1, d_2, ...\}$ is a set of data elements whose values may be set or modified during flow execution. Each data element d is associated with a value domain $DOM(d)$.

- $T = \{T(n_1), T(n_2), ...\}$ is a set of *triggers*, one for each node $n \in N$. $T(n)$ is a logical expression over D and A_n, where $A_n \subset A$ is the set of input arcs of node n.

Example.   We recast the Diagnosis flow procedure shown in Figure 18.4 in the preceding definition as follows:

- ◇ N: {StartDiag, Exam, XRay, Biopsy, BloodTest, Analysis, EndDiag}, where the start node is StartDiag and the end node is EndDiag

- ◇ A: {StartDiag → Exam, Exam → EndDiag, Exam → XRay, Exam → Biopsy, Exam → BloodTest, XRay → Analysis, Biopsy → Analysis, BloodTest → Analysis, Analysis → EndDiag}

- ◇ D: {NeedBloodTest: Boolean, NeedXRay: Boolean, NeedBiopsy: Boolean}

- ◇ T(Exam): TRUE

---

[5]The syntax of ObjectFlow's flow definition language decomposes the trigger expression into two components: a router and an in-trigger. The router of a node specifies conditionals that dictate whether a follow-on node needs to be evaluated when this node terminates; the in-trigger of a node specifies the condition required for the node to fire on being evaluated. This syntactic difference is not discussed further in this chapter.

◇ $T(\text{XRay})$: NeedXRay

◇ $T(\text{Biopsy})$: NeedBiopsy

◇ $T(\text{BloodTest})$: NeedBloodTest

◇ $T(\text{Analysis})$: (NeedXRay $\Rightarrow$ XRay $\rightarrow$ Analysis) AND (NeedBiopsy $\Rightarrow$ Biopsy $\rightarrow$ Analysis) AND (NeedBloodTest $\Rightarrow$ BloodTest $\rightarrow$ Analysis)

◇ $T(\text{EndDialog})$: (NeedBloodTest OR NeedXRay OR NeedBiopsy) =¿ (Analysis $\rightarrow$ EndDiag)

Execution Semantics. A noncyclic flow procedure $g = \langle N, A, D, T \rangle$ is executed according to the semantics defined as follows.

◇ *Flow State.* A flow is created by an instantiation request. The instantiation request provides the initial data values for data items in D. In addition, the flow contains the following state variables: binary node states, *fired* (TRUE) or *not fired* (FALSE), for each node n in N and binary arc states, *signaled* (TRUE) or *not signaled* (FALSE), for each arc a in A. All node states are initialized to not fired; all arc states are initialized to not signaled.

◇ A flow instantiation request is valid if, for every node n targeted by an output arc of the start node, node n's trigger $T(n)$ can be evaluated assuming that all output arcs of the start node are signaled . (A trigger cannot be evaluated if its value is unknown due to references to data items that have not received values). If the instantiation request is valid, a flow is created and it

   o fires the start node by setting its state to be fired,

   o sets all output arcs of the start node to be signaled,

   o for every node n targeted by an output arc of the start node, node n is fired if its trigger is evaluated to be TRUE. When a node is fired, a unique fire-instance identifier is assigned.

Otherwise, the instantiation request is rejected and the flow is not created.

◇ **Processing Event**. The instantiated flow now goes through a *node-termination event* processing loop. The event comes from the agent that has performed the activities that correspond to the fired node. The event includes updates to data items in D. On receiving a node-termination event for node n, the flow validates the event. The event is valid if

   ◇ node n is in the fired state, and the event identifies a current fire-instance identifier for node n (i.e., the event is not a stale event);

   ◇ for each output arc a of n, let nl denote the target of a. Then nl's trigger can be evaluated assuming the updates to D are carried out.

If the event is valid then the flow processes the event as follows:

- mark the current fire instance of node n as stale
- set all output arcs of node n to be signaled
- apply updates to data items in D
- for every node nl targeted by an output arc of n, node nl is fired if it is currently *not fired* and if its trigger is evaluated to TRUE

Otherwise the event is rejected.

◇ **Termination**. If any of the node nl being fired during an event processing is the end node, then the flow terminates.

We illustrate trigger evaluation as follows.

Example of EvalT(). Consider the Diagnosis flow. Assume that the flow state is such that,

◇ NeedXRay = NeedBiopsy = TRUE

◇ NeedBloodTest = FALSE

◇ NodeState[StartDiag] = NodeState[Exam] = NodeState[XRay] = NodeState[Biopsy] = fired

◇ NodeState[BloodTest] = not fired

◇ ArcState[XRay $\rightarrow$ Analysis] = TRUE

◇ ArcState[Biopsy $\rightarrow$ Analysis] = ArcState[BloodTest $\rightarrow$ Analysis] = FALSE

Then EvalT(Analysis) = FALSE, since ArcState[Biopsy $\rightarrow$ Analysis] = FALSE

Now assume that Biopsy has just terminated. Then

◇ ArcState[Biopsy $\rightarrow$ Analysis] = TRUE,

which in turn allows EvalT(Analysis) = TRUE, and therefore the node Analysis fires.

The Progress Property. The noncyclic model allows us to rigorously assert a fundamental property for flows, the *progress* property. Progress is one of the key notions germane to a business process. In contrast, the classic $ACID$ property has proven to be difficult to apply directly in business processes, although business processes and extended transactions have many similarities (e.g., see [5, 13].)

A node in a noncyclic flow fires at most once. This follows directly from the execution semantics, which says that a node whose state is Fired cannot be fired even if additional input signals have been received.

Definition 2. A node in a noncyclic flow is *expired* if it will never fire.

A node n in a noncyclic flow is expired if it is not fired and $\forall n' s.t. n' \rightarrow n \in A, n'$ *is either terminated or expired*. This follows because the noncyclic flow procedure is acyclic and a node cannot fire unless it can receive at least a signal on its input arc.

Definition 3. The *position* of a flow at time t, denoted as $P(t)$, consists of the set of nodes that are terminated, expired, or active.

Intuitively, $P(t_1) \subseteq P(t_2)$ implies that the flow execution has advanced in some way from t_1 to t_2, as the set of nodes for which the state are known has increased in size.

Definition 4. A flow execution is said to satisfy the *progress property* if for all time t_1 and t_2 during its execution, if $t_1 < t_2$, then $P(t_1) \subseteq P(t_2)$.

Proposition: *The execution of a noncyclic flow satisfies the progress property. This follows from the previous discussions and the fact that every node-termination event can only produce knowledge that adds to the position, and cannot possibly subtract from the current position.*

Other Properties. Additional properties can be defined for flows. We informally describe some of them in what follows.

- *Termination*: A flow procedure is said to satisfy the termination property if the end node will eventually be triggered. That is, the flow will not "hang."

- *Precedence Preserving*: A flow procedure is said to be precedence preserving if the node firing sequence is compatible with α.

The noncyclic flow execution does not guarantee either one of these two properties. The conditions under which a noncyclic flow execution will satisfy these properties are beyond the scope of this chapter.[6]

---

[6] In particular, the ECHO flow model satisfies both the termination and precedence preserving property. It is a refinement of the flow model described in this chapter.

18.2.3   Cyclic Flows, or Conditional Rollback

Business processes often encounter situations that require revisiting previously terminated or expired nodes. This requirement is modeled by adding a set of backward arcs to our noncyclic flow procedure model.

Definition 5. *A cyclic flow procedure* g *is a 6-tuple* $\langle N, A, D, T, A_{bwd}, T_{bwd} \rangle$, *where* $N, A, D, and T$ *are as defined in noncyclic flows, and*

- $A_{bwd} = \{b_1, b_2, ...\}$ is a set of *backward arcs* s.t. b_i is not in the transitive closure of the graph $\langle N, A \rangle$ (recall that the graph $\langle N, A \rangle$ is acyclic). *Restrictions:* Let $b_i = n_j \to n_i$ be a backward arc. We require that all nodes that are ordered after n_i in α must also be ordered with n_j, and all nodes that are ordered before n_j in α must also be ordered with n_i (this essentially states that the region covered by the backward movement must be isolated).

- $T_b wd = \{T_b(n_1), T_b(n_2), ...\}$ is a set of *backward routers*, one for each node. $T_b(n)$, for a node n, is a *list of routing conditions* $tb_1, tb_2, ...$, each of which associates a backward output arc of the node n with a logical expression over D. Let C denote the set of all logical expressions over D. Thus, we have tb: $A_{bwd} \to C$. *Restrictions:* If a node has multiple backward output arcs, the routing conditions associated with these backward arcs must be such that at most one of them can be true when the node terminates during run time.

Example. Consider the PatientCare flow shown in Figure 18.3. All arcs in the flow are forward arcs except for the arc *Outpatient* $\to$ *Diagnosis*. The backward router of the Outpatient node is:

$$\{tb_{Outpatient \to Diagnosis}: \text{NeedsReexamination}\}$$

where "NeedsReexamination" is a Boolean datum. $\square$

For a cyclic flow procedure, when a node terminates, if the routing condition for a backward arc is evaluated to true, then the flow state must be reset. The execution semantics shown before for noncyclic flows is extended to handle this possibility. We extend the execution semantics with the following procedures to handle backward events:

$\Diamond$ *Process Backward Event:* On receiving a *node-termination event* for node n, if the node-termination event results in a backward arc $n \to n_1$ being selected, then the flow validates the event (i.e., check that the event is not a stale event).

$\Diamond$ If the event is valid, then the flow processes the event as follows:

- o mark the current fire instance of node n as stale
- o for all nodes n_2 s.t. $n_1 \, \alpha = n_2 \, \alpha = n$, if NodeState[$n_2$] = TRUE, then reset its node state and its output arc states to FALSE

∘ apply updates to data items in D

◇ Otherwise, the event is rejected.

The model does not trigger *compensation actions* [7] as a node's state is restored from fired to not fired. The notion of compensation will be investigated in application contexts to determine its applicability.

Execution of a noncyclic flow procedure does not guarantee the progress property. When a rollback event is processed, nodes that were previously fired or expired may be reset to unknown again, thus violating the progress definition. However, if one segments the execution such that each occurrence of a regression request starts a new segment of execution, then each segment itself is progress-preserving. We have defined a notion of *virtual execution history* (the detail is beyond the scope of this chapter) that essentially "erases" the part of the execution history that has been rolled back by the regression movement of the flow. When a flow terminates, the virtual execution history shows a flow that executes from the start node, and is progress-preserving.

18.3   Nested and Dynamic Subflows

18.3.1   Primitive Versus Compound Nodes

A node in our basic model is further refined into node types. These refinements extend the basic execution semantics specified in our abstract model in a straightforward manner. The primitive node type is a step node or a milestone node. A step node is directly linked to a business activity. A step-node-termination event must be reported before the node is terminated. A milestone node is a control node that does not require external execution of a business activity, but is simply there to provide more structure to the flow layout. A milestone node is terminated on trigger and its routing conditions evaluated immediately.

A subflow node is a compound node. It is a node that is linked to a subflow procedure defined within the flow. When a subflow node n is triggered in a flow f, f instantiates a subflow f_s, and f_s executes the subflow procedure the same way a flow executes a main flow procedure. In the simplest case, f_s shares all the data contained in f. When the end node of the subflow procedure is triggered, f_s stops, and the subflow node n in f terminates.[7]

Example. In the PatientCare flow shown in Figure 18.3, the Diagnosis and the Inpatient nodes are subflow nodes. The subflow procedure corresponding to the Diagnosis node is shown in Figure 18.4. □

Dynamic Subflow. A dynamic subflow node is a special type of compound node which allows for additional specification of iteration (sequentially spawning multiple instances) and fanout (concurrently spawning multiple instances). The exact

---

[7][10] describes the nested execution model in more detail.

dimension of iteration or fanout can be evaluated or controlled during execution time.

Iteration. When a dynamic iterative subflow node n is triggered, a subflow f_1 is instantiated that executes the appropriate subflow procedure. When f_1 stops, if the condition for exiting the iteration has been satisfied, then node n terminates and the parent flow proceeds as usual. Otherwise, another subflow f_2 is instantiated to execute the same subflow procedure again, and node n remains active. Note that the dynamic iterative subflow node is fundamentally different from the notion of flow regression or rollback explained previously.

Fanout. Similarly, when a dynamic fanout subflow node n is triggered, a number of subflows f_1, f_2, ... , f_m are instantiated concurrently. Each of these subflows executes the same subflow procedure. Whenever a subflow f_i stops, if a completion rule of node n is now satisfied, then node n is terminated and the parent flow proceeds as usual. Otherwise, node n remains active.

In essence, a simple subflow node embeds a single subbusiness process. A dynamic subflow node embeds multiple (0 to n) subbusiness processes. From the recovery point of view, each subflow can have its own "redo" arcs defined. During run time, each instance of the subbusiness process may cause a "redo" arc to be activated, and the state of that subprocess instance is recovered in a similar manner, as described in the case of a main flow.

18.3.2   Applications, Data Flow, and Data Recovery

A step node of a flow procedure is linked to a business activity that is typically carried out by some application. The flow definition model contains simple primitives for describing the activity to be performed. This includes an identity of the application object, and the data to be passed back and forth.

Data needed to locate and invoke the application object are carried in the flow as the context data. Applications participating in a business process use the flow object as the repository to obtain input data from the upstream applications, and to store the output data to be passed to the downstream applications. To the applications, the flow's context data area is a bulletin board with which they communicate with each other without a need for direct communication channels among themselves.

The input and output data specification for each step node application also defines the potential change in the *data state* of the flow. When a step node terminates, the termination event also reports updates in the data elements. On invocation of a "redo" arc, therefore, the data state also needs to be recovered. The updates performed by the intervening nodes are "rolled back" and the data values are restored to be those at the start of the node to be redone.[8]

---

[8] Data recovery was not supported in DWA V1.0 or ObjectFlow V1.0; however, ObjectFlow keeps the new data states at each state transition of the flow in the flow history database, and these data states can be used to recover the data state on a "redo" occurrence.

18.3.3   Execution Control

A set of flow manipulation primitives is provided in our flow model to accommodate actions resulting from unplanned conditions. They either temporarily alter the prescribed course of execution (i.e., temporarily adding arcs and overriding the trigger and backward router specifications) or they alter the flow procedure itself.

Change Course. On submitting a node-termination event for node n, the agent can optionally specify a command to change course to a different node n_1. The effect is as if an arc $n \rightarrow n_1$ has been temporarily inserted (if not already existent) in the graph, and the effect depends on the intention of the change:

1. *Forward*: This requires that n *alpha* n_1, and it results in a trigger $T(n_1) :=$ TRUE to be temporarily inserted. All other output arcs of n are temporarily ignored. This action "fast forwards" the progress. The progress property is not violated.

2. *Rollback*: This requires that n_1 α n, and it results in a backward arc and a backward router $T_b(n) := \{tb_{n \rightarrow n_1}: \text{TRUE}\}$ to be temporarily inserted. This is treated as a backward movement. The restrictions on the use of backward arcs apply. Like the backward arc activation, this use of the Change Course primitive is generally nonprogress-preserving. Jump: This generates the same effect as Forward; however, it is generally not progress-preserving, and is primarily designed to jump to a currently inactive part of the graph that handles exceptions.

Modify Flow Procedure by Dynamically Extending a Procedure. On submitting a node-termination event for node n, the agent can optionally specify a command to chain a new node n_1 right after n. The effect is that the flow procedure for the flow is altered as follows:

1. Add a new arc $n \rightarrow n_1$

2. $T(n_1) := \text{TRUE}$; {new node is triggered by n.}

3. For all output arcs of n of the form $n \rightarrow n_2$ in the original graph, replace it with $n_1 \rightarrow n_2$ and replace all references to n in the arc expressions of n_2's trigger expressions to refer to n_1 instead of n.

The chain command is most useful when the sequence of the activities within a flow is not fully understood prior to flow execution. The flow procedure may start out with a single node n in between the start and end nodes. When an agent terminates node n, it uses the chain command to add the next node in sequence, thus developing a flow procedure dynamically.

Asynchronous Exceptions. Asynchronous exceptions can occur at any point in the normal course of a flow (but typically do not occur). For example, a patient may decide to transfer to another hospital half way through his normal course of patient care flow. Although it is difficult to predict when and whether this would occur, it is possible to plan the procedure (e.g., a patient transfer subflow) to be taken on occurrence of the exception condition. This part of the procedure can be included as an additional path in the flow procedure preceded with a milestone node whose trigger is defined as the condition under which this procedure is to be activated. An agent performs the following on detecting the exception condition to transfer control to the exception handling path:

1. Abort active node(s) in the normal flow.

2. Use the *Change Course-Jump* primitive discussed previously and target it at the milestone node associated with the exception handling procedure. This causes the exception handling path to be activated.

18.3.4   Role Resolution

The flow model contains primitives that authorize operations on a node in a flow procedure to a *role*. Resources that satisfy the specification of the role can operate on the node. This authorization process is called *role resolution*.

Example. In the Diagnosis flow procedure shown in Figure 18.4, the node Exam is authorized to a role Doctor. A rule that defines the role Doctor to be anyone whose JobCode is 400 has also been specified in the flow procedure. During flow execution, if a resource x requests to execute the node Exam, the request is granted only if x's job code is 400. □

In ObjectFlow, the attributes used to specify the role resolution rules are customizable. For example, an organization may have Skill and ManagerName as attributes for the role resolution, but not JobCode.

18.4   STRUCTURE AND IMPLEMENTATION OF OBJECTFLOW

To support third-generation workflow applications, a workflow enabler ought to open the specifications of application programming interfaces, flow definition languages, data schemas, and protocols in order to allow integration of application development and execution environments and tools. The workflow enabler needs to support atomicity and durability of well-defined state transitions in a flow. Furthermore, it needs to support transactional consistency when such an atomic state transition is integrated with production data. This section defines the client-server structure of a workflow system and the various components comprising a workflow enabler. It also describes the implementation of ObjectFlow–its system configuration and how system-level recovery for atomic state transitions of workflow is accomplished.

18.4.1 Structure of a Workflow System

Figure 18.4 shows the structure of ObjectFlow, which was designed to meet the earlier requirements.[9].

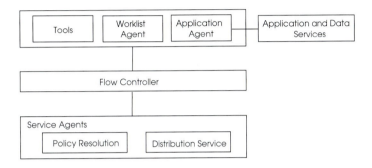

Figure 18.4. Structure of a Workflow system.

The flow controller provides services for defining, creating, executing, and monitoring business processes. It manages installed flow descriptions, active flows, and histories; it enforces constraints and policies, handles exceptions, and pushes flows forward until proper termination; it offers these services to flow agents (see what follows) via application programming interfaces.

Flow agents are customizable clients to the flow controller on behalf of resources. Flow agents integrate the flow controller with end-user tools and environments. Flow agents can be thought of as the "glueware" of the workflow system: Application- or domain-specific flow agents can be plugged in to work with the flow controller and create a variety of workflow environments. We distinguish between two classes of agents: worklist agents and application agents.

Worklist agents provide work notification to resources. They provide views on active flows and steps waiting to be performed and allow users to select work. They can automatically invoke application agents. Workflow system for knowledge workers implement flexible worklist agents that give the worker the freedom to choose the workitems to work on. More rudimentary worklist agents might display only one workitem at a time. PDAs might integrate the personal work-to-do lists with workitems that the flow controller pushes. In manufacturing applications, the worklist agent might execute the workitems according to specified policies without human intervention.

Application agents provide a step execution environment. They are invoked by a resource to execute a step, or are automatically invoked by a worklist agent.

---

[9]This structure is defined in the Distributed Workflow Architecture ([12]). The architecture provides a model, a specification, and common terminology for workflow management products. The flow controller service interface is specified using CORBA's interface definition language ([1]). ObjectFlow conforms to this architecture.

Application agents might rely on other services (e.g., data management services) to provide additional data to users. They may invoke applications. Applications are treated as modules that can be modified, replaced, or reused.

Some workflow systems require an integrated view of data managed by a document management service and data managed by the flow controller. The application agent is chartered to retrieve workflow data and object data and presents both by means of an integrated user interface.

Tools offer user interfaces and utilities for flow development and management. They may be integrated with other desktop utilities and development environments. Examples of tools are workflow designer tools (e.g., ObjectFlow's Designer), workflow inspection tools (e.g., ObjectFlow's Inspector), and workflow simulation tools.

Service agents extend the flow services provided by the flow controller. Examples of service agents are policy resolution service and distribution service.

18.4.2   Workflow Execution Framework

The flow controller component implements the domain and the flow object. Resources are accountable participants in a flow, and an agent is an authenticatable representative of a resource. The agent, domain, and flow objects interact according to a workflow execution framework:

1. The agent identifies itself to a flow control domain.

2. The agent requests that a flow be instantiated in that domain.

3. A flow object is created that executes a flow procedure already defined to (i.e., installed in) the flow control domain; as the flow executes, it fires its nodes according to the procedure description; fired nodes (i.e., steps) are active in the flow.

4. A participating agent obtains a list of (active) flows and steps in that domain that are of interest to the resource represented by it, this list is called a *worklist*

5. The agent selects an activity from the worklist to work on.

6. The agent requests for information about the flow from the flow object; the request is granted only if the resource is authorized to perform the work corresponding to the node.

7. The agent performs the work, possibly launching an application program and passing relevant flow data to and from the application.

8. The agent posts a step-termination event (with flow data updates) to the flow, or posts exception events and requests for exception handling;

9. The flow continues its execution, firing nodes and handling events, until it reaches the end of the flow procedure, at which point it terminates.

An agent can operate on a step or flow only if the resource on whose behalf the agent is making requests satisfies the specification for the role authorized to the node. The organization database is external to a flow control domain. A flow control domain must be able to access an organization database in order to perform role resolution; an organization database may be used for role resolution in multiple flow control domains.

An agent, on selecting a step to work on, can obtain the step descriptions associated with the node and invoke the application directly on behalf of the resource. Note that to the application object, the identity of the invoker is the resource whom the agent represents, not the flow control domain. Agents with generic worklist handling and application object invocation capabilities (e.g., via CORBA, Microsoft's OLE2), combined with a flow control domain from which the agents obtain the context data needed to invoke the application objects, allow a business process to be configured and reconfigured from a set of resources and application objects without extensive development effort.

18.4.3   API and Distributability

The ObjectFlow Engine implements the architected ObjectFlow APIs. The flow agents (clients) create flows and execute steps by invoking the APIs. The ObjectFlow API is specified as the interface definitions of the ObjectFlow object classes, and is implemented as a standard C binding of the definitions. Each object class corresponds to a CORBA *interface*. There are three primary object classes: Domain, Work (flow and step), and Worklist.

By leveraging on the CORBA service, the flow agent (the client) can be remote from the Engine code. In the current design, the CORBA name service infrastructure is used by a flow agent to locate, and to connect to a server for a Domain object. This connection then allows the flow agent to operate on the Work objects and the Worklist objects within the domain. Direct connection between a flow agent and a domain (and all work and worklist objects in that domain) across any distance accessible to a CORBA service is possible with this design. The current design also enables the client to reside on any client platform that can access the CORBA service.

18.4.4   Atomic State Transitions and System Recovery

The ObjectFlow Engine is expected to become part of the "middle-ware" layer. Layering on standard components and becoming a standard service for higher-level tools and applications was a main goal of its design.

The ObjectFlow Engine is a client of the DBMS that stores the work flow information. The engine instances are expected to be distributed clients of the DBMS. The ObjectFlow Engine design relies on the DBMS to maintain any persistent state. This allows an ObjectFlow Engine instance to appear stateless during failure and recovery situations.

The design chosen uses transactional semantics and a database to provide atomicity of flow state changes and durability of the recorded states across failures. Each API has a well-defined effect on the persistent state of the engine. If an API can change the persistent state, then its effect is atomic - the call either succeeds and all its effect is made persistent, or none of its effect is captured.

ObjectFlow defines flow state transitions at the point of *open* and *close* API calls. When a step in a flow is opened, the flow transitions to a "locked" state, where the opened step owns the lock.[10] If the *open-step* API call succeeds, then the step is opened (by the identifiedy agent) and this fact is securely captured. If the API call fails, then the step is not opened and the flow does not have a transition.

After a step (or a flow) is opened, the agent performs additional API calls to read and update the data elements, read and update the states of the step and the flow, as well as issuing commands such as execution control commands. However, effects of all these calls are only captured temporarily in the engine. When a step in a flow is closed, the flow transitions to a new flow state with the step node marked as fired and the data elements updated; any additional actions and commands that were issued during the time when the step was open are also captured and processed. The engine also triggers the firing of subsequent nodes or carrying out any exception detection and handling. If the *close-step* API call succeeds, then all these effects are made in an atomic fashion to the flow state, and they are made secured. If this API call fails, then none of the effects is captured or made durable, and the flow essentially remains at the state when the step was opened.

In the engine implementation, SQL Begin and Commit or Rollback Transaction requests are used to ensure that the open and close actions are atomic. All user API interaction between an open and a subsequent close is volatile. The only persistent record is made within the transaction that bounds the close activity.

Figure 18.5 shows three different configurations supported by the ObjectFlow Engine.

1. In Configuration 1, the ObjectFlow Engine and the active agent (i.e., an application processing a step of a work flow) are in the same processor. The database management system would be on a server system. Using the Object Request Broker (ORB) interface, even though the active agent and the engine are in the same processor, they would be in different processes. The alternative is to allow the interface to be linked directly, which allows the engine to be packaged as a Dynamic Link Library on the client platform.

2. In Configuration 2, the active agent is in a client processor, and communicates with the ObjectFlow Engine through the Object Request Broker. The

    ObjectFlow Engine is on the same processor as the DBMS. The ObjectFlow Engine's interface with the DBMS is a standard client-server interface, so the placement of the engine is one of convenience, rather than structure.

---

[10] A lock on a flow is a semantic lock at the flow model level and is not the same as a lock used in the underlying database systems to perform concurrency control. Additional APIs are provided to authorized users to explicitly unlock a locked flow should the lock be held for too long.

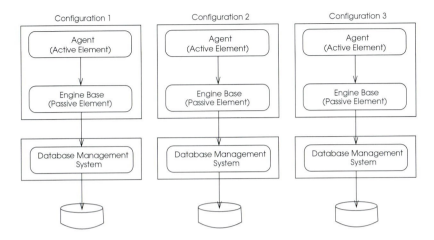

Figure 18.5. System configurations.

3. In Configuration 3, the active agent, the ObjectFlow Engine, and the DBMS all exist on different processors.

18.5   CONCLUSIONS

Many believe that workflow computing represents a major shift in the computing paradigm. Through intelligent process models and tools, it attempts to narrow the gap between services offered by conventional data processing and those needed by business end users in a competitive world.

The design and implementation of ObjectFlow kept a focus on a common code base for the ObjectFlow Engine and ObjectFlow Tool set, and has resulted in a true system service in support of business process engineering. The system structure is open and extensible. The flow model is rigorous, intuitive, and flexible. Additional business rules can be first added as plug-in service agents, and then migrated to the base engine.

This chapter provides a general description of ObjectFlow and discusses the recovery issue in workflow systems. It distinguishes between business process recovery and system recovery, and discusses how ObjectFlow's flow model and implementation address these issues.

ObjectFlow can be extended in many dimensions. Along the recovery dimension, the business process recovery semantics can be refined, based on deployment experience, to capture more semantics (e.g., whether compensation actions up one "redo" should be supported). If execution control commands such as "change course" or "add new step" has been used in a flow, and it encounters a "redo" invocation further down the road, whether those previous changes to the flow map should be maintained or forgotten needs to be looked at.[11] More efficient techniques to implement process rollback will also be very useful. For example, the current implementation, which relies on retrieving information in the history database to support data state rollback, may also need to be refined to avoid the need to keep a very large history database. Finally, an elegant and efficient approach to allow a workflow state transition to be atomically committed together with commit of applications is required. In this regard, the use of an open transaction manager will be required for a general solution, and a capability is needed to allow the application agent to drive the workflow engine and the application in committing together. Many challenging issues remain in the design and implementation of these services.

Acknowledgments

This chapter reflects the work of many people. We like to thank all members of the ObjectFlow implementation teams for pioneering and developing these concepts and for implementing ObjectFlow. We want to thank Dieter Gawlick for promoting and supporting this project for many years, and Barry Rubinson for helping to position and deliver the product. We also wish to thank team members of the ECHO project, the Team Route project, and the WFM project for their invaluable insights in workflow requirements that lead to ObjectFlow's architecture and model.

References

[1] The Common Object Request Broker: Architecture and Specification, OMG Document Number 93.xx.yy, Revision 1.2, Draft, December 1993.

[2] Organizing Long-running Activities with Triggers and Transactions, *Proc. ACM SIGMOD*, May 1990.

[3] Dunham R., Business Design Technology Software Development For Customer Satisfaction, *Proc. 24th Annual Hawaii International Conference on Systems Sciences*, 1991.

[4] De Antonellis V., and Zonta B., Modelling Events in Data Base Applications Design, *Proc. Intl. VLDB Conf.*, 1981.

[5] Elmagarmid A.K., Editor, Database Transaction Models for Advanced Applications, Morgan Kaufmann Publishers, 1992.

[6] Foster D., EDI, E-mail, and Workflow Automation, EDI World, April 1993.

[7] Garcia-Molina H., Salem K., Sagas, *Proc. ACM SIGMOD Conf.*, May 1987.

[8] Grunbauer D., General Descriptions: Case Plan Model, ECHO document suite Reference No. 1.2.5.3.1.7, Draft 1.10, Digital Equipment Corporation, October 1992.

---

[11] See, for example, [20], which studies the dynamic change control in detail.

[9] Hammer M., and Champy J., Reengineering the Corporation, A Manifesto for Business Revolution, HarperBusiness, Harper Collins Publishers, 1993.

[10] Hsu M., Ghoneimy A., Kleissner K., An Execution Model for an Activity Management System, presented at *Workshop on High Performance Transaction Systems*, September 1991.

[11] Hales K., Lavery M., Workflow Management Software: The Business Opportunity, Published by Ovum Ltd. 1991.

[12] Hsu M., Distributed Workflow Architecture: System Model, Digital Equipment Corporation, December 1992.

[13] Hsu M., Editor, *IEEE Data Engineering, Special Issue on Workflow and Extended Transaction Systems*, June 1993.

[14] Leymann F., Altenhuber W., Managing Business Processes As Information Resource, *ITL IRM Conference*, October 1993 (also to appear in IBM Systems Journal).

[15] Lin W.K., Ries D.R., Blaustein B.T, Chilenskas R.M., Office Procedures as a distributed database application, *Proc. Workshop on Databases for Business and Office Applications*, ACM-SIGMOD Database Week, 1983.

[16] McCarthy J.C., and Bluestein W.M., Workflow's Progress, *The Computing Strategy Report*, 8(12), Forrester Research, Inc., October 1991.

[17] Process Managers: Flow-Control Requirements, Gartner Group, February, 1994.

[18] McCarthy D.R., Sarin S.K., Workflow and Transactions in InConcert, *IEEE Data Engineering*, 16(2) (June 1993).

[19] Medina-Mora R., Wong H.T., Flores P., ActionWorflow as the Enterprise Integration Technology, *IEEE Data Engineering*, 16(2) (June 1993).

[20] Reichert M., Perter, D., ADEPT - Supporting Dynamic Changes of Workflows Without Losing Control. Submitted for publication.

[21] Reuter, A., Schwenkreis. F. Con Tracts - A Low-Level Mechanism for Building General-Purpose Workflow Management Systems. In: *IEEE Data Engineering, Special Issue on Workflow Systems*, 18(1), (1995)

[22] Zisman M.D., Use of Production Systems for Modelling Asynchronous, Concurrent Processes, in Pattern Directed Inference Systems, Waterman and Hayes-Roth (eds.), Academic Press, 1978.

Chapter 19

The Case for Safe RAM

George Copeland, Tom Keller, Ravi Krishnamurthy, and Mark Smith

Abstract

Battery-backed-up $DRAM$ memories can be configured today to be almost as reliable as disk. This chapter argues that it is cost-effective to employ Safe RAM in computer systems that support reliable updates. Safe RAM allows systems that support reliable updates, such as database and transaction processing systems, to perform more efficiently. We show how response time improvement can always be realized and how throughput improvement can be realized to the extent that a system has had to limit disk utilization to achieve adequate response time. We also show that Safe RAM is cost-effective today for most applications and will become increasingly cost-effective as more caching is used, and as $DRAM$ standby power and disk active power decrease.

19.1 INTRODUCTION

This chapter investigates whether it is cost-effective to employ in computer systems a memory that is made almost as reliable as disk, which we call *Safe RAM*. We define Safe RAM as a memory having enough backup power to keep both the memory and disk alive long enough to copy the memory to disk, as well as adequate protection from runaway software. Some Safe RAM eatures are available in some systems today.[1] However, a convincing argument has not yet been made for the cost-effectiveness of Safe RAM. A major area of opportunity for Safe RAM is in

---

[1] Tandem, Stratus, HP, DEC's Mira, IBM disk caches, and Amdhal RAM disks have the capability of keeping memory alive during power failure. The IBM AS400 has an option that allows both the memory and disk to continue operation for several minutes.

support of reliable updates that must be made atomic and persistent. Although other benefits may exist for Safe RAM (e.g., improved availability), we base our cost-effectiveness arguments only on reliable updates.

Many computer systems, such as database and transaction processing systems, must support reliable updates. Such systems typically employ several conventional techniques or amortizing disk I/O across multiple transactions. The most common, caching (i.e., memory buffering for disk reads), amortizes reads. The addition of logging and cleckpointing amortizes reliable data writes [7, 9]. The further addition of group commit amortizes log writes [4, 6]. A common thread among these techniques is that the disk is assumed to be a stable mass storage and RAM is not, so that a transaction must commit its reliable updates by forcing either the updated data pages or logs containing the updates out to disk. A performance limitation of this assumption is that a transaction must wait on at least one disk write for the log.

We can overcome this limitation by the strategy of spooling all data and/or log pages containing reliable updates into safe RAM. A transaction can then safely commit after having written its updates to the Safe RAM, thus avoiding the need for forcing logs or pages containing reliable updates to disk during the critical path of a transaction. Pages are written from the Safe RAM to disk by a background task whenever the disk has no other I/0 to perform. This strategy allows all disk writes for reliable updates to be removed from the critical path of any transaction. This gives Safe RAM a performance advantage for disk-bottlenecked systems, which can be applied at different points along the throughput and response time continuum. We show that a response time improvement can always be realized, and that a throughput improvement can be realized to the extent a system has had to limit disk utilization to achieve adequate response time.

The performance advantages of Safe RAM increase in time as technology progresses. Safe RAM is of marginal advantage in processor-bottlenecked systems; however, processor MIPS are becoming cheaper at a much faster rate than disk arms. Also, *DRAM* standby power and disk active power, which contribute to the cost of Safe RAM, are decreasing at a rapid rate. Thus, *the reasons why Safe RAM may not have been a good idea in the past are rapidly diminishing.*

We first discuss the feasibility and cost of Safe RAM using conventional technologies in Section 19.2. In Section 19.3, we review conventional techniques for reliable updates and show how they can be easily extended to use Safe RAM. Sections 19.4 and 19.5 quantify the performance impact of this Safe RAM extension to the best of the conventional techniques and show when it is cost-effective. Throughout this comparison, we make assumptions that are pessimistic for Safe RAM. Section 19.6 discusses some related issues. Section 19.7 provides a summary.

19.2   FEASIBILITY AND COST OF SAFE RAM

In this section, we first describe how Safe RAM can be realized using conventional RAM, UPS(uniterruptible power supply), and memory-protection technologies using either of two physical organizations. Then, we describe how the additional cost involves only a few percent of the system cost. We use this cost later as a basis for determining cost-effectiveness.

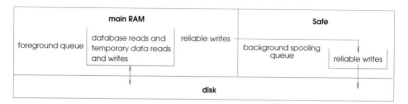

Figure 19.1. A storage hierarchy with Safe RAM.

19.2.1   Realization with Conventional Technology

We view the storage hierarchy of the system as shown in Figure 19.1. It consists of (1) a main conventional RAM, (2) a Safe RAM which we call the Safe, and (3) a conventional disk. The main RAM contains code, system files, temporary results, transaction workspaces, and a cache for the most frequently used pages of the database. The Safe is used as a stable intermediate storage for reliable updates to disk, such that the pages in the Safe are almost as resilient to system and power failures as pages in disk[2]. We use a foreground (i.e., high-priority) disk queue for database reads and 1/0 for temporary data, and a background (i.e., low-priority) queue to spool reliable data and log writes.

Although the Safe is built using off-the-shelf RAM technology, it must be made *almost as safe as disk*. A disk is nonvolatile and is protected by requiring access through a controller. Making RAM almost as safe as disk requires roughly comparable nonvolatility and protection.

Nonvolatility is accomplished by using a UPS for the Safe, the disk, and the disk controller. Upon UPS detection of power failure, these components are switched to UPS battery power and the Safe's contents are written to disk.When normal power is reinstated, recovery requires no special procedure. The UPS power requirement is the total active power of these components plus the standby power of the Safe's $DRAM$. The UPS energy ($energy = power \times time$) requirement is dependent on the time to write the Safe to disk.

Safe RAM is a storage medium. The physical failure rate of equally priced disk and parity-based RAM subsystems are roughly equivalent [2]. Any of the conventional recovery techniques used for disk media failure in conventional systems can be used to protect against Safe RAM media failure as well. Most database systems use a checkpoint and log technique for recovery from disk media failure, which writes a log of updates for each transaction before the transaction is allowed to commit and periodically writes a checkpoint of the database, both to a separate

---

[2][7] makes the historical note that database systems using core memories, which were nonvolatile, assumed that the contents of in-core logs survived system crashes.

media than those containing the database [7]. Some database systems offer an optional mirrored-disk technique for recovery from disk media failure, which maintains copies of the database on separate disks by applying writes to both disk copies [10]. The mirrored-technique improves availability because it recovers much faster than the checkpoint and log technique, but increases cost.The choice of whether to use this technique is based on the application's availability and cost requirements and the expected frequency of disk media failure. In systems that use the mirrored-disk technique, the checkpoint and log technique is usually also used as a backup for media recovery and recovery from user and system errors that commit incorrect updates to the database. *A similar choice whether to use a mirrored Safe for recovery from Safe media failure is possible.*

19.2.2 Physical Realizations

Figure 19.2 illustrates two physical realizations of the Safe. The *Separate Safe* realization employs a Safe that is separate from the main RAM and requires a separate mode of access (e.g., through a controller in a "silicon disk" implementation). The *Integrated Safe* realization makes the entire main RAM safe, so that the Safe pages can be distributed throughout the main RAM, intermixed with other pages (e.g., workspace and cache pages).

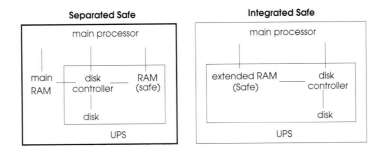

Figure 19.2. Physical realization.

The advantages of the Separate Safe are as follows:

- No additional protection requirements are needed, because the separate mode of access to the Separate Safe by the main processor protects the Safe from runaway system errors that result in undesired writes to memory. For the Integrated Safe, additional memory protection may be required to reduce the frequency of recovery. Conventional memory-protection techniques (e.g., generous use of process virtual address spaces, write-protection mechanisms available in conventional MMUs, shadow memory pages, or mirrored processor and memory pairs) can be used to ensure that only very limited types of system or user-program errors can damage Safe contents.

- Only the disk controller, the Safe, and the disk require battery power and energy during the time required to write the Safe to disk. The Integrated Safe requires all of memory to be refreshed during this time.

The advantages of the Integrated Safe are as follows:

- The size of the Safe in Integrated Safe can be dynamically varied up to the size of main memory. The size of the Separate Safe is fixed at a smaller moderate size and therefore requires the additional complexity of handling the case where the size of the Safe is exceeded (e.g., by forcing writes to the disk instead of the Safe until room becomes available in the Safe). Also, the cost of additional memory for the Integrated Safe to accommodate the Safe contents is limited to the average Safe size, instead of a maximum Safe size as in the case of the Separate Safe.

- By copying pages between workspaces, the cache and the Safe is not necessary. Instead, pointers and protection status can be updated to reflect the move without physically copying the pages. The Separate Safe requires transfers between the main RAM and the Safe using a different, and probably slower, mode of access. This advantage is important for throughput if the processor is the bottleneck (since less work is required) and for response time (because copying takes place during the critical path of this transaction). On the other hand, the copying required by the Separate Safe can reduce data contention because copying is considerably shorter than disk I/O and the page must be read locked during this time to ensure that a consistent copy of the page is written to disk.

For brevity, we will assume a Separate Safe for this chapter. An analysis that includes the Integrated Safe may be found in [3].

19.2.3   Assumptions About Technology

The technology estimates relevant to this chapter concern $DRAM$ (dynamic RAM) cost, standby power and active power, processor active power, disk cost, speed and active power, and UPS cost, power, and energy. In Table 19.1, we provide estimates for both 1987 and 1993 for the sake of comparison. In particular, notice the rapid rate of decline of $DRAM$ standby power [5, 15] a trend that favors a Safe RAM approach. We arrived at these estimates by simple extrapolation from historical trends and from various popular periodicals. We have pessimistically assumed that UPS costs will remain constant. The purpose of these numbers is not to make accurate predictions about technology. Instead, we use them to roughly calibrate various curves and provide ballpark estimates for several parameters. The conclusions that we draw in this chapter are not highly sensitive to the accuracy of these estimates and our calculations can be easily redone by the reader with different technology characterizations and cost estimates as they become available.

Table 19.1. Technology Assumptions

Storage	Parameters	1987	1993
DRAM	Cost/MB	$500/MB	$25/MB
	Standby power	2 watts/MB	10 watts/GB
	Active power	10 watts	10 watts
Microprocessor	Active power	5 watts	5 watts
Fast disk + controller	Form factor	8 in.	5.24 in.
	Unit cost	$5000	$2000
	Cost/MB	$10/MB	$2/MB
	Track capacity	25KB	50KB
	Average seek time	0.018 sec	0.010 sec
	Rotation time	0.015 sec	0.010 sec
	Cost/access/sec for track for sector	$165/access/sec $130/access/sec	$40/access/sec $30/access/sec
	Active power	100 watts	50 watts
UPS	Cost/power	$1/watt	$1/watt
	Time of power	20 min (1200 sec)	20 min (1200 sec)
	extra batteries	$0.5/KW-sec	$0.5/KW-sec

19.2.4 Cost of Safe RAM

In this section, we estimate the cost of the Separate Safe physical realization in both 1987 and 1993. We define the Safe as *cost-effective* if it can improve throughput by at least some *CostRatio* (ratio of system cost with Safe to without Safe) without increasing response time. For example, we determine later that the CostRatio is 1.043 for the Separate Safe realization using 1987 technology. This means that to be cost-effective, Safe would have to increase Throughput by more than 4.3%, without sacrificing response time. The CostRatios that we calculate in this section are pessimistically high because of the following assumptions:

- We assume a single disk system. The required Safe size for n disks is significantly smaller than n times the size required for one disk.

- We only include disk in the base cost. Including processor and memory in the base cost would reduce the CostRatio required to make Safe RAM cost-effective.

- We include a large memory size in the standby power requirements of the Integrated Safe. The UPS power requirements for RAM standby power are proportional to RAM size.

- Only a very small percentage of the UPS energy is actually required to support Safe RAM, but we include the full cost of this unused energy in the CostRatio.

For the Separate Safe in 1987, the power required is about 116 watts, including a 100-watt disk, a 5-watt microprocessor, a $DRAM$ with active power of 10 watts, and one hundred 2-KB pages of Safe $DRAM$ at 2 watts/MB for standby power (0.4 watt). The time to write 100 sector-sized pages of Safe at 0.026 sec/access is 2.6 sec (assuming random writes to sectors). This is only about 0.2% of the energy capacity of the UPS, so that no additional battery energy is needed. This results in $116 worth of UPS. The additional RAM cost for the Safe would be $100. Thus, the total additional cost for the Safe is about $216. Because disk cost is $5000, the CostRatio is 1.043.

For the Separate Safe in 1993, the power required is about 65 watts, including a 50 watt disk, a 5 watt microprocessor, a $DRAM$ with active power of 10 watts, and one hundred 2-KB paces of Safe $DRAM$ at 10 watts/GB for standby power (6.002 watts). The time to write 100 sector-sized pages of Safe at 0.016 sec/access is 1.6 sec (assuming random writes to sectors). This is only about 0.1% of the energy capacity of the UPS, so that no additional battery energy is needed. This results in $65 worth of UPS. The additional RAM cost for the Safe would be $5. Thus, the total additional cost for the Safe is about $70. Because disk cost is S2000, the CostRatio is 1.035. Obviously, even for today's technology, only a negligible improvement in throughput is required to recover the dollar cost of Safe RAM because the dollar cost is so small.

19.3   HISTORY OF RELIABLE UPDATES TECHNIQUES

In this section, we summarize the historical evolution of conventional techniques for reliable updates and show how they can be easily extended to use Safe RAM. In the simplest technique for reliable updates, a transaction reads pages from the public database and updates copies of the pages in the cache or a local workspace. When the transaction is ready to commit, a log of the updates is forced to disk, denoting the commit point. Then, the updated database pages are forced to disk to reflect the transaction-consistent state. The disk I/Os in the critical path of each transaction in this simple technique can be characterized by three variables:

- Dr: the number of read I/Os for pages that were not in the cache (and 1/0 for temporary data)

- Dw: the number of write I/Os for pages containing reliable updates

- Dl: the number of log I/Os of reliable updates at commit time

Some pages are read only once and discovered in cache by subsequent transactions, that amortize reads. In the simple technique, a page may be overwritten on disk many times if that page is updated by many transactions. Many techniques have been proposed to amortize the writes over many transactions. Two such techniques are *checkpointing* (CP) which amortizes data writes, and *group commit* (GC) which amortizes log writes.

In CP techniques [7, 9, 13], only the log, is forced to disk at commit time of the transaction. A database page is written to disk only when that page is swapped out by the cache-replacement algorithm. As a result, a database page may be written to disk only once after many updates. To recover from failure, the system must reconstruct a consistent state of the database using the log. To avoid a recovery having to go arbitrarily far back in the log, checkpointing is periodically done, wherein all the updated pages still in the cache are forced to disk at the end of a checkpointing interval. This strategy incurs the following I/Os *in the critical path* of each transaction: (1) Dr, (2) Dw' (I/O for swapping out dirty pages for allocating memory for later transactions), (3) Dl, and (4) checkpointing overhead. Due to cache locality, Dw' is usually smaller than Dw (for the simple technique) and checkpointing overhead is amortized over many transactions. Although checkpointing *reduces* the I/O for reliable updates, the data writes still lie in the critical path of some later transaction, because the cache-replacement algorithm will write pales out to allocate memory for later transactions. Thus, every write of an updated page is done in the critical path *some* transaction.

After reducing the number of read and write I/Os per transaction via caching and checkpointing (perhaps close to zero for systems supporting memory-resident data), the log I/O cost becomes significant. In GC techniques [4, 6, 13], transactions are held up until a full log page can be written or a time out occurs. Thus, the log write is amortized over a group of transactions. This strategy incurs the following I/Os in the critical path of each transaction: (1) Dr, (2) Dw', (3) Dl', and (4) checkpointing overhead. Dl' is usuilly less than Dl (in the simple and CP techniques), because the logs are amortized over several transactions. Further, a log I/O still lies in the critical path of each transaction, data I/Os still lie in the critical path of some later transaction, and each transaction is also held up for a period of time (waiting to commit) in its critical path. Consequently, the response time of each transaction reflects these I/O and waiting overheads.

Recall that in both the CP and GC techniques, dirty data pages are written out to disk by the cache-replacement algorithm to reallocate memory during the critical path of some later transaction. Alternatively, *spooling* can be used to migrate these dirty pages to disk. The advantage of spooling is that the dirty pages are written to disk as a background operation when no read I/O request is pending, instead of during the critical path of some transaction. The GC technique can be extended to use such a spooling mechanism to further improve performance. When this extension is made, checkpointing is usually also further optimized by making a log entry containing system status information (e.g., which pages are "dirty" and the status of transactions) instead of actually flushing the updated (dirty) pages, because spooling will keep the updated pages young enough so that a recovery does not have to go very far back in the log.

We consider Safe RAM a natural next step in this migration toward improved performance. Although Safe RAM may eventually influence the design of recovery algorithms, the use of Safe RAM does not necessarily require changing existing recovery algorithms provided that the Safe is treated the same as disk. Safe RAM can be used productively in conjunction with the most efficient, conventional, and reliable update techniques (e.g., GC with spooling). In Sections 19.4 and 19.5, we compare the performance impact of Safe RAM on GC with spooling. In this context, the advantage of Safe RAM is that amortizing log writes via grouping does not cause a delay in commit times. This removes the log writes from the critical path of transactions. We quantify when this justifies the cost of Safe RAM.

19.4 MODELING

This section provides guidelines for the size of the Safe and provides equations for throughput and response time, which we use in Section 19.5 to show cost-effectiveness. We compare the best of the conventional reliable update techniques (e.g., GC with spooling) with and without the Safe. Throughout this section, we assume that the disk is the system bottleneck. We also make a number of assumptions, which we refer to as "pessimistic assumptions," that have a negative effect on the performance model for Safe RAM (e.g., overestimating the required size of the Safe and underestimating its improvements in response time and throughput). As a result, we get a *lower bound* for the improvement using Safe RAM, so that our cost-effectiveness argument is conservative.

19.4.1 Size of Safe

We are interested in determining the required size of the Safe given disk loading and how the load is made up of reads and writes. We will do this by defining two metrics, the mean time to overflow the Safe ($MTTO$) and the mean time to recover from the overflow ($MTTR$), and then, for given loads and Safe sizes, determining these means and seeing if they are acceptable. We show that even under extremely pessimistic assumptions, a moderate-sized Safe results in acceptable $MTTO$ and $MTTR$. We model the system by a single $M/M/1$ queue, making the following pessimistic assumptions in order to guarantee that the calculated $MTTO$ will be far smaller than would be observed in an actual implementation:

- *All* disk I/Os are writes. The higher the proportion of reads to writes, the smaller the Safe needs to be. (If all disk I/Os were reads, then no Safe would be required.)

- Disk service times are exponentially distributed. This distribution has a variance higher than usually encountered in disk systems, resulting in longer queue-length distributions (and thus a shorter $MTTO$).

For simplicity, we assume Poisson arrival rates. We assume a Safe of k pages (capable of holding k writes) and arrival and service rates characterized by means λ and μ. The probability of having exactly k writes in the queue is $(1-\rho)\rho^k$, where

$\rho = \lambda/\mu$, the average utilization [11, 12]. The steady-state probability of having more than k writes in the queue (an overflowed Safe) is simply ρ^{k+l}. The probability of having k or fewer writes in the queue is $1 - \rho^{k+l}$. The average rate at which the Safe overflows is

$$\lambda Prob\,[\text{a full Safe given that we started with a nonfull Safe}] =$$
$$\lambda Prob\,[\text{k writes in the queue given that we started with} \le \text{k writes in the queue}]$$
$$= \lambda \frac{(1-\rho)\rho^k}{1-\rho^{k+1}} \quad = \quad \frac{(1-\rho)\rho^{k+1}\mu}{1-\rho^{k+1}}$$

The mean time between overflows is the inverse, or

$$MTTO = \frac{1}{\mu}\frac{1-\rho^{k+1}}{(1-\rho)\rho^{k+1}}$$

Similarly, the mean rate at which the system exits the overflow state is

$$\mu Prob\,[\text{k}+1 \text{ writes in the queue given that we started with k writes in the queue}]$$
$$= \mu \frac{(1-\rho)\rho^{k+1}}{\rho^{k+1}} = (1-\rho)\mu$$

The inverse yields $MTTR$, or

$$MTTR = \frac{1/\mu}{1-\rho}$$

Notice that MTTR is independent of k.

Figure 19.3 illustrates how $MTTO$ (plotted on a log scale) depends exponentially on ρ for a given Safe size of k. We use a mean disk service time of $1/\mu = 26$ msec for the plot. Note that for even (unrealistically) high disk utilizations (e.g., 0.90), the *pessimistic* bound of $MTTO$ yields 10,800 sec = 3.0 hours for $k = 100$. The bound of $MTTR$ for this case is 0.26 sec. To summarize this extreme example, *if one implemented this system and ran an exclusively write workload on an overutilized disk with mean utilization of 90%, then one could expect a 100-page Safe to require writes to be forced to disk instead of the Safe for 0.26 sec once every 3 hours.*

19.4.2 Performance Model

This section develops the throughput and response-time equations with and without Safe RAM. We assume the following:

- Only disk I/O is included in our throughput and response-time equations. Processor delays are assumed to be negligible.

- The logs of $G(G \ge 1)$ transactions are grouped into one page.

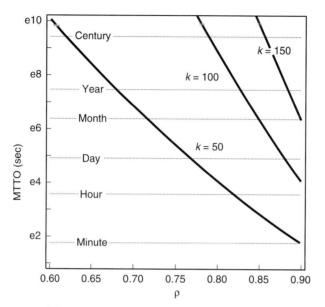

Figure 19.3. Mean time to overflow the safe

- Reliable writes are spooled for both the Safe and non-Safe case. We assume these spooled writes are removed from the critical path of any transaction. This assumption is justified by the short length of the spooling queue described in Section 4.1 and by the fact that these pages will have a recently used cache status at the time they are put into the queue. These writes are nonpreemptive, so that the foreground queue must wait on any spooling I/Os that have already begun,

- There is a single database disk characterized by service rate μ and utilization ρ.

- There is a single log disk characterized only by service rate μ. Safe RAM never requires waiting for the log write, so that this response-time delay is eliminated and a high log-disk utilization can be tolerated. Without Safe RAM, we optimistically assume that the log disk is never the system bottleneck and has low enough utilization so that its response time equals its service time of $1/\mu$. We also optimistically assume that a log write can be accomplished in a single 1/0, regardless of how large Dw and G are. These optimistic assumptions are correspondingly pessimistic for Safe RAM.

- For simplicity, we ignore any checkpointing overhead, which is typically quite small.

When Safe RAM is not used for either disk, the commit time of multiple (G) transactions are delayed for a group commit, so that their logs can be written to the log disk with a single log write. We assume each transaction causes a total of D disk I/Os to the database disk, so that the maximum number of transactions per second without Safe RAM is

$$TPSo = \frac{\lambda_o}{D} = \frac{\rho_o \mu}{D}$$

where ρ_o is the database disk utilization without the Safe. The Dr reads are placed in the database disk's foreground queue, the Dw writes are placed in the database disk's spooling queue, and the log writes are placed in the log disk's foreground queue. Thus, the transaction response time has three terms.

First, each transaction must wait on Dr I/Os in the database disk's foreground queue. The average response time (queue wait plus service) for each of these I/Os is given in [11] as

$$\frac{\rho_o/\mu}{1 - \rho_r} + \frac{1}{\mu}$$

where

$$\rho_r = \frac{D_r}{D}\rho_o$$

is the disk utilization due to the foreground queue.

Second, each transaction must wait on the other transactions in its group. This average group delay lies within the range:

$$\frac{1}{2}\frac{1}{TPS_o}(G-1) = \frac{D}{2\rho_o\mu}(G-1) > \frac{D}{2\mu}(G-1)$$

The first expression assumes that each transaction is delayed for an average of half of the *average interarrival time* of G–1 transactions (we assume the last transaction does not have to wait). The second expression assumes that each transaction is delayed for an average of half of the *burst-service time* of G–1 transactions. We use the second expression for group delay because it is lower and thus is pessimistic for Safe RAM (i.e., it underestimates the savings due to Safe RAM).

Third, each transaction must then wait on the log write in the log disk's foreground queue, which we assume is $1/\mu$. As a result, the average transaction response time without Safe RAM is

$$RTo = Dr\left(\frac{\rho_o/\mu}{1 - (Dr/D)\rho} + \frac{1}{\mu}\right) + \frac{D}{2\mu}(G-1) + \frac{1}{\mu}$$

When Safe RAM is used for both data and log disks, the logs of multiple (G) transactions are grouped within the Safe containing the log disk's spooling queue so that they can later be written to the log disk with a log write, but without requiring the commit-time transaction to be delayed. Each transaction causes a total of D I/Os to the database disk, so that the maximum TPS with Safe RAM is

$$TPSs = \frac{\lambda_s}{D} = \frac{\rho_s \mu}{D}$$

where ρ_s is the database disk utilization with the Safe. The Dr reads are placed in the database disk's foreground queue, the Dw writes are placed in the database disk's spooling queue, and the log writes are placed in the log disk's spooling queue. Thus, each transaction must wait on Dr I/Os in the database disk's foreground queue. This is described by the first term in RTo, except that ρ_s is used instead of ρ_o. Safe RAM avoids the delays for group commit and log writes (second and third terms in RTo). As a result, RT with Safe RAM is

$$RTs = Dr \left(\frac{\rho_s / \mu}{1 - (Dr/D)\rho_s} + \frac{1}{\mu} \right)$$

19.5   WHEN IS SAFE RAM COST-EFFECTIVE?

In this section, we quantify the performance improvements of Safe RAM and show when it is cost-effective.

19.5.1   Comparison Methodology

The performance improvement due to Safe RAM can be applied at different points along the throughput and response-time continuum. We examine throughput ratios (with Safe RAM over without Safe RAM) while constraining the response time with Safe RAM to be at least as good as without it. We also examine response-time ratios (without Safe RAM over with Safe RAM) while constraining throughput to be equal. The numerators and denominators of these throughput and response-time ratios are chosen to conveniently indicate that Safe RAM is better when either of the ratios is greater than 1. We define

$$TPSs/o \equiv \frac{TPSs}{TPSo} \bigg| RTs \leq RTo \quad \text{and} \quad RTo/s \equiv \frac{RTo}{RTs} \bigg| TPSo = TPSs$$

We define $cost - effective$ to mean that TPSs/o is greater than the CostRatio described in Section 19.2.4.

It is easy to prove that $RTo/s > 1$ and $TPSs/o \geq 1$ for all values of Dr, Dw, G and ρ_o, and that $TPSs/o > 1$ when $\rho_o < \rho_m$, where ρ_m is the maximum allowable disk utilization even when the Safe is employed. The remaining questions are: By how much do these ratios exceed I. When is Safe RAM cost-effective (i.e., when $TPSs/o > CostRatio$)?. We derived $TPSs/o$ and RTo/s analytically and plotted them using the following values:

D_r	D_w	D	D_r/D
3	4	7	0.43
0.3	0.4	0.7	0.43
6	1	7	0.86
0.6	0.1	0.7	0.86

$\times$

G
1
4

$\times$

ρ_m
0.9
0.7

The first case is the DebitCredit benchmark without caching [1]. The second case constrains Dr/D to be the same as the first case while decreasing D via caching. The third case constrains D to be the same as the first case while increasing Dr/D. The fourth case constrains Dr/D to be the same as the third case while decreasing D via caching. We use G values of 1 (no grouping) and 4. We varied ρ_o from 0.2 to 0.9 and allowed ρ_s to go as high as 0.9 and 0.7. We included $\rho_m = 0.9$ to represent the upper bound on disk utilization for any system. We also included $\rho_m = 0.7$ to represent systems that require spare disk utilization for other purposes (e.g., disk mirroring).[3]

19.5.2   The Comparison

For the case when grouping is not used ($G = 1$), Figure 19.4 illustrates the effect of Safe RAM on throughput when response time with Safe RAM is constrained to be at least as good as without it. The $TPSs/o$ curves are shown in solid lines for $\rho_m=0.9$. $TPSs/o = \rho_m/\rho_o$ except when ρ_s is forced to be below ρ_m by the response-time constraint. The dashed line shows the $0.7/\rho_o$ curve. For $\rho_m = 0.7$, the curves are the minimum of the $0.7/\rho_o$ curve and the solid curves. The higher of the two CostRatios (1.043) is also shown by the dotted line. Figure 19.6 illustrates $TPSso$ when grouping is used ($G = 4$). Figures 19.4 and 19.6 illustrate the following:

- As Dr is reduced (either by reducing Dr directly or by reducing D with Dr/D held constant), the curves come closer to the ρ_m/ρ_o curve, because the response-time constraint becomes easier to meet. For $G = 1$ and $\rho_m = 0.9$, the (0.3, 0.4) curve is the same as the $0.9/\rho_o$ curve. For $G = 1$ and $\rho_m = 0.7$, the (0.3, 0.4) and (0.6, 0.1) curves are the same as the $0.7/\rho_o$ curve. For $G = 4$ and $\rho_m = 0.9$, all but the (6,1) curve are the same as the $0.9/\rho_o$ curve. For $G = 4$ and $\rho_m = 0.7$, all of the curves are the same as the $0.7/\rho_o$ curve.

---

[3] For example, if disk mirroring were used with DebitCredit without caching (the first case), then Dr, Dw, and D become

Mode of operation	Dr	Dw	D
During normal operation	3	8	11
While one of the disks is out	6	8	14

To support the same arrival rate while one of the disks is out, maximum utilization during normal operation must be reduced below $11/14 = 0.79$ in order to keep utilization while one of the disks is out below 1.0.

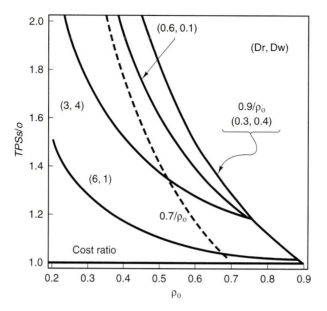

Figure 19.4. Throughput improvement

- As G is increased, the throughput improvement due to Safe RAM becomes much larger. This is because Safe RAM eliminates the delay involved in group commit.

- As ρ_o approaches ρ_m, there is less room left for TPS improvement, but the RT improvement increases. For the case when grouping is not used ($G = 1$), Figure 19.5 illustrates the effect of Safe RAM on response time with throughput held constant. The RTo/s curves are shown in solid lines for $\rho_m = 0.9$. For $\rho_m = 0.7$, the portion of the curves to the right of the dashed line do not apply. Figure 19.7 illustrates RTo/s when grouping is used ($G = 4$).

The a dvantage of Safe RAM comes from the following:

- Log writes can be put in a spooling queue in addition to the data writes, so that the single log write is taken out of the response time's critical path. This advantage diminishes when Dr and po increase (the foreground queue wait time dominates) or when D and G increase (the group delay dominates).

- Response time is not delayed in order to exploit the grouped log writes. This advantage improves as G and D increase (the group delay dominates) and diminishes as Dr and ρ_o increase (the foreground queue wait time dominates). It has been argued that a group-commit time out value is typically much shorter (e.g., 50 to 100 msec) than the required response time (e.g., 1 sec), so that Safe RAM provides little advantage. However, in such systems, Safe

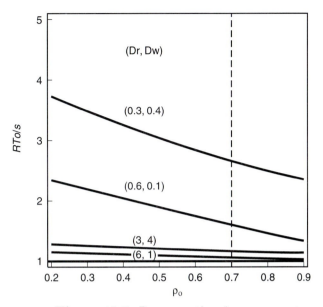

Figure 19.5. Response time improvement

RAM would allow a much larger G without impacting response time, so that more of the advantages of grouped log writes would be possible. Also, parallel systems often tend to centralize logging to exploit the maximum throughput advantage from group commit without increasing its response-time penalty. Safe RAM allows more parallelism for logs, so that the maximum throughput advantage from group commit can be obtained without adding to transaction response time.

Our most significant point is: *Even with pessimistic assumptions, Safe RAM is cost-effective for systems that support reliable updates and have had to limit disk utilization to achieve adequate response times, provided that Dr is reasonably small.*
Safe RAM is expected to become increasingly cost-effective in the future because of the following:

- The CostRatio is expected to decrease in the future because of reduced $DRAM$ standby power and cost per bit and reduced active disk power, even though we assumed that disk unit cost will decrease and UPS cost will be unchanged.

- The continuous improvements in $DRAM$ cost per bit will cause caching to substantially increase in the future, so that Dr will decrease.

When viewing Figures 19.4 through 19.7, it is useful to recall the assumptions that we have made that are pessimistic for Safe RAM:

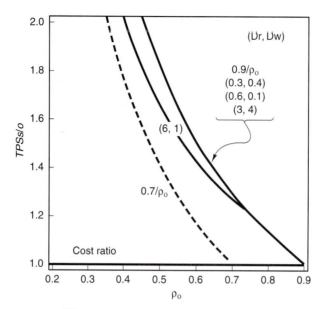

Figure 19.6. Throughput improvement

- The COSLRatios were inflated because

  - we included the higher of the two CostRatios in the $TPSs/o$ figures

  - we assumed a single disk system

  - we only included disk in the base cost

  - we include a large memory size in the standby power requirements of the integrated Safe

  - we included the full UPS energy cost even though only a tiny percentage of the UPS energy is required to support Safe RAM

  - we overestimated the size of the Safe

- We assumed that the log disk's delay without the Safe was a minimal $1/\mu$ due to low utilization (even though a log disk employing Safe RAM could tolerate a very high utilization) and regardless of how large G and D were (even though large G and/or D would cause multiple log writes).

- The group commit delay was based on burst service time instead of average interarrival time.

The accumulative effect of these assumptions can be quite significant.

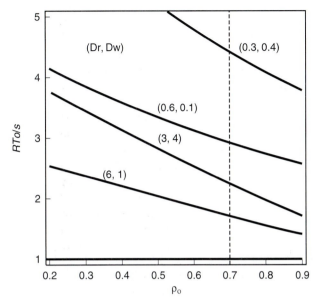

Figure 19.7. Response time improvement

19.6 SOME RELATED ISSUES

This section describes several open issues concerning Safe RAM.

We showed that a typical existing UPS has considerably more capacity than is required to realize Safe RAM. (The energy requirements of Safe RAM could be even further reduced by writing the pages in the Safe to contiguous disk locations during power failure and making the appropriate updates to disk page-mapping tables.) This suggests that a UPS with less energy and lower cost would suffice to realize Safe RAM. In fact, a *large-capacitance power supply might suffice*. Otherwise, the excess energy could be used to keep memory alive during power outage, so that subsequent disk reads of the data that were in memory at the time of power failure are unnecessary. The most cost-effective amount of energy for such higher availability could be calculated using an analysis similar to the 5-minute rule (Gra87] to trade off UPS energy cost for disk arm cost. Further, the excess energy could be used to keep the entire system alive during power outage to increase availability.

An interesting variation of the Separate Safe physical realization is the *Controller Safe*, which includes the Safe within the disk controller. This realization would allow today's systems that do not use group commit and that support reliable updates to plug in such a disk controller *transparently to the rest of the system* to achieve performance improvements. For the Integrated Safe realization with a large cache, a separate spooling queue for cache-resident data (i.e., fixed in memory) with lower priority than the disk-resident data (i.e., subject to *LRU* swapping) has two advantages. One advantage is a significant reduction in the size of the spooling queue, because the separate spooling queue for cache-resident data can consist of pointers to cache-resident pages instead of the pages themselves. A second advantage is more efficient buffer management. Cache-resident data require cache space anyway, whereas disk-resident data needs to be written out as early as possible to avoid being allocated by the LRU mechanism, which would cause a disk I/O during the critical path of some later transaction.

19.7   SUMMARY

We argued the feasibility of Safe RAM using conventional technologies and estimated the additional cost required in both 1987 and 1993 using a physical realization called Separate Safe. We then described how Safe RAM can be used in conjunction with the most efficient conventional recovery techniques for improved performance. Finally, we quantified the performance effect of Safe RAM and described how, even with very pessimistic assumptions, Safe RAM Is cost-effective today for systems that support reliable updates and have had to limit disk utilization to achieve adequate response times, provided that there are a reasonably small number of disk reads per transaction. Even though we assumed that disk unit cost will decrease and UPS cost will be unchanged, we showed how Safe RAM will be increasingly cost-effective in the future because caching will increase (due to $DRAM$ cost per bit improvements) and because $DRAM$ standby power and disk active power will decrease.

Acknowledgment

Thanks to Jim Gray for his encouragement and helpful suggestions.

References

[1] Anon. et al, "A Measure of Transaction Processing Power," *Datamation*, April 1, (1985).

[2] J. Bell, private communications concerning experience as a Field Engineer and a Quality Assurance Manager (1988).

[3] G. Copeland, R. Krishnamurthy and M. Smith, "The Case For Safe RAM," *MCC Technical Report* No. ACA-ST-080-88 (February 1988).

[4] D.J. DeWitt, R.H. Katz, F. Olken, L.D. Shapiro, M. R. Stonebraker and D. Wood, "Implementation Techniques for Main Memory Database Systems," *Proceedings of the ACM SIGMOD Conference on Management of Data*, Boston (June 1984).

[5] S. Fujii et al, "A 50-μA Stancibv 1NIxi/256Kx4 CMOS *DRAM* With High-Speed Sense Amplifier," *IEEE Journal of Solid-State Circuits*, 21(5), (October 1986).

[6] D. Gawlick and D. Kinkade, "Varieties of Concurrencv Control in INfS/VS Fast Path," *IEEE Quarterly Bulletin on Database Engineering*, 8(2), (June 1985).

[7] J.N. Gray, "Notes on Database Operating Systems," in Operating Systems: An Advanced Course, Springer-Verlag, New York (1978).

[8] J.N. Gray and F. Putzolu, "The 5 Minute Rule for Trading Memorv for Disc Accesses and the 10 Bvte Rule for Trading Memorv for CPU Time," *Proceedings of the ACM SIGMOD Conference*, San Francisco (May 1987).

[9] T. Haerder and A. Reuter, "Principles of Transaction-Oriented Database Recovery," *ACM Computing Surveys*, 15(4) (December 1983).

[10] J.A. Katzman, "A Fault-Tolerant Computing system," *Proceedings of the Eleventh Hawaii Conference on System Sciences*, January 1978.

[11] L. Kleinrock, *Queueing Systems, Volume 1: Theory, and Queueing Systems*. New York, John Wiley & Sons, (1976).

[12] L. Kleinrock, *Volume 2: Computer Applications*. New York, John Wiley & Sons, (1976).

[13] C. Mohan, D. Haderle, B. Linsav, H. Pirahesh and P. Schwarz, "ARIES: A Transaction Recovery Method Supporting Fine-Granularicv Locking And Partial Rollbacks Using Write-Ahead Logging," *IBM Research Report* RJ6649, San Jose, (January 1989).

[14] T. Ohsawa et al, "A 60-ns 4-Mbit C-NIOS DRAM With Built-In Self-Test Function," IEEE Journal of Solid-State Circuits, 22(5) (October 1987).

[15] K. Sawada et al, "A 30-μA Data-RecenLion Pseudostatic RAM With Vir-Luallv Static RAM mode." *IEEE Journal of Solid-Slare Circuits*, 1-3(1) (February 1988).

Chapter 20

Recovering from Main-Memory Lapses

H.V. Jagadish, Avi Silberschatz, and S. Sudarshan

Abstract

Recovery activities, like logging, checkpointing, and restart, are used to restore a database to a consistent state after a system crash has occurred. Recovery-related overhead is likely to form a bottleneck in a main-memory database, since I/O activities are performed for the sole purpose of ensuring data durability. In this chapter we present recovery algorithms that reduce recovery-related overheads in main-memory databases. The benefits of our algorithms include the following: Disk I/O is reduced by logging to disk only redo records during normal execution. The undo log is normally resident only in main memory, and is garbage collected after transaction commit. Checkpoints need not be transaction-consistent; uncommitted data can be written to disk by also writing out relevant parts of the undo log. Contention on the system log is reduced by having per transaction logs in memory. And, finally, the algorithms make only a single pass over the log during recovery. Thus, our recovery algorithms combine the benefits of several techniques proposed in the past. The ideas behind our algorithms can be used to advantage in disk-resident databases as well.

20.1 INTRODUCTION

Current computer systems are able to accommodate a very large physical main memory. In such an environment, it is possible, for certain type of applications, to keep the entire database in main memory rather than on secondary storage. Such a database system is referred to as a main-memory database (MMDB). The potential

548

for substantial performance improvement in an MMDB environment is promising, since I/O activity is kept at minimum. Because of the volatility of main memory, updates must be noted in stable storage (on disk) in order to survive system failure. Recovery-related processing is the only component in a MMDB that must deal with I/O, and hence it must be designed with care so that it does not impede the overall performance.

The task of a *recovery manager* in a transaction processing system is to ensure that, despite system and transaction failures, the consistency of the data is maintained. To perform this task, bookkeeping activities (e.g., checkpointing and logging) are performed during the normal operation of the system and restoration activities take place following a failure. To minimize the interference to transaction processing caused by recovery-related activities, it is essential to derive schemes where the length of time it takes to do a checkpoint as well as the time to recover from system failure are very short. It is the aim of this chapter to present one such scheme, tailored to main-memory databases.

For simplicity, we assume that the entire database is kept in main memory, and a backup copy is kept on disk and is only modified when a checkpoint takes place. However, the ideas behind our algorithms can be used profitably in disk-resident databases as well, where parts of the database may need to be flushed to disk more often in order to make space for other data. A checkpoint dumps some fraction of the database residing in main memory onto the disk. A write-ahead log is also maintained to restore the database to a consistent state after a system crash. The key features of our scheme are as follows:

- The write-ahead log on disk contains only the redo records of committed transactions; this minimizes recovery I/O. We maintain in main memory the redo and undo records of active transactions (i.e., transactions that have neither committed nor aborted). Redo log records as well as undo log records of transactions are kept in a per transaction log. The redo log records are flushed to the system redo log only when the transaction commits, thereby reducing contention on the log tail.

  Undo records of a transaction are discarded once the transaction has committed; we call this feature *transient undo logging*. Undo as well as redo records of a transaction are discarded once it has has aborted. The undo records of a transaction are written to disk only when a checkpoint takes place while the transaction is active. By writing out undo records thus, we are able to perform checkpointing in a state that is action consistent but not transaction-consistent.[1]

- The recovery actions after a system crash make only a single pass over the log. The usual backwards pass on the log to find "winners" and "losers" and undo the actions of losers is avoided by keeping the undo log separate from the redo log.

---

[1] The issue of action-consistency is important if logical operation logging is used.

- Our algorithms can be used with physical as well as logical logging.

- Checkpoints need only be action-consistent, and the database can be partitioned into small segments that can be checkpointed separately. Interference with normal transaction processing is thereby kept very small.

No assumptions are made regarding the availability of special hardware such as nonvolatile RAM or an adjunct processor for checkpointing. Consequently, the scheme proposed here can be used with any standard machine configuration.

Since an earlier version of this paper appeared in [13], the algorithms described here have been extended in several ways. In particular, in [6], the algorithms have been extended to support repeating of history, completely "fuzzy" checkpointing to minimize interference with updates, and support for multilevel recovery [17, 23]. The extended algorithm is used in the Dalí main-memory database system [12]. Further extensions to support recovery in client-server and shared-disk environments are described in [5]. Section 20.8 briefly outlines these extensions.

The area of recovery for main-memory databases has received much attention in the past. We present the connections of the present work to earlier work in the area in Section 20.9.

The remainder of this chapter is organized as follows. In Section 20.2, we present our system model. In Section 20.3, the basic checkpoint and recovery scheme is presented. The correctness of the scheme is established in Section 20.4. Various extensions to the basic scheme, including segmentation of the database and logical logging, are presented in Sections 20.5, 20.6, and 20.7. Section 20.8 summarizes the extensions described in [5] and [6]. Section 20.9 describes related work, and concluding remarks are offered in Section 20.10.

20.2 SYSTEM STRUCTURE

In this section, we present the system model used in this chapter, and describe how transaction processing is handled.

20.2.1 System Model

The entire database is kept in main memory, and a backup copy, possibly out of date and not transaction-consistent, is kept on disk. We assume that serializability is achieved through the use of a rigorous two-phase locking (R2PL) protocol, where all locks are released only after a transaction either commits or aborts. The use of the R2PL protocol also ensures that the commit order of transactions is consistent with their serialization order. The granularity of locking is irrelevant to our algorithm; it can be at the level of objects, pages, extents, or even the entire database.

The system maintains a redo log on the disk, with the tail of the log in main memory. Information about actions that update the database, such as writes, is written to the redo log. At various points in time, the tail is appended to the log on the disk. We refer to the portion of the redo log on the disk as the *persistent*

Trans. ID	Start Addr.	Length	Data

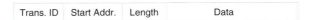

Figure 20.1. Structure of a physical log record.

redo log (or as the *persistent log*) and the portion of the redo log in main memory as the *volatile redo log*. The entire redo log is referred to as the *global redo log* (or as the *global log*).

The global log consists of all the redo records of the committed transactions, and the redo records of a committed transaction appear consecutively in the global log. This is in contrast to traditional logs where the log records of different transactions are intermingled. To achieve this, the redo records of an active transaction are kept initially in a private redo log in main memory, and these redo records are appended to the global log only when the transaction begins its commit processing. (This aspect of the model is not central to our algorithms, and later we discuss extensions that allow redo records to be written directly to the global log tail.) We say that a transaction *commits* when its commit record hits the persistent log. When this occurs, the system can notify the user who initiated the transaction that the transaction has committed.

Initially, we assume that the only actions that modify the database are writes to the database, and writes are logged to the redo log. The structure of a typical physical log record is shown in Figure 20.1. The transaction ID field identifies the transaction, the start address and length specify the start and length of a range of bytes that have been modified, and the data field stores the new byte values of the range of bytes. There is also a type field to identify the log record type, which is not shown. Later, we consider actions that are encapsulated and treated as a unit for the purpose of logging.

For ease of exposition, we initially require that the following condition hold; in Section 20.6, we shall relax this restriction.

Condition LA1. Actions logged are idempotent and are atomic; that is, repetition of the actions in a state where the effect of the actions is already reflected is harmless, and any stable image of the database is in a state after an action finished execution or in a state before the action started execution.

The backup copy of the database on disk is updated only when a checkpoint is taken. We allow a checkpoint to be taken at any time, which implies that the backup copy may contain pages with uncommitted updates. The possibility of having pages with uncommitted updates on the backup copy implies that we need to be able to undo the effect of those transactions that were active when the checkpoint took place, and that have since aborted. We do so by keeping in memory, for each active transaction, a private log consisting of all the undo records of that transaction. The private undo log of a transaction is discarded after the transaction either commits or aborts. The undo logs of all the active transactions are flushed to disk when a checkpoint takes place (see Section 20.3.1). An overview of our system model is presented in Figure 20.2.

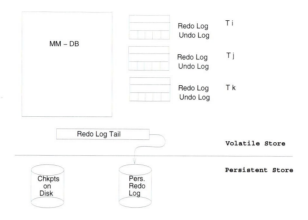

Figure 20.2. System model.

Some recovery algorithms proposed in the past to do away with undo logging assume deferred updates [3]. Deferred updates require a mechanism to note updates done on an object by an uncommitted transaction without executing them, and redirecting further accesses on the object to the updated copy instead of the original. A mechanism to install the deferred updates after commit is also required. In an object-oriented database, the redirecting of accesses may be particularly troublesome.[2] Our recovery algorithms do not assume the use of deferred updates (i.e., they allow in-place updates), and are thus more general.

20.2.2   Commit Processing

When a transaction T_i starts its execution, it is added to the list of active transactions, and the record $\langle start\ T_i \rangle$ is added to the private redo log of T_i. While the transaction is executing, its redo and undo records are maintained in the private logs. When T_i finishes executing, it *precommits*, which involves the following steps:

Precommit Processing

1. Transaction T_i is assigned a commit sequence number, denoted by $csn(T_i)$, which is a unique spot in the commit order.

2. Transaction T_i is marked as "committing" and its commit sequence number is noted in the active transaction list.

3. The record $\langle commit\ T_i, csn(T_i) \rangle$ is added to the private redo log, and the private redo log is appended to the (in-memory) global log. (The commit

---

[2]Shadow paging can remove the lookup overhead by making use of virtual-memory address mapping, but carries with it a space cost as well as a time overhead for creating shadow pages.

record is the last log record of a transaction to be appended to the global log.)

4. Transaction T_i releases all the locks that it holds.

Transaction T_i actually commits when its commit record hits the disk. After this has occurred, the system executes the following postcommit processing steps.

Postcommit Processing

1. Notify the user that transaction T_i committed (and pass back any return values).

2. Remove T_i from the list of active transactions.

3. Delete the volatile undo log created for T_i.

Figure 20.3. Steps in transaction processing.

Figure 20.3 outlines the sequence of the main steps in redo logging and commit processing.

We are in a position to state several key properties of our scheme. Before doing so, however, we need to define some terms.

Definition 1. We say that two database states are *equivalent* if they cannot be distinguished by any transactions. The definition accounts for abstract data types that may have different internal structures but that cannot be distinguished by any operations on the abstract data types. □

The redo log records for a transaction must satisfy the following condition.

Condition RP1. Consider the set of objects accessed by a transaction T_i that is executing alone in the system. Suppose that transaction T_i finds this set of objects in state s when first accessed, and its execution takes the set to state s'. Then replaying the redo log of transaction T_i starting from state s takes the set of objects to a state equivalent to s'.

Since the R2PL protocol ensures that the commit order is the same as the serialization order, and since we write out redo records in commit order, the following two key properties hold:

- The order of transactions in the persistent log is the same as their serialization order.

- The commit order of transactions is the same as the precommit order of transactions. Further, a transaction commits only if all transactions that precede it in the precommit order also commit.

The preceding properties, along with condition RP1, ensure that replaying the redo log starting from the empty database (and executing only redo actions of committed transactions) is equivalent to a serial execution of the committed transactions in an order consistent with their serialization order (i.e., the two bring the database to equivalent states). After presenting the checkpointing algorithm, we will discuss ways to recover from a system crash without replaying the entire log.

Discussion. The use of private redo logs reduces contention on the global log tail, as noted in [14]. The log tail is accessed only when a transaction has precommitted, and repeated acquisitions of short-term locks on the log tail are eliminated. Although writing out private redo records at the end of the transaction can slow down the commit process for transactions that write many log records, it speeds up processing of transactions that write only a few (small) log records. It is not hard to extend the algorithm to allow redo records (but not commit records) to be written ahead for large transactions (e.g., whenever there is a pageful of redo records), and ignored on restart if the transaction does not commit.

The release of locks on precommit allows a transaction T_i to access data written by an earlier transaction T_j that has precommitted but not committed. However, T_i has to wait for T_j to commit before it can commit. This is not a problem for updaters (since they have to wait to write out a commit record in any case). However, for read-only transactions that have read only committed data, such a wait is unnecessary. Read-only transactions may fare better under an alternative scheme that holds all locks until commit, since read-only transactions as before can commit without being assigned a spot in the commit sequence order.

The benefits of the two schemes can be combined by marking data as uncommitted when a precommit releases a lock, and removing the mark when the data have been committed. Then, read-only transactions that do not read uncommitted data do not have to wait for earlier updaters to commit. Refining the scheme further, uncommitted data can be marked with the commit sequence number of the transaction that last updated the data. A read-only transaction can commit after the commit of the transaction whose *csn* (commit sequence number) is the highest *csn* of uncommitted data read by the read-only transaction.

20.2.3   Abort Processing

Undo logging is implemented as follows. The undo records are written to the volatile undo log ahead of any modification to memory. The undo log records are not written to disk except when a checkpoint is taken. The undo log records of each transaction are chained so that they can be read backwards. After a transaction commits, the volatile undo log of the transaction may be deleted. (Similarly, the undo log may be deleted after a transaction aborts; see the description of abort processing below.)

We require the following condition on undo logs:

Condition UL1. The effect of a transaction that has not precommitted can be undone by executing (in reverse order) its undo log records.
Abort processing is done as follows.

Abort Processing. When a transaction T_i aborts, its undo log is traversed backwards, performing all its undo operations. Each undo action is performed and its undo record is removed from the undo log in a single action (atomic with respect to checkpointing). After all the undo operations have been completed, the record $\langle abort\ T_i \rangle$ is added to the global log. The transaction is said to have *aborted* at this point. After a transaction has aborted, it releases all the locks that it held.

We do not require the global log to be flushed to disk before declaring the transaction aborted. Also, since we assumed R2PL, there is no need to reacquire any locks during abort processing. The use of the abort record in the persistent log will be made clear once we discuss the checkpoint scheme.

20.3 CHECKPOINTING AND RECOVERY

In this section, we describe the main details of our checkpointing and recovery scheme. For ease of exposition, we describe first an algorithm for an unsegmented database; we call this algorithm A1. Algorithm A1, however, could cause transactions to wait for an inordinately long time. In Section 20.5, we address the problem by extending algorithm A1 to permit segmented databases where each segment is checkpointed separately; we call the extended algorithm A2. In such an environment, the length of time for which transactions are delayed is reduced correspondingly. Section 20.6 describes extensions to the algorithm to handle logical (operation) log records; we call the extended algorithm A3.

20.3.1 Checkpointing

In recovery algorithm A1, checkpointing is done in an *action-consistent* manner (i.e., no update actions are in progress at the time of the checkpointing). Action-consistency implies that the database and the undo log are frozen in an action consistent state during the course of the checkpoint. The set of active transactions and their status is not changed during the checkpoint. We discuss alternative ways of implementing freezing after presenting the basic algorithm.

Checkpoint Processing–A1

1. Freeze all accesses to the database and to the undo log in an action-consistent state.

2. Write the following out to a new checkpoint image

    (a) A pointer to the end of the persistent log

(b) The undo logs of all active transactions

(c) The main-memory database

(d) The transaction IDs and status information of all transactions that are active at the end of the checkpoint[3]

(e) The last assigned commit sequence number

3. Write out the location of the new checkpoint to the checkpoint location pointer on stable store. After this, the old checkpoint may be deleted.

We assume that there is a pointer in stable store to the latest checkpoint. The last action performed during a checkpoint is the update of this pointer. Thus, we follow a ping-pong scheme (see [22]), keeping up to two copies of the database. Partially written checkpoints are ignored in the event of a crash, and the previous (complete) checkpoint is used for recovery. Thus, the writing of the checkpoint is in effect atomic (i.e., it either happens completely or appears to have not happened at all).

It is not hard to see that the preceding protocol ensures the following two conditions:

1. The *undo log record* is on stable store before a checkpoint with the corresponding update is completed (by updating the pointer to the latest checkpoint), so that the update can be undone if necessary.

2. Every *redo log record* associated with a transaction is on stable store before a transaction is allowed to commit, so that its updates can be redone if necessary.

Discussion.   Although in the preceding description the main-memory database is written out to disk, it is simple enough to apply standard optimizations such as spooling out a copy to another region of main memory, and writing the copy to disk later, and further optimizing the scheme by spooling using copy on write [21]. These techniques, together with the segmented database scheme described later, reduce the time for which the database activities (or accesses to parts of the database, in case segmenting is used) are frozen.

In contrast to most other checkpoint schemes, our algorithms do not require the redo log to be flushed at checkpoint time (although they do require the undo log to be checkpointed). As a result, the (backup) database on disk may be updated before the redo log records for the corresponding updates are written out.

However, the checkpoint processing algorithm makes the following guarantee: Any redo records that occur in the persistent log before the pointer obtained before have their effects already reflected in the database. Thus, they need not be replayed (and are not replayed). But commit records do not have this consistency guarantee,

---

[3]Although we assume here that access to the database is frozen, during checkpointing, we relax the assumption later, so the set of active transactions can change during checkpointing.

since the status of active transactions may still need to be changed. There may be redo operations reflected in the database, but that appear after the persistent log pointer in the checkpoint. We describe later how to handle both cases in the recovery algorithm.

Some checkpointing schemes such as that of Lehman and Carey [14] require checkpoints to be taken in a transaction-consistent state, and the redo log to be flushed to disk at checkpoint time. However, transaction-consistent checkpoints can lead to lower concurrency and a longer checkpoint interval, especially if long transactions are executed.

To implement freezing of access in an action-consistent manner, we can use a latch that covers the database and the undo log. Any action has to acquire the latch in shared mode at the start of the action, and release it after the action is complete. The checkpointer has to acquire the latch in exclusive mode before starting the checkpoint, and can release it after checkpointing is complete.

Action consistency is not required in the case of physical logging, since physical undo/redo actions can be performed even if a checkpoint was made at a stage when the action was not complete. However, we require the following:

Condition UL2. Insertion/deletion of records in the undo log does not occur during checkpointing.

This condition ensures that the undo log written at checkpoint time is in a consistent state.

The checkpointing algorithm described here writes out the entire database. An optimization to write out only pages that have been updated is described in Section 20.8.

20.3.2 Recovery

The recovery algorithm is executed on restart after a system crash, before the start of transaction processing. Unlike most other recovery algorithms, our recovery algorithms are essentially one pass, going forward in the persistent log. Our first recovery algorithm is described in what follows.

Recovery Processing–A1

1. Find the last checkpoint.

2. From the checkpoint, read into main memory:

   (a) The entire database

   (b) The pointer to the end of the persistent log at checkpoint time

   (c) The transaction IDs and status information of all transactions that were active at checkpoint time

   (d) The undo logs of all transactions active at checkpoint time.

   (e) The last assigned commit sequence sequence number at checkpoint time

3. Go backward in the persistent log from the end until the first commit/abort record is found. Mark the spot as the end of the persistent log, and delete records after that spot.

4. Starting from the persistent log end noted in the checkpoint, go forward in the log, doing the following:

   (a) If a redo operation is encountered, Then
       If the operation is a physical redo operation,
       Then perform the redo operation.
       Else /* Steps to handle logical redo operations are discussed later */

   (b) If an abort record is encountered, Then
       If the transaction was not active at the time of checkpoint,
       Then ignore the abort record.
       Else find checkpoint copy of (volatile) undo log for the
           transaction, and perform the undo operations as before.

   (c) If a commit record is encountered,
       Then read its commit sequence number and update the last commit
       sequence number.

5. Perform undo operations (using the checkpointed undo log) for all those transactions that were active at the time the checkpoint took place, and whose commit records were not found in the redo log, and that are not marked committing. After performing the undo operations for a transaction, add an abort record for the transaction to the global log.

6. Perform undo operations (using the checkpointed undo log), in reverse commit-sequence-number order, for all transactions that were active at the time of checkpoint such that (i) their commit records were not found in the redo log, and (ii) they are marked committing and their commit sequence number is greater than the commit sequence number of the last commit record in the log. After performing the undo operations for a transaction, add an abort record for the transaction to the global log.

Discussion. We need to skip any redo records at the end of the persistent log that do not have a corresponding commit record. In our implementation, instead of traversing the redo log backwards to skip them, we only go forward in the log, but we read all the records for a transaction (these are consecutive in the log) before performing any action. If the commit or abort record for the transaction is not found, we ignore the log records of the transaction that were read in earlier. Thereby, we avoid the need for atomic writes of individual log records (i.e., log records can cross page boundaries), and the need to keep back pointers in the log.

By the use of commit sequence numbering, our recovery algorithm can find the transactions that have committed without looking at the commit records in the persistent log preceding the pointer. Alternative schemes, such as using the address of the record in the persistent log instead of the commit sequence number, can also be used to similar effect. There may be redo records after the persistent log pointer stored in the checkpoint, whose effect is already expressed in the checkpointed database. Replaying, on restart, of such log records is not a problem for physical log records due to idempotence. When we discuss logical logging, we describe how to avoid replaying logical log records whose effect is already expressed in the checkpoint.

This completes the description of the basic version of our recovery scheme. In the following sections, we will extend the functionality of the recovery scheme. First, however, we establish the correctness of the basic recovery scheme.

20.4 CORRECTNESS

The following theorem is the main result that shows the correctness of our recovery scheme.

Theorem 1. If rigorous two-phase locking is followed, recovery processing using algorithm A1 brings the database to a state equivalent to that after the serial execution, in the commit order, of all committed transactions. **Proof:** The redo log notes the points at which transactions committed or aborted. Actual undo operations are stored in the checkpoint image. We first show that undo actions are carried out correctly during recovery. We do this via the following claims: (a) We correctly undo the actions of every transaction that did not commit before system crash, *and* (b) we do not undo the actions of any transaction that did commit before system crash.

To show (a), we need to show that we undo the effects of every transaction whose updates are reflected in the checkpoint, and further we perform the undo actions in the correct order. Consider any action that has dirtied the checkpoint and did not commit. There are four cases.

Abort Finished Before Checkpoint. Such transactions may still be present in the active transaction list. However, since the abort finished, the effects of the transaction have been undone, and the undo log of the transaction must be empty. Hence, no further undo actions are carried out.

Abort Finished After Checkpoint But Before Crash. If the transaction started after the checkpoint, it could not have affected the checkpoint, and no undo log for it can be present. Otherwise, it must figure in the checkpointed active transaction list. We will find its abort record, and undo its effects starting from the checkpoint state. (If the transaction aborted due to an earlier crash, and its effects were undone on an earlier recovery, an abort record would have been introduced into the global log at the time of the earlier recovery. If any transaction committed afterwards, the abort log would also have been flushed to disk, so we will reexecute the abort before reexecuting actions of any transaction that started after the previous restart.) It is safe to perform the undo operations at the point where the abort record is found since the transaction must have held locks up to that point (again, logically, a transaction that aborted due to a crash can be viewed as having aborted at recovery time without releasing any locks).

Did Not Precommit. The transaction did not precommit and did not abort. Hence, it must have held all locks to crash time. The effects of all such transactions are undone at the end of recovery. But no two of them can conflict since all held locks till the crash. (Recall that we assume rigorous two-phase locking.)

Precommitted But Did Not Commit. This means that not all redo records were written out, so the transaction must be rolled back at recovery. We detect such transactions, since they are marked "committing" but have larger sequence numbers than the last committed transaction. These must have been serialized after the last committed/aborted transaction, and we roll these back in the reverse of the commit-sequence-number order, after those that did not precommit. Hence, their effects are undone in the correct order.

This completes the proof of claim (a).

To prove claim (b), we need to show that if a transaction commit record hit stable store before crash, it is not rolled back. There are again several cases:

Commit Happened Before Checkpoint. It may still be the case that the transaction is in the active transaction list. But then it must be marked "committing", and its commit sequence number is less than or equal to that of the last one that committed. We will then not roll it back.

Commit Happened After Checkpoint. Even if the transaction is in the active transaction list, we find the commit record while processing the redo log, and hence we will not roll back the transaction.

This completes claim (b).

We have shown that all required undo operations are executed and no others. No undo action is executed more than once, since there is no repetition during recovery, and any undo operation carried out earlier as part of abort processing is deleted from the undo log atomically with the undo action. It then follows from UL1 that undo operations are replayed correctly.

Redo records are written out to disk in the commit order, and are replayed in the commit order, which is also the serialization order since we assumed rigorous 2PL. Hence, they are replayed in the correct order. Every redo operation that is not reflected in the checkpointed segment is replayed, since the redo log of each transaction is flushed to persistent log after transaction precommit, while we noted the end of the redo log as of the start of checkpointing. (Some operations already reflected in the checkpoint may be redone.) Every redo operation that hits the persistent redo log before the checkpoint is reflected in the checkpoint, since the transaction must have precommitted. Hence, the action can be considered to have been replayed already. Thus, we have shown that we, in effect, replay all necessary redo actions in the correct order. Since physical actions logged are all idempotent, this guarantees that the desired database state is reached.

This completes the proof. □

20.5   SEGMENTING THE DATABASE

Until now, we had assumed that the entire database is checkpointed at one time, and all transactions are frozen. Now we consider how to perform recovery when we divide the database into units that we call *segments*. The database is divided into segments for two reasons. First, to allow the database to be partitioned logically, so that only partitions that are needed at any time are resident in memory. Second, to reduce the overhead of checkpointing the entire memory-resident database at once, and the resultant delays of transactions if the checkpoint has to be action-consistent.

A segment can be a page, or a set of pages. With small segments, checkpointing a segment will have overhead comparable to page flushing in a disk-resident database. We require the following condition to hold:

Condition AS1. Each database action that is logged, as well as the actions to redo or undo it, access data resident in only one segment.

The preceding condition is required so that different segments may be checkpointed independently. Otherwise, during restart, if a single logical redo or logical undo action accesses different segments checkpointed separately, it could see an inconsistent database state.

Recovery algorithm A2 is defined as follows. The algorithm uses the logging, checkpointing, and recovery techniques of algorithm A1 with the following changes:

- The undo log of each transaction is split into a set of undo logs, one for each segment it accesses. Since each action affects only one segment, it is straightforward to do so. The undo log records of a transaction are chained together as before, allowing them to be scanned backwards. Redo logging is done as before.

- Checkpointing is done one segment at a time. There is no requirement that segments are checkpointed in any particular order, although some performance benefits of ordering are discussed later. To checkpoint a segment, all accesses to the segment are frozen in an action-consistent state. For all active transactions, the undo logs corresponding to the segment are written out, instead of the entire undo logs.

  Instead of a single pointer to the end of the persistent log, each checkpointed segment has its own pointer to the end of the persistent log. Similarly, instead of a pointer to the database checkpoint in stable store, a table of pointers, one per segment, is maintained in stable store, and these pointers are updated when the checkpoint of a segment (or of a set of segments) is completed.

- We use a latch that covers the segment and its undo log to implement action-consistent checkpointing of a segment. Any action on the segment has to acquire the latch in shared mode at the start of the action, and release it after the action is complete.

As in algorithm A1, the redo log need not be flushed when checkpointing a segment, although the undo log must be checkpointed. Thereby, the overhead of checkpointing a segment is reduced, which is particularly beneficial if segments are small.

Recovery is done as in algorithm A1 with the following changes: The log is scanned from the minimum of the end-of-persistent-log pointers across all segment checkpoints. For each segment, we ignore the persistent log records before the persistent log pointer in its last checkpoint.

Discussion.   The list of active transactions that have updated the segment but have not committed must not change while checkpointing the segment. This is ensured since a persegment, pertransaction undo log has to be created before a transaction updates a segment, and has to be deleted before a transaction aborts.

Logged operations must be kept small enough or segment sizes should be made large enough to ensure that Condition AS1 is satisfied. If a segment is large, we can use techniques like the black/white copy on the update scheme of [20] to minimize the time for which the segment is inaccessible for transaction processing. Segments need not be predefined, and could be possibly extended dynamically to ensure Condition AS1.

A benefit of segmenting the database, noted in [14], is that segments containing hot spots (i.e., regions that are accessed frequently) can be checkpointed more often than other segments. Recovery for such segments would be speeded up greatly, since otherwise a large number of redo operations would have to be replayed for the segment.

20.6   LOGICAL LOGGING

Logging of higher-level "logical" actions as opposed to lower-level or physical actions, such as read/write, can be beneficial in a database system (see [10]). There are actually two kinds of logical logging, logical redo logging, and logical undo logging that have different motivations.

Logical Undo Logging.   With most extended concurrency control schemes, such as multilevel transactions [17, 23], physical undo logging cannot be used to rollback transactions–an object may have been modified by more than one uncommitted transaction, and a compensating logical operation has to be executed to undo the effect of an operation. Thus, the undo information for a completed action must be logical, not physical. For instance, such is the case with space allocation tables, which we cannot afford to have locked till the end of the transaction.

Logical Redo Logging. Logical logging of redo information can significantly reduce the amount of information in the log. For example, an insert operation may change a significant part of the index, but a logical log record that says "insert specified object in index" would be quite small.

If redo logging is done logically and not physically, checkpoints must be in an action-consistent state, which means fuzzy checkpointing cannot be used. In some cases, there could also be a trade-off between recomputation at the time of recovery and extra storage for physical log records. Logical redo logging is therefore not as widely used as logical undo logging.

20.6.1 Model of Logical Logging

Conceptually, we view a logical operation as an operation on an abstract data type (ADT). For example, an index, or an allocation table can be considered an ADT, and operations such as "insert a tuple" or "allocate an object" can be considered as logical operations. We make the following assumption:

LO1. Each logical operation affects exactly one data item (although the data item may be large, e.g., an index).

Typically, the ADT performs its own concurrency control scheme internally, which may not be R2PL (and may not even be 2PL). Some form of higher-level locking is used to ensure serializability of transactions.

On system restart, our recovery algorithm

1. performs redo and undo operations in serialization order (since the operations are initially added to local logs, which in turn are appended to the system log only at commit time)

2. omits operations that were rolled back before the checkpoint

The design of an ADT that uses logical logging and supports redo in serialization order must ensure that when performing redo and undo operations in serialization order, rather than in the order in which they actually occurred, (i) each redone operation has the same result as when it originally executed, and (ii) the ADT is brought to a "consistent" state at the end of restart; that is, a state that is equivalent (in an application-specific sense) to one where the operations corresponding to committed transactions are executed in serialization order. Also, the ADT must be able to undo any operation until transaction commit.

For an intuitive idea of what these requirements signify, consider the case of a space allocator. The redo log should contain not only data stating that an allocate request was made, but should also contain data that say what the location of the allocated space was (the location is the return value of the allocation operation). When performing a redo, the allocator must ensure that the same location is allocated. Further, the space allocator must be able to undo both allocate and deallocate requests. To undo a deallocate request, the deallocated space should be reallocated, and its value restored, which means the space should not be allocated to any other transaction until the transaction that performs the deallocate commits. At the end of recovery, the state of the allocation information should be such that all space that was allocated as of the end of recovery is noted as allocated, and all that was free is noted as free. The state may not be exactly the same as if only actions corresponding to committed transactions were executed, since the exact layout of the tables may be different. But any difference in the layout is semantically irrelevant, assuming that an allocation request (not a redo of an allocation request) may return any space that was free.

An alternative to the preceding is to log operations directly to the system redo log, rather than to the transaction local redo logs. This approach is more complicated to implement, but has the obvious benefit of greatly simplifying the design of the ADT. Such extensions are described in [6], and summarized in Section 20.8.

20.6.2   Logical Logging and Rollback

A logical operation may take a good deal of time to complete. To accommodate such logical operations, we relax assumption LA1 further here, by allowing checkpointing in the middle of a logical operation. To understand how this can be done, logical operations are best understood as multilevel nested transactions (e.g. [2, 17, 23], or see [10]).

In order to roll back partially completed logical actions, we create undo logs for the nested transaction. We create redo log records for logical actions and hence do not need to create redo log records for the nested transaction.

The undo log for the nested transaction, with an identifier i, is embedded in the undo log of the main transaction as follows:

1. A "⟨ begin operation i ⟩" is written to the undo log.

2. The undo operations of the nested transaction are written to the undo log.

3. An "⟨ end operation i ⟩" record, with any information necessary for logical undo, is written to the undo log. The nested transaction is said to commit as soon as the "⟨end operation i ⟩" record enters the undo log. The insertion of the log record is done in an atomic fashion.

On system restart, logical redo operations should not be executed repeatedly, since they may not be idempotent, and the "⟨ end operation i ⟩" records are used to ensure nonrepetition, as described later. We require the following properties of the undo log:

Condition NT1. The effects of a nested transaction that has not committed can be undone by executing (in reverse order) the undo log records of the nested transaction.

Condition NT2. At any point after the commit of a nested transaction, but before the commit of the main transaction, the effects of logical operation i can be undone by executing the logical undo operation specified in the "⟨ end operation i ⟩" record.

Redo logging in the case of logical actions is the same as with physical actions. We now present versions of the abort processing and recovery processing algorithms that work correctly, even with logical logging.

Abort Processing–A3. When a transaction aborts, its undo log is traversed backwards, performing all its undo operations. If an "⟨ end operation i ⟩" record is encountered, the logical undo operation is performed, and undo actions of the corresponding nested transaction are ignored. Otherwise, the undo actions of the nested transaction are executed. In any case, an undo action is performed and its undo record is removed from the undo log in a single atomic action.

After all the undo operations have been completed, the transaction logs an *abort record* in the shared (redo) log. The transaction is said to have *aborted* at this point. (Note, in particular, that it is not necessary to wait for the abort record to reach the persistent log.) After a transaction has aborted, it can release all its locks.

The requirement that logical undo actions are performed and the undo record removed from the log in one atomic action essentially says that checkpointing should not take place while these actions are in progress.

It is important that the designer of the ADT ensures that logical undo operations will never run into a deadlock when acquiring the (lower-level) locks that they need. If such a situation were to arise, another abort may be needed to break the deadlock, which can lead to a cycle that leaves the system hung forever.

20.6.3 Checkpointing and Recovery

We now present a modification to the checkpoint processing and recovery processing techniques given in Section 20.3.

Checkpoint Processing–A3. Checkpoint processing is done as before, except that if a logical action is implemented as a nested transaction, with its own undo log, checkpointing can be done in a state that is action-consistent with respect to the nested transaction's actions. Thus, checkpointing need not be suspended for the entire duration of the logical action.

Recovery processing with logical logging differs from recovery processing with physical logging only in the way logical log records are handled. We describe in what follows the relevant steps of the recovery processing algorithm.

Recovery Processing–A3

1. Find the last checkpoint. /* As before */

2. ... as before, read in checkpoint data.

3. ... as before, find the end of the persistent log.

4. Starting from the persistent log pointer noted in the checkpoint, go forward in the log:

   (a) If a redo operation (numbered, say, i) is encountered, Then
   > If the operation is a physical redo operation,
   >> Then perform the redo operation
   >> Else /* it is a logical action */
   >>> If there is an "end operation i" record in the checkpointed undo log,
   >>>> Then ignore the redo operation.
   >>>> /* the effect of the operation has been reflected in the checkpointed segment and it should not be reexecuted. */
   >>> Else
   >>>> If there are undo log records from a nested transaction for the logical redo action, then execute the undo operations.
   >>>> Execute the logical redo operation.
   >>>> /* Executing the redo operation creates undo log records as described earlier */

   (b) ... handle abort records as before.

   (c) ... handle commit records as before.

5. ... perform undo operations, as before.

20.6.4 Correctness

The correctness arguments of the scheme with logical logging are similar to the correctness arguments for the scheme with physical logging. The primary additional concern is that we have to prove that at recovery time, we do not redo any action whose effect is already reflected in the checkpoint, and that is not idempotent.

Either a record "$\langle$ end operation i $\rangle$" is present in the checkpointed undo log or it is not. In the first case, we do not replay the logical operation, and its effect is already reflected in the checkpointed segment. In the second case, one of two things is possible. Either the operation had not finished at the time of the checkpoint, and by condition NT1, it is safe to use the undo log of the nested transaction corresponding to the logical action to undo any partial effects of the transaction. The recovery algorithm does the undo, and at this stage, the state is equivalent to the state (in a serial replay) just before when the action was initially performed. The recovery algorithm then replays the redo action. Hence, at this stage, the redo operation has been correctly replayed, and the database state reflects the execution of the action. The other case is that the operation had finished at the time of the checkpoint. But the absence of the "end-operation" record then implies that the transaction must have committed or aborted before the checkpoint, and in either case, we could not have found a redo operation in the persistent log after the persistent log pointed in the checkpoint. In any case, the return values of the redone operations are exactly the same as that of the original operations, and the ADT is in a consistent state at the end of recovery.

20.7 EXTENSIONS

In this section, we consider several extensions of the algorithms described so far.

20.7.1 Database Bigger Than Memory

We assumed earlier that the database fits into main memory. We can relax this assumption by using virtual memory. Alternatively, we could use the checkpointer to flush some segments, in order to make space for other segments. Doing so may be preferable to writing pages to swap space since we get the benefit of checkpointing with roughly the same amount of I/O. In fact, our algorithm can be used for disk-resident databases as well, and will be efficient provided most of the data in use at any point of time fits into main memory. The idea of writing undo logs only when flushing segments that are not transaction-consistent can be used in disk-resident databases as well, and our basic algorithm can be used with some minor modifications even in cases where data do not fit into main memory.

20.7.2 Partitioning the Redo Log

We can partition the redo log across segments (assuming that every log operation is local to a segment). Partitioning the redo log permits segments to be recovered independently, transactions can start executing before all segments have been recovered, and segments can be recovered on demand. To commit a transaction, we write a "prepared to commit" record to each segment redo log, and then flush each segment redo log. After all segment redo logs have been flushed, we can write a commit record to a separate global transaction log; the transaction commits when this record hits stable storage. Abort records are written to each segment redo log and to the global transaction log. During recovery, the global transaction log is used to find what transactions committed and what transactions did not commit.

To recover a segment, we bring the segment into main memory and use recovery processing as before on it but using its local redo log, and doing either redoing or undoing the actions of the transaction at the point where the "prepared to commit" or abort log record is found, depending on whether the commit record is in the global transaction log or not.

Partitioning the redo log per segment permits efficient support for segments to be recovered independently, and to allow new transactions to begin operating on segments that have been recovered, even while recovering other segments. Although it is possible to recover segments independently with a single redo log, multiple passes would be required on the whole log.

Lehman and Carey [14] present a redo log partitioning technique where the log tail is written unpartitioned into a stable region of main memory, and later a separate processor partitions the log tail. However, the technique appears to depend on the availability of stable main memory for the log tail.

20.7.3   Miscellaneous

If checkpointing is done cyclically on the segments (i.e., in a round-robin fashion), we can use a bubble propagation scheme to keep segment checkpoints (almost) contiguous on disk. The idea is to all have segment checkpoints contiguous, except for a single bubble. The bubble is used to create a new checkpoint image for the segment whose old checkpoint is just after the bubble. Once the checkpoint is complete, the bubble is moved forward, replacing the old checkpoint of the segment. The bubble can be used to checkpoint the next segment. Since the undo log that is written out with each segment is not of a predetermined size, some fixed amount of space can be allocated for the undo log, and if the log is too big, any excess can be written in an overflow area.

20.8   DISCUSSION

An extended version of our recovery scheme is described in [6] (and also briefly outlined in [5]). This extended scheme is used in the Dalí main-memory database system [12]. The extensions include the following:

- Repeating of history with physical redo and logical undo. As part of repeating history, redo logging is performed even when performing undo (whether physical or logical). Redo records are added to the system redo log on operation completion. The design of ADTs for logical actions is greatly simplified by repeating of history, since operations during recovery will occur in exactly the same order as during the earlier execution.

  Logical undo logging permits some locks, such as index locks, to be released early when an operation completes. Once locks are released, logical undos are performed by executing compensating actions.

- Completely fuzzy checkpointing, without even requiring transactions to acquire latches when updating a page. Thereby, interference due to checkpointing is almost completely eliminated.

  To support completely fuzzy checkpointing, a log flush is performed after writing the contents of memory to disk, before declaring the checkpoint committed. The special treatment of precommitted transactions is also simplified somewhat as a result, since the log flush ensures that any transaction noted as precommitted in the checkpoint image will actually be committed before the checkpoint completes.

- Dirty-page-only checkpointing. This feature allows the checkpointing algorithm to only write out pages that have been updated, and avoid writing pages that never changed.

  To support this feature, checkpoints are performed alternately on two copies of the checkpoint on disk. When writing to a copy, *only* those pages are written that have changed since the last time that copy was written. A dirty-page table is maintained to detect which pages have been written to since the last checkpoint. Entries in the dirty-page table are updated when appending redo log records to the system log.

- Postcommit actions. These are actions that can be registered by a transaction, and are guaranteed to be executed if and only if the transaction commits. Sending a success message to a client system is an example of such an action. Postcommit actions are implemented in a manner very similar to logical undo; the main difference is that they are performed on commit, whereas undo operations are performed on abort.

- Multilevel recovery. Multiple levels of operations are supported, permitting very high concurrency. The extra concurrency can be important due to long transactions, two-phase commit, or waits for human actions.

The extended recovery algorithm retains the benefits of the techniques described in this paper such as transient undo logging, pertransaction redo and undo logs to reduce system log contention, and single-pass recovery.

The preceding scheme has been further extended to handle client-server systems and shared-disk parallel systems; the extensions are described in [5]. Two approaches are described: one where pages are shipped between processors, and the other where log records are shipped between processors, and applied on the local copy of data at each processor to keep it up to date.

20.9   RELATED WORK

For a detailed description of the issues related to main-memory databases, and how they differ from disk-resident databases, see [9]. In this section, we concentrate on issues related to checkpointing and recovery. There has been a considerable amount of work on checkpointing and recovery schemes for main-memory databases. Salem and Garcia-Molina [21] and Eich [7] provide surveys of main-memory recovery techniques.

Main-memory databases differ from disk-oriented databases in several ways. The most important differences that we exploit in the present chapter are as follows. (a) Segments with uncommitted data are not flushed to disk as often as pages with uncommitted data are flushed to disk in a disk-based system. (b), The redo and undo logs of uncommitted transactions can be kept in memory and modified without incurring any disk I/O. As a result of (b) we are able to modify the logs and write out to disk only what is absolutely needed to be written to disk, and thus reduce log I/O and recovery time. The benefit of (a) is that undo logs of most transactions never need be written to disk if the transaction runs to completion without any of its dirty pages being written out.

There are other techniques that can be used to avoid undo logging [3]. The benefits of redo-only logging are clear–recovery time is speeded up by eliminating an analysis pass on the log, and undo operations do not have to be replayed. Li and Eich [16] present an analysis that underscores the benefits of not having undo logging. However, previous techniques paid a high price for this benefit, since checkpointing had to be transaction consistent if undo logging was not done. For example, in the algorithm of Lehman and Carey [14], in order to checkpoint a segment, the checkpointer has to obtain a read lock on the segment. This can adversely affect performance in the case of database hot spots, since the checkpointer will cause contention with update transactions. Levy and Silberschatz [15] also require transaction-consistent checkpointing, as do the redo/no-undo techniques described in [3], and the EOS storage manager [4]. If the database does not fit entirely into main memory, our technique can checkpoint a segment with uncommitted updates, and swap it at any time, in contrast to other techniques, such as that of Lehman and Carey, that require transaction-consistent checkpoints.

The most important contribution of our technique is that it permits the use of redo-only logging while permitting action-consistent checkpointing. We believe that our technique will have significant benefits in the presence of "hot" pages/segments, which are updated by many transactions. Transaction-consistent checkpointing of the hot pages/segments would interfere greatly with regular processing since checkpointing would have to acquire a read lock on the page/segment.

Our algorithms support action-consistent checkpointing by permitting pages with uncommitted updates to be written out, but writing corresponding undo log records to the checkpoint. Independently, a similar technique is described in [18], in the context of the Rdb/VMS, shared-disk, parallel database system. Unlike the technique of [18], our technique permits fine-gr anularity locks and the release of locks on precommit. Further, their technique does not support logical redo or undo logging. Finally, checkpointing in [18] is done in a transaction-consistent state (although pages with uncommitted updates may be flushed to disk), whereas we permit action-consistent checkpointing. On the other hand, their technique handles shared-disk parallel systems. More recently, in [5], we have extended our recovery algorithm to handle both client-server and shared-disk systems.

In the Oracle database system, pages are locked into memory and thereby prevented from being flushed for the entire duration of certain kinds of transactions ("discrete transactions"). We believe that undo logs are not written to disk for such transactions, and the TPC benchmark numbers from Oracle indicate the resultant benefits [1]. However, the Oracle scheme forces a bound on the number of discrete transactions that can be executed concurrently, since the pages cannot be flushed to disk. In contrast, our scheme permits the pages to be flushed to disk.

An alternative, proposed by Eich [8], is not to checkpoint the primary copy of the database, but instead to replay redo logs of committed transactions continually on a secondary stable copy of the database, and have transactions execute on the primary copy only. This would double the storage and processing requirements. Moreover, replaying could become a bottleneck, since it is in effect replaying the committed actions of the main-memory database on the disk database, in serialization order, and could require a considerable amount of I/O. Hagmann [11] allows fuzzy checkpointing, but logical undo logging cannot be supported by his technique, and transient undo logging is not supported.

Some of the details of our recovery scheme are similar to those of Lehman and Carey [14]. Both schemes propagate only redo information of committed transaction to the stable log, and both schemes keep the redo log records of a transaction consecutive in the log. Lehman and Carey also support segmented databases with independent checkpointing for each segment, and logical logging. However, as mentioned earlier, their scheme requires transaction -consistent checkpointing.

The algorithms of [14] and [8] *require* stable main memory. Our algorithms are not dependent on the availability of stable main memory. This will enable our algorithms to be used on standard workstations without hardware modifications, which is very beneficial. However, if stable main memory is available, we can use it for storing the log tail, and thereby achieve better performance in a manner similar to [14] and [8].

Our algorithms have some benefits over Aries [19]. The main benefits include transient undo logging, and per-transaction redo and undo logs to reduce system log contention. Our basic algorithms have some drawbacks as compared to ARIES, such as not supporting checkpointing of only dirty pages, and not fully supporting repeating of history. However, the extensions described in Section 20.8 remove these drawbacks, and provide further advantages such as completely fuzzy checkpointing.

20.10   CONCLUSION

With the general availability of dozens to hundreds of megabytes of main memory on relatively inexpensive and widely used systems, it is rapidly becoming the case that many useful database applications today fit entirely (or largely) within the available main memory. A major factor in performance, and almost the sole cause of disk I/O, is the recovery subsystem of the database, responsible for maintaining the durability of the transactions.

In this chapter we have presented a recovery scheme for main-memory databases that exploits the characteristics of main-memory databases to provide important benefits such as transient undo logging, per transaction redo and undo logs, and fast recovery. The techniques described here have since been extended to support a variety of new features, and are used in the Dalí main-memory database system.

Acknowledgments

We would like to thank Mike Franklin, Alex Biliris, Narain Gehani, and Dan Lieuwen for their comments on an earlier version of this chapter, and Ken Salem for providing us information about System M.

References

[1] Anderson, J. *Data management: Benchmarking facts of life and why Oracle now comes up a winner*, Open Systems Today, April 1993.

[2] C. Beeri, H.-J. Schek, and G. Weikum. "Multi-level transaction management: theoretical art or practical need?," In *International Conference on Extending Database Technology, Lecture Notes on Computer Science*, Vol. 303. Springer Verlag, 1988.

[3] P. A. Bernstein, V. Hadzilacos, and N. Goodman. *Concurrency Control and Recovery in Database Systems*. Addison-Wesley, 1987.

[4] Biliris, A., and E. Panagos. *EOS User's Guide, Release 2.0.0*, Technical report, AT&T Bell Labs, 1993. BL011356-930505-25M.

[5] P. Bohannon, J. Parker, R. Rastogi, S. Seshadri, A. Silberschatz, and S. Sudarshan. "Distributed multi-level recovery in main-memory databases," In *Procs. of the International Conference on Parallel and Distributed Information Systems (PDIS)*, 1996.

[6] P. Bohannon, R. Rastogi, A. Silberschatz, and S. Sudarshan. "Multi-level recovery in the Dali main-memory storage manager," submitted for publication, February 1996.

[7] M. Eich. "A classification and comparison of main memory database recovery techniques," In *Proceedings of the Third International Conference on Data Engineering, Los Angeles*, 1987.

[8] M. Eich. "Main memory database recovery," In *1986 Proceedings ACM-IEEE Fall Joint Computer Conference, Dallas*, 1986.

[9] H. Garcia-Molina and K. Salem. "Main memory database systems: An overview," *IEEE Transactions on Knowledge and Data Engineering*, 4(6) (December 1992).

[10] J. Gray and A. Reuter. *Transaction Processing: Concepts and Techniques*. Morgan Kaufmann, San Mateo, California, 1993.

[11] R. B. Hagmann. "A crash recovery scheme for memory-resident database system," *IEEE Transactions on Computers*, C-35(9) (September 1986).

[12] H.V. Jagadish, Dan Lieuwen, Rajeev Rastogi, Avi Silberschatz, and S. Sudarshan. "Dali: A high performance main-memory storage manager," In *Procs. of the International Conf. on Very Large Databases*, 1994.

[13] H.V. Jagadish, Avi Silberschatz, and S. Sudarshan. "Recovering from main-memory lapses," In *Procs. of the International Conf. on Very Large Databases*, 1993.

[14] T. J. Lehman and M. J. Carey. "A recovery algorithm for a high-performance memory-resident database system," In *Proceedings of ACM-SIGMOD 1987 International Conference on Management of Data, San Francisco*, 1987.

[15] E. Levy and A. Silberschatz. "Incremental recovery in large-memory database systems," *IEEE Transactions on Knowledge and Data Engineering*, 4(6) (December 1992).

[16] Xi Li and Margaret H. Eich. "Post-crash log processing for fuzzy checkpointing main memory databases," In *International Conf. on Data Engineering*, 1993.

[17] David Lomet. "MLR: A recovery method for multi-level systems," In *Procs. of the ACM SIGMOD Conf. on Management of Data*, 1992.

[18] David Lomet, Rick Anderson, T. K. Rengarajan, and Peter Spiro. *How the Rdb/VMS data sharing system became fast*, Technical Report CRL 92/4, Digital Equipment Corporation, Cambridge Research Lab, May 1992.

[19] C. Mohan, D. Haderle, Bruce Lindsay, Hamid Pirahesh, and P. Schwarz. "ARIES: A Transaction Recovery Method Supporting Fine-Granularity Locking and Partial Rollbacks Using Write-Ahead Logging," *ACM Transactions on Database Systems*, 17(1) (March 1992).

[20] C. Pu. "On-the-fly, incremental, consistent reading of entire databases," *Algorithmica*, (1) 1986.

[21] K. Salem and H. Garcia-Molina. *Crash recovery for memory-resident databases*, Technical Report CS-TR-119-87, Princeton University, Computer Science Department, 1987.

[22] K. Salem and H. Garcia-Molina. "System M: A transaction processing testbed for memory resident data," *IEEE Transactions on Knowledge and Data Engineering*, 2(1) 1990.

[23] G. Weikum, C. Hasse, P. Broessler, and P. Muth. "Multi-level recovery," In *Procs. of the ACM Symp. on Principles of Database Systems*, April 1990.

Chapter 21

Fuzzy Checkpointing Alternatives for Main-Memory Databases

Margaret H. Dunham, Jun-Lin Lin, and Xi Li

Abstract

The goal of checkpointing a database is to save the database state in nonvolatile storage in order to reduce the amount of work during the restart operation after a failure. *Fuzzy checkpointing*, due to its low interference with other database activities, has been shown to be one of the best checkpointing approaches for main-memory databases (MMDB). This chapter introduces two variants of the fuzzy checkpointing approach targeted for high transaction throughput MMDB systems where recovery time is crucial. The first approach, *dynamic segmented fuzzy checkpointing (DSFC)*, divides the main memory into segments automatically to adapt to changing run-time conditions. The checkpointing process checkpoints each segment in a round-robin fashion. The second approach, *partition checkpointing (PC)*, assumes that main memory is divided into partitions based on frequency of update. Partitions are checkpointed independently at rates proportional to the update frequency. A global checkpoint across all partitions is performed implicitly when each of the updated partitions has had a local checkpoint. Both approaches incur minimal overhead during transaction processing with the potential of saving much time during recovery in the event of system failure.

21.1 INTRODUCTION

In a *main-memory database (MMDB)*, all or a major portion of the database is placed in main memory. What is important is the perception of where data resides. With an MMDB, the DBMS software is designed assuming the data are memory-resident. With a *disk-resident database (DRDB)*, the DBMS is designed assuming the data are stored on disk and I/O is required to access the data. The permanent copy of DRDB data is assumed to be on disk, and that of MMDB data is assumed to be in main memory. The impact of the primary location of data on the DBMS design includes differences in recovery techniques, data structures, query processing algorithms, and concurrency control [9, 15].

An MMDB, as the primary copy of the database, resides in main memory and is more vulnerable to failures. Power loss, chip burnout, hardware errors, or software errors can corrupt the primary copy of the database [16]. A stable backup of the database on secondary storage must be maintained in order to restore the memory copy after a failure. Checkpoint techniques provide an important way to refresh the backup database and keep the amount of log data processed at recovery small. An MMDB checkpoint writes out memory data to secondary storage. With a large main memory, the efficiency of the checkpointing method becomes crucial. This can significantly impact database processing in a high-throughput MMDB environment or a real-time database system with deadline schedules for transactions.

Many researchers have examined this problem [8, 13, 14, 16]. Hagmann first presented fuzzy checkpointing for main memory databases in [13]. In his fuzzy checkpointing scheme, there are two methods to write main-memory pages to secondary storage: Either all the pages or only dirty pages are copied out during checkpointing. Lehman proposed an interesting checkpointing scheme that checkpoints a page at a time based on number of updates to the page or time since the last checkpoint [16]. In this scheme, however, checkpoints are executed as normal transactions and read locks are held on the database pages when checkpoint transactions are invoked. Levy proposed a technique based on the application of log records to the backup disk [8]. In his approach, a dedicated processor directly applies log information in log tails to a backup database. However, synchronization control is required between updates from the normal page replacement and the log processing of the recovery processor. Jagadish et al. [17] proposed an action-consistent checkpointing scheme. When checkpointing, the undo-log-records of active transactions are first written to the log, and then dirty pages are flushed to disks to enforce the WAL protocol. During normal transaction processing, the logger only writes the redo-log-records of the committed transactions to the log. This approach reduces the size of the log, since not all the undo-log-records are written to the log. However, in order to achieve action consistency, no update actions can be in progress when checkpointing. This not only affects the throughput, but also causes an intolerable delay when checkpointing. This approach was originally used in Dali, a main-memory database server developed at AT&T Bell Labs [22]. Tests conducted with this recovery algorithm led to a restructuring of Dali's recovery algorithm to include fuzzy checkpointing [3]. Fuzzy checkpoints were implemented due to the poor performance of the original action-consistent ones.

We have two goals for any successful MMDB checkpoint technique: It should cause little or no interference to normal database processing, and it should reduce restart time after a crash. Salem studied several checkpoint algorithms and demonstrated that fuzzy checkpointing requires little or no synchronization with normal processing [14]. Therefore, we consider fuzzy checkpointing as the basic approach for checkpointing a large main-memory system.

In this chapter, we discuss two variants of a fuzzy checkpointing technique for large-memory systems. The first technique, namely, *dynamic segmented fuzzy checkpointing (DSFC)*, divides the MMDB into segments based on the transaction-access pattern. The checkpointing activity proceeds according to the order of segments in a round-robin fashion. Unlike the conventional fuzzy checkpointing approach that constructs a complete checkpoint interval only after checkpointing the entire database, DSFC constructs a new complete checkpoint interval whenever a segment has been completely checkpointed. Thus, DSFC is able to provide the restart operation with more up-to-date information, and to yield better recovery performance. Moreover, DSFC automatically adjusts the way the database is segmented to ensure better recovery performance since the transaction access pattern changes from time to time. The database administrators (DBAs) do not have to decide how to segment the database. This self-adjustable feature makes DSFC extremely desirable for real-world applications.

The second technique, namely, *partition checkpointing*, is based on prior knowledge (or estimates) of data-update patterns in databases. The idea of a *partition checkpoint* is that the checkpoint method no longer treats the entire database as a single object, but as a collection of smaller data partitions, each with different update frequency. The checkpoint/recovery mechanism checkpoints data partitions based on frequency of update. The partitions with a high frequency of update are checkpointed more often. This reduces the number of log items that need to be processed by the recovery component for installing effects of committed actions not present in the checkpoint of hot-set partitions. That is, as far as recovery is concerned, checkpointing a hot-set page has more *recovery value* than checkpointing some other page, because the former installs more updates into persistent archive. Any updates not installed into the persistent archive need to be installed by the recovery process in the case of a crash. Partition checkpointing attempts to maximize the *recovery value* of the checkpointing activity. It has the potential to greatly reduce reload time after system failure, and thus bring up high-performance MMDB systems faster than would be possible with normal checkpointing. Partition checkpointing actually consists of two types of checkpointing: checkpointing at the partition level, which is called a *local checkpoint*, and checkpointing across all partitions which is called a *global checkpoint*. The global checkpoint is required to recover the MMDB to a transaction-consistent state.

The rest of this chapter is organized as follows. Section 21.2 describes a general MMDB architecture. Section 21.3 presents the DSFC approach. Section 21.4

presents the partition checkpointing and associated recovery algorithms. Section 21.5 gives a brief comparison among several checkpointing techniques. Finally, in Section 21.6, we conclude with a summary.

21.2   MMDB ARCHITECTURE

In this chapter we assume that the MMDB architecture is composed of one or more CPUs, volatile main memory, log buffer, archived disks, and log disks. For simplicity, we assume that the size of main memory is large enough to hold the entire database, and the primary copy of the database resides in the main memory. Thus, there is no disk I/O due to page faults. The *archived disks* are used as *archive memory* to store the nonvolatile version of the database.

Log records are first written to the *log buffer*, and then flushed to the *log disks*. We assume the *immediate-update* scheme is used, that is, a transaction can update the main-memory database before it reaches the *commit* state. Thus, the *recovery manager* needs to maintain both the *redo-log-records* and the *undo-log-records* for each transaction. To ensure *durability* of committed transactions, a transaction cannot commit until all of its redo-log-records have been flushed to the nonvolatile log. This is called the *Redo Rule* [10]. On the other hand, to ensure all aborted transactions can be rolled back after a system failure, the undo-log-records of an update operation must be flushed to the nonvolatile log ahead of flushing the updated result to the archived disks. This is called *write-ahead-logging (WAL)* protocol [12]. We assume the logging activity follows both the Redo Rule and the WAL protocol.

We denote the *redo-point* as the position in the log from which the restart operation begins the forward redo processing. To facilitate the restart operation in determining the redo-point, we also assume the logging activity follows the *logging-after-write (LAW)* protocol, which requires that the redo-log-records of an update operation are flushed to the nonvolatile log after updating the main memory database [18]. With LAW and the Redo Rule, the redo-point is at the beginning point of the most recent complete checkpoint interval [18]. Notice that this may not be true if LAW is violated; Figure 21.1 gives an example.

In Figure 21.1, a transaction T updates the content of a data item X, and then commits. The checkpointing process is running in parallel with the execution of T. For clarity, the undo logging activity is not shown in Figure 21.1, since it does not affect where the redo-point is. If the system crashes after taking a complete checkpoint and committing T, but before flushing the update of T to the archived disks, then the redo-point is not the begin-chkpt record of the most recent complete checkpoint; otherwise, the update of the T will be lost, since the redo log record of T precedes the begin-chkpt record in the log. For more detailed discussion about the LAW protocol, refer to [2, 18, 19].

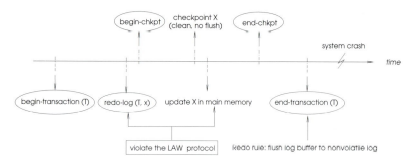

Figure 21.1. A logging scenario where the redo-point is not at the beginning point of the most recent complete checkpoint due to violating the LAW protocol.

21.3   DYNAMIC SEGMENTING FUZZY CHECKPOINTING

In this chapter we discuss dynamic segmented fuzzy checkpointing. First, let us consider a conventional fuzzy checkpointing scheme for MMDB as follows:

Algorithm CFC: Conventional Fuzzy Checkpointing

1. forever **do** {

2.   check all pages in the database, flush dirty ones,
        and update dirty-page-bitmap accordingly;

3.   write a chkpt-record into log buffer, and flush log buffer;

4.   store the address of the chkpt-record in the restart file;

5. } /* end of do */

Recall from Section 21.2, with LAW and the Redo Rule, the redo-point is the beginning point of the most recent complete checkpoint interval. Accordingly, for CFC, the redo-point is at the second most recent chkpt-record. We denote the size of the log from the redo-point to the end of the log as R, and use R to measure the recovery performance. Assuming log records are generated at a constant rate, and the time required to complete a checkpoint is constant, then the value of R increases at a constant rate, but drops 50% whenever a chkpt-record is written to the log (except at the first chkpt-record), as shown in Figure 21.2, where t1, t2, t3, t4, t5, and t6 denote the time a chkpt-record is written to the log. We denote the size of the log generated within a complete checkpoint interval as S_{cfc}. With CFC, if the system fails right before writing a chkpt-record to the log, the value of R is at its maximum. As a result, the recovery time is quite long.

To mitigate this problem, we introduce a checkpointing scheme, called segmented fuzzy checkpointing (SFC), to reduce both the maximum value and the average

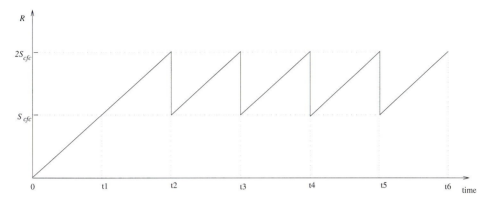

Figure 21.2. R vs. time in CFC.

value of R. With SFC, the checkpointer controls the order in which pages are checkpointed such that overlapping checkpoint intervals is possible. A complete checkpoint interval requires all memory pages be checked at least once, whereas there is no restriction concerning the order in which pages are checkpointed. By dividing the main memory into segments and checkpointing each of them in a round-robin fashion, we can overlay the adjacent complete checkpoint intervals. The SFC algorithm works as follows [23]:

Algorithm SFC: Segmented Fuzzy Checkpointing

1. $i \leftarrow 1$; /* segment counter */

2. forever **do** {

3.   check all pages in Segment i, flush dirty ones, and update dirty-page-bitmap accordingly;

4.   write a chkpt-record into log buffer, and flush log buffer;

5.   store the address of the chkpt-record in the restart file;

6. $i \leftarrow (i+1) \bmod n$;

7. } /* end of do */

With SFC, the redo-point is at the $(n+1)$st most recent chkpt-record, and the most recent complete checkpoint interval is from the redo-point to the most recent chkpt-record. To show why SFC can recover faster than CFC, we also calculate the value of R for SFC. Assuming log records are generated at a constant rate, and the time required to checkpoint each segment is the same, then the value of R increases at a constant rate, but drops by $1/n + 1$ whenever a chkpt-record (except the first

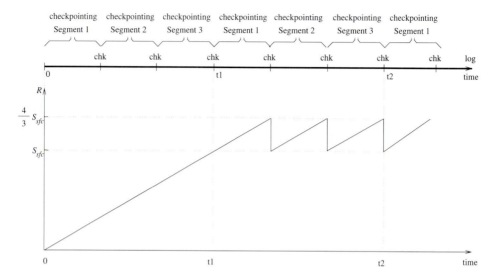

Figure 21.3. R vs. time in SFC. Here, the database is divided into three segments.

n chkpt-records) is written to the log, as shown in Figure 21.3. If the size of the log generated with in a complete checkpoint interval in CFC (denoted as S_{cfc}) is equal to that in SFC (denoted as S_{sfc}), both the maximum and average values of R are smaller in SFC than in CFC. Although, in reality, S_{sfc} is slightly greater than S_{cfc} due to the extra overhead of SFC, SFC still has smaller R because this overhead is very small.

The SFC algorithm has some difficulties in practice. Since the transaction access pattern changes from time to time, a fixed segmenting pattern cannot guarantee to provide better recovery performance all the time. Thus, a dynamic version of SFC is needed, which automatically adjusts the segmenting pattern in response to the change of transaction access pattern. We will show how this is achieved next after discussing how to segment the MMDB.

21.3.1　Segmenting Main-Memory Databases

In what follows, we assume the entire database is memory-resident. Also, we assume the size of the log (not including the chkpt-records) generated within a complete checkpoint interval is independent of the way the database is segmented. Table 21.1 shows the parameters and derived formulas.

Lemma 1:　For a fixed number of segments, if the size of the log (not including the chkpt-records) generated within a complete checkpoint interval is independent of the way the database is segmented, and the size of the log generated when checkpointing a segment is the same for each segment, then the average size of the log from the redo-point to the end of the log is minimum.

Table 21.1. Analysis of Segmented Fuzzy Checkpointing Scheme

Param.	Description	Derived Formula
n	Number of segments	
s_{chk}	Size of a chkpt-record	
s_i	Size of log generated (when checkpt Segment i) (excluding chkpt-records)	
S'	Size of log within a complete checkpt interval (excluding chkpt-records)	$S' = \sum_{i=1}^{n} s_i$
S	Size of log within a complete checkpt interval (including chkpt-records)	$S = S' + s_{chk} \times (n+1)$
P_i	Probability of crash when checkpointing Segment i	$P_i = \frac{s_i}{S'}$
r_i	Avg. size of log for redo if system fails when checkpointing Seg. i	$r_i = S + \frac{s_i}{2}$
R_{avg}	Avg. size of log for redo	$R_{avg} = \sum_{i=1}^{n} P_i \times r_i$ $= \sum_{i=1}^{n}(s_i + \frac{s_i}{S'} \times s_{chk} \times (n+1) + \frac{s_i^2}{2 \times S'})$ $= S' + s_{chk} \times (n+1) + \frac{1}{2 \times S'} \sum_{i=1}^{n} s_i^2$

Proof: From the derived formula of R_{avg} in Table 21.1, the value of R_{avg} is minimum when $s_1 = s_2 = s_3 = \cdots = s_n$. □

Lemma 2:   If the size of the log (not including the chkpt-records) generated within a complete checkpoint interval, denoted as S', is independent of the way the database is segmented, and the size of the log generated when checkpointing a segment is the same for each segment, then, when the number of segments equals to $\lfloor \sqrt{S'/(2 \times s_{chk})} \rfloor$, where s_{chk} is the size of a chkpt-record, the average size of the log from the redo-point to the end of the log is minimum.

Proof: According to Lemma 1, we can further derive R_{avg} and the value of n that yields minimum R_{avg} as follows:

$$
\begin{aligned}
R_{avg} &= S' + s_{chk} \times (n+1) + \frac{1}{2 \times S'} \times n \times (\frac{S'}{n})^2 \\
&= S' + s_{chk} \times (n+1) + \frac{S'}{2 \times n}
\end{aligned}
$$
(21.1)

$$
\frac{\partial R_{avg}}{\partial n} = s_{chk} - \frac{S'}{2} \times n^{-2} = 0
$$

$$\Longrightarrow n_{opt} = \lfloor \sqrt{\frac{S'}{2 \times s_{chk}}} \rfloor \qquad (21.2)$$

where n_{opt} denotes the value of n that yields minimum R_{avg}.   □

Lemma 2 provides a simple way to estimate the value of n, and Lemma 1 provides a guideline about how to segment the database. Both are used to develop the dynamic segmented fuzzy checkpointing approaches discussed next.

21.3.2   Dynamic Segmented Fuzzy Checkpointing

The SFC algorithm discussed earlier has some difficulties in practice. First, the database administrators (DBAs) may have problems deciding how to partition the database. Second, whenever the transaction access pattern and/or the transaction arrival rate change, the current segments may no longer satisfy the conditions in Lemma 1 or 2 to achieve better recovery performance. Third, it is sometimes impossible or very costly to find a segmenting pattern that strictly follows Lemmas 1 and 2.

Consequently, to make SFC a practical solution for checkpointing MMDBs, there are three other issues that must be considered, that is, *automaticity*, *adaptability*, and *sensitivity*. Automaticity refers to the system's ability to automatically decide the segmenting pattern, and thus relieve the burden from DBAs. Adaptability refers to the system's ability to detect a change in transaction access pattern and arrival rate, and adjust the segmenting pattern accordingly. Sensitivity decides how sensitive the checkpointer should be, in terms of constructing new segmenting patterns, to a change in transaction access pattern and arrival rate. Although the objective of changing segmenting patterns is to improve the recovery performance, changing the segmenting patterns too often could negatively impact performance during run time.

With these three issues in mind, in what follows, we present the dynamic versions of the SFC algorithm (DSFC). The basic ideas behind dynamic segmented fuzzy checkpointing (DSFC) are listed in what follows:

- Dynamically calculate the size of the log generated within a complete checkpoint interval, denoted as S'.

- Use Equation 21.2 to calculate a proper value for the number of segments, denoted as n,

- Once the value of n has been decided, follow Lemma 1 to partition the database.

For ease of exposition, we use the following notations. The size of the log generated when checkpointing Segment i, denoted as s_i for $i = 1$ to n, is updated when Segment i has been completely checkpointed. If the value of s_i varies by a predefined amount σ, the checkpointer will recompute the number of segments n, and reconstruct the segmenting pattern after checkpointing Segment n. The segmenting pattern is defined in the segment boundary variables, denoted as $boundary[i]$ for $i = 2$ to n. Here, $boundary[i]$ contains the beginning address of Segment i. Both s_i and $boundary[i]$ are stored in main memory. The size of the log (not including the chkpt-records) generated within a complete checkpoint interval, denoted as S', is also stored in main memory.

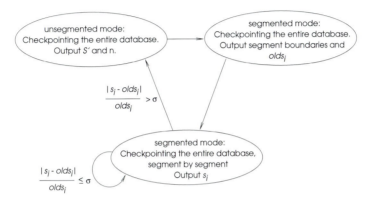

Figure 21.4. State transition in DSFC.

With DSFC, the checkpointer is operating in one of the three modes: **unsegmented, segmenting,** and **segmented,** as shown in Figure 21.4. When the system is first brought up, it is set to the **unsegmented** mode. In the **unsegmented** mode, the checkpointer works like the conventional fuzzy checkpointing approach to checkpoint the entire database. After completing a checkpoint, the value of S' can be easily calculated by subtracting the addresses of the two most recent chkpt-records.[1] Then we use the value of S' and Equation 21.2 to compute n. Finally, the checkpointer switches to the **segmenting** mode.

In the **segmenting** mode, the checkpointer checkpoints the entire database, and at the same time, decides the segment boundaries using the values of S' and n, such that Lemma 1 is approximately satisfied. This is achieved by setting the value of $boundary[i]$ to the current checkpoint address when the size of the log increases by more than S'/n. At this moment, the checkpoint writes a chkpt-record to the log, and calculates the value of $olds_{i-1}$ by subtracting the addresses of the two most recent chkpt-records. Note that log records might be generated at quite different speeds in the current **segmenting** mode than in the previous **unsegmented** mode. Sometimes, adjustment of n is needed in order to segment the database, since the value of n is calculated based on the S' of the previous **unsegmented** mode, not based on the S' of the current **segmenting** mode. Thus, the number of segments is not decided until all the segment boundaries have been decided (see algorithm

---

[1]If there is only one chkpt-record in the log, we can use 0 as the address of the second most recent chkpt-record.

DSFC which follows for details). Once the segment boundaries have been decided, the checkpointer switches to the **segmented** mode.

In the **segmented** mode, the checkpointer works like the SFC algorithm discussed earlier. After checkpointing Segment i, the value of s_i is calculated by subtracting the addresses of the two most recent chkpt-records. If $|s_i - olds_i|/olds_i$ is greater than some predefined value σ, the checkpointer switches back to **unsegmented** mode after checkpointing Segment n; otherwise, it stays in the **segmented** mode.

For recovery purpose, we need to know the number of segments used when a chkpt-record was written to the log. Thus, the number of segments is included in each chkpt-record. We denote a chkpt-record as $chk(n)$ if it is written to the log when the number of segments is n. Note that in the **unsegmented** mode, the number of segments is 1. Also, since the number of segments in the **segmenting** mode is not known until all the segment boundaries have been decided, all chkpt-records (except the last one) generated within **segmenting** mode are denoted as $chk(0)$. When writing the last chkpt-record to the log in **segmenting** mode, the number of segments has been decided. Thus, this chkpt-record is in the form of $chk(n)$, instead of $chk(0)$, assuming the number of segments is n. The algorithm for DSFC follows.

Algorithm DSFC: Dynamic Segmented Fuzzy Checkpointing

```
mode ← unsegmented; boundary[1] ← 0
forever do {
  if (mode = unsegmented)
    fuzzy chkpt the entire database, write chk(1) into log buffer
    and flush log buffer
    store the address of the chk(1) in the restart file
    compute S' by subtracting the addresses of the two most recent chkpt-recs.
    n ← ⌊√(S'/2 × s_chk)⌋
    mode ← segmenting
  else if (mode = segmenting)
    i ← 1
    while (i ≤ n) {
      if (i < n)      /* before segment n */
        fuzzy chkpt the database starting at address boundary[i]
        until either the size of log increases by more than S'/n or
        the end of the database is reached
        if (database end is reached)   /* n is too big, needs adjustment */
          n ← i
          write chk(n) into the log buffer, and flush the log buffer
          store the address of the chk(n) in the restart file
        else
          write chk(0) into the log buffer, and flush the log buffer
```

```
              store the address of the chk(0) in the restart file
              compute olds_i by subtracting the addresses of
              the two most recent chkpt-recs.
              i ← i + 1
              boundary[i] ← current checkpointing main-memory address
           else /* segment n */
              fuzzy checkpoint the rest of the database
              write chk(n) into log buffer, and flush log buffer
              store the address of the chk(n) in the restart file
              compute olds_i by subtracting the addresses of
              the two most recent chkpt-recs.
              i ← i + 1
        } /* end of while */
        mode ← segmented
        flag ← NoChange
        i ← 1
     else /* mode = segmented */
        check all pages in seg. i, flush dirty ones
        update dirty-page bitmap accordingly
        write chk(n) into log buffer, and flush log buffer
        store the address of the chk(n) in the restart file
        compute s_i by subtracting the addresses of the two most recent chkpt-records
        if ( |olds_i - s_i| / olds_i > σ) then flag ← Change
        if (i = n) and (flag = Change) then mode ← unsegmented
        else i ← (i + 1) mod n
  } /* end of do */
```

Assume the most recent chkpt-record is $chk(i)$. Then the redo-point and the most recent complete checkpoint interval can be determined as follows:

- If there are less than two chkpt-records in the log that are in the form of $chk(x)$, where $x \neq 0$, then the redo-point is at the beginning of the log.

- If $i \neq 0$ and none of the i most recent chkpt-records is $chk(1)$, then the redo-point is at the $(i+1)$st most recent chkpt-record, and the most recent complete checkpoint interval is from the redo-point to the most recent chkpt-record.

- If $i = 0$ or at least one of the i most recent chkpt-records is $chk(1)$, then the chkpt-record right before the most recent $chk(1)$ is the redo-point. The redo-point and the most recent $chk(1)$ construct the most recent complete checkpoint interval.

In DSFC, the value of σ decides the sensitivity of the checkpointer: The smaller the value of σ, the more sensitive the DSFC checkpointer is to the change of transaction access pattern and arrival rate. Overall speaking, DSFC consumes slightly more CPU time and log space than CFC does, but DSFC offers better recovery performance than CFC. Here, we give a simplified logging example for DSFC in Figure 21.5.

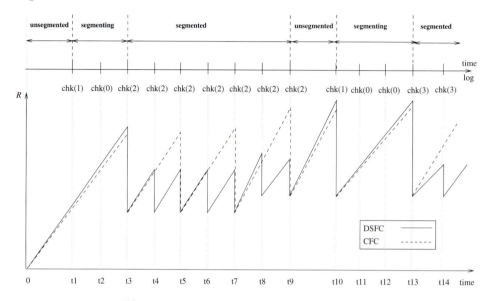

Figure 21.5. A logging example for DSFC.

The upper half of Figure 21.5 shows the status of the checkpointing activity, and the lower half shows the corresponding R vs. time curve (in solid line) for DSFC. Here, R denotes the size of the log from the redo-point to the end of the log. After a new segmenting pattern at time t_3 is constructed, the checkpointer stays in the **segmented** mode until time t_9. Notice that at time t_7, the transaction pattern starts to change, and thus the checkpointer switches back to the **unsegmented** mode at time t_9 to prepare constructing a new segmenting pattern.

In practice, the number of segments is usually much larger than that in this example. For ease of comparison, we also show the R vs. time curve for CFC in the dashed line in the lower half of Figure 21.5. Here, the dashed line also indicates that the transaction pattern starts to change at time t_7. The average value of R, denoted as R_{avg}, is smaller in DSFC than in CFC, since the value of R is smaller during the **segmented** mode in DSFC. However, DSFC offers no improvement on the value of R within the **unsegmented** and **segmenting** modes. Actually, the maximum value of R in DSFC is slightly greater than that in CFC due to the extra overhead of DSFC.

21.3.3   Further Improvement of DSFC

The DSFC algorithm discussed earlier offers no improvement on the value of R within the **unsegmented** and **segmenting** modes. In the following, we discuss how to reduce the value of R by eliminating the **unsegmented** mode and by overlapping two consecutive segmenting patterns in the **segmenting** mode.

Eliminating Unsegmented Mode. The **unsegmented** mode serves two purposes in DSFC. First, it separates two consecutive segmenting patterns with a chkpt-record, $chk(1)$. Second, it provides the values of S' and n to be used in the subsequent **segmenting** mode for constructing a new segmenting pattern. Eliminating the **unsegmented** mode, we need to calculate the value of S' and n within the **segmented** mode. When the system is first brought up, the database is in the **segmented** mode with only one segment. A new segmenting pattern starts at the beginning of a **segmenting** mode, which is preceded by a **segmented** mode of another segmenting pattern. As in the DSFC algorithm, the chkpt-records generated within the **segmenting** mode are $(n-1)$ chkpt-records in the form of $chk(0)$ followed by a chkpt-record in the form of $chk(n)$. Here, n is the number of segments, and n could be 1. Thus, we can use the last chkpt-record generated at the end of the **segmented** mode to separate two consecutive segmenting patterns. This chkpt-record can be easily identified since it will be followed by either $chk(0)$ or $chk(1)$ generated within the **segmenting** mode.

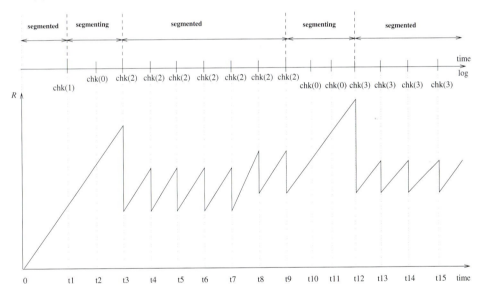

Figure 21.6. A logging example for DSFC without the **unsegmented** mode.

The upper half of Figure 21.6 gives a logging example for the resulting DSFC without the **unsegmented** mode, and the lower half shows the corresponding R vs. time curve. The transaction access pattern and/or arrival rate starts to change at time t_7, and thus the checkpointer switches to the **segmenting** mode at time t_9. Notice that the average value of R, denoted as R_{avg}, is reduced, since there is no **unsegmented** mode, where the value of R is large. But the value of R within the **segmenting** modes is still large, which can be improved by overlapping the consecutive segmenting patterns discussed next.

Overlapping Two Consecutive Segmenting Patterns.   To reduce the value of R within the **segmenting** mode, we use a *construct-before-abandon* technique to control when to switch to a new segmenting pattern. Note that the checkpointer begins and finishes constructing a new segmenting pattern at the beginning and the end of the **segmenting** mode respectively. With the *construct-before-abandon* technique, the checkpointer does not abandon the current segmenting pattern until the new segmenting pattern has been completely constructed. As a result, two consecutive segmenting patterns can overlap in time during the **segmenting** mode: one is inherited from the preceding **segmented** mode, and the other is the new segmenting pattern under construction. To avoid confusion, we shall call the former the *current* segmenting pattern, and the latter the *new* segmenting pattern. This is different from the DSFC algorithm discussed earlier, where the checkpointer abandons the current segmenting pattern at the same time starting to build the new segmenting pattern.

In order to distinguish the chkpt-records generated within any two overlapped segmenting patterns, we attach a color (*black* or *white*) to each chkpt-record. The idea is to ensure that all chkpt-records generated in the same segmenting pattern have the same color, and that chkpt-records generated in any two consecutive segmenting patterns have different colors. Thus, we denote a chkpt-record as $chk(n, color)$, where n is the number of segments, and $color$ is the color of the chkpt-record.

During the **segmenting** mode, the checkpointer writes at most three kinds of chkpt-records to the log. According to the new segmenting pattern, n_{new} chkpt-records in the form of $chk(0, color_{new})$ followed by a $chk(n_{new}, color_{new})$ are generated. At the same time, according to the current segmenting pattern, at most $(n_{current} - 1)$ chkpt-records in the form of $chk(n_{current}, color_{current})$ are generated. By adding the chkpt-records according to the current segmenting pattern, we can overlap segmenting patterns to avoid the recovery performance gap during the **segmenting** mode. Notice that we write a $chk(0, color_{new})$ to the log at the beginning of the **segmenting** mode. That is why there are n_{new}, instead of $(n_{new} - 1)$, chkpt-records in the form of $chk(0, color_{new})$ in the **segmenting** mode. This chkpt-record indicates where the **segmenting** mode (and the new segmenting pattern) starts. Without overlapping segmenting patterns, we can use the last chkpt-record generated in the **segmented** mode for this purpose, but we are unable to do the same here since the same kind of chkpt-records in the **segmented** mode also occurs in the subsequent **segmenting** mode.

The upper half of Figure 21.7 gives a logging example for DSFC with overlapping segmenting patterns and without **unsegmented** mode, and the lower half shows the corresponding R vs. time curve. Three kinds of chkpt-records are written to the log during the **segmenting** mode from time t_{10} to t_{15}, that is, $chk(2, b)$, $chk(0, w)$, and $chk(3, w)$. The value of R during **segmenting** mode is reduced due to overlapping the segmenting patterns.

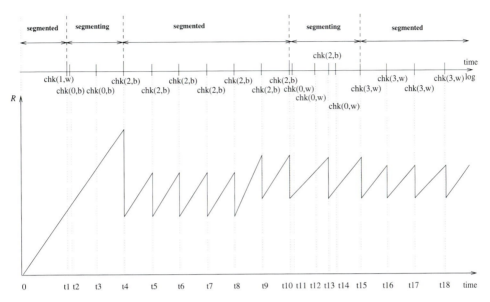

Figure 21.7. A logging example for DSFC with overlapping segmenting patterns and without the **unsegmented** mode.

21.3.4 Performance of DSFC

To do a thorough performance study on the proposed DSFC algorithms, four simulation models have been implemented: one without any checkpointing in progress (denoted as NFC), one using CFC, one using DSFC without unsegmented mode (denoted as DSFC-2), and one using DSFC with overlapping segmenting pattern and without unsegmented mode (denoted as DSFC-3). Plain DSFC is not implemented since it does not work as efficiently as DSFC-2 and DSFC-3. The simulation models are implemented using SLAM II simulation language [24]. The main objective of this simulation study is to compare the performance of DSFC (DSFC-2 or DSFC-3) and CFC. The parameters used in the simulation models are shown in Table 21.2. The default value will be used, unless specified otherwise. The simulation models are similar to the one in [4], and the default values of all the time-related parameters in Table 21.2 are based on the values used in [4], except the time required to transfer a database page or log page to disk (denoted as TRANSFER and LOGIO_TM, respectively) is quoted from [13].

The MMDB system simulated is completely memory-resident, that is, the entire database can be loaded into the main memory. The archived copy of the database is stored in a set of archived disks. Thus, the size of the MMDB is the same as the size of the archived disks, and the number of pages in main memory is equal to the

Table 21.2. Parameters

Parameter Name	Notation	Default Value
Number of archived disks	NUM_AM	10
Size of an archived disk (MB)	SZ_AM	40
Database page size (KB)	PAGE_SZ	4
Number of database pages	NUM_PAGES	$\frac{NUM\_AM * SZ\_AM * 1024}{PAGE\_SZ}$
Transaction arrival time distribution		Poisson
Average transaction arrival rate (tps)	TR_RT	300
Maximum number of operations per transaction	MAX_OP	10
Minimum number of operations per transaction	MIN_OP	5
Probability of write operations	PROB_WR	0.2
Multiprogramming level	MPL_MAX	10
Accessed page distribution		exponential
Mean of accessed page distribution		2
Number of bytes per word	WORD_SZ	4
Size of a BT log record (bytes)	SZ_BT	4
Size of an ET log record (bytes)	SZ_ET	4
Size of a undo-log-record (bytes)	SZ_BFIM	8
Size of an redo-log-record (bytes)	SZ_AFIM	8
Time to initialize log I/O (sequential, msec)	INTIO_TM	0.01
Log page size (bytes)	LOGPG_SZ	2048
Time to write a log page to disk (msec)	LOGIO_TM	1
Time to preprocess a transaction (msec)	PRETRAN	1.25
Time to preprocess a operation (msec)	PREOP	0.005
Time needed to get a lock (msec)	LOCK_TM	0.025
Time needed to release a lock (msec)	UNLK_TM	0.025
MM access time per word (msec)	MM_ACCESS	0.0001
Search for a page in MM (msec)	MM_SEAR	MM_ACCESS*3
Log buffer access time per word (msec)	SM_ACCESS	0.00011
Time to finish up a transaction (msec)	ET_TM	1.25
Time to find a 1 in bitmap (msec)	BMAP_TM	0.00011
Time to allocate a page (msec)	ALLOC_TM	0.05
Time to release an MM page (msec)	RELEASE_TM	0.05
Time to copy an MM page to an MM buffer (msec)	COPY_TM	$\frac{MM\_ACCESS * 2 * PAGE\_SZ * 1024}{WORD\_SZ}$
Time to send a r/w request to/from AM (msec)	AMREQ_TM	0.02
Average seek time (msec)	SEEK	16
Average latency (msec)	LATENCY	8.3
Time to transfer a page to disk (msec)	TRANSFer	1
Time to access 1 data page from AM randomly (msec)	AM_ACCESS	SEEK+LATENCY+TRANS
Size of an EC log record (bytes)	SZ_EC	2*MPL_MAX+1
Sensitivity factor	σ	0.05

size of archived disks divided by the size of a database page. The configuration of the archived disks is defined by the number of archived disks, and the size of each archived disk. Disk I/Os are handled on a first-come, first-serve basis.

To prevent the recovery activity from affecting normal transaction activity, we assume the system contains two processors: one for normal transaction processing, and one for logging and checkpointing [20]. Transactions are generated according to the following parameters: the distribution of time between transaction arrival, the average transaction arrival rate (denoted as TR_RT), maximum and minimum numbers of operations per transaction (respectively denoted as MAX_OP and MIN_OP), and the probability of write operations (denoted as PROB_WR). The number of operations per transaction is uniformly distributed between MIN_OP and MAX_OP. Transactions are processed concurrently, and the multiprogramming level is defined in parameter MPL_MAX. The concurrency control between transactions is achieved using strict two-phase locking with preclaiming. That is, a transaction must acquire all needed locks before it can be processed, and it must release all its locks at the commit time. The locking granularity is at page level. The accessed page number is exponentially distributed with mean equal to 2. A transaction writes the 'BT' (Begin Transaction) and 'ET' (End Transaction) records to the log to indicate the point when the transaction starts and when it commits. The immediate-update scheme is used. The logging activity follows the WAL and LAW protocols and the Redo Rule. Also, the nonvolatile log buffer is used to avoid I/O when transactions are committed. This speeds up the system performance and simplifies the logging activity. Thus, prior to updating a data item in main memory, a transaction writes a undo-log-record for this update to the nonvolatile log buffer, and the transaction cannot write the corresponding redo-log-record to the nonvolatile log buffer until the data item in main memory has been updated. Also, a transaction cannot commit until its 'ET' record is written to the nonvolatile log buffer.

Table 21.3. Testing Sets.

Testing set	Testing parameter(s)	Testing values	Algorithms
1	SZ_AM	10, 20, 30, 40, 50, 60, 70, 80, 90, 100	NFC, CFC, DSFC-2, DSFC-3
2	NUM_AM	2, 4, 6, 8, 10	CFC, DSFC-3
3	(SZ_AM, NUM_AM)	(3, 80), (4, 60), (5, 48), (6, 40), (8, 30), (10, 24)	CFC, DSFC-3

Three simulation testing sets are performed. We focus on the performance of DSFC as the configuration of the archived disks and the size of the MMDB change (see Table 21.3). We assume the size of the MMDB is the same as the size of the archived disks. Thus, the size of the MMDB is the product of the number of archived disks (NUM_AM) and the size of each archived disk (SZ_AM). Testing sets 1 and 2 respectively evaluates the effect of NUM_AM and SZ_AM, and testing set 3 varies both NUM_AM and SZ_AM but keeping their product a constant. We provide an overview of the results here. For a more thorough treatment, see the literature [1].

Testing Set 1: Varying the Size of each Archived Disk. In testing set 1, we vary the size of each archived disk (SZ_AM) from 10 to 100 MB, while keeping the total number of archived disks (NUM_AM) a constant, 10. This will also cause the MMDB under test to change its size from 100 to 1000 MB since we assume the size of MMDB equals to SZ_AM * NUM_AM. This experiment gives us some ideas about the performance of DSFC for different sizes of MMDB, whose archived copy is stored in the same number of disks.

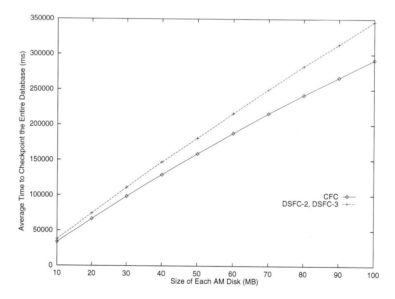

Figure 21.8. Average time to checkpoint the entire database v.s. SZ_AM.

We denote the *average* time to checkpoint the entire database as T_{chk}. Here, the time to checkpoint the entire database is measured from starting checkpointing Segment 1 to finishing checkpointing Segment n, assuming Segment n is the last segment. Figure 21.8 shows that CFC takes less time to checkpoint the entire database than DSFC-2 and DSFC-3 do. This is attributed to the overhead of generating more chkpt-records in DSFC-2 and DSFC-3 than in CFC. Compared with CFC, as SZ_AM increases from 10 to 100, both DSFC-2 and DSFC-3 increase T_{chk} by the range from 11.9% to 18.49%. Figure 21.8 also shows that T_{chk} is approximately linearly proportional to SZ_AM. This is expected since the larger the database, the longer it takes to complete a checkpoint. Note that this might not be true if NUM_AM is not kept constant (see testing sets 2 and 3).

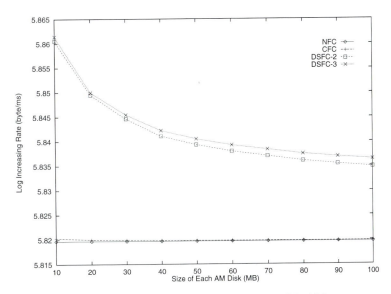

Figure 21.9. Log increasing rate vs. SZ_AM.

Figure 21.9 shows the comparison of log increasing rate: NFC < CFC < DSFC-2 < DSFC-3. NFC has the smallest log increasing rate since it does not generate any chkpt-record. Also, since the transaction arrival rate and write probability are kept constant in this experiment, the log increasing rate for NFC is constant, independent of the value of SZ_AM. The log increasing rate of CFC is slightly larger than that of NFC because CFC generates chkpt-records but NFC does not. For CFC, the log increasing rate decreases by less than 0.001 byte/msec, as SZ_AM increases from 10 to 100. This is because CFC writes one chkpt-record per checkpoint interval, and the checkpoint interval get larger as the size of the MMDB increases due to larger SZ_AM (see Figure 21.8). DSFC-2 has a larger log increasing rate than CFC since DSFC-2 generates more chkpt-records than CFC. Similarly, the log increasing rate of DSFC-3 is slightly larger than that of DSFC-2 since DSFC-3 generates more chkpt-records during the **segmenting** mode than DSFC-2 does. Overall speaking, compared with CFC, DSFC-2 increases the log by the range from 0.69% to 0.26%, and DSFC-3 by the range from 0.7% to 0.28%, as SZ_AM increases from 10 to 100. Thus, as SZ_AM increases, the chkpt-records are written to the log at a lower rate. This explains why the log increasing rate decreases in DSFC-2 and DSFC-3 as SZ_AM increases, as shown in Figure 21.9.

Figure 21.10 shows the frequency of moving the redo-point: DSFC-3 > DSFC-2 > CFC. Recall that the redo-point is moved forward when a new complete checkpoint interval is constructed. Thus, this frequency depends on the frequency of writing chkpt-records to the log. Therefore, the result in Figure 21.10 is similar to that in Figure 21.9.

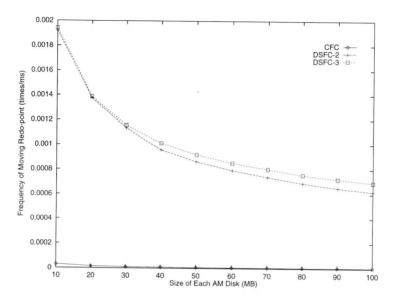

Figure 21.10. Frequency of moving the redo-point vs. SZ_AM.

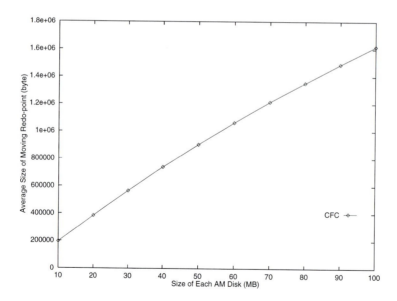

Figure 21.11. Average distance of moving the redo-point vs. SZ_AM.

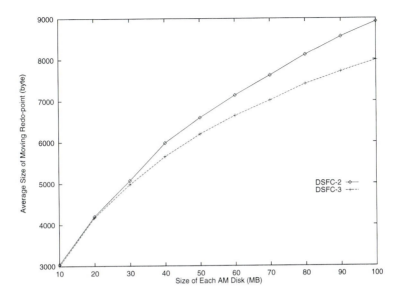

Figure 21.12. Average distance of moving the redo-point vs. SZ_AM.

Figures 21.11 and 21.12 show the average distance of moving the redo-point: CFC > DSFC-2 > DSFC-3. The distance for CFC is much larger than that in DSFC-2 and DSFC-3. In all three cases, the distance increases as SZ_AM becomes larger. According to the algorithm of CFC, this distance is approximately equal to S', which is approximately linearly proportional to SZ_AM. This is consistent with Figure 21.11. According to the algorithms of DSFC-2 and DSFC-3, this distance is approximately equal to S'/n, which is approximately linearly proportional to $\sqrt{\text{SZ\_AM}}$. This is consistent with Figure 21.12.

Figure 21.13 shows the average size of the log for redo during recovery: CFC > DSFC-2 > DSFC-3. Compared with CFC, DSFC-2 reduces R_{avg} by the range from 24.28% to 21.86%, and DSFC-3 by the range from 24.47% to 23.74%, as SZ_AM increases from 10 to 100. In all cases, R_{avg} increases as SZ_AM increases. This is consistent with our analysis that follows. In CFC, R_{avg} is estimated to be $S' + S'/2$, which is approximately linearly proportional to SZ_AM. In DSFC-2 and DSFC-3, R_{avg} is estimated to be $S' + S'/n$, where S' is approximately linearly proportional to SZ_AM, and S'/n is approximately linearly proportional to $\sqrt{\text{SZ\_AM}}$.

Our simulation results indicate that the throughput is the same in all cases. This is because the system is not heavily loaded with transactions. Figure 21.14 shows that the checkpointing process (CFC, DSFC-2, or DSFC-3) increases the response time by about 0.2 msec. The response times for DSFC-2 and DSFC-3 are almost the same; both are about 0.02 msec slower than CFC. Compared with CFC, both DSFC-2 and DSFC-3 increase the response time by about 0.4%. The value of SZ_AM does not have much effect on the response time.

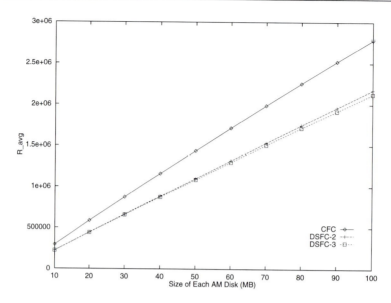

Figure 21.13. Average size of the log for redo during recovery vs. SZ_AM.

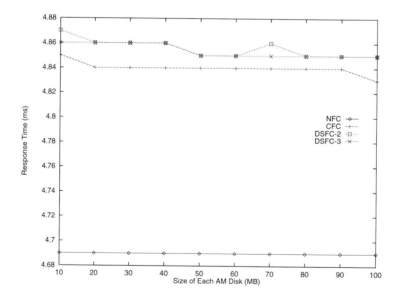

Figure 21.14. Response time vs. SZ_AM.

In summary, testing set 1 shows that the value of SZ_AM does not change the relative order of CFC, DSFC-2, and DSFC-3 in terms of the time required to checkpoint the entire database, log increasing rate, frequency and average distance of moving the redo-point, average size of the log for redo during recovery, and response time. The results show that DSFC-3 moves the redo-point more frequently (see Figure 21.10) but at a smaller distance (see Figures 21.11 and 21.12), and thus yields a smaller R_{avg} (see Figure 21.13). Therefore, DSFC-3 has the best recovery performance among DSFC-3, DSFC-2, and CFC. On the other hand, DSFC-3 incurs the highest log size overhead (see Figure 21.9). The performance of DSFC-2 is similar to that of DSFC-3, except DSFC-2 has a slightly less log size overhead and larger R_{avg} than DSFC-3. Thus, for the rest of the testing sets, we will not include DSFC-2 in our discussion. Also, since this performance study is to evaluate the performance of DSFC vs. CFC, we will not include NFC for the rest of the testing sets.

Testing Set 2: Varying the Number of Archived Disks. In testing set 2, we vary the number of archived disks (NUM_AM) from 2 to 10, while keeping the size of each archived disk (SZ_AM) a constant, 40 MB. Similar to testing set 1, as the value of NUM_AM increases, the size of MMDB increases accordingly. Also, since the checkpointing process can flush dirty pages to different archived disks in parallel, we can evaluate the effect of parallel I/O.

In summary, testing set 2 shows that NUM_AM does not change the relative order of CFC and DSFC-3, just like SZ_AM in testing set 1. DSFC-3 has better recovery performance but larger log overhead. Also increasing SZ_AM (as in testing set 1) and increasing NUM_AM (as in testing set 2) both increase the size of the MMDB, and thus tends to increase T_{chk}. But increasing NUM_AM also increases the degree of parallel I/O that tend to reduce T_{chk}. The results show that the effects of NUM_AM on T_{chk}, the log increasing rate, frequency and the average distance of moving the redo-point, and average size of the log for redo during recovery, are just the opposite of the effect of SZ_AM in testing set 1.

Testing Set 3: Varying SZ_AM and NUM_AM. In testing set 3, we vary both NUM_AM and SZ_AM, while keeping their product constant. Consequently, the size of MMDB is constant. We focus on how the degree of parallelism of I/O affects the checkpointing process.

CFC takes less time to checkpoint the entire database than DSFC-3 does. Also, similar to testing set 2, T_{chk} decreases as NUM_AM increases, but at a faster rate. Recall that increasing the MMDB size tends to increase T_{chk}, whereas increasing NUM_AM tends to decrease T_{chk}. Since the MMDB size is kept constant in testing set 3, but it is linearly proportional to NUM_AM in testing set 2, T_{chk} decreases faster in testing set 3 than in testing set 2. Other testing results for testing set 3 are similar to that in testing set 2. However, the measured data are more sensitive to (NUM_AM, SZ_AM) in testing set 3 than NUM_AM in testing set 2. Increasing NUM_AM favors the recovery performance but also causes more log size overhead in DSFC-3.

21.4 PARTITION CHECKPOINTING

In this section, we describe algorithms needed to implement partition checkpointing [21] in MMDBs. With partition checkpointing, the volatile main memory (denoted as MM) is divided into partitions. A *partition* in the MM is composed of one or more database pages. In this study, we choose the frequency of update as the only criterion in partitioning an MMDB. Thus, partitions are allowed to be variable-length data segments. Furthermore, according to the general database reference pattern, there may be only a few database pages that have a high update frequency. Thus, the partitions with higher update frequencies may be much smaller than partitions with lower update frequencies.

In applications where the partition of data access frequency arises naturally, a partition may correspond to a database object (relation, index, or system data structure). It is possible that several relations may share one partition. (Our discussions assume the relational data model, however, our approach is at a lower level than the data model and any logical data model may be used.) In some applications, tuples in a relation happen to have different update frequencies. we may split the relation into several parts and put each part into a different partition. Thus, relations may span partitions. There is no restriction in partitioning an MMDB, and there is also no restriction on how transactions access partitions. Transaction access may span partitions. We assume that the concurrency control component ensures that transactions access the data in a consistent manner.

With partition checkpointing, each partition is checkpointed independently of the others. We call the action of flushing a partition a *local checkpoint*. A local checkpoint is initiated by writing a *Begin-Checkpoint, BC(local)*, record to its local log, and it then moves out all the dirty pages in its partition to archive memory (denoted as AM). The local checkpoint terminates by writing an *End-Checkpoint, EC(local)*, record in the local log and sets the corresponding bit in the checkpoint bit map. These actions are actually intermixed with logging and transaction activities. No locking or quiescing of the system is needed.

The entire database is checkpointed by global checkpoints. A *global checkpoint* is accomplished only when each partition in MM has been checkpointed at least once. (Only exceptions are those partitions that are never modified or that do not need to be checkpointed.) A global checkpoint is initiated when a BC(global) record is written to the global log, and all the bits in the checkpoint bit map are cleared to indicate the beginning of a new global checkpoint. Local checkpoints are then invoked on partitions based on one of several strategies which are introduced in Section 21.4.4. A global checkpoint is signaled when all bits in the checkpoint bit map are set. Thus a global checkpoint is implicitly requested. The global checkpoint has been completed when a EC(global) record is appended to the global log.

21.4.1 MMDB Architecture for Partition Checkpointing

To support partition checkpointing, each partition must have its own local log and dirty bitmap. Also, a global log is needed. Thus, we extend the MMDB architecture discussed in Section 21.2 by adding a global log, and using a local log and a dirty bitmap for each partition, as shown in Figure 21.15. We also assume all log buffers are nonvolatile, implemented via a battery-backed RAM (or use of UPS). Using nonvolatile log buffer avoids I/O actions when transactions are committed, and thus is essential to performance in MMDBs [20, 16]. The tail end of the log is in nonvolatile log buffer; enough nonvolatile log buffer to hold at least the log information for active transactions is assumed in this architecture. A logger processor flushes the log buffer asynchronously to the corresponding local log disk.

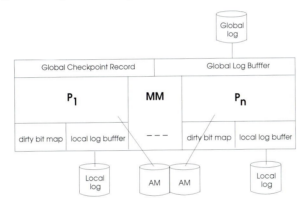

Figure 21.15. Partition MMDB.

With the partition checkpointing MMDB, the log information is divided into two parts: global log and local logs, and there may be separate log disks for each local log and the global log. Since separate IO channels are used for checkpointing and logging, we assume there is no IO traffic contention during checkpointing and log buffer management. The *global log* contains information about transaction initiation and termination, such as *Begin-Transaction (BT)* and *End-Transaction (ET)* records. The global log preserves transaction serialization history. At the time of recovery, the global log is used to generate lists of committed and uncommitted transactions (active and aborted transactions). Besides transaction information, the global log contains information about global checkpoints. Table 1 lists the types of log items in the global log. We assume that the BC record contains a list of transactions active when the global checkpoint was started. This is needed at recovery time to determine which transactions need to be undone.

In the MMDB BFIM/AFIM *(BeFore IMage, AFter IMage)*, log records are grouped according to their corresponding partitions, and a *local log* is maintained for each partition. Thus, each log consists of data information local to that partition. We assume physical logging. Physical logging is essential for a fuzzy checkpointing

Table 21.4. Log Types in the Global Log

BT	TID
ET	TID
BC	Chkpt-id (global) + Active TIDs
EC	Chkpt-id (global)

MMDB. This because fuzzy checkpointing in MMDBs simply copies out pages of MM to AM without any synchronization. The idempotent property of physical logging can ensure that redo and undo operations are repeatable in the sense that doing them several times produces the same result as doing them once as long as they are done in the right order. With the idempotent property, the log processing can apply every log record in the log to the database without checking the status of actions; thus the postcrash log processing is greatly simplified. Besides BFIM/AFIM values, each local log also saves BT records for transactions. Since transaction access may span partitions, BFIMs of a transaction may be distributed among all the local logs. In the undo recovery process, the recovery procedure must apply BFIMs of uncommitted transactions in each local log to the corresponding partition. When all of the BFIMs of a transaction in every local log have been processed, the rollback process of this transaction is done. To determine whether the rollback process of a transaction in a partition has been completed, the BT records of transactions are required in every local log. Table 21.2 shows the record types in local logs.

Table 21.5. Log Types in Local Logs

BT	TID			
BFIM	TID	Len	Laddr	VAL
AFIM	TID	Len	Laddr	VAL
BC	Chkpt-id (local)			
EC	Chkpt-id (local)			

global address	P_1			P_n	
	1	local address		0	local address
checkpoint bit map	0	local address		1	local address

Figure 21.16. Global checkpoint record.

There is a *global checkpoint record* in stable memory (see Figure 21.16) that supports the partition checkpointing technique, and keeps information about the most recent local checkpoints. A *global address* field is used to denote the location on the global log where a global checkpoint is initiated. Each partition has one entry in this global checkpoint record, and each entry has two items corresponding to the two last local checkpoints for this partition. A partition item is composed of a current bit field and local log address field. The *current bit* indicates whether this checkpoint is the most recent, and the *local log address field* identifies the location on the local log where the local checkpoint starts. The global checkpoint record also contains a *checkpointing bit map* that denotes whether a partition has been checkpointed during the current global checkpoint. When all bits in the checkpointing bit map are set, a global checkpoint has implicitly been completed. We assume that global checkpoints are never explicitly requested. However, only a slight modification is needed to support explicit global checkpoint requests. An explicit global checkpoint request would cause uncheckpointed partitions to checkpointed.

21.4.2 Partition Checkpointing Algorithms

Checkpoints are executed in the background and invoked continuously. Once a global checkpoint is finished, the next one is started. Within a global checkpoint, local checkpoints may be scheduled according to many different algorithms. The number of local checkpoints that occur within a global checkpoint and the order in which partitions are checkpointed can be varied. The key feature of the partition checkpointing approach is the ability to checkpoint partitions based on the frequency of update. In general, hot-set partitions should be flushed out more frequently than cold-set partitions. In a global checkpoint, a hot-set partition may have been flushed out to AM several times, whereas a cold-set partition probably would be checkpointed only once. The objective of a local checkpoint scheduling algorithm is to minimize normal overheads of checkpointing yet still improve the postcrash log processing performance.

When a local checkpoint is signaled, a BC (local) record is written to the local log. Then the recovery component saves the position of this log record, so that at the time of recovery, the recovery procedure can easily locate a proper starting point for the undo and redo activities. The address is kept in the global checkpoint record. As stated earlier, only dirty pages are dumped out to AM during checkpointing. For each page, if the dirty bit is on in the bit map, then the page is copied to the fixed location in AM for that page. The procedure for a local checkpoint is presented as follows:

Algorithm LC: Local Checkpoint (P_i)
Input   : database pages in this partition
Process   :
1   write the BC(local) record in the local log
2   save the location of the BC(local) record in the global checkpoint record.
3   **While** there is a database page unchecked **Do**

3.1   if the page is dirty, then reset the bit in the dirty bit map;
                copy data to the IO buffer;
                request IO to flush this page to its location in AM.
           end of while.
4   write the EC(local) record in the local log.
5   switch current bits in the global checkpoint record.
6   set checkpoint bit map.
7   if all bits in the checkpoint bit map are on then execute algorithm GC.

Notice that the global checkpointing is triggered in step 7 once all partitions have been checkpointed. The algorithm for a global checkpoint in a partition checkpointing MMDB is as follows:

Algorithm GC: Global Checkpointing $(P_1, \ldots, P_n)$
Input   : MM partitions: $P_1, \ldots, P_n$.
Process :
1   reset the checkpointing bit map
2   write the EC(global) record in the global log.
3   write the BC(global) record in the global log.

With the partition checkpointing technique, the schedule of local checkpoints in a global checkpoint is important for the performance of recovery. For example, there are two extreme situations in setting the sequence of local checkpoints in a global checkpoint. One is that hot-spot data are always moved to AM, but cold-set data are ignored for a long period of time. In such a case, the amount of the log data to be processed for hot-spot partitions will be small. However, there would be too many updates accumulated in cold-set partitions. Since the recovery time for cold-set partitions is increased, the overall performance of system recovery is negatively impacted. The second kind of extreme case is when each local checkpoint is invoked once and only once within a global checkpoint. Thus, the number of local checkpoints in a global checkpoint is evenly distributed over all partitions. With such a scheduling algorithm, the partition checkpoint technique degenerates to the normal fuzzy checkpoint method.

21.4.3   Recovery Algorithm

With the partition checkpointing MMDB, the redo-point for each local log is the BC record of the last complete local checkpoint, and the undo transactions are those transactions that have been active since the earliest BC record of all the last complete local checkpoints.

To restore a partition in the MMDB, the global recovery procedure applies BFIM/AFIM values in the local log to the MM that has been reloaded with the current AM state. To direct the redo and undo activities, the lists of committed transactions *Commit List (CL)* and uncommitted transactions *Aborted list (AL)* are maintained in the MMDB at the time of recovery. The restoration for a partition in the MMDB proceeds as follows:

Algorithm LRE: Local Recovery (P_i, LBC, CL, AL)

Input   : The local log of Partition P_i

              LBC is the BC record of the last complete checkpoint in P_i

              CL list of committed transactions that should be redone

              AL list of uncommitted transactions that should be undone

Process :

1   read a block in the local log from the end of the log. // undo process

2   **While** the AL is not empty **Do**

2.1   **For** each log record in the block **Do**

              if it is BFIM and its TID is in AL, then move BFIM to MM

              if it is BT and its TID is in AL, then remove its TID from AL

2.2   read in the next block in the local log

3   read a block starting from the LBC in the local log.// redo process

4   **While** the end of the local log is not reached **Do**

4.1   **For** each log record in the block **Do**

              if it is AFIM and its TID is in CL, then move AFIM to MM

4.2   read in the next block in the local log

To generate the CL and AL, the recovery procedure scans the global log backward and categorizes transactions by the values of the BT and ET records. In addition, any transactions not found in either the CL or AL that are found in the global BC must be added to the AL. To locate the BC record of the last complete checkpoint for an MM partition, the recovery procedure examines the bits of the current fields in the global record. For a local checkpoint, if its current bit is set and it has been finished, then it is the desired one. Otherwise, the last complete checkpoint is identified as the other checkpoint that is kept in the global checkpoint record. Once the last complete checkpoint has been identified, it is easy to locate from the global checkpoint record the position of the LBC in the local log.

The partition checkpointing scheme supports two kinds of recovery methods. One is the usual *complete recovery*. With the complete recovery method, the system can be started only after all the logs have been processed and the complete database recovered to a transaction consistent state. Transaction processing and the postcrash log processing cannot be executed in parallel. (Note that this is the situation with traditional recovery techniques.) The second approach to recovery is *partial recovery*. With this approach, the system does not wait until all the logs have been processed. Instead, only portions of the database need be recovered. The system can be brought up when hot-spot partitions have been recovered. For the rest of the database, the postcrash log processing can be performed on a demand basis or after the system is up. This flexible method allows transaction processing and general recovery to proceed in parallel. In this chapter, we assume that the

MMDB adopts the usual recovery scheme, and the system can be started only after the entire database is reloaded and the redo and undo recovery have been finished. Future work will examine partial recovery in more detail. The recovery algorithm for a partition checkpointing MMDB is a follows. We assume AM has already been loaded into MM.

Algorithm CR: Complete Recovery $(P_1, \ldots, P_n)$
Input   : the global log
             MM which has been reloaded using AM
Process :
1   identify the last complete ckpt and LBC for each partition in MM.
2   initiate CL and AL list.
3   read a block in global log from the end of the log.
4   **While** the earliest point of all local ckpts in all partitions is not reached **Do**
4.1   **For** each log record in the block **DO**
             if it is ET, then add its TID in CL
             if it is BT and its TID is not in CL, then add its TID in AL
4.2   read in the next block from the global log.
5   Add to the AL any TIDs which are in the BC record but not in the CL.
6   **For** $P_1, \ldots, P_n$ **Do**
             LRE(P_i, LBC,CL,AL), where $1 \leq i \leq n$.
7   bring up system.

The category of a transaction is unambiguously identified from the global log in the recovery algorithm described earlier. Hence, if a transaction is in CL, the restoration for a partition redoes the actions of the transaction, and the effects of the transaction have been installed in the partition after system recovery. Since the partition checkpointing MMDB invokes the restoration procedure for all the partitions in the MMDB, the effects of committed transactions are ensured to be installed in all of the partitions. Therefore, all of the effects of committed transactions are reflected in the recovered database. The atomicity of committed transactions is thus guaranteed by the recovery algorithm described earlier. For a transaction in AL, its actions are undone in every partition by the recovery algorithm. The atomicity of uncommitted transactions is guaranteed.

21.4.4   Scheduling Algorithms for Local Checkpoints

In the previous sections, we have described an MMDB architecture that supports the partition checkpointing technique, and we have presented some associated recovery algorithms for this approach. In this section, we describe several algorithms for scheduling local checkpoints within a global checkpoint.

A scheduling algorithm in a partition checkpointing MMDB addresses issues in the arrangement of local checkpoints in a global checkpoint, including the numbers of local checkpoints for each partition and the order of local checkpoints. The objective of the scheduling is to achieve better performance for checkpointing and recovery. We present three algorithms for scheduling local checkpoints within a global checkpoint. An additional algorithm, round-robin checkpoint Scheduling, was examined but is not covered in detail here. With this approach, local checkpoints are invoked one by one. After the local checkpoint to one partition has been finished, the recovery component immediately schedules the local old checkpoint to the next partition.

Frequency Scheduling. To take advantage of hot spots in databases, the frequency of local checkpoints should be proportional to their frequency of update. The frequency scheduling algorithm takes frequency of update in MMDB partitions into account. Its purpose is to invoke local checkpoints proportional to their frequency of update. Thus, the hot-spot partitions will be flushed out more frequently. Hence, the MMDB improves the recovery performance for these partitions.

Suppose MMDB partition $P_1, P_2, \ldots, P_n$ has frequency of updates $f_1, f_2, \ldots, f_n$. We want an algorithm such that partition P_i is checkpointed with frequency f_i, for each i from 1 to n.

One frequency scheduling algorithm is described in what follows. We assume that given the frequencies $f_1, \ldots, f_n$, there is a function $\mathcal{F}$ that chooses the integer i with frequency f_i, for i from 1 to n. It is easy to define such a function based on a random-number generator. For example, let $\mathcal{G}$ be a function that generates integers uniformly in the range 0 to $\sum_{i=1}^{n} f_i$ and let $\mathcal{F}$ choose i if $\mathcal{G}$ generated an integer in the closed interval of length f_i starting at 0 if i is 1, and starting at $\sum_{j=1}^{i-1} f_j$ otherwise.

Algorithm FS: Frequency Scheduling
Input   : MM partitions $P_1, \ldots, P_n$
          : checkpoint frequency $f_1, f_2, \ldots, f_n$
Process :
1   Loop FOREVER
1.1   Let i = value returned by $\mathcal{F}$;
1.2   invoke local checkpoint $LC(P_i)$;
         end of Loop.

Interleaved Frequency Scheduling. The interleaved frequency scheduling algorithm works very similarly to the frequency scheduling algorithm, and local checkpoints to a partition are invoked proportional to the frequency of their update in the partition. However, this algorithm invokes the MMDB partitions in an interleaved fashion. The algorithm is described as follows.

Algorithm IFS: Interleaved Frequency Scheduling
Input   : MM partitions $P_1, \ldots, P_n$
          : checkpoint frequency $c_1, c_2, \ldots, c_n$
Process :

```
i=1;
For partitions P_1,..., P_n Do
    invoke local checkpoint LC(P_i) if c_i > 0;
    c_i^{--};   i^{++};
end of for;
until (c_1 = c_2 = ... = c_n = 0).
```

Dynamic Scheduling. This algorithm invokes a partition's local checkpoint based on the actual updates to that partition. Thus, during transaction processing each partition must keep a counter that is incremented with each update. When the number of updates in a partition reaches a predetermined threshold, a local checkpoint in the partition is triggered. The algorithm of dynamic scheduling is described as follows.

Algorithm DS: Dynamic Scheduling
Input   : MM partitions $P_1, ..., P_n$
              : number of updates in partitions $P_1\_no, ..., P_n\_no$
Process   :
        IF there is $P_i\_no \geq threshold$ then
            invoke local checkpoint $LC(P_i)$;
            $P_i = 0$;
        end of if.

The frequency scheduling algorithms described depend on prior knowledge of the MMDB updates. In contrast, with the dynamic algorithm, the scheduling of local checkpoints is based on the actual update information in the MMDB.

21.4.5   Performance Analysis for Partition Checkpointing

In this section, we examine the performance of the partition checkpointing approach. The objective is to validate it as a viable checkpointing/logging scheme for MMDB systems and to highlight the potential benefits to be achieved. Using a simple analytic approach, we examine the space and time requirements for partition checkpointing, and compare it to that used by a fuzzy checkpointing scheme without partitioning. Results are indicative of overhead and savings, but are not intended to be exact. Future studies will examine the performance in more detail, using simulations. To examine the performance, we look at the checkpointing algorithms themselves, the requirements for logging, as well as the recovery aspects. We evaluate three performance measures: the total overhead for the partition checkpointing approach as compared to a fuzzy technique without partition checkpointing, the savings in log processing at recovery time, which the partition approach provides, and finally a comparison of these two measures to predict when the partitioning approach is a valid alternative.

Table 21.3 shows the performance parameters to be used throughout this section. Here N_{tran} represents the number number of transactions with a BT record in the last complete checkpoint. We use this to approximate the number of transactions that need to be undone and redone. Our study centers around calculating the additional overhead (during logging and checkpointing) for the partition checkpointing scheme and the savings (during recovery), which partition checkpointing produces, compared to fuzzy checkpointing. We assume that one global checkpoint is performed in the partition scheme and one complete checkpoint is taken with the fuzzy approach.

Table 21.6. Performance Parameters

Parameter	Description	Default	Range
N_{tran}	No. of transactions (trans.)		200–1000
N_{BFIM}	Number of BFIM records	calc	
N_{AFIM}	Number of AFIM records	calc	
N_{part}	Number of partitions		1,5,10
$N_{locchkpt}$	Number of local checkpts	calc	
P_{upd}	Prob. that an operation is update	0.1	0.1–0.4
P_{abort}	Prob. that a tran. does not commit	0.03	
S_{BT}	Size of BT record	2	
S_{ET}	Size of ET record	2	
S_{BC}	Size of BC record	2	
S_{EC}	Size of EC record	2	
S_{BFIM}	Size of BFIM record	5	
S_{AFIM}	Size of AFIM record	5	
S_{tran}	No. of operations in trans.	5	5–25
$S_{partlog}$	Total size of log for partition checkpting	calc	
$S_{fuzzlog}$	Total size of log for fuzzy checkpting	calc	
$S_{parttran}$	No. of log words to identify trans. status for partition scheme	calc	
$S_{fuzztran}$	No. of log words to identify trans. status for fuzzy scheme	calc	
$S_{partrecov}$	No. of log words to perform redo for partition scheme	calc	
$S_{fuzzrecov}$	No. of log words to perform redo for fuzzy scheme	calc	

21.4.6 Partition Checkpointing Overhead

We first compare the total log size for partition checkpointing $S_{partlog}$ to that for fuzzy checkpointing $S_{fuzzlog}$. The size of the log for the partition checkpointing approach includes both the local logs and the global log. The global log contains one BC and EC record, a BT for each transaction, and an ET for each committed transactions. In addition, each local checkpoint log has a BT for each transaction, BFIM and AFIM records for all updates, and a BC and EC for each checkpoint performed:

$$
\begin{aligned}
S_{partlog} &= (S_{BC} + S_{EC}) + (N_{tran} * (S_{BT} + ((1 - P_{abort}) * S_{ET}))) \\
&+ (S_{BT} * N_{part} * N_{tran}) + (N_{BFIM} * S_{BFIM}) \\
&+ (N_{AFIM} * S_{AFIM}) + (N_{locchkpt} * (S_{BC} + S_{EC}))
\end{aligned}
$$

where $N_{BFIM} = N_{AFIM} = N_{tran} * S_{tran} * P_{upd}$.

The total size for the fuzzy checkpointing log is one BC and one EC record, a BT for each transaction, an ET for each committed transaction, and the same number of BFIM and AFIM records:

$$
\begin{aligned}
S_{fuzzlog} &= (S_{BC} + S_{EC}) + ((S_{BT} + (S_{ET} * (1 - P_{abort}))) * N_{tran}) \\
&+ (N_{BFIM} * S_{BFIM}) + (N_{AFIM} * S_{AFIM})
\end{aligned}
$$

We thus see that the additional log space overhead for the partition approach is:

$$
(S_{BT} * N_{part} * N_{tran}) + (N_{locchkpt} * (S_{BC} + S_{EC}))
$$

The partition checkpointing scheme has, in addition, the overhead for the global checkpoint record. This additional space overhead is $2 * r * N_{part}$, where r is the size of a global checkpoint record.

This follows since each partition has two entries. In our calculations that follows we assume r = 1.

Figure 21.17 shows the total overhead for partition checkpointing per each global checkpoint. This overhead is shown in terms of additional words needed for the partition approach. Thus, it indicates the space and also the CPU overhead. This figure shows results for 1, 5, and 10 partitions, respectively. The number of local checkpoints is calculated assuming a frequency scheduling approach. Calculating the number of local checkpoints with the frequency approach depends on the frequency of updates. We assume that for a partition i, that the number of local checkpoints per global checkpoint is i. Thus, overall we have $N_{locchkpt} = (N_{part} * (N_{part} + 1))/2$. However, since the type of local scheduling algorithm has little impact on the overhead, results are similar for other scheduling techniques.

21.4.7   Savings to Identify Transaction Status

We now examine the savings from the partition checkpointing scheme. As examined in Section 21.3 and the last subsection, there is small time and space overhead during transaction processing due to the BT records written to the local logs. The actual savings for the approach are realized during recovery time that come from (1) reduction in the number of log items to be processed, and (2) reduction in the time required to identify the status of transactions for recovery. The former is discussed in the next subsection, here we examine the latter. The partition checkpointing

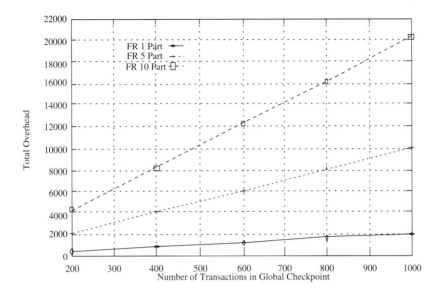

Figure 21.17. Total overhead for partition checkpointing.

scheme identifies the status of transactions by examining the global log, and a traditional fuzzy scheme must examine the whole log. The partition checkpoint scheme only uses time proportional to the number of global log records:

$$S_{parttran} = (S_{BC} + S_{EC}) + ((S_{BT} + ((1 - P_{abort}) * S_{ET})) * N_{tran})$$

while the fuzzy scheme uses time proportional to the total log size:

$$S_{fuzztran} = S_{fuzzlog}$$

Thus the total savings to identify transaction status in the partition checkpointing scheme is $(N_{BFIM} * S_{BFIM}) + (N_{AFIM} * S_{AFIM})$

In Figure 21.18, we see the savings to determine the status of transactions at recovery time. Here, the saving is independent of the number of partitions; it depends only on the number of operations within the transactions. This figure looks at transactions with 5, 10, 15, 20, and 25 operations per transaction. When comparing Figure 21.18 to Figure 21.17, we observe that the savings with 20 operations per transaction is about the same as the overhead with 10 partitions, and the savings with 10 operations is approximately that of the overhead with 5 partitions. The exact break-even point depends on the probability that an operation is updated, which we have assumed to be 10%.

21.4.8 Recovery Savings Due to Reduced Log Processing

Savings in processing cost exist at recovery time due to the reduced number of log records that need to be examined and installed into the reloaded checkpoints. The

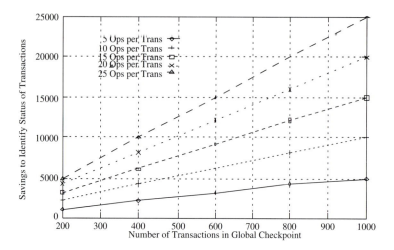

Figure 21.18. Savings at recovery time to determine the status of transactions.

exact savings depend on how the partitions are created, the number of operations in the logs, and the scheduling of local checkpoints within a global checkpoint. At the extreme case of the round-robin scheduling, there is no savings at all. Thus, the partition checkpointing scheme should not be used unless some attempt at partitioning and scheduling local checkpointing based on frequency of update is used. We thus assume this to be the case. For example, suppose that we have three partitions where the updating probabilities are 10%, 40%, and 50%. We expect, then, that the frequency of local to global checkpoints is 1, 4, and 5, respectively. This frequency of taking local checkpoints has the effect of evening out the size of the local logs to be examined during recovery. The expected number of updates to be examined during log processing per partition is then the same for all partitions and is equal to the expected number of log records in the least frequently updated partition. This can result in a substantial savings in recovery processing cost.

To determine the potential savings at recovery time, we must look at both the undo and redo functions. The undo logic for both the partition and regular fuzzy technique are the same. Each must undo all aborted or active processes. In this section, then, we concentrate on the redo portion for recovery. We assume that the number of local checkpoints for partition i is i. Thus, for recovery purposes, only $1/i$ of the corresponding local log needs to be examined for recovery redo. To determine the savings during the redo phase, we assume the sum of the update probabilities for each partition is 1 and that the frequency of update depends on the partition number. That is, the update probability for partition i is i times that of the first partition. Since the sum of the probabilities must be 1, we have:

$$1 = (N_{part} * (N_{part} + 1)/2) * x$$

where x is the update probability for the first partition. Solving this equation we find that the update probability for the first partition is:

$$2/(N_{part} * (N_{part} + 1))$$

Using this formula and the fact that a partition i only has to examine 1/i of its local log for redo, we estimate the total fraction of the local logs that must be examined at redo time to be

$$2/(N_{part} + 1)$$

We can now calculate the size of the log to be examined during the redo phase:

$$
\begin{aligned}
S_{partrecov} \;=\; & (2/(N_{part} + 1)) * ((S_{BT} * N_{part} * N_{tran}) + (N_{BFIM} * S_{BFIM}) \\
& + (N_{AFIM} * S_{AFIM}) + (N_{part} * (S_{BC} + S_{EC})))
\end{aligned}
$$

The number of log records to be examined during redo processing for a fuzzy technique is the same as the total log size:

$$S_{fuzzrecov} = S_{fuzzlog}$$

Thus, the savings with the partition scheme is

$$
\begin{aligned}
S_{fuzzlog} - S_{partrecov} \;=\; & ((S_{BC} + S_{EC}) + ((S_{BT} + (S_{ET} * (1 - P_{abort})))) * N_{tran}) \\
& + (N_{BFIM} * S_{BFIM}) + (N_{AFIM} * S_{AFIM})) \\
& - (2/(N_{part} + 1)) * ((S_{BT} * N_{part} * N_{tran}) \\
& + (N_{BFIM} * S_{BFIM}) + (N_{AFIM} * S_{AFIM}) \\
& + (N_{part} * (S_{BC} + S_{EC})))
\end{aligned}
$$

Figure 21.19 shows the savings at recovery time to read the log assuming a frequency scheduling of local checkpoints. When comparing this figure to that for Figure 21.17, it can be seen that the savings for one partition is about the same as the overhead for one partition, whereas the savings for the other partitions is less than the overhead. The actual savings, of course, depends not only on the number of partitions, but the size and type of the operations.

21.4.9 Total Savings for Partition Checkpointing

In this section, we examine the overall savings versus the total cost. The total cost was stated in Section 21.4.8 to be

$$(S_{BT} * N_{part} * N_{tran}) + (N_{locchkpt} * (S_{BC} + S_{EC})) + 2 * N_{part}$$

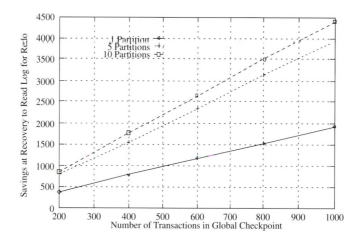

Figure 21.19. Savings at recovery time to read logs.

The total savings assuming a frequency scheduling of local checkpoints is the sum of the savings to identify the status of the transactions and to read the logs at recovery:

$$((S_{BC} + S_{EC}) + ((S_{BT} + (S_{ET} * (1 - P_{abort}))) * N_{tran}) + (2 * N_{BFIM} * S_{BFIM}) + (2 * N_{AFIM} * S_{AFIM})) - (2/(N_{part} + 1)) * ((S_{BT} * N_{part} * N_{tran}) + (N_{BFIM} * S_{BFIM}) + (N_{AFIM} * S_{AFIM}) + (N_{part} * (S_{BC} + S_{EC}))),$$

assuming frequency scheduling.

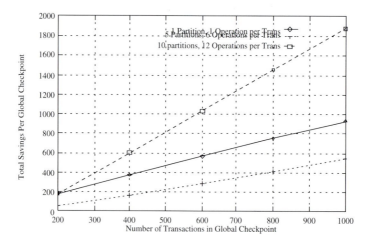

Figure 21.20. Total savings per global checkpoint assuming recovery.

Figure 21.20 shows the total savings per global checkpoint assuming a frequency scheduling. In this figure, we show the savings assuming the size of a transaction is 1 with 1 partition, 6 with 5 partitions, and 12 with 10 partitions. The actual savings depends on the number of operations and number of partitions. Under these conditions, there is always a savings. However, with a fewer number of operations per transaction, there may or may not be a savings. We have seen in the last two sections that there is always a savings with the partition checkpointing scheme at recovery time. We now see, however, that this saving does not always outweigh the overhead incurred during normal processing. Future studies will further examine this situation to identify precisely when the partition scheme savings outweighs the overhead. However, the additional overhead is small and the potential savings is large. In a high-performance system this savings in time to recover and thus reduce the downtime of the system after a crash, may far outweigh any slight overhead.

21.5 COMPARISON AND EXTENSION

The DSFC and partition checkpointing approaches have many similarities. They are both variations of the basic fuzzy checkpointing algorithm. Both divide main memory into segments (partitions). With both, a complete global checkpoint is achieved when all of the segments has been checkpointed at least once. Both shorten recovery time by reducing the size of the log, which needs to be examined during recovery. However, this is where the similarity ends. Table 21.5 shows the differences between the two approaches.

Table 21.7. Differences between DSFC and Partition Checkpointing

	DSFC	Partition Checkpointing
Segments	Dynamic	Static
Checkpointing	Global	Local and global
Scheduling	Round robin	Several
Logs	One	Local and global
Dirty Bit Map	Global	Local and global
Recovery	Global	Local and global

The major differences are caused by the fact that the partition checkpointing approach has both local and global logs. This results in local and global checkpointing, bit maps, and recovery algorithms. In addition, it facilitates a partial recovery of MMDB. That is, only the desired partitions need be recovered prior to bring the system on-line after a crash. Since the local logs are separate, only the logs for the target partitions need to be processed during this recovery. This is not possible with the DSFC approach, as only one log exists. Thus, the partition checkpointing technique is targeted for MMDB systems where this feature is needed.

In a sense, both SFC and partition checkpointing try to move the redo-point forward whenever possible. But the determination of the redo-point (both local and global) relies on the use of the LAW protocol. Without the LAW protocol, we cannot simply use the begin-chkpt-record of the most recent complete checkpoint interval as the redo-point [2]. One way to decide a proper redo-point without enforcing LAW protocol is a backward scan on the log starting from the begin-chkpt-record of the most recent complete checkpoint interval. This approach certainly reduces the performance of recovery in the MMDB. A second approach requires the checkpointing process to store some information in the chkpt-records during run time in order to determine a proper redo-point if a system failure occurs. ARIES [11] falls into this category. With ARIES, each main-memory page maintains a recovery log sequence number (denoted as REC-LSN). When a page is about to be updated, the REC-LSN of that page is assigned to be the current end-of-log log sequence number. Each chkpt-record contains minimum(REC-LSNs of all dirty pages), and the redo-point is determined as minimum(LSN of begin-chkpt record, minimum(REC-LSNs of all dirty pages)).

Without LAW, this REC-LSN mechanism can be combined with DSFC to determine a redo-point in a straightforward manner. For partition checkpointing, we need to maintain LSNs for each local log, and REC-LSN for each page in main memory, and there is no need to maintain LSN for a global log. Each local log determines a local redo-point based on the minimum of the REC-LSN of the EC(local) and the LSN of BC(local). The rest of the checkpointing and recovery algorithms still apply.

21.6   CONCLUSIONS

In this chapter, we have presented the DSFC approach. In most cases, the DSFC approach can speed up the log processing time by more than 20%, compared to the CFC approach. Furthermore, the DSFC approach segments the database without human intervention, which makes it very appropriate for real-world applications. Also, DSFC does not incur much overhead, and it is flexible and easy to design. DSFC is the first checkpointing algorithm proposed with the ability to segment the database dynamically to ensure better recovery performance.

Also, we have introduced the partition checkpointing scheme, which makes use of hot-spot information to improve the recovery performance of MMDBs. Caching, data migration, prefetching, replication, and data reloading are examples of performance improvement techniques that can take advantage of hot-spot information [4, 5, 6, 7]. This is the first hot-spot based checkpointing technique to be proposed. By incurring a slight increase in logging and checkpointing, the partition checkpointing scheme can improve processing time at system recovery by reducing the number of log records that need to be processed.

---

[2] A relaxed LAW that requires the redo-log-records go to the *volatile* log buffer prior to updating the main memory database, can still use the beginning point of the most recent complete checkpoint interval as redo-point [2]

Acknowledgment

The authors wish to thank Ashley Chaffin Peltier for the comparison to Memory Lapses.

References

[1] J. L. Lin and M. H. Dunham. *A Performance Study of Dynamic Segmented Fuzzy Checkpointing in Memory Resident Databases*, Southern Methodist University, Dept. of Computer Science and Engineering, Dallas, TX, Technical Report, No. 96-CSE-14, 1996.

[2] J. L. Lin and M. H. Dunham and X. Li. *Efficient Redo Processing in Main Memory Databases*, Southern Methodist University, Dept. of Computer Science and Engineering, Dallas, TX, Technical Report, No. 96-CSE-13, 1996.

[3] Philip Bohannon and Rajeev Rastogi and Avi Silberschatz and S. Sudarshan. *Multi-Level Recovery in the Dali Storage Manager*, AT&T Bell Labs Internal Report, 1995.

[4] Le Gruenwald and Margaret H. Eich. "MMDB Reload Algorithms," *Proceedings of ACM-SIGMOD 1993 International Conference on Management of Data*, 1991.

[5] Kenneth Salem and Daniel Barbara and Richard J. Lipton. "Probabilistic Diagnosis of Hot Spots," *IEEE 8th International Conference on Data Engineering*, 1992.

[6] G. Sacco and M. Schkolnik. "A Mechanism for Managing the Buffer Pool in a Relational Database System Using the Hot Set Model," *Proceedings of the Conference on Very Large Databases*, 1982.

[7] G. Sacco and M. Schkolnik. "Buffer Management in Relational Database Systems", *ACM Transactions on Database Systems*, 11(4) 1986.

[8] Eliezer Levy and Abraham Silberschatz. "Log-Driven Backups: A Recovery Scheme for Large Memory Database Systems", *Proceedings of the 5th Jerusalem Conference on Information Technology*, 1990.

[9] Margaret H. Eich. "Main Memory Databases: Current and Future Research Issues", *IEEE Transactions on Knowledge and Data Engineering*, 4(6) 1992.

[10] P. A. Bernstein and V. Hadzilacos and N. Goodman. *Concurrency Control and Recovery in Database Systems*, Addison-Wesley (Reading MA), 1987.

[11] C. Mohan and D. Haderle and B. Lindsay and H. Pirahesh and P. Schwarz. "ARIES: A Transaction Recovery Method Supporting Fine-Granularity Locking and Partial Rollbacks Using Write-Ahead Logging", *ACM Transactions on Database Systems*, 17(1) 1992.

[12] J. N. Gray. *Notes on Data Base Operating Systems*, Operating Systems: an Advanced Course, Springer-Verlag, NewYork, Vol. 60, 1978.

[13] Robert B. Hagmann. "A Crash Recovery Scheme for a Memory-Resident Database System", *IEEE Transactions on Computers*, C-35(9) 1986.

[14] K. Salem and H. GarciaMolina. "Checkpointing Memory-Resident Databases", *Proc. IEEE CS Intl. Conf. No. 5 on Data Engineering*, Los Angeles, 1989.

[15] H. Garcia Molina and K. Salem. "Main Memory Database Systems: An Overview", *IEEE Transactions on Knowledge and Data Engineering*, 4(6) 1992.

[16] T. J. Lehman and M. J. Carey. "A Recovery Algorithm for a High Performance Memory-Resident Database System", *Proceedings of ACM-SIGMOD 1987 International Conference on Management of Data, San Francisco*, 1987.

[17] H. V. Jagadish and A. Silberschatz and S. Sudarshan. "Recovering from Main-Memory Lapses", *Proceedings of the 19th Conference on Very Large Databases*, Dublin, 1993.

[18] X. Li and M. H. Eich. *A new logging protocol: LAW*, Technical Report No. CSE9221, Southern Methodist University, Dept. of Computer Science and Engineering, Dallas, TX. 1992.

[19] X. Li and M. H. Eich. "Post-crash Log Processing for Fuzzy Checkpointing Main Memory Databases", *Proc. IEEE CS Intl. Conf. No. 9 on Data Engineering*, Vienna, 1993.

[20] M. H. Eich. "MARS: The Design of A Main Memory Database Machine", *The 5th International Workshop on Database Machines*, 1987.

[21] X. Li and M.H. Eich and V.J. Joseph and Z. Gulzar and C.H. Corti and M. Nascimento, "Checkpointing and Recovery in Partitioned Main Memory Databases", *Proc. IASTED/ISMM International Conference on Intelligent Information Management Systems*, Washington, DC., 1995.

[22] H. V. Jagadish and D. Lieuwen and R. Rastogi and A. Silberschatz and S. Sudarshan. "Dali: A High Performance Main Memory Storage Manager", *Proceedings of the 20th Conference on Very Large Databases*, Santiago, Chile, 1994.

[23] J.L. Lin and M.H. Eich. "Segmented Fuzzy Checkpointing for Main Memory Databases", *Proceedings of the 11th Annual Symposium on Applied Computing (SAC '96)*, Philadelphia, Pennsylvania, 1996.

[24] A. Alan and B. Pritsker. *Introduction to Simulation and SLAM II*, 3rd ed., Systems Publishing Corporation, 1986.

Chapter 22

Performance Measurement of Main-Memory Database Recovery Algorithms Based on Update-in-Place and Shadow Approaches

Vijay Kumar and Albert Burger

Abstract

In the recent past, the price of volatile random access memory (RAM) have declined rapidly, and the trend is expected to continue. With such a downward trend in the price of memory, the idea of a memory resident database system is rapidly gaining momentum. In such systems the data movement between disk and main memory from the transaction execution path is completely eliminated. It is expected that the elimination of such I/O traffic would bring a significant performance improvement. With a memory resident database, however, recovery becomes more complex mainly due to the volatility of main memory. In a disk based database system, it is the disk copy representing the stable database is restored after a failure, but in main memory database systems (MDBSs), the RAM copy of the database must be recovered. An MDBS recovery algorithm, therefore, would have to do much more than the disk based recovery algorithm to guarantee atomicity and durability of transactions. This chapter discusses the recovery issues in MDBSs and presents a somewhat detailed performance study of two recovery algorithms, one using a *shadow* approach and the other *update-in-place*.

Our results show that in MDBSs, *shadow* approach performs better than *update-in-place*. We introduce minor improvements to the *shadow* scheme and show that the modified algorithm does offer further performance improvement.

22.1   INTRODUCTION

The increasing demand on transaction processing capability and the programming complexity of current database systems have stimulated much recent interest in MDBS. In MDBSs the entire database is treated as a main memory (RAM) object. By making the entire database a RAM object, an MDBS eliminates I/O from the transaction execution path, which is likely to gain significant performance improvement. Furthermore, other complexities which arise due to interaction with the disk will not be present, thus increasing the availability of the CPU for transaction processing. This will be especially useful for relational database systems where time consuming operations like *product*, *join*, and so on, can then be performed entirely in RAM as well as for object-oriented databases which are process oriented. In [13] the relationship between Prolog and relational database systems has been addressed. It was argued there that having efficient algorithms for relational operations in RAM could be useful for processing queries in future logic programming language implementations. The direct addressing capability of MDBSs is likely to minimize data retrieval time and increase CPU availability which can be utilized in increasing the level of concurrency. It seems then that there is much to be gained by making the database a RAM object in order to avoid interaction with the disk and the buffer manager to the maximum extent possible. The usefulness of MDBSs has motivated research in the area of main memory data structures, concurrency control, recovery algorithms and many other aspects.

In this chapter we concentrate on the recovery aspects of MDBSs. In MDBSs, recovery becomes more complex mainly due to the volatility of RAM and the elimination of the separation of data storage and data processing locations. The volatility of RAM necessitates the use of non-volatile storage (mainly disk) for saving necessary information for database recovery after a failure (transaction or system). The disk copy of the database serves as a database archive and it is the creation and maintenance of the archive database that make the recovery process tricky and complex. An MDBS recovery algorithm, therefore, must do much more than the disk based recovery algorithm to guarantee *ACID* properties [10] of transactions and database integrity without sacrifying the performance advantages of MDBSs. The recovery manager's requirements (I/O, logging, checkpointing etc.) must, as far as possible, not hinder normal transaction processing, that is, the execution of recovery transactions (system initiated transactions for database recovery) and normal transactions should be highly asynchronous. In this chapter, we present a somewhat detailed performance study of two MDBS recovery algorithms. We concentrate our investigation on the following problems:

- What is the cost of supporting database recovery, that is, how much time does the system spend in preparing and saving data necessary for recovery?

- How do *shadowing* and *update-in-place* strategies perform in a MDBS environment?

- How does demand recovery (recovering desired entities when asked for by normal transactions along with undemand recovery) compare with initial recovery followed by a resumption of normal transaction processing policy?

- How should an efficient load balancing be achieved if there are more than one CPU used in transaction processing and database recovery?

22.1.1 A Review of earlier works on MDBS Recovery

In this section, first we present a brief review of MDBS recovery algorithms that have appeared recently in the literature [1, 2, 4, 6, 8, 9, 12]. We then select two algorithms for our performance study.

In MDBSs, the volatility of RAM makes maintaining the *log* and *checkpointing* difficult and time consuming. An up to date copy of the *log* (*redo/undo*) must be saved on some stable storage and be available to the recovery system when necessary. *Checkpointing* may be required more frequently to minimize the recovery overhead. Recovery overhead should not be prohibitively expensive and the recovery transaction should execute asynchronously with normal transactions. Recent work on recovery mechanisms for MDBSs has identified and addressed these issues. All the algorithms we have reviewed in this chapter, make use of a reasonable sized nonvolatile RAM (NVRAM) for saving log. There are different types of NVRAM with different survival capacities. A detailed description of the different types can be found in [3].

A recovery algorithm based on *pre-committed* transactions has been presented in [2]. A transaction is called *pre-committed* if its log record has been successfully written to a stable part of the main memory. A *pre-committed* transaction's dirty pages (modified but not written to the final database) are available to other transactions for processing. To maintain *serializability*, transactions are committed (in a log dump operation a group of *pre-committed* transactions commits) in a dependency order. In this way the frequency of writing the log to the disk is reduced, and transactions do not wait for other transactions' commits to be completed. *Checkpointing* is done occasionally and asynchronously with transaction processing thus eliminating the need to quiesc the system. In a *checkpointing* operation, first the set of pages that have been updated since the last *checkpoint* is saved on a separate disk, and then this set of pages is moved to the database disks. If a system failure occurs during *checkpointing*, then these of set of pages is used in recovery. The recovery algorithm based on *pre-commit* transactions seems efficient particularly in a high update transaction environment, which can generate a large number of updated pages between *checkpointing*. There are three points that may affect the performance of the system: (1) the effect of dependency, (2) the extra RAM to hold the *checkpointing* pages, and (3) the extra disk required to hold the *checkpointing* pages and the time to save them. The response time of a transaction may suffer since it has to wait for other transactions it depends on to commit and transactions must spend additional time waiting for their commit groups to assemble. A short read-only transaction may unnecessarily be held up before it can commit. In the case of system failure while *checkpointing*, the entire database has to be recovered from the *checkpointing* disk, making the database unavailable for asynchronous transaction processing.

The recovery mechanism suggested in [12] is based on hardware logging (HALO). It tries to eliminate the need for dependency commit and introduces a separate hardware device for *logging* and *checkpointing*. This device uses an internal nonvolatile buffer and frees the CPU from all logging functions. When a CPU performs a write operation on the data, HALO takes responsibility for updating the database from the CPU. It then creates the log in the nonvolatile buffer, saves the old and new values of the data, and uses a spare RAM cycle to perform the write. In the event of a system crash, HALO restores the database with the help of the CPU. The dependency commit is no longer required since the locked entities are released only after a transaction has committed. *Checkpointing* is done at regular intervals by the CPU. In *checkpointing*, the pages are first copied to a special checkpointer buffer before flushing them to the disk. This ensures that the partial updates by a transaction are not flushed to the *checkpointing* disk. It seems a good idea to have a special hardware unit for database updates and recovery. However, such a unit may be expensive and its continuous interaction with the CPU may reduce its availability for transaction processing. Furthermore, *checkpointing* is still performed by the CPU, again affecting transaction response time.

The recovery algorithm suggested in [6] uses a *fuzzy* dump [11] and log compression to save the current state of the memory database for recovery from failure. Frequently a *fuzzy* dump of the entire RAM is taken on the disk and at system failure, with the help of the *log*, the dump is processed to acquire the last consistent state of the database, which is then loaded into RAM. The algorithm does not use any stable buffer to save log information and both *undo* and *redo* logs are saved on the log disk. A transaction failure is handled as is done on a disk based system, that is, the transaction is *undone* using an *undo* log, but after a system failure a global *redo* is initiated. This mechanism does not require extra hardware. However, the recovery processing is complex. The *log* has to be compressed and then processed for recovery to achieve acceptable performance.

In [8] a recovery technique is proposed that uses two processors, the main CPU and a recovery CPU, and supports *undo* and *redo*. The main CPU is responsible for transaction processing, *logging* into the stable log buffer, *checkpointing* and transaction *undo*. The recovery CPU is responsible for transaction commit and system recovery. In the technique proposed by [4], main memory shadow pages are used to eliminate transaction *undo*. Pages to be modified by transactions are duplicated in the stable memory before they are updated, that is, their after images (*AFIMs*) are created. We describe these two algorithms in detail later in this chapter.

The outline of the chapter is as follows. Section 22.2 presents our criteria for selecting two recovery algorithms for investigation and describes the selected algorithms. Section 22.3 explains our simulation models, Section 22.4 discusses the results, and, finally, Section 22.5 presents our conclusions.

22.2 ALGORITHMS INVESTIGATED

Two commonly known recovery approaches are *update-in-place* and *shadowing*. A *shadow* approach generally offers a poor performance in a disk-based system and the *update-in-place* scheme is commonly used. We wanted to verify how these two different approaches behave in the MMDB environment. We selected Eich's[1] algorithm [4] since to our knowledge no other recovery algorithm has used the shadow approach and investigated its behavior in MMDBs. We selected Lehman's [8] algorithm since it uses the *update-in-place* approach and its performance has been studied in detail in [8].

22.2.1 Lehman's Algorithm

The algorithm uses a main CPU and a recovery CPU. The stable memory is divided into "stable log buffer" and "stable log tail". Database and log records are archived on a set of checkpoint disks and a set of log disks respectively. RAM contains the entire database. The algorithm supports redo and undo for transaction and database recovery. The main CPU (MCPU) is responsible for logging in the stable memory and saving log records on log disks. Undo log records are maintained in RAM and redo log records are written to the stable log buffer. Log records in stable log buffer are organized in lists of fixed-size log pages (one list for one transaction). When a transaction commits, the recovery CPU (RCPU) copies all its log records from the stable log buffer to stable log tail. In stable log tail, log records of a partition (a partition is a unit of access and is similar to a page) are grouped together. Grouping by partition is done for the following reasons:

- It allows easy location of all log records of a partition during recovery. All log records for one partition are collected in a list of log pages and when a log page in the stable log tail becomes full, it is flushed to the log disk

- It allows amortization of the cost of checkpointing for a partition over many update operations. Log records for each partition are counted. A checkpoint transaction for a partition is triggered when a certain number of log records for that partition have been collected.

- Stripping redundant address information from the log records.

---

[1] Formerly Margaret Eich. Her current name is Margaret Dunham. However, we will continue to her former name in this chapter

Checkpointing. Checkpointing is done for a partition at a time. A partition may be checkpointed if it has accumulated a predefined number of log records or because of its age. The log space on the disk holding active log information is of fixed size and is called the log window. When new log pages are written to the disk and the active log information exceeds the log window size, the oldest partition in the log window falls out of the log window and must be checkpointed (checkpoint by age). A checkpoint transaction for a partition first requests a read lock on the partition to be checkpointed. When the read lock is granted, it copies the partition to a temporary buffer in RAM. It releases the partition, updates catalogues, flushes the temporary buffer to the checkpoint disk, and releases the temporary buffer.

Recovery from a transaction failure. In a transaction recovery *undo* records, saved in the main memory, are used. At the end of the recovery, *undo* and *redo* records for that transaction are deleted from RAM and from the stable log buffer respectively.

Database recovery. The database recovery process first restores catalogues and their indices and then begins database recovery. The database recovery is initiated by recovery transactions. A normal transaction during execution initiates a recovery transaction to recover the entity it requires. One recovery transaction is initiated for one partition. The recovery transaction reads the latest checkpoint copy of the partition from the checkpoint disk into RAM and all its log records (which were written after the last checkpoint for that partition) from the log disk into the stable memory. It then restores the last consistent state of the partition by applying the log records. In parallel with demand recovery, normal (not on demand) recovery transactions continue to run as low priority background jobs to recover other partitions. This means that at any time there are four types of transaction running simultaneously: normal transactions, checkpoint transaction, recovery transactions, and background recovery transactions.

22.2.2   Eich's Algorithm

The algorithm uses a database processor (DP or MCPU) and a recovery processor (RP or RCPU). Both processors have their own area of memory. They also share RAM containing the entire database and NVRAM where log records are initially written. Further, there exist disks (AM - archive memory) for log records and for the archive database. NVRAM consists of shadow memory, archive database directory, checkpoint bitmaps and log record buffer. Shadow memory is accessed associatively and transactions modify database entity in shadow memory creating AFIMs. The bit map is used by the checkpointing transactions to identify modified data pages waiting to be checkpointed. The log record buffer contains log records of committed transactions. Logging database updates are done by MCPU in the stable memory. A transaction commits when all its log records have been saved in the stable log buffer. MCPU notifies RCPU about transaction commit which then copies the log records to the log buffer, releases the space in the shadow area, and updates the checkpoint bitmap. When a log buffer block is full, CPU transfers all log records to the log disk. These blocks are written to the log disk in sequence.

Checkpointing. RCPU is responsible for checkpointing which is done periodically. In checkpointing the bit map is copied to a safe place and reinitialized. All modified pages since the last checkpoint, indicated by the bit map, are copied from RAM to the checkpoint disk (AM). The beginning and the end of a checkpoint operation is recorded in the log buffer.

Recovery from a transaction failure. The recovery processor simply removes all AFIMs of data items modified by a transaction from the shadow memory. The RCPU then notifies the MCPU to clear any locks held by the transaction.

Database Recovery. In a system failure the entire RAM is lost. During a recovery process RAM is formatted according to the AM directory. Priorities for loading segments into RAM are determined based on the access frequency of segments. Log records are loaded from the log disks to the stable memory and applied on the desired data items in the shadow area, and the recovered segments are loaded form the checkpoint disks (AM) into RAM. Regular transaction processing is resumed after log records have been applied to the data items in the shadow area. Data items involved in the recovery are locked in shared mode until the corresponding segments are recovered and loaded in RAM. In a recovery process highest priority is given to segments requested by transactions.

22.3 BASIC ASSUMPTIONS AND SIMULATION MODELS

22.3.1 Basic Assumptions

We have tried to evaluate these algorithms under a common transaction processing environment for a meaningful comparison of their performance. The model assumptions are:

- The size of RAM is infinite in the sense that regardless of the size of the database, it entirely fits there.

- The size of NVRAM is large enough to hold desired data for manipulation and log records.

- We assume that the underlying concurrency control mechanism is based on a two-phase locking[2] policy [5]

- Database access is uniform, that is, every entity of the database is equally likely to be accessed by normal transactions.

- The access time of NVRAM is about half times slower than that of the RAM

---

[2] [8] and [4] explained their algorithms under a two-phase locking concurrency control mechanism.

- The size of the RAM is sufficiently large to hold the entire database and the size of NVRAM is large enough to hold desired information and it does not fail

- Stable memory is slower by a factor of 2 than RAM

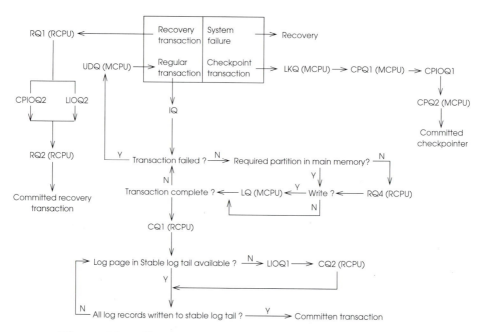

Figure 22.1. Simulation model of Lehman's recovery algorithm.

22.3.2   Simulation Model of Lehman's Algorithm

The simulation model of [8] is given in Figure 22.1. We identify regular, recovery and checkpoint transactions. Regular transactions are issued by the user, and the recovery and checkpoint transactions are initiated by the system.

Regular transactions flow. A regular or normal transaction, after going through the scheduler, waits for the MCPU (main CPU) in the IQ (Initialization Queue). It is picked up from here by MCPU for execution. If the transaction fails, then it moves to UDQ (UnDo Queue) and waits here to be rolled back by MCPU. A rolled-back transaction is moved to IQ to be restarted. If the transaction does not fail, then it looks for the required partition in RAM. The transaction, then moves into RQ4 (Recovery Queue) if the desired partition is not recovered. When the recovery is complete, the transaction from RQ4 is scheduled for execution, and if the next database access is a write operation, then the transaction enters LQ (Log Queue) queue. From LQ, a transaction is picked up by the MCPU for writing log record for the update operation. At the end of processing, the transaction enters CQ1 (Commit Queue) and waits there to be committed. The RCPU picks up a transaction from CQ1 and transfers its log records from regular stable log buffer to stable log tail. If free log pages are available then all log records are written otherwise the transaction must wait for free log pages to be available by going through LIQ1 (Log IO Queue) and CQ2 (Commit Queue) to complete the transfer of log records to stable log tail. The transaction commits when all log records are written to stable log tail.

Recovery transactions. A recovery transaction is initiated either by a regular transaction that requires a data item that has not yet recovered or for low-priority background recovery after a system crash. In both cases a recovery transaction enters RQ1 (Recovery Queue) from where it is picked up by RCPU. The recovery transaction is divided into two independent parts, one enters CPIOQ2 (CheckPoint IO Queue) and waits here for the checkpoint disk and the second enters LIOQ2 the log disk. The recovery transaction then enters RQ2 which is then picked up by RCPU to be committed. Checkpoint transaction: A checkpoint transaction first moves into LKQ (LocK Queue) and waits here for a read lock to be granted on the partition to be checkpointed. It enters CPQ (CheckPoint Queue) from LKQ and waits here for MCPU. When MCPU is available, the checkpoint transaction is moved to CPIOQ1 (CheckPoint IO Queue) where it waits for the checkpoint disk. At the end of checkpoint operation it waits for MCPU in CPQ2 to be committed. System recovery: After a system crash the recovery mechanism performs several recovery steps as described earlier. However, there are no queueing situations since all concurrent transaction activities are not resumed until the system recovery part is completed.

22.3.3   Simulation model of Eich's algorithm

The simulation model of [4] is given in Figure 22.2. We identify regular transactions, checkpoint transactions and a special recovery transaction. We describe the flow of these transactions through our model during a recovery process. A regular transaction when scheduled goes to LQ1 (Log Queue) or RQ3 (Recovery Queue) and waits for MCPU for performing a write operation. If the required page is locked (a page remains locked if during its update a system crash occurred and it has not been recovered), it waits in RQ3 for the page recovery to complete. From RQ3 it moves to LQ2 and waits for MCPU. In case a transaction wants to read an item which is neither in the shadow area nor in the main memory, it waits in RQ2 (Recovery Queue) for the corresponding segment recovery to complete. A transaction from RQ2, LQ1 or LQ2 goes to CQ1 (Commit Queue) and waits there for RCPU to be committed. An incomplete transaction resumes the execution cycle by going through RQ2, LQ1 or LQ2. A failed transaction enters UDQ (Undo Queue) and waits to be undone by RCPU. Undo operation in this algorithm is simple; RCPU simply removes the AFIMs of the failed transaction from the stable memory and re-scheduled for execution. A transaction from CQ1 commits if all log records are

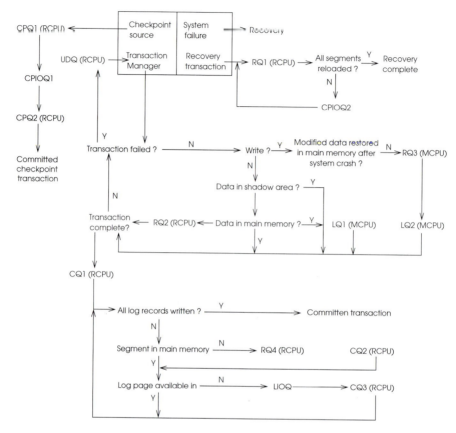

Figure 22.2. Simulation model of Eich's recovery algorithm.

written in the stable log. If a page that needs to be updated has not yet been recovered the transaction enters RQ4 (waiting for the recovery to finish). Upon exit from RQ4 it enters CQ2 and waits there for RCPU. In the the absence of free log page in the log buffer, the transaction waits in LIOQ (Log IO Queue) for log page to become available. It then moves to CQ3 (Commit Queue) and waits for RCPU to be committed. The transaction commits when all log records are written into the log buffer. Checkpoint transactions are triggered at fixed time intervals. All modified pages since the last checkpoint are written to the checkpoint disk. A checkpoint transaction first enters CPQ1 (Checkpoint Queue) and waits there for RCPU. Upon exit, it enters CPIOQ1 (Checkpoint IO Queue) where it waits for the checkpoint disk to become available. Finally, it enters CPQ2 (Checkpoint Queue) from where it is picked up by RCPU and is committed.

The system, after a system failure, performs several activities (as described earlier) before regular transactions are allowed to, enter the system. The recovery transaction, which runs asynchronously to the regular transactions, enters RQ1 (Recovery Queue) once for each segment to be recovered. It cycles through CPIOQ2 (Checkpoint IO Queue), each time waiting for the checkpoint disk to become available) until all segments are reloaded in RAM. After all segments are reloaded and recovered, the recovery transaction terminates.

22.4 SIMULATION RESULTS AND DISCUSSION

Our simulation evaluates the behavior of these algorithms with and without transaction and system failures. In the first set of experiments, we measure the logging time, checkpointing activity, commit time, and the response time of normal transactions under different arrival rates selected from Poison arrival. As mentioned before, we assume a concurrency control mechanism based on two-phase locking to serialize the execution of transaction, but we do not measure their effect on database recovery. Although the underlying concurrency control does have some effect on the recovery but their exclusion from performance study does not discredit the results. In the second experiment, we introduce transaction and system failures and measure the effect of such failures on logging, transaction undo, commit, checkpointing and transaction response. Our aim has been to see the difference in the behavior of logging, checkpointing, commit and transaction undo, in particular, the cost increase in preparing for system recovery. A comparison of the results of these two sets illustrates that the shift in the behavior of certain activities is significant when the system has to cope with these failures, but for certain activity there is no difference. We first present the performance results in the absence of any failure and then with failure. We identify Lehman's curves by the letter L and Eich's curves by the letter E.

Table 22.1 lists the simulation parameters and their values that were estimated using instruction counts. A similar method was used for this purpose in [8]. Our aim has been to investigate how efficiently these algorithms manage the recovery operation under an identical system failure environment. We did not want to investigate how their performance changes, for example, with page size or with checkpoint frequencies, and so on. For these reasons and since each algorithm has an exclusive set of parameters, we kept their values constant. We created an identical failure environment by keeping the transaction arrival and transaction size (average size of 12 entities) and type (read and write) the same. We varied the failure environment by changing the percentage of transactions that failed during processing. The times are given in units where one unit can be interpreted as 10 msec.

22.4.1 No-Failure Case

Figure 22.3 shows the relationship between transaction arrival rate and response time. Response time is a combination of logging and commit time. The graph illustrates a marked difference between the behavior of Lehman's and Eich's algorithms. The overall response time of Eich's algorithm is significantly lower than Lehman's

Table 22.1. Simulation Parameters and Their Values

Parameters for Lehman Algorithm	Time units	Parameters for Eich Algorithm	Time units
Allocate a page for undo	0.003	Update AFIM in shadow area	0.003
Allocate a page for redo	0.003	Create AFIM in shadow area	0.004
Memory update	0.002	Delete AFIM in shadow area	0.002
Write a redo/undo log record	0.003	Read AFIM in shadow area	0.002
Commit phase 1	0.002	Prepare commit	0.002
Commit phase 2	0.005	Update in main memory	0.002
Copy ALB to SLT	0.002	Update bitmap	0.001
Log disk I/O	0.050	Write a log record	0.003
Discard undo/redo page	0.004	Copy AFIM to log	0.005
Checkpoint phase 1	0.824	Log disk I/O	2.050
Checkpoint phase 2	0.008	Copy a bitmap	2.030
Checkpoint I/O overhead	4.050	Initialize a bitmap	0.020
Main-memory undo	0.008	Checkpoint I/O overhead	4.050
Initiate a recovery transaction	0.004	Restore catalogue and indexes	0.400
Initiate checkpoint and log I/O	0.016	Initiate an I/O	0.008
Apply one redo log record	0.007		
Restore catalogue and indexes	0.400		
Read lock a partition	0.005		

algorithm. At higher arrival rates (e.g., after 10) the response time of Lehman's algorithm increases sharply but in Eich's case there is no significant rise at any arrival rate.

We examine the logging and commit times individually to discover which has dominating effect on the response time. Figure 22.4 shows the relationship between logging and arrival rate and Figure 22.5 shows the relationship between arrival rates and commit time (time taken to commit a transaction), which includes log transfer time from one part of the stable store to another but does not include logging time). At all arrival rates, logging time is much higher in Lehman's algorithms than in Eich. The commit time is higher in Eich than in Lehman's algorithm. In Eich, a transaction commit involves accessing RAM database twice for each updates. The update process goes through the memory management twice; once to copy the BFIMs of data items in the stable store and then again to install the AFIM in the database. This delays transaction commit unnecessarily. In Lehman, on the other hand, a transaction goes through the memory management only once since it updates data items in-place. This seems to be the main reason for increased commit time in Eich's algorithm. In the case of logging, Lehman creates undo log

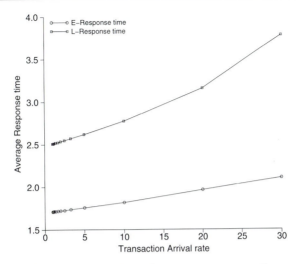

Figure 22.3. Arrival rate vs. response time.

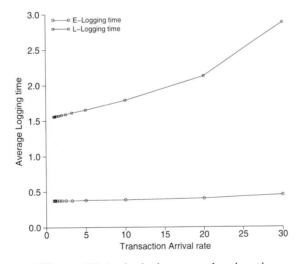

Figure 22.4. Arrival rate vs. logging time.

in RAM and redo log in the stable log store. Eich on the other hand, creates log at only one place. Figure 22.4 shows a significant difference in the logging time in these two algorithms. The response time (Figure 22.3), however, indicates that the higher logging time in Lehman's case eliminates the advantage gained in the commit time. The logging operation in Lehman's algorithm completes in two steps (logging in stable log and then in log tail) before a transaction can commit. In Eich's algorithm a transaction can commit as soon as all its log records have been written to the stable log. In this way the logging in Eich's case is a one level operation.

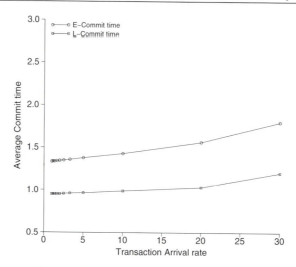

Figure 22.5. Arrival rate vs. commit time.

One level logging in Eich's algorithm manages to save significant amount of time thus giving it a distinct advantage over Lehman's algorithm.

In Lehman's algorithm, for each operation on data, an undo log record is created in RAM and a redo log record in stable memory. The undo log records are discarded if the transaction completes successfully. On the other hand, in Eich's algorithm, there is no undo log record and only NVRAM is used for logging. In this way, the logging in Eich's case is a one-level operation that manages to save a significant amount of time, thus giving it a distinct advantage over Lehman's algorithm. In Eich, a transaction commit involves accessing the RAM database and creating log records in the log buffer. On the other hand, in Lehman, log records are created in the stable log tail only during commit time. The higher workload in a transaction commit accounts for higher commit time in Eich's algorithm. However, the logging overhead in Eich's algorithm is much lower since it only has to create an AFIM of each data item it writes. In Lehman, as explained previously, the logging has to update RAM, write an undo record in RAM, and write a redo log record in the stable log buffer.

22.4.2 Failure Case

Figure 22.6 shows the relationship between transaction arrival rate and response time (logging plus commit plus undo times) under transaction failure percentages 10, 30, 50, and 60. In Figure 22.7, which shows the relationship between arrival rates and *undo* times, we see that after the arrival rate of 20, the undo time in Lehman's algorithm rises faster than it does in Eich's case. We also observe that in the latter case, it does not depend very much on failure percentage. The reason for the difference in behavior (Figures 22.6 and 22.7) is the way these algorithms

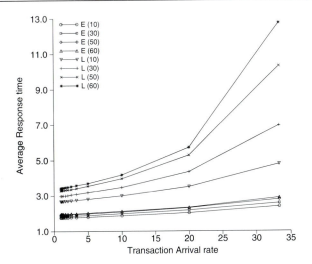

Figure 22.6. Arrival rate vs. response time.

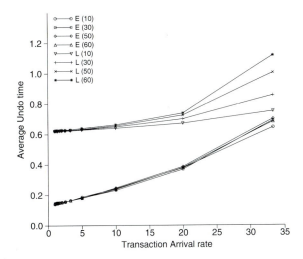

Figure 22.7. Arrival rate vs. undo time.

manage the logging operation. Lehman uses update-in-place, which requires undo for transaction recovery. In an undo, the system accesses RAM, thus increasing transaction recovery time. In Eich, shadowing makes transaction recovery easier since the undo becomes an external to transaction recovery. All operations; commit, logging, and undo contribute significantly to the response time in Lehman's algorithm. This is not the case in Eich where a visible rise in the response time with arrival rate seems mainly due to commit and logging.

22.4.3   CPU Utilization

The entire database operations (transaction processing and database recovery) in these algorithms are managed by RCPU and MCPU. In Eich, MCPU is responsible for logging, and undo, commit and checkpointing are done by RCPU. In Lehman, on the other hand, MCPU is responsible for logging, checkpointing and undo, and RCPU for commit.

The utilization of KCPU and MCPU for 10, 60, and 100% failure is shown in Figures 22.8 and 22.9, respectively. The MCPU in Eich's case is underutilized, but the RCPU is heavily utilized. This is because MCPU is responsible for logging only the least time-consuming activity among commit and checkpointing. However, when regular transaction processing, which is managed by MCPU in both algorithms, is taken into account, Eich's load distribution seems to be a balanced one. In Lehman, on the other hand, the MCPU is overutilized without transaction processing load (Figure 22.9). It may become a bottleneck if transaction processing is also considered. A better load distribution in Lehman would be to allocate MCPU for transaction processing and undo, and logging, commit, and checkpointing to RCPU.

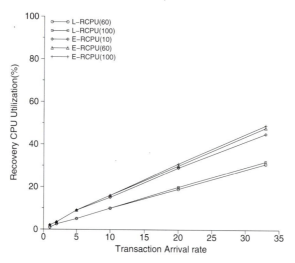

Figure 22.8. Arrival rate vs. RCPU utilization.

The way the two CPUs are used in these algorithms introduces some idle time (Figures 22.8 and 22.9). We wanted to see how many CPUs were sufficient to provide an improved performance. We provided a pool of CPUs (1 to 5) and allocated a free CPU from this pool whenever the resource was needed. Our result indicates that the performance of both algorithms improves noticeably when the pool size is increased from 1 to 2 and then it did not increase with pool size. We conclude that there is likely to be an optimal ratio between the workload and the pool size that should be obtained to gain the highest performance with minimum idle time. We

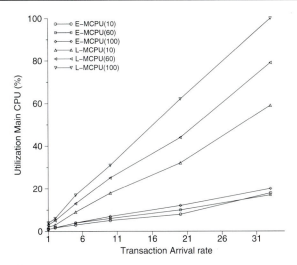

Figure 22.9. Arrival rate vs. MCPU utilization.

make two additional observations. First, Lehman's approach gains a relative higher improvement by adding CPUs, indicating that CPU availability is a more serious problem for Lehman's proposal than it is for Eich (Figure 22.10). Second, even if we do not take into consideration the degree of CPU availability, Eich's algorithm seems to outperform Lehman's algorithm. A better approach, we believe, is to remove the distinction among CPU resources, making them activity independent. This will allow any free CPU to be allocated on demand to any type of activity.

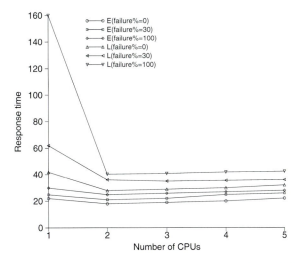

Figure 22.10. Response time vs. a pool of CPUs.

22.4.4   The Behavior of the System After a Crash

We have measured the system behavior in terms of transaction response after a system crash. In both algorithms, after a crash, the system spends some time in setting up the recovery environment (creating catalogue, setting up directories etc.). Normal transaction processing can begin as soon as this initial set up is complete. From this point on database recovery (on demand and background) and transaction processing go in parallel. We have investigated the the performance under the following scenario: (1) Each data access goes to a different segment. This means a transaction access a segment for one data item only. We identify this access pattern with access cluster value equal to 0. (2) All database accesses of a transaction are confined to one segment (in Lehman's case different partitions within a segment). We identify this access pattern with a cluster value equal to 1.

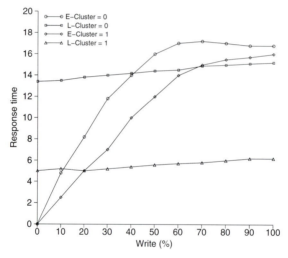

Figure 22.11. Response time vs. write percentage.

Figure 22.11 shows the relationship between write lock percentage (average number of write locks applied by a transaction) and the response time for an average arrival rate of 10 transactions per unit time. We observe a significantly different behavior in these two algorithm in this environment. In Eich's case, read only transactions can get the consistent data items in the stable memory since it survives system failure. In the case of read/write transactions, on the other hand, for a write operation the desired segment must be loaded into the main memory. It is possible that all pages modified but not checkpointed prior to a system crash. These pages are locked by the recovery transaction and remained locked until the recovery transaction commits. This implies that the response time would increase with write percentage. We see that graph 8 supports our observation. The entire recovery operation, therefore, may delay normal transaction processing and locks may be applied to a large portion of the database.

In Lehman's algorithm the read/write ratio does not have any significant effect on the response time. Both operations (read and write) require RAM database to be recovered before access to it is granted. In the case of no clustering, all partitions required by a transaction must be recovered in RAM before the transaction can commit. In this situation a transaction may have to wait for a long time before the recovery of of the last partition is complete. In the case of clustering, the situation is much better since each transaction requires only one partition to be recovered before it can commit. The recovery transaction response time is obviously not strongly influenced by the regular transaction arrival rate. The effect of a system crash on regular transaction decreases with a lower arrival rate. The bottleneck during RAM recovery is the checkpoint disk. This leads to a low utilization of the MCPU during that period, which causes the low priority recovery process to trigger recovery transactions for all partitions within a short period of time. Hence, within a short period after the system crash recovery transactions for all partitions are started, independent of the transaction arrival rate. This leads to the high value in the recovery transaction response time. If the arrival rate of regular transactions is low only a few of them will be processed within that high intensive recovery time and therefore the overall average overhead per transaction decreases.

22.4.5   Modification to Eich's Algorithm

We observed (Figure 22.11) that Lehman's mechanism achieves better results after a system crash if transactions accesses are locally bounded (cluster = 1). This is because Lehman's algorithm recovers database partitions individually. We modified Eich's algorithm so that individual portions of the database can be recovered as is done in Lehman's algorithm. As expected, in the modified method (Figure 22.12), the response time is significantly reduced for cluster = 1. This suggests that the approach of recovering parts of the database individually, as is done in Lehman's algorithm, is a better choice.

22.5   CONCLUSION

In this paper MDBS recovery issues were discussed in general and the result of a somewhat detailed performance study of MDBS recovery algorithms was presented. We investigated two main memory recovery algorithms; one based on redo/undo policy and the other uses shadow approach. Our aim was to investigate how update in-place and shadow strategies perform in main memory database environment. We used two algorithms, one proposed by Lehman [8] and the other by Eich [4]. Lehman's algorithm uses update in-place whereas Eich's approach is based on shadowing. Our investigation indicates that the shadow approach, as used in [4], has some advantages over the update in-place strategy of Lehman. The shadow approach has faster response of normal transactions even though transaction commit is slower compared to update in-place approach. The other important activities such as logging, checkpointing, undo etc., are much faster and give shadow approach

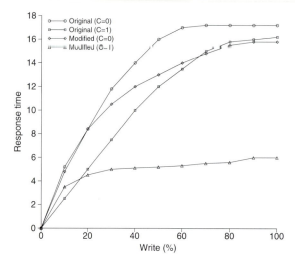

Figure 22.12. Response time vs. write percentage.

some desirable properties. In the recovery algorithms we investigated, multiple processors have been used to handle recovery and normal transaction processing. The use of multiple processors is not a part of the algorithm but it affects their performance. Such use of processors raises the problem of load sharing. We conclude in this experiment that irrespective of the recovery algorithm an efficient load balancing plays an important part in the performance of the system. It is, however, true that a recovery algorithm may imply a load balancing most suited to the set of operations supported by this algorithm. In spite of this fact, we suggest that there should not be a predefined load sharing strategy but processors should be allocated to any kind of activity on a demand basis.

References

[1] A. C. Amman, M. B. Hahrahan, and R. Krishnamurthy, "Design of a memory resident DBMS," *Proc. IEEE Spring Coinp. Conf.*, 1985.

[2] D. J. DeWitt et al., "Implementation techniques for main memory database systems", *Proc. 1984 ACM SIGMOD Conf*, June 1984.

[3] Eich, M. H. *Nonvolatile Main Memory: An Overview of alternatives*, Technical report 88-CSE-6, Dept. of Comp. Sc. and Eng., Southern Methodist University.

[4] M. H. Eich, "MARS: The design of a main memory database machine", *Proc. 5th Int. Workshop on Database Machines*, Oct. 1987.

[5] K.P. Eswaran, K. P., et al., "The Notions of Consistency and Predicate Locks in Database Systems", *Comm. of the ACM*, 19(11) (November 1976).

[6] R. B. Hagmann, "A crash recovery scheme for a memory-resident database system," *IEEE Transactions on Computers*, Vol. C-35, Sept. 1986.

[7] V. Kumar and A. Burger, "Performance measurement of some main memory database recovery algorithms," in Proc. 7th *IEEE Int. Conf. on Data Engineering*, Kobe, Japan, Apr. 8-12, 1991.

[8] T. J. Lehman, "Design and performance evaluation of a main memory relational database system", Ph. D. dissertation, Univ. of Wiscon Madison, Aug. 1986.

[9] C. Pu, "On-the fly, incremental,. consistent reading of entire database", *Algorithmita*, Vol. 1, 1986.

[10] Hearder, T., A. Reuter. "Database Recovery", ACM Computing Surveys, 15(4) (December 1983).

[11] Rosenkrantz, D. "Dynamic Database Dumping", *ACM Proceedings of SIGMOD*, Austin, 1978.

[12] K. Salem, "Failure recovery in memory resident transaction processing systems," Ph.D. dissertation, Princeton Univ., Jan. 1989.

[13] Warren, D. H. D. "Efficient Processing of Interactive Relational Database Queries Expressed in Logic", *Proc. 7th Conf. VLDB*, Cannes, France, September, 1981.

Chapter 23

Recoverable Mobile Environment: Design and Trade-Off Analysis

P. Krishna, N. H. Vaidya, and D. K. Pradhan

Abstract

The mobile wireless environment poses challenging problems in designing fault-tolerant systems because of the dynamics of mobility and limited bandwidth available on wireless links. Traditional fault-tolerance schemes, therefore, cannot be directly applied to these systems.Mobile systems are often subject to environmental conditions that can cause loss of communications or data. Because of the consumer orientation of most mobile systems, run-time faults must be corrected with minimal (if any) intervention from the user. The fault-tolerance capability must, therefore, be transparent to the user.

Presented here are schemes for recovery on a failure of a mobile host. This chapter portrays the limitations of the mobile wireless environment and their impact on recovery protocols. Toward this, adaptation of well-known recovery schemes are presented that suit the mobile environment. The performance of these schemes has been analyzed to determine those environments where a particular recovery scheme is best-suited. The performance of the recovery schemes primarily depends on (1) the wireless bandwidth, (2) the communication-mobility ratio of the user, and (3) the failure rate of the mobile host.

23.1 INTRODUCTION

A distributed system with mobile hosts is composed of a static backbone network and a dynamic wireless network [5]. A node that can move while retaining its network connection is referred to as a *mobile host*. A static network is comprised of the fixed hosts and the communication network. Some of the fixed hosts, called *base stations*, are augmented with a wireless interface, providing a gateway for communication between the wireless and the static network. Because of the limited range of the wireless transceivers, a mobile host can communicate with a base station only within a limited surrounding region, referred to as a base station's *cell*. A mobile host can reside in the cell of only *one* base station at any time. Because of mobility, an active mobile host moves from cell to cell. Thus, when a mobile host moves from one cell to another, the base station responsible for the mobile host must be changed. This process, known as a *handoff*, is transparent to the mobile host. Thus, end-to-end connectivity in the dynamically changing network topology is preserved transparently.

A mobile host may become unavailable due to (1) failure of the mobile host, (2) disconnection of the mobile host, and (3) wireless link failure [5]. Limitations in battery power make disconnections from the network very frequent. Because of their frequency, disconnections must be treated differently than failures. The difference between disconnection and failure is its *elective* nature. Disconnections can be treated as *planned* failures, which can be anticipated and prepared for [5]. The wireless link is equivalent to an intermittently faulty link, which transmits the correct message during fault-free conditions, and which stops transmitting upon a failure. Disconnections and weak wireless links primarily delay the system response, whereas a host failure affects the system state. Strategies are developed in this chapter that tolerate failure of the mobile host. Transient failures that affect the mobile host, as well as permanent failures, are handled. It may be noted that the wireless link failure can be treated as a host failure as well. When a mobile host fails, it results in a loss of its volatile state. The mobile host is assumed to be *fail-silent*, that is, the base station is able to detect the failure of the mobile host. One way to implement it is to require that an active mobile host send periodic beacons to the base station.

It will now be discussed why traditional fault-tolerance schemes cannot be applied to a mobile wireless environment. Some of the differences between static and mobile networks are enumerated in Table 23.1.

Traditional fault-tolerance schemes like checkpointing and message logging [6, 8] require a stable storage for saving the checkpoint and the logs. It has been pointed out [3] that while the disk storage on a static host is stable, the stability of any storage on a mobile host is questionable, for obvious reasons such as dropping of laptops or effect of airport security systems [1]. Thus, a mobile host's disk storage cannot be considered stable and is uniquely vulnerable to catastrophic failures. Moreover, all mobile hosts are not necessarily equipped with disk storage. Thus, we need the stable storage to be located on a static host. An automatic candidate is

Table 23.1. Difference Between Static Wired and Mobile Wireless Networks: Recovery Perspective

Category	Static Wired Networks	Mobile Wireless Networks
Network char.	Uniform, nonvarying	Nonuniform, varying
Host's local disk	Stable	Unstable
Stable storage location	Static	Mobile
Key performance parameter	Failure rate	Failure rate, wireless bandwidth, mobility
Performance metrics	State-saving cost, recovery cost	State-saving cost, recovery cost, handoff time

the "local base station," where the local base station is the base station in charge of the cell in which the mobile host is currently residing. Traditional recovery schemes are not applicable because these mobile hosts move from cell to cell. Thus, a mobile host does not have a fixed base station to communicate with. Also, recovery is complicated because successive checkpoints of a mobile host may be stored at different base stations. This dynamic topological situation warrants formulation of special techniques to recover from failures. Also, some of the failure modes are peculiar to the mobile network not present in a static network.

Traditional fault-tolerant schemes do not consider the disparity in the network characteristics (bandwidth, error, etc.) of the static network and the wireless network. Moreover, the network characteristics (bandwidth, error) of the wireless network also vary with the type of network used (infrared, packet relay, satellite, etc.). Over a length of a connection, the mobile host might be employing different types of wireless networks. For example, within a building, infrared will be used; in a campus environment, packet relay will be used; and in a remote region, satellite will be used. Available wireless bandwidth and error conditions will be different in each of these wireless networks. Thus, the appropriate recovery protocol needs to be determined adaptively, based on the characteristics of the underlying wireless network.

Performance of traditional recovery schemes primarily depends on the failure rate of the host [9, 12]. However, in a mobile environment, due to mobility of the hosts and limited bandwidth on the wireless links, parameters other than failure rate of the mobile host play a key role in determining the effectiveness of a recovery scheme. A mobile environment is determined by the mobility, wireless bandwidth, and the failure rate. This chapter presents the following:

- User-transparent recovery with mobile host failure

- Trade-offs for the recovery schemes proposed

- Optimal recovery scheme for an environment

We propose several schemes for recovery from a failure of a mobile host. These proposed schemes have two major components: a *state-saving* scheme and a *handoff* scheme. We propose two schemes for state saving, namely, (1) *No Logging* (N) and (2) *Logging* (L), and three schemes for handoff, namely, (1) *Pessimistic* (P), (2) *Lazy* (L), and (3) *Trickle* (T). We denote a recovery scheme that employs a combination of a state-saving scheme, X ($X \in \{N, L\}$), and a handoff scheme, Y ($Y \in \{P, L, T\}$), as XY. For example, LL is a recovery scheme that uses a combination of the logging scheme for state saving and the Lazy scheme for handoffs.

Each combination provides some level of availability and requires some amount of resources: network bandwidth, memory, and processing power. Through analysis, we show that there can be no single recovery scheme that performs well for all mobile environments. However, we determine the optimal recovery scheme for each environment, as shown in Table 23.2.

Table 23.2. Optimal Recovery Scheme

Mobility	Wireless Bandwidth	Failure Rate	Optimal Scheme
High	Low	Low	LL
		High	NT
	High	All	LT
Low	All	All	LL

This chapter is organized as follows: Section 23.2 overviews related work. Section 23.3 presents the recovery strategies. Section 23.4 gives the performance analysis of the recovery strategies, and conclusions are found in Section 23.5.

23.2   RELATED WORK

Research in mobile computing primarily has focused on mobility management, database system issues, network protocols, disconnected operation, and distributed algorithms for mobile hosts [5, 7]. Work on fault-tolerance issues is very limited.

Alagar and Venkatesan [2], demonstrate schemes to tolerate base station failures by replicating the information stored at a base station at several "secondary" base stations. Strategies for selecting the secondary base stations were shown. These schemes can be easily integrated with the recovery schemes presented in this chapter, to provide a system that tolerates both base station and mobile host failures.

Rangarajan at el. [10] present a fault-tolerant protocol for location directory maintenance in mobile networks. The protocol tolerates base station failures and host disconnections. Logical timestamps are used to distinguish between old and new location information. The protocol also tolerates the corruption of these logical timestamps.

Acharya at el. [1], identify the problems with checkpointing mobile distributed applications, presenting an algorithm for recording global checkpoints for distributed applications running on mobile hosts.

In this chapter, however, we consider protocols to recover from failure in a mobile host, independent of other hosts in the system. Also, we study the effect of mobility and wirelessness on such recovery protocols.

23.3   RECOVERY STRATEGIES

A recovery strategy essentially has two components: a state-saving and a handoff strategy. This section presents two strategies for saving the state and three strategies for handoff to achieve fault tolerance. Strategies for saving the state are similar to traditional fault-tolerance strategies.

23.3.1   State Saving

State-saving strategies presented in this chapter are based on traditional check-pointing and message-logging techniques. In such strategies, the host periodically saves its state at a stable storage. Thus, upon failure of the host, execution can be restarted from the last-saved checkpoint.

It was indicated earlier [3] that a mobile host's disk storage cannot be considered stable. Thus, our algorithms use the storage available at the base station for the cell in which the mobile host is currently residing, as the stable storage.

Multiple hosts (both static and mobile) will take part in a distributed application. Such applications require messages to be transferred between the hosts, and might also require user inputs at the mobile hosts. Whereas the user inputs may go directly to the mobile host, the messages will first reach the base station in charge of the *cell* in which the mobile host currently resides. The base station then forwards the messages to the corresponding mobile host. Likewise, all messages sent by a mobile host will first be sent to its base station, which will forward them to the destination host (static or mobile).

Two strategies to save the process state [6] will be discussed here: (1) *No Logging* and (2) *Logging*. It is assumed that the mobile host remains in one cell during the length of the application. This is followed by a discussion of three schemes that address the recovery steps needed because of mobility.

- *No-Logging* Approach (denoted as N): The state of the process can be altered, either on receipt of a message from another host or on user input. The messages or inputs that modify the state are called *write* events. (If the semantics of the message is not known, in the worst case, we might have to assume that the state is altered on receipt of every message or user input.) In the *No-Logging* approach, the state of the mobile host is saved at the base station on every *write* event on the mobile host data.

  After a failure, when the mobile host restarts, the host sends a message to the base station, which then transfers the latest state to the mobile host. The mobile host then loads the latest state and resumes operation. Importantly, need for frequent transmission of state on the wireless link is a limiting factor for this scheme.

- *Logging* Approach (denoted as L): This approach is rooted in "pessimistic" logging [4], used in static systems. In this scheme, a mobile host checkpoints its state periodically. To facilitate recovery, the *write* events that take place in the interval between checkpoints are also logged. As defined earlier, the messages or inputs that modify the state of the mobile host are called *write* events. If a *write* message is received from another host, the base station first logs it and then forwards it to the mobile host for execution. Likewise, upon user input (write event), the mobile host first forwards a copy of the user input to the base station for logging. After logging, the base station sends back an acknowledgment to the mobile host. The mobile host can process the input while waiting for the acknowledgment, but cannot send a response. Only upon receipt of the acknowledgment does the mobile host send its response.

The preceding procedure ensures that no messages or user inputs are lost due to a failure of the mobile host. The logging of the write events continues until a new checkpoint is backed up at the base station. The base station then purges the log of the old write events along with the previous checkpoint.

After a failure, when the mobile host restarts, the host sends a message to the base station, which then transfers both the latest backed-up checkpoint of the host, as well as the log of write events, to the mobile host. The mobile host then loads the latest backed-up checkpoint and restarts executing by replaying the write events from its logs, thus reaching the state before failure. In what follows, the recovery steps are considered that are needed, arising due to mobility of the hosts.

23.3.2   Handoff

The mobility warrants a special *handoff* process, described in what follows. The key problem to be addressed is how a recovery can be effected if a mobile host moves to a new cell, as illustrated in the following example.

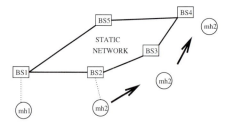

Figure 23.1. Handoff in the middle of an execution.

Consider the system in Figure 23.1. *BSi* denotes *i*th base station, and *mhi* denotes *i*th mobile host. Here, mobile hosts *mh1* and *mh2* are executing a distributed algorithm. The mobile host *mh2* has saved both its checkpoint and message log at *BS2*. In the middle of the execution, *mh2* moves to the cell of *BS3*, and then to the cell of *BS4*. Handoff occurs at both the boundaries of *BS2* and *BS3*, and *BS3* and *BS4*. Let a failure of the mobile host *mh2* occur on reaching the cell of *BS4*. Had *mh2* remained in the cell of *BS2*, the system would have recovered because the checkpoint and the logs are saved at *BS2*. But since no state saving took place at *BS3* or *BS4*, and since *BS4* does not know where the last checkpoint of *mh2* is stored, the recovery procedure will now have to identify the base station where the checkpoint is saved. This will warrant additional steps to identify the base station. Therefore, what is proposed is transferring during the handoff process some *information* regarding the state of the mobile host. The following delineates three ways to transfer this information during the *handoff* process: (1) *Pessimistic*, (2) *Lazy*, and (3) *Trickle*.

Pessimistic Strategy (*P*).   When a mobile host moves from one cell to another, the checkpoint is transferred to the new cell's base station during handoff. If the logging strategy is being used, then in addition to the checkpoint, the message log is also transferred to the new cell's base station. Upon receipt of the checkpoint and/or the log, the new cell's base station sends an acknowledgment to the old base station. The old base station, upon receiving the acknowledgment, purges its copy of the checkpoint and the log, since the mobile host is no longer in its cell.

The chief disadvantage to this approach is that it requires a large volume of data to be transferred during each handoff. Potentially, this can cause long disruptions during handoffs. However it can be avoided if we use the *Lazy* or *Trickle* strategy, as will be explained.

Lazy Strategy (*L*).   With the *Lazy* strategy, during handoff, there is no transfer of checkpoint and log. Instead, the *Lazy* strategy creates a *linked list* of base stations of the cells visited by the mobile host. The mobile host may be using either one of the state-saving strategies (No Logging or Logging) described earlier. If the mobile host is using the No-Logging strategy, the checkpoint is saved at the current cell's base station after every *write event*. On the other hand, if the Logging strategy is used, a log of *write* events is maintained, in addition to the last checkpoint of the mobile host at the base station. Upon a handoff, the new cell's base station keeps a record of the preceding cell. Thus, as a mobile host moves from cell to cell, the corresponding base stations effectively form a linked list. One such linked list needs to be maintained at the base station for each mobile host.

This strategy could lead to a problem if the checkpoint and logs of the mobile host are unnecessarily saved at different base stations. To avoid this, on taking a checkpoint at a base station, a notification is sent to the last cell's base station to purge the checkpoint and logs of the mobile host, if present. If a checkpoint is not present, this base station forwards the notification to the preceding base station in the linked list. This process continues, until a base station with an old checkpoint of the mobile host is encountered. All base stations receiving the notification purge any state associated with the particular mobile host.

The *Lazy* strategy saves considerable network overhead during handoff, compared to the *Pessimistic* strategy. Recovery, though, is more complicated. Upon a failure, if the base station does not have the process state, it obtains the logs and the checkpoint from the base stations in the linked list. The base station then transfers the checkpoint and the log of write events to the mobile host. The host then loads the checkpoint and replays the messages from the logs to reach the state just before failure.

Trickle Strategy (T). Importantly, in the *Lazy* strategy, the scattering of logs in different base stations increases as the mobility of the host increases, potentially making recovery time-consuming. Moreover, a failure at any one base station containing the log renders the entire state information useless.

To avoid this, a *Trickle* strategy is proposed. In this strategy, steps are taken to ensure that the logs and the checkpoint are always at a nearby base station (which may not be the current base station). In addition, care is taken so that the handoff time is as low as with *Lazy* strategy.

We make sure that the logs and the checkpoint corresponding to the mobile host are at the "preceding base station" of the current base station.[1] (The preceding base station is the base station of the previous cell visited by the mobile host.) Thus, assuming that neighboring base stations are one hop from each other (on the static network), the checkpoint and the logs are always, at most, one hop from the current base station.

To achieve the preceding, during handoff, a control message is sent to the preceding base station to transfer any checkpoint or logs that had been stored for the particular mobile host. Similar to the *Lazy* strategy, the current base station also

---

[1] Variations of this scheme are possible where the checkpoint and logs are at a *bounded* distance from current cell.

sends a control message to the new cell's base station identifying the preceding cell location of the mobile host. Thus, the new cell's base station just retains the identification of the mobile host's preceding cell.

If a checkpoint is taken at the current base station, it sends a notification to the preceding base station that has the last checkpoint and logs to purge the process state of the mobile host. During recovery, if the current base station does not have a checkpoint of the process, it obtains the checkpoint and/or the logs from the preceding base station.[2] The base station then transfers the checkpoint and/or the log to the mobile host. The mobile host then loads the checkpoint and replays the messages from the logs, to reach the state just before failure.

23.4 PERFORMANCE ANALYSIS

Basically, six schemes (combinations of state saving and handoff) are possible. This section analyzes these schemes, determining which combination is best-suited for a given environment.

23.4.1 Terms and Notations

The following terminology is used, the significance of which will be clearer later in this Section.

- The term *operation* may refer to one of (1) checkpointing, (2) logging, (3) handoff, or (4) recovery.

- *Cost* of an operation quantifies the network usage of the messages due to the operation.

- λ: Failure rate of the mobile host. We assume that the time interval between two failures follows an exponential distribution with a mean of $1/\lambda$.

- μ: Handoff rate of the host. We assume that the time interval between two handoffs follows an exponential distribution with a mean of $T = 1/\mu$.

- The time interval between two consecutive write events is assumed to be fixed and equal to $1/\beta$. Write events are comprised of user inputs and messages from other hosts. Since we are only interested in the performance penalty due to fault tolerance of the various schemes proposed, this assumption will not significantly affect the results.

- r: Communication-mobility ratio, defined as the expected number of write events per handoff, equal to β/μ. For a fixed β, a small value of r implies high mobility, and vice versa.

---

[2]If the No-Logging strategy was used for state saving, the checkpoint will be transferred. On the other hand, if Logging is used, the checkpoint and the log are transferred.

- ρ: Fraction of write events that are user inputs. If ρ is 1, then all the write events are user inputs. This means that the application is not distributed in nature, and that the mobile host is the only participant in this execution.

- T_c: Checkpoint interval, defined as the time spent between two consecutive checkpoints executing the application. T_c is fixed for all schemes under consideration. Specifically, T_c is $1/\beta$ for No-Logging schemes.

- k: Number of write events per checkpoint. For the Logging schemes, $k = \beta T_c$. For the No-Logging schemes, k is always equal to 1.

- α: Wireless network factor. This is the ratio of the cost of transferring a message over one hop of a wireless network to the cost of transferring the message over one hop of a wired network. The higher the value of α, the costlier is the wireless transmission relative to the wired transmission.

- $N_c(t)$: Number of checkpoints in t time units.

- $N_l(t)$: Number of messages logged in t time units.

- C_c: Average cost of transferring a checkpoint state over one hop of the wired network.

- C_l: Average cost of transferring an application message over one hop of the wired network

- γ: Relative logging cost. It is the ratio of the cost of transferring an application message to the cost of transferring a checkpoint state over one hop of the wired network (C_l/C_c).

- C_m: Average cost of transferring a control message over one hop of the wired network. The size of a control message is typically assumed to be much less than the size of an application message.

- ϵ: C_m/C_c = Relative control message cost. It is the ratio of the cost of transferring a control message to the cost of transferring a checkpoint state over one hop of the wired network.

- C_h: Average cost of a handoff operation.

- C_r: Average cost of a recovery operation.

- C_t: Average total cost per handoff.

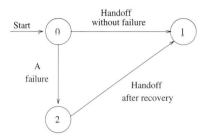

Figure 23.2. Markov chain representation.

23.4.2   Modeling and Metrics

The interval between two handoffs is referred to as a *handoff interval*. A handoff interval can be represented using a three-state discrete Markov chain [11, 12], as presented in Figure 23.2.

State 0 is the initial state when the handoff interval begins. During the handoff interval, the host receives messages and/or user inputs (write events). Depending on the state-saving scheme, the host either takes a checkpoint or logs the write events. A transition from State 0 to State 1 occurs if the handoff interval is completed without a failure. If a failure occurs during the handoff interval, a transition is made from State 0 to State 2. After State 2 is entered, a transition occurs to State 1 once the handoff interval is completed. To simplify the analysis, we have assumed that, at most, one failure occurs during a handoff interval. This assumption does not significantly affect the results when the average handoff interval is small, compared to the mean time to failure.

The transition probability P_{02} is the probability that a failure occurs within a handoff interval. Let t_f be the time of failure, and t_h be the time of handoff. Then:

$$P_{02} = P(t_f < t_h) = \int_0^\infty \int_{\tau_f}^\infty \lambda \mu e^{-\lambda \tau_f} e^{-\mu \tau_h} \; d\tau_h \, d\tau_f$$

Solving the preceding, we get

$$P_{02} = \frac{\lambda}{\lambda + \mu}$$

The expected duration from the beginning of the *checkpoint* interval until the time when the failure occurred, given that a failure occurs before the end of the checkpoint interval, is

$$T_{cexp} = \int_0^{T_c} \frac{t \lambda e^{-\lambda t}}{1 - e^{-\lambda T_c}} \; dt = \frac{1}{\lambda} - \frac{T_c e^{-\lambda T_c}}{1 - e^{-\lambda T_c}}$$

As stated earlier, $N_c(t)$ and $N_l(t)$ denotes the number of checkpoints and messages logged in t time units, respectively. Cost C_{01} of transition $(0,1)$ is the expected total cost of operations that occurs during the time spent in State 0 before making the transition to State 1. C_{01} is as follows: (Recall that T is the mean handoff interval.)

$$C_{01} = (\alpha C_c) * N_c(T) + (\alpha C_l) * N_l(T) + C_h \tag{23.1}$$

Performance metrics for the proposed schemes are as follows:

- **Handoff Time:** The handoff time is the *additional time* required to transfer the state information from one base station to other, with the overhead of fault tolerance. Basically, it is the difference in the time duration of a handoff operation with fault tolerance and the time duration of a handoff operation without fault tolerance.

- **Recovery Cost:** Upon a failure, this is the expected cost incurred by the recovery scheme to restore the host to the state just before failure.

- **Total Cost:** This is the expected cost incurred during a handoff interval with and without failure. The total cost is determined as follows:

$$C_t = C_{01} + P_{02}C_r \tag{23.2}$$

The costs will depend on the state-saving and handoff scheme used. We denote the total cost of a scheme that employs a combination of a state-saving scheme, X ($X \in \{N, L\}$), and a handoff scheme, Y ($Y \in \{P, L, T\}$) as C_{tXY}.

Now, we will derive the costs C_{01}, C_r, and the handoff time for each scheme. The total cost C_t for each scheme can be determined by replacing the costs C_{01} and C_r obtained in Equation (23.2). Our analysis assumes that the cost of transmitting a message from one node to another depends on the number of hops between the two nodes. We also assume that neighboring base stations are at a distance of one network hop from each other.

23.4.3   No-Logging Pessimistic (NP) Scheme

A checkpoint operation takes place on every write event. Thus, on every write event, the checkpoint is transferred over the wireless network to the base station, incurring a cost of αC_c, on average. There are r write events during a handoff interval. Since there is no logging operation involved, $N_l(t) = 0, t \geq 0$. During a handoff, the last checkpoint is transferred to the new base station, and, in reply, an acknowledgment is sent. Therefore, the cost of handoff $C_h = C_c + C_m$. Thus from Equation (23.1) we get $C_{01} = (r\alpha + 1)C_c + C_m$.

During recovery, the process state will be present at the current base station. Therefore, the recovery cost is the cost of transmitting a request message from the mobile host to the base station, and the cost of transmitting the state over one hop of the wireless link. Thus:

$$C_r = \alpha(C_c + C_m)$$

23.4.4   No-Logging–Lazy (NL) Scheme

The checkpoint and logging operations are similar to the NP scheme in Section 23.4.3. However, upon the first checkpoint operation at the current base station, a control message is sent to the base station that has the last checkpoint, requesting it to purge that checkpoint. Let that base station be, on average, N_h hops from that current base station. Thus, the average cost of purging is $N_h C_m$. A handoff operation includes setting a pointer at the current base station, and transferring a control message between the current and the new base stations. Since setting a pointer does not involve any network usage, the cost of handoff, C_h, is equal to the cost, C_m, of transferring a control message between the two base stations. Thus:

$$C_{01} = r\alpha C_c + N_h C_m + C_m$$

Since a checkpoint operation takes place upon every write event, and the checkpoint is not transferred to the new base station upon a handoff, the location of the last checkpoint will depend on the number of handoffs since the last write event. The upper bound on the number of hops traversed, to transfer the last checkpoint to the current base station, will be the number of handoffs between two write events (or, in this case, checkpoints). In addition to this, the cost of transferring the checkpoint over the wireless link is incurred: αC_c. The average number of handoff operations completed since the last write event (or checkpoint event) until the time of failure is N_h, where

$$N_h = \mu T_{cexp} \tag{23.3}$$

A cost is also incurred due to the request message from the mobile host for the checkpoint. The cost is $(\alpha + N_h)C_m$. Thus, an upper bound on the recovery cost is

$$C_r = (N_h + \alpha)(C_c + C_m)$$

We will use this C_r to evaluate C_{tNL}. As this C_r estimated is an upper bound, C_{tNL} estimated here is somewhat pessimistic.

23.4.5   No-Logging–Trickle (NT) Scheme

The checkpoint and logging operations are the same as for the NP and NL schemes described in Sections 23.4.3 and 23.4.4. As in the NL scheme, the handoff cost is the cost of transferring a control message from the current to the new base station. In addition to this, a control message is sent to the previous base station, requesting it to transfer any state corresponding to the mobile host. This ensures that the maximum number of hops traversed, to transfer the state during recovery, is 1. The cost of the handoff operation is, thus, the sum of the cost of transferring the state over one hop of wired network, and the cost of sending two control messages. Thus, $C_h = C_c + 2C_m$. It should be noted, however, that the handoff time is only determined by C_m, for the transfer of a control message between the current and the new base station. The time spent due to the transfer of state is transparent to the user.

Upon the first checkpoint operation at the current base station, a control message is sent to the base station that has the last checkpoint, requesting it to purge that checkpoint. Let that base station be, on average, N'_h hops from the current base station. Therefore, the cost of purging is $N'_h C_m$. Thus:

$$C_{01} = (r\alpha + 1)C_c + 2C_m + N'_h C_m$$

As stated earlier, during the recovery operation, the number of hops traversed to transfer the state is, at most, 1. Thus:

$$C_r = (N'_h + \alpha)(C_c + C_m)$$

where

$$N'_h = 1(1 - e^{-\mu T_c}) + 0(e^{-\mu T_c}) = (1 - e^{-\mu T_c}) , \tag{23.4}$$

where $e^{-\mu T_c}$ is the probability that the last checkpoint took place at the current base station.

23.4.6 Logging-Pessimistic (LP) Scheme

For this scheme, the state of the process will contain a checkpoint and a log of write events. The message log will contain the write events that have been processed since the last checkpoint. The logging cost will involve only those write events that have to traverse the wireless network to be logged at the base station. Only the user inputs need to traverse the wireless network to be logged. On the other hand, write events received from other hosts in the network come via the base station anyway, so they get logged first, and then forwarded to the mobile host. Thus, no cost is incurred due to logging of write events from other hosts. As stated earlier, ρ is the fraction of write events that are user inputs. Thus, ρr is the number of user inputs between two handoffs. This is also the number of logging operations in a handoff interval. For each logging operation, there is a cost for the acknowledgment message sent by the base station over the wireless network. The cost of each acknowledgment message is αC_m.

The handoff cost will now include the cost of transferring the state as well as the message log, and the cost of transferring an acknowledgment. Let ν denote the average log size during handoff. Then, the average handoff cost will be $(\nu C_l + C_c + C_m)$. Under the assumption of handoffs being a Poisson process, $\nu = \frac{k-1}{2}$. (Recall that k is the number of write events per checkpoint.) Thus:

$$C_{01} = \frac{r\alpha C_c}{k} + \rho r\alpha C_l + \rho r\alpha C_m + \nu C_l + C_c + C_m$$

During recovery, the checkpoint and the log are present at the current base station. Therefore, the recovery cost is the cost of transmitting a request message from the mobile host to the base station, and the cost of transmitting the checkpoint and log over one hop of the wireless network. The expected size of the log at the time of failure is ν'. For Poisson failure arrivals, $\nu' = \frac{k-1}{2}$. Therefore:

$$C_r = \alpha(\nu'C_l + C_c + C_m)$$

23.4.7 Logging-Lazy (LL) Scheme

The checkpoint and logging operations are the same as for the LP scheme described in Section 23.4.6. When a checkpoint takes place, the old checkpoint and logs at the different base stations are purged. As also determined earlier in Section 23.4.4, the purging cost is $N_h C_m$, and the handoff cost is C_m.

$$C_{01} = \frac{r\alpha C_c}{k} + \rho r\alpha C_l + \rho r\alpha C_m + N_h C_m + C_m$$

As determined earlier, the expected number of write events completed until the time of failure since the last checkpoint is $\nu' = \frac{k-1}{2}$. This is distributed over different base stations. The last checkpoint and the logs have to traverse, on an average, N_h (see Equation 23.3) hops on the wired network to reach the current base station, and an additional wireless hop to reach the mobile host. A cost of $(N_h + \alpha)C_m$ is also incurred due to the request message for the checkpoint and the logs (same as for NL scheme). Therefore,

$$C_r = (N_h + \alpha)(\nu'C_l + C_c + C_m)$$

23.4.8 Logging-Trickle (LT) Scheme

The checkpoint and logging operations are the same as in LP and LL. The cost of handoff operation is, thus, the sum of the cost of sending two control messages (same as for the NT scheme), and the cost of transferring checkpoint and logs over one hop of wired network. Thus, $C_h = \nu C_l + C_c + 2C_m$. The cost of purging is $N'_h C_m$. Thus:

$$
\begin{aligned}
C_{01} &= \frac{r\alpha C_c}{k} + \rho r\alpha C_l + \rho r\alpha C_m + \nu C_l + C_c + 2C_m + N'_h C_m \\
C_r &= (N'_h + \alpha)(\nu'C_l + C_c + C_m)
\end{aligned}
$$

23.4.9 Results

The preceding equations have been normalized with respect to C_c. Recall that γ is the relative logging cost and is equal to C_l/C_c. Thus, $C_l = \gamma C_c$. Recall that ϵ is the relative control message cost and is equal to C_m/C_c. We assume that $C_m \ll C_c$ (which is the case, in practice). We replace $C_c = 1$, $C_l = \gamma$, and $C_m = \epsilon$ in the preceding equations and determine the handoff time, recovery cost, and the total cost. The rate of writes β is set to 1.

For our analysis, we assume that $\rho = 0.5$. (Recall that ρ is a fraction of write events that are user inputs.) This means that the write events comprise an equal percentage of user inputs and messages from other hosts. For our analysis, we fix the relative control message cost, $\epsilon = 10^{-4}$.

Optimum Checkpoint Interval. An optimum checkpoint interval is required to be determined only for the Logging schemes. Recall that for a No-Logging scheme, a checkpoint takes place upon every write event. However, for a Logging scheme, a checkpoint takes place periodically every T_c units of time. Since the rate of writes β is equal to 1, the number of write events per checkpoint (k) is equal to T_c. A "good" value for k needs to be chosen for the Logging schemes. We define a good value of k to be the one that offers the minimum total cost. This value of k (say, $k_{opt_{LY}}$, for a Logging scheme that uses scheme Y for handoffs: $Y \in \{P, L, T\}$) is a function of the failure rate λ, relative logging cost γ, wireless network factor α, and communication-mobility ratio r. Let us consider the LL scheme as an example. The value of $k_{opt_{LL}}$ for the LL scheme is obtained as a solution of

$$\frac{\partial C_{tLL}}{\partial k} = 0 \quad \text{and} \quad \frac{\partial^2 C_{tLL}}{\partial^2 k} < 0$$

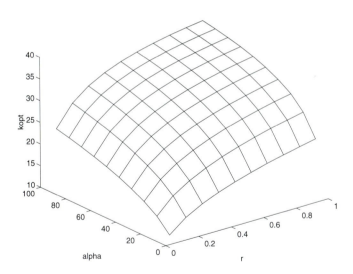

Figure 23.3. $k_{opt_{LL}}$ vs. r and α: $\lambda = 10^{-2}$ and $\gamma = 0.1$.

Figure 23.3 illustrates the variation of $k_{opt_{LL}}$ with r and α for $\lambda = 10^{-2}$ and $\gamma = 0.1$. It is shown that $k_{opt_{LL}}$ increases as r and α increase. For a given k, as r increases, the number of checkpoints per handoff increases. This increases the total cost. As α increases, the cost due to a checkpoint increases. Thus, to lower the

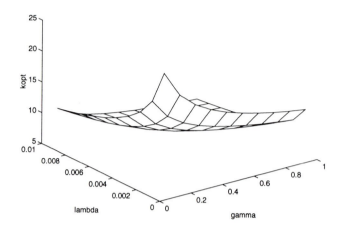

Figure 23.4. $k_{opt_{LL}}$ vs. γ and λ: $\alpha = 10$ and $r = 0.1$.

total cost, k should also increase. Therefore, as r and/or α increases, $k_{opt_{LL}}$ also increases.

Figure 23.4 illustrates the variation of $k_{opt_{LL}}$, with γ and λ for $r = 0.1$ and $\alpha = 10$. It is shown that $k_{opt_{LL}}$ decreases as γ and λ increase. As γ increases, the cost of the logging operation increases. Thus, checkpoint interval size has to be reduced to decrease total cost. Therefore, $k_{opt_{LL}}$ decreases as γ increases. As λ increases, the probability of failure increases. Therefore, the fraction of recovery cost in the total cost increases. The recovery cost for the Logging schemes depends on the average log size during failure. The average log size, in turn, depends on checkpoint interval size. To decrease the recovery cost, we need to reduce the checkpoint interval size. Thus, as λ increases, $k_{opt_{LL}}$ decreases.

Similar behavior was observed for the LP and LT schemes. We used $k = k_{opt_{LY}}$ for the analysis of the Logging scheme, which uses scheme Y for handoffs, where $Y \in \{L, P, T\}$. We assume that relative logging cost $\gamma = 0.1$. We vary α to represent different classes of wireless networks. We vary λ to represent different failure rates. We vary r to represent different user-mobility patterns. We will now illustrate the performance of each of the proposed schemes.

Handoff Time.   Recall that the handoff time is the *additional* time required, due to the transfer of state information by the fault-tolerance scheme during the handoff operation. Let BW be the bandwidth of a link on the wired network. Table 23.3 illustrates the handoff cost and (handoff time $\times BW$) of the various schemes. The Pessimistic handoff schemes incur a very high handoff *time* compared to the Lazy and Trickle handoff schemes. This is because in the Lazy scheme, there is no state transfer during handoff. In the Trickle scheme, the state transfer is performed separately from the handoff. It can be noticed, however, that for a given state-

Table 23.3. Handoff Cost and ($\times BW$ Handoff Time)

Scheme	Handoff Cost	($\times BW$ Handoff Time)
NP	$1 + \epsilon$	$1 + \epsilon$
NL	ϵ	ϵ
NT	$1 + 2\epsilon$	ϵ
LP	$1 + \nu\gamma + \epsilon$	$1 + \nu\gamma + \epsilon$
LL	ϵ	ϵ
LT	$1 + 2\epsilon + \nu\gamma$	ϵ

saving scheme, the handoff *cost* of the Trickle handoff scheme is almost equal to the Pessimistic handoff scheme.

Recovery Cost. In Figure 23.5, we plot the recovery cost for all the schemes for $\alpha = 10$ and $\lambda = 10^{-2}$. Similar behavior was observed for other values. As expected, the recovery cost of the Logging schemes is more than the No-Logging schemes. The recovery cost of the NP scheme is independent of r. The NP scheme incurs the lowest cost for all values of r. This is because the last checkpoint state is always present at the current base station. The recovery cost of the NT scheme is a constant for low r $(r < 1)$ and slightly more than the NP scheme. This is because the last checkpoint of the host is always available one hop from the current base station. As stated earlier, β is fixed for the analysis. For a fixed β, as μ (i.e., mobility) decreases, r $(= \beta/\mu)$ increases, and the probability of the last checkpoint being available at the current base station increases. Therefore, at high values of r $(r > 1)$, the costs of NT and NP converge.

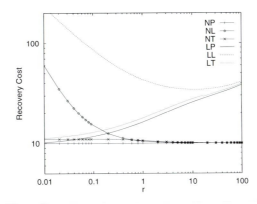

Figure 23.5. Recovery cost: $\lambda = 10^{-2}$ and $\alpha = 10$.

The recovery cost of the LP and the LT schemes is proportional to the size of the log before failure. The size of the log depends on k. Since k ($= k_{opt_{LP}}$ or $k_{opt_{LT}}$) increases with r, the recovery cost also increases. Similar to NP and NT schemes, at low values of r ($r < 1$), the recovery cost of the LT scheme is slightly higher than LP scheme. However, at high values of r, the costs of LP and LT schemes become similar.

For low values of r ($r < 1$), it can be noticed that the recovery cost of the Lazy handoff (LL and NL) schemes are much larger than for the Pessimistic and the Trickle handoff schemes. This is because the checkpoint state might not be at the current base station. Second the log of write events might be distributed at different base stations. Thus, the cost of recovery will include the cost of transferring the checkpoint state and the log from the various base stations to the current base station, and then forwarding them to the mobile host over the wireless link. The LL scheme incurs a very high recovery cost for low r. The lower the value of r, the greater the amount of scatter of recovery information. As r increases, the possibility of a checkpoint operation taking place at the current base station increases. Thus, the recovery cost decreases as r increases. However, as r increases, k ($= k_{opt_{LL}}$) also increases. Thus, after some value of r, the recovery cost starts increasing. On the other hand, the recovery cost of the NL scheme continues to decrease as r increases. At high values of r ($r > 1$), the cost of NL converges to NP and NT. Similarly, the cost of the LL scheme becomes similar to LP and LT.

As expected, at high values of r (i.e., low mobility), the recovery cost becomes almost independent of the handoff scheme used with the state-saving scheme determining the recovery cost.

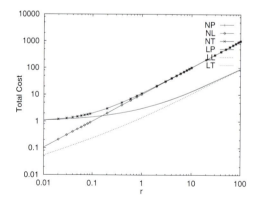

Figure 23.6. Total cost: $\lambda = 10^{-2}$ and $\alpha = 10$.

Total Cost. Figure 23.6 illustrates the variation of total cost of various schemes with r, for $\lambda = 10^{-2}$ and $\alpha = 10$. The total costs is comprised of the failure-free cost and the recovery cost. The total cost of the Pessimistic handoff scheme and the Trickle handoff scheme are almost equal ($NP \approx NT$ and $LP \approx LT$). The Lazy handoff scheme incurs a lower total cost at low values of r ($r < 1$). At high values of r, the total cost of the different handoff schemes converge. However, the difference in the total costs of the Logging and No-Logging schemes remains. The total cost of No-Logging scheme is higher than the Logging scheme for all values of r. The LL scheme incurs the lowest total cost for all r.

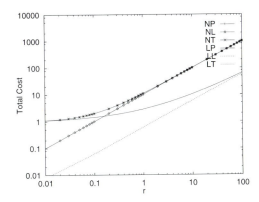

Figure 23.7. Total cost: $\lambda = 10^{-5}$ and $\alpha = 10$.

Figure 23.7 illustrates the variation of the total cost with r, for $\lambda = 10^{-5}$. Comparison of Figures 23.6 and 23.7 indicates that for the same α, as λ decreases, the cost difference between the handoff schemes for the Logging state-saving scheme increases. As the probability of failure decreases, the Lazy handoff scheme becomes more justified. The total costs of the Trickle and the Pessimistic handoff schemes are almost always equal, and both are higher than the Lazy scheme.

Figure 23.8 illustrates the variation of the total cost with r, for $\alpha = 500$. The total cost increases with α. Comparison of Figures 23.6 and 23.8 indicates that for the same λ, as α increases, the cost difference between the handoff schemes reduces. Thus, the performance of a scheme becomes more dependent on the state-saving scheme used than on the handoff scheme.

23.4.10   Discussion

Handoff time of Pessimistic handoff schemes is very high, and unacceptable for applications that require connection-oriented services. During a handoff period, there are no packets sent or received by the mobile host. Thus, if handoff time is very high, the communication protocols used for these connection-oriented services might time out and/or the mobile host might notice long disruption in service during handoffs [5].

Some applications might require a very quick recovery, and some other applications might require a very low total cost to be incurred by the recovery schemes. Some hosts might be running the application in a high-failure-rate environment, and some in a very low-failure-rate environment. As can be observed from the re-

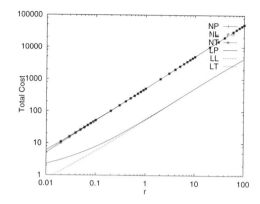

Figure 23.8. Total Cost: $\lambda = 10^{-2}$, $\alpha = 500$

sults, there is no single recovery scheme that performs best (lowest total cost, lowest recovery cost and lowest handoff time) for all environments.

We will now determine the environments where a particular recovery scheme is best suited. We classify the environment into low-failure-rate and high-failure-rate environments.

In a low-failure-rate environment, failures occur very infrequently. The primary goal of a recovery scheme in such an environment is to incur low-failure-free cost. The LL scheme incurs low-failure-free cost for all values of r. However, for high α values, the difference in the failure-free costs of the LL and LT schemes reduces. Since the recovery time (as determined by recovery cost) of the LT scheme is much lower than for the LL scheme for low values of r, it is preferable to choose LT for high α values.

In a high-failure-rate environment, failures occur very frequently. The primary goal of a recovery scheme is to incur low-failure-free cost and low recovery cost. For low r values, the recovery costs of the LL and NL schemes are very high. Thus, we need to choose between NT or LT. When α is low, NT incurs a low-failure-free cost (slightly more than LT), and provides a quicker recovery than LT. However, when α is high, LT becomes preferable. For high r values, LL is preferable over other schemes.

23.5 CONCLUSIONS

Mobile computing's popularity is rapidly increasing. The new mobile wireless environment presents many challenges due to the mobile nature of the hosts and the limited bandwidth on the wireless network. Presented in this chapter are recovery schemes for a mobile wireless environment. The recovery schemes are a combination of a state saving strategy and a handoff strategy. Two strategies for state-saving, namely, (1) *No Logging* and (2) *Logging*, and three strategies for handoff, namely,

(1) *Pessimistic*, (2) *Lazy*, and (3) *Trickle* are discussed.

Our main goal here is to present the limitations of the new mobile computing environment, and its effects on recovery protocols. The trade-off parameters to evaluate the recovery scheme were identified. It was determined that in addition to the failure rate of the host, the performance of a recovery scheme depended on the mobility of the hosts and the wireless bandwidth. We analyzed the performance of the various recovery schemes proposed in this chapter, and determined those mobile environments where a particular recovery scheme is best-suited.

Currently, we are at work on other problems related to fault-tolerance issues in mobile computing, such as recovery from failure of a base station, fault-tolerant broadcast/multicast protocols, and development of new and efficient distributed recovery schemes.

Acknowledgment

We would like to thank Fred Meyer for his help and insightful comments.

References

[1] A. Acharya and B. R. Badrinath, "Checkpointing Distributed Applications on Mobile Computers," *IEEE Conf. on PDIS*, Sep. 1994.

[2] S. Alagar and S. Venkatesan, "Tolerating Mobile Support Station Failures," Comp. Sc. Tech. Report, Univ. of Texas, Dallas, Nov., 1993.

[3] R. Alonso and H. Korth, "Database System Issues in Nomadic Computing," *SIGMOD*, June, 1993.

[4] A. Borg et al., "A Message System Supporting Fault Tolerance," *ACM SOSP*, Oct., 1983.

[5] G. H. Forman, et al., "The Challenges of Mobile Computing," *IEEE Computer*, Apr. 1994.

[6] Pankaj Jalote, "Fault Tolerance in Distributed Systems," Prentice Hall, 1994.

[7] P. Krishna, "Performance Issues in Wireless Networks," Ph.D. Diss., Department of Computer Science, Texas A&M University, 1996.

[8] Dhiraj K. Pradhan, Fault Tolerant Computer System Design, Prentice Hall, 1996.

[9] D. K. Pradhan and N. H. Vaidya, "Roll-Forward Checkpointing Scheme:A Novel Fault-Tolerant Architecture," *IEEE Trans. on Computers*, 43(10) (Oct. 1994).

[10] S. Rangarajan et.al., "A Fault-Tolerant Protocol for Location Directory Maintenance in Mobile Networks," *FTCS*, June, 1995.

[11] K. S. Trivedi, Probability and Statistics with Reliability Queueing and Computer Science Applications, Prentice Hall, 1982.

[12] N. H. Vaidya, "On Checkpoint Latency," *Pacific Rim Fault Tolerant Sys.*, December, 1995.

Chapter 24

Fault Tolerance and Recovery in Mobile Computing Systems

Elisa Bertino, Elena Pagani, and Gian Paolo Rossi

24.1 INTRODUCTION

Through wireless networks, mobile personal machines have the ability to access data and services that can be located on both mobile and wired servers. Unlike wired hosts, mobile hosts can be temporarily unreachable as a consequence of their moving across different cells, their energy limitation or unavailable wireless channels. Mobility forces mobile hosts to alternate connected and disconnected work. When connected, they perform personal communications and access shared data and services; when disconnected, they can process locally cached data objects.

As for wired networks, data replication is the key element to ensure high data availability and to increase performance. However, disconnected work and the uncertainties of the underlying wireless network introduce new challenging issues that have been recently discussed in the literature. There are three main aspects that we wish to discuss in this chapter:

1. how to provide a fault-tolerant architecture that addresses data access and management despite mobility and disconnected work

2. how to manage data replication to ensure data consistency, integrity, and durability according to the application requirements

3. the extend to which the general requirement of network independency can be met or otherwise the application awareness of mobility can be effectively exploited to provide the level of quality of service needed

In this chapter, we investigate how the problem of managing a distributed database and guaranteeing data consistency is affected by the characteristics of the mobile setting. We discuss the impact of mobility and disconnections on fault tolerance and recovery. We investigate how fault-tolerance can be ensured, by analyzing some of the algorithms proposed for database management in mobile systems.

This chapter is organized as follows. In Section 24.2, we describe the mobile environment and introduce data management issues in such an environment. In Section 24.3, we present the system architecture to which we refer in the remainder of the discussion, and in Section 24.4, we characterize mobile applications. In Section 24.5, we investigate how fault tolerance is affected in mobile environments and how the ACID properties can be re defined to guarantee data correctness in a mobile setting. In Sections 24.6 and 24.7, we discuss some of the approaches proposed for managing distributed databases. Finally, in Section 24.8 we report some performance evaluation results concerning some of the described algorithms.

24.2 DISTRIBUTED SYSTEMS WITH MOBILE HOSTS

Unlike computer networks with fixed stations (FHs), a mobile host (MH) can retain its network connection even *while* moving. This is possible because of the use of different network technologies, such as radio links, satellite networks, and infrared links [35, 36], that do not impose any physical constraint to the hosts, that is, they are *wireless*.

Wireless networks may be classified in *single-hop* [3, 13, 23, 24, 27, 28] and *multi-hop* [11, 12]; in the latter case, all the machines in the system are mobile, whereas in the former, both mobile and fixed stations are involved.

In the sequel, we restrict our attention almost only to single-hop systems, as they are the most considered in the literature.

Single-hop networks are organized as shown in Figure 24.1: Some of the fixed hosts, denoted as *Mobile Support Stations* (MSSs) [1, 2, 4, 24] are equipped with a wireless interface; they support communication between the MHs that reside in a *cell* and the MHs in different cells. The cell is the area in which the signal generated by the MSS can be received by the MHs. The messages generated by a given MSS are broadcast within the cell. The MHs filter the messages according to their destination address; on the contrary, a MH can communicate with another MH of the same cell only by sending its message to the cell MSS that executes the broadcast. FHs and MSSs are connected through a *wired* network, whose topology is static and used to support the communication between cells. Because of movements, the topology of the wireless network may change over time.

The diameter of the cells may vary according to the wireless technology foe example, it spans from a few meters for infrared technology to 1 to 2 miles for radio or single-hop satellite networks [36]. Moreover, the technology also affects the available bandwidth: LANs that use infrared technology have transfer rates on the order of 1 to 2 Mbps (up to 100 Mbps in the recent experiments [36]); on the contrary, WANs have poorer performance, as they usually provide bandwidths in

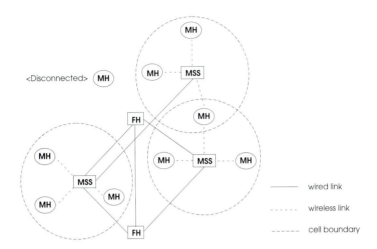

Figure 24.1. Example of a single-hop network

the range 14.4 to 64 Kbps. Wireless networks that offer around 100-Kbps services are under development [36]. Finally, wireless networks are supposed to be less reliable than wired ones: It has been estimated that the failure rate will increase at least of one order of magnitude with respect to the current wired networks.

Cells may overlap. Hence, a MH may be contemporarily in more than one cell although it refers to only one MSS a time. In most systems, MHs choose their current MSS according to the highest signal they receive [1, 13]. When the MH_m moves from MSS_1 to MSS_2, a *handoff* (or *handover*) procedure [4, 24] is activated between MSS_1 and MSS_2 to transfer the state information about MH_m to MSS_2. A *mobility assumption* [1, 2] is required to ensure system liveness: MH_m resides in a cell at least for the time sufficient to complete the handoff procedure and to allow the MSS to deliver to MH_m at least one of the messages that were still pending at MSS_1; in this way, we guarantee that messages do not starve.

In their wandering, MHs could move to places that are out of the cell *coverage*, that is, become *disconnected*. This depends on the system capability to cover a given geographical area. In the United States [36], the wireless service with the broadest coverage is Ardis, which reaches more than the 80% of the U.S. population and spans around 90% of the metropolitan areas and the $30 - 40\%$ of the rest of the country. As a counterpart, Ardis has a very low bandwidth; it offers 4.8-Kbps connections. Other wireless networks exist but because of the current lack of standards, it is not possible to exploit the services of different wireless networks to gain a greater coverage.

Disconnections can also occur because of several events, for example, the MH may exhaust its battery charge, it can be lost, or it can crash.

MHs can be classified as either *dumb terminals* or *walkstations* [24]. The former ones are diskless hosts (such as, for instance, palmtops) with reduced memory and computing capabilities. They can receive from the wireless network, but they are not able to send messages. Walkstations are comparable to classical workstations and can both receive and send messages on the wireless network. We will focus our considerations on this latter type of MHs.

Despite their computing resources, MHs are mainly constrained by the short lifetime of batteries [8] that are heavily affected by the communications over wireless channels. To reduce the energy waste, MHs enter a *doze mode* when they are not involved in sending or receiving packets. A doze MH only has the network interface active, which is able to filter the messages broadcast in the cell on the basis of the destination address. If a message is observed that is addressed to the MH, the system is awakened to revert to the normal operation mode.

The described system behaviors impact on the design of distributed applications. To our purposes, the most relevant are

- the high failure rate requires to address both the fault-tolerance and the recovery issues

- the energy-saving argument generates some new constraints that must be considered while designing the services to support distributed applications

24.3   SYSTEM ARCHITECTURE

Figure 24.2 helps us to identify the main functional modules that compose a MH architecture [29]. The hardware interface provides the physical access to the network and also filters the messages broadcast in the cell according to their destination address.

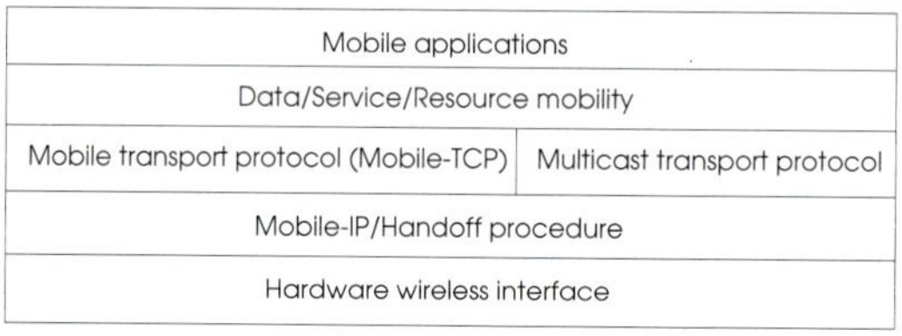

Mobile applications	
Data/Service/Resource mobility	
Mobile transport protocol (Mobile-TCP)	Multicast transport protocol
Mobile-IP/Handoff procedure	
Hardware wireless interface	

Figure 24.2. Reference architecture of a mobile host.

On top of it, the Network layer, for example, through the Mobile-IP [31] protocol, provides transparent addressing of MHs and executes the handoff procedure [6, 38].

Communication over the wireless network is unreliable, that is, packets are lost, corrupted, or duplicated, and the transmission delay is highly variable due to different wireless technologies and load conditions. Hence, a wireless network may be considered as an asynchronous system; this implies the unpredictable duration of transaction processing. The transport layer masks network uncertainties to upper layers and provides some sort of reliable, point-to-point, or multicast [1, 2] channels amongst MHs. Certain multicast transport channels (e.g., [1, 2]) can ensure FIFO order in the message delivery.

The higher layer provide the value-added services to directly support the application communication requirements. These services mainly address the management of the data objects and files in the presence of mobility. They are also responsible for negotiating with MSSs the quality of the service according to both user requirements and services actually supplied by the wireless network [7, 13, 15, 22, 28, 29, 32].

The problem of *locating* MHs, i.e. of knowing their current position to allow the routing of the messages, has received great attention [5, 25] and is emphasized by the trend of reducing the cell's size to improve the communication bandwidth. Location service is architecturally located within the network layer, although some interesting evolution of the basic location service are oriented to allow their direct use by mobile applications (see, e.g., [41]).

24.4 MOBILE APPLICATIONS

Applications that run on mobile hosts are likely to have different requirements with respect to those designed for traditional environments. Most users will use MHs for personal communications (e.g., e-mail, around 25%) and for mobile office activities (around 45%) [36]. The latter possibility implies the ability of porting existing applications on MHs and of allowing them to access and share remote data objects.

In [23, 24] a first attemp to classify mobile applications has been introduced based on the locality of the data the application accesses. In *vertical* applications, the users access the data within a specific cell and the access is denied to users that are out of that cell, for instance, data concerning the availability of parking places in that cell, the position of the nearest doctor, or the personal identities of the other users in the cell. On the contrary, *horizontal* applications handle data that span over users being distributed on the whole system; typically, they are applications whose users cooperate toward a common task, in spite of their movements, or multimedia applications such as conferencing.

The nature of the applications impacts on the pattern of access in reading and writing the data; in particular, in [23, 24] the following classes of data have been identified:

Private Data: They are maintained, accessed, and managed by a single user, the owner; no other users may access the data.

Public Data: One user may update them, and all the users of the system can read them. Consider, for instance, applications such as weather forecast, news bulletins, or broadcast of financial data. Another important kind of information in this category is *location* data [41], that is, data concerning the identity of the cell in which a MH currently resides. In [41], data have been further classified into three categories according to their semantics, which reflects the frequency of their updating: (1) *terminal mobility data*, which concern the location of the host; (2) *personal mobility data*, which concern the user's identity and are used for the user authentication and (3) *service mobility data*, which describe the users' profiles, regarding, for instance, the customization of the applications they use or the subscribed services.

Shared Data: They are accessed both in read and write by a group of users cooperating to a common task (e.g., cooperative workgroup) or managing multiple copies of the data to achieve availability and reliability.

Whereas public data are mainly managed by vertical applications, the use of shared data in the framework of horizontal applications introduces a general and complete range of fault-tolerance and recovery issues that mainly concern the topics of this chapter. In this work, we will mainly consider this setting.

To ensure the service availability and to improve the performance, shared data can be *replicated*. Copies may be located both in fixed and mobile stations. Mobility introduces new challenging issues in the design of the mechanisms that guarantee data consistency and integrity. The *scalability* of these mechanisms over a possibly large amount of MHs is also an important issue.

24.5   FAULT TOLERANCE IN MOBILE DATABASE PLATFORMS

As the mobile setting highly differs from the fixed setting, it is necessary to redefine what a failure is, and what "fault tolerance" means in this new context.

In general, a system is fault-tolerant if it guarantees to behave correctly with respect to its service specification despite malfunctions; in the case of database systems, correctness is usually defined in terms of *ACID properties*. In this section, we explore the approaches to fault-tolerance in database management and show some examples of normal MHs behaviours that may be misinterpreted as failures. We discuss the impact of these behaviours on the correct operation of the system and show how fault-tolerance may be redefined according to these considerations, and how to achieve it. In the following, we do not consider the failures on the wireless network because their detection and recovery are the responsibility of the transport protocol. A reliable transport service is observed at the interface with the transport protocol (see Section 24.2). The services we consider throughout this chapter are built on top of such reliable transport protocol.

24.5.1   Transaction Execution in Mobile Database Systems

The characteristics of MHs introduce new fault-tolerance issues in transaction management. Among these issues, the capability of tolerating the disappearance of MHs from the cells is of primary concern because of mobility and disconnections. Whether the MHs store the entire database or part of it, and actively participate in the management of the database, is a design choice that impacts on the effects that failures may have.

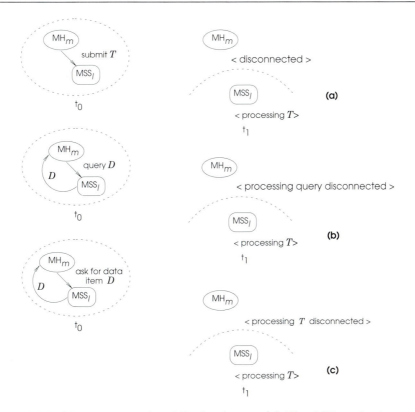

Figure 24.3. Management of mobile databases. (a) The MH_m submits a transaction T according to the transaction proxy approach. (b) The MH_m submits a query on the data D according to the read-only transaction approach. (c) The MH_m submits a transaction T according to the weak transaction approach.

Most approaches assume that copies of data on MHs are *secondary* copies, whereas *primary* copies are maintained at FHs and MSSs. As we will see in Section 24.6, different approaches may be used that give more or less autonomy to MHs in operating on the database. Almost all these approaches, however, force MHs to perform periodic checkpoints and to maintain their backups on FHs. The adopted approaches may be classified as follows:

Transaction Proxy: The MHs do no execute any computation, but instead ask the MSSs to execute transactions on their behalf [13, 27, 44]. Therefore, the MSSs always hold the consistent database, and MHs do not need to execute any update action on the data objects nor to keep any data object in their caches, see Figure 24.3(a).

Read-Only Transactions: MHs only cache data objects for queries, and updates are performed as in the preceding case, see Figure 24.3(b).

Weak Transactions: Besides performing queries on cached data, MHs may update data objects in their caches even while disconnected [7, 28, 30, 40] see Figure 24.3(c). In this case, they must *stabilize* their updates as soon as they re-connect, that is, they have to globally commit the updates in order to re-establish consistency and to guarantee durability. For the purpose of stabilizing the disconnected transactions or *undoing* them in the event of an abort, a *log* is maintained in secondary storage at the MH, recording the actions executed by uncommitted transactions [28, 30]. The log of each transaction is sent to the MSS on reconnection, so that the MSS can reexecute the transaction on its primary copy, to verify whether it can safely commit.

It should be evident that in the case of the weak-transaction approach, applications have to deal with more difficult fault-tolerance problems than in the transaction proxy approach, because of the maintenance of data objects stored by the MHs. In the weak-transaction approach, recovery mechanisms must be designed by properly taking into account the scarce availability of storage resources of walkstations.

24.5.2 Impact of mobility on transaction correctness

In section 24.2, we have shown that a mobile environment is characterized by hosts that can be temporarily unreachable, because of entering the doze mode, disconnecting or moving to uncovered zones, and by the intrinsic asynchrony of the underlying network environment. In this section, we discuss how these features may lead to the violation of ACID properties or may jeopardize the liveness of the system even in the absence of failures.

Figure 24.4 shows two cases. In the first case [Figure 24.4(a)], MH_m caches a set D of data objects while being in cell l, and then it disconnects and continues to process its transactions while being disconnected. When it later reconnects to the same or to a different MSS, its copy of the data is inconsistent with respect to the one held at MSSs. The same problem also arises when the MH_m caches data for read-only transactions because of the updates carried out by other FHs or MHs, whereas MH_m is unreachable.

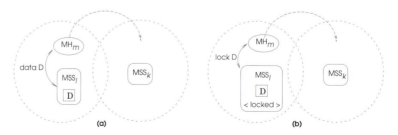

Figure 24.4. Example of possibly incorrect behaviurs in the case of movement of an MH.

To solve this problem, MH_m can lock the data objects D at the MSS_l site while executing local transactions, thus preventing concurrent execution of other transactions originating from the MSS_l or other MHs [Figure 24.4(b)]. If MH_m disconnects or cannot be reached for a long time, it can be suspected of having failed. If MSS_l maintains the lock, problems arise in the event of actual crashes or long-lived disconnections. If the MSS_l releases the lock after a time out the problem arises of inconsistent copies [Figure 24.4(a)].

The preceding problems arise because of the difficulty in distinguishing a temporaneous unreachability from a crash. It is possible,however, to distinguish between planned and sudden disconnections [4]. The former are predictable. When the MH becomes doze, or it disconnects either to recharge the batteries or to save power, some safety actions can be performed to tolerate such a temporary disconnection. For instance, the pending transactions can be moved to the destination MSS, where an *agent* can execute them on behalf of the mobile application to allow the MH to obtain the results on reconnection, as proposed in [13]. Another approach allows MHs to *prefetch* in the cache the data they require while being disconnected. Appropriate algorithms are designed to reestablish consistency among the existing copies of the data when the MH reconnects.

24.5.3   Transaction Correctness in Mobile Computing Systems

The ability of working in a mobile context must coexist with the possibility that even normal system conditions may lead to the violation of the database correctness. As a consequence, the efforts to achieve fault tolerance have been addressed to redesign the notion of correctness rather than to redefine the notion of failure. A number of alternative definitions of ACID properties have been proposed [15, 21, 30, 33] that weaken one or more of the properties. In general, their goal is to guarantee the MHs a certain degree of autonomy in transaction processing during disconnections, and to preserve the (modified) system correctness by allowing bounded inconsistencies among the data copies.

In the following, we describe how each property has been redefined in some proposals in the scientific literature. Usually, only one property is considered at a time. The weakening of a given property, however, may impact the other ACID properties.

ATOMICITY PROPERTY.   The first step toward fault tolerance in mobile systems is allowing MHs to submit "*pieces*" of transactions in different cells according to their movements. Several alternative methods are described in [21]. This approach weakens the classical formulation of atomicity and requires the ability of breaking a transaction so that *subtransactions* can be concurrently executed and interleaved with subtransactions of other transactions while guaranteeing other ACID properties. These mobile transaction models are based on extended transaction models developed for long-duration transactions, such as Open Nested Transactions (ONT) [16] and Saga Transactions [18]. For instance, in the ONT model, the abort of one or more subtransactions does not necessarily imply the abort of the entire transaction. Hence, when a transaction T commits, only some of its operations may have been actually executed.

The decomposition of a transaction in subtransactions can be performed according to different principles and at different levels of granularity. Different approaches to decomposition have been proposed for each of the three transaction models discussed in Section 24.5.1. In the case of transaction proxies and read-only transactions, transactions may be either submitted as a whole at a unique MSS [13, 44], or they may be *split* during processing (Kangaroo model, [21]) following the movements of the MH that submitted the transaction. In the latter case, communication costs are reduced by relocating computations as near to the MH as possible.

In the case of weak transactions, a transaction T is decomposed into mutually independent subtransactions. This decomposition ensures that the subtransactions of a transaction T can be *concurrently* processed at the different MSSs to which they have been submitted, and that their execution order does not impact on the successful commit of T. Independence may be guaranteed, for instance, according to Bernstein's conditions [9]. Each subtransaction S_i has a write set W_i and a read set R_i. Every two subtransactions S_i and S_j of a transaction T satisfy the following conditions:

$$W_i \cap W_j = \emptyset \qquad\qquad R_i \cap W_j = \emptyset \qquad\qquad W_i \cap R_j = \emptyset$$

that guarantee their independence (Reporting and Co-transaction model [21]). This approach is based on the Split Transaction Model [34]. A run-time support must exist that computes the decomposition by determining an appropriate partition of the read and write sets of the transaction.

Another approach is based on fragmenting a transaction T so that each of its subtransactions S_i executes operations that are *commutative* with those of the other subtransactions of T [21].

Both in the Kangaroo model and in the Reporting and Co-transaction model, the handoff procedure must be extended to involve the transfer of information concerning pending transactions generated by the MH. These models imply a redefinition of the other ACID properties. Both isolation and durability are restricted to subtransactions instead of global transactions. In the case of weak transactions the consistency property is also affected, and a mechanism is required to merge copies and reestablish consistency on reconnection.

CONSISTENCY PROPERTY. An approach alternative to that of weakening the atomicity property consists in the redefinition of the consistency property. Under this approach, the database is considered partitioned in *clusters*, either according to semantics-based criteria (e.g., data objects related by integrity constraints belong to the same cluster) or to location proximity (clustering model [21, 33]). Data in the same cluster must be strictly consistent, whereas a *bounded* degree of inconsistency is tolerated amongst clusters, according to some definition of consistency. Hence, clustering can, for instance which support multiversion databases or tolerate divergences between the secondary copy of the data maintained at a MH (that constitutes a cluster) and the primary copies on FHs. MHs are therefore allowed to process transactions while being disconnected. According to this approach, two classes of primitives are used to update data:

1. *weak-write* and *weak-read* that modify data only in the local cluster, thus possibly causing inconsistencies with respect to other clusters

2. *strict-write* and *strict-read* that modify data in the global database, thus maintaining consistency

These primitives are executed so that operations that work on the same cluster do not conflict. Conflicts are prevented by locking mechanisms. In assigning locks, the usual lock compatibility modes are applied. Moreover, to guarantee that weak operations do not observe intermediate results produced by strict operations, strict-write locks and weak-read locks conflict. By contrast, strict-read and weak-write operations are not conflicting operations. The implementation must only guarantee that a strict-read operation reads the value written by the last strict-write operation.

A consequence of the redefinition of the consistency property is a more complex notion of serializability. Strict transactions must serialize with respect to each other according to one-copy serializability [17]. Moreover, let the *projection* of a strict transaction T on a MH_m be the subtransaction of T that operates on the data objects held at the MH_m. Weak transactions processed at MH_m must serialize always according to the one-copy serializability with respect to each other and with respect to the projections on MH_m of the strict transactions.

The degree of inconsistency can be defined, for instance, in terms of the maximum number of versions of the same data objects that can exist at the same time or the maximum number of weak operations that can be executed on a copy of a data without being propagated to the other copies [32]. A timestamp can be associated with each datum so that locks on that data are automatically released after the expiration of a time out (time-based consistency model [21]). This way, MHs can operate disconnected for a limited interval of time.

ISOLATION PROPERTY. Some transaction models have been devised for mobile environments in which the isolation property is not guaranteed, that is, intermediate results of a transaction T can be observed by other transactions. This is usually a side effect of the relaxation of other ACID properties.

We have observed in the previous paragraph that isolation can be enforced by properly modifying conflict rules amongst locks, in the case of operations that work on data having different degrees of consistency.

By contrast, if a transaction model is adopted such as those mentioned in the discussion on atomicity, the isolation property only holds for subtransactions. If a subtransaction S_j of a transaction T_j is processed at a MSS after that subtransaction S_i of a transaction T_i has been processed at the same MSS, then S_j can observe the result of S_i, that is, an intermediate result of T_i. Helal et al. observe in [21] that the sharing of partial results amongst transactions, for example, by means of *Reporting Transactions*, may be desirable for some applications. On the other hand, enforcing isolation property is probably expensive in that it may severely restrict concurrency among transactions.

DURABILITY PROPERTY.   Durability of committed transactions is mainly affected by the possibility MHs have of autonomously operating on data. In some transaction models, MHs can execute transactions on locally stored data even while being disconnected (Reporting and Co-transaction model, Clustering model [21]). If a MH_m operating in the disconnected mode fails before *stabilizing* the results of its committed transactions on the primary copies of the database, these results could be never recovered (for example, in the case of a media failure).

To ensure fault tolerance, in the CODA file system [28, 30], the durability property is relaxed by providing two types of transactions and two degrees of commitment. *First-class transactions* are those executed by either connected MHs or users on FHs, and *second-class transactions* are those processed by disconnected MHs.

A disconnected MH can only commit a transaction *locally* if this transaction does not conflict with other transactions executed on the *same* host while the host is disconnected. On reconnection, the transactions are *globally* committed, unless they conflict with already committed first-class or second-class transactions executed on different MHs.

Hence, first-class transactions have one level of commitment

- a first-class transaction can commit if it is serializable with respect to all the transactions previously committed

By contrast, second-class transactions are subject to two levels of commitment:

- *local commitment*: the transaction can commit if it is serializable with respect to all the previously committed second-class transactions executed on the same host

- *global commitment*: the transaction can commit if it is serializable with respect to all the committed transactions in the system

Two levels of commitment have also been adopted for the weak transactions described in the consistency paragraph [33]. The global commitment allows to detect possible inconsistencies caused by weak transactions on reconnection. A locally committed transaction however can globally abort. The durability of locally committed transactions is *not* guaranteed until these transactions globally commit.

24.5.4   Recovery in Mobile Databases

Transaction recovery deals with the capability of ensuring *failure atomicity* [14]. It concerns the durability and the atomicity properties. Recovery mechanisms guarantee that these properties are satisfied in spite of failures.

As in most proposals found in the current literature, we assume that the fixed network is reliable. We therefore focus on the problem of recovering MHs. As in the case of fault tolerance, we must understand which situations require recovery.

Moreover, we investigate how recovery could be achieved according to the limited computing and storage resources of the MHs.

According to [20], we may classify failures in three categories:

Transaction Failures: A transaction may abort because the MH was disconnected, as in the read-only transactions and weak-transaction approach. On reconnection, the invalidation of its cache is communicated to the transactions or a conflict is raised between the updates of the transaction and the updates of other, possibly already committed, transactions

Site Failures: The MH crashes, but the content of its permanent storage is not lost.

Media Failures: The loss of part or all the secondary storage holding the database can occur.

Recovery in general makes of a *log* file recording information on the operations executed by both committed and still uncommitted transactions, the last safe state, and what else is needed to rebuild a consistent database in case of failures. This information is used during recovery to *undo* the partially executed transactions (atomicity property) and to *redo* the committed transactions (durability property) based on the last safe state.

As we have seen in the previous section, atomicity in mobile environments is affected by failures when a MH_m either (1) processes transactions while being disconnected, or (2) submits subtransactions. In the latter case, a subtransaction S may have to be undone whose results have been observed by other subtransactions, possibly belonging to an already committed transaction. In [21], this situation is dealt with by executing *compensating* transactions that *semantically* undo the effects of S (Saga model [21]). This solution however is not always viable because some operations are inherently non-compensatable.

If the MH_m carries some data and autonomously operates on them, as in case (1), other MHs could concurrently update the same data. Hence, if MH_m recovers from a failure, the undo of pending transactions produces an obsolete version of the database.

For this reason, under the most widely adopted solution, the recovered MHs refetch the updated version of the data objects to report their database view to a consistent state.

The durability property is ensured only on fixed stations. The problem is to determine when the data maintained at MHs need to be recovered and the most appropriate recovery technique according to the adopted transaction management policy. With respect to the classification presented in Section 24.5.1, the recovery mechanisms are as follows:

Transaction Proxy: As MHs do not maintain any data object, none of the above failure modes needs a MH recovery.

Read-Only Transactions: The MH_m cache may become out of date during disconnections, movements, or crashes. Usually, data have a version number [28] or timestamp [21], so that invalid caches can be detected on reconnection. When MH_m reconnects, it is sent an invalidation message from the MSS (*server callback*). Such a message could result in query aborts. It is up to the MH_m to refetch the invalidated data and to reexecute the aborted queries. A different approach is taken in *data-broadcasting* algorithms [10, 26], where MSSs broadcast either the whole database or the more frequently accessed data objects and MHs autonomously keep up to date. We further discuss these algorithms in Section 24.6.

Weak Transactions: If the disconnected transactions cannot globally commit, according to the definitions we gave in Section 24.5.3, a transaction failure occurs. The problem here is how to make durable the locally committed (but globally aborted) transactions. The recovery procedures that can be adopted range from the automated refetch of the updated data and reexecution of the globally aborted transaction, to the user notification, to the execution of an application-dependent algorithm [30]. Such an algorithm has the purpose of understanding whether the globally aborted transaction can be dropped, or only a part of it can be reexecuted, or one of the two previous solutions can be adopted, according to the application semantics [30]. The redo is performed according to the recorded log file. After the redo is completed, a global commit is tried again. Site failures do not affect either the redo of globally aborted transactions or the global commit. By contrast, media failures that cause the loss of the log file are unrecoverable. Transactions not yet globally committed are lost, and the failure has to be reported to the application.

In Section 24.6, we describe some of the algorithms that have been proposed and the recovery mechanisms they implement. An important question is that in mobile systems, because of mobility, disconnections, and higher failure rates than in static environments, recovery procedures are likely to be executed more frequently. Hence, besides being lightweight in terms of the required MH resources, recovery procedures should support a fast transaction restart.

24.6 CLASSES OF SOLUTIONS

We discussed in the previous sections how fault-tolerance and recovery concepts are adapted to a mobile environment. In this section, we describe algorithms for managing replicated data in mobile environments. The aim of this description is to highlight the capability of a given approach to satisfy the previously mentioned fault-tolerance requirements.

24.6.1   The "Data-Broadcasting" Approach

The data-broadcasting approach is a special case of the *read-only transactions* approach in which MHs can only query data. The database resides on one or more FHs; a MSS holding a copy of the database periodically broadcasts this copy to the MHs in the cell (Figure 24.5). The broadcast database version corresponds to a checkpoint at a given time; updates are performed between two successive broadcasts. ACID properties are guaranteed on FHs and mobile queries cannot cause inconsistencies.

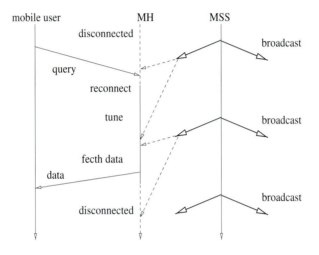

Figure 24.5. Layout of the data-broadcasting approach.

This approach requires that an MH stay active by listening to all the incoming messages until it receives the desired data. Some improvements to this approach have been proposed that allow MHs to *tune* in when data are transmitted to save energy. This is achieved by broadcasting only the *hot-spot* data, that is, the most frequently accessed data, and by periodically broadcasting an *index*, or *directory*, of the database. Indexes are interleaved with blocks of data and allow MHs to determine which data will be sent next.

The broadcast of frequently accessed data is based on the principle of *data access skew*, that is, on the hypothesis that data objects are not accessed with the same frequency (80 : 20 rule) [19]. Less accessed data can be retrieved *on demand*. Explicit requests of data are recorded by MSSs and used to adapt the hot -spot composition accordingly.

The reader can find in [10, 26] details on how to interleave index information with data in order to optimize the amount of time an MH has to be connected before receiving the data.

By adopting the data-broadcasting approach, MHs cannot suffer transaction failures. Simple fault-tolerant mechanisms are required to ensure consistency of the data that MHs are likely to cache. The introduction of proper information about the modified data in the index results in an efficient policy to selectively update cached data while a MH is connected [26]. In the event of a disconnection or a crash, the consistency is achieved by refetching the data copies in the MH cache. The periodic broadcast of index and data guarantees that an MH eventually receives the required information despite network packet loss and corruptions.

The main advantage of this approach is simplicity and low complexity at the MHs. These advantages are, however, obtained at the price of low performance and high-bandwidth consumption. It is suitable for applications that involve simple MHs, for example, dumb terminals, accessing public data on FHs.

24.6.2   The "proxy" approach

Under the transaction proxy approach, MHs can generate both queries and transactions. Data are maintained at FHs.

Two methods may be distinguished for managing transactions: (1) MHs submit the transactions or subtransactions [13, 44]; (2) MHs submit the requests for read or write-locks on the required data objects [27].

Under the former method, MHs do not maintain data. MHs submit transactions or subtransactions to the MSSs they visit while moving. Fixed stations are in charge of enforcing correctness properties on data by adopting proper fault-tolerant mechanisms. If an MH fails while submitting the query, the failure does not affect the database. By contrast, under the latter method, MHs can maintain local data. The locks on the data, however, are recorded and managed at the MSSs.

In [13], the database is assumed to be fully replicated at the MSSs and the MHs can submit transactions to their current MSS. The ISIS system provides the required fault tolerance within the group of MSSs. The ISIS ABCAST primitive is used to ensure a total order in the delivery of the multicast messages that transport transactions. MH status information is partially replicated over cluster of MSSs centered around the current location of the MH. Both status and location data are considered and managed as the database objects.

In [44], MHs can submit subtransactions and are free to distinguish between a *global database* and a *local database*, which is locally maintained and accessed. The global database is replicated over the group of MSSs. Data correctness is guaranteed among the copies of the global database. Suppose that a global transaction or subtransaction T_g is executed that precedes a local transaction T_l that satisfies some integrity constraints between global and local databases. If T_l causally precedes another global transaction T_{g1}, the group of MSSs database servers must process T_{g1} after T_g. To enforce this causality in the transaction processing order, global transactions or subtransactions carry a *ticket*, that is, a *timestamp*.

The method described in [27] is quite similar to the one in [44]. If that is unlikely, it assumes that MHs can require read and write locks to "handle" the data according to a revised version of the *optimistic two-phase-locking*. Before accessing a data item, an MH_m must require the appropriate lock to the current MSS (MSS1);

read locks are immediately granted, whereas write locks are postponed at commit time.

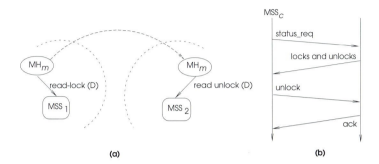

Figure 24.6. Optimistic 2-phase-locking for mobile systems

Because of mobility, locks may be requested to different MSSs. Lock information could be transmitted together with the MH state during the handoff procedure. To improve performance, however, read locks and unlocks are maintained at the MSSs to which they have been required, up to the commit time; see Figure 24.6(a). At this point, before granting write locks, the current MSS checks for the existence of conflicting locks on the other MSSs. The procedure is shown in Figure 24.6(b), where MSS_c is the current MSS. It sends a status request to the other copies and waits for *all* the replies, reporting the locks and unlocks recorded at those sites. MSS_c tries to *match* each read lock with a corresponding unlock. If it succeeds and no other write lock already exists, it releases all the existing read locks on the other copies and, after receiving their acknowledgments, it grants the write lock to the MH. A copy sending the acknowledgment records at the same time to be write-locked.

An MH failure or disconnection can leave some data unlocked. This problem can be handled by associating a *time out* with each lock. On expiration of the time out the lock is unilaterally released. The timeout may be specified by the user. Once the time out is expired, the MSS that drops the lock must inform the other copy holders that the transaction has aborted. The MH is notified on reconnection, to make its state consistent and to preserve the atomicity property.

Serializability is guaranteed by associating version numbers with the data. Moreover, each copy must record a write-intent lock when it receives a status-request message by MSS_c.

The described methods are suitable to manage both public and shared data and can support both vertical and horizontal applications. The algorithm described in [44] also considers the possibility of combining private and global data that have some integrity relationship.

24.6.3   The "Disconnected" Approach

The disconnected approach has been introduced with the CODA file system [28, 30] and has been adopted in other algorithms to manage either file systems [39, 40] or databases [32]. It uses the weak transaction approach and enforces correctness by relaxing either the isolation property [28, 30] or the consistency property [32, 39, 40], as we described in Section 24.5.3.

The mentioned algorithms assume that the database is fully replicated on the MSSs. MSS copies are considered *first-class replicas*, whose consistency is always guaranteed. The MHs can host *second-class replicas* of the database or of a part of it.

MHs and MSSs can execute transactions on the database according to an *optimistic* concurrency control strategy.

Transactions initiated by connected MHs are executed so that the usual definition of the ACID properties is satisfied. MHs work on the data they have cached up to commit time. In [32], these *strict* transactions are processed guaranteeing one-copy serializability. When a strict transaction commits, all the first- and second-class copies are updated accordingly, thus automatically guaranteeing cache consistency. In CODA, only fixed hosts apply the changes to their copies; hence, data maintained on MHs can become inconsistent. Cache coherence is enforced among connected MHs with a protocol based on *callback* primitives. The MH whose cache has been invalidated or that experiences a cache miss during transaction processing can obtain the updated data on demand from its MSS.

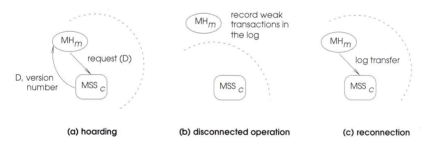

(a) hoarding   (b) disconnected operation   (c) reconnection

Figure 24.7. Weak transactions in the CODA file system.

Disconnected MHs can rely only on the contents of their caches. The problem of cache management in mobile environments has been widely discussed in [42, 43]. To this purpose, CODA includes the special-purpose module *Venus*. The Venus module is located at the MH and operates to maintain in cache the most recently used data. While preparing for a disconnection (*hoarding* phase), it can also use user's hints to fetch in the cache the data that are likely to be needed once disconnected; see Figure 24.7(a). Data are tagged with *version numbers* that are also stored in the cache.

A disconnected (*weak*) transaction $\mathcal{T}$ is processed so that it *locally* serializes with the other weak transactions executed on the same host (Section 24.5.3). In the approach proposed in [32], weak transactions can also be executed by connected MHs. Therefore, communication on the wireless network is reduced, but there is the additional requirement that weak transactions cannot observe partial results of strict transactions. Operations executed on the database by disconnected transactions are recorded in a *log file* together with the data version numbers; see Figure 24.7(b). The log file is stored in permanent storage together with the cached data. This allows the MHs to survive long disconnections in spite of the reduced size of the volatile storage. The effects of weak transactions are not permanent until they *globally commit*.

The global commitment is executed when MH_m reconnects; see Figure 24.7(c). The log file is transferred to the current MSS_c, which checks for conflicts by comparing the version numbers recorded in the log with those currently associated with its copy of the data. MSS_c detects conflicts by building and analyzing a *precedence graph* amongst the weak transactions and the previously committed strict transactions. If no conflicts are detected, the MSS_c locks all the data on which disconnected transactions operated, and *redos* these transactions according to the trace in the log. A *commit* message is sent to MH_m and the results are propagated to all the connected hosts holding a database copy. Locks on data are released. Otherwise, an *abort* message is sent to MH_m; *cascading* abort only affects pending disconnected transactions executed on MH_m. In CODA, a *reply file* is sent together with the abort message, containing the results of the MSS_c attempt and the current state of the database at the MSS_c.

If a transaction aborts during the global commitment phase, three solutions are proposed in [28, 30]: (1) the abort is notified to the application; (2) MH_m refetches the updated data and reexecutes the aborted transaction; (3) application-dependent algorithms are executed. These algorithms examine the reply file to decide whether one between solutions (1) and (2) is appropriate or whether the transaction can be only partially redone.

Transaction failures can also be experienced by MHs on local commitment. A disconnected transaction aborts when a cache miss occurs or the cache overflows as a consequence of either the increase in the log size or the creation of new data. In these cases, the MH has to suspend transaction processing waiting for reconnection.

Since these algorithms are able to tolerate long disconnections of the MHs without either blocking the system or jeopardizing the correctness of the primary copies of the database, the same mechanisms allow them to tolerate both MHs site and media failures.

From the point of view of MH recovery, site failures are not harmful. The transport protocol ensures that the log transfer is performed as an atomic action. Hence, the MH fails either before the transmission be successfully completed or after that. In the former case, the global commitment of pending transactions is executed when MH recovers from the crash. In the latter case, the MSS autonomously proceeds in its processing and the message containing the outcome of the global commitment is delivered to MH when it recovers.

On the contrary, media failures causing the loss of the log and the cached data cannot be recovered and the failure has to be notified to the application.

These algorithms can be executed by MIIs having nonnegligible computing and storage capabilities, such as walkstations. They can be used to manage both public and shared data, and to support both horizontal and vertical applications. In the last case, however, the database cannot always be replicated at all the MSSs, and an MH_m must reconnect in a cell in which the access to the database is supported to stabilize its weak transactions. Finally, since processing is executed locally, both long and interactive transactions are supported for MHs.

24.6.4 The "Distributed" Approach

This approach adopts the weak-transaction model as the previous one. It differs from the disconnected approach in that it supports only strict transactions that require cooperation among the hosts holding a copy of the database. The correctness notion used in this approach is based on the usual definition of ACID properties. In the literature, only [7] describes an algorithm that follows this approach; hence, we refer to it in the following description.

Copies of the database are maintained at both FHs and MHs. Copies are classified as *core* (primary) ones and *cached* (secondary) ones, according to their consistency degree. This classification however is independent from the type of the host in which a copy resides. It rather depends on whether the host actively participates in the data management or not. Cached copies are maintained at the hosts where applications run that can tolerate inconsistent data. Only queries can be executed on cached copies. On the contrary, hosts requiring consistent data or wishing to generate transactions must belong to the group of core sites. Core nodes periodically generate multicast messages containing the current version of the data to bring up to date the cached copies. The delivery of these messages must serialize with the queries processed at the cache sites.

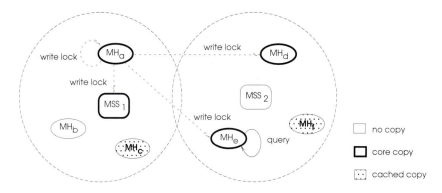

Figure 24.8. Layout of the distributed approach: read-one-write-all method; MH_e makes a query while MH_a requires write locks for a transaction.

Transactions generated by core sites are processed according to existing algorithms used in wired networks; in particular, in [7], the following approaches to transaction processing are considered:

1. **Primary/Backup:** Transactions are sent to a coordinator node (the *primary*) that processes them on its local copy and propagates the result to the other core sites (the *backups*);

2. **Read-One-Write-All:** The host that generates a transaction T must lock all the core copies before processing T, whereas a query can be performed on the local copy when this copy is not locked (Figure 24.8).

3. **General Quorums:** A *weight* is assigned to each core copy; quorums are defined for both read and write operations. The host that generates a transaction must lock enough core copies before processing it, so that the sum of their weights equals the appropriate quorum.

4. **Majority Quorum:** This is a special case of the preceding approach. Each core copy has weight 1 and a majority of the weights must be obtained for both read and write operations.

In both approaches (3) and (4), the results of transactions are propagated to all the unlocked core copies. The preceding approaches guarantee the ACID properties as they do in wired networks.

Note that the preceding approaches do not distinguish between FHs and MHs. A mobile station that generates a transaction is required to stay connected up to commit time.

Information on the acceptable quorums is recorded in a *directory*. In [7], the authors suggest that the best technique to manage the directory is to maintain a copy of it at each core site, that is, at the hosts that need to read the directory. The copies of the directory can be updated as if they were user data, for example to modify the quorums. Transactions modifying the directory must serialize with the queries to the directory made by transactions accessing the database, according to one-copy serializability.

The directory also contains information about the membership of the group of core sites. The core group can dinamically change. An MH_m that either voluntarily disconnects or observes a degradation in the wireless communications must renounce its core copy. It can either become a cached copy or give up. In both cases, MH_m must update the directory to publish the exit of this core copy from the core group. A transaction on the directory is executed by MH_m on its local copy, and only affects the data concerning MH_m (*primary-by-row* update algorithm). Therefore, problems of consistency and concurrency among transactions on the directory are avoided. The result is then propagated to the other core sites.

The preceding procedure allows us to manage planned disconnections. By contrast, the algorithm in [7] does *not* tolerate sudden disconnections of core nodes, whichever is the method used to execute transactions. In the primary/backup case, the failure of the primary node causes the loss of all the transactions queued at it waiting for processing. With the read-one-write-all method, the system is blocked in the presence of even only one node failure. In cases (3) and (4), quorums may become unreachable in consequence of one or more disconnections, thus leaving the system blocked. Sudden disconnections include site and media failures.

Transaction failures occur when either a host contacts the wrong primary site or tries to lock an unacceptable quorum, because it has read an old version of the directory and is still unaware of the last updates. These failures are recovered by reexecuting the aborted transaction.

As for the disconnected approach, the distributed approach is suitable for all mobile applications.

24.7   COMPARISON

In this section, we qualitatively compare the characteristics of the algorithms described in Section 24.6 and we leave some quantitative analysis to be discussed in Section 24.8. The analysis concerns

- features of the services offered to the applications (Section 24.7.1)

- requirements on the underlying system (Section 24.7.1)

- power saving issues (Section 24.7.1)

Fault tolerance and recovery aspects are separately considered in Section 24.7.2.

The main characteristics of the described approaches are summarized in Table 24.1. In the table we report the following items:

- the number of generated wireless messages
- whether MHs can be disconnected during transaction processing
- whether MHs can autonomously process transactions
- whether the approach guarantees fault-tolerance
- the kind of application for which each approach is more suitable
- the type of data that are better managed by each approach
- whether the data copies are kept consistent
- whether the approach requires an underlying location service
- the amount of time a MH has to remain connected and active
- whether transactions may abort as a consequence of conflicts
- the type of MH more suitable for each approach
- the communication pattern in which MHs are involved
- the amount of computation executed on MHs

24.7.1   Qualitative Analysis

The approaches proposed to address the problem of data management in distributed systems with MHs widely differ under several respects. Differences arise because of the different system features on which the developers of the various systems have

Table 24.1. Summary of the Described Approaches.

Approach	data-broadc.	trans. proxy	disconnected	distributed
Wireless messages	1	1 - 2	2	$O(n)$
Disconnected work	Yes	Yes	Yes	No
MH's autonomy	No	No	Yes	Yes
Fault tolerance	Yes	Yes	Yes	No
Applications	Vertical	Horizontal	Horizontal	Horizontal
Data	Public	Shared	Shared	Shared
Data consistency	Yes	Yes	No	Yes (core); No (cached)
Location problem	No	No	No	Yes
MH's activity	Trans. process.	Trans. submiss.	Trans. process.	Always
Conflicts	No	No	Yes	No
MH's type	Dumb/walkst.	Dumb/walkst.	Walkstation	Walkstation
MH's communica.	Point-to-point	Point-to-point	Point-to-point	Multicast
MH's computation	Low	Low	High	High (primary or quorums); low ($\neq$ primary)

focused their attention, as well as the different mobile application requirements they have considered. In this section, we discuss and compare the described approaches.

Service Features

The different characteristics of the described approaches impact on the features of the services that each approach can support. Our discussion is based on the consideration that mobile applications have varying requirements and characteristics:

- applications may require that a group of MHs operate tightly coupled or, on the contrary, that they can work disconnected

- applications may be characterized by short or long and conversational transactions

- applications may involve several users that simultaneously access the same data (such as, e.g., in cooperative workgroup applications). On the contrary, the concurrency degree amongst users may be low

If MHs are dumb terminals, they can bear a low degree of **autonomy** because of their reduced computing and storage resources. The choice of moving transaction processing to MSSs is justified by the computational costs of the protocols. Hence, the data-broadcasting and the transaction proxy approaches must be adopted. By contrast, the application requirement of autonomous work can be satisfied by fully exploiting the potential of walkstations. This is achieved by adopting either the disconnected or the distributed approaches.

Applications exist whose transactions intrinsically have a **long** duration. Moreover, in the mobile setting, transactions are likely to have longer duration than in the fixed setting, because of the intrinsic asynchronicity of the system. Under these conditions, the distributed approach can be unsuitable. In fact, it forces each core site to stay connected throughout the whole transaction execution, even if the site has not initiated a transaction. The length of the connection time makes the distributed approach costly in terms of power consumption. The disconnected and the transaction proxy approaches are better suited than the distributed approach in the case of long transactions.

The described approaches differ in their capability of supporting **conversational** (interactive) transactions. Conversational transactions are not possible in the transaction proxy approach if MHs are forced to submit whole transactions to MSSs [13]. On the contrary, if transactions are split into subtransactions, interactive transactions can be submitted. Moreover, in this case, the requirement that subtransactions of the same transaction must be independent can be relaxed. In fact, consider a subtransaction S_i of a conversational transaction T, initiated by a user on MH_m. Let S_i be generated as a result of an interaction of the user with the mobile application. Then, S_i is necessarily processed after the MH_m has received the results of the previously submitted subtransactions. Hence, no concurrent processing is possible between S_i and the other subtransactions of T on which S_i depends. No inconsistency can arise even if S_i is not independent from the previous subtransactions.

The ability of exploiting **concurrency** among transactions is interesting for both the increase in the throughput and the possibility the MHs have of working autonomously from each other, possibly in the disconnected mode. In the case transaction processing is carried out by FHs, such as in the transaction proxy approach, the usual concurrency control policies are used. In the distributed approach, the degree of the achieved concurrency depends on the locking policy. For instance, in the read-one-write-all approach, all the queries submitted at different core MHs can be executed concurrently. This does not occur in the majority quorum approach. The disconnected approach, in spite of the high degree of achievable concurrency among disconnected MHs, is heavily affected by conflicts among transactions. In fact, as pointed out in [28, 30], this approach is not adequate for databases in which a fine-granularity level is used for locks and highly concurrent applications are executed. A better load balancing of transactions can be achieved in **multiversion** databases, if applications can tolerate data not up to date.

Required Underlying Services

To fully evaluate each approach, it is important to consider which services each approach requires to the underlying protocol layers and which assumptions it makes on the characteristics of the underlying system. All of the approaches that use the wireless communication within a single cell do not require any underlying service.

The distributed approach described in [7] requires some form of **group-addressing** and **group-oriented services**. The multicast protocol proposed in [1, 2] could be used to this purpose. Such protocol guarantees an exactly once reliable and ordered message delivery service to a group of mobile hosts. Furthermore, if the quorum or the read-one-write-all methods are chosen, an **agreement** protocol is required. To avoid system deadlocks, the core copies must agree on the order at which they have to satisfy the lock requests.

A **location service** [5, 25] is also required. As long as the hosts that store core copies do not disconnect, the copies can be moved across cell boundaries. Hence, the initiator of a transaction on a host MH_m, which must lock other core copies, has to know their current location. This service is generally provided at the network layer.

Protocols using timestamps [21, 44] to check the validity of data require some form of **synchronization** among all the hosts. This property however, is quite difficult to achieve in a mobile environment.

The previously mentioned requirements restrict the applicability of the described approaches to those systems that provide the required services. An interesting question is whether and to which extent these protocols affect the performance of the upper, layer algorithms for database management. As far as we know, no investigations have been reported on this issue.

Power Saving

An important comparison aspect concerns the ability of carefully managing the available power resources. In the remainder of this section we list the characteristics of the approaches that allow energy to be saved, together with some considerations about how they are fulfilled by the different approaches.

Use of the Wireless Network. As pointed out in Section 24.2, the use of the hardware interface to the wireless network implies high power consumption. Hence, MHs should stay disconnected as long as possible.

Under this point of view, the most expensive approach is the distributed approach, in which communications can span over different cells.

On the contrary, in both the transaction proxy approach and the disconnected approach communications take place *inside* the cell of the MH_m that submitted a transaction. However, in the last case, the size of the exchanged messages can be larger, because they contain either the data, which are needed during the disconnection, or the log file that reports the activities being carried out by weak transactions and still globally uncommitted.

The use of server callbacks [21, 28, 30] to invalidate MH caches optimizes the use of the wireless network because, as long as the cache remains valid, no communication is required. The relocation of the computation as near as possible to the current location of the submitting MH_m has a similar effect, because wireless communication is confined inside a cell.

Possibility of Supporting Disconnections. This issue involves two requirements: (1) the possibility of working in a disconnected mode, thus reducing power consumption, and (2) the possibility of staying in the doze mode or disconnected every time the MH_m is not directly involved in transaction processing. These requirements are not satisfied by the distributed approach, as we have seen before.

Computation Load on MHs.   Although walkstations have computing capabilities comparable to those of fixed workstations, the use of these computing resources implies power consumption. According to the requirements of the applications regarding MHs autonomy, it is preferable to maintain the computation on FHs as longer as possible. This goal is achieved by the data-broadcasting and the transaction proxy approaches. Moreover, if the MHs are actively involved in the computation, only the MHs directly concerned with the transactions (i.e., their initiators) should process the transaction. This guideline has not been met in the distributed approach. Moreover, the choice of the lock policy in the distributed approach affects the distribution of the computation load. With the primary/backup method, the entire computation is carried out by the current primary site, whose power resources are heavily used. By contrast, with the quorum methods, the load of submitted transactions can be balanced among different subsets of hosts.

24.7.2 Fault tolerance and Recovery Issues

In a mobile environment, where the MHs failures are indistinguishable from disconnections, fault tolerance is guaranteed by redefining the correctness notion, namely, the ACID properties, to properly meet different application requirements. In the resulting fault-tolerant architecture, the achievement of the needed level of consistency, durability, and availability over replicated data is solved at the application level according to the well known end-to-end argument [37]. All the described approaches follow this schema which seems to be more flexible and efficient than the construction of a middleware layer that provides some general-purpose data management services. The transport protocol is still responsible of detecting and recovering failures over wireless channels.

24.8 PERFORMANCE EVALUATION OF RECOVERY TECHNIQUES

The data management techniques introduced in Section 24.6 cannot be meaningfully compared with respect to performance, because they differ both in the system assumptions and in the application requirements they address. However, it is of some interest to compare the four techniques that apply to the distributed approach, because they directly derive from wired systems and because they require tightly coupled and connected operations. As a consequence, these techniques are prone to be somehow affected by mobility. In line with that, we used simulations to observe the following indexes:

Throughput: The number of transactions that commit in the system per time unit. It depends on both the specific transaction management policy and the concurrency control method. It is affected by (1) the amount of communication on the wireless network and the size of the exchanged messages; (2) the amount of computation on the Mhs; and (3) the need of locating MHs within the system as a consequence of mobility.

Latency: It can be observed at the interface with the application processes and it is computed as the elapsed time between the transaction generation time and the commit time. It depends on the same factors that influence the throughput. Moreover, latency can be negatively affected by the possibility of conflicts among transactions. The conflict probability depends on both the concurrency degree among users and the rate between read and write operations.

Scalability: The capability of scaling is fundamental in the mobile environment, where the number of hosts involved in a distributed protocol is expected to be higher than in the fixed setting. It is easy to notice that the most scalable among the described approaches is the data-broadcasting approach. Indeed, only one broadcast message is required inside a cell m to satisfy all the waiting queries, independently from the number of listening MHs within m.

Our measures concern:

    i the primary/backup method with the primary site residing on a FH (P_FH)

    ii the primary/backup method with the primary site residing on a MH (P_MH)

    iii the read-one-write-all method (R.o.w.a.)

    iv the majority quorum method (Maj.)

Cases (1) and (2) allow the evaluation of the impact of the use of the wireless network. Case (i) strictly resembles the transaction proxy approach in which MHs must submit whole transactions to their MSSs.

The main difficulty derives from the determination of the appropriate parameters that characterize the mobile environment. Examples of these parameters are the number of MHs that can simultaneously be involved in the same distributed application, and the concurrency level among MHs in accessing the database (e.g., in terms of the rate between queries and updates). The difficulty in estimating the parameters is a consequence of the lack of experience on real mobile systems and applications. We believe, however, that these parameters do not differ much from those in the fixed setting.

The system we considered is composed of 5 MSSs and 200 MHs, among which core copies are uniformily distributed. The ratio we used between the bandwidth of the wired and the wireless links is 1 : 3. In particular, we simulated a wireless network having a bandwidth of 19.2 Kbps and a wired network having a bandwidth of 64 Kbps; clearly, results would change if faster existing technologies were considered.

Core copies can move from one site to another. We chose appropriate parameters to model a system in which core sites change three to four times a minute, much higher than in real systems. We did not model sudden disconnections, because the distributed approach does not tolerate them. The load in terms of transactions is decided by comparing the value of a random variable, generated according to a β distribution, with 0.71.

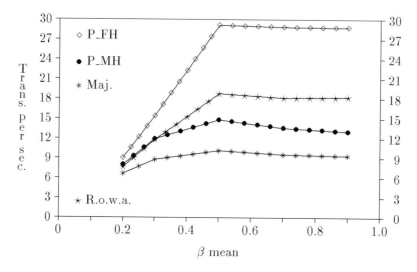

Figure 24.9. Throughput of the lock methods vs. load under access pattern of 70% read operations and 30% write operations.

In Figure 24.9, we compare the throughput produced by the various methods under different load conditions. On the x axis we report the mean of the β distribution. A group of five core sites has been simulated, whose access pattern to the database consists of 70% of read operations (queries) and 30% of write operations (update transactions).

The P_FH approach takes great advantage of its reduced use of the wireless network with respect to all the other approaches. In fact, messages are never exchanged between a pair of MHs. The P_MH approach seems to suffer from the growing load on the wireless link. This is a consequence of the multicast protocol we used. This protocol guarantees a reliable, ordered message delivery. Under this protocol, a MSS uses blocking primitives to send the messages to the MHs in its cell. For this reason, in the event of write operations, the primary MH wastes more time than the primary FH in receiving the acknowledgments to the backup messages, from the other core sites. The overhead grows with the increase in the transaction load thus leading to system congestion.

Both the distributed methods generate the highest number of messages that traverse wireless links. However, the majority quorum method is further penalized because it does not exploit concurrency among read operations.

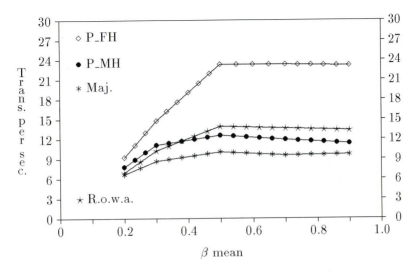

Figure 24.10. Throughput of the lock methods vs. load under access pattern of 50% read operations and 50% write operations.

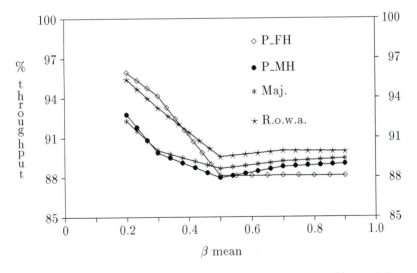

Figure 24.11. Percentage of throughput in presence of 10% link failures.

These considerations are confirmed by the results shown in Figure 24.10, where the rate of read and write operations has been respectively set to 50% and 50%. The throughput is lower for almost all the approaches because of the exchange of a higher amount of backup messages generated as consequence of write operations. The read-one-write-all method is more sensitive to the higher amount of write operations

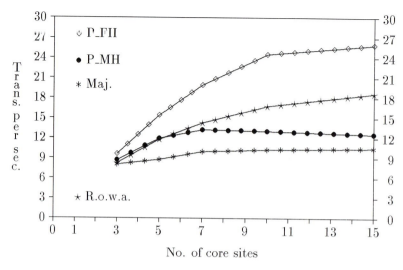

Figure 24.12. Throughput vs. number of core sites as a measure of scalability.

because MHs are not able to fully exploit concurrency among read operations. The majority approach shows the same behavior in the two cases because backup messages are sent together with the unlock messages. As a consequence, the number of messages is independent from the access pattern.

In the experiments reported in Figure 24.11, we introduce a 10% of failure probability on each wireless link, whereas the wired network is still reliable. We report the observed throughput as the percentage of the throughput obtained in the reliable case, under the same conditions of Figure 24.9. As a consequence of failures, the throughput decreases according to the increase in a transaction load. The read-one-write-all method results to be less sensitive to failures than the other approaches because it generates the lowest amount of messages. On the contrary the P_FH approach shows the worst performance.

To evaluate the scalability, we performed the same measures of Figure 24.9 varying the number of core sites at a fixed β mean (0.3). Results are reported in Figure 24.12. The increase in the number of core sites has the same effect of the increase in the load. The methods show a comparable behavior, as shown in Figure 24.9.

In Figures 24.13 and 24.14, we report the time spent by the different methods to complete a query, Figure 24.13 or an update Figure 24.14. Measures have been taken under the same conditions of Figure 24.12. The observed performance clearly differentiates the P_MH and majority quorum approaches from the P_FH and read-one-write-all approaches. The P_MH and the majority quorum approaches are affected by the high number of exchanged messages. Figures 24.13 and 24.14 confirm that the P_MH method is also affected by the congestion on the wireless links when backup messages are generated as a consequence of write operations. By contrast,

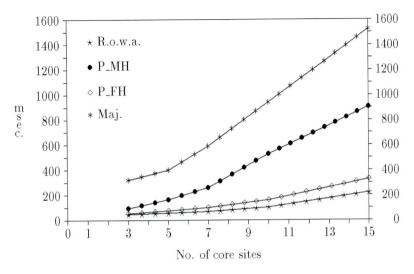

Figure 24.13. Comparison amongst lock methods with respect to the latency for read operations.

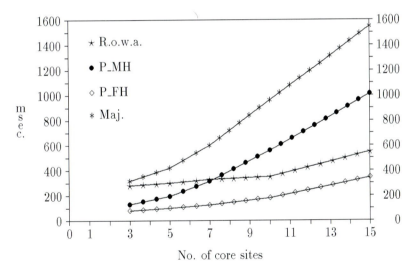

Figure 24.14. Comparison amongst lock methods with respect to the latency for write operations.

the increase in the number of generated backup messages has a lower impact on the latency in the case of the P_FH method, because of the reduced use of the wireless network. As we could expect, the read-one-write-all method has a very different behavior when executing either read or write operations. The queries submitted at different hosts can be all processed concurrently. Hence, the measured time only accounts for the concurrency with write operations and thus the delay in acquiring the grant to lock the local copy of the database.

24.9   CONCLUSIONS

In this chapter, we have investigated database management issues in a mobile computing environment. We have described the characteristics of the mobile setting and we have illustrated how these characteristics impact the algorithms for data management. We have discussed and compared some of the approaches proposed for guaranteeing proper data maintenance in spite of mobility and disconnections. We have analyzed the performance of some of the described approaches.

The simulation results highlight that the effect that the presence of the wireless network has on the algorithms is the increase of latency. The development of new technologies will enable faster communications, and the reliability of the wireless links can be improved by using appropriate transport protocols, thus reducing latency. Also mobility seems to have no other effect than the introduction of delays.

The impact of disconnections depends on the approach adopted for data management. In the disconnected, the transaction proxy and the data-broadcasting approaches disconnections are supported to improve efficiency in power savings. By contrast, the distributed approach does not tolerate sudden disconnections.

In turn, the choice of a specific approach depends on the characteristics of the application. For instance, the distributed approach is probably the most suited for managing data accessed by highly concurrent users, for example, in cooperative workgroup applications, in spite of its cost. If, however, the probability that the same data be simultaneously accessed by more than one user is low, the disconnected approach should be preferred. When conflicts are rare, the disconnected approach allows a better resource usage than the distributed approach. The choice of an approach is also driven by the characteristics of the system. When MHs are dumb terminals, only the data-broadcasting and the transaction proxy approaches are possible.

Several research issues remain open. Extensive performance measurements should be carried out to further analyze and compare the existing approaches. In particular, it would be interesting to estimate the time a MH has to stay connected for transaction processing according to the different approaches. These evaluations would allow to determine a trade-off between the possibility of disconnected work and the probability that a weak transaction has to be reexecuted after having globally aborted because of conflicts.

Protocols could be designed to add fault tolerance to the algorithms that implement the distributed approach, so that sudden disconnections are tolerated. Such protocols should probably run underneath the data management algorithms.

The distributed approach deserves much attention, because it is the most suitable for multihop networks. Since this approach makes no distinction between MHs and FHs, nor relies on some characteristics specific to FHs for its correctness, all the involved hosts could be MHs. On the contrary, the other approaches could be used in multihop networks only by assuming the existence of particularly reliable and powerful MHs that could act as FHs with respect to the other hosts in the system.

References

[1] Acharya A., Badrinath B. R. "Delivering Multicast Messages in Networks with Mobile Hosts," *Proc. 13th Intl. Conf. on Distributed Computing Systems*, May 1993.

[2] Acharya A., Badrinath B. R. "A Framework for Delivering Multicast Messages in Networks with Mobile Hosts," ACM/Baltzer Journal of Wireless Networks, Special Issue on *Routing in Mobile Communication Networks*, Vol. 1, 1996. ftp://athos.rutgers.edu/pub/acharya/mcast_winet.ps.Z.

[3] Badrinath B. R., Acharya A., Imielinski T. "Designing Distributed Algorithms for Mobile Computing Networks," To appear in Computer and Communications, 1996. ftp://athos.rutgers.edu/pub/acharya/algos_journal.ps.Z.

[4] Badrinath B. R., Acharya A., Imielinski T. "Impact of Mobility on Distributed Computations," *ACM Operating Systems Review*, 27(2) (April 1993).

[5] Badrinath B. R., Imielinski T. "Replication and Mobility," *Proc. 2nd IEEE Workshop on Management of Replicated Data*, November 1992.

[6] Balakrishnan H., Seshan S., Katz R. H. "Improving Reliable Transport and Handoff Performance in Cellular Wireless Networks," *ACM Wireless Networks*, 1996.

[7] Barbará D., Garcia-Molina H. "Replicated Data Management in Mobile Environments: Anything New Under the Sun ?," *Proc. IFIP Conf. on Applications in Parallel and Distributed Computing*, Caracas, Venezuela, April 1994.

[8] Bassak G. "Brainy, Brawny Batteries," *Byte*. Special Issue on "Mobile Computing," June 1995.

[9] Bernstein A. J. "Program Analysis for Parallel Processing," *IEEE Transactions on Electronic Computers*, EC-15(5) (Oct. 1966).

[10] Chen M., Yu P. S., Wu K. *Index Allocation for Sequential Data Broadcasting in Wireless Mobile Computing*, IBM T. J. Watson Research Center Technical Report, 1994.

[11] Chlamtac I., Weinstein O. "Distributed 'Wave' Broadcasting in Mobile Multi-Hop Radio Networks," *Proc. 7th Intl. Conf. on Distributed Computing Systems*, 1987.

[12] Chlamtac I., Weinstein O. "The Wave Expansion Approach to Broadcasting in Multihop Radio Networks," *IEEE Transactions on Communications*, 39(3) (March 1991).

[13] Cho K., Birman K. P. "A Group Communication Approach for Mobile Computing," *Proc. Mobile Computing Workshop*, Santa Cruz, CA, December 1994.

[14] Coulouris G., Dollimore J., Kindberg T. "Distributed Systems: Concepts and Design - 2nd Edition," Addison-Wesley, 1994.

[15] Duchamp D., Tait C. D. "An Interface to Support Lazy Replicated File Service," *Proc. 2nd IEEE Workshop on Management of Replicated Data*, Monterey, CA, November 1992.

[16] Elmagarmid A. K. Database Transaction Models for Advanced Applications, Morgan Kaufman.

[17] Eswaran K. P., Gray J. N., Lorie R. A., Traiger I. L. "The Notions of Consistency and Predicate Locks in a Database System," *Communications of the ACM*, 19(11) (1976).

[18] Garcia-Molina H., Salem K. "Sagas," *Proc. ACM Conf. on Management of Data*, May 1987.

[19] Gray J., Reuter A. Transaction Processing: Concepts and Techniques, Morgan Kaufmann, 1993.

[20] Haerder T., Reuter A. "Principles of Transaction-Oriented Database Recovery," *ACM Computing Surveys*, 15(4) (December 1983).

[21] Helal A., Balakrishnan S., Dunham M., Elmasri R. *A Survey of Mobile Transaction Models*, Technical Report CSD-TR-96-003, Department of Computer Science, Purdue University, February 1996.

[22] Huang Y., Wolfson O. "Object Allocation in Distributed Databases and Mobile Computers," *Proc. 10th Intl. Conf. on Data Engineering*, Houston, TX, February 1994.

[23] Imielinski T., Badrinath B. R. "Mobile Wireless Computing: Challenges in Data Management," *Communications of the ACM*, Vo. 37, No. 10, 1994.

[24] Imielinski T., Badrinath B. R. *Mobile Wireless Computing: Solutions and Challenges in Data Management*, Rutgers University Tech. Rep. DCS-TR-296/WINLAB-TR-49, 1994.

[25] Imielinski T., Badrinath B. R. Querying Locations in Wireless Environments, *Wireless Communications: Future Directions*, J. M. Holtzmann, D. J. Goodman. Kluwer 1993.

[26] Imielinski T., Viswanathan S., Badrinath B. R. "Energy Efficient Indexing on Air," *ACM SIGMOD*, May 1994.

[27] Jing J., Bukhres O., Elmagarmid A. "Distributed Lock Management for Mobile Transactions," *Proc. 15th Intl. Conf. on Distributed Computing Systems*, Vancouver, British Columbia, June 1995.

[28] Kistler J. J., Satyanarayanan M. "Disconnected Operation in the Coda File System," *ACM Trans. on Computer Systems*, 10(1) (February 1992).

[29] Liu G., Marlevi A., Maguire G. Q. "A Mobile Virtual-distributed System Architecture for Supporting Wireless Mobile Computing and Communications," *Proc. ACM MOBICOM '95*, November 1995.

[30] Lu Q., Satyanarayanan M. "Isolation-Only Transactions for Mobile Computing," *ACM Operating Systems Review*, 28(2) (April 1994).

[31] Perkins C. IP Mobility Support Draft 12. IETF Mobile-IP Draft, 1995,

[32] Pitoura E., Bhargava B. "Maintaining Consistency of Data in Mobile Distributed Environments," *Proc. 15th Intl. Conf. on Distributed Computing Systems*, Vancouver, British Columbia, June 1995.

[33] Pitoura E., Bhargava B. "Revising Transaction Concepts for Mobile Computing," *Proc. 1st IEEE Workshop on Mobile Systems and Applications*, Santa Cruz, CA, December 1994.

[34] Pu C., Kaiser G., Hutchinson N. "Split-transactions for Open-ended Activities," *Proc. 14th VLDB Conference*, 1988.

[35] Reinhardt A. "From Here to Mobility," *Byte, Special Issue on "Mobile Computing"*, June 1995.

[36] Salamone S. "Radio Days", *Byte. Special Issue on "Mobile Computing"*, June 1995.

[37] Saltzer J. H., Reed D. P., Clark D. D. "End-to-End Arguments in System Design," *ACM Transactions on Computer Systems*, 2(4) (November 1984).

[38] Seshan S., Balakrishnan H., Katz R. H. *Handoffs in Cellular Wireless Networks: The Daedalus Implementation and Experience*, Technical Report, Dept. of Electrical Engineering and Computer Science, Univ. of California at Berkeley, 1995.

[39] Tait C. D., Duchamp D. "An Efficient Variable-Consistency Replicated File Service," *Proc. USENIX File Systems Workshop*, Ann Arbor, MI, May 1992.

[40] Tait C. D., Duchamp D. "Service Interface and Replica Management Algorithm for Mobile File System Clients," *Proc. 1st IEEE Intl. Conf. on Parallel and Distributed Information Systems*, Miami, FL, December 1991.

[41] Wirth P. E. "Teletraffic Implications of Database Architectures in Mobile and Personal Communications," *Computer Networks and ISDN Systems*, 28(5) (March 1996).

[42] Wong M. H., Leung W. M. *A Caching Policy to Support Read-Only Transactions in a Mobile Computing Environment*, Technical Report, Dept. of Computer Science, Chinese Univ. of Hong Kong, 1994.

[43] Wu K., Yu P. S., Chen M. *Energy-Efficient Caching for Wireless Mobile Computing*, IBM T. J. Watson Research Center Technical Report, 1994.

[44] Yeo L. H., Zaslavsky A. "Submission of Transactions from Mobile Workstations in a Cooperative Multidatabase Processing Environment," *Proc. 14th Intl. Conf. on Distributed Computing Systems*, Poznan, Poland, June 1994.

Chapter 25

Advanced Recovery Techniques in Practice

David Lomet

Abstract

Over the past 10 years, the way that database systems achieve recovery, both from system crashes and transaction aborts, has undergone a major advance. Prior techniques severely impeded concurrency and resulted in large amounts of data being written to the log. The new techniques now permit early release of locks, hence improving concurrency; and logical operations, hence avoiding the need to physically copy data to the log. This technology has found its way into database systems currently available in the marketplace. In this chapter, we briefly sketch the techniques being exploited, which are described fully elsewhere in this book, and illustrate them by describing how they solve the problem of B-tree recovery.

25.1 INTRODUCTION

Early database systems picked among those recovery techniques that forced compromises among concurrency, amount of data written to the log, and pauses in normal system operation and expensive checkpointing. In some cases, a single technique could lose in both concurrency and in the amount of data written to the log. Checkpointing, whose goal is to shorten recovery by truncating the log (advancing the redo scan start point) can be expensive in disk writes and in the system interruption needed, in some cases, to produce an atomic checkpoint.

Although it is possible to provide recovery without using a log-based technique (e.g., read an old master copy–write a new master copy), no commercial database system uses such techniques. All exploit logs, and follow the write-ahead log protocol to ensure that the log truly reflects all changes that might have been or need to be captured in the stable database. Our discussion then focuses only on log-based techniques.

25.1.1 Requirements for Log-Based Recovery

All log-based methods assume that the operations used are atomic and that they appear on the log in the order in which they executed. In addition, with transactional recovery, they are tagged in some way with the transaction that performed the action captured by the operation. Finally, a transaction commit record indicates that the transaction involved was completed and should be guaranteed to be durable (the changes will persist) or, if not present, that the transaction did not complete and hence that the effects of the transaction should not appear in the stable system state.

To guarantee durability of committed transactions, log-based methods must force (write synchronously) to the durable log all log records of the transaction, including the transaction commit record. They must further, and frequently with much more difficulty, ensure that replaying the logged operations against the version of the stable database that exists at the time of the crash is possible and results in a correct database state that includes the changes of all committed transactions. This can be a nontrivial requirement.

To guarantee the rollback of uncommitted transactions requires that recovery guarantee that it is possible to execute successfully all undo operations recorded on the log, in inverse order. It is not acceptable to abort a transaction undo, so this guarantee has to include the absence of a permanent abort. Think of this as the need to guarantee that the transaction must "commit" with a guarantee of reaching an acceptable state. The minimal acceptable state is that the transaction have no effect. States in which partial executions become durable are not acceptable.

25.1.2 Why Recovery Is Difficult

What is needed is for the recovery method to provide what was called in [7] a REDO test, which we now informally extend to undo recovery as well and rename as an EXECUTE test. The EXECUTE test must satisfy the following conditions:[1]

1. Safety: If the test returns true, then (a) the operation is applicable to the state (the part of the state it sees is the state it either saw originally or that it needs) and (b) its execution and modification of the state will not make it impossible to execute other logged operations that are needed to recover the system.

2. Liveness: When recovery encounters the operation while processing the log, and it needs to be executed for successful recovery, then the test returns true.

---

[1] Conditions called "determinable execution" and "operation consistency" were used in [5] to characterize the requirements for undo recovery. But these are stronger than necessary.

Recovery is hard not because of our inability to construct an appropriate EXE-CUTE test. We know how to leave information in the state to help us to TEST the state appropriately. Rather, it is the difficulty of ensuring that the state of the system at the time that a logged operation is to be executed has the desired properties. We must orchestrate cache management, concurrency control, and recovery so as to *guarantee* that the state against which we execute logged operations is guaranteed to be the state that we need. Because this is so difficult in general, recovery systems have simplified the problem by restricting the kinds of operations that they log.

25.1.3   The Choice of Log Operations

Log-based recovery systems have to choose the form of operation that they support, and then map the actions of the database system into those operations. The mapping step is clearly important, but is not the subject of this chapter. In describing recovery, we deal only with the successful redo or undo of logged operations, and assume that the mapping between actual database activities and logged operations has been done correctly.

We further restrict our attention precisely to the impact of the form of logged operation on the performance characteristics of the recovery system. More complete descriptions of the requirements and organization of recovery systems are found elsewhere in this book, and in [1, 3, 8].

Section two explores what has become the standard set of options when choosing logged operations. There are two "extremes," logical recovery and physical recovery. We briefly describe them to give a flavor of why the recovery problem has been difficult. We then introduce physiological recovery [3, 8], which is a carefully crafted limited form of logical recovery tailored to the block oriented organization of the disk. Recovery in most industrial database systems is based on physiological recovery.

Although physiological recovery is an enormous improvement on its predecessors, work continues on further improvements. It is the advancements beyond physiological recovery that are the subject of this chapter. There are two techniques that we describe, one for undo recovery and one for redo.

Undo: Multilevel transactions [10] and their recovery [5, 11] make it possible to release locks before the end of transaction while preserving serializable executions. The multilevel recovery is described in Section three, where we show how to enhance concurrency for B-tree structure changes.

Redo: More logical redo permits us to avoid logging state changes when new pages are initialized and substantial data are moved. "Logical" redo, in which an operation can span database pages [7], is explained in Section four, where we show how it can reduce the data logged during a B-tree split.

It is worth emphasizing here (though we do not provide citations) that both the preceding techniques have appeared in commercial database systems. So this is not a discussion of theoretical recovery methods, but rather of pragmatic ones.

25.2   STANDARD LOGGED OPERATIONS

25.2.1   Physical Operations

Recovery when using physical (state-based) operations is very simple indeed. Log records contain the new and old states. One performs redo by simply installing the new states and undo by installing the old states of uncommitted transactions. There are very few requirements on the cache manager as to how to order the posting of changes to the stable database state. Any page can be flushed at any time. But there are two serious shortcomings, log space consumption and limited concurrency.

Since states are being logged, one needs to capture that state. The unit of recovery is frequently the page, which is the unit of transfer between cache and disk. Hence, every page change, no matter how small, requires the saving of two pages of information on the log, the before and after images of the page. Because of this explosion of log space, recovery systems frequently log only partial pages, indicating the bytes on the page that have changed. This is at best a partial solution, as many small changes, such as inserting a new record into a vector of records in key order can change an average of half a page. This helps, but there is still a large amount of log data per update.

Potential concurrency is also reduced. Physical logging requires physical locks. These are transaction-duration locks that prevent one transaction from updating a page on which a second transaction has already made a change. High-performance transaction systems usually cannot live with this page-level granularity of locking.

25.2.2   Logical Operations

At the other extreme from logging physical operations or state-based "value setting" operations is the logging of operations that may be much closer to what a user thinks of as his operations. For example, a user might wish to execute the following logical step:

insert record into B-tree-table

One could choose to log this as a < redo, undo > pair of operations that update multiple pages should the table containing the record be stored as a B-tree. Should the B-tree structure change, multiple pages would be changed as the result of this operation. Operations that read and write multiple pages have been difficult to deal with. One needs to understand when the operation's effects have been included in the stable system state, and one needs to ensure that cache managment always maintains the stable state in such a way that either the effects of the operation are fully included in the state or that recovery can successfully reexecute the operation and update the parts of the state not yet containing the operations results. This can be very difficult and complicated. It is referred to as the action consistency problem [3], and can arise for both redo and undo operations.

To solve this problem while providing operations that may touch multiple pages, System R [2] periodically installed operation- consistent checkpoints. These checkpoints required that execution of the operational system be temporarily suspended so that the results of all operations since the last checkpoint could be atomically installed (via a shadow technique) into the database state. After installation, normal operation was resumed. It is this very large checkpoint cost that has caused logical logging to fall out of favor for redo recovery.[2]

25.2.3   "Physiological" Operations

The recovery technique that is at the core of recovery in current industrial database systems is what is called in [3] physiological logging. The operations are specific to a page, the unit of transfer between cache and disk, but the operations are logical, not physical. That is, the operations represent state transitions, not state values. Page-based, state-transition operation logging was not described in the research literature until [3, 8], but it had been used in some commercial systems substantially before.

Physiological logging, like logical logging, requires that the state needed by an operation be identifiable. This led to the notion of state identifiers called log sequence numbers, or LSNs. The log record has an LSN (its address on the log) and the page has an LSN (called the page LSN or pLSN) that identifies the log record of the last operation that updated the page. During redo recovery, one scans the log and compares log record LSN with the pLSN of the page updated by the logged operation. There are two outcomes:

log LSN ≤ pLSN: The update is already incorporated into the page; bypass this operation.

log LSN > pLSN: The update is not yet in the page; redo the operation and update the page.

The current recovery paradigm with physiological logging is to repeat history [8] by performing redo first using all logged updates. This brings the system to a state as of the last logged operation. Then one applies undo to roll back uncommitted operations, where the undo can be of the same form as for handling transaction abort during normal operation. This simple pattern provides high assurance that the method actually results in correct recovery.

Physiological logging has a number of advantages. The amount of information logged is modest since an entire page state (or even a part thereof) need not be captured. Second, page locks can be dropped after the operation is complete, with only the locks needed by the operation retained, for example, record locks. Thus, the unit of lock granularity can be the record. (This is actually a trivial instance of a multilevel transaction, which is described more fully in the next section.) Thus, physiological logging substantially improves on space consumption and concurrency limitations of physical logging.

Like physical logging, physiological logging does not require a systemwide action-consistent checkpoint. The cache manager can write changed pages to the disk incre-

---

[2]The situation for undo recovery is different, as we shall see.

mentally and in any order. This technique thus avoids the substantial complication of logical logging.

It is not surprising that most industrial systems have settled on physiological logging as the core recovery mechanism. What is less appreciated is that many industrial systems enhance this basic mechanism to further improve concurrency and reduce log-space consumption. We describe these enhancements in the next two sections.

25.3   MULTILEVEL UNDO RECOVERY

25.3.1   Multilevel Transactions

Concurrency control and recovery theory suggests [1] that strict two-phase locking is required to serialize *and* recover transactions. Strict locking means holding all locks until a transaction commit so that one can ensure that the transaction can be successfully aborted should that be necessary. (Indeed, abort is the one transaction outcome that a database system guarantees.) But the fact is that no industrial database systems use strict two-phase locking because they cannot tolerate the restricted concurrency. All of them use some flavor of multilevel transaction [10] that permits locks to be released early without compromising either serializability or recovery.

A multilevel transaction is another form of subtransaction, more powerful than a nested transaction. Nested transactions can lock objects held by the parent transaction and return all their locks to their parent when they commit. Multilevel transactions exploit layers of abstraction. At the lower level, within the subtransaction, low level operations may require low-level locks. But when the a multilevel subtransaction commits, it drops these low-level locks, and passes to itsparent only the high level locks necessary to serialize and ensure undo at the higher level of abstraction [5, 11] in this volume. This is effective exactly because of the different levels of abstraction.

Database systems that do physiological recovery all use a trivial form of multilevel transaction to ensure that only one operation can change a page at a time. Typically, a transaction takes an exclusive latch on the page to prevent other transactions from seeing an intermediate state of an update. Once the update is complete, a record lock is retained for the record changed, and the page latch is dropped. This commits the multilevel subtransaction. This form of multilevel transaction does not impact recovery because the page being changed is "pinned" in the cache (is prevented from being flushed to disk) for the duration of the subtransaction. Hence, no intermediate states of the subtransaction ever appear in the stable system state. So recovery need not deal with them.

25.3.2   B-Tree Need for Multilevel Recovery

When a subtransaction updates multiple pages, it can be difficult or impossible to avoid materializing intermediate states on the disk. Then a more explicit subtransaction is needed, coupled with recovery that ensures that the lower-level abstraction being exploited is well-formed.

This is what is involved when high B-tree concurrency is required. High B-tree concurrency requires that locks on B-tree nodes that protect the tree while it is being updated or restructured be held for much less than the duration of a user transaction. If this is not done, and a long transaction were to change the tree and leave locks in place, the entire subtrees affected would be locked. Conceivably, the entire tree might be locked, preventing all concurrent access by way of the tree.

So high-concurrency B-tree implementations release B-tree node locks early. This early release of node locks permits multiple transactions to be concurrently updating different parts of the tree, including within the subtree whose root is being split. These updates may be uncommitted at the time of a system crash. If these updates have been moved because of a completed structure change lower in the tree, they will need an undo that requires a tree search involving a path that includes the node whose split is incomplete.

The multilevel way of looking at this is that there are two levels of abstraction, an ordered record abstraction and the B-tree implementation that supports it. The logical operations (undos in this case) are expressed in terms of the ordered record abstraction. For these operations to execute correctly, the path that they need from root to leaf must be well-formed. But the B-tree implementation layer is being changed as well, via a page split in this case. We must guarantee that the changes leave the path well-formed when we need to perform the record-level undos. This means that incomplete structure changes on such paths need to be recovered before the record-level operation is undone.

25.3.3   Ordering Problems for B-Tree Restructuring

We assume here that our recovery method performs redo recovery first, repeating history, during a forward pass over the log. Then it performs undo by starting at the tail of the log and scanning backwards, undoing operations of uncommitted transactions and of uncommitted B-tree restructurings, until all required undo operations have been executed.

Recall that a B-tree split will touch multiple pages, and hence there will be multiple log records, spread out among other operations on the log. Further, some of the changes produced by the split may have been flushed to the disk. Despite this, if all log records describing a B-tree restructuring on a path are naturally guaranteed to occur later on the log than the log records for the logical record-level operations that require the path to be well-formed, then no extra care is required. But this is not guaranteed, as the example in Figure 25.1 makes clear.

Sequence of activity.

- T1 begins update activity and traverses past node A

- T2 follows T1 down the tree to perform an update

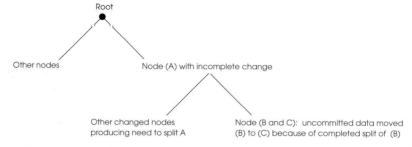

Figure 25.1. An example of a corrupted path to data requiring logical undo. The path through node A must be well formed before logical undo can succeed. But here the structure change involving A begins before the update to B, and hence appears earlier on the log.

- T3 performs an update elsewhere that results in node splits on another path that includes A, and must split A as a result

- T3 BEGINS splitting A

- T1 updates record R in B

- T2 makes an update that causes B to split, moving record R to C

- T2 commits

- The system crashes

During the redo scan, the state of the B-tree will be exactly restored as of the time of the crash, with node A in transition and hence paths through A not well-formed. For example, the version of A on the disk might have been flushed after half its contents were moved, and node A', which is expected to contain the other half, has not yet been flushed. Hence, half of the tree previously accessible via A is not currently accessible.

Eventually, A will be restored to its original form because its split subtransaction did not complete, and undo operations early on the log will restore the missing contents. But A will not be restored at the time when we need to undo the update to R, because the update to R occurs later on the log than the start of the subtransaction for the split of A.

25.3.4 Solutions

There are two fundamental forms of solution to the above difficulty.

Prevention: We prevent log records from structure modifications from being earlier in the log than the undo operations that need them, by restricting how record operations and structure changes are ordered.

Out-of-Sequence Undo: We undo incomplete B-tree structure changes needed
by operations that are later on the log before we undo the later operations,
hence not processing the log strictly from the tail backward.

We describe these solutions below. Several commercial database systems use solutions from the set described below to realize highly concurrent B-trees.

Restrict B-tree Modification Interactions. The log reflects the order in which
operations are performed. Thus, our way of controlling where on the log operations can occur is by using concurrency control to restrict the sequence in which
operations are performed. Industrial database systems use locking for concurrency
control. The granularity of the lock and its lock mode conflicts will determine how
much concurrency is possible.

The basic ARIES/IM [9] B-tree method provides a single structure modification
lock (SMO), which is locked in exclusive (X) mode when a structure modification
is in progress. Only a single modification can be active at a time. As indicated
in Figure 25.1, we need two structure modifications on a common path in order to
produce the problem. If the split of A precedes the split of node B, the split of A
would be completed by the redo phase before we tried to undo the record update
moved by the split of B. If the split of A follows the split of B, then undo would
encounter this incomplete split and undo it prior to trying to undo the update to
record R.

The ARIES/IM authors knew this was much more restrictive than required. As
a concurrency enhancement, they suggested acquiring the SMO lock in X mode only
for non-leaf nodes. The lock is acquired in IX mode for leaf structure modifications,
which are hence permitted to occur in parallel because IX is compatible with IX.
But the conflict between IX and X means that an interior node cannot be split
while a leaf or other interior node is being split.

At the cost of more intention locks, one could lock nodes down the path to a
split with IM locks (denoting intention to modify nodes lower in the tree on this
path). IM locks conflict with the M mode locks that indicate the modification of
the tree at a node, i.e. splitting the node. But IM locks are compatible with all
other lock modes, including X, so these modes impede no other activity except a
structure modification. This prevents multiple active structure modifications on
the same path, which is precisely what needs to be prevented to provide effective
recovery.

Both of the more adventurous methods do not guarantee deadlock avoidance.
Hence, one must use heavy duty locks managed by the lock manager, not latches,
for the structure modification locks. This raises the normal lock overhead involved,
while providing higher concurrency. And, of course, occasionally, transactions will
be aborted to cope with deadlocks.

Out-of-Sequence Undo. Maximum concurrency permits B-tree structure modifications to occur simultaneously, whether on the same path or not. The bottom up
method described in [6] permits this, and with no risk of deadlock. Hence, latches

can be used This method exploits a side link a la the B-link tree of [4] to restructure the tree without fear of deadlock. The structure modification operations are sometimes called half-splits, and each can be protected with a single latch specific to the splitting node. However, even half splits can have multiple log records per structure modification. Hence they have visible duration on the log. So an incomplete structure modification might not be recovered properly before the logical record operation needing an intact path is undone.

Recovery designed to cope with multi-level subtransactions are designed specifically for situations like these. Instead of performing undo recovery from the log tail back in a single sequential pass of the log, multi-level methods [11, 5] perform undo recovery level by level, begining at the lowest level of abstraction. In the case of B-trees, this ensures that the B-tree is fully recovered prior to undoing logical record operations that need well-formed paths.

The MLR method [5] extends to an arbitrary number of levels. Using MLR, B-tree structure modifications can be incorporated into any scheme involving multiple levels of abstraction, regardless of the number of other levels. It uses a single log, exploits physiological operations for redo, and repeats history a la ARIES.

25.4   MORE POWERFUL REDO OPERATIONS

B-tree node splitting is a challenge for logging as well as concurrency. Logging physiological operations is very effective for many forms of record updating. Only the change involving the record itself need be logged. But when a B-tree node splits, this is an operation involving the entire node, and can result in the need to write large portions of the node to the log.

In this section, we describe first what the by now standard phsiological operations need to log in order to redo and undo B-tree half-splits. A half-split is the part of a B-tree node split that divides the entries of a node into two parts, the low order part that stays in the old node, and the high order part that is moved to a new node. It is this part of the B-tree node split that requires writing a large amount of data to the log. We then describe how logging more powerful operations can eliminate the need for logging most of that data. [3]

25.4.1   Physiological Half-Split Operations

Each page needs a physiological operation on the log to describe the changes to be made to the page. Further, each page needs to provide operations for both redo and undo recovery. The undo and redo operations for a given page are usually stored within a single log record for the page. But information needed by both of these operations needs to be stored in this log record.

For a B-tree half-split, two pages are involved, the old full page and a new page.

---

[3] Updates to several parts of system state occur when performing a full B-tree split. So using a subtransaction mechanism will usually be required even when we exploit more powerful log operations.

The log records for each of those pages must stand on their own because there is no guarantee that both will be written. Thus, the log record for the old page must contain all information necessary to

- redo the split given the original state of the old page, meaning removing the half of the data higher than the split key. This is easy as it merely requires that we identify the operation as a node split, page to be split, and the key to be used for the split.

- undo the split given the new state of the old page, meaning restoring the half of the data higher than the split key to the page that now does not include this data. In addition to the information needed for redo, this incurs the cost of logging the records that were removed by the split so that they can be put back during the undo. This is approximately half a page of data.

The log record for the new page similarly has both redo and undo information. In this case, the record must contain the necessary information to

- redo the half-split given the original state of the new page, which is the null state. This requires the identification of the operation as the initialization of a new page, the page involved, and the initial contents of the page, which is the collection of records that are being moved from the old page to the new. This is approximately half a page of data.

- undo the half-split given the new state of the new page. This is easy as it merely requires that we restore the identified page to its original unallocated state.

Logging these operations on old and new nodes of the B-tree requires then the writing of approximately a full page of data to the log in addition to the usual information needed for physiological operations. For large B-tree nodes, this can be 4K bytes or 8K bytes. While B-tree page splitting only occurs once in every 10 or 20 updates, depending on the number of records contained in the B-tree leaf, this amount of logging adds substantially to the cost of using a B-tree as the storage structure for database records. [4]

25.4.2   Multi-Page Half-Split Operations

The recovery framework in [7] explains how, in general, the nature of log operations imposes requirements on cache management. A multi-page operation requires that the cache manager order flushes of pages to disk. Here we only explain the specific example of a multi-page half-split operation.

What we desire is not to have to write any of the moved data to the log. We want to simply specify a log operation that captures the half-split as a single logical operation. This operation will not be a physiological one, however, because two

---

[4]A node of data is written to the log for every new node that is added to the B-tree.

pages (nodes) are involved. Thus, we describe the split logically as an allocation of the new node, and a move of all entries with keys greater than the split key from the original node to the new node. This completely describes the split. It contains sufficient information for the undo of the split as well, indicating where to find the contents that are needed to restore the original node. The problem, as we shall see, is that it can be difficult to ensure that the undo operation can be replayed after a system crash.

Hence, our "split" log record needs to contain sufficient information to

- redo the half-split given the original state of the old node. This is easy as all the moved data is still present in the old node. We need merely indicate the split key in addition to identifying page and operation. Since all information needed for the new page is acquired from the old page, we are indifferent as to whether the new page was updated or not.

- undo the half-split given a state that includes one or both of the pages containing the results of the operation. This presents no problem in the two out of three cases below:

  1. the new node in its new state is present on the disk, but not the original node. We simply reset the state of the new node to "unallocated".

  2. both original node and new node in their new states are present on the disk. We move the contents of the new node back to being the high order entries of the original node, hence restoring it to its original state. We then reset the state of the new node to "unallocated"

The undo case that cannot be handled is when the change made to the original node is on the disk but the new node in its new state is not on the disk when the system crashes. Then we have lost the high order records from the original node that are needed to restore it to its pre-split state. We need help from the cache manager to prevent this from happening.

25.4.3   Consequences for Cache Management

A necessity of using log operations that read and write multiple pages is that the cache manager must be careful to flush pages to disk in the correct order. The correct order for the split (and its undo operation, the "unsplit") is derived from the pattern of reads and writes. For our purposes, we need only describe read-write conflicts between operations and how they impose a flush order on the pages. Any write-read conflicts do not impact recovery as inverting the flush order does not prevent the redo of the earlier operation. Write-write conflicts are technically more difficult to reason away, but can nonetheless be ignored [7] for the split operations that we deal with here.

A split operation reads the original node O, and writes both O and a new node N. Thus, it makes two separate updates, to O and to N, and further, there is are read-write edges between the update to O and both the update to N and to itself. That is, the update to O writes into the variable O that it read. When a single operation has multiple updates, we must install an update writing into its read set last. Otherwise, we make it impossible for the operation to be redone so as to replay the other updates. In the case of the node split operation, the update to N must be flushed before the update to O.

For the "unsplit" operation, executed during undo, it reads from O and N and writes to O and to N. But its write to N does not depend on what is read. Indeed, if "unsplit" is to be executed, it does not matter what is the value of N before the operation, as after the operation, it will be in an original unallocated state. The write of N during undo can thus be though of as a separate operation (and logged that way if compensating log records are used).

The read-write conflict between the updates for the split operation results in the need to flush N before O is flushed. During undo, the upsplit read-write conflicts result in the need to flush O before N. The framework of [7] lead directly to these requirements (with appropriate explanation to deal with the B-tree undo recovery situation. At least one commercial database system logs a half-split as a single operation. To avoid complicating the cache manager, the resulting flush order dependency is discharged by immediately flushing the page required to be flushed first. Cache manager operation can freely exploit the usual steal policy subsequently.

25.5   DISCUSSION

We have seen how advanced recovery techniques have been adapted to solve existing problems within commercial database systems. The future role of these techniques should be even more interesting.

Multi-level transaction undo recovery: New forms of resource managers can be realized which, rather than being built from scratch, can exploit existing transactional record managers. For example, one could build a transactional queue on top of a database kernel. Further, workflow systems, which usually require ways to provide compensation actions, are naturally supported via multi-level transactions.

Multi-page operations for redo recovery: Having applications as well as committed transactions survive across system crashes would be a substantial boon for long running applications such as workflows. It is multi-page operations and their recovery that may make this recovery possible at an affordable execution cost.

References

[1] P. Bernstein, V. Hadzilacos, and N. Goodman. *Concurrency Control and Recovery in Database Systems*. Addison-Wesley Publishing, Reading, MA, 1987.

[2] J. Gray, P. McJones, M. Blasgen, B. Lindsay, R. Lorie, T. Price, and F. Putzolu. "The recovery manager of the System R database manager," *ACM Computing Surveys*, 13(2) (June 1981).

[3] J. Gray and A. Reuter. *Transaction Processing: Concepts and Techniques.* Morgan Kaufmann, 1993.

[4] Lehman, P., Yao, S.B., "Efficient locking for concurrent operations on B-trees," *ACM TODS*, 16(4) (December 1981).

[5] D. Lomet. "MLR: A recovery method for multi-level systems," In *Proceedings of the 1992 ACM SIGMOD International Conference on Management of Data*, ACM, June 1992.

[6] Lomet, D. and Salzberg, B. "'Concurrency and Recovery for Index Trees," In *Proceedings of the 1992 ACM SIGMOD International Conference on Management of Data*, ACM, June 1992.

[7] Lomet, D. and Tuttle, M. "Redo Recovery after System Crashes," *VLDB*, Zurich, Switzerland, September 1995.

[8] Mohan, C., Haderle, D., Lindsay, B., Pirahesh, H., and Schwarz, P. "ARIES: A transaction recovery method supporting fine-granularity locking and partial rollbacks using write-ahead logging," *ACM TODS*, 17(1) (March 1992).

[9] Mohan, C. and Levine, F. "ARIES/IM: An efficient and high concurrency index management method using write-ahead logging," In *Proceedings of the 1992 ACM SIGMOD International Conference on Management of Data*, ACM, June 1992.

[10] G. Weikum. "A theoretical foundation of multi-level concurrency control," In *Proceedings of the 5th Annual ACM Symposium on Principles of Database Systems*, March 1986.

[11] G. Weikum, C. Hasse, P. Broessler, and P. Muth. "Multi-level recovery," In *Proceedings of the 9th Annual ACM Symposium on Principles of Database Systems*, April 1990.

Chapter 26

Logging and Recovery in Commercial Systems

Ron Obermarck

26.1 INTRODUCTION

Logging and recovery is well documented in the literature. Much good information is found in Part Five [2]. This chapter concentrates on two of the high-end database and transaction processing systems in the commercial market. IBM's IMS[1] product was developed in the late 1960s in a proprietary environment. It has evolved over the years.

The IMS Fast Path Feature deserves discussion on its own. It is a performance and availability feature that has had a unique effect on the IMS product. IMS Fast Path Feature was introduced in 1977. It has evolved as well.

The Oracle RDBMS and product set are more modern offerings, designed for client server operation in an *Open* environment. This chapter discusses the approach of each of the products to logging and recovery, not to look at which is better or worse, but to contrast the specific problems each has overcome.

26.2 IMS

The IMS program product has evolved from IMS/360 Version 1 in 1968, designed to execute in a System/360 computer with 256K (yes, kilobytes) of memory and 0.05 MIPS, to IMS/ESA Version 6, which is targeted to operate under MVS/ESA SP

---

[1] System/360, MVS/ESA, IMS/360, IMS/VS, and IMS/ESA are registered trademarks of the International Business Machines Corporation. Oracle is a registered trademark of the Oracle Corporation.

Version 4, Release 3 [IBM Announcement Letters (US)–Document 296-330, September 10, 1996].

26.2.1 Logging and its interaction with the system

IMS logging evolved from magnetic tape logging to disk logging. IMS used a write-ahead log, and force at commit protocol. In fact, the database buffers modified by the transaction were forced to disk at the transaction's commit. This was in contrast to the modified message queue buffers, which were forced to disk during system checkpoint. As pointed out in [2], IMS did physiological logging. However, the logging was heavily on the side of physical images of the before and after images of the changes. In many cases, the before and after images were compressed into a single record. When Program Isolation was introduced in 1973, a second, temporary log (the *dynamic back-out data set*) was implemented as a backing store for cached transaction undo records. The undo records were written to the tape log, but cached to allow transaction undo for failed transaction programs.

As disk capacity increased, there were requests to do disk logging. Because of the log write-ahead and force at commit protocols used by IMS, the log was forced frequently. Average rotational delay was on the order of 18 milliseconds, so forcing the log was a huge performance impact. A search was made for a way to improve the latency associated with synchronizing writes to disk. A group devised a way of trading disk space for rotational delay time, and the *write-ahead data set (WADS)* was invented. Gray describes this in [2].

Briefly, the method used a track per forced write. All tracks were formatted with fixed-length blocks and a single search key. By using the key search of the count key data architecture disks, the write was done to the next block to come under the read-write heads. Each write was done to a different track on the disk allocated for this purpose. In this way, writes to the real disk log could be done for full, very large blocks. As part of log-oriented performance enhancements, log records were minimized. The overhead associated with each log record was reduced by putting more data into a log record when that avoided having to write a second log record. Compression was applied to the IMS log in 1988's IMS/ESA Version 3.

The next evolution in IMS logging was to transmit a copy of the log to a stand-by system for faster recovery. This was one of the aspects of the Extended Recovery Feature first announced in 1986. The first use required the stand-by machine to be close to the one executing, but failover times under heavy load were reduced to less than a minute.

In 1995, the Remote Site Recovery feature of IMS/ESA Version 5 was announced and made generally available. This feature ships log data as it is produced to a remote system. The remote system may be an archive or may do full database shadowing. Extensive synchronization capabilities were implemented to allow uninterrupted operation of the transmitting site (and catch-up at the receiving site) in the case of transmission or receiving system failures.

26.2.2   Commit Behavior

IMS has evolved from a single-phase commit through several stages to support the X-Open-defined XA commit protocols, as well as the System Network Architecture (SNA) (Logical Unit) LU6.2 (CIP-C and APPC) two-phase commit protocols. In 1987, IMS/VS Version 2 Release 2 announced support as a transaction manager for IBM's DB2 relational database product. Both transactions executing standard IMS message processing, and those using the Fast Path feature were included. Two-phase commit protocols were used to maintain consistency between the resource managers. IMS use of formal two-phase commit was a product support decision more than a technical decision. Other products from IBM (e.g., CICS) used the formal two-phase commit protocol in SNA in the late 1970s. IMS, being a combined database and transaction manager, with its application support separated by its message queues from direct interaction with communications, was slower to accept other resource managers.

26.2.3   Checkpoints

The IMS online system has always done checkpoints. Initially, the checkpoints required terminating everything except polling of the terminals. The transaction processing applications were controlled by the IMS control region, and were easily quiesced. However, making all processing wait from the time a checkpoint was internally signaled until the last application completed processing caused severe performance problems.

IMS changed first to a quiesce of transaction applications at a synchronization (commit) point. This left independently scheduled (batch message processing programs) in an unsynchronized state. The checkpoints were fuzzy with respect to those applications. It was decided that the checkpoints would be done without quiescing the transaction processing programs either. Instead, the checkpoint identity prior to the point at which the longest-running application had done its last commit was recorded as part of the checkpoint data. That became the checkpoint at which the system would be restarted.

The database buffers were forced to disk at application commit. However, the message queue buffers were not forced at that time. In the early 1980s, IMS was supporting networks of several thousand terminals, and executing hundreds of transactions per second of the TPC-A variety. The message queue processing had to use a steal, no-force protocol. The message queue data was forced to disk as part of each checkpoint.

Checkpoint of the message queue buffers, to protect from failure of the queue data sets, was done as a special type of termination checkpoint. The queue data was rebuilt (reorganized from data on the log) when a restart was done from that checkpoint. This became a performance problem at restart time, so a physical image was written as a checkpoint on the log. This allowed restart to occur more quickly when a failure did not damage the message queue data sets.

26.2.4   Relationship to Recovery and Restart

The dynamic back-out data set also became the repository of undo log records during recovery-restart. As most of the transactions were short enough for all the undo log information to exist in the cache, this was a performance enhancement at restart time. The log had to be read only in the forward direction, as opposed to forward to the end, then backward to apply undo records for uncommitted transactions. The WADS was a very difficult dataset to read, to extract the log tail information. So a restart control dataset was created. As the system failed, functional recovery routines were invoked:

1. An attempt was made to force the log buffers to the real log, and then to close the log datasets. If this was successful, a record was written to the recovery dataset.

2. An attempt was made to force all modified buffers in the database cache to disk. If this was successful, another record was written to the restart control dataset.

3. An attempt was made to force the undo log records for uncommitted transactions to the dynamic back-out dataset. Again, a record was written to the restart control dataset.

The restart control dataset was read during restart. The mode of recovery was determined from information recorded there. If the system had been shut down normally, then a normal warm start would be done. If the system had not been shut down normally, an emergency restart would be done. Depending on how many actions were recorded as successfully completed, less work had to be done during the restart itself. The package was called fast restart, although there were those who indicated that it really should be called slow shutdown. The amount of bookkeeping was minimal, and the benefit of the first part was great.

The need to begin the recovery at the correct checkpoint, and to include all volumes of the log, was exemplified by problems in the message queue recovery. Assumptions were made in the message queue recovery that were not always met. Nearly all transaction processing used the message queue, as did nearly all terminal traffic. If a failure occurred, and a cold start was done instead of a recovery restart, the message queue data was compromised. A simple recovery restart (after the operator error had been discovered) with the original logs would seem to correct the problem, but the message queue structures on disk would be in error. This usually resulted in a failure that would cause the system to be unrecoverable.

The restart control dataset helped avoid this type of situation by automating the recovery restart process. Another addition to the message queue restart code validated the message queue data at the completion of restart. Invalid message queue information was logged and eliminated, leaving the message queues correct. Although the routine was put in as a required recovery step, it became optional (again because of restart performance).

26.3   IMS FAST PATH FEATURE

The IMS Fast Path Feature was introduced as an add-on to the IMS on-line system in 1978. The feature was focused on high-volume, simple banking transaction processing. It was designed to be highly available, with a combination of batch and transaction processing. The requirement to limit the impact of disk failures and reorganization operations led to the horizontal partitioning of the data-entry databases.

26.3.1   Logging and Its Interaction with the System

Fast Path avoided log forces by queuing work against the writing of log blocks. When an action required synchronization with the log (e.g., for log write-ahead of data block writes), the assumption was that system activity would cause the log block to be written soon enough, so the activity would wait for either the natural write to complete or a timer. If the timer woke the action, the log would then be force-written. In a busy system, the log was nearly always ahead of the timer.

Fast Path initiated a no-steal buffer management scheme. Fast Path did not have to log before images, and did not have to synchronize the log to database I/O at commit time as tightly as did standard IMS.

26.3.2   Commit Behavior

In Fast Path transaction processing, the request to commit disconnected the application from the commit process, allowing the application to immediately begin processing the next transaction. The system became responsible for the context of the committing transaction, either to commit or abort the work. If the transaction failed to commit, the original message was presented to the application as a new transaction. If the transaction committed, the output message was sent as part of the commit processing.

Fast Path used group commits wherever possible. The changes requested for the main storage database were processed during commit. The database was locked, the changes were validated to ensure the conditions specified in the change still held, and the commit record was written to the log. Then the changes were applied to the main storage database, and the database unlocked. Note that the log was not forced at this time. Access and changes made by following transactions did not violate the rule of atomicity, because the results of a transaction were not externalized until the commit record was written to the physical log. Because the log was a sequential stream, operations were always serialized. This second aspect was called *Fast Commit* [1]. The fast commit and group commit techniques combined to enhance Fast Path's performance by eliminating a major bottleneck in transaction processing.

26.3.3   Checkpoints

Main storage databases were synchronized with the normal IMS checkpoint by keeping two copies of the database in sequential files. A fuzzy dump was written to alternate files with each checkpoint The latest completed dump was used at restart, and redo was applied from the corresponding checkpoint to the end of log.

26.3.4   Relationship to Recovery and Restart

The IMS Fast Path feature was designed to avoid many of the recovery and reorganization bottlenecks in standard IMS. The feature implemented vertical partitioning in its data-entry databases, so that a single failure (or batch operation like recovery) would not make the whole database unavailable.

In addition, each partition of the database was allowed to be defined as multiple-copy, with up to seven copies written. If one copy became unavailable, it was moved off-line, and processing continued with the remaining copies. When the disk was repaired, or another disk was allocated, the copy was refreshed from an up-to-date copy. A streaming read/write was done in sections. While a section was being streamed, that section was effectively locked from current execution. When the section was competed, the new copy became part of the write set for changes through the end of that section, and the section was released for processing. When the copy included the last section, it was marked as available for reading as well.

Note that this process could be done in anticipation of failure. If a disk was nearing the time at which it required preventive maintenence, it could be taken off-line and replaced by a fresh disk without bringing down the partition.

The IMS Fast Path feature was the impetus for other availability features, including the IMS/XRF (eXtended Reliability Feature). By using two processors connected to the same disk and terminal controllers, with one processor acting as a backup for the other, restart recovery times for very large systems are on the order of seconds. Combined with database multiplexing, this feature provides the high availability required by on-line banking.

26.4   ORACLE

The Oracle relational database management system is a high-end DBMS. Oracle is designed for *open systems*, which includes both high-end and much smaller systems. The database server is a multiple process server, with parallel, large-cluster environments in mind. The system is expected to scale from small, single processor systems to massively parallel systems consisting of hundreds of processors. (This is deliberately vague, because Oracle runs very well on large SMP systems connected together to form large clusters.)

The Oracle RDBMS supports data warehouses as well as OLTP environments. In the parallel-server configuration, the failure of an instance (node) is detected and recovered without bringing down the database. Remote stand-by systems are supported to protect against data loss in disaster situations.

The Oracle Corporation web page (http://www.oracle.com:81/corporate/html/who.html) describes the history of the company, founded 20 years ago, as a database and information management company.

The architecture of the Oracle database avoids locking for read operations. This is accomplished by saving undo in the database, and using that to create a consistent view of changed data as of a point in time. When a block is accessed that has changes beyond the reader's *point in time*, the undo information is used to roll back a copy so the reader sees a consistent view.

Because blocks are shared across all instances of the DBMS, a global system change number (SCN) is maintained to localize changes of each instance to any given database block. A block that is accessed in multiple instances is logically moved from the cache of one instance to that of another by writing the block if necessary, purging it from the holding instance's cache, and reading the block from disk to the cache of the new instance. The SCN is managed such that any changes to the block in the receiving instance will have a higher SCN than that of the releasing instance.

26.4.1 Logging and Its Interaction with the System.

Each instance of the Oracle RDBMS has its own log stream, which may consist of up to four copies of each log. The copies are software-managed copies, and each may be on RAID devices, providing a further level of redundancy. The log is written in groups of sectors with each sector being a verifiable block. All copies of each group of sectors are written in parallel. During recovery, the log is read, and a read error causes an automatic switch to the next readable copy. A read error may be signaled on detection of a logically corrupt block or as part of the end-of-log detection.

Redo information written to the log is grouped into records, which are the atomic units of log data. Each record consists of one or more *change vectors* that make up a consistent, undoable modification to the database. The change vectors may (usually do) refer to different database blocks, which must be changed together for logical consistency. The most common configuration of a log record consists of a change vector describing a forward change and a change vector describing the undo change, both of which must be applied to the database. Note that both change vectors are processed the same during forward recovery. Undo for transaction rollback, and for creating consistent versions of read-only data, is maintained as part of the database. The rollback of data for uncompleted transactions is performed following the redo recovery.

On-line logs are required for recovery from instance failure. The on-line logs are switched as they are filled. The candidate log file is checked to ensure that it is overwritten, before it is selected. A log file may be overwritten if it is not required for an instance recovery, and if it has been archived if archiving for media recovery is being done.

26.4.2 Commit Behavior

Commit consists of writing the transaction commit record to the database, and to the log. The commit is considered complete when the record is known to be on the log. The log write is strongly suggested by the commit process, after which the process waits for the log write to complete. This allows multiple commits to group in a given force of the log. Distributed two-phase commit is supported, with the transaction state maintained in the database. The state of in-doubt transactions is queryable, and a process is allocated to manage the resolution of in-doubt transactions.

26.4.3 Checkpoints

Each instance takes checkpoints at regular intervals. As part of the checkpoint, an attempt is made to synchronize the log with a database write state. This is done by trying to write all blocks dirty at checkpoint 1 time to the database by the next checkpoint's completion. An instance has a checkpoint initiated whenever it switches active log files, and also when either a given volume of log has been written or a specified length of time has passed. If the database has not been synchronized when the next checkpoint starts, the prior checkpint is abandoned, and a new synchronization attempt is initiated. This allows the number of logs required for instance recovery to vary, but does not impact a busy system.

Data files are also checkpointed at specific times. For example, if a file is to be taken off-line, all instances coordinate to write any altered buffers, and the SCN is recorded as the file's checkpoint. When the system is taken down normally, a file checkpoint of all files is done.

26.4.4 Relationship to Recovery and Restart

The log is an important part of recovery from process failure. If a process dies in the act of modifying the database, the cache copy of the blocks that were being changed may be inconsistent. The change was recorded in the log in its entirety before modification of the buffer cache started. Therefore, the process that notes the failure will do a limited forward recovery from the log for the failed transaction. If this recovery is successful, the remainder of the processing can continue as for any transaction abort.

Recovery from instance failure is done in the parallel server configuration by the first live instance to become aware of the failure. Recovery from the failure of all instances is called crash recovery. The first instance to start begins crash recovery when the later database open command is issued. The control file is used to determine the active instances that require recovery before the database can be used for normal processing, and an instance recovery is done for each of them in turn.

Only one instance recovery is done at a time. In the case of a crash recovery, the instance with the highest checkpoint SCN is chosen as the first instance to recover, and the remaining instances are recovered in descending order of their checkpoint SCN. This allows the database checkpoint to be advanced when the last instance is recovered. When all instances have been recovered, the database may be opened for processing.

Instance recovery consists of reading the on-line log(s) for the failed instance, and applying the change vectors in the redo log records. The log is positioned to the point at which the last checkpoint was completed. A check is made with each change vector, to determine whether the change is included in the disk copy of the block. This is done by comparing a system change number (and sequence number) in the block to that associated with the change. If the change did not make it to disk, it is applied. This continues until the end of the log is reached.

The recovery done so far is automatic. Process and instance recoveries require no outside intervention. Crash recovery requires a command to start and open the database, but no further intervention, as the current log files are known for all instances. Media recovery can require external intervention, such as locating and supplying files that may not be on-line.

Recovery from media failures is done with a file restore from full and incremental backups followed by the merge of all logs (archived and on-line) that have modified the file (or files) since the backup occurred. The set of files is locked and the appropriate backups are restored. The log files are merged by SCN and all changes are applied from the selected set of files to be recovered.

26.5   CONCLUSIONS

IBM's Information Management System is a high-end database and transaction processing system. It supports terminal networks of tens of thousands of terminals, processing thousands of transactions per second. Recovery and restart have been the watchword of IMS since its first release. In 1969, it was enough to be able to recover a database and to restart transaction processing without gaining or losing messages. Today, IMS supports continuous operation in the face of failures. It is well into its support of continuous operation across all events, including system redefinition. The use of two-phase commit allows participation in distributed transactions on open systems. Checkpoints are generally nondisruptive from the standpoint of performance impact. Restart of a failed system, or recovery of a damaged database, is not only close to a completely automated process, it can be transparent to the users of the system.

The IMS Fast Path Feature started as the high-volume OLTP (on-line transaction processing) feature. It also was the feature that pioneered many high-availability aspects later generalized into the remainder of IMS. Customers still look to IMS and the IMS Fast Path Feature for extremely high-end transaction processing. The major trade-offs are the proprietary nature of the system, platform on which it runs, and the difficulty of generalized access.

Oracle is an open relational database management system. It is designed for a client-server operation in a wide range of environments, including massively parallel processing. It excels in data warehousing applications as well as OLTP. Oracle parallel-server configurations provide automatic recovery of node failures for availability. Oracle provides a wide range of recovery functionality on all of its supported platforms.

Each of the systems serve high-end customers. The specific problems they address, and the environments for which the answers were developed, have led to different internal solutions. From an external view, the systems supply similar functionality in the realm of logging and recovery. As soon as the function and performance questions are answered in a satisfactory manner, the reliability and availability of the systems become the differentiating factor. As each new version or release is presented, more emphasis is placed on reliability and availability. Logging and recovery will advance in the future as it has in the past.

References

[1] Gawlick, D., and D. Kinkade. "Varieties of Concurrency Control in IMS/VS Fast Path" *IEEE Database Engineering.*, 8(2) (1985).

[2] Gray, Jim, Andreas Reuter. *Transaction Processing: Concepts and Techniques*, San Matéo, CA: Morgan Kaufmann, 1993.

Chapter 27

The Recovery Manager of the System R Database Manager

Jim Gray, Paul McJones, Mike Blasgen, Bruce Lindsey, Raymond Lorie, Tom Price, Franco Putzolu, and Irvin Traiger

Abstract

The recovery subsystem of an experimental data management system is described and evaluated. The transaction concept allows application programs to commit, abort, or partially undo their effects. The *do-undo-redo* protocol allows new recoverable types and operations to be added to the recovery system. Application programs can record data in the transaction log to facilitate application-specific recovery. Transaction undo and redo are based on records kept in a transaction log. The checkpoint mechanism is based on differential files (shadows). The recovery log is recorded on disk rather than tape.

27.1 INTRODUCTION

27.1.1 Application Interface to System R

Making computers easier to use is the goal of most software. Database management systems, in particular, provide a programming interface to ease the task of writing electronic bookkeeping programs. The recovery manager of such a system in turn eases the task of writing fault-tolerant application programs.

System R [1] is a database system that supports the relational model of data. The SQL language [4] provides operators that manipulate the database. Typically, a user writes a PL/I or COBOL program that has imbedded SQL statements. A collection of such statements is required to make a consistent transformation of the

```
FUNDS_TRANSFER: PROCEDURE;
  BEGIN_TRANSACTION;
      ON ERROR DO; {in case of error}
          RESTORE-TRANSACTION; {undo all work}
          GET INPUT MESSAGE; {require input}
          PUT MESSAGE ('TRANSFER FAILED'); {report failure}
          GO TO COMMIT;
      END;
      GET INPUT MESSAGE; {get and parse input}
      EXTRACT ACCOUNT-DEBIT, ACCOUNT-CREDIT, AMOUNT FROM MESSAGE;
      UPDATEACCOUNTS{dodebit}
          SETBALANCE = BALANCE - AMOUNTWHEREACCOUNTS.NUMBER =
ACCOUNT - DEBIT;
      UPDATE ACCOUNTS {do credit}
          SET BALANCE = BALANCE + AMOUNT WHERE ACCOUNTS. NUMBER =
ACCOUNT-CREDIT;
      INSERTINTOHISTORY < DATE, MESSAGE >; {keepaudittrail}
      PUTMESSAGE('TRANSFERDONE'); {reportsuccess}
      COMMIT : {commitupdates}
  COMMIT-TRANSACTION
  END; {end program}
```

Figure 27.1. A simple Pl/I-SQL program that transfers funds from one account to another.

database. To transfer funds from one account to another, for example, requires two SQL statements: one to debit the first account and one to credit the second account. In addition, the transaction probably records the transfer in a history file for later reporting and for auditing purposes. Figure 27.1 gives an example of such a program written in pseudo-PL/l. The program effects a consistent transformation of the books of a hypothetical bank. Its actions are either to

- discover an error

- accept the input message

- produce a failure message

or to

- discover no errors

- accept the input message

- debit the source account by AMOUNT, credit the destination account by AMOUNT

- record the transaction in a history file

- produce a success message

The programmer who writes such a program ensures its correctness by ensuring that it performs the desired transformation on both the database state and the outside world (via messages). The programmer and the user both want the execution to be

- *atomic* : either all actions are performed (the transaction has an effect) or the results of all actions are undone (the transaction has no effect)

- *durable* : once the transaction completes, its effects cannot be lost due to computer failure

- *consistent* : the transaction occurs as though it had executed on a system that sequentially executes only one transaction at a time

In order to state this intention, the *SQL* programmer brackets the transformations with the SQL statements, *BEGIN_TRANSACTION* to signal the beginning of the transaction and *COMMIT_TRANSACTION* to signal its completion. If the programmer wants to return to the beginning of the transaction, the command *RESTORE_TRANSACTION* will undo all actions since the issuance of the *BEGIN_TRANSACTION* command (see Figure 27.1).

The System R recovery manager supports these commands and guarantees an atomic, durable execution.

System R generally runs several transactions concurrently. The concurrency control mechanism of System R hides such concurrency from the programmer by a locking technique [6, 9, 15] and gives the appearance of a consistent system.

27.1.2   Structure of System R

System R consists of an external layer called the research data system (RDS), and a completely internal layer called the research storage system (RSS) (see Figure 27.2).

The external layer provides a relational data model, and operators thereon. It also provides catalog management, a data dictionary, authorization, and alternate views of data. The RDS is manipulated using the SQL language [4]. The SQL compiler maps SQL statements into sequences of RSS calls.

The RSS is a nonsymbolic record-at-a-time access method. It supports the notions of *file, record type, record instance, field within record, index* (B-tree associative and sequential access path), *parent-child set* (an access path supporting the operations PARENT, FIRST_CHILD, NEXT_SIBLING, PREVIOUS_SIBLING with direct pointers), and *cursor* (which navigates over access paths to locate records). Unfortunately, these objects have the nonstandard names "segment," "relation," "tuple," "field," "image," "link," and "scan" in the System R documentation. The former, more standard, names are used here. RSS provides actions to create instances of these objects and to retrieve, modify, and delete them.

The RSS support of data is substantially more sophisticated than that normally found in an access method; it supports variable-length fields, indices on multiple

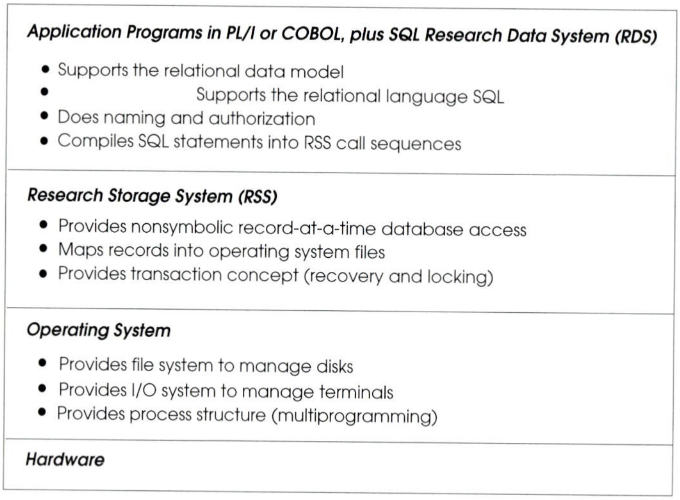

Application Programs in PL/I or COBOL, plus SQL Research Data System (RDS)

- Supports the relational data model
- Supports the relational language SQL
- Does naming and authorization
- Compiles SQL statements into RSS call sequences

Research Storage System (RSS)

- Provides nonsymbolic record-at-a-time database access
- Maps records into operating system files
- Provides transaction concept (recovery and locking)

Operating System

- Provides file system to manage disks
- Provides I/O system to manage terminals
- Provides process structure (multiprogramming)

Hardware

Figure 27.2. System R consists of two layers above the operating system. The RSS provides the transaction concept, recovery notions, and a record-at-a-time data access method. The RDS accepts application PL/I COBOL programs containing SQL statements. It translates them into COBOL or PL/I programs plus subroutines which represent the compilation of the SQL statements into RSS calls.

fields, multiple record types per file, interfile and intrafile sets, physical clustering of records by attribute, and a catalog describing the data, which is kept as a file that may be manipulated like any other data.

Another major contribution of the RSS is its support of the notion of transaction, a unit of recovery consisting of an application-specified sequence of RSS actions. An application declares the start of a transaction by issuing a BEGIN action. Thereafter all, RSS actions by that application are within the scope of that transaction until the application issues a COMMIT or an ABORT action. The RSS assumes all responsibility for running concurrent transactions and for assuring that each transaction sees a consistent view of the database. The RSS is also responsible for recovering the data to their most recent consistent state in the event of transaction, action, system, or media failure or a user request to cancel the transaction.

A final component of System R is the operating system. System R runs under the VM/370 [7] and the MVS operating system on IBM S/370 processors. The System R recovery manager is also part of the SQL/DS product running on DOS/CICS. The operating system provides processes, a simple file system, and terminal management.

System R allocates an operating system process for each user to run both the user's application program and the System R database manager. Application programs are written in a conventional programming language (e.g., COBOL or PL/1) augmented with the SQL language. A SQL preprocessor maps the SQL statements to sequences of RSS calls. Typically, a single application program or group of programs (main and subroutines) constitute a transaction. In this chapter we ignore the RDS and assume that application programs, like those produced by the SQL compiler, consist of conventional programs that invoke sequences of RSS operations.

27.1.3 Model of Failures

The recovery manager eases the task of writing fault-tolerant programs. It does so by the careful use of redundancy. Choosing appropriate redundancy requires a quantitative model of system failures.

In our experience, about 97Of the remainder, almost all fail because of incorrect user input or because of user cancellation. Occasionally (much less than 1transactions are aborted by the system as a result of some overload such as deadlock. In a typical system running one transaction per second, a transaction undo occurs about twice a minute. Because of its frequency, a transaction undo must run about as fast as forward processing of transactions.

Every few days, the system restarts (following a crash). Almost all crashes are due to hardware or operating system failures, although System R also initiates crash and restart whenever it detects damage to its data structure. The state of primary memory is lost after a crash. We assume that the state of the disks (secondary and tertiary storage) is preserved across crashes, so at restart, the most recently committed state is reconstructed from the surviving disk state by referencing a log of recent activity to restore the work of committed and aborted transactions. This process completes within a matter of seconds or minutes.

Occasionally, the integrity of the disk state will be lost at restart. This may be caused by hardware failure (disk head crash or disk dropped on the floor) or by software failure (bad data written on a disk page by System R or other program). Such events are called media failures and initiate a reconstruction of the current state from an archive version (old and undamaged version of the system state) plus a log of activity since that time. This procedure is invoked once or twice a year and is expected to complete within an hour.

Table 27.1. Frequency and Recovery Time of Failures

Recovery manager trade-offs		
Fault	Frequency	Recovery time
Transaction abort System restart Media failure	Several per minute Several per month Several per year	Milliseconds Seconds Minutes

If all these recovery procedures fail, the user will have lost data because of an unrecoverable failure. We have very limited statistics on unrecoverable failures. The current release of System R has experienced about 25 years of service in a variety of installations, and to our knowledge almost all unrecoverable failures have resulted from operations errors (e.g., failure to make archive dumps) or from bugs in the operating system utility for dumping and restoring disks. The fact that the archive mechanism is only a minor source of unrecoverable failure probably indicates that it is appropriately designed. Table 27.1 summarizes this discussion.

If the archive mechanism fails once every hundred years of operation, and if there are 10,000 installations of System R, then it will fail someone once a month. From this perspective, it might be underdesigned.

We assume that System R, the operating system, the microcode, and the hardware all have bugs in them. However, each of these systems does quite a bit of checking of its data structures (defensive programming). We postulate that these errors are detected and that the system crashes before the data are seriously corrupted. If this assumption is incorrect, then the situation is treated as a media failure. This attitude assumes that the archive and log mechanism are very reliable and have failure modes independent of the other parts of the system.

Some commercial systems are much more demanding. They run hundreds of transactions per second, and because they have hundreds of disks, they see disk failures hundreds of times as frequently as typical users of System R (once a week rather than once a year). They also cannot tolerate downtimes exceeding a few minutes. Although the concepts presented in this chapter are applicable to such systems, much more redundancy is needed to meet such demands (e.g., duplexed processors and disks, and utilities that can recover small parts of the database without having to recover it all every time). The recovery manager presented here is a textbook one, whose basic facilities are only a subset of those provided by more sophisticated systems.

The transaction model is an unrealizable ideal. At best, careful use of redundancy minimizes the probability of unrecoverable failures and consequent loss of committed updates. Redundant copies are designed to have independent failure modes, making it unlikely that all records will be lost at once. However, Murphy's law ensures that all recovery techniques will sometimes fail. As seen in what follows, however, System R can tolerate any single failure and can often tolerate multiple failures.

27.2   DESCRIPTION OF SYSTEM R RECOVERY MANAGER

27.2.1   What Is a Transaction?

The RSS provides actions on the objects it implements. These actions include operations to create, destroy, manipulate, retrieve, and modify RSS objects (files, record types, record instances, indices, sets, and cursors). Each RSS action is atomic – it either happens or has no effect – and consistent–if any two actions relate to the same object, they appear to execute in some serial order. These two qualities are ensured by (1) undoing the partial effects of any actions the fail and (2) locking necessary RSS resures for the duration of the action.

RSS actions are rather primitive. In general, functions like *hire an employee* or *make a deposit in an account* require several actions. The user, in mapping abstractions like *employee* or *account* into such a system, must combine several actions into an atomic transaction. The classic example of an atomic transaction is a funds transfer that debits one account, credits another, writes an activity record, and does some terminal input or output. The user of such a transaction wants it to be an all-or-nothing affair, in that he does not want only some of the actions to have occurred. If the transaction is correctly implemented, it looks and acts atomic.

In a multiuser environment, transactions take on the additional attribute that any two transactions concurrently operating on common objects appear to run serially (i.e., as though there were no concurrency). This property is called consistency and is handled by the RSS lock subsystem [6, 8, 9, 15].

```
BEGIN        BEGIN        BEGIN
READ         READ         READ
WRITE        WRITE        WRITE
READ         READ         READ
  .            .            .
  .            .            .
  .            .            .
WRITE        ABORT      ⟸ SYSTEM ABORTS TRANSACTIONS
COMMIT
```

Figure 27.3. The three possible destinies of a transaction: commits, aborts, or is aborted.

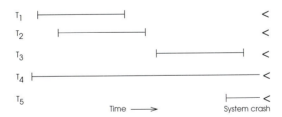

Figure 27.4. Five transactions. The effects of actions by transaction T_1, T_2, and T_3 will survive a system crash because they have committed. This is called durability. But the effects of transactions T_4 and T_5 will be undone because they were in progress at the time of the crash (had not yet committed).

The application declares a sequence of actions to be a transaction by beginning the sequence with a BEGIN action and ending it with a COMMIT action. All intervening actions by that application (be it one or several processes) are considered to be parts of a single recovery unit. If the application gets into trouble, it may issue the ABORT action that undoes all actions in the transaction. Further, the system may unilaterally abort in-progress transactions in case of an authorization violation, resource limit, deadlock, system shutdown, or crash. Figure 27.3 shows the three possible outcomes–commit, abort, or system abortion–of a transaction, and Figure 27.4 shows the outcomes of five sample transactions in the event of a system crash.

If a transaction either aborts or is aborted, the system must undo all actions of that transaction. Once a transaction commits, however, its updates and messages to the external world must persist–its effects must be durable. The system will *remember* the results of the transaction despite any subsequent malfunction. Once the system commits to "Open the cash drawer" or "retract the reactor rods," it will honor that commitment. The only way to undo the effect of a committed transaction is to run a new transaction that compensates for these effects.

27.2.2 Transaction Save Points

The RSS defines the additional notion of a transaction save point. A save point is a firewall that allows transaction undo to stop short of undoing the entire transaction. Should a transaction get into trouble (e.g., deadlock or authority violation), it may be sufficient to back up only as far as an intermediate save point. Each save point is numbered, with the beginning of a transaction being save point 1. The application program declares a save point by issuing a SAVE action specifying a save point record to be entered in the log. This record may be retrieved if and when the transaction returns to the corresponding save point.

```
      Ticket Agent      Application program
    input message  ⇒    BEGIN
                        SAVE (state)
                        ⟨actions to reserve first hop⟩
                        SAVE (state)
                   ⇐    new screen
        next hop   ⇒    SAVE (hop)
                        ⟨actions to reserve next hop⟩
                        ⋮
        last hop   ⇒    SAVE (hop)
                        ⟨actions to reserve last hop⟩
    printed ticket ⇐    COMMIT ⟨reservation⟩
```

Figure 27.5. A multihop airlines reservation transaction using save points. If the application program or ticket agent detects an error, the transaction can undo to a previous save point and continue forward from there.

Figure 27.5 illustrates the use of save points. It describes a conversational transaction making a multihop airline reservation involving several ticket agent interactions, one per hop. The application program establishes a save point before and after each interaction, with the save point data, including the current state of the program variables and the ticket agent screen. If the ticket agent makes an error or if a flight is unavailable, the agent or program can back up to the most recent mutually acceptable save point, thereby minimizing the agent's retyping. Once the entire ticket is composed, the transaction commits the database changes and prints the ticket. The Program can request a return to save point N by issuing the UNDO N action. Of course, all the save points may be washed away by a system restart or serious deadlock, but most error situations can be resolved with a minimal loss of the ticket agent's work.

The System R save point facility is in contrast to most systems in which each message causes the updates of the transaction to be committed. In such systems, either the agent must manually delete previous steps of the transaction when something goes wrong or the application program must implement recovery by keeping an undo log or deferring all updates until the last step. Such application program recovery schemes complicate the program and may work incorrectly because locks are not held between steps (e.g., the lost update problem described in [8]).

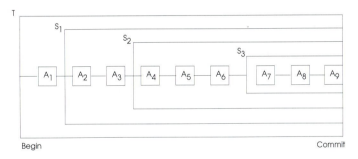

Figure 27.6. An example of nested transactions using save points. The transaction T consists of RSS actions A_1, ..., A_9. Actions A_2, A_4, and A_7 are defined as save points S_1, S_2 and S_3, which become nested subtransactions of T. There are probably RDS actions which consists of several RSS actions. Each RSS action is a minitransaction on the RSS state. If the RSS action gets into trouble, it backs up to the beginning of the action and retries. If that fails, undo propagates to the nearest save point that can resolve the issue. This is the spheres of control notation of [5].

Save points are used by the RDS to implement certain complex operations. Some RDS operations require many RSS operations, and the RDS guarantees that each SQL statement is atomic. The RDS supports atomic SQL statements by beginning each such complex operation with a save point and backing up to this save point if the RSS or RDS fails at some point during the operation. Figure 27.6 illustrates the use of save points.

27.2.3   Summary

To summarize, the RSS recovery manager provides the following actions:

- BEGIN designates the beginning of a transaction.

- SAVE designates a firewall within the transaction. If an incomplete transaction is backed up, undo may stop at such a point rather than undoing the entire transaction.

- READ_SAVE returns the data saved in the log by the application at a designated save point.

- UNDO undoes the effects of a transaction to an earlier save point.

- ABORT undoes all effects of a transaction (equivalent to UNDO 0).

- COMMIT signals successful completion of transaction and causes updates to be committed.

Using these primitives, the RDS and application programs using the RDS can construct groups of actions that are atomic and durable.

This model of recovery is a subset of the recovery model formulated by Davies and Bjork [2, 5]. Unlike their model, System R transactions have no parallelism within a transaction (i.e., if multiple nodes of a network are needed to execute a single transaction, only one node executes at a time). Further, System R allows only a limited form of transaction nesting via the use of save points (each save point may be viewed as the start of an internal transaction). These limitations stem from our inability to find an acceptable implementation for the more general model.

27.3   IMPLEMENTATION OF SYSTEM R RECOVERY

27.3.1   Files, Versions, and Shadows

All persistent System R data are stored in files. A user may define any number of files. A file, for our purposes, is a paged linear space of up to 68 billion (2^{36}) bytes, which has been dynamically allocated on disk in units of 4096-byte pages. A buffer manager maps all the files into a virtual memory buffer pool shared by all System R users. The buffer manager uses a Least Recently Used (LRU) algorithm to regulate occupancy of pages in the pool. The buffer pool is volatile and presumed not to survive system restart.

Each file carries a particular recovery protocol and corresponding overhead of recovery. Files are dichotomized as shadowed and nonshadowed. Nonshadowed files have no automatic recovery. The user is responsible for making and storing redundant copies of these files. System R simply updates nonshadowed file pages in the buffer pool. Changes to nonshadowed files are recorded on disk when the

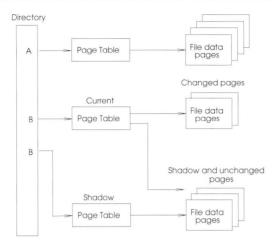

Figure 27.7. The directory structure for nonshadowed and shadowed files. File A is not shadowed. File B is shadowed and has two directory entries, a current version and a shadow version.

pages are removed from the buffer pool (by the LRU algorithm) and when the file is saved or closed.

By contrast, the RSS maintains two on-line versions of shadowed files, a shadow version and a current version. RSS actions affect only the current version of a file and never alter the shadow version (except for file save and restore commands). The current version of a file can be SAVED as the shadow version, thereby making the recent updates to the file permanent; the current version can also be RESTORED to the shadow version, thereby "undoing" all recent updates to the file (see Figure 27.7). If data are spread across several files, it is desirable to save or restore all the files "at once." Therefore, file save or restore can apply to sets of shadowed files.

Although the current version of a file does not survive restart, because recent updates to the file may still reside in the buffer pool, the shadow version of a file does. Hence, at RSS restart (i.e., after a crash or shutdown) all nonshadowed files have their values as of the system crash (modulo updates to central memory that were not written to disk) and all shadowed files are reset to their shadow versions. As discussed in what follows, starting from this shadow state, the log is used to remove the effects of aborted transactions and to restore the effects of committed transactions.

The current and shadow versions of a file are implemented in a particularly efficient manner. When a shadow page is updated in the buffer pool for the first time, a new disk page frame is assigned to it. Thereafter, when that page is written from the buffer pool or read into the buffer pool, the new frame is used (the shadow is never updated). Saving a file consists of writing to disk all altered pages of the file currently in the buffer pool and then writing to disk the new page table, and freeing superseded shadow pages. Restoring a file is achieved by discarding pages of that file in the buffer pool, freeing all the new disk pages of that file, and returning to the (old) shadow page table. Lorie [13] describes the implementation in greater detail.

27.3.2   Logs and the DO, UNDO, and REDO Protocol

The shadow-version/current-version dichotomy has strong ties to the old-master/new-master dichotomy common to most batch EDP systems in which, if a run fails, the old master is used for a successive attempt; if the run succeeds, the new master becomes the old master. Unfortunately, this technique does not seem to generalize to concurrent transactions on a shared file. If several transactions concurrently alter a file, file save or restore is inappropriate because it commits or aborts the updates of all transactions to the file. It is desirable to be able to commit or undo updates on a per transaction basis. Such a facility is required to support the COMMIT, ABORT, and UNDO actions, as well as to handle such problems as deadlock, system overload, and unexpected user disconnect. Further, as shown in Figure 27.4, selective transaction backup and commit are required for system restart.

Figure 27.8. A transaction log is the sequence of changes made by this transaction.

We were unable to architect a transaction mechanism based solely on shadows that supported multiple users and save points. Instead, the shadow mechanism is combined with an incremental log of all the actions a transaction performs. This log is used for transaction UNDO and REDO on shared files and is used in combination with shadows for system checkpoint and restart. Each RSS update action writes a log record giving the old and new value of the updated object. As Figure 27.8 shows, these records are aggregated by transaction and collected in a common system log file (which is optionally duplexed).

Table 27.2. Recovery Attributes of Files

	No shadow	Shadow
No log	Contents unpredictable after crash	Contents equal shadow after crash
Log	Not supported	All updates logged transaction consistent after a crash

When a shadowed file is defined by a user, it is designated as logged or not logged. The RSS controls the saving and restoration of logged files and maintains a log of all updates to logged files. Users control the saving and restoration of non-logged shadowed files. Nonshadowed files have none of the virtues or corresponding overhead of recovery (see Table 27.2).

In retrospect, we regret not supporting the LOG and NO SHADOW options. As explained in Section 27.4.8, the log makes shadows redundant, and the shadow mechanism is quite expensive for large files.

Each time a transaction modifies a logged file, a new record is appended to the log. Read actions need not generate log records, but update actions on logged files must enter enough information in the log so that, given the log record at a later time, the action can be completely undone or redone. As seen in what follows, most log writes do not require I/O and can be buffered in central memory.

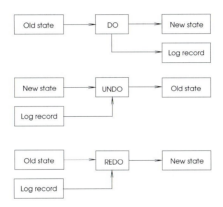

Figure 27.9. Three aspects of an action: Action DO generates a new state and a log record. Action UNDO generates an old state from a new state and a log record. Action REDO generates a new state from an old state and a log record.

Every RSS operation on a logged file must be implemented as a set of operations (see Figure 27.9):

- a DO operation, which does the action and also writes a log record sufficient to undo and redo the action

- an UNDO operation, which undoes the action given the log record written by the DO action

- a REDO operation, which redoes the action given the log record written by the DO action

- optionally, a DISPLAY operation, which translates the log record into a human-readable format

To give an example of an action and the log record it must write, consider the record update action. This action must record the following in the log:

- file name

- record identifier

- old record value

- new record value

The log subsystem augments this with the additional fields:

- transaction identifier

- action identifier

- timestamp

- length of log record

- pointer to previous log record of this transaction

The UNDO operation restores the record to its old value and appropriately updates associated structures such as indices and storage management information. The REDO operation restores the record (and its associated structures) to its new value. The display operation returns a text string giving a symbolic display of the log record.

Once a log record is recorded, it cannot be updated. However the log manager provides a facility to open read cursors on the log that will traverse the system log or traverse the log of a particular transaction in either direction.

27.3.3   Commit Processing

The essential property of a transaction is that it ultimately commits, aborts, or is aborted, and that once it commits, its updates persist, and once it aborts or is aborted, its updates are suppressed. Achieving this property is nontrivial. In order to ensure that a transaction's effects will survive restarts and media failures, the system must be able to redo committed transactions. System R ensures that uncommitted transactions can be undone and that committed transactions can be redone as follows:

1. The transaction log is written to disk before the shadow database is replaced by the current database state.

2. The transaction commit action writes a commit log record in the log buffer and then forces all the transaction's log records to disk (with the commit record being the last such record).

A transaction commits at the instant its commit record appears on disk. If the system crashes prior to that instant, the transaction will be aborted. Because the log is written before the database (item 1), System R can always undo any uncommitted updates that have migrated to disk. On the other hand, if the system crashes subsequent to the writing of the commit record to disk, then the transaction will be redone, from the shadow state, using the log records that were forced to disk by the commit. In the terminology of Gray [9], item 1 is the *write-ahead log protocol.*

27.3.4 Transaction UNDO

The logic of action UNDO is very simple. It reads a log record, looks at the name of the action identifier in the log record, and invokes the undo operation of that action, passing it the log record. Recovery is thereby table-driven. This table-driven design has allowed the addition of new recoverable objects and actions to the RSS without any impact on recovery management.

The effect of any uncommitted transaction can be undone by reading the log of that transaction backward, undoing each action in turn. Clearly, this process can be stopped halfway, returning the transaction to an intermediate transaction save point. Transaction save points allow the transaction to backtrack.

From this discussion it follows that a transaction's log is a push down stack; writing a new log record pushes it onto the stack, and undoing a record pops it off the stack (see Figure 27.8). To minimize log buffer space and log I/O, all transaction logs are merged into one system log, which is then mapped into a log file. But the log records of a particular transaction are chained together as a linked list anchored off of the transaction descriptor. Notice that UNDO requires that the log be directly addressable while the transaction is uncommitted. For this reason, at least one version of the log must be on disk (or some other direct-access device). A tape-based log would be inconvenient for in-progress transaction undo.

27.3.5 Transaction Save Points

A transaction save point records enough information to restore the transaction's view of the RSS as of the save point. The user may record up to 64 kilobytes of application data in the log at each save point.

One can easily restore a transaction to its beginning by undoing all its updates and then releasing all its locks and dropping all its cursors (since no cursors or locks are held at the beginning of the transaction and since a list of cursors and locks is maintained on a per transaction basis). To restore to a save point, the recovery manager must know the name and state of each active cursor and the name of each lock held at the save point. For performance reasons, changes to cursors and locks are not recorded in the log. Otherwise, every read action would have to write a log record. Instead, the state of locks and cursors is only recorded at save points. Assuming that all locks are held to the end of the transaction, transaction backup can reset cursors without having to reacquire any locks. Further, because these locks are kept in a list and are not released, one can remember them all by remembering the lock at the top of the list. At backup to a save point, all subsequent locks are released.

27.3.6   System Configuration, Startup, and Shutdown

A System R database is created by installing a "starter system" and then using System R commands to define and load new files and to define transactions that manipulate these files. Certain operations (e.g., turning dual logging on and off) require a system shutdown and restart, but most operations can be performed while the system is operational. In particular, we worked quite hard to avoid functions like SYSGEN and cold start.

A monitor process (a task or virtual machine) is responsible for system startup, shutdown, and checkpoints and for servicing system operator commands. If several instances of System R (several different databases) are running on the same machine, each instance will have a monitor. System R users join a particular instance of System R, run transactions in the users' process, and then leave the system. In theory, 254 users may be joined to a system at one time.

27.3.7   System Checkpoint

System checkpoints limit the amount of work (undo and redo) necessary at restart. A checkpoint records information on disk that helps locate the end of the log at restart and correlates the database state with the log state. A checkpoint saves all logged shadow files so that no work prior to the checkpoint will have to be redone at restart. If checkpoints are taken frequently, then restart is fast, but the checkpoint overhead is high. Balancing the cost of checkpoints against the cost of restart gives an optimum checkpoint interval. Because this optimum depends critically on the cost of a checkpoint, one wants a cheap checkpoint facility.

The simplest form of checkpoint is to record a transaction-consistent state by quiescing the system, deferring all new transactions until all in-progress transactions complete, and then recording a logically consistent snapshot. However, quiescing the system causes long interruptions in system availability and hence argues for infrequent checkpoints. This, in turn, increases the amount of work that is lost at restart and must be redone. System quiesce, consequently, is not a cheap way to obtain a transaction-consistent state.

The RSS uses a lower level of consistency, augmented by a transaction log, to produce a transaction-consistent state. The RSS implements checkpoints that are snapshots of the system at a time when no RSS actions are in progress (an action-consistent state). Since RSS actions are short (less than 10,000 instructions), system availability is not adversely affected by frequent checkpoints. (Long RSS actions, e.g., sort or search, occasionally "come up for air" in an action-consistent state to allow checkpoints to occur.)

Checkpoints are taken after a specified amount of log activity or at system operator request. At checkpoint, a checkpoint record is written in the log. The checkpoint record contains a list of all transactions in progress and pointers to their

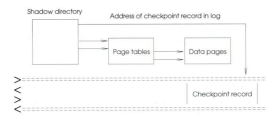

Figure 27.10. The directory root points at the most recent checkpoint record in the log.

most recent log records. After the log records are on disk, all logged files are saved (current state replaces shadows), which involves flushing the database buffer pool and the shadow-file directories to secondary storage. As a last step, the log address of the checkpoint record is written as part of the directory record in the shadow version of the state [13]. The directory root is duplexed on disk, enabling the checkpoint process to tolerate failures while writing the directory root. At restart, the system will be able to locate the corresponding checkpoint record by examining the most recent directory root (see Figure 27.10).

27.3.8 System Restart

Given a checkpoint of the state at time T along with a log of all changes to the state made by transactions prior to time $T + E$, a transaction-consistent version of the state can be constructed by undoing all updates, logged prior to time T, of transactions that were uncommitted or aborted by time $T + E$. and then redoing the updates, logged between time T and time $T + E$, of committed transactions.

At system restart, the system R code is loaded and the file manager restores any shadowed files to their shadow versions. If a shadowed file was not saved at shutdown, the then current version will be replaced by its shadow. In particular, all logged files will be reset to their state as of the most recent system checkpoint.

The recovery manager is then given control and it examines the most recent checkpoint record (which, as Figure 27.10 shows, is pointed at by the current directory). If there was no work in progress at the time of the checkpoint and if the checkpoint is the last record in the log, then the system is restarting from a shutdown in a quiesced state. No transactions need be undone or redone, and restart initializes System R and opens up the system for general use.

On the other hand, if work was in progress at the checkpoint, or if there are log records after the checkpoint record, then this is a restart from a crash. Figure 27.11 illustrates the five possible states of transactions at this point:

- T_1 began and ended before the checkpoint

- T_2 began before the checkpoint and ended before the crash

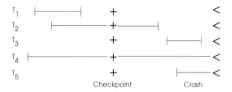

Figure 27.11. Five transaction types with respect to the most recent checkpoint and the crash point.

- T_3 began after the checkpoint and ended before the crash

- T_4 began before the checkpoint but no commit record appears in the log

- T_5 began after the checkpoint and apparently never ended

To honor the commit of T_1, T_2, and T_3 transactions requires their updates to appear in the system state (done). But T_4 and T_5 have not committed and so their updates must not appear in the state (undone).

At restart, the shadowed files are as they were at the most recent checkpoint. Notice that none of the updates of T_5 is reflected in this state, so T_5 is already undone. Notice also that all of the updates of T_1 are in the shadow state, so it need not be redone. T_2 and T_3 must be redone from the checkpoint forward. (The updates of the first half of T_2 are already reflected in the shadow state.) On the other hand, T_4 must be undone from the checkpoint backward. (Here we are skipping over the following anomaly: If, after a checkpoint, T_2 backs up to a save point prior to the checkpoint, then some undo work is required for T_2.)

Restart uses the log as follows. It reads the most recent checkpoint record and assumes that all the transactions active at the time of the checkpoint are of type T_4 (active at checkpoint, not committed). It then reads the log in the forward direction, starting from the checkpoint record. If it encounters a BEGIN record, it notes that this is a transaction of type T_5. If it encounters the COMMIT record of a T_4 transaction, it reclassifies the transaction as type T_2. Similarly, T_5 transactions are reclassified as T_3 transactions if a COMMIT record is found for that transaction. When it reaches the end of the log, the restart manager knows all the T_2, T_3, T_4, and T_5 transactions. T_4 and T_5 type transactions are called "losers" and T_2 and T_3 type transactions are called "winners." Restart reads the log backward from the checkpoint, undoing all actions of losers, and then reads the log forward from the checkpoint, redoing all actions of winners. Once this is done, a new checkpoint is written so that the restart work will not be lost.

Restart must be prepared to tolerate failures during the restart process. This problem is subtle in most systems, but the System R shadow mechanism makes it fairly straightforward. System R restart does not update the log or the shadow version of the database until restart is complete. Taking a system checkpoint signals the end of a successful restart. System checkpoint is atomic, so there are only two cases to consider. Any failure prior to completing the checkpoint will return the restart process to the original shadow state. Any failure after the checkpoint is complete will return the database to the new (restarted) state.

27.3.9 Media Failure

In the event of a system failure that causes a loss of disk storage integrity, it must be possible to continue with a minimum of lost work. Such situations are handled by periodically making a copy of the database state and keeping it in an archive. This copy, plus a log of subsequent activity, can be used to reconstruct the current state. The archive mechanism used by System R periodically dumps a transaction-consistent copy of the database to magnetic tape.

It is important that the archive mechanism have failure modes independent of the failure modes of the on-line storage system. Using duplexed disks protects against a disk head crash, but does not protect against errors in disk programs or fire in the machine room.

In the event of a single media failure, the following occurs:

- If one of the duplexed on-line logs fails, then a new log is allocated and the good version of the duplexed log is copied to the new one.

- If any other file fails, the most recent surviving dump tape is loaded back into the database, and then all committed update actions subsequent to the checkpoint record of the archive state are redone using the log.

Recovery from an archive state appears to the recovery manager as a restart from a very old checkpoint. No special code has been written for archive recovery.

The most vulnerable part of this system is the possible failure of both instances of the on-line log. Assuming the log software has no bugs, we estimate the mean time between such coincident failures at about 1000 years. As mentioned in the Introduction, operational errors are much more frequent, and so make log failure a minor source of unrecoverable errors.

Although performing a checkpoint causes relatively few disk writes and takes only a short time, dumping the entire database is a lengthy operation (10 minutes per 100 megabytes). Maintaining transaction quiesce for the duration of the dump operation is undesirable, or even impossible, depending on the real-time constraints imposed by system users. Lorie [13] describes a scheme based on shadows for making an archive dump while the system is operating. Gray [9] describes a *fuzzy* dump mechanism that allows the database to be dumped while it is in operation (the log is later used to focus the dump on some specified time). IMS and other commercial systems provide facilities for dumping and restoring fragments of files rather than whole databases. We did not implement one of these fancier designs because the simple approach was adequate for our needs.

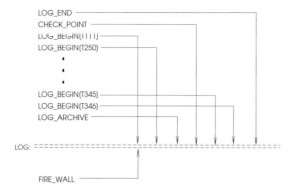

Figure 27.12. Bytes betweeen FIRE_WALL and LOG_END are needed for system restart and hence are kept in the log ring buffer.

27.3.10   Managing the Log

The log is a very long sequence of pages, each with a unique sequence number. Transactions undo and redo need quick access to the log but most of it can be kept off-line or discarded. Figure 27.12 illustrates the bookkeeping of the on-line log. The online log file is used to hold the "useful" parts of the log. It is managed as a ring buffer, with LOG_END pointing just beyond the last useful byte of the log and CHECK_POINT pointing at the most recent checkpoint. Clearly, all records since the checkpoint must be kept on-line in support of transaction redo. Further, transaction undo needs all records of incomplete transactions on-line (LOG_BEGIN(I) for active transaction I). Last, one cannot free the space occupied by a log record in the ring until the database is archived (this point is addressed by LOG_ARCHIVE). So at restart, the system may need records back to the FIRE_WALL, where FIRE_WALL is the minimum of LOG_ARCHIVE, CHECK_POINT, and LOG_BEGIN(I) for each active transaction I. Bytes prior to FIRE_WALL need not reside in the on-line ring buffer. If the on-line ring buffer fills, it is because (1) archiving of the log is required, (2) a checkpoint is required, or (3) a transaction has been running for a very long time (and hence has a very low LOG_BEGIN). The first two problems are solved by periodic archiving and checkpoints. The third problem is solved by aborting very old transactions. For many applications, dual on-line logs of 1 megabyte are adequate, although 10 to 100 megabytes are more typical. Duplexing of the log is a system option that may be changed at each restart. Duplexing is transparent above the log interface; reads (usually) go to one instance of the log, and writes go to both instances. If one instance fails, the other is used at restart (on a page-by-page basis).

27.3.11   Recovery and Locking

Recovery has implications for and places requirements on the lock subsystem. In order to blindly undo the actions of one transaction without erasing subsequent updates by other transactions, it is essential that all transactions lock all updates in the exclusive mode and hold all such locks until the transaction is committed or undone. In fact, System R automatically acquires both share and exclusive locks and holds them all until the end of the transaction. See [8] for a detailed discussion of the various locking options supported by System R. A second issue is that transaction undo cannot tolerate deadlock (we do not want to have to undo undo's). Undo may take advantage of the fact that it only accesses records the transaction locked in the do step; hence, it need not re request these locks. (This is a consequence of holding all exclusive locks until the end of the transaction.) But transaction undo may have to set some locks because other RSS actions are in progress and because RSS actions release some locks at the end of each RSS action (e.g., physical page locks when logical record locking is the actual granularity). To solve this problem, transactions that are performing transaction undo are marked as "golden." Golden transactions are never chosen as deadlock victims; whenever they get into a deadlock with some other transactions, the other transactions are preempted. To assure that this rule does not produce unbreakable deadlock cycles (ones containing only golden transactions), the additional rule is adopted that only one golden transaction can execute at a time (and hence that no deadlock cycle involves more than one golden transaction). A special lock (RSSBACKUP) is requested in exclusive mode by each golden transaction before it begins each undo step. This lock is released at the end of each such undo step. During restart, locking is turned off. Essentially, the entire database is locked during the restart process, which sequentially executes actions in the order they appear in the log (making an undo pass followed by a redo pass).

27.4   EVALUATION

We were apprehensive on several counts when we first designed the System R recovery system. First, we were skeptical of our ability to write RSS actions that could always undo and redo themselves. Second, we were apprehensive about the performance and complexity of such programs. And third, we were concerned that the added complexity might create more crashes than it cured. In retrospect, the recovery system was comparatively easy to write and certainly has contributed to the system's reliability.

27.4.1   Implementation Cost

The RSS was designed in 1974 and 1975 and became operational in 1976. Since then, we have had a lot of experience with it. Writing recoverable actions (ones that can undo and redo themselves) is quite hard. Subjectively, writing a recoverable action is 30requires about 20action. In addition, the recovery system itself (log management, system restart, checkpoint, commit, abort, etc.) contributes about

15However, the RSS is less than half of System R, so these numbers may be divided in half when assessing the overall system implementation cost, leaving the marginal cost of implementing recovery at about 10

27.4.2   Execution Cost

Another component of cost is the instructions added to execution of a transaction to support recovery (frequently called "path length"). Fortunately, most transactions commit and hence make no use of the undo or redo code. In the normal case, the only cost imposed by recovery is the writing of log records. Further, only update operations need write log records. Typically, the cost of keeping a log is less than 5execution cost, associated with recovery, of periodic checkpoints is minimal. Restart is quite fast, typically running ten times faster than the original processing (primarily because updates are infrequent). Hence, if the checkpoint interval is 5 minutes, the system averages 15 seconds to restart. As described in the next section, checkpoint is I/O-bound.

27.4.3   I/O Cost

A third component of recovery cost is I/O added by the recovery system. Each transaction commit adds two I/Os to the cost of the transaction when the duplexed log is forced to disk (as part of the commit action). This cost is reduced to one extra I/O if dual logging is not selected. Log force is suppressed for read-only transactions. Depending on the application, log force may be a significant overhead. In an application in which each transaction is a few (50) RSS actions, it constitutes a 20transaction of Figure 27.1 would have about a 25I/O overhead. In another application in which the database is all resident in central memory, the log accounts for all of the disk I/O. IMS Fast Path solves this problem by logging several transactions in one I/O so that one gets less than one log I/O per transaction. The shadow mechanism when used with large databases often implies extra I/O, both during normal operation and at checkpoint. Lorie's estimates in [13] are correct: A checkpoint requires several seconds of I/O after 5 minutes of work on a 100-megabyte database. This work increases with larger databases and with high transaction rates. It becomes significant at 10 transactions per second or for billion-byte files.

27.4.4   Success Rate

Perhaps the most significant aspect of the System R recovery manager is the confidence it inspires in users. During development of the system, we routinely crashed the system knowing that the recovery system will be able to pick up the pieces. Recovery from the archive is not unheard of, but it is very uncommon. This has created the problem that some users do not take precautions to protect themselves from media failures.

27.4.5   Complexity

It seems to be the case that the recovery system cures many more failures than it introduces. Among other things this means that everybody who coded the RSS understood the do-undo-redo protocol reasonably well and that they were able to write recoverable actions. As the system has evolved, new people have added new recoverable objects and actions to the system. Their ability to understand the interface and to fit into its table-driven structure is a major success of the basic design. The decision to put all responsibility for recovery into the RSS made the RDS much simpler. There is essentially no code in the RDS to handle transaction management beyond the code to externalize the begin, commit, and abort actions and the code to report transaction abort to the application program.

27.4.6   Disk-Based Log

A major departure of the RSS from other data managers is the use of a disk-based log and its merging of the undo and redo logs. The rationale for the use of disk is that disks cost about as much as tapes (typically, $30,000 per unit if controllers are included), but disks are more capacious than tapes (500 megabytes rather than 50 megabytes per unit) and can be allocated in smaller units (a disk-based log can use half of the disk cylinders; it is not easy to use half of a tape drive). Further, a disk-based log is consistent with the evolution of tape archives such as the IBM 3850 and the AMPEX Terabit Store. Last, but most important, a disk-based log eliminates operator intervention at system restart. This is essential if restart is to occur automatically and within seconds. Since restart is infrequent, operators are likely to make errors during the restart process (even if they have regular "fire drills"). A disk-based log reduces opportunities for operator error. Several systems observe that the undo log is not needed once a transaction commits. Hence, they separate the undo and redo log and discard the undo log at transaction commit. Merging the two logs causes the log to grow roughly twice as fast but leads to a simpler design. Since transactions typically write only 200 to 500 bytes of log data, we do not consider splitting the undo and redo logs to be worth the effort.

27.4.7   Save Points

Transaction save points are an elegant idea that the RSS can implement cheaply. Transaction save points are used by the RDS to undo complex RDS operations (i.e., make them atomic). However, transaction save points are not available to application programs using the SQL language. Unfortunately, the RDS implementors let PL/I do most of the storage control, so the RDS processor does not know how to save its state and PL/I does not offer it a facility to reset its state even if the RDS could remember the state. The RDS, therefore, does not show the RSS save point facility to users. Supporting save points is an unsolved language-design issue for SQL. If SQL were imbedded in a language that supported backtrack programming, save points might be implemented rather naturally. INTER-LISP is a natural candidate for this [16], since it already supports the notion of undo as an integral part of the language. We had originally intended to have system restart reset in-progress transactions to their most recent save point and then to invoke the application at an exception entry point (rather than abort all uncommitted transactions at restart). (CICS does something like this.) However, the absence of save point support in the RDS and certain operating system problems precluded this feature.

27.4.8   Shadows

The file shadow mechanism of System R is a key part of the recovery design. It is used to create and discard user scratch files, to store user work files, and to support logged files. A major virtue of shadows is that they ensure that system restart always begins with an RSS action-consistent state. This is quite a simplification and probably contributes to the success of system restart. To understand the problem that shadows solve at restart, imagine that System R did not use shadows but rather updated pages in place on the disk. Imagine two pages P_1 and P_2 of some file F, and suppose that P_1 and P_2 are related to one another in some way. To be specific, suppose that P_1 contains a reference R_1 to a record R_2 on P_2. Suppose that a transaction deletes R_2 and invalidates R_1 thereby altering P_1 and P_2. If the system crashes, there are four possibilities:

1. Neither P_1 nor P_2 is updated on disk.

2. P_1 but not P_2 is updated on disk.

3. P_2 but not P_1 is updated on disk.

4. Both P_1 and P_2 are updated on disk.

In states 2 and 3, P_1 and P_2 are not RSS-action-consistent: Either the reference, R_1, or referenced object, R_2, is missing. System restart must be prepared to redo and undo in any of these four cases. The shadow mechanism eliminates cases 2 and 3 by checkpointing the state only when it is RSS-action-consistent (hence, restart sees the shadow version recorded at checkpoint rather than the version current at the time of the crash). Without the shadow mechanism, the other two cases must be dealt with in some way. One alternative is the *write-ahead log (WAL)* protocol used by IMS [10]. IMS log records apply to page updates (rather than to actions). WAL requires that log records be written to secondary storage ahead of (i.e., before) the corresponding updates. Further, it requires that undo and redo be restartable: Attempting to redo a done page will have no effect and attempting to undo an undone page win have no effect, allowing restart to fail and retry as though it were a first attempt. *WAL* is extensively discussed by Gray [9]. There is general consensus that heavy reliance on shadows for large shared files was a mistake. We recognized this fact rather late (shadows have several seductive properties), so late in fact that a major rewrite of the RSS is required to reverse the decision. Fortunately, the performance of shadows is not unacceptable. In fact, for small databases (fewer than

10 megabytes), shadows have excellent performance. Our adoption of shadows is largely historical. Lorie implemented a single-user relational system called XRAM, which used the shadow mechanism to give recovery for private files. When files are shared, one needs a transaction log of all changes made to the files by individual users so that the changes corresponding to one user may be undone independently of the other users' changes. This transaction log makes the shadow mechanism redundant. Of course the shadow mechanism is still a good recovery technique for private files. A good system should support both shadows for private files and log-based recovery for shared files. Several other systems, notabley QBE [11], the DataComputer [14], and the Lampson and Sturgis file system [12] have a similar use of shadows. It therefore seems appropriate to present our assessment of the shadow mechanism. The conventional way of describing a large file (e.g., over a billion bytes) is as a sequence of allocation units. An allocation unit is typically a group of disk cylinders, called an extent. If the file grows, new extents are added to the list. A file might be represented by 10 extents and the corresponding descriptor might be 200 bytes. Accessing a page consists of accessing the extent table to find the location of the extent containing the page and then accessing the page. By contrast, a shadow mechanism is much more complex and expensive. Each page of the file has an individual descriptor in the page table. Such descriptors need to be at least 4 bytes long and there need to be two of them (current and shadow). Further, there are various free-space bit maps (a bit per page) and other housekeeping items. Hence, the directories needed for a file are about 0.2 percent of the file size (actually 0.2 percent of the maximum file size). For a billion-byte file this is 2 megabytes of directories rather than the 200 bytes cited for the extent-oriented descriptors. For large files, this means that the directories cannot reside in primary storage; they must be paged from secondary storage. The RSS maintains two buffer pools: a pool of 4-kilobyte data pages and another pool of 512-byte directory pages. Management and use of this second pool added complexity inside the RSS. More significantly, direct processing (hashing or indexing single records by key) may suffer a directory I/O for each data I/O. Another consequence of shadows is that "next" in a file is not "next" on the disk (logical sequential does not mean physical sequential). When a page is updated for the first time, it moves. Unless one is careful, and the RSS is not careful about this, getting the next page frequently involves a disk seek. (Lorie in [13] suggests a shadow scheme that maintains physical clustering within a cylinder.) So it appears that shadows are bad for direct (random) processing and for sequential processing. Shadows consume an inconsequential amount of disk space for directories (less than 1On the other hand, in order to use the shadow mechanism, one must reserve a large amount (2space to hold the shadow pages. In fact, some batch operations and the system restart facility may completely rewrite the database. This requires either a 100operation must be able to tolerate several checkpoints (i.e., reclaim shadow) while it is in progress. This problem complicates system restart (its solution was too complex to describe in the system restart section). The RSS recovery system does not use shadowed files for the log; rather, it uses disk extents (one per log file). However the recovery system does use the shadow

mechanism at checkpoint and restart. At checkpoint, all the current versions of all recoverable files are made the shadow versions. This stops the system and triggers a flurry of I/O activity. The altered pages in the database buffer pool are written to disk, and much directory I/O is done to free obsolete pages and to mark the current pages as allocated. The major work in this operation is that three I/Os must be done for every directory page that has changed since the last checkpoint. If updates to the database are randomly scattered, this could mean three I/Os at checkpoint for each update in the interval between checkpoints. In practice, updates are not scattered randomly and so things are not that bad, but a checkpoint can involve many I/Os. We have devised several schemes to make the shadow I/O asynchronous to the checkpoint operation and to reduce the quantity of the I/O. It appears, however, that much of the I/O is inherent in the shadow mechanism and cannot be eliminated entirely. This means that the RSS (System R) must stop transaction processing for seconds. That in turn means that user response times will occasionally be quite long. These observations cause us to believe that we should have adopted the IMS-like approach of using the WAL protocol for large shared files. That is, we should have supported the log and no-shadow option in Figure 27.9. If we had done this, the current and shadow directories would be replaced by a much smaller set of file descriptors (perhaps a few thousand bytes). This would eliminate the directory buffer pool and its attendant page I/O. Further, a checkpoint would consist of a log quiesce followed by writing a checkpoint record and a pointer to the checkpoint record to disk (two or three I/Os rather than hundreds). WAL would not be simpler to program (e.g., WAL requires more detailed logging). But the performance of WAL is better for large shared databases (bigger than 100 megabytes).

27.4.9   Message Recovery, an Oversight

As pointed out by the examples in Figures 27.1 and 27.4, a transaction's database actions and output messages must either all be committed or all be undone. We did not appreciate this in the initial design of System R and hence did not integrate a message system with the database system. Rather, application programs use the standard terminal I/O interfaces provided by the operating system, and messages have no recovery associated with them. This was a major design error. The output messages of a transaction must be logged and their delivery must be coordinated by the commit processor. Commercial data management systems do this correctly.

27.4.10   New Features

We recently added two new facilities to the recovery component and to the SQL interface. First, the $COMMIT$ command was extended to allow an application to combine a $COMMIT$ with a $BEGIN$ and preserve the transaction's locks and cursors while exposing (committing) its updates. $COMMIT$ now accepts a list of cursors and locks that are to be kept for the next transaction. These locks are downgraded from exclusive to shared locks, and all other cursors and locks are released.

A typical use of this is an application that scans a large file. After processing the A's, it commits and processes the B's, then commits and then processes the Cs, and so on. In order to maintain cursor positioning across each step, the application uses the special form of commit that commits one transaction and begins the next. A second extension involved support for the two-phase commit protocol required for distributed systems [9]. A PHASE-ONE action was added to the RSS and to SQL to allow transactions to prepare to conunit. This causes the RSS to log the transaction's locks and to force the log. Further, at restart there are now three kinds of transactions: winners, losers, and in-doubt. In-doubt transactions are re-done and their locks are reacquired at restart. Each such transaction continues to be in doubt until the transaction coordinator commits or aborts it (or the system operator forces it). During the debugging of this code, several transactions were in doubt for 2 weeks and for tens of system restarts. At present, our major interest is in a distributed version of System R. We are extending the System R prototype to support transparent distribution of data among multiple database sites.

Acknowledgments

We have had many stimulating discussions with Dar Busa, Earl Jenner, Homer Leonard, Dieter Gawlick, John Nauman, and Ron Obermarck. They helped us better understand alternate approaches to recovery. John Howard and Mike Mitoma did several experiments that stress tested the recovery system. Jim Mehl and Bob Yost adapted the recovery manager to the MVS environment. Tom Szczygielski implemented the two-phase commit protocol. We also owe a great deal to the recovery model formulated by Charlie Davies and Larry Bjork.

References

[1] Astrahan, M. M., Blasgen, M. W., Chamberlin, D. D., Eswaran, K. P., Gray J. N., Griffiths, P. P., King, W. F., Lorie, R. A., McJones, P. R., Mehl, J.W., Putzolu, G. R., Traiger, I. L., Wade, B. W., and Watson, V. "System R: A relational approach to database management," *ACM Transactions on Database System* 1(2) (June 1976).

[2] Biork, L. "Recovery scenario for a DB/DC system," *Proc. of ACM National Conference*, 1973, pp. 142-146.

[3] Blasgen, M. W., Gray, J., N., Mitoma, M., and Price, T. "The convoy phenomenon," *ACM Operating System Reviews* 14(2) (April 1979).

[4] Chamberlin, D. D., Astrahan, M. M., Eswaran, K. P., Griffiths, P. P., Lorie, R. A., Mehl, J. W., Reisner, R., and Wade, B. W. "SEQUEL 2: A unified approach to data definition, manipulation and control," *IBM J Research Dev.* 20(6) (Nov.1976).

[5] Davies, C. T. "Recovery semantics for a DB/DC system," *Proc. ACM National Conference*, 1973.

[6] Eswaran, K. E., Gray, J. N., Lorie, R. A., and Traiger, I. "The notion of consistency and predicate locks in a relational database system," *Communication of the ACM* 19(11) (Nov. 1976).

[7] Gray, J. N., and Watson, V. "A shared segment and interprocess communicationfacility for VM/370," *IBM San Jose Re-search Lab. Rep.* RJ 1679, May 1975.

[8] Gray, J. N., Lorie, R. A., Putzolu, G. F., and Traiger, I. "Granularity of locks and degrees of consistency in a shared data base," *Modeling in data base management systems*, G. M. Nijssen, Ed., North-Holland, Amsterdam, 1976, (also IBM Research Rep., RJ 1706.

[9] Gray, J. N. "Notes on data base operating systems, in Operating systems-an advanced course," R. Bayer, R. M. Graham, and G. Seegmuller, Ecls., Springer Verlag, New York, 1978. also *IBM Research Rep.* RJ 2188, Feb. 1978.

[10] IBM "Information management system/virtual systems (IMS/VS), programming reference manual," IBM Form No. SH20-9027-2, sect. 5.

[11] IBM "Query by example program description/operators manual," IBM Form No. SH20-2077.

[12] Lampson, B. W., and Sturgis, H. E. "Crash recovery in a distributed data storage system," *Communications of the ACM* to appear

[13] Lorie, R. A. "Physical integrity in a large segmented database," *ACM Transactions Database System* 2(1) (March 1977).

[14] Marill, T., and Stern, D. H. "The Datacomputer: A network utility," *Proc. AFIPS National Computer Conference*, Vol. 44, AF-IPS Press, Arlington, Va., 1975.

[15] Nauman, J. S. "Observations on sharing in database systems," IBM Santa Teresa Lab. Tech. Rep. TR 03.047, May 1978.

[16] Teitleman, W. "Automated programming-The programmer's assistant," *Proc. Fall Jt. Computer Conference*, Dec. 1972.

Chapter 28

Implementing Crash Recovery in QuickStore: A Performance Study

Seth J. White and David J. DeWitt

Abstract

Implementing crash recovery in an object-oriented database system (OODBMS) raises several challenging issues for performance that are not present in traditional DBMSs. These performance concerns result both from significant architectural differences between OODBMSs and traditional database systems and differences in OODBMS's target applications. This chapter compares the performance of several alternative approaches to implementing crash recovery in an OODBMS based on a client-server architecture. The four basic recovery techniques examined in the chapter are called page differencing, sub page differencing, whole-page logging, and redo-at-server. All of the recovery techniques were implemented in the context of QuickStore, a memory-mapped store built using the EXODUS Storage Manager, and their performance is compared using the OO7 database benchmark. The results of the performance study show that the techniques based on differencing generally provide superior performance to whole-page logging.

28.1 INTRODUCTION

This chapter examines the performance of several alternative approaches to implementing crash recovery in QuickStore [18], a memory-mapped store for persistent C++ that was built using the EXODUS Storage Manager (ESM) [3]. Providing recovery services in a system such as QuickStore raises several challenging implementation issues, not only because it is a memory-mapped storage system, but also because of the kinds of applications that object-oriented database management Systems (OODBMs) strive to support, that is CAx, GIS, OIS, and so on. Furthermore, since QuickStore is implemented on top of the EXODUS Storage Manager (ESM), it is a client-server, page shipping system [5]. This raises additional performance concerns for recovery that are not present in database systems based on more traditional designs, that is, centralized DBMSs or systems based on a query-shipping architecture.

The chapter examines four basic recovery techniques that are called page differencing, subpage differencing, whole-page logging, and redo-at-server. All of the recovery techniques were implemented in the context of QuickStore/ESM so that an accurate comparison of their performance could be made. The performance study was carried out using the OO7 object-oriented database benchmark [2]. The performance results illustrate the impact of different database sizes, update patterns, and available client memory on the relative performance of the various techniques. In addition, the number of clients accessing the database is varied in order to compare the scalability of the different recovery algorithms.

The remainder of the chapter is organized as follows. Section 28.2 presents a detailed discussion of the factors (briefly mentioned earlier) that make recovery in QuickStore a challenging problem. Section 28.3 describes several alternative techniques for implementing recovery in QuickStore. Next, Section 28.4 describes the performance study that was carried out to compare the performance of the different recovery schemes. Section 28.5 presents the performance results. Section 28.6 discusses related work. Finally, Section 28.7 presents our conclusions and some proposals for future work.

28.2 CHALLENGES FOR RECOVERY

One challenge faced by QuickStore recovery results from the way that persistent objects are accessed under its memory-mapped architecture. As described in [18], QuickStore supports a comprehensive pointer swizzling strategy that allows application programs to manipulate persistent objects directly in the ESM client buffer pool by dereferencing normal virtual memory pointers. This strategy allows applications to update persistent objects at memory speeds with essentially no overhead, but it also makes detecting the portions of objects that have been updated more difficult than in systems that use traditional implementation techniques. For example, in OODBMSs that do not perform pointeer swizzling or that implement pointer swizzling using traditional software-based techniques, a function that is a part of the database run-time system is typically called to perform each update. This provides a hook that the system can use to record the fact that the update has occured. We note that this approach requires special compiler support to insert function calls for updates into the application code in order to make updates transparent.

A second factor affecting the design of a recovery scheme for QuickStore is that

QuickStore, like most OODBMSs, is designed to handle nontraditional database applications, for example, CAD, geographic information systems (GIS), and office information systems (OIS). Applications of this type typically read objects into memory and then work on them intensively, repeatedly traversing relationships between objects and updating the objects as well. This behavior differs dramatically from that exhibited by relational database systems, which usually update an individual tuple just once during a particular update operation. For example, giving all the employees in a company an annual raise requires only a single update to each employee tuple. Since relational database systems typically update each tuple only once, they generate a log record for recovery purposes for each individual update. However, such a strategy is not practical in an OODBMS where an object may be updated many times during a single-method invocation. Here it is necessary to batch the effects of updates together in order to achieve good performance by attempting to generate a single log record that records the effects of several updates to an object.

A final consideration in the design of a recovery scheme for QuickStore arises because QuickStore is based on a client-server architecture in which updates are performed at the client workstations. This raises the issue of cache consistency between the clients and the server [8] since both the client and the server buffer pools can contain cached copies of a page that has been updated. In addition, to increase availability, the stable copy of the transaction log is maintained by the server, so clients are required to ship log records describing updates over a network to the server before a transaction can commit. This differs from the traditional approached used in centralized database systems, where updates are performed at the server and log records are generated locally at the server as well.

28.3   RECOVERY STRATEGIES

This section describes the four basic recovery schemes that were implemented and evaluated using QuickStore: page differencing, subpage differencing, whole-page logging, and redo-at-server. We begin by describing the implementation of recovery in ESM since several of the techniques are built on top of or involve modifications to the underlying ESM recovery scheme. It should be noted that although the recovery algorithms are discussed in the context of QuickStore, they are not QuickStore-specific and, in general, are applicable to any similar client-server OODBMS.

28.3.1   Recovery in ESM

The EXODUS Storage Manager is a client-server, page-shipping system [5] in which both clients and servers manage their own local buffer pools. When a client needs to access an object on a page that is not currently cached in its local buffer pool, it sends a request (usually over a network) to the appropriate server asking for the page. If necessary, the server reads the page from secondary storage into main memory, sends a copy of the page to the client, and retains a copy of the page in its own buffer pool as well.

Objects are updated at clients and clients also generate log records that describe updates for recovery purposes. Log records for updates contain both redo and undo information for the associated update operation. For example, if a range of bytes within an object is updated, then the log record will contain the old and new values of that portion of the object. Log records are collected and sent from a client to the server a page at a time. For simplicity, ESM enforces the rule that log records generated for a page are always sent back to the server before the page itself is sent. Thus, the server never has a page cached in its buffer pool for which it does not also have the log records describing the updates present on the page.

The ESM server manages a circular, append-only log on secondary storage and uses a STEAL/NO-FORCE buffer management policy [10]. Clients can cache pages in their local buffer pools across transaction boundaries. However, intertransaction caching of locks at clients is not supported. Also, all dirty pages are sent back to the server at commit time in order to maintain cache consistency between the clients and the server and simplify recovery. The log records generated on behalf of a transaction must be written to the log by the server before the transaction commits, but the dirty pages themselves are not forced to disk. [9] contains a more detailed description of the ESM recovery scheme.

28.3.2   The Page-Differencing Approach

The ESM recovery mechanism handles the generation of log records for updates. However, if recovery were done in a straightforward way using the basic services provided by ESM, then each time an update is performed, a log record would be generated. This is a situation that we would like to avoid, if possible. Furthermore, there is no obvious way for a QuickStore application to detect that an update has occurred since application programs are allowed to update objects by simply dereferencing standard virtual memory pointers.

Enabling Recovery for Page Differencing.   The problems mentioned above can be addressed by employing a page-differencing (PD) scheme to generate log records. This approach works as follows. QuickStore gives application programs access to persistent data by mapping a range of virtual memory (using the Unix mmap system call) in the address space of the application process to the location in the client buffer pool of a particular database page when it is cached in main memory [18]. We refer to the range of virtual memory that has been mapped to a page as a *frame* of virtual memory. Virtual memory frames are contiguous and uniform in size (8 KB). Read permission is enabled on a virtual frame that is mapped to a page in the buffer pool so that persistent objects located on the page can be accessed by the application process. Objects on the page are accessed by dereferencing standard virtual memory pointers into the virtual frame. However, write access is not automatically enabled on a virtual frame that has been mapped. In particular, write access is never enabled when the actions necessary to *enable* recovery for a particular page have not been taken. Thus, any attempt by an application program to update an object on a page for which recovery is not enabled will result in a page fault, causing the QuickStore fault-handling routine to be invoked.

The QuickStore run-time system maintains an in-memory table that contains an entry (called a page descriptor) for each virtual frame that has been associated with a page in the database. The in-memory table is implemented as a height-balanced binary tree. When the fault-handling routine is invoked, it begins by searching the in-memory table for the page descriptor corresponding to the virtual memory address that caused the fault. By inspecting status information contained in the page descriptor entry, the fault-handler will detect that the access violation is due to a write attempt. If recovery is not already enabled on the page, it may be if paging in the buffer pool is taking place, then the fault handler copies the page into an area in memory called the *recovery buffer* and sets the page descriptor entry to point to the copy. The fault handler also obtains an exclusive lock on the page from ESM, if needed, and enables write access on the virtual frame that caused the fault. At this point, all the work needed to enable recovery on the faulted page is complete, so control is returned to the application program, which can then proceed to update objects on the page directly in the client buffer pool.

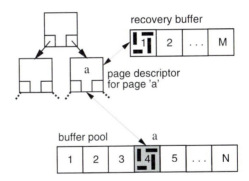

Figure 28.1. The page-diffing approach.

Figure 28.1 shows the effect of the actions described before on the in-memory data structures maintained by QuickStore. In Figure 28.1, page a, which is cached in the client buffer pool, is shaded to show that it has been updated. A copy containing the value of page a before recovery was enabled has been placed in the recovery buffer, and the page descriptor for page a has been set to point to the copy. As Figure 28.1 shows, the recovery buffer contains room for M pages, where M is fixed and $1 \leq M \leq N$ (where N is the number of pages in the ESM client buffer pool.) Since M is fixed, the recovery buffer can become full, so it may be necessary to free up space periodically when an additional page is updated, by generating log records for a page that has already been copied into the recovery buffer. Space in the recovery buffer is managed using a simple FIFO replacement policy.

Generating Log Records for Pages   At transaction commit time, when paging in
the buffer pool occurs, or when the recovery buffer becomes full, the old values
of objects contained in the recovery buffer and their corresponding updated values
in the buffer pool are compared (diffed) to determine if log records need to be
generated. The actual algorithm used for generating log records is slightly more
sophisticated than the simple approach of generating a single log record for each
modified region of an object. This simple approach was rejected since it has the
potential to generate a great deal of unnecessary log traffic. For example, consider
an object in which the first and third words (1 word = 4 bytes) have been updated.
The simple approach would generated two log records for the object. Since each
ESM log record contains a header of approximately 50 bytes, the total space used
in the log would be 116 bytes (50 bytes for each log header plus 4 bytes for each
before and after image). On the other hand, if just one log record were generrated,
only 74 bytes would have been used (50 bytes plus 12 bytes for each before and
after image), providing a 36%, saving in the amount of log space used.

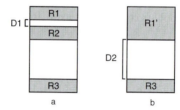

Figure 28.2. Combining modified regions in an object.

   The algorithm for generating log records uses diffing to identify consecutive
modified regions in each object on a page; if only one region exists, then a single log
record is generated for the object. (Log records could, in principle, span objects but
the current implementation of recovery in ESM does not allow this.) For example,
Figure 28.2(a)shows an object that contains three modified regions, labeled $R1$, $R2$,
and $R3$. The diffing algorithm starts from the beginning of the object, so initially
it would identify the two modified regions $R1$ and $R2$. It is easy to show, given
the before-image/after-image format of log records in ESM, that if the distance $D1$
between $R1$ and $R2$ satisfies the equation $2 \times size(D1) > H$, where H is the size
of a log record header, then generating separate log records for each region will
generate the least amount of log traffic. If this were the case in the example, then
the algorithm would generate a log record for $R1$ before proceeding to consider
additional regions. However, a log record for $R2$ is not immediately generated,
since it may be advantageous to combine $R2$ with some region that has not yet
been discovered. If, on the other hand, $2 \times size (D1) \leq H$, that is, the distance
between $R1$ and $R2$ is small, then the algorithm combines the two region into a
single rregion. Figure 28.2(b) illustrates the second case. here, $R1$ and $R2$ have
been combined into a single region $R1'$. Again, no log record is generrated at this

step, as the algorithm may decide to combine $R1'$ with additional regions.

In either case mentioned before, the algorithm continues by identifying the next modified region in the object (if there is one) and repeats the previous check using the newly discovered region and either the combined region from the previous iteration or the region from the previous iteration for which no log record has yet been generated. In the example shown in Figure 28.2(b), the algorithm would next examine regions $R1'$ and $R3$ to see if they should be logged separately or combined. Since the distance between $R1'$ and $R3$ is large, the algorithm will generate seperate log records for $R1'$ and $R3$. Finally, we note that the decision concerning whether to combine consecutive modified regions depends only on the distance between them and not on their size, so the order in which the rregions are examined does not matter. Thus, the algorithm is guaranteed to generate the minimum amount of the log traffic.

28.3.3   The Subpage-Differencing Approach

The page-differencing recovery scheme described in the previous section has some potential disadvantages. The most obvious disadvantage is that the CPU overhead for copying and diffing a whole page may be fairly high, especially when very few updates have actually been performed on the page. In addition, page diffing has the potential to waste space in the recovery buffer by copying a whole page when only a few objects on the page have been updated. This can increase the number of log records generated during a transaction, if the recovery buffer becomes full. However, the pagewise granularity of the page-diffing scheme is necessary if applications are allowed to update objects via normal virtual memory pointers as virtual memory is page-based.

An alternative approach is to interpret update operations in software. One way that this can be accomplished, in general, is by compiling persistent applications using a special compiler that inserts additional code to handle update operations. This code can simply be a function call that replaces the usual pointer dereference at the points in the application program where updates occur. In our case, the function that is invoked is part of the QuickStore run-time system. This approach yields a system in which objects may be read at memory speed using standard virtual memory pointers, but in which update operations are more heavyweight, requiring a function call and other software overhead. The hope when using such an approach is that the extra cost incurred on each update will be repaid through reduced recovery costs.

Figure 28.3 illustrates the in-memory data structures used by QuickStore to implement the subpage-differencing (SD) approach. Under the SD approach, each page is divided into a contiguous sequence of regions called blocks. Blocks are uniform in size. (We experimented with block sizes ranging from 8 to 64 bytes.) As Figure 28.3 shows, the page descriptor for a page that has been updated holds a pointer to an array containing pointers to copies of blocks that have been modified. There is one entry in the array for each block on the page, and array entries for

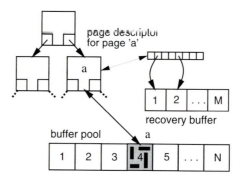

Figure 28.3. The subpage-diffing approach.

unmodified blocks are null. Blocks were used as the subpage unit of copying and diffing instead of objects for two reasons. First, it is cheaper in terms of CPU cost to identify the block on a page that is being updated than it is the object, when an update occurs (see what follows). And second, objects within a page may be rather big (i.e. up to 8 KB in size). If this is the case, then the advantages of the subpage, diffing approach will be lost when updates are sparse.

28.3.4 Enabling Recovery for Subpage-Differencing

Each time the QuickStore update function is called, it looks up the page descriptor of the appropriate page using the address of the memory location that is being updated (which is passed as a parameter). Once the page descriptor is found, a check is made to see if the block that is about to be updated has been copied. This check is relatively inexpensive since the address of the location in memory being updated can be used to index the array of block pointers contained in the page descriptor (after applying some simple logical operations). If a copy of the block has not yet been made, then a copy is placed in the recovery buffer. In addition, the status flags in the page descriptor are examined to see if an exclusive lock has been acquired for the page, and write access is enabled on the virtual frame mapped to the page (if it is not already). Finally, the update itself is performed. We note that write access could be enabled automatically on virtual frames when using the subpage approach. We chose not to do this because not enabling write access allows the run-time system to catch erroneous writes to virtual frames that have not been updated, and because the extra cost of the approach we used is very low.

Generating Log Records for Subpages Like the page-diffing approach, the SD approach generates log records at transaction commit time, when a modified page is paged out by the buffer manager, or when the recovery buffer becomes full. Log records can be generated by diffing the original values of the blocks contained in the recovery buffer with the modified versions of the same blocks located in the buffer pool, using the diffing scheme described in Section 28.3. In addition, one could avoid the expense of diffing altogether by simply logging entire blocks. We experimented with both techniques, and refer to the subpage approach without diffing as subpage logging (SL) in the upcoming discussion on performance.

28.3.5 The Whole-Page logging approach

This section describes the third recovery algorithm included in the study. This algorithm is called whole-page logging (WPL) since entire modified pages are written to the log instead of log records for updated regions of objects. We note that WPL is also the basic approach used in ObjectStore [12], a commercial OODBMS product. The advantages of WPL are that it avoids the client CPU cost that is incurred by the two diffing schemes for copying and diffing. WPL also avoids the memory overhead at clients for storing the original values of pages/blocks. This can potentially improve performance by allowing WPL to allocate more memory to the client buffer pool and, thereby, generate fewer log records. Finally, WPL allows applications to update objects at memory speeds by dereferencing normal virtual memory pointers, so the cost of actually performing updates is low.

The disadvantage of whole-page logging is that it logs entire after images of dirty pages at the server. This means that all of the pages dirtied by a transaction must be forced to the log at the server before the transaction commits. We note, however, that the cost of shipping dirty pages back to the server does not add any additional costs in ESM since its recovery algorithm always sends updated pages back to the server when a transaction commits (see Section 28.3). The WPL scheme does not rely on the support provided by ESM for recovery as the difffing schemes do. Thus, WPL differs from the previous schemes in the actions taken at both clients and the server to support recovery.

28.3.6 Actions Performed at Clients

The whole-page logging algorithm works as follows at the clients. When an application first attempts to update a page at a client, a page fault is signaled, as usual. The QuickStore page-fault handling routine marks the copy of the page cached in the buffer pool as dirty, in addition to requesting an exclusive lock if necessary, and enables write access on the virtual memory frame that is mapped to the page. Control is then returned to the application program. Dirty pages are shipped back to the server.

Actions Performed at the Server.   When the server receives a dirty page, it appends the page to the log and caches a copy of the page in its own buffer pool. The server does not allow the original copy of the page on disk to be overwritten with the new copy of the page until after the transaction that updated the page commits. If paging in the server buffer pool causes a dirty page to be replaced during a transaction, then the page is read from the log if it is reaccessed during the same transaction. When a transaction reaches its commit point, the original values of any updated pages are still located on disk in their permanent locations, and the updated values of the pages have been flushed to the log together with a commit log record for the transaction. This makes it possible to abort a transaction at any time before the commit point is reached by simply ignoring from then on any of its updated values of pages located in the log or cached in memory. No undo processing for updates is required.

A page updated by a committed transaction must be maintained in the log until one of two things happens. The first is that the page is read from the log and used to overwrite its permanent location on disk. The log space for the page can then be reused since the copy of the page contained in the log is no longer needed for recovery. The reason for this is fairly obvious. For example, suppose that transaction T updates page P and then commits, that is, P is forced to the log. If a cr Space for a page in the log can also be reused if a subsequent transaction updates the page and commits, thereby forcing a new copy of the page, say, $C2$, to the log, before the initial copy of the page $C1$ in the log overwrites the permanent location of the page. In effect, $C1$ is not needed at this point, since following a crash $C2$ will be used. Note, however, that both $C1$ and $C2$ must be maintained in the log until the transaction that wrote $C2$ commits.

The server maintains an in-memory table, called the WPL table, to keep track of pages contained in the log that are needed for recovery purposes. Figure 28.5 shows the format of a table entry. Each table entry contains the page ID (PID) of the page, which identifies its permanent location on disk. Entries also contain the log sequence number (LSN) of the log record generated for the page. The LSN identifies the physical location of the page in the log. Additional fields stored in each entry include the transaction ID (TID) of the transaction that last dirtied the page and some additional status information. When a page is initially written to the log, the status information records the fact that the transaction that dirtied the page has not yet committed. Finally, table entries contain a pointer that refers to the entry for a previously logged copy (if any) of the same page if that copy is still needed for recovery.

The server also maintains a list, for each active transaction, of the pages that have been logged for that particular transaction. When a transaction commits, the WPL table entry for each page on this list is updated to show that the transaction that modified the page has committed. In order to reclaim log space, there is a background thread that asynchronously reads pages modified by committed transactions from the log. (As an optimization, pages modified by a transaction that are still cached in the server buffer pool at commit time are simple marked as having been read.) Once a page has been read from the log, the server is free to flush the page to disk at any time. Once this happens, the entry for the page in the WPL table is removed.

Recovering from a Crash

In order to be able to recover from an unexpected crash, the server periodically takes checkpoints. At checkpoint time, the WPL table is written to the log. In order to recover from an unexpected failure, the server must be able to reconstruct the WPL table so that it contains entries for all of the pages that have been updated by committed transactions, but not yet written to their permanent disk locations. Once this is done, the server can resume normal operation.

Restart after a crash requires a single pass through the log that begins at the end of the log and proceeds backward to the most recent checkpoint record. At the start of the pass, a list that records committed transactions, called the committed transactions list (CTL), is initialized to empty. During the pass, a transaction is added to the CTL when a commit record for the transaction is encountered during the backward scan. When a log record for a modified page is encountered, an entry for the page is inserted into the WPL table if the transaction that updated the page is in the committed transaction list. Otherwise, the modify record is ignored since the associated transaction did not commit before the crash.

When the checkpoint record is reached, the committed transaction list contains an entry for each transaction that committed after the checkpoint was taken. The contents of the checkpoint record itself are then examined. Entries in the checkpoint record that pertain to members of the CTL, or which are marked as pertaining to transactions that committed before the checkpoint was taken, are added to the newly constructed WPL table. At this point, the WPL table has been fully reconstructed and normal processing can resume.

28.3.7 The Redo-at-Server Approach

The final recovery algorithm that we examined is called redo-at-server (REDO). This algorithm is a modification of the ARIES-based recovery algorithm used by ESM in which clients send log records, but not dirty pages, back to the server. (Recall that the usual EXODUS recovery algorithm sends both log records and dirty pages back to the server, although only log records are forced to disk before commit.) Under REDO, when a log record is received at the server, the redo information in the log record is used to update the server's copy of the page. The disadvantage of REDO is that the server may have to read the page from secondary storage in order to apply the log record.

In addition to the obvious advantage of not having to ship dirty pages from clients to the server, REDO is also appealing from an implementation standpoint. It simplifies the implementation of a storage manager by providing cache consistency between clients and the server [8]. REDO is currently being used in the initial version of SHORE [1], a persistent object system being developed at Wisconsin. Since REDO only involves changes at the storage manager level, it can be used in combination with any of the recovery schemes mentioned previously that make use of the recovery services provided by EXODUS. Here we will study its use in conjunction with the PD scheme.

28.3.8   Implementation Discussion

Each of the four recovery schemes described in this section has been implemented in the context of QuickStore/ESM. The two diffing schemes did not require any changes to the base recovery services provided by ESM. Instead of modifying the gnu C++ compiler, *the gnu compiler was used to compile the QuickStore application code* to insert function calls for updates to support the subpage-diffing approach, the necessary function calls were inserted by hand at the application level to save time. In implementing whole-page logging we made use of the existing ESM recovery code whenever possible. For example, ESM already supported whole-page logging for newly created pages. The changes made to the ESM client to support WPL were therefore fairly minor. The changes made to the server were more substantial, and involved tasks such as maintenance of the WPL table (Section 28.3.5) and rereading pages from the log. Implementing redo-at-server was also relatively easy. The ESM server already supported redo as part of the ARIES-based recovery scheme that it uses, and it was not hard to get the server to apply each log record to the appropriate page as log records were received by inserting a function call in the appropriate spot in the server code.

28.4   PERFORMANCE EXPERIMENTS

This section describes the performance study that was conducted to compare the performance of the recovery algorithms described in the previous section. The OO7 object-oriented database benchmark was used as a basis for carrying out the study [2].

28.4.1   OO7 Benchmark Database

The structure of the OO7 database benchmark is discussed in detail in [2], but we describe it briefly here for completeness. The OO7 database is intended to be suggestive of many different CAD/CAM/CASE applications. A key component of the database is a set of *composite parts*. Each composite part is intended to suggest a design primitive such as a register cell in a VLSI CAD application. Associated with each composite part is a *document* object that models a small amount of documentation associated with the composite part. Each composite part also has an associated graph of *atomic parts*. Intuitively, the atomic parts within a composite part are the units out of which the composite part is constructed. One atomic part in each composite part's graph is designated as the "root part." Each atomic part is connected via a bidirectional association to three other atomic parts. (This can be varied.) The connections between atomic parts are implemented by interposing a connection object between each pair of connected atomic parts.

Additional structure is imposed on the set of composite parts by a structure called the "assembly hierarchy." Each assembly is either made up of composite parts (in which case it is a *base assembly*) or it is made up of other assembly objects (in which case it is a *complex assembly*). The first level of the assembly hierarchy consists of *base assembly* objects. Each base assembly has a bidirectional association with three composite parts that are chosen at random from the set of all com Each assembly hierarchy is called a *module*. Modules are intended to model the largest subunits of the database application. Each module also has an associated *Manual* object, which is a larger version of a document.

Table 28.1. 007 Benchmark Database Parameters

Parameter	Small	Big
NumAtomicPerComp	20	20
NumConnPerAtomic	3	3
DocumentSize (bytes)	2000	2000
Manual Size (Kbytes)	100	100
NumCompPerModule	500	2000
NumAssmPerAssm	3	3
NumAssmLevels	7	8
NumCompPerAssm	3	3
NumModules	5	5

We included two different database sizes in the study, called small and big. Table 28.1 shows the OO7 parameters used to construct the two databases. We note that the parameters used here do not correspond exactly to the "standard" OO7 database specification of [2]. As indicated in Table 28.1, a module in the small database here is the same size as a module in the small database of [2]; however, modules in the big database differ from the small database in that they contain 2000 composite parts instead of 500, and there are eight levels in the assembly hierarchy in the big database versus seven in the small database. Both the small and big database here contain five modules, as the number of clients that access the database will be varied from 1 to 5. During a given experiment, each module will be accessed by a single client, so a module represents private data to the client that uses it. We decided not let the clients share data in order to avoid locking conflicts and deadlocks, both of which can have a major effect on performance. Removing these effects simplified the experiments and allowed us to concentrate on the differences in performance that were due to the recovery mechanisms being studied.

Table 28.2 lists the total size of the databases and the size of a module within each database. The size of a module in the small database is 6.6 MB, which is small enough that an entire module can be cached in main memory at a client (12 Mb). In addition, the total size of the small database (33 Mb) is small enough that it fits into main memory of the server (36 Mb). Thus, the experiments performed using the small database test the performance of the recovery algorithms when the

Table 28.2. Database Sizes (in megabytes)

	Small	Big
Module	6.6	24.3
Total	33.3	121.5

entire database can be cached in main memory. The size of a module in the big database, however, is larger than the main memory available at any single client. In addition, when more than a single client is used the amount of data accessed is also bigger than the memory available at the server. Experiments performed using the big database test the relative performance of the algorithms when a significant amount of paging is taking place in the system.

28.4.2   OO7 Benchmark Operations

This section describes the OO7 benchmark operations used in the study. Since the goal of the study is to examine recovery performance, we only include the OO7 tests that perform updates. In addition, some of the OO7 update tests stress index updates these tests are also not included in the study as they did not shed any additional light on the performance of the recovery algorithms.

The experiments were performed using the T2A, T2B, and T2C OO7 traversal operations. The T2 traversals perform a depth-first traversal of the assembly hierarchy. As each base assembly is visited, each of its composite parts is visited and a depth-first search on the graph of atomic parts is performed. Each T2 traversal increments the (x, y) attributes contained in atomic parts as follows and returns a count of the number of updates performed:[1].

T2A: Update the root atomic part of each composite part.
T2B: Update all atomic parts of each composite part.
T2C: Update all atomic parts four times.

During each experiment, the traversals were run repeatedly at each client, so that the steady-state performance of the system could be observed. Each traversal was run as a separate transaction. The client and server buffer pools were not flushed between transactions, so data were cached in memory across transaction boundaries.

---

[1] [2] specifies that the (x, y) attributes should be swapped. We increment them instead so that multiple updates of the same object change the object's value. This guarantees that the diffing schemes always generate a log record for each modified object.

28.4.3   Software Versions

We experimented with several QuickStore recovery software versions. Table 28.3 shows the names used to identify the different versions in the performance section. Each name generally consists of two parts. The first part identifies the scheme used for generating log records (PD, SD, or SL), and the second specifies the underlying recovery strategy that was used (ESM or REDO). In addition, the size of the recovery buffer given to the diffing schemes is sometimes appended to the name of these systems. For example, PD-REDO-4 denotes a system using page diffing with a 4 MB recovery buffer in combination with redo-at-server recovery. In the case of whole-page logging, the name has only one part (WPL). We note that the subpage, diffing (SD) versions shown in the performance section use a block size of 64 bytes. We experimented with other block sizes, but their performance was similar.

Table 28.3. Example Software Versions

Name	Description
PD-ESM	Page diffing, ESM recovery
SD-ESM	Subpage diffing, ESM recovery
SL-ESM	Subpage logging(no diffing), ESM recovery
PD-REDO	Page diffing, REDO recovery
WPL	Whole-page logging

28.4.4   Hardware Used

As a test vehicle, we used six Sun workstations on an isolated Ethernet. A Sun IPX workstation configured with 48 megabytes of memory, two 424-megabyte disk drives (model Sun0424), and one 1.3-gigabyte disk drive (model Sun1.3G) was used as the server. One of the Sun 0424s was used to hold system software and swap space. The Sun 1.3G drive was used by ESM to hold the database, and the second Sun 0424 drive was used to hold the ESM transaction log. The data and recovery disks were configured as raw disks. For the clients we used five Sun Sparc ELC workstations (about 20 MIPS) configured with 24 megabytes of memory and one 207-megabyte disk drive (model Sun0207) each. The disk drives were used to hold system software and as swap devices.

28.5   PERFORMANCE RESULTS

This section presents the performance results. We first present and analyze the results obtained using the small database and then turn to the results obtained using the big database.

28.5.1   Unconstrained Cache Results

This section presents results for experiments using the small database. All systems were given 12 megabytes of memory at each client to use for caching persistent data. For the systems that do diffing, 8 MB was allocated for the client buffer pool and 4 MB for the recovery buffer. This allocation of memory allowed all of the persistent data (modified and unmodified) accessed by a client to be cached completely in the client's main memory. Since the small database was used, all of the data accessed by the client could be cached in the server buffer pool as well.

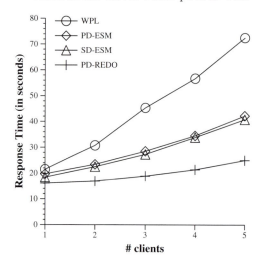

Figure 28.4. T2A, small database.

Figures 28.4 and 28.5 show the response time and throughput versus number of active clients for the T2A traversal for several software versions. PD-REDO (page diffing using redo recovery) has the best performance overall, whereas WPL (whole-page logging) has the worst. WPL is 22% slower than PD-REDO when one client is used, but its performance relative to the other systems steadily worsens as the number of clients increases. At five clients, WPL is 2.4 times slower than PD-REDO. WPL has slow performance in this experiment because T2A does sparse updates, causing WPL to write significantly more pages to the log than the other systems.

Figure 28.9 shows the total number of pages (data and log) and the number of log record pages shipped from each client to the server on average during a transaction. The results in Figure 28.9 are labeled according to the underlying recovery scheme used, since that determined the number of pages sent for each system, for example, PD-ESM and SD-ESM had the same write performance, since when no paging occurs at the clients, they always generate the same number of log records and dirty pages. The main difference between PD-ESM and SD-ESM in this case is in the amount of data copied into the recovery buffer and diffed per transaction. The

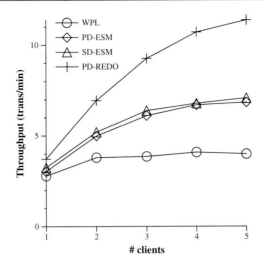

Figure 28.5. T2A, small database.

number of pages written to the log by the server was very close to the total number of pages shipped for WPL, and it was also close to the number of log pages shipped for the other systems. Figure 28.9 shows that WPL writes 435 pages back to the server on average during T2A, whereas PD-REDO writes just 5. Thus, the diffing scheme used by PD-REDO is very effective at reducing the amount work required at the server for recovery in this case.

The performance of PD-ESM and SD-ESM lies between that of the other two systems in Figure 28.4. Surprisingly, the overall response time of SD-ESM is only slightly faster than PD-ESM (6.5% at 1 client, 3.3% at 5 clients), as the savings in CPU cost provided by SD-ESM were only a small part of overall response time in this experiment. The absolute difference in response time between SD-ESM and PD-ESM did not change significantly as the number of clients varied, and was roughly 1.3 seconds. This amounted to a savings of 3 milliseconds for SD-ESM for each page that was updated. The difference in CPU usage between PD-ESM and SD-ESM in Figure 28.4 was approximately 8% throughout, which was also quite low. We believe the small difference in CPU usage was caused partly by the CPU overhead at clients for shipping dirty pages back to the server. The response time for SL-ESM is not shown in Figure 28.4 since it was basically the same as SD-ESM. This was because the number of additional log pages generated by SD-ESM relative to SD-ESM was very small during this experiment.

The throughput results shown in Figure 28.5 mirror the response-time results in Figure 28.4. Figure 28.5 shows that although the throughput increases with the number of clients for the systems that use diffing, WPL becomes saturated when more than two clients are used. The increase in throughput for PD-ESM is 56%, and for PD-REDO it is 67% as the number of clients increases from 1 to 5.

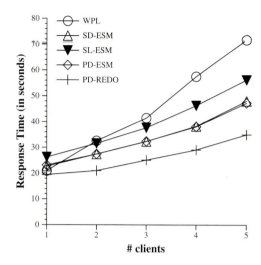

Figure 28.6. T2B, small database.

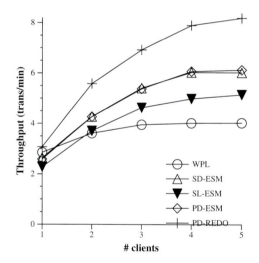

Figure 28.7. T2B, small database.

We turn next to Figures 28.6 and 28.7, which show the results of the T2B traversal. Comparing Figure 28.6 with Figure 28.4 shows that the difference in performance between the systems is smaller during T2B, as T2B performs significantly more updates per page than T2A slowing the performance of the diffing schemes. PD-REDO again has the best overall multiuser performance, however, the difference in performance between PD-REDO and WPL ranges from just 5% to 41% as the number of clients increases since PD-REDO must write a significant number of log records to disk per transaction (Figure 28.9). WPL is faster than the remaining systems when a single client is used, but its performance degrades more swiftly than the other systems since writing log records at the server is more of a bottleneck for WPL.

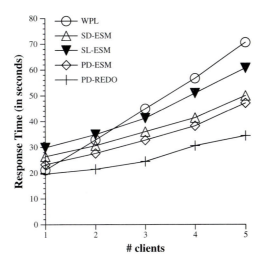

Figure 28.8. T2C, small database.

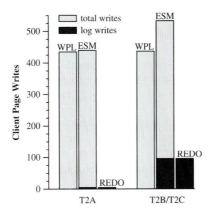

Figure 28.9. Client Writes, small database.

Interestingly, the performance of PD-ESM and SD-ESM are nearly identical during T2B because the client CPU usage of the two systems were the same.The performance of SD-ESM is a bit worse relative to PD-ESM during T2B because T2B updates more objects on each page that is updated, causing SD-ESM to do more copy and diffing work. In addition, since more updates are performed, the cost of actually doing the updates is more of a factor for SD-ESM, since each update incurs the cost of a function call and other CPU overhead, as described in Section 28.3. The performance difference between SL-ESM and SD-ESM is approximately 14% in all cases in Figure 28.6, showing that it is indeed worthwhile here to diff the 64-byte blocks copied by the subpage-diffing scheme. Lastly, Figure 28.7 shows that the transaction throughput begins to level off after four clients for most of the systems, with WPL showing no increase in throughput beyond three clients.

Figure 28.8 shows the response-time results for the T2C traversal. The response time for PD-ESM, PD-REDO, and WPL did not change significantly relative to T2B because these systems allow applications to update objects by dereferencing normal virtual-memory pointers. The performance of both SD-ESM and SL-ESM was 3.5 seconds slower, independent of the number of clients, due to the higher cost of performing updates in these systems. The overhead for performing the updates themselves is significant during T2C since a total of 1,049,760 additional updates are performed per transaction relative to T2B. Thus, the performance of PD-ESM is between 12% (1 client) and 6% (5 clients) faster than the performance of SD-ESM in Figure 28.8. The throughput results for T2C are not shown since they were also similar to those for T2B and can be deduced from the response-time results of Figure 8. In addition, the number of pages (total pages and log record pages) sent from the client to the server during T2C was the same as during T2B (Figure 9).

28.5.2   Constrained Cache Results

This section presents results obtained by running the various systems with a restricted amount of memory at each client. As in the previous section, the small database is used, but each client is given only 8 megabytes of memory to use for caching persistent data here. For the systems that do diffing, 7.5 Mb was allocated for the client buffer pool and 0.5 Mb for the recovery buffer. This allocation of memory results in a client buffer pool that is large enough to avoid paging. So, for example, the performance of WPL here is the same as in the previous section. However, now there is insufficient space in the recovery buffer to hold all of the data required by the diffing schemes until commit time. Figures 28.10 and 28.11 show the response time and throughput for traversal T2A in the constrained case. SD-ESM has the best performance in Figure 28.10. SD-ESM is 31% faster than PD-ESM and 40% faster than WPL at five clients. PD-ESM is slower than SD-ESM in this case because it experiences more contention in the recovery buffer. This causes PD-ESM to generate 4 times as many pages of log records on average per transaction as did SD-ESM (see Figure 28.14). WPL has competitive performance when the number of clients is low, but it has the worst performance when three or more clients are used. The performance of WPL degrades faster than the performance of the other systems, as before, because server performance is more of a limiting factor for WPL. On the other hand, the diffing schemes benefit from their ability to perform more work at the clients, which allows them to scale better.

The performance of PD-REDO appears to be approaching that of SD-ESM as

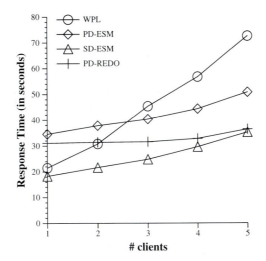

Figure 28.10. T2A, small, constrained cache.

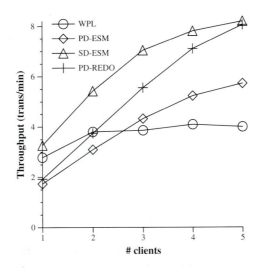

Figure 28.11. T2A, small, constrained cache.

the number of clients increases. PD-REDO scales better than the other systems here because it does not suffer from the overhead of shipping dirty pages back to the server. PD-REDO thus has the second best performance when two or more clients are used and is only 3% slower than SD-ESM at five clients. The throughput results shown in Figure 28.11 show that transaction throughput increases for all of the systems, except WPL (which becomes saturated), as the number of clients increases. SD-ESM and PD-REDO show the biggest increases in throughput. The throughput of SD-ESM increases by 2.5 times when the number of clients is increased, and the throughput for PD-REDO increases by a factor of 4.2.

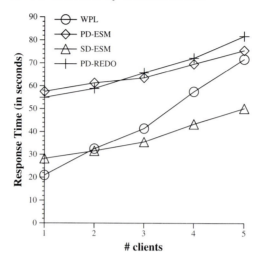

Figure 28.12. T2B, small, constrained cache.

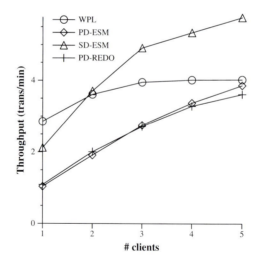

Figure 28.13. T2B, small, constrained cache.

We now turn to Figures 28.12 and 28.13, which show the response time and throughput, respectively, for traversal T2B. WPL has the best performance at one client, where it is 27% faster than SD-ESM (which is the next best performer). Beyond two clients, however, SD-ESM has the best performance, and at five clients, SD-ESM is 30% faster than WPL. SD-ESM scales better than WPL because it performs most of its recovery work at the clients, whereas WPL relies more heavily on the server. The page-diffing systems, PD-ESM and PD-REDO, have the worst performance in Figure 12. The reason for this can be seen in Figure 28.14 which shows the number of page writes per transaction for the systems. In Figure 28.14, PD-ESM produces 2.2 times as many log pages per transaction as does SD-ESM during T2B. In addition, the number of log pages produced by PD-ESM is approaching the number of pages written to the log per transaction by WPL due to the high level of contention in the recovery buffer for PD-ESM.

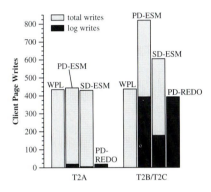

Figure 28.14. Client writes, small, constrained cache

PD-REDO is slightly faster than PD-ESM when the number of clients is low, but for more than three clients, PD-ESM has better performance. PD-REDO does not scale as well as PD-ESM in Figure 11 because of the CPU overhead of applying log records at the server for PD-REDO. The results for T2C are not shown for this experiment because they were similar to the results for T2B. The only difference in the times for T2C was that SD-ESM was consistently slower by a few seconds relative to its times for T2B.

28.5.3   Big Database Results

This section contains the results of the experiments that were run using the big database. In these experiments, all of the systems were given 12 Mb of memory at each client to use for caching persistent data. For the systems that do diffing, two alternative strategies for partitioning the memory between the client buffer pool and the recovery buffer were explored. Some of the systems were given 8 Mb of memory to use as the client buffer pool, and the remaining 4 Mb was used for the recovery buffer. Others were allocated 11.5 MB for the buffer pool and just a 0.5 MB for the recovery buffer.

Figure 28.15 shows the average response time for each system when performing traversal T2A. Surprisingly, WPL has the fastest response time when the number of clients is less than 4; however, when four or more clients are used, PD-ESM-1/2 has the best performance. PD-ESM-1/2 is 17% faster than WPL for five clients.

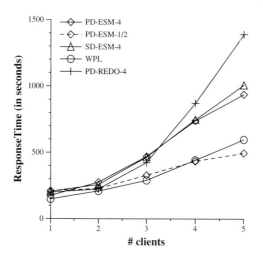

Figure 28.15. T2A, big database.

Overall, WPL has fast performance in this experiment because it is able to devote all of available memory at the clients to the buffer pool, thereby, decreasing the amount of paging in the system and lessening the burden placed on the server. However, the server log disk becomes a bottleneck for WPL as the number of clients increases, and eventually PD-ESM-1/2 performs better. As in previous experiments, the diffing scheme (PD-ESM-1/2) appears to scale better since it makes use of the clients' aggregate processing power to lessen the burden placed on the server's log disk and CPU.

Comparing the performance of PD-ESM-1/2 and PD-ESM-4 in Figure 28.15 shows the importance of choosing a good division of memory between the client buffer pool and the recovery buffer. PD-ESM-4 has better performance than PD-ESM-1/2 when one client is used, but for multiple clients, when paging between the client and the server becomes relatively more expensive, PD-ESM-1/2 is always faster. Indeed, as Figure 28.16 shows, the systems that were given smaller client buffers pool begin to thrash significantly when more than two clients are used, while the throughput for PD-ESM-1/2 continues to increase as the number of clients increases (although the increase is very small for more than two clients).

Interestingly, there is little difference in performance between PD-ESM-4 and SD-ESM-4 in Figure 28.15. This is because there is a significant amount of paging going on in the client buffer pool in Figure 28.15 (paging in the buffer pool is exactly the same in both systems), and each time a modified page is replaced in the client buffer pool, the same number of log records is generated by both PD-ESM-4 and SD-ESM-4. Thus, subpage diffing does not save nearly as much in terms of the number of log records generated in Figure 28.15 as it did in the small, constrained experiment (Figure 28.10). In fact, SD-ESM-4 only generates 10% fewer log records than does PD-ESM-4 in Figure 28.15, as opposed to generating 75% fewer log records in Figure 28.10. Finally, we note that although PD-REDO-4 is competitive with PD-ESM-4 when fewer than three clients are used, its performance grades more quickly than the other systems when the number of clients increases beyond 3. This is because a larger number of pages must be reread from disk at the server by PD-REDO-4 as the number of clients increases, so that log records describing updates to the pages can be applied.

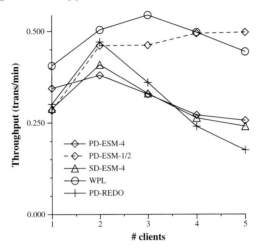

Figure 28.16. T2A, big database.

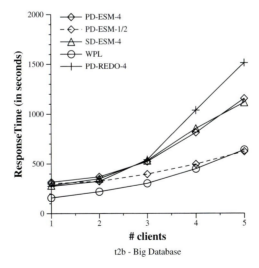

Figure 28.17. T2A, big database.

Comparing the results shown in Figure 28.15 to those of Figure 28.17, we see that the relative performance of the systems during T2B (dense updates) and T2A (sparse updates) is similar for the big database. WPL does somewhat better relative to PD-ESM-1/2 during T2B, as T2B updates a much larger number of objects per page, thus causing PD-ESM-1/2 to generate more log records. However, PD-ESM-1/2 scales better than the other systems (including WPL) and the performance of PD-ESM-1/2 appears to surpass that of WPL when five or more clients are used. The performance of SD-ESM-4 and PD-ESM-4 is almost identical in Figure 28.17 (as it was in Figure 28.15). Again, this is because SD-ESM-4 generates almost as many log records as PD-ESM-4, and because the savings in client CPU cost provided by SD-ESM-4 for performing less diffing and copying work does not provide any noticeable benefit in terms of performance. The scalability of the REDO algorithm is again the worst overall in Figure 28.17 as it was in the sparse update case (Figure 28.15). When five clients are used, PD-REDO-4 is 25% slower than PD-ESM-4.

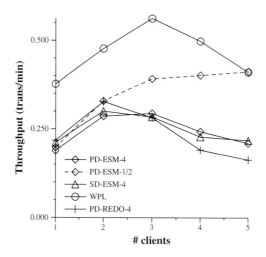

Figure 28.18. T2B, big database.

Figure 28.18 shows the throughput for the dense traversal run on the big database. Not surprisingly, the throughput results for the dense traversal are similar to those for the sparse traversal (Figure 28.16). Figure 28.18 highlights the fact that the systems that were given a larger client buffer pool (WPL, PD-ESM-1/2) scale better than the systems that were given smaller buffer pools (SD-ESM-4, PD-ESM-4, PD-REDO-4). This is because avoiding paging between the client and the server when using the big database is more important for achieving good performance than avoiding the generation of additional log records as is done by PD-ESM-1/2 and WPL. Even though WPL was given a large (12 Mg) client buffer pool, it begins to thrash for more than three clients, as the server becomes more of a performance bottleneck.

28.6 RELATED WORK

This section discusses related work that has been done on the design and implementation of recovery algorithms for client-server database systems. We also compare the study presented here with other studies that have dealt with the issue of recovery performance.

[9] describes the design and implementation of crash recovery in the EXODUS Storage Manager (ESM). In addition, [9] discusses the issues that must be addressed when implementing recovery in a client-server environment. The recovery algorithm described in [9] is based on ARIES [13], and supports write-ahead logging and a STEAL/NO-FORCE buffer management policy at the server. However, the ESM currently requires that all dirty pages be shipped from a client to the server before a transaction commits. This could be termed a force-to-server-at-commit policy. We note here that although ESM addresses the recovery issues raised by a client-server architecture, it does not address the issues discussed in Section 28.2, for example, issues that are specific to object-oriented systems and memory-mapped stores.

More recently, [14] has presented an algorithm called ARIES/CSA that also extends the basic ARIES recovery algorithm to the client-server environment. ESM differs from ARIES/CSA in that it supports fine-granularity locking, which ESM currently does not. ARIES/CSA also supports unconditional undo. Another difference between the two approaches is that clients in ARIES/CSA take their own checkpoints in addition to checkpoints taken by the server, whereas in ESM, checkpoints are only performed at the server. In principle, the recovery techniques described in Section 28.3 that use ESM could also be used in conjunction with ARIES/CSA. However, it is not clear how features such as fine-granularity locking that are supported by ARIES/CSA would be used by a memory-mapped storage system such as QuickStore since the memory-mapped approach is inherently page-based.

A related study on recovery performance appears in [11]. The study presented in [11] differs from the study presented here, in that it is only concerned with alternative methods for detecting and recording the occurrence of updates. We consider these issues as well, and also examine different strategies for processing log records in a client-server environment, that is, ARIES-based schemes, whole-page logging, and redo-at-server. An interesting note about the study presented here is that our results differ substantially from the results presented in [11]. Some of the variation in the results is undoubtedly due to architectural differences between the systems examined in the two studies. For example, in [11], the transaction log is located at the client machine instead of at the server as in ESM. The advantage of locating the log at the server as ESM does is that it increases system availability, since if a client crashes, the server can continue processing the requests of other clients. Placing the log at the server impacts performance because log records must be sent from clients to the server (usually over a network) before they are written to disk. Thus, differences in alternative techniques for generating log records will be smaller in a system in which the log is located at the server than in a system where log records are written to disk at the client.

Other reasons for differences in the results have to do with implementation details. For example, both [11] and our study examine the trade-offs involved in detecting the occurrence of updates in software versus using virtual-memory hardware support. However, [11] uses a *copy* architecture in which objects are copied one-at-a-time as they are accessed from the client buffer pool into a separate area in memory called the *object cache*. The hardware-based recovery scheme used in [11] requires that the virtual memory page in the object cache that will hold an object unprotected and then reprotected each time an object is copied into the page emproducing a substantial amount of overhead (up to 100%), even for read-only transactions. Under the approach used in QuickStore (in-place access, page-at-a-time swizzling) a page's protection is only manipulated once, when the first object on the page is updated. Thus, our results show that the hardware-based detection scheme does much better than do the results presented in [11]. In particular, the scheme used in QuickStore does not impact the performance of read-only transactions.

[11] also examines several schemes (called *card marking*) that are similar to the subpage approach examined here. The results presented in [11] show that the size of the subpage region used for recovery has a great impact on performance. The difference in performance reported in [11] is because using a small subpage unit for recovery can reduce diffing costs when updates are sparse. The results presented in this study, on the other hand, show that the size of the sub-page region used for recovery has a great impact on performance. The difference in performance reported in [11] is due to the fact that using a small sub-page unit for recovery can reduce diffing costs when updates are sparse. The results presented in this study, on the other hand, show that the size of the sub-page blocks is important, not because of savings in CPU costs when the block size is small, but because smaller block sizes can result in the generation of fewer log records when space in the recovery buffer is tight. [11] does not consider this case. We believe the differences in the results are because fact that we use an in-place scheme whereas [11] uses a copy approach, and to the cost for supporting concurrency control (the system examined in [11] is single-user system that do not support concurrency). The study presented here also differs from [11] in that we examine the scalability of the various recovery schemes as the number of clients accessing the database increases. We also examine the performance of the different recovery techniques when a large database is used and a significant amount of paging (object replacement) is taking place in the system. [11] does not consider these issues. We also note the performance study contained in [17] also contains some results concerning recovery performance. However, the systems compared in [17] (ObjectStore and E/EXODUS) were not built on the same underlying storage manager, so it is not possible to accurately measure the performance differences due to recovery in [17].

Although several OODBMSs are commercially available, very little has been published concerning the recovery algorithms they use. The O_2 system [4] also uses an ARIES-based approach to support recovery. O_2 differs from ESM and ARIES/CSA in that it uses shadowing to avoid undo. The most popular commercial OODBMS is ObjectStore [12], which, like QuickStore, uses a memory-mapping scheme to give application programs access to persistent data. ObjectStore currently uses whole-page logging to support recovery. The basic idea of this approach is that dirty pages are shipped from a client to the server and written to the log before a transaction is allowed to commit. This differs from the ARIES-based schemes mentioned before that only require that the log records generated by updates be written to disk at commit time. [19] describes the Texas storage manager, which also uses a memory-mapping scheme. [19] was the first to propose the use of differencing to detect updates of persistent data. Finally, we note that the whole-page logging approach to recovery was first described in [6], which presents the design of the *database cache*.

28.7 CONCLUSIONS

This chapter has presented an in-depth comparison of the performance of several different approaches to implementing recovery in QuickStore, a memory-mapped storage manager based on a client-server, page-shipping architecture. Each of the recovery algorithms was designed to meet the unique performance requirements faced by a system like QuickStore. The results of the performance study show that using diffing to generate log records for updates at clients is generally superior in terms of performance to whole-page logging. The diffing approach is better because it takes advantage of the aggregate CPU power available at the clients to lessen the overall burden placed on the server to support recovery. This provides much better scalability, as it prevents the server from becoming a performance bottleneck as quickly when the number of clients accessing the database increases.

The study also compared the performance of two different underlying recovery schemes on which the diffing algorithms were based. These included the recovery algorithm used by the EXODUS Storage Manager and a simplified scheme termed redo-at-server (REDO). Although the REDO approach provided significant performance benefits in some cases when using a small database, while producing only a moderate number of log records per transaction, it failed to perform well when the database was bigger than the server buffer pool, and when the volume of log records sent to the server per transaction was high. The results presented in the study show that REDO can suffer from both disk and CPU bottlenecks at the server. System builders will have to decide whether the simplifications in system design and coding are worth the poor scalability of REDO in certain situations.

Finally, the study compared the performance of page-based and subpage-diffing techniques. Surprisingly, the subpage-diffing techniques provided very little advantage in terms of performance over the page-based approach. This is apparently due because diffing is a relatively inexpensive operation compared to the other costs involved in the system, such as network and disk access costs. The subpage-diffing approach did pay off in one situation, that is, when the amount of memory that could be devoted to recovery was very low. System designers will have to decide whether this situation is likely to arise often enough in practice to justify using subpage diffing. In addition, it was shown that subpage diffing can have worse performance than page diffing when updates are performed repeatedly. This fact must be weighed against the mild advantages of the technique when deciding on an implementation strategy. Finally, the results showed that diffing is even worthwhile when subpage granularity is used for recovery. Systems that used a sub-page granularity, but which did not use diffing always had comparable or worse performance than the systems that used diffing.

In the future, we would like to explore improvements to the recovery schemes based on differencing to see if the diffing approach can be enhanced to better adapt to dynamic workload changes. One class of techniques that we would like to explore involves dynamically varying the amount of memory allocated to the buffer pool and the recovery buffer of a client during and across transactions.

References

[1] M. Carey, D. DeWitt, M. Franklin, N. Hall, M. McAuliffe, J. Naughton, D. Schuh, M. Solomon, C. Tan, O. Tsatalos, S. White, M. Zwilling, Shoring Up Persistent Applications, *Proc. ACM SIGMOD Conference*, Minneapolis, MN, May 1994.

[2] M. Carey, D. DeWitt, J. Naughton, The OO7 Benchmark, *Proc. ACM SIGMOD Conference*, Washington, DC, May 1993.

[3] M. Carey et al., *Storage Management for Objects in EXODUS*, in Object-Oriented Concepts, Databases, and Applications. W. Kim and F.Lochovsky, eds., Addison-Wesley, 1989.

[4] O. Deux et al., The O2 System, *Comm. of the ACM*, 34(10) (October 1991).

[5] D. DeWitt, P. Futtersack, D. Maier, F. Velez, A Study of Three Alternative Workstation-Server Architectures for Object-Oriented Database Systems, *Proc. 16th VLDB Conference*, Brisbane, Australia, August, 1990.

[6] K. Elhardt, R. Bayer, A Database Cache for High Performance and Fast Restart in Database Systems, *ACM Trans. on Database System*, 9(4) (December 1984).

[7] J. Eliot B. Moss, Working with Persistent Objects: To Swizzle or Not to Swizzle, *IEEE Trans. on Software Eng.*, 18(8) (August 1992).

[8] M. Franklin, *Caching and Memory Management in Client-Server Database Systems*, Ph.D. thesis, University of Wisconsin-Madison, Technal Report No.1168, July 1993.

[9] M. Franklin et al., Crash Recovery in Client-Server EXODUS, *Proc. ACM SIGMOD Conference*, San Diego, California, 1992.

[10] T. Haerder, A. Reuter, Principles of Transaction Oriented Database Recovery - A Taxonomy, *Computing Surveys*, 6(1) (February 1988).

[11] A. Hosking, E. Brown, J. Moss, Update Logging in Persistent Programming Languages: A Comparative Performance Evaluation, *Proc. 19th VLDB Conference*, Dublin, Ireland, 1993.

[12] C. Lamb, G. Landis, J. Orenstein, D. Weinreb, The ObjectStore Database System, *Comm. of the ACM*, 34(10) (October 1991).

[13] C. Mohan, D. Haderle, B. Lindsay, H. Pirahesh, P. Schwartz, ARIES: A Transaction Recovery Method Supporting Fine-Granularity Locking and Partial Rollbacks Using Write-Ahead Logging, *ACM Trans. on Database System*, 17(1) (March 1992).

[14] C. Mohan, I. Narang, ARIES/CSA: A Method for Database Recovery in Client-Server Architectures, *Proc. ACM SIGMOD Conference*, Minneapolis, MN, 1994.

[15] J. Richardson, M. Carey, and D. Schuh, The Design of the E Programming Language, *ACM Trans. on Prog. Lang. and System*, 15(3) (July 1993).

[16] D. Schuh, M. Carey, and D. Dewitt, Persistence in E Revisited— Implementation Experiences, in *Implementing Persistent Object Bases Principles and Practice, Proc. 4th Int'l. Workshop on Pers. Obj. System*, Martha's Vineyard, MA, Sept. 1990.

[17] S. White and D. DeWitt, A Performance Study of Alternative Object Faulting and Pointer Swizzling Strategies, in *Proc. 18th VLDB Conference*, Vancouver, British Columbia, August 1992.

[18] S. White, D. DeWitt, QuickStore: A High Performance Mapped Object Store, *Proc. ACM SIGMOD Conference*, Minneapolis, MN, May 1994.

[19] P. Wilson, S. Kakkad, Pointer Swizzling at Page Fault Time: Efficiently and Compatibly Supporting Huge Address Spaces on Standard Hardware, *Proc. Int'l. Workshop on Obj. Orientation in Operating System*, Paris, France, Sept. 1992.

Chapter 29

Disk Array Striping

Peter M. Chen and Edward K. Lee

Abstract

Redundant disk arrays are an increasingly popular way to improve I/O system performance. Past research has studied how to stripe data in non redundant, RAID Level 0 disk arrays; this chapter focuses on how to stripe data in redundant, RAID Level 5 disk arrays. We create simple design rules to select a striping unit that guarantees the best possible performance for a specified range of synthetic workloads. We then validate the synthetically derived design rules using real workload traces to show that the design rules apply well to real systems.

We find no difference in the optimal striping units for RAID Level 0 and 5 for read-intensive workloads. For write-intensive workloads, in contrast, the overhead of maintaining parity causes full-stripe writes (writes that span the entire error-correction group) to be more efficient than read-modify writes or reconstruct writes. This additional factor causes the optimal striping unit for RAID Level 5 to be four to six times smaller for write-intensive workloads than for read-intensive workloads.

We examine how the optimal striping unit varies with the number of disks in an array, both when concurrency is known and when it is not known. We find that the optimal striping unit for reads in a RAID Level 5 varies inversely to the number of disks, but that the optimal striping unit for writes varies with the number of disks. Overall, we find that the optimal striping unit for workloads with an unspecified mix of reads and writes is independent of the number of disks. Together, these trends lead us to recommend two simple design rules:

- If concurrency is known, choose a striping unit of $1/8 \times$ average disk positioning time $\times$ disk transfer rate $\times$ (concurrency $- 1$) $+ 1$ sector. This achieved at least 85% of the best possible performance for all workloads (average performance 96%) at that concurrency for disk arrays of 5 to 33 disks.

- If concurrency is not known, choose a striping unit of $1/2 \times$ average disk positioning time $\times$ disk transfer rate. This achieved at least 60% of the best possible performance for all workloads (average performance 84%) for disk arrays of 5 to 33 disks.

29.1 INTRODUCTION

For the past several decades, input/output (I/O) performance has not kept up with advances in processing speeds. Disk arrays have been proposed and used to increase aggregate disk performance by ganging together multiple disks in parallel [2, 10]. Redundant disk arrays add errorcorrecting codes to improve reliability. One popular type of redundant disk array interleaves data in block-size units known as striping units and uses parity to protect against failures. This type of disk array is known as a RAID Level 5 (Figure 29.1) [10]. This figure illustrates how data are distributed in a round-robin manner across disks in a RAID Level 5-disk array. Each number represents one data block; the size of each data block is called the striping unit. Parity blocks have the same size and are rotated between the disks. Each parity block contains the parity for the data blocks in its row. For example, P0 contains the parity computed over data blocks 0 to 3. The specific data distribution shown here (and used throughout the chapter) is called the left-symmetric distribution [8].

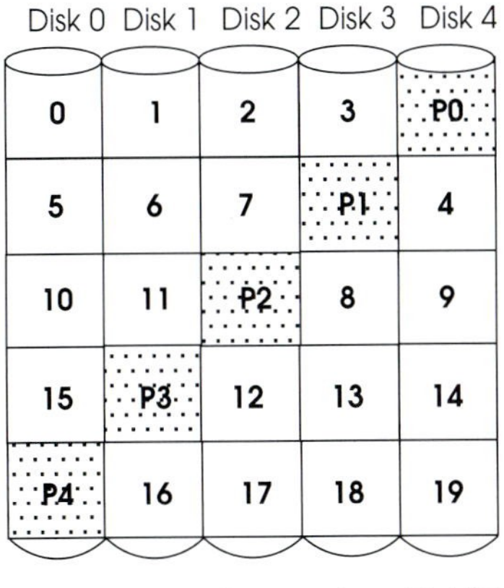

Disk 0 Disk 1 Disk 2 Disk 3 Disk 4

0	1	2	3	P0
5	6	7	P1	4
10	11	P2	8	9
15	P3	12	13	14
P4	16	17	18	19

Figure 29.1. Data and parity layout in a RAID Level 5-disk array.

One of the most crucial parameters in designing a disk array is the size of the striping unit. The striping unit determines how a logical request from a user is broken up into physical disk requests to the disks. This distribution profoundly affects a disk array's performance—[1] shows that performance of a nonredundant disk array (RAID Level 0) can vary by an order of magnitude depending on the striping unit.

Several papers address how to choose the striping unit in nonredundant disk arrays [1, 7, 12], but none has yet examined how to choose it in a RAID Level 5.

The overhead of maintaining parity in a RAID Level 5 leads to additional factors in choosing the best striping unit. The goals of this chapter are to

- quantify the effect these additional factors have in choosing the striping unit

- create simple design rules for determining the best striping unit for a range of workloads

- quantify how the number of disks in the array affects the optimal striping unit.

Our key results, found by using synthetic workloads and verified by using real-world traces, are as follows:

- Concurrency is the single most important feature of a workload. Knowing concurrency allows one to choose a single striping unit that achieves near-optimal performance for a range of request sizes. That striping unit is $S \times average\ positioning\ time \times disk\ transfer\ rate \times (concurrency - 1) + 1\ sector$. We graph S as a function of the number of disks for read workloads, write workloads, and read/write workloads. S for read/write workloads is 1/8 and is independent of the number of disks.

- Even without knowing concurrency, one can still choose a striping unit that guarantees at least 60% of optimal performance for any concurrency and request size. That striping unit is $Z \times average\ positioning\ time \times disk\ transfer\ rate$. We graph Z as a function of the number of disks for read workloads, write workloads, and read/write workloads. Z for read/write workloads is 1/2 and is independent of the number of disks.

- As the number of disks in the array varies, the best striping unit for reads increases, but the best striping unit for writes decreases. These two trends effectively cancel and the striping unit that guarantees the highest performance over a mix of reads and writes is independent of the number of disks.

- Design rules for choosing the striping unit depend only on the product of a disk's average positioning time and transfer rate.

This chapter is organized as follows: Section 29.2 reviews previous research on disk-array striping and describes qualitatively how RAID Level-5 disk arrays change the optimal striping unit. Section 29.3 describes the experimental setup that we use in this chapter. In Sections 29.4 and 29.5, we use synthetic workloads to derive simple design rules for striping data in RAID Level-5 disk arrays given varying amounts of workload information and disks. We then validate the synthetically derived design rules in Section 29.6 using real workload traces to show that the design rules apply well to real systems.

29.2 BACKGROUND AND PREVIOUS WORK

29.2.1 Nonredundant Disk Arrays (RAID Level 0)

We define the striping unit as the amount of logically contiguous data stored on a single disk (Figure 29.1). A large striping unit will tend to keep a file clustered together on a few disks (possibly one); a small striping unit tends to spread each file across many disks.

Parallelism describes the number of disks that service a user's request for data. A higher degree of parallelism increases the transfer rate that each request sees. However, as more disks cooperate in servicing each request, more disks waste time positioning (seeking and rotating) and the efficiency of the array decreases. We define the degree of concurrency of a workload as the average number of outstanding user requests in the system at one time. A small striping unit causes higher parallelism but supports less concurrency in the workload; a large striping unit causes little parallelism but supports more concurrency in the workload.

Fundamentally, disk striping affects the amount of data that each disk transfers before repositioning (seeking and rotating to the next request). This amount of data has a drastic impact on disk throughput. For a Seagate Elite3 disk, if a disk transfers one sector per random request, throughput will be 0.03 MB/s; if it transfers one track per request, throughput will be 1.79 MB/s; if it transfers one cylinder per request, throughput will be 4.16 MB/s. The choice of striping unit should maximize the amount of useful data each disk transfers per request and still make use of all disks. Large striping units maximize the amount of data a disk transfers per access but require higher concurrency in the workload to make use of all disks. Small striping units can make use of all disks even with low-workload concurrency, but they cause the disks to transfer less data per access.

Chen and Patterson investigated these trade-offs in a RAID Level 0 with 16 disks [1]. They found that the choice of striping unit depends heavily on the workload concurrency and only minimally on the workload's average request size. If concurrency is known, they found that it is possible to choose a striping unit that guarantees good performance to workloads with that concurrency over a wide range of sizes. Good performance in this context means getting over 95% of the throughput at the optimal striping unit. Chen and Peterson's choice of striping unit was expressed as $S \times$ (average disk positioning time) $\times$ (disk transfer rate) $\times$ (workload concurrency - 1) + 1 sector, where S is called the "concurrency-slope coefficient" and is found to be approximately 1/4 to 1/2 for a 16-disk array.

If concurrency is unspecified, a good choice for striping unit can still be made, although the performance guarantees are weaker than when concurrency is specified. Chen and Patterson found a good choice of striping unit to be $Z \times$ (average disk positioning time) $\times$ (disk transfer rate), where Z is called the "zero-knowledge coefficient", since it applies when no workload information is given, and is found to be approximately 2/3 for a 16-disk array.

Note that the preceding two equations can be rewritten to depend on only one composite disk parameter: (average disk positioning time) × (disk transfer rate). We call this the disk's "bandwidth-delay product", similar to the bandwidth-delay product of a network.

In this chapter we extend the work of [1] to RAID Level-5 disk arrays. Section 29.2.2 describes how the choice of striping unit in a RAID Level 5 differs from that in a RAID Level 0 due to the effect of maintaining parity when performing writes in a RAID Level 5.

Lee and Katz [6, 7] developed an analytic model of nonredundant disk arrays and derived an equation for the optimal striping unit to be

$$\sqrt{\frac{bandwidth - delay\ product \times (concurrency - 1) \times request\ size\ \sigma}{number\ of\ disks}}$$

Taken together, [1] and [6, 7] concluded that the striping unit depends on the bandwidth-delay product and concurrency. [6, 7] concluded that the optimal striping unit depends on request size, but [1] showed that this dependence can be ignored with less than a 5% performance penalty.

Scheuermann, Weikum, and Zabback show moderate performance improvements by allowing different striping units for different files [12, 14]. This performance improvement comes at the cost of additional complexity and assumes a priori knowledge of the average request size and peak throughput of applications accessing each file.

29.2.2   Block-Interleaved, Parity Disk Arrays (RAID Level 5)

Like RAID Level 0, RAID Level-5 disk arrays interleave data across multiple disks in blocks called striping units (Figure 29.1). To protect against single-disk failures, RAID Level 5 adds a parity block for each row of data blocks. These parity blocks are distributed over all disks to prevent any single disk from becoming a bottleneck. The group of data blocks over which a parity block is computed is called a parity group or stripe. In Figure 29.1, data blocks 0 to 3 and parity block P0 compose a stripe.

Note that the distribution, or rotation, of parity blocks among the disks in the array is independent of the striping unit. The amount of contiguous parity on a disk is called the parity striping unit. All current disk arrays set the parity striping unit equal to the striping unit.

Reads in a RAID Level 5 are very similar to accesses (both reads and writes) in a RAID Level 0. Writes in a RAID Level 5, however, are quite different because they must maintain correct parity. There are three types of writes in a RAID Level 5, depending on how the new parity is computed.

- *Full-stripe writes*: writes that update all the stripe units in a parity group. The new parity value for the associated parity block is computed across all new blocks. For instance, in Figure 29.1, writing blocks 0 to 3 would be a full-stripe write. No additional read or write operations are required to compute parity, and hence full-stripe writes are the most efficient type of writes.

- *Reconstruct writes*: writes that compute parity by reading in the data from the stripe that are not to be updated. Parity is then computed over this data and the new data. For instance, writing data blocks 0 to 2 in Figure 29.1 could lead to a reconstruct write. The disk array software would read the values of data block 3, and then compute parity over the new data (blocks 0 to 2) and data block 3. Reconstruct writes are less efficient than full-stripe writes because they perform more I/Os per byte written.

- *Read-modify writes*: writes that compute the new parity value by (1) reading the old data blocks from the disks to be updated, (2) reading the old parity blocks for the stripe, (3) calculating how the new data are different from the old data, and (4) changing the old parity to reflect these differences. For instance, writing block 0 in Figure 29.1 could be done as a read-modify write. To compute the new parity, the disk-array software reads the old value of block 0 and the old value of parity block P0. It would then compute parity by seeing how the old value of block 0 was different from the new value and applying these differences to the old parity block to generate the new value of parity block P0. Read-modify writes are less efficient than full-stripe writes because they must read the old values of the data and parity blocks. Note that read-modify writes could be performed as reconstruct writes. We assume the system chooses the method that minimizes the total number of I/Os.

The method used to compute parity depends on the size of a request and its starting location. In general, writes that span a larger fraction of the stripe are more efficient than writes that span a smaller fraction. This factor tends to make the choice of striping unit for writes in a RAID Level 5 smaller than for reads. This chapter uses simulation to study the effects of the preceding factors and determine guidelines for selecting the best striping unit.

29.3 EXPERIMENTAL DESIGN

29.3.1 The Disk Model

We model several types of disks in our study. The default disks are IBM Lightning 3.5-inch disks [5]. In order to maintain the same disk-array capacity, we use only the first 300 MB of each disk. Thus, the effective average seek time for the Seagate Elite3 disks is three times faster than if we had spread requests over the entire disk. All disks in the array are rotationally synchronized, that is, sector 0 passes under the read/write head at the same time for all disks. Table 29.1 summarizes the relevant parameters for the disks we model in this study.

Table 29.1. Disk Model Parameters

	IBM Lightning	Seagate Elite3	Seagate Wren4
Bytes per sector	512	512	512
Sectors per track	48	99	53
Tracks per cylinder	14	21	9
Cylinders per disk	949	2627	1549
Disk capacity (MB)	311	2667	361
Revolution time (ms)	13.9	11.1	16.7
Single cylinder seek time (ms)	2.0	1.7	5.5
Average seek time (ms)	12.5	11.0	16.5
Max-stroke seek time (ms)	25.0	22.5	35.0
Sustained transfer rate (MB/s)	1.8	1.8	1.6
Effective (simulated) capacity	300	300	300
Effective average seek time (ms) (first 300 MB of disk)	12.2	4.1	14.9
Effective average positioning time	19.2	9.7	23.2
Effective bandwidth-delay product	33	43	37

Average seek time is the average time needed to seek between two equally randomly selected cylinders. Sustained transfer rate is a function of bytes per sector, sectors per track, and revolution time. IBM Lightning is the IBM 0661 3.5 inch SCSI disk drive; Seagate Elite3 is the Seagate ST-43400N 3.5 inch SCSI disk drive; and Seagate Wren4 is the Seagate ST-4350N 5.25 inch SCSI disk drive. The seek profile for each disk is computed as $seekTime(x) = a \times \sqrt{x-1} + b \times (x-1) + c$, where x is the seek distance in cylinders, and a, b, and c are chosen to satisfy the single-cylinder seek time, average seek time, and max-stroke seek time, respectively. The square-root term in the preceding equation models the constant acceleration/deceleration period of the disk-head and the linear term models the period after maximum disk head velocity is reached. We have compared the model to the seek profile of the Amdahl 6380A [13] and IBM Lightning and have found the model to closely approximate the seek profile of the actual disk. We did not model zone-bit recording; instead, we assumed an average transfer rate over all cylinders.

29.3.2   The Workload

The primary workload we use in this chapter is stochastic and characterized by three parameters: degree of concurrency, request size, and read/write mix. In Section 29.6, we verify our results using traces. We chose to primarily use a stochastic workload for the following reasons:

- Our goal of synthesizing design rules as a function of workload required an extremely flexible workload. In particular, we needed to be able to independently vary each of three workload parameters: concurrency, request size, and read/write mix. A stochastic workload allowed us to easily explore many different workloads. Traces, in contrast, can provide a realistic snapshot of a system and workload, but their fixed characteristics would have unduly limited our study.

- One goal of this chapter is to compare our choice of striping units for RAID Level 5 with the choice of striping units for RAID Level 0 from previous studies. Previous studies were done using stochastic workloads, so our use of a stochastic workload enabled a direct comparison.

Concurrency controls the load on the system by specifying the number of independent processes that are simultaneously issuing requests. The number of processes is fixed during each simulation run and each process repeatedly issues an I/O request, waits for its completion, and immediately issues the next request. We simulate concurrencies between 1 and 20. Unless the striping unit is much smaller than the average request size, concurrency 1 leaves most disks idle. On the opposite extreme, workloads with concurrency 20 keep all the disks busy.

Request size controls the amount of data for each logical access. We use the following five distributions of request size:

- exp4KB: an exponential distribution with a mean of 4 KB

- exp16KB: an exponential distribution with a mean of 16 KB

- norm100KB: a normal distribution with a mean and standard deviation of 100 KB

- norm400KB: a normal distribution with a mean and standard deviation of 400 KB

- norm1500KB: a normal distribution with a mean and standard deviation of 1500 KB

The smaller distributions model requests generated by time-sharing and transaction processing applications and the larger distributions model requests generated by scientific applications. Request sizes are always a multiple of a kilobyte and are always at least a kilobyte in size; zero and negative request sizes are not allowed. The means of the target distributions are adjusted so that the actual mean request size seen by the array is 4, 16, 100, 400, or 1500 KB. In all cases, requests are aligned on kilobyte boundaries and are uniformly distributed throughout the disk array.

Other workload parameters are possible, such as disk skew, sequentiality, and burstiness. Skew between the disks of a round-robin interleaved array is likely to largely absorbed by higher-level caches if those caches can hold multiple striping units worth of data. The underlying sequentiality of a workload is included in the request-size parameter-sequential disk accesses often are simply single, large logical requests that have been broken down (and can be easily recombined by a disk-array controller). Burstiness can be thought of as a workload whose concurrency varies with time. During a burst, concurrency is high; between bursts, concurrency is low. We synthesize rules for choosing a single striping unit that achieves good performance for a mix of workloads of both high and low concurrency.

29.3.3   The RAID Simulator

Our study is conducted using a detailed simulator of the disk system. We opted for a simulation-driven study rather than a queueing-model study because read-modify writes and reconstruct writes in a RAID Level 5 create synchronization constraints that are very difficult to model analytically.

The RAID simulator, *raidSim*, is an event-driven simulator developed at Berkeley for modeling nonredundant and redundant disk arrays. It consists of a module for implementing a variety of RAID levels, a module for modeling disk behavior, and a module for generating synthetic I/O requests. The only resources modeled are disks. In particular, resources such as the CPU, disk controllers, and I/O busses are ignored. This allows us to focus on the intrinsic performance effects of using multiple disks. *RaidSim* simulates each workload until the mean response time is within 5% of the true mean at a 95% confidence level. This typically requires simulating several thousand requests. The disks support request merging (as is provided by an on-disk cache [11]). That is, if a disk receives two consecutive requests for two adjacent disk blocks, it services these requests as though they had been one large request.

29.3.4   Metrics

Common disk system performance metrics are throughput and response time. With a fixed level of concurrency and a specific request size, higher throughput always leads to faster response time (Little's law implies that Throughput = average_request_size × average_concurrency/response_time, so response time can be easily calculated for each workload from its throughput [4]). In this chapter, we use throughput as the main performance metric. Most throughput values will be given as a percentage of the maximum throughput over all striping units. For example, given a particular workload, if the maximum throughput over all striping units is 10 MB/s, and a striping unit S yields a throughput of 3 MB/s, then the throughput for striping unit S will be given as 30% of maximum throughput.

29.4   CHOOSING THE STRIPING UNIT

Figures 29.2 and 29.3 show the throughput versus the striping unit for reads and writes over a range of sizes and concurrencies. As expected, the throughput increases as request sizes or concurrencies increase. Note that a write throughput is uniformly lower than a read throughput (Figure 29.2), due to the extra overhead of maintaining parity in a RAID Level 5.

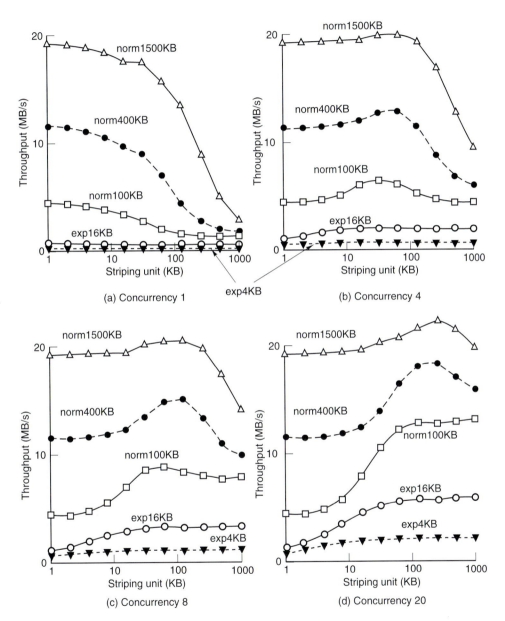

Figure 29.2. Read throughput for a range of sizes and concurrencies.

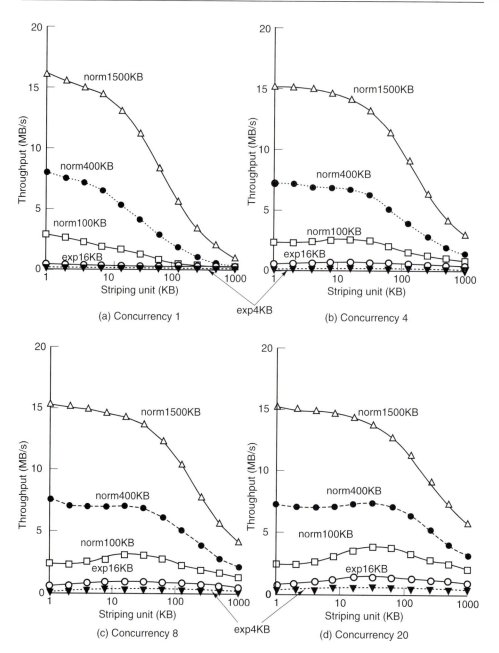

Figure 29.3. Write throughput for a range of sizes and concurrencies.

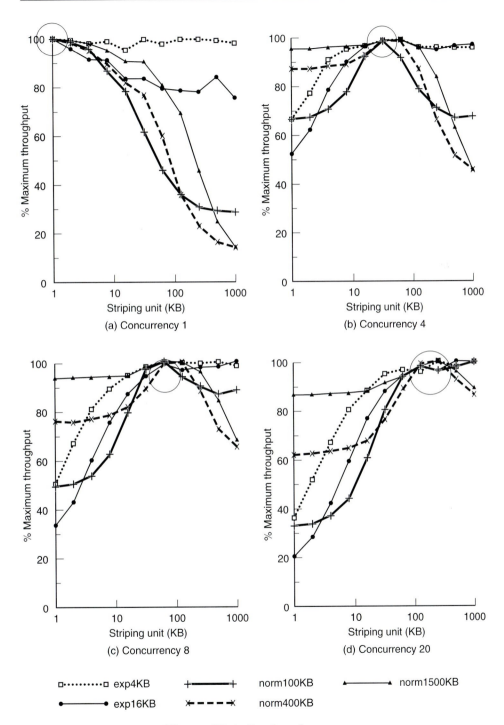

Figure 29.4. Read performance

These results are for 17 IBM Lightning disks. We vary the striping unit from 1 KB to 1 MB and make the following observations.

- At any fixed striping unit, the throughput increases with larger request sizes and higher degrees of concurrency. Increasing request sizes allow each disk to access more data per request; higher degrees of concurrency are able to make use of more disks.

- Reads perform uniformly better than writes due to the extra overhead of maintaining parity when writing data.

In order to compare trends from different workloads more easily, we scale the throughput of each workload, expressing it as a percentage of the maximum throughput. The percentage of maximum throughput for a range of sizes and concurrencies are shown as a function of the striping unit in Figures 29.4 and 29.5. The circled point on each graph indicates the striping unit that guarantees the highest percentage of maximum throughput to all workloads shown on that graph. Note that increasing concurrency leads to larger optimal striping units. Note that the optimal striping unit for write- intensive workloads is smaller than for the read-intensive workloads in Figure 29.4.

If one knows the parameters of a workload, that is, the request-size distribution, concurrency, and read/write mix, one can use Figures 29.4 and 29.5 to choose the striping unit that yields the maximum possible performance (100%) for that workload. In real systems, however, some of the workload parameters (size, concurrency, and read/write mix) may be unspecified. Thus, it is desirable to be able to choose a good striping unit with as little knowledge about the workload as possible. In this chapter, we strive to maximize the *minimum percentage throughput over a range of workloads*. In other words, we wish to guarantee the highest percentage of maximum throughput to all workloads in consideration, and the number of workloads under consideration *increases* as our knowledge about the workload *decreases*. For example, if we know the workload is 100% reads with concurrency 4, but we do not know the request size, we can use Figure 29.4(b) to choose a striping unit. In Figure 29.4(b), over a wide range of request sizes, the striping unit that maximizes the minimum percentage throughput is 40 KB. At that striping unit, all workloads considered yield at least 98% of their maximum possible throughput.

We begin with a fairly complete specification of the workload and gradually limit our knowledge of the workload. At each stage, we synthesize a simple design rule for how to choose the striping unit to guarantee the highest possible performance to all workloads being considered.

29.4.1 Knowing Concurrency

In [1], we found that request size was the least important workload parameter to know when choosing the striping unit for RAID Level 0. We found it possible to guarantee nearly 100% performance to a workload, even without knowing its request

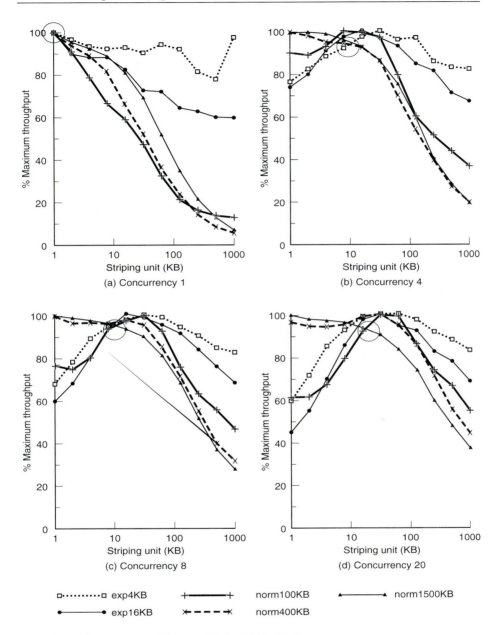

Figure 29.5. Write Performance

size. In this section, we verify this result for RAID Level-5 read and write workloads and calculate the concurrency-slope coefficient for choosing a good striping unit. It is shown in Figure 29.6, that the range of striping units that yield at least 95%

(reads) or 90% (writes) of the maximum throughput for all request sizes (exp4KB, exp16KB, norm100KB, norm400KD, and norm1500KD) for reads and writes. The range for reads is marked by + signs; the range for writes is marked by signs. The dashes show that the lines fit to lie entirely in the displayed range.

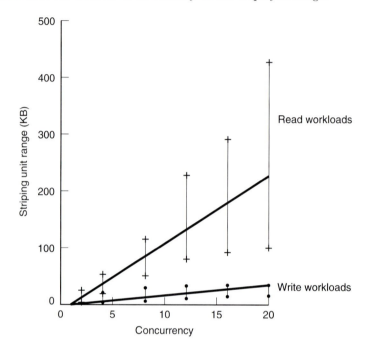

Figure 29.6. Striping unit chosen versus concurrency–17 IBM Lightning disks.

We start by focusing on performance of reads in a RAID Level 5. As in [1], if we know the concurrency of a read workload, it is possible to choose a striping unit that guarantees over 95% of the maximum throughput for any request sizes. In fact, there is a *range* of striping units that guarantee 95% of maximum throughput to workloads with any request size. Figure 29.6(a) shows the range of these striping units for read workloads as vertical lines delineated by + signs. Note that higher concurrencies lead to larger striping units. This is expected from the discussion in Section 29.2.2. Higher concurrencies inherently use all disks, so we can then use larger striping units to maximize the amount of data each disk transfers per logical request.

We can express our choice of striping unit as a linear function of workload concurrency by (1) fixing the striping unit choice for a concurrency of one at 1 sector (0.5 KB), and (2) measuring the slope of the striping unit versus concurrency line that lies entirely in the displayed range (if there is a range of possible slopes, we choose the midpoint of the range). Our choice of striping unit in Figure 29.6 can then be expressed as *Striping unit = slope × (concurrency − 1) + 1 sector.*

Table 29.2. Values of Concurrency-Slope and Zero-Knowledge coefficients for three disk types. The values of the various coefficients useful in choosing the striping unit are shown. For three very different disks, the values of each coefficient are relatively independent of disk type.

Disk type	Read Workloads		Write Workloads		Read and Write Workloads	
	S_r	Z_r	S_w	Z_w	S_{rw}	Z_{rw}
17 Lightnings	0.36	0.73	0.061	0.18	0.11	0.48
17 Elite3	0.34	0.67	0.072	0.19	0.12	0.58
17 Wren4	0.28	0.68	0.056	0.17	0.10	0.46
Average	0.33	0.69	0.063	0.18	0.11	0.51

The slope term can be expressed as $S_r \times$ (bandwidth-delay product), where S_r is the concurrency-slope coefficient and can be shown to be independent of disk technology (Table 29.2 and Appendix 1) [1]. For 17 IBM Lightning disks, the slope of this line is 12 KB/concurrency and hence S_r is 0.36. These values match the results in [1], verifying that reads in a RAID Level 5 using the left-symmetric parity placement [8] lead to identical striping unit choices as I/Os in a nonredundant disk array.

We next turn to writes in a RAID Level 5. From the discussion in Section 29.2.2, we expect that the best striping unit for write-intensive workloads will be smaller than those for read-intensive workloads. Figure 29.6 shows the range of optimal striping units for writes as vertical bars delineated by (●). For write-intensive workloads, it is not always possible to choose a striping unit for a specific concurrency that yields 95% performance for all request sizes, so we relax the performance criterion until it is possible to fit a line through the range of striping units that meet the criterion (which occurred at a criterion of 90%).

The range of optimal striping units in Figure 29.6 is uniformly lower for writes than for reads, as expected. Writes perform better when striped across more disks, since they then require less accesses to compute the new parity. Smaller striping units thus lead to more efficient writes; this makes the range of optimal striping units lower for write-intensive workloads than the range for read-intensive workloads. Also note that even very high-concurrency workloads do not lead to very large optimal striping units. This ceiling on the optimal striping unit arises because writes yield better performance when they utilize all the disks by issuing full-stripe writes rather than by utilizing the workload concurrency. Of course, this must be balanced by the fact that the disk array is more efficient when a disk transfers a larger amount of data for a logical request.

We can again use a simple linear equation to describe our choice of striping units at each concurrency. The lower, dashed line in Figure 29.6(b) describes the following equation for striping unit: S_w × bandwidth-delay product × (concurrency - 1) + 1 sector, where S_w is the concurrency-slope coefficient for writes and is equal to 0.061. Thus the slope for writes is approximately six times shallower than the slope for reads. Table 29.2 shows that the values of S_w for different disks is relatively constant over a wide range of disk technologies.

By further relaxing the performance criterion, the ranges for reads and writes (Figure 29.6) widen and eventually overlap. This makes it possible to find a range of striping units that gives good performance to both reads and writes at a given concurrency. This criterion is approximately 85% and leads to a slope coefficient S_{rw} of 0.11. That is, a striping unit of S_{rw}× bandwidth-delay product × (concurrency - 1) + 1 sector guarantees at least 85% performance to all workloads at a given concurrency (over all mixes of reads and writes and over all request sizes), where S_{rw} is 0.11 for 17 disks.

These equations guarantee at least the criterion performance to all applicable workloads; that is, they are a worst-case guarantee. The *average* performance seen over the range of workloads we used was even higher: 99% for reads using S_r, 97% for writes using S_w, and 96% for reads and writes using S_{rw}.

29.4.2   Not Knowing Concurrency

Next let us consider the case where we know the workload is 100% reads but have no information about the concurrency or request size. In this case, we can choose a good compromise striping unit by superimposing all the graphs in Figure 29.4, as shown in Figure 29.7(a), and using the striping unit that guarantees the highest percentage of maximum performance to all workloads. As in [1], we express this choice as Striping unit = Z_r × bandwidth-delay product.

The circled point on each graph (see Figure 29.7 indicates the striping unit that guarantees the highest percentage of maximum throughput to all workloads shown on that graph. Note that the optimal striping unit for (b) write-intensive workloads is smaller than for (a) the read-intensive workloads.

For 17 IBM Lightning disks, the compromise striping unit for reads is 24 KB and hence Z_r is 0.73. This striping unit guarantees at least 70% of the maximum performance to workloads with any request size or concurrency. Again, this matches closely to previous results. Table 29.2 lists results for different disk types and shows that Z_r and S_r are independent of disk technology.

We can choose a good compromise striping unit for write-intensive workloads as we did for reads. We superimpose all graphs in Figure 29.5, as shown in Figure 29.7(b), and choose the striping unit that guarantees the highest percentage of maximum performance to all workloads. For write-intensive workloads on 17 IBM Lightning disks, this compromise striping unit is 6 KB, so Z_w, which is the optimal striping unit divided by the bandwidth-delay product for IBM Lightning disks, is 0.18. A 6 KB striping unit guarantees at least 73% of maximum performance to

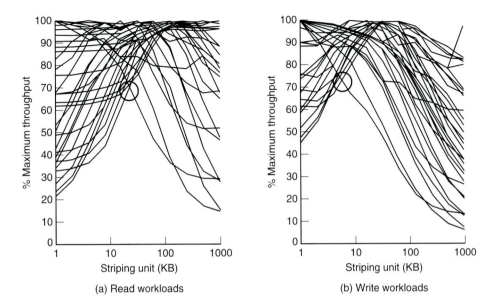

Figure 29.7. Choosing the striping unit without knowing concurrency.

all workloads tested. We tabulate the values of Z_w using other disk technologies and find that Z_w is independent of disk type. These equations guarantee a certain percentage of the maximum throughput for each workload. Again, the average performance seen over the range of workloads we measured was much higher: 89% for reads using Z_r, 90% for writes using Z_w, and 84% for both reads and writes using Z_{rw}.

Note that it is possible to guarantee 85% performance to all workloads by knowing concurrency, but it is possible to guarantee only 70% performance by knowing the read/write mix. We can thus order the workload parameters in terms of how important they are in optimizing performance: Concurrency is the most important parameter, read/write mix is the second most important, and request size is the least important parameter. When tuning performance on a given system, concurrency is thus the first workload parameter to measure.

In many situations, the workload is completely unspecified. For example, a disk-array manufacturer may want to ship the system with a good default striping unit, suitable for a wide range of workloads. We recommend a striping unit for this situation by superimposing the graphs in Figure 29.7 and looking for the striping unit that guarantees the best performance to all read or write workloads of arbitrary concurrency and request size. This striping unit is 16 KB for 17 IBM Lightning disks and guarantees 60% of maximum throughput to workloads with any request size, concurrency, and mix of reads and writes. We express this choice in terms of the bandwidth-delay product as Striping unit = Z_{rw} × Bandwidth-delay product, where Z_{rw} is 0.48. Thus, for a 17-disk array and in the absence of any workload information, we recommend a striping unit of approximately half the product of the average positioning time and the single-disk transfer rate.

29.5   VARYING THE NUMBER OF DISKS

We have expressed our recommendations for striping unit for a 17-disk array in terms of coefficients S and Z and the bandwidth-delay product. Disk arrays with more or less than 17 disks will have different values for these coefficients, because the number of disks affects the trade-offs discussed in Section 29.2.2. With more disks, smaller striping units are needed to ensure that all disks are used. Conversely, with fewer disks, each disk is more precious, leading to larger striping units to avoid tying up too many disks. Thus, we expect that the coefficients will vary inversely to the number of disks in the array. Figure 29.8 shows that varying the number of disks affects the striping unit differently for read and write workloads. When concurrency is known, the best striping unit is $S \times$ Bandwidth-delay product $\times$ (concurrency - 1) + 1 sector. When concurrency is not known, the best striping unit is $Z \times Bandwidth - delay\ product$. In both situations, the striping unit varies proportionately with the coefficient (S or Z). For read-intensive workloads, S_r and Z_r decrease as the number of disks increases because smaller striping units are needed to ensure that all disks are used. For write-intensive workloads, S_w and Z_w decreases as the number of disks decreases because the extra overhead of read-modify writes becomes prohibitive when there are less disks. These two trends effectively cancel each other out, and so the striping unit that maximizes performance without knowing the read/write mix is independent of the number of disks. When concurrency is known, the best striping unit is $1/8 \times$ Bandwidth-delay product $\times$ (concurrency -1) + 1 sector. When concurrency is not known, the best striping unit is $1/2 \times$ Bandwidth-delay product. The performance guaranteed in (a) is approximately 95% for reads (using S_r), 90% for writes (using S_w), and 80-85% for reads and writes (using S_{rw}). The performance guaranteed in (b) is approximately 70% for reads (using Z_r), 70% for writes (using Z_w), and 60% for both reads and writes (using Z_{rw}). [6, 7] predict that the striping unit will vary inversely to the square root of the number of disks. We find empirically that the optimal striping unit for read-intensive workloads varies inversely to the cube root of the number of disks.

Surprisingly, S_w and Z_w increase as the number of disks increases. This trend means that as the number of disks in the array decreases, the optimal striping unit also decreases, and each write request is best striped over more disks. To understand this, recall that limiting a write request to a few disks causes more read-modify writes. These read-modify writes cause extra read operations to the parity and data blocks, which increases disk utilization by a factor of approximately 2. In a disk array with less disks, this increased disk utilization ties up a higher fraction of the disks and severely hinders performance. Thus, the optimal striping unit is smaller with less disks to cause more full-stripe writes and hence decreases

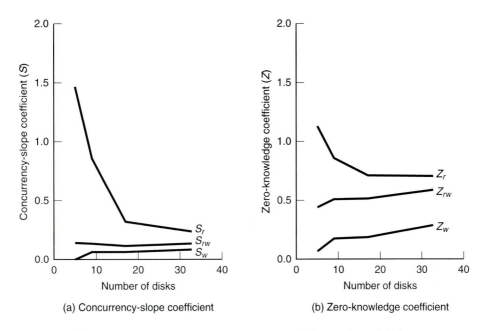

Figure 29.8. How striping units vary with number of disks.

the number of read-modify writes.

The combination of these trends leads to a fairly constant values for S_{rw} at $1/8$ and for Z_{rw} at $1/2$. Thus, if one knows the workload concurrency for an array with any number of disks, one should choose a striping unit of $1/8 \times$ Bandwidth-delay product $\times$ (concurrency - 1) + 1 sector.

And without any workload knowledge about request size, concurrency, or mix of reads and writes, one should choose a striping unit equal $1/2 \times$ Bandwidth-delay product.

For our three disk types (using the true seek time, not the shortened seek time of the first 300 MB of each disk), the optimal striping unit in the absence of any workload information is 18 KB for the IBM Lightning disks, 38 KB for the Seagate Elite3 disks, and 20 KB for the Seagate Wren4 disks.

29.6 VERIFICATION USING TRACES

In this section, we use I/O traces from real systems to validate the design rules derived using synthetic workloads, verifying that our recommended striping unit performs well under specific workloads. The traces we use come from Miller and Katz's supercomputing workload study and capture the I/Os from a range of climate modeling, aerodynamic, turbulence, and structural dynamics applications [9]. The traces are at the file system level and did not capture the disk location of each access, so we processed the traces using a simple, extent-based file allocation. Each file is allocated as a single, contiguous extent in the disk array's logical address space. Concurrencies greater than one are simulated by running multiple instantiations of the same trace at the same time, using disjoint file spaces and starting each trace after a random delay.

In Figure 29.9, we see that for a trace with predominantly large I/Os, small striping units perform best over a range of concurrencies. The vertical shows the striping unit we recommend without any advance workload information. Though it guarantees reasonable performance to all concurrencies (66%), it can certainly be improved upon with more specific workload knowledge.

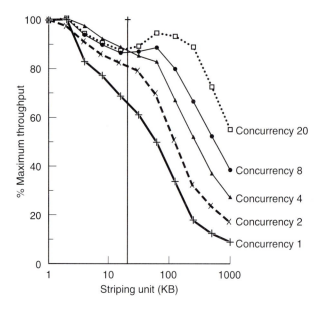

Figure 29.9. Performance of venus trace.

We first simulated each trace separately on an array of 17 Seagate Elite3 disks and found that they fell into one of two main categories. Traces in the first category, represented by venus (simulation of venus' atmosphere), perform large (approximately 400-KB) I/Os. Traces in the second category, represented by ccm (community climate model), perform relatively small (16 to 32-KB), highly sequential I/Os. The performance of the ccm trace, comprised mostly of relatively small (32-KB) sequential requests. The workload with concurrency one achieves much higher performance with small striping units because they allow the disks to service multiple sequential requests without seeking. The same workload after grouping is used to combine multiple sequential requests into a few large ones. No single striping unit achieves good performance for all workloads, though our recommended striping unit (shown as a vertical line) does about as well as any other. Our recommended

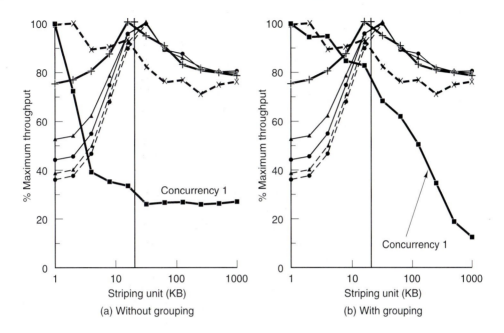

Figure 29.10. Performance of ccm trace.

striping unit achieves almost 80% of the best possible performance for each individual workload. The vertical lines in Figures 29.9 to 29.11 show the striping unit we recommend if no workload information is given (21 KB for the Seagate Elite3 disks with the 300-MB capacity limit). As for the ccm trace, no single striping unit guarantees good performance for all concurrencies, though our recommended striping unit (21 KB) performs as well as any other (circle A). For concurrency one, the best striping unit is small. For all others, our recommended striping unit guarantees at least 85% of the best performance foreach workload (circle B).

Figure 29.9 shows that workloads with all large I/Os perform best with very small striping units over all concurrencies. This agrees with the workloads with large requests in Figures 29.4 and 29.5. Our recommendation of 21 KB performs reasonably well. Although we know in advance that the request size is large, at least 66% of the maximum possible performance for each concurrency would certainly make it possible to achieve higher performance.

Figure 29.10(a) shows that no single striping unit performs well for workloads with relatively small sequential I/Os. Our recommendation yields close to the best possible performance, but this only guarantees about 30% of the maximum possible performance to each concurrency. This low-performance guarantee is due to the workload with concurrency one. Because most of the I/Os in the trace were sequential, a workload with only one process can achieve much better performance by using a small striping unit. With a small striping unit, all disks always seek and

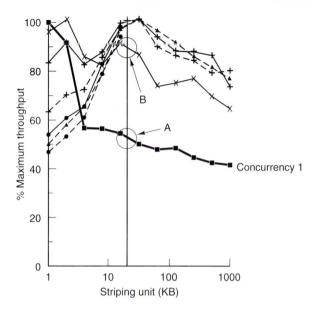

Figure 29.11. Performance of composite trace.

transfer in parallel. Because the workload is sequential, using small striping units does not cause extra seeks. In contrast, when one process runs on a disk array with large striping units, a single disk seeks and transfers the data, then another disk seeks and transfers the next request, and so on. In essence, having a small striping unit allows the disk array to overlap the seeks for all 17 disks, even with only one process issuing I/Os. This phenomenon does not occur at concurrencies higher than one, since multiple interleaved processes disrupt the workload sequentiality and prevent the disks from servicing more than one request after each seek.

There are several ways to prevent this sharp performance drop-off for workloads with concurrency one, although workloads that leave many disks idle are poor candidates to run on disk arrays. The best way, though often impractical, is to modify the application or the operating system to group multiple I/Os together into a single larger I/O (a form of prefetching). With larger requests, disk arrays with large striping units can achieve the same disk parallelism that arrays with small striping units can. An easier solution that does not require modifying the application is to have all idle disks seek to the same position as the active disk. This overlaps the seeks, but not the transfers, of multiple disks. Figure 29.10(b) shows the performance resulting from grouping multiple sequential requests into a single large one for one process. We see that our recommended striping unit is able to perform much better here, guaranteeing 80% performance to all concurrencies.

Finally, we merged all the traces into a single composite trace and explored how the composite trace performed under different concurrencies. Figure 29.11 shows that, similar to Figure 29.10(a), no single striping unit performs well for all concurrencies. Again, concurrency one performs differently than other concurrencies, but for a different reason. Mixing the traces removes all sequentiality between requests, but small striping units still perform significantly better than large ones for concurrency one. The reason is that performing only full-striped I/Os allows the disk arms to seek in unison, even when not performing sequential requests. This is faster than synchronizing 17 randomly positioned disk arms and improves performance. No workload transformation can change this phenomenon–it is simply a benefit of very small striping units (RAID Level 3).

Figure 29.11 shows that if you place high value on workloads with concurrency one, choose a small striping unit. However, if you value workloads with both high and low concurrencies, then our recommendation of half the bandwidth-delay product performs as well as any other striping unit. And if you do not value concurrency one workloads, this chapter's recommended striping unit provides excellent performance to all workloads, guaranteeing at least 85% of the best possible performance. These results agree with the major results of Section 29.4: (1) knowing concurrency enables one to choose a near-optimal striping unit, and (2) without knowing workload concurrency, the best striping unit is approximately $1/2 \times$ average positioning time $\times$ disk transfer rate (21 KB for the 300-MB capacity Seagate Elite3 disks).

29.7   CONCLUSIONS

We have investigated how to stripe data in a RAID Level-5 disk array for a variety of workloads, both synthetic workloads and application traces. We found that reads in a RAID Level 5 behaved similarly to reads and writes in a nonredundant disk array. The resulting optimal striping unit for reads traded off two factors: (1) making use of all the disks in the array and (2) having each disk transfer as much as possible before repositioning. Write-intensive workloads, on the other hand, achieved optimal performance at smaller striping units (1/4 to 1/6 the size for a 17-disk array) on RAID Level 5 than on RAID Level 0. This was because full-stripe writes performed better than read-modify or reconstruct writes. Smaller striping units led to more full-stripe writes and correspondingly better performance.

For both reads and writes in a RAID Level 5, concurrency was the most important workload factor in choosing an optimal striping unit. The optimal striping unit increased with concurrency for both reads and writes, but the rate of increase was approximately six times more gradual for writes than for reads. Again, this was due to full-stripe writes performing better than read-modify or reconstruct writes. We also noted that even infinite levels of concurrency did not lead to arbitrarily large striping units for writes. This ceiling on the striping unit for writes occurred because writes "prefer" to utilize all the disks by issuing full-stripe writes rather than by depending on the workload's concurrency.

Next, we investigated the effect of varying the number of disks in a RAID Level 5. We found that the striping unit for read-intensive workloads decreased as the number of disks increased, but that the striping unit for write-intensive workloads increased as the number of disks increased. Both these trends sought to lower the number of disks each request occupied as the number of disks in the array decreased. The combined effect of these opposing trends was that, without any workload knowledge of the read/write mix, the optimal striping unit stayed fairly constant at half the bandwidth-delay product. Thus, in the absence of any workload knowledge, we recommend a striping unit of $1/2 \times$ average positioning time $\times$ disk transfer rate for RAID Level-5 disk arrays with any number of disks. If concurrency is known, we recommend a striping unit of $1/8 \times$ average positioning time $\times$ disk transfer rate $\times$ (concurrency - 1) + 1 sector.

Last, we validated our main design rule by using I/O traces gathered from a range of scientific workloads. As found using stochastic workloads, specific workloads can achieve their best performance by using a carefully tailored striping unit. This was especially true for workloads with very large requests or concurrency one. For systems that run a range of workloads, the traces verified that our simple design rule accurately selects a near-optimal striping unit.

References

[1] Peter M. Chen and David A. Patterson. "Maximizing Performance in a Striped Disk Array," *International Symposium on Computer Architecture*, May 1990.

[2] Peter M. Chen, Edward K. Lee, Garth A. Gibson, Randy H. Katz, and David A. Patterson. "RAID: High-Performance, Reliable Secondary Storage," *ACM Computing Surveys*, 26(2) (June 1994).

[3] Peter M. Chen and Edward K. Lee. "Striping in a RAID Level 5 Disk Array," *ACM SIGMETRICS Conference on Measurement and Modeling of Computer Systems*, May 1995.

[4] Peter J. Denning and Jeffrey P. Buzen. "The Operational Analysis of Queueing Network Models," *ACM Computing Surveys*, 10(3) (September 1978).

[5] *IBM 0661 Disk Drive Product Description-Model 371*, IBM Technical Report, July 1989.

[6] Edward K. Lee and Randy H. Katz. *An Analytic Performance Model of Disk Arrays and its Applications*, Technical Report UCB/CSD, 91/660, University of California at Berkeley, 1991.

[7] Edward K. Lee and Randy H. Katz. "An Analytic Performance Model of Disk Arrays," *ACM SIGMETRICS Conference on Measurement and Modeling of Computer Systems*, May 1993.

[8] Edward K. Lee and Randy H. Katz. "The Performance of Parity Placement in Disk Arrays," *IEEE Transactions on Computers*, 42(6) (June 1993).

[9] Ethan L. Miller and Rand Katz. "Input/Output Behavior of Supercomputing Applications," *Supercomputing*, November 1991.

[10] David A. Patterson, Garth Gibson, and Randy H. Katz. "A Case for Redundant Arrays of In- expensive Disks (RAID)," *ACM SIGMOD*, June 1988.

[11] Chris Ruemmler and John Wilkes. "An Introduction to Disk Drive Modeling," *IEEE Computer*, March 1994.

[12] Peter Scheuermann, Gerhard Weikum, and Peter Zabback. *Automatic Tuning of Data Placement and Load Balancing in Disk Arrays. Database Systems for Next-Generation Applications: Principles and Practice*, DBS-92-91, 1991.

[13] Jean Thisquen. *Seek Time Measurements*, Technical report, Amdahl Peripheral Products Division, May 1988.

[14] Gerhard Weikum and Peter Zabback. "Tuning of Striping Units in Disk-Array-Based File Systems," *2nd International Workshop on Research Issues on Data Engineering: Transaction and Query Processing*, 1992.

Appendix 1 - Why Results Depend Only on the Disk Bandwidth-Delay Product

In all our results, the only dependency the optimal striping unit had on disk technology was the disk's bandwidth-delay product (*single disk transfer rate × average positioning time*). This appendix argues why that is the case.

First, consider a simulator that uses exactly two constants to model the disk: *positioningTime* and *transferRate*. Since these are the only two performance model parameters that contain units of time, multiplying *positioningTime* by 1000 and dividing *transferRate* by 1000 is equivalent to changing the unit of time from seconds to milliseconds. Therefore, although the performance results of the model would now have to be interpreted in milliseconds rather than seconds, the true, unit-adjusted value of the result remains unchanged and the optimal striping unit would be unchanged. That is, multiplying *positioningTime* by N and dividing *transferRate* by N must yield the same performance results and the same optimal striping units.

Hence the performance of the system depends only on the relative sizes of *positioningTime* and *transferRate*, that is, *positioningTime × transferRate* (the bandwidth-delay product). Systems with equal bandwidth-delay products must have equal optimal striping units, so any equation for the optimal striping unit must use only the bandwidth-delay product to express dependency on disk technology.

The *raidSim* simulator contains many other disk parameters besides *positioning Time* and *transferRate* (rotational speed, minimum seek, maximum seek, for example). If we modeled different disks by scaling all parameters by the same factor, the above argument would hold exactly. To model a wider variety of disks and disk geometries, we vary each parameter independently, so the above argument does not hold exactly. However, since it is possible to model different disks fairly accurately by scaling all disk speed parameters by the same factor, the above argument explains why we found empirically that striping unit depended only on $averagePositioningTime \times single\ disk\ transfer\ rate$.

Chapter 30

RAID5 Disk Arrays and Their Performance Evaluation

Alexander Thomasian

Abstract

High data availability is critical for the operation of everyday applications such as automatic teller machines, among many others with this requirement. RAID5 disk arrays provide a cost-effective solution to this problem by dedicating the capacity of one of $N+1$ disks to parity blocks containing the exclusive OR of the contents of the corresponding N blocks on the other disks in the array. Parity blocks that are uniformly distributed among all disks make it possible to recreate the contents of any one of the $N+1$ disks if it fails. The updating of an individual data block requires three extra disk accesses to read the old values of data and parity blocks and to write the updated parity block. We review several methods to cope with the so-called small write syndrome. The need for manual load balancing to eliminate access skew in RAID5 disk arrays is alleviated through striping, that is, allocating partitions of a file onto consecutive disks. We describe analytic solution methods based on queueing theory, which utilizes parameters obtained from trace-driven simulations, such as the disk cache hit ratio, to estimate RAID5 performance in various operating modes. RAID5 performance in normal mode (with no disk failures) is inferior to an unprotected array because of the parity-update overhead. This degradation in performance is tolerably small for some realistic workloads when a nonvolatile cache is provided that allows (1) fast writes, that is, a write is considered completed when it is written into the cache; (2) the exploitation of disk geometry for the efficient destaging of dirty blocks; and (3) reads to have a higher priority than destages. In degraded mode, that is, with one disk failed, the load on surviving disks increases sharply, for example, it doubles when all requests are reads. In the rebuild mode, the reconstruction of the contents of a failed disk introduces extra load, which is however given a lower priority than user requests. We extend the analysis for the normal mode to degraded and rebuild modes, since disk-array performance in these two modes is especially critical. We summarize results from our earlier performance evaluation studies. The solution methods provided in this chapter can be readily extended to analyze the performance of other disk-array implementations, some of which are described in this chapter.

30.1   INTRODUCTION

High data availability is a prerequisite for many everyday applications, such as airline reservation systems, point-of-sale terminals, networks of automatic teller machines, video-on-demand systems, and web servers, to name just a few. Our discussion is concerned with highly available data storage subsystems for database applications. We are not concerned here with scientific applications, that require high I/O bandwidths to access large data volumes [27]; specialized environments such as video-on-demand systems, where the data layout is geared to meeting the performance requirements of the system in the presence of data failures (see, for example, [2, 53]); and network-based disk systems [19, 36].

Protecting disk data through parity is proposed in [33]. The term *Redundant Array of Independent Disks–RAID* is coined in [55], which also defines various RAID levels. Different types of RAID systems are described in the following two sections, but the emphasis is on RAID Level 5 or RAID5. RAID1 or disk mirroring is introduced as a special case. The interested reader is referred to [37] for a classification of RAID systems and definitions of associated terminology.

Disk mirroring, which has appeared in several commercial systems [70], has the potential to minimize the response time for read requests, for example, by processing a read request at the disk incurring a shorter seek time. A large nonvolatile storage (NVS or NVRAM) cache can be used as a *write-only disk cache* (see [64] for a discussion of disk caches and their performance), which buffers writes and processes them when the disk arm is in the "vicinity" of the data block to be written out [66]. In *distorted mirrors*, the data are updated in place on the primary disk, but the *write anywhere* policy is used on the secondary disk [65]. This requires the controller to maintain a data structure to locate the data. Furthermore, only the primary disk is suited for processing long sequential requests. The need for NVS can be relieved by allowing the write anywhere policy on the secondary disk [52]. The two mirrored disks alternate in processing read requests and being updated by write requests accumulated in an NVS cache [56]. The performance gain is in the more efficient processing of writes, plus the fact that a *fast write* capability exists due to NVS [40], that is, a disk write is considered completed as soon as it is written to the NVS cache.

Interleaved declustering implemented in the Teradata DBC/1012 shared-nothing architecture [71] duplicates the data on disks and achieves a balanced processor load after failure. One or more disks (constituting a logical disk) attached to a processor constitute a node. Each (logical) disk has a primary and secondary area, where the data in the primary area of a disk is duplicated on the secondary area of another disk in the same cluster of N nodes. If one of the nodes in a cluster fails, the increase in the load at the processors of other nodes in the cluster is $1/(N-1)$.

The *chained declustering* method in [25] is proposed for the Gamma database machine, which also has a shared nothing architecture with a total number of N' disks. Each disk has a primary and secondary area. The data on each disk attached to a processor are duplicated on the (secondary) area of the following disk (modulo the number of disks). The processor at each node processes the data in the primary area of the disk at that node when there are no failures. When a node fails, the chained declustering paradigm increases the load on surviving nodes by $1/N'$. When node 1 fails, processor 2 is assigned the load on disk 1 (residing on the secondary area on disk 2) plus $1/N'$ of its own load to access the primary data on disk 2. Processor 3 processes $(N'-1)/N'$ of the load for processor 2 and $2/N'$ of its own load, and so on. The increase in the load with chained declustering is much smaller than that with interleaved declustering, because the total number of disks (N') is much larger than the number of disks in a cluster (N).

A RAID4 disk array has $N+1$ disks, where the last disk holds the exclusive-OR (XOR) of the contents of the first N disks. This collection of disks is referred to as a *stripe*, which is a subset of the disks in the disk subsystem. If one of the first N disks is determined to be failed, for example, through the error-detection codes associated with the disk, a disk page to be read from the failed disk can be reconstructed by exclusive ORing (XORing) the corresponding bits from the $N-1$ surviving disks and the parity disk. Thus, protection against disk failures is possible with an overhead of one disk for each N disks, that is, much more efficiently than earlier duplication-based solutions. Updating a disk block or page requires the updating of the corresponding page on the parity disk. Instead of recomputing the parity from all the blocks in the stripe, the effect of the old block is removed by an XOR with the parity block followed by an XOR of the new block, that is, $P_{new} = P_{old} \oplus D_{old} \oplus D_{new}$, where D and P designate data and parity pages, respectively. This is accomplished by reading the old value of the data and parity blocks and XORing them with the new data block to compute the new parity block. In the extreme case of a workload with random writes that are not preceded by reads, the number of accesses to the parity disk is N times the number of accesses to the other disks. RAID5, which is described in the next section, is a solution to this problem. RAID3 is (usually) a synchronized RAID4, where a bloc ksize of one byte is used to allow high-bandwidth disk transfers [55].

Briefly, a RAID Level-2 system consists of *data disks* and *check disks*, where the check disks may contain a Hamming error-correcting code [15] computed over the contents of the data disks. Self-identifying failed components are referred to as *erasure channels* as opposed to *error channels*. An error-detecting code for an error channel becomes an error-correcting code for an erasure channel [15], which is the case for disk failures since they are self-identifying. RAID2 works on this principle, but some disk-array implementations do not take advantage of this error-correction capability [21].

Reliability and availability modeling of disk arrays is beyond the scope of this discussion, but is addressed in numerous studies (see, for example, [15]). An array of $2M$ disks, where disk pairs constitute mirrors, can tolerate the failure of up to M disks as long as they do not belong to the same mirrored pair. In interleaved declustering, it takes the failure of two disks in a cluster, whereas in chained declustering, it takes the failure of two consecutive disks for data loss to occur. Most RAID systems can only tolerate a single failed disk per stripe, although some schemes that tolerate multiple failures are discussed in Section 30.2.

Readers are referred to [8, 15, 60, 63, 81] for general information on disk technology. Detailed discussions of disk arrays appear in [8, 15, 21].

The chapter is organized as follows. Section 30.2 provides a brief introduction to RAID5 disk arrays and their operating modes: normal, degraded, and rebuild. In Section 30.3, we give an overview of analytic and simulation studies of RAID5 disk arrays. In Section 30.4 we describe the model used in analyzing RAID5 disk arrays. Analytic solution methods from queueing theory, which are applicable to the analysis are discussed in Section 30.5. We proceed to discuss the analysis of RAID5 disk arrays in the normal and degraded modes in Section 30.6 and in rebuild mode in Section 30.7. A summary of results from earlier analytic and simulation studies by the author appears in Section 30.8. Conclusions appear in Section 30.9.

30.2   RAID5 DISK ARRAYS

A RAID5 disk array is a set of disk drives and a controller that can automatically recover data when one drive in the set fails. A *parity or redundancy group* or a stripe in RAID5 comprises $N + 1$ *striping units* or *stripe units*, which are partitions of successive areas of a file allocated on N consecutive disks plus a parity striping unit containing the XOR of the previous striping units [15]. Unlike RAID4, parity blocks in RAID5 are uniformly distributed over the $N + 1$ disks, such that a uniform distribution of data block updates will result in a uniform distribution of parity block updates [55]. This alleviates the potential bottleneck in writing parity blocks associated with RAID4 disk arrays.

RAID was originally proposed as an inexpensive (hence, the original "I" in RAID) replacement for the then prevalent large form-factor and expensive disks [55]. It turns out that this argument is no longer true, that is, smaller form-factor disks have replaced larger form-factor disks at all levels of computing systems. Although disk form factors are decreasing, at any point in time, there is a prevalent disk technology (3.5 inches at the time of this writing), that provides a target overall disk capacity at a lower cost, superior disk performance, and at a higher system reliability. Smaller and less expensive disks may not provide the most cost-effective solution over the lifetime of a system, for example, the reliability of the disk array is lowered since a larger number of disks are required to attain the same capacity.

The same level of reliability is attainable when both RAID5 and non-RAID systems use the same disk technology. High data availability is still quite desirable, since disk failures can be masked. A RAID5 (or RAID4) disk array can tolerate single disk failures, as determined by error-detection codes normally associated with the data on individual disks. The data on a failed disk are recreated by XORing the corresponding blocks on the surviving N disks. The performance of the system is poor because each read intended for the failed disk entails an access to all surviving disks. A spare disk in hot-standby mode may be provided for reconstructing data on the failed disk as soon as it fails or its failure is imminent, as determined by *predictive failure analysis* [12]. If a spare drive is not provided, the reconstruction of the data on the failed drive should await its repair (that is, replacement), which increases the chances of data loss (due to a second disk failure) compared to a hot sparing system. Thus, a hot-standby minimizes the probability of data loss, reduces the duration of degraded mode operation, may be shared among several disk arrays, and makes low-cost periodic repair possible.

We have described *dedicated sparing*, where as shown in Table 30.1a, the disk array consists of $N + 1$ primary disks holding data and parity striping units, whose size may correspond to one or multiple sectors (usually 512 bytes), 4-Kbyte disk blocks or pages, disk tracks, or even cylinders. A small striping unit might be beneficial since it allows higher bandwidth for large data transfers, but this increase in bandwidth is only significant when the disks are synchronized (as in RAID3). Otherwise, the completion time of a disk request is the maximum of the response times of the requests on individual disks. The increase in bandwidth available to a single application is at the cost of the involvement of a large number of disks to satisfy a single request. This tends to be unacceptable in a multiprogramming environment, where efficient processing of disk requests is required for achieving a higher aggregate throughput. The processing efficiency of a disk is defined as the fraction of the maximum disk transfer rate, which is achieved for sequential disk accesses. A smaller striping unit is attractive from the viewpoint of eliminating access skew, but trace-driven simulation studies have shown that relatively large stripe units corresponding to one or more cylinders introduce little skew and allow the efficient processing of sequential requests.

The following actions are required to update the parity block corresponding to a modified 4-KBlock. Read the old values of the data and parity blocks from disk and XOR them with the new data block to obtain the new parity block. The writing of a data block is considered complete when both the parity and data block are written onto disk. The reading of the old values of data and parity blocks is not required if they are cached.

If all the corresponding blocks in a stripe are updated, then the parity block can be computed by XORing these data blocks. If more than one-half of the blocks in a stripe are updated, it may be more efficient to read the remaining blocks to compute the parity block [9]. The analysis of disk reference traces indicates that such *reconstruct writes* are lightly used, unless there are a large number of dirty blocks in the disk cache [78].

In *distributed sparing*, there are $N + 2$ online disks with a fraction $N/(N + 2)$ of the tracks dedicated to data, $1/(N+2)$ dedicated to parity blocks; and $1/(N + 2)$ to

Table 30.1. Distributed Parity RAID5

		RAID5 disk array plus a spare disk					System in normal & degraded mode (disk 3 has failed)					System after rebuild			
DISK#		1	2	3	4	5	1	2	3	4	5	1	2	4	5
C#	T#														
1	1	D	D	D	P	S	D*	D*	X	P*	S	D	D	P	D
1	2	D	D	P	D	S	D	D	X	S	D	D	D	P	D
1	3	D	P	D	D	S	D	P	X	D	D	D	P	D	D
1	4	P	D	D	D	S	P*	S	X	D*	D*	P	D	D	D
2	1	D	D	D	P	S	S	D*	X	P*	D*	D	D	P	D
2	2	D	D	P	D	S	D	D	X	D	S	D	D	D	P
2	3	D	P	D	D	S	D*	P*	X	S	D*	D	P	D	D
2	4	P	D	D	D	S	P	D	X	D	D	P	D	D	D
3	1	D	D	D	P	S	D*	S	X	P*	D*	D	D	P	D
3	2	D	D	P	D	S	S	D	X	D	D	P	D	D	D
3	3	D	P	D	D	S	D*	P*	X	D*	S	D	P	D	D
3	4	P	D	D	D	S	P*	D*	X	S	D*	D	D	D	D
4	1	D	D	D	P	S	D	D	X	P	D	D	D	P	D
4	2	D	D	P	D	S	D	S	X	D	D	D	P	D	D
4	3	D	P	D	D	S	S	P*	X	D*	D*	D	P	D	D
4	4	P	D	D	D	S	P*	D*	X	D*	S	P	D	D	D
5	1	D	D	D	P	S	D*	D*	X	S	P*	D	D	D	P
5	2	D	D	P	D	S	D	D	X	D	P	D	D	D	P
5	3	D	P	D	D	S	D*	S	X	D*	P*	D	D	D	P
5	4	P	D	D	D	S	S	D*	X	D*	P*	D	D	D	P
				(a)					(b)					(c)	

There are $N + 2 = 5$ disks, 5 cylinders per disk and 4 tracks per cylinder. From left to right we have: (a) A RAID5 disk array plus a spare disk. (b) Shows the effect of distributing the spare tracks. Tracks displaced in this manner are moved to disk 5. The '*'s show the required accesses to recreate data on disk 3, which is presumed to have failed. (c) System in pseudo-normal mode after rebuild is completed.

spare blocks, such that the surviving $N+1$ disks have enough spare capacity to hold the contents of a failed disk [42]. One advantage of distributed sparing with respect to dedicated sparing with an on-line spare is the increase in the disk bandwidth by a factor of $(N + 2)/(N + 1)$. Distributed sparing thus provides a higher degree of parallelism for rebuild processing than dedicated sparing [42]. The wasted capacity and bandwidth of the spare disk in dedicated sparing is reduced when the spare disk is shared among several arrays.

The data layout for a RAID5 disk array with distributed sparing can be derived from that of a dedicated sparing system [77]. Table 30.1a, depicts a dedicated sparing disk array with $N + 1 = 4$ disks plus a spare disk with the rotated parity or *left-symmetric* layout, which has several desirable properties [34, 15], for example, that sequential reads can progress at full speed by utilizing all disks. The striping unit in the table is postulated to be one disk track to simplify the discussion. Distributed sparing allocates the spare tracks evenly among all disks, such that they replace data and parity tracks, which, as shown in Table 30.1b, are displaced to the spare disk. It will be shown that the resulting configuration provides: (1) an even distribution of parity and spare tracks in normal mode, (2) a balanced load in degraded mode, and (3) an even distribution of parity striping units after rebuild.

A dedicated sparing system operates in three modes as follows. (1) *normal mode* with all nonspare disks operational (the spare disk may or may not be operational); (2) *degraded mode* with one of the nonspare disks failed (there is a significant increase in system load, since, for example, reads targeted to the failed disk require the reading of $N - 1$ surviving primary disks); and (3) Rebuild mode, which should be started immediately after a disk failure occurs for two reasons; (a) the system is susceptible to data loss if a second disk failure occurs before the data on the failed disk is reconstructed, and (b) to improve system performance by returning it to normal operating mode.

A distributed sparing system operates in four modes as follows [42]: (1) *The normal mode*; (2) *The degraded mode* with one failed disk. Assuming that a disk has failed, Table 30.1b indicates accesses generated due to reads (respectively writes) to the failed disk to recreate lost data blocks (respectively to compute and write the parity blocks). It is observed that this load is evenly distributed over surviving disks. (3) *The rebuild mode* is the first of two rebuild steps that leads to the *pseudo-normal mode* of operation, basically converting the array into a dedicated sparing system (with a failed spare disk), that is, data and parity blocks are materialized on $N + 1$ rather than $N + 2$ disks. The initial allocation of striping units in Table 30.1b ensures the even distribution of parity blocks after the rebuild is completed, as can be observed from Table 30.1c. In the pseudo-normal mode, the system can sustain an additional disk failure and continue operation in degraded mode, with the load on surviving disks remaining evenly distributed. (4) *The copyback mode* is the second of the two rebuild steps during which the tracks of the failed disk are read from the spare areas of the surviving $N + 1$ disks and are written to a new disk, such that the spare areas become available again.

In, the rebuild mode, the system sequentially reads consecutive tracks of data from surviving disks, XORs bits on associated tracks to reconstruct lost tracks, and then writes them onto the spare tracks. This "disk-oriented" scheme outperforms a "stripe-oriented" scheme, which reads all the required tracks from surviving disks before proceeding to the next track in a lock-step manner [21, 23]. This is due to the synchronization effect imposed by the second scheme. In effect, we have a fork-join synchronization delay in reading each disk track. Note that a disk-oriented rebuild scheme is considered in [39, 75].

Rebuild options for dedicated sparing are described in [47]. These options are applicable to a distributed sparing system with the obvious modifications. Note that in the rebuild mode, writes of data and parity blocks targeted to the failed disk are carried out on the spare areas if the block has been reconstructed:, otherwise they are ignored. The *rebuild with read redirection*, as opposed to the *baseline rebuild procedure*, reads reconstructed data blocks from spare areas (the spare disk in dedicated sparing) rather than recreating them on demand. Note that this is possible because reconstructed blocks are kept up to date. In discussing the following options, we assume that read redirection is in effect, since it reduces the utilization of surviving disks and hence rebuild time [22, 47, 75], unless the spare disk in dedicated sparing constitutes a bottleneck (see discussion of clustered RAID in what follows). The *piggybacking rebuild* utilizes materialized data blocks (to satisfy read requests) to write missing blocks. A similar option is to write data blocks intended for the failed disk, which are otherwise deferred and carried out by the rebuild process as noted earlier. The piggybacking scheme does not improve performance, which is because the writing of a reconstructed block can be done at no extra cost (in processing time) as part of the writing of remaining blocks on the track [22, 23]. It is therefore not considered further in this study.

The *split-seek* option with read redirection allows the preemption of a rebuild read after a seek is completed [75]. The split latency/transfer option allows a preemption at sector boundaries during both the latency and transfer phases of a track read [74].

Numerous variations to RAID5 disk arrays are possible, which are discussed at this point.

A *clustered* or a *declustered parity* RAID system differs from a regular RAID5 dedicated sparing system in that the size of the parity group G is less than the number of disks $N + 1$. This has the advantage of offering a higher maximum bandwidth than a regular RAID5 disk array in degraded mode [22, 23, 47]. For example, disk utilization in RAID5 is doubled when all requests are reads, whereas with clustered RAID, it increases by the *declustering ratio:* $\alpha = (G - 1)/N$, that is, the increase in system load can be reduced by choosing G to be much smaller than N, but this is at the cost of additional redundancy. A combinatorial block design approach for data allocation for this purpose is reported in [22, 23, 48, 51] for a dedicated sparing system and in [21, 51] for a distributed sparing system as well. An alternative method for declustering is proposed in [44], which is based on random permutations. It has the disadvantage of requiring a relatively large amount of computation to generate each block address as compared to the block design approach [23].

One method to cope with the problem of multiple disk failures in a RAID5 disk array with a large number of disks is to partition the array into a number of smaller arrays, since they are less susceptible to multiple disk failures in the same array (see Eq. 30.18 in Section 30.7). This is at the cost of extra parity overhead; on the other hand, spare disks may be shared among different arrays. A disk array may be designed to tolerate multiple disk failures. At least $n+1$ writes to disks are required to tolerate n failures [16] and additional space is required for this purpose. Multiple failure tolerance is required for applications where data loss is catastrophic and to deal with *latent sector failures* [21]. This is a situation where data loss is not detected until rebuild time, because the data are rarely accessed. Thus, the correction of two errors is required to complete the rebuild.

Two disk failures can be tolerated by arranging n^2 data disks in a square configuration and providing $2n$ parity disks arranged vertically and horizontally, such that each data disk is protected by two parity disks [15] (this idea was also proposed in [33]). The failure of up to $2n-1$ disks can be tolerated by this scheme, but the failure of only four disks whose coordinates constitute a rectangle will result in a system crash. This data layout has the inefficiency associated with RAID4, that is, the parity disks may limit the system throughput for a write-intensive workload. An efficient placement method for tolerating two disk failures is proposed in [54]. The "crosshatch" disk array proposed in [50] addresses double failures not just for disks, but also for controllers and cabling.

Two check digits for the data digits on two data disks A and B can be computed as follows $P = (A+B)mod4$ and $Q = (A+2B)mod4$. In case the data disks fail, their contents can be recomputed as $A = (2P-Q)mod4$ and $B = (Q-P)mod4$ [15]. A commercially available system using $P+Q$ coding based on Reed-Solomon codes uses 4 bit symbols to provide double erasure correction for up to 13 data disks [15].

Two parity blocks are associated with each stripe in [4], where the first parity block (as in RAID5) corresponds to $N-1$ data blocks, and the second parity block is obtained over the $N-1$ data blocks and the first set of parity blocks. This method which tolerates two disk failures, is shown to be optimal with respect to update penalty and extra disk space requirement. Another advantage of this method is that unlike $P+Q$ coding, it only requires Boolean operations.

Several studies have considered using an NVRAM as a disk cache to improve the efficiency of writes. One of the effects that results in an improvement in performance with an NVRAM is the overwriting of dirty blocks [61]. A second advantage is the ability to reorder the writing out (or destaging) of the blocks cached in the buffer, for example, to minimize the seek time in writing out multiple updated blocks. The latter issue was discussed in the context of mirrored disks in Section 30.1. A combined NVRAM and a cache-disk (not a disk cache, but a real disk), which is written sequentially to reduce seek overhead, is used in [26] for caching disk writes. The cache-disk provides adequate capacity for caching data blocks when the disk array is highly utilized, in order to temporarily relieve its load. The cached data blocks are used to update blocks in their home locations at a later time.

According to the high/low-mark algorithm proposed in [3], destages to disk are enabled when the occupancy of the cache exceeds the high mark and disabled when it falls below the low mark. It is shown in [78] that increasing the cache space allocated to dirty blocks may reduce the effective disk service time for updates by an order of magnitude. On the other hand, this disk space may be more effectively used for caching reads, that is, the buffer allocation is workload-sensitive. The high and low marks in this case were set to 5% and 4% of the cache size, respectively. The linear threshold scheduling paradigm varies the rate of destages according to cache occupancy reported in [79], which then uses a trace-driven simulation to compare the performance of this scheme with the high/low-mark algorithm.

Numerous techniques have been proposed to reduce the overhead due to the small write syndrome. A technique based on *floating parity* is proposed in [41], which provides for a limited form of write-anywhere paradigm noted earlier (also see [43], which also considers the write anywhere paradigm for data blocks). *Parity logging* is another approach described in [68], which basically first logs a parity update record, that is, the XOR of the old and new value of the data block. The parity blocks can be updated efficiently at a later time, when a sufficiently large number of parity update blocks have been accumulated. Multiple updates to the same page require only one disk write.

The *log-structured file system (LFS)* paradigm [59] is applicable to RAID5 disk arrays. In the LFS, user writes are deferred and written out with great efficiency (that is, incurring a single initial seek) onto an empty area on disk only when sufficiently large chunks of data are available. This paradigm is applicable to RAID5 disk arrays by accumulating a stripe's worth of data and writing it out after computing the parity block. An additional advantage of this method is that it allows the application of data compression, since we are not constrained by the write in-place paradigm (that the updated data do not fit in the space previously allocated to them). A disadvantage of this method is that, for example, sequential access to a relational table, which is usually clustered by its primary index, may not be possible after it has been updated by transactions. This method incurs an additional overhead to consolidate empty spaces on disk (referred to as segment cleaning [59]). A performance comparison of this scheme with RAID5 appears in [38]. It is noted that although there is a degradation in the efficiency of sequential accesses to a file, there is an improvement in response time when the requests to access the required blocks are initiated in parallel (this is also true for RAID5 when the striping unit is appropriately small). The LFS paradigm also allows an improvement in performance by writing hot objects onto the middle disk cylinders in order to minimize seek time. Similar techniques have been considered for reorganizing data on disks for improved performance [1].

In *virtual striping*, the location of a stripe is not fixed and it can be written anywhere on its home disk (its location is held in a table) [46]. In order to reduce the parity update overhead, it is best to carry out a full stripe write, which is possible according to this paradigm. A garbage collection process is used to create empty stripes by copying the contents of almost empty stripes elsewhere.

The *variable-scope parity protection* scheme reduces the overhead of parity updates by designating unused disk blocks as unprotected from the parity viewpoint [13, 14]. The writing of data blocks to such pages will therefore not require the reading of the previous value of the data block. Further efficiency is gained by writing dirty blocks to consecutive free blocks on a stripe for which the parity block is cached and can be readily updated. The previous location of an updated data block is at first designated dirty, but its status is changed to unprotected by a periodic process that updates the parity blocks when the system is less busy. Simulation results quantify the reduction in disk accesses with respect to a RAID5 disk array as a function of disk space utilization [13].

Our discussion so far has been concerned with disk failures, but system failures should also be considered to ensure the integrity of disk contents. Techniques similar to database logging can be used to assure successful crash recovery. For example, in a P + Q system, an inconsistent state may arise when the writing of one or more of the parity blocks is not completed after the data block is written. Thus, a P + Q system is more vulnerable to inconsistent states due to system crashes than an ordinary RAID5. An NVS cache can be used to alleviate the writing of state information required for recovery from system crashes to disk. Techniques to cope with system crashes in a "software-based RAID5" without a specialized disk controller for RAID5 operation are described in [58].

30.3   OVERVIEW OF ANALYTICAL AND SIMULATION STUDIES

Performance evaluation studies of disk arrays can be broadly categorized into analytic and simulation studies. There are very few reported measurement studies of disk arrays [7]. In what follows, we review studies dealing with the performance of RAID5 disk arrays.

Several rebuild schemes for a *clustered RAID*-dedicated sparing system are proposed and their rebuild times compared in [47]. That some of the optimizations proposed in [47] have a negative effect on performance is shown through detailed simulation studies in [21, 22, 23]. For example, it is shown that piggybacking does not result in an improved performance (an intuitive reason for this is given in Section 30.2) and that read redirection may result in an increase in rebuild time with a small declustering ratio when the utilization of surviving disks is low, such that the spare disk is saturated (the mean response time is always improved). Redirected reads also result in extra seeks, which are otherwise unnecessary in writing consecutive tracks on the spare disk.

A simulation study to compare the performance of the following four RAID organizations is reported in [6]: (1) dedicated sparing; (2) distributed sparing; (3) a special case of clustered RAID; and (4) *parity sparing*, which merges two redundancy groups into one to utilize the space occupied by parity blocks for sparing. It is shown that the block-design approach and parity sparing provide the best performance, depending on system parameters.

An approximate analysis with exponential disk service times to estimate the disk response time and the time to read each disk for rebuild is reported in [39] for a RAID5 disk array with dedicated sparing. A similar analysis is used in [42] to compare the performance of dedicated and distributed sparing and *parity sparing* [48]. Parity sparing handles failures by combining parity groups, that is, using one of the two parity groups to materialize the data that resided on the failed disk (the other parity blocks are recomputed). A performance analysis of a clustered RAID with the $M/G/1$ queueing model is reported in [44]. A two-moment approximation for $M/G/1$ queueing systems is used to analyze performance in the rebuild mode, which differs from other studies in that rebuild requests are processed one at a time and at the same priority as user requests, rather than at a lower priority.

A simulation study to determine a desirable *rebuild unit*, that is, the unit of reconstructing lost blocks from the failed disk, concludes that a track constitutes an acceptable compromise between rebuild efficiency and disk response times [24]. A larger rebuild unit, for example, a cylinder, allows rebuild processing to proceed more efficiently than a smaller rebuild unit, for example, a track, in that it incurs a single seek to process all the tracks on a cylinder. This will result in a reduction in the rebuild time, but the disk response time to user requests will be considerably higher. In the limit, with the rebuild unit set to the capacity of a disk, the processing of user requests is stopped in favor of quickly completing rebuild processing. This is of course not possible in an OLTP (on-line transaction processing) system with stringent response-time requirements. Preemptions of rebuild read requests is discussed in [74] and Section 30.6.

A queueing analysis that uses detailed disk characteristics to compare the performance in the normal mode of operation of RAID5 disk arrays with the *parity striping* option [18] is reported in [9] for multiblock requests spanning multiple disks. In *parity striping*, data are not striped at all and manual load balancing is required, although it tends to be unreliable. The analysis in [9] postulates a small striping unit for RAID5 such that multidisk accesses are required to satisfy a single request. This biases the comparison in favor of parity striping. A trace-driven simulation study comparing RAID5 (with a striping unit of one cylinder) and parity striping concludes that RAID5 provides better performance [78].

In this chapter we describe the analytic solution methods reported in [75] and [77] for RAID5 with dedicated and distributed sparing, respectively. We also summarize the conclusions of numerical investigations in these papers and [73] and [74]. We consider analytic solution techniques based on "intermediate" queueing theory (using the classification in [31]). An $M/G/1$ queueing model [31, 69], whose service time captures detailed disk characteristics, is used to evaluate RAID5 performance in normal, degraded, and rebuild modes. The *vacationing server model* with multiple vacations of different types for $M/G/1$ queues [69] is used in [75] to analyze the performance of a dedicated sparing system in rebuild mode. The analysis of the rebuild processing mode in RAID5 with distributed sparing is an extension of this approach [77]. Analytic results in both cases are validated against detailed simulations and shown to be quite accurate. Although balanced disk loadings are considered in this study, the analysis can be extended to handle skewed accesses possible with parity striping.

Accurate performance results can only be obtained through trace-driven simulations on a detailed simulator [60], since the inclusion of certain details required in modeling modern disk systems is not possible via analysis. Analytic models are usually based on a rather simplified workload model, whereas the trace-driven simulation method is one way to avoid the workload characterization problem, but this approach has limitations of its own, for example, it is difficult to vary the arrival rate of requests to study the effect of increased load on system performance. Justifications for using an analytic solution versus simulation are given at this point. The reader should note that some of the points in the following discussion will become clearer after reading the rest of this chapter.

1. Although trace-driven simulation studies of single disks have been carried out successfully (see, for example, [60]), the cost of simulating a disk subsystem comprising multiple disk arrays with nonhomogeneous workloads is prohibitively expensive. This is also true for random-number-driven simulations for higher disk utilizations, where lengthy simulation runs are required to obtain statistically accurate results.

2. The disk subsystem is usually analyzed as a component of a computer system model, where the main interest is in user-level performance measures, such as mean transaction response time. In a hierarchical solution method, the analysis of the rest of the system generates the arrival rate to the disk subsystem, and the analysis of the disk subsystem is used to obtain the delay due to disk I/O in modeling the rest of the system (see, for example, "Inclusion in a System Model" in [5]). Iterative solutions developed for this purpose require the response time of the disk subsystem to be determined for different arrival rates, which can be done efficiently only through an analytical solution method.

3. Optimizing the allocation of data files in RAID5 requires the evaluation of its performance for a very large number of cases to find the "optimal" configuration. An analytical solution is indispensable for a fast computation of mean response times for a given configuration in this case, for example, to which array should a file be allocated in a multiarray system.

4. Certain insights that can be gained from a closed-form analytic solution cannot be gained readily from simulation results. For example, the mean response time of user accesses in the rebuild mode increases by the residual delay associated with reading the rebuild unit (see Eq. 30.3 in Section 30.5). In a lightly loaded system with a rebuild unit of one track (as recommended in [24]), the mean extra delay to disk accesses is equal to one-half of the disk rotation time. The mean response time for disk accesses can be improved significantly in this case by introducing preemption [74]. Analysis similarly shows that preemption will introduce little improvement in response time to user requests in a heavily utilized disk array. This is because the response time of user requests is degraded due to queueing effects with respect to each other, rather than the delay due to the in progress-track reads.

5. A hybrid method can be adopted. Simulation of disk cache behavior through trace analysis can be used to extract certain destage parameters, which can then be used in a performance evaluation study of RAID5 (based on analysis or simulation). In fact the same paradigm is followed in, [39, 77], where the effect of caching is incorporated through parameters determining the destage workload.

6. Detailed simulations tend to be complex and prone to error. The validity of results obtained from such simulations can be ascertained through the analytic solution of a possibly simplified system model.

30.4   MODELING ASSUMPTIONS AND PARAMETERS

We initially consider a *noncached* RAID5 disk array consisting of $N + 1 + \delta$ disks, where $\delta = 0$ (respectively $\delta = 1$) in the case of dedicated (respectively distributed) sparing. A relatively small striping unit is postulated in this study, which implies an evenly balanced load. This is not always possible with parity striping as noted earlier. Note that RAID5 does not alleviate the need for load balancing across arrays. Whereas the actual size of the striping unit is immaterial for the analysis in normal mode, the striping unit is assumed to be large enough such that almost all disk requests are satisfiable by accessing one disk

We analyze the performance of the system with an OLTP workload, since such workloads have stringent performance requirements, for example, the debit/credit transactions that access a few data blocks. That most database accesses are to small disk blocks is confirmed by the analysis of database traces for an airline reservations system in [57]. The distribution of disk accesses is simplified in [22] as 80% 4K reads, 16% 4K writes, 2% 24K reads, and 2% 24K writes. Only 4K disk accesses are considered here for the sake of brevity. Additional database workloads are characterized in [78], where it is observed that multiblock sequential and list (noncontiguous sequential) accesses (to read and write) are also quite common in DB2 workloads.

An open rather than a closed system is considered in this study, which is tantamount to arrivals from an infinite rather than a finite number of sources. This assumption is justifiable because we are interested in the performance of the disk subsystem, rather than the overall system, which would have required additional modeling details. Furthermore, as in nearly all queueing models of secondary storage systems, we assume a time-homogeneous Poisson process [31]. This assumption further simplifies the analysis, because closed-form analytic expressions for performance measures of interest are available in this case [69].

The disk-array controller processes various I/O requests that vary in pathlength based on whether it is a cache hit or miss, etc. Disk controller delays are ignored in this study. Path contention in I/O subsystems has been reported in numerous earlier studies (see, for example, [5]). We assume a high-bandwidth packet-switched bus with prioritized transmission of disk I/O commands with respect to data transmissions, such that queueing delays in initiating a disk I/O are negligible and are ignored in this study. Rotational Positional Sensing (RPS) misses, which result in increased latency in the form of additional rotations when the path for transmitting data from disk is busy, are alleviated by providing a *track (segmented) buffer* [78] or an *on-board buffer* [82] to temporarily hold data read from a disk. The associated analytic model should be modified to take into account the fact that the reading of a block may entail a full track read or the reading of the remainder of the track depending on the prefetching policy. The track buffer is expected to have limited effect on the cache hit ratio when disk accesses are random. This effect is ignored in this study, but can be taken into account by an off-line simulation of the trace of a given workload. The bus bandwidth might be a limiting factor in degraded mode and especially in rebuild mode, since the number of disks attached to a bus is usually determined by normal mode processing. An adequate bus bandwidth is postulated for all cases. The time to compute the parity is negligible, since we assume that specialized hardware is used for this purpose.

A disk subsystem usually consists of multiple arrays, but only one array is considered here, with an arrival rate K. In a system with multiple arrays with different workloads, the overall response time is a weighted sum according to the fractions of the arrival rates to the arrays and their mean response time. The maximum arrival rate K_{max} to an array is determined by the bottleneck resource in the system, which is the resource with the highest utilization. The utilization of a resource is the fraction of time it is busy, which is the product of the arrival rate of requests and their mean service time [31]. This is a special case of Little's result, which states that the mean number of requests in a system is the product of their arrival rate and the mean time spent in the system, which may correspond to the queue, server, or both [31]. Since the utilization of a resource cannot exceed one, K_{max} is equal to the reciprocal of the mean disk service time (determined in what follows). The response time of a disk increases sharply as the disk approaches full utilization (see Section 30.5), but an acceptable mean response time to read requests is possible at very high utilizations if certain precautions are taken, for example, giving a lower priority to disk writes with respect to read requests, since write response time is not critical (see Section 30.5).

The fraction of reads and writes in the arrival stream is f_r and $f_w = 1 - f_r$, respectively. A read request accesses a 4K block, which is a Simple-Read-Write (SRW) access. The writing of a data block requires the old values of data and parity blocks to compute the new parity. The reading and writing of noncached blocks can be accomplished more efficiently by using Read-Modify-Write (RMW) disk accesses, that is, the reading of a block is followed by its writing after one disk rotation [39]. The separation of these two actions is inefficient, since it introduces an extra seek, but there is the potential for reduced latency. We assume that the read and write steps for a RMW are issued atomically, as one independent request after another. In a cached disk array with NVS, the processing of reads at a higher priority than destage requests is preferable because of the improved read response time. This may result in the separation of the two steps of a RMW. Nonpreemptive read priorities are considered in [78, 73], whereas preemptive processing of reads with respect to destage requests is discussed in [73] and in Section 30.6.

The arrival rate of requests in normal mode to each disk is $\lambda_1 = f_r K/(N+1+\delta)$ for SRW disk requests for reads and $\lambda_2 = 2f_w K/(N+1+\delta)$ for RMW requests for data and parity blocks. The overall arrival rate to each disk is $\Lambda = \lambda_1 + \lambda_2 = (2-f_r)K/(N+1+\delta)$.

The arrival rate of requests to surviving disks in the rebuild mode varies according to the fraction of materialized data on the spare areas (denoted by σ). The arrival rate in the degraded mode corresponds to $\sigma = 0$. When read redirection is in effect, the arrival rate to each surviving disk with dedicated sparing is [75, 39]: $(2-\sigma)f_r K/(N+1)$ reads; $2(N-1+\sigma)f_w K/N(N+1)$ RMW accesses for data and parity (when data and parity blocks are both available); $(1-\sigma)f_w K/(N(N+1))$ data writes (when the parity block on the failed disk has not been reconstructed yet); and $(1-\sigma)f_w K/(N+1))$ data reads or parity writes (when the data block on the failed disk has not been reconstructed yet).

In distributed sparing, the arrival rates of different types of requests to each disk are [77]:

- Arrival rate for data reads (with read redirection option):

$$\lambda_0'(\sigma) = \frac{[1+\sigma+(2-\sigma)N]f_r K}{(N+1)(N+2)}$$

- Arrival rate for RMW requests for writing data and parity blocks on surviving disks:

$$\lambda_1'(\sigma) = \frac{2(N+2\sigma)f_w K}{(N+1)(N+2)}$$

- Arrival rate for simple writes when the parity block is missing:

$$\lambda_2'(\sigma) = \frac{(1-\sigma)f_w K}{(N+1)(N+2)}$$

- The arrival rate of requests to read data blocks from $N-1$ surviving disks and simple writes of parity blocks, when the data block is not available:

$$\lambda_3'(\sigma) = \frac{(1-\sigma)Nf_w K}{(N+1)(N+2)}$$

The arrival rate of requests to each nonfailed disk in degraded and rebuild modes is $\Lambda'(\sigma) = \sum_{i=0}^{3}\lambda_i'(\sigma)$. The ratios $\lambda_i'(\sigma)/\Lambda'(\sigma)$ are the fractions of different types of requests processed by the disks. The disk utilization is simply the sum of the products of the arrival rates and corresponding service times, which are obtained in what follows.

The disk service time is modeled as a general distribution, since it is not just the mean but also the second moment of the service time that affects the mean waiting time (see discussion in Section 30.5). The random variables for the three main components of disk service time: seek, search, and transfer time are x_S, x_L, and x_T, respectively, such that the disk service time is $x = x_S + x_L + x_T$. The Laplace-Stieltjes Transform LST (see, for example, [69]) $\mathcal{X}^*(s)$ for the probability density function (pdf) of disk service time ($f_X(x)$) can be expressed as the product of the LST's for seek, search, and transfer time, since they are assumed to be independent (the dependence between latency and transfer time is discussed in what follows), $\mathcal{X}^*_{type}(s) = \mathcal{X}^*_S(s)\mathcal{X}^*_L(s)\mathcal{X}^*_T(s)$. $\mathcal{X}^*_T(s)$ corresponds to the transfer time of a block (respectively the transfer time of a block plus a disk revolution) when the request type is a SRW (respectively a RMW). The LST for disk service time is used to analyze the vacationing server model in Section 30.5 [69].

Let $\overline{X^i}_{SRW}$ and $\overline{X^i}_{RMW}$ denote the ith moment for the SRW and RMW service time, respectively. The ith moment of disk service time is given by $E[x^i] = E[(x_S + x_L + x_T)^i]$. Even with the independence assumption (see, for example, [9]) this leads to relatively cumbersome expressions for the higher moments of disk service time, which are not given here for the sake of brevity. Alternatively, given the LST for the components of disk service time: $E[x^i] = (-1)^i d^i \mathcal{X}^*(s)/ds|_{s=0}$. The mean, variance, and second moment of disk service time for SRW requests are $X_{SRW} = X_S + X_L + X_T$, $Var[X_{SRW}] = Var[X_S] + Var[X_L] + Var[X_T]$, and $\overline{X^2}_{SRW} = Var[X_{SRW}] + X^2_{SRW}$. The expression for RMW requests uses the transfer time of a block plus rotation time. The moments of service time when the system is operating in normal (respectively rebuild) mode are $\overline{X^i}_{normal} = g\overline{X^i}_{SRW} + (1 - g)\overline{X^i}_{RMW}$ (respectively $\overline{X^i}_{rebuild}(\sigma) = h(\sigma)\overline{X^i}_{SRW} + (1 - h(\sigma))\overline{X^i}_{RMW}$), where $g = f_r/(2 - f_r)$ (respectively $h(\sigma) = 1 - \lambda'_1(\sigma)/\Lambda'_1(\sigma)$). In the degraded mode $h(\sigma)$ is computed with $\sigma = 0$.

The disk service time LST in the rebuild mode with a fraction σ of the data materialized is similarly $\mathcal{X}^*(s) = h(\sigma)\mathcal{X}^*_{SRW}(s) + (1 - h(\sigma))\mathcal{X}^*_{RMW}(s)$. The ith moment for the service time of rebuild writes onto the spare areas of surviving disks is denoted by $\overline{X^i}_{w-rbld}$. For rebuild writes, we consider the two extremes of zero and an average seek for writing a track.

IBM 0661 Model 370 (Lightning) disks are used in generating the numerical results in our studies, but the conclusions are expected to apply to other disks. The characteristics of Lightning disks can be summarized as follows [22]: 326.5 MB capacity; $C = 949$ cylinders per disk; 14 tracks per cylinder; the number of tracks per disk is therefore $N_{track} = 13.286$; the number of 512-byte sectors per track is $N_{ST} = 48$; with an RPM (rotations per minute) of 4317.8; the rotation time is $T_R = 13.9$ msec; the sector time is $T_S = T_R/48$. The number of sectors in a 4K block is $N_{SB} = 8$ and hence there are $N_{ST}/N_{SB} = 6$ blocks per track.

Zero-latency or *roll-mode* read/write capability is assumed, that is, disk transfers can start at a sector boundary with a mean latency of $T_S/2$ for full-track reads. There is a 4 (respectively 7) sector track (respectively cylinder) skew to make time for head switching to allow the uninterrupted reading of sequential tracks (for rebuild) possible.

We will compute the rotational latency by first noting that it tends to be smaller when the zero-latency option is in effect. The probability that the read/write head is located inside (respectively outside) the block to be read is $r = N_{SB}/N_{ST}$ (respectively $1 - r$). If we ignore sector latencies to simplify the discussion, we have the following composite distribution for latency alone: $T_R - T_B = (1 - r)T_R$ with probability r and a uniform distribution over $(0, (1 - r)T_R)$ with probability $1 - r$, which implies a mean latency of $(1 - r^2)T_R/2$. We approximate the rotational latency to access 4K blocks by a uniform distribution over $(0, T_R)$, which implies $X_L \approx T_R/2$. This approximation becomes more accurate as r decreases with the number of sectors per track increasing, but is exact when roll-mode disk transfers are not available. The ith moment of latency and its LST can be approximated by $\overline{X_L^i} = T_R^i/(i + 1)$ and $\mathcal{X}_L^*(s) = (1 - e^{-sT_R})/(sT_R)$, respectively. The latency for roll-mode reading of tracks is uniform over $(0, T_S)$ and its LST is given by $\mathcal{X}_{L-sector}^*(s) = (1 - e^{-sT_S})/(sT_S)$.

The transfer time for 4K blocks for SRWs is $T_B = T_R/N_{SB} = 2.3$ msec. Hence the mean, variance, ith moment, and LST of transfer time for 4K blocks are $X_T = T_B$, $Var[X_T] = 0$, $\overline{X_T^i} = T_B^i$, and $\mathcal{X}_{T_B}^*(s) = e^{-sT_B}$, respectively. The transfer time for an initial track read is $X_{T-track1} = T_R$ and for successive track reads $X_{T-track2} = 13T_R/12$ (due to the four-sector track skew).

The seek-time equation derived from the seek-time characteristic is $t(d) = 2.0 + 0.01(d - 1) + 0.46\sqrt{d - 1}, 1 \leq d \leq C - 1$ [22]. Denoting the probability of a zero-seek with p, the seek distance probability mass function for nonzero seeks can be specified as

$$P_{SD}[d] = (1 - p)\frac{2(C - d)}{C(C - 1)}, \quad 1 \leq d \leq C - 1 \tag{30.1}$$

Given $t(d)$ and $P_{SD}[d]$, the moments of seek time $(\overline{X_S^i})$ can be computed easily. Disk cylinders are expected to be accessed uniformly by an OLTP workload with small reads and writes. The mean seek time in this case with $p = 1/C$ is $X_S = \sum_{d=1}^{C-1} t(d)P_{SD}[d] = 12.7$ msec. The number of sectors per track varies with *zoned bit recording* or zoning for short, since the number of recorded bits per track can be made to be higher on the outer tracks than the inner tracks [63, 60]. The seek distance (in cylinders) for uniform access to sectors are derived in [77].

The analysis of the $M/G/1$ queueing model used in this chapter is based on the assumption that successive service times are independent [69]. This is not so for disk service times, since seek times are *positively correlated,* for example, a long seek implies that the arm is near the edges and that provided seeks are uniformly distributed the next seek will have a mean of $C/2$ cylinders, while a seek from the middle of the disk will result in a mean seek of $C/4$. An analytical solution method that takes this correlation into account appears in [20], but we have opted for the simpler method because it tends to be quite accurate for modern disk-drive parameters.

To derive $\mathcal{X}_S^*(s)$, we first use a piecewise linear approximation to the seek-distance versus seek-time characteristic (inverse function to $t(d)$) with K line segments with endpoints $(T_k, D_k), 1 \leq k \leq K+1$ (with $D_1 = 1$ and $D_{K+1} = C-1$). The equation for the kth line segment is $d = \alpha_k t - \beta_k$ with $\alpha_k = (C_k + 1 - C_k)/(T_k + 1 - T_k)$ and $\beta_k = \alpha_k T_k - C_k$. The disk seek-time LST taking into account zero seeks is given by

$$
\mathcal{X}_S^*(s) \;=\; p + \frac{2(1-p)}{C(C-2)} \sum_{k=1}^{K} \Big\{ \alpha_k (C + \beta_k) \frac{e^{-sT_k} - e^{-sT_{k+1}}}{s}
$$
$$
- \alpha_k^2 \left[\frac{T_k e^{-sT_k} - T_{k+1} e^{-sT_{k+1}}}{s} - \frac{e^{-sT_k} - e^{-sT_{k+1}}}{s^2} \right] \Big\} \qquad (30.2)
$$

30.5   ANALYTIC RESULTS

In Section 30.5.1, we outline the analysis of a queueing model for individual disks. In Section 30.5.2, we analyze the vacationing server model that is applicable to analyzing the system in rebuild mode. In Section 30.5.3, we outline an approach to estimate the completion time of fork-join requests required for the analysis in the degraded mode.

30.5.1   Analysis of $M/G/1$ Queueing Systems

An $M/G/1$ queue has a single server with Markovian or Poisson arrivals with rate λ and a General service time distribution with random variable b, pdf $b(t)$, whose LST is $\mathcal{B}^*(s)$, and its ith moment b_i. The server utilization is $\rho = \lambda b_1 < 1$. The random variable for waiting time is w. The ith moment of waiting time with a FCFS discipline is denoted by $\overline{W^i}$. The mean queue length, which is another performance measure of of interest, follows from Little's result as λW.

By using a simplified notation for the first moment, the mean response time is $R = W + b_1$. More generally, the ith moment of response time is $\overline{R^i} = E[(b + w)^i]$. The variance of response time is $\sigma_R^2 = \overline{R^2} - R^2$ and its coefficient of variation squared is $c_R^2 = \sigma_R^2/R^2$. The expression for $\overline{R^i}$ can be simplified provided w is independent of b, that is, for queueing disciplines that serve requests without taking into account the service time if it is known a priori. SJF (shortest job first) is a nonpreemptive scheduling discipline, which minimizes response time by giving a higher priority to the processing of shorter requests. Two disk-scheduling disciplines that are approximations to SJF are the shortest seek time first (SSTF) [20] and the shortest access time first (SATF), which also takes into account rotational latency [82].

In a *vacationing server queueing system*, the server takes a vacation after a busy period is completed. On returning from vacation, the server checks the queue, and according to the *multiple vacation model*, it takes another vacation if it is empty; otherwise, it starts processing requests [69]. Figure 30.1 shows the processing of requests and the taking of vacations as time progresses. The ith moment of

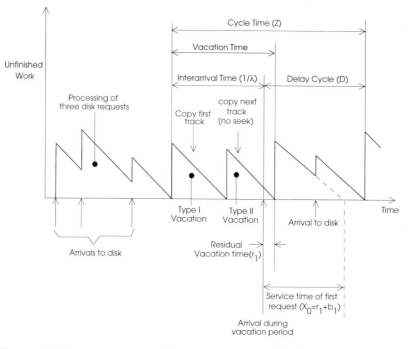

Figure 30.1. Delay cycles and vacations in an $M/G/1$ queueing system.

the vacation time with a probability distribution function (PDF) $V(t)$ is denoted by γ_i. The mean residual vacation time is $r_1 = \gamma_2/2\gamma_1$ and its ith moment is $r_i = \gamma_{i+1}/(i+1)\gamma_1$. The first two moments of waiting time in this system are [69]

$$W = r_1 + \frac{\lambda b_2}{2(1-\rho)} = r_1 + \frac{\lambda b_1^2(1+c_b^2)}{2(1-\rho)}, \tag{30.3}$$

$$\overline{W^2} = r_2 + \frac{\lambda b_2}{1-\rho}r_1 + \frac{\lambda b_3}{3(1-\rho)} + \frac{(\lambda b_2)^2}{2(1-\rho)^2} \tag{30.4}$$

The first two moments of waiting time for the case when there are no vacations (a basic $M/G/1$ queueing system) can be obtained from the preceding equations by setting $r_i = 0, i \geq 0$. Note that in order to obtain the ith moment of waiting time, we need the $(i+1)$st moment of service time, which is the reason for providing the higher moments of the components of disk service time in Section 30.4. The exponential service-time distribution for disks will tend to overestimate the mean waiting time (W), since the coefficient of variation of disk service time (c_b in the second expression for W) tends to be less than one. Appropriate bounds in queueing theory can be used when the arrival process is not Poisson. In this case, the mean waiting time is proportional to the sum of the squared coefficients of variations of the interarrival and service time $(c_a^2 + c_b^2)$. The validation of performance estimates based on an $M/G/1$ analysis (with $c_a^2 = 1$ for the exponential interarrival time distribution) has supposedly only been possible in some experiments after setting c_b^2 to a negative value, which in effect compensates for the fact that $c_a^2 < 1$.

The LST for the response-time distribution is given by [31, 69]

$$\mathcal{R}^*(s) = \frac{s(1-\rho)\mathcal{X}^*(s)}{s - \lambda + \lambda\mathcal{X}^*(s)} \tag{30.5}$$

The LST for the density function is then $\mathcal{R}^*(s)/s$ [31].

A special analysis is required for a dedicated "sparing system", where user requests are given a higher priority than rebuild requests on the spare disk. A similar situation arises at all surviving disks in a distributed sparing system. In both cases, the arrival of rebuild writes is assumed to be according to a Poisson process. The first two moments of waiting time for the higher priority (class one) requests in a system with two priority levels with multiple vacations are as follows [69]:

$$W_1 = P_V r_1 + \frac{U_2}{1 - \rho_1} \tag{30.6}$$

$$\overline{W_1^2} = P_V r_2 + \frac{U_3}{3(1 - \rho_1)} + (\lambda_1 b_{2,1} + 2W'_1)W_1$$

where $P_V = (1-\rho)/(1-\rho_1)$, $U_i = \sum_{k=1}^{2} \lambda_k b_{i,k}/2$, with $b_{i,k}$ denoting the ith moment of service time for the kth priority level, $\rho_k = \lambda_k b_{k,1}, 1 \leq k \leq 2$, and $\rho = \rho_1 + \rho_2$. W'_1 is given in what follows.

Reads may be given a higher priority than destage operations in a cached disk array with NVS (see Section 30.6). The mean waiting time for the higher-priority class 1 requests with the assumption that the arrival of destage requests is random is given by

$$W'_1 = \frac{U_2}{1 - \rho_1} \tag{30.7}$$

A *busy period* in $M/G/1$ begins with an arrival to the system and ends when the processing of all requests is completed. A *delay cycle* is a busy period started by an *exceptional request* (with mean b_0), whose mean duration is [69]

$$D = \frac{b_0}{1 - \rho} \tag{30.8}$$

30.5.2 Analysis of the Vacationing Server Model for $M/G/1$

In order to estimate the mean time to read a disk for rebuild we need to compute the mean cycle time, which, as shown in Figure 30.1 is the sum of the mean duration of a delay cycle and the time from the completion of a delay cycle to the beginning of the next delay cycle (this is simply the interarrival time $1/\lambda$). The mean processing time of the initial request is the sum of the mean residual delay due to vacations and the mean service time $b_0 = r_1 + b_1$. The mean cycle time is then $Z = 1/\lambda + D$, where D is given by Eq. 30.8.

Different vacation types are required to model the behavior of the system. Figure 30.1 shows an $M/G/1$ system with two vacation type and specifies some of the parameters required by the analysis. Following [11], we first consider infinitely many vacation types which are taken according to the sequence $\{V_i\}_{i=1}^{\infty}$, that is, the server returning from V_1 starts V_2 if there are no requests, and so on. Given that $V_j(t)$ is the PDF of the jth vacation and q_j the fraction of type j vacations, the distribution of a typical vacation is $V(t) = \sum_{j=1}^{\infty} q_j V_j(t)$. The ith moment of a type j vacation is denoted by $\gamma_{i,j}$.

Let p_j denote the probability that the first request starting a new busy cycle arrives during the jth vacation. Noting that the probability of no arrival (respectively an arrival) in a time interval t is $e^{-\lambda t}$ (respectively $1 - e^{-\lambda t}$) and unconditioning with respect to $V_j(t)$, $j \geq 1$, yields

$$p_j = \left[1 - \int_0^{\infty} e^{-\lambda t} \, dV_j(t) \right] \prod_{j=1}^{i-1} \int_0^{\infty} e^{-\lambda t} \, dV_j(t) = \left[1 - V_j^*(\lambda) \right] \prod_{i=1}^{j-1} V_i^*(\lambda) \quad (30.9)$$

where the integrals correspond to an LST with a parameter λ. The mean number of vacations per idle period is $\overline{J} = \sum_{j=1}^{\infty} j p_j$. It follows that $q_j = \sum_{i=j}^{\infty} p_i / \overline{J}$. In the case of a system with two types of vacations, an initial vacation of type I and all remaining vacations of type II, we have

$$p_1 = 1 - V_1^*(\lambda), p_i = [1 - V_2^*(\lambda)]V_1^*(\lambda)[V_2^*(\lambda)]^{i-2}, \quad i \geq 2 \quad (30.10)$$

The mean number of vacations in this case is

$$\overline{J} = \frac{1 + V_1^*(\lambda)}{1 - V_2^*(\lambda)} \quad (30.11)$$

It follows that

$$q_1 = \frac{1 + V_1^*(\lambda)}{1 - V_2^*(\lambda)}$$

and the ith moment of vacation time is

$$\gamma_i = \sum_{j=1}^{\infty} q_j \gamma_{i,j} = \frac{[1 - V_2^*(\lambda)] \gamma_{i,1} + V_1^*(\lambda) \gamma_{i,2}}{1 - V_2^*(\lambda) + V_1^*(\lambda)} \quad (30.12)$$

A vacationing server model with three vacation types is required to analyze rebuild with the split-seek option [75], whereas the split latency/transfer option is difficult to analyze and its behavior is investigated through simulation in [74].

30.5.3 Analysis of Fork-Join Requests

A fork-join request generates K requests on its arrival to the system and is considered completed when all its components have finished their processing at the K servers. The expected maximum of the K components (R_K^{max}) is an upper bound to the expected value of the fork-join response time [49]. When regular (nonfork-join) requests contribute heavily to the utilization of individual disks, the components of fork-join response time are almost independent, which is attributable to the variability in queue lengths encountered by associated fork-join requests [72]. In this case R_K^{max}, in addition to being an upper bound to $R_K^{F/J}$, is also a good approximation to it. This assertion was verified for several distributions through simulation studies reported in [72, 76]. The expected value of the maximum of a set of K independent random variables with PDF $R_i(t), 1 < i < K$, is given by

$$R_K^{max} = \int_0^\infty \left[1 - \prod_{i=1}^{K} R_i(t) \right] dt \qquad (30.13)$$

In the special case of identical response-time distributions, $R_i(t) = R(t), 1 < i < K$. Different response-time distributions are possible when (1) requests have different service times, such as SRW and RMW disk accesses; (2) service times are the same but, the disks utilizations are different, which may be due to access skew in parity striping [18].

Numerical integration can be used to obtain R_K^{max} from the preceding equation. Since the integral can be evaluated when the response time PDF is expressible as an exponential, one method to simplify the computation of R_K^{max} is to match the first two moments of the response-time distribution for read requests to an Erlang or hyperexponential distribution, depending on whether the coefficient of variation $c_R < 1$ or $c_R > 1$, or the Coxian distribution regardless of the value of c_R [31]. The coefficient of variation of response time can be obtained using the expressions for the moments of response time. This is particularly simple when we consider a read-only workload with SRW requests. Using R_{SRW} and $\sigma_{SRW}^2 = \overline{R^2}_{SRW} - R_{SRW}^2$, we have

$$c_R^2 = \frac{\sigma_{SRW}^2}{R_{SRW}^2} = \frac{c_X^2 + \frac{\rho s_X}{3(1-\rho)} + \rho \frac{1+c_X^2}{4(1-\rho)^2}}{1 + \rho \frac{1+c_X^2}{1-\rho} + \rho \frac{1+c_X^2}{4(1-\rho)^2}} \qquad (30.14)$$

where $c_X^2 = \overline{X^2}_{SRW}/X_{SRW}^2 - 1$ and $s_X = \overline{X^3}_{SRW}/X_{SRW}^3$. For $\rho = 0$ (respectively $\rho \to 1$) $c_R = c_X$ (respectively $c_R \to 1$). The coefficient of variation c_R tends to be less than one for SRW requests and the same is true for the overall disk response time for the system and workload parameters considered in Section 30.3. The Erlang distribution has a coefficient of variation smaller than one and it is hence suitable for approximating the response-time distribution.

The PDF for a k-stage Erlang distribution is given by

$$F(t) = 1 - e^{-\mu t} \sum_{j=0}^{k-1} \frac{(\mu t)^j}{j!} \qquad (30.15)$$

Its mean, variance, and coefficient of variation squared is given by k/μ, k/μ^2, and $1/k$, respectively.

The mean of the maximum of K random variables with an Erlang distribution is given by Eq. 30.13

$$R_K^{max} = \int_0^\infty \left\{ 1 - \prod_{i=1}^{K} \left[1 - e^{-\mu_i t} \sum_{j=0}^{k_i-1} \frac{(\mu_i t)^j}{j!} \right] \right\} dt \qquad (30.16)$$

In the case of two queues with different response times and parameters, $\mu_1 = 1/R_1$, $\mu_2 = 1/R_2$, k_1, and k_2, we have

$$R_2^{max} = R_1 + R_2 - \sum_{m=0}^{k_1-1} \sum_{n=0}^{k_2-1} \frac{(m+n)!}{m!n!} \frac{\mu_1^m \mu_2^n}{(\mu_1+\mu_2)^{m+n+1}} \qquad (30.17)$$

Given that $R_i(\rho)$ and $\sigma_i^2(\rho)$ are the mean and standard deviation of the ith response time, respectively, the parameters of the corresponding Erlang distribution can be determined as follows. The mean number of stages for the ith Erlang distribution is $Y_i = R_i^2(\rho)/\sigma_i^2(\rho)$ and the rate of each stage is $\mu_i = Y_i/R_i(\rho)$. The following interpolation is applicable when Y is noninteger $R_Y^{max} = R_{J_2}^{max}(J_1 - Y) + R_{J_1}^{max}(Y - J_2)$, where $J_1 = ceil(Y)$ and $J_2 = floor(Y)$. R_K^{max} for higher values of K can be obtained from a generalization of Eq. 30.17, but the computational cost increases rapidly with K and the number of stages Y. When the computational cost of this method is excessive, R_K^{max} can be approximated by its upper bound using the method in [17].

Alternatively, we may match the first two moments of disk response time to an extreme value distribution [28]: $Pr[X < x] = exp\left[-e^{-(x-a)/b}\right]$ with a mean $a + \gamma b$ and variance $(\pi b)^2/6 \approx 1.64483 b^2$. Note that no assumption about c_R is required in this case. Because of its form the maximum of K random variables with an extreme value distribution also follows this distribution with a mean $a + \gamma b + b ln(K)$, which leads to $R_K^{max}(\rho) = R(\rho) + \sqrt{6}\sigma(\rho)ln(K)/\pi$. The advantage of this method is its low computational cost.

A technique described in [32] for estimating fork-join response times is also worthy of mention. It is based on approximating the service time of an $M/G/1$ queueing system with an Erlang distribution [31]. The distribution of response time (or virtual waiting time) for an $M/E_r/1$ queueing system can be computed using the method in [29]. The method in [17] is then used to estimate R_K^{max}. Approximating the response-time distribution with an Erlang, hyperexponenetial, or Coxian distribution provides more flexibility in that it can be applied to different service-time distributions.

More accurate estimates for the mean fork-join response time can be obtained by interpolating between the mean of its maximum value (obtained using the forementioned methods) and the mean of its minimum value, when there are no interfering requests. An empirical equation for the mean response time in the latter case and a methodology based on curve fitting to simulation results to estimate the parameters of the equation is provided in [72, 76]. Further experimentation is required to determine the weights for interpolation, but this effort may not be warranted since there is not much difference between the two bounds.

30.6 ANALYSIS OF RAID5 IN NORMAL AND DEGRADED MODES

We first outline the analysis of a system without a cache in normal and degraded modes. The analysis of a system with a cache, part of which may be nonvolatile is outlined at the end of this section. We note that the analyses for dedicated and distributed sparing are quite similar in this case. Furthermore, the analysis is applicable to clustered RAID with appropriate modifications, for example, in terms of the number of blocks to be read to recreate a lost data block.

The writing of data and parity blocks is somewhat complicated in that if the RMW requests for both are initiated at the same time, the new parity block cannot be computed in time to be written to disk if due to queueing delays the *old* value of the data block is not available yet. One solution to this problem is to allow additional rotations to write the parity block. This wasted processing can be alleviated by initiating the RMW request for the parity block only *after* the data block to be written has been read. This is at the cost of a higher mean response time for writes (at lower disk utilizations), but this is of little concern since write response times do not directly affect application response times, for example, a transaction is considered completed as soon as its log records have been written. The *before-service* policy initiates the access to the parity block only when the write request for the data block reaches the head of the queue [9]. A higher priority may be given to parity block accesses to compensate for the delay in initiating the request.

The mean response time for read and write requests are then $R_r = R_{SRW}$ and $R_w = R_{SRW} + R_{RMW}$, with $R_{SRW} = X_{SRW} + W$ and $R_{RMW} = X_{RMW} + W$, where W is obtained using Eq. 30.3 with $r_1 = 0$ in Section 30.5.1. Substitutions of system-specific parameters into the queueing equations are not given here for the sake of brevity. The read (SRW) response-time distribution and its percentiles are also of interest and can be obtained by inverting the associated LST; (see Eq. 30.6 in Section 30.5.1). For example, the 90th and 95th percentile of response time can be approximated by $W + 1.3\sigma_W$ and $W + 2.0\sigma_W$, respectively.

In the degraded mode, a read targeted to the failed disk will entail reading the N corresponding data and parity blocks from the N (respectively $N + 1$) surviving disks in the case of dedicated (respectively distributed) sparing (note that one of the disks in distributed sparing holds a spare striping unit). Such reads correspond to fork-join requests, whose mean response time $(R_N^{F/J})$ is the mean completion time of all N requests. For a write targeted to the failed disk, the system reads the corresponding $(N-1)$ data blocks, computes the parity block, and then writes it. $R_K^{F/J}$ is approximated by R_K^{max} in obtaining numerical results.

The mean read response time in the case of a dedicated sparing system is a weighted sum of the mean response time of reads directed to surviving disks and the fork-join accesses substituting requests to the failed disk $R_r = (NR_{SRW} + R_N^{max})/(N+1)$. The mean response times for the three types of writes are as follows: (1) both the data and parity disk survived the crash $R_w^1 = R_{SRW} + R_{RMW}$; (2) the data disk crashed $R_w^2 = R_{SRW}$; (3) the parity disk crashed: $R_w^3 = R_{N-1}^{F/J} + R_{SRW}$. The overall write response time is $R_w = [(N-1)R_w^1 + R_w^2 + R_w^3]/(N+1)$.

In a distributed sparing system, we have $R_r = [(N+1)R_{SRW} + R_N^{F/J}]/(N+2)$. The mean response times for the three types of writes are as follows: (1) Both data and parity disk survived: $R_w^1 = R_{SRW} + R_{RMW}$. (2) The parity disk crashed: $R_w^2 = R_{SRW}$. (3) The data disk crashed: $R_w^3 = R_{N-1}^{F/J} + R_{SRW}$. To derive the mean response time for write requests, let $\Lambda_w = \Lambda f_w$ denote the arrival rate of requests to write data blocks on all disks. The arrival rate of writes to the $N+1$ surviving disks is $(N+1)\Lambda_w/(N+2)$ of which $N/(N+1)$ (respectively $1/(N+1)$ have parity blocks on the remaining surviving disks (respectively the failed disk). The rate of requests to write data blocks on the failed disk is $\Lambda_w/(N+1)$. Thus, the weights associated with R_w^1, R_w^2, and R_w^3 are $N/(N+2)$, $1/(N+2)$, and $1/(N+2)$, respectively. The overall write response time is $R_w = (NR_w^1 + R_w^2 + R_w^3)/(N+2)$.

The writing of a data block in a cached disk array without NVS requires both the data and parity blocks to be written before it is considered completed. In this case, the writing process upon a write miss is similar to what was described earlier for a system without a disk cache. When there is a cache hit for the data block, the write request for the data block and the RMW requests for the parity blocks can be initiated simultaneously. Although a cache hit is also possible for parity blocks, we assume that parity blocks are not cached, that is, they are read on demand and written out as part of the destage operation. This is because it is more efficient to cache data rather than parity blocks [78].

A write hit means that a clean copy of the block to be updated is in the cache. Since h_w usually applies to the time of the initial write, then we implicitly assume that the clean block is pinned, because this block may be LRUed out by the time it is scheduled to be destaged (this scheme was shown to yield an improvement in performance according to the trace-driven simulation study in [78]). Further updates of the same block overwrite the dirty version of the block. The analysis for fork-join requests developed in Section 30.5.3 can be used to determine the completion time of the data and parity block writes, since the RMW for the parity block can be initiated immediately

Provided that the old version of a data block is cached, which occurs with probability h_w, the data block can be written with an SRW access. Otherwise a RMW access is required. The three types of requests to each disk and the associated frequencies are as follows: (1) Read requests $f_r(1 - h_r)$. (2) Writes of a data block when the old data block is cached $f_w h_w$. (3) RMW accesses for data and parity blocks $f_w(2 - h_w)$. These frequencies can then be used to determine the moments of disk service time required for the analysis.

Fast writes are possible in the case of a cache with NVS, that a write is considered completed as soon as it is written to the NVS cache (also defined in Section 1). There are several options in processing the writing of a data block when the old value of the data block is cached. Overwriting it will require a future disk read in order to compute the parity. The *save-old-data-value* method [40] allocates a new block, which has the disadvantage of allocating two cache blocks to the same disk block. In fact, two copies of the block in separately powered NVS caches may be written to assure higher reliability [40]. Since the data blocks written onto NVS are considered to be safe, they can be destaged asynchronously at a lower priority than read requests.

When the two steps of a RMW are separated, an extra seek may be required for the write operation of a RMW (although the associated latency is expected to be smaller than what would be encountered otherwise). This is taken into account approximately by estimating the probability that a read request arrives while the read segment of a RMW is in progress, that is, $p_{arrive} = \mathcal{X}^*_{SRW}\left[\Lambda f_r(1 - h_r)/(N + 1)\right]$. The mean seek time for the write phase of a RMW, which is treated separately from its first phase, equals $p_{arrive}T_S$ and its mean latency is $p_{arrive}(1 - r^2)T_R/2 + (1 - p_{arrive})(1 - r)T_R$.

With NVS, there are two opportunities to reduce disk utilization due to destage activity as noted in Section 30.2. The analyses reported in [39, 77] used the parameters capturing these effects for a disk-access trace for an IMS OLTP workload.

1. A dirty block may be updated several times before it is propagated to disk. The fraction of writes to clean pages was determined to be $f_{Clean}(= 0.4)$, which implies that the rate of write requests to the array is $f_{Clean}K f_w$.

2. The destaging of multiple blocks of data can be carried out with a higher efficiency by taking advantage of disk geometry, including destage locality, that applies to data and corresponding parity blocks. It follows from trace analysis that on the average $\overline{n}_{block}(= 2)$ blocks can be destaged on each track, which implies that one seek is required to destage $\overline{n}_{block}$ blocks. We furthermore assume that the (two) blocks to be written out are contiguous on the track.

30.7 ANALYSIS OF RAID5 IN THE REBUILD MODE

In this section we first introduce the simpler analysis for dedicated sparing system for RAID5 [75] and then extend it to the analysis of a distributed sparing system [77].

Estimating rebuild time is important because it determines the duration of time during which disk response time is high (it is at its highest when rebuild starts).

It also affects the availability measure of the disk array, which is the fraction of time the system provides access to all data, that is, $MTTF_{system}/(MTTF_{system} + MTTR_{disk})$, where the $MTTF_{system}$ and $MTTR_{disk}$ are the mean time to system failure (data loss) and mean disk repair time, respectively. A system failure due to data loss occurs if a disk fails before rebuild is completed. The $MTTF_{system}$ of a RAID5 disk array assuming that the disk failure and repair processes are exponentially distributed with means equal to $MTTF_{disk}$ and $MTTR_{disk}$ respectively is [15, 55]

$$MTTF_{system} = \frac{MTTF_{disk}^2}{(N+1) \times N \times MTTR_{disk}} \qquad (30.18)$$

However, once a hotspare is provided, which is the assumption made in this study, rebuild time is not very critical from the second viewpoint, since disk MTTFs tend to be quite large (150 Kilohours for Lightning disks [15]), unfortunately failures in disk arrays tend to be correlated [15].

Mean rebuild time can be approximated by the mean disk reading time (as justified in what follows), which is in turn determined by disk idleness, such that mean rebuild time equals $N_{track}X_{track-read}/(1-\rho)$, where $X_{track-read}$ is the mean time to read a track. Since $X_{track-read}$ is unknown a priori, an upper (respectively lower) bound to rebuild time can be obtained by assuming that all track reads incur an average (respectively no) seek. A rough estimate of disk copying time can be obtained by noting that the lower (respectively upper) bound is applicable at lower (respectively higher) disk utilizations. The analysis that follows is then concerned with estimating the fraction of track reads that incur a seek.

The reading of tracks for rebuild is carried out in parallel using the disk-oriented scheme in [23]. Disk blocks are read into a buffer, which is postulated to be large enough to ensure that there is no need to throttle the reading process due to buffer space exhaustion. Once all the tracks associated with a lost track are available in the buffer, they are XORed to recreate the lost track, which is then written onto a spare track. Alternatively, only a one-track buffer is required if the contents of newly read tracks can be XORed with the contents of the buffer at the time they become available. The completion of a rebuild in any case is determined by the finishing of the reading of the last track.

When a hotspare is available, the rebuild process is initiated immediately at idle surviving disks and delayed on busy disks, until they become idle. The rebuild process makes a seek to an appropriate disk cylinder (where the rebuild process was last interrupted) and reads successive disk tracks until a user request arrives. As noted earlier, a disk track is an appropriate rebuild unit [24]. Disk rebuild is modeled as an $M/G/1$ queueing system with multiple vacations of different types (see Section 30.5.2). The reading of the first track incurs a seek, whereas the reading of each one of the following tracks does not require a seek. These correspond to type I and II vacations, respectively. In addition, roll-mode or zero-latency reads result in a mean latency of half a sector time in the reading of the first track, whereas due to track skew further track reads incur a four-sector latency in addition to the transfer time. Combining the results in Sections 30.4 and 30.5 we have the following LSTs for the first and second vacation types: $\mathcal{V}_1^*(s) = \mathcal{X}_S^*(s)X_{L-sector}^*(s)\mathcal{X}_{T-track1}^*(s)$ and $\mathcal{V}_2^*(s) = \mathcal{X}_{T-track2}^*(s)$. Setting s in $\mathcal{V}_i^*(s)$'s equal to the arrival rate to surviving disks provides the values for evaluating Eq. 30.10 and Eq. 30.12.

A disk alternates between processing user requests and reading disk tracks for rebuild. The fact that the processing required by the user workload varies during rebuild is a complicating factor in computing the rebuild time as well as the response time for user requests. The analysis for rebuild is carried out for varying fractions of data read from the disks (σ) and materialized data on the spare disk (or spare areas in the case of distributed sparing). As discussed in what follows, the second variable tracks the first one rather closely. We consider I intervals during which the data are reconstructed, setting σ to the midpoint value during that interval $\sigma_i = (i - 0.5)/I, 1 < i < I$. The seek distance for the first user request (interrupting the rebuild process) is affected by the disk arm position. For example, the mean seek distance is $C/4$ when rebuild is in progress in the middle of a disk and it is $C/2$ when the rebuild is at its edges. An improvement in response time for user requests is only noticeable at lower user disk utilizations [74], since otherwise a very small fraction of disk accesses are affected by the initial position of the disk arm. On the other hand, a smaller seek distance is required for rebuild reads and writes when rebuild is in progress on the middle cylinders of a disk. The number of intervals can be chosen to be arbitrarily large, since the computational cost per interval is negligibly small. Note that due to the reduction in the additional processing on surviving disks, the intervals are successively shorter. This is because more and more reads (with the read redirection option in effect) are processed *directly* rather than as fork-join requests.

For each interval i, we compute the mean cycle time (Z_i) and the mean number of tracks read per cycle ($\overline{N^i}_{copy}$, where i is a superscript). Noting that the number of tracks per disk is N_{track}, the mean reading (copying) time of a disk is

$$T_{copy} = \frac{N_{track}}{I} \sum_{i=1}^{I} \frac{Z_i}{\overline{N^i}_{copy}} \qquad (30.19)$$

where $\overline{N^i}_{copy} = \overline{J}$ ($\overline{J}$ is the mean number of vacations per idle period, which is given by Eq. (11) in Section 5.2). In the case of the split-seek option $\overline{J}$ is derived in [75]. The rate at which tracks are copied onto the spare disk is

$$\lambda_{copy}^i = \overline{N^i}_{copy}/Z_i, \quad 1 \le i \le I \qquad (30.20)$$

Given λ_{copy}^i and the minimum time required for writing tracks onto the spare disk, for example, without incurring seeks, the disk utilization can be used to determine whether for a given declustering ratio in clustered RAID, the spare disk potentially constitutes a bottleneck or not. With read redirection, the heaviest load on the spare disk is when $i = I$. This is because as rebuild progresses, the load to recreate lost data blocks decreases on surviving disks, whereas the load on the spare disk increases as more blocks are materialized on it. This effect is less significant due to updates of materialized blocks only, when read redirection is not in effect.

Up to this point, we have computed the expected value of the random variable t_{copy}. However, the mean rebuild time is determined by the completion of rebuild reads at all surviving disks: T_N^{max}, which is the expected value of the maximum of the N random variables t_{copy}. The difficulty of carrying out this step analytically is discussed in [77]. Fortunately, simulation results have shown that t_{copy} has very little variability (except at very heavy loads due to user accesses) and hence its mean value is a good approximation for the maximum [77].

A remaining factor is that rebuild is considered completed when all rebuild writes are done. In the case of a dedicated sparing system, it is easy to see that the spare disk is not a bottleneck, since its utilization approaches that of the remaining disks as it is fully rebuilt, but this is not so in a clustered RAID5 system [47, 22, 44, 23]. Rebuild writes are therefore completed in a few cycles after rebuild reads are finished. In distributed sparing, rebuild writes are uniformly distributed over all disks, such that unless the disk utilization is very high, rebuild writes are completed in a few cycles after rebuild reads are finished.

A disk-oriented rebuild scheme is used in the case of distributed sparing as well, since this scheme provides a shorter rebuild time [23]. Rebuild writes similarly to rebuild reads are carried out at the track level, since parity and spare striping units are assumed to be rotated at the track level. The rate of rebuild writes at each disk is determined by noting that rebuild writes are carried out one track at a time and that spare tracks are uniformly distributed over the surviving $(N + 1)$ disks. Rebuild writes are given a lower priority than user requests to improve the response time to user requests, but a higher priority than rebuild reads to reduce the buffer space requirements for the rebuild process. Rebuild writes in this case elongate the rebuild read process at each disk. On the other hand a fraction $(N + 1)/(N + 2)$ of the N_{track} tracks of each disk need to be read. Note that the same amount of data is transferred in both cases.

The analysis in [77] considers two extreme cases where a rebuild write incurs an average seek and when no seek is incurred. The motivation for the second option is the expected affinity between tracks being read and the associated spare areas. In the case of no seeks, the delay due to track skew is taken into account. In this case we also expect only one seek to be incurred by the rebuild process, since the track to be reconstructed is expected to be in the vicinity of tracks being read. This is handled by setting the probability of a zero seek to the fraction of cases rebuild reads are interrupted by rebuild writes, rather than user requests.

The rate of rebuild writes for a given value for σ is $\lambda_{w-rbld}(\sigma) = \lambda_{copy}(\sigma)/(N + 1)$, since the spare data tracks are distributed evenly over all disks. Since $\lambda_{w-rbld}(\sigma)$ (for each σ) is not known a priori, it is initialized to zero and determined by an iterative solution, which is given in [77] and will not be repeated here for the sake of brevity.

A detailed simulator was written for validating the few approximations introduced by the analysis, especially for the fork-join queuing system. The simulator models the position of the arm with respect to disk cylinders, but not the angular position, since we do not consider schemes that take advantage of this information. Simulation was also used in estimating performance measures that cannot be computed analytically, such as the effect of a limited buffer size and buffer space allocation policies on the rebuild process. Destage processing with NVS (respectively rebuild processing) was simulated in [73] (respectively [74]).

30.8   CONCLUSIONS FROM NUMERICAL STUDIES

The workload specified in Section 30.4 with uniformly distributed read and write accesses to 4 KB blocks is used in preliminary performance studies, with reads constituting 75% of accesses, and $N + 2 = 10$ disks.

Mean response times in normal, degraded, and rebuild modes in dedicated and distributed sparing versus the arrival rate of requests show a pattern typical of $M/G/1$ queues, that is, the mean response time increases with the disk arrival rate and goes to infinity as the disks reach saturation (note that we assume a balanced load, so that disks are equally utilized). The same maximum throughput is attained in degraded and rebuild modes, which is smaller than the maximum throughput in normal mode. The maximum attainable throughput is halved in the worst case when all user requests are reads. The mean read response when rebuild starts is higher than degraded mode by the mean residual rebuild processing time (see Eq. 30.3 in Section 30.5.1).

Rebuild takes approximately 3 minutes when disks are idle, which is the time to read the disks described in Section 4. There is a tenfold increase in rebuild time at 87.5% disk utilization, but a half-hour rebuild time is acceptable (given that a hotspare is provided so that rebuild can start immediately after a disk failure occurs), since disk failure rates tend to be small.

Read redirection provides a better response time to user requests than baseline rebuild as would be expected [74, 75]. This is also so in clustered RAID, but read redirection may result in an increased rebuild time when the spare disk in dedicated sparing constitutes a bottleneck. The split-seek option allows the preemption of a rebuild read after a seek is completed, whereas the split-latency/transfer option allows a preemption at sector boundaries during both the latency and transfer time of a track read. Numerical results show that the split-latency option results in a significant improvement in response time at lower disk utilizations (due to user requests), but at higher disk utilizations, the increase in rebuild time associated with the split-seek and split-latency/transfer option with respect to read-redirection makes these options less desirable. This is because at higher loads, the mean response time of user requests is degraded mainly due to the interference among the requests rather than the extra delay due to rebuild processing (see Eq. 30.3 in Section 30.5.2. Given the trade-off between the decrease in response time and the increase in the duration of the rebuild interval, we define a single performance metric *the excess cumulative response time* for this purpose. It is the difference between the expected value of response time of user requests processed on the average in the rebuild mode and the same number of requests in the normal mode. Simulation results in [74] have shown that the split-latency/transfer option (respectively read redirection) is the best (respectively worst) performer with respect to this metric at lower (respectively higher) arrival rates.

We next consider the effect of caching and especially an NVS cache on the performance of a distributed sparing in normal mode [77]. Two workloads are considered for this purpose, the first one of which is cache-friendly with $f_r = 0.875$ (7 reads per write), a read (respectively write) hit ratio of 0.7 (respectively 1.00). Workload II is cache-unfriendly with $f_r = 0.5$ (one write for each read) and a read (respectively write) hit ratio of $h_r = 0.20$ (respectively $h_w = 0.50$).

In the case of a cache with NVS, rather than destaging dirty blocks continuously, a control strategy may be used to maintain the contents of the NVS portion of the cache in a certain range (see Section 30.2). An analytical solution is possible if it is assumed that the destaging of data blocks is initiated at random instants of time. The rate of destages is determined by the rate of writes, but taking into account the effect of repeated writes and destage locality (the latter is tantamount to the writing of two blocks to the same track; see Section 30.4. The *relative* frequency of the three types of accesses to the disks are as follows (1) read requests $f_r(1 - h_r)$; (2) writes of data and parity blocks with a write hit for the data block $f_w h_w f_{Clean}/\overline{n}_{block}$; (3) writes of data and parity blocks with a write miss for the data block $f_w(1 - h_w)/\overline{n}_{block}$, that is, repeated writes are assumed to only occur in the case of a write hit. Eq. 30.8 in Section 30.5.1 for higher-priority requests in a nonpreemptive priority queuing $M/G/1$ system is used to compute the mean response time for read requests.

The mean overall response time ($R = f_r R_r + f_w T_w$) follows the mean read response time (R_r), because the mean response time for fast writes (R_w) and read hits (R_r^{hit}) is negligibly small for a sufficiently fast disk controller, such that $R \approx f_r R_r$ with $R_r = (1 - h_r)f_r R_r^{miss}$. The mean read response time due to cache misses (R_r^{miss}), remains relatively flat up to the point of full disk utilization for the two workloads being considered. This is because read requests have a higher priority at the disks than destage operations and the fraction of disk utilization due to read requests is moderate.

The following observations can be made. A cache without NVS results in a significant improvement in performance, especially when reads have a high hit ratio. The mean response time for reads and the overall response time improves when an NVS cache is provided, because the response time for writes is negligible with the fast write capability and reads can be processed at a higher priority than destages.

There is no improvement in the disk array throughput available to user requests when there is no destage locality and there are no repeated updates (to dirty blocks), since the amount of disk processing remains the same as it was in a system without NVS. This, however, is usually not the case and a significant increase in the disk throughput is possible.

More aggressive methods prioritizing the processing of disk reads with respect to destage processing are considered in [73]. These methods include the split-seek and split-latency options considered in the context of rebuild processing [74, 75] (with the small difference with the split-latency/transfer option that once the transfer of a block is started, it is not preempted). Simulation results in [73] quantify and compare the improvement in performance attainable by the different options. Furthermore, it follows from simulation results and the analysis of an appropriate vacationing server model that the reduction in the maximum throughput attainable by the system due to preemptions is rather small. Increased sizes for NVS allowing a larger number of dirty blocks should lead to a higher efficiency in destage processing, but this is highly workload-dependent and little destage locality was observed in the analysis of disk reference traces reported in [78].

Finally, it is interesting to compare the performance of the cached distributed sparing system with $(N + 2 = 10)$ disks with the performance of a cached array without parity protection (that is, RAID0) with 10 disks. In both cases, the caches are equipped with NVS, so that fast writes and efficient destaging is possible (the parameters in Section 30.4 are used for this purpose). There is a slight degradation in response time for RAID5 with respect to RAID0, but more importantly there is a reduction in the maximum throughput, which is 15% (respectively 60%) for workload I (respectively II). The performance degradation to achieve fault tolerance via RAID5 is expected to be closer to that due to workload I than workload II.

30.9 CONCLUSIONS AND FUTURE WORK

We develop an accurate analytic solution for the performance of RAID5 disk arrays, utilizing results for $M/G/1$ queues for the analysis in the normal and rebuild modes and an approximate analysis to estimate the fork-join response time in the degraded mode. As verified by simulation results, the analysis provides very accurate estimates for performance measures of interest for the RAID5 disk array under consideration for different operating modes.

The analysis can be easily extended to allow skewed disk accesses as in parity striping [18]. The analysis presented in this work is geared to a certain implementation of RAID5 disk arrays. but it can be easily extended to others. For example, the vacationing server model is suitable for analyzing log-structured arrays [38], where the vacations correspond to the background processing required for preparing clean stripes.

The idea that multiple RAID configurations may coexist in the same array is attractive from the viewpoint of accommodating different access requirements for data. In [45] the space in the disk array is partitioned such that hot (respectively cold) data blocks are stored according to a RAID1 (respectively RAID5) configuration. The HP AutoRAID also provides such a combination [80]. A scheme combining replication and parity to tolerate multiple disk failures is proposed in [35]

Prior to RAID5, manual balancing was used to allocate files in a disk subsystem, because disk accesses had a tendency to become highly skewed otherwise. Although striping in RAID5 is supposed to alleviate this problem, there is the issue of balancing the load across stripes in a multiarray system, possibly through on-line data reorganization to attain "disk cooling" [02]. A major application for an analytic solution is as a capacity planning tool for disk arrays.

Data prefetching is a desirable approach for dealing with the data-latency problem associated with disk drives (see, for example, [30]). The application of prefetching in the context of disk arrays requires further investigation.

Rather simple methods are used for data declustering in RAID disk arrays. A set of more sophisticated methods that facilitate efficient access to multidimensional data are reviewed in [67], but the practicality of these methods remains to be determined.

References

[1] S. Akyurek. *Adaptive disk management*, Computer Science Technical Report CS-TR-3315, University of Maryland, College Park, MD, July 1994.

[2] S. Berson, L. Golubchik, and R. R. Muntz. "Fault tolerant design of multimedia servers," *Proc 1995 ACM SIGMOD Int'l Conf. on Management of Data,* San Jose, CA, May 1995.

[3] P. Biswas, K. K. Ramakrishnan, and D. Towsley. "Trace driven analysis of write caching policies for disks," *Proc. 1993 ACM SIGMETRICS Conf. on Measurement and Modeling of Computer Systems,* Santa Clara, CA, May 1993.

[4] M. Blaum, Journal Brady, Journal Bruck, and Journal Menon. "Evenodd: An optimal scheme for tolerating double disk failures in RAID architectures," *IEEE Transactions on Computers,* 44(2) (February 1995).

[5] A. Brandwajn. "Models of disk subsystems with multiple access paths: A throughput driven approach," *IEEE Transactions on Computers,* 32(5) (May 1983).

[6] Journal Chandy and A. L. Narasimha Reddy. "Failure evaluation of disk array organizations," *Proc. 13th Int'l Conf. on Distributed Computing Systems,* Pittsburgh, PA, May 1993.

[7] P. M. Chen, E. K. Lee, A. L. Drapeau, K. Lutz, E. Miller, S. Srinivasan, K. Shirriff, D. A. Patterson, and R. H. Katz. "Performance and design evaluation of the RAID-II storage server," *Distributed and Parallel Databases* 2(3) (July 1994).

[8] P. M. Chen, E. K. Lee, G. A. Gibson, R. H. Katz, and D. A. Patterson. "RAID: High-performance, reliable secondary storage," *ACM Computing Surveys,* 26(2) (June 1994).

[9] S. Z. Chen and D. Towsley. "The design and evaluation of RAID 5 and parity striping disk array architectures," *Journal Parallel and Distributed Computing*, 10(1/2) (January/February 1993).

[10] D. Journal DeWitt, S. Ghandeharizadeh, D. A. Schneider, A. Bricker, H. I. Hsiao, and R. Rasmussen. "The Gamma database machine project," *IEEE Transactions Knowledge and Data Engineering*, 2(1) (February 1990).

[11] B. T. Doshi. "An M/G/1 queue with variable vacations," in *Modeling Techniques and Tools for Performance Analysis '85*, N. Abu el Ata (editor), North-Holland, Amsterdam, 1985.

[12] L. W. Emlich and H. D. Polich. "A fault manager implementation," *Digital Technical Journal*, 8(2) (February 1989).

[13] P. A. Franaszek and Journal T. Robinson. "On variable scope of parity protection in disk arrays," *IEEE Transactions on Computers*, 46(2) (February 1997).

[14] P. A. Franaszek, Journal T. Robinson, and A. Thomasian. *RAID level 5 with free blocks parity cache*, United States Patent Number 5.522,032, May 1996.

[15] G. A. Gibson. *Redundant Disk Arrays: Reliable, Parallel Secondary Storage*, The MIT Press, 1992.

[16] G. A. Gibson, L. Hellerstein, R. Karp, R. Katz, and D. Patterson. "Coding techniques for handling failures in large disk arrays," *Proc. Int'l Conf. on Architectural Support for Programming Languages and Operating Systems*, Boston, MA, May 1989,

[17] A. Gravey. "A simple construction of an upper bound for the mean of the maximum of N identically distributed random variables," *Journal Applied Probability*, Vol. 22, (1985).

[18] Journal Gray, B. Horst, and M. Walker. "Parity striping of disk arrays: Low-cost reliable storage with acceptable throughput," *Proc. 16th Int'l Conf. on Very Large Data Bases*, Brisbane, Australia, (Augugust 1990).

[19] Journal H. Hartman and Journal K. Ousterhout. "The Zebra striped network file system," *ACM Transactions on Computer Systems*, 13(3) (August 1995).

[20] M. Hofri. "Disk scheduling: FCFS vs. SSTF revisited," *Communication of the ACM*, 23(11) (November 1980).

[21] M. C. Holland. *On-line reconstruction in redundant disk arrays*, Ph.D. Thesis, Dept. of Computer and Electrical Engineering, Carnegie-Mellon University, 1994.

[22] M. Holland and G. A. Gibson. "Parity declustering for continuous operation in redundant disk arrays, *Proc. 5th Architectural Support for Programming Languages and Operating Systems,* Boston, MA, October 1992.

[23] M. Holland, G. A. Gibson, and D. P. Siewiorek. "Architectures and algorithms for on-line failure recovery in redundant disk arrays," *Distributed and Parallel Databases,* 11(3) (July 1994).

[24] R. Y. Hou, Journal Menon, and Y. N. Patt. "Balancing I/O response time and disk rebuild time in a RAID5 disk array," *Proc. Hawaii Int'l Conf. on System Sciences,* Vol. I, Honolulu, Hawaii, January 1993.

[25] H. Hsiao and D. DeWitt. "Chained declustering: A new availability strategy for multiprocessor database machines," *Proc. 6th Int'l Conf. on Data Eng.* Los Angeles, CA, February 1990.

[26] Y. Hu and Q. Yang. "DCD– Disk caching disk: A new approach for boosting I/O performance," *Proc. 23rd Int'l Symp. on Computer Architecture,* Philadelphia, PA, May 1996.

[27] R. Jain, Journal Werth, and Journal C. Browne (editors). *Input/Output in Parallel and Distributed Computer Systems,* Kluwer Academic Publishers, 1996.

[28] N. L. Johnson and S. Kotz. *Distributions in Statistics: Continuous Univariate Distributions-I,* John-Wiley and Sons, 1970.

[29] C. Kim and A. Agrawala. *Virtual waiting time of an Erlangian single server queueing system,* Technical Report UMIACS-TR-1986-6, University of Maryland, College Park, MA, Dec. 1985.

[30] T. Kimbrel, A. Tomkins. R. H. Patterson, B. Bershad, P. Cao, E. Felton, G. A. Gibson, A. S. Karlin, and K. Li. "A trace-driven comparison of algorithms for parallel prefetching and caching," *Proc. 2nd USENIX Symp. on Operating System Design and Implementation,* Seattle, October 1996.

[31] L. Kleinrock. *Queueing Theory, Vol. I: Theory* John-Wiley and Sons, 1975.

[32] A. Kuratti and W. H. Sanders. "Performance analysis of the RAID5 disk array," *Proc. Int'l Computer Performance and Dependability Symp.* Erlangen, Germany, April 1995.

[33] F. D. Lawlor. *Efficient mass storage parity recovery mechanism,* IBM Technical Disclosure Bulletin, 24(2) (July 1981).

[34] E. K. Lee and R. H. Katz. "Performance consequences of parity placement in disk arrays," *Proc. 4th Int'l Conf. on Architectural Support for Programming Languages and Operating Systems,* Santa Clara, CA, April 1991.

[35] C.-S. Li, M.-S. Chen, P. S. Yu, and H.-I. Hsiao. "Combining replication and parity approaches for fault-tolerant disk arrays," *Proc. 6th IEEE Symposium on Parallel and Distributed Processing*, Dallas, TX, November 1994.

[36] D. Long, B. Montague, and L.-F. Cabrera. "Swift/RAID: A distributed RAID system," *Computing Systems*. The USENIX Association, 3(7) (1994).

[37] P. Marsaglia (ed.). *The RAIDbook: A Source Book for Disk Array Technology*, Fourth Edition, The RAID Advisory Board, St. Peter, MN, Sept. 1994.

[38] Journal Menon. "Performance comparison of RAID5 and log-structured arrays," *Proc. 4th IEEE Int'l Symp. on High Performance Distributed Computing*, Washington, D.C., August 1995.

[39] Journal Menon. "Performance of RAID5 disk arrays with read and write caching," *Distributed and Parallel Databases* 11(3) (July 1994).

[40] Journal Menon and Journal Cortney. "The architecture of a fault-tolerant cached RAID controller," *Proc. 20th Annual Int'l Symp. on Computer Architecture*, San Diego, CA, May 1993.

[41] Journal Menon and Journal Kasson. "Methods for improved update performance of disk arrays," *Proc. Hawaii Int'l Conf. on System Sciences*, Honolulu, HA, January 1992.

[42] Journal Menon and D. Mattson. "Comparison of sparing alternatives for disk arrays," *Proc. 19th Annual Int'l Symp. on Computer Architecture*, Brisbane, Australia, May 1992.

[43] Journal Menon, Journal Roche, and Journal Kasson. "Floating parity and data disk arrays," *Journal Parallel and Distributed Computing*, 10(1/2) (January/February 1993).

[44] A. Merchant and P. S. Yu. "Analytic modeling of clustered RAID with mapping based on nearly random permutation," *IEEE Transactions on Computers*, 45(3) (March 1996).

[45] K. Mogi and M. Kitsuregawa. "Hot mirroring: A method of hiding parity update penalty and degradation during rebuilds for RAID5," *Proc. 1996 ACM SIGMOD Int'l Conf. on Management of Data*, Montreal, Que., Canada, June 1996.

[46] K. Mogi and M. Kitsuregawa. "Virtual striping: A storage management scheme with dynamic striping," *IEICE Transactions on Information and Systems*, E79-D(8), August 1996.

[47] R. R. Muntz and Journal C. S. Lui. "Performance analysis of disk arrays under failure," *Proc. 16th Int'l Conf. on Very Large Data Bases*, Brisbane, Australia, August 1990.

[48] A. L. Narasimha Reddy, Journal Chandy, and P. Banerjee. "Design and evaluation of gracefully degradable disk arrays," *Journal Parallel and Distributed Computing* 17(1/2) (January/February 1993).

[49] R. Nelson and A. Tantawi. "Approximate analysis of fork-join synchronization in parallel queues," *IEEE Transactions on Computers*, 37(6) (June 1988).

[50] S. W. Ng. "Crosshatch disk arrays for improved reliability and performance," *Proc. 21st Annual Int'l Conf. on Computer Architecture*, Chicago, IL, April 1994.

[51] S. W. Ng and R. L. Mattson. "Uniform parity distribution in disk arrays with multiple failures," *IEEE Transactions on Computers*, 43(4) (April 1994).

[52] C. Orji and Journal Solworth. "Doubly distorted mirrors," *Proc. 1993 ACM SIGMOD Int'l Conf. on Management of Data*, Washington, D.C. June 1993.

[53] B. Ozden, R. Rastogi, P. Shenoy, and A. Silberschatz. "Fault-tolerant architectures for continuous media servers," *Proc. 1996 ACM SIGMOD Int'l Conf. on Management of Data*, Montreal, Que., Canada, June 1996.

[54] C. I. Park. "Efficient placement of parity and data to tolerate two disk failures in disk array systems," *IEEE Transactions on Parallel and Distr. Systems*, 6(11) (November 1995).

[55] D. Patterson, G. Gibson, and R. H. Katz. "A case for redundant arrays of inexpensive disks (RAID)," *Proc. 1988 ACM SIGMOD Int'l Conf. on Management of Data*, Chicago, Illinois, June 1988.

[56] C. Polyzois, A. Bhide, and D. Dias. "Disk mirroring with alternating deferred updates," *Proc. 19th Int'l Conf. on Very Large Data Bases*, Dublin, Ireland, August 1993.

[57] K. Ramakrishnan, P. Biswas, and R. Karedla. "Analysis of file I/O traces in commercial computing environments," *Proc. Joint ACM SIGMETRICS Conf. on Measurement and Modeling of Computer Systems and Performance 92*, Newport, RI, (June 1992).

[58] Journal Riegel and Journal Menon. "Performance of recovery time improvement algorithms for software RAIDs," *Proc. 4th Int'l Conf. on Parallel and Distributed Systems*, Miami Beach, FL, Dec. 1996.

[59] M. Rosenblum and Journal K. Ousterhout. "The design and implementation of a log-structured file system," *ACM Transactions on Computer Systems*, 10(1) (February 1992).

[60] C. Ruemmler and Journal Wilkes. "An introduction to disk drive modeling," *IEEE Computer*, 27(3) (March 1994).

[61] C. Ruemmler and Journal Wilkes. "UNIX disk access patterns," *Proc. of Winter USENIX Conf.,* San Diego, CA, January 1993.

[62] P. Scheuermann, G. Weikum, and P. Zabback. ""Disk cooling" in parallel disk systems" *Data Engineering Bulletin* 17(3) (Sept. 1994).

[63] H. M. Sierra. *An Introduction to Direct Access Storage Devices,* Academic Press, 1990.

[64] A. Journal Smith. "Disk cache: Miss ration analysis and design considerations," *ACM Transactions Computing Systems,* 3(3) (August 1985).

[65] Journal Solworth and C. Orji. "Distorted mirrors," *Proc. First Int'l Conf. on Parallel and Distributed Information Systems,* Miami Beach, FL, Dec. 1991.

[66] Journal Solworth and C. Orji. "Write-only disk caches," *Proc. ACM SIGMOD Int'l Conf. on Management of Data,* Atlantic City, NJ, May 1990.

[67] Journal Srivastava, T. M. Niccum, and B. Himatsingka. "Data declustering in PADMA: A PArallel Database MAnager," *Data Engineering Bulletin,* 17(3) (Sept. 1994).

[68] D. Stodolsky, G. Gibson, and M. Holland. "Parity logging: Overcoming the small write problem in redundant disk arrays," *Proc. 20th Annual Int'l Symp. on Computer Architecture,* San Diego, CA, May 1993.

[69] H. Takagi. *Queueing Analysis, Vol. 1: Vacation and Priority Systems, Part 1,* North-Holland, 1991.

[70] Tandem Database Group. "NonStop SQL: A distributed, high-performance. high-reliability implementation of SQL," *High Performance Transaction Systems,* D. Gawlick et al. (editors), Springer-Verlag, 1987.

[71] Teradata Corp. *DBC/1012 Database Computer System Manual,* Release 2, November 1985.

[72] A. Thomasian. "Approximate analyses for fork/join synchronization in RAID5," *Computer Systems: Science and Engineering,* to appear in 1997.

[73] A. Thomasian. "Priority queueing in RAID5 disk arrays with an NVS cache,". *MASCOTS'95: Int'l Workshop on Modeling, Analysis and Simulation of Computer and Commun. Systems,* Durham, NC, January 1995.

[74] A. Thomasian. "Rebuild options in RAID5 disk arrays," *Proc. 7th IEEE Symp. on Parallel and Distributed Systems,* San Antonio, TX, Oct. 1995. **

[75] A. Thomasian and Journal Menon. "Performance analysis of RAID5 disk arrays with a vacationing server model for rebuild mode operation," *Proc. 10th Int'l Conf. on Data Engineering,* Houston, TX, February 1994.

[76] A. Thomasian and A. Tantawi. "Approximate solutions for M/G/1 fork-join synchronization," *Proc. Winter Simulation Conf.*, Orlando, FL, Dec. 1994.

[77] A. Thomasian and Journal Menon. "RAID5 performance with distributed sparing," *IEEE Transactions on Parallel and Distributed Systems*, 8(5) (June 1997).

[78] K. Treiber and Journal Menon. "Simulation study of cached RAID5 designs," *Proc. First IEEE Symp. on High Performance Computer Architecture*, Raleigh, NC, January 1995. (more details can be found in *IBM Research Report*, RJ 9823, May 1994.

[79] A. Varma and Q. Jacobson. "Destage algorithms for disk arrays with n0n-volatile storage," *Proc. 22nd Annual Int'l Symp. on Computer Architecture*, Santa Margherita Ligure, Italy, June 1995.

[80] Journal Wilkes, R. Golding, C. Staelin, and T. Sulivan. "The HP AutoRAID hierarchical storage system," *Proc. 15th ACM Symp. on Operating System Principles*, Copper Mountain Resort, CO, Dec. 1995.

[81] C. Wood and P. Hodges. "DASD trends: Cost, performance, and form factor," *Proc. of the IEEE*, 81(4) (April 1993).

[82] B. L. Worthington, G. R. Ganger, and Y. L. Patt. "Scheduling for modern disk drives and non-random workloads," *Proc. ACM SIGMETRICS 1994 Conf. on Measurement and Modeling of Computer Systems*, Nashville, TN, May 1994.

Chapter 31

A Performance Comparison of RAID5 and Log-Structured Arrays

Jai Menon

Abstract

In this chapter, we compare the performance of the well-known RAID5 arrays to that of *log-structured arrays* (LSA), on transaction processing workloads. We begin by analyzing the performance of RAID5 arrays with non-volatile caching using an analytical model. Next, we examine LSA, a newer type of array architecture. LSA borrows heavily from the *log-structured file system* (LFS) approach pioneered at University of California, Berkeley, but is executed in an outboard disk controller. Since outboard controllers do not understand files, it is more appropriate to think of LSA as a log-structured track manager than a log-structured file system. The LSA technique we examine combines LFS, RAID, compression, and non-volatile cache. In LSA, updated data is written into new disk locations instead of being written in place. We use an analytical model to show the kind of performance that can be expected from LSA. In addition to improved transfer times, performance benefits result because by storing compressed data in the subsystem cache, we get an effectively larger cache. We look at sensitivity of LSA performance to the amount of free space on the physical disks and to the compression ratio achieved. We conclude by comparing the performance of LSA to standard RAID5, and to a RAID5 design that supports compression in cache.

847

31.1   INTRODUCTION

A nice description of five types of disk arrays called RAID Levels 1 through 5 is given in [18], and a sixth type of disk array is described in [8].

For this chapter, we are primarily interested in the RAID Level-5 disk array and in a newer array architecture called a log-structured array (LSA). A RAID Level-5 array uses a *parity* technique described in [13, 5, 18] to achieve high reliability. We illustrate the array parity technique in what follows on a $4 + P$ disk array. In Figure 31.1, P_i is a parity block that protects the four data blocks labeled D_i.

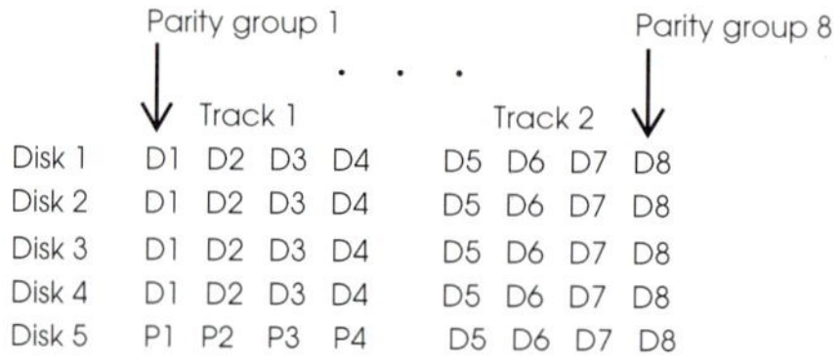

```
        Parity group 1                    Parity group 8
              │            · · ·                  │
              ↓     Track 1        Track 2        ↓
      Disk 1  D1  D2  D3  D4     D5  D6  D7  D8
      Disk 2  D1  D2  D3  D4     D5  D6  D7  D8
      Disk 3  D1  D2  D3  D4     D5  D6  D7  D8
      Disk 4  D1  D2  D3  D4     D5  D6  D7  D8
      Disk 5  P1  P2  P3  P4     D5  D6  D7  D8
```

Figure 31.1. Array parity technique on a $4 + P$ disk array.

We show only two tracks (each with four blocks) on each of the disk drives (disks for short). A column consisting of 4 data blocks and a parity block is called a *parity group*. There are eight parity groups in the figure shown. The *parity width* of the array is the number of blocks per parity group, 5 in our example. In the figure, P_1 contains the parity or exclusive-OR of the blocks labeled $D1$ that are in the same parity group. Similarly, P_2 is the exclusive-OR of the blocks labeled D_2, P_3 the exclusive OR of D_3's, and so on. Such a disk array is robust against single disk crashes; if disk 1 were to fail, data on it can be recreated by reading data from the remaining four disks and performing the appropriate exclusive-OR operations.

We are also interested in log-structured arrays (LSA), a newer type of array architecture. LSA borrows heavily from the log-structured file system (LFS) approach pioneered at University of California, Berkeley [19], but is executed in an outboard disk controller. The LSA technique we examine combines LFS, RAID, compression, and non-volatile cache. In LSA, updated data is written into new disk locations instead of being written in place. The STK Iceberg project ([4]) appears to have some similarities, but the details we know about it are sketchy; what we have defined as LSA in this chapter may bear no resemblance to Iceberg's design.

We begin by analyzing the performance of RAID5 arrays with non-volatile caching using an analytical model. Next, we use an analytical model to show the kind of performance that can be expected from LSA. In addition to improved transfer times, performance benefits result because by storing compressed data in the subsystem cache, we get an effectively larger cache. We look at sensitivity of LSA performance to amount of free space on the physical disks and to the compression ratio achieved. We conclude by comparing the performance of LSA to standard RAID5, and to a RAID5 design that supports compression in cache.

31.2   RAID5 PERFORMANCE ANALYSIS

We proceed to evaluate the performance of cached RAID Level-5 arrays [16] in transaction processing environments where the workload consists of small random accesses. Our cached RAID analysis extends the work we originally reported in [15]; the model is more accurate. We also use more realistic workloads than we have used before in [15] and in [20]. Nonetheless, we emphasize that simplifying assumptions have been made to keep the analysis tractable, so there is no claim that the analysis is highly accurate. For example, the analysis does not model disk characteristics as accurately as [20]. However, we believe that the analysis is accurate enough for performance comparisons between RAID and LSA subsystems, which is the main goal of this paper. Simulations, not reported here, have been used to verify various aspects of our analysis for accuracy.

The RAID controller is assumed to have a non-volatile read and write cache. We assume an array has $N+1$ disk, storing N disks worth of data and one disks worth of parity. Cached RAIDs use a technique called *fast write*. In this technique, all disk, array controller hardware such as processors, data memory (memory containing cached data blocks and other data buffers) and control memory (memory containing control structures such as request control blocks, cache directories, request queues, etc.) are divided into at least two disjoint sets, each set on a different power boundary. The data memory and the control memory are either battery-backed or built using non-volatile storage (NVS) so they can survive power failures. When a disk block to be written to the disk array is received, the block is first written to data memory in the array controller, in two separate locations, on two different power boundaries. At this point, the disk, array controller signals successful completion of the write to the host. In this way, from the host's point of view, the write has been completed quickly without requiring any disk access. Since two separate copies of the disk block are made in the disk, array controller, no single hardware or power failure can cause a loss of data.

Disk blocks in array controller cache memory that need to be written to disk are called *dirty*. Disk blocks in cache memory that are identical to their counterparts on disk are called *clean*. Clean blocks do not need to be written to disk. Also, unlike dirty blocks for which we keep 2 copies in cache memory, only 1 copy of clean blocks are kept in cache memory. Dirty blocks are written to disk in a process we call *destaging*. When a block is destaged to disk, it is also necessary to update, on disk, the parity block for the data block. This may require the array controller to read the old values of the data block and the parity block from disk, XOR them with the new value of the data block in cache, and then write the new value of the data block and of the parity block to disk. Therefore, a destage may require two disk reads and two disk writes. Since many applications first read data before updating them, we expect that the old value of the data block might already be in an array controller cache. Therefore, the more typical destage operation is expected to require one disk read and two disk writes.

To summarize, the use of fast write in disk array controllers has three advantages:

it will eliminate disk time from the write response time as seen by the host; It will eliminate some disk writes due to overwrites caused by later host writes to dirty blocks in cache and it will reduce disk seeks because destages will be postponed until many destages can be done to a track or cylinder.

31.2.1   Analysis of Cached RAIDs

We assume that the RAID controller consists of multiple (p) processors (also called storage directors in IBM parlance [17]). One of the jobs of these microprocessors is to examine a shared, non-volatile cache for hits and misses on read and write requests. We refer to the non-volatile cache as NVS (non-volatile store). The NVS only contains data blocks; parity blocks are not cached. If the block requested by a read is in cache, it is considered a *read hit*; otherwise it is a *read miss*. Read hits are satisfied directly out of the cache: read misses require access to the disks. If the block written by a write request is in cache, it is a *write hit;* otherwise it is a *write miss*. On a write hit or miss, the data block is accepted from the system and placed in the non-volatile cache after which the write is considered "done." This block is destaged to disk (pushed from NVS and written to disk) at some later time, along with other blocks that also need to be destaged and that are in the same cylinder. Disks only see read misses and destages. However, remember that a destage operation of a data block also requires the corresponding parity block to be updated; this requires either 3 or 4 disk operations: Read the old value of the data block if it is not already in cache, read the old value of the parity block, write the new value of the data block and compute and write the new value of the parity block (new parity is computed as "old data XOR new data XOR old parity").

Write hits may be divided into hits on dirty blocks (blocks that have been previously written by the host system and are sitting in the cache waiting to be destaged) and hits on clean blocks. We call the fraction of write hits that are to dirty blocks the *NVS hit ratio*. If the system request rate is K, the fraction of requests that are write hits to clean blocks is C and the fraction of requests that are write misses is D; then $KC + KD$ is the rate at which new dirty blocks are created in cache. This is because write misses and write hits to clean blocks are the only 2 ways of increasing the number of dirty blocks in cache. In steady state, $KC + KD$ must also be the rate at which dirty blocks are destaged from cache. If X blocks are destaged per destage operation (e.g., due to clustering on the same physical track for), the destage rate can be expressed as $(KC + KD)/X$ destages/sec. If B is the fraction of requests that are read misses, then there are KB read misses/sec.

This system is modeled as an $M/M/p$ system (to represent the p storage directors managing the cache) that generates read misses and destages at some rate to be handled by $N + 1$ disks each of which is represented by 2 queues, one for read misses and one for destages. We assume that read misses have higher priority than destage requests at the individual devices, since [11] shows that this is important for performance. This is why there are two queues at each device, a high priority queue into which the read misses go, and a low-priority queue into which the separate operations constituting the destage are sent. We assume a nonpreemptive priority queuing discipline; a low-priority operation will commence only if there are no high-priority operations waiting, but once a low-priority operation starts, it will not be preempted by a high-priority operation. The situation is shown in Figure 31.2. There are four types of requests from the system: read hits, read misses, write hits, and write misses. Read hits, write hits, and write misses are satisfied directly by the cache in the controller; hence, their response time is modeled as the response time of an $M/M/p$ system. Read misses first pass through the $M/M/p$ system with some response time, and then enter the read miss queue of one of the (N+1) devices with equal probability. A destage is treated as 3 or 4 separate disk operations: read old parity, write new parity, optionally read old data and write new data. For simplicity, let KB, the read miss rate be R, let KC the destage rate due to write hits on clean pages be D_1, and let KD the destage rate due to write misses be D_2. Then, each device gets $R/(N+1)$ read misses per second, and it also gets $3D_1/(N+1) + 4D_2(N+1)$ destage operations per second. We are mainly interested in the read miss response time. The response time of a destage is not reported. The destage rate must keep up with the write rate from the system, but since the system does not wait for the destage to be completed, reporting the response time for the destage is of little interest. On a read miss, we assume that the requested block and all remaining blocks following it in the rest of that track are staged into cache as in done in the IBM 3990 disk controller ([17]). The response time of the read miss only includes the time to retrieve the block requested; the staging of the rest of the track is done in the background and keeps the device busy, but does not contribute directly to read miss response time. The utilization of the devices is calculated easily, since the read miss rate and the destage rate are known, and the service time for a read miss and the service time for a destage are also known.

All the quantities needed to calculate the read miss response time at the devices is thus known. The total read miss response time is calculated as the sum of the response time through the cache ($M/M/p$ queue) and the response time at the device (a server with 2 classes of jobs, each with Poisson arrivals and general service times, and a nonpreemptive priority discipline). The response time at the device consists of a waiting time and a service time. The waiting time is given by the equation ([6])

$$\frac{\lambda_1 E(ST_1{}^2) + \lambda_2 E(ST_2{}^2)}{2 \times (1 - \rho_1)}$$

where λ_1 and ST_1 are the arrival rate and service time of read misses, respectively and λ_2 and ST_2 are the arrival rate and service time of destage operations, respectively, and ρ_1 is the device busy due to read misses. In Appendix A, we include a derivation of how we calculate $E(ST_1{}^2)$, the second moment of the read miss service time, and $E(ST_2{}^2)$, the second moment of the destage service time. The average request response time may now be calculated as a function of read hit response time, write hit response time, write miss response time, and read miss response time.

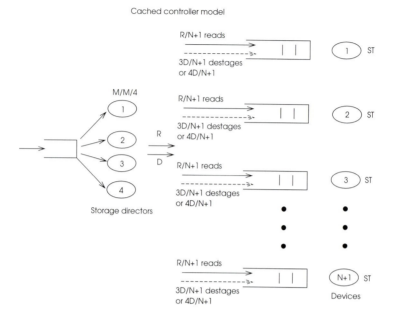

Figure 31.2. Cached array model.

31.3   PARAMETERS USED IN PERFORMANCE COMPARISONS

31.3.1   Disk, Controller, and Channel Parameters

We have largely used the IBM Model 0664-M1 disk-drive characteristics as the basis for choosing performance parameters for the disk drive in our study. So, we have picked an average seek time of 10 msec, a data rate of 4.2 MB/sec, and a latency of 5.56 msec. We also assume the device is capable of *roll-mode* operation, that is, following a seek to the track containing the requested data, the device does not wait until the first of the requested sectors rotates under the read head. Rather, it waits only until *any* one of the requested sectors rotates under the read head, and then returns the requested sectors in an order possibly different from the normal sequential order of these sectors. For example, if we request sectors 10 through 20 from the disk, a roll-mode read might cause the sectors to be returned in some other order such as 14 through 20, then 10 through 13. We assume the disk is capable of roll-mode operation on both reads and writes. For the controller, we have assumed an overhead of 0.5 msec, and for the channel that attaches the controller to the host system, we have assumed a data rate capability of 18 MB/sec.

For p, the number of storage directors, we choose a value large enough so that the storage director processing does not turn out to be the bottleneck to throughput. We did this deliberately, because our intent in this chapter is to understand fundamental

RAID issues without having the results distorted by processing overheads in the storage-director.[1]

31.3.2   Workload Parameters

We are particularly interested in the performance of the subsystems for database and transaction processing applications. Our experience with such applications indicates that some of these workloads are dominated by single-block read and write requests. Therefore, our entire analysis assumes single-block accesses to the arrays. The workload parameters we have used are largely those obtained by analysis of *IMS* customer traces ([9]). The average block size read or written is set to 4096 bytes. The number of blocks destaged together per track is set at 2, that is, when a block is destaged, we assume there is one other block on that same track that may also be destaged at the same time. We also assume that the 2 blocks on a track that are destaged together are 0.3 of a revolution of the disk apart on the track.

Seek affinity for a given workload is defined as the ratio between the average seek time for that workload and the average seek time for a pure random workload. Seek affinity for a pure random workload is, therefore, 1. Seek affinity on workloads with locality of reference are less than 1. On non-RAID IMS systems, we see a seek affinity of 0.4. The data striping done by RAID5 does impact seek affinity, so we use a seek affinity of 0.6 for the RAID subsystems (obtained from simulation).

Skew between disk drives is very related to seek affinity. The smaller the seek affinity, the more the skew. The following is a typical skew we have seen on a 28-device IMS system.

0.378;0.17;0.10;0.068;0.050;0.038;0.03;0.025;0.020;0.017;0.014;0.012;0.011;0.009;0.008;
0.007;0.006;0.005;0.0046;0.004;0.0037;0.0032;0.0028;0.0026;0.0022;0.002;0.0018;0.0016

That is, we see the busiest disk getting 37.8% of the I/O activity, and the least busy disk getting only 0.16% of the activity. It has been shown before [11] that data striping eliminates skew within an array. So, for a four array subsystem, we assume a flat skew within the devices of the array. However, there is skew between the arrays, since we do not stripe data across arrays, only within arrays. The skew 0.472; 0.246; 0.162; 0.12 is used across arrays.

The NVS hit ratio (the fraction of write hits that are hits on dirty blocks) is set to a constant of 0.6.

---

[1] However, we feel it is important to point out that, in our experience, the throughput achievable by a RAID is often limited by the processing power in the storage directors and not by the disks. This means that the results we present may be optimistic, since they assume throughputs are limited by the disks, when, in fact, they could be limited by the processors.

31.4   IMPORTANCE OF DESTAGE ASSUMPTIONS IN CACHED RAID PERFORMANCE

Our standard destage assumption is that one track is destaged at a time, and that when a track is destaged, two blocks on the track are dirty and can be destaged together. We also assumed that the two blocks on a track that are destaged together are .3 of a revolution of the disk apart on the track. Finally, we assumed that the NVS hit ratio was 0.6. These assumptions are known to be true for IMS workloads with small (4-MB) write (NVS) caches. We will refer to these as the normal destage assumptions. With larger caches, it is possible that more blocks can be destaged together at destage time and that the NVS hit ratios are higher. To test the robustness of cached RAID5 performance to variations in destage assumptions, we considered two extremes - one case in which the NVS hit ratio was 0.8, and four records occupying 0.6 of a revolution of a track could be destaged together; and a second case where the NVS hit ratio was 0 and only one record could be destaged per track. The first can be considered an optimistic extreme and the second can be considered a pessimistic extreme. We have analyzed a pessimistic extreme before in [20], on a less realistic workload without skew and seek affinity, but we have not analyzed the optimistic extreme before.

In Figure 31.3, we show the results of our comparisons for a workload with a read-to-write ratio of 7:1, a read hit ratio of 0.7, and a write hit ratio of 1^2. For this case, the maximum throughput for the pessimistic extreme is 1800 I/Os/sec and for the optimistic extreme it is 3400 I/Os/sec (maximum throughput under normal destage assumptions is 2900 I/Os/sec). Our results indicate that very pessimistic destage assumptions can impact both response time and throughput significantly (confirming similar analysis of [20], which assumed a less realistic workload). However, we find that very optimistic destage assumptions do not improve response time significantly compared to the destage assumptions we made in the previous section (it does improve throughput somewhat).

We feel that the assumptions we made about destage in the previous section are reasonable. The actual situation is not likely to be worse; if anything, the actual situation is likely to be better because of larger write caches. Since better

---

[2] The preceding read and write hit ratios are for an unarrayed subsystem and are adjusted downward for the cached RAID5 subsystem. This is because the RAID5 cache must contain both the old and new values of data blocks in cache until the block is destaged, whereas normal caches only contain one value of any block of data. For example, consider a write hit to a clean block. In this case, the array controller allocates a new page in cache to hold the new block just received from the host. The old value of the block (the clean block) is preserved, since it is needed to calculate new parity at destage time. We estimate (results from trace studies) that array controllers need approximately a 17% larger cache to achieve the same hit ratio as an unarrayed controller, because it uses 17% of its cache space to hold the old values of data blocks. So, to calculate the read and write hit ratios for the RAID5 controllers, we assume that we have effectively a cache that is only 0.83 as large as the cache for the unarrayed case. We then use the empirical result in [14] that miss ratios are inversely proportional to the cube root of cache sizes. For example, this means that if the unarrayed controller has a read hit ratio of 10%, the arrayed controller will be assumed to have a hit ratio of about 4.3% for the same size cache.

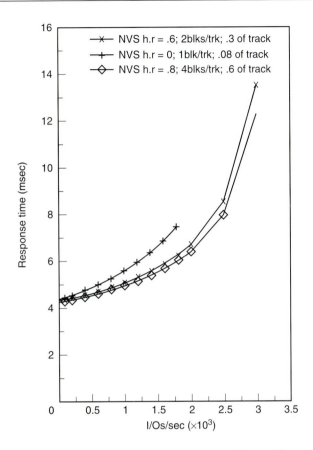

Figure 31.3. Impact of Destage assumptions - Case 2.

assumptions do not improve performance much, we feel comfortable in using the destage assumptions of the previous section for all the results in this chapter.

31.5   COMPRESSION IN RAID SUBSYSTEMS

LSA is an approach to combine LFS, RAID, non-volatile caching and compression in the storage subsystem. We are calling the approach LSA (log-structured arrays), because it borrows several concepts from the LFS (log-structured file system) approach of University of California, Berkeley ([19]). Similar approaches are apparently used in the STK Iceberg project ([4]), but because Iceberg's details are sketchy, our LSA approach may turn out to be significantly different. Because LSA is implemented in an outboard controller that has no understanding of files, it is more appropriate to think of LSA as a log-structured track manager rather than a log-structured file system. In this respect, LSA has some similarities to Loge [7] and to Logical Disk [10], both of which are implemented below the file system. Loge does not use logstructuring, compression, RAID or NVS and Logical Disk does not use RAID or NVS. In what folows, is a description of the LSA approach we model.

31.5.1 Overview of LSA

In LSA, data are stored on disks in compressed form. A lossless form of compression is used, so that no information is lost. For example, a form of the Liv-Zempel (LZ) algorithm is used for compression. A feature of data compression is that the amount of compression achieved is data-dependent. After a piece of data is updated, it may not compress as well as it did before it was updated, so it may not fit back into the space that had been allocated for it before the update. The implication is that we can no longer have fixed, static locations for all the data. This, in turn, implies that the subsystem must keep a directory that it uses to locate data items in the subsystem.

The host system writes (logical) records to the subsystem. The record is compressed as soon as it reaches the subsystem. As a result, compressed records are stored in the controller cache. We assume a non-volatile cache and the use of fast write (as for RAID5). That is, as far as the host system is concerned, the write is considered done as soon as the data are in the controller cache. When the record needs to be written to disk (destaged), it is written along with other records of the same logical track. Therefore, a logical track always appears as a contiguous entity on disk, and is stored as a set of compressed records on physical sectors of a disk. If, when a record needs to be written to disk, the other records of the track are already in cache, no disk access is needed to fetch these other records. Otherwise, the controller will first need to fetch the remaining records of the track from disk. When the host system tries to read a record, we fetch the entire logical track containing that record from disk. This entire track is stored in the controller cache; the requested record alone is decompressed and sent to the host. Since entire tracks are fetched on read misses, a subsequent update to this track will not need to fetch any data from disk.

A log-structured array (LSA) that supports compression operates as follows. The LSA consists of $N + 1$ physical disks, where each disk is divided into large consecutive areas called segment-columns. A segment-column is typically as large as a physical cylinder on a physical disk. Corresponding segment-columns from the $N + 1$ disks constitute a segment. The array has as many segments as there are segment-columns on a disk in the array. One of the segment-columns of a segment contains the parity (XOR) of the remaining segment-columns of the segment. For performance reasons, the parity segment-columns are not all on the same disk, but are rotated among the disks. Logical devices are mapped and stored in this log-structured array. A Logical track is stored, as a set of compressed records, entirely within some segment-column of some physical disk of the array; many logical tracks can be stored in the same segment-column. The location of a logical track in an LSA changes over time. A directory, called the LSA directory, indicates the current

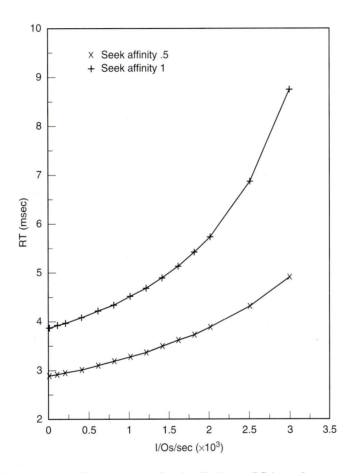

Figure 31.4. Importance of seek affinity to LSA performance.

location of each logical track. It has an entry for each logical track. The entry has the logical track number, the physical disk and segment-column number within the disk that it is mapped to, the starting sector within the column at which the logical track starts, and the length of the logical track in physical sectors. Given a request to read a logical track, the controller examines the LSA directory to determine the physical disk, starting sector number, and length in sectors to which the logical track is currently mapped; it then reads the relevant sectors from the relevant disk. Because we use a logical track as the unit of data that is maintained contiguously, we essentially have a log-structured track manager. Although it is possible to use a unit that is smaller than a logical track, this increases the size of the directory that needs to be maintained, and hurts seek affinity.

The entire LSA directory is maintained in NVRAM in the disk controller, to avoid disk accesses when searching the directory. For reliability reasons, the LSA directory is replicated; two copies are kept of each entry, and the two copies are on two separate power boundaries.

Writes to the array operate as follows, using a section of controller memory, logically organized as $N+1$ segment-columns called *the memory segment*. It consists of $N+1$ memory segment-columns; N data memory segment-columns, and 1 parity memory segment-column. When all or part of a logical track is updated by the system, the entire logical track is written into one of the N data memory segment-columns (and the host is told that the write is done). When the memory segment is full (all data memory segment-columns are full) and cannot hold any new logical tracks from the system, we XOR all the data memory segment-columns to create the parity memory segment-column, then all $N+1$ memory segment-columns are written to an empty segment on the disk array. All logical tracks that were just written to disk from the memory segment must have their entries in the LSA directory updated to reflect their new disk locations. If these logical tracks had been written before by the system, the LSA directory would have contained their previous physical disk locations; otherwise the LSA directory would have indicated that the logical track had never been written, so has no address[3]. Note that writing to the disk is more efficient in LSA than in RAID5, where four disk accesses were needed for an update. However, LSA needs to do a process called *garbage collection*, since holes (garbage) form in segments that previously contained one or more of the logical tracks that were just written. To ensure that we always have an empty segment to write to, the controller garbage collects segments in the background. It selects for garbage collection those segments that have lots of holes (garbage) and/or those segments that are not anticipated to produce more holes for a long time. All logical tracks from a segment selected for garbage collection that are still in that segment (are still pointed to by the LSA directory) are read from disk and placed in a memory segment. It may be placed in the same memory segment used for destaging logical tracks written by the system or it may be placed in a different memory segment of its

---

[3]In LSA, logical tracks that have never been written by the system take up no physical space on disk.

own. In any case, these logical tracks will be written back to disk when the memory segment fills. Garbage-collected segments are returned to the empty segment pool and are available when needed. Well-known techniques need to be used to ensure that the memory segment is not a single point of failure. Also, it is possible to begin writing portions of the memory segment to disk before the memory segment fills, but, for simplicity, this chapter assumes that we wait until a memory segment fills before writing it out to a segment on disk.

To improve performance, we assume the LSA controller has a large, nonvolatile (NV) cache memory, in addition to the memory segment that we had discussed earlier. The NV cache is interposed between the host system bus and the memory segment, and holds both updated logical tracks received from the host system and clean logical tracks read from disk. A write received from the host system is first written into NV cache and the host is immediately notified that the write is done. The NV cache is organized in the traditional LRU fashion. The fraction of cache occupied by modified tracks is monitored by the controller. When this fraction exceeds some threshold, some number of modified tracks are moved (logically) to the memory segment, from where they are written (destaged) to disk. When cache memory is needed to hold new logical tracks read from disk, or new logical tracks received from the host system, LRU clean tracks can be overwritten in cache.

The use of an NV cache alleviates a problem of loss of seek affinity with a log-structured array to some extent, since writes are not immediately written to the memory segment and then to disk. Rather, they are first written to an NV cache where they can spend a fair bit of time. If other writes to adjacent tracks are received into the NV cache from the system before the first track is selected for pushing out from the NV cache to the memory segment, all logically adjacent modified tracks can be pushed out at the same time into the same memory segment-column of the memory segment. This will ensure that if adjacent tracks are modified within some window of time proportional to the size of the NV cache, they will still be placed contiguously on disk, and no seek affinity will be lost.

31.5.2   Seek Affinity and Skew in LSA

Current disk controllers not organized as log-structured arrays tend to see reasonably good seek affinity, even on workloads that have mostly random content, such as database workloads. This is because, if we consider some short interval of time, some one dataset or file tends to get most of the activity on any particular disk. Even if accesses to the dataset are random, the disk arm only needs to move within the small range of cylinders that contains that dataset. For the purposes of this chapter, we call such a very active dataset a *hot dataset*. At any one time, we typically only see one hot dataset per disk arm, because the database administrator has carefully separated the datasets and placed them on disks in such a way that multiple datasets on a disk do not usually get active (hot) simultaneously. Of course, there can be multiple, hot datasets in the subsystem as a whole, but they tend to be on different disks. The good seek affinity of current disk controllers comes at the expense of device skew, that is, in any short interval of time, the accesses are not spread evenly among the disks of the subsystem.

In a log-structured array, because of the way writes are handled, datasets are not stored on one disk, but tend to be stored on multiple disks. As a result, we see a flattening of the device skew, similar to what we saw with RAID5. In fact, if we allow data to be written to any one of the disk arrays in the subsystem, we find that the skew flattening can be even better than for RAID5; in RAID5 we obtained skew flattening within an array but not across arrays; with LSA, we get skew flattening both within and across arrays. However, as for RAID5 with a small striping unit, there is a loss of seek affinity. The loss of seek affinity is even worse than for RAID5, because with LSA, two consecutive logical tracks can be far apart on disk if one is updated (and so moved) and the other is not. In our comparisons for IMS, we set the seek affinity of LSA to 0.8, which is worse than the 0.6 we assume for RAID5.

31.5.3   A Performance Model of LSA

As for RAID5, we assume that the controller consists of multiple (p) processors or storage directors. These processors examine a shared, non-volatile cache for hits and misses on read and write requests. As before, the NVS only contains data blocks; parity blocks are not cached. Read hits, read misses, write hits, and write misses are defined as for RAID5. On a write hit or miss, the data block is accepted from the system and placed in the non-volatile cache after which the write is considered "done." This block is destaged to disk (pushed from NVS to memory segment and then written to disk) at a later time. All blocks of a logical track are written to disk at the same time, so the logical track is always together on disk. If only a portion of a logical track is updated by the system, and the rest of the logical track is not in cache, it is read from disk and combined with the updated portion before being destaged. During garbage collection, disk segments are read, garbage data are eliminated, and the remaining data are written into different disk segments. Disks see read misses, destage writes, reads of logical tracks that are not in cache and partially updated (reads due to write misses), garbage-collection-reads and garbage-collection writes.

Write hits may be divided into hits on dirty blocks and hits on clean blocks. If the system request rate is K, the fraction of requests that are write hits to clean blocks is C and the fraction of requests that are write misses is D; then $KC + KD$ is the rate at which new dirty blocks are created in cache. In steady state, this must also be the rate at which dirty blocks are destaged from cache. If there are X blocks per logical track in cache when the logical track is being destaged, the destage rate can be expressed as $(KC + KD)/X$ tracks/sec. If B is the fraction of requests that are read misses, then there are KB read misses/sec.

This system is modeled as an $M/M/p$ system that generates read misses, destages, garbage collection reads and writes, and logical track reads of partially updated tracks (reads due to write misses) at various rates to be handled by $N + 1$ disks, each of which is represented by two queues, one for read misses and one for all other types of requests. Of the two queues at each device, the read miss queue has higher priority than the second queue, which is used for all other types of requests. As before, we assume a nonpreemptive-priority queuing discipline.

There are four types of requests from the system: read hits, read misses, write hits, and write misses. Read hits, write hits, and write misses are satisfied directly by the cache; hence, their response time is modeled as the response time of an $M/M/p$ system. Read misses first pass through the $M/M/p$ system with some response time, and then enter the read miss queue of one of the $N+1$ devices with equal probability.

To calculate device utilization, we need to know the read miss rate, the destage rate, the garbage-collection read and write rates, and the reads due to write miss rate. We earlier calculated the read miss rate as KB/sec and the destage rate as $(KC + KD)X$ tracks/sec. The reads due to the write miss rate is easily seen to be KDX. So, we only need to calculate the garbage-collection read and write rates. We will defer this calculation briefly and proceed assuming we know the garbage-collection rates.

On a read miss, we assume that the entire logical track containing the requested block is staged into cache. The response time of the read miss only includes the time to retrieve the block requested; the staging of the rest of the track is done in the background and keeps the device busy, but does not contribute directly to the read miss response time.

As before, we know that the read miss response time at the device consists of a waiting time and a service time. The waiting time is given by the equation ([6])

$$\frac{\lambda_1 E(ST_1{}^2) + \lambda_2 E(ST_2{}^2)}{2(1 - \rho_1)}$$

where λ_1 and ST_1 are the arrival rate and service time of read misses, respectively, and λ_2 and ST_2 are the arrival rate and service time of requests to the low-priority queue, respectively, and ρ_1 is the device busy due to read misses. In Appendix A, we include a derivation of how we calculate the second moment of the read miss service time ST_1 and the first and second moments of the service time ST_2 of the low-priority queue. With that, all the quantities needed to calculate the read miss response time at the devices is thus known. The total read miss response time is calculated as the sum of the response time through the cache ($M/M/p$ queue) and the response time at the device. The average request response time may now be calculated as a function of the read hit response time, write hit response time, write miss response time, and read miss response time.

Earlier, we had deferred calculating the garbage-collection rate. We now proceed to do this.

31.5.4 Calculating the Garbage-Collection Rate

This is done in three steps. First, we calculate the average segment occupancy (ASO). This is the average amount of live data (not holes or garbage) in a segment. Then, we calculate the occupancy of the segment with the least amount of data, since that is the segment whose garbage should be collected when space is needed, since it will return the maximum amount of space.[4] Finally, we calculate the garbage-collection rate. The lower the average segment occupancy, the lower the occupancy of the least occupied segment and the lower the garbage collection rate. The most direct way to reduce the amount of garbage-collection activity is to reduce the average segment occupancy.

The average segment occupancy is calculated is follows. Let there be S sectors per physical disk. Then there are $N * S$ sectors for storing data in the $N + 1$ LSA array.[5] Let L logical devices be mapped to this array, each with T logical tracks of uncompressed size U sectors. Let the average compression and compaction ratios for a logical track be C. Compaction on a track is achieved whenever the system uses only a fraction of the logical track to store data. Compression is achieved on the actual data stored by the system in the used fraction of the logical track. For example, the system may store data only in the first 50% of a track. If this data compresses 2:1, then C is 4.[6] Then L logical devices need $(L \times T \times U)/C$ sectors. Assume that the host system has only allocated a fraction F of the tracks on the L logical devices. Since, in LSA, only allocated tracks take up disk space, the allocated tracks from the L logical devices only need $(L \times F \times T \times U)/C$ disk sectors. Then the average segment occupancy (ASO) is $(L \times F \times T \times U)/(C \times N \times S)$.

Note that there are several separate factors that go into the calculation of the average segment occupancy. One is the number of logical devices that are mapped to the set of $N+1$ physical devices. The fewer the number of logical devices mapped to the array, the lower the average segment occupancy. The second factor is the fraction of logical tracks allocated by the host system from the set of mapped logical devices. Again, the smaller the fraction of logical tracks allocated, the lower the average segment occupancy. The third factor is the degree of compression and compaction achieved per allocated track. The higher the compression compaction achieved, the lower the average segment occupancy. The first factor is something over which we have some limited control as subsystem designers, since we can limit the number of logical devices per $N+1$ physical devices. The second factor is something over which the host system administrator has some control. The host system administrator also has some control over the third factor to some extent, though the compression ratio, which is data-dependent cannot be controlled. Together, these factors can be controlled to impact the ASO and, hence, the garbage-collection rate.

Next, we calculate the best segment occupancy (BSO). This is the occupancy of the segment with the least amount of live data (most holes or garbage). Only a simple outline of the derivation is given here. The derivation is based on steady-

---

[4] The actual criteria we use for deciding which segment to garbage collect are somewhat more complicated, but this assumption is accurate enough for analysis.

[5] Some of these sectors will be used to store the LSA directory, but the fraction of sectors used for this purpose is small enough to be ignored for our analysis.

[6] We will continue to refer to C as the compression ratio, though it is more accurate to call it the compression and compaction ratios on an allocated track.

state equilibrium analysis. Let the capacity of a segment in compressed logical tracks be Z. Define a function N such that, in steady state, let there be $N(Z)$ segments with Z logical tracks, $N(Z-1)$ segments with $Z-1$ logical tracks, and so on; $N(Y)$ segments with Y logical tracks, where YZ is the occupancy of the least occupied segment, or BSO. Steady-state arguments tell us that the number of tracks in segments with Z tracks must be equal to the number of tracks in segments with $Z-1$ tracks, and so on. That is, $Z \times N(Z) = (Z-1) \times N(Z-1) = \ldots = Y \times N(Y)$. The reasoning is as follows. Assume that the preceding is true in steady state. One of the segments with Y tracks is picked for garbage collection. To form a full segment, $Z-Y$ more tracks must be rewritten by the system, which when added to the Y tracks whose garbage was collected, will form a full segment. Let's assume that these $Z-Y$ tracks currently occupy random locations in the segments of the LSA array[7]. Assuming these $Z-Y$ tracks are picked at random, we expect 1 track is currently in a segment with Z tracks, 1 track is currently in a segment with $Z-1$ tracks, and so on, and 1 track is currently in a segment with $Y+1$ tracks. Therefore, 1 segment currently with Z tracks will have 1 fewer track and become a segment with $Z-1$ tracks, 1 segment currently with $Z-1$ tracks will have 1 fewer track and become a segment with $Z-2$ tracks, and so on, and 1 segment currently with $Y+1$ tracks will have 1 fewer track and become a segment with Y tracks. So, at the end of this step when a new segment with Z tracks (Y garbage collected, $Z-Y$ newly rewritten) is created, the number of segments with Z tracks remains the same (increases and decreases by 1), the number of segments that has $Z-1$ tracks remains the same (increases and decreases by 1), and so on, the number of segments with Y tracks increases and decreases by 1. In other words, if the proposition is true to begin with, it continues to remain true[8]. Also, we know that the total number of logical tracks in all segments is $L \times T \times F$. These equations can be solved to get

$$ASO = \frac{(1 - BSO)}{Log_e(1/BSO)}$$

For example, if ASO = 0.6, then BSO = 0.324. That is, if the average segment occupancy is 0.6, then the segments with the lowest (best) occupancy has an occupancy of 0.324[9].

Now, we proceed to calculate the garbage-collection rate as follows. When a segment's garbage is collected we get BSO $\times Z$ live logical tracks from it. These are grouped with (1-BSO) $\times Z$ new logical tracks written by the system and written into a new segment. How long does it take the system to generate (1-BSO) $\times Z$ dirty logical tracks for writing to disk? Well, we know that dirty tracks for destaging are

---

[7] If these $Z-Y$ tracks are not randomly picked, it will make some difference to the BSO and to the garbage-collection rate, but the difference to overall LSA performance is small enough to be ignored for the purposes of this chapter.

[8] This result has been verified with simulations by Larry Stockmeyer.

[9] We thank Jim Roche for this derivation. Larry Stockmeyer has verified this equation to be accurate through simulations.

created at the rate of $(KC + KD)/X$ tracks/sec. So a segment is written and a segment is read at the rate of $(KC + KD)/[X \times (1 - \text{BSO}) \times Z]$ segments/sec. All the reading of segments is attributable to garbage collection. Only a fraction BSO of the writing of segments is attributable to garbage collection the rest is attributable to destage.

31.5.5   LSA Performance Results

With this model of LSA, we are in a position to understand the impact of various parameters on LSA performance.

Effect of Seek Affinity.   We begin by studying the impact of loss of seek affinity on performance. Figure 31.4 shows two curves of LSA performance on an IMS workload that reads and writes 4 KB. As in previous calculations for RAID5, we assume a read to write ratio of 7:1, a read hit ratio of 0.7, a write hit ratio of 1, and an NVS hit ratio of 0.6[10]. A $2 \times (7 + P)$ array subsystem is studied. It is assumed that we can get 3:1 compression on the user's data. In such a subsystem, we assume we are trying to store the same amount of data as we can in a $4 \times (7 + P)$ RAID5 subsystem. This is possible because we are getting 3:1 compression. Any extra space we have left over is used to lower the average segment occupancy and, hence, the garbage-collection rate. The figure shows that loss of seek affinity can have a significant negative impact on performance. For example, we see that the performance (response time) of LSA without seek affinity (seek affinity = 1) is 50% higher at low I/O rates and 100% higher at high I/O rates than that of LSA with 0.5 seek affinity. We conclude that it is important to control the placement of data in LSA so all seek affinity is not destroyed.

Effect of Free Space.   Next, we study the impact of free (storage) space on LSA performance for the same IMS workload as preceding. The more free space, the lower the average segment occupancy, and the lower the garbage-collection rate. In our experiments, we assume that we want to store as many logical tracks in a $2 \times (7 + P)$ LSA as we can in a $4 \times (7 + P)$ RAID5, and we assume we can get 2:1 compression. This implies that if the system allocated 100% of the logical tracks, the LSA system will have no free space left (it needs to store only $\frac{1}{2}$ as much data as the RAID5 system, but has only $\frac{1}{2}$ as many disks). To study the impact of free space on LSA performance, we consider two values for the fraction of logical tracks allocated by the host, 0.7 and 0.9. Figure 31.5 shows that reducing the amount of free space available for LSA by assuming 0.9 of the tracks allocated

---

[10] The preceding read and write hit ratios are for unarrayed subsystems, and are adjusted for LSA as follows. We assume some fraction (say, 17%) of the cache is used to hold the LSA directory. So, to calculate the read and write hit ratios for the LSA controller, we assume that we have effectively a cache that is only 0.83 as large as the cache for the unarrayed case. If we get 2:1 compression, then we assume we have effectively a cache that is 1.66 as large as the cache for the unarrayed case. We then use the empirical result in [14] that miss ratios are inversely proportional to the cube root of cache sizes.

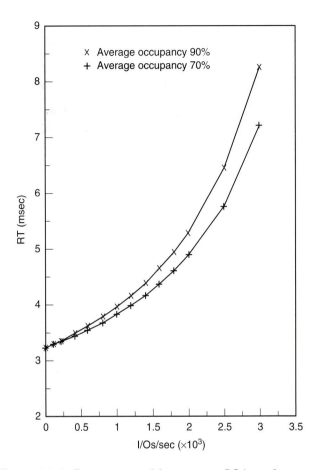

Figure 31.5. Importance of frr space to LSA performance.

can lead to worse response times. The reduced free space leads to higher garbage-collection rates, which in turn leads to higher device utilizations and, therefore, worse response times. Figure 31.6 shows that garbage collection is responsible for as much as 30% of the device utilization when the fraction allocated is 0.9. In fact, the total device utilization is actually slightly greater than 1 at 3000 I/Os/sec (indicating that the system is actually not capable of handling this high an I/O rate).[11] Figure 31.7 shows that garbage collection is responsible for only about

---

[11] In systems with cached RAIDs, and where we have a high-priority and a low-priority queue, the response-time graphs do not curve up toward infinity even when device utilization is almost 100%. This is because the device utilization seen by read misses is less than 100% even when total device utilization is 100%, since read misses are given higher priorities over destages. What this means is that it will appear as if the subsystem can handle more read misses/sec beyond what it could when device utilization was 100%, but this is only because the controller is letting destage work accumulate and is no longer destaging fast enough to keep up with the system. After a while,

10% of the device utilization when the fraction allocated is 0.7, and the device utilization is only 76% at 3000 I/Os/sec. In fact, when the fraction allocated is 0.7, the LSA system can handle I/O rates as high as 3900 IOs/sec (not shown), which is almost 25% higher than when the fraction allocated is 0.9. In general, we believe that an LSA subsystem should have an average segment occupancy of 0.8 or less for performance to be reasonable. At occupancies higher than 0.8, the increased garbage collection rate can cause rapid decreases in performance.

31.5.6   Effect of Compression Ratio.

A related parameter is the compression ratio. Improved compression ratios help in two ways. First, the better the compression ratio, the greater the free space, and, hence, the better the performance. Second, the better the compression ratio, the better the cache hit ratios. This second factor affects performance quite significantly, particularly at low I/O rates where it has a bigger impact than the first factor. In our next study, graphed in Figure 31.8, we assumed the host system allocates 100% of the tracks. Again, we assume a $2 \times (7 + P)$ LSA that is storing as much information as a $4 \times (7+P)$ RAID5. This means that the compression ratio has to be better than 2:1, so we have some free space to do garbage collection. We varied the compression ratio from 2.1:1 to 3:1. In this study, we assumed that no compaction was achieved per allocated track; all reduction in the size of the allocated track on disk was assumed to be because of compression. The average segment occupancies for the three cases we study in the figure are 95%, 83%, and 67%. The maximum sustainable I/O rates for these 3 cases (not possible to see from the figure) are 2250, 4000 and 5000 I/Os/sec. As before, we see that when the occupancy is high (95%) because the compression ratio is low (2.1:1), there is a very significant impact on both response time and throughput.

We conclude, again, that occupancies much higher than 0.8 are to be avoided for LSA.

31.5.7   RAID5 with Compression in Cache

LSA has an advantage over standard RAID5 in that the data are compressed in the controller cache, so it appears to have an effectively larger cache. It is also possible to implement a version of RAID5 in which data are stored compressed in cache. The approach would be as follows. When a record is written by the system, store it in compressed form in the cache. When the record is written to disk, write it in compressed form, but leave enough pad after it to be able to store the full uncompressed form of the record. This ensures that we can always do an update in place. With this approach, no disk space is saved and no LSA directory is needed, but improved performance or lower cost is possible because the data is stored compressed in cache. We call this approach *RAID5 with compression*.

---

the write cache will be full and the subsystem will no longer be able to do fast writes.

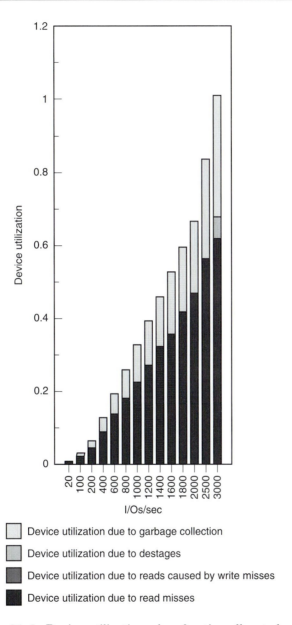

Figure 31.6. Device utilization when fraction allocated = 0.9.

31.6   RAID5 VERSUS LSA

Now we are ready to compare the performance of three systems: a RAID5 system, a RAID5 system with compression, and an LSA system. In understanding these

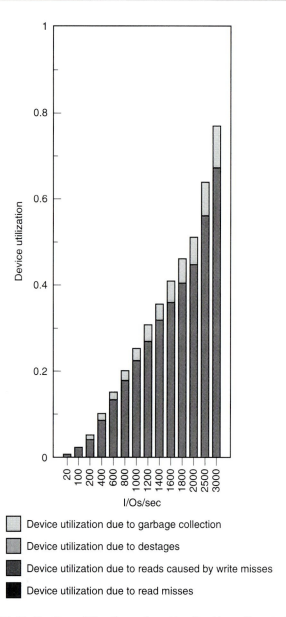

Figure 31.7. Device utilization when the fraction allocated = 0.7.

comparisons, keep in mind the following assumptions: (1) The storing of old data for RAID5 and the LSA directory for LSA are both assumed to take 17% of the cache, so only 83% of the cache is used for other purposes. (2) Schemes that store compressed data in cache have an effectively larger cache. (3) RAID5 has a flat

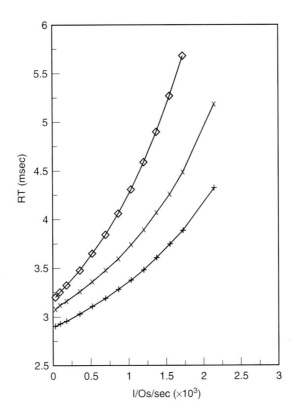

Figure 31.8. Importance of comparison ratio to LSA performance.

skew within an array but has some skew between arrays, LSA has no skew within or across arrays (4) Only LSA obtains better transfer times due to compressed data on disk. (5) RAID5 has better seek affinity than LSA.

31.6.1 Comparison on an IMS-like Workload

Results of one such comparison are shown in 31.8 for a workload that reads and writes 4 KB We assume a $4 \times (7 + P)$ RAID5 system. For LSA, if we get 3:1

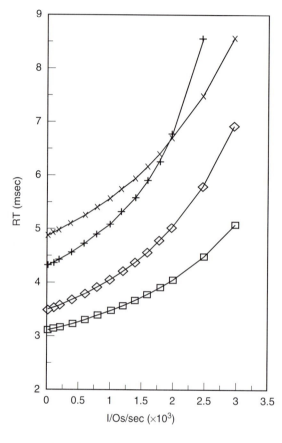

+   4*(7+P) RAID-5; seek aff. .6
◇   2*(7+P) LSA; seek aff .6, 3:1 comp.
□   4*(7+P) RAID-5; 3:1 comp; seek aff. .6
×   4*(7+P) LSA, seek aff. .6, 1:1 comp.

Figure 31.9. LSA vs. RAID-5.

compression, we can use a $2 \times (7+P)$ subsystem. Otherwise, if we get no compression (1:1), then we assume a $4 \times (7 + P)$ LSA subsystem. In any case, we assume that the host allocates 70% of the logical tracks. We also assume that no compaction was achieved per allocated track; so all reduction in the size of the allocated track on disk is assumed to be caused by compression. Effectively, the $2 \times (7 + P)$ LSA system with 3:1 compression has 53% free space and the $4 \times (7 + P)$ system with 1:1 compression has 30% free space. We set LSA seek affinity to 0.8 (worse than

0.6 for RAID5). If we get no compression (data are already compressed in the host), the LSA subsystem can have worse response time and the same cost as a RAID5 subsystem. If we do get 3:1 compression, the LSA subsystem can have better performance (primarily because of improved cache hit ratios) and lower cost than a RAID5 subsystem. However, it has worse performance and better cost than a RAID5 subsystem with compression. This shows us again how important getting good compression ratios are for LSA performance. We could have an LSA with twice as many devices ($4 \times (7 + P)$ LSA versus $2 \times (7 + P)$ LSA) and give up all the advantage of having twice as many arms if we do not get good compression. In summary, LSA performance can be better or worse than standard RAID5, though we generally expect it to be better and have lower cost. However, LSA performance is not as good as compressed RAID5 performance. Similar results are obtained in Figure 31.10 for a workload with more writes.

In discussing performance so far, we mainly focussed on response time. For the curves in Figure 31.10, the maximum throughputs achievable by the different RAID5 and LSA cases are as follows (not shown in the figure): $4 \times (7 + P)$ RAID5 with seek affinity of 0.6 has a maximum throughput of 2890 I/Os/sec; $2 \times (7 + P)$ LSA with seek affinity of 0.8 and a 3:1 compression ratio has a maximum throughput of 4100 IOs/sec; $4 \times (7 + P)$ RAID5 with 3:1 compression and a seek affinity of 0.6 has a maximum throughput of 3855 I/Os/sec; $4 \times (7 + P)$ LSA with seek affinity of 0.8 and a 1:1 compression ratio has a maximum throughput of 4280 I/Os/sec. This shows us that LSA throughputs are always better than that of RAID5 and slightly better than that of RAID-5 with compression. This is because of the higher destage overheads for RAID5 compared to the destage and garbage collection overheads for LSA and because of better skew flattening with LSA. Response times for RAID5 with compression look reasonable because the destage is given lower priority; however, beyond a certain throughput, total device utilization reaches 100% and this point is reached sooner for RAID5 than for the LSA cases.

The maximum throughputs for the curves of Figure 31.11 are as follows. $4 \times (7 + P)$ RAID5 with a seek affinity of 0.6 has a maximum throughput of 1400 I/Os/sec; $2 \times (7 + P)$ LSA with seek affinity of 0.8 and a 3:1 compression ratio has a maximum throughput of 2500 I/Os/sec; $4 \times (7 + P)$ RAID5 with 3:1 compression and a seek affinity of 0.6 has a maximum throughput of 1800 I/Os/sec; $4 \times (7 + P)$ LSA with a seek affinity of 0.8 and a 1:1 compression ratio has a maximum throughput of 2100 I/Os/sec. Once again, LSA throughputs are always better than that of RAID5 or RAID5 with compression.

In comparing the curves of Figure 31.9 with those of Figure 31.10, we notice that the second set of curves has better response times but worse throughputs than the first set of curves. That is, when the fraction of writes in the workload is higher, the response times are better (because of fast write), but the maximum throughput is lower (because of more disk activity due to destaging).

Our results for IMS workloads may be summarized as follows. RAID5 with compression has better response time and throughput than RAID5 without compression, so we should try to do the former whenever possible. This means, that

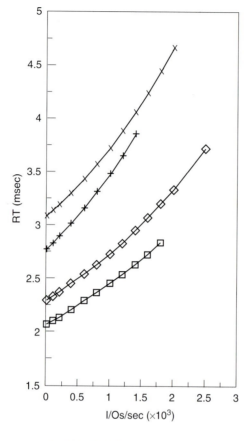

+   4*(7+P) RAID-5; seek aff. .6
◇   2*(7+P) LSA; seek aff .6, 3:1 comp.
□   4*(7+P) RAID-5; 3:1 comp; seek aff. .6
×   4*(7+P) LSA, seek aff. .6, 1:1 comp.

Figure 31.10. LSA versus RAID5.

the choice is really between LSA and RAID5 with compression.

If data are already precompressed by the host, then RAID5 with compression performs exactly like RAID5. In this case, LSA has worse response time and better throughput. Of course, LSA does not have much of a cost advantage in this case, since advantages can only accrue due to track compaction and less than 100% track allocation.

If data are not already precompressed, we expect to get about 3:1 compression. Combined with track compaction and less than 100% track allocation, we could try to build an LSA that is two times cheaper than the equivalent RAID5 with compres-

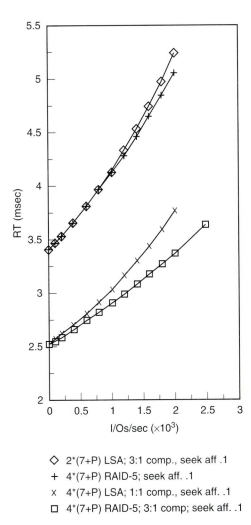

Figure 31.11. LSA versus RAID-5.

sion. Such an LSA has much worse response time but slightly better throughput than RAID5.

31.6.2 Comparison on a Workload with Flat Skew

The LSA throughput advantage is a consequence of the skew flattening between arrays achieved by LSA. This advantage should disappear if the original workload already has flat skew to begin with. We conclude our comparisons of LSA and RAID5 by considering a workload with flat skew. It appears that Unix workloads may be of this type, hence the comparisons are interesting. Results are shown in Figure 31.10. For RAID5 and LSA, we assume that the seek affinity is 1, since this is a random workload with flat skew. For LSA, we also assume that the host allocates 70% of the logical tracks and that no compaction is achieved per allocated track.

If the data does not compress at all (1:1 compression), then LSA and RAID5 are seen to have practically the same response time. In terms of maximum throughput, RAID5 gets 2250 I/Os/sec and LSA gets 2000 I/Os/sec, so they are about the same.

If the data do compress (3:1 compression), then the LSA response time is slightly worse than RAID5 with compression. In terms of maximum throughput, RAID5 with compression gets 2800 I/Os/sec and LSA with seek affinity of 1 gets 2200 I/Os/sec. So, LSA has a slightly worse response time and maximum throughput than RAID5 with compression.

LSA and RAID-5 performance are nearer each other than they were for IMS. RAID5 loses some of its response time advantage because it no longer has better seek affinity; and LSA loses its throughput edge because it no longer has a skew advantage. RAID5 with compression is now a clear performance winner.

31.7   CONSLUSIONS

In this chapter, we began by looking at cached RAID performance. We looked at sensitivity of cached RAID performance to destage assumptions, extending work reported in [20].

Next, we described our approach to supporting compression and cached RAIDs called log-structured arrays (LSA). We showed the importance of seek affinity and compression ratio to LSA performance. We also showed the importance of carefully selecting the correct amount of free space to leave in an LSAdesign and concluded that leaving less than 20% free space was not to be recommended.

Finally, we showed some performance comparisons of RAID5designs that support compression only in the cache (not on disk) versus LSA designs that support compression on disk and in cache. These designs were also compared against RAID5designs that did not support compression at all. In these results, we assumed that the controller microprocessor was not a bottleneck. We also assumed that the controller overheads were similar for RAIDand LSA systems.[12] With these assumptions, for IMS workloads, we found that if we get no compression (data are already compressed in the host) and seek affinity is 0.8, the *LSA* subsystem can have worse response time (though better throughput) and the same cost as a RAID5 subsystem. If we do get 3:1 compression, the LSA subsystem can have better throughput though worse response time, and lower cost than a RAID5 subsystem, even a RAID5 with compression. In comparing LSA to RAID5 with compression, seek affinity and skew are crucial. If LSA can improve its seek affinity, it would have better response time. Also, an LSA design that allows the home of a data item to wander across ar-

---

[12]Results can be quite different if our assumptions are incorrect.

rays (rather than only wander within one array) is important; that is, what flattens skew across arrays for LSA and gives it a throughput edge over RAID5.

For workloads with flat skew (Unix workloads), we found that LSA and RAID-5 performance are nearer each other than they were for IMS. RAID5 loses some of its response time advantage because it no longer has better seek affinity; and LSA loses its throughput advantage edge because it no longer has a skew advantage. RAID5 with compression is now a clear performance winner.

An interesting side result of our analysis was that we showed situations in which one subsystem can have consistently better response times than another subsystem, while having a lower maximum throughput. This is possible only in cached systems with NVS caching and disks with priorities. In uncached systems, one subsystem (A) can have lower response time than another (B) at low I/O rates, but the response time curves of the two subsystems will eventually cross if A has lower maximum throughput than B.

We only compared RAID5 and LSA on random workloads; we expect RAID5 to be better on sequential workloads. Future work remaining to be done includes considering the effect of preemptive disk priorities rather than nonpreemptive disk priorities, and accounting for the controller microprocessor overheads more accurately.

Acknowledgments

I wish to thank Jim Brady who has been a leader in the design of RAID and LSA subsystems that are modeled in this chapter. I also want to acknowledge design contributions by Alden Johnson, Steve Gerdt, and Paul Burton. Thanks to Jim Roche and Larry Stockmeyer for their contributions to the analysis of LSA garbage collection rate. Finally, Alex Thomasian helped make the performance analysis more rigorous and correct. He also developed the method used in the Appendix for determining if the write portion of a destage would need a seek in a RAID5 array.

Appendix A. Calculating Second Moments of Service Time for Cached RAIDs and LSA

Calculating the Second Moment of Read Miss Service Time

On a read miss, some fraction f of the track (typically, 0.7 for the IMS workload) needs to be read. The service time consists of an overhead O, an average seek S, then a roll-mode read R. First, we calculate R as follows. When the seek completes, with probability f, we are in the middle of the requested fraction of data, and with probability $1 - f$, we are outside the requested fraction of data. If we land in the middle of the requested data, it takes us 1 revolution to get all the data read. If we land outside the requested data, it takes us on average $(1 - f)/2$ of a revolution to get to the beginning of the requested data and then another fraction f of a revolution to get all the data read. Let rev be the time for 1 revolution of the disk. Then,

$$E(R) = f \times 1 + (1 - f) \times \left(\frac{1-f}{2} + f \right) \times rev$$

which simplifies to:

$$E(R) = \left(\frac{1}{2} + f - \frac{f^2}{2} \right) \times rev$$

Also,

$$E(R^2) = f \times rev^2 + (1 - f) \times rev^2 \times \frac{(1-f)^2}{3} + f^2 + f \times (1 - f)$$

Finally, the variance of R, $VAR(R)$ is

$$VAR(R) = E(R^2) - E(R)^2$$

which simplifies to

$$VAR(R) = rev^2 \times \left(\frac{-f^4}{4} + \frac{3 \times f^2}{2} - 2 \times f + \frac{3}{4} \right)$$

since the overhead is a constant, its variance is 0.

Finally, we model seek time S as follows. We define a fraction called sf (seek affinity) which is the fraction of non-zero seeks. $1 - sf$ then is the fraction of zero seeks. Also, let the average seek time be sk. Then, $E(S) = (1 - sf) \times 0 + sf \times sk$ and $VAR(S) = sk^2 \times sf \times (1 - sf)$. Then, the variance of the read miss service time is $VAR(O) + VAR(S) + VAR(R)$ and, after some simplification, the second moment of the read miss service time is

$$sk \times sf \times (1 + sk) + rev^2 \times (-f^3 + 2 \times f^2 - f + 1) + O^2 + rev \times \left(0.5 + f - \frac{f^2}{2} \right) +$$
$$sk \times sf \times rev \times (1 + 2 \times f - f^2) \text{ where } O \text{ is the overhead.}$$

Calculating the Second Moment of Service Time of Requests to Low-Priority Queue

For RAID5: The low-priority queue is the one that sees destage requests. As we have discussed before, destaging a block requires either three disk operations (if old data are already in cache) or four disk operations (if old data are not in cache). We assume that destages are done by a physical track and that there may be as many as X dirty blocks that can be destaged together on a physical track. We assume that these X blocks occupy a fraction d of the physical track. In many of our performance results, we set $X = 2$ and $d = 0.3$ which we have found to be true for an IMS workload. For our analysis, we also make the simplifying assumption that either all the X blocks to be destaged on a track require old data to be read, or that all the X blocks do not require old data to be read. Simulation results prove this to be a reasonable assumption. Finally, when a track is destaged, there is some probability that another track at the same cylinder position can also be destaged. To account for this, we assume a certain seek affinity for the seek that takes us to the track to be destaged.

The four (3) destage operations needed to destage a track are read a fraction d of the data track, write a fraction d of the data track, read a fraction d of the parity track (optional), write a fraction d of the parity track. On the surface, it appears that the low-priority queue sees only two types of requests the read part of a destage operation (read a fraction d of track) and the write part of a destage operation. Actually, there are three types of requests seen by the low-priority queue (a) the read part of a destage operation ; (b) the write part of a destage operation, which is like and (c) the write part of a destage operation where the write happens in the next revolution after the corresponding read for destage. The reason for two different types of writes is because preemption (by a higher-priority read miss request) is possible between the read and the write part of a destage operation. If preemption occurs, the write request sees an average seek similar to the average seek for the read; otherwise it takes 1 disk revolution. Let the respective service times for these three types of requests be $STa4$, STb and STc, STa and STb are the same. STc is equal to 1 revolution of the disk. A write for destage request is of (type b), the preceding if a read miss arrives at the high priority queue when the read part of a destage operation is being serviced in the low-priority queue; otherwise, if no read miss arrives when the read part of a destage operation is being serviced in the low-priority queue, then the write request is of type c above and will happen in the next revolution following the read for destage.

Let D_1 be the destage rate due to write hits on clean pages and D_2 be the destage rate due to write misses. Also, let λ be the arrival rate of read misses to the high priority queue. Then, $e^{-\lambda \times STa}$ is the probability that no read miss arrives during a read for destage operation (assuming read miss arrivals are Poisson). By remembering that each destage due to a write hit on a clean page takes three accesses, whereas each destage due to a write miss needs four disk accesses, it is easy to see that the fraction of type (a) or (b) requests to the low priority queue is

$$f_a = \frac{(3 - e^{-\lambda \times STa}) \times D_1 + (4 - 2 \times e^{-\lambda \times STa}) \times D_2}{3 \times D_1 + 4 \times D_2}$$

and the fraction of type c requests is

$$f_c = \frac{e^{-\lambda \times STa} \times D_1 + 2 \times e^{-\lambda \times STa} \times D_2}{3 \times D_1 + 4 \times D_2}$$

The second moment of service time is now

$$f_a \times E(STa^2) + f_c \times E(STc^2)$$

If d is the fraction of track destaged, STa and its second moment can be computed exactly like we computed the read miss service time and its second moment (except for replacing fraction f with fraction d). The second moment of STc is rev^2.

For LSA: A segment consists of many segment-columns, one segment column per disk. A segment-column consists of many physical tracks. In many of our results, we assume 15 physical tracks per segment-column. As discussed before, activity on the low-priority queue includes the reading and writing of segment-columns, and the reading of logical tracks on a write miss. Reading/writing a segment column is not executed as a single disk operation, since a high-priority read miss might have a long wait if it arrived during such an operation. Instead, we assume that this is broken up into 15 (for example) "read/write a physical track" operations. The first of these 15 requests will incur an average seek (with some seek affinity); the remaining 14 may or may not incur seeks, depending on whether preemption occurs because of a higher priority read miss.

It should now be clear that there are three types of requests as seen by the low-priority queue: (1) read or write a physical track with an average seek, (2) read or write a physical track without an average seek, and (3) read a logical track on a write miss. Let the respective service times for the 3 types of requests be S_1, S_2 and S_3. S_1 consists of an overhead, an average seek, and 1 revolution of the disk. So, $E[S_1] = O + rev + sf \times sk$ and $E[S_1{}^2] = sf \times sk \times (sk + 2 \times O + 2 \times rev) + (O + rev)^2$ Also, the first and second moments of S_2 are rev and rev^2. Finally $E[S_3]$ and $E[S_3{}^2]$ are calculated as for read miss, with the fraction f replaced by the fraction which represents the ratio between the logical track size and the physical track size. If the respective fractions of these 3 types of requests are $f1$, $f2$ and $f3$, we know that the second moment of the service time is $f1 \times E[S_1{}^2] + f2 \times E[S_2{}^2] + f3 \times E[S_3{}^2]$

To calculate the fraction of physical track readwrites with average seek versus those without a seek, we reason as follows. Let $E[S_1]$ be k, and $E[S_2]$ be k' Let λ be the arrival rate of read misses to the high-priority queue. Let $q = e^{-\lambda \times k}$ be the probability of no read miss arriving during a physical track readwrite with seek and $r = e^{-\lambda \times k'}$ be the probability of no read miss arriving during a physical track read/write without seek. If reading/writing the ith physical track of a segment takes time k with probability p and time k' with probability $(1 - p)$, then it is easy to see that reading/writing the $(i + 1)$th track takes time k with probability $p \times (1 - q) + (1 - p) \times (1 - r)$ and takes time k' with probability $pq + (1 - p)r$. For $i = 0$, we know $p = 1$. Then, we know that for $i = 1$, $p = 1 - q$, and so on. Knowing the number of tracks in a segment column (15, typically), the required fractions may be calculated.

References

[1] American National Standards Institute (ANSI). *Small Computers Systems Interface (SCSI)*, ANSI Standard X3.131. New York: ANSI, 1986.

[2] Chen, P. M., Gibson, G. and Patterson, D., An Evaluation of Redundant Arrays of Disks Using an Amdahl 5890, *Proc. ACM SIGMETRICS Conf. on Measurement and Modeling of Computer Systems*, CO. May 1990.

[3] Chen, P. M. and Patterson, D. A., Maximizing Performance in a Striped Disk Array, *17th International Symposium on Computer Architecture*, 1990

[4] Chen, P. M. et. al. RAID: High-Performance, Reliable Secondary Storage," *ACM Computing Surveys*, 26(2) (June 1994).

[5] Clark, B. E. et. al. *Parity Spreading to Enhance Storage Access*, United States Patent, Vol. 4,761,785, August 1988.

[6] Conway, R. W., Maxwell, W. L. and Miller, L. W. *Theory of Scheduling*, Reading, MA: Addision-Wesley, 1967.

[7] English, R. M. and Stepanov, A. A. Loge: A Self-Organizing Disk Controller," *Proc. USENIX 1992 Winter Conference*, San Francisco, August 1992,

[8] Gray, J. N., Horst, B. and Walker, M. *Parity Striping of Disk Arrays: Low-Cost Reliable Storage With Acceptable Throughput*, August 1990' Brisbane, Australia, *Tandem Computers Technical Report*

[9] Hyde, J. Personal Communication, IBM SSD Performance Group, 1990.

[10] Jonge, W., Kaashoek, M.F. and Hsieh, W. C. The Logical Disk: A New Approach to Improving File Systems," *Proc. of 14th ACM Symposium on Operating System Principles*, Asheville, Dec. 1993.

[11] Kent, T. and Menon, J. Simulation Study of Cached RAID5 Designs," *First International Symposium on HPCA*, Raleigh, January 1995.

[12] Kleinrock, L. *Queueing Systems, Vol. I*, New York: John Wiley, 1975.

[13] Lawlor, F. D. *Efficient Mass Storage Parity Recovery Mechanism*, IBM Technical Disclosure Bulletin, 24(2) (July 1981).

[14] McNutt, Bruce A Simple Statistical Model of Cache Reference Locality," *CMG Proceedings*, 1991.

[15] Menon, J. Performance of RAID5 Disk Arrays With Read and Write Caching *Journal of Distributed and Parallel Databases*, 2(3), 1994.

[16] Menon, J. and Cortney, J. The Architecture of a Fault-Tolerant Cached *RAID* Controller *20th Annual International Symposium on Computer*, San Diego, May 1993.

[17] Menon, J. M. and Hartung, M. The IBM 3990 Disk Cache," *Compcon*, San Francisco, June 1988.

[18] Patterson, D., Gibson, G. and Katz, R. H. Reliable Arrays of Inexpensive Disks (RAID)," *ACM SIGMOD Conference*, Chicago, June 1988

[19] Rosenblum, M. and Ousterhout, J. Design and Implementation of a Log-Structured File System," *SOSP-91*, Monterey, 1991.

[20] Thomasian, Alexander and Menon, Jai *RAID5 Performance With Distributed Sparing*, IBM Research Report No. RJ 9878, August 1994.

SELECTED BIOGRAPHIES

The following biographies were available at the time of final manuscript submission.

Phil Bernstein

Dr. bernstein obtained his PhD in Computer Science from the University of Toronto in 1975. From 1976 to 1983, he was a computer science professor at Harvard University. From 1983-85, he served as VP at Sequoia Systems. From there he moved to Wang Institute of Graduate Studies as a professor and worked there from 1985 to 1987. After working as a Senior Consulting Engineer at Digital from 1987 to 1994, he moved to Microsoft where he is an Architect. His areas of specialization are transaction systems, database systems, repositories, etc.

Contact coordinates

Microsoft Corporation
One Microsoft Way
Redmond, WA 98052-6399

Email: philbe@microsoft.com
Phone: (425)936-2838

Peter M. Chen

Peter M. Chen is an Assistant Professor in the Department of Electrical Engineering and Computer Science at the University of Michigan. He is at present directing the Rio (RAM I/O) project at the University of Michigan, which is investigating how to implement and use reliable memory. His research areas are disk arrays, file systems, fault tolerant systems, transaction processing, and distributed systems.

Asit Dan

Asit Dan received his Ph.D. from the University of Massachusetts, Amherst, in Computer Science and Computer Engineering, respectively. His doctoral dissertation on "Performance Analysis of Data Sharing Environments" received an Honorable Mention in the 1991 ACM Doctoral Dissertation Competition and was subsequently published by the MIT Press.

Since 1990 he has been a Research Staff Member at the IBM T.J. Watson Research Center, Yorktown Heights, NY. He has published extensively on the design and analysis of video servers as well as transaction processing architectures, and participated in the design and development of video servers on various IBM platforms. He holds several top rated patents in these areas and has received IBM Outstanding Innovation Awards for his work in both the areas.

His current research interests include Internet based transaction processing, secure sandbox execution environment, and innovative multimedia applications. Dr. Dan has served on various program committees and is currently serving as a guest editor for the IBM Journal of Research and Development.

Contact coordinates

H4-C10, IBM T.J. Watson Res.Center   Email: asit@watson.ibm.com
30 Sawmill River road   Phone: (914) 784-6677
Hawthorne, NY 10532   Fax : (914) 784-7455

Margaret (Maggie) H. Dunham

Margaret (Maggie) H. Dunham received her Ph.D. in computer science from Southern Methodist University in 1984.

She is an associate professor in the department of Computer Science and Engineering at Southern Methodist University in Dallas. Maggie served as Associate Chairman of the department from 1992 to 1994. She also served as as President of the SMU Faculty Senate during 1996-1997. In addition to her academic experience, Professor Dunham has nine years industry experience.

Professor Dunham's research interests encompass Main Memory Databases, Distributed Heterogeneous Databases, Temporal Databases, and mobile computing. She directs the SMU Database Research Group and is responsible for the design of MARS, a high-throughput main memory database system.

Dr. Dunham served as editor of the ACM SIGMOD Record from 1986 to 1988. She has served on the program and organizing committees for many ACM and IEEE conferences. She served as guest editor for a special section of IEEE Transactions on Knowledge and Data Engineering devoted to Main Memory Databases as well as a special issue of the ACM SIGMOD Record devoted to Mobile Computing in databases.

Contact coordinates

Dept. of Computer Science and Eng.   Email: mhd@seas.smu.edu
Southern Methodist University   Phone: (214) 768-3087
Dallas, Texas 75275   Fax: (214) 768-3085

Michael Franklin

Michael Franklin is an Assistant Professor in the Department of Computer Science at the University of Maryland. His research focuses on the architecture and performance of distributed and parallel information systems. He received the Ph.D. from the University of Wisconsin-Madison in 1993. At Maryland, Dr. Franklin leads the DIMSUM project to develop a flexible query processing architecture for local and wide-area networks, and is a co-developer of the Broadcast Disks data dissemination paradigm. Dr. Franklin has worked on several well known research database systems including the EXODUS and SHORE systems at Wisconsin and the BUBBA parallel database system at MCC. More recently he has been an Invited Professor at INRIA-Rocquencourt and has worked with industrial researchers at AT&T Research and Bellcore. He is the author of the book "Client Data Caching: A Foundation for High Performance Object Database Systems", published by Kluwer in 1996, is Editor-In-Chief of the ACM SIGMOD Record, and is an Associate Editor of ACM Computing Surveys, and the IEEE Data Engineering Bulletin. Dr. Franklin is a 1995 recipient of the NSF CAREER award.

Contact coordinates

Dept. of Computer Science
A.V. Williams Building
University of Maryland
College Park, MD 20742

Email: franklin@cs.umd.edu
Phone: 301-405-6713
Fax: 301-405-6707

Hector Garcia-Molina

Hector Garcia-Molina is the Leonard Bosack and Sandra Lerner Professor in the Departments of Computer Science and Electrical Engineering at Stanford University, Stanford, California. He is currently the Director of the Computer Systems Laboratory at Stanford. From 1979 to 1991 he was on the faculty of the Computer Science Department at Princeton University, Princeton, New Jersey. His research interests include distributed computing systems and database systems. He received a BS in electrical engineering from the Instituto Tecnologico de Monterrey, Mexico, in 1974. From Stanford University, Stanford, California, he received in 1975 a MS in electrical engineering and a PhD in computer science in 1979. Garcia-Molina is a Fellow of the ACM.

Contact coordinates

Department of Computer Science
Stanford University
Gates Hall 4A, Room 434
Stanford, CA 94305

Email: hector@cs.stanford.edu
Phone: (650) 723-0685
FAX: (650) 725-2588

Paulo B. Goes

Paulo B. Goes is an Associate Professor of Operations and Information Management, University of Connecticut. Dr. Goes obtained his Ph.D. in Computers and Information Systems from the University of Rochester in 1991. His research interests are in the areas of database recovery and security, computer networking, technology infrastructure, Internet and electronic commerce. His research methodology generally involves applying mathematical models and artificial intelligence techniques to solve complex problems.

His publications have appeared in IEEE Transactions on Computers, IEEE Transactions on Communications, INFORMS Journal on Computing, Decision Support Systems, Queueing Systems: Theory and Applications, Journal of the Operational Research Society and International Journal of Flexible Manufacturing Systems.

Dr. Goes is currently a Larry Ackerman Scholar in the School of Business Administration at the University of Connecticut. He is a member of ACM and INFORMS.

Contact coordinates

Associate Professor   Email: paulo@sbaserv.sba.uconn.edu
Operations and Info. Management   Phone: (860) 486-2379
School of Business Administration   Fax: (860) 486-4839
Box U-41 IM
University of Connecticut
Storrs, CT 06269

James N. Gray

Dr. Gray is a specialist in database and transaction processing computer systems. At present he is the Manager of Microsoft's Bay Area Research Lab (BARC). At Microsoft his research focuses on scaleable computing: building super-servers and workgroup systems from commodity software and hardware. Prior to joining Microsoft, he worked at Digital, Tandem, IBM and AT&T on database and transaction processing systems including Rdb, ACMS, NonstopSQL, Pathway, System R, SQL/DS, DB2, and IMS-Fast Path. He is editor of the Performance Handbook for Database and Transaction Processing Systems, and coauthor of Transaction Processing Concepts and Techniques. He holds doctorates from Berkeley and Stuttgart, is a Member of the National Academy of Engineering, Fellow of the ACM, a member of the National Research Council's Computer Science and Telecommunications Board, Editor in Chief of the VLDB Journal, Trustee of the VLDB Foundation, and Editor of the Morgan Kaufmann series on Data Management. He frequently lectures at universities, and often reviews application designs. He has been a McKay Fellow at UC Berkeley. His current activities are Research on fault-tolerant, parallel, and distributed database systems.

Contact coordinates

Microsoft Research   Email: Gray@Microsoft.com
301 Howard St #830   Phone: 415-778-8222
SF CA 94133.   Fax: 415-778-8210

Abdelsalam A. Heddaya

Dr. Heddaya received his Ph.D. in computer science from Harvard University, in 1988.

Dr. Heddaya has served on the program committees of the 10th IEEE International Conference on Distributed Computing Systems, and the 2nd IEEE International Symposium on Computers and Communications. He has given numerous invited talks both in industrial and academic settings. Dr. Abdelsalam A. Heddaya is co-founder and vice president for research and architecture of InfoLibria, Inc. He is currently on leave from Boston University, where he serves as associate professor of computer science. Dr. Heddaya's research in distributed systems focuses on high availability and high performance. Recently, he co-authored a book titled "Replication Techniques in Distributed Systems" (Kluwer, 1996). He has led project WebWave for large scale internet-wide caching, and project Mermera, which produced a model and system for specifying, reasoning about, and programming mixed-coherence distributed shared memory. Other works of his were on congestion control, and bulk-synchronous parallelism.

Contact coordinates

Computer Science Dept   Email: heddaya@cs.bu.edu
BostonUniversity   Phone: 617-353-8922
111 Cummington Street
Boston, MA 02215

H. V. Jagadish

H. V. Jagadish obtained his Ph. D. degree from Stanford University in 1985 and has since been with AT&T Labs, where he currently heads the Database Research Department.

Contact coordinates

AT&T Labs, A119   Email: jag@research.att.com
180 Park Ave.   Phone: (973) 360-8750
Florham Park, NJ 07932   FAX: (973) 360-8871

Henry F. Korth

Henry F. Korth is the head of the Database Principles Research Department at
Bell Laboratories, Lucent Technologies Inc. He was previously a Vice President
of Panasonic Technologies, Inc. and Director of the Matsushita Information Technology Laboratory. For nine years, he was on the faculty of the Department of
Computer Sciences of the University of Texas at Austin where he was an Associate
Professor. Prior to that, he was on the research staff of the IBM Watson Research
Center and earned his Ph.D. at Princeton University. He is co-author of the textbook Database System Concepts, an associate editor of the VLDB Journal and
co-editor of the book Mobile Computing. His research interests include real-time
and high performance database systems, transaction processing, mobile computing,
data warehouses, and parallel and distributed computing. He is co-author of the
1985 paper "A Model of CAD Transactions" chosen as "Most Influential Paper from
the Proceedings of Ten Years Ago: at the 1995 International Conference on Very
Large Data Bases.

Contact coordinates

Room 2T-216   Email: hfk@research.bell-labs.com
Bell Laboratories   Phone: 908-582-7791
Lucent Technologies Inc.   Fax: 908-582-1239
700 Mountain Avenue
Murray Hill, NJ 07974

David Lomet

Dr. Lomet received his Ph.d from the Moore School of Electrical Engineering at
the University of Pennsylvania.

David Lomet has been a Senior Researcher and manager of the Database Research Group at Microsoft Research in Redmond, Washington since January, 1995.
He consults actively with the SQL Server development team on database kernel
technology. Earlier, he was a researcher at the IBM Thomas J. Watson Research
Center in Yorktown, a professor of Information Technology at the Wang Institute
of Graduate Studies, and a Senior Consulting Engineer at the Digital Equipment
Corporation, first in the Database Systems Product Group and subsequently at
the Cambridge Research Lab. His database technical interests are in the areas of
recovery, concurrency control, and access methods. The Phoenix Project at Microsoft Research, which he leads, is aimed at providing application robustness using
database recovery techniques.

His work, both in research and in product development, has involved programming languages, compilers, machine architecture, and the architecture and algorithms of database and transaction processing systems. During a sabbatical at the
University of Newcastle-upon-Tyne, Dr. Lomet invented the notion of atomic action, later seen to be essentially the same as the notion of serializable transaction

developed at about the same time.

Dr. Lomet has published extensively in the leading conferences and journals of the database field. He serves as Editor-in-Chief of the Data Engineering Bulletin and as an associate editor of both the VLDB Journal and the Journal of Distributed and Parallel Databases. He has served on the program committees of all the leading database conferences and has participated in a number of NSF Lagunita Workshops and an ACM workshop whose purposes were to chart an agenda for future database research. He holds 11 patents, including five in the area of recovery.

Contact coordinates

Microsoft Research   Email: lomet@MICROSOFT.com
One Microsoft Way   Phone: (206)703-1853
Redmond, WA 98052   Fax: (425)936-7329

Kenneth Salem

Kenneth Salem is an associate professor in the Department of Computer Science at the University of Waterloo. He joined the department in 1994, after spending a year there as a visitor. Before coming to Waterloo, Dr. Salem was a faculty member at the University of Maryland and a staff scientist at CESDIS, NASA's Center of Excellence in Space Data and Information Sciences. He received his BSc in electrical engineering and applied mathematics from Carnegie-Mellon University in 1983, and his PhD in computer science from Princeton University in 1989. His research interests are in the areas of data management and operating systems.

Contact coordinates

Department of Computer Science   Email: kmsalem@uwaterloo.ca
University of Waterloo   Phone: (519)888-4567, x3485
Waterloo, Ontario N2L 3G1, Canada   Fax: (519)885-1208

Avi Silberschatz

Avi Silberschatz, who earned his doctorate from the State University of New York at Stony Brook, is the director of the Information Sciences Research Center at Bell Laboratories in Murray Hill, New Jersey. Prior to joining Bell Labs, he held a chaired professorship in the Department of Computer Sciences at the University of Texas at Austin. Dr. Silberschatz is a Fellow of the ACM. He is recognized as a leading researcher, educator, and author in operating systems, database systems, and distributed systems. His writings have appeared in numerous ACM and IEEE publications, as well as in other journals and proceedings of professional conferences. He is the coauthor of the textbooks Operating System Concepts (Fifth Edition, Addison Wesley, 1998) and Database System Concepts (Third Edition, McGraw-Hill, 1997).

Contact coordinates

Information Sciences Research Center   Email: avi@bell-labs.com
MH 2T-210   Phone: 908-582-4623
Bell Laboratories
600 Mountain Ave.
Murray Hill, NJ 07974

S. Sudarshan

S. Sudarshan received his B.Tech. from IIT Madras in 1987 and his Ph.D. from the
University of Wisconsin, Madison in 1992. He is currently an assistant professor
in the Department of Computer Science and Engineering at the Indian Institute of
Technology, Bombay. Earlier, he was a member of the technical staff at the AT&T
Bell Laboratories, Murray Hill, New Jersey from 1992 to 1995. His research interests
include query processing, query optimization, and failure recovery in main-memory
databases. He was a member of the original design team for the Coral deductive
database system at Wisconsin, and initiated (with Avi Silberschatz and H.V. Jagadish) the Dali main-memory database system project while at Bell Laboratories.
He is a co-author of the book "Database System Concepts", by Avi Silberschatz,
Henry F. Korth, and S. Sudarshan, McGraw-Hill, 1997.

Contact coordinates

Dept. of Computer Science and Eng.   Email: sudarsha@cse.iitb.ernet.in
I.I.T. Bombay   Phone: +91 22 578 2545 ext 7714
Powai, MUMBAI 400076, India

Ushio Sumita

He received his Ph.D. in 1981 from the William E. Simon Graduate School of
Business Administration, the University of Rochester, Rochester, New York, and a
second Ph. D. in 1987 from Tokyo Institute of Technology, Tokyo, Japan.

Ushio Sumita is the Dean and Professor at the Graduate School of International
Management, the International University of Japan (IUJ), Niigata, Japan. Prior
to joining IUJ as the Dean, he worked for various organizations and universities in
the U.S., including Xerox Corporation, the Laboratory for Information and Decision Systems at Massachusetts Institute of Technology, GTE Laboratories, Syracuse
University, the Simon School of the University of Rochester, and the Stern School of
New York University. His primary research interest includes appplied probability,
stochastic processes, queueing theory, operations management, database management systems, distributed database systems, and performance evaluation of com-
puter/communication and manufacturing systems. He has published more than 80
papers in leading archive journals in these areas. Recently, he has been analyzing the

characteristic differences between the US capitalism and the Japanese capitalism, explaining different management approaches in the two countries. He frequently writes articles on organizational issues surrounding globalization in Nikkei Business and other Japanese business journals.

Contact coordinates

Associate Professor
Operations and Information Management
School of Business Admn., Box U-41 IM
University of Connecticut
Storrs, CT 06269

Phone: (860) 486-2379
Fax: (860) 486-4839

Alexander Thomasian

Alexander Thomasian received the Ph.D. degree in computer science from University of California at Los Angeles in 1977. He was a faculty member at Case Western University and the University of Southern California, and has served as an adjunct faculty at Columbia University. He was a Senior Staff Scientist at the Burroughs Corp. before joining IBM's T. J. Watson Research Center in 1985.

He is now affiliated with the Networked Data Systems Dept., where he is doing research in the area of digital libraries. He has also done research in performance modeling and analysis of transaction processing systems, concurrency control methods, parallel and distributed computer systems, and disk arrays. He has received IBM's Invention Achievement and Outstanding Innovation Awards.

He has published over 90 papers and is the author of "Database Concurrency Control: Methods, Performance, and Analysis" by Kluwer Publ. in 1996. He has given tutorials on high-performance query and transaction processing systems. Dr. Thomasian is a Senior Member of IEEE, Member of ACM, and an area editor for IEEE Transactions on Parallel and Distributed Systems. He has been on the program committees of the IEEE Int'l Conf. on Distributed Computing Systems, IEEE Int'l Symp. on High Performance Distributed Computing, IEEE Int'l Conf. on Data Engineering, and IEEE Int'l Conf. on Information and Knowledge Management.

Contact coordinates

IBM T. J. Watson Resaerch Center
30 Saw Mill River Rd
Hawthorne, NY 10532

Email: ATHOMAS@watson.ibm.com
Phone: (914)-784-7299

William E. Weihl

William E. Weihl is a senior research scientist at DIGITAL's Systems Research Center (SRC), where he has been working on a variety of areas including computer architecture, performance measurement, and program optimization techniques. As of this writing (1997), he is leading a project exploring profile-driven optimizations for improving program performance on high-speed processors, with particular emphasis on performance problems due to memory access latencies. The project has produced a profiling system, the DIGITAL Continuous Profiling Infrastructure, that provides accurate detailed instruction-level information about the stalls incurred by individual instructions yet incurs minimal overhead (around 1 to 3%).

Dr. Weihl received a Bachelor of Science degree in Mathematics in 1979 from the Massachusetts Institute of Technology (MIT). In 1980 he received Bachelor of Science and Master of Science degrees in Computer Science, also from MIT, and in 1984 he received a Doctor of Philosophy degree in Computer Science from MIT.

From 1984 through 1996, Dr. Weihl was a member of the computer science faculty at MIT, where his research focused on distributed and parallel systems. He was a key contributor to the Argus programming language and system for building reliable distributed systems and to the Mercury system for building heterogeneous distributed systems. He also made fundamental advances in the design of high-performance transaction-processing systems, developing a number of new concurrency control and recovery techniques for multi-level systems comprised of abstract data objects. His research group produced the Proteus multiprocessor simulation system, which made it possible to simulate a wide range of parallel architectures while making a range of tradeoffs between accuracy and performance of the simulation. His group also produced the Prelude programming language and system for building efficient yet portable parallel programs; Prelude embodied a number of important ideas for controlling the placement and migration of data and computation.

Since 1994, Dr. Weihl has been a member of the research staff at SRC. Prior to his current work on profile-driven optimizations, he has worked on tools for measuring, testing, and debugging performance, and on devices to facilitate reading text online. His research interests cover a wide range of topics in systems, including concurrent and distributed systems, computer architecture, and programming language design and implementation.

Contact coordinates

DIGITAL Systems Research Center   Email: weihl@pa.dec.com
130 Lytton Avenue   Phone: 415/853-2197
Palo Alto, CA 94301

Seth White

Seth White received his Ph.D. in Computer Science from the University of Wisconsin-Madison. Since completion of his Ph.D. degree in August 1994, Seth has been employed at Sun Microsystems, Inc. in Palo Alto, California. Seth is currently working in the Javasoft division at Sun where he is responsible for the evolution of the JDBC (Java Database Connectivity) API. His interests include: accessing enterprise data from Java, distributed computing in intranet environments, object-oriented and object-relational databases, and database middleware.

Contact coordinates

JavaSoft
901 San Antonio Road
Mailstop UCUP02-201
Palo Alto, CA 94303

Email: seth.white@eng.sun.com
Phone: 408/343-1628

Index

U

U-NR 220, 222
U-R 221
undo 128, 131, 148, 219, 339
undo log shipping 484
undo pass 424
undo-redo 220
uninterpreted 447
unsegmented 587
unsolicited-vote 387
update hit 349
update-in-place 27, 73, 83, 619

V

volatile 111
voluntarily aborts 472

W

WAL 117, 132, 154, 339, 421
Walkstations 664
WALT 3
weak-transaction 668
well-formedness 81
whole-page logging 750
wireless 638, 639, 640, 643
wireless networks 662, 664
workflow 505, 506, 520
worklist agents 521
write-ahead log 14, 488, 549
write-invalidate 489
write-write 105, 106, 114

Y

Yes-Vote 373